WITHDRAWN

VIRGINIA LEE FISHER

Theory and Problems
of
Child Development

Second Edition

David P. Ausubel, M.D., Ph.D.
Office of Research and Evaluation
City University of New York

Edmund V. Sullivan, Ph.D.
The Ontario Institute for Studies in Education
Toronto, Canada

GRUNE & STRATTON New York · London

To Our Parents

Grune & Stratton, Inc.
757 Third Avenue
New York, New York 10017

First Edition
© Grune & Stratton, Inc. 1957
Second Edition
© Grune & Stratton, Inc. 1970

Library of Congress Catalog Card Number 72-102029
International Standard Book Number 0–8089–0641–0

Printed in the United States of America (PC–B)

Contents

PART III. PERSONALITY DEVELOPMENT

PART IV. LINGUISTIC AND COGNITIVE ASPECTS OF DEVELOPMENT

PART V. PHYSICAL AND MOTOR ASPECTS OF DEVELOPMENT

Preface

This book represents a revision of the first author's conceptualization of theory and methods in child development which was originally published in 1958. The years subsequent to the publication of the first edition have witnessed significant changes in almost all areas of child development research. In spite of these significant changes, much of the materials from the first edition have been incorporated into the revised edition. The review of recent publications and the writing of the second edition was the responsibility of the second author. The editing of chapters in the revised textbook was the joint responsibility of both authors. In general, the revised edition is consonant with the theoretical orientation of the first edition, e.g., the theoretical treatment of personality development and the interactional view of the nature-nurture problem. In addition, many of the first author's views on language and cognitive development, that have been advanced in more recent works, have been incorporated in this second edition where appropriate.

This book represents and attempts to organize and interpret the empirical findings in this field in relation to a general treatise on the nature of human development. Throughout, the approach has been to treat development as a process requiring explanation as well as description—to examine the factors that control and regulate it, the conditions under which it occurs, and its distinguishing properties and characteristics. Occupying a central place in the theoretical discussions in this book are such issues as the relative contributions of biological and social factors to the regulation of development, the existence and interpretation of "human nature", the meaning of maturation and "cultural relativism", continuity and discontinuity and reversibility and irreversibility in development, the nature of developmental regression, sources of uniformity and difference in developmental sequences, parallelism and unevenness in the component aspects of development, generality and specificity and integration and differentiation in the developing organization of behavior and personality.

The scope of the theoretical problems involved in issues such as these transcends characteristic doctrinal divisions among the different schools of psychological thought. Hence, the basic theoretical need is less for an organization or interpretation of data in terms of the general doctrinal orientations of various broad-based systems of psychology (or even in terms of an eclectic selection of doctrines) than for a body of relatively doctrine-free theory dealing exclusively with the major kinds of generalizations that can be made about the nature and regulation of development as a process. This would consist of an integrated and self-consistent set of propositions consonant with the empirical findings, the logical inferences, and the more self-evidently valid theoretical constructs in the various disciplines comprising child development. Thus it follows that although the views of numerous writers will be examined when appropriate to a particular discussion, this book does not purport to review and appraise systematically the major theoretical positions in the field; this latter task would constitute a volume in itself. Our primary concern is with the elaboration and exposition of a substrate of developmental theory for an interdisciplinary field of knowledge rather than with a history or critique of the application of general psychological theories to developmental problems.

This substrate consists of two recognizably distinct although not unrelated bodies of theory: (a) general principles dealing with the nature and regulation of development as a whole, and (b) principles of personality development. The former is wider in scope and includes personality as well as other areas of development. The latter attempts to provide a theoretical framework for the interpretation of those sequential changes in the more central aspects of personality structure (e.g., self-concepts, motives, values, interests, emotions, etc.) which accompany developmental fluctuations in biosocial status.

The organization of subject matter is based on the premise that cognitive learning represents a process of progressive differentiation or relatively undifferentiated fields of knowledge. We submit that human beings do not easily learn materials that are neatly segregated by virtue of topical or categorical homogeneity into discrete chapters and treated throughout at a uniform level of conceptualization. The ideational content of a particular field naturally imposes a logical sequence and mode of organization that cannot be summarily violated; but this does not preclude the simultaneous adoption of a scheme of presentation that attempts to conform to the actual cognitive steps by which facts and concepts are most effectively integrated into a coherent and stable body of knowledge. Hence, an overview of general principles is provided before more detailed information is introduced and previously presented concepts are reintroduced when they become relevant in new contexts.

The argument for fluidity of boundaries between topics is further buttressed by the obvious fact that single aspects of human development never occur in isolation from the total growth matrix. Nevertheless some artificial compartmentalization of material into separate chapters is self-evidently necessary for purposes of convenience, since everything cannot be simultaneously discussed and related to everything else.

The two theoretical portions of the book already alluded to above are Part 1, *Theoretical Foundations of Child Development*, and Part 3, *Personality Development*. Parts 2, *Beginnings of Development*, Part 4, *Linguistic and Cognitive Aspects of Development*, and 5, *Physical and Motor Aspects of Development* are concerned with less general problems and therefore contain fewer implications for development as a whole.

Part 1 deals with the general theoretical and methodological issues in child development: description and delimitation of the field, historical trends regarding the control and regulation of development, general issues involved in the interaction between heredity and environment, the nature of developmental processes, and research problems and methods in child development.

Part 2 considers the origins, raw materials and beginning status of behavior and capacity. It is concerned with such topics as the psychological aspects of pregnancy and lactation, prenatal development, the birth process, maturity at birth, neonatal behavior and capacities. A significant omission in this revised edition is a chapter strictly devoted to infant care practices and their implications for personality development. The enormous amount of research literature coupled with the confusion of theory and results seemed to indicate that this area of child development, as presently conceptualized, is going nowhere theoretically or empirically. Recent reviews of this literature are available and the reader should consult these sources if he deems it necessary (e.g., Caldwell, 1964).

Part 3 deals with the general theory of personality development. Separate chapters are devoted to ego development, emotional development, parent-child relationships, and moral development, the impact of culture on personality, and relationships with peers. Considerations of space made it necessary to abandon the original plan of including a chapter on the interpretation and management of the common behavior problems and disorders of childhood. However, in view of the abundance of opinion and the relative dearth of empirical data in this field of knowledge this chapter was considered most expendable in a volume devoted primarily to theoretical issues and problems in the normative aspects of child development.

Part 4 is concerned with the following special aspects of development, which are relatively more peripheral and less ego-related than the topics listed in the preceding paragraph: development of language, perceptual and cognitive development, and the growth of intelligence. In a larger sense, of course, these latter areas are also significant components of personality structure which constitute in addition extremely important independent variables affecting the more control stratum of personality development considered in Part 3. The second edition breaks cognitive development into two separate chapters; one dealing with more general aspects of cognitive development (e.g., stage theory) and the other treating more specific processes (e.g., memory).

Finally, Part 5 is solely concerned with physical and motor development.

A word of caution is indicated regarding the applicability of the generalizations and empirical data in this book to practical problems of child rearing, child guidance, and curriculum development. Although such data and generalizations have obvious implications for these problems, immediate and wholesale extrapolation is not only unwarranted but also extremely dangerous. At the very best, child development may be considered one of the basic sciences underlying these applied or engineering sciences—in the same sense that physiology and bacteriology are basic sciences for medicine or pediatrics. Thus, before the practical implications of child development can be legitimately and validly applied in guidance and educational settings, extensive preliminary research at the engineering level of operations is obviously required. The generalization that neuromuscular development proceeds in a proximo-distal direction to the detailed planning of a physical education curriculum is as far a cry as the antibiotic action of streptomycin in a petri dish and its therapeutic use in tuberculous meningitis. Partly to discourage the prevailing tendency toward rash and uncritical extrapolation, partly to conserve space, and partly because they are so frequently accepted as evidence rather than as interesting illustrative matter, case histories and anecdotal material have not been included in this volume.

Also, as a space conserving measure, and because of an impression that in many instances they serve more to simulate an atmosphere of scientific precision than to facilitate genuine conceptual understanding, figures and tables have been utilized only when it was felt that they could convey meanings more succinctly and effectively than could language. Considerations of space likewise precluded reference to all available empirical studies, thereby requiring the exercise of fallible subjective judgment regarding relative merit and significance whenever selective choice became necessary.

Finally, as should be abundantly clear from the material itself, there is need for great tentativeness and considerable humility in the statement of generalizations concerning psychological development. Compared to other developmental sciences such as embryology and geology, relatively little that is definite and conclusive is known about the psychological development of children.

This book is primarily intended as an advanced textbook for graduate students in psychology and education although in some instances it might be appropriately used by mature undergraduates with adequate preparation in psychology as well as in the biological and social sciences. It is intended too as a reference work for educators, pediatricians, clinical psychologists, psychiatrists, social workers, and other persons whose professional work brings them into contact with children.

We are especially indebted to Mrs. Mary Stager and Mrs. Nancy Taylor who scrupulously combed the abstracts for appropriate material for this volume. Their editorial assistance was appreciated and a word of thanks here is also appropriate to Peter Tomlinson. We would like to thank some of our colleagues for reading some of our chapters and criticizing them. Special thanks here goes to David Brison, William Fowler, David Hunt, Larry Kohlberg, David Olson and Floyd Robinson. Finally, we would like to thank Mrs. Diane Hansen and Mrs. Helena Webb for their assistance in typing the manuscript.

David Ausubel, New York
Edmund Sullivan, Ontario
1970

Theoretical Foundations of Child Development

CHAPTER 1

The Field of Child Development

DEFINITION OF THE FIELD

AT FIRST BLUSH it might seem that the question of what constitutes the proper field of child development is a glaringly self-evident proposition. Closer inspection, however, reveals that the scope, concerns and objectives of this subdivision of knowledge are far from being a settled matter. For example, wide differences of opinion prevail as to whether child development is a natural or experimental science, whether description or explanation of development is desired, whether understanding, prediction and control of *individual* behavior is one of its legitimate concerns. Should child development specialists focus on the *behavior* of children at different age levels as an end in itself or merely as preliminary data from which growth trends may be abstracted and studied? In what sense are those "fundamental mechanics and dynamics of the developing person," that hold true irrespective of age level, appropriate matters of concern in child development. To what extent is the developmental psychologist concerned with the reciprocal impact of organism and environment upon each other (Anderson, 1954; Cronbach, 1958; Kessen, 1960)? In measuring and explaining development, should emphasis be placed upon the overt and objective aspects of change in the organism or upon their subjective, psychological meaning to the individual (Bijou & Baer, 1961; Kessen, 1962; Lewin, 1954)? Does child development encompass any unique content or goals that justify and make desirable the retention of its present status as a separate field of specialization or would scientific progress be better served if it were reabsorbed by its parent disciplines?

These and many other unresolved issues concerning the field of child development will be discussed in an effort to arrive at some tentative and defensible conclusions.

Developmental versus "Contemporaneous" Sciences

By way of introduction a useful distinction may first be made between "contemporaneous" and developmental sciences, or more precisely between "contemporaneous" and developmental phenomena within a given science. Time is naturally a dimension in which both kinds of phenomena occur. But in the first instance it is only of nominal or incidental interest in relation

1

to the phenomenon under investigation; whereas in the second instance, *change* as a function of time is itself the phenomenon under investigation.

Thus, for example, in the characteristic kinds of contemporaneous phenomena studied in chemistry, physics, physiology, psychology, sociology, ethnology, etc., scientists are concerned with describing and explaining events and relationships which for all practical purposes undergo no significant change during the conventional time interval in which they are considered. On the other hand, in each of these broad areas of science, when the focus of interest shifts to how and why matter, form, organisms, behavior, institutions, and civilizations are different from one point in time to another, we are confronted with such developmental phenomena as constitute the subject matter of geology, embryology, biological evolution, genetic psychology, philology, and history.

It is important to note that in this distinction the crucial consideration is not the duration of the time interval involved but whether change as a function of time is the primary phenomenon under investigation. Developmental phenomena may encompass less than a day (e.g., the life cycles of unicellular organisms) or millions and billions of years (e.g., geological events, biological evolution). And, similarly, as long as phenomenological constancy over time may be conventionally assumed for the purposes of a given investigation, tremendous variability may prevail with respect to the temporal span of events conceived as occurring within a contemporaneous frame of reference.

The Content and Goals of Child Development

In the light of the foregoing discussion, child development as a field may be best defined as that branch of knowledge concerned with the nature and regulation of significant structural, functional and behavioral changes occurring in children as they advance in age and maturity. However, the fact that it deals with the characteristics of children is not the essential reason for classifying it among the developmental sciences. Childhood, after all, constitutes but a single segment in the total life cycle of the ever-developing human being. Thus, scientists who restrict the scope of their inquiries to this particular age period are not necessarily specialists in child development. They may simply be anatomists, physiologists, pathologists, psychologists, physicians or anthropologists who specialize in children.

Neither do attempts to establish the descriptive characteristics of children at different age levels necessarily imply concern with developmental processes. It frequently happens that the collection of normative data is regarded as an end in itself and leads to no subsequent effort to discern or account for growth trends. To be sure, such trends can only be abstracted from the measured properties and capacities of children occupying different positions on an age continuum. But unless the normative investigator takes the further steps of treating these temporally separated phenomena as successive stages of a continuous sequence in which the elaboration of each phase is lawfully related to its precursor, he is dealing less with the nature of change than with a discrete series of unrelated contemporaneous events. In short, the ultimate goal of child development is not simply to produce a series of composite portraits of the child at ages one, three, five, seven, or nine—his physical dimensions and bodily functions, how he eats, sleeps, plays, thinks, feels, and responds to others—but to identify the sequential steps between two levels of maturity, to explain how one is transformed into the other, to discover the variables that effect the transformation, the factors that either facilitate or retard its occurrence, and the uniformities and differences by which it is characterized.

By definition, therefore, the concept of development presupposes that some degree of lawful continuity prevails between successive stages of an ongoing growth process and that the properties of prior phases contribute in part to the form and substance of subsequent phases (Kessen, 1962). Furthermore, in as complex a field as child development, in which innumerable over-lapping areas are simultaneously undergoing change, it is evident that successive chronological ages are representative of more than a series of uniformly spaced points in time. They represent, in addition, progressive stages in the developmental status of the *total* organism* which are also lawfully related to subsequential phases in any *particular* aspect of growth.

The definition of the field formulated above also requires some restatement of several traditionally accepted goals of child development, If, for example, the nature of developmental change is made the primary focus of inquiry in child development research, it follows that the variables contributing to such change become legitimate objects of study only insofar as they are implicated in the developmental process, and not as ends in themselves. This holds true for both environmental factors and for such endogenous variables as the basic structural and functional properties of human beings that remain relatively constant over the age span. How these latter factors influence, direct, and limit growth is obviously a matter of great concern to the child development specialist. But the "mechanics and dynamics" of these properties in their own right—how they are governed and how they operate apart from their relationship to development—constitute "contemporaneous" phenomena which rightfully belong in the domain of anatomy, physiology, biochemistry and psychology.

---

*These two different interpretations of the meaning of chronological age in the conventional growth curve (in which performance or capacity is plotted against age) introduce a possible source of confusion. Unless it is clearly appreciated that chronological age, when interpreted as representative of total development status, is only one of many independent variables operating during the time interval in which growth is studied, all of the measured change may be erroneously attributed to its influence. See Kessen (1960) for a more detailed discussion of this issue.

A somewhat different but related question is the extent to which child development is concerned with the reciprocal influence of organism and environment upon each other. (Anderson, 1954; Kessen, 1960). Since environment is undoubtedly an exceedingly important collective variable participating in the control and regulation of development, one may properly refer to its "impact on the organism." It might be more precise, however, to conceive of the developmental influence wielded by the environment in more indirect terms—as constituting but one of many regulatory vectors which, by interacting, generate in turn the growth matrix that actually determines the direction of development. On the other hand, although the impact of the developing organism on the wider social environment is of great import in social psychology and sociology, it normally lies beyond the scope of child development. It becomes a matter of relevant interest only to the extent that by significantly influencing his more immediate environment in certain cases (e.g., parents, teachers, peers) the child contributes to the external factors shaping his development.

Lastly we would hold that the assessment of the *individual*, either genetically or at a given horizontal level, is not a function indigenous to child development as a field. At this juncture we would invoke the well-established distinction between basic and applied sciences. Thus, as a basic science, child development is concerned with discovering—as an end in itself—growth trends that characterize a designated universe of children. Individual assessment, however, not only leads to no valid generalizations about children, but also implies primary concern with rendering such practical services as guidance, training and therapy. And although the child development specialist can hardly object to the collection of developmental data for single individuals and their subsequent utilization for practical ends, he should in all propriety leave these tasks to appropriately trained specialists in the applied disciplines.

Child Development as a Natural Science

Many of the characteristics of child development as a field, as well as many of its theoretical and methodological problems, stem from the fact that by virtue of its phenomenological content it is primarily a natural rather than an experimental science.

The experimental method has proven eminently satisfactory for the solution of scientific problems in which the crucial variables involved could first be clearly identified and then systematically varied under controlled laboratory conditions. Unfortunately, however, it is neither possible nor feasible to apply experimental procedures to many very significant problems in science. This is especially true when the phenomena under investigation are extremely complex, spatially gross, or of unusually long duration, and when the conditions under which they occur are difficult to identify, control, and reproduce—even by means of miniature scale models. Under these circumstances, the scientist has no other choice but to describe, measure and relate phenomena as they occur naturally in uncontrived situations. Geology, meteorology, astronomy, ecology, sociology and anthropology are typical examples of sciences in which such naturalistic procedures have been employed with great success.

Child development is a natural science for many of the reasons indicated above. Apart from the great number and complexity of the variables involved and the difficulty in identifying, isolating and controlling them under experimental conditions, it is impossible in many instances to create in laboratories situations which exist in real life (Sanford, 1965). Some of the most significant aspects of human development—parent-child relationships, the assimilation of cultural values, relationships with peers, etc.—involve such extended periods of time, such a wide variety of situations, and the cumulative impact of so many repetitive and interlocking experiences, that adequate simulation by experiment would be physically and administratively impossible.

But, even if the latter feat were within the realm of human contrivance, many practical considerations would still render the experimental method unfeasible and ethically undesirable for such problems. We could not synthesize and manipulate human emotions, attitudes, values and interests at will for any length of time and still hope to simulate convincingly their real-life counterparts. Investigators could not in good conscience instruct mothers to reject some children and accept others, to overdominate one sibling and underdominate another, etc. And if they conceivably were rash and unethical enough to make the attempt, would mothers be able and willing to comply with such requests? Similarly, children could not be subjected experimentally to the prolonged and extreme experiences of physical deprivation, emotional frustration, and social abuse that unfortunately occur so frequently under natural auspices. In all of these instances it would be sounder and more practicable to follow the lead of the epidemiologist who studies the incidence, distribution, and etiology of naturally occurring diseases in relation to relevant, naturally occurring conditions (Watson, 1958). This approach is so much more defensible and self-evidently valid that it is extremely unlikely that the epidemiologists ever toy with the idea of creating real epidemics in situ for research purposes or of simulating small scale models of epidemic conditions in the laboratory.

Serious misunderstandings have arisen in the past about the principal reason for the infrequent use of experimental methods in the natural sciences. It is not, as has so frequently been claimed, that the natural scientist has any deep-seated aversion to the fact of simulation per se, i.e., to the element of unnaturalness or artificiality that inheres in transferring a natural phenomenon to a laboratory setting. It is rather that he is unable to simulate *adequately* in his laboratory the conditions that are necessary for studying the significant problems in his field. From the standpoint of scientific method, the truly objectionable aspect of artificiality is not that natural events are contrived by man at arranged times and in arranged places, but that the attempted simulation is not complete or accurate enough to reproduce the essential features and conditions of the problem under investigation. Considered in this light, the more faithfully arrangements can be simulated, the less artificial they become.

Thus, no one looks askance at the artificiality of studying the life cycle and adaptive capacities of bacteria cultured in petri dishes. But should the comparable venture be attempted for tigers in zoos, the hue and cry that would be raised about artificiality would be deafening. And similarly, experimental methods in child development are not necessarily artificial just because they are employed in laboratories. They are only artificial when they are invalidly and inappropriately employed. That is, to the extent that they inadequately represent the conditions or phenomena they purport to simulate in the real-life problem under investigation.

As a matter of fact, as will be pointed out in Chapter 5, in the form of standardized tests, unstructured projective devices, manipulated stress experiences, etc., experimental techniques have an important place among the recognized research methods in child development. In accordance with accepted usage, however, the laboratory or test procedure is not designed to constitute in itself a representative sample of complex, prolonged, or cumulative real-life situations. Rather they are used either (a) to measure the effects of such naturally occurring situations on behavior, capacity, perception, and response tendency, or (b) to simulate a relatively simple and episodic type of real-life situation.

Apart from the question of its intrinsic adequacy for these latter purposes in particular research studies, a related problem obviously bearing on the validity of the laboratory procedure is whether or not it appears artificial to children. But here the relevant criterion of naturalness or artificiality is not the degree of functional equivalence between simulated (laboratory) and natural experience or the extent to which the former is either realistically acted out with the customary props or merely "imagined." All that is required for the appearance of naturalness is sufficient congruence with the child's conception of the universe to permit a reasonable degree of self-involvement in the situation.

We may conclude, therefore, that although experimental techniques do have a legitimate auxiliary place in child development research, answers to the basic problem of how children actually develop in a complex interpersonal, social, and cultural environment will be obtained only as rapidly as adequate and sophisticated naturalistic methods of investigation are evolved. This requires greater acceptance of such methods in child development. It also means coming to grips with the following issues stemming from the status of child development as a natural science: (a) the avoidance of unsystematic, unprecise and biased observations, (Chapter 5); (b) the relationship between theoretical and empirical approaches; (c) the distinction between subjective and objective levels of analysis; and (d) the avoidance of unjustifiable extrapolation in the interpretation of naturalistic data.

Descriptive and Explanatory Levels of Analysis. Ecological investigations of children are not necessarily developmentally oriented simply because they deal with behavior in natural settings—even when they focus in normative fashion upon successive stages in the life cycle. The study of development first begins when normative data, naturalistic or otherwise, are *deliberately* collected or analyzed for the purpose of describing and explaining the *changes* that have occurred in the organism between various designated points in time. It is possible, therefore, to distinguish between two distinct levels of analysis: descriptive and explanatory.

Descriptive analysis takes place completely within the framework of frankly normative studies. Starting only with the assumption that development involves both continuity and a lawful process of transformation, data from single individuals or from entire age groups are first arranged in chronological sequence. The principal characteristics, both quantitative and qualitative, of successive age levels are then tabulated and described as coherently as possible. This preliminary procedure permits the abstraction of common trends and of sequential uniformities and differences between individuals. Similarities and differences between age levels may be pointed out or the data may be subjected to further analysis in terms of various characteristics of subgroups, situational contexts, etc.

Explanatory analysis begins with the questions raised but left unanswered by the normative data. How did the changes occur? What variables were responsible? How did the variables interact with each other and with the prevailing state of the organism? Were some factors more critical than others in effecting transformation? Did susceptibility to change vary from one stage to the next? Were some changes relatively more discontinuous and irreversible than others? Questions such as these lead to explanatory hypotheses and the design of new studies that can test them. Inability to manipulate variables experimentally is a disadvantage but does not necessarily preclude the planning and satisfactory performance of such research. By means of appropriate matching and statistical procedures, sufficient "control" may be established to uncover many significant explanatory relationships among naturally occurring phenomena. Psychological experiments in nature are occurring every day and we need only the proper techniques and facilities to take advantage of them. (Barker, 1965).

Ordinarily, therefore, in the field of child development, descriptive analysis based upon normative studies must be considered logically prior to the planning of explanatory or hypothesis-based research. Before we can attempt to explain how or why certain changes take place during the course of development we need precise information about the actual changes that *do* occur. Otherwise we not only fail to identify the phenomena requiring explanation, but can also do little more than speculate about speculations (i.e., about the nature of hypothesized events) instead of testing hypotheses that might explain demonstrably occurring events. The futility of the latter procedure was clearly evident in the area of children's cognitive development until Piaget's work on children's emergent cognitive development was rediscovered in the late 1950's. Piaget's contribution to child development constitutes the most extensive accumulation of normative data on children's cognitive development to date. Piaget's stage formulation must now be subjected to more rigorous hypotheses centering around the rules of transition (i.e., What are the environmental conditions, predispositional variables, etc., and their interaction, which moves the child from one stage to the next?) (Kessen, 1962).

Despite the fact, that more rigorous hypotheses are tested after normative data is gathered, this does not rule out the utilization of intuitive theorizing in guiding the collection of normative data. Popper (1958-1959) is sharply critical of what he calls the *empiricist fallacy*, that is, the exclusion of theory until empirical observations are gathered.

"The scientist's imagination does not roam about casting up random hypotheses to be tested by him. He starts by thrusting forward ideas he feels to be promising because he senses the availability of resources that will support them—and his imagination then goes on to hammer away in directions felt plausible, bringing up material that has a reasonable chance of confirming these guesses . . . It is a mistake to think of heuristic surmises as well-defined hypothetical statements which the scientist proceeds to test in a neutral and indeed critical spirit. Hunches often consist in narrowing down the originally wider program of inquiry (Polyani 1968; pp. 40-41)."

If theorizing necessarily followed the *empiricists' dictum*, then the imaginative meta-theory which stems from Piaget's background in mathematics, philosophy and biology (Piaget, 1960) would be ruled out of the scientific arena.

Relationship between Empirical and Theoretical Approaches. It is possible in .a sense to regard the preceding discussion as one aspect of the contrast between empirical and theoretical approaches. Explanatory hypotheses obviously deal with more theoretical matters and issues than the descriptive data from which they are derived. Ordinarily, however, a theoretical orientation refers to an organized structure of abstractions and propositions in relation to which a vast array of descriptive and explanatory data as well as interlocking hypotheses and postulates may be systematized and interpreted in meaningful fashion. Theories serve at least three important functions in science: (a) they serve as a guide in the collection of normative data, (b) they make possible the orderly integration of seemingly miscellaneous and unrelated facts and fragments of knowledge under more inclusive generalizations, (c) they lead to a greater economy of research effort by structuring specific explanatory hypotheses along lines that are consistent with a larger body of interrelated principles and empirical findings. In this way hypotheses are both less likely to constitute aimless shots in the dark and to eventuate in data that are difficult to interpret and relate to other findings.

Of course, theoretical formulations in child development may themselves differ widely with respect to the level of generalization at which they are stated. They may deal with the developmental process as a whole or with a relatively circumscribed area of sub-area of growth. Somewhat intermediate between these extremes are theories that attempt to encompass and interrelate developmental changes in the more central, ego-related areas of personality that follow from or contribute to the shifting biosocial status of the individual in his social milieu.

As in all other sciences, empirical and theoretical approaches in child development are interdependent. Unrelated to a comprehensive theoretical framework, hypothesis-based research is wasteful and uneconomical; both the data from which it is derived and the findings it yields, considered as ends in themselves, are chaotic and unintelligible. On the other hand, specific explanatory hypotheses as well as larger bodies of theory that are not anchored to and continually corrected by empirical data are dealing with phenomena and problems the very existence of which is purely speculative.

Fruitful interaction between the two approaches occurs at still another point in the research process. After explanatory hypotheses are related to both descriptive normative data and to theory, preliminary exploratory studies may be profitably conducted before large-scale representative investigations of a longitudinal or cross-sectional nature are launched. (Anderson, 1954; Kessen, 1960). By testing both the general sense of the hypotheses and the feasibility of the proposed methods, this procedure may effect necessary and valuable improvements in conceptualization, design, and measuring instruments. In this way the irrevocable commitment of excessive amounts of time, effort and money to theoretically unsound or practically unfeasible research ventures may be prevented.

In addition to being congruent with the implications of available data, adequate and fruitful theories in child development should conform to the law of parsimony and should be so formulated as to be testable by means of naturalistic investigation. Self-evident or face validity, as well as credibility in terms of the actual reactive capacities of *children*, are also highly desirable attributes of hypothetical constructs, especially in areas where empirical confirmation is difficult or impossible. Lastly, as Lewin suggests, a fundamental objective of theoretical inquiry in a field such as child development is to identify "genotypic" clusters of antecedent regulatory conditions (or states of the organism) the developmental or behavioral products of which are relatively homogeneous in terms of basic origins, even if markedly different in terms of phenotype (i.e., overt appearance). Thus, for example, developmental disequilibrium, in periods of abruptly discontinuous personality growth, is a genotype which may alternately give rise to such diverse phenotypes as resistiveness and ultraconformity (see p. 357). And, on the other hand, the same phenotype of emulatory behavior may, at different stages of development, or in basically different personalities, be a manifestation of such different genotypes as the need for dependence and independence respectively (see p. 251). To use phenotypic similarity as the basis of classification is to reduce this essential tool of scientific systematization to little more than a convenient but arbitrary filing system, and to subvert its primary function of categorizing phenomena in accordance with their underlying commonalities.

Avoidance of Extrapolation. A serious methodological and theoretical hazard confronting all research in the behavioral and social sciences, naturalistic or otherwise, is the almost inevitable tendency to extrapolate unwarrantedly from one phenomenological level to another in observing and interpreting events and relationships. Nevertheless, the utilization of familiar frames of reference and conceptual models for understanding and ordering new sets of experienced relationships is an inescapable fact of cognitive life which hardly merits condemnation. When situations or phenomena are sufficiently comparable to warrant the tentative extension of generalizations from one area to another, new explanatory hypotheses are generated in the simplest possible fashion. In any event before a decision can be reached that direct analogy is unwarranted and that radically new models or frames of reference are required, preliminary examination of similarities and differences and a genuine attempt at reconciliation are first necessary.

Hence, as an *exploratory* procedure in conceptualizing new relationships, extrapolation is by all accounts an unavoidable and desirable process. It is also perfectly legitimate in a more terminal sense if, on the basis of a reasonable degree of comparability between two situations, it leads to the formulation of analogous explanatory hypotheses. It first becomes objectionable (a) if the stage of preliminary and deliberate exploration is by-passed and analogies are accepted automatically or uncritically, (b) if analogous hypotheses are generated in the absence of sufficient essential comparability, and (c) if the extrapolated generalizations are regarded as self-evidently valid propositions rather than as hypotheses to be proven by further research.

The problem, therefore, of deciding whether the terminal phases of extrapolation are justifiable is very similar to the problem of deciding whether experimentally arranged conditions in the laboratory adequately simulate events in nature. An important difference, however, is the fact that in extrapolating one assumes, by definition, the existence of a greater gap between analogous situations as a result of the differential operation of one or more significant variables. Hence, the explanatory generalizations suggested by familiar and approximately comparable models not only always require confirmation by means of additional research in the new contexts to which they are applied, but the relevance (comparability) of the models is also more frequently open to question. The latter problem tends to arise when the introduction of significantly new or different variables creates a qualitatively different order of phenomenology which renders two situations no longer comparable and the application of the original explanatory principles pointless and unprofitable, (Sanford, 1965).

Variability in the relevance of conceptual models is illustrated by the relationship between animal and child development. Many of the same kinds of developmental conditions confront children and the young of infra-human mammals. This is true in situations where the influence of culture is relatively minimal and where the unique reactive capacities of human beings are as yet undeveloped or are not fully called into play. Here generalizations respecting mammalian development may (in the form of explanatory hypotheses) be properly extended to children. But when neither of these conditions prevail, analogies are not apt to prove fruitful, since the mammalian principles when applied to children hold true only in a substrate sense and at a level of generality that has little explanatory value for the particular phenomenon under investigation.

Other typical illustrations of extrapolation in child development include (a) the interpretation of the child in terms of an adult frame of reference or in terms of a synthetic stereotype of a "primitive" adult, and (b) ethnocentric interpretation of the behavior of children in other cultures and subcultures. Thus by attributing mature reaction capacities to infants and children, investigators have "observed" differentiated emotional responses in neonates (Watson, 1919). They have hypothesized the occurrence of anxiety in response to the implications of separation present in the birth experience (Freud, 1936; Rank, 1929), and have "perceived" the operation of complex, adult-like sex drives (including the object of libidinal interest) during the first year of life (Spitz, 1950).

Although it is probably impossible to rid completely the observation and interpretation of children's behavior from the contaminating influence of unwarranted extrapolation, two suggestions may be offered for minimizing it. First, *awareness* of the extrapolating process and *deliberate* use of it as a preliminary conceptualizing technique in the formulation of explanatory hypotheses undoubtedly serve to hold in check the tendency uncritically to accept far-fetched and basically untenable analogies. Second, if the development of children at a given stage of maturity is *first* interpreted from the standpoint of their known perceptual, cognitive, and reactive capacities, and in relation to the known environmental context in which it occurs, the aptness of using generalizations from other fields as the basis of explanatory hypotheses may be judged more explicitly, and appropriate modifications of the latter may be made.

Objective and Subjective Dimensions of Development. In studying the development of the child, it is possible to focus either on the more objectively observable aspects of growth such as physical size and motor capacity, intellectual and language performance, and overt emotional and social behavior, or on the more subjective aspects of psychological experience such as perceptions, feelings, motives and attitudes. Although the former can undoubtedly be investigated more directly and with greater validity, it cannot for this reason be considered more indigenous to the field. As a matter of fact, many of the more significant aspects of development are concerned precisely with subjective meanings and reactions.

The subjective content of children's behavior and development may in turn be divided into two main categories of experience: (a) children's perceptions of the environment, and (b) their non-overt, conscious reactions to these perceptions. The perceptual world has been variously referred to as the psychological life-space or habitat. (Barker 1965; Lewin 1954). It, rather than the stimulus world, is the proximate external determinant of both the subjective and objective components of behavior. That is, the individual responds to the world as it exists for him, not to its objectively ascertainable stimulus characteristics. His subjective reactions to these perceptions are feelings, attitudes, values and aspirations. Thus, for example, loss or gain in social status is an objective event in the real world; but an individual only responds to it with subjective feelings of adequacy or inadequacy in terms of the status change that he *perceives*.

Subjective aspects of development may also be approached from the standpoint of descriptive or explanatory analysis. Normative investigation, for example, may establish that "the world in which the newborn, the one-year-old, and the ten-year-old child live are different even in identical physical and social surroundings." (Lewin 1954). The crucial explanatory problem, however, is to discover how and why the objective world is perceived differently at successive points in the life cycle. How do perceptual maturity, general developmental status, and personality factors interact with the stimulus properties of the environment to produce characteristic age-level differences in perception? Similarly, it is important to go beyond a simple statement of relationship and to ascertain how and on what basis certain perceptions interact with the existing capacities and personality structure of the individual to generate various feelings, motives, attitudes and values, (Harvey, Hunt and Schroder, 1961). This latter (reactive) aspect of subjective experience never involves a *direct* relationship to the "material-cultural world," although superficially this may seem to be the case since the intervening process of perceptual mediation is seldom observed. *

The investigation of subjective dimensions of development is naturally fraught with grave methodological hazards. The observer can never share directly the content of a child's experience but must always resort to inferences from his behavior and verbalizations. To really make contact with the subjective stratum of experience, however, he must attempt to relate himself to the child, to participate in his experiences, to empathize with him, to perceive the world through his eyes, and to react to such perceptions from the standpoint of the latter. Observations made in this way are, of course, always subject to the contaminating influence of extrapolation, particularly from the observer's own experience and adult frame of reference. Here extrapolation already enters the picture at the stage of obtaining descriptive data, even before explanatory analysis is attempted. Other methods of investigation include direct verbal (introspective) reports from the child and the indirect elicitation of subjective content by means of projective devices. These techniques are discussed in Chapter 5.

Justification as a Separate Field of Specialization

In recent years the question of whether child development constitutes a legitimate field of specialization has been raised with increasingly greater insistence. Are the interests of scientific progress best served by the present arrangement, or would it be more desirable to reorganize the subject matter it presently encompasses under the various component disciplines and subdisciplines from which it is derived? Answers to this question can only be framed in terms of such criteria as convenience, developmental trends in the history of science, and the potentiality of a given organizational scheme for solving significant problems in a unique area of scientific inquiry and, hence, for ultimately facilitating the solution of problems of practical importance in human affairs.

---

*In a negative sense, however, the environment may be considered to exert a direct limiting influence on the subjective components of behavior. The absence of certain physical or social conditions in the lives of particular individuals of groups need not be perceived in order to be related to a corresponding lack of subjective reactive experience or growth.

One familiar argument for abolishing child development as a separate field is based on the premise that, as human beings, children are subject to the same physiological and behavioral laws that govern all individuals irrespective of age. This, of course, is true for a great number of functions such as intracellular oxidation, the formation of urine in the kidneys, the basic optical phenomena underlying vision, and the temporal and reinforcement arrangements affecting the establishment of conditioned reflexes. On the other hand, there are a whole host of physiological, immunological, nutritional and behavioral phenomena which undergo marked qualitative as well as quantitative change over the course of childhood. The identification of these changes as a function of age and the discovery of their nature and regulation constitute the distinctive subject matter of child development, whereas the former category of phenomena belong in the realm of "contemporaneous" science. And as already noted it is the concern with the properties of *change* rather than with children as an age category of characteristically functioning individuals that stamp the field as developmental in orientation.

A second type of argument disputing the desirability of retaining child development as a field of specialization does not challenge the easily demonstrable fact that many structural, functional and behavioral properties of children vary with developmental status. Instead, the point is made that the changes attributable to age (like those related to other independent variables such as sex and socioeconomic status) could be adequately and more advantageously considered under other recognized fields of specialization, e.g., physical anthropology, medicine, psychology and its various subdivisions. However, while this arrangement would undoubtedly suffice for specialists in these other areas it would constitute a highly inconvenient, scattered, and fragmentary organization of knowledge for persons primarily interested in human development. It would hardly provide an integrated picture of how *many* different functions change with age, of the interrelationships among them, or of *total* developmental status at a given age level. But perhaps the most serious disadvantage of all is the fact that studied adjunctively in this fashion, changes related to age would tend to be analyzed on a descriptive rather than on an explanatory level; and with developmental findings scattered over many fields, it would be difficult indeed to abstract general principles of development transcending particular functions.

Child Development versus Child Psychology. Although often used interchangeably to describe the same field, child psychology and child development are actually quite different in at least two important respects. First, child development covers a much broader and more interdisciplinary canvas, dealing with *all* the facets of childhood, not merely with phenomena that are psychological in nature. Strictly speaking, therefore, it includes such topics as the physiological, nutritional and immunological changes occurring with

increasing age, age changes in response to disease-producing and therapeutic agents, etc. However, because courses in child development are
generally designed for students in psychology, education and home economics, these more medically oriented aspects of development are customarily reserved for treatises on pediatrics. The actual field and technical
literature are broader and more interdisciplinary than is apparent from text
books in child development. Yet latter works are traditionally restricted to
the different aspects of psychological development supplemented by a consideration of prenatal development, the birth process, physical (primarily
skeletal) growth and motor development. Even so, they draw on data from
such diverse fields as genetics, embryology, physical anthropology, pediatrics,
psychology, psychiatry, education, sociology, and ethnology. Second, the
emphasis in child psychology more usually (although not necessarily) tends
to be on the characteristic behavior and conscious processes of different age
levels of children as ends in themselves rather than on the nature and regulation of the intervening changes. In this sense, a particular aspect of the child
(i.e., the psychological) in contradistinction to its developmental history in
childhood serves as the primary focus of concern and the distinctive feature of
the specialty. In short, child development may be considered that branch of
developmental anatomy, physiology, psychology, etc., dealing with the early
phases of the life cycle, whereas child psychology deals with only one aspect of
the child and not necessarily in terms of a developmental approach. As a field
the latter is more comparable to pediatrics and child psychiatry.

Age Periods in Child Development. For purposes of convenience it has been
found worthwhile to divide human development into the four age periods of
childhood, adolescence, maturity and senescence. This classification, of
course, is somewhat arbitrary, but can be rationalized on the grounds of the
relative homogeneity of both biosocial status and of the rate of change
characterizing development at each of these stages. On the basis of the same
criteria, child development in turn may be subdivided into the following six
age periods; *prenatal*, from conception to birth; *neonatal*, the first two to four
weeks of life; *infancy*, the remainder of the first two years; *preschool*, ages two
to six; *middle childhood* or primary school, ages six to nine; and *preadolescence*,
age nine to the onset of adolescence.

Applications of Child Development

As a basic science, child development is concerned with the discovery of
general laws in its area of special concern as an end in itself. Ultimately, of
course, such laws have self-evident implications for the realization of certain
practical goals which have social value. These include better understanding
of individual children, more desirable methods of child rearing, the guidance
and treatment of deviant children, and the improvement of education.

However, because of widespread misunderstanding of the relationship between child development and these problems of *applied* science, much unwarranted and premature extrapolation of findings has taken place. It is
necessary, therefore, to deal more explicitly with the limitations and hazards
involved in applying such data and generalizations to the solution of problems for which they were not originally intended. Two separate issues involving different degrees of extrapolation require consideration here:
(a) the utilization of child development generalizations for interpreting and
predicting the development of the *individual* and evaluating his current
behavior (this type of diagnostic and prognostic use is a necessary preliminary step in child rearing, guidance and therapy); and (b) the application of knowledge form child development research in devising efficacious
educational and guidance procedures for individuals or groups.

Interpreting and Predicting Individual Development. Many generalizations in
child development are statements of uniformities and differences and of
relationships between variables that apply to a designated universe of individuals. They are directly applicable to the understanding of the development of individual members of the universe for which they hold in the sense
that prediction from one variable to another (e.g., from antecedents to
consequences or vice versa) is possible within a certain margin of error.
However, because we almost always deal with multiple causality in as complex a field as child development, predictions for individuals must be made
from multiple regression equations. For example, assuming that the respective degrees of relationship between a majority of significant causal factors
and the occurrence of a given outcome were established, it would be possible
to predict, with a fair degree of accuracy, the probability with which the
event in question would occur in a particular individual, providing that the
specific values of these factors in the latter were known. This type of prediction, of course, is implicit in the original statement of relationship. Extrapolation is not required unless generalizations are invoked involving variables
and relationships that are only indirectly related to the problem of development for which individual predictions are sought.

Unfortunately, however, the limiting conditions inherent in this modest
statement of applicability are frequently ignored. Child development
specialists are often embarrassed and dismayed when credited with omniscience by persons who seek precise developmental diagnoses and prognoses
of children's behavior deviations on the basis of very inadequate data. At
least five common misunderstandings are involved in this practice. First, it is
seldom realized that more than one variable contributes to the condition
under discussion; hence, no information is furnished about many other
significant factors. Second, even if such data are available, reliable assessment of the status of all relevant variables in the particular individual is

necessary before diagnosis or prognosis can be attempted. This implies first-hand evaluation by a trained person rather than casual judgment based upon hearsay evidence of unknown reliability by a presumed expert who may very well lack experience in the specific problem. Third, it is not fully appreciated that because child development is primarily concerned with general growth trends, most research findings are only highly tangential to many practical problems and developmental deviations in individuals. Thus, greater caution than is customarily employed is indicated if unwarranted extrapolation is to be avoided. Fourth, generalizations are frequently applied to individuals who cannot even remotely be considered members of the universe for whom they are valid. Lastly, many uncritical enthusiasts tend to accept diagnoses and prognoses as absolute pronouncements of fact rather than as the conditional statements of probability which they really are.

In addition to generalized statements of relationships, *normative* findings in child development are also directly applicable to the understanding of the individual child. In evaluating his *current* behavior, it is imperative that we first place it in its appropriate developmental setting, i.e., assess it in terms of the maturational standards and range of variability that prevail for children passing through the comparable period of development. Otherwise, gross distortions in interpretation are inevitable. However, this procedure obviously does not provide in itself a complete explanation of a given sequence of individual behavior. Other necessary information includes the unique personality attributes of the individual as well as significant characteristics of the immediate situation and of the wider cultural setting.

Relationship to Child Rearing, Guidance and Education. Somewhat more indirect than the application of child development research to the understanding of individual development and behavior, is its application to the *manipulative* aspects of child rearing, guidance, and education. Developmental generalizations are obviously germane to the aims and methods of these applied sciences. In a very general sense, for example, they indicate the effects of different interpersonal and social climates on personality development and the kinds of methods and subject matter content that are most compatible with capacity and mode of functioning at a given stage of growth. But at the applied level, specific ends and conditions are added which demand *additional* research before such basic science generalizations become explicitly useful in practical situations. Thus, for example, the principle of developmental readiness in learning is of little practical value to the teacher unless tendered more specific in terms of different backgrounds, subject matters, levels of difficulty, and techniques of instruction.

On the more positive side, however, it can be stated that although child development findings do not ordinarily provide explicit answers to specific problems in these applied disciplines, they are extremely useful in other more indirect ways. First, as already indicated, they contribute to the evaluation of the individual child's behavior and development—a necessary precondition for employing rational child rearing, guidance and educational measures on an individual basis. Second, they constitute part of the basic theoretical background required for intelligent professional work in the above applied disciplines. Third, they provide a general theoretical orientation for devising research hypotheses and interpreting empirical data in the applied fields which ultimately raises the level at which such research can be performed.

Reasons for Studying Child Development

By way of summary the following reasons may be offered for studying child development:

First and foremost, an understanding of the nature and regulation of developmental processes in children based upon a critical interpretation of the empirical evidence is regarded as an important end in itself, quite apart from its applicability to practical problems. Such knowledge certainly holds as much intrinsic interest for most persons as do other developmental sciences (e.g., embryology, biological evolution) which are generally pursued without regard for their immediate utility in everyday life.

Second, provided that certain precautions are observed, generalizations in child development are applicable to the understanding and prediction of the development of particular children.

Third, normative child development findings make possible the evaluation of an individual's current behavior in terms of the maturational standards and of the distinctive developmental tasks and problems of his age group.

Lastly, by virtue of the previous two reasons, and because it provides a general theoretical orientation for professional and research workers in related applied fields, child development may be considered one of the basic sciences for such disciplines as child guidance, child psychiatry, pediatrics and education. Thorough grounding in the scientific literature of child development presumably fosters a cautious and critical attitude toward transitory fads in child care and promotes the search for sound and rational procedures in the management of practical problems. And because of developmental continuity, knowledge of child development is obviously valuable for educators, psychologists, psychiatrists, social workers and others whose professional concern is with adolescents and adults.

CHAPTER 2

Historical Overview of Theoretical Trends

Both on historical grounds and for purposes of convenience, the major theoretical issues in child development may be divided into two main categories: (a) issues dealing with the *control* and *regulation* of development, and (b) issues dealing with all of the other (i.e., *nonregulatory*) properties, of the developmental process. The first category is concerned with the factors that determine development, their interaction and relative influence. Of paramount importance here is the regulation of developmental uniformities and differences prevailing between individuals exposed to similar and dissimilar cultural settings, and the respective contributions of heredity and environment to different developmental acquisitions. Subsumed under this general issue are such problems as the theory of recapitulation, the nature of maturation, the origin of drives, similarities and differences between animal and human endowment, and the meaning of human nature and cultural relativism. The second general class of theoretical issues, on the other hand, is concerned with such problems as continuity and discontinuity in the maintenance of developmental individuality. It is also concerned with reversibility and irreversibility in development, the organization of behavior, characteristics of transitional periods in development, parallelism and unevenness in the component aspects of growth, developmental regression, etc.

Both categories of issues will be discussed in every chapter of the book in relation to personality and various special aspects of development. But as already described elsewhere, for purposes of providing an integrated substrate for a general theory of child development, an overview of the regulatory issues will be presented in Chapter 3 and of other developmental principals in Chapter 4. The present chapter will be devoted to a brief historical survey of various trends and currents of thought dealing with the nature of the child and the control of development. It is primarily intended as a conceptual introduction to the more detailed discussion in Chapter 3.

The regulation of human development is still very much of a live and highly controversial issue. The nature-nurture controversy as such has abated somewhat in the sense that the two factors are now seldom regarded as mutually exclusive or as operative on an either-or basis. Interaction between them in determining the direction of growth is widely accepted in many quarters. Nevertheless much disagreement still persists, regarding their relative influence with respect to particular aspects of development, and very little is known about the mechanisms through which such interaction is mediated. Furthermore, the same basic issue of the regulation of development turns up in relation to many other theoretical problems in which it is often only dimly perceived as being relevant. These include the doctrines of maturation and recapitulation, psychoanalytic theories of personality, hypotheses regarding the nature of drives, various conceptions of cultural relativism, etc. For these reasons, therefore, more explicit consideration of the historical roots of and relationships between different ideological trends bearing on this issue may prove rewarding.

PREFORMATIONIST APPROACHES

Historical analysis shows that an interactional point of view regarding the role of internal and external determinants of development is of relatively recent origin. Over the past few centuries, and even in our own time, the theories of development that have wielded most influence have either stressed (a) an environmentally oriented *tabula rasa* approach or (b) a preformationist or predeterministic approach emphasizing the contributions of endogenous and innate factors.

The fundamental thesis of preformationism is a denial of the essential occurrence and importance of development in human ontogeny. The basic properties and behavioral capacities of man—his personality, values and motives, his perceptual, cognitive, emotional and social reaction tendencies —are not conceived as undergoing qualitative differentiation and transformation over the life span, but are presumed to exist preformed at birth. Nothing need develop as a result of the interaction between a largely undifferentiated organism with certain stipulated predispositions and his particular environment. Instead everything is already prestructured, and either undergoes limited quantitative modification with increasing age or merely unfolds sequentially on a prearranged schedule.

The origins of preformationist thinking are not difficult to trace. On the one hand, it is obviously related to theological conception of man's instantaneous creation and to the widespread belief in the innateness of the individual's personality and sense of unique identity as a person. A quaint prescientific embryological counterpart of this point of view is the formerly popular homuncular theory of human reproduction and prenatal gestation. It was seriously believed that a miniature but fully-formed little man (i.e., an homuculus) was embodied in the sperm, and when implanted in the uterus simply grew in bulk, without any differentiation of tissues or organs, until full-term fetal size was attained at the end of nine months.

On the other hand, the disposition to perceive the infant or child as a miniature adult is largely an outgrowth of the ubiquitous tendencey toward extrapolation or anthropomorphism in interpreting phenomena remote from own experience or familiar explanatory models. What is easier than to explain the behavior of others in terms of one's own response potentialities? In order to extend this orientation to the interpretation of the child's behavior, it was necessary, of course, to endow him with the basic attributes of adult motivation, perceptual maturity and reaction capacities. Modern and extreme expressions of this tendency include such widely accepted psychoanalytic views that the prototype of all later anxiety lies in the psychological trauma of birth (Freud, 1936; Rank 1929), that infantile and adult sexuality are qualitatively equivalent (Freud, 1935) and that infants are presumably sensitive to the subtlest shadings of parental attitudes.

The theological variety of preformationism, allied as it was to a conception of man as innately sinful, inspired a rigid, authoritarian and pessimistic approach to education. Since ultimate form was assumed to be prestructed and complete in all of its essential aspects, one could at best only improve slightly on what the individual already was or was fated to become. Hence, it was unnecessary to consider the child's developmental needs and status, the conditions propitious for development at a given stage of maturity, or readiness for particular experience. Because he was not perceived as qualitatively different from the adult or as making any significant contribution to his own development, the arbitrary imposition of adult standards was regarded as self-evidently defensible.

Innate Ideas

Philosophically, in the realm of cognition, preformationism was represented by the doctrine of innate ideas, i.e., ideas existing independently of individual experience.* Vigorously combatted, by John Locke (1632-1704) and other empiricists, this notion consistently waned in influence and all but disappeared from view until revived and made popular by psychoanalytic theorists. Jung (1928) for example, postulated the existence in the "racial unconscious" of such inborn ideas as eternality, omnipotence, reincarnation, male and female, mother and father. And Freud's (1935) analagous "phylogenetic unconscious" included—as the basis for resolving the Oedipus complex— an inherited identification with the like-sexed parent prior to any opportunity for actual interpersonal experience.

---

*The content and validity of this and other historically important concepts will be considered more fully elsewhere in this chapter and in Chapter 3. Here we are only concerned with gaining historical perspective.

Human Instincts

On a behavioral level, preformationist doctrines have flourished in various theories of instincts and innate drives. Influenced by studies of inframammalian behavior and by the early nativistic implications of Mendelian genetics, psychologists, represented by such notable figures as McDougall (1914) and Thorndike (1919) devised elaborate lists of human instincts, e.g., mating, maternal, acquisitive, pugnacious, gregarious. These were conceived an unlearned, complexly patterned, sequentially organized responses, perfectly executed on initial performance, that either unfolded in due course or were triggered off by appropriate environmental cues. But undermined by the rising tide of behaviorism in the 1920's, by demonstrations of numerous forms of conditioned responses, and by research findings in infrahuman primate development, ethnology, and sociology which pointed to the acquired, experiental basis of such behavior, this variety of instinct theory as applied to human behavior has long since passed into oblivion.

Primary and Libidinal Drives

Doctrines deeply rooted in cultural tradition do not die easily. Rejected in one guise, they subsequently gain reacceptance in other more palatable forms. Thus, instinctual theories reappeared respectively in stimulus or viscerogenic constructs of "primary drives" and in psychoanalytic conceptions of libidinal drives. The former notion, which was more compatible with the prevailing behavioristic and biologically oriented climate of psychological opinion, assumed the existence of a certain irreducible number of states of physiological disequilibrium which supposedly constituted in themselves the innate, energizing basis of motivated behavior. These states (i.e., primary drives) were, by definition, conceived of as innate and inevitable since their operation was simply a function of the presence of persistent visceral or humoral stimuli within the organism or of intense external stimuli (e.g., pain) to which the organism invariably responded in predetermined ways.

Libidinal drives, in contrast, were conceptualized as innate, substantive sources of energy virtually independent of internal or external stimulation. Because the uninhibited expression of such drives seemed to engender a conflict of interest between biologically related needs of the individual and the mores of his culture, and because their sequential appearance was couched in terms of pyschosexual "development," this point of view was more congruent than other instinct theories with the theoretical leanings of the more dynamically oriented psychiatrists, clinical psychologists and social anthropologists. Actually, however, no more development was envisaged than in any other orthodox, preformationist concept of instinct, for the energizing aspect of the libidinal drives, their locus, mode, and object of expression, and the sequential order of their appearance were all prestructured in advance; and although the emergence of later-appearing drives necessarily had to be latent at first, their eventual unfolding was assured without any intervening process of transformation or interaction with individual experience.

Thus, despite their differences with respect to the source and nature of the fundamental drives, both "primary" and libidinal drive theorists agreed that the energizing basis of human behavior was innate and inevitable. Furthermore, both groups tended to regard the preformed drives as original and all other drives as derived from them through the various mechanisms of conditioning, symbolic equivalence, and sublimation. In other words, the environment was not conceived as capable of independently generating drives but only as repressing, modifying, differentiating and re-channeling innate drives.

Freud and his followers also derived the other two layers of personality, the ego and superego (i.e., conscience), from the libidinal instincts as they came into contact with a repressive reality and had to adapt to its demands. Similarly, character traits were conceptualized as symbolical derivatives of fixated libido at one of the stages of infantile psychosexual development following inordinate experiences of frustration or gratification. In all of these latter instances, it is true, preformationist concepts as such were not employed. Environmental vicissitudes were granted a share in the developmental process, but only in the sense of modifying or accentuating a preformed product rather than of participating crucially in the directional regulation of new patterns.

PREDETERMINISTIC APPROACHES

In contradistinction to preformationism, predeterministic doctrines satisfy the minimal criteria of a developmental approach. Successive stages of the organism are not merely regarded as reflective of a sequential unfolding of preformed structures or functions forever fixed at conception or birth, but as the outcome of a process of qualitative differentiation or evolution of form. Nevertheless, because the regulation of development is conceived as so prepotently determined by internal factors, the net effect is much the same as if preformationism were assumed. Interaction with the environment and the latter's influence on the course of development is not completely ruled out; but its directional role is so sharply curtailed that it never crucially affects eventual outcome, accounting at the very most for certain minor limiting or patterning effects.

Rousseau and the Educational Philosophers

The first definitive predeterministic theory of child development was elaborated by the famous French philosopher, J. J. Rousseau (1712-1778). Rousseau postulated that all development consists of a series of internally regulated sequential stages which are transformed, one into the other, in conformity with a prearranged order and design (Rousseau, 1895). According to this conception of development, the only proper role of the environment is avoidance of serious interference with the processes of self-regulation and spontaneous maturation. It facilitates development best not by imposing restrictions or setting coercive goals and standards, but by providing a maximally permissive field in which, unhampered by the limiting and distortive influences of external constraints, the predetermined outcomes of growth are optimally realized. Consistent with this orientation was Rousseau's belief that the child is innately good, that society constitutes the source of all evil, and that a return to a less inhibited and less socially restrictive method of child rearing would necessarily result in the unfolding of the individual's inherently wholesome and virtuous developmental proclivities.

The educational implications of these doctrines, which in essence were shared by such distinguished followers of Rousseau as Pestalozzi (1746-1827) and Froebel (1782-1852), were in marked contrast to those of the preformationists (Froebel, 1896; Pestalozzi, 1895). Prominent recognition was given to the child's contributions to his own development, to his developmental needs and status, to his expressed interests and spontaneously undertaken activities, and to the importance of an unstructed, noncoercive instructional climate. This point of view has, of course, exercised tremendous influence on all subsequent educational theory and practice, and is essentially identical and, in a sense, historically continuous with present-day movements advocating a nondirective and child-centered approach to the training, education, and guidance of children.

The Doctrine of Recapitulation: G. Stanley Hall

An especially fanciful but historically significant facet of Rousseau's (and later of Froebel's) conception of development was the theory that the child, in progressing through the various stages of his growth toward maturity, recapitulates the phylogenetic and cultural history of the human race. The analogy was only crudely drawn. However, it served the purpose of providing a seemingly plausible explanation (a) for the hypothesized internal regulation of development, and (b) for the predetermined inevitability of its outcome in a direction which presumably paralleled the ascending spiral of cultural evolution. More than a century later, G. Stanley Hall (1846-1924) elaborated and refined this theory in great detail, postulating many ingenious and specific parallelisms between various hypothetical epochs in the history of civilization (e.g., arboreal, cave-dwelling, pastoral and agricultural) and supposedly analogous stages in the development of the behavior and play interests of the child (Hall, 1904).

These speculations, which were advanced with great skill, comprehensiveness and internal consistency, acquired considerable vogue and many enthusiastic adherents. Their initial favorable reception was attributable, perhaps, to the fact that they were in accord with the prevailing evolutionary approach to cultural anthropology, and superficially, at least, seemed congruous with certain broad generalizations linking embryology and biological evolution. They were also bolstered by the prevalent beliefs that the thought processes of the civilized child are comparable to those of a stereotyped "primitive" adult (the "primitive mind" fallacy) and that the cultures of contemporary primitive peoples are analogous to the early stages of more advanced civilizations. Later, following more searching examination in the light of emerging data in comparative child development, and of changing concepts regarding the complex interrelationships between cultural environment, genetic endowment and individual development, this theoretical orientation was no longer accepted as a parsimonious and potentially fruitful approach to problems in developmental psychology (see p. 35).

Theory of Maturation: Arnold Gesell*

With the collapse of Hall's elaborate theory of recapitulation, predeterministic theories of development received a serious setback, but they by no means disappeared from the scene. They simply assumed other forms more compatible with the prevailing theoretical climate. Perhaps the most influential and widely accepted of all present-day predeterministic approaches is Arnold Gesell's theory of maturation which reiterates Rousseau's emphasis upon the internal control of development, but discards the specific parallelisms between cultural history and individual development which made Hall's position so vulnerable to attack.

Gesell's theory also capitalized on its general resemblance to the empirically demonstrable concept of maturation which had gained considerable acceptance among behavioral scientists, educators and the lay public. Actually, the latter concept dealt with the non-learning (as distinguished from the learning) contributions to enhancement in capacity, rather than with the more general issue of the relative importance of internal and external regulatory factors in development irrespective of the role of learning. Operationally it merely referred to increments in functional capacity attributable to structural growth, physiological change or the cumulative impact of incidental experience, in contradistinction to increments attributable to specific practice

---

*See Ausubel, D. P.: Theory and Problems of Adolescent Development, 1954.

experience (i.e., learning). Gesell, however, used the term *maturation* in a very special and more global sense to represent the endogenous regulatory mechanisms responsible for determining the essential direction of *all* development, including that conditioned in part by learning and enculturation.

In essence, Gesell proposed an embryological model for all aspects of human growth—structural, physiological, behavioral and psychological—which "are obedient to identical laws of developmental morphology" (Gesell, 1954). In *all* of these areas alike, a growth matrix consisting of endogenous factors supposedly determines the basic direction of differentiation and patterning, whereas "environmental factors (merely) support, inflect and modify, but . . . . do not generate the progressions of development" (Gesell, 1954). These intrinsic regulatory factors correspond to "ancestral genes" which in general reflect the evolutionary adaptive achievements of the race, but neither refer to specific epochs in cultural history nor condition the development of analogous ontogenetic phases (Gesell, 1933).

Because phylogenetic genes by definition have a species-wide distribution and are unusually potent in their effects, Gesell theorized that developmental sequences are relatively invariable in all areas of growth, evolve more or less spontaneously and inevitably, and show basic uniformities even in strikingly different cultural settings. Like Hall before him, he taught that certain undesirable stages in behavioral development were inevitable by virtue of the child's phylogenetic inheritance, and could be handled best by allowing them spontaneously to run their natural course without interference. Since comparable endogenous factors assured the eventual unfolding of more acceptable behavior, permissiveness and patience on the part of the parents, and self-regulation and self-discipline on the part of the child could be confidently relied upon to correct the situation. The application of parental expectations, demands, limitations and controls was not only regarded as unnecessary but also as calculated to increase negativism and to impair the parent-child relationship (Gesell and Ilg, 1943).

This embryological model is basically tenable when applied to the development of structures, functions and behaviors which are phylogenetic in nature, i.e., which characterize all individuals of a given species. It could apply to the total development of members of lower phyla, to the prenatal behavioral development of human beings and of much of the sensori-motor growth that occurs during human infancy.* But as far as the greater part of postnatal

---

Gesell's (1933) embryological model does not deny that environmental events have some effects. His position on the role of the environment is that it inflects and modifies development but does not determine it. The effects of deleterious environmental influences during gestation (Mussen, Conger and Kagan, 1963; McClearn, 1964) and severe postnatal experiences (Dennis, 1960; Fowler, 1965) which clearly alter the normal pattern of development during pregnancy and later motor development, does not necessarily contradict Gesell's model since his position takes these extreme environmental effects into consideration. Such influences arrest or distort the genically determined direction of development (e.g., abortion, still birth, prematurity, malformation) but do not initiate any development progressions of their own, i.e., do not determine the direction of development.

psychological development in the human species is concerned, unique factors of individual experience and cultural environment make important contributions to the direction, patterning and sequential order of all developmental changes. Not only is there significantly greater variability in the content and sequence of development, but also the uniformities that do occur (both intra- and interculturally) largely reflect the existence of common problems of physical and social adaptation and common culturally derived solutions to these problems.

Theory of Intellectual Development: Piaget

In contemporary developmental theory, Piaget's formulation of intellectual development can also be characterized as predeterministic with certain qualifications and reservations (Piaget, 1960, 1964, 1965).* Piaget has postulated that cognitive development proceeds through a fixed sequence of stages from infancy to adulthood. Intellectual development emerges through three main stages and also various substagtes:† (1) *Sensori-motor* (birth to 2 years); (2) *Pre-operational* (2 to 7 years) which is subdivided into the earlier *preconceptual* stage (2 to 4 years) and later *intuitive* stage (4 to 7 years); (3) *concrete operational* (7 to 11 years) and (4) the *later formal operational stage* (11 to 16 years). The development through these stages moves from concrete, stimulus modes of thinking to more abstract, stimulus controlled modes of thinking. The essential component of his stage motion is not age, but the fixed order of succession (Inhelder, 1953, 1962). Piaget is aware of the effects of cultural differences, social class, intelligence, etc., (cited in Ausubel, 1968) which change the age parameters of his stages.

In delineating the factors which effect transition through his stages of intellectual development, Piaget subscribes to an interactional position. He postulates four main factors to explain the development from one stage to another (Piaget, 1964, 1965): (1) *Maturation* in Gesell's sense is important, since development is a continuation of embryogenesis. The effects of maturation have the same qualifications as seen in Gesell since:

> Maturation of the nervous system *can do* no more than determine the totality of possibilities and impossibilities at a given stage. A particular social environment remains indispensable for the realization of these possibilities; it follows that their realization can be accelerated or retarded as a function of cultural and educational conditions (Inhelder & Piaget, 1958, p. 337).

(2) *Social Interaction* effects stage development through transmission in the broad sense of language and education: (3) *Physical experience* in the sense of acting upon objects and drawing some knowledge about the objects by abstractions from the objects, as well as the converse, where the knowledge is

---

*See Sullivan (1968) for a more extensive discussion af Piagets' predeterministic position.

†Piaget at different times has outlined his stages in different ways than from those stated above. This is not a discrepancy however, since the different stage breakdowns are still concerned with the same observations.

not drawn from object, but derived by the actions effected upon the objects, and finally: (4) *Equilibration* (self-regulation) considered by Piaget the most fundamental, subsuming the others, and defined as the progressive interior organization of knowledge in a step-wise fashion. In order to clarify Piaget's notion of equilibration, (self-regulation) it is necessary to consider it within the general framework of his definition of intelligence. Piaget (1960) defines intelligence (functionally) as a process of adaptation and organization. Adaptation is seen as an equilibration (equilibrium)* in the organism's interaction with its environment. Organization is a concept which is structural and this involves the constant organization, reorganization, and integration of what Piaget calls the schemas. Schemas are defined as essentially repeatable, psychological units of intelligent action (Piaget, 1960). The best interpretation of this definition is that schemas are types of "programs" or "strategies" that the individual has at his disposal when interacting with the environment.

Adaptation involves the two invariant processes of assimilation and accommodation. Assimilation is the incorporation of the environment into present patterns of behavior. Accommodation is the change in the intellectual structures (schemas) which are necessary in order for the person to adjust to demands which the external environment make on the individual.

Equilibration involves a balance between the two invariant processes of assimilation and accommodation. When imbalance occurs the organism is forced to change its schemas (i.e., strategies) in order to adjust to the demands of the external environment (adaptation). When the organism attempts to adapt to the environment with the already existing schemas assimilation is said to be in operation. The postulation of schemas as mental processes by which past experiences are stored and made partial determinants of present behavior is significant, because it implies that the organism perceives the environment in terms of its existing organization. Disequilibration or imbalance exists when assimilation is unsuccessful. Accommodation occurs as a result of disequilibration and the alteration or emergence of new schemas ensues. Cognitive development is marked by a series of equilibration-disequilibration states. Stages such as those postulated by Piaget's theory may be considered as particular sets of strategies (schemas) which are in a relative state of equilibration at some point in the child's development. The development from one stage to the next in Piaget's framework involves a hierarchical organization of preceding and successive stages. Simply stated, the lower stage is coordinated and integrated into the next higher stage.

---

*In a more recent article Piaget has expressed a preference for equilibration over equilibrium which he feels has a static connotation. For purposes of consistency we will use the word equilibration (Piaget, 1965).

The classification of Piaget as a predeterminist (despite his interactional profession) comes from the relative weight that he attributes to the previously mentioned factors. It is clearly evident that Piaget (1964) places prime importance and prominence on the equilibration factor. In explaining how developmental transition occurs, Piaget and his followers (e.g., Smedslund, 1961) deny that specific learning experience or training (practice), particularly of a verbal nature, or for that matter, education generally has any significant influence on the emergence of stages of intellectual development. The effects of *social interaction* is only given lip service in his theory.

Piaget's (1964) dichotomy between development and learning further emphasizes the previous point. *Development* is a spontaneous process tied to embryogenesis, while *learning* is induced by external situations. Piaget (1964) contends that the development of knowledge (stage transition) is a spontaneous process tied to the whole of embryogenesis. Like Gesell, he notes that *embryogenesis* not only concerns bodily development, but also the nervous system and mental functions; thus *development* is a process which involves the totality of the structures of knowledge. *Learning* is a much more restricted process in Piaget's framework provoked by situations (e.g., didactic teaching, psychological experimenters, etc.) and is limited to *single* problems of *single* structures.

Piaget is thus regarded as predominantly a predeterminist because of his rather consistent emphasis on the *spontaneous* aspects of development, and his complete subordination of learning to this unfolding of genic factors and spontaneously occurring self-regulation (internal ripening). The sharp line that he draws between the child's ideas of reality developed mainly through his own mental efforts (equilibration) and those that are decisively influenced by the external environment (learning) is further highlighted by his distinction between *spontaneous* and *nonspontaneous* concepts.

Vygotsky (1962) appears to have driven to the very heart of this dichotomy when he states that:

> There are errors in Piaget's reasoning that detract from the value of his views. Although he holds that the child in forming a concept stamps it with the characteristics of his own mentality, Piaget tends to apply this thesis only to spontaneous concepts and assumes that they alone can truly enlighten us on the special qualities of child thought; he fails to see the interaction between the two kinds of concepts and the bonds that unite them into a total system of concepts in the course of the child's intellectual development." (Vygotsky, 1962, p. 84).

The similarities between Gesell's position on "internal ripening" and Piaget's "self-regulation" should now be apparent. Piaget's view of "equilibration" subsumes maturation (internal genetic factors) as well as self-regulated *incidental* learning, (Piaget, 1964, 1965). He is thus more inclusive than Gesell whose notion of maturation centers around merely the process of "internal ripening" (genic factors). Thus Piaget's position allows him to go one step further toward accounting for interindividual, intraindividual, and intercultural differences in the age at which stages occur in the content area in which they are manifested by inclusion of incidental, spontaneous learning experiences, (Ausubel, 1968). At the same time, the convergence of thought in Piaget and Rousseau are rather striking; both center on the idea that the role of the external environment is simply in avoiding serious interference with the process of self-regulation and spontaneous maturation.

As stated earlier, this characterization of Piaget's position is made with certain qualifications and reservations. There appears to be no inherent necessity in his formulation which dictates that he be labelled a pre-determinist except for his consistent reiteration of the relatively minor role of the external environment on development. The confusion arises because of Piaget's (1964, 1965) conflicting statements about the four factors which influence cognitive development. At first, he seems to adopt an *interactionist* point of view, and then constantly undermines the role of social transmission (previously noted), as well as physical experience:

> The logical structure is not the result of physical experience. It cannot be obtained by external reinforcement. The logical structure is reached only through internal equilibration, by self-regulation . . . ." (Piaget, 1964, p. 16).

Vygotsky (1962) again has a cogent criticism of Piaget on this point:

> It is one of the basic tenets of Piaget's theory that progressive socialization of thinking is the very essence of the child's mental development; but if his views on the nature of nonspontaneous concepts were correct, it would follow that such an important factor in the socialization of thought as school learning is unrelated to the inner developmental process. This inconsistency is the weak spot of Piaget's theory, both theoretically and practically. (Vygotsky, 1962, p. 85).

Earlier writings of Piaget (1926, 1932b) indicate that his position was much more flexible in admitting the role of the social environment in the child's development. Thus, for example, in the case of moral judgments of the child (Piaget, 1932b) the movement from *heteronomous* to more *autonomous* modes of moral thoughts resulted from decrease in the unilateral respect for adults with a corresponding increase of mutual respect and solidarity among peers.

Supporting Biological Trends

Related biological trends influenced and bolstered predeterministic concepts of child development in at least two important ways. First, they helped create a general climate of scientific opinion which affected the acceptability of the latter theories. Second, various biological concepts suggested, modified, or reinforced the specific content of predeterministic theories.

That these supportive effects and conceptual resemblances were often based on popular misconceptions, outdated formulations, and even on basically irreconcilable contradictions with allegedly analagous biological models, does not in the least minimize the historical fact or importance of their occurrence. The three fields of biology that exercised most influence on pre-deterministic theories of child development were evolutionary theory, embryology, and genetics— concerned respectively with the origin of species, prenatal development, and the mechanisms of inheritance. In more recent years, advances in these fields have belatedly influenced a trend toward a more interactional approach to human development.

Biological Evolution. In 1859, Charles Darwin proposed the revolutionary theory that biological evolution was a consequence of gradual and cumulative developmental changes in species resulting from the selective survival and transmission of small inherited variations that furnished adaptive advantages in relation to prevailing environmental conditions. The environment, he believed, could not directly induce structural, functional or behavioral changes in the organism that were transmissible to its offspring*. It merely played a role in the determination of which of a number of naturally occurring variations was most adaptive and, hence, selectively favored for representation in future generations by virtue of a differential rate of survival and ultimate self-perpetuation. The impetus for and the regulatory mechanisms of biological organic evolution, resided, therefore, in existing and spontaneously occurring variability ascribable to hereditary endogenous factors rather than to environmental factors.

Applied to the development of human behavior, this latter principle was frequently misinterpreted in ways that supported the predeterministic position. It was not fully appreciated that although the environment could not directly induce changes that were transmissible to offspring, and, hence, could not initiate phylogenetic differentiation (i.e., the development of new species), it could still influence ontogeny (i.e., developmental sequences in the life cycle of individual members of a species). Thus, the Darwinian position was frequently misrepresented to mean what was never intended, namely, that environmental factors were also incapable of exercising a direct

---

According to J. B. Lamarck (1744-1829) and his followers, "acquired characters" were transmissible to offspring. This doctrine however, is in conflict with modern genetic theory which holds that ordinary, environmentally-wrought changes in the phenotype are not accompanied by corresponding changes in the genotype. Although there is "no proof that Lamarckian inheritance is impossible . . . no incontrovertible evidence in favor of it has been brought forward." Weismann's famous experiments (1889), which have been widely accepted as conclusively disproving Lamarck's hypothesis, actually did not adequately test it. The acquired traits, which are hypothesized by Lamarck as inheritable, were conceived as products of prolonged exposure or adaptive exercise over many generations, and could hardly be equated with such artificial, instantaneous insults as Weismann's snipping off of several generations of animals' tails.

effect on ontogenesis. Unfortunately this misinterpretation was reinforced and rendered more credible by the fact that it was not too far afield in relation to lower organisms with a more or less stereotyped pattern of adaptive behavior in response to environmental vicissitudes. Here individual experience is actually not much more crucial for the ontogeny than for the phylogeny of behavior. However, in higher species, particularly in man, adaptation is characteristically a function of a learned and flexible organization of behavior modified by individual and cultural experience. Thus, the predeterministic tendency to discount the impact of experience on human ontogeny was seriously tainted with error and distortion. The preformationists, starting from the same position, denied behavioral development altogether, equating man's socially learned behavior in Western civilization with a catalogue of king-sized inframammalian instincts.

Embryology. Early knowledge of embryology also reinforced predeterministic doctrines by pointing to more or less invariable sequences of development regulated predominantly by endogenous factors. Even when slightly qualified by later research showing that gestational environment was not entirely inconsequental for the outcome of development, the embryological model as such, when projected into postnatal life, still proved highly inapplicable to most problems of human development. In the first place it dealt almost exclusively with developmental acquisitions that characterized the species as a whole. Second, it was concerned with development in a relatively constant physiological environment largely insulated from external stimulation. It was, therefore, an analogy heavily loaded in favor of predeterministic conceptions, thereby confirming the bias of theorists, who, like Gesell, minimized the contribution of individual experience to ontogeny.

Actually these latter considerations interpreted in the light of numerous findings in experimental embryology should have led to precisely the opposite conclusions. All of the research of the past forty years indicates (a) that marked and even less extreme variations in the intrauterine environment such as rubella, irradiation, drugs, or advanced age of the mother, etc., are associated with developmental abnormalities in the fetus (Mussen, 1963), and (b) that structural growth and functional development of embryonic neural tissue are affected by many factors in the internal fetal and intrauterine environments. Much experimental work (Munn, 1965; Mussen et al., 1963) point to the conclusion that structural differentiation and the sequential development of function in different portions of the nervous system are influenced in part by differential concentrations of biocatalysts, by quantitative levels of various metabolites and hormones in the fetal blood stream, by mechanical and other external stimulation communicated to the child in utero, and by the presence and functioning of adjacent tissues. This last-mentioned effect has been variously explained in terms of regional differences in metabolic activity (gradients), the organizing potential of certain embryonic cells in promoting tissue differentiation (organizers), and the operation of electrodynamic fields induced by biological activity.

We may conclude, therefore, that the internal (intrafetal and gestational) environment plays an important contributory role in embryological development, and that the preservation of its constancy is important for uniformity of developmental outcome—even with respect to species characteristics. If this is so, it would be reasonable to expect that the directional influence of the environment on the development of intra-species differences would be infinitely greater once the individual were exposed to the tremendously wide spectrum of extrauterine variability in stimulation.

Genetics. The rediscovery of Mendel's laws in 1900 and the early subsequent work of geneticists had tremendous repercussions on theories of human development. The demonstration of a physical basis for heredity in the form of relatively stable, self-reproducing, discrete genes, which were resistant to ordinary environmental influences and which seemingly exercised an inevitable, unconditional, and one-to-one effect on the determination of specific traits, naturally favored prevailing predeterministic conceptions regarding the development of human behavior. And, of course, quite apart from this latter influence, the new science of genetics provided an urgently needed model for explaining the mechanisms underlying (a) *phylogenetic* inheritance as manifested in both biological evolution and in the embryological development of the individual, and (b) the *familial inheritance* operative in numerous studies of animal breeding, of the recurrent incidence of various "hereditary" diseases in certain human families, and of trait relationships between individuals differing in degree of consanguinity.

Later research in genetics showed that the model of single major genes with gross effects on variability, completely and invariably influencing the development of specific traits, was greatly over-simplified. It was convincingly demonstrated that "the phenotype of an organism is not a mere mosaic of independently expressed single-gene effects . . . [but] depends on developmental interactions involving the entire aggregate of genic material." (David & Snyder, 1951). Thus it is now known that the effects of many single genes are modified by other genes, and that most normal (and less extreme pathological) genetic variability in human beings is produced by constellations of polygenes. The latter exert "individually minute but cumulatively appreciable [and] . . . quantitatively equivalent effects" resulting in continuous rather than in conspicuously discontinuous distributions of phenotypic variability" (David & Snyder, 1951).

More important perhaps was the undermining of the older genetic view supporting the established belief (mistakenly derived from Darwinian theory and from exaggerated instinct approaches to animal behavior) that the environment does not appreciably influence ontogeny. Modern genetics fully support the proposition that the phenotype "is the result of a developmental 'trajectory' which is determined by the complex interaction of both genetic and environmental factors" (McClearn, 1964). This, of course, does not mean that environmental factors ordinarily alter genes but that they alter the expression of genes. The effect of genes on the development and patterning of morphological traits is frequently contingent upon the presence of a restricted range of such environmental conditions as moisture, temperature, and diet. In other cases, environmental influences are similarly operative only within a restricted range of genotypes; and sometimes the effects of heredity and environment on development are more nearly independent, additive, or complementary. Finally, "the effects of certain genes appear to be expressed with great uniformity within any range of environmental conditions," (McClearn, 1964), and, conversely, the effects of certain environmental conditions are manifested in practically all genotypes.

According to modern conceptions of genetics, therefore, the influence of genes on development is never complete or absolute, but always reflects to a variable extent the influence of the intracellular, intercellular, gestational or external environments. The phenotypic consequences of genetic action are presently conceived of in such terms as probabilities of determination, degrees of regularity and completeness of expression, and limiting the threshold values of response and attainment. As will be pointed out later, this shift in theoretical orientation played an important role in resolving dichotomous views of the nature-nurture controversy and in generating an interactional approach to problems of human development. Nevertheless, exaggerated notions of the simplicity, specificity, prepotency and inevitability of genetic effects continued to flourish and influence predeterministic formulations. For example, over-enthusiastic supporters of the latter point of view uncritically accepted much fragmentary and unreliable evidence from pedigree studies which purported to show that an amazing variety of feeble-mindedness, mental disease, social delinquency, moral waywardness, and personality inadequacy was exclusively or predominantly the effect of genes inherited from a single and remote defective ancestor (Goddard, 1912).*

The ultimate in emphasis upon the pre-eminent importance of genetic factors in human development is embodied in the eugenics movement. Its program is predicated on the belief that the soundest and surest method for improving the lot of mankind lies in upgrading the genetic endowment of large populations through the rigorous application of principles of selective

---

*In reaching these conclusions little attention was paid to such obvious considerations as the representativeness of the sample, comparisons with a control population, the accuracy and equivalence of diagnoses made over an extended time span, the reliability of herasay evidence, and the influence of substandard family and social conditions which invariably accompany and compound such conditions.

and restrictive mating. However, even if men and women could be induced to choose their mates on the basis of eugenic considerations, it would still require vastly greater knowledge about the mechanisms of human genetics than is presently available before such a program could be successfully inaugurated. Furthermore, from the study of cultural history it is clearly evident that profound changes in the behavior of human beings and in the quality of their civilization can be effected by social, economic, technological, scientific, and educational advances within several generations. On the other hand, comparable examination of human evolution indicates that significant changes in the genic basis of human behavior and capacity could only be expected over time periods measuring tens or hundreds of thousands of years. Negative eugenics, i.e., the reduction and elimination of physical and psychological abnormalities by sterilizing the grossly unfit, is unfortunately not much more realistically grounded. Most of the more common and less extreme human defects that have an appreciable hereditary component are polygenically determined; and the relatively few and uncommon defects that are attributable to the effects of single genes are extremely rare "recessives" the incidence of which would not be significantly altered by sterilization.

Relationships Between Biological Evolution and Embryology. The existence of many obvious parallels between biological evolution and embryological development inevitably led to much speculation about how these two phenomena are related. As a result, many biological and biocultural concepts of recapitulation were elaborated, varying greatly in degree of empirical substantiation and theoretical credibility.

The biological theory of recapitulation embodied in Ernst Haeckel's (1834-1919) famous proposition that ontogeny recapitulates phylogeny was predicated upon certain gross sequential parallelisms in morphogenesis between the biological evolution of a species in geologic time and the embryological development of its members. This proposition is compatible with the fact that biological evolution is characterized by both continuity and modification; that is, in addition to well-marked lines of divergence, there is also much structural and functional continuity between a given species and its evolutionary forbears. Genetically speaking, therefore, it could be anticipated that each species would inherit and transmit genes reflecting such commonalities and divergences, and hence, that its members would tend to recapitulate in their early ontogeny the course of its descent from earlier forms of animal life.

That such parallelisms are not exact and do not embody all previous stages is not at all surprising. In the first place, the line of descent typically zig-zags instead of following a directly vertical course. Second, considering the difference in the relative time scales involved in each process and the undoubted influence of the more recent genic material on older morphogenic sequences, considerable telescoping and modification of ontogenetic phases could reasonably be expected to occur.

However, *biogenetic* theories of recapitulation (e.g., Rousseau's, G. Stanley Hall's), although superficially resembling Haeckel's proposition, were actually an entirely different breed of cat. The analogy was extended to include the *cultural* history of the race and the *postembryological behavioral* development of the individual. We have already noted that the latter kind of development (in contrast to embryological morphogenesis) is both less insulated from environmental influence and is characterized more by intraspecies differences in ontogenesis resulting from unique individual experience. In addition, these theories are not substantiated by any convincing evidence, and are based on the untenable assumptions (a) that cultures universally undergo a parallel sequence of evolutionary changes, and (b) that such cultural acquisitions are genically transmissible, and hence universally recapitulated.

Both on empirical and theoretical grounds, the once fashionable notion of universal stages of cultural evolution is now thoroughly discredited. Some gross developmental sequences may conceivably be parallel in different cultures because of "recurrent causal relationships in independent cultural traditions." (Steward, 1953). For example, the evolution of certain levels of social organization may almost universally be dependent upon the prior attainment of supporting levels of technology. However, apart from such limited parallels, and in the absence of significant cultural diffusion, the cumulative impact of differences in geography, climate, history, values, institutions, etc., typically leads to progressively greater divergence in the development of cultural forms. We must conclude, therefore, that all human beings, reagrdless of cultural membership, hold their biological descent in common and undergo the same embryological development, but by no means share a cultural history which reflects the operation of substantially identical processes of social evolution.

But even if cultures everywhere did undergo the same evolutionary process, what effect would this have on the genetic constitution of Man? It will be remembered from the preceding discussion (see p. 30) that ordinarily only spontaneous, genetically induced structural or behavioral variability is inheritable, and that the main contribution of the environment to phylogeny is its role in natural selection. Although environmental factors influence profoundly the development of the human individual during his lifetime,*

---

*It may be noted that predeterministic theorists tend to reject the quite modest proposition that the environment significantly influences human ontogeny. Yet, paradoxically enough, they accepted the primacy of certain internal regulatory factors, the very existence of which presupposed the validity of the much more extreme environmentalistic position that cultural experience directly influences phylogeny by affecting the genotype.

the changes they induce do not effect his genes and, hence, are only culturally rather than genically transmissible to his offspring. It is clearly evident,
therefore, the the genetic assumptions of biocultural recapitulation are
incompatible with modern conceptions of biology.

Thus, despite the vast changes that have occurred in man's behavior and
cultural level since the emergence of Homo sapiens a quarter to half a million
years ago, it is not probable that the biological basis of human abilities has
appreciably changed during this period. (de Chardin, 1961; David, et al.,
1951; Dobzhansky, 1962; La Barre, 1954). And it is even more certain that
all contemporaneous groupings of human beings—irrespective of past
cultural history—share the same genic potentialities for psychological and
cultural development.

In a very limited and quite different sense of the term, concepts of psycho-
cultural recapitulation might hold promise of manifesting somewhat greater
face validity. If, for example, we conceive of a trend toward increased use of
symbols and abstractions as characteristic of cultural development, it would
appear that at later stages in the history of most cultures, the intellectual
development of the individual would tend to be extended beyond the point
which generally prevailed when the ideational level of the culture was lower.
In a sense, therefore, the historically later-born individual might be said to
be "recapitulating" the intellectual development of his culture as he gradually grows in intellectual capacity. However, parallel development would
occur in this instance not because certain cultural sequences were written
into his genes and merely needed to unfold, but (a) because a trend from
concrete to symbolic ideation happens to characterize the course of intellectual development in both individual and culture, and (b) because the limits
of individual growth are dependent in part upon the level of cultural
achievement.

Thus, the greater attained intellectual capacity of individuals in more
highly advanced civilizations would not be indicative of cultural alternation
of genotypic endowment, but of the greater phenotypic achievement that is
possible with a constant genotype under conditions of enriched cultural
stimulation. Its occurrence would in no sense be inevitable but would be
dependent upon actual ontogenetic exposure to the necessary experience.
Hence, if twentieth century American children were artificially insulated
from all ideational stimulation, their prospects for advanced intellectual
development would hardly be brighter than those of prehistoric men.

"TABULA RASA" APPROACHES

In marked contrast to the preformationist and predeterministic doctrines
we have been discussing are such movements as humanism, behaviorism,
"situational determinism" and certain varieties of cultural relativism. If we

consider the former approaches as constituting one extreme of a continuum embracing the various theories concerned with the regulation of human development, the latter ideological movements would have to be placed at the other extreme of the same continuum. They are referred to as *tabula rasa* (literally, "blank slate") approaches because they minimize the contributions of genetic endowment and of directional factors coming from within the individual, and concomitantly emphasize the pre-eminent role of the environment in determining the outcome of development.* The analogy which likens the neonate to a *tabula rasa* is aptly representative of their general thesis that no fundamental predispositions are inherent in the raw material from which behavior and personality develop, and that human beings are infinitely malleable. All of the patterning, differentiation, integration, and elaboration of specific and general behavioral content that emerges during the course of development is accounted for in terms of the unique stimulus conditions to which the individual is or has been subjected.

It should be noted, however, that the term *tabula rasa* is being used here in a very general sense, and only to denote such extreme environmentalist positions as described above. In the more specific sense of the term, as employed by John Locke, the "blank slate" only referred to the *ideational* state of affairs at birth and not to the *complete* absence of developmental predispositions; as a matter of fact in his discourses on education he placed much emphasis on the need for restraining the natural impulses of children. Furthermore, in the light of modern conceptions of cognitive and behavioral development, neither Locke's *tabula rasa* proposition nor more recent dissatisfaction with the notion of human instincts could be regarded as indicative of an extreme position with respect to the nature-nurture controversy. Hence, although theories of innate ideas, instincts and instinctual drives must be categorized as essentially preformationist in orientation, disavowal of these constructs does not necessarily constitute a *tabula rasa* approach to human development.

Humanism and Related Approaches

The humanistic movement in philosophy and education has consistently championed the environmentalist position that given proper conditions of nurturance, man's developmental potentialities are virtually unlimited in

---

We have already referred to Lamarckianism as an example of the extreme environmentalist position in biology since it is based on the assumption that the genotype as well as the phenotype can be altered by prolonged exposure to certain environmental conditions. However, the most basic feature of the tabula rasa approach is its emphasis on the plasticity of human beings (i.e., the absence of significant or enduring predispositions) rather than on the importance of environmental determinants of development. Certain more recent tabula rasa orientations, e.g., client-centered therapy, stress the notion of plasticity, but assign the main directional control of significant personality change to self-directed cognitive and motivational processes.

scope or direction. Implicit in this optimistic appraisal is (a) the belief that "human nature" is essentially amorphous and can be molded to whatever specifications man chooses to adopt as most compatible with his self-chosen destiny, and (b) unbounded confidence in the possibility of attaining this objective through appropriate educational procedures.

Of course, the humanistic conviction that man can deliberately select and take steps to insure the realization of whatever goals he chooses, and, hence, is the master of his own fate, would be a perfectly defensible proposition if it were related to and qualified by the actual psychological capacities of human beings. More often than not, however, it is merely stated as an unqualified philosophical desideratum. This is especially detrimental to its acceptability since it is becoming increasingly more evident that the extent of developmental plasticity is no longer a question which can be settled by speculative fiat. Furthermore, it is extremely unlikely that one blanket generalization could ever suffice to cover all aspects of development. In the modern era this issue is more properly regarded as a matter for empirical determination. And regardless of the ultimate outcome of particularized research inquiry, any realistic statement of human objectives and potentialities should presently be formulated within the framework of the limitations imposed by man's genetic endowment as currently conceived in the light of all relevant data.

Although predicated upon quite different theoretical premises, the humanistic program of education was strikingly similar in spirit and content to the preformationist (theological) approach already described (see p. 20). Despite the fact that one school viewed the infant as a formless entity wholly at the mercy of his environment and the other conceived of him as essentially prestructed in advance, both were in agreement (a) that the individual himself contributes little to his own development, (b) that the child in essence is a miniature adult, and (c) that improvement of man's nature could be best effected through the imposition of a stern and rigorous regimin of training and education. Preformationists reached this conclusion by both denying that any significant developmental changes occur in the first place, and by conceding that some quantitative improvement of prestructed attributes could result if superimposed from without by proper authority. Humanists, on the other hand, arrived at the same position more directly by attributing all developmental changes in an originally amorphous creature to the all-important influence of environmental factors, and by conceiving of such changes as occurring in quantitative steps rather than by qualitative stages.

Typically, therefore, the humanistic approach to education was rigidly academic, traditional and authoritarian. Severe and arbitrary standards were imposed and strictly enforced by the application of physical punishment and other extrinsic motivational devices. If necessary, rationality and classical erudition were literally pounded into the resistive or reluctant individual.

Age level differences in capacity and in developmental needs and status were largely ignored and little or no attention was paid to individual differences in ability or temperament. Humanistic educators did not seriously attempt to enlist the child's voluntary participation, encourage his spontaneity or appeal to endogenous motivation. The contribution of ongoing personality to behavior and cognitive development was regarded as inconsequential, and the learner was granted no directive role or responsibility in the educative process.

Behaviorism shared many of the environmentalist biases of humanism but conceptualized them in more psychological terms. Consistent with its *tabula rasa* emphasis upon behavioral plasticity was its denial of subjective experience (except as a form of subliminal behavior), its rejection of all developmental predispositions (except for reflexes and certain emotional responses) and its conception of the human organism as a noncognitive response mechanism subservient to the control of conditioned stimuli. Similarly in the area of child care and education, its advocacy of impersonal handling, strictness, regularity, and the importance of habit training was strikingly reminiscent of humanistic practices (Watson, 1928).

However, it need not be thought that a *tabula rasa* conception of human nature is necessarily or inevitably associated with a concomitant emphasis upon the pre-eminence of environmental determinants of development. The currently flourishing school of client-centered therapy (Rogers, 1951), for example, combines a clinical estimate of extreme human plasticity with an emphasis upon endogenously derived needs, goals, insights, responsibility, initiative for change, etc., in a maximally, permissive and nonauthoritarian therapeutic environment. As long as this relationship between endogenous and exogenous influences prevails, the possibilities for reorganizing personality on a more wholesome and constructive basis are held to be virtually unlimited, irrespective of existing personality structure or previous developmental history.

This point of view is obviously very close to the educational position of those predeterminist theorists (e.g., Rousseau, Hall, Gesell) who stressed the importance of permissiveness and self-direction in child rearing. Its principal point of departure from the older approach is that it conceives of these latter conditions as essential for the active *self-creation* of a personality with almost limitless possibilities for self-realization (or for the therapeutic reconstruction of an environmentally distorted personality) rather than for the optimal unfolding of a developmentally prestructured personality. However, we must reiterate again that the plasticity of the human personality and its responsiveness to reorganization are not issues that can be resolved by doctrinal assertion, but are matters for explicit empirical determination. And although self-direction is undoubtedly important for many aspects of both therapeutically facilitated and more normative sequences of development, there is little reason to believe that directional influences originating in the environment are unnecessary, unimportant, or typically detrimental.

Cultural and Situational Determinism

The growth of empirical cultural anthropology during the first four decades of this century led to the formulation of a more explicit environmentalist position in conjunction with the conception of infinite human plasticity. Studies of modal behavior, socialization, and enculturation in different primitive cultures impressed ethnologists with the remarkable homogeneity of these phenomena within cultures, with their tremendous diversity from one culture to another, and with the apparent absence of intercultural uniformities. The almost inevitable outcome of such conclusions was the emergence of a concept of cultural determinism i.e., the notion that the human being is "well-nigh an empty vase into which culture and social prescriptions are poured," (Sherif, 1951) and that his behavior and personality development, therefore, are simply a function of the particular sociocultural stimuli which impinge on him. The personality-culture and the individual society dichotomies were thus "resolved" by the simple expedient of virtually abolishing the categories of individual and personality. *

As long as intracultural differences in behavior were ignored, there was no pressing need to acknowledge the contributions of enduring response tendencies, selective perceptual sensitivities, and differential thresholds of reactivity established by the interaction between the individual's unique genotype and experiential history; and likewise, as long as cross-cultural similarities in development were disregarded, it seemed quite unnecessary to

---

*We have already referred to social instinct theories which resolved the same dichotomies in opposite fashion by deriving culture and society from the preformed patterned behavior of individuals. Spiro (1951) is respresentative of a new trend in social science theory which seeks to reduce both personality and culture to a unique configuration of cumulatively learned individual behavior in an interpersonal setting; hence, according to this view "there are as many cultures as there are personalities." This reductionism is based on the propositions that the locus of culture resides in the behavior of its individual members, that the acquisition of culture can only be conceived as a learning (internalization) process occurring in particular individuals, and that individuals typically modify their cultural heritage. However, one can accept all three propositions as valid without necessarily reaching the conclusion that personality and culture are one and the same thing. Although "culture" as such is an abstraction derived from a nonhomogenous totality of individual behaviors, their interactions, and products (and can obviously enjoy no existence independently of the persons who comprise, internalize, influence, and are influenced by it), it still is a conceptually (if not functionally) independent phenomenon external to personality. The consensuses, commonalities, and uniformities to which it refers are real (e.g., actual shared values, beliefs, social customs), distinguishable from those of other cultures, and are sufficiently stable to be studied as if existing in their own right (Herskovits, 1948). They affect and are acquired by the individual as a result of influencing and being internalized by the particular cultural representatives (e.g., parents, teachers, peers) with whom he interacts in the course of his enculturation.

search for those panhuman regularities (of genic, physiological, psychological, or interpersonal origin) that serve to limit and channel the impact of cultural influences on the human growth matrix along ontogenetic lines that are roughly parallel in terms of process from one culture to another.

Fortunately, expressions of this extreme *tabula rasa* version of cultural determinism are less commonly heard today. Most anthropologists, although still not greatly impressed by intercultural uniformities, have become much more cognizant of the importance of intracultural differences. However, the battle line they abandoned is still vigorously manned by various sociologists and sociologically oriented social psychologists who explain *all* such differences on the basis of subcultural membership or situational variables, and steadfastly deny the existence of stable, enduring antecedent predispositions to behavior or development. The situational *determinism* they advocate shifts the locus of personality structure from an organized system of underlying behavioral predispositions ("under the skin") to a series of behavioral *acts* manifested under specified socio-situational conditions. Whatever needs or motives are required to initiate or sustain behavior are derived intracurrently from the situation itself. Personality, as the more extreme of these theorists conceive it, is not a continuing, self-consistent structure exhibiting generality over situations, but a transitory configuration of individual behavior that is purely a function of the particular social stimulus conditions which evoke it.

This view of personality is rationalized on the grounds that since an individual's behavior does in fact vary *every time* the situational context is altered, it must therefore be determined by the latter variable *alone*. It is hardly necessary to point out, however, that the demonstration of behavioral change associated with variability in one factor does not necessarily preclude the possibility that other variables are simultaneously operative. In fact, by simply reversing the picture, i.e., keeping the situation constant and varying the individuals exposed to it, one could just as easily emerge with the equally one-sided conclusion that only personality factors determine behavioral change. However, when a number of persons are studied in a diversity of situations, it becomes quite evident that both factors contribute to the obtained variability in behavior. This is shown by the fact that intercorrelations among behavioral measures in different situations are neither zero nor unity but somewhere in between, and that they tend to become higher when either the situations themselves or the subjects' degree of ego-involvement in them are made comparable (see pp. 114, 281).

The situational approach to personality not only strips it of any explanatory implications, but also renders futile any search for the genotypic bases of behavior. If personality has neither stability nor generality, there is certainly little point in considering the possible effects it might have on behavior, and even less point in attempting to trace the course of its development. And similarly, if overt behavior cannot possibly be related to under-lying predispositions in personality structure, behavioral taxonomy must be based entirely on phenotypic similarities and differences irrespective of their genotypic references (see p. 10).

It might also be noted at this point that in practice (if not theoretically) nondirective schools of therapy tend to support the situational concept of personality. Although they do not explicitly deny the influence of ante-cedent response tendencies on ongoing behavior, they minimize their im-portance (a) by regarding them as almost invariably reversible, (b) by con-sidering the discovery of their developmental origins as irrelevant for therapy, and (c) by placing major emphasis on the current adjustive situation.

Cultural Relativism

Viewed in historical perspective, cultural relativism must undoubtedly be reckoned the outstanding component and moving force behind the concept of cultural determinism discussed above. However, for purposes of concep-tual clarity, it would be desirable for several reasons to consider the former movement separately. First, cultural determinists need only assume that the behavior of human beings is both plastic and crucially influenced by cultural factors; they need *not* accept the relativistic position that it is *completely unique* in every culture. In fact, if significant parallels of custom and tradition are demonstrable from one culture to another, to be perfectly consistent with the logic of cultural determinism one would have to postulate a corresponding parallelism in the area of behavior and personality development. Second, cultural relativism has been associated historically with an empirical, field study approach to ethnology and with a non-evolutionary, non-individualistic interpretation of cultural change* that are by no means indigenous to the position of cultural determinism. Third, because of these historical associa-tions cultural relativism has come to represent an extreme point of view with respect to such issues as the plasticity, cultural uniqueness, intracultural homogeneity, and intercultural heterogeneity of behavior, that is not necessarily inherent even in a relativistic position. Thus, many theorists who would readily agree that behavior and development are relative to and determined by the cultural environment in many important respects still

---

*Since we are only concerned here with individual development, this issue naturally lies outside the scope of our inquiry. However, it is important to point out that the methodological approach of the relativists, which emphasized the empirical study of behavior in particular cultures (as opposed to the logical analysis of cultural institutions and products in relation to a universal concept of cultural evolution) predisoposed them toward a conception of uniqueness in considering the impact of culture on behavior and persnality (Spiro, 1951). Their non-evolutionary view of cultural change similarly pre-disposed them in this direction; but since similarity in cultural development is only one of many factors affecting cross-cultural uniformities in personality, the two positions (the anti-evolutionary and the relativistic) are not necessarily co-extensive.

hold views on these latter issues that are much less extreme than is implied in a more doctrinaire statement of cultural relativism.

Cultural relativism, of course, provided a much needed corrective against the ethnocentric social instinct and biogenetic doctrines that flourished during the same and preceding decades. It denied that complex social behavior is ever innately patterned by virtue of universal instincts, or that intra- and intercultural uniformities ever reflect the operation of an identical species-wide genotype with prepotent and invariable directional influence in the content and sequence of development. In accounting for behavioral regularities within a culture, it pointed to the obvious importance of considering commonalities in social conditioning; however in explaining cross-cultural similarities, it advanced the less convincing hypothesis of cultural diffusion. Most important, however, by demonstrating that the cultural patterning of innumerable aspects of behavior and development is characterized by an extremely wide range of variability, it completely demolished the ethnocentric preformationist view that distinguishing features of personality structure in Western civilization are mainfestations of an immutable "human nature" and hence must be universally distributed. Instead it advanced the thesis that the unique values, traditions, institutions, and historical development of each culture give rise to a distinctive personality type. In so doing it established the beginnings of the now flourishing research area concerned with empirical investivation of the personality-culture problem.

Of course, even cultural relativists could not assume complete behavioral plasticity. Certain limitations imposed by man's species membership and by his biological and psychological needs, capacities, and mechanisms were recognized as constraining the impact of culture on behavior. But within the framework of these highly general limits, all patterning, differentiation, and selectivity in behavioral development were considered a function of cultural variables. Thus, for example, culture was conceived as determining the kinds of stimuli evoking a particular emotion and the manner in which it is expressed, and as selecting through differential rewards and punishments which potential capacities and personality traits of man are either emphasized or neglected in a particular cultural setting.

Relationship to Psychoanalytic Theory. To a very great extent the full impact of cultural relativism on conceptions of personality development was blunted by the considerable influence exerted by psychoanalytically oriented ethnologists and by psychoanalytic theorists concerned with the problem of the individual in society. The partial fusion of these two currents of thought (i.e., psychoanalysis and cultural relativism) probably reflected the prevailing absence of a satisfactory body of competing psychological theory in the area of personality as well as some dissatisfaction with the extremeness of the relativistic view. In any event it occurred despite the presence of the following serious conceptual incompatibilities between the two positions*: First, psychoanalysis reintroduced the anthropologically suspect doctrine of instinct in the somewhat more palatable form of patterned psychosexual drives, and established the latter as the new basis of intercultural uniformities. Nevertheless, this conception of drives as innately prestructured and biogenetically transmitted entities was in direct conflict with the relativistic principle that all significant and detailed psychological patterning is determined by unique factors of cultural conditioning; and projected universally as it was from an unrepresentative sample of neurotic individuals in our own society, it naturally ran afoul of the rigorous relativistic strictures directed against ethnocentrism. Second, the psychoanalytic view of society as basically frustrating was incompatible with the proposition implicit in any form of cultural determinism that the social order not only provides the means of gratifying the individual's biologically instigated drives but is also capable of independently generating in its own right highly significant drives of interpersonal origin. Lastly, the psychoanalytic school explained intercultural differences in personality structure almost exclusively on the basis of differential parental practices influencing the course of psychosexual development. Cultural relativists, on the other hand, have necessarily taken a much broader view of the potential range of interpersonal and sociocultural factors that are significant for personality development in a given society and have recognized that aspects of personality structure other than erogenous impulses are subject to societal influence.

IMPLICATIONS OF HISTORICAL TRENDS FOR MODERN CONCEPTIONS OF DEVELOPMENT

We can summarize most helpfully the implications of the foregoing historical trends for modern conceptions of developmental regulation by indicating briefly in what general ways both predeterministic and *tabula rasa* approaches to human development are theoretically untenable. These considerations will point up the desirability of adopting the emerging interactional approach that will be presented in Chapter 3. Since the main issue here is the extent of behavioral plasticity, we may properly subsume preformationist views under the predeterministic category.

---

*Basic incompatibilities in viewpoint with respect to the development of cultural institutions are not pertinent to the present discussion. In general, however, Freudian interpretations of cultural forms and practices as institutionalized mechanisms of repressing of symbolically expressing psycho-sexual drives have not won as much acceptance from ethnologists as have psychoanalytic formulations regarding the influence of culture on personality development.

Summary Critique of Predeterministic Approaches

1. Except for simple responses of a reflex nature, there is little substantial basis in either logic or empirical data for the belief that *any* psychological aspect of human functioning is preformed at birth, *completely* independent of subsequent environmental experience. Even the initial, unpatterned psychological repercussions of intense visceral and hormonal stimuli (i.e., drive states) are influenced by the effects of prior experiences and by concurrent internal and external stimulation; and under extremely unfavorable social auspices, it sometimes happens that certain "primary" drives (e.g., sex) may *never* be generated, regardless of the adequacy of gonadal output. Where complex patterning is involved, the possibility of prestructured psychological entities is, of course, still less credible. But although the existence of human instincts is no longer taken seriously by most behavior scientists, the quite comparable notion that patterned affectional-sex drives exist preformed in a biogenetically inherited id has won much acceptance in many quarters.

The most anachronistic of all present-day preformationist thinking is exemplified in the psychoanalytic theory of innate ideas (e.g., cosmic identification, reincarnation, omnipotence) lodged in a phylogenetic unconscious. Supports of this doctrine point to the widespread occurrence of these themes in the mythologies of historically unrelated cultures and in the ideational outpourings of deeply regressed psychotics. The first phenomenon, however, is more parsimoniously explained by the independent cultural generation of common ideological solutions to such universal problems as death and supernatural control of the environment, and the second by regression to an earlier ontogenetic stage of ego development (see pp. 257-259).

2. Equally unsubstantiated is the embryological model of psychological development which is not predicated upon preformationism, but asserts nevertheless that developmental sequences and outcomes are basically predetermined and inevitable because of the propotent influence of internal (genic) directional factors. Actually, this conception only holds true for the relatively few and simple behavioral acquisitions which in terms of specificity of content and sequential appearance characterize every member of the human species (e.g., locomotion). For all other behavioral traits, the contribution of unique environmental conditions to developmental regulation is considerably greater; and, hence, both the kinds of growth changes that take place and the sequence in which they occur are more variable by far. It is quite erroneous, therefore, (a) to underestimate the impact of culture and individual experience on almost any psychologically significant aspect of human development; (b) to minimize the extent and significance of culturally conditioned diversity in individual development; and (c) to overlook cultural

commonalities operative in the life histories of individuals, and attribute all observed developmental uniformities both within and between cultures solely to the influence of similar genic factors.

Biogenetic theories of recapitulation hypothesizing specific parallelisms between successive stages in the psychological development of the individual and various inferred stages in the cultural evolution of mankind are insupportable on both empirical and theoretical grounds. They rest on the discredited assumptions that cultures everywhere evolve in parallel sequence and that the cultural acquisitions of a people are genically transmissible to their offspring.

Summary Critique of "Tabula Rasa" Approaches

1. Not content with having successfully cast doubt on the validity of preformationist and predeterministic doctrines, tabula rasa theorists unfortunately veered to the opposite extreme and asserted that human behavior is infinitely plastic and malleable to environmental influences. Although they were probably correct in assuming that some aspects of behavior (e.g., social roles and attitudes) are almost entirely determined by cultural variables, they stood on palpably less solid ground in refusing in recognize that other facets of psychological development are patterned in many significant ways by various selective predispositions, limitations, capacities and potentialities arising from within the individual. Because these internal factors (which either directly or indirectly have a genic basis) do not characteristically exercise solitary, highly specific, and invariable effects on the content and sequence of development, tabula rasa theorists fallaciously concluded that they do not even operate as partial or general determinants.

2. Hence, for example, extreme cultural relativists and situational determinists failed to appreciate (a) that many intracultural differences in behavioral development are conditioned by genotypic diversity as well as by subcultural, familial and individual differences in background experience; and (b) that numerous intercultural uniformities in psychological development are undoubtedly determined in part by various aspects of man's genic endowment which both relate him to and differentiate him from other species.* Thus, the unique ontogeny of human beings is more than a reflection of their uniqueness in being the only species in nature whose development happens to be systematically molded by a culture. It is also a reflection of the fact that they are the only species genetically capable of responding to cultural stimuli in ways that characterize the development of a cultural organism. No amount of cultural stimulation could possibly make chimpanzees develop like human beings.

---

*See p. 66 for a listing of both genic and environmental factors contributing to intercultural uniformities in development.

48 THEORY AND PROBLEMS OF CHILD DEVELOPMENT

3. In addition to overlooking the genic basis of intercultural uniformities in behavioral development, cultural relativists also failed to appreciate that many of these uniformities (e.g., general stages in personality development) are induced by numerous "common denominators" in culture itself. The latter in turn are derived from universal features in man's physical and interpersonal environment and from his adaptations thereto, as well as from panhuman biological and psychological characteristics (Kluckhohn, 1953; Murdock, 1945).

4. As will be pointed out in later chapters, many cultural relativists (under the influence of psychoanalytic and stimulus theories of drive), paradoxically relapsed into some of the most serious errors they berated in their adversaries. For example, in assuming that sex drives are either preformed or inevitably generated by gonadal hormones, they surprisingly underestimated the characteristic plasticity of human beings in responding to factors that induce and pattern drive states. And in defining a basic human capacity such as guilt in terms of the particular conditions under which it arises and the specific forms it adopted in our own culture, they reached the surprising ethnocentric conclusion that individuals in most other cultures exhibit shame rather than guilt.

CHAPTER 3

The Regulation of Development: Interaction Between Heredity and Environment

---

THE NATURE-NURTURE CONTROVERSY is much less acrimonious today than a consideration of the historical trends in Chapter 2 would indicate. As a result of research and theoretical progress in the fields of embryology (see p. 30), genetics (see p. 33), intellectual growth (see Chapter 17) and social anthropology, current formulations of the respective roles of heredity and environment in development are couched in less dichotomous and more interactional terms. Nevertheless, as long as the interactional position is restricted to a general statement of bipolar determination, the hub of the controversy merely shifts from "all-or-none" propositions to conflicting estimates of overall relative importance. *The pseudo-issue underlying the controversy can only be eliminated by specifying in more precise and detailed fashion how the interaction takes place and the relative weight of each factor in determining the course and outcome of particular kinds of development.* When this approach is adopted, the irrelevancy of dichotomous or overall estimates becomes apparent, and we are left with a genuine scientific problem which can be formulated in terms of theoretical postulates that are both meaningful and empirically testable.

In the present chapter, therefore, we shall attempt an interactional interpretation of the problem of developmental regulation that deals more explicitly with the directional influence, mode of operation, and relative weight of both genic predispositions and environmental conditions. We shall first consider these regulatory factors systematically and relate them to the similarities and differences in developmental sequence to which they give rise. Then, reversing the procedure, we shall survey intercultural uniformities, intracultural regularities, and intracultural differences, and try to identify their determinants. Lastly, we shall conclude the chapter with a discussion of two issues traditionally associated with the heredity-environment problem, namely, maturation and the neutral correlates of development.

INTERACTIONAL BASIS OF DEVELOPMENTAL REGULATION

In studying the development of children, the concepts of heredity and environment are no more than convenient abstractions or categories of variables that only theoretically can be disentangled from each other. What we actually observe as development takes place is change in a given direction when certain internal or external influences impinge on an individual with existing properties and predispositions. The latter already represent the resultants of innumerable prior interactions between hereditary and environmental factors. What was once originally environmental or outside the inherited genic material is now inextricably bound up with it as the organism's contribution to the course of development.

In the first portion of the present section, therefore, we shall examine this interdependency between heredity and environment which renders them phenomologically inseparable and guarantees the bipolar determination of all developmental processes. At a purely abstract level of analysis, however, it is legitimate to inquire about the "relative contribution of variation in genes and variation in life history to variation" in developmental outcomes (Anastasi, 1958; Fuller, 1954); and we shall, immediately afterwards, turn our attention to this aspect of the problem.

Bipolar Determination of Development

Human development is always a product of continuous interaction between various stimulating factors and a prevailing growth matrix consisting of selective predispositions both to undergo change and respond to the environment in particular ways (Murphy, 1963). This latter matrix naturally encompasses directional tendencies representing the total outcome of all preceding developmental history. It is synonymous with the genotype of the individual only at the moment of conception. Thereafter, it itself, and the development progressions it generates, are always interactional products.

Genotype, Phenotype, Growth Matrix and Constitution. The "genotype" of the individual refers to his genic endowment or to the totality of all his inherited elements. It consists of the potentialities inherent in the 23 chromosomes inherited from each of his parents and represented in every somatic cell of his body. Barring exposure to such atypical stimulation as massive doses of x-rays, the genotype remains intact, throughout the life span of the individual. At any given point during this period, and especially during the prenatal and early postnatal phases of development, it constitutes a major determinant of the growth matrix. But although it itself remains unchanged, the directional influence it contributes to the growth matrix is naturally modified in varying degrees from the very beginning of the organism's existence. Strictly speaking, therefore, the predispositions established by genes are never absolute or inevitable in their effects on development; their actualization is always a function both of their relative strength and of various environmental considerations. Thus, regardless of whether final phenotypic outcome closely approximates or is far removed from genic endowment, it can never be said that genes determine traits and capacities, but only that they determine the potentialities for developing traits and capacities.

It is not always apparent that the impact of the genotype on development is operative over the entire life history of the individual. In many cases, of course, the consequences of its influence are overtly observable at birth and in the developmental sequences that progressively follow. In other cases, however, the initial products of genic determination are either years in the making (e.g., gonadal maturation) or cannot be manifested until a certain level of development is already achieved. Thus, for example, considerable time must elapse from birth before any but the grossest kinds of genically conditioned temperamental traits became evident in personality structure.

The "phenotype" on the other hand, is a "description of the organism in terms of its observable qualities" (Fuller, 1954). "The phenotype is always the resultant of the interaction between a certain genotype and a certain environment" (Boyd, 1953). Although the latter cannot alter the properties of genes, it not only limits and modifies their expression but also independently initiates many directional trends of its own.

A genotype must have an environment in which to develop a phenotype. But the same genotype can produce quite different phenotypes, depending on the environments in which it may develop. Furthermore, a given environment can nurture quite different phenotypes, depending on the genotypes which may develop there. . . . So, while environment makes an undeniably important contribution to the particular values obtained in phenotypic measurements, consideration of particular environments should not change our general picture of population structure. Without an appreciation of the genotypic structure of populations, the behavioral sciences have no basis for distinguishing individual differences that are attributable to differences in previous history from those that are not, and no basis for understanding any differences whatsoever where there is a common history (Hirsch, 1963, p. 1442).

As already indicated, the "growth matrix," like the phenotype, is a product of all prior interactions between heredity and environment. It not only consists of "the immediately observable qualities of the organism" (i.e., the phenotype), but also of all *covert* factors within the individual which at any given time predispose the nature of his response to the environment and contribute to the current direction of his development. The products of the latter event, in turn, include new phenotype, new developmental predispositions and, hence, a new growth matrix.

The term "growth matrix" was introduced in this discussion because the special meaning to which it refers is conceptually distinct from that of both genotype and phenotype. The genotype is a stable, ordinarily unmodifiable structural entity which in an abstract sense is synonymous with all of the inherited potentialities of the organism; but the particular directional predispositions to which it contributes and which are *actually* operative at any given stage in the course of development are reflective of genotypic endow-ment *alone* only at the moment of conception. Thereafter, it is not pure genotypic tendencies which interact with current stimulating conditions to determine developmental outcome, but the former tendencies as modified by extragenic protoplasm, by other bodily tissues and agents, and by prior influences from gestational and external environments. The phenotype, which is an interactional product and describes the *manifest* appearance of the organism at a given point in its life cycle, comes closer than the genotype to indicating what is meant by the growth matrix; but it only includes *overt* properties of the individual entering the interactional process, and makes no reference to the equally important *covert* developmental predispositions.

Within the framework of the particular developmental sequence in which it is operative, the growth matrix manifests the same regulatory properties as the hereditary and environmental factors that determine it. That is, it exerts limiting, directional (patterning), and selective influences on development. And its modifiability is similarly dependent upon its own resistance to change and upon the strength of the environmental variables with which it interacts.

In the entire field of genetics and development, there is no more confusing term than that of "constitution." It has been variously defined as synonymous with the genotypic endowment of the individual, with all of his phenotypic characteristics, with multifactorial protective elements in his genic organiza-tion that facilitate his adaptation to the environment and increase his re-sistence to disease (Kallman, 1947), and with his "basic physiological makeup . . . at a given time" (Kluckhohn and Murray, 1949). In the broadest sense of the term, however, its meaning is most adequately and consistently conveyed by the coneept of growth matrix as delineated above.

Constitution therefore, refers to the totality of the individual's relatively stable predispositions, at a given point in his life history, to respond in par-ticular ways to environmental influences affecting his structural, functional, or behavioral development. By virtue of traditional usage, however, it is usually restricted to predispositions established by body type, by physiological characteristics (especially those related to metabolic, endocrinological and autonomic functions), by genically conditioned aspects of temperament and susceptibility to different physical and mental disorders, and by the various interrelationships among these latter factors. It includes those aspects of personality with strong genic loading as well as response predispositions that are morphological, biochemical, immunological, etc., rather than behavioral or psychological in nature. Existing correlations between these different categories of constitutional variables have been explained on the basis of (a) "pleiotropic or linked genes," (b) genically regulated mediating mecha-nisms (autonomic nervous system, endocrines) with dual effects on psychological and bodily functions, and (c) experientially established reciprocal relationships between certain physical and temperamental traits such as muscular hypertrophy and enjoyment of motor activity (see p. 76).

Manipulation of Developmental Regulation. The problem of developmental regulation also has important practical implications. As our knowledge of the relevant determinants expands, it becomes increasingly possible to manipulate them in ways that are most conducive to optimal or desired outcomes. If we rule out eugenic procedures at the present time (see p. 34), contemporary attempts at manipulation must necessarily assume the existence of a constituted and fixed genotype. For this reason, only in relation to the environmental determinants of a given trait, can intervention be effected *directly* and with hope of achieving significant positive changes in patterning or level of functioning. It is only necessary in such cases—to the extent that is compatible with the plasticity of the trait and with the possibility of modifying the physical, interpersonal and social environments—to provide those environmental conditions that are correlated with optimal development* in the desired direction.

The above statement conflicts in no way with the previous description of genotypic predispositions as subject to modification. It must be realized, however, at the present level of maturity in genetic research, that modification can only be affected indirectly by the operation of the environmental determinants of a given trait rather than directly by any change in its genetic structure in the future because:

"A method may some day be discovered to induce directed mutations, i.e., to change specific genes in desired ways. This would enable one to alter certain genes in the sex cells or in the body cells, and thus "cure" hereditary diseases by removing their causes." (Dobzhansky, 1962, p. 333).

The possibility in the future of direct modification of genetic dispositions, may center around the research focused upon the chemical nature of the genes. Present research evidence suggests that the essential "hereditary" chemical is deoxyribonucleic acid (DNA) (Dobzhansky, 1962; Hirsch, 1967; Munn, 1965; McClearn, 1964; Sutton, 1965). DNA constitutes about 40 percent of the chromosomes, and it is not present in other parts of the cell (McClearn, 1964), The function of DNA appears to be in *"coding"* genetic information which other constituents of the chromosome *"translate"* into action by transforming the cytoplasmic material. Ribonucleic acid (RNA) appears to be the translator of the coded message and "carries the genetic information in the DNA to the cytoplasm where it serves as a template for

---

What are optimal conditions for development will, of course, apply generally to only certain kinds of growth; for other types of growth these conditions will vary for different categories of individuals. Genic determinants of traits, on the other hand, cannot be influenced directly or in the same positive sense.

the specific alignment of amino acids" (Sutton, 1965). The amino acids become linked to a protein chain, which is then released from the RNA and becomes available to fulfill its role in cellular biochemical processes. The possibility of direct alteration of this process may prove to be most important in alleviating certain genetic anomalies in man (e.g., sickle cell anemia is an anomaly which appears to be due to a certain type of hemoglobin which is not found in normal individuals). "Genetic studies have shown that the difference is due to one locus. Studies of the molecular nature of hemoglobin have shown that it is a large molecule composed of some 560 amino acids, and it has been found that the sickle cell hemoglobin differs from normal hemoglobin only in the substitution of valine for glutamic acid in one particular location." (McClearn, 1964, p. 451).

Direct intervention (possibly induced by mutation via high energy radiation* or chemical means) is important here since the genetic differences at one locus result in the change of only one amino acid in a complex molecule, yet the difference appears to be a matter of life and death.*

In less extreme cases, the environment can, at best, indirectly mitigate or circumvent the negative consequences of genotypic inadequacies. It cannot exert a more positive influence on development by generating genic predispositions that do not already exist as, for example, it can generate new exogenously derived predispositions. To counteract the effects of genic insufficiency, either optimal environmental conditions can be brought to bear on development, or phenotypic deficiencies can be compensated for nondevelopmentally by employing substitutive measures (e.g., supplying diabetics with insulin they can not produce, having diets free of phenylalanine for those who suffer from phenylketonuria, administering reserpine to people with Huntington's chorea) or surgical procedures.

Regulatory Functions of Heredity and Environment in Development. The respective roles of hereditary and environmental factors in the bipolar regulation of development may be summarized in the following listing of the ways in which each participates in the developmental process:

1. Genic factors set absolute *limits* of growth for both individual and species which cannot be exceeded in any environment, as well as determining capacity for profiting from environmental stimulation. Environmental factors similarly *limit* the extent to which existing genic potentiality can be realized in individuals or species. In a generally optimal environment, phenotypic actualization of the genotype is enhanced for everyone, and the prevailing range of variability is widened.

The vast majority of mutations produced by non selective massive radiation are lethal in nature. Although this consideration is irrelevant in radiating plant seeds to produce one beneficial mutation in perhaps a million, the method is obviously proscribed in human genetics.

2. Both factors in varying degrees contribute to the *patterning* of traits, i.e., determining the direction, differentiation, content, and sequence of development.

3. Genic variables make the individual *selectively* sensitive to or more prone to prefer certain aspects of the environment to others. Environmental variables, on the other hand, in accordance with cultural needs and values, differentially *select* from the total range of genic potentiality certain capacities and traits for maximal development and others for relative oblivion.

4. To a certain extent, the genetically conditioned temperamental characteristics of an individual help determine his environment by differentially affecting the attitudes and reactions toward himself of significant persons in his interpersonal milieu.

Determination of Relative Influence

Now that we have defined the different interactional variables and products involved in the developmental process, we are ready to consider the relative contributions of hereditary and environmental factors. Our aim is to go beyond the indisputable but unilluminating generality that all development is the product of heredity *and* (rather than *or*) environment. Obviously, as abundant research data have already demonstrated, there is and can never be any overall solution to the question of relative influence. The weight of each factor in the resulting phenotype is not only different for every conceivable trait, but also for every individual in a given population. However, if we wish to derive some meaningful generalizations from data bearing on such relationships, it will first be necessary to deal with the "average effects [of heredity and environment] upon individual differences," and to establish various quantitative classes of relative influence, i.e., categories of development regulated predominantly by either factor or by varying proportions of the two factors. The next step is to establish criteria for traits that may be placed in each of these categories and to relate them to different models of genic organization* and of heredity-environment interaction.

Before attempting these latter tasks, it will be helpful to note that in general the greater the relative influence of genic factors is upon the development of a given trait the less variable it tends to be in its phenotypic expression. This inverse relationship between degree of genic regulation and extent of expressed variability is a function of two related factors. First, more potent genic effects are, by definition, more resistant to environmental influence than relatively less potent genic effects. Hence, the resulting phenotype tends to reflect mostly the impact of genic sources of variability in the

---

The detailed properties, organization and effects of genes are obviously beyond the scope of this volume. For more detailed treatments see Boyd, 1953; Hirsch, 1967; Penrose, 1961; Snyder and David, 1957; Sutton, 1961; Waddington, 1957.

former instance and of both genic and environmental sources in the latter instance. Second, traits referable to more prepotent, environmentally resistant genic effects generally illustrate the operation of single or major genes which genotypically exhibit very little variability and phenotypically are distributed in either uniform or dichotomous fashion among members of a species (e.g., almost all human beings have two eyes which tend to be blue or brown in color). On the other hand, traits referable to less prepotent and more environmentally susceptible genic effects are generally polygenic in nature (see p. 33) and, hence, are genotypically more variable from one individual to another (except in monozygotic twins), and phenotypically are continuously distributed (e.g., height, I.Q.). Thus, traits that are more heavily determined by hereditary factors tend to be less variable on two counts: they not only reflect less the influence of environmental variability but also are less variable in terms of their genic components.

It is true, of course, that traits predominantly influenced by environmental factors also reflect only a single source of variability. However, this solitary source of variability is usually greater than in the analogous situation of traits determined predominantly by heredity, since the latter traits tend to be expressions of single-gene effects. Nevertheless, although environmental diversity is more striking than genotypic diversity (even where polygenes are involved), it is quite obvious that there are uniformities as well as differences in the environments of individuals, and that all developmental uniformities cannot be ascribed to genic factors alone.

The Ontogenetic-Phylogenetic Continuum

The bottom row of figure 1 presents a classification of categories reflective of varying relative weights of heredity and environment (modified from Boyd, 1953), arranged in the form of a continuum. At one end of the continuum are traits that are so prepotently determined by heredity that they appear almost invariably in *any* environment favorable enough to sustain life. At the other end of the continuum are traits that are analogously determined in prepotent fashion by the environment. In between are categories of traits the developmental direction of which is either (a) primarily determined by one factor, contingent upon certain restrictive conditions in the other, or (b) the additive or vectorial resultant of more nearly independent influences provided by both factors.

In relation to this continuum, a useful qualitative distinction can be drawn between two great classes of traits—phylogenetic and ontogenetic—under which can be placed the entire spectrum of phenotypic characteristics (morphological, physiological and behavioral) manifested by a given species. *Phylogenetic* traits are fundamental developmental acquisitions that are both characteristic of the species as a biologically distinct class of organisms and

Genic Mechanism	Identical single – gene effects	Dichotomous single – gene effects	Polygenic	Polygenic	Polygenic
Susceptibility of Genotype to Environmental Influence	Practically zero	Slight	Moderate	Great	Very great
Phenotypic Range of Variability	Practically zero	Dichotomous	Continuous with moderate range	Continuous with wide range	Continuous with very wide range
←———————————————————————————————————→					
	Phylogenetic Traits	←——————— Ontogenetic Traits ———————→			
Relative Determination of Phenotype	Genetic for almost any environment	(a) Genetic within a restricted range of environmental conditions	(b) Bipolar (additive or vectorial effects of heredity and environment)	(c) Environmental within a restricted range of genotypes	(d) Environmental for almost any genotype

FIGURE 1. Schematic representation of a hypothetical ontogenetic-phylogenetic continuum showing relative influence of heredity and environment on the development of a given trait.

essentially independent of individual experience. Hence, they are essentially identical for all members of the species. *Ontogenetic* traits, on the other hand, are also present or potentially present in almost all members of the species, but differ from one individual to another in accordance with both genic and environmental sources of variability. They constitute the entire range of characteristics by which individual representatives of the species can be distinguished from each other in contradistinction to the fund of characteristics they share in common.

As illustrated in figure 1, phylogenetic traits tend to be homogeneously determined by single-gene effects that are highly resistant to environmental influence and, both genotypically and phenotypically, are practically identical for all individual members of a given species. Ontogenetic traits, on the other hand, are extremely heterogeneous with respect to the degree of their genic determination. They include (a) single-gene effects, only slightly susceptible to environmental influences, that are expressed with considerable regularity and completeness and result in dichotomous phenotypic distributions (e.g., brown versus blue eyes; ovaries versus testes); (b) polygenic effects, moderately susceptible to environmental influences, that are irregularly and incompletely expressed and result phenotypically in relatively wide continuous distributions (e.g., height, weight, IQ); and (c) traits almost completely determined by environmental factors (e.g., social and cultural attitudes).

The acquisition of phylogenetic traits by the individual is extremely important for the realization of "his racial inheritance" (Gesell, 1954). In human beings, the vast majority at such traits develop during prenatal life and early infancy and include morphological, physiological and behavioral characteristics essential for viability or species membership. Behaviorally, they are for the most part restricted to reflex, sensory, sensori-motor, and neuromuscular acquisitions (e.g., tendon reflexes, vision, sitting, walking, vocalization). On the whole, these traits develop "autogenously," i.e., without the benefit of cultural tutelage, and, barring *unusual* environmental pressures, they emerge at approximately the same age and in the same sequence in all sociocultural environments, thereby rendering the basic developmental features of infancy universal in spite of tremendous diversity in child-rearing practices (Dennis & Dennis, 1940). Even a practice as severe as cradling, for example, does not materially delay the age of walking among Hopi infants (Dennis, 1940), and pronounced socioeconomic differences do not affect the acquisition of neuro-muscular and sensori-motor capacities during the first 36 weeks of life* (Gilliland, 1951). On the other hand, marked cultural pressures and taboos may effect some changes in the sequential patterning of locomotor development. Balinese infants do not crawl in the course of learning to walk, and unlike American infants squat before they are able to stand (Mead & Macgregor, 1951).

At either extreme of the ontogenetic-phylogenetic continuum, literal insistence on the bipolar determination of development is confusing, although as the aforementioned examples indicate, some interaction always takes place. Throughout the greater range of the continuum, however, the bipolar determination of such ontogenetic traits as temperament and intelligence is clearly evident. Sometimes, nevertheless, when one determinant is not completely prepotent and the directional influence of the other is only minimal, the latter's contribution to development is overshadowed and tends to be disregarded entirely. Hence, the fact that a given trait (e.g., temperamental factors associated with sex membership) is not universally distributed but appears to be determined by specific cultural factors does not definitely eliminate the possibility that relatively weak panhuman genic predispositions might be operative but overwhelmed by sociocultural variables. It is similarly easy to overlook the contribution of relatively noncrucial environmental factors when hereditary influences appear all-important (e.g., as in prehensile and locomotor development). Also, although cross-cultural universality of a behavioral trait (e.g., nuclear family groupings), coupled with

---

*It should be noted however, that as early as 13½ months, premature negro children of both sexes score significantly lower than full term infants on a standardization test of gross motor development (Braine, Hermer, Wortis, Freedman, 1966).

occurrence among infrahuman primates, is strong presumptive evidence of considerable genic determination, much of the uniformity may be a product of universally limited environmental or social possibilities (Sells, 1963).

Intra-species Uniformities, Differences and Limits of Variability. From the foregoing considerations, it is evident that the following sources of developmental *uniformity* exist within a species: First, all members of a species develop phylogenetic traits (e.g., reflexes, sitting) that are almost identical in sequence and detailed content because of the operation of prepotent identical genes. Second, uniformities with respect to *general* process and sequence of development (e.g., language, cognitive) arise as a result of commonalities in polygenic make-up. Superimposed on these uniformities, however, are genically conditioned individual differences in rate of growth, ultimate level of attainment, and detailed content and sequence of development. Lastly, commonalities in *environmental* conditioning give rise to comparable kinds of process and sequence uniformities in the development of ontogenetic traits, (Sells, 1963). It is extremely important to note at this point that because phylogenetic traits pertaining to behavioral aspects of development are relatively rare in human beings beyond the first year of life, few developmental generalizations about the behavior of children could ever be formulated if these latter two sources of uniformities did not exist. We would, otherwise, have to regard development in each individual as practically unique and as a law unto itself.

Intra-species *differences* in phenotypic outcome are similarly attributable to both hereditary and environmental factors. Differences of genic origin are either dichotomously distributed in the case of single-gene effects or continuously distributed in the case of polygenic effects. Environmentally conditioned differences, in turn, reflect variation in familial and cultural setting as well as in the idiosyncratic experience of individuals, and are characteristically distributed within a wide range of continuous variability.

The limits of developmental variability within a species are determined by the interaction between two factors: (a) a characteristic range of genotypic diversity for a given trait setting maximal and minimal points of potential attainment at the extremes of the distribution*; and (b) the prevailing range of environmental diversity, which both determines the degree of realization of genotypic potentialities that is possible and more independently influences the patterning of traits. In instances of minimal genic determination of development, the potential range of phenotypic variability is as unlimited as environmental variability itself, subject, of course, to constraints imposed by limitations in other relevant traits.

The adult stature of most human beings, for example, varies between four feet, ten inches and six feet, eight inches.

Method of Determining Relative Weight

The precise determination in quantitative terms of the proportionate influence of heredity and environment upon the development of a given trait is naturally fraught with serious difficulties. In the first place, all empirical approaches to this problem presuppose the possibility of working with known and measurable degrees of genotypic and environmental similarities and differences. Actually, this requirement can at best be met only indirectly and approximately for both kinds of variables. The genotype, for example, can never be measured directly; its properties must always be inferred from its effects, which invariably, even at the moment of birth, have already been influenced to an undeterminable extent by fetal, gestational, and external environments. Even in the case of monozygotic twins it is unwarranted to assume complete genotypic equivalence. And when it comes to equating or estimating environmental variability, the difficulties of establishing adequate controls and obtaining accurate measures are even greater. Differential specification of the environment may lead to different relationships with varied traits. Thus, the physical and health environmental differences are more closely related to the trait of *weight*, whereas educational environmental differences are more clearly related to I.Q. (Bloom, 1964; Newman, Freeman and Holzinger, 1937; Smith, 1965). Second, in many research areas such as the development of intelligence, personality, and behavior disorders, the above methodological hazards are further compounded by the unavailability of completely reliable and valid measures of the trait under investigation (Fuller and Thompson, 1960; Jones, 1954). Finally, the quantitative estimates of the relative influence of heredity and environment can be validly applied only to populations that are reasonably comparable (in terms of level and variability of the two factors) to the sample from which they were derived (Fuller *et al*, 1960; Jones, 1954; Smith, 1965).* And since these highly fallible estimates naturally refer to "average effects upon individual differences, or to differences between groups" (Jones, 1954), their probable errors, when applied to particular individuals must obviously be high enough to impair seriously their usefulness for prognostic purposes.

Co-Twin Method. All methods of determining the proportionate weight of heredity and environment attempt to ascertain the variation in a given trait attributable to variability in each of the two factors. In the co-twin method, variability with respect to each factor is introduced separately while the other is held constant. When the co-twin method is being utilized, the relative influence of heredity would be adjudged greater than that of environment

---

Smith (1965) found that dizygotic twin families are more frequently observed to be of lower socio-economic status than are monozygotic families. This difference in overall environment of the two types may in turn influence intra-pair differences.

(a) if *much* variation occurred in the phenotypic outcome of a trait as genic constitution was varied in a relatively homogeneous environment, and (b) if *little* variation occurred in trait outcome as environmental setting was varied for relatively homogeneous genotypes. In the first instance, holding family environment for sibling pairs constant, small mean intra-pair trait differences would be associated with relative genotypic equivalence (monozygotic twins), and large trait differences with genotypic diversity (like-sex dizygotic twins). In the second instance, holding heredity constant, extremely divergent environmental settings would *not* be associated with much larger mean intra-pair trait differences than would relatively similar environmental settings (monozygotic twins reared together versus monozygotic twins reared apart).

In interpreting co-twin studies, it is important to keep several methodological and theoretical considerations in mind (Fuller *et al*, 1960).* (1) Are all twin pairs from a homogeneous sample of adequate size? Comparison between monozygotic pairs of one age and dizygotic pairs of another are spurious, since age may have an important effect on the trait measured. (2) Accurate diagnosis of zygosity is of critical importance. Dizygotic opposite sexed twins are generally not used in psychological genetics because sex differences introduce complications in comparison with necessarily like-sexed monozygotic pairs. (3) The possibility of *overestimating* the importance of heredity in monozygotic twins when compared with dizygotic twins because monozygotic pairs tend to be together more and to select similar surroundings and common friends to a greater extent than do dizygotic twins. In many instances, monozygotic twins are treated more alike, and may even be confused by parents and associates. The obvious physical similarity of monozygotic twins may influence judges' ratings in underestimating psychological differences. (4) The possibility of *underestimating* the importance of heredity in monozygotic twins when compared with dizygotic twins can occur, if rebellion against identification with an identical twin leads to the adoption of different personality roles. Sensitivity of judges to the previous problem of *overestimation* may influence the ratings on monozygotic co-twins by picking out minor differences between them as important. (5) Finally, there is the impossibility of keeping genetically different dizygotic twins in as close step developmentally as is possible with a pair of monozygotic twins. The different genotypes of dyzygotic pairs must interact differentially with environment, and the responses lead to further differentiation accumulated upon a genotypic base. If monozygotic twins are placed in objectively different environments, it is conceivable that they will select similar parts for attention and effectively reduce the psychological consequences of environmental variability.

---

*See Fuller & Thompson (1960) for a more detailed discussion of these questions.

More specific findings illustrating the use of these various research methods will be provided later in this chapter and in the discussion of the nature-nurture problem as it relates to intellectual development (see Chapter 17). For our present purposes it will suffice to give several examples showing that the relative influence of heredity and environment varies greatly depending upon the particular trait under investigation. Preliminary evidence from twin studies, in which both genic and environmental sources of variability were considered, indicates that physical traits (except for body weight and muscular development) are least affected and that intellectual attainment and personality traits (especially those associated with values and interests) are most affected by environmental variability.* Somewhere between these two extremes are such psychological characteristics as intelligence and temperamental traits related to susceptibility to personality disorder. Environmental variability results in relatively small differences between separated monozygotic twins in the incidence of schizophrenia (Fuller *et al*, 1960).

Multi-Abstract-Variance-Analysis. New statistical techniques are now being suggested in order to explore the relative influence of heredity and environment and their interaction. An important shortcoming of the statistics utilized in the co-twin method is that they do not take into consideration the relationship between hereditary and environmental influences (Cattell, 1963, 1965). Furthermore, the twin method gives only the ratio for quite specific "within" family hereditary variation and the quite peculiar environmental differences between twins (Cattell, 1965). A Multi-Abstract-Variance Analysis (M.A.V.A.), which is a type of analysis of variance, is suggested (Cattell, 1963, 1965) for future behavior genetic research because it takes into account the variability of hereditary and environmental concomitancy and extends beyond the twin study method of considering only "within" family heredity variation, by also including "between" family heredity variation, the salient feature of the M.A.V.A. method. Discussions of different quantitative methods in this research area are available (Fuller and Thompson, 1960; McClearn, 1962; Vandenberg, 1965). The present discussion is included simply to provide an illustration of how one particular method (M.A.V.A.) is attempting to go beyond the twin method models. It is the selection of various types of families whose variances may be considered as combinations of the fundamental variances. The equations are grouped in sets such that solutions for certain variance terms and correlations are possible (Fuller and Thompson, 1960). It is possible to examine a greater variety of situations with this method when compared with co-twin

*Similar findings are reported by Clark, 1956 in the American Journal of Human Genetics 8: 49-56, 1956 and by Bloom (1964). For a current example of a co-twin study see Brown, Stafford, and Vandenberg (1967).

analysis. In addition to the analysis of (1) identical twins reared together; (2) identical twins reared apart; (3) sibs reared together and (4) sibs reared apart, one can also examine situations such as (5) half-sibs reared together; (6) half-sibs reared apart; (7) unrelated children reared in the same family and, finally, (8) unrelated children reared apart.

Let us consider the comparison between two situations that cannot be examined by the co-twin method: (1) unrelated children reared together (σ^2 UT), the case of foster families and, (2) siblings raised together (σ^2 ST). For practical purposes the important hereditary and environmental variances are those "within" families *genetic* and *environmental* differences (σ^2 wg and σ^2 we), and those "between" families *genetic* and *environmental* differences (σ^2 bg + σ^2 be). To illustrate, the components of the family variance in these two situations would be as follows:

$$\sigma^2 \text{ UT} = \sigma^2 \text{ wg} + \sigma^2 \text{ we} + \sigma^2 \text{ bg} + (2r \text{ wg, we wg we} + 2r \text{ we, bg we wg})$$
$$\sigma^2 \text{ ST} = \sigma^2 \text{ wg} + \sigma^2 \text{ we} + (2r \text{ wg, we wg we}) \qquad (\sigma = \text{variance})$$

The terms in the parentheses represent the interactions between the simple component variances. The solution for the fundamental variance is the separation of the one variance term (σ^2 bg) which is not common to both situations. Thus $\sigma^2 \text{ bg} = \sigma^2 \text{ UT} - \sigma^2 \text{ ST}$.

The M.A.V.A. method is valuable for getting at developmental laws in situations where experimental control is impractical. The method has more potential significance for the general nature-nurture problem than the results of twin studies because of the diversity of family types it can treat (Cattell, 1965).*

DETERMINATION OF INTRA- AND INTERCULTURAL UNIFORMITIES AND DIFFERENCES

In the preceding section we have seen how it is possible to integrate meaningfully a large number of complex interrelationships among genic mechanisms, relative potency of heredity and environment, and degrees of expressed phenotypic variability by postulating the existence of a continuum of ontogenetic-phylogenteic traits (see figure 1). This paradigm defines in highly general terms the interactional nature of developmental regulation for a wide range of traits and species representation along a phyletic scale. It is this very generality of its applicability, however, that makes it unsuitable for conceptualizing the regulatory relationships governing the vast majority of developmental phenomena considered in this volume. Human development is characterized by various special features that make desirable the

---

*In principle, the method can be broadened to include other heredity units than the family, such as kith groups and races and also other environmentally uniform groups, e.g., cultures, social status strata, etc. (Cattell, 1965).

introduction of additional organizing concepts. The latter, however, supplement rather than supplant or invalidate the previously established biological classification.

The unmodified ontogenetic-phylogenetic paradigm cannot handle adequately problems of human development for the following reasons:

First, because human beings are biologically unique in undergoing development under distinctive cultural auspices, it is not very meaningful to talk about *intra-species* uniformities and differences as such. It is more illuminating to inquire why and in what ways development (a) is alike in all cultures, (b) differs from one culture to another, (c) is essentially similar for most individuals within a culture, and (d) varies for individual representatives of a particular culture.

Second, relatively few of the uniformities characterizing human behavioral development can be referred to the phylogenetic end of the continuum. Hence, in contrast to infrahuman, and especially infraprimate species, the overwhelming proportion of uniformities that do occur involve ontogenetic traits, are more variable in sequence, are both genically and environmentally determined, and are more reflective of process than content of development.

Third, within the range of ontogenetic behavioral traits, environmental factors are much more important determinants of both developmental uniformities and differences among human than among infrahuman individuals. At the lower phyletic levels, more of the basic patterns and processes of behavioral development are regulated by genic effects that are relatively resistant to environmental variability, thereby limiting the potential impact of the environment to comparatively inconsequential developmental sequences. This pre-emption of the more significant aspects of infrahuman behavioral regulation by genic factors obviously reduces the possible incidence of environmentally conditioned uniformities more than it does that of environmentally conditioned differences—since uniformities, unlike differences, characteristically occur at the level of general process rather than at the level of specific details of patterning. Furthermore, environmentally conditioned behavior in animals tends to be quite idiosyncratic to the individual. In human beings, on the other hand, not only are more basic patterns of behavior susceptible to environmental influence, but the culture also standardizes and institutionalizes the environment. We may conclude, therefore, that environmental factors primarily give rise to developmental differences in behavior among infrahumans, whereas among humans they also constitute a significant source of intra- and intercultural uniformity.

The very same behavioral plasticity of human beings also accounts for their potentially greater range of environmentally conditioned developmental differences (both intra- and intercultural). In the absence of this plasticity, the greater environmental variability induced by cultural factors could never be reflected in behavioral development.

In order to deal more adequately with these special developmental characteristics of human behavior, the following supplementary classification will be employed to categorize traits in terms of uniformities and differences exhibited within and between cultures: (a) The term *psychobiological* will refer to intercultural uniformities in development. Except for phylogenetic traits, which exhibit both process and content similarities, this category ordinarily includes only those ontogenetic traits that manifest a certain amount of genically and/or environmentally determined panhuman uniformity in the process of development (irrespective of specific differences in form, content, or degree attributable to cultural variation). (b) The term *psychosocial* will encompass intercultural differences and their reciprocal intracultural uniformities in development. It refers to those relatively more plastic and environmentally determined ontogenetic traits that reflect the influence of the particular or unique customs, values, institutions and social conditions prevailing within a given culture. It is self-evident, of course, that the very psychosocial traits that differentiate individual behavioral development from one culture to another (i.e., interculturally) constitute *intraculturally* the uniformities characterizing the development of individuals who share the same cultural membership. (c) The term *idiosyncratic* will refer to all of the differences in developmental outcome and process among individuals within the same culture. It includes ontogenetic traits which are either not completely plastic to environmental influences or which reflect the impact of that unique combination of experiences which is idiosyncratic for each individual representative of a particular culture.

Sources of Psychobiological Traits

In general, intercultural uniformities in behavioral development (i.e., psychobiological traits) are determined by the interaction between (a) certain genic predispositions and potentialities which all human beings share in common, and (b) certain universal features of their physical, interpersonal and cultural environments. At the outset, however, it should be noted that the concept of psychobiological traits is a far cry from the theory of universal cultural evolution. In the first place, the former concept refers to successive changes in the life cycles of *individual* representatives of the culture and not to historical changes in cultural forms and practices. Second, cultural evolution ordinarily refers to a complicated chain of events set off by intricate social and economic phenomena. The processes of cultural change are, interculturally, much more divergent than they are similar; and insofar as they influence individual development, they tend to give rise to psychosocial rather than psychobiological traits.

Man differs in his development from infrahuman species not only in being uniquely stimulated by a rich cultural environment, but also in possessing a genic endowment that enables him to acquire culture and to respond to it in particular ways. This same endowment, of course, enables him to invent and acquire a culture in the first place, and to continually modify and expand it. The essential culture-giving attributes of his genic make-up are: (a) the fact that so many of his basic behavioral adaptations are not prepotently determined by hereditary influences, thereby leaving room for invention and making his survival dependent upon it; and (b) the fact that he possesses the cognitive and other capacities that make possible the original invention and transmission of learned adaptations within a cultural framework and their subsequent acquisition by later generations.

Table 1 presents in highly condensed form the sources (determinants) of psychobiological traits. Actual examples or manifestations of such traits will be considered later under the heading of "human nature."

TABLE 1—*Sources of Psychobiological Traits**

I. Genetic Sources

A. Patterning Predispositions

1. Predispositions toward relatively invariable process and content ("phylogenetic") uniformities in development (e.g., locomotion, prehension).
2. Predispositions toward more variable ("ontogenetic") process uniformities:
   a. General predispositions governing sequence of development in motor, emotional . and cognitive development (e.g., the "concrete-to-abstract" trend in cognitive development).
   b. Predispositions resulting in unlearned sensory preferences (e.g., sweet over bitter) and hierarchies of drive-reducing responses (e.g., sucking over kicking in hunger).
   c. Predispositions toward various responses to particular endocrine stimulation (e.g., selective lowering of thresholds for perceptual and behavioral responses; increased motility and irritability).
   d. Predispositions toward random, general activity.
   e. Predispositions to react to certain kinds of situations (e.g., frustration, pain, perceptual disorientation) with emotional instability.
   f. Predispositions toward specific motor expression of various emotional states (e.g., facial expressions in anger, fear, joy).
   g. Predispositions to respond to frustration and anxiety in particular ways (e.g., perseveration, stereotypy, regression, defense and escape mechanisms).
   h. Predispositions toward certain primate temperamental-social traits; gregariousness; tendency to form social aggregations†; desire for companionship; dislike of social isolation; curiosity; imitativeness. etc.

**Based on reference data (Hallowell, 1953; Harlow, 1953; Kluckhohn, 1953; Kluckhohn and Murray, 1949; Leuba, 1954; Murdock, 1945; Scott, 1953; Spiro, 1951). The listing of the various sources of psychobiological traits is intended to be illustrative rather than exhaustive.*

†*Harlow (1953) observes that in contrast to New World primates, the Old World primate stock (from which man and the anthropoid apes are descended) exhibits many antisocial temperamental traits, such as brutality, aggressiveness, self-centeredness, and ruthless dominance patterns, which are not ideally suited to the functioning of complex social organizations. However, even if such predispositions are operative at the human level, they are obviously not singly determinative as evidenced by the tremendous intercultural variability in the expression of these traits.*

B. Potentialities for Developing Various Capacities

1. Potentialities for developing species-characteristic capacities and mechanics of biological and psychological functioning that are basically stable over the life span (e.g., most reflex activity).

2. Potentialities for acquiring species-characteristic capacities that fluctuate more on a developmental basis: ranges of sensory sensitivity; gross motor skills; perceptual, memory, discriminative functions; primary drives and emotions.

3. Potentialities for various types and mechanisms of social behavior exhibited by primates, e.g., affection, loyalty, identification, helpfulness, mutual dependence, rivalry, possessiveness, differentiated interpersonal roles and status.

4. Potentialities for various types and mechanisms of learning, e.g., conditioning and problem solving; incidental, intentional, goal-directed and drive-reduction learning; imitation and identification; rote and meaningful verbal learning, etc.

5. Potentialities for developing unique human capacities making possible and facilitating the invention and acquisition of culture.†

   a. Unusual capacity for behavioral plasticity, i.e., for learning major behavioral adaptations to the environment (e.g., for improvising mechanisms of satisfying biological needs, institutionalizing social relationships, inventing tools).

   b. Greater capacity for mechanical dexterity (dependent in part upon opposing thumb and erect posture).

   c. Capacity for inventing and acquiring language‡, making possible more complex conceptualization, commonality of meanings and values, indirect communication of ideas, and continuity of traditions (dependent upon spontaneous vocalization, superior mimicry and ability to articulate sounds, and superior symbolical intelligence).

   d. Greater capacity for higher-order conceptualization and problem solving involving the manipulation of symbols.

   e. Capacity for symbolical adjustive mechanisms (e.g., rationalization).

   f. Greater capacity for time perspective, delay of overt response, and anticipation of consequences.

   g. Greater capacity for self-awareness, making possible complex ego attitudes and motivations (e.g., self-esteem, levels of aspiration) and self-evaluation in relation to internalized group norms (necessary for conscience formulation).

---

†*It is generally agreed that human culture, in contradistinction to animal societies, is characterized by more variable, learned adaptations; the institutionalization of interpersonal relationships; the possibility of indirect (other than face-to-face) communication between individuals and groups; continuity of learned adaptations from one generation to another; an invented symbolical language; intergroup relationships, etc.*

‡*Studies of chimpanzee and human infants reared alike (Hayes, 1951; Kellogg & Kellogg, 1933) show that their rate of acquiring habits is quite comparable with respect to such learnings as use of the toilet, utilization of eating utensils, dressing, etc. The former, however, exhibit little spontaneous vocalization and, for all practical purposes, fail to acquire linguistic sounds and language. In evaluating the comparability that does exist, it should also be borne in mind that the chimpanzee matures more rapidly and ordinarily attains adult maturity at a much earlier age.*

II. Environmental Sources

A. Universal Interpersonal Problems, Needs, and Conditions of Adaptation to the Physical and Social Environments

1. Intrafamilial needs, problems, and conditions of adaptation:
    a. Occurrence of early development within nuclear family group assuming responsibility for child's physical survival, rearing and enculturation.
    b. Basic structural conditions of family organization: two sexes; more than one child; individuals of different age, sex, status, and capacity in the same group.
    c. Long period of biosocial and emotional dependence on parents facilitating socialization, identification, and internalization of parental norms.
    d. Necessity for intrafamilial differentiation of roles and status, regulation of sexual access, and socialization of child.
    e. Universally limited possibilities in basic dimensions of parent attitudes (e.g., accepting or rejecting; over- or underdominating. etc.); uniformities in modification of parental demands and expectations with increasing maturity of child.
    f. Uniform shifts in kinds of biosocial status (derived or primary) available to child at different states of maturity, with accompanying transitional stages in personality development.

2. Social or extrafamilial needs, problems and conditions of adaptation:
    a. Satisfaction of group's biological needs and problems of physical survival; regulation of sexual access.
    b. Invention of stable and organized systems of social interaction and differentiation of roles and status (e.g., division of labor, privileges, responsibilities).
    c. Need for socialization and personality maturation of child in the direction of greater independence and frustration tolerance, inhibition of immediate impulses, self-subordination to group norms, internalization of moral obligations, acceptance of social responsibility.
    d. Integrative system of communication, some mutuality of values, minimal reciprocity of behavior and expectations.

B. "Universal Categories of Culture" and Cultural Needs

1. Commonality in customs, practices, and adaptive solutions (e.g., the universality of kinship systems, codified language, incest taboos, institutionalization of status relationships and of child rearing practices, division of labor).
2. Needs for cultural survival: protection against external threats and internal disruption, recognition of limited life span, provision for indoctrination and training of younger generation.

Two general categories of determinants, genic and environmental, are delineated. The former in turn are broken down into (a) predispositions toward specified kinds of developmental patterning, and (b) potentialities for developing certain capacities or mechanisms of biological and psychological functioning that both limit and make possible the kinds of development that can take place. Some of the predispositions and capacities are shared with man's primate relatives; others are unique to man and account for culture as a biological emergent. They are deduced from developmental comparisons between man and other primates in their natural habitat, in controlled situations, and in simulated human environments. It must be borne in mind, however, that genic predispositions toward various temperamental traits are much more plastic in man than in other primates and are subject to cortical modification in the light of all kinds of situational and cultural variables. Nevertheless they are still operative as partial determinants and at least furnish the alternatives from which cultural selection is made.

The environmental sources of psychobiological traits are grouped under *interpersonal* (both intra- and extrafamilial) and *cultural* categories. The former category includes universal *needs, problems* and *conditions* of adaptation to the physical and social environments that are characteristic of man as a social animal and both antedate and coexist with culture. Cultural sources of psychobiological traits, on the other hand, consist of a common body of customs or adaptive *solutions* to the above needs and problems as well as universal new needs generated by culture itself. The "common denominators" of culture, as already noted, reflect the operation of the same genic and interpersonal uniformities giving rise to psychobiological traits. In addition, they are attributable to universal features of the physical environment, to common limitations in available solutions, and to certain gross parallels in cultural development. *

Human Nature. The conception of psychobiological traits,† i.e., intercultural uniformities in development transcending specific differences in cultural conditioning, corresponds to what has traditionally been referred to as "human nature." This latter concept, however, has long since fallen into disrepute because of certain unwarranted assumptions that had been made about the source of these uniformities. Predeterminists accounted for them on the basis of prepotent, genically determined predispositions for all human beings, irrespective of cultural milieu, to develop in uniform ways. Preformationists invoked the concept of hereditary, prestructured, species-wide instincts. Further difficulty was generated by the ethnocentric tendency to identify as panhuman behavior (i.e., as part of human nature) some of the distinctive subcultural or psychosocial traits prevailing within our own culture (e.g., desire for prestige). Thus, when it became evident that such ethnocentric projections had no intercultural basis in fact, that no complexly

---

*We are only concerned here with "universal categories of culture" as determinants of psychobiological traits. Sophisticated discussions of the factors generating these universal categories are available (Hallowell, 1953; Kluckhohn, 1953; Lindsey, 1967; Murdock, 1945) and in Chapter 2 (Steward, 1953).

†Examples of psychobiological traits include developmental sequences in locomotion and prehension, directional gradients in neuromuscular coordination, gross stages in personality development, general characteristics of personality maturation (see Chapter 8), general trends in cognitive development (see Chapter 15), etc.

patterned behavior is ever preformed, and that many intercultural uniformities are environmentally determined, these conceptions of human
nature became insupportable. Unfortunately, however, the baby was discarded with the bath. Instead of merely rejecting the untenable theories of
human nature, the valuable and necessary concept of human nature itself
was dismissed as invalid.

Much of the difficulty with the concept of human nature arose from a failure to distinguish between intercultural behavioral uniformities and their
sources or determinants. Both were loosely referred to as "human nature."
From the restricted perspective of instinctual or predeterministic theory, the
distinction between uniformities of innate origin and innate determinants of
uniformities was obviously not very important. However, when environmental determinants entered the picture, the broader distinction could no
longer be logically ignored without giving rise to serious misunderstandings.
Hence, it was not always as clear as it should have been (a) that if the term,
human nature, were to be applied to developmental uniformities, *both* genic and
environmental determinants had to be recognized, and (b) that if it were still
desired to reserve the human nature concept for the "raw material" or
hereditary basis of human behavior, the term could not refer to panhuman
commonalities in behavioral development but only to their genic
determinants.

In choosing between these alternative meanings, we have decided to use
the term *human nature* to refer to psychobiological traits, i.e., to the uniform
ways in which human beings actually develop everywhere, irrespective of
cause, for the following reasons: (a) This connotation is somewhat more
consistent with historical usage. (b) Intercultural uniformities in development can be identified directly by conducting cross-cultural research, whereas
their genic determinants can only be inferred indirectly and tentatively from
inter-species comparisons.* For example, the similarities observed between
human beings and chimpanzees, each in their own habitat, could be caused
by comparable interpersonal variables as well as by genic commonalities;
and the differences between human and chimpanzee infants reared in the
same environment are not necessarily determined by uniquely human genic
potentialities, but could be attributed, in part, to the disadvantages experienced by chimpanzees in being exposed to an environment structured for
and by human beings.

---

*The method of determining the relative influence of hereditary and environmental factors described
above (see page 60) can only be applied intraculturally where it is possible to work with relatively
known and measureable degrees of genotypic and environmental variability.*

The method of cross-cultural comparison can be used only to identify a human nature defined in terms of intercultural developmental uniformities. It cannot be employed to provide data about an original nature referable to genic endowment. In conducting such comparisons, all we are doing is separating that which is culturally universal (psychobiological) from that which is specific to particular cultures (psychosocial). Since it is true, as Margaret Mead (1942) points out, that we are holding "human nature constant" here, it is valid to infer that observed intercultural differences are culturally determined. But at the same time we cannot conclude that the residual intercultural uniformities are genically determined. What we are holding constant is not just genotypic endowment alone, but also the interpersonal and cultural determinants of panhuman uniformities.

In accordance with our usage of the term, the only criterion that can be employed for designating a particular developmental sequence as characteristic of human nature is virtual universality of occurrence. This universality simply indicates that either genic or environmental commonalities (or the interaction between them) are sufficiently salient to induce process uniformities in development despite cultural diversity. The absence of universality, therefore, does not necessarily signify that particular hereditary or environmental factors are not operative but that they are insufficiently potent to be overtly determinative of psychobiological traits.

Observable changes in human nature, as we have defined it, are of course, inconceivable in terms of the usual historical time scale of centuries and millenia. But fortunately, neither the progress of civilization, significant betterment in the development of individuals, nor substantial improvement in interpersonal and intergroup relationships are as dependent upon the modification of human nature as is frequently alleged to be the case. The constraints imposed upon behavioral development by the determinants of human nature must certainly be realistically reckoned with, but they need not be exaggerated out of all proportion to their actual influence. Despite the virtual constancy of human nature, tremendous change and diversity in cultural forms have occurred—even in the relatively infinitesimal fraction of evolutionary time that is spanned by recorded history. It is quite apparent, therefore, that such changes must be brought about by complex social, economic, scientific, technological and ideological factors that exhibit an impressive range of variability within the framework of a stable human nature. And since man's psychosocial traits can be altered in the space of a single generation by conspicuous cultural change, considerable room for rapidly shifting variability in human behavioral development prevails within the same framework of psychobiological constancy.

Sources of Psychosocial Traits *

Now that we have examined the determinants of pan-human uniformities in development (i.e., psychobiological traits), the analagous problem may be raised in relation to psychosocial traits. Why is it that individuals who share the same cultural tradition also share certain developmental commonalities that set them apart from individuals in other cultures? What properties of culture † account for the relative intracultural standardization of so many features of behavior and development? At this point we shall be concerned only with the different *sources* or determinants of psychosocial traits and not with the *mechanisms* whereby the distinctive customs, values, and institutions of a particular culture find uniform representation in a corresponding set of developmental processes, content, and outcomes among its individual members. The actual *mediating* mechanisms responsible for the acquisition of cultural norms (e.g., external sanctions, imitation, identification, internalization of obligations, prestige suggestion) and for their selective perpetuation once acquired (e.g., canalization, reaction-sensitivity, perceptual structuralization, symbolization) will be elaborated in succeeding chapters. Only by the study of these latter mechanisms can we learn how and why "the members of society . . . *want to act as they have to act* and at the same time find gratification in acting according to the requirements of the culture" (Fromm, 1949).

In consequence of the growth of empirical cultural anthropology and the correction of earlier ethnocentric bias, many features of development that were formerly regarded as genically determined and universally distributed can now be categorized as psychosocial in origin. Nevertheless, so influential has the doctrine of maturation been, that many developmental uniformities are still widely accepted as inherently and inevitably characteristic of "Five" or "Nine," even though they could be much more credibly attributed to the fact that the children to whom they refer all happen to grow up in American middle-class families living in a medium-sized New England city.

---

*The term, psychosocial, customarily refers to the psychological accompaniments or consequences of social phenomena. In this volume, however, its meaning is restricted to those aspects of development that reflect the operation of practices unique to a given culture or group of cultures. Hence, depending on the level of generality (universality) involved, social factors may give rise to either psychobiological or psychosocial traits.

†Because "persons who live in the same culture are more likely to have the same genes than are persons who live far apart," it is theoretically possible that some psychosocial traits are genically determined (Kluckhohn & Murray, 1949). Actually, however, the possibility is quite remote since the only type of inheritance conceivable in the case of these relatively plastic characteristics is the polygenic variety; and the degree of genic segregation necessary for the uniform expression of polygenically determined traits within a culture never occurs in the absence of natural selection except in extremely small and isolated populations (David, 1951). We are quite safe, therefore, in attributing the source of psychosocial traits to environmental (predominantly cultural) factors.

On the other hand, the concept of psychosocial traits must be qualified in several important respects. First, all of the developmental uniformities found within a culture are not necessarily of psychosocial origin. In the absence of cross-cultural investigation, it is impossible to distinguish definitively between regularities conditioned by the specific intracultural standardization of the environment and regularities that are panhuman (intracultural) in scope. Second, the same psychosocial traits could be anticipated in all cultures in which similar kinds of institutionalized role and status relationships prevail (Kluckhohn & Murray, 1949). In instances where certain generalized aspects of these relationships approach universality (e.g., some dimensions of parent-child interaction), we would, in fact, be dealing with psychobiological traits. Last and most important, because culture itself is only an abstraction referring to *modal* behavior, values, norms, etc., the developmental uniformities it induces can be regarded only as approximate rather than as identical. Herein lies the source of many of the idiosyncratic traits to be discussed below. "Few institutions apply without exception to every member of a society" (Hands, 1949). In addition to "universals," i.e., beliefs, values, and aspirations shared by practically all members of a culture, there are "specialities" (skills, values, and behaviors restricted to a particular age, sex, status or occupational group) as well as culturally tolerated *alternative* value systems that cut across these latter groupings (Linton, 1936). And if one looks closely enough at the norms that hold for any one of these three categories, discrepancies will almost certainly be found from one situation to another and between the officially professed ideology and the actual behavior that prevails.

The nonuniversal properties of culture give rise to psychological traits in two ways—by limiting and patterning the course of individual development. Because the level of cultural stimulation to which human beings are exposed limits the actualization of their genic endowment, cultures differ quantitatively among each other in the extent to which various potentialities are realized in the modal individual. The differential level of cultural achievement itself may either be determined by technological and historical factors, or may be reflective of a prevailing set of cultural values which influence the selection of certain human capacities (e.g., art, motor skill, mechanical invention) for maximal development in preference to others.

The second inevitable outcome of cultural diversity—and source of psychosocial traits—is differential cultural patterning of the content, sequence and outcome of development: (a) By virtue of cultural tradition, certain aspects of drive and emotion are uniquely differentiated with respect to eliciting stimuli, mode and conditions of expression, adequacy of opportunity for gratification, need for repression, etc. Sensory preferences and favored modes of adjustment within a culture are similarly determined.

(b) Each culture has its own way of institutionalizing relationships with respect to age, sex, status and occupational differentiation. The particular choices it adopts have profound implications for such aspects of personality structure as security and adequacy feelings, levels of aspiration and anxiety, and attributes of masculinity and femininity. (c) The central values of a culture, i.e., whether emphasis is placed on mercantile, artistic, spiritual, competitive, or cooperative endeavors, shape the goals of its members and help determine which personality traits are encouraged and rewarded. The modal or basic personality type of a particular culture is partly determined by these latter two factors and partly by various technological, economic, political, and historical considerations that influence the frustration and anxiety levels of individuals and the quality of interpersonal relations.

Sources of Idiosyncratic Traits

Since all of the individuals within a culture do not develop in the same way or reach the same terminus of development, we propose to examine briefly in this section both the genic and environmental sources of idiosyncratic traits and the different mechanisms mediating the influence of genes on behavioral and personality development.

Genic Sources. Geneticists are in agreement that genotypically (apart from some physical traits), the populations of different cultures are substantially alike with respect to the range and central tendency of most individual differences. Hence, it is quite defensible to assume that genic factors are not responsible for intercultural differences or intracultural uniformities in behavioral development. But this does not mean, despite frequent claims to the contrary, that genotypic diversity plays no role whatsoever in determining differences among individuals *within* a culture. It is obvious, of course, that genic factors are not singly determinative of behavioral, intellectual, and temperamental differences,* that they interact with environmental variables at every stage of development, and that the significance of their phenotypic effects is contingent upon cultural values. Thus, although many genically determined temperamental predispositions are undoubtedly eclipsed by and subordinated to the influence of more weighty cultural factors, others are sufficiently potent to modify appreciably the impact of the social environment on individual development, and sometimes even to produce a personality who deviates seriously from the expectations of his culture.

The most obvious genic source of idiosyncratic traits are hereditary factors influencing such capacities as intelligence, gross motor skills, mechanical

We shall not consider here genic determinants of physical variability which indirectly influence personality development by affecting the social acceptability of an individual, since the ultimate outcome of such variability is almost completely a function of sociocultural factors.

dexterity, artistic ability, various sensory acuities, etc. Genic differences not only limit the terminal level of attained capacity and the relative rate of growth in these particular areas of development, but also differentially influence the individual's interests and responsiveness to various kinds of environmental stimulation and the quality of his adjustment and inter-personal relations. It is also conceivable that in certain extreme cases, quantitative differences in capacity may give rise to qualitative differences in the processes of development.

Many opportunities are also present for genically determined *tempera-mental* differences to influence the course of personality development. It could be anticipated, of course, that greater leeway would exist for the operation of such differences in those areas of behavior that are "relatively less institutionalized, more variable from generation to generation and socially less consequential" (Hanks, 1949). The influence of culture is truly pervasive; nevertheless innumerable aspects of private life are left relatively uncharted by social norms. But even in more highly institutionalized aspects of behavior, "each person's selection from and reaction to cultural teachings have an individual quality" (Kluckhohn *et al.*, 1949). In accordance with his temperamental proclivities he interprets cultural prescriptions slightly differently from his neighbors and improvises minor variations of his own on major cultural themes; and as long as his deviancy is passably discreet and conforms overtly to accepted ways, it is usually accorded a reasonable measure of social tolerance. In still other instances, culturally institutional-ized alternatives are available, making it possible for him to choose values and activities most compatible with his temperamental inclinations.

Human beings, therefore, are more than helpless puppets dangling from the ends of cultural strings. In the formation of their personalities, innate temperamental characteristics always interact with social pressures; and depending upon the relative strength of the variables concerned, complete or partial conformity or outright resistance and rebellion ensue. And in a sense their peculiar temperamental qualities even help determine their social environments by eliciting differential responses from significant individuals in their interpersonal orbits.

Types of Evidence for Genic Determination of Individual Differences in Behavioral Development. In some areas the evidence for the contribution of genotypic diversity to intracultural differences in behavior is conflicting, ambiguous, and difficult to interpret. In general, however, there can no longer be any serious doubt about the fact that some of the observed variance in psycho-logical capacities, behavior, and personality structure must be attributable to genic differences. *Direct* and relatively unequivocal evidence comes from pedigree studies of such rare causes of feeble-mindedness as amaurotic familial idiocy, sex-linked idiocy, phenylketonuric amentia, and micro-cephaly (Fuller *et al.* 1960; Hirsch, 1967; McClearn, 1962, 1964); from Huntington's chorea (Fuller *et al.* 1960; McClearn, 1962, 1964), schizo-phrenia (Bender & Grudelt, 1956; Kallman, 1947, 1953; Kallman & Roth, 1956; Slater, 1956), male homosexuality (Kallman, 1952); and from twin studies of such nonpathological behavioral traits as intelligence (Fuller *et al.* 1960; Newman, Freeman & Holzinger, 1937), numerous verbal and motor abilities (Blewett, 1954; Strandskov, 1954), and locus and degree of auto-nomic reactivity (Hirsch, 1967; Jost & Sontag, 1944).

Indirect sources of evidence for the genic determination of behavioral de-velopment are much more equivocal when considered individually but are quite convincing in their totality: (a) The finding of consistent individual differences among neonates in such temperamental factors as kinetic level, irritability and reaction to stress (see p. 123) can only be explained on a nongenic basis if all of the variability is ascribed to such factors as the uterine environment. (b) Lower mammalian species can be selectively bred for many temperamental traits including emotionality, spontaneous activity, tameness and aggressiveness, and maze brightness (McClearn, 1962). Although analogous genic predispositions in man are undoubtedly subject to greater experiential and ideational modification (Snyder *et al.*, 1951), in the total context of evidence from related sources it is highly improbable that they are not operative at all. (c) Meaningful relationships between various personality traits and variability in endocrine and autonomic functioning (see below) can be explained most plausibly by assuming the existence of genically regulated differences in the reactivity of the latter mechanisms (or their "target" tissues) with resulting parallelism in their behavioral and physiological effects. (d) Obtained correlations between body-type, on the one hand, and temperament (Bayer & Reichard, 1951; Garn *et al.*, 1960; Hanley, 1951; Osborne & De George, 1959; Rees, 1950; Sanford, 1949; Selzer, 1945; Sheldon, 1942), neurotic and psychotic trends (Rees, 1950), and hormonal and autonomic functioning (Rees, 1950; Sanford, 1949; Selzer, 1945), on the other hand, suggest that the relationship between body type and temperament* is mediated either by "linked genes" (with direct effects on physical characteristics and the neuroendocrine basis of tempera-ment) or through genically regulated hormonal and autonomic mechanisms with parallel secondary effects on morphology and behavior.

---

*Some reported correlations between body-type and temperament have undoubtedly been inflated by (a) "halo effect" in rating, (b) the fact that the temperamental traits under investigation (e.g., "active," "energetic") are stereotyped psychological equivalents of bodily characteristics (e.g., well-developed muscles), and (c) experientially determined mutual reinforcement as a result of conforming to socially stereotyped expectations (e.g., "fat and jolly") or of a circular relationship between organ (muscular) hypertrophy and frequent, satisfying (motor) activity. Nevertheless, significant but lower correlations still remain when the first two sources of spuriousness are removed.

Mediation of Genic Influences on Behavior. Except for some of the relatively rare neuropathological causes of amentia and behavior disorder (e.g., amaurotic idiocy, Huntington's chorea), variability in the normal and in the more common of the abnormal behavioral traits is undoubtedly related to polygenic rather than to single-gene inheritance (David *et al.*, 1951; Fuller, 1954; Fuller *et al.*, 1960; Hirsch, 1967; McClearn, 1962, 1964). Individual differences in such traits, therefore, reflect the cumulative effect of many positive and negative factors. However, in certain instances, the phenotypic appearance of a trait (e.g., schizophrenic symptoms) may depend upon exceeding for a given environment a critical threshold value of the polygenic influences concerned. Such all-or-none phenomena may obscure the continuous nature of the susceptibility gradient (Fuller, 1954). If, for example, an individual's genic threshold for psychotic breakdowns were high, much environmental stress would be needed to precipitate a psychosis; if it were low, the opposite would hold true. In the more median ranges of susceptibility, relatively small shifts in environmental stress would be determinative of phenotypic outcome.

As in the case of any other trait, genes do not influence behavioral development in some mystical fashion but through a series of intermediate mechanisms. The latter are probably initiated by some effect (of genes) on chemical reactions and rates of reaction in the developing organism (Boyd, 1953; Hirsch, 1967; McClearn, 1962, 1964). Preliminary evaluation of available evidence indicates that the following kinds of intermediate mechanisms may be operative between genic effects and behavior: Most directly, in the case of single-gene inheritance, behavioral defects may be caused by the defective structure of an intracellular enzyme (phenylpyruvic amentia) (McClearn, 1964), by cerebral agenesis, or by gross organic brain lesions (amaurotic idiocy, Huntington's disease). More indirectly, the effect of genes may be mediated through the autonomic nervous system. Young infants, for example, vary in their degree of visceral or somatic responsiveness to excitatory stimuli (Jones, 1930). Even the locus of maximum autonomic reactivity may be genically determined as shown by the greater resemblance between monozygotic twins than between siblings in autonomic patterning (Jost and Sontag, 1944), and by individual consistency in types of autonomic response to different kinds of stress (Lacey, Bateman & Vanlehn, 1952). Wenger (1947) has demonstrated that parasympathetic (as contrasted with sympathetic) predominance in autonomic balance is associated with such traits as diminished emotional excitability, less fatigability and suggestibility, and high dominance.

A similar type of mediating mechanism may be provided by endocrine secretions. The relationships between general activity and thyroid functioning, between motherliness and blood levels of prolactin and estrogen are well known. Benedek (1952) has been able to relate psychological aspects of sex drive to different histological phases of the menstrual cycle. More recently, the tissue-damaging and tissue-protecting roles of various humoral responses to stress situations have been elucidated (Selye, 1950). The possibility that genically determined hyperreactivity in the destructive aspects or of deficiency in the defensive aspects of reaction to stress is related to incidence of psychotic breakdown is suggested by the facts that (a) schizophrenics do not respond adequately to stress tests with enhanced corticosteroid output (Friedlander, 1951), (b) that schizophrenic patients with poor prognosis and poor response to shock therapy do not respond therapeutically to ACTH (Friedlander, 1951), and (c) that normal children and children with behavior problems differ in their EEG and autonomic response patterns to physiological stress stimuli (Ellingston, 1953). It is quite conceivable, however, that in the case of both endocrine and autonomic mechanisms, differential reactivity is related to genically determined differences in the responsiveness of "target" tissues rather than to differences in the level of stimulation per se. Clues regarding the mechanisms mediating many other genically regulated predispositions are presently unclear. In this category belong differential sensitivity to stimulation in particular sensory modalities; differences in intelligence and in motor, mechanical and artistic abilities; and many temperamental differences such as self-sufficiency, self-assertiveness, etc.

We are by no means suggesting that these genically determined capacities and temperamental factors operate *directly* in influencing the course of personality development or the genesis of behavior disorder. However, it does not seem unreasonable to suppose that they interact with other interpersonal, situational and cultural factors in differentially determining personality outcomes. It is not difficult, for example, to appreciate how the temperamental traits of dominance, self-assertiveness, and strength of hedonic drives might affect ease of socialization and disposition to assume dependent or independent roles. Such traits as level of affectivity, self-sufficiency, and being "tender" or "tough-skinned" are self-evidently related to introversion-extroversion, ability to relate to reality and to other persons, and to choice of escape and defense mechanisms. Similarly, frustration tolerance, level of energy and intelligence, and availability of other adaptive resources affect the quality of an individual's adjustment and his susceptibility to behavior disorder.

Environmental Sources. The social and cultural environments both limit and furnish the ways in which individuals can differ from each other intraculturally. Irrespective of the degree of genotypic diversity that exists, variability can never be expressed phenotypically in the absence of those environmental determinants essential for the development of a given trait or capacity. The culture also establishes the limits of tolerance for deviancy and provides the necessary instrumentalities for the expression of individual differences, whether these are tailor-made, institutionalized alternatives or uniquely improvised innovations. Even "the political revolutionary does not refuse to cast his revolutionary songs in the modal structure and the scale progressions of the culture he is in the process of changing." (Herskovits, 1951).

The environmental sources of idiosyncratic traits are interpersonal, cultural and situational. No culture can ever institutionalize interpersonal relationships so thoroughly that all of the temperamental qualities of the participants as well as their affective reactions to each other are completely squeezed out of the transaction. Especially in their early formative years, and to a lesser extent in adult life, individuals are continually influenced by these culturally unstandardized aspects of the feelings and personalities of parents, siblings, and other associates. Furthermore, no two persons are ever ground through the same cultural mill. Each of us is exposed to a unique conception of cultural reality by the biased sample of cultural representatives we encounter in the course of our experience.

Lastly we must consider situational factors, i.e., unplanned events that "just happen to people." Such situations are by definition unique in their "number, kinds and temporal order" for any particular individual (Kluckhohn et al., 1949). When to this situational uniqueness is added a unique genotype, a unique familial upbringing, unique exposure to the institutionalized aspects of culture, unique interpersonal transactions with others, and the unique resultant of the interaction among all of these various factors, it is difficult indeed to appreciate how the existence of intracultural differences in development could have ever been seriously denied.

MATURATION

Maturation has long been the central theoretical issue in child development dealing with the nature-nurture problem. However, ever since the concept was first introduced, its meaning has been clouded by ambiguity and by the diversity of connotations with which it has been endowed. The latter are presently predominantly predeterministic in accordance with the immense influence on professional and lay opinion wielded by Gesell and the Yale school who regard the term as descriptive of a process whereby *all* development is essentially regulated by endogenous factors, (see pp. 25-27). Most other writers have taken a less global position, equating maturation with either the acquisition of "readiness" in *certain* capacities as a consequence of internally directed "ripening," or with changes in the anatomical and physiological substrate of behavior. Because of the resulting semantic confusion it might even have been advisable to dispense with the term altogether. But in view of its great historical importance in the theory and research of child development, it was deemed preferable to redefine it rigorously in operational terms and to clarify its meaning in relation to such concepts as development, growth, learning and readiness.

The Meaning of Maturation

We shall use the term, "maturation," to refer to any instance of development (i.e., change in the status or underlying process of a behavioral trait) that takes place in the demonstrable absence of specific practice experience.* It should be noted that so defined it is neither restricted to development occurring independently of environmental influence (internal ripening), nor is uniquely identified with enhancement in capacity resulting from alteration of the neuro-anatomical or neurophysiological substrate of behavior. Also, in contrast to Gesell's usage of the term, this definition does not equate maturation with an endogenous process regulating all development (including that in which learning is determined). It simply designates those particular components or aspects of a developmental sequence in which the influence of specific practice can be operationally or logically excluded, in contradistinction to those aspects in which it is a determining factor. Apart from historical considerations the main justification for retaining the concept of maturation is that this distinction has obviously important implications for education and other related disciplines.

Since most developmental sequences consist of both maturation and learning, it is frequently difficult to distinguish between the two components. Nevertheless, in most instances it is possible and practically useful to order various developmental sequences in accordance with the relative contributions of genic factors, incidental experience, and specific practice to increment or change in capacity. Categorization of traits on this basis can, in turn, be related to the ontogenetic-phylogenetic and psychobiological-psychosocial continua discussed previously: (a) At one end of the continuum (psychosocial traits), specific practice is always essential, genic factors are of negligible significance, and incidental experience may or may not be important. (b) At the opposite end of the continuum (phylogenetic traits), development is largely regulated by prepotent genic factors, specific practice is not involved, and incidental experience similarly plays a supportive role. (c) Between these two extremes, in the case of psychobiological traits that are ontogenetic in character, the regulatory picture is more variable: all three determinants are implicated, and their relative importance varies with the nature and complexity of the particular developmental sequence involved.

---

*Maturation has a special meaning in biology (i.e., meiosis), designating the process whereby the number of chromosomes in the ovum or sperm are reduced in half as a result of one member of each homologous pair being segregated into each of two daughter cells. In personality theory, maturation usually refers to the child's gradual acquisition of the character traits typical of adult members of the culture.

Hence, under the heading of maturation can be subsumed that portion of any increment or change in capacity referable to genic influence and/or incidental experience. Development in phylogenetic traits is wholly maturational with emphasis upon the former component. The latter component assumes greater salience in the ontogenetic variety of psychobiological traits and also plays a role in psychosocial traits. Learning (specific practice), on the other hand, is the most important determinant of psychosocial traits, does not influence phylogenetic traits at all, and is of variable significance in psychobiological traits that are not phylogenetic.

Differentiation from Development, Growth, and Readiness. One important source of confusion regarding the meaning of maturation has resulted from the failure to distinguish between two entirely independent dimensions of development. The first, dealing with the participation and relative importance of specific practice (learning) versus genic influences and incidental experience (maturation) as determining factors, has already been discussed. The second concerns the question of whether or not structural and functional changes in the nervous system accompany developmental modifications of "overt behavior" (Milner, 1967). In a strictly technical sense the term, *growth*,* may be used to designate relatively permanent changes in the neuroanatomical and neurophysiological substrate of behavior. Development is inclusive of both dimensions of behavioral change—of substrate and overt aspects as well as of maturation and learning. Growth, on the other hand, refers only to the substrate correlates of overt developmental change irrespective of whether it is attributable to maturation or learning.

Many writers have attempted to differentiate between maturation and learning by identifying the former with the substrate changes we have just defined as growth. However, this distinction is unwarranted because such changes occur in both maturation and learning. In the first instance they are effected by genic factors and incidental experience, and in the second instance by practice. In both maturation and learning, the achievement of substrate adequacy is an essential prior or limiting condition for the emergence of any nontransitory overt change in behavioral development. However, this does not necessarily mean that "structure precedes function" since both incidental experience and practice contribute to as well as reflect substrate adequacy.

The fact that the existing status of a capacity affects its responsiveness to regulatory influences requires the introduction of still another term. *Readiness* signifies that the current developmental status of an organism is such that a reasonably economical increment in capacity may be anticipated in response

As used here, growth refers only to substrate changes associated with behavioral development. Obviously, much anatomical and physiological growth, both inside and outside the nervous system, has no effect whatsoever on behavior. Kresch (1968) has reported several studies which indicate the effects of stimulating and non-stimulating environments on underlying growth indicators (e.g. brain size, number of cells etc.) in rats.

to adequate stimulation—irrespective of how this status is achieved or the type of stimulation that is applied. In either case, maturation, learning or a combination of the two factors may be involved. Thus, for example, because of inadequate readiness, an individual may fail to profit from either practice or incidental experience; and the deficiency in readiness, in turn, may be reflective of insufficient learning as well as of insufficient maturation. On the same grounds, although the outcome of most developmental sequences depends on the operation of both maturation and learning, it is inaccurate to state that the two processes are necessarily mutually interdependent. Either one could occur in the absence of the other if sufficient readiness ascribable to one of the two factors alone prevailed.

Evidence Regarding Maturation

By controlling the opportunity for and the timing and amount of specific practice affecting development, it is possible to demonstrate empirically that maturation does occur. However, since nonspecific environmental determinants are operative from the very moment of conception, the relative contributions of genic influences and of incidental experience can be estimated only approximately. In certain instances the organism seems ready and able to perform a given behavior at the very first opportunity without the benefit of prior experience. Relatively complex behaviors of this type do occur in lower phyla and are called instincts. These are not preformed, but for all practical purposes are predetermined, developing during embryonic life. In man, however, only simple responses of a reflex nature are fully organized at birth. Undoubtedly, in the case of such developmental acquisitions, as well as in the case of phylogenetic traits acquired postnatally, environmental factors play a supportive rather than a crucially determinative role. But beyond these primitive developmental sequences of early infancy, the relative importance of incidental experience increases tremendously.

In general three kinds of empirical data support the occurrence of maturation: (a) evidence of developmental progress when opportunity for practice is experimentally or otherwise restricted; (b) evidence indicating that specific practice has no effect whatsoever on development until a certain stage of readiness is achieved in the absence of intervening practice; and (c) evidence indicating that when intervening practice is excluded, training at a later age is more efficacious than at any earlier age.

Restriction of Practice. The consistent emergence in unvarying sequential order of such neuromuscular acquisitions as movement of various bodily parts, prone progression, sitting, and postural adjustment (Gesell & Halverson, 1942; McGraw, 1943; Shirley, 1931), lends support to the view that these phylogenetic traits are acquired through maturation. It is true, of course that in these instances the possibility of specific practice is not experimentally excluded. Nevertheless, there is little reason for believing that a significant degree of parental tutelage is furnished in any culture. Furthermore, cross-cultural studies (Dennis et al., 1940; Mead et al., 1951), indicate that (barring extreme deprivation or cultural pressures) these as well as several simple social and emotional developmental sequences are substantially identical from one culture to another in the first year of life in spite of considerable diversity in child rearing practices.

More rigorous evidence is provided in an experiment by Dennis in which fraternal twins were reared under conditions of artificially restricted practice and minimal social stimulation. Despite lack of encouragement, reward, example, or opportunity for the usual degree of self-initiated experience, only slight retardation in motor development occurred, the latter being attributed to deprivation of self-directed activity (Dennis, 1941). In the same vein are findings that cradling does not delay the onset of walking (Dennis, 1940), that smiling appears spontaneously in the absence of social example (Dennis et al., 1940), and that the facial expressions of laughter, fear, and anger develop no differently in blind than in seeing children (Thompson, 1941).

More drastic and controlled restriction of practice has naturally been possible in animal experiments. In general these studies show that many phylogenetic capacities develop almost normally despite restriction of function "beyond the expected period of their manifestation," although they do not necessarily "emerge at a peak of perfection" (e.g., pecking in chickens) (McGraw, 1946). The latter qualification, of course, does not invalidate the maturational hypothesis since incidental experience falls within the scope of maturation. Typical of these experiments is Carmichael's demonstration that the swimming capacity of salamander embryos is not adversely affected as a result of immobilization in an anesthetic solution during the period in which bodily movements ordinarily develop.* It should be noted, however, that deprivation of ordinary environmental experience impedes development in certain functions and can cause retardation in any area if prolonged "beyond a critical period" (Birney & Teevan, 1961; McGraw, 1946). For example, pigeons do not develop optokinetic nystagmus in the absence of vision (Mowrer, 1946), infant chimpanzees isolated from normal tactual stimulation show defective kinaesthetic learning and cutaneous localization (Nissen, Chow, Semmes, 1951), and chimpanzees reared in darkness fail to fixate or recognize familiar objects or to blink in response to a threatening object (Riesen, 1947). Examples of more permanent retardation following severe deprivation will be given later.

---

*For a review of animal studies, see Birney & Teevan (1961); McGraw (1946); Hess (1962); Munn (1965).

Effects of Premature Practice. The occurrence of maturation can also be demonstrated by showing that practice which is useless or relatively ineffective at one stage of development becomes more efficacious at a later stage despite isolation from a given activity in the intervening period. McGraw has shown that specific practice has little if any effect on the acquisition of phylogenetic traits; development simply proceeds at its own pace in response to genic influences and incidental experience. She gave systematic daily toilet training to one member of each of two sets of identical twins after the first few weeks of life. Nevertheless, they failed to achieve bladder control any earlier than their co-twins whose training was postponed until they indicated responsiveness to same (McGraw, 1940). Similarly, in a pair of fraternal twins, Johnny and Jimmy, practice in such activities as sitting, walking and standing did not accelerate Johnny's development and only modified minor aspects of sequence and patterning (McGraw, 1935). On the other hand, practice was found to be essential in the acquisition of psychosocial skills and to accelerate their development provided that it was administered when the child was maturationally ready for it; prior to such time it was just as ineffective as in the case of phylogenetic traits. Much variability prevailed from one skill to another with respect to the age at which readiness developed. For example, Johnny was an accomplished skater by sixteen months but profited little from early practice in tricycling (McGraw, 1935).

Numerous experiments have been conducted in which practice of training at an early age has been shown to be much less efficient than at a later age when increased readiness attributable to maturation was present. In such studies an experimental group or identical twin is given extended early practice, whereas an equated control group or co-twin is given a shorter period of practice at a later age. The relative superiority of the latter procedure (i.e., the same gain in capacity after considerably less practice) has been demonstrated for such motor activities as buttoning, stair and ladder climbing, cutting with scissors, tossing rings, cube building, and throwing a ball at a moving target (Gesell *et al.*, 1929; Hicks, 1930; Hicks & Ralph, 1931; Hilgard, 1932, 1933). It is also more effective for tasks of a more cognitive nature such as learning vocabulary (Gates & Taylor, 1925; Hilgard, 1933) and memorizing digits.

Neural Correlates of Behavioral Development

Corresponding to all overt changes in behavioral development are substrate changes in the nervous system.* The latter constitute the characteristic

---

*Reviews and reports of original investigations are available in this area (Carmichael, 1954; Conel, 1939, 1955a, 1955b, 1959; Eichorn, 1963; Kresch, 1968; McGraw, 1943, 1946; Milner, 1967; Peiper, 1963; Scheibel & Scheibel, 1964; Volokhov, 1959).

form of growth associated with behavior, in the same sense that certain quantitative and qualitative changes in bone and muscle mark the course of skeletal development. Depending on the level of behavior involved (i.e., phylogenetic, ontogenetic, psychosocial), neural growth may reflect genic influences, incidental experience or specific practice.

Unfortunately, the determination of the neural correlates of behavioral development is beset by numerous difficulties. One approach is to measure the electroencephalographic changes that occur with increasing age (Scheibel *et al.*, 1964; Milner, 1967). Until the fifth fetal months, EEG activity is not recordable, and between the fifth to eight fetal months EEG is subcortical in origin. Cortical activity (EEG) emerges for the first time about the eighth fetal month and does not change appreciably until the end of the first post-natal month. Postnatally, EEG activity has been recorded almost entirely in the primary sensory-motor area during the first months. Frequency is irregular during this period, with no alpha wave recording and a predominance of delta waves. Asynchrony of wave forms between hemispheres is typical of the infant's record, but synchrony increases during the first several years. Initially, the EEG record shows no difference between waking or sleeping; but by three years of age this differentiation approaches adult patterns. Individual differences in EEG can be detected in premature infants by their slower and more irregular waves than full term infants or full term normals, and sex differences show consistently faster development for females (Milner, 1967). When cortical activity is evoked, the postnatal infant is unable to produce more than one of two sequences of activation at any one time (Schiebel *et al.*, 1964): these methods however, at best, furnish an extremely limited and superficial picture of neural organization and functioning.

A much more basic approach is through elaborate histological analysis of the brains of children who die at various ages. The disadvantages of this method are (a) the enormous technical labor involved, and (b) the impossibility of obtaining behavioral and morphological data from the same subjects (McGraw, 1946). Nevertheless, such studies (Conel, 1939, 1947, 1955a, 1955b, 1959; McGraw, 1943), have identified many histological developments that take place in the course of neural maturation. At birth, an orderly laminated arrangement of cells, divisional differentiation of function, and fissurization are present. During the ensuing months, cortical cells become increasingly more differentiated, their processes became longer and more elaborate, further localization of function takes place, and the presence of myelin and neurofibrils becomes more evident. The anatomic findings and the onset of function in different portions of the brain, indicate that the immaturity at birth is not evenly extended over the brain; the ontogenetically and phylogenetically oldest sections of the brain are histologically most mature (Peiper, 1963). Maturation progresses from the medulla oblongata over the basal ganglia and mesencephalon, toward the cortex of the cerebral hemispheres. The ontogenetically younger tracts also show a retarded development when compared with older sections. Those brain hemispheres that have to fulfill a vital function are usually most mature. This applies particularly to the region of the respiratory centers in the medulla oblongata (Peiper, 1963). In general, these changes are demonstrable at an earlier age in those regions of the cortex that become functional first in terms of overt behavior, appearing earlier in the motor than in other areas, and earliest in the cephalic portion of the motor cortex.*

On the basis of these findings and correlative observations of infant behavior, McGraw has formulated a credible neurobehavioral theory of early motor development (1943). She holds that behavior in the first few months of life is essentially regulated by subcortical nuclei, and increasingly thereafter by the cerebral cortex. In support of this view are (a) the earlier neural maturation of the lower centers, (b) the fact that acephalic monsters manifest normal neonatal behavior (Dennis, 1951), and (c) the fact that certain reflexes (Moro, Babinski, grasp), which conceivably have vestigal phylogenetic significance, are active shortly after birth but are then inhibited and replaced by more mature responses. On the other hand, it is difficult to reconcile evidence of learning, conditioning, and localization of cutaneous stimuli in neonates with the *complete* absence of cortical functioning (Pratt, 1954). However, the greater participation of the cortex in subsequent behavioral development is unequivocally evident in the inhibition of primitive reflexes (which may reappear after cortical injury), the emergence of voluntary motor sequences, and the parallelism between the cephalocaudal trend in neuromuscular development and the order in which different portions of the motor cortex reach maturity (Volokhov, 1959). The successive stages of subcortical reflex dominance, cortical inhibition, and voluntary cortical control postulated by McGraw are in agreement with empirical findings regarding the development of swimming movements, prone progression and postural adjustment (McGraw, 1943, 1946). Sitting, however, which "is of recent phylogenetic origin" starts at a cortical level" (McGraw, 1946).†

Although there is general agreement that these histological changes are characteristic of neural maturation, difference of opinion prevails regarding which structural changes are essential for functioning. Tracts tend to become myelinated in order of their phylogenetic development and functional readiness, but function may antedate myelinization. Different workers have attributed "the essential basis of functional activity in the nervous system" to the appearance of neurofibrils, to differentiate thresholds at the synaptic junctures between neurons, or to critical concentrations of choline esterase in neutral tissue (Carmichael, 1954).

†It is interesting to note that this interpretation of motor development is in marked contrast to Piaget's formulation of the ontogenesis of behavior during the first 18 months of life. Piaget's basic assumptions about early motor development is that there is a functional comparability and developmental continuity between reflex and nonreflex sequences. See Ausubel (1966) for a more extensive critique.

Vygotsky's Theory of Development: An Interactionist's Approach

The main thesis of the present chapter has been the development of an *interactionist* point of view, in contrast to the *predeterministic* and *tabula rasa* models discussed in the previous chapter. The presentation of Vygotsky's (1962) theory of conceptual development here, serves to illustrate an interactionist position in contrast to the *predeterministic* and *tabula rasa* approaches, and also anticipates the subsequent discussion on "readiness" and its educational implications.

Vygotsky's (1962) approach toward the understanding of concept formation involves the distinction between "*spontaneous*" and "*nonspontaneous*" concepts. Spontaneous concepts refer to those concepts of reality that are developed mainly through the child's own mental efforts (i.e., incidental experience). In operating with spontaneous concepts (e.g., house, dog, red, etc.), the child is not conscious of the concepts because attention is centered on the object to which the concept refers, but never on the act of thought itself. Spontaneous concepts are characteristic of the preoperational stage of development.

Nonspontaneous concepts (i.e., scientific) are those which are acquired in school and are characterized by consciousness and deliberate control over the act of thought itself. Nonspontaneous concepts are characteristic of the operational stages of development.

Vygotsky (1962) developed his "*interactionist*" position by asking two main questions concerning the development and interrelationship between the above mentioned concepts:

> What happens in the mind of the child to the scientific concepts he is taught in school? What is the relationship between the assimilating of information and the internal development of a scientific concept in the child's consciousness? (Vygotsky, 1962, p. 82).

Vygotsky commences by criticizing two prevailing schools of thought, because of the way they treat the above mentioned condepts. The "*tabula rasa*" position, which is exemplified by associationist theorists (e.g., Thorndike) hold that scientific concepts have no inward history and are absorbed ready-made through a process of understanding and assimilation. Vygotsky maintains that this viewpoint fails to stand up under scrutiny, either theoretically or practically, since investigations of the process of concept formation reveal that a concept is more than the sum of its associative bonds formed by memory, and mental habit;* it is also a complex act of thought that cannot be taught by drilling. Learning scientific concepts is accomplished only when the child's mental development has reached the requisite level.

> The development of concepts, or word meanings, presupposes the development of many intellectual functions: deliberate attention, logical memory, abstraction, the ability

---

Contemporary neobehaviorists, although introducing complex mediational processes in concept formation, still hold to this associationist position (see Osgood, 1957; Staats, 1961).

to compare and differentiate. These complex psychological processes cannot be mastered through initial learning alone. (Vygotsky, 1962, p. 83).

Because instruction and development are treated as identical, there is no question of the relationship between scientific and spontaneous concepts.*

Predeterministic approaches to concept formation, although recognizing the distinction between scientific and spontaneous concepts, are criticized because they fail to see the interaction between the two kinds of concepts in the course of the child's intellectual development (see pp. 27-30). Spontaneous concepts, acquired through incidental experience (i.e., self-regulation), assume primary importance in Piaget's theorizing and are considered as the primary indicators of intellectual development. Vygotsky (1962) in commenting on this viewpoint, notes that the theory considers instruction and development to be mutually independent.

> Development is seen as process of maturation subject to natural laws, and instruction as the utilization of the opportunities created by development. Typical of this school of thought are its attempts to separate with great care the products of development from those of instruction, supposedly to find them in their pure form.   (Vygotsky, 1962, p. 93).

Vygotsky believes that the two processes (i.e., development of spontaneous and scientific concepts) are related and constantly influence each other. Because *spontaneous concepts* develop through the incidental experience of the child, while scientific concepts result from school instruction, it is felt that they must differ in their development as well as in their functioning. However, these two variants of the process of concept acquisition must influence each other's evolution. The interrelation of scientific and spontaneous concepts is a special case within a much broader subject: the relation of school instruction to the mental development of the child.

It is important to recognize and take account of the highly significant interaction that takes place between many scientific concepts and their subverbal or intuitive precursors. As Vygotsky (1962) notes, the elementary-school child, in acquiring assimilated concepts, is greatly assisted by the existence in his cognitive structure of analogous spontaneous concepts at the preoperational level which he uses nondeliberately and with relatively little cognitive awareness.† These provide a springboard for the acquisition of "scientific" concepts and for their "downward" exemplification and everyday reference. But although these spontaneous concepts undoubtedly enhance the meaningfulness of their analogous assimilated counterparts, and probably discourage rote reception learning (tabula rasa), they may also,

---

*General contemporary theories of instruction still treat the acquisition of these concepts as synonymous (see Bereiter & Engelmann, 1966; Gagné, 1967).

†"Work", for example, is both a spontaneous concept acquired from direct experience and a more formal, abstract concept with precise criterial attributes.

because of their primacy and vividness, interfere with the learning of more precise and categorical criterial attributes. The same kinds of relationships also undoubtedly prevail between the more precise and abstract concepts acquired at the secondary-school level and their more intuitive elementary-school precursors.

Both Piaget and Vygotsky agree that awareness of the cognitive operations involved in concept acquisition does not develop until the child approaches and has been exposed to considerable systematic instruction in scientific concepts.

> In operating with spontaneous concepts the child is not conscious of them because his attention is always centered on the object to which the concept refers, never on the act of thought itself. . . .
> A concept can become subject to consciousness and deliberate control only when it is part of a system . . . In the scientific concepts that the child acquires in school, the relationship to an object is mediated from the start by some other concept . . . A superordinate concept implies the existence of a series of subordinate concepts, and it also presupposes a hierarchy of concepts at different levels of generality . . . Thus the very notion of a scientific concept implies a certain position in relation to other concepts . . . The rudiments of systematization first enter the child's mind by way of his contact with scientific concepts and are transferred to everyday concepts, changing their psychological structure from the top down. (Vygotsky, 1962, pp. 92, 93).

Awareness of concept acquisition develops late, Vygotsky (1962) believes, because it requires awareness of similarity. This, in turn, presupposes "a more advanced structure of generalization and conceptualization than awareness of difference."

Nevertheless, even though a child cannot use a word like "because" deliberately in a test situation, and does not really grasp causal relations except in a very primitive and intuitive sense, he is able to use "because" correctly in everyday conversation. The rules of syntax, too, can generally be employed correctly by young children despite complete lack of awareness of the nature of these rules. However, deliberate use of such words as "because" is possible in relation to *scientific* concepts because the "teacher, working with the pupil, has explained, supplied information, questioned, corrected, and made the pupil explain" (Vygotsky, 1962, p. 107). It is hardly surprising, therefore, that awareness of concept acquisition and deliberate use of concepts arise earlier in relation to scientific than to spontaneous concepts.

In teaching scientific concepts, therefore, it is essential to take account of the nature of their spontaneous precursors, i.e., explicitly to contrast the two sets of criterial attributes and to indicate why the adoption of the more abstract and precise set is preferable. Within the limits imposed by developmental readiness, systematic verbal instruction in abstract concepts at the elementary-school level, combined with appropriate use of concrete-empirical props, is pedagogically feasible and can greatly accelerate the acquisition of higher-order concepts. It is unnecessary and educationally wasteful to wait for such concepts to evolve spontaneously from direct experience. Further, many abstract concepts (e.g., "photosynthesis," "ionization") can only be acquired verbally since they are not susceptible to direct experience. Other, more concrete concepts (e.g., "house," "dog," "red," "hot"), on the other hand, are practically meaningless in the absence of actual experience with the objects or phenomena in question (Ausubel, 1968).

The presentation of Vygotsky was designed to contrast an *interactionist* position with "*predeterministic*" and "*tabula rasa*" approaches. His theory has also prepared us for a discussion of the principle of "readiness" which is ignored in tabula rasa positions and confused with maturation in predeterministic positions.

The Principle of Readiness: Educational Implications

The principle of readiness, that attained capacity (irrespective of how it is achieved) limits and influences an individual's ability to profit from current experience or practice, is one of the conceptual cornerstones of child development with important implications for education and other applied disciplines. Unfortunately, however, because of the predeterministic connotations associated with the term, it has been seriously misinterpreted to mean that readiness is solely the product of maturation and that it is fixed by an endogenous (genic) timing mechanism wholly unresponsive to external influences. Readiness is a cumulative developmental product reflecting the influence of all prior genic effects, all prior incidental experience, and all prior learning on cognitive patterning and the growth of cognitive capacities. Thus it reflects the effects of subject-matter learning as well, but only its *general* effects on̄ *cognitive capacities* or mode of *cognitive functioning*, as distinguished from the acquisition of the *particular* learnings that constitute the basis of subject-matter readiness. In any particular instance of readiness, any one or all of these factors may be involved. Readiness may be general in the sense that an individual manifests a certain level of cognitive functioning required for a wide range of intellectual activities. On the other hand, it may be limited to the highly particularized cognitive capacities necessary for the learning of a narrow segment of new subject matter, and even to the particular teaching method employed in acquiring that knowledge.

The Nature of Readiness. Cognitive readiness refers to the adequacy of existing cognitive processing equipment, or capacity, for coping with the demands of a specified cognitive learning task. Empirically, readiness is indicated by ability to profit from practice or learning experience. An individual manifests readiness when the outcomes of his learning activity, in terms of increased knowledge or academic achievement, are *reasonably commensurate* with the amount of effort and practice involved. Readiness, in the developmental sense of the term, is a function of general cognitive maturity. General cognitive maturity, in turn, largely reflects age-level differences in intellectual capacity or stage of intellectual development. In any particular individual, of course, it also reflects individual differences in genic potentiality, incidental experience, intellectual stimulation, and educational background.

The particular kind of subject matter that an individual studies induces two main classes of effects: On the one hand, it determines his *specific* readiness for *particular* other kinds of subject-matter learnings, i.e., transfer. On the other hand, it also contributes to *general* changes in cognitive readiness that are, at least in part, independent of the kind of subject matter studied. For example, the study of elementary-school science prepares a pupil for high-school science, and the study of elementary-school grammar prepares a pupil for high-school grammar. In addition, however, experience with each subject contributes to his *general* cognitive development and helps determine the general level of his cognitive functioning. Thus, in appraising cognitive readiness, we would consider all relevant age-level changes in ability to cope with different kinds and levels of subject matter that are reflective of growth in cognitive capacity or mode of cognitive functioning. Examples of such changes in cognitive capacity that influence learning, retention, and thinking processes, and hence influence developmental readiness for learning different kinds and levels of subject matter, include the following: increased widening and complexity of the cognitive field; increased familiarity of the psychological world; greater differentiation of cognitive structure; greater precision and specificity of meanings; the possession of more abstract, higher-order concepts and transactional terms; greater ability to comprehend and manipulate abstractions and relationships between abstractions—without recent or current references to concrete-empirical experience; greater ability to deal with general propositions apart from particularized contexts; decreased subjectivity in approach to experience; increased attention span; and increased differentiation of intellectual ability. Some of these changes in cognitive sophistication (e.g., increased differentiation of cognitive content, structure, and intellectual ability; greater precision and specificity of meanings) have self-evident implications for general developmental readiness insofar as it bears on the breadth-depth issue in curriculum.

There is little disagreement about the fact that cognitive readiness always crucially influences the efficiency of the learning process, and often determines whether a given intellectual skill or type of school material is learnable at all at a particular stage of development. Most educators also implicitly accept the proposition that an age of readiness exists for every kind of learning. Postponement of learning experience beyond this age of readiness wastes valuable and often unsuspected learning opportunities, thereby unnecessarily reducing the amount and complexity of subject-matter content that can be mastered in a designated period of schooling. On the other hand, when a pupil is prematurely exposed to a learning task before he is adequately ready for it, he not only fails to learn the task in question (or learns it with undue difficulty), but also learns from this experience to fear, dislike, and avoid the task.

Up to this point, the principle of readiness—the idea that attained developmental capacity limits and influences an individual's ability to profit from current experience or practice—is empirically demonstrable and conceptually unambiguous. Difficulty first arises when it is confused with the concept of *maturation*, and increases when the latter concept, in turn, is equated with a process of "internal ripening." The concept of readiness simply refers to the adequacy of existing cognitive capacity or level of cognitive functioning (not knowledge) in relation to the demands of a given learning task. No specification is made as to how this capacity is achieved—whether through prior learning activities, through incidental experience, through genically regulated changes, or through various combinations of these factors. Maturation, on the other hand, has a different and much more restricted meaning. It encompasses those increments in capacity that take place in the demonstrable absence of specific practice experience, i.e., those increments that are attributable to genic influences and/or incidental experience. Maturation, therefore, is not the same as readiness, but is merely *one* of the two principal factors (the other being learning) that contribute to or determine the organism's developmental readiness for coping with new learning tasks. Whether or not readiness exists, in other words, does not necessarily depend on maturation alone; in many instances, it is solely a function of cumulative prior learning experience, and most typically it depends on varying proportions of maturation and learning.

To equate the principles of readiness and maturation not only muddies the conceptual waters, but also makes it difficult for the school to appreciate that insufficient readiness may often reflect cognitive immaturity on the part of pupils that is attributable to a generally unstimulating, inappropriate, or inefficient educational environment. "Lack of maturation" can thus become a conveniently available scapegoat whenever children manifest insufficient developmental readiness to learn; and the school, which is thereby automatically absolved of all responsibility in the matter, consequently fails to subject its instructional practices to the degree of self-critical scrutiny necessary for continued educational progress. In short, while it is important to appreciate that the current readiness of pupils determines the school's current choice of instructional methods and materials, it is equally important to bear in mind that this readiness itself is partly determined by the general appropriateness and efficiency of the previous instructional practices to which pupils have been subjected. The quality of education a pupil receives, in other words, is a significant determinant of his *developmental* readiness, as well as of his subject-matter readiness, for further learning (see Kresch, 1968, previously cited in footnote, p. 81).

The conceptual confusion is further compounded when maturation is interpreted as a process of "internal ripening" essentially independent of *all* environmental influences, that is, of *incidental experience* as well as of learning. Readiness then becomes a matter of simple genic regulation, unfolding in accordance with a predetermined and immutable timetable; and the school, by definition, becomes powerless to influence developmental readiness—even through a preschool or kindergarten program of providing incidental background experience preparatory to the introduction of more formal academic activities.

It is hardly surprising, therefore, in view of the tremendous influence on professional and lay opinion wielded by Gesell and his colleagues, that many educators conceive of readiness in absolute and immutable terms, and thus fail to appreciate that, except for such traits as walking and grasping, the mean age of readiness can never be specified apart from relevant environmental conditions. Although the modal child in contemporary America may first be ready to read at the age of six and one-half (Morphett and Washburne, 1931), the age of reading readiness is always influenced by cultural, subcultural, and individual differences in background experience, and, in any case, varies with the method of instruction employed and the child's IQ. Middle-class children, for example, are ready to read at an earlier age than lower-class children because of the greater availability of books in the home, and because they are "read to" and "taken places" more frequently (Milner, 1951). Exposure to television has undoubtedly decreased the age of readiness for reading in recent years, but even so, the typical child of average intelligence is not ready for formal instruction in reading prior to entering kindergarten (Kinsella, 1965).

Pedagogic Applications of the Readiness Principle. By virtue of his distinctive degree of cognitive sophistication at every age level, the child has a characteristic way of approaching learning material and "viewing the world" (Bruner, 1960). The pedagogic problem in readiness is to manipulate the learning situation in such a way that one takes account, and optimal advantage, of existing cognitive capacities and modes of assimilating ideas and information, as for example, the learner's objectivity-subjectivity, his level of generality or particularity, and the abstractness and precision of his conceptualizations. "The task of teaching a subject to a child at any particular age is one of representing the structure of that subject in terms of the child's way of viewing things. The task can be thought of as one of translation" (Bruner, 1960).

The objection has been offered that we can have no *direct* knowledge of an individual's state of developmental readiness, and that we would therefore be better advised to ignore this factor and manipulate other learning varia-ables about which we have more direct knowledge and over which we have more direct control, e.g., situational and interpersonal variables, reinforce-ment, attributes and organization of the learnng task, and the conditions of practice. All of these latter variables can be manipulated independently of any reference to the existing cognitive capacities of the learner. But although it is true that we can have no *direct* knowledge of and control over his state of readiness, we should not be unduly discouraged. We can still make some fairly shrewd and accurate inferences about existing cognitive readiness from detailed knowledge of the learner's family, cultural, social-class, and educa-tional background, and from the use of diagnostic testing procedures. Furthermore, we can also exercise some control over the readiness factor by providing a pertinent background of incidental experience or special pre-paratory learning activities at the desired level of sophistication.

Much more significant in terms of pedagogic applications is the serious dearth of research on the cognitive aspects of readiness. We desperately need studies indicating that certain kinds, components, and levels of subject matter which cannot be learned efficiently at one age level, can be learned efficiently at another age level; studies which, by taking general or par-ticularized readiness factors into account, achieve, thereby, superior learning and achievement; and studies showing that more difficult kinds and levels of subject matter—ordinarily not learnable at younger ages—can be learned successfully and without inordinate effort if appropriate changes in teaching methods are made. Until the principle of readiness is particularized in each academic discipline with respect to the various subareas, levels of difficulty, and methods of teaching that can be most advantageously employed at each level of development, the principle will have little pedagogic utility.

What light can the field of human growth and development throw on the issue of "What shall the schools teach?" We earnestly wish that it were possible to list and discuss a dozen or more instances in which developmental principles have been validly utilized in providing definitive answers to questions dealing with the content and organization of the curriculum. Unfortunately, however, it must be admitted that at the present time this discipline can only offer a limited number of very crude generalizations and highly tentative suggestions bearing on this issue. In a very general sense, of course, it is undeniable that concern with child development has had a salutary effect on the educational enterprise. It alerted school administrators to the fact that certain minimal levels of intellectual maturity are necessary before various subjects could be taught with a reasonable degree of efficiency and hope of success; and it encouraged teachers in presenting subject matter to make use of the existing interests of pupils, to consider their point of view, and to take into account prevailing limitations in command of language and grasp of concepts. On the other hand, premature and wholesale extrapolation of developmental principles to educational theory and practice has also caused incalculable harm. It will take at least a generation for teachers just to unlearn some of the more fallacious and dangerous of these over-generalized and unwarranted applications.

Much of the aforementioned difficulty proceeds from failure to appreciate that human growth and development is a "pure" rather than an "applied" science. As a pure science it is concerned with the discovery of general laws about the nature and regulation of human development *as an end in itself*. Ultimately, of course, such laws have self-evident implications for the realization of practical goals in such fields as education, child rearing, and guidance. In a very *general* sense, for example, they indicate the effects of different interpersonal and social climates on personality development, and the kinds of teaching methods and subject-matter content that are most compatible with developmental capacity and mode of cognitive functioning at a given stage of growth. Thus, because it offers important insights about the changing intellectual and emotional capacities of children as developing human beings, child development may legitimately be considered one of the basic sciences underlying education and guidance, and as part of the necessary professional preparation of teachers—in much the same sense that anatomy and bacteriology are basic sciences for medicine and surgery.

Highly detrimental in their effects on pupils and teachers, however, have been the consequences of far-fetched and uncritical extrapolation to educational practice of developmental generalizations that either have not been adequately validated, or which apply only to a very restricted age segment of the total span of children's development. Two illustrations of the latter category of unwarranted extrapolation of highly limited generalizations—the "internal ripening" theory of maturation and the principle of "self-selection"—have already been discussed. An example of a widely accepted but inadequately validated developmental principle, frequently cited to justify general or overall ability grouping of pupils, is the proposition that a "child's growth and achievement show a going-togetherness" (Olson and Hughes, 1943). Actually, except for a spuriously high correlation during infancy, the relationship between physical status and motor ability, on the one hand, and intelligence and intellectual achievement on the other hand, is negligible and declines consistently with increasing age. Even among the different sub-tests of intelligence and among the different areas of intellectual achievement, the weight of the evidence indicates that as a child grows older his component rates of growth in these various functions increasingly tend to diverge from each other.

Postponement and Premature Learning. Intellectual training should not be postponed merely on the theory that an older child can invariably learn anything more efficiently than a younger child. Instruction in typing (Wood and Freeman, 1932), for example, is more successful at age seven than at age five, but this is insufficient reason, in and of itself, to postpone this activity for two years. *Adequate* readiness rather than age per se is the relevant criterion. Waiting beyond the point of adequate readiness means that certain specific learnings, (as well as the accompanying more general gains in capacity) that could easily have been acquired in the interim, if attempted, unnecessarily fail to take place.

The acquisition of many intellectual achievements that lie within the capability of children, but for which they are not adequately ready, can be accelerated by providing suitable contrived experience specially geared to their cognitive capacity and mode of functioning. The age at which children *can* learn a given intellectual task (like the age of readiness itself), is, after all, not an absolute, but is always relative, in part, to the method of instruction employed (Gates, 1937). By taking advantage of the preschool child's curiosity and urge to explore, by placing extensive reliance on overt manipulative activity in understanding and using symbols, and by programming stimulation at appropriate rates and in suitable forms, Montessori (Rambusch, 1962), O. K. Moore (Pines, 1963), and Fowler (1962) have been able to advance considerably the typical age of reading and writing.*

Similarly, by using an intuitive approach, it is possible successfully to teach the elementary-school child many ideas in science and mathematics (Arnsdorf, 1961; Brownell, 1960; Bruner, 1960; O. L. Davis, 1958; Dienes, 1964) that were previously thought much too difficult. However, one must balance against the possible advantages of early intuitive learning, the high risk of failure and expensive time and effort cost involved in many *premature* instances of such learning. Where genuine readiness is lacking, it is more feasible in the long run to postpone entirely the introduction of particular subject-matter fields until children are cognitively more mature. The decision regarding readiness must be based, in each case, upon the findings of particularized research. In one progressive school, for example, children who learned no formal arithmetic until the fifth grade equalled matched controls in computation by the seventh grade, and surpassed them in arithmetic reasoning (Sax and Ottina, 1958).

A good case can be made for the proposition that modern nursery schools and kindergartens fail to provide children with sufficient intellectual stimulation, or that preschool children are *adequately ready* for more than they are

---

That preschool children are able to learn to read is not so surprising when one considers that they do, after all, learn spontaneously to understand and use representational auditory stimuli (i.e., the denotative and syntactical meaning conveyed by words and sentences).

taught (Pines, 1963; Wann, Dorm and Liddle, 1962). Enrichment of the preschool curriculum so that it is more commensurate with existing levels of readiness is therefore quite defensible. But:

Even if it be demonstrated that young children *can* learn this or that "advanced" process, we should still need to decide whether it is desirable and appropriate for them to do so. Sociologically, we may ask whether this is the best way for children to spend their time and energy. Intellectually, we may ask whether this is the most suitable preparation for future intellectual activities. Emotionally, we may ask whether "early" systematic instruction in reading, mathematics, or what have you, will have a harmful effect upon motivation, or upon personal and social behavior . . . The point we are trying to make here is simply this: Just the fact that children *can* learn this or that does not *by itself* mean that we, therefore, must *require* them to do so at some young age or in some early grade. (F. T. Tyler, 1964, pp. 223-224).

The crucial issues, in other words, are whether such early learning is reasonably economical in terms of the time and effort involved, and whether it helps children *developmentally* in terms of their total educational careers.

CHAPTER 4

The Nature of Developmental Processes

THIS CHAPTER is concerned with the general characteristics of development as a process apart from its determinants or from the factors that control and regulate it.

CONTINUITY AND DISCONTINUITY*

Second only to the nature-nurture controversy in historical importance has been the great debate over whether development in a process of gradual, quantitative and continuous change, or whether it is characterized by abrupt, uneven and discontinuous changes which are qualitatively different from one another. However, in recent years, paralleling in large measure the fate of the first great controversy, this issue has all but disappeared from the current theoretical arena. In both instances, the decline in interest and theoretical salience has resulted from general appreciation of the fact that each issue, as originally stated, constituted a false dichotomy; but unfortunately, in the excess of enthusiasm over this discovery, both the genuine (as well as many of the pseudo) aspects of this issue were discarded. For even after the "either-or" and "all-or-none" formulations are rejected as untenable, the tasks of determining the relative contributions of heredity and environment in particular developmental sequences and of identifying those aspects that are relatively continuous or discontinuous still remain.

No living organism is ever in a state of complete developmental equilibrium. Nevertheless, the changes that transpire from one interval to another are hardly homogeneous in either kind or degree. For both practical and theoretical reasons it is important to distinguish between periods of intra- and interstage development. Both types of change are equally characteristic of the developmental process; and whether growth is quantitative and continuous or qualitative and discontinuous is partly a function of the rate at which it is taking place. When the rate of change is slow, development tends to occur within the framework of qualitative constancy. All forms are consolidated or modified slightly to meet new conditions, and new elements are incorporated without any necessity for fundamental reorganization. A state of relative equilibrium and stability prevails. But when the rate of change is

*A short review of recent research on this topic may be found in Emmerich (1967).

more rapid, qualitative differentiation also tends to occur. Established patterns must either be discarded or undergo radical revision. Together with recently introduced components, they are reorganized into a qualitatively different Gestalt which is discontinuous with the antecedent condition of the organism; and until consolidation occurs, a state of relative instability and disequilibrium exists. In other instances, however, because of the operation of cushioning mechanisms, qualitative interstage growth is accomplished gradually without abruptness.

Factors Making for Development Continuity

The greater portion of any developmental process tends to be continuous rather than discontinuous in nature. When, for example, height, strength, masculinity-femininity, or androgenic-estrogenic secretion are plotted against age, the resulting growth curves are smooth except for one or two indications of marked acceleration or deceleration. These abrupt quantitative changes do not disturb the continuity aspect, whereas qualitative changes of content also reflect discontinuity in development. (Werner, 1957). Other growth curves (e.g., general intelligence) appear to be completely continuous, although this is partly attributable to the fact that they represent the average attainment of many individuals with respect to a battery of heterogeneous functions. Nevertheless, even if a given sequence can be divided into several qualitatively different phases, it is self-evident that the total duration of intra-stage growth will usually exceed that of transitional periods of development.

Apart from the absence of conditions that precipitate sudden rapid growth, many factors inherent in the developmental process operate either to cushion the abruptness of this continuous change or to maintain continuity. The first possibility is illustrated by the fact that a sharp line of demarcation can seldom be drawn between the relinquishment of an established pattern and the acquisition of a new pattern of behavior. Instead, a long period of co-existence tends to be the rule. Creeping and walking occur alternately in varying proportions until the latter practice predominates and gains ascendency. Sometimes a preview of the more mature behavior appears sporadically long before it is ready to function. Thus, a ten-month-old infant may take several steps and then not make another attempt at walking for another month. Eventually, however, the new pattern becomes a subsidiary accompaniment of the old and undergoes gradual perfection before partial and later total replacement occur. In a sense the earlier phase of a new activity may be regarded as a preparatory stage of the terminal phase. This sequence of events not only takes place autogenously in nature, but is also deliberately induced as an instrument of parental or cultural child-rearing policy. For example, much of the training which children receive is not intended for immediate application but as an investment in the future—to be available when needed in adult life. In either case, however, this overlapping of current and future patterns mitigates the abruptness of developmental discontinuity.

Cushioning of the content as well as of the execution of discontinuous change is also possible. This occurs when an old behavior pattern can be retained or re-established but requires radical reconstruction because of significant alteration in the larger setting in which it takes place. This would apply to certain areas of sexual behavior, to the quest for primary or derived status in ego development, and to many forms of dependence and immature behavior that are acceptable at a later stage of development, provided that they are recast in a qualitatively different form. Thus, early dependency in girls is acceptable at later stages in their development, provided that this dependency does not have the same characteristics as it had in its earlier stages. Nevertheless, the change is not nearly as discontinuous as would be the case if the content were completely new.

A more fundamental source of continuity that goes beyond mere cushioning of abrupt qualitative change is inherent in the possibility of perpetuating established patterns of behavior in quantitatively different contexts *without* any basic need for reorganization of content or process. For example, most of the motor skills of early childhood (e.g., swimming, bicycling) are retained intact for a lifetime despite gross changes in size, strength, and body proportions. Similarly, the moral and religious values of adults are fundamentally identical in content with those of children despite marked shifts in the basis of acceptance.

Factors Making for Developmental Discontinuity

Because biological and behavioral equilibria are maintained by a complex system of regulatory devices, once established they are not easily disrupted. Generally speaking, organisms react to changing conditions by modifying themselves or the environment in ways that tend to perpetuate the constancy of the prevailing adaptive mechanisms. In the absence of compelling reasons for drastic change, only minor and qualitatively homogeneous adjustments are made; and even when coercive reasons are operative, the cushioning factors described above frequently temper the abruptness of change. Hence, the only *essential* criterion of discontinuity is a qualitative break in the content, organization, or functional basis of a phenomenon. It need not necessarily be ushered in abruptly or represent a complete departure from previous practice, although acceleration in the rate of change obviously forces disequilibrium and reorganization.

Crises in personality development satisfy both criteria of discontinuity. They are generated by a relatively sudden introduction of compelling new variables with a catalytic or consummatory impact on an ongoing developmental process (see pp. 116 and 260). The threshold phenomenon—developmental acquisitions that do not become overtly functional until a certain level of substrate change is exceeded—offers another case in point. Many long-range learning processes and endocrinological changes illustrate this type of development. Here the occurrence of gradual continuous change merely results in quantitative, nonfunctional modification over the greater proportion of a given range of variability. Then, with the reaching of threshold value, the last unit of quantitative change generates a qualitatively discontinuous state of affairs culminating in the apparently sudden emergence of a new function.

When the determining factors of development are less dramatic or when cushioning is more effective, this continuity in process or content still occurs but the mode of transformation of the extent of change is less abrupt. In response to new demands, expectations, or developing capacities, qualitatively different levels of functioning are achieved by the accumulation of small, continuous changes. Many successful and highly rewarding behavior patterns of long standing (e.g., creeping, hand feeding, executive dependence on parents) are gradually abandoned or revived in this manner. The changeover itself is effected gradually and continuously, despite the fact that the new patterns are qualitatively distinct and even antithetical to the old. In phylogenetic activities, such changes may occur quite spontaneously without any cultural pressure, but it cannot be assumed that the same holds true for ontogenetic traits as well. The abruptness of change in other instances is lessened by the duplication of content, even though extensive qualitative restructuring is required.

Criteria for Stages of Development*

A concept closely related to the issue of continuity and discontinuity is the legitimacy of identifying different stages of development. The notion of stages of development has been historically attacked by criticis on the grounds that for stages of development to exist it is necessary to assume (a) that they are spontaneous and inevitable products of endogenous factors and (b) that no overlapping of process occurs among children of different ages. Following from these assumptions, the 1950's saw Piaget's description of different stages of causal thinking dismissed on the grounds that both mature and immature responses are found at all age levels.† The most recent criticisms of *stage* theory formulations have come from theorists of the American

---

*Provocative discussions of criteria for stages of development may be found in Kessen (1962), Kohlberg (1968), and Turiel (1968), Van den Daele, (1969).

†It should be noted that earlier critics of Piaget's precausal thinking use different criteria and methods in replicating his early studies. Recent replications, closely allied to his methodology, have replicated his earlier findings (Laurendeau and Pinard, 1962).

neobehaviorist tradition. Researchers in the Skinnerian tradition, for example, reject cognitive stage formulations, because they detract from the assumption that behavior is under *"stimulus control"* and that responses are quantitative and continuous (Bijou, 1968; Bijou & Baer, 1961; Skinner, 1953). Stage theories have also been criticized because they emphasize interindividual variability over time and similarities among individuals at specifiable age periods (Bandura & Walters, 1963b). Finally, stage theoretical formulations, which have a clear developmental orientation, are criticized because of their apparent divorce from "general behavior theory". In general, this criticism centers around the fact that, in many instances, stage descriptions have not emphasized the experimental testing of hypotheses derived from a "theory" of behavior (Bijou, 1968; McCandless & Spiker, 1956; Russell, 1957; Spiker, 1966; Zigler, 1963).

In general, these criticisms are usually centered around the dichotomy between two different psychological traditions (i.e., predeterministic versus tabula rasa approaches). By emphasizing the most extreme elements in predeterministic positions when discussing stage theory, the baby is thrown out with the bath water. Recent criticisms by American psychologists and educators, for example, have been sharply critical of Piaget's stages or designation of stages for the concrete-abstract dimension of cognitive development. They argue that the transitions between these stages occur gradually rather than abruptly or discontinuously (Bandura and Walters, 1963b; Bandura and McDonald, 1963); that variability exists both between different cultures and within a given culture with respect to the age at which the transition takes place; that fluctuations occur over time in the level of cognitive functioning manifested by a given child; that the transition to the abstract stage occurs at different ages both for different subject-matter fields and for component sub-areas within a particular field; and that environmental as well as endogenous factors have a demonstrable influence on the rate of cognitive development. For all of these reasons, therefore, they deny the validity of Piaget's designated stages.

Actually, developmental stages imply nothing more than identifiable sequential stages in an orderly progression of development that are *qualitatively* discriminable from adjacent phases and generally characteristic of most members of a broadly defined age range. As long as a given stage occupies the same sequential position in all individuals and cultures whenever it occurs, it is perfectly compatible with the existence of intra-individual, interindividual, and intercultural differences in age levels of incidence and in subject-matter fields. It reflects the influence of both genic and environmental determinants, and can occur either gradually or abruptly. Hence, all of the aforementioned arguments disputing either the legitimacy of Piaget's stages of intellectual development seem quite irrelevant.

Although stages of development are qualitatively discontinuous in *process* for preceding and succeeding stages, there is no reason why their *manner of achievement* must necessarily be abrupt or saltatory. This is particularly true when the factors that bring them into being are operative over many years and are cumulative in their impact. Unlike the situation in physical, emotional, and personality development, cognitive development is not marked by the sudden, dramatic appearances of discontinuously new determinants. In Piaget's theory of cognitive development, he is much more cognizant of the continuity-discontinuity question than his detractors imply. Thus, in relation to a stage theory formulation of cognitive development, Inhelder (1962) notes:

> A theory of stages remains incomplete, however, as long as it does not clarify the contradiction between two concepts of development—the one stressing the complete continuity, and the other the absolute discontinuity, of stages. Our first longitudinal investigations led us to a third position (as a hypothesis), namely, that in the development of intellectual operations, phases of continuity alternate with phases of discontinuity. Continuity and discontinuity would have to be defined by the relative dependence or independence of new behavior with respect to previously established behavior. Indeed, it seems as if during the formation of a structure of reasoning (characteristic of stage A) each new procedure depends on those the child has just acquired. Once achieved, this structure serves as a starting point for new acquisitions (characteristic of stage B). The latter will then be relatively independent of the formative process of the former structure. It is only in this sense, that there would be discontinuity in passage from one stage to another. (p. 24).

It is also unreasonable to insist that a given stage must occur at the same age in every culture. Since the rate of development is, at least in part, a function of environmental stimulation, the range in which a stage occurs tends to vary from one culture to another. Thus, considering the marked differences between Swiss and American school systems, it would be remarkable indeed if comparable stages of development took place at the same ages. Similarly, within a given culture, a particular stage cannot be expected to occur at the same age for all individuals. When a particular age level is designated for a given stage, it obviously refers to a mean value and implies that a normal range of variability prevails around the mean. This variability reflects differences in intellectual endowment, experiential background, education, and personality. Thus a certain amount of overlapping among age groups is inevitable. A particular stage may be generally characteristic of five- and six-year-olds, but also typically includes some four- and seven-year-olds and even some three- and eight-year-olds. Piaget's age levels, like Gesell's, are nothing more than average approximations set for purposes of convenience. Hence, to attack the concept of developmental stages on the grounds that a given stage includes children of varying ages, instead of taking place at the precise age designated by Piaget, is simply to demolish a straw man.

One also cannot expect complete consistency and generality of stage behavior within an individual from one week or month to another, and from one subject matter or level of difficulty to another. Some overlapping and specificity are inevitable whenever development is determined by multiple variable factors. A particular twelve-year-old may use abstract logical operations in his science course in October, but may revert for no apparent reason to a concrete level of cognitive function in November, or even several years later when confronted with an extremely difficult and unfamiliar problem in the same field. Furthermore, he may characteristically continue to function at a concrete level for another year or two in social studies and literature (Stone, in press). Since transitions to new stages do not occur instantaneously but over a period of time, fluctuations between stages are common until the newly emerging stage is consolidated (Piaget, 1967; Turiel, 1968). In addition, because of intrinsic differences in level of subject-matter difficulty, and because of intra- and interindividual differences in ability profiles and experiential background, it is hardly surprising that transitions from one stage to another do not occur simultaneously in all subject-matter areas and sub-areas. Abstract thinking, for example, generally emerges earlier in science than in social studies because children have more experience manipulating ideas about mass, time, and space, than about government, social institutions, and historical events. However, in some children, depending on their special abilities and experience, the reverse may be true. In any developmental process where experiential factors are crucial, age *per se* is generally less important than degree of relative experience. Finally, stages of development are always referable to a given range of difficulty and familiarity of the problem area. Beyond this range, individuals commonly revert (regress) to a former stage of development.

Neither is the concept of developmental stages invalidated by the demonstration that they are susceptible to environmental influence. It is erroneous to believe that stages of intellectual development are exclusively products of "internal ripening" and hence that they primarily reflect the influence of endogenous factors.* Gesell's embryological model of development has little applicability to human development beyond the first year of life when environmental factors become increasingly more important determinants of variability in developmental outcome. In fact, as the educational system improves, we can confidently look forward to earlier mean emergence of the various stages of cognitive development.

Particularly related to specific theoretical and methodological strategies, it should be noted that Piaget's use of *stages* as part of his explanatory apparatus

---

*It should be noted, that in Piaget's stage theory of development, the interpretation of predeterminism may arise because of his emphasis on equilibration as the primary factor in stage transition. (see Chapter 2, p. 27).

is reflective of a preference for such concepts over shear explanation on the basis of "*stimulus control*". This position is held in contradistinction to extreme tabula rasa approaches (i.e., Skinnerians). Thus, Piaget's mental operations which are characteristic of a particular stage, in a sense, will partially determine how the stimulus will be processed or interpreted. To say, then, that the child is at the formal operational stage is more than just saying he is such and such an age, or that he can solve such and such a problem. There is included in the statement, based on theory, that his approach to, and competence with, all problems demanding abstract operations will be of a particular and specific kind (Kessen, 1962). A stage, from this point of view, is a mediator between stimulus-response events. On this account, Piaget should not be criticized because he holds to an alternative position when contrasted with Skinnerians. In point of fact, Piaget's stage descriptions of cognitive development may be the initial accomplishment of what Gollin (1965) calls the primary task of developmental research:

. . . to provide observations which will be useful in clarifying the character and properties of central processes and in establishing their role in the determination of functional relations between stimulus and response events throughout development (p. 161).

Finally it is rather ludicrous to accuse theorists with a developmental bent of divorcing themselves from "general behavior theory" tradition. In Piaget's case, it is an historical fact that his findings from the 1930's to the late 1950's were curiously ignored due to the predominant interest given to behaviorism in American psychology. The myopia of American psychology during this period would seem to have precipitated this divorce more than exclusiveness on the part of developmentalists, especially in Piaget's case. Moreover, to restrict hypothesis testing simply to manipulative experiments places serious limitations on the scientific endeavour. To test the "hypothesis" of invariance of sequential stages, it seems more appropriate to use longitudinal studies rather than manipulative experiments. Cross-sectional studies of stage sequence appear to substantiate this hypothesis in sensory-motor development (Decarie, 1965) and causal thinking in childhood (Laurendeau and Pinard, 1962).

The most recent clarification of the notion of *stages* may further elaborate and clarify the potential future utility of this concept of psychological research (Kessen, 1962, 1966; Kohlberg, 1968). Thus, stages may be considered as descriptions of states—as specifications of individual differences—and as statements of transition rules. By this distinction, it may be said that Piaget's description of stages is an adequate description of developmental states. The criticism that Piaget does not specify individual differences within states (Bandura & Walters, 1963b) is an unfair criticism both because a theorist should only be held responsible for the constructs that he specifies

(Hall & Lindsey, 1957), and because such differences are in no way precluded by his stages. Piaget's justification of the "rules of transition" (determinants of change) from one stage to another (i.e., equilibration) is most
vulnerable to criticisms and needs further clarification through research
(Flavell, 1962; Kessen, 1962; Sullivan, 1967; see also Ch. 2, pp. 27-30). Indeed, it is in this aspect, that experimental manipulative designs may prove
to be most appropriate and should further articulate the continuous and discontinuous aspects of development.

LONG-RANGE STABILITY OF INDIVIDUALITY

A related but different kind of developmental continuity from the type
we have just been discussing has to do with the long-range stability of individual differences. Here we are not concerned with the continuity or discontinuity of normative developmental sequences but (a) with the problem
of whether individuality in personality organization is maintained over
extended periods of time, and if so, (b) with the factors responsible for same.

Evidence for Stability

The discussion of long-range stability of individuality in personality
organization has both theoretical and methodological problems related to
the types of measuring devices used at different times in the life cycle. For
example, in studying long-term consistency of aggression, it is necessary to
develop a theoretical rationale for relating phenotypically different early
measures of aggression with later follow-up measures. Obviously, the face
validity of using the same instruments for both initial and follow-up measures
will be greater for some traits (e.g., intelligence) than for others (e.g.,
aggression). It is therefore imperative, in this type of research, to specify the
consistency between traits in more dynamic terms (Yarrow & Yarrow, 1964).
Thus:

> If personality formation is seen as a process of personality change, the phenotypic concept
> of personality consistency, which assumes an isomorphic identity in traits or behavior
> throughout the life cycle, is not a very meaningful one. Much more meaningful is the
> concept of dynamic continuity in which changes in overt characteristics are seen as
> developmental transformations which are dynamically related to earlier personality
> patterns (Yarrow, 1964, p. 69).

Notwithstanding the fact that equating phenotypically different response
measures as indicative of the same underlying trait is open to serious theoretical and methodological difficulties, it is still necessary to proceed in this
fashion if the question of long-term stability is to be fruitfully explored.

Examination of the available evidence points unequivocally to an affirmative answer to the first question of long-range stability of personality organi-

zation. Temperamental differences are both marked at birth and stable throughout infancy and the preschool period. Consistency of a dimension called "reactivity", characterized by *instability* and *activity level*, is reported for the first two years of life (Thomas et al., 1963); and moderate success has been achieved in predicting from *high activity* level at two years to weak impulse control at five years (Escalona and Heider, 1959). Earlier studies on irritability and activity level report similar findings (Gesell and Ames, 1937; Shirley, 1933, 1941)*. Stability of a wide variety of personality traits is evident from early infancy to adulthood (Manheimer and Mellinger, 1967; Sontag, 1963). A general dimension of activity-passivity shows long-term consistency from early childhood to adolescence and adulthood in girls (Bayley, 1964; Bloom, 1964; Kagan and Moss, 1962; Honzik, 1964; Macfarlane, 1964.)† Short term stability of such dimensions as aggression-dominance have been reported for two years of nursery school (Emmerich, 1966; Stott, 1958), and longer stabilities on a dimension of passivity-dominance has been found between the ages of five and sixteen years (Bronson, 1966, 1967).

Apropos of the discussion of the dynamic consistency hypothesis, the trait dimension of *ascendence-submission* shows stability from nursery school years to adulthood when retrospection and adult ratings are used at 26 years (Jayaswal and Stott, 1955) but no stability when a later authoritarian scale is used (Jaiswal, 1955). Stability of the trait dimension of *aggression* has been reported for males between the ages of eight and fourteen years using T.A.T. responses (Kagan, 1959; Kagan and Moss, 1962; Moss and Kagan, 1964), and earlier preschool stabilities have been reported by Bloom (1964) and Emmerich (1966). Similar findings to the above have been reported for achievement motivation (Kagan, 1959; Kagan and Moss, 1959; Bloom, 1964). Moreover, moderate stability for achievement motivation has been reported from childhood into the late twenties (Moss and Kagan, 1961). Longitudinal studies (Kagan, 1960; McKinnon, 1942; Paulson, 1953) for the age periods ranging from three years to twenty years indicate moderate

---

*The persistence of many single temperamental traits, such as laughing, crying, smiling, aggressiveness, perseveration, etc., during this period and the prenatal period have been reported by several investigators (Anderson, 1948; Sontag, 1963).

†The studies reported here, in many instances, are categorized under one general conceptual category (e.g., activity-passivity) for summary purposes. Thus, Bayley (1964) reports a dimension of active introverted-passive introverted while Kagan and Moss (1962) report a simple dimension of dependence-passivity. Because of conceptual differences, a comparison of results of different studies rests on the interpretation of the probable equivalence or similarity of concepts. Even when the same construct is apparently used, "differences in operational definitions or in the specification of the meaning of the construct make an evaluation of consensus questionable" (Schaffer, 1964). Thus our summary here, is simply an attempt to bring to the reader a variety of studies which indicate long-range stability of personality organization.

to marked individual differences in general approach to social situations and in Rorschach variables despite developmental changes implicating the group as a whole. Where shifts occurred, they were in the direction of tendencies that were evident but less pronounced at an earlier age. Stability of popularity and peer reputation has been reported throughout the elementary-school years (Tuddenham, 1959). Follow-up studies of Shirley's infant subjects (Mowrer and Kluckhohn, 1944) and of Gesell's infant twins T and C 15 later indicated that many of the earlier differences in total personality pattern or style of life were still maintained. Even more remarkable was the finding that ratings of children on 30 out of 35 character traits remained approximately the same when they were independently rated on the same traits 50 years later (Smith, 1952).

These data by no means point to the long-life "freezing" of childhood personality structure. In fact, as we shall indicate shortly, many of the more desirable personality outcomes of favorable early upbringing can be partly vitiated by undue deprivation, severe interpersonal conflict, or crippling disease in later childhood, adolescence and adult life. Nevertheless, they do indicate that a sizable nucleus of stubborn individuality remains relatively intact in the face of environmental vicissitudes.

Sources of Stability

How can such consistency in individual personality development be explained? Three kinds of factors seem to be involved: those originating from within (a) the child himself and (b) his environment, and (c) various integrative and self-perpetuating mechanisms involved in the organization of personality. The child furnishes a cluster of genically determined temperamental predispositions (see p. 123) which, in accordance with their strength and resistiveness to environmental modification, help perpetuate the sameness of his response to social experience. These predispositions may even be strong enough in certain cases to persist despite considerable training and cultural pressure in the opposite direction (Shirley, 1933, 1941). In addition, different children respond differently to the same pattern of parental behavior, and thereby serve either to change or reinforce the latter. A self-assertive child, for example, reacts differently than an apathetic child to parental overdomination. Lastly, the child's temperament in and of itself selectively evokes differential responses from significant persons in his environment; and to the extent that his genically conditioned traits and the reactions of parents, teachers, and associates to same are relatively consistent, an additional source of long-range continuity is provided. Everyday experience indicates that irritability or peevishness in a child "tends to arouse impatience and annoyance in others, and by so doing . . . helps to produce an environment that fosters his peevish ways." (Jersild, 1954).

The parent contributes to the continuity of the child's individuality by providing a relatively constant interpersonal environment during the important formative years of the latter's personality development. This constancy, of course, is a function of the longitudinal consistency of the parent's own personality and child-rearing attitudes. Moreover, sex differences in the twin dimensions of aggression and passivity "show long term stability if that behavior is congruent with the cultural definition of the sex role of the individual" (Kagan and Moss, 1962). The fact that boys maintain their position on the aggressive continuum and girls on passive dependency hints at possibly genically determined biological determinants (Honzik, 1964). Children showing stability come from families which are homogeneous, stable, and free from traumatizing vicissitudes (Murphy, 1964). It is true that sooner or later the child is directly exposed to extrafamilial values in the culture which are at variance with those of the home; but in general, by virtue of prior conditioning and differential exposure, he tends to be selectively influenced by the particular value judgments emanating from the social class and other institutional affiliations of his parents.

Perpetuation of the formative effects of early (post-infantile) experience may be attributed in part to their initially deep entrenchment. The family-biased sample of the culture exerts disproportionate influence on the child's personality development because the restricted nature of his early environment and the unstructured condition of his major value and attitude systems make him maximally susceptible to any form of recurrent, pervasive, and affectively toned patterning influence. Then, once established, canalization and reaction-sensitivity tend to impose further restrictions on the theoretical array of behaviors open to any individual. What would otherwise constitute just one of many potentially adequate ways of meeting a need or solving a problem becomes the *only* adequate way (Murphy, 1947). "Habitual modes of reaction," in turn, "sensitize" the individual "to certain aspects of his experience and dull him to others. When he enters new surroundings and meets new people, he is more ready to respond in one direction than another, and this readiness itself acts selectively to bring him more of similar kinds of experience." (Cameron, 1947).

Once organized on a stable basis, distinctive personality structure, like any developmental equilibrium, tends to remain intact in the absence of substantial cause for change. The child does not start from scratch in each new situation, but brings with him a precipitate of all past learnings. He attempts to maintain the same orientations, habits, adjustive mechanisms, and modes of striving and interacting with others that he used before. Even if change occurs in the objective properties of a situation (e.g., parent attitudes), habitual apperceptive sets may be strong enough in certain cases

to force altered stimulus content into preconceived perceptual molds*
("perceptual constancy"). When this kind of perceptual manipulation is
precluded by major change in the environmental situation, the child attempts first to respond in terms of his existing personality organization and
to utilize habitual adjustive techniques found successful in the past before he
ventures to reorganize his personality or to improvise basically new patterns
that are no longer appropriate or acceptable at higher age levels, e.g.,
temper tantrums, "baby talk," enuresis, motor helplessness in an eight
year old.

Finally, the longitudinal continuity of individuality can be attributed to
the fact that certain central dimensions of personality play a crucial integrative role in its development and organization:

> As a result of characteristic ways of interacting with significant persons in the environ-
> ment, more or less permanent constellations of ego needs and habitual modes of self-
> evaluation arise. Examples of such constellations are differential feelings of security and
> adequacy, and needs for ego status and independence that emerge in crucial develop-
> mental s quences like satellization† or failure to undergo devaluation. These constella-
> tions give rise to propensities for characteristic modes of learning, aspiring, socialization,
> ego-defense, and attitudes toward authority and group demands (Ausubel, 1954).

It would be surprising indeed if the prior existence and operation of such
salient aspects of individual uniqueness did not leave some functional residue
in personality structure. The latter could affect directly the kind of current
biosocial status an individual seeks and the basis on which he assimilates
values. "Thus, for example, although an adult who satellized as a child
obtains most of his current status from primary rather than from derived
sources, some satellizing patterns [could] still remain operative in adult life
and furnish a subsidiary source of status, e.g., satellizing-like relationships
with boss, spouse, pastor, physician, membership group, etc." (Ausubel,
1957). In addition, a residue of prior satellizing experience could conceivably constitute an inner core of self-acceptance which would be independent of situational success and failure. Although this would not function
as a subsidiary source of currently generated status, it could exercise a substrate influence serving to keep his ego aspirations within realistic limits and
to protect him from catastrophic impairment of self-esteem.

-----

*This "freezing" of perception despite change in stimulus content is facilitated further by the
acceptance of general categorical propositions which dispose individuals to ignore the information
supplied by first-hand experience. Once general categories of objects and relationships are established,
the properties of currently experienced stimuli are simply inferred on the basis of their categorical
membership.

†A form of dependent identification with superordinate figures as a result of which an individual
acquires derived status if he is accepted and intrinsically valued by the former.

CONTEMPORANEOUS CONSISTENCY IN PERSONALITY ORGANIZATION

Even more basic perhaps to the concept of personality than the longitudinal continuity of individuality is its internal consistency at a given horizonal level. It is self-evident that the former can be no more than a developmental outgrowth of the latter. As already pointed out, the entire concept of personality would be meaningless if it did not refer to a relatively stable and consistent organization of individually unique behavioral predispositions (see p. 42); behavior could otherwise be explained completely in terms of general reaction capacities, situational determinants, and transitory motivations generated in the course of current experience.

Both contemporaneously and longitudinally, consistency in personality structure is largely a function of the fact that behavioral traits become organized and hierarchically ordered in relation to certain of its central unifying gradients or core aspects. In human beings, the ego, a functionally interrelated constellation of attitudes, motives, values, aspirations, and orientations toward other persons and groups—all having significant self-reference—plays this crucial integrative role in personality organization and development. (Ausubel 1954; Murphy 1947; Sherif 1953). It constitutes in itself a self-consistent, integrated, and enduring system; and further consistent development is insured by the tendency to assimilate new trait trends compatible with it and, hence, with each other. As a result, generality in responding to a host of objects, persons, values, and institutions in an unending variety of concrete situations becomes possible (Sherif 1953), and syndromes of functionally and developmentally meaningful personality traits can be identified.

Evidence of Limited Consistency in Children

In children, for reasons which we shall examine shortly, the evidence indicates that although a nucleus of horizontal consistency does exist, considerable tolerance for inconsistency in personality organization is also present but probably diminishes with increasing age. Sanford, et al (1943) were able to identify twenty meaningfully constituted personality syndromes in school children based upon intercorrelations among traits that averaged about .5 within each syndrome. However, these syndromes were quite phenotypic in nature, the intersituational generality of the various trait measures was unknown, and relatively little stability over a three-year period was maintained. Ferguson and Maccoby (1966) have also demonstrated relationships between interpersonal traits and differential cognitive abilities (i.e., high social interaction children and high numerical ability). Even here, however, differential-abilities groups do not suggest that a great deal of variance in measures of ability is accounted for by interpersonal factors. Similarly, high-prejudice children, when compared to a low-prejudice group show more spontaneous hostility, see virtue in their own group, and score lower on inductive reasoning tasks. (Kutner 1958).

Research devoted to "cognitive style" may also be considered as another aspect of contemporaneous consistency in personality organization. "Cognitive style" refers to self-consistent and enduring individual differences in cognitive organization and functioning. The term refers both to individual differences in general principles of cognitive organization (e.g., simplification and consistency trends), and to various self-consistent idiosyncratic tendencies (e.g., reflective vs. relational thinkers, field dependent vs. field-independent) that are not reflective of human cognitive functioning in general. It reflects differences in personality organization as well as in genically and experientially determined differences in cognitive capacity and functioning; and in a very real sense, it mediates between motivation and emotion, on the one hand, and cognition on the other (Paul, 1959).*

General studies with children have demonstrated relationships between category styles of analytic-reflective vs. impulsive thinking (Kagan and Henker, 1966). In a study of six-year-olds of both sexes, analytic-reflective children in contrast to impulsive children, on a figure-sorting task, were superior on inductive reasoning tasks and response uncertainty items (Kagan, Pearson, and Welch, 1966). It was also found that analytic-reflective styles are more stable over time and have greater inter-task generality (Kagan, Rosman, and others 1964). Autonomic correlates of the analytic attitude reveal cardiac deceleration, increased respiratory rate, and decreased respiratory variability when attending to visual and auditory inputs (Kagan and Rosman 1964).

Bruner and Tajfel (1961) and Tajfel, Richardson and Everstein (1964) report consistent preferences for *broad* or *narrow* categorization. Narrow categorizers show greater preference than broad categorizers for taking the risk of being wrong as stimulus situations change (Bruner, *et al*, 1961). With rare exceptions, a serious methodological weakness common to many of the studies in this area is the fact that intra-or intertask generality of function of the measures which they use for cognitive style, its determinants, and its functional consequences has not been adequately established. It is questionable, in most cases, therefore, whether these measures are actually indicative

---

Short summaries of the literature on cognitive style may be found in Kagan, Moss, & Sigel, (1963) and Kogan and Wallach (1965).

of stable and generalized cognitive traits. Furthermore, for both theoretical and methodological purposes:

. . . there is an urgent need for systematic studies to determine the relation among the various cognitive style variables used by individual investigators and for the translation of local terms into a more general language (Kagan and Henker, 1966, pp. 26-27).

A component aspect of personality organization involves moral, character, and value traits. Hartshorne and May obtained correlations of .4 to .5 for different objective measures of deceit within the same kind of situation but considerably less generality of function from one situation to another. (Hartshorne & May, 1928). Similar findings to the above have been found for 5-year-olds. Further exploration of the Hartshorne and May data using factor analysis, however, reveals a small general factor in various experimental tests of classroom cheating (Burton, 1963). Moreover, comparable studies on character formation range from low positive correlations between tests, where repetition of the same test showed substantial similarity (Weinberger in Sears 1960), to a fair amount of intersituational generality in children for truthfulness (Slaght 1928) and honesty (Barbu, 1951). In studying satellizing and nonsatellizing trends in such related areas as explanations of moral behavior, agreement with perceived parent opinions, identification with heroes, and notions of omnipotence, Ausubel and others found relatively high inter-item generality for each instrument but low intercorrelations among the different variables in a population of ten year olds. (Ausubel, Schiff, & Zeleny 1954, 1956). Children characterized as *humanistic* as opposed to *conventional* on moral judgments gave more guilt responses on a story completion test. (Hoffmann, 1963; Hoffmann & Salzstein, 1960). Delay of gratification discriminated cheaters from non-cheaters with IQ and age controlled (Mischel 1963).

Moral character and value traits, however, probably provide too rigorous a test of trait generality in children. Much of the inconsistency is undoubtedly indicative (a) of insufficient cognitive ability with which to subsume specific situations under general value propositions (Ausubel, 1952; Hoffman, 1963; Kohlberg, 1964); and (b) of the chaotic and conflictful state of moral education in our culture. In contrast, extremely high generality over trials was obtained for such motivational measures as goal discrepancy scores (level of aspiration), goal tenacity scores, (Ausubel, *et al*, 1954) and responsiveness to prestige incentives, (Ausubel 1951), and for responsiveness to prestige suggestion (Ausubel, *et al*, 1956); and in the case of the first three variables, generality coefficients of .4 to .9 were found, depending on the degree of similarity between the tasks used. (Ausubel, 1951; Ausubel, *et al*, 1954).

Sources of Inconsistency

Consistency is a measure of the compatibility of parts with the whole and with each other. Hence, since the child's personality is relatively unformed and is changing rapidly, there is obviously less basis for consistency than in the adult. Until a crystallized and stable representation of individuality is achieved, many divergent trends are compatible within the existing total organization. Furthermore, since the child requires some experience with a given kind of behavior before he can judge its congruence with his major goal and value systems, he is apt to give many ultimately unsuitable patterns a "provisional try" before he finally rejects them. With increasing age, however, a more characteristic portrait of the individual emerges and a clearer standard for gauging compatibility becomes available. Many alternatives experimented with on a tentative basis are found wanting and are sloughed off. Thus, by a process of progressive "acquisition of dislikes by individuals whose initial attitude is favorable toward everything," personality organization becomes increasingly more integrated and self-consistent. Even in the turbulence of adolescence such character traits as honesty, responsibility, and moral courage acquire considerably more generality than in childhood. (Havighurst & Taba 1949). And the adolescent and young adult who consistently over- or underestimates his forthcoming performance does likewise with his past performance, (Ausubel, *et al*, 1953), his I.Q. (Gilinsky 1949), and his sociometric status (Schiff 1953).

We do not wish to imply that judgments of consistency are necessarily deliberate; very frequently they are made quite incidentally. Yet with advancing age, as the child's personality takes more definite shape and as he develops a clearer conception of it and greater capacity for perceiving incompatibility, the need for preserving self-consistency gradually increases. Unlike the young child, the older individual employs a conscious monitoring system which, by virtue of selective assimilation, retention, and rejection, helps maintain congruence between his personality structure and his self-concept; (Ausubel 1957); but since unbiased conscious control is often insufficient for this purpose, he also utilizes such supplementary mechanisms as perceptual and logical distortion, repression, and the isolation of beliefs in logic-tight compartments. Nevertheless, even the well-integrated adult displays considerable tolerance for consciously appreciated inconsistency. The widespread belief that all inconsistency must necessarily be "unconscious" or below the threshold of awareness is one of the major psychological myths of our time.

Relatively recently it has also been recognized that some of the apparent lack of trait generality in children, as well as in adults, is spurious because of the failure to hold ego-involvement constant. It stands to reason that trait behavior in different situations is not comparable unless degree of self-implication is approximately equivalent. For example, level of aspiration in laboratory (Harvey & Sherif 1951; McCandless 1967; McGehee 1940; Preston & Bayton, 1940), and "real-life" (Ausubel, *et al*, 1953) tasks, tendency to cheat, responsiveness to prestige incentives (Ausubel 1951), memory for completed as against incompleted tasks (Rosenzweig 1941), level of confidence in a variety of tasks (Klein & Schoenfeld 1941), and tenacity of vocational goals (Ausubel, *et al*, 1953) all increase with magnitude of ego-involvement.

Lastly, some of the apparent inconsistency in children's personality structure is merely a reflection of the grossness and invalidity of existing measuring instruments. In the absence of subtle measures capable of penetrating beneath (a) normative commonalities characterizing all children at a particular stage of development, and (b) different phenotopic expressions of the same genotype tendency, spurious inconsistency is inevitably added to that which already exists. Thus, to advocate dismissal of research on contemporaneous trait consistency in personality (Brim 1960), is an attempt at premature closure on a problem which is just beginning to show its research possibilities (Cronbach 1957).

TRANSITIONAL PERIODS OF DEVELOPMENT

We have already indicated that one of the chief types of developmental discontinuity is brought about by significant and relatively rapid shifts in the individual's biosocial status. The periods in which qualitatively new and discontinuous (inter-stage) changes in personality organization are being formulated may be designated as transitional phases or developmental crises. "During these transitional periods the individual is in the marginal position of having lost an established and accustomed status and of not yet having acquired the new status toward which the factors impelling developmental change are driving him (Ausubel 1954). He is not without any status whatsoever, but that which he does enjoy is "vague, ambiguous, and rapidly changing" (Ausubel 1954).

Causes of Developmental Crises

What is responsible for critical shifts in biosocial status and the developmental crises they precipitate? Although it is true that some of the determining factors may be endogenous or the product of incidental experience, no transitional period is ever completely divorced from external pressures or solely a reflection of "spontaneous maturation." * It is also important to bear

---

In some nonpersonality areas of development (e.g., neuromuscular development in infancy), transitional periods may be conceived as of maturational. (McGraw 1943).

in mind that preparatory or predisposing influences are usually operative for a long time before consummatory or catalytic factors are brought into play, and that the factors responsible for inaugurating developmental crises are not necessarily the same ones required for their satisfactory resolution.

In general, transitional stages in personality organization are precipitated by two kinds of factors: (a) an urgent need within the culture for a fundamental modification of the social and personality status of an entire group of individuals who are in a given stage of developmental equilibrium; (b) and the occurrence of marked changes within the individual—changes in physical make-up, basic drives, competencies, perceptual ability—which are so crucial that present status becomes incompatible with his altered appearance, capacities, needs and perceptions. (Ausubel 1954, p. 66). An example illustrating the operation of and interaction between these variables is afforded by the crisis of devaluation separating infancy from childhood. It is precipitated by the consolidation of sufficient motor, intellectual, and social skill to make possible a greater measure of self-help and conformity to parental direction. The parents in turn are motivated by a desire to gain the volitionally ascendent role in the relationship that the conditions of dependency warrant, and to rear their child in the traditions of the culture. And lastly, the child's perceptual capacity becomes sufficiently acute to appreciate more realistically his role and status. (Ausubel 1952).

Characteristics of Transitional Periods

There are many reasons for believing that transitional periods in personality development must be difficult and productive of stress. First, an individual's biosocial status provides an over-all frame of reference for the organization of his attitudes, values, goals, and standards of conduct. Hence, it is quite understandable that profound *disorientation* should occur when it is abruptly cast aside and replaced by another. As he is thrust into "new and uncharted psychological fields the landmarks . . . of which are obscure and hazy," the familiar and differentiated roles that he had learned in relation to an earlier pattern of social expectations and the cues that he had employed with confidence in interpreting his interpersonal environment suddenly become useless and confusing. Second, considerable *anxiety* is engendered by the threat to self-esteem inherent in forfeiting current status while the attainment of new status is still uncertain. He is required to discard a painfully acquired portion of his identity, the security of established roles and status prerogatives, and frequently a sheltered and protected position; and in return he is permitted to strive for a potentially more satisfactory type of biosocial status. But in connection with this striving looms the ever-present threat of disappointment and failure, the pull of conflicting loyalties and the awesome responsibilities of freedom and autonomy.* (Jersild 1954). And whenever he is forced to choose between two alternatives, each of which offers disadvantages (e.g., parents or peers, dependence or independence, conformity or individuality), a choice in favor of one inevitably frustrates needs and inclinations referable to the other and gives rise to regret and self-recrimination.

A third source of the stressfulness of transitional periods is the inevitable abruptness with which they are inaugurated. The very suddenness of discontinuous changes in the rate or direction of development adds to disorientation and anxiety and affords insufficient opportunity for the acquisition of adaptive responses; "and when the developmental process is sufficiently complex to encompass several constituent aspects, discrepancies in rate of growth are practically inevitable" (Ausubel 1954). Fortunately, however, the abruptness of developmental crises is often mitigated by the cushioning mechanisms described in the first section of this chapter.

Marginality of status is a characteristic feature and still another source of transitional stress. It is a product of natural overlapping in developmental sequences (as when preparatory or training periods coexist with older patterns of behavior), of inertia and resistance to change, and of developmental regression. Inertia refers to the various regulatory devices that tend to perpetuate sameness of personality organization and to adapt established response patterns to new conditions, i.e., canalization, reaction sensitivity, perceptual constancy, the preferential use of habitual adjustive techniques, and the tenacity of central organizing dimensions of personality. Resistance to change arises from anticipated anxiety and disorientation in connection with developmental crises, from threatened loss of immediate status, from ambivalence about exchanging an established and familiar status for one that is insecure and uncertain, and from resistiveness to insistent environmental pressures. By opposing irresistible forces impelling redirection of development, it makes the transition more traumatic and conflictful. Lastly, regression (see following section), a common adjustive response to the hazards and frustrations of developmental transition, reinstates outmoded behavior patterns and prolongs the period of overlapping.

Marginality—whether of overt status or of needs and loyalties—generates an uncomfortable and unstable state of psychological ambiguity, tentativeness, uncertainty, and indecision. Unquestionably, "many conflicts in childhood are due to forces corresponding to the various groups to which the child belongs. Such conflicts are particularly important for children in

---

It also seems likely that the aura of uncertainty regarding the acquisition of potential status is deliberately fostered by the culture in order to encourage a high and sustained level of individual motivation in meeting new social expectations.

marginal positions, that is, for children who are standing on the boundary between two groups. . . . Uncertainty of the ground on which the child stands leads to an alternation between the values of the one and of the other group, to a state of emotional tension, and to a frequent fluctuation between overaggression and overtimidity." (Lorenz 1935). Transitional periods of personality development, in which biosocial status and major identifications and anchorages are substantially marginal and indefinite, are necessarily self-limited in duration. Beyond a period of weeks or months they become intolerable. Hence, if further prolongation is required, as, for example, during adolescence in most complexly organized cultures, "it becomes necessary to formalize a definite interim status" with various distinctive characteristics of its own. This acquires relative stability, and "provides the adolescent with some recognized social standing, an opportunity for acquiring some current self-esteem, and a tangible frame of reference for selectively accepting certain attitudes, values, and goals and rejecting others." (Ausubel 1954).

A component aspect of the general discussion of transitional periods in personality organization involves the continuity-discontinuity issue in stages of intellectual development (p. 101). In contrast to the *crises* precipitated by discontinuity in other aspects of development, stages of intellectual development, although qualitatively discontinuous in process from one another, do not appear in their manner of *achievement* as abrupt and saltatory. This is particularly true when the factors that bring them into being are operative over many years and are cumulative in their impact. Thus, unlike the situation in physical, emotional ,and personality development, cognitive development is not marked by the sudden, dramatic appearance of discontinuously new determinants. *

PARALLELISM AND DIVERGENCE IN COMPONENT ASPECTS OF DEVELOPMENT

There can be little argument about the fact that different aspects of development must of necessity be interrelated. Since any organism functions and develops as a whole rather than as a collection of discrete and isolated

---

*It should be pointed out that in the most widely discussed stage theory of intellectual development (i.e., Piaget), understanding of transitional periods is hampered by his tendency to ignore such obvious and crucial considerations as extent of intersituational generality and relative degree of intra- and inter-stage variability in delineating stages of development. Moreover, his use of cross-sectional observations to measure developmental change (i.e., observations on different age groups of children, (see Chap. 5, p. 142), are particularly ill-adapted for his purposes. The transitional stages and qualitative discontinuities he purports to find can be convincingly demonstrated only by longitudinally extended studies of the same children. Logical inference is not an adequate substitute for empirical data in naturalistic investigation.

capacities, growth or retardation in any one area obviously affects (i.e., stimulates or limits) growth in all other areas. However, even though such interrelatedness makes for a significant degree of functional and developmental interaction, and limits the extent of disparity between component rates of growth, it does not necessarily insure *parallelism* between different functions. In effect this means that although physical and intellectual development, for example, mutually influence each other, there is no necessary relationship between their respective rates of growth in a *particular* individual. Thus, if Johnny is physically advanced for his age, the probability that his intellectual development will be similarly accelerated is little better than chance.

The Evidence

Studies of the relationship between physical status and motor ability, on the one hand, and intelligence or intellectual ability, on the other hand, show negligible or zero correlations throughout adolescence and adult life (Bloom 1964). Relatively high positive correlations are found during infancy (Bayley, 1933; Shirley, 1931), but these decline consistently with increasing age (Abernathy, 1936; Bayley, 1933, 1940). Moreover, even the initially high relationship is largely spurious. Since intelligence has few cognitive outlets in infancy, many of the tests of "intellectual" ability included in infant intelligence scales really measure sensori-motor or neuromuscular skills. Body size measures have low correlations with metabolic and endocrine measures and a large number of mental and behavioral measures (Abernathy, 1936; Ljung, 1965; Tanner, 1960, 1962). However, fat-free or lean body mass are related to differences in nursery school behavior (Douglas, Ross, and Simpson, 1965, Ljung, 1965). In relation to neuromuscular skills, taller children tend to walk earlier (Norval, 1947).

The positive relationship between intelligence and physical-motor status demonstrated at the extremes of intellectual ability also reflects the operation of extraneous factors. In extreme cases of intellectual deficit, children frequently do not possess sufficient general intelligence to learn even simple motor skills; and intellectually gifted children tend to be taller and heavier and to become pubescent earlier (Ljung, 1965; Tanner, 1960, 1962; Terman, 1939) largely because the same superior socioeconomic status they tend to enjoy provides both better nutrition and more intellectual stimulation. A direct test of the organismic age concept in children at three grade levels showed no tendency for acceleration in mental age to be accompanied by similar acceleration in weight, skeletal age or dental age (Blommers, Knief, and Stroud, 1955). Even in the case of body size, "the correlation is not simply explained by an advancement in physical development being associated with an advancement in intellectual development" (Douglas *et al*,

1965). Summaries of the effects of language development on cognitive, perceptual, and motor skills must also proceed with the same caution in interpretation; as Ervin-Tripp (1966) points out in summary: "Both verbal skills and other cognitive schema change with age. Verbalization can sometimes interfere by distraction or false emphasis. Language seems to be of greatest value in aiding the coding and storage of information but has less effect on sensory perception, new concept attainment, and basic cognitive operations" (p. 85).

In view of these findings, the generalizations reached by Olson and Hughes (1943) that "a child's growth and achievement show a 'going-together-ness' " and that "achievement is a function of the organism as a whole," hardly seem justified. That they are supported by isolated cases selected from a given population proves little indeed since such occasional concomitance could be expected merely on a chance basis. Furthermore, much of the obtained parallelism can be accounted for by the presence of common general factors *within* the two main categories of functions measured by these workers. For example, it is hardly surprising that reading age, spelling age, language usage and educational age are positively intercorrelated, or that height, weight, strength of grip, skeletal age, and dental age are similarly related to each other.

Factors Making for Divergence

Logical analysis confirms the empirical findings cited above. Since each area of development is regulated by a different set of determinants, there is no *a priori* reason for supposing that parallelism should exist. "It is extremely unlikely that the particular constellation of genic and environmental factors regulating the development of any given trait or capacity would completely overlap the set of regulatory factors involved in the development of any other trait or capacity." (Ausubel, 1954). During transitional periods of development, discrepancies between the relative status of different functions tend to widen since all components are not equally sensitive to the factors precipitating developmental crises. Skeletal and neuromuscular growth, for example, are extremely conspicuous during infancy, level off in childhood, and enjoy another spurt in adolescence. Emotional and social development are also marked by periods of slow and rapid growth, whereas the course of intellectual development is relatively smooth and even.

The general trend in development is toward increasing divergence of existing differences in the component capacities of an individual. In intellectual development, for example, intelligence becomes increasingly more differentiated, as shown by the decreasing intercorrelations among the subtests of intelligence scales as children advance in age (see Chapter 17). Another indication of the progressive trend toward differentiation of abilities is the fact that ten year old boys of high socioeconomic status make higher scores than ten year old boys of low socioeconomic status on tests of both verbal and mechanical ability, but at age sixteen are only superior on the verbal tests (Havighurst and Janke, 1944).

This trend toward differentiation and divergence reflects the operation of a selective process which accentuates initial acceleration or retardation in a given function. Since all potential abilities cannot be maximally developed, individuals tend to exercise those capacities in which they excel and succeed, and to avoid those activities in which they are relatively inferior and experience failure. Thus, as a result of a circular relationship between use and proficiency, original discrepancies in ability are progressively widened.*

Factors Making for Parallelism

As already suggested, although the interrelatedness of development does not necessarily insure parallelism, it does limit the extent of divergence that is possible. Serious intellectual deficiency, for example, inevitably spreads to all other aspects of development. Another type of limiting effect is illustrated by the fact that acceleration in one area must frequently be halted until growth in other supportive areas catches up sufficiently to permit further progress. Thus, relative to his limited motor and verbal capacities, an infant's social behavior is quite precocious; but until he learns to locomote and communicate more efficiently, more mature forms of social experience are beyond his reach. Rapid development in one area may also serve to stimulate growth in antother, thereby tending to reduce the discrepancy between them. This sequence of events is seen during transitional periods of development that are precipitated when the capacities of an age group are seriously at variance with the type of biosocial status it enjoys. The period of infancy, for example, is brought to a close when parents decide that a child is mature enough in a motor and cognitive sense to surrender some of his volitional independence (i.e., to submit to their direction) and to manifest more executive independence (self-help).

Parallelism in rate of growth of capacities within an individual sometimes occurs because of particular social values or stereotypes. Since educational and motor retardation affect adversely a child's social acceptability among his peers, it would be reasonable to expect that this retardation would spread to the social sphere as well. Similarly, by virtue of expectations generated by the cultural association of leadership ability with a commanding appearance, tall, well-built children are more apt to seek and be chosen for positions of leadership (see p. 352).

---

*In compensating for deficiencies it is only natural to seek success in conspicuously different activities. Conformity to such cultural stereotypes as athlete or scholar also helps to promote dichotomization and divergence in the development of abilities.

INDIVIDUAL DIFFERENCES IN RATE AND PATTERNING OF DEVELOPMENT

In the present section we shall consider some general issues concerned with individual differences in development. This discussion, of course, deals with much different problems than the advisability of using the individual as a source or subject of application of developmental data and insights (see pp. 15 and 147).

Normative Growth versus Individual Differences

Despite the occurrence of individual differences and overlapping between age groups in rate, sequence, and patterning of growth, many uniformities characterize development as a process. Except for phylogenetic traits, these regularities are attributable to commonalities in polygenic make-up and in environmental influences. If they did not occur, few generalizations indeed could ever be formulated about the development of children, and each child's growth would have to be considered completely unique. Fortunately, however, it is possible to discover developmental laws that express in equation form the relationships of different variables to each other. In relation to such laws individual differences have to be conceived of as various, specific values which these variables have in a particular case.

It is equally important to emphasize the converse of the above proposition. That is, despite the existence of normative uniformities, it is possible to identify both wide variations within the range of normality and innumerable individual patterns of development. As children advance in age, they tend to maintain their individuality as well as to undergo the normative changes that characterize their respective age groups. This is easily demonstrable in many areas where the relative status of an individual's capacity can be expressed in quantitative form, e.g., I.Q.; in other instances normative changes of a qualitative nature are so salient that in the absence of extremely subtle measuring instruments, individual differences are completely obscured. In any case, however, it is never safe to assume qualitative equivalence between the mean status of a given age group and the status of accelerated younger or retarded older individuals. For example, the intellectual status and functioning of children aged four, eight, and sixteen who possesss the same mental age of eight are hardly comparable (see Chapter 17). Similarly, an extremely independent preadolescent is not necessarily self-assertive on the same basis as the modally independent adolescent.

Because of the strikingly more rapid rate of development in children than in adults, both variance from one age level to another and uniformity within a given age level *appear* much more conspicuous than intra-age group variability. For example, the fact that all ten year olds in our culture enjoy an overtly dependent biosocial status which is not commensurate with their biosocial competence does much to obscure and confound marked and possibly consistent individual differences (Ausubel, *et al*, 1954). However, this restricted range of intra-age group variability in children is actual as well as relative to greater inter-age group variability, since the former tends to increase with age in most functions (Bayley, 1956). The widened range of variability in older individuals can be explained by the greater differentiation within a given stage of development that is possible when the rate of growth decreases, and by the greater cultural tolerance for nonconformity in adults than in children.

Developmental norms are valuable because they provide a standard or frame of reference for evaluating and interpreting the status or current behavior of an individual. They can be abused if the range of variability is overlooked; if expectations for all children are geared to group averages; if substantial parallelism is expected between component rates of growth; if they are unwarrantedly applied to individuals who could not be included in the sampling population; and if individual guidance is predicated upon normative comparisons alone to the exclusion of information regarding individual patterning. They are also abused if they are regarded as inevitable and immutable products of maturation or as necessarily desirable. But because an instrument is subject to abuse is no reason for declaring it valueless or urging its abolition as some over-zealous but misguided exponents of the "clinical" approach have suggested.

Early Manifestations of Individuality

There is no such thing as absolute identity in nature. Behavioral differences are demonstrable in infants from the very moment of birth—even in monozygotic twins (Gesell, 1928; Gesell, *et al*, 1937). Such differences are determined by polygenic factors, uterine environment, length of gestation, type and duration of delivery, and perhaps, by minor variations in early handling. Genotypic diversity is probably the most important determining factor in the case of ordinary siblings and unrelated children, and cannot be discounted even in the case of single-egg twins.

Six main categories of distinct and stable individual differenes have been identified in infants during the early months of life. These may be grouped as follows: (a) placidity and irritability (Escalona & Heider, 1959; Rosenblith, 1966; Scarr, 1966; Thomas, *et al*, 1963); (b) activity level and distribution of activity (Bell, 1960; Escalona, 1963; Kessen, Williams, & Williams, 1961; Scarr, 1966; Schaffer, 1966; C. E. Walters, 1965); (c) tone, length, and vigorousness of crying (Fisichelli & Karelitz, 1966; Schaffer & Emerson, 1964; Walters & Parke, 1965); (d) tolerance of frustration or discomfort and reaction to stress situation and under- and over-stimulation (Campbell &

Kalafat, 1966; Klatskin, *et al*, 1966; Salk, 1962; Walters & Parke, 1965); (e) differential sensitivity to stimulation in various sense modalities (Bayley, 1964; Kagan & Lewis, 1964; Lewis, Bartels, Campbell, & Goldberg, 1967; Walters & Parke, 1965); and (f) smiling and other types of positive emotional responses (Ambrose, 1961; Escalona, 1965; Kistlakovskaia, 1965; Shaffer, 1963; Schaffer & Emerson, 1964; Walters & Parke, 1965). The demonstration of differences such as these does not, of course, preclude the existence of other genically conditioned differences in temperament (e.g., introversion-extroversion) which can first be manifested only after a certain stage of maturity is reached. Many of the studies reported here do not preclude the effects of environmental differences, but at a later age it is much more difficult to assess their genic origin because of the operation of many more environmental factors during the interim.

Individual Differences in Rate of Growth

Normative investigations which concentrate on *mean* changes in capacity or behavior with increasing age frequently tend to obscure individual differences in rate of growth. However, in longitudinal studies, where repeated measurements of the same subjects are made over an extended period of time, and where individual scores as well as measures of central tendency are plotted against age, individual patterns of development are clearly evident. Except for extreme cases of mental deficiency, few individuals are uniformly accelerated or retarded in all growth functions. Even within a single area such as intelligence, most children achieve basal age scores on some subtests and over- or underage scores on others.

In general, three principal methods of expressing rate of growth are currently utilized: (1) an individual may serve as his own unique basis of comparison, (2) his status may be compared to that of the *mean* child of like age, or (3) his status may be assessed in terms of the progress achieved by the particular sub-group of his age mates in which his level or rate of growth in a given function place him. In the first instance, the individual's status at a particular stage of development is represented by the percentage of his adult or maximum growth attained at that age level. This expression does not indicate his relative status or rate of growth in terms of his age group but in relation to his own terminal achievement. It is undoubtedly the most meaningful way of assessing an individual's developmental progress in the light of his own idiosyncratic pattern of growth.

In the second method, the child's current status is generally expressed as a *developmental age* (e.g., skeletal age, mental age) or as a *developmental quotient* (e.g., I.Q.). An individual's developmental age in a given function corresponds to the chronological age at which the mean attainment of a representative sample of children equals his current status in that function. If this expression is divided by his chronological age, a developmental quotient is obtained. Needless to state, developmental age units for a given function are not comparable (equivalent) from one period to another unless differences in variability at successive age levels are taken into account. Otherwise, they artificially tend to impose an appearance of straight-line progress on basically uneven growth sequences.

By using standard scores,* relative status can be rendered comparable from one age level or function to another. Nevertheless, additive treatment of component individual scores representing different areas of development is still unwarranted. Since the latter are largely independent of each other, both functionally and in terms of their determinants, there is no defensible basis for using a standard score version of the organismic age concept which implies that the constituent elements are qualitatively homogeneous or that their rate of growth is regulated by a common set of factors. The major disadvantage of using standard scores is that because of the restricted range of variability in the early years of life, relatively small differences in capacity can give rise to relatively large differences in score values. This tends to magnify the effect of any adventitious situational or testing variable operative for one series of measurements but not for another, and hence to give an exaggerated impression of instability in rate of growth.

The third method listed above represents a compromise between the normative and uniquely individual approaches. Several typical patterns of development in a given function are first identified, and then the individual's growth is appraised sequentially in relation to the particular category in which he falls (see Chapter 18).

Each of the three methods of expressing the current developmental status and rate of growth of an individual provides valuable information from a particular standpoint of assessment. Used conjunctively, they supplement each other in the task of interpreting and evaluating the processes of growth in children (Bayley, 1954).

Constancy of Individual Rate of Growth. How constant is an individual's rate of growth in a given function? Does he tend to retain the same relative status among his age-mates from one age level to another? Here we are referring to quantitative longitudinal constancy, not to long-range consistency in personality traits or in the organization of personality. We shall return to this topic again in Chapter 18 in discussing growth in stature and intelligence. It will suffice to point out here that individual rates of growth in these functions tend to remain relatively constant (probably because of the relative stability of their genic and environmental determinants), and that whatever inconsistency does exist tends to be normally distributed. That is,

A standard score is the difference between individual score and group mean divided by the standard deviation of the group.

with respect to a given function, most individuals tend to be only slightly variable in rate of growth from one age level to another, a smaller number tend to be moderately variable, and a still smaller number tend to be extremely variable.*

Fluctuations in rate of growth may be cause (a) by factors relating to the standardization, reliability, and validity of the measuring instrument or to situational variability associated with test administrations (see Chapter 17), (b) by significant changes in environment, and (c) by idiosyncratic irregularities in the processes of growth that occur even in a relatively constant environment. At this point we shall only consider the second and third factors. Mention has already been made of the genuine inconsistency that is indigenous to extremely rapid periods of growth, and of the spurious appearance of inconstancy attributable to restricted intra-age group variability. Both of the latter conditions apply to infancy and early childhood and account for much of the striking instability of most functions during those age periods (e.g., intelligence).

In general, such fluctuations in the environment of children as frequency of illness, health status, nursery school attendance, and separation from parents show conflicting results when correlated with measures of general intelligence. However, even in the cases where negative results are obtained, the impact of these variables on the intellectual growth of individual children could conceivably be obscured in the correlational analysis of group data by the simultaneous operation of compensatory factors. By carefully studying individual mental growth curves and accompanying life histories, various investigators have shown that conspicuous fluctuations in intelligence test scores frequently correspond in time to incidence and recovery from emotional and environmental perturbations (Bayley, 1940; Despert & Pierce, 1946; Honzik, MacFarlane & Allen, 1948; Sontag, Baker, & Nelson, 1958). However, a note of caution in accepting these latter findings at face value is indicated by the demonstration that the reported fluctuations in one of these studies (Despert & Pierce, 1946) do not differ significantly from the deviations in test scores that could be ordinarily anticipated on the basis of test unreliability (Harris & Thompson, 1947). Such caution is justified by the fact that "In general, detailed studies of the influence of the relationship of emotional disturbance and characteriological deviations to intellectual development and functions are lacking. Such studies should probably be carried out with due consideration for age, sex, and clinical diagnosis." (Levine, 1966).

Much of the idiosyncratic patterning in rate of growth can undoubtedly be attributed to individual differences in genotypic makeup of experiential

---

*Approximately one-half of the I.Q.'s of elementary school children do not deviate more than five points from original score on retesting.

background. For example, in analyzing the mental growth carreers of 48 children over a period of nine years, Bayley found that eight children maintained a fairly constant rate of growth, eight lost and eight gained ground consistently, eight maintained a decelerating pace in early childhood and an accelerating pace in later childhood, eight did just the opposite of the latter, and eight did not conform to any recognizable pattern (Bayley, 1940). A similar study carried out on 200 children from the time of birth until the twelfth year also demonstrates marked differences in rate of mental growth, as reflected in the I.Q. from year to year (Sontag et al, 1958). Some children maintain approximately the same I.Q. from year to year throughout the period studied, while others exhibit an increasing I.Q. or a declining one. The contributing factors to changes in rate of I.Q. growth are still not clear, with some investigators attributing it to "complex environmental causes" (Sontag et al, 1958), while others place greater emphasis on genic origins (Bayley, 1955). Characteristic patterns in the velocity of mental growth also appear to be related to the intellectual status of children. In comparison to their brighter contemporaries, dull children tend to gain a larger proportion of their eventual intellectual attainment during the early years (see Chapter 17). In general, Bayley's (1955) conclusion on the factors which are determinants of individual rates of growth in I.Q. may also serve as a tentative conclusion for rates of growth in other areas of development:

> Slight irregularities may reflect temporary conditions of motivation, health, or emotional factors. The more constant shifts require other explanations, though they result from prolonged emotional or environmental influences, they may also express inherent tendencies to develop at different rates. I suspect that each child is a law unto himself—in some instances certain factors are more important, while in others, different factors play the determining role (p. 815).*

REVERSIBILITY AND IRREVERSIBILITY IN DEVELOPMENT

Physical, chemical, biological and psychological reactions vary tremendously in the extent to which phenomenological change is reversible. The factors affecting the occurrence of reversibility, the conditions under which it occurs, and the nature of the developmental processes that render it possible or impossible are obviously matters of the greatest theoretical and practical importance. For, depending on the outcome of research findings in this crucial area of inquiry in developmental psychology, many issues affecting child rearing, guidance, education, and therapy will be resolved.

Reversibility commonly has two quite different meanings. In the physical sciences it refers to the possibility of reversion to an antecedent or alternative condition. In the behavioral sciences reversibility more usually refers to the possibility of modifying the direction of behavior or personality development

_____
*See our discussion of the "growth matrix" in Chapter 3.

once a given type of conspicuous change has taken place; the former meaning is conventionally considered under the heading of regression. Reversibility may also be classified with respect to whether it is partial or relatively complete, peripheral or central, covert or overt. Some developmental changes for example, repudiate almost completely antecedent phases of growth (e.g., walking, the acquisition of adult executive independence). Other developmental experiences, such as satellization in early childhood, leave a permanent residue in personality structure that either affects adult behavior covertly or is perpetuated more overtly as a current form of adult status-seeking activity.

Generally speaking, few developmental phases in human beings are ordinarily irreversible, especially in those instances in which environmental determinants are influential. Despite the tendency for personality equilibria to resist reorganization, the typical course of development is for one stage to be succeeded by another as significant changes in biosocial status occur. This is less true for development in infrahuman species and in embryonic life; here it is more difficult for subsequent experience to alter the direction of development because of the relatively prepotent influence exerted by genic factors.

Types of Irreversibility

Three fundamentally different mechanisms help account for developmental irreversibility in animals and human beings. First, relative irreversibility of behavioral organization may be a function of extreme susceptibility to specific kinds of stimulation during those brief critical periods in ontogeny when certain types of behavior normally are shaped and molded for life.* (Hess, 1962; Scott, 1963; Walters & Parke, 1965). By the same token, if the individual is deprived of the necessary stimulation during the critical period, when he is maximally susceptible to it in terms of actualizing particular potential capacities or developing in new directions, it is held that some degree of permanent retardation is inevitable (i.e., that he never or only partly can attain the capacities in question). Learnings established during such periods may be maximally resistive to change because of the unstructured state of the organism's behavior, the absence of competing responses, and the pre-emptive effects of canalization; and once established, certain

---

*This hypothesis is logically and historically related to research findings in experimental embryology which indicate that the developmental susceptibility of transplanted tissues to the cellular environment in which they are embedded is limited to relatively restricted periods of time. However, it would be unwise to extend this analogy too far since few developmental sequences in postinfantile human beings are as prepotently determined by genic factors. More specific discussion of the "critical periods hypothesis" as it relates to infant deprivation studies and long-term deficit in intellectual skills due to early deprivation, will be taken up in Chapters 14 and 15 respectively. Irreversibility in personality organization will be discussed in Chapter 12.

types of early experience influence later behavior by structuring the individual's perceptual capacities. Also, since he lacks an adequate experiential
background and adjustive repertoire with which to interpret and respond to
environmental trauma and frustration, the younger individual is more
vulnerable to the damaging effects of such experience than the mature
member of the species, provided, of course, that he is sufficiently mature to
be susceptible in the first place. And by the same token, if he is deprived of
necessary stimulation during the critical period when he is maximally
susceptible to it, in terms of actualizing potential capacities or developing in
new directions, it is quite conceivable that some degree of retardation will
result.

An implicit form of the "critical periods" hypothesis was applied to
intellectual development many years ago by Montessori and her followers to
justify the particular graded series of learning tasks which children are set in
Montessori schools (Rambusch, 1962). More recently it has been invoked by
advocates of the proposition that young children can learn many intellectual
skills and kinds of subject matter more efficiently than adults can. The
argument in both instances is that since there are allegedly optimal (i.e.,
critical) periods of readiness for all kinds of cognitive acquisitions, children
who fail to learn the age-appropriate skills at the appropriate time are forever handicapped in acquiring them later.

Serious difficulties, however, lie in the path of extrapolating the "critical
periods" hypothesis to human cognitive development (Ausubel, 1965b). In
the first place, it has been validated only for infant individuals in infra-human
species, and in relation to those kinds of rapidly-developing perceptual,
motor, and social traits that are largely regulated by genic factors. In human
individuals, expecially beyond the prenatal period and first year of life,
environmental determinants of development are more important, and the
rate of maturation is significantly slower. Second, it has never been empirically demonstrated that *optimal* readiness exists at particular age periods
for specified kinds of *intellectual* activities, and that if adequate conditions for
growth are not present during those periods, no future time is ever as advantageous, thereby causing irreparable developmental deficit.

A more credible explanation of the possible irreversibility in cognitive
development are the possible deleterious consequences that result from prolonged cultural deprivation (Ausubel, 1965b). We refer to the tendency for
existing developmental deficits to become cumulative in nature, since
current and future rates of intellectual growth are always conditioned or
limited by the attained level of development. The child who has an existing
deficit in growth incurred from past deprivation is less able to profit developmentally from new and more advanced levels of environmental
stimulation. Thus, irrespective of the adequacy of all other factors—both

internal and external—his deficit tends to increase cumulatively and to lead to permanent retardation.

New growth, in other words, always proceeds from the existing phenotype, that is, from already actualized capacity, rather than from potentialities inherent in the genotype (genic structure). It makes no difference in terms of this limiting influence whether the attained deficiency is attributable to inferior genic endowment or to inadequate environment. If, as a result of a consistently deprived environment during the early formative years, potential intellectual endowment is not actualized, the attained deficit in functional capacity significantly limits the extent to which later environmental stimulation, even if normal in quantity and quality, can increase the rate of cognitive growth. Hence, an individual's prior success or failure in developing his intellectual capacities tends to keep his future rate of growth relatively constant. Initial failure to acquire adequate language, information-processing, and problem-solving abilities, for example, limits the later growth of cognitive capacities and of cognitive functioning.

A second source of relative developmental irreversibility lies in diminished plasticity or increased rigidity of personality structure.* Aside from factors already mentioned as enhancing resistance to personality reorganization (see p. 110), Kounin has demonstrated that "degree of rigidity is proportional to chronological age and hence to degree of feeblemindedness for any given mental age level" (Kounin, 1943). Recent studies summarized by Zigler (1966) attempting to explicitly test the Kounin model have, with rare exceptions (Budoff and Pagell, 1965) failed to provide support for it. Even in the studies which support the hypothesis that degree of rigidity and differentiation increase independently as a function of advancing age, it is just as plausible to hypothesize that growing rigidity is largely a reflection of the restricted range of variability that necessarily results as behavior and potential genotypic capacity become progressively more committed in specific directions during the course of differentiation.

Lastly, some aspects of personality structure are relatively irreversible because of the strength of their genic determinants, the recurrent aspects of certain interpersonal experience, and the operation of various perpetuating mechanisms in personality organization. The latter have already been considered in discussing the long-range continuity of individuality (see p. 110). It is important not to confuse irreversibility of such origin with the type that results from the persistent influence of less continuous but more dramatic experience during crtical periods of susceptibility. The discussion of "irreversibility" borders on many topics in the field of mental retardation; however, elaborate treatment of this topic is beyond the scope of this book.

---

*A thorough summary of recent theories and research in mental retardation may be found in Zigler (1966).

Factors Affecting Reversibility

In the light of the foregoing mechanisms accounting for relative developmental irreversibility, what variables must be considered as affecting behavioral modifiability? First is the matter of susceptibility at the time of original exposure to the experience in question. In the absence of minimal psychological susceptibility, the most traumatic experiences can have little lasting effect. Thus, because he is insufficiently mature in a cognitive sense to appreciate the meaning of threat, the young infant is insulated from much psychological trauma; and even if he were sufficiently mature, there would still be no definite ego to which threat could be referred. Since he cannot distinguish among persons (Spitz and Wolf, 1946) and offers no resistance to or fear of inoculation before the age of six months* (Levy, 1951), it is fanciful indeed to suppose that "birth trauma," hunger, or separation from the original mother figure can leave permanent emotional consequences. In general, it is safe to assume that until he gains in perceptual maturity the young infant will be susceptible to only the grosser aspects of interpersonal relations, and will not be affected by subtleties of parent attitude; in this respect he is even less susceptible than mammals of comparable chronological age who already display a relatively keen sense of social perception. And even beyond this age, retention of specific experience is bound to be poor unless it is recurrent or singularly dramatic (see Chapter 16). Thus the applicability of the "critical periods" hypothesis must be tempered by the fact that:

... the disruption of a specific attachment can have no particular significance until a specific attachment is formed. Evidence that infants under 6 months of age are not greatly disturbed by separation from their mothers, whereas older infants show much more disturbance ... provides support of the hypothesis that most infants do not develop specific attachments until the second half of the first year of life, but does not have a crucial bearing on the critical-periods hypothesis. Moreover ... severity of a reaction to a disruption of an established affectional competence depends on disposition to seek out and secure alternative sources of rewarding experiences. In this respect, infants are probably little less handicapped than elderly persons for whom separation may also have acute and relatively long-term deleterious effects ... (Walters & Parke, 1965, p. 85).

A second important factor affecting reversibility of development is the particular trait or experience involved. For reasons that will be elaborated in later chapters, there are credible grounds for believing that the effects of extrinsic valuation by parents are less reversible than those of rejection, and that failure to learn adequate techniques of self-assertion is more permanently damaging than is the learning of excessive self-assertion (see pp. 312 and 317). Much depends also on the importance of a given type of experience for overall personality development at the particular stage in the life cycle when it

---

Naturally, the designation of such normative ages does not imply applicability to all infants since individuals undoubtedly differ in degree of susceptibility to particular kinds of experience.

occurs. In general, one would expect unfavorable experience to be most damaging when it interferes with the dominant personality changes taking place at a given phase of development. Hence, gross emotional neglect and loss of succorance are most serious in their consequences in the last quarter of the first year and in the second year of life when initial socialization occurs; more subtle rejection and extrinsic valuation by parents are most damaging in the preschool period when satellization ordinarily takes place; and parental overprotection and underdomination have most detrimental after-effects in middle childhood and pre-adolescence when they impede the preparatory phases of adult maturation. In all of these instances, of course, duration and severity of trauma, and constitutional and normative differences in resistance to stress are crucial variables.

Finally, we must take into account the nature of subsequent experience that counteracts the impact of previous events. It makes a difference whether such experience (e.g., re-education) occurs early or late, within or beyond the period of maximum susceptibility; whether it is consistent or sporadic, intensive or superficial, gentle or insistent; whether the organism is rigid or retains a reasonable measure of plasticity in responding to particular environmental influences.

CHAPTER 5

Problems and Methods of Research
In Child Development

IN THIS CHAPTER we propose to discuss some general methodological problems and issues of a theoretical nature that confront the research worker in child development. It should be understood at the outset that we cannot possibly deal here with (a) the design of psychological studies, (b) the various types of research methods and measuring instruments available in psychology, or (c) all of the many specific research techniques that have been designed for obtaining data about the behavior and development of children. Many excellent textbooks and papers covering these latter areas are currently available.* Considerations of space only permit discussion of crucial methodological issues indigenous to child development as a field,† and of selected research methods employed in research with children that are not covered adequately in treatises on psychological measurement.

GENERAL PROBLEMS OF METHOD

The scientific standing of any field of knowledge depends upon the reliability, validity and definitiveness of the empirical evidence on which its generalizations are based. Depending on these criteria, the latter are qualified by varying degrees of tentativeness, assuming the status of laws, theories, or hypotheses. Historically speaking, two poles-apart approaches to the problem

---

*Good discussions of design of psychological studies and their relation to theories may be found in Cronbach, 1957; Cronbach & Meehl, 1955; Mandler & Kessen, 1959; Marx, 1963; Underwood, 1957. Research design more specifically related to child development is discussed in Anderson, 1954; Baldwin, 1960; Gollin, 1965; Kessen, 1960. Discussions of reliability and validity of research instruments is found in Anastasi, 1968; Cronbach, 1960. Statistical procedures in research design are found in Hays, 1963; Winer, 1962. Discussion of specific research techniques used in child development research may be found in Mussen's 1960 Handbook of Research Methods in Child Development. Specific chapters of this handbook are written by psychologists in their own area of research specialization.

†Many of these issues have already been discussed in defining the field of child development, namely, its status as a natural science, the appropriateness and difficulty of exercising experimental control, descriptive versus explanatory levels of analysis, the relationship between theory and data, the problem of extrapolation, objective and subjective aspects of development, and the hazards associated with investigating the latter (see pp. 6-17).

of evidence were adopted in child development. On the one hand, extreme "empiricists" engaged in the collection of discrete data and isolated measurements unrelated to any comprehensive or systematic theories of development. On the other hand, psychoanalytic theoreticians, unconstrained by rigorously obtained data from representative populations of children, enjoyed a speculative field day in developmental psychology. Theories that are not founded upon or testable by naturalistic data are not far removed from idle speculation and have little heuristic value. And data that are not derived from integrative hypotheses can hardly be expected to shed much definitive light on crucial problems.

The shortcomings of the earlier approaches to child development have led to a shift in more recent child development research:

> . . . first and foremost, the gathering of data for data's sake seems to have lost favor. The major concern in today's developmental research is clearly with inferred processes and constructs. Moreover, as the level of abstraction has risen, the focus of interest has often been sharpened with the result that entire chapters are now addressed to particular constructs, such as aggression, dependency, and anxiety. . . . Nor is the presentation of methods or descriptive material lacking, but they are closely interwined with problems of construct validity and hypothesis-testing. In other words, the trend toward closer articulation between theory and empirical work has continued (Bronfenbrenner, 1963, pp. 527-528).

The evaluation of child development research is indicative of a movement toward greater sophistication; one example is the constant endeavor to identify and validate behavioral constructs. Concerning the latter example, Bronfenbrenner (1963) raises a major issue for future researchers. Piaget and his workers are investigating and utilizing changes in the child's performance at different age levels as a means of isolating behavioral constructs. At the same time, social scientists pay little attention to such differences but are concerned rather with differences of sex, social class, and other variables. Bronfenbrenner recommends that the two "schools" cooperate for the benefit of further research.

> . . . given this perspective, the further growth of developmental theory appears to call for a convergence between the approach of Piaget and that of social learning, with each incorporating and applying the concepts and concerns of the other (p. 541).

Desired Kinds of Generalization from Data

The principal aim of child development research is to formulate—as ends in themselves—generalizations about different aspects of the development of children. Although such generalizations may be employed for making diagnoses and prognoses about the development of *particular* children, this use represents an application outside the ordinary scope of the field and should be restricted to properly qualified clinicians. It is true, of course, that research workers in child development expend much effort in studying individual growth patterns. However, their interest stems from concern with discovering general principles regarding individuality and variability in different areas of development rather than from concern with understanding a particular child as such or with influencing his development.

Although many investigators in the past "have worked backward from behavior outcomes to antecedent factors," more satisfactory generalizations could be obtained if studies moved "from context to behavior, not from behavior to context"* (Anderson, 1954). The "backward-working" approach has been traditional in clinical and ethnological studies. However, even in these areas, more careful research planning and control of relevant variables would be possible if the independent variables (environmental conditions) were ordered first and the dependent variables (behavioral outcomes) measured later in the research sequence. This latter approach offers the additional advantage of avoiding the serious pitfalls associated with the retrospective collection and interpretation of data.

Realistically oriented research in child development also avoids seeking generalizations based upon the "fallacy of the single cause" (Anderson, 1954; Baldwin, 1960; Cronbach, 1957; Kessen, 1960).

Appropriateness of Method for Age Group

To a very great extent, the appropriateness of a given research method is a function of the age of the children under investigation. In the case of infants and young children, direct observation is the most feasible method. The investigator is greatly handicapped by the limited language ability of the young child, the difficulty with which he follows directions, his frequent unwillingness to cooperate, his distractibility and limited span of attention, and by his disconcerting tendency to respond to other aspects of the stimulus field than the ones designated by the experimenter. Also, to elicit a satisfactory number of meaningful responses test stimuli must be relatively concrete and highly structured. Older children are more cooperative and attentive, can respond better to more abstract and unstructured stimulus situations, can be tested by procedures requiring reading and writing, and can report verbally their perceptions, attitudes, feelings and emotions. On the other hand, they are less ingenuous and more disposed and better able to conceal responses that they feel will meet with disapproval.

---

*Behavior at any moment is the result of the child's history and of the stimulation present. The concept of simple and single causes must be replaced by concepts of multiple causation, reciprocal relations, and the progressive cumulation of effect (Anderson, 1954).

Difficulties in Obtaining Evidence in Child Development

Difficulties Shared with Psychology. Human behavior is so extremely complex that it is very difficult even to identify the relevant variables that are operative in a given situation. Furthermore, the great number and complexity of the variables involved makes it difficult to keep some factors constant while varying others. But even when control is theoretically possible, humanitarian considerations rule out the imposition of many experimental conditions that are injurious to children (e.g., extreme deprivation, frustration, etc.). Partly for this latter reason, ecological methods are mandatory in many areas of developmental research (see p. 5).

The phenomenological content of psychology also makes for research problems not found in other disciplines. Most important of these is the difficulty of obtaining reliable and valid measures of behavior or conscious processes. First, many psychological functions and traits such as intelligence, motivation, interest, anxiety, etc., must be measured *indirectly* by eliciting responses to a representative sample of stimuli that are supposedly indicative of the trait or function in question. However, it is often somewhat questionable to what extent such instruments measure what they purport to measure since criteria of validity are usually just as indirect as the measures themselves. In many instances, also, the subject's sincerity, honesty, cooperativeness and ability to communicate his actual feelings and ideas are difficult to evaluate, although in recent years many ingenious devices have been employed to check objectively these aspects of his test behavior.

Second, because human behavior is so complex and is influenced by so many transitory factors, measurements tend to be unstable and inconsistent from one session or test component to another; and because of the tremendous range of intra-group variability characterizing most behavioral indices, measures of control tendency tend to have relatively large standard errors. Finally, before many kinds of psychological findings can be generalized to a wider population, it is necessary to choose an experimental sample that is reasonably representative of the population about which generalizations wish to be made. Consideration must be given to a veritable host of socio-economic and other variables that could influence behavior or development differentially. Such serious sampling problems do not ordinarily arise when the properties of molecules, bacteria, or muscle fibers are under investigation.

Special Difficulties in Developmental Research. In addition to the foregoing difficulties, special methodological problems arise in developmental studies. First since behavioral change over *extended* intervals of time is the phenomenon under investigation, experimental control is obviously much more difficult than when a relatively contemporaneous or situational event is studied, even if it were possible and desirable to simulate nature successfully. Second, if it is necessary to make use of retrospective data, there are problems of simple and selective forgetting, purposeful and "unconscious" distortion, and the sheer impossibility of an adult recalling and interpreting childhood events as they actually appeared to him at the time of their occurrence. Even if it is possible to collect and record data contemporaneously, they are not easy to interpret five, ten, or twenty years later in a changed context, especially if the personnel of a research project has turned over several times in the interim. *Third, because developmental studies are usually intensive and extensive in scope and involve repeated and frequent measurements, practical difficulties frequently arise in obtaining an experimental population. Parents, teachers and school administrators are reluctant to contribute the necessary time, often fail to appreciate the value or ultimate usefulness of such investigation, or object to "using children as guinea pigs." Fourth, sampling considerations are more important in developmental studies than in other types of psychological research because of concern with making normative statements about various age groups of children and interpreting the nature of the developmental differences between them. For many types of contemporaneous phenomena, on the other hand, when higher order relationships between variables or basic processes are under investigation, almost any subjects are equally representative of human beings.†

Finally, the measurement of change and rate of change presents many serious methodological problems. Suppose that we wished to determine whether three- and four year old children differ significantly with respect to a given capacity or type of behavior. The significance of the measured difference would vary depending on the size and composition of our sample, the degree of variability among our subjects, the research strategy utilized, and the discriminating power of our instrument (e.g., whether it was an "all or none" measure or reflected partial or subliminal status, whether it provided adequate "ceiling" for the older groups, etc.). The age difference itself could also be an important factor. It is quite conceivable that by simply using six months older children in both groups or by increasing the age difference slightly, significant results could be rendered nonsignificant or vice versa.‡

---

*If it is possible to curtail some of the above shortcomings of "retrospective" reports, this approach has certain advantages over long term longitudinal studies in its immediate field of data. Thus, if a researcher is studying stranger anxiety, he may observe his subjects in nursery school to determine dependency scores and interview the children's mothers in establishing the level of stranger anxiety observed in the past. (Kessen, 1960). A theoretical article which presents both the positive and negative aspects of "retrospection" vis-a-vis "prospective" methods may be found in Bell (1960).

†When there are small but reliable changes in behavior of subjects over age, the longitudinal study is a more sensitive estimate of developmental change when contrasted with the cross-sectional study. (Kessen, 1960).

‡Of course, by reducing the interval between two measurements sufficiently it would never be possible to obtain a significant indication of growth. Hence, the consistency of a trend in a given direction is more important than the significance of a difference between any two points on a growth curve.

Moreover, the determination of age differences assumes that the measuring instrument yields scores that are comparable in the sense of measuring qualitatively equivalent capacities or behavior, If, for example, we use one battery of sub-tests for measuring intelligence at age four and different batteries at ages six, eight, ten, twelve and fourteen, plotting scores against chronological age assumes that all of the batteries are equally representative of general intelligence. Baldwin (1960), addressing himself to the problem, notes that:

> . . . when the individual growth curves on mental age are plotted, it is quite common to find considerable variability from one time to another. These are frequently attributed to environment but such an interpretation is not the only possibility. Bayley . . . . , for example, suggests that such variation may well be due to the fact that intelligence tests measure different abilities at different age levels (p. 25).

On the other hand, if the measures do not vary in content from one age level to another, they may for this very reason provide a distorted picture of growth if the *capacities* or behaviors in question undergo qualitative change over the age span.

Even if the foregoing assumptions with respect to the measurement of behavioral change are adequately satisfied, the mean performances of different age groups may still not be comparable (a) unless relevant environmental factors are relatively equivalent for the two age groups, and (b) unless measures are expressed in units that are quantitatively equivalent at all points on the scale. Thus, it makes considerable difference whether developmental status is expressed in terms of raw scores, age scores, standard scores, or percentages of mature capacity. Raw scores and age scores are obviously not comparable from one age level to another since degree of variability does not remain constant from infancy to adolescence. All the criteria that affect the validity of measured differences between adjacent age groups naturally apply also to comparisons made in the *rate* of developmental change or to the slope of the growth curve.

When units of measurement are available that are quantitatively and qualitatively comparable, meaningful growth curves may be constructed by plotting successive scores of individuals or groups against chronological age. If such units are *not* available, marked differences in the form of a given growth function will result depending on the instrument and type of score employed. Age scores (e.g., mental age), for example, will by definition yield linear growth curves since one year of functional gain is calibrated in terms of the mean increment attained in a calendar year. However, when intellectual status is measured as a percentage of total adult achievement, several studies show similar negatively accelerated curves despite sampling differences and differences in the type of measuring instrument used (Bayley,

1965; Jones & Conrad, 1944). The same findings are reported for growth curves based on standard deviation scaling (Odom, 1929; Richardson & Stokes, 1935; Thorndike *et al*, 1926; Thurstone & Ackerson, 1929).

Although a negatively accelerated curve is characteristic of growth in many different areas of development, it can by no means be considered *the universal* growth curve. Some types of growth (e.g., skeletal, genital), for example, are marked by spurts and plateaus; others show a gradual or precipitous decline after maximum attainment.

Evaluation of Difficulties. The research problems described above certainly complicate the task of obtaining valid developmental data, but by no means remove child development from the realm of science. The least common denominators making for research difficulty are the variability and complexity of human beings. Because of these factors it is difficult to identify and control relevant variables, to construct reliable and valid measuring instruments, and to obtain representative and statistically significant findings. However, these problems are not unique to developmental psychology. In varying degrees they characterize all sciences. Identity does not exist in nature—not even in the case of two sodium atoms. In ascending order of the complexity and variability of their phenomenological content, the different sciences may be ordered as follows: physics, chemistry, biology, psychology and sociology.

Hence, comparable difficulties may be found in all sciences. Absolute control is a research ideal that can be approached but never attained. At best one can hope to control the most important and relevant variables. Sampling errors occur even in physics and chemistry but are sufficiently small to be ignored safely. The same applies to errors of measurement obtained with micrometers and stop watches. Statistical significance can also never be more than a statement of probability that defines the *relative* degree of confidence which may be placed in a given finding. In child development these problems are more serious than in the physical and biological sciences. However, by the use of judicious sampling techniques, special control procedures, ingenious measuring devices, and large groups of subjects, it is possible to obtain research findings that satisfy the criteria of scientific data.

Problems of Sampling

The reasons for the greater importance of sampling problems in child development than in other areas of psychology have already been discussed. Although child development specialists always wish to generalize beyond their experimental population, this does not necessarily mean that generalizations applying to *all* children are always sought. More frequently, because of the practical considerations involved, it is necessary to restrict the scope of applicability to a particular culture, subculture or socioeconomic group.

Sometimes also, an investigation is concerned with a special kind of population, e.g., physically handicapped, intellectual gifted, or social maladjusted children. In the latter instances, care need only be taken to choose a sample representative of the particular subpopulation.

Sampling considerations are not as important in some aspects of child development as in others. Normative investigations of children and of developmental changes in capacity obviously require highly representative experimental populations. Before certain emotional, social, cognitive, and psychosexual behaviors can be characterized as typical of designated age levels of children, much greater attention must be paid to problems of sampling than Gesell, Freud, Piaget and their followers have acknowledged as necessary. The same holds true for many of the conditions and factors affecting development. However, certain physiologic and phylogenetic aspects of development (see p. 57) and many higher order relationships between antecedent conditions (e.g., parent attitudes) and personality outcomes are relatively uninfluenced by cultural and socioeconomic factors. For example, anterior pituitary and gonadal hormones probably influence skeletal development, and *gross* emotional deprivation probably affects personality development in much the same ways in all cultural settings; but height and child rearing norms and their relationship to social adjustment obviously vary tremendously from one culture to another. Hence, rigid insistence on sampling control of the same variables (e.g., intelligence, socioeconomic status, paternal occupation) in all studies is just as indefensible as is total neglect of sampling in purely normative investigations.

The operation of numerous selective factors in the social and cultural environments makes it extremely difficult to obtain a representative sample by merely choosing children at random (Kessen, 1960). By procuring subjects solely from within a given socioeconomic level, from a particular section of a city, or from either exclusively rural or urban areas, it is quite possible to select a highly distorted sample of the population for which an estimate of capacity or a statement of relationship is sought. Randomized sampling is only feasible when extremely large experimental populations are employed or either when there is substantial reason for believing that variability in the function under investigation is not distributed selectively, i.e., is relatively unaffected by social stratification. Ordinarily, therefore, the experimental sample should be deliberately stratified in advance so as to duplicate as nearly as possible the major characteristics of the total population.

Statements regarding the statistical significance of differences between age levels or other groups of children are obviously misleading if they are based upon data secured from unrepresentative samples. In many instances, expedience forces the researcher into use of "unsampled" subjects, and it is important to come to terms with this problem by replication. As Kessen (1960) points out:

... aside from the practical problems most as great as those of random sampling, the kind of information that would indicate the variables to be used for appropriate stratification is frequently not available. The result of these constraints is the almost universal use of "unsampled" subjects in developmental research; the researcher uses children who are available when he needs them. often without convincing evidence of their representativeness in relation to some larger population. This necessary compromise with ideal standards sets two demands on child development research: First, that replication with more than one sample take place in order to provide empirical support for the generalization of findings from unsampled groups; and, second, that we seek out information that will tell us what variables can be disregarded in the selection of subjects and what variables must be controlled by more sophisticated sampling techniques (p. 40).

Thus replications across culture gives further support for Piaget's stages of intellectual development. In relation to Kessen's (1960) second suggestion, it should be apparent that categories used as a basis for selecting a stratified sample of a particular age level of children vary with the relationships that are being studied. In general, stratification need only be concerned with population characteristics that might be expected to influence the variables under investigation. Since the two sexes differ significantly with respect to many developmental functions, it is always advisable to use an equal number of boys and girls and to analyze the data separately by sex. Socioeconomic status affects so many developmental phenomena that it is usually desirable to stratify the sample by paternal occupation. In some studies, the experimental sample should take into account the additional factors of race or ethnic origin, religion, geographical location, and urban or rural residence. School grade and I.Q. are also relevant sampling considerations in a substantial number of studies.

MEASUREMENT OF DEVELOPMENTAL CHANGE*

In addition to the difficulties already discussed as complicating the measurement of developmental change (see pp. 136-139), another major problem still remains to be considered. Since behavioral development refers to change in performance or capacity occurring between two designated points in the

---

*Although the strategies for assessing developmental change constitute one of the most important topics in child development, it is beyond the scope of this volume to consider them in detail. Methodological considerations of the advantages and disadvantages of longitudinal and cross-sectional studies may be found in Anderson (1954), Baldwin (1960), Bayley (1965), Bell (1953), Chess and others (1960), Jones (1958, 1960), Kessen (1960), Kodlin and Thompson (1958), Kotaskova (1966), Kuhlen (1963), Stott (1955), Thomas et al, (1963). Descriptive summaries of various longitudinal studies may be found in Bayley (1965), Kagan (1964), and Stone and Onque (1959) and the Annual Review of Psychology.

life cycle, it is essential that successive age levels of experimental subjects be comparable in all respects except for chronological age. Two different approaches may be employed here—*cross-sectional* and *longitudinal*. The former investigates the growth of a particular function by comparing mean measurements of *different* groups of children varying in age. The latter approach utilizes successive mean measurements made on the *same* individuals at regularly prescribed intervals. The objectives of the study should determine the type of design utilized: an example of a relevant question to ask might be: Does the stated objective of the study demand measurement of the relationship (a) between successive observations, as, for example, a measurement of correlation between stature at successive ages; or (b) between "early" events and the variable trait under study at a subsequent point of time, as for example, a measurement of correlation between early illness history and performance on mental or physical tests at maturity?

If the answer is "yes," it means that only a longitudinal approach can achieve the objective stated. If the answer is "no" that is, if it is desired only to obtain the average stature of children at specific ages, or the average increments in growth at successive ages, then the longitudinal approach may be unnecessary. An unequivocal answer to this question requires a precise and detailed statement of the objectives of the study (Kodlin and Thompson, 1958, p. 9).

Cross-Sectional Study

The cross-sectional approach offers many attractive advantages. First, it is relatively easy to obtain access to large groups of subjects for short-term research projects particularly in large urban centers. Second, cross-sectional studies are relatively inexpensive and require no continuity of or long-term cooperation between research workers. Third, data need not be "frozen" over long periods of time until subjects complete their development before interpretation and publication are possible. Lastly, uniform sampling procedures can be used throughout the age or level series; selective loss of subjects does not occur as in a longitudinal population (Bayley, 1965; Kessen, 1960; Kuhlen, 1963).

However, carefully executed stratified sampling is necessary before successive age levels of different subjects can be rendered truly comparable. Matching different groups for even the important identifiable variables can at best be only approximate . . . in school populations increasing age itself tends to operate selectively in such important variables as intellectual ability since many duller pupils become academic casualties (Ausubel, 1954).

Cross-sectional studies do not provide the researcher with indications of the direction of the changes taking place within his groups. For example, if dependent children become more dependent during the mother's pregnancy and independent children become more independent; the cross-sectional study can only tell you the variance of dependency changes, never that there is a systematic direction in the change (Kessen, 1960). Furthermore, because children grow at different rates and reach similar developmental levels at different times, a cross-sectional study places together at the thirteen-year age level many girls well past puberty and many girls months away from puberty (Anderson, 1954). The averaging of individual curves in a cross-sectional study may conceal the growth spurt that is taking place (Anastasi, 1958a; Kessen, 1960). Finally, the effects of social change renders noncomparable the respective backgrounds of different age groups of children. Consider, for example, a cross-sectional study of night fears or response to sudden awakening among adolescents. London children may show striking changes at ages 15 to 18, not necessarily because of some growth characteristic of late adolescence but moreso, because these 18 year-old children had been through the battle of Britain (Kessen, 1960). Relating to the broader problem of cultural change, the problem is intensified by the fact that different aspects of culture do not change to the same degree or in the same directions over the same period of time (Kuhlen, 1963). Thus, in an analysis of children's readers there is a marked curvilinear relationship over time in the pressure put upon children for achievement. The analysis suggests an increase in achievement pressure from 1800 to 1890, a steady decrease thereafter through the 1940's and a recent increase in the last few years (de Charms and Moeller, 1962). If a relationship as the above characterized the life span of individuals now living, then cultural change will have a differential impact upon different age groups in cross-sectional studies (Kuhlen, 1963).

Longitudinal Approach

In longitudinal studies, although the comparability of serial age levels of the *same* individuals is affected by selective loss of the residentially less stable subjects, it is obvious that in all other respects greater comparability prevails. Hence, not only is matching of different groups unnecessary, but also many different studies can be performed on the same population. However, because of the need for stability of the subject population, certain types of sample biases may be introduced. In many instances samples are drawn from a population whose lives are less likely to be subject to violent upheavals or geographical instability. However, even if generality is sacrificed, there are strong arguments for maximizing the chances of finding something before worrying about the generality of what is found (Baldwin, 1960). It is also possible with longitudinal data to plot individual growth curves and increments and to analyze in detail the inter-relationship between growth processes, both maturational and experiential, because all data have been obtained on the same children (Jones, 1958). This is especially important in studies of the cumulative effect of antecedent conditions on the personality development of children, where there is no satisfactory substitute for intensive longitudinal measurement, particularly if individual growth curves are desired. A further advantage is that longitudinal findings allow one

> . . . to trace the development of special subgroups within the total population, thus pointing up differential trends that would otherwise become obliterated in computing measures of central tendency for the group. It is also possible, of course, to use cross-sectional data in studying the development of subgroups, by first identifying and making comparable in other respects varying age samples of the subgroups; but unless the criteria for identification are relatively unambiguous and homogeneous in nature (e.g., race, sex, physical characteristics), such comparisons cannot be relied upon to provide as accurate a picture of differential development as would be possible with data on the same group of special individuals available over a period of years. If, for example, we wish to study the social development of preadolescents who as children were rejected by their parents, it would not be very satisfactory to obtain our data from different age groups of rejected children. In either instance, however, comparison with a control group would be necessary before a significant differential trend could be concluded (Ausubel, 1954, p. 33).

The longitudinal study is most suited to studying the problems of continuity and discontinuity in development e.g., irritability, dependency, aggression, intelligence. As Kagan (1964) points out

> . . . it is necessary that psychologists obtain more precise accounts of the developmental history of selected response systems. For many research endeavours find themselves in cul-de-sacs because of untenable assumptions, regarding behavioral continuities. . . . The occurrence of transformations of early responses must be acknowledged. For development is a cryptograph in which early appearing responses often lead to behaviors which are phenotypically unlike the original response but theoretically derived from the original habit. The discovery of such lawful transformations seems impossible without a longitudinal approach (p. 2).

When there are small, but reliable changes in the behavior of subjects over age, the longitudinal study provides, because of the matching characteristics, more sensitive estimates of such changes. Thus the study of age functional relationships in which relatively small but individually stable changes over age are expected is best. Moreover, the longitudinal study, because of the extended time duration, serves not only as a data-collection device, but also as a source of hypotheses for the researcher. Thus, in many instances, the longitudinal study opens up new areas for fruitful study (Kessen, 1960). The problem of cultural or social change, which is present in the cross-sectional study, can to some extent be controlled in the longitudinal study. The longitudinal study, because of its extended time, puts the investigator in a better position to assess the impact of shifts in milieu when compared to the investigator who studies cross-sectionally at one time the behavior of age-differing groups of children (Kessen, 1960).

Lastly, longitudinal data enable the investigator to measure more adequately the impact on development of events (e.g., pubescence, confirmation, initial school attendance, death of parent) which do not occur at the same age for all children. For example, with longitudinal data the emotional or intellectual status of individuals one, two, three, or four years after pubescence can be measured and the data pooled regardless of whether pubescence occurred at 10 or 17.

The longitudinal approach also has some serious disadvantages. From a practical standpoint, it is much more expensive, requires continuity of research personnel and postpones publication of findings for many years (Sontag, 1959). In many instances the shift in personnel to other research jobs and to teaching leaves analysis of data to persons other than those who had instigated their collection (Sontag, 1958). A change in investigators characteristically brings investigators with a new set of values, skills, and interests. Much material that has been laboriously collected by one person with certain well-considered goals, may seem to the new investigator to be of little value, or outside the range of his skills and interests (Bayley, 1965). Furthermore, it is difficult to obtain a cooperative population which is willing to be studied intensively and repeatedly for a decade or more; and almost by definition, such a population constitutes a highly unrepresentative sample (Bayley, 1965). Original errors in sampling or in the omission of crucial variables, hypotheses and newly originated methodological devices can never be corrected (Bayley, 1965; Jones, 1960). Many subjects drop out because of illness, death, removal from the area, financial catastrophy, or simply because they are "fed up" (Bayley, 1965). Those who remain come from atypically cooperative and stable families or may be affected by repeated measurement per se and, hence, are no longer representative of the population at large; and unless the original data of subjects who drop out are discarded, the different age levels are no longer comparable (Baldwin, 1960; Bayley, 1965). Even if the sample is carefully selected as generally representative, this does not assure maintenance of sample constancy. One of the limitations of longitudinal research is the difficulty in testing every child at every scheduled testing on every item to be tested.

Children get sick (one case of measles on a projected testing date could ruin a rigid research design); they become upset and the measure must be omitted; they refuse to comply on some items . . . Sometimes if the original sample is large enough, it is possible to select for a given age-span, a subsample which meets certain criteria of representativeness (Bayley, 1965, p. 187).

Finally, if the span of years covered by the research includes an unusual social or economic phenomenon, such as war or depression, growth curves may be distorted. Thus,

. . . depression, changing cultures, and technological advances all make considerable impact. What are the differential effects on two-year-olds, of parents with depression-caused worries and insecurities, of TV or no TV; of the shifting climate of the baby-expert advice from strict-diet, let-him-cry, no-pampering schedules, to permissive, cuddling (enriching) loving care? On the other hand, as in some studies, one might eliminate this chronological problem by adding from five to ten new born infants each year and then making comparisons according to age of the child and not the calendar year (Bayley, 1965, p. 189).

In any event, it is clear that the elaborate longitudinal studies as well as refined sampling techniques are wasteful before meaningful and testable hypotheses related to a comprehensive, theoretical orientation can be formulated.

. . . beyond this, several further supports for theory-directed research can be stated. The first has to do with the broad scientific question of inter-relationships among empirical findings. An explicit set of hypotheses permit the researcher to set out on a program of study, with the end in view of bringing his data together in a coherent statement. Traditional studies of child development may be liable to the charge that they lack organization and present a failure to establish linkages between one set of relationships and another. We know a great deal about the development of children; what sometimes appears to be missing is a conceptual framework on which this knowledge can be ordered and extended (Kessen, 1960, p. 59).

Thus in the absence of specific questions to be asked of the data, all kinds of information that could be obtained about the subjects of the study have, at times, been unselectively accumulated.

. . . it seems curious to speak of having too much information about a group of subjects, but as the longitudinal researcher works over a period of years to collect observations that he considers relevant to his research goals, he may find himself in possession of a staggering array of data and with no end in sight. The issue is somewhat further complicated by the fact that the researcher cannot turn to the analysis of the data he has already collected because he is spending full time collecting new material on his subjects. For those studies that extend over decades rather than years, the danger of being overwhelmed by the weight of data is by no means mythical (Kessen, 1960, pp. 65-67).

It is highly desirable, therefore, first to test, redefine and reformulate preliminary hypotheses and measuring instruments by cross-sectional methods on less precisely selected populations (Kodlin and Thompson, 1958). If it turns out that the hypothesis finds no support in the cross-sectional data, it is probably not one which should be used in subsequent studies. Comprehensive cross-sectional data should suggest new relationships among phenomena and enable the investigator to examine not only the specific relationships between two factors as hypothesized, but numerous additional variables which may modify, inhibit, or facilitate the emergence of the behavior in question (Kessen, 1960).

Several new designs have been suggested to overcome the shortcomings of both the longitudinal and cross-sectional methods. Bell (1953) suggests a "convergence approach" in which:

. . . cross-sectional studies are made of different age groups so spaced in age that re-measurement of the same group after a period of time provides information on the nature of changes occurring over the entire age period as well as data which will permit an answer to the question of whether the shorter curves for each stand may reasonably be combined into a curve covering the entire age period . . .

The convergence approach appears to have greatest utility in two types of situations: (a) in investigations basically oriented toward a cross-sectional approach, but in which there is reason for concern over the comparability of the experimental groups relative to the dependent variables on the factors other than age, and in which it is possible to make limited remeasurements of these groups; (b) for investigations oriented toward the longitudinal approach but faced with problems of transient or less cooperative groups or with possibilities of undesirable contamination of the experimental population by extensive observation (Bell, 1953, p. 152).

A similar approach is suggested by Schaie (1965) in which the research can be designed in such a way that the data can be collected concurrently for both longitudinal and cross-sectional age-specific comparisons. Thus, growth rates of children between successive one-year intervals can be compared for children born in 1956 and children born in 1960 or 1964. Five-year-olds tested for the first time can be compared with five-year-olds tested for the second, third or fourth time. Furthermore, one can obtain measures on cross-sectional samples of children of different ages all measured at the same time. The design is an attempt to assess the effect of changes in cultural context, differences in life experiences previous to the time of measurement, or genetic changes from one cohort group to the next. *

Other similar, essentially cross-sectional approaches that include longitudinal components are (a) Mead's (1954) method of studying different age levels grouped about a transitional stage of development, (b) Lasswell's (1937) method of "interlapping observation" in which transitional phases between different adjacent age groups are observed and (c) Kuhlen's (1963) method of introducing cross-sectional checks periodically in a longitudinal study to assess the effects of cultural change.

Because the focus of attention is on developmental phenomena that occur relatively rapidly, much valuable intra-group longitudinal data can be collected in the space of a single year to supplement the data on inter-age group differences. Furthermore,

. . . the shorter the elapsed time of data collection the less will be the attrition of the sample, and the greater the ease of maintaining the same staff and measuring instruments and procedures. Annual increments can still be studied, and the effects of different life experiences can be cancelled out or measured and statistically controlled (Bayley, 1965, p. 189).

Case Study Approach

The case study method may be considered a special variant of the longitudinal approach. Here, too, emphasis is placed on accumulating develop-

---

*Cohorts *are individuals born at the same point or interval in time.*

mental data—both measurements of antecedent conditions and of outcomes—on the *same* individuals over a span of years. Ordinarily the unit of
study is an individual rather than a group of subjects, and the purpose of the
study is to shed light on some problem of adjustment for which diagnosis,
therapy and prognosis are desired. Hence a much greater quantity of
personal data from a wider diversity of sources is usually assembled for a
single case study than ever becomes available for an individual subject in a
longitudinal group. Not only are more biographical and interview data
utilized in addition to the usual objective measures, but also the focus of
inquiry is the unique growth pattern of a single individual rather than
developmental trends characterizing children in general.

> From the intimate knowledge thus gained of the interrelationship between significant
> aspects of an individual's developmental history, personality structure and overt behavior,
> it is often possible to acquire valuable insights into the nature of personality development
> and behavioral adjustment. But apart from their applicability to the individual from
> whom they are derived, such insights enjoy at best the status of hypotheses which can be
> tested either by an analysis of a *series* of case studies or by normative group studies (Ausu-
> bel, 1954, p. 35).

Simple application of the methodological principles elaborated above indicates why although the attempt is frequently made, no definitive generalizations about human development can be drawn from one individual. First is
the matter of sampling. Case studies are not typical of children generally but
largely of maladjusted children whose parents are either financially poor
enough to qualify for free treatment in clinics or sufficiently wealthy to
afford the high cost of private therapy.

In relation to a single case it is also impossible to determine whether an
obtained difference or finding of relationship is statistically significant or is
merely a chance occurrence. One reads, for example that delinquent Johnny
came from a "broken home." But it is very simple to cite case studies of
children from broken homes who never became delinquent and of children
from intact homes who did. It is also self-evident that in the absence of
systematic control of other relevant variables, which is impossible in the
single case approach, no statement of relationship or causal inference can be
generalized to a wider population.

Another limitation of case-study methods only applies when the data involved are derived from retrospective reports of the subject.* The problem
of selective distortion of memory, when attempting to study personality
growth, makes the type of introspection a highly questionable technique
(Mead, 1954).

*Some case-studies, e.g., cumulative records, "simultaneous life histories (Anderson, 1954; Greene,
1952; Mead, 1954; White, 1952) utilize data in which subjects offer contemporaneously recorded
verbalizations regarding current aspects of their life situation. Such accounts can be checked against the
memories of other persons for historial accuracy and related to objective indices of behavior.

A final criticism of the case study method relates to an extremely wide-spread practice which, however, is not necessarily indigenous to this approach. This is the common error of citing single case studies as proof rather than as illustrative of a given theory of personality development. Were this error not multiplied countless times every year it would hardly bear repetition that genuine empirical evidence in support of a theoretical orientation can only come from empirical studies concerned with such matters as sampling, control, reliability and validity of instruments, tests of statistical significance, and exclusion of alternative theories. Permitted to select a "typical" case of their own or even using the very same case material psychologists of ten different schools could find equally credible support for their particular theories.

In conclusion, the *single* case study is useful only as a source of hypotheses or as an illustration of a particular theoretical viewpoint or previously validated generalization. *Series* of case studies, on the other hand, can be used in much the same way as longitudinal data, provided, of course, that the usual methodological requirements are observed.

Developmental-Manipulative Designs *

The focus of most psychological research centers around two major research strategies; correlational and experimental designs. These strategies, taken singly or combined, constitute the major portion of child development research in both longitudinal and cross-sectional studies of child development. Correlational analysis is a statement of relationship (i.e., co-variation) between two or more variables; e.g., anxiety and aggressiveness, age and concept acquisition, age and achievement). In the vast majority of early child development research, this method constituted the major research strategy. Thus, the variable *age* has been correlated with *intelligence, achievement, language, activity level,* and *motor behavior,* etc. Anyone of these characteristics or behaviors is said to be developmental if it is related to age in an orderly or lawful way (Kessen, 1960). Developmental lawfulness, in a correlational study, is signified by a significant positive or negative correlation of some characteristic or behavior with age. The major shortcoming of the correlational study is *inference* possibilities. The fact that variables are related in no way constitutes an explanatory statement for the relationship. Thus the statement of a substantial positive relationship between *age* and *language facility* does not allow one to infer that age is an antecedent condition for

*The problem of design of experiments—use of control groups, matched pairs of children, co-twin control, etc., and of experimental and statistical methods of systematically varying, holding constant, replicating and analyzing the effects of and interaction between various determinants of behavior—is beyond the scope of this volume. This brief discussion of Experimental-Manipulative designs is presented here because of its sketchy treatment in many of the sources discussing problems of methodology. See footnote (p. 133) for further references of the general topic.

increasing language facility. The two variables may co-vary because of other known or unknown variables (i.e., certain learning experiences take time to happen, and thus increase in language facility may be occurring because of these learning experiences which occur over a temporal interval).

In child development research however, the fundamental variable for consideration is *age* and

> Theories of child development are, in a sense, systems of proposals about the processes that lie behind changes in behavior with age but we are so far from an acceptable general theory of development that we must continue for some time the slow accumulation of evidence that is expressed in age-functional generalizations. (Kessen, 1960, p. 38).

At the same time, age should be considered the starting point for developmental research, keeping in mind the fact that investigation of simple age functions are naive, and must be bolstered, where possible, with designs which involve the interaction of age and environmental changes or the analysis of age functions in special populations (Kessen, 1960).

Experimental designs gain in importance when there is an attempt to study the interaction of age with environmental changes due to experimental manipulation or variation in condition.* Experimental manipulation of environmental antecedents in its purest form, constitutes fundamentally the experimental design. The experimental procedure involves the systematic manipulation of specified antecedent conditions and detailed observation of the consequences. The major advantage of this technique in child development research is the possibility of random assignment to groups treated differentially. Random assignment eliminates the problem of correlated differences when assignment to subgroups is made purely by chance (Kessen, 1960). This procedure is called an experiment because an environmental manipulation is being given to at least one of the randomly selected set of subject groups.†

Historically, experimental manipulations were rare in developmental research, with the exception of the co-twin studies discussed previously (pp. 60-63). The developmental-manipulative perspective in these studies was achieved not by a "random assignment" but by attempting to control "maturational" changes by employing identical twins assuming identical genetic makeup. More recently, attempts at combining age related developmental factors with experimental manipulative designs have been stressed by

---

*For ethical reasons it is not always possible to manipulate the child's environment (e.g., subject some children to maternal deprivation, etc.). See Ausubel quote on page 144 for an example of a variation in condition design.

†For a review of laboratory-experimental techniques with children see Bijou and Baer (1960). In many instances, the designs reported here are simply using children as subjects. At most, they constitute short term longitudinal studies. See Chapter 1 for discussion of contemporaneous designs.

several authors (Cronbach, 1957; Gollin, 1965; Harvey, Hunt and Schroder, 1961; Kessen, 1960).* Thus, the longitudinal study can combine with manipulative designs by randomly assigning some of the subjects to an experimental treatment (e.g., language enrichment program) while maintaining an appropriate "control group" for purposes of comparsion. Significant differences between experimental and control groups over age (i.e., increasing language facility of the experimental group over the control group) would tend to indicate some of the environmental factors which influence age related changes on some characteristic or behavior. Similar designs may be employed in cross-sectional studies where age differences are seen as important in the learning of more complex learning skills (Gollin; 1965). The fact that older subjects are able to learn more complex impression formation tasks is indicative of the fact that this is an important variable for consideration even in experimental designs (Gollin, 1965).

More complex *developmental-manipulative* designs may be generated by combining age variables with differences in population, and experimental manipulations (Baldwin, 1960; Cronbach, 1957; Harvey *et al*, 1961; Kessen, 1960). The recent research on inducing *"stage"* changes in Piaget's theory by experimental manipulation (e.g., conservation research, Chapter 15) illustrates the combination of particular populations of children (i.e., consideration of children at certain *stages* of cognitive development as opposed to others) with particular experimental manipulations. Thus manipulation procedures for conservation are not considered appropriate or interesting for the specific population of children who have reached the stage of *formal operations*, whereas they are of paramount importance for populations of children at the *pre-operational* stage. Age changes are important here since stage of development is highly correlated with age. Another illustration of the age, population experimental-manipulative design is seen in populations of children over age (e.g., High-Achievement—Low-Achievement) with performance on some learning tasks.

The use of more sophisticated developmental-manipulative designs proceeds on the assumption that:

> . . . the organism, or, in our case, the person, has a number of properties or characteristics. Because of these characteristics he behaves the way he does in the situation. On the other hand, it is equally valid to say that he behaves the way he does because of the characteristics of the situation. The same organism behaves differently in different situations; different organisms behave differently in the same situation. The behavior is, therefore, a function of the characteristics of the person and the characteristics of the situation (Baldwin, 1960, p. 20).

Developmental-manipulative designs constitute what Cronbach (1957) calls the combination of correlational with experimental designs.

METHODS OF MEASUREMENT

In this section we shall consider some of the more important methods of psychological measurement utilized in child development research. Naturally many of the same measurement techniques and considerations applying to adult behavior apply to children as well. Hence, the more general aspects of these methods will not be discussed unless they deserve special emphasis. *

OBSERVATIONAL TECHNIQUES†

The key role of observation in all natural sciences, including child development, has already been considered at length. But whereas systematic and rigorously controlled observation yields valuable scientific data, the scientific value of incidental and impressionistic observations (except for suggesting new hypotheses) is practically nil. Most anecdotal (baby diaries) kept by fond parents fall into the latter category. The early baby biographies written by such famous figures in the early history of child psychology as Tiedemann (1787), Preyer (1888), Pestalozzi (1895) and Shinn (1900) were handled somewhat more systematically and provided a continuous, longitudinal, and multidimensional picture of simultaneous and successive factors in the behavior and circumstances of an individual child (Wright, 1960). The principal aim of the child diaries has been not the idiographic one of describing and understanding this special behavior of each child subject, but the normative one of discovering behavior traits of children by and large at different ages and stages of development. Piaget's (1951, 1952) description of his own children in their infancy is obviously intended for normative purposes.

Nevertheless, these biographical efforts suffered from many of the understandable methodological shortcomings that could be expected at this early stage in child development research. Observations were often made haphazardly and at irregular intervals, resulting in biased selection of incidents. The kinds of behavior to be observed were not determined in advance, and the precision of observations in terms of setting, antecedent conditions, and properties of eliciting stimuli were not always adequate. Common criteria for recording a given instance of behavior were the special and often fluctuating

---

*No attempt, also, will be made to consider rating, ranking, questionnaire and interview methods, definitively. These are handled adequately in the following references. (Anastasi, 1968; Anderson, 1954; Cronbach, 1960; Kessen, 1960; Sarason, 1962). Inventory methods and standardized tests will not be considered at all, since they are usually treated quite exhaustively in courses in psychological measurement. Infant developmental scales and preschool tests of mental ability are discussed in Chapter 12. Parent-child interaction techniques are discussed in Chapter 15.

†A judicious methodological review of observational tehhniques in child study may be found in Wright (1960). For observational methods and research on socialization processes see (Yarrow and Rauch, 1962).

interests of the observer and the uniqueness or precocity of the performance. The latter tendency was enhanced by the fact that the biographers were usually highly educated and proud parents whose objectivity and comparability to the population at large were obviously open to question. Much of the recording was also done retrospectively and was subject to selective forgetting; and since observations were not always distinguished from interpretations, the former were distorted by preconceived notions, particularly by the attribution of adult response capabilities to children. Lastly, these data share all of the disadvantages of single case studies, insofar as generalizability to wider populations was concerned.

Ecological Observation. Ecological observation is concerned with the description of behavior in natural or contrived situations in which the observer does not attempt to manipulate the stimuli impinging on the subject. Strictly speaking, it is limited to in situ field studies in our own or other cultures.

Adequate ecological techniques demand attention to the following methodological points. First, the range of situation and behavior to be observed should be explicitly defined and limited in advance to prevent undesirable dispersion and nonuniformity of observational efforts. Observation should also be conducted at regularly determined intervals and under uniform conditions of time, place and setting. Second, it is essential to use trained and unbiased observers; and to make possible an estimate of observer reliability, several different observers should be used. Complete absence of bias, of course, is an unattainable ideal. Appraisals of the same behavior vary considerably from one observer to another because of differential projection of observer attitudes into behavior settings (Wright,1960). Hence, an important part of the training of observers lies in techniques of minimizing and holding constant the involvement of the observer in the subject's behavior (Wright, 1965). Barker and Wright (1949) also recommend half-hour observation periods for a single observer because the alertness required to perceive and remember the multitude of simultaneous and sequential occurrences is fatiguing.

Third, observations should be recorded in full *immediately after* they are made from notes taken during the observation. Retrospectively recorded observations, are not only less accurate and more biased but also are only as valuable as the questions which were already formulated in the investigator's mind (Mead, 1954; Wright, 1960). Simultaneous records, on the other hand, contain a great deal more spontaneous observations and they yield to analysis and reanalysis not only by the investigator but also by other investigators (Mead, 1954; Wright, 1960). Ambiguities and omissions in the observational report can be corrected by later interrogation of the observer (Wright, 1960).

Fourth, long rather than short behavioral sequences maximize the continuity in behavior and minimize the possibilities of biased selection and interpretation of incidents (Barker, 1965). *Immediate* inferences regarding the motivations and feelings of the subject should also be made. Extreme objectivists must face the fact that they have to deal with the direction, the goals and the meaning of behavior when they study psychosocial development, and that these can never be perceived directly. The utility of recording long sequences of both directly observed and inferred behavior stems from the fact that it appears to be the best basis for constructing a *final* true record of the events (Barker and Wright, 1949). Furthermore, more global and inferred observations appear to have greater reliability when compared with molecular-literal interpretations (Wright, 1960). Although observations and inferences may be recorded simultaneously in time, they must be carefully distinguished from each other. Also, all interpretation other than first order inferences from the behavior itself, should be excluded from the record.

Fifth, the influence of the observer must be kept minimal and constant. The observer is almost always a part of the subject's psychological situation and hence influences his behavior in some degree. This is an inevitable limitation of most naturalistic observations (Barker, 1963, 1964, 1965; Wright, 1960). Some, but not all of this contamination, can be reduced by allowing for an initial period of habituation (Wright, 1960). One-way screens and hidden microphones are useful for this purpose but can only be utilized in relatively few natural (non-laboratory) settings. Records may also be supplemented by simultaneous sound-moving pictures (Wright, 1960). However, this adds greatly to the technical difficulties and expense of the operation and accentuates the presence of the observer and the self-consciousness of the subject.

The ecological method is exemplified best by field studies. Since these long-range investigations are concerned with the evolution of inter-personal and inter-group relationships, group structure, and role behavior, it is advantageous for the observer to serve as a participant in the community activities of the population of subjects under investigation (Wright, 1960). This enables him to gain access to much data and to acquire many insights that would ordinarily be inaccessible to a detached observer. In studies involving more circumscribed kinds of behavior non-participation of the observer is more appropriate (Baker, 1965; Lafore, 1945; Wright, 1960). If, in certain instances, more direct and immediate quantification of observational data is desired, several alternative procedures are afforded the investigator:

. . . specimen description covers intensively and continuously the behavior and situation of the child during more or less extended behavior sequences. Time-sampling records record selected aspects of behavior if and as they happen within precisely limited time spans. Event sampling singles out naturally segregated behavioral events of one or another class and records these events as they arise and unfold. . . . Crate ratings select dimensions of behavior and base judgments about them on observations during extended sequences of behavior. (Wright, 1960, pp. 73-75).

Time Sampling for example, enables the investigator to quantify his data readily and to determine the generality of observed behavior. He simply enumerates the number of times a particular type of recurring behavior (e.g., quarrelling, cooperative behavior, aggression) is manifested by a given child in a constant, systematically spaced interval of time. It must be borne in mind, however, that such enumeration of response patterns, independent of context, may lump many genotypically diverse behaviors into the same phenotypic category. Also, the descriptive data they yield do not necessarily shed any light on the nature of the behavior or on the determining factors involved. From a methodological standpoint, the ecological approach in child development has been employed most definitively by Barker and Wright.* These investigators defined a large number of discriminable (psychological habitats) which tend to arise uniformly in particular kinds of behavioral settings.

The *behavior setting* is defined as a physical or social part of the non-psychological world that is generally perceived as appropriate for particular kinds of behavior. For example, the Sunday school, the day school, the drug store, are particular kinds of behavior settings which coerce the children who enter them to behave in relatively homogeneous ways regardless of the individual characteristics of the children (Barker and Wright, 1949). Furthermore, one property of behavior settings which varies widely and is widely believed to have an important consequence for the functioning of settings and for the behavior of persons within them, is the number components (Barker, 1965).

. . . in fact, we had long been intrigued by sandlot baseball games in the midwest with varying numbers of players: a game with four players on a side has manifestly different consequences for the players than a game with nine players on a side; it makes no difference who the players are, once a boy becomes part of a four-man team, he plays four-man baseball, with all of its privileges (of frequent batting, for example) and all of its burdens (such as wide, fatiguing field to cover). Baker, 1965, p. 10).

The "psychological habitat," on the other hand, represents the psychological life-space or situation of a particular individual in a behavior setting. Barker (1965) reviews many of the studies on psychological habitats of different age levels of children (and hence their "psychosocial development") by observing meaningful, goal-directed behavior units ("episodes") occurring in such standardized behavior settings, and by making judgments of children's subjective reactions to various objective determinants of frustration, satisfaction, success, failure and constraint.

A summary of ecological observations techniques and reference sources to this method up to the present may be found in Barker (1965).

Controlled Observation. A modified form of ecological observation results when a limited degree of control is imposed on a situation in which subjects are observed. This may vary from the extremely general kinds of constraint placed upon behavior, as would be implicit in the physical and social arrangements found in nursery schools and playgrounds, to much more specific attempts at manipulating the types of stimuli in situations to which children are exposed (e.g., play techniques, experimental situations, psychometric and personality tests). A great deal of the normative data in child development is a product of the former approach (Bühler, 1930; Gesell and Ilg, 1943; Shirley, 1931). In infant and nursery school laboratories, the typical use of one-way vision screens makes the children unaware of the fact that they are being observed. Sound motion pictures have also been used to supplement the observational record (Wright, 1960).

When situations and stimuli are selected, structured, or manipulated more specifically, the method of controlled observation tends to shade into the laboratory type of experimental investigation. For example, if number, age, and sex of children, and type and number of toys are systematically varied in order to determine the relationship of these variables to ascendent behavior (Jack, 1934), if control variability in "social climate" is related to group cohesiveness and expression of aggression (Lippit, 1940), if regressive behavior is induced by observer manipulated frustration (Barker, Dembo and Lewin, 1941), the essential features of the ecological approach are largely replaced by those of experiment. Such experiments, of course, can yield valuable data about the social, emotional, and intellectual behavior and development of children, particularly when the impact of situational variables is studied or when the experimental study is used to *elicit* and measure *existing* response tendencies and capacities. By means of carefully designed experiments, it is possible to determine the effects of an interaction between particular variables that are not likely to operate frequently in isolation under natural auspices. However, the futility of attempting to use experimental situations to simulate the cumulative *effect* of many kinds of complex, recurrent and long-term aspects of the natural interpersonal environment has already been discussed at length (see pp. 5-6). Moreover, the contrived aspects of the experimental situation may seriously alter the response that the child makes (Barker, 1965). For example, frustration induced by contrived means occurs at different rates when compared to the real life situations of children (Fawl, 1963). Specimen records of children's everyday behavior where the situations are not contrived reveal that: "frustration was rare in the children's days, and when it did occur, it did not have the behavioral consequences observed in the laboratory. It appears that the earlier experiments simulated frustration very well as we defined and prescribed it for our subjects (in accordance with our theories); but the

experiments did not simulate frustration as life prescribes it for children"
(Barker, 1965, p. 5).

More structured and controlled observations, but less rigidly controlled
than experimental situations, are various *play techniques*. These differ from
other *projective devices* in presenting a wider and less controlled range of stimulation that evokes more spontaneous responses. Originally employed in the
diagnosis and treatment of emotionally disturbed children, this method has
also been used for a decade or more as a research tool for investigating the
normal child's perceptions, concepts, feelings and attitudes (Miller, 1960). Its
chief advantage is that it makes possible the elicitation of existing attitudinal
and response tendencies in simulated real-life situations that could otherwise
not be elicited at all because of the limitation in the young child's verbal
capacities. Standardized stimulus objects and figures (e.g., doll families and
furniture) are utilized to enable the subject to dramatize and fantasy the
type of behavior he might ordinarily express (or repress) in relation to the
actual figures represented by the dolls. As a source of valid generalizations
about the children's behavior and attitudes, the use of play techniques is
warranted to the extent that careful attention is paid to such matters as
standardization of materials, experimenter-child interaction, duration of
play sessions, conditions preceding play sessions, recording of observations,
reliability and validity of measures, etc.* For example, the studies related to
doll-play aggression support the construct validity of doll-play measures, but
the relationship between aggression and doll play and natural social situations has not yet been widely investigated (Bronfenbrenner *et al*, 1960).

Extreme caution is indicated in the interpretation of children's responses
to play interviews. Specific and invariable relationships between a child's
handling of play material and particular aspects of child rearing cannot be
expected. For example, the same attitude of parental rejection may in different children (or under different conditions in the same child) give rise to
overt play aggression against the offending parent, to displaced aggression
directed against self or another adult, to complete inhibition of aggressive
response (Winstel, 1951). It is also important to guard against projection of
observer bias or theoretical orientation. Psychoanalytically oriented thera-
pists tend to generalize impressionistic interpretations of isolated play session
episodes to all children (Davidson and Fay, 1953; Erikson, 1940, 1951;
Freud, 1928; Fries, 1937; Klein, 1932). Ignoring such obvious considerations
as sampling, observer reliability, statistical significance, the laws of parsimony
and exclusion of alternative hypotheses, they present *illustrations* of doll play
dealing with erogenous zones as "evidence" for the Freudian theory of

---

*Treatment of these methodological problems is available in the following references (Anastasi,
1968; Bach, 1945; Bronfenbrenner and Ricciuti, 1960; Sears, 1947; Winstel, 1951).*

psychosexual development. For the less doctrinaire observer, however, there is no self-evident connection between a little boy pushing a miniature auto into a toy garage and incestuous desires for sex relations with his mother, or between the "oral and anal stages of personality development" and ubiquitous interest of four-year-olds in nursing bottles and toy toilets.

Cross-Cultural Studies. Cross-Cultural investigations represent a special variant of intracultural field studies. Although mainly utilized in the past to disprove ethnocentric overgeneralizations regarding child development, they can serve the more positive function of extending our knowledge of the possible range of human behavior, and thereby lead to empirical differentiation between those aspects of development (psychobiological) that are universal in distribution and those aspects (psychosocial) that are referable to unique factors of sociocultural conditioning (see pp. 65-68). In this regard they offer the following special advantages: (a) they include a broader sample of child rearing practices and other conditions affecting personality development than is available in our own culture; (b) they encompass varieties of social systems which we could neither produce experimentally nor derive by extrapolation from known forms (Mead, 1954).

The focus of interest in most cross-cultural studies seems to follow a particular historical *zeitgeist*. Thus, the 1930's and 40's saw the proliferation of I.Q. tests given in many parts of the world, while the 1950's saw the exploration of Freudian hypotheses and other effective domains by means of projective techniques (Greenfield & Bruner, 1966). Early cross-cultural tests of intelligence were attacked on the ground that they put many cultures at a disadvantage and the tests were used to the advantage of the source culture (Strodtbeck, 1964). This criticism precipitated a wave of research attempting to devise a "culture-free" test of intelligence.

The failure of cross-cultural studies to measure up to their earlier promise in the 50's is largely attributed to two factors: First, there had been a lack of adequate conceptualization in terms of which broad hypotheses with respect to personality development and socialization could be formulated, tested, and related to the vital distinction between psychobiological and psychosocial processes and mechanisms of development. This step should obviously precede the organization of long-term and expensive field studies in which precise observations and measures are brought to bear on relatively specific problems (Berrien, 1967; Mead, 1954). Instead, ethnologists have been preoccupied with disproving ethnocentric overgeneralizations or stereotypes of "the primitive mind" or with finding discrete illustrations of child rearing practices or outcomes that "prove" or "disprove" various aspects of Freudian theory (Mead, 1954).

Second, and equally important, was an incredible degree of methodological confusion regarding the nature of scientific evidence. Numerous investigators had made sweeping generalizations about the relationship between various specific items of infant care and adult personality on the basis of impressions gleaned from a single culture or from a small unrepresentative sample of cultures. These impressions were used to "prove" (rather than illustrate) various psychoanalytic formulations regarded as self-evidently valid. In general they ignored such elementary considerations as adequate sampling, statistical significance, and control of other relevant variables. They have failed to consider the possibilities of accidental concomitance and of multiple causality. Observations have frequently been recorded retrospectively and developmental generalizations made from the retrospective accounts of older individuals, the authenticity of which could not be checked.

The current focus of cross-cultural studies in child development, seems to be in the areas of child rearing practices, language development, and cognitive development. For example, the recent interest in Piaget's stage theory of cognitive development has made cross-cultural studies a means of replication of his findings in Switzerland. As Piaget himself (1966) points out:

... comparative studies in the field of genetic psychology are indispensable for psychology in general and also for sociology, because only such studies allow us to separate the effects of biological or mental factors from those of social and cultural influence on the socialization of individuals. (Piaget, 1966, p. 3).

The present replications of Piaget across divergent cultures (Goodnow, 1962; Greenfield et al, 1966; Hyde, 1959; Price-Williams, 1961), indicate the invariance in sequence of Piaget's stages, with differences in speed of transition from one stage to another. These studies have attempted to address themselves to the vital distinction between psychobiological and psychosocial processes and mechanisms of development. The distinction is clear in the conclusion of one of the studies:

... some environments "push" cognitive growth better, earlier, and longer than others. What does not seem to happen is that different cultures produce completely divergent and unrelated modes of thought. The reason for this must be the constraint of our biological heritage (Greenfield et al, 1966, p. 105).

Notwithstanding the distinct improvements over earlier cross-cultural studies in terms of the important distinction between psychobiological and psychosocial factors, current cross-cultural studies in the area of language and cognitive development as well as studies on child-rearing attitudes and practices, still face formidable methodological problems. Because of difficulties in communication, ecological and controlled observation, nonverbal psychometric tests, projective devices, play techniques, infant developmental scales, and physiological measures are the most feasible methods of investigation in studying the development of children in other cultures. First, care must be taken to attempt a fair comparison between two cultures by using similar educational or social levels (Berrien, 1967; Bharucha-Reid, 1962). The comparison of children from families of university graduates in one culture with working class children of another culture may be an inadequate representation of both cultures.

Second, where inferences are being drawn about the population between cultures, care must be taken to draw from representative samples (Berrien, 1967). Thus the sample from both cultures should not be idiosyncratic to its culture on the question being researched, but an adequate representative of the whole population.

Third, the research question of interest in the one culture must also be of interest and researchable in the comparison culture (Berrien, 1967).

...the general proposition is that significant researchable problems within one culture may not be researchable within another, merely because societal taboos and levels of abstractions themselves are so vastly different. This clearly implies that even at the very early stages of any cross-cultural project, it becomes necessary to establish relationships between researchers who are representative of the culture to be compared, to ensure that the issues to be examined are, in fact, relevant and researchable in the respective areas. (Berrien 1967, pp. 37-38).

Fourth, comparability of research instruments between the same culture and the comparison culture demands that:

...prerequisite to the transferring of diagnostic measures from one culture to another is, thus, an investigation of the extent to which the original medium of the instrument is accepted and commonly understood in the second culture, too, with respect to the subject-matter which it transmits. If no cultural differences exist in this field, the original stimuli may be used. (Ortar 1963, p. 222).*

Moreover, the "construct validity" of a particular dimension being explored must be seen in the light of the different cultures being compared. For example, exploring the parental dimension of "*control*"; German parents may indicate "control" by severely punishing such areas as toilet training, table manners, etc., while United States parents illustrate it in the areas of personal hygiene, sex behavior, and sports, etc. (Wesley & Carr, 1966).

Finally, particularly in child development research, contemporaneous testing should be tempered by the fact that the variables under consideration may change with age (Wesley *et al*, 1966). Thus, in surveying mother's attitudes as to the most important attributes of child rearing, German mothers of six-year old boys ranked "obedience" while mothers of fourteen-year-olds listed "protective" and "steering" attitudes. A survey of U.S. mothers found a different pattern (i.e., "getting along with peer") and no age change between six and fourteen year olds (Wesley *et al*, 1966).

This problem is historically centered around the production of "culture-free", "culture-fair" test. Further discussions may be found in Greenfield et al (1966), Berrien (1967), Cesa-Bianchi (1966), Mead (1954), Wesley & Carr (1966).

Rating Methods

In quantifying observational data on the behavior of children, an almost inevitable step involves abstracting discriminable traits or capacities and rating them on a quantitative continuum of frequency, more or less, better or worse, etc. If the original observations were not made in reference to an evaluative scale or in accordance with a "time sampling" technique, the rating is done at a later date on the basis of a series of prior observations. Sometimes, and preferably, the ratings emerge from comparative content analysis of simultaneously recorded protocols of systematically observed behavior. More frequently, however, they represent a cumulative impression in which the rater reviews retrospectively in his mind the behavior of the ratees as he remembers it, or expresses a mere formulated judgment of the trait in question. This latter type of rating is naturally more contaminated by subjective bias, retrospective error, and lack of consistent, systematic and temporally equivalent relationships to the actual behavior of the different subjects being rated. Hence, ratings should not be used when more direct measures or more objective indirect indices of behavior or capacity are available.

Ratings are more valid when raters are trained in advance (i.e., briefed on the nature of the trait; permitted to ask questions, to make a trial run of ratings, to compare and discuss their ratings with others; instructed on how to distribute their ratings over the entire scale). The rater must be in a position to observe subjects frequently with respect to the trait being measured, and the trait itself should be tangible, accessible to observation, and objectively assessable on the basis of concrete behavior considered in its situational context. "Halo effect" can be minimized by having the rater judge each item on the scale for the entire group before proceeding to the next item. A mean rating by five observers is more reliable than a single rating; if this is not possible, a mean of successive ratings by a single observer should be used. Reliability may be determined by intercorrelating the ratings of different observers or the successive ratings of the same observer. *

Self-Report Methods†

A major departure from observational techniques, objective and psycho- metric tests, experimental situations and rating methods is taken by pro- cedures which rely on information that is provided by the subject himself

---

*A methodological discussion of rating and ranking procedures is available in the references. (Anastasi, 1968; Cronbach, 1960; Levine, 1966; Wright, 1960),

†To a very great extent, the same problems also apply to observational data. Parents, for example, are motivated to impress observers favorably regarding their child-rearing practices. The identical issue of whether a parent's verbal report of his attitudes toward his children represents a true sample of his actual attitudes arises when the validity of observations of his child rearing behavior is examined. In neither case is there a genuinely independent or direct validating criterion available.

rather than being inferred from observation or measurement of behavior and performance. Although such data present serious difficulties with respect to the sincerity, honesty and authenticity of the data supplied by the subject, promising attacks have been made on many of these problems.*

Furthermore, self-report methods frequently constitute the only *direct* approach to the investigation of the subjective life of human beings, their attitudes, values, motives, beliefs, perceptions, etc. Natural science methods that ignore these crucial areas of human behavior and development would, by definition, be ruling out some of the most important aspects of the phenomenological field. The distinctive feature of the ecological approach is not the fact that it relies on observational techniques but its concern with studying behavior in naturally occurring settings. In subhuman species, observation and experiment are the only feasible methods of investigation because animals cannot verbalize their subjective experience. Among human beings, however, not only is such verbalization possible, but the kinds of subjective experience that can be verbally communicated also happens to be the most significant aspects of their behavior broadly conceived.

The use of self-report methods in child development presupposes that the child is sufficiently mature in a cognitive sense to supply the desired kinds of information. Hence, they are inapplicable to infants and can only be employed in a very limited sense in the preschool child. These methods include the face-to-face interview, the questionnaire, inventory, diary and perceptual inquiry. Sometimes pictorial materials may be used to illustrate the concepts about which inquiry is made, e.g., race relations, awareness of interpersonal relations.

Interview. Interviews may be either structured or unstructured. The latter are conducted informally; appropriate questions are asked at opportune moments. To avoid inhibiting the subject, only brief notes are made if at all. In recent years, with the advent of sound recording devices, such interviews are usually transcribed and then studied or analyzed at a later date. Although they make for better rapport and often yield richer data, they present serious disadvantages when used for research rather than for clinical purposes. The same ground is not covered and questions are asked in a different sequence and situational context for each subject. Since there is no standardized way of phrasing questions, variability in response will be indeterminably influenced by such difference in phrasing. Difficulty also arises in quantifying the data; simple categories such as "approve"-"disapprove" present no unique problem but qualitative data of the sort obtained in open-ended interviews require special techniques for translating the data to a form of statistical treatment (L. Yarrow, 1960). One possible method is to subject

---

*A methodological review of self-report techniques may be found in Miller (1960). L. Yarrow (1960). and M. R. Yarrow (1960).

the protocols to content analysis and obtain independent ratings from qualified judges which can then be inter-correlated for a determination of reliability (Sears, 1950; L. Yarrow, 1960).

Structured interviews correspond more to questionnaires except they make possible more detailed responses, and tend to discourage indifferent and careless replies. They do not generate as much rapport as do unstructured interviews, but, on the other hand, yield more uniform, comparable and quantifiable data. Subjects are generally more inhibited and suspicious and are often disturbed by the verbatim recording of their replies. The interviewer also has to adhere closely to his schedule of questions and is unable to pursue unexpected leads.

Questionnaire. The questionnaire is a frequently used and abused research instrument in child development. However, it can provide valid data if certain precautions are rigorously observed. The questions should be tangible, precise, specific and unambiguous. Unless opinions and attitudes are the objects of investigation, questions should refer to matters of fact that are accessible to the subject and recent enough to be remembered accurately. It is also essential that respondents be sufficiently mature and intelligent to grasp the meaning of questions and under no undue pressure to give particular kinds of answers. Some measure of the authenticity and sincerity of replies should be used. This may consist of a spot check against available objective records or the use of built-in devices that detect insincerity and carelessness in responding. It goes without saying that careful sampling is necessary before any reliance can be placed on normative or interpretive findings.

A very common error in the interpretation of questionnaire data is the investigator's tendency to equate frequency with saliency. For example, children may be asked to mention the school subjects or games they like best, the reasons for selecting particular vocational choices, etc. Responses are then tabulated and ordered in frequency of mention. Thereupon the unwary investigator may conclude that the most frequently mentioned items or reasons are the most important. It is entirely possible, however, that because of purposeful forgetting, repression, lack of insight, desire to impress the examiner favorably, or miscellaneous situational factors, frequency of report reflects conventionality rather than saliency of subjective content. Hence, some independent index of sincerity of response is essential before much credence can be placed on questionnaire data.

Inventories. Inventories are more complete, detailed, and standardized questionnaires dealing with the attitudes, interests, personality traits, or adjustive behavior of respondents. However, the data they provide are not used as ends in themselves but to furnish an indirect measure of a more generalized trait or ability. Hence they correspond to psychometric and indirect personality tests. *

Diaries. Diaries provide useful sources of developmental data if a sufficient number of such autobiographical accounts are available to make possible the application of suitable sampling criteria and tests of statistical significance. Quantification by means of content analysis is only possible if the diaries are "written under essentially the same conditions and for the same purposes," and if particular categories of events and subjective reactions occur with sufficient frequency (Anderson, 1954).

Direct Subjective Inquiry. Direct subjective inquiry includes a wide variety of methods in which the subject reports his own perceptions, attitudes and judgments. He may rate perceptions of himself or others on a scale (e.g., self-ratings, predictions of individual or group responses). He may express interpersonal attitudes or preferences (e.g., sociometric choices), categorize prepared statements on a judgmental continuum into discriminable steps in terms of a designated criterion or dimension of subjective experience (Q-sort), (Medinnus, 1961) or select persons who best fit a given description ("guess who"), or compare his own perceptions or judgments systematically to each other (method of paired comparisons). Customarily, these methods are shorter and more restricted in scope than the questionnaire or interview, but obviously have much in common with the latter techniques. They differ from projective devices in yielding data (perceptions, judgments or attitudes) which constitute in themselves the phenomena under investigation rather than *indirect* measures of more global capacities or traits. Hence, since they are not "tests" in the usual sense of the term, the customary criterion of validity, i.e., the extent to which they accurately reflect or sample the larger and more general universe of behaviors they purport to measure does not apply. The only relevant question that can be raised regarding their validity is the extent to which verbal reports of subjective content correspond to actual subjective content. Correspondence to objective stimulus reality is not a relevant criterion of validity since perceptual instruments only purport to measure perceptions, not the stimuli that evoke them. But since no genuinely independent measure of the actual content of perception can ever be obtained, the best available criterion of validity is test reliability as measured by stability over successive administrations or by generality over items.

Perceptual measures are especially important in studies of children's personality development. For example, in studying the impact of parent attitudes on children's personality growth it is reasonable to suppose that "although parent behavior is an objective event in the real world it affects

---

A discussion of the principles of test construction, scaling, reliability and validity is available in Anastasi (1968), Anderson (1954), Cronbach (1960), Mussen (1960).

the child's ego development only to the extent and in the form in which he receives it." (Ausubel *et al*, 1954). Second, there is reason to believe

... that children's perceptions of parent behavior and attitudes can be measured more validly than those latter phenomena themselves. In relation to such emotionally loaded issues as acceptance-rejection and intrinsic-extrinsic valuation, both verbal responses by parents to structured or unstructured interview questions and ratings of actual parent behavior by observers are inevitably contaminated by the parents' understandably strong motivation to perceive their role behavior in a favorable light and similarity to impress others. Furthermore, the intent of such inquiries can be more effectively disguised from children; and because of their relative inexperience in such matters, the responses of the latter are less likely to be devious representations of actual feelings. (Ausubel *et al*, 1954, p. 173, 174.)

By means of an attitudinal inquiry device such as sociometry (Thompson, 1960; Sherif, 1964), it is possible to obtain valuable developmental data regarding group structure, social distance, and interpersonal relationships within peer groups. (Marshall, 1957; McCandless & Marshall, 1957; Thompson, 1960; Sherif, 1964). Patterns of choices, social stratification, clique formation, leadership, popularity, sex and race cleavage, deviancy, reciprocity, etc., can be studied effectively by means of sociograms. It is important to realize, however, that sociometric choices vary depending on the particular activity for which one child selects another. A child's sociometric status also varies depending on whether it is computed from the number of times he is chosen or from the mean social distance (acceptability) rating he receives from all members of the group. Sociometric scores show both stability over time and generality over persons (Glidewell, Kantor, Smith and Stringer, 1966); and since they are direct measures, they are as valid as they are reliable (Pepinsky, 1949).

If children are asked to predict the attitudes or responses of others, and if measures of the latter are available, various other dimensions of interpersonal perception can be investigated. For example, at the same time that children rate each other sociometrically, they can predict the sociometric ratings they will receive from their age mates as well as the sociometric status of the latter. It then becomes possible to measure accuracy in perceiving own and others status, tendency to over- or underestimate own and others' status, the degree to which individuals actually reciprocate acceptance and tend to assume that such reciprocity exists, and the extent to which an individual is both similar to the group in accepting or rejecting other persons and tends to assume similarity in this respect. Such measures of interpersonal perception in peer groups (sociempathy) have been shown to possess considerable generality over persons and to be significantly correlated with other judgmental aspects of personality (Ausubel, 1953; Ausubel & Schiff, 1955; Ausubel, Schiff & Gasser, 1952).

Objective Tests of Behavior and Personality

Objective tests of behavior and personality differ from projective and psychometric tests in being direct measures, and from direct subjective inquiry in dealing with overt behavior. Unlike the former, the behavior measured is the actual object of measurement and not an indirect representation of a more generalized trait or capacity. In common with projective techniques, however, the purpose of the test is generally concealed, thereby increasing the likelihood that obtained responses are genuinely representative of actual response tendencies. Hence, test data constitute samples of everyday behavior which are difficult to obtain in uncontrived situations either because they occur infrequently under relatively standardized conditions or because they tend to be disguised to avoid censure and punishment. In the former sense they are quite comparable to experimental situations, differing principally in elaborateness of standardization and concealment of purpose and in emphasis upon yielding reliable individual scores.

Typical of objective measures of conduct are tests of deceit in which subjects are given an opportunity to steal, cheat or lie and are led to believe that detection is difficult or impossible (Grinder, 1961; Hartshorne & May, 1928). Objective measures of motivational behavior include level of aspiration techniques, measures of goal persistence (length of time in persevering in an exceedingly difficult or impossible task (Ausubel et al, 1954; Crandell, 1963), responsiveness to prestige versus anonymous or to cooperative versus competitive motivational conditions (Maller, 1929) and goal tenacity (tendency to maintain high levels of aspiration in relation to prior success-failure experience) (McCandless, 1967). These tests manifest very high inter-item generality, but intersituational generality, however, not only reflects the actual tentativeness of personality structure in children, but also such spurious determinants of specificity as inability to generalize abstract moral propositions and variability in ego-involvement. For example, degree of responsiveness to a prestige incentive depends on degree of ego-involvement in the type of test material employed. Thus, although the trait itself may be general in nature and the objective measure of it perfectly adequate, an individual child's scores will naturally vary from task to task unless ego-involvement is kept constant. The solution to this problem is not to discard objective measures of personality but to construct tests utilizing a wide variety of situations and to weight subscores in accordance with degree of ego-involvement. This weighting may be done on the basis of the subject's own ratings, or if subscores are converted into standard scores and then combined into a composite standard score, they are automatically weighted in terms of ego-involvement (subjects make higher standard scores in tasks in which they are highly ego-involved and vice versa).

The great advantage of objective over projective tests of personality is the directness of the former: there is no ambiguity regarding the trait or dimension of personality being measured, the aspect of the stimulus field to which the subjects are responding, the particular character in a story or picture with which he is identifying, and whether the identification is mild or intense, positive or negative. The widely cited disadvantage of situational specificity has been greatly exaggerated. As already pointed out, much of the apparent specificity reflects an actual lack of generality in children's character structure, and much of the remaining test specificity is spurious and correctable. A more inferential objective test of personality in children is illustrated by the use of physiological indices (e.g., pulse rate, blood pressure, respiration rate, psychogalvanic reflex) (Lipton et al, 1966), and a behavioral rating scale (e.g., non-adjustive activity, substitutive responses, withdrawal, regression) to measure frustration tolerance in children (Bandura & Walters, 1963a & b). Since behavioral and physiological indicators are never specific to a single motivational or emotional state or to a particular personality trait, they can only be used when the personality variable under investigation can be inferred unambiguously from the test situation or when it is desirable to corroborate or scale in intensity test responses derived from other methods.

Projective Personality Measures*

In recent years projective techniques have been used with increasing frequency in child development research. In fact, the uncritical enthusiasm with which they have been greeted in some quarters—as a panacea for all methodological difficulties—has many of the earmarks of a fad. To a certain extent this enthusiasm reflects the influence of clinical approaches, especially psychoanalysis. In part it reflects disillusionment with objective personality measures and other techniques for investigating personality such as paper and pencil inventories, which have adhered more closely to traditional

---

*A volume in itself would be required to present pertinent descriptive and evaluative data on the tremendous number and variety of projective techniques currently available. Hence, the following discussion will only consider general methodological problems and issues involved in the use of projective techniques in child development research—their distinguishing characteristics, the special difficulties they present with children, and research versus clinical use. General discussions of projective methods in developmental research may be found in the following sources: (Anastasi, 1968; Bronfenbrenner & Ricciuti, 1960; Henry, 1960; Kagan, 1960; Lindzey, 1960); Rorschach test, (Ames, 1960; Hayworth, 1962; Levine, 1966; Magnussen & Cole, 1967; Miller, 1960; Rickers-Ovsiankina, 1960); Thematic tests, (Murstein, 1963; Rabin & Hayworth, 1960); children's art work and other special techniques (Ames & Ilg, 1962; 1964; Hayworth 1961, 1962). For the use of projective methods in "motive" assessment (i.e., achievement etc.,) and "cognitive style" (Crandell, 1963; Levine, 1966; Kagan & Moss, 1961; Bronfenbrenner & Ricciuti, 1960; Wallach & Kogan, 1965). The methodological problems of reliability and validity are adequately discussed in other sources and will not be discussed here, (see Anastasi, 1968; Levine, 1966). Specific references previous to 1958 may be found in the "first edition" of this book.

psychometric principles. Because of their relatively nonverbal nature, projective devices also have unique appeal to investigators working with young children.

Like any other measure of personality, the usefulness of projective techniques in child development research depends on their ability to delineate different age levels or stages of personality organization, to indicate the nature of the changes that occur from one stage to another (and the determinants and conditions thereof), and to identify individual differences among children at the same level of development. Only if both inter- and intra-age level differences are distinguishable is it possible to differentiate between what is uniquely characteristic of the individual child and what is characteristic of his age group; and only in the light of the norms referable to his own age level is it possible to evaluate and place in perspective the developmental deviations that occur in any particular child.

General Characteristics. Like objective personality tests and play techniques, the purpose and psychological significance of projective measures are disguised from the subject. They are designed to elicit personality trends that are covert or not immediately observable, to make self-revelation possible with a minimum of awareness, repression, dissimulation and self-embellishment. Although they typically present subjects with a more restricted or standardized range or stimulation than do play techniques, they too are relatively unstructured in three important respects. First, the stimulus content itself is relatively ambiguous (lacks explicit meaning), and hence is subject to wide variability in interpretation. This does not mean, of course, that external test stimuli play no role whatsoever in determining perceptual responses. It simply means that because the external determinants of perception are indefinite in form and structure, the influence of internal personality determinants is maximized; and since standardized stimulus cues are presented to all subjects, individual differences in response presumably reflect variability in the internal determinants of perception. Subjects either react differentially to the same set of cues or respond selectively to a different constellation of cues in the stimulus field.

A second aspect of unstructuredness inherent in projective tests is the fact that they permit the subject to react *simultaneously* to many different, nonspecific attributes of the stimulus field. Hence he tends to reveal various generalized aspects or organizing features of his personality structure rather than specific traits or attitudes with substantive content. Projective measures, therefore, are especially useful for providing a global picture of the person as an interrelated whole, for sketching in broad outlines the uniqueness of his individuality. They indicate the quality of his adjustment and his adjustive resources; his organizing potentialities and his characteristic way of attacking problems; his level of integration and his awareness of reality. They also indicate the extent to which he is original, spontaneous, and creative or rigid, inhibited, and restricted; his drive and emotionality; his relatedness to other persons; his degree of achievement motivation; his "cognitive style" in organizing his experience; the characteristic degree of tension under which he is operating.

A third related feature of projective measures that contributes to their unstructuredness is the freedom they allow the subject in organizing his responses. Since he is neither required to focus on a restricted portion of the field in deriving his perceptions nor to direct his perceptual impressions along specified lines, many different dimensions of personality are simultaneously implicated.

Special Limitations in Use with Children. One of the chief difficulties encountered in using projective techniques with children is the relatively meager, matter of fact responses they give to unstructured stimuli. This is partly a reflection of the minimal degree of generality and self-consistency characterizing their personality organization (see pp. 111-115). On *a priori* grounds alone, one could hardly anticipate richness of response to the more diffuse and less well organized aspects of the stimulus field that ordinarily implicate the global organizing features of more mature personalities. Of course, where differences between groups are great enough, as in normative studies, relative impoverishment of response is not as serious a drawback as in relational studies of personality organization within a restricted age range. In the latter instance individual differences tend to be obscured by commonalities referable to the group as a whole. Nevertheless, a significant range of individual variability is found within each of the age levels on the Rorschach test; and as children mature they not only participate in the age level changes shown by their fellows but also tend to maintain with some consistency earlier evidences of individuality with respect to many of the global traits measured by this instrument (Ames *et al*, 1952, 1959; Ledwith, 1959).

In order to overcome this and other disadvantages many investigators have modified the projective method by both making the stimulus content more explicit and highly structured and by restricting freedom of response. For example, instead of merely asking the subject to invent a story about an ambiguous picture, the investigators may supply much of the narrative content and then ask specific open-ended questions or provide several alternative endings or interpretations from which the subject is required to choose the one that seems most appropriate to him. In addition to tapping individual differences more effectively, this approach involves less subjectivity of interpretation and yields data more relevant and specific to the particular variables under investigation. It also permits inquiry into the more substantive aspects of personality and makes determination of inter-item generality possible. By definition, however, less global features of personality are evoked in this type of perceptual response, and the purpose of the test becomes more transparent.

Research versus Clinical Use. Because many of the research disadvantages of projective instruments do not apply to clinical use, clinicians tend to be less conversant than research workers with their limitations. Clinical diagnosis is admittedly a highly subjective process involving special skills and sensitivities. Hence, for clinical practice, it is less important to eliminate subjective diagnostic instruments requiring special intuitive talents than it is to eliminate practitioners who lack these talents. Also, since more abundant life history data are available in clinical settings, subjective interpretation (even of substantive content) tends to be more valid and individual differences within an age group more identifiable. Furthermore, in clinical practice, isolation of relevant variables is not important since the object is to obtain a view of the individual as an interrelated whole and not to compare individuals on a series of personality traits for relational purposes.

In any event as long as projective tests are only used as supplementary sources of information or as adjunctive diagnostic tools they can obviously be no more invalid than the very procedure of clinical diagnosis itself. In a sense they can be considered a diagnostic short-cut for the interview method, especially in the clinical handling of children where difficulties in communication are formidable indeed. However, it is one thing to use instruments of questionable validity in a setting where the exigencies of the situation demand that something be done immediately for a disturbed individual (and nothing better is available) and quite another to use them as sources of purportedly valid generalizations about intra- or inter-age group differences among children.

In conclusion, unstructured projective techniques are most suitable for clinical practice and for normative and longitudinal research study of children. They are inappropriate for isolating substantive personality variables and their reliability and validity are not easily established. Nevertheless, they are less adversely affected by limited degrees of reliability and validity and by meagerness of response, and require less subjectivity of interpretation when used for measuring normative and intra-individual longitudinal trends than when used for identifying interindividual differences within an age group. As screening devices, for differentiating between grossly contrasting populations, they find ready applicability to many research, clinical and personnel problems. Obviously a much higher order of reliability and validity is necessary before dependable individual predictions can be made with respect to smaller and more subtle personality differences. For reasons indicated above, *structured* projective instruments appear to be more promising than unstructured devices for investigating interindividual personality trends of a substantive nature in children. In any event because of the relative trait specificity, the relatively uncrystallized state of children's personality organization, and the all pervasive influence of normative similarities within an age group, methodological difficulties constitute the principal bottleneck in research on children's personality development. Hence it has not yet been possible to devise sufficiently valid, reliable, and subtle instruments that reveal the individuality of children in many of the crucial substantive aspects of personality organization.

PART II

The Beginnings of Development

CHAPTER 6

Prenatal Development and the Birth Process

SURVEY OF PRENATAL DEVELOPMENT

IN SEARCHING for the origins and early developmental phases of behavior we must start with the fetus, not with the neonate. Before the baby is born many of the raw materials of behavior have already been patterned in certain very definite ways to constitute the antecedents of later forms of development. By studying these antecedents the nature of subsequent developmental processes becomes more comprehensible, providing that we do not assume that *all* aspects of "later performance [are necessarily] implicit or hidden in earlier types of response"; much can intervene in the interim to account for essential features of more mature behavior that were not even suggested in beginning phases (Carmichael, 1954).

Although genic predispositions present at conception are modified somewhat by fetal, gestational, and external factors during the course of prenatal development, their influence still tends to be prepotent. Thus the embryological model of development fits well: the environment is relatively constant, and even if variability does occur it has little effect unless extreme. During this period of development, the acquisition of "phylogenetic" traits (intra-species uniformities referable to identical single-gene effects) is most conspicuous. Nothing is preformed, but since the genic contribution to the growth matrix is disproportionately great, the basic outlines of development are virtually predetermined. Growth is not independent of environment, but environment, within very broad limits, does not play a crucially determinative role in the regulation of development.

Method of Study

Four general methods are available for studying the prenatal development of human behavior: (1) observation of development in infrahuman species, the embryos of which are more accessible to observation (e.g., birds) and from which large samples of individuals at various stages of growth can be obtained at will: (2) observational and motion picture study of nonviable human fetuses removed surgically under local anesthesia while still alive (for medical reasons) and placed in saline solution at body temperature; (3) study of

175

prematurely born, viable human fetuses delivered spontaneously or opera-
tively; and (4) study of the spontaneous or induced activity of the intact
unborn fetus and of its responsiveness to stimulation from reports of the
mother and by means of apparatus (e.g., stethoscope) applied to her abdominal wall.

Each of these methods has its advantages and limitations. When the data
they yield are pooled they provide complementary and confirmatory evidence from which a coherent picture of prenatal behavioral development
can be constructed. Animal specimens are more available and sometimes
more accessible to observation; but the viviparous species which most closely
resemble the human are equally as inaccessible. In any event, the problem of
extrapolation invariably arises, particularly in the case of the oviparous
lower species which offer the advantage of greater accessibility. Surgically
removed fetuses can be stimulated and observed directly—but obviously
under conditions quite different from those of uterine life. Instead of being
suspended in amniotic fluid under constant pressure and temperature, and
largely insulated from stimulation, they are placed in a different, more
variable, and generally more stimulating environment. Even more important perhaps are the impact of recent operative insult and the effects of
gradual asphyxiation that first increase and then inhibit the very activity
which the investigator is seeking to elicit in response to controlled stimulation.

These latter disadvantages are absent when the spontaneously delivered,
viable premature infant is studied. On the other hand, the disparity in this
instance between uterine and external environments is even greater; and
fetal-maternal circulatory, respiratory, alimentary and excretory arrangements are not merely disrupted but are replaced by a modified set of independent arrangements. Furthermore, viability is generally impossible before
the fetus is twenty-six weeks old, and relatively little new development,
especially in the motor sphere, occurs between that age and full-term. All of
these contaminating factors can, of course, be avoided by studying the unborn fetus in utero, but the barrier to direct stimulation and observation
imposed by abdominal and uterine walls and by fetal membranes is formidable indeed, especially in the early months of pregnancy.

Another difficulty common to all methods is the impossibility of ascertaining accurately the age of the fetus. If age is inferred from fetal length, using
the table of mean age-length equivalents, two sources of error enter into the
determination of the age of a particular fetus—variability in rate of growth
and the original error in estimating age in the sample of fetuses used in
constructing the table. Hence, it is more straightforward to determine fetal
age by simply using whatever method is employed in making the estimate
in the first place. True age, of course, would be measured from the moment
of conception, but since there is no way of ascertaining when this occurs, it

can only be inferred from the date of ovulation preceding fertilization. Unfortunately, however, the occurrence of this event cannot be determined directly with any exactitude. In practice, therefore, it is necessary to use a formula which, on the basis of related histological and biochemical evidence, assumes that the ovulation prior to pregnancy occurs two to three weeks after the first day of the last menstruation. Moreover, in addition to the possible error of one week stemming from variability in the time of ovulation, uncertainty about the date of effective insemination and about the viability span of both ova and spermatozoa contributes further to the error or estimate.

Timetable of Embryological Highlights*

By way of general orientation to fetal behavioral development, the following overview of major embryological highlights based largely on studies of surgically removed fetuses may be offered:

By the end of the *third week* humoral integration of the organism is made possible as the fetal circulatory system becomes functional. Neural development is marked by the appearance of the medullary groove and of the cerebral and optic vesicles. Limb buds are already in evidence, and maternal-fetal circulatory interchange is firmly established through the placenta and umbilical vessels. By the *second month* the fetus becomes recognizably human; almost all bodily organs, including the special sense organs, are present. The muscles respond to direct electrical stimulation, but no neurally-mediated responses are possible as yet.

At the beginning of the *third month* all of the components necessary for neuromuscular behavior at the simple, segmental reflex arc level are functionally available. The earliest neurally-mediated response to tactile stimulation occurs when the oral-nasal regions innervated by sensory fibres of the trigeminal nerve are stimulated; but the response is highly diffuse, implicating practically all effector units that are functional at this time. Whether or not spontaneous, generalized movements of an uncoordinated nature precede or follow this diffuse type of response to stimulation is still an open question (Carmichael, 1954; Hooker, 1943, 1952, 1958). During the course of this month practically all of the various kinds of motion possible at each of the joints appear. The fetus responds to proprioceptive and vestibular stimulation and palmar and plantar reflexes can be elicited. The mature form of the kidney is present and minimal function is indicated by the appearance of urea in the amniotic fluid.

During the *fourth month* tactile stimulation at any point on the body surface becomes capable of eliciting reflex response. By this time most of the discrete responses manifested by the neonate (including swallowing and abdominal

---

*Based on available references. See Carmichael (1954); Gesell (1945); Hooker (1943, 1951); Montagu (1962); Millen (1963); Munn (1965); Sontag (1966); Windle (1940).

reflexes) are at least partially developed except for functional "respiration, voice, grasp, suctorial response, tendon reflexes, and special sense responses (Hooker, 1943). A wide repertoire of both spontaneous and elicited responses appear which are also less mechanical, generalized, and sterotyped and more specific, graceful, and delicate.

Unequivocal and gross signs of fetal activity in utero become evident during the *fifth* month: the mother "feels life" and the fetal heart beat becomes audible. Grasp and Babinski reflexes appear and weak respiratory movements can be evoked by applying stimulation to the thoracic wall. During the *sixth month* synergetic movements and tendon, sucking, Moro, and corneal reflexes make their appearance. Toward the end of this period and the beginning of the *seventh month* the fetus becomes viable and is able to cry weakly. In terms of response capacities, little change occurs during the *last two* months of pregnancy although fetal activity decreases during the last month (Walters, 1964). The fetus gains principally in strength, fat, and volume of neuromuscular activity. Individual differences in degree of spontaneous activity may have initial prognostic value inasmuch as more active fetuses tend to rank higher posnatally on such behaviors as motor and liguistic as measured by the Gesell Developmental Scale as late as the 36th month (Richard and Nelson, 1938; Sontag, 1966; Walters, 1965). Sex differences in fetal activity appear to be negligable (Bernard, 1964). In comparison to fullterm infants the visual responsiveness and ocular movements of the prematurely born are poorly developed.

Influence of Gestational Factors*

Through what mechanisms does uterine experience influence fetal behavior and contribute (along with the genotype) to the growth matrix regulating the direction of development? How crucial is the influence of extragenic, environmental factors during the prenatal period? Four different categories of gestational variables must be considered: (1) humoral communication between mother and fetus through the placenta; (2) the uterine environment—considered as both a gestational habitat and as a source of stimulation; (3) external stimuli penetrating the uterine wall and impinging upon the fetus; and (4) stimuli originating within the fetus itself. Also, apart from whatever other effects it may have on fetal development, receptivity to intrafetal, uterine, and external stimulation introduces the possibility of acquiring new behavior patterns (learning) or modifying existing patterns.

Communication through the Placenta. The placenta is a special organ of circulatory interchange derived from both the uterine mucosa and from the chorionic villi of the fetus. These villi, vascularized by terminal branches of

---

*A more complete treatment of this topic may be found in Montagu (1962).

the umbilical artery and vein, penetrate branches of the uterine artery. Through this semipermeable barrier, selective interchange of practically all substances found in plasma occurs between the circulatory systems of mother and fetus. This includes water, blood proteins, glucose, amino acids, blood fats, oxygen, carbon dioxide, non-protein nitrogen, hormones, vitamins, antibodies, antigens, electrolytes, drugs, viruses, bacteria, etc. In this way it is possible for the mother to supply the fetus' needs for oxygen and nutritive elements and to remove carbon dioxide and nitrogenous wastes. Nevertheless, a certain amount of selectivity of interchange is maintained; the concentration of various substances (e.g., vitamin E, glucose, antibodies) is less in fetal than in maternal blood (Hagerman & Viller, 1952; Montagu; 1962; Vahlquist, Lagercrantz and Nordbring, 1950; Windle, 1940), and the opposite is true in the case of fructose (Hagerman et al, 1952).

Ordinarily the placental barrier is not permeable to the formed elements of the blood, i.e., red and white corpuscles and platelets. This is indeed fortunate since it reduces by almost twenty times the incidence of erythroblastosis in mothers whose own red blood cells do not contain the Rh factor (Rh negative) but whose offsprings' red blood cells do contain this factor (Rh positive). In this disease Rh agglutinogens in fetal red blood cells manage to penetrate the placental barrier and enter the maternal blood stream. Since the mother does not have the Rh agglutinogen in her red cells, it acts as an antigen and stimulates the production of specific antibodies (agglutinins) capable of agglutinating Rh positive red cells. These agglutinins have no difficulty in entering fetal circulation and destroying large numbers of red blood corpuscles. Severe anemia and jaundice results, and sometimes lesions in the basal ganglia, abortion, and fetal or neonatal death (Pasamanick and Knobloch, 1966). It is evident, however, that in all instances in which the placental barrier is normally impermeable to red blood cells this disease will not occur despite disparity between mother and fetus with respect to the Rh factor.

The concentration of metabolites in the fetal blood stream maintains a remarkable degree of constancy despite great variability in maternal diet and nutrition. The fetus obtains much more than its proportionate share of nutritive elements when maternal diet is inadequate. Nevertheless, because it is developing and growing at such a rapid rate, it apparently suffers more than the mother from the consequences of malnutrition (Burke et al, 1943; Drillien, 1957; Ebbs et al, 1942; Montagu, 1962; Pasamanick & Knobloch, 1966; Sontag, 1960). Unsatisfactory nutrition in the mother is associated with lower fetal and infant weight, with occurrence of fetal rickets, and with a higher incidence of abortion, stillbirth, malformations, infant mortality, and of such diseases as infant rickets, anemia and tetany (Burke et al, 1943; Ebbs et al, 1942; M'Gonigle & Kirby, 1936; Sontag, 1960; Tisdell, 1945;

Murphy, 1947; Montagu, 1962; Pasamanick & Knobloch, 1966; Warkany, 1947).*

Because of maternal-fetal circulatory interchange, the development of the fetus is affected by many pathological conditions in the mother which influence the composition of her blood plasma. It may develop allergies from allergens in her diet. Large doses of quinine, morphine and barbituates may have an adverse effect on the fetus (Sontag, 1960). Such infectious diseases as measles, mumps, chickenpox, erysipelas, syphillis, tuberculosis, and rubella (German measles) are transmissable through the placenta. The last mentioned, when occurring in the first trimester of pregnancy not infrequently results in stillbirth, premature birth, abortion and in such abnormalities as cataract, deafness, and mental deficiency (Montagu, 1962; Sivan, 1948; Wesselhoeft, 1949). Various non-infectious maternal conditions such as hypertension and diabetes are associated with a higher incidence of abortion, stillbirth, neonatal death and oversized infants (Barns & Morgans, 1948; Chesley and Annetto, 1947; Gaspar, 1945; Montagu, 1962; Sontag, 1960).

It is also entirely conceivable that through the neurohumoral bond between them (Montagu, 1962), maternal activity, fatigue, emotion, and personality may influence the irritability, activity level, and autonomic functioning of the fetus (Montagu, 1962; Sontag, 1960; 1966; Pasamanick & Knobloch, 1966). Excessive activity and fatigue in the mother alters the lactic acid and carbon dioxide levels of fetal blood, thereby increasing fetal activity and pulse rate. Fear, rage, and anxiety in the mother have similar effects on the fetus by virtue of the sympathomimetic effects of adrenalin and its tendency to lower all response thresholds. In fact, prolonged and intense maternal anxiety may cause autonomic imbalance and dysfunction in the immature and susceptible fetal gastrointestinal tract, as well as chronic generalized lowering of motor response thresholds. This may carry over into neonatal life in the form of pyloric spasm, cardiospasm, excessive irritability, emotional maladjustment, mongoloidism, epilepsy, cerebral palsy, reading disability, and increased frequency of allergic reactions (Davids et al, 1963; Drillien, 1963; Halliday, 1948; Ottinger et al, 1964; Pasamanick & Knobloch, 1966; Sontag, 1941, 1944, 1946, 1960, 1966; Stott, 1959). Indirectly, abnormal emotional states in the mother decrease her intake, absorption, and utilization of food, thereby affecting adversely the nutritional status of the fetus (Montagu, 1962; Sieve, 1949; Sontag, 1946, 1966). And insofar as cultural variables influence the activity level and emotional responsiveness of expectant mothers, it is possible to account for some of the discrepancies between cultures in the typical amount of fetal activity reported by pregnant women.

---

*See section on prematurity (pp. 201) for further references on this topic.

Uterine Environment. The gestational habitat provided by the uterus, fetal membranes, and amniotic fluid tends to provide a relatively stimulus-free environment under constant pressure and temperature. A more important source of intrauterine variability, therefore, consists of various endocrine and local tissue factors that enable the mother to maintain the fetus intact throughout the gestational period, inhibit premature contraction of the uterus, and prevent disintegration or premature separation of the placenta. Thus, older mothers who presumably are less adequate in these respects, conceive fetuses who are more predisposed toward abortion, stillbirth, neonatal mortality, hydrocephalus, and mongolism (Kuder and Johnson, 1944; M'Gonigle *et al*, 1936; Montagu, 1962; Pasamanick & Knobloch, 1966). Substantiating this interpretation is the fact that the last-mentioned condition also tends to occur more frequently in infants whose mothers have a prior history of menstrual and hormonal abnormalities, difficulty in becoming pregnant, uterine pathology, and habitual abortion (Benda, 1949; Sontag, 1960). Abnormalities of fetal position and knots in the umbilical cord may also result in deformities and strangulation.

Responsiveness to Intrafetal and External Stimulation. Evidence regarding fetal responsiveness to stimulation comes from surgically removed fetuses, from prematurely born fetuses, and from studies of fetuses in utero. All such evidence is pertinent in considering the extent to which the fetus *could respond* to particular kinds of stimulation. This is one question which we will want to consider. An entirely different issue, however, is the extent to which intrafetal and external stimulation influence the course of fetal development. This depends not only on absolute sensory capacity but on whether and to what degree the fetus actually *does respond* to various types of stimulation under typical conditions of intrauterine life. Hence, in evaluating the pooled data presented below as it relates to the latter issue, it is necessary to bear in mind that extrauterine sources of tactile, pressure, vibratory, pain and auditory stimulation are largely buffered or muffled by fetal membranes, amniotic fluid, uterus, and maternal abdominal wall; that these various layers are completely impenetrable by light; that adequate stimuli for taste, smell, pain, and visceral sensation rarely if ever impinge on the fetus; and that the range of variability in intrauterine temperature is extremely small and never discriminable.

In view of all these formidable barriers to stimulation from without, it seems likely, therefore, that the fetus itself serves as its own principal source of sensory experience. Most effective stimulation during the gestational period originates within the fetus and is picked up by proprioceptive, vestibular, and visceral interoceptors. Of the extroceptors, only the non-distance tactile receptors are actually functional in prenatal life; and for the most part tactile stimulation is provided as moving fetal parts come into apposition with each other. Energy changes in the environment for which the human organism has no adequate receptors will not be considered here, although such phenomena (e.g., massive doses of x-ray) may have deleterious effects on development, gestation, and on the genotype itself, giving rise to malformations, abortion, and imbecility (Montagu, 1962; Murphy, 1929, 1947). In the present atomic age, these potential consequences of radiation need to be taken more seriously.

Proprioceptive receptors in muscles, tendons, and joints are well developed in the early months of prenatal life (Carmichael, 1954; Hooker, 1951; Windle, 1940). A continuous source of proprioceptive stimulation is provided by normal muscle tonus, by movement of bodily parts, and by shifts in postural tonus induced by positional changes of the entire fetus. The latter postural shifts, including accompanying eye movements, are probably mediated by vestibular stimulation, although it is difficult to exclude the contribution of proprioceptive stimuli associated with changes in positional orientation. Because of adequate fetal experience, prematurely born infants respond just as adequately as full-term infants to both kinds of stimulation. Rhythmic activity and tonus changes in the nonstriated muscles of the respiratory and gastrointestinal systems probably account for some visceral-proprioceptive stimulation in utero, but this is obviously minimal compared to what is generated when these systems become functional after birth. Nevertheless, since the receptors themselves are well developed, the premature infant is highly responsive to visceral stimuli.

The tactile components (touch and pressure) of cutaneous sensibility are both well-developed and well-exercised during prenatal life. Beginning in the oral-nasal area in the third month, the acquisition of sensitivity spreads rapidly and is almost complete by the fourth month. A wide variety of reactions of both reflex and nonreflex nature occur in response to tactile stimulation, and gradually become more specific and localized with age. Fetal responsiveness to pain, however, is minimal both because of little actual uterine experience with pain and because of the important role of cortical, apperceptive, and emotional factors; for the latter reasons, responsiveness is not markedly increased shortly after birth in either premature or full-term infants. In the case of thermal sensitivity, on the other hand, the afferent mechanism is well developed and quite functional in the premature infant, but fails to be stimulated in utero. The same holds true for taste and smell; amniotic fluid is not a good medium for transmitting olfactory stimuli, and does not vary sufficiently in chemical composition to provide adequate gustatory stimulation.

The auditory apparatus is also ready to function during the last two months of fetal life and in premature as well as in full-term infants. However, because of closure of the external auditory meatus and Eustachian tubes and the presence of a gelatinous substance in the middle ear, sounds of ordinary intensity are not effective prior to birth. Loud music, a doorbell buzzer placed close to the fetal head, and pure tones transmitted through air to the maternal abdomen evoke convulsive, startle-like responses in the fetus and result in cardiac acceleration (Johansson, Wedenburg & Westin, 1964; Dwornicka, Jasienska, Smolarz and Wawryk, 1964; Sontag, 1960, 1966; Sontag & Richards, 1938; Windle, 1940), but it is not clear whether these responses are caused by auditory or vibratory stimulation (Bernard & Sontag, 1947). Development of the visual mechanism starts early in fetal life, but the morphological changes involved are not completed until after the normal gestational period (Carmichael 1954; Windle, 1940). Thus, although the prematurely born neonate can differentiate between light and dark and responds to illumination with the iris reflex, he does not manifest pursuit, pupillary distance, and convergence responses (Carmichael, 1954; Windle, 1940). Even if light could penetrate the uterus the fetus would be relatively unresponsive to it.

Importance of Gestational Factors. To what extent is this summary of the evidence dealing with the effects of gestational influences on prenatal development compatible with our preliminary conclusions that genic factors are relatively prepotent during this stage of growth? We have seen that for the most part the fetus is enveloped in a relatively constant gestational environment and is exposed to very little variability in stimulation, either through the placental circulation or through penetration of the fetal habitat by extra-uterine stimuli. This degree of variability is both too great to account for the remarkable uniformity prevailing in the development of phylogenetic traits and too little to contribute much to the development of ontogenetic traits. Hence, it seems likely that intra- and extrafetal gestational factors ordinarily play a supportive rather than a crucial directional role in development. Only when these factors are extreme or pathological in nature do they seem to make a difference; and even then their effect tends to be negative. That is, instead of providing *new* direction for growth, they merely produce malformations by retarding or arresting development, or else create conditions that are unfavorable for continued fetal life or gestation (stillbirth, abortion, premature birth, fetal and neonatal death or disease).

Furthermore, even if gestational variables are extreme, their detrimental effects on fetal development still seem to be partly contingent upon the presence of other special factors. In the case of phylogenetic traits, pathologic conditions affect principally those organs or organ systems which are developing most rapidly at the time when the disturbance is operative; or, stated conversely, susceptibility to the adverse effects of gestational pathology in a given organ is largely limited to a brief "critical period" when developmental differentiation is most rapid. Thus, by knowing the timetable of fetal development and the date when uterine disturbance occurs, it is possible to predict the site and type of developmental malformation that will result.* German measles, for example, produces defects chiefly in certain portions of the central nervous system and in the auditory and visual apparatus; however, it will only do so if the mother contracts the disease in the early months of pregnancy when these regions are in a critical stage of development (Montagu, 1962). In view of the highly damaging effects of anoxia, particularly on the central nervous system and on rapidly developing tissues, it is possible that oxygen deprivation is the common mechanism through which the damaging effects of many different pathological conditions are mediated (Montagu, 1962).

Ontogenetic traits are more responsive to extreme variability in the gestational environment than are phylogenetic traits, and are also more affected by less extreme degrees of variability. There is reasons to believe, however, that uterine disturbances primarily affect prenatal development in instances where a strong genic predisposition toward disease or dysfunction already exists in the first place. The stronger an unfavorable genic predisposition is, the less intense and prolonged the cumulative environmental insult must be before the defect in question becomes overtly manifest. Thus one would tend to suspect strong genic loading in those neonates showing marked symptoms of hyperirritability and autonomic inbalance following exposure to maternal anxiety during gestation; genically determined inadequate ACTH responses to stress (e.g., to maternal adrenalin) could conceivably fail to protect organs against damage and dysfunction, particularly physiologically immature organs (e.g., gastrointestinal) which first begin functioning after birth. It is also possible that strong genic predispositions may be responsible for most fetal and neonatal deaths. This is indicated by the fact that whereas environmental improvement over the past forty years has resulted in a phenomenal drop in infant mortality, the corresponding reduction in neonatal mortality has been negligible (Bundesen, 1953; World Health Organization Chronicle, 1967).

Because sensory experience in utero is so restricted it is hardly likely that it plays a significant directional role in prenatal development. Some sense modalities are quite well developed but fail to provide the fetus with much sensory experience since *adequate* stimuli are not available. This applies to taste, smell, hearing, temperature, and visceral sensibility; in the case of vision and pain, not only are adequate stimuli lacking, but responsiveness itself is highly limited. Only the proprioceptive, vestibular, and cutaneous modalities are reasonably functional during prenatal life, and these do not furnish the type of sensory impressions from which clear percepts can be

---

*For a comprehensive survey of the evidence in support of this theory see T. H. Ingalls; Journal of the American Medical Association 161: 1047-1951, 1956.

formed. Hence it seems reasonable to infer that stimuli impinging on these modalities mostly evoke available responsiveness, and only to a very meager extent give rise to clearly defined mental content that influences the course of behavioral development.

Development of Prenatal Behavior

Learning Versus Genic Regulation. In the previous section we have considered intrafetal and extrauterine sources of stimulation as factors evoking available sensory and motor responsiveness and as potential determinants of conscious experience. Implicit in this discussion was the assumption that the determination of which patterns of response are associated with which types of stimulation is a matter that, for all practical purposes, is controlled by genic factors and is not essentially influenced by specific experience. This proposition, as suggested earlier, follows from the remarkable degree of intra-species uniformity in prenatal behavioral development in the absence of sufficiently determinative and uniform regulatory influences from without.

Nevertheless, in view of the fact that receptivity to stimulation and potentiality for establishing sensori-motor connections exist in the fetus, it is necessary to examine more fully the position of Holt (1931) and others that the neonate's behavioral repertoire is largely acquired as the product of specific intrauterine experience. In support of this notion, Holt presents the development of the grasp reflex as a paradigm illustrating how purportedly unlearned reflexes could conceivably be acquired by a process of conditioning. As part of the fetal posture of generalized flexion, the muscles of the hand are flexed, generating proprioceptive impulses which tend to perpetuate finger closure. Concomitantly, the tips of the fingers touch the palm. Eventually, according to Holt, after many contiguous occurrences, the tactile stimulus alone becomes adequate for eliciting the grasp reflex. That this type of conditioning is theoretically possible was demonstrated in fetuses 26 to 34 weeks old. After about twenty contiguous presentations of a loud sound and tactile vibration to the maternal abdomen it was possible to elicit fetal movement with the latter (originally inadequate, conditioned) stimulus alone (Spelt, 1948). Sontag (1960) has also demonstrated what would appear to be a learned *habituation response* resulting from repeated vibratory stimulation in the latter part of the fetal period.

Dennis (1943), however, lists many convincing reasons for not regarding such evidence as adequately substantiating the thesis that fetal behavior is learned. First, the grasp reflex is the only possible illustration that can be offered where this theory fits easily; applied to any other instance of fetal behavior it is highly implausible. Second, although certain conditioned reflexes can be established *experimentally* during fetal life, the minimal conditions essential for conditioning are not ordinarily present in utero. Auditory and vibratory stimulation, for example, are seldom intense enough to arouse fetal responsiveness, and do not normally occur with sufficient contiguity or repetitiveness to make conditioning possible. Only proprioceptive and tactile stimuli are reasonably adequate during fetal life, and only in the case of the grasp reflex does contiguity occur frequently and regularly enough to lend credence to this explanation. Third, many reflexes can be elicited perfectly or nearly perfectly at birth even though the neonate had not previously been exposed to the evocative stimuli in question, e.g., ocular pursuit movements in response to a roving visual stimulus, crying in response to intense heat, cold, or smell. This eliminates any possibility of learning or conditioning. Fourth, for a conditioned response to be established the response itself must be available so that it can be associated with an originally inadequate stimulus; but some responses, like crying, do not appear until after birth.

Fifth, even if the conditioning hypothesis were applicable in some instances it would still not account for *all* fetal stimulus-response behavior patterns, since an unconditioned response must obviously exist before conditioning itself is possible. Sixth, the suggestion that the behavior patterns developed in the last few months of antenatal existence are conditioned derivatives of earlier developed responses is not very convincing because most discrete responses, except for sucking, crying, respiration, and tendon, grasp, and visual-motor responses, are already present by the fourth month; and since, in the latter instances (except for the grasp and tendon reflexes), neither the responses nor the adequate stimuli are available, learning is out of the question. To hypothesize that the early tactile reflexes are themselves learned would assume that learning is possible nine weeks following conception.

Finally, the absence of significant cortical participation in fetal and neonatal behavior patterns, as demonstrated experimentally and in the case of acephalic monsters, makes the learning hypothesis extremely unlikely. Subcortical learning is difficult indeed in human beings. The few acephalic monsters who do survive after birth show no evidence of learning. Thus, "if prenatal development occurs by virtue of a sort of subcortical learning, one wonders why such learning [does] not continue to occur in [the] acephalous infant." (Dennis, 1943).

In conclusion, therefore, the weight of the evidence indicates that the emergence of fetal and neonatal behavior patterns is a function of neural maturation. It is regulated for the most part by prepotent genic predispositions for particular kinds of afferent input to be linked with designated types of efferent output. Except for certain isolated instances, the conditions of fetal existence are not propitious for the uniform acquisition of such connections on the basis of specific experience.

Organizational Trends. Quite apart from the relative contributions of genic and experiential factors to the development of fetal behavioral capacities is the long-standing and controversial issue of sequential trends in the organization of these capacities. Are independently controlled part-activities individuated out of total responses of the entire organism, or are single part-activities combined to form more complex whole activities? From his study of behavioral development in the salamander, Coghill concluded both that the direction of organization is invariably from total to part activity and that original total responses are integrated from the very start. He showed that swimming movements implicating the entire organism precede independent motion of single limbs, and that lateral rotation of the entire body, in response to a stimulus in one visual field, precedes simple rotation of the eyeballs alone (Coghill, 1929, 1936).

These findings were later applied by Coghill and others to encompass the direction of behavioral organization in all species. Critical examination of the evidence, however, indicates that the generalizations holding true for the salamander probably do not apply to human beings: too much disparity exists between the two species in rate of behavioral development and in degree of cortical control over integrated activity. The developmental situation, therefore, is much more complicated in the human infant. First, although individuation of part activities out of total responses does precede the knitting together of simple parts into more complex wholes, the latter type of organizational trend (e.g., coordinated and sequential reflexes, learned motor performance) is *also* very characteristic of human behavioral development. Second, the original form of total activity is uncoordinatedly diffuse rather than integrated. Individuation proceeds from a diffuse type of mass activity; and integration is only achieved subsequently—when the individuated parts are synthesized into a new coordinated whole.

Furthermore, qualitatively different kinds of individuation seem to take place and to occur at different rates. The earliest type of diffuse response to stimulation is apparently displaced by discrete, and invariable stimulus-response connections; this sequence corresponds to the development of simple reflexes and is presumably regulated by potent genic factors. On the other hand, stimulus-elicited behavior that is more variable in nature, spontaneous behavior, and finally volitional behavior, appear to be individuated from a different type of precursor. Development in these latter instances does not follow the seemingly predetermined and inevitable pattern of attaining greater discreteness and invariability; instead diffuseness is replaced by greater specificity, directedness, and localization, but never by a stereotyped set of responses (Hooker, 1958). This type of individuation also begins later and is by no means completed in fetal life.

Other directional trends in prenatal behavioral development are axial in nature. The emergence of neuromuscular responsiveness, control, and coordination follows a proximo-distal and cephalo-caudal sequence. That is, sensori-motor function appears earlier in cranial than in sacral areas of innervation, and sooner in muscle groups that are close to, rather than distant from, the longitudinal axis of the body. These axial trends also persist in postnatal motor development.

PREGNANCY, CHILDBIRTH, LACTATION AND MATERNAL BEHAVIOR

Maternal behavior begins before the child is born. Genetically speaking it starts as soon as the mother-to-be as a child forms her first concept of parenthood. More proximately it begins with her reactions to ongoing pregnancy and anticipated childbirth. Here the dominant considerations are factors that increase or decrease the desire for motherhood. After birth takes place, the problem of caring for an infant who is now an insistent reality elicits actual parent behavior that is determined by a related but different set of physiological, cultural, personal, and situational variables.

Psychological Reactions to Pregnancy

In all cultures powerful social and psychological forces operate to increase a woman's desire for motherhood and to generate positive attitudes regarding pregnancy. Wherever children are supportable, they are desired for a wide variety of reasons: to help in the economic support of the family; to perpetuate the culture; to carry on the family name; to enhance the dignity and social standing of the parents; to succor them in their old age; to attend to their burial; to mourn for them, and to care for their departed spirits; and, especially where the material level of the culture is high, children are also desired for their own sake—for the psychological joys and satisfactions of parenthood. The sterile woman is frequently an object of cultural scorn. Sterility creates dissatisfactions in marital life, undermines the woman's position in the home, and frequently jeopardizes the very legal status of her marriage.

Because motherhood fulfills important biological and social sex roles in a woman, it constitutes a source of considerable ego satisfaction that tends to place pregnancy and its successful culmination in a very favorable anticipatory light. It enables her to prove her biological adequacy and to achieve parity with other women (Schopbach et al, 1952), to satisfy an unconscious desire for immortality (Deutsch, 1944), to avoid the cultural reproach of sterility (Deutsch, 1944), and to look forward to a companion whose personality she can mold. It is no wonder then that pregnancy is a period of pride, exhilaration, and increased zest for many women and is regarded as the beginning of a rewarding and challenging experience (Jersild *et al*, 1949). Nevertheless, even for the normal woman who looks forward with enthusiasm to motherhood, pregnancy gives rise to many stresses and tensions; and for the woman who is emotionally unstable or who abhors the prospect of maternity, it is a period of genuine crisis.

How a woman will respond to the stresses and strains of pregnancy is naturally a function of the personality structure she brings with her into this experience. It is reasonable to expect a continuation of the same level of adjustment and of the same type of adjustive devices that prevailed prior to this time. Hence, pregnancy may be regarded as a period of more or less stress that tests the adequacy of the prepregnancy personality rather than as a discontinuously new and unpredictable cause of behavior disorder. Deviant psychological reactions to pregnancy are seldom unheralded in the past history of the expectant mother (Bibring, Dwyer and others, 1961; Harvey and Sherfey, 1954; Schopbach *et al*, 1952; Victoroff, 1952).

Sources of Tension during Pregnancy. Counteracting the more positive motivations and wholesome attitudes regarding pregnancy and maternity are numerous other factors that make for tension and conflict. The social stigma attached to sterility (the blame for which is almost invariably placed on the woman) may be great enough to coerce a woman into a pregnancy for which she is not quite ready or create undue apprehension about its successful outcome. A comparable type of unwholesome situation exists when pregnancy is perceived as necessary to retain the husband's affection or to rescue a faltering marriage. Under such circumstances the felt need for pregnancy may be sufficiently intense to precipitate pseudocyesis, a hysterical condition in which a non-pregnant woman believes she is pregnant and presents such characteristic signs and symptoms of pregnancy as cessation of menses, morning sickness, sensation of fetal movements, enlargement of breasts, uterus and abdomen, and labor pains (Parks, 1949; Schopbach *et al*, 1952). In instances where a woman has doubts about remaining married to her husband, pregnancy often carries implications of finality and is, therefore, resented for restricting her freedom of decision.

Even in the absence of unusual pressures, expectant motherhood has its characteristic hazards and adjustive difficulties. For every woman there is always the statistical possibility of protracted illness, disability, and death in connection with childbirth; of abortion or fetal death; of giving birth to a monster or an idiot, to a deformed infant or a child with a dread hereditary disease (Thompson, 1942). All pregnant women have to face the ordeal of labor and delivery—both the genuine, tissue sources of pain and the emotional sources derived from fearful anticipation of these events as they are represented in the embroidered tradition of folklore. For prudish women there is the additional shame and humiliation of exposure before physicians and nurses and of discussing signs and symptoms of an intimate bodily nature (Thompson, 1942). Motherhood invariably brings new duties and responsibilities, the curtailment of personal freedom, and limited opportunities for enjoying rest, relaxation, and leisure-time activities. In many instances it creates serious financial difficulties* and interrupts or even ends a woman's vocational career. As a matter of fact, in terms of the practical and emotional readjustments involved, parenthood makes more of a difference than marriage in the lives and daily routine of most persons.

Expectant motherhood may also reactivate latent conflicts and guilt feelings that a woman experiences in the course of her relationship with her own mother (Deutsch, 1944; 1949). It signifies the expression of emotional independence and the enactment of a mature adult role that is directed toward the establishment of new primary attachments. Hence it carries implications of disloyalty and threatens the dependency ties of an over-dependent woman to her own parents; whereas in the case of women who are still resentful of their parents' former authority, the same situation provides a consummate opportunity for self-assertion. This latter motivation plus the desire to inflict punishment on the parents are often found in cases of repeated illegitimate pregnancy (Bowlby, 1966; Cappon, 1954; Clifford, 1962). The stigma attached to such pregnancy in our culture commonly leads to acute anxiety, shame, guilt, and resentment, culminating frequently in self-induced or illegally committed abortion, infanticide, suicide, hysterical denial of pregnancy, or psychotic states (Parks, 1949).

The most serious types of disturbed psychological reactions to pregnancy (persistent vomiting and gestational psychosis) occur in women who by virtue of personality structure are strongly predisposed to regard prospective motherhood with apprehension, anxiety, ambivalence, or outright rejection (Brekstad, 1966; Davids et al, 1963; Osterkamp & Sands, 1962; Ottinger and Simmons, 1964; Singer et al, 1968). The characteristic symptoms of these syndromes (e.g., vomiting, denial of or amnesia for the act of parturition, delusions of infant death, fear of or projection of own homicidal impulses onto the child, and over-solicitude are generally interpreted as reflective of extreme disinclination for motherhood (Cappon, 1954; Davids et al, 1963; Ferreira, 1960; Harvey et al, 1954; Osterkamp, 1962; Parks, 1949; Victoroff, 1952). Psychiatric study shows that one or more of the following personality trends underlie such reactions: (a) narcissistic self-preoccupation, (b) resentful rejection of the feminine role in life as incompatible with basic ego aspira-

---

*That reluctance for children in marriage is less often a function of actual financial incapacity than of social class values, competing vocational ambitions, and high standards of what constitutes an acceptable minimal family income is shown by the inverse relationship between socioeconomic status and number of children in the family.

tions, (c) an immature attitude of passive irresponsibility and parasitic dependence on others, and (d) feelings of anxiety and depression stemming from lack of self-confidence in handling the anticipated responsibilities of motherhood (Cappon, 1954; Deutsch, 1949; Harvey *et al*, 1954; Parks, 1949; Victoroff, 1952).

Reactions to Childbirth

A woman's anticipations of and actual experiences during childbirth are, of course, determined in part by the actual content of the three stages of labor (uterine contractions and dilation of the cervix, expulsion of the fetus, delivery of the afterbirth).* In large measure, however, it is also influenced by culturally determined concepts and practices of childbirth. The intensity of pain experience, for example, depends in part on the degree of threat perceived in a given situation and on the degree of emotional response made to such threat. Hence, in accordance with the traditions in their culture, women react to the same physiological experience of childbirth in a large variety of ways. At one extreme, childbirth is accepted very casually; expectant mothers work in the fields until active labor begins, are unattended throughout, sever the umbilical cord by themselves, walk home with the infant immediately after delivery, and then go about their daily routines. At the other extreme, as in our culture, pregnancy has more or less the status of a debilitating disease, childbirth is regarded as an excruciatingly painful ordeal and as a hospital or quasisurgical procedure, and elaborate prenatal and postnatal measures are observed.

In recent years a new concept of "natural childbirth" has arisen in obstetrical practice (Goodrich, 1950; Mandy, 1952; Read, 1953; Thomas, 1950). It is based on the premise that pregnancy and childbirth can be made less fearsome and more emotionally satisfying experiences by counteracting cultural factors that heighten the *emotional* determinants of pain and discomfort. Despite popular misconceptions to the contrary, no claim is made that labor and delivery are "naturally" free of all pain and discomfort, or that the latter experiences are *entirely* emotional in origin. It is pointed out, however, that the tissue basis of pain is enhanced tremendously by such culturally derived sources of fear as anxious anticipation of unbearable pain, lack of knowledge of what to expect in the course of labor and delivery (due to ignorance of the underlying anatomy and physiology and of hospital routines), isolation of the "patient" from others in the delivery room, the absence of opportunity to explore her fears with informed persons, and the conspiracy of silence surrounding her condition and progress during labor.

Such experience naturally varies in duration and severity depending on the size and position of the fetus; pelvic dimensions; condition of uterine, perineal and abdominal musculature and of other soft parts; parity of the mother, etc.

These emotional components of fear are combatted psychologically by an appropriate program of education during pregnancy, by the continuous attendance of and sympathetic reassurance from trained personnel throughout labor, and by keeping the patient informed of her progress. The pain and discomfort of pregnancy and labor are also reduced by an adjunctive program of breathing control, muscular relaxation, and exercises that relieve the postural backache of pregnancy and strengthen the abdominal muscles for pushing during the second and third stages of labor. These procedures generally make it possible for the obstetrician to eliminate entirely, or to reduce considerably, the need for anesthesia or analgesia during labor. As a result, although consciousness during delivery is not necessary for the success of this method, it is often achievable, thereby eliminating amnesia for the experience of childbirth and allowing the woman to cooperate more actively. She is able to enjoy the exhiliaration that comes from immediate and first-hand knowledge that partly through her own efforts her pregnancy has been brought to a successful conclusion.

Initial Maternal Behavior

The nature of early maternal behavior in the human female is still a highly unsettled and controversial matter. The once fashionable notion of "maternal instinct," either in the sense of an innately determined "drive" or of a ready-made pattern of complex behavior inevitably released at childbirth, has long since fallen into disrepute—even for explaining the post-pregnancy behavior of infrahuman mammals (Hamburg & Lunde, 1966). Tremendous variability from one culture to another in the basic characteristics of the mother's early behavior toward her offspring demonstrates quite unequivocally that social variables determine in large measure both the genesis and intensity of maternal drive and the specific content of maternal behavior (D'Andrade, 1966). Nevertheless, despite widespread belief to the contrary, this does not mean that culture is the *only* determining variable. Physiological, personality, experiential, and situational factors all play supportive and sometimes extremely significant roles; and in the case of the first two variables mentioned, genes (both "phylogenetic" and "ontogenetic") are also regulatory factors.

Physiological Aspects and Lactation. The relationships between maternal behavior and lactation are complex indeed. Both phenomena are determined in part by the same physiological factors. Lactation occurs in the general context of and probably enhances maternal behavior. Positive attitudes toward breast feeding correlate with the ability to produce milk for breast-feeding infants (Newton, 1968). Mothers who breast-feed consider the baby happier with the breast, while bottle-feeding mothers appear to be influenced by such values as convenience, freedom, and appearance (Brown, Liberman,

Winston and Pleshette, 1960). The ability of the mother to lactate can also be influenced by cultural attitudes (Newton, 1968).

The breasts of non-pregnant women do not ordinarily contain sufficient glandular tissue to make lactation anatomically possible. During pregnancy, however, this defect is remedied as estrogens and progesterone, secreted by the placenta, act as priming agents stimulating the necessary tissue growth. Thus, by the end of pregnancy, the breasts are able to produce milk when stimulated adequately by prolactin, a hormone secreted by the anterior pituitary. Nevertheless, because of the inhibitory influence of high blood levels of estrogen and progesterone on the secretory *function* of the breast, lactation does not occur until about 24 hours after birth, when removal of the placenta allows the blood levels of these hormones to fall.* If the infant is placed at the breast immediately after birth, his sucking may help stimulate later milk flow, but at the time he obtains colostrum, not milk.

In addition to stimulating lactation, prolactin also tends to lower the threshold for the elicitation and acquisition of maternal attitudes and behavior. That is, it facilitates the release of maternal tendencies and responses that have already been acquired by cultural indoctrination or actual experience, as well as facilitates the elaboration of maternal responses from initial bodily and suctorial contacts. It does not establish by itself any recognizable pattern of maternal behavior (Schneirla, 1951). The breast-feeding situation in turn leads to such mutually stimulative and tension-relieving effects as the provision of bodily warmth, the satisfaction of hunger, and the reduction of mammary gland engorgement. In infrahuman mammals this constitutes a nucleus of highly rewarding behavior, in part reflexly and physiologically determined, which under the influence of prolactin facilitation can be expanded into a more complex pattern of learned maternal responses (Leuba, 1954; Schneirla, 1951). At the human level, the satisfying experiences associated with breast feeding undoubtedly reinforce existing, and promote the acquisition of new, maternal dispositions; but because human maternal tendencies and practices are part of the cultural heritage and do not have to be fashioned anew by each individual from personal learning experience superimposed upon more or less inevitable tactual-suctorial mother-child interactions, their acquisition is not dependent upon the latter core of experiences.

Since prolactin is a common determinant of both lactation and maternal attitude, and since the breast-feeding situation probably enhances maternal responsiveness, it is hardly surprising that women who are judged as more motherly in attitude also produce more milk (Newton, 1950, 1968). It is

---

Sometimes even the infant himself secretes milk since his breasts may be both enlarged from prenatal exposure to placental hormones and functionally stimulated by removal from these hormones at birth.

unjustifiable, however, to conclude from this positive relationship that motherliness necessarily increases milk flow, although it may obviously influence disposition (rather than ability) to continue breast-feeding.

Other Determinants. Cultural standards and concepts of maternal role crucially influence the development of the mother's attitudes toward the neonate. Such standards of what constitutes appropriately maternal attitudes, duties, functions, and responsibilities are related in turn to more general moral and religious values in the culture and to the cultural valuation of children and of child rearing. In certain extreme instances they even provide moral sanction for such apparently unmaternal practices as infanticide and child barter (Klineberg, 1935). Although some intracultural variability does prevail in these latter practices, and in the extent to which consanguinity (i.e., biological motherhood as opposed to adoption) is regarded as important for the development of maternal feelings, most of the variance in the expression of such behavior seems to be inter- rather than intracultural.

In most aspects of maternal behavior, however, considerable intracultural variability is the rule. The perceived cultural norm constitutes the ideological core of the individual's maternal value system, but this core is modified substantially by personality and idiosyncratic experiential factors; and in the actual expression of maternal behavior, the situational and physiological considerations operative at the moment must also be taken into account (Newton, 1968). A woman's first concept of motherhood is based upon her perceptions as a child and upon her *own* mother's behavior. In accordance with her affective reaction to these perceptions and memories—matter-of-fact acceptance, idealization, or rejection—she tends to impart to different components of the cultural prescription her own peculiar emphases and personal flavor. Motherliness, to a certain extent, is also a reflection of a constellation of temperamental traits bearing on the individual's capacity for bestowing affection, tenderness, and solicitude on a helpless creature who is dependent on her. Since it is positively correlated with duration of menstrual flow (Levy, 1942), these traits are probably determined in part by level of estrogenic secretion, as well as by other genic and experiential factors. Their expression is also undoubtedly influenced by such ego-related personality traits as level of ego aspiration, acceptance of feminine role in life, tendency toward narcissistic self-preoccupation, level of anxiety, feelings of adequacy, notions of volitional and executive independence, ability to postpone hedonistic self-indulgence, and sense of moral responsibility. Depending on the strength of some of the latter trends, the infant will be accepted warmly for his own sake, rejected as a nuisance or as a barrier to the mother's vocational career, overprotected, or regarded as a potential source of vicarious ego aggrandizement. Women with pronounced anxiety reactions and attitudes of rejection toward motherhood not only tend to have more physical and emotional symptoms of maladjustment during pregnancy and delivery, but also experience more difficulty in adjusting psychologically to their newborn infants (Osterkamp *et al*, 1962; Zemlick & Watson, 1953).

Numerous situational factors also impinge on the evolution of maternal behavior from the moment the child is born. Absence of breast feeding deprives the mother of the initial reinforcement of maternal impulses that this satisfying, tension-relieving experience ordinarily effects. Isolation of the infant in the hospital nursery may leave her with a sense of strangeness and remoteness about the reality of her relationship to him, and may generate overwhelming feelings of apprehension or inadequacy about her ability to cope with the routines of child care when she is home on her own with no immediate source of help or advice (Escalona, 1950; Newton, 1968). In addition, upon arriving home from the hospital she must face again the countless household responsibilities from which she had been given a temporary respite, as well as satisfy other demands on her affectional resources. The emotional needs of her husband and other children must somehow be integrated with her care of the newcomer—otherwise he may be justifiably regarded as an intruder and become an object of resentment. Then too, she has her own dependency needs as a wife and as a person who has just passed through what the culture generally regards as a harrowing, crisis-like experience in her life (Escalona, 1950). She wants to receive emotional support as well as extend it, to lean on others, and to be relieved of some of the responsibility of caring for her child. Because she feels entitled to some self-indulgence she may resent the actual or perceived unwillingness of relatives to shoulder part of her new burdens (Escalona, 1950). If her family situation is essentially wholesome, such problems are inevitably resolved in the course of time. If, on the other hand, it is beset by marital discord, these problems tend to become worse, to aggravate existing relationships with her husband, and eventually to involve the child as a pawn, a scapegoat, a compensatory source of affection, or an object of competition between his parents.

An integral part of the immediate situation shaping the mother's early attitudes toward the neonate emanates from the latter himself. His very helplessness is, in a sense, his greatest ally, but his apparent fragility may also constitute a source of considerable maternal anxiety. He also helps or hinders his own cause, as the case may be, depending on whether his sex and general appearance conform to what had been desired and anticipated. Because of the mother's lack of sophistication about infant care, or her susceptibility to the more morbid insinuations of baby folklore, she may become unduly alarmed about such natural occurrences as startle reactions or the shallowness of his breathing (Escalona, 1950). For similar reasons she may exaggerate the hazards of bathing and the dangers of suffocation, or blame herself un-reasonably about her inability to interpret the uninterpretable and predict the unpredictable, i.e., the significance of and the reason for all of his crying (Escalona, 1950).

In conclusion, therefore, it seems likely that cultural factors furnish the substantive and ideological core from which maternal attitudes are fashioned, and account for both some major intercultural uniformities as well as some conspicuous intercultural differences. Within a given culture, variability in maternal attitudes is related to idiosyncratic individual experience, to temperamental, physiologically-determined, and ego-related personality traits influencing motherliness, and to specific situational factors emanating from the marital and family situations, from the lying-in experience, and from the infant himself. In all cultures hormonal variables facilitate the expression of existing maternal dispositions, determine ability to lactate, and indirectly provide reinforcement for maternal behavior through the tension-relieving properties of the breast-feeding situation. However, neither hormonal facili-tation nor the nursing situation necessarily insures the development of maternal behavior in the human female; and evidence from the child-rearing behavior of foster mothers, and from fathers generally, indicates that psycho-logical parenthood is possible without the facilitating influence of hormones, breast feeding, or the notion of consanguinity.

THE BIRTH PROCESS

Birth represents a transition from a parasitic type of sheltered existence in a relatively invariable environment to a physiologically autonomous ex-istence in a less protected and highly variable environment. During the course of less than a day, the fetus is catapulted from a restricted fluid world of constant warmth, darkness, and muffled sounds to a vastly expanded world of air, light, noise, taste, smell, and temperature, as well as ever-present contact with stimuli outside himself. He is suddenly required to obtain his own oxygen, ingest and digest his own food, excrete his own wastes, and regulate his own temperature. Hence, many organ systems and sense modalities, although capable of functioning at an earlier date, are first brought into actual use at this time, thereby facing an initial period of adaptation before they can operate efficiently. Another group of organ sys-tems and sensory mechanisms, on the other hand, (e.g., cardiovascular, endocrine, neuromuscular, vestibular) have already been functioning effectively for some time and merely undergo varying degrees of adjustment to changed conditions of life.

Major Physiological Changes*

Respiration. The sudden need for obtaining his own oxygen supply at birth makes the inauguration of functional respiration a critical condition for the continued survival of the neonate. More than half of all natal deaths are attributable to asphyxiation (Block *et al*, 1942). At least five to ten per cent of newborn infants have difficulty establishing respiration after birth, and an unknown number have been exposed to oxygen reduction during fetal life (Graham, Caldwell, Ernhart, Pennoy & Hartmann, 1957). After some pre-liminary gasping, breathing movements become strong enough for the first time to inflate the lungs and permit oxygen to pass from the pulmonary air spaces to the infant's blood stream (Pratt, 1954). They are initiated both (a) by cutaneous and thermal stimulation from the environment, and (b) by the humoral stimulation of the medullary respiratory center that results when disturbance of the placental circulation during delivery increases the carbon dioxide content of fetal blood. The first functional inspiration is accompanied by mechanical stimulation of the vocal cords, causing them to vibrate. This is the physiological basis of the well-known "birth cry" which marks so dramatically the onset of the infant's career as a physiologically autonomous organism. At birth respirations are mostly of the abdominal type, and even during sleep average about thirty-two per minute as compared to twenty in the adult (Halverson, 1941).

The change from fetal to natal respiration also happens to be adaptive at this time because the former method is not adequate for the full-term fetus' intracellular tissue needs. As embryonic tissue becomes more mature it shifts to a more aerobic type of respiration in which a greater percentage of the source of energy (glucose) is oxidized completely into carbon dioxide and water rather than being converted to an intermediary product such as lactic acid. Although this results in a more economical utilization of glucose and makes possible a reduction in caloric intake per pound of body weight, it necessitates an increase in oxygen supply. During the last few weeks of prenatal life, however, the amount of oxygen available from the placental circulation becomes insufficient to satisfy these increased demands, leading to severe anoxia if pregnancy is prolonged beyond term (Clifford, 1954). The high mortality rate in post-mature infants may be a result of this oxygen deficit (Zwerdling, in press). To compensate in part for the relatively low oxygen tension, the number of circulating red blood corpuscles increases. After birth, when the oxygen supply is adequate again, the additional red cells are no longer needed and are destroyed releasing a rich supply of iron

---

*A detailed description of recent research methods applied to the psychophysiology of infancy may be found in Lipton and Steinschneider (1964).

for future use and sometimes sufficient bile pigment (bilirubin) to create a mild, temporary condition of jaundice.

Circulation. The two major cardiovascular changes at birth are (a) termination of the placental circulation that links maternal and fetal blood systems, and (b) obliteration of the shunts that channel fetal blood away from the lungs. In prenatal life, since fetal oxygen requirements are taken care of by the mother, and since the lungs in any case contain no air, pulmonary circulation of blood is unnecessary and is by-passed by means of two shunts that divert venous blood directly from the right side of the heart into the systemic circulation. At birth, when the fetus is obliged to oxygenate his own blood and the lungs are inflated with air, these shunts are obliterated and pulmonary circulation commences (Gairdner, 1958). The trend toward increased cardiac output that begins in prenatal life (Vallbona, Desmond and others, 1963) continues after birth and is reflected in a progressively increasing blood pressure and decreasing pulse rate. Neonatal pulse rate is approximately twice as rapid as that of the adult, and blood pressure is correspondingly only half as high as the adult (Halverson, 1941).

Nutrition and Excretion. For all practical purposes, ingestion and digestion of food occur for the first time after birth when nutritive elements are no longer available to the infant from the mother's blood stream. Prior evidence of gastrointestinal activity, such as fetal stools, is attributable to the swallowing of amniotic fluid. Neonatal stomach contractions tend to be more vigorous than in the adult and to occur about three hours after nursing despite the fact that the stomach takes four to five hours to empty (Pratt, 1954). Emptiness of the stomach, therefore, does not seem to be essential for gastric contractions; and as we shall see later, gastric contractions, themselves, are not the only determinants of hunger. The neonate typically loses weight during the first few days of life but tends to regain his birth weight by the end of the first week. The weight loss is probably a reflection of dehydration due to initial restriction of fluid intake and inefficient absorption of what fluid is ingested.* The kidneys also become functional at this time since nitrogenous wastes can no longer be disposed of through the placental circulation. In the total absence of sphincter control it is not surprising that an average of nineteen urinations and four to five defecations occur in the course of a day (Halverson, 1940).

Physical Trauma

Even normal uncomplicated birth is a prolonged and violent phenomenon. It involves much pushing and squeezing through extremely narrow quarters

As fluid intake increases, some of the initial, extreme dehydration (and weight loss) is reversed. In general, however, gradual but progressive dehydration of the tissues is a regular concomitant of the aging process.

and a sudden drastic change in environment and in basic physiological processes. Yet there is no reason to believe that it ordinarily exceeds the infant's capacity for withstanding stress or that it leaves lasting consequences. Instances of prolonged and difficult labor, however, (especially where forceps are applied high in the birth canal) are quite another matter. Asphyxia is a common complication under these circumstances, and such serious injuries as skull fracture, intracranial hemorrhage, and cerebral laceration may result. Anoxia appears to be correlated with later complications such as hyperexcitability (Honzik, Hutchings and Burnip, 1965, Ucko, 1965), lower developmental quotient scores in the first two years (Stechler, 1964), perceptual and psychomotor defects (Corah, Anthony and others, 1965; Wunderlin & McPherson, 1962), and schizophrenia (Taft & Goldfarb, 1964). Intracranial injury may lead to convulsive disorders, cerebral palsy, and mental retardation (Doll, 1946; McKhann, Belnap and Beck, 1951; Malzberg, 1950; Sugawara, 1965). Less serious consequences, such as loss in auditory acuity (Pratt, 1954), disturbed osseous growth (Sontag and Harris, 1938), slower breathing (Prechtl, 1963), and less initial activity following birth (McGrade, Kessen & Leutzendorf, 1965), may occur in cases of difficult and protracted labor in which no obvious signs of injury or dysfunction are present at birth.

The possibility also exists that mild degrees of cerebral damage due to birth complications may have a delayed effect in later years. For example, the behavior disorders of children with a history of birth complication tend to be characterized by hyperirritability and general psycho-motor problems (Goussis, 1958; Honzik, Hutchings & Burnip, 1965; Klatsin, McGarry & Steward, 1966; Schroeder, 1929; Wile & Davis, 1941); and in monozygotic twins suffering from mental disease, the member of a twin pair with the more serious form of the disorder is more likely to have had the more difficult birth experience (Slater, 1953). Drugs and medication given for birth complications appear to lower the child's attention level (Stechler, 1964). Medication administered to the mother appears to affect the child; the chronic use of opiates by mothers is associated with congenital narcotic addiction in babies (Cobrinik, Hood & Chusid, 1959).

Lest the significance of physical trauma at birth be exaggerated, the foregoing facts should be qualified by the following considerations: First, the vast majority of deliveries are not unduly protracted or difficult and fall well within the infant's capacity for withstanding trauma. Second, many of the typical manifestations of birth injury may also be caused by other, entirely unrelated conditions. For example, marked vitamin K deficiency in the mother may give rise to intracranial hemorrhage in the fetus, hereditary cerebral agenesis is responsible for much cerebral palsy, and nuclear jaundice (associated with incompatibility of the Rh factor) results in varying degrees of spasticity. Lastly, even in these instances in which labor and delivery are unduly difficult, other predisposing factors such as prematurity or genic susceptibility to disease may be operative. If this were not the case, all children exposed to a given degree of birth trauma would be adversely affected by it.

Psychological Trauma

Less credible than the possibility of physical trauma at birth are the metaphysical claims of psychological birth trauma advanced by the psychoanalytic school. It is alleged that uterine existence is experienced as a paradisaic state in which the fetus shares a mystical and undefined "oneness" with the mother; that a nostalgic desire for return to the serenity of the womb pervades behavior until death; that birth is catastrophically traumatic because it interrupts the Nirvana-like bliss and separates the child from unity with his mother; and that the "helplessness" and "insecurity" experienced as a result of the separation constitute the primal basis for and the prototype of all later anxiety (Freud, 1936). Clinical "evidence" of the reality of these feelings, desires, and reactions is even brought forward from the dreams of adult patients (Fodor, 1949).

It hardly needs to be pointed out that before an individual could conceivably appreciate the blissfulness of the womb, enjoy "oneness" with the mother, or react traumatically to the implications of separation, he would first require a varied background of experience, much cognitive sophistication, and the speculative abilities and proclivities of a philosopher. Life in the uterus might appear very attractive to a battle-weary and philosophically minded veteran of life. Unfortunately, however, the neonate has neither the experiential perspective nor the intellectual equipment to enjoy his alleged good fortune. As is true of the vaunted "peace of the grave," prenatal existence could be enjoyable indeed—*if* only the necessary sensibilities for enjoyment were available. Furthermore, reactions of helplessness, insecurity, and anxiety presuppose that the neonate possesses functional concepts of self and self-esteem, appreciates his own executive incompetence, is mature enough to feel threatened, and is able to think in terms of the future. As we shall see later (see Chapter 12), unequivocal evidence for even the much simpler emotion of fear is not present before the fifth month of life.

MATURITY AT BIRTH

Because of variability in the length of gestation and in the rate of prenatal development, children naturally vary in degree of maturity at birth. Although the precise duration of the gestational period can never be ascertained for a particular child (see p. 176), the *mean* length of gestation is estimated to be 280 days, with an upper limit of 334 and lower limit of 180 days (Carmichael,

1954). The lower limit is set by the age of viability and corresponds to the minimal degree of structural and functional maturity necessary to sustain life outside the uterus; in accordance with the generally observed "margin of safety" characterizing most biological processes, this occurs well in advance of the age at which parturition typically takes place. The upper limit is set by the inability of the placenta to satisfy increased fetal needs for food and oxygen, especially in the wake of degenerative changes that develop after full-term. Approximately one-third of all postmature infants fail to survive if the mother is primiparous and over 26 years of age (Clifford, 1954).

In actual practice when we refer to "prematurely born" infants, what we actually mean is that they are "immature" (Drillien, 1964). The commonly employed criterion of prematurity is not reduced length of gestation (which can only be estimated), but developmental status inferior to that of a full-term infant. Such immaturity, of course, could be caused by slow rate of development as well as by delivery prior to term. Since the characteristics and management of this condition are the same irrespective of the cause, it is not too important to make the distinction provided that "immaturely-born" is understood when the conventionally accepted term "prematurely-born" is used.

The Prematurely Born Infant*

Prematurely born infants constitute five to ten per cent of all live births (Arey and Dent, 1950). With very few exceptions viability is not possible prior to 26 weeks of age or under a birth weight of two and one-half pounds. Thereafter, if special care is provided, such infants may be kept alive, their chances of survival varying directly with weight and gestational age (Knobloch & Pasamanick, 1966; Wiener et al, 1965). Prematurity is associated with unwed motherhood, primiparity, and advanced age of the mother (Drillien & Ellis, 1964; Montagu, 1962; Shirley, 1938b); with maternal rubella, congenital syphillis, and incompatibility of the Rh factor (Arey & Dent, 1959); with congenital anomalies of the fetus such as anencephaly (Arey & Dent, 1959); and with inadequate maternal nutrition (Ebbs et al, 1942; Weiner, 1962). For the latter reason the incidence is higher among Negroes and lower socioeconomic groups (Block et al, 1942; Braine et al, 1966; Kagan & Henker, 1966; Knobloch & Pasamanick, 1966; Pasamanick & Knobloch,

---

*No attempt will be made here to discuss in detail the vast literature on prematurity and its complications. Reviews are available (Kagan & Henker 1966; Weiner, 1962). The following references are not quoted in the text but are pertinent to the subject of prematurity. Bell, Taylor & Dockrell, 1965; Caplan et al., 1963; Cavanaugh et al., 1957; Crosse, 1961; Crump, Gore & Horton, 1958; De Hirsch, Jansky & Langford, 1966; Izmozi, 1963; McDonald, 1966; Oppe, 1960; Parmelee, 1963; Rossier, 1962; Rothschild, 1967; Silverman, Fertig, & Berger, 1958; Wortis, Heimr, Braine, Redlo & Rue, 1963; Wortis & Freedman, 1965; Zapella, 1963.

1966; Robinson & Robinson, 1965). In general, premature infants have a greater susceptibility to physiological and anatomical anomalies (Braine *et al*, 1966; Cutler, Heimer, Wortis & Freedman, 1965; Kagan *et al*, 1966; Robinson & Robinson, 1965). As might be expected, the mortality rate among prematurely born infants is exceedingly high because of their susceptibility to asphyxia and intracranial hemorrhage. Birth trauma is less important here than immaturity of the respiratory center, capillary fragility, and softness of the skull and brain. Prematurity is a causal factor in more than half of all neonatal deaths (Arey & Dent, 1950).

Characteristics. From the standpoint of response capacities, the viable, prematurely born infant is relatively well developed. All of the discrete responses of the full-term infant are elicitable, but level of general activity is lower and the more recently acquired responses tend to be rudimentary in nature. Thus, his respirations are shallow, his cry is weak, and he is unable to suck and swallow well or to regulate his body temperature efficiently. For reasons already indicated (see p. 182), his sensory status, except for vision, does not compare unfavorably with that of the full-term infant at birth (because he is one to three months younger) and he is more highly developed nine months after conception than is the latter because of exposure to the more stimulating environment outside the uterus during the last few months of this period.

The actual diagnosis of prematurity is made on the basis of various physical signs, the most important of which is birth weight under five and one-half pounds. Other physical criteria include softness of the cartilages of the nose, absence of centers of ossification in the lower extremities, crown-rump length less than 32 cm, head circumference less than 33 cm., scalp hairs shorter than 2 cm., and characteristic posture, limb movements, reflexes, and muscle tone (Dawkins & MacGregor, 1965; Ellis, 1951).

Special Care. The prematurely born infant requires a special environment designed to compensate for his adaptive immaturity and to satisfy his distinctive metabolic needs. Because of his poor temperature control and precarious breathing, a constant, warm atmosphere high in oxygen and low in humidity is necessary. He must be spoon-fed because of inadequate sucking and swallowing responses. Unlike the full-term infant, his relatively anaerobic intracellular oxidation requires a daily caloric intake of 120 rather than 45 calories per pound. His diet should be rich in calcium and vitamins C and D because ossification of bone normally begins in the last two months of prenatal development; and since he does not experience the typical compensatory increase in red blood corpuscles in the latter weeks of intrauterine life (followed by their destruction after birth with release of iron), he is more dependent upon dietary sources of iron.

Later Development. Prematurely born infants normally experience retardation. primarily in the postural, locomotor, and manipulative areas. The effects of retardation appear to be a function of the extent of the prematurity. Thus moderately premature infants, as opposed to extreme prematures and normal infants, are more gregarious, exhibitionistic, and aggressive between the fifth and seventh years (Koch, 1964). Prematurity at birth is correlated with various later complications such as hyperactivity, excessive distractibility, hypersensitivity to sound, impaired intellectual capacities, personality disturbance, cerebral palsy, visual defect, and reading deficiencies (Braine et al, 1966; Cutler et al, 1965; Drillien, 1964; Hirschi, Levy & Litvak, 1948; Knobloch & Pasamanick, 1966; Lubchenco, Horner and others, 1963; Moore, 1965; Shirley, 1938, 1939; Wiener et al, 1965). Some of these symptoms (e.g., hyperirritability, hyperactivity, distractibility) point to the possibility of mild but diffuse brain injury at birth.

CHAPTER 7

Neonatal and Early-Infant Behavior and Capacities*

THE NEONATAL PERIOD is generally regarded as comprising the first two weeks or month of postnatal life. It is a transitional phase of physiological and psychological adaptation from a parasitic fetal to a more autonomous post-embryonic existence. In most respects the study of the neonate merely carries us one continuous step beyond the fetus in the search for antecedents of behavior. No new organic developments take place, essentially no new sensory or response capacities emerge, and subcortical centers continue to dominate behavioral activity (McGraw, 1943; Milner, 1967; Peiper, 1963; Saint-Anne Dargassies, 1960). The principal change is in exposure to a new environmental milieu which requires the exercise of latent vegetative capacities, and provides more frequent and adequate stimulation and greater freedom of movement for the activation of available but hitherto unused or little used sensori-motor functions (Kessen, 1963; Pratt, 1954). The demonstration of competence in some of these sensori-motor functions in the neonate has moved the area of infant research away from purely *tabula rasa* interpretations of infant development (Kessen, 1963; Lipsitt, 1966).

Nevertheless, despite this exposure to a richer and more variable environment, genic factors play, as they did in prenatal life a rather prepotent role in the regulation of development. The most essential neurological difference between newborn and adult will gradually be compensated for in the course of the first year of life, as the location of the functional centers switches from the pallidum to the cerebral hemispheres (Peiper, 1963). The observation that the rate of early development appears to be inversely proportional to the eventual complexity and degree of cortically controlled behavior partially explains why the period of subcortical dominance is more prolonged in human infancy than in the infancy of any other species (Hofstaetter, 1951).

In some respects the behavior of neonates may be studied with greater facility than the behavior of older infants and children. Experimental backgrounds are more nearly equal, the current environment is more restricted

---

The tremendous growth of research literature on neonatal and infant development necessitates a rather selective treatment in order to present a coherent picture of the area. Brackbill's (1967) handbook on infancy and early childhood is an excellent reference source. See also Brackbill and Thompson (1967); Foss (1961, 1963, 1966) and Peiper (1963).

and easier to control, differential social and interpersonal factors are minimal, and behavior is relatively simple and, therefore, more amenable to complete observation, description, and analysis. On the other hand, since the neonate is unable to verbalize his sensations, perceptions, and feelings, we are dependent upon inferences from behavior for clues about the subjective content of his experience (Lewis, 1967). This naturally opens the door wide to adultomorphic speculations concerning what is going on in infancy (Richmond, 1964). This situation has led to the use of more physiological methods in infant assessment (Lipton & Steinschneider, 1964; Richmond, 1964).

GENERAL APPEARANCE AND PHYSICAL CHARACTERISTICS

The first month of postnatal existence is by far the most dangerous period of life (Pasamanick & Knobloch, 1966). Reduction of neonatal mortality, particularly in the first few days has been substantially less over the past four decades than one might have anticipated from the dramatic lowering of infant mortality in general. This discrepancy, however, is not surprising when one considers that the effects of such factors as prematurity, birth injury, difficult labor, initial delay in respiration, congenital malformation, and genically determined susceptibility to stress are primarily reflected in the neonatal death rate (Pasamanick & Knobloch, 1966). It is true, of course, that the higher incidence of neonatal mortality among non-white groups in the United States suggests that some of these early deaths could be prevented by better prenatal care, by more careful management of labor, and by improved handling of the prematurely born (Pasamanick & Knobloch 1966).

The neonate's general appearance is by no means prepossessing. His head and eyes are disproportionately large and his trunk and limbs disproportionately small in relation to later childhood standards. As a result of "molding" of the skull bones and subcutaneous swelling or hemorrhage (due to pressure contact in passing through the narrow birth canal) his head may be misshapen. Not the least disappointing to an unprepared mother is the red, wrinkled, and ill-fitting skin covered with a cheesy substance. Fortunately at this point positive maternal attitudes are facilitated by the secretion of prolactin.

Mean weight at birth is between seven and seven and one-half pounds and mean length is 20 inches (Landreth, 1967). Consistent average differences prevail between various racial and ethnic groups (Meredith, 1963). Male infants are slightly heavier and larger in all bodily dimensions (Cates and Goodwin, 1936; Garn, 1966; Singer, Westphal & Niswander, 1968), and first-born infants tend to be smaller at birth than the infants they precede in birth order, although this relationship is reversed in later childhood

(Meredith, 1950). Probably because birth weight and size are affected by poor maternal health and nutrition, infants from lower socioeconomic levels tend to be smaller and lighter at birth.

BEHAVIORAL ORGANIZATION AT BIRTH

The organization of behavior in the neonate is a reflection of organizational changes occurring during the preceding prenatal period. The distinction, which is quite apparent even in fetal behavior and development, between reflex and nonreflex activity (see pp. 207, and 209), becomes sharper after birth. Because of the conventional tendency to lump together all fetal and neonatal behavior (reflex and non-reflex) under the ambiguous term "response" (often used interchangeably with "reflex") incalculable conceptual confusion has arisen in the past. This looseness in terminology obscures basic differences in rate, patterning, and regulation of development, as well as the salient generalization that motor development as it is generally understood is an outgrowth of non-reflex activity.

Because individuation of reflex activity has almost reached completion, a large number of discrete reflexes may be elicited in the neonate. Individuation of nonreflex activity, of the type of behavior that will eventually be voluntary and cortically controlled, has first begun. It is characterized by much diffuse mass activity and by relatively little and only partially localized specific movements. Hence, until more precise control of these latter movements is attained, much integrated whole behavior on a non-reflex basis cannot be expected; most of the integrated behavior displayed by the neonate consists of coordinated reflexes. Thus, the general picture of neonatal behavioral organization is epitomized by the striking contrast between the highly developed segmental and coordinated reflexes regulated by spinal and subcortical centers and the relatively diffuse, amorphous non-reflex responses that have yet to be brought under efficient cortical control.

Non-Reflex Behavior

Mass Activity. Although a number of reflexes can be discerned at birth, many investigators of neonatal development have been impressed by the amount of apparently unintegrated, diffuse, non-reflex behavior (Gordon & Bell, 1961). These diffuse behaviors, which are differentiated from reflexes, have been given the label mass activity (Irwin, 1930). This type of behavior tends to increase in quantity during the first ten days of life (Irwin, 1930). Most observers attribute it to the absence of the degree of cortical inhibition and control that is necessary both for precise and directed specific movements on a non-reflex level and for integration and coordination of such movements into more complex patterns (Irwin, 1930; Peiper, 1963; Pratt, 1954; Wolf, 1966).

Mass activity can be instigated by a variety of stimuli and consists of highly generalized and largely irrelevant movements (Pratt, 1954; Pratt, Nelson & Sun, 1930). The whole body or large parts of it are simultaneously involved. Head, trunk, hips, arms, legs, hands, feet, toes and fingers all are moving at once to the accompaniment of sucking or smacking movements of the lips or violent crying (Irwin, 1930). Although either internal or external stimuli may release mass activity, the greater part of it seems to be instigated by viscerogenic or humoral excitants, particularly those originating in or related to gastro-intestinal functions. This is evident from the intensification of general motility during bowel evacuation, intestinal disturbance, and regurgitation (Irwin, 1930), and from its progressive increase during the interval between feedings (Irwin, 1932b; Wolff, 1966). Intense, abrupt, prolonged, or noxious stimuli from without also increase mass activity (Crowell, 1967; Pratt, 1954), whereas mild external stimulation (such as provided by clothing, swaddling or moderate and continuous illumination or sound) tends to reduce it (Brackbill, Adams and others, 1966; Crowell, Yasaka & Crowell, 1964; Irwin & Weiss, 1934a, 1934b; Lipton, Stein-schneider & Richmond, 1960; 1965; Weiss, 1934), possibly by inhibiting vicerogenic excitation.

Full appraisal of the meaning of the apparently random and disorganized nature of mass activity demands consideration of contributing factors (other than lack of cortical control) that help determine its distinguishing properties. First, the extent to which responses are specific or generalized is partly a function of the intensity of stimulation involved; less intense stimuli tend to be associated with more specific movements (Delman, 1935). Thus, some of the wide spatial dispersion of mass activity must certainly be attributed to the intensity ordinarily characterizing visceral stimulation. Second, since such stimulation tends to be diffusely distributed (and is localized with difficulty even by adults), it is not surprising that (in the absence of reasons to the contrary) the responses thereto should be equally diffuse and irradiated. Third, general bodily activity is undoubtedly facilitated by the general lowering of *all* response thresholds caused by humoral factors operative during hunger and excitement. Fourth, limitations in the available data concerning correlates of mass activity make it difficult to trace individual origins. No relationships have been found thus far between motility and sex or race, body temperature, change in environmental temperature, physical measurements or nutritional status (Crowell, 1967). Nevertheless, individual differences in "activity level" present at birth persist up to two years (Thomas, Chess, Birch & Hertzig, 1960).

Finally, mass activity and specific movements are not to be considered as mutually exclusive or contradictory (Irwin, 1930). Reflective of some beginning progress toward individuation, mass activity is not completely disorganized but is characterized by a certain degree of patterning and by the inclusion of some segmental responses (Delman, 1935; Pratt, 1954). The fact that mass activity in the neonatal "startle" varies inversely in frequency with other types of motor activity (Wolff, 1959; Brownfield, 1956) suggests that there may be many components of activity lumped together under one apparently diffuse response (Gordon & Bell, 1961). Certainly the present status of the "mass activity" research suggests that:

> . . . there may be an irreducible core of unintegrated, diffuse activity in the newborn after best efforts have been made to isolate components, but it is apparent at this stage of research that not enough attention has been devoted to this type of analysis. . . . It will be costly for the over-all movement of research in this area to ignore the possibility that qualitatively different components exist in what is now vaguely referred to as the activity of the newborn. (Gordon & Bell, 1961, p. 113).

Specific Movements. In contrast to the mass activity described above, *specific non-reflex* behavior involves a localized or segmental response of the organism characterized by more precision of movements and occurring at a rate slow enough to be observed and analyzed in detail. It includes the following kinds of simple segmental responses: rolling of the trunk; all of the varieties of motion that are possible about any of the joints of the extremities (e.g., extension, flexion, abduction, adduction, rotation); backward, forward and sideways movement of the head; opening and closing of the eyelids; pursing, licking, and smacking of the lips; sucking, whimpering, and vocalizing (Dennis, 1934; Irwin, 1930). Most of the utterances of the neonate, however, are crying sounds which do not occur alone but as accompaniments of mass activity (Irwin, 1930). In addition, the neonate's behavioral repertoire contains several more complex, specific movements, such as smiling, pursuit movements of the eyes, a characteristic sleeping posture, and alternate extension and flexion of the legs, that involves some bilateral, contralateral, or intersegmental coordination (Dennis, 1934; Irwin, 1930). As in mass activity, specific movements are instigated by both internal and external stimuli. For example, Turkewitz, Gordon and Birch (1965) report increases in specific head turning responses when the mouth region is stimulated. Irwin (1930) contends that specific integrated movements are infrequent when external stimuli are constant. At present, however, the issue of stimulation of specific movements is an open research question. The study of individual differences in specific movements in the neonate has hardly been touched upon. The importance of this area of investigation is illustrated by the one existing study which reported that boys lift their heads higher than girls in a prone position (Bell & Darling, 1965).

Both on the stimulus and response sides, specific behavior in the neonate is not nearly as specific as the name implies (Jensen, 1932; Pratt, 1954; Pratt, Nelson & Sun, 1930). The lack of specificity to which we are alluding here is not variability in locus and occurrence of stimulus-elicited response but rather *irrelevancy* in stimulus-response connections; by definition non-reflex behavior is variable in both former respects. Some segmental responses are triggered off by completely irrelevant stimuli; and conversely, a single stimulus may evoke several irrelevant as well as relevant responses. The *sucking response*, for example, may be elicited by pulling the infant's hair or by pinching his toes; and leg flexion may be accompanied by sucking and thrashing of the arms when the sole of the foot is stimulated. Nevertheless, a specific movement tends to be elicited most reliably by its normally appropriate stimulus. And although other irrelevant movements may be implicated in the segmental response to a particular stimulus, they tend to be less vigorous than the relevant components of the behavior in question (Peiper, 1963).

Reflex Behavior

Reflex behavior shares many of the aforementioned properties of the more specific variety of non-reflex behavior. It too consists of precise, clearly defined and isolatable units of activity that are localized and segmental in nature. The stimulus-response connections, however, appear to be more strongly predetermined by genic factors and are more specific and stereotyped. They are also more invariable, both with respect to the locus and type of response to a particular stimulus and with respect to the elicitation of the response (provided, of course, that the stimulus is adequate). Furthermore, reflex behavior is stimulus-bound in the sense that it can only be initiated by stimulation, never volitionally, and is not ordinarily or completely subject to voluntary inhibition.*

Although individuation of reflex responses is quite far advanced prior to birth, some terminal aspects of the process remain to be completed during the neonatal period. Further shrinkage of reflexogenous zones takes place, and with increasing age there is progressively less involvement of the organism in the response (Pratt, 1954). Reflex activities in the neonate, however, are not nearly as nonspecific as even the more specific components of non-reflex activity. And far from being substantially complete at this time, individuation of non-reflex behavior is a continuing aspect of motor development, both in the early "phylogenetic" states dominated by neural maturation and in the later "ontogenetic" stages dominated by practice.

Regional Survey. By way of illustrating the large repertory of reflex behavior in the neonate, the more important and commonly observed reflexes will first be listed and described briefly. Three of these reflexes (plantar, grasp and Moro), which have been the object of particularly extensive investigation and which undergo significant developmental changes during early infancy, will then be described in greater detail.

Some neonatal reflexes, although never brought under voluntary control, are regularly and permanently inhibited some months later by higher neural centers, thus disappearing from the behavioral repertoire of older infants. Reflexes, therefore, are not necessarily fixed or permanent.

The following is a summary of reflex responses in the neonate classified according to organ of the body (Crowell, 1967; Dennis, 1934; Irwin, 1930; Thompson, 1962; Peiper, 1963)* (1) *Eyes:* eyelid closure in response to illumination or a blast of air; pupillary contraction and dilation in response to change in illumination or in the distance of the object of fixation from the eyes; nystagmus in response to bodily rotation or to cold stimulation in the external auditory meatus; imperfect coordinate movements of the eyes imperfect convergence of the eyeballs in fixating an approaching object. (2) *Upper respiratory and gastrointestinal tract:* salivation, swallowing, sneezing, coughing, yawning, gagging. (3) *Abdominal and pelvic viscera:* hiccoughing, vomiting, urination, and defecation.† *Head and neck:* balancing movements of the head in response to change in bodily position, tonic neck reflexes in the supine position (Gesell, 1954). (5) *Arm and hand:* arm flexion in response to a sudden blow against the hand; the grasp reflex. (6) *Trunk:* abdominal and cremasteric reflexes (contraction of the recti muscles and retraction of the scrotum respectively in response to tactile stimulation of the lower abdominal wall and of the inner surface of the thigh). (7) *Leg and foot:* knee and ankle jerks in response to tapping of the patellar and Achilles tendons; stepping movements when the neonate is supported under the armpits with the soles of his feet touching a hard surface; the plantar reflex. (8) *Coordinate responses:* creeping and swimming movements of the neonate when lying prone with resistance offered to the soles of his feet; the Moro reflex; hand-mouth coordinate reflexes (Crowell, 1967).

The plantar reflex per se consists of flexion of the big toe when the outer edge of the sole of the foot is stimulated. In neonates and young infants, such stimulation often evokes extension of the big toe and fanning of the other toes (the Babinski reflex) and frequently retraction of the foot, leg and thigh (the mass reflex) (Crowell, 1967; McGraw, 1937; Peiper, 1963; Pratt, 1954; Richards & Irwin, 1934; Sherman & Flory, 1936). The Babinski is diagnostically important since it occurs in adults with pyramidal tract lesions (Peiper, 1963). The relative frequency of the Babinski and plantar reflexes in the neonate, and the age until which the former reflex can be elicited in normal infants, are matters of some dispute. Discrepancies between equally competent observers may be attributed to differences in the type of stimulus employed, to variability in the posture of the toes prior to stimulation, and to differences in the wakefulness of the subjects (Pratt, Nelson & Sun, 1930; Richards & Irwin, 1934; Sherman *et al.*, 1936). It does seem clear, however, that with increasing age both the mass and Babinski reflexes become progressively more infrequent until only the plantar reflex is elicited

---

*Peiper (1963) discusses the reflex system in detail and offers many illustrations and examples.

†Only the reflex aspects of these activities are referred to here. Both the urethral and anal external sphincters, currently non-functional, are brought under voluntary control during later infancy.

(Pratt *et al.*, 1930; Richards & Irwin, 1934; Sherman *et al.*, 1936). Since the Babinski reflex reappears following lesions of the pyramidal tract, and since extensive neural maturation of the cortex takes place during the early period of postnatal life (see p. 84), we may infer that the developmental waning of this reflex is reflective of cortical inhibition.

The grasp or palmar reflex exhibits a developmental history that is very similar to that of the Babinski reflex. Descriptively, in stimulus-response terms, it is homologous to the plantar reflex; the palm and four fingers (but not the thumb) close in response to tactile stimulation. Approximately ten per cent of all neonates can support their own weight by grasping a thin rod in this fashion (Sherman et al., 1936). Gradually, during the first four to six months of postnatal existence, the grasp reflex is replaced by volitional grasping which is both less invariable and characterized by conspicuous involvement of the thumb (Halverson, 1937). This developmental trend may also be interpreted as an indication of increased cortical control and of inhibition of a subcortically regulated reflex, especially since the grasp reflex may be reactivated after injury to the premotor area of the cortex.

The Moro reflex is still another in this group of subcortically mediated reflexes which are progressively subjected to cortical inhibition. It is a coordinate response, more complex than the grasp or Bakinski, consisting of initial bilateral extension of the arms and legs, followed by return to the middle line of the body. The response is elicited by intense stimuli, such as pounding of the table surface near the infants' head, by lifting the head and releasing it, or by pulling the baby from a supine to a sitting position and partially releasing the arms so the head drops suddenly (Crowell, 1967). The same kind of stimulation may also evoke a startle reflex which makes it difficult to discriminate the type of response elicited (Parmelee, 1964). The startle response, however, appears to be a more restrained flexion response and has a somewhat shorter latency time (Landis & Hunt, 1939; McGraw, 1943); But, whereas the Moro reflex tends to disappear after four to six months of life, the startle reflex remains indefinitely (Clarke, 1939; Landis & Hunt, 1939; Morgan & Stellar, 1950; Peiper, 1963). Although they resemble fear, it is improbable that either the Moro or the startle reflex per se are accompanied by any subjective emotional content; the latency time between stimulus and response is much too short and the organism returns much too instantaneously to its prior motor and visceral state. This does not mean, however, that these reflexes and generalized excitement (or at a later date, fear) are necessarily mutually exclusive. If the eliciting stimulus is sufficiently prolonged or intense, the Moro reflex in the neonate may be followed by all of the bodily signs of excitement including crying (McGraw, 1943); and similarly if the older child perceives the stimulus evoking the startle reflex as threatening, he reacts shortly afterwards with fear.

Subsequent Organizational Trends

Once maximal specificity and discreteness are attained, reflex behavior undergoes relatively little developmental change after the neonatal period. The vast majority of discrete reflexes remain intact throughout the life span. From time to time, of course, depending on particular idiosyncratic experience, conditioning may occur. As already indicated, some subcortically regulated reflexes, especially those which are intersegmental (mass reflex, Moro reflex) and which are suggestive of vestigial prehensile (grasp reflex) and locomotor (stepping, swimming and creeping movements) functions, are subjected to cortical inhibition; they are replaced by more segmental or restricted reflexes (plantar, startle), and by voluntary, cortically controlled prehensile and locomotor responses (McGraw, 1943; Peiper, 1963; Saint-Anne Dargassies, 1960). But except for chronological antecedence and superficial resemblance in the kind of behavior involved the subcortical reflex stage of these activities bears little relationship to the cortical voluntary stage which follows. The latter is not a functional outgrowth of the former, but merely a later-occurring, phenotypically similar activity dependent upon intervening neural maturation.

All other behavioral change generally subsumed under motor development occurs in the area of non-reflex activity which includes both stimulus-elicited and voluntary responses. With increasing age such responses become more localized, economical in extent of involvement, and relevant in relation to their eliciting stimuli, but never as invariable or as stereotyped as true reflexes. However, this narrowing down of the range of stimuli that can elicit a particular response and of the range of responses that are made to a particular stimulus cannot be interpreted in strictly quantitative terms. Actually, in the course of learning, many new and originally inadequate stimuli tend to become adequate as a result of conditioning, and many new and different responses are made to familiar stimuli. Hence the restriction that occurs constitutes an increase in the selectivity rather than a decrease in the quantity of stimulus-response connections. It is true that the number of irrelevant connections decreases, but at the same time new learning experiences continually establish new relevancies. And taking place concomitantly or alternately with this process of individuation in the acquisition of new motor skills in the complementary process of integration of individuated activities into new complex patterns (McGraw, 1935).

In interpreting the meaning of "stages" in later motor development, it is important to distinguish between phylogenetic and ontogenetic acquisitions In the first place, the occurrence and the sequence of stages is much more invariable in the phylogenetic group; deviations from a panhuman norm will only be minor in nature except under extremely atypical environmental conditions. Second, whereas incidental learning and practice are important for *both* the inter-and intra-stage changes occuring in ontogenetic traits, they can only account for *intra*-stage changes in phylogenetic traits. Before the organism can go on to a new stage in the development of the latter traits, a higher level of neural organization must first be achieved. Thus, in the development of phylogenetic traits, although lower stages of neural integration are sometimes (but not necessarily) prerequisite for the emergence of higher stages of neural integration, lower stages of *performance* cannot be considered functionally prerequisite for the emergence of higher stages of performance. In other words, the individual could conceivably proceed from one stage of motor development to another solely on the basis of neural maturation, without actually having experienced the performance aspects of the earlier stage. In the genesis of ontogenetic motor traits, on the other hand, discontinuously new (inter-stage) changes in performance are developmental outgrowths of and functionally dependent upon prior levels of performance at the time of their emergence.

The above interpretation is clearly in contrast to Piaget's formulations regarding the ontogenesis of motor behavior during the first 18 months of life (Piaget, 1952). One of Piaget's basic assumptions about early motor development is that there is functional comparability and developmental continuity between reflex and non-reflex behavioral sequences. For example, he derives more advanced forms of cortically controlled prehension (e.g., primary circular reactions, hand-mouth coordinations, visual-manual coordinations) from the primitive, subcortically regulated grasping reflex via such mechanisms as "generalizing assimilation", "differential assimilation" and "reciprocal assimilation" to the "grasping schema" (Piaget, 1952). The theoretical difficulty here arises from the paradoxical fact that Piaget, of all persons, who ordinarily overelaborates stage differences far beyond his data, appears to ignore the fundamental distinction between reflex and non-reflex activity (Ausubel, 1966). As a result, his description and explanation of early motor development obscure basic differences in rate, patterning, and regulation characteristic of these two forms of behavior as well as the salient generalization that motor development, as it is generally understood, is an outgrowth of non-reflex rather than the reflex activity. This theoretical difficulty, of course, applies less to developmental sequences, such as sucking and visual pursuit movement, that are non-reflex in nature from the very beginning than to sequences that are reflex in nature from the very beginning.

MAJOR NEONATAL BEHAVIORAL PATTERNS

Another approach to the behavior of the neonate, apart from analyzing it in terms of its differential organizational elements, consists of identifying the major functional areas, in which his response patterns are distributed. Here our concern is with describing and interpreting those aspects of his behavior that constitute the greater portion of his activity day as a total functioning organism. Four such salient patterns that dominate neonatal behavior are crying, feeding responses, sleeping, and response to pain.

Crying

Crying and whining are almost the only sounds that the newborn is able to utter (Peiper, 1963) and are invariably accompanied by mass activity (Irwin, 1930). Crying is not apparently under cortical control, serves no communicative purposes, and is spectographically different from speech sounds (Rebelsky, Starr & Luria, 1967). Observers are unable to distinguish reliably between cries evoked by some different stimuli as hunger, pain, and cold (Blanton, 1917), and show little agreement in identifying an emotional state accompanying crying unless they know what the evocative stimuli are (Sherman, 1927b). Nevertheless, crying is the most effective response the infant can make in relieving discomfort caused by unsatisfied bodily needs or by noxious stimulation; it is an unlearned adaptive response that summons help from his interpersonal world. At this point it is completely involuntary; but later on as its causal relationship to need reduction is perceived, it is employed deliberately for this purpose.

A sterotyped pattern of pre-crying behavior precedes actual vocalization by several seconds. The forehead wrinkles, the jaws are depressed, the eyes are shut tight, tongue and nose are flattened, the mouth opens and unilateral kicking begins (Ames, 1941). If these pre-crying cues are recognized and the infant's needs promptly satisfied, it might be possible to forestall both the early involuntary and later volitional crying (Rosenzweig, 1954). During the first week of life infants cry on the average about two hours a day, but wide individual differences prevail with respect to amount, loudness, and intensity of crying (Aldrich, Sung & Knap, 1945a, 1945b). Sound analysis at this time shows that front vowels predominate over the rear vowels and that consonants are infrequent. (Irwin & Curry, 1941; Peiper, 1963). Hunger accounts for approximately one-third of all crying, the incidence of crying being greatest just prior to feeding; observers have attributed the cause of the remainder equally to wetting and soiling and to unknown factors respectively (Aldrich *et al.*, 1945b; Peiper, 1963). Contrary to general belief the crying of one infant in a nursery does not tend to stimulate crying on the part of other infants (Aldrich *et al.*, 1945a). Crying ceases when the discomfort which evokes it is removed directly (e.g., by feeding or change of diapers), or when substitute satisfactions habitually associated with need reduction (e.g., holding by adult, swaddling, etc.) are provided (Lipton *et al.*, 1960; Peiper, 1963; Wolff, 1959). In addition, infants cry less when there is some type of auditory stimulation present (Brackbill, Adams *et al.*, 1966) and if they are kept in a prone position (Keital, Cohen &

Harnish, 1960). It increases when parents or other attendents are too busy to identify the cause of discomfort and remedy it either directly or indirectly (Aldrich *et al.*, 1945a; Stewart *et al.*, 1954), and appears to be higher in incidence in infants whose mothers have been highly anxious before birth (Ottinger & Simmons, 1964).

Feeding Responses

When stimulated in the oral-facial region, the neonate turns toward the stimulus, opens his mouth and begins to suck. Stimulation of the lips is most effective in eliciting this series of responses, other stimuli varying in effectiveness with distance from the lips (Pratt *et al.*, 1930). Practically any kind of stimulation will release searching and sucking behavior in the newborn, but with increasing age the areas of stimulation start to diminish, and stimulation becomes effective only in the immediate region of the mouth (Crowell, 1967). At present there are conflicting theories concerning the mechanism for this sequence; they stress either learning or instinct explanations (Prechtl, 1958; Turkewitz *et al.*, 1965). Neonates suck when they are awake or aroused, regardless of degree of hunger (Bridger, 1962; Levin & Kaye, 1965). Sucking rate also varies with the stimulus presented, a bottle nipple eliciting more sucking than an ordinary tube (Levin & Kaye, 1965). Nevertheless, the nature of the contact stimulus that initiates sucking is relatively nonspecific and the infant will ordinarily suck on anything that is soft. It is sheer adultomorphism therefore to attribute to him any initial purpose in searching for the breast as such or any foreknowledge of its function. Human mothers place their infants at the breast; but the young of other mammalian species reach this goal through purely trial and error efforts (as would the unaided human infant), and perish if they are unsuccessful. Indicative of the importance of the sucking mechanism for survival is the fact that the pad of fat constituting the sucking cushion is selectively resistive to absorption, remaining intact even after the body as a whole is thoroughly emaciated (Gesell, 1954).

Each infant tends to maintain a characteristic and regular sucking rhythm that is coordinated with breathing and swallowing (Peiper, 1963). Hence, for swallowing to take place it is unnecessary for either breathing or sucking to cease (Pratt, 1954). During sucking the thoracic cavity typically expands, the abdominal cavity contracts (Halverson, 1944), and general motility decreases (Kessen, Leutzendorff, Stoutsenberger, 1967; Jensen, 1932). With continued exercise of the feeding responses, various signs of inefficiency attributable to initial use tend to disappear. As lip control improves, leaking of milk from the corners of the mouth decreases (Gesell & Ilg, 1937). The older neonate sucks more vigorously and is less responsive to irrelevant stimuli (Pratt, 1954); and eventually the young infant learns to swallow food without simultaneously swallowing air.

Hunger is an extremely salient experience in the neonate. Strong gastric contractions are probably related to hunger pangs, but are typically induced by humoral factors (low blood sugar, "hunger hormone") rather than by emptiness of the stomach (Richards, 1936; Taylor, 1917). However, since typical hunger behavior can be induced in a satiated gastrectomized animal by the injection of blood from a starved animal, it seems evident that humoral substances can affect this behavior by directly lowering response thresholds as well as indirectly increasing the amplitude of gastic contraction. The behavioral response to hunger is four-fold: (a) increased sucking and responsiveness to stimuli inducing sucking (selective lowering of relevant response threshold) (Marquis, 1943; Pratt, 1954; (b) increased mass activity (Hendry & Kessen, 1964; Irwin, 1932a, 1932b; Marquis 1941; 1943; Peiper, 1963) (generalized lowering of all response thresholds); (c) undifferentiated excitement, including crying (Aldrich et al., 1945a; Marquis, 1943); and (d) more marked cardiac reactions (Richmond & Lipton, 1959). As previously noted, interpretations of hunger cries as indicative of rage, fear, or insecurity are undoubtedly adultomorphic projections.

With increasing age, hunger contractions decrease in frequency (Taylor, 1917) and, accordingly, infants on a "self-demand" schedule demand food less frequently (Gesell & Ilg, 1937; Simsirian & McLendon, 1942; 1945; Peiper, 1963). This evidence, plus the fact that neonates on a three-hour feeding schedule are less restless than neonates on a four-hour feeding schedule, seems to indicate that a flexible regimen of progressively less frequent feedings is more compatible with the physiological needs of the newborn infant than a fixed regimen (Marquis, 1941). Nevertheless, even in the neonatal period, infants appear capable of adapting to a four-hour feeding interval; by the tenth day of this regimen, the typically sharp increase in activity and crying between the third and fourth hours tends to diminish. This is in marked contrast to the abrupt rise in activity that occurs during the same interval when infants habituated to a three-hour schedule are suddenly shifted to a four-hour regimen (Marquis, 1941). Finally, "breast-fed" babies tend to be more agitated and show more sucking than "bottle-fed" babies (Bell, 1966; Waldrop & Bell, 1966).

Sleeping

A rule of thumb on sleeping is that the younger an infant is the longer he sleeps (Parmelee, Wenner and Schulz, 1964; Peiper, 1963). Although the neonate is judged to be asleep from 16 to 20 hours a day (Parmelee, Schulz and Disbrow, 1961; Pratt, Nelson & Sun, 1930), the state of sleep is even more difficult to define than in the adult. Sleeping and waking states are not dichotomous and have been described in terms of relative degrees of irritability and motility (Brown, 1964; Dittrichova, 1962; Dittrochova & Lapackova, 1964; Prechtl & Beintema, 1964; Wolff, 1959; 1966; Wagner, 1937)*. The most precise physiological criteria of sleep are electrical brain waves (EEG) that are correlated with the behavioral states of attention, consciousness, wakefullness and sleep (Bartoshuk, 1962; Scheibel & Scheibel, 1964). Two types of sleeping phases have been identified behaviorally (Aserinsky & Kleitman, 1953; 1955a; 1955b): one is a phase of rapid eye movements (REM) and the other is marked by the absence of rapid eye movements (NREM). The REM phase is concomitant with continuous muscle contractions and the NREM phase is essentially devoid of muscular activity (Roffwarg, Muzio & Dement, 1966). The EEG supports the notion that these phases are distinct patterns (Aserinsky & Kletman, 1953) and a cycle of alteration between these states has been found in newborns (Parmelee, Schultz, Akiyama, Wenner & Stern, 1967). The neonate's characteristic pattern is REM and this diminishes with chronological age and the maturation of the nervous system (Roffwarg et al., 1966). The reason for this developmental shift is as yet not clearly understood and two theories have been advanced (Roffwarg et al., 1966; Snyder, 1966). Roffwarg et al., 1966 contend that the REM state reflects a barrage of random stimulation which serves the fetus as replacement for external stimuli, thus helping the growth of the nervous system. Snyder (1966) advances the hypothesis that REM sleep provides moments during sleep in which danger signals may be appreciated. At present, both theories do not give adequate accounts of why REM sleep declines during the course of life (Campbell & Thompson, 1968).

Despite the fact that the neonate spends a preponderant portion of his day in sleep, individual periods of sleep are relatively short, approximately three hours in duration (Pratt, Nelson & Sun, 1930). At birth, almost equal amounts of sleep occur during day and night, but by the sixteenth week twice as much sleep occurs at night as during the day (Parmelee, Wenner & Schulz, 1964). With increasing age, the sleep and waking states tend to become more dichotomous, and the total amount of time spent in sleep decreases; most of this decrease occurs during the first three months of life (Buhler, 1930; Parmelee, Wenner & Schulz, 1964). In addition individual periods of sleep and wakefulness become longer in the older infant (Buhler, 1930).

Response to Pain

The infant's sensitivity to pain can be tested electrically or by means of pin pricks (Peiper, 1963). Sensitivity to painful stimuli increases rapidly during the first four days of life. This is shown by the marked decrease in the

---

*Wolff (1966) for example, has described a seven point continuum ranging from regular sleep through irregular sleep, periodic sleep, drowsiness, alert inactivity, and waking activity, to crying.

minimal intensity of stimuli necessary to evoke a response (Kaye & Lipsitt, 1964; Lipsitt & Levy, 1959; Sherman, Sherman & Flory, 1936). Habituation to certain types of painful electro-tactual stimuli can occur, however, where response thresholds are raised by the intervening stimulation (Gullickson & Crowell, 1964). Sensitivity is greater in the cephalic than in the caudal region of the body (Sherman & Sherman, 1925; Sherman et al., 1936) and is appreciably diminished when the infant is asleep or nursing (Pratt, 1954). From the available evidence, therefore, there is little reason to doubt that painful experience associated with noxious and intense stimulation (typically of visceral origin) is a major cause of excitement, mass activity, and crying in the neonate (Peiper, 1963). Nevertheless, from the fact that operations such as circumcision are performed at one week of age without anesthesia and do not precipitate surgical shock, we can infer that the experience of pain is less intense in the neonate that in older individuals.

Various theoretical considerations also lead to the same conclusion. First, because of immaturity of the cerebral cortex and paucity of apperceptive background, the coritical threshold for pain perception is probably high; much pain sensation is undoubtedly experienced at a crude thalamic level. Second, pain experience is not enhanced by anticipatory anxiety or by emotional reaction to the threatening implications of pain, since it is unlikely that the neonate is sufficiently mature to perceive threat; and even if he were able to do so, he has no functional concept of self to which of perception of threat could be referred. Finally, because he is asleep most of the day and nursing a good part of the remainder, his threshold for pain is typically much higher than its lower physiological limit.

THE DEVELOPMENT OF THE NEONATAL
SENSORY-RESPONSE APPARATUS*

Except for late occurring anatomical and physiological changes, the sensory capacities of the neonate are little different from those of the viable fetus (see pp. 181-183). The main difference lies in the greater degree of exposure to adequate stimuli in postnatal life.

The investigation of sensory experience in the newborn is fraught with numerous methodological difficulties. Foremost among these is the unavailability of verbal reports of subjective experience and the necessity for relying completely on overt responses to stimuli. It is evident, therefore, that the neonate's failure to respond to a given stimulus may be less indicative of sensory incapacity than of the inappropriateness of the experimental arrangements for peculiarities in his sensory, response, and the attentional

*Reviews of the literature on this topic are available: see Peiper (1963) and Spears and Hohle (1967).

capacities.* Interpretation of overt responses is further complicated by the simultaneous occurrence of mass activity and specific movements induced by internal stimuli.

Vision

All parts of the neonate's eye which are necessary for seeing, with the exception of the fovea centralis in the retina, are completely formed at birth (Peiper, 1963). This foveal immaturity, combined with difficulties in accomodation and ocular imbalance, results in poor fixation (Peiper, 1963; Spears & Hohle, 1967).   At birth, the eyes appear to function independently, monocular fixation predominating during the first six weeks and given way to binocular fixations thereafter (Peiper, 1963; Spears & Hohle, 1967)†. Neonatal accommodation to distance targets is minimal but improves rapidly by the fourth month (Haynes, White & Held, 1965). The readiness with which the neonate responds to illumination leaves little doubt about his visual sensitivity. Intense stimuli of short duration elicit pupiliary contraction, eyelid closure, the Moro and startle reflexes, the ocular-neck reflex, E.E.G. changes, and changes in circulatory and respiratory responses (Lipton & Steinschneider, 1964; Peiper, 1963; Pratt, 1954; Spears and Hohle, 1967; Steinschneider, 1967). Full term infants show E.E.G. patterns in the occipital area in response to a brief light flash (Ellingson, 1958), and the response latencies decrease (Ellingson, 1960) while the amplitudes increase (Dustman & Beck, 1966) with age. Brightness discrimination undergoes rapid development in the first two months of life (Doris & Cooper, 1966). *Continuous* illumination tends to inhibit mass activity, the degree of inhibition increasing (within limits) with the intensity of the stimulation, and stimuli of intermediate brightness are preferred over dim or bright objects (Hershinson, 1964).

It is one thing, however, to show that light can release various subcortical responses in the neonate, and quite another to define the properties of his visual experience. Does he visually apprehend discrete objects, how clear are the images he sees, does he experience different colors? Through the use of newer methods for studying infant perception it is apparent that the neonate perceives shape, forms, and patterns (Spears & Hohle, 1967). Although perceptual processes are apparent from birth, his visual acuity will increase with age through the adolescent years (Gough and Delcourt, 1969).

---

*The consideration of the infant's "state" has become an important topic in infant research. See Brown (1964), Wolff (1966). Campbell & Thompson (1968) refer to several sources that consider the infant's "state" as an experimental variable.

†Although monocular fixation in newborns is apparently the predominent response, nevertheless newborns tend to converge more on some patterns (stripes) than on others (grey stimulus) (Wickelgren, 1967). This suggests that human judgments of neonate ocular orientation may not reliably indicate stimulus discrimination and preference in infants. See also Dayton & Jones (1964).

The neonate however, from as early as five days shows preferences for patterns, forms, shapes, and faces (Fantz, 1963; 1965; Fantz & Nevis, 1967; Fantz, Ordy & Udelf, 1962; Lang, 1966; Salapatek & Kessen, 1966). At about two and one half months there is a qualitative shift in visual perferences for "social objects" over other types of stimuli (Wolff, 1965). Early infancy after the neonatal period is also characterized by preferences for "faces" over "designs" (Lewis, Kagan & Kalafat, 1966; McCall & Kagan, 1967) and for familiar rather than distorted faces (Kagan, Henker, Hen-Tov, Levine & Lewis, 1966). At present, there appears to be contradictory evidence concerning infants' preferences for complexity (Berlyne,1958; Fantz, Ordy & Udelf, 1962; Thomas, 1965). The findings clearly indicate that the neonate discriminates patterns, forms, shapes etc., but at present the stimulus dimensions and attributes governing preference are largely unknown (Spears & Hohle, 1967). The beginnings of depth perception can be measured by approximately two months (Polak, Emde, & Spitz, 1964b), but the problems of binocular coordination at this time impose serious limitations. Perception of movement (optokinetic nystagmus) appears to be present in the neonate (Dayton & Jones, 1964; Tauber & Koffler, 1966).

The question of color vision is an unsettled issue, as yet hardly explored. It appears, however, that the ability of the neonate to pursue a spot of color moving against a background of another color, equated for brightness, provides presumptive but not definite evidence of color discrimination (Chase, 1937). The fact that electroretinograms (E.R.G.) indicate neonates have both photopic (cone) and scotopic (rod) vision (Barnet, Lodge & Armington, 1965; Spears & Hohle, 1967) is also indirect evidence for the possibility of color discrimination at this time. By the fourth month of infancy we see preferences for color over shape (Spears, 1966).

The fact that visual perception appears at birth raises again the question of the primacy of genic (Franz, 1963) over learned (Thomas, 1965) factors (and vice versa) in the appearance of these capacities in the neonate. No clear evidence favors either interpretation and the importance of the interaction of genic factors with environmental stimulation is seen by the fact that greater contact and handling by adults produces more visual exploration in infants (White, Castle & Held 1964). This issue will be raised again in greater detail in chapter eleven.

Hearing

The auditory system of the human neonate is essentially complete by the later stages of fetal development with the exception of the middle ear cavity which at birth is filled with a residue of connective tissue restricting full movement of the ossicles (Peiper, 1963; Spears & Hohle, 1967). This lack of mobility of the middle ear structures has led to the erroneous conclusion that the infant is deaf at birth (Peiper, 1963; Spears & Hohle, 1967). Summaries of the studies on prenatal and early neonatal auditory development leave little doubt that there is a variety of reflex responses to auditory stimuli at this time (Peiper, 1963; Spears & Hohle, 1967). Although the neonate is more responsive than the full-term intrauterine fetus to auditory stimulation, nevertheless his auditory acuity is still relatively poor, probably because of the presence of amniotic fluid or mucous in the middle ear, external auditory meatus, and Eustachian tubes. The types of responses made to auditory stimulation in the neonate range from behavioral to physiological measures (e.g., auro-palpebral reflex, Moro reflex, kicking, head and eye turning, cardiac acceleration or deceleration, G.S.R. and E.E.G.) (Spears & Hohle, 1967; Steinschneider, 1967).

The comparison of neonates with older infants and adults reveals the neonate to be less sensitive to sounds (Spears & Hohle, 1967). The degree of these differences in auditory sensitivity however, is unknown at this time (Spears & Hohle, 1967).

As in the case with vision, when auditory stimuli are of short duration, an increase in their intensity tends to release more overt responses such as eyelid reflexes, general bodily movement, crying, changes in respiration and circulation, cardiac responses, and Moro or startle reflexes (Bartoshuk, 1964; Pratt, 1954; Pratt, Nelson & Sun, 1930; Steinschneider, 1967; Steinschneider, Lipton & Richmond, 1966; Stubbs, 1934). The duration of the stimulation and its effect is an open question because of conflicting experimental results (Kagan & Henker, 1966). Early studies simply indicated that sounds of over approximately ten seconds resulted in adaptation to the sound stimulus (Stubbs, 1934). Recent research has led to conflicting findings; changes in sucking behavior in response to an auditory stimulation were found at ten second but not at two second durations (Eisenberg, Griffen, & Coursin Hunter, 1964). Levin & Kaye's (1964) results conflict with the above findings; sounds of at least fifteen seconds were necessary for auditory responsivity. The resolution of this conflict may lie in the study of "states" such as differences in wakefulness (Kagan & Henker, 1966)*.

The earlier findings on *continuous* auditory stimulation producing a reduction in level of activity and arousal in the infant (Weiss, 1934) are consistent with summaries of the contemporary research (Spears & Hohle, 1967). Moreover, with extended stimulation, human auditory mechanisms undergo a reduction in responsiveness (adaptation and habituation) which does not appear to be the result of fatigue (Bartoshuk, 1962a, 1962b; Bronshtein & Petrova, 1952; Spears & Hohle, 1967), and the absence of which is

---

*The importance of "infant state" is shown by the findings that crying infants are less responsive to auditory stimulation (Stubbs, 1934). Also, children in R.E.M. sleep are less responsive to auditory stimuli than are children in N.R.E.M. sleeping states (Weitzman, Fishbein & Graziani, 1965).

indicative of communication disorders (Eisenberg, Coursin & Rupp, 1966). Finally, the presence of sound localization is subject to the types of measures utilized. Earlier studies using eye movements to test sound localization (with the exception of Wertheimer, 1961) have yielded negative results. Using methods employing habituation-dishabituation techniques, however, indicates that sound localization is present in the neonate (Bronshtein & Petrova, 1967; Leventhal & Lipsitt, 1964).

Taste and Smell

Compared with adult standards, gustatory and olfactory sensitivity in the neonate is minimal despite exposure to more adequate stimuli than in fetal life (Pratt, Nelson & Sun, 1930). The neonate reacts positively (i.e., by continual sucking) to a sweet solution, whereas salt, bitter and sour solutions induce cessation of sucking, negative facial grimaces, and irregularities in respiration and circulation (Jensen, 1932; Pratt, Nelson & Sun, 1930). It is doubtful whether differentiation of the four taste qualities exists as such, apart from this distinction between positive and negative reactions. The neonate's taste sense cannot distinguish between food that will agree and food that will disagree with him; sweetness apparently is the main criterion (Peiper, 1963). Taste discrimination tends to improve during the neonatal period (Pratt *et al.*, 1930), and to be sharper in a moderately full than in a hungry infant (Jensen, 1932).

Because of methodological difficulties, evidence regarding olfactory sensitivity in the neonate is rather sparse. The receptors for olfaction are located in a small area at the very top of the nasal cavities where they come into contact with a small portion of all air passing through the nostrils (Spears & Hohle, 1967). Response indicators of olfactory sensitivity that have been used include gross negative reactions to odorous substances (e.g., crying, squirming, grimaces, changes in respiration and circulation) and calibrated sucking and motility as measured by a stabilimeter (Spears & Hohle, 1967). Earlier studies had indicated that neonates only react to such stimuli as ammonia and acetic acid (Pratt, Nelson & Sun, 1930); but since these substances also irritate the nasal mucosa, it is entirely possible that their behavioral effects are wholly or partly produced by pain receptors. Also, a greater percentage of response to stimulation is reported for a variety of odorous substances than for pure air, but the responses to these different odors are indistinguishable from each other and do not vary with age (Disher, 1934).

More recent studies, using more sophisticated methodology, have demonstrated that the neonate is much more sensitive olfactorily than heretofore appreciated (Engin, Lipsitt & Kaye, 1963; Lipsitt, Engen & Kaye, 1963). The neonate responds to at least one odor (asafaetida) shortly after birth and the olfactory thresholds for this odor decreases drastically over the first few days of life, with the infant becoming increasingly responsive to chemical stimuli administered nasally (Lipsitt *et al.*, 1963). Engen, Lipsitt and Kaye, (1963) have also found neonatal sensitivity in different degrees to acetic acid, asafaetida, phenylethyl alcohol, and anise oil. Conflict with the earlier studies is attributed to the fact that these studies typically presented the stimulous odors within the same session, possibly causing response habituation and/or decreasing sensitivity due to adaptation (Lipsitt *et al.*, 1963) *.

Thermal Sensitivity †

Neonates respond to thermal stimuli that deviate markedly from physiological zero, i.e., from the temperature of the body surface that is being stimulated. Both the upper and lower thresholds beyond which thermal stimuli first become adequate are relatively distant from physiological zero but vary considerably for different part of the body (Pratt, 1954; Pratt, Nelson & Sun, 1930). Although threshold values also vary widely from one individual to another, they tend to be quite stable within a particular individual (Jensen, 1932). Generally speaking the neonate is relatively insensitive to small differences within the range of adequate thermal stimuli, but here too there is much variability among individuals. The major response to thermal stimulation consists of movements of the body part which is stimulated, but other more generalized movements and changes in respiration and circulation may occur as well. When the oral cavity is stimulated thermally, the sucking rhythm becomes irregular (Jensen, 1932). Warm stimuli lead to adient responses whereas cold stimuli more usually result in withdrawal.

Ability to maintain a constant body temperature is relatively deficient in the neonate. He is less able than the older child or adult to adjust to extremes of environmental temperature, especially to heat. Since increased motility is one way of adjusting to cold, body activity tends to be inversely related to room temperature. Thermoregulation mechanisms for cold are not completely effective at birth; effective regulation starts between the first six to ten days (Mestyan & Varga, 1960). Because of inefficient temperature control and a relatively large body surface for his weight (both of which factors promote heat loss) the neonate's basal metabolic rate is high.

Other Sense Modalities

Cutaneous, proprioceptive, and vestibular sensitivity in the neonate is little different from that previously described for the fetus (see p. 181). By virtue of early structural and physiological development and frequent exercise in

The plausibility of this hypothesis appears to receive support from recent studies testing these possibilities. See Engen & Lipsitt, 1965; Engen et al., 1963.

†*See reviews by Peiper, 1963; Pratt, 1954; and Spears & Hohle, 1967.*

intrauterine life, these modalities are highly developed at birth. As already indicated in the discussions of mass activity, hunger, and crying, visceral stimulation becomes an important determinant of behavior when gastro-intestinal and excretory systems become physiologically autonomous subsequent to birth.

DIAGNOSTIC AND PROGNOSTIC IMPLICATIONS OF THE NEONATAL SENSORY-RESPONSE SYSTEM

Thus far in this chapter consideration of behavioral organization at birth, neonatal behavioral patterns, and sensory-response apparatus has demanded a rather voluminous summary of empirical findings with very little theoretical integration apparent. With the exception of the theorizing on the role of cortical and subcortical functioning in reflex behaviors (e.g., McGraw, 1943), very little integrative theorizing concerning this period of life has been done. Wolff's (1966) comment on this theoretical vacuum is typical when he notes that:

> It is surprising . . . with the notable exception of Piaget's work, no comprehensive psychological theory has systematically assimilated the empirical data on infancy, and that infant investigators themselves have formulated no comprehensive theory that integrates their findings. On the one hand, an extensive body of information exists without theoretical coherence; on the other hand, major theoretical systems, when they are concerned with early development, either ignore what is known about infancy, or else select isolated observations out of context to corroborate their reconstructions (Wolff, 1966; p. 1).

It appears that fears of "adultomorphism" have hampered theory construction in infant research and have encouraged empirical studies. With the improvement in methodology in recent investigations on infant capacities, however, impetus for studies on individual differences may give us a better understanding of the development of emotion, personality, and psychophysiological pathology (Steinschneider, 1967). The possibilities for using these early infant assessment devices for prognostic and diagnostic purposes seems most promising. Threshold and latency for crying in response to a pain can distinguish normal from brain-damaged children; brain-damaged children have longer latencies and higher thresholds (Fisichelli & Karelitz, 1963; Karelitz & Fisichelli, 1962; Karelitz, Karelitz & Rosenfeld, 1960). Neonatal measures on activity level, adaptability, intensity of reaction, etc. show patterns of individual differences at birth which are discernable after two years (Thomas, Chess, Birth & Hertzig, 1960. Newborns with pregnancy complications are inferior to normals on certain reflex responses (e.g., Moro reflex etc.) and excitability, and these differences are predictive two to four years later (Prechtl & Dijkstra, 1960). Tests to distinguish normal from traumatized infants (the latter suffering from anoxia and other prenatal and paranatal complications) have utilized pain thresholds, vision, muscular tension, irritability etc. (Graham, Matarazzo & Caldwell, 1956; Rosenblith, 1961, 1966) and have had some diagnostic success. Comparison, using the Graham Scale of anoxic and normal infants revealed that degree of impairment in test performance reflected severity of clinical condition (Graham, Pennoyer, Caldwell, Greenman & Hartmann, 1957).

The use of these early neonatal indices for prognostic and diagnostic purposes have obvious practical utility in discriminating early infant complications which may have extended effects in later personality development. Thus, even when theory is lacking, empirical studies which are methodologically adequate can justify their existence when they have diagnostic and prognostic promise*.

EMOTIONS

The distinguishing characteristic of emotion is a special kind of intense subjective experience consisting of strong feeling tones. This experience is usually accompanied by some perceptual awareness of the instigating stimulus and is followed by a generalized lowering of response thresholds and visceral and somatic reactions. Afferent reports of the latter responses, in turn, reinforce, enhance, perpetuate and modify the original subjective state. The "subjective experience" is obviously the most troublesome and controversial aspect of emotional experience and evidence for its existence in the neonate can at best be presumptive (Ricciuti, 1968). Nevertheless, it is a fair inference, that the evident excitement (violent mass activity and crying) exhibited by infants when aroused by intense noxious and prolonged stimuli is analogous in intensity of feeling tones to the emotional states of older infants. It is equally clear, however, that this excitement is completely undifferentiated with respect to quality of feeling tones (fear, rage, anxiety), instigating agents, and mode of expression.

Watson's (1919) theory of three innate emotions, rage, fear, and love (aroused respectively by restraint, loud noises or loss of support, and stroking the skin), is only remembered today as a vivid illustration of adultomorphic interpretation of infant behavior. Sherman (1927a; 1927b) demonstrated conclusively that observers show little agreement in identifying specific emotional patterns in neonates unless they are aware of the instigative stimuli. The Moro and startle reflexes are frequently released by loud noises but can also be evoked by other abrupt and intense stimuli (Crowell, 1967); furthermore they are elicited and dissipated much too instantaneously to have any emotional content. Instantaneous smiling in the neonate is probably an unlearned biologically based response (Freedman, 1964; 1965; Wolff, 1963); however, because of the wide variety of evocative stimuli ininvolved, it cannot be considered a reflex (Gewirtz, 1965). Restraint also

---

*See Peiper (1963) for a more detailed discussion of this topic.

fails to evoke any consistent response (Taylor, 1934). If it is rough, it precipitates undifferentiated excitement as does any intense stimulus (Dennis, 1940); if it is mild (such as the effect of clothing) it has a quieting effect (Dennis, 1940; Irwin & Weiss 1934a). And finally, what Watson called "love" can be most parsimoniously interpreted as quiescence or physiological satiety. It is extemely doubtful whether the initial feeling of pleasantness associated with this latter state is sufficiently intense to qualify as the emotional reciprocal of excitement (Sherman, 1928). Behaviorally, it appears that excitement is the only emotional state found in the neonate (Bridges, 1932).

That patterned emotions should be absent in the neonate is entirely consistent with theoretical considerations pertaining to ego development. First, it is highly improbable that differential emotional responses could be made to threat, frustration, or protection against threat in the absence of sufficient cognitive sophistication to perceive and understand the significance of these conditions that ordinarily determine the distinctive quality of feeling tones. The evidence that the subcortical centers associated with emotion are fully developed in the neonate (Scheibel & Scheibel, 1964) does not detract from the fact that the undeveloped cortical areas and limited apperceptive background severely limit the possibility of highly differentiated emotional responses. Second, unless a functional concept of self to which perceptions of threat and frustration can be referred is available, such perceptions lack the salient implications necessary to arouse strong feeling tones. Obviously, if a neonate does not have a sense of identify he cannot be frightened by threat (even if it were possible for him to perceive and appreciate its significance).

It is interesting to note that in young infants slightly past the neonatal period, the intensity of the visceral components of emotional response (as measured by the psychogalvanic reflex) is not highly correlated with the vigorousness of the motor and vocal components (Jones, 1930). Since this correlation is much improved in preschool children (Jones, 1935), it appears that integration of the different aspects of emotional expression is dependent in part upon maturation (substrate growth and incidental experience). This evidence also suggests that the degree of excitement inferred from the violence of the neonate's crying and bodily activity is often exaggerated since it is not necessarily accompanied by the extent of visceral involvement necessary for reinforcing and prolonging emotional reactions (Jones, 1930).

LEARNING*

Since ability to learn is pre-eminently a cortically regulated function (see p. 185) we cannot anticipate impressive amounts of learning in the neonate.

*Recent reviews on learning in the neonate and early infancy are available. See Brackbill & Koltsova (1967); Horowitz (1968); Lipsitt (1963, 1966); and Sameroff (1968). Brackbill and Koltsova (1967) also extensively discuss the different techniques and methods used in infant learning experiments.

However, if learning is broadly defined as more or less permanent modification of behavior caused by repeated exposure to similar experience, the newborn individual undoubtedly manifests it to a limited extent. This indicates either that some learning can occur on a subcortical level (Marquis, 1931) or that the neonate's cortex is not completely lacking in function. Two kinds of learning in the neonate—simple association and temporal conditioning—have already been alluded to in the discussion of crying (see p. 214) and feeding (see p. 215). The infant who ceases to cry when held, even before he is fed, has learned to associate preliminary contact with the feeding situation. Being held, therefore, serves as a signal of imminent need reduction and may even result in some anticipatory satisfaction. In due time, by virtue of repeated association with actual reduction of hunger, contact may also acquire some substitutive satisfaction value in its own right, in addition to heralding the approach of food. Temporal conditioning is shown by neonates who gradually learn to "expect" food every three hours after nine days of habituation to such a schedule (Marquis, 1941). The adaptation of neonates to a four-hour schedule, on the other hand, involves the learning of tolerance for an initially frustrating situation (as a result of habituation) as well as temporal conditioning.

The occurrence of classical conditioning in the neonate is still a controversial topic. Some studies on classical conditioning have been divided into classical aversive and classical appetitive conditioning (Brackbill & Koltsova, 1967; Lipsitt, 1963) since these two types of conditioning appear to be differentially effective in the neonate. Classical conditioning is demonstrated when a previously neutral or conditioning stimulus (CS), after being temporarily paired with an already adequate or unconditioned stimulus (UCS), elicits the response or some component of the response which was formerly typical of the reaction to the UCS (Lipsitt, 1963). Classical aversive conditioning usually involves a defensive response (e.g., withdrawal, blinking, etc.) to an aversive stimulus (UCS) (e.g., shock, pinching, etc.) being ultimately elicited by a previous neutral stimulus (CS) (e.g., tone). Appetitive conditioning occurs when an appetitive response (e.g., sucking) which is normally elicited by the presence of the unconditioned stimulus (UCS) (e.g., food, pacifier, etc.) is elicited by a previously neutral stimulus (CS) (e.g., tone).

Wenger (1936) reported classical aversive conditioning in the neonate by obtaining conditioned responses (eyelid reflex, limb withdrawal, and respiration), which were normally elicited only by unconditioned aversive stimuli, to a neutral stimulus. The results of this study were not definitive because they were based on a small number of subjects and because the experimental and control groups overlapped. Furthermore, Wickens & Wickens (1940) have found that they were apparently able to condition leg withdrawal to a buzzer by first pairing the latter (originally inadequate) stimulus repeatedly with electric shock; however, members of a control group who received shock *alone* (unpaired with the buzzer) during the training period also responded positively to the buzzer alone when tested for conditioning. The investigators suggest that after repeated elicitation of the leg withdrawal by shock the response becomes "sensitized"; that is, the muscles involved are in a state of readiness and may be tripped off by almost any extraneous stimulation, and not exclusively by the stimulus which had been previously inadequate and then experimentally paired with shock. With few exceptions (Kasatkin, 1952; Polikanina, 1961), the vast majority of studies on aversive classical conditioning have produced negative results (Brackbill & Koltsova, 1967; Lipsitt, 1963; Morgan & Morgan, 1944; Rendle & Short, 1961; Sameroff, 1968). Lipsitt (1963) tempers this conclusion by noting:

> While it cannot be argued that all possible techniques for the establishment of classical aversive conditioning in the human neonate have been attempted, it must certainly be concluded that such conditioning is at best difficult to obtain (p. 162).

Studies on classical appetitive conditioning in the neonate appear to have had more positive results (Brackbill & Koltsova, 1967; Lipsitt, 1963). The earliest study by Marquis (1931) purports to have conditioned a sucking response (nipple in mouth as the unconditioned stimulus) to a buzzer, although Wenger (1936) was unable to replicate the study and criticized it for lacking adequate controls and utilizing a subjective response-assessment procedure. Moreover, the status of the conditioned response is further complicated by the fact that it is somewhat more analogous to instrumental conditioning or to associative learning in the holding-feeding situation than to classical conditioning. That is, the sucking response made to the conditioned stimulus (buzzer, holding) is not merely an acquired response to an originally inadequate stimulus but also leads to need reduction as well. Hence, the buzzer, in addition to being a conditioned stimulus for sucking, may also (by signalling imminent need reduction) provide some anticipatory satisfaction, or may even acquire some substitutive satisfaction value of its own. It is also understandable that inasmuch as satiety ordinarily raises the threshold of the sucking response in relation to its unconditioned stimulus, it also does so in relation to a conditioned stimulus. Thus in infants six weeks to four months old, Kantrow (1937) found that the conditioned sucking response is rarely elicitable immediately after nursing.

The most recent studies on classical appetitive conditioning have attempted to control for some of the previous criticism leveled against the earlier studies (Lipsitt, 1963). Lipsitt & Kaye (1964) in a carefully executed study were able to demonstrate conditioned sucking to a loud tone. The sucking to the tone was greater in infants who received paired presentations of the tone with insertion of a nipple in the mouth than in infants who received unpaired presentations of the same stimuli*. Conditioned head turning and auditory discrimination were demonstrated in the newborn by pairing a buzzer and tone as positive and negative stimuli (Siqueland and Lipsitt, 1966). The procedure involved the pairing of auditory stimuli with the tactual stimulus of being stroked near the mouth eliciting head turning. On the trials of the positive stimulus pairings with tactual stimulation, the infant was rewarded for head turning with glucose solution; however, the negative stimulus trials resulted in no reinforcement for head turning. The study demonstrated auditory discrimination in neonates because they increased their response to the tactual stimulus on the trials in which the positive auditory stimulus was presented. Two other studies reported by the same authors were less successful (Sequeland & Lipsitt, 1966). By simply pairing a buzzer with the tactual stimulation, they were unable to obtain conditioning to the buzzer, and by demanding that a turn to opposite sides be made for the positive and negative auditory stimulus, they were unable to obtain auditory discrimination (Siqueland & Lipsitt, 1966). In contrast to these negative results, Papousek (1967) was able to condition a head turning response to a bell after three weeks of life. These discrepant results might be explained by the facts that the infants in the latter study (Papousek, 1967) were older than those in the previous studies (Sigueland & Lipsitt, 1966) and that the ascendance of cortical regulation increases as the neonate grows older. It is puzzling to note, however, that the learning of an apparently more complex auditory discrimination can occur earlier than simple auditory conditioning. Nevertheless, the results on classical appetitive conditioning have been generally positive when compared with classical defense conditioning (Brackbill & Koltsova, 1967; Lipsitt, 1963; Sameroff, 1968); the negative results found in appetitive conditioning in studies by the Russians (Lipsitt, 1963), however, demand further explorations into the parameters and mechanisms for appetitive classical conditioning at this time.

Classical conditioning, other than aversive or appetitive, has also been recently demonstrated in newborns with the Babkin reflex (Kaye, 1965). The Babkin reflex involves opening the mouth and turning it downward to the stimulus of pressing the neonate's palms; the CS consisted of transporting the arms of the infant from his sides over his head just prior to pressing his palms. The experimental group had five baseline trials of air-lifting alone, thirty-five conditioning trials, and ten extinction trials. The control group

---

*The controls for sensitization to the CS and extinction trials are clearly an improvement over the previous studies. Sameroff (1968) however, questions whether conditioning studies using sucking responses are really classical conditioning. He notes that the conditioned mouth movement without a nipple is a response quite different from sucking on a nipple and it is impossible to make the C.R. totally identical with the U.C.R. In spite of this criticism, it is hard to understand why the underlying associative process is questioned.

had the same baseline trials as the experimental group, followed by thirty-five trials of simple palm-pressing with the arms held in an upward position and by fifteen extinction trials. The results of this rather ingeneous technique indicated that the experimental group gave reliably more Babkin responses during the extinction period.

Turning from classical conditioning, there have been several recent studies which appear to be employing operant conditioning techniques although they are sometimes mixed with classical conditioning procedures (Sameroff, 1968). Prior to this decade, there had been no systematic studies on operant conditioning in early infancy (Lipsitt, 1963). In the instrumental or operant paradigms, the associative connection can be made between the response and its after-effect normally referred to as the reinforcement or response consequence (Lipsitt, 1963). Depending on whether the response consequence is rewarding or punishing, the response will either increase or decrease. Response differentiation may occur when some components of the response are rewarded while others go unrewarded. Sameroff (1968) demonstrated response differentiation in the neonate by rewarding the child with milk either for mouthing or sucking. When the mouthing was simply reinforced, the sucking component diminished or disappeared. Similar results have been found with infants one month and older (Bruner, 1968). Lipsitt, Kaye and Bosack (1966) increased a low sucking rate made to a tube by adding a dextrose solution through the tube hole. Finally, several studies have reported success with operant conditioning of head-turning (Sameroff, 1968; Siqueland & Lipsitt, 1966). The rate of head-turning increased in two groups which were reinforced for this response and decreased in a third group which was reinforced for holding the head still (Sameroff, 1968). Head-turning to tactual stimulation of the cheek increased as a result of reinforcement and was differentially effective in getting the infant to turn his head more to one side (Siqueland & Lipsitt, 1966). This study was also combined, in a manner described earlier, with a classical conditioning procedure. Operant response differentiation in these experiments differs from Skinner's "shaping" in that an already organized pattern of behavior is strengthened and enhanced as a result of reinforcement (Sameroff, 1968).

The presence of "associative" processes in the human neonate appears to be partially substantiated by the recent studies on instrumental (operant) *and* classical appetitive conditioning.* Horowitz (1968) interprets the recent findings as follows:

---

*Because we have referred to learning as an "associative" process we have purposely omitted the neonatal studies on habituation and response adaptation. Many of these studies are reviewed or discussed in the following sources: Brackbill & Koltsova (1967); Horowitz (1968); Lipsitt (1963); Sameroff (1968).

It could be maintained that in the last ten years research on infant learning has been largely involved in demonstrating on methodologically sounder grounds the claims of the '20s and '30s that conditioning can be made to occur in neonates and very young human infants . . . One area that touches on a variety of problems concerns the sensory modality of external stimulation involved in conditioning. First, it is clear that much information is yet to be gathered on auditory, visual, tactual, and kinesthetic sensitivity (p. 110).

The presence of learning in the neonate does not detract from the thesis that earliest infant activity is primarily subcortical and reflexive and gradually gives way to more cortically controlled activities (McGraw, 1943; Peiper, 1963). It would be useless to deny however, the possibility that some of infants' activity at birth is regulated by the cortical areas. The possibility that further maturation of the nervous system is occurring in the early months is bolstered by the fact that there is a negative correlation between age and number of reinforced trials necessary to achieve a conditioned response (Brackbill & Koltsova, 1967). Maturation, here, need not be interpreted as simply a genic unfolding of the nervous system, since even at this early stage an *interactionist* position is plausible. The effect, of the stimulation of early learning probably enhance the further growth of cortical hemispheres; *and this in turn facilitates further learning.* The findings of Krech (1967) on the further development, in the rat, of the cerebral hemispheres as a result of stimulus enrichment (see p. 81) is just one indication of the possible effect that early environmental stimulation has on the further growth of the neonatal system.*

INFANT CARE PRACTICES IN THE NEONATAL AND INFANCY PERIODS

Thus far, we have been considering the infants' capacities as relatively independent of the surrounding environment. It is true that the utilization of the neonate's sensory-motor system is an event which can occur without interpersonal contact, but this is the exception rather than the rule. Clearly, the stimulus of the interpersonal world occurs with the beginning of infant care practices.

Historically, infant care practices have centered around such considerations as breast-versus-bottle feeding, toilet training and demands for sphincter control, and maternal contact (e.g., "rooming-in" vs. other types of hospital procedures). The preoccupation with such topics as orality and anality is due to the influence of psychoanalysis in the study of infant care practices.

---

*Sameroff (1968) has presented an "interactionist" position which interprets most of the early neonatal learning findings within a Piagetian framework. Although his theorizing is provocative, he falls prey to Piaget's obliteration of the distinction between reflexive and non-reflexive behaviors (see p. 86).

The prescriptions made by child care specialists were marked by rather radical shifts in ideology over the years. Thus, the decades of the 1940's and 50's was characterized by a tolerance toward the child's autoerotic impulses, while from 1914 to 1921 severe curtailment of these impulses was advocated. The changes in ideology over the years was couched in dogmotic notions and fads about the nature of desirable infant care and about the personality implications of such care. In the past, this field was characterized more by ex cathedra dogma than was any other branch of medicine, psychiatry, or psychology. The term "dogma" is used because the assertions and opinions expressed were largely empirically unvalidated and yet were dispensed with the authority and confidence befitting indisputably proven scientific fact.

The critical reviews of the effects of these practices (Orlansky, 1949; Vincent, 1951; Wolfenstein, 1953), combined with the waning influence of psychoanalysis in the study of infants has finally led to a decrease in dogmatic attitudes. Thus, the 1963 version of *Infant Care* is characterized by a complete absence of dogmatism about the influence of a specific practice and a recognition of the possibility of alternative modes of infant response to similar forms of infant stimulation (Caldwell, 1964) *.

Contemporary research on infant care practices appears to be abandoning the older emphasis on a limited number of variables of material care (e.g., breast-versus-bottle fed, rooming-in, feeding and weaning etc.) because there are dimensions of the neonate's and infant's environment that are of much greater significance than such variables as weaning and toilet training (Yarrow, 1963). Certainly, many of the currently prescribed practices (e.g., self-demand feeding, delayed toilet training, rooming-in) may be recommended because of practical advantages associated with their use in the day-to-day management of infants. They take into account maturational readiness, recognize individual differences among children and diurnal fluctuations within the same child, avoid the imposition of unnecessary frustrations, enhance the child's perception of his environment as generally dependable and benevolent, and encourage parents to develop confidence in their own judgment. Thus, in general, they have an immediate impact upon child behavior serving to eliminate many causes of unnecessary friction between parent and child, to increase the latter's frustration tolerance, and to reduce the incidence of behavior problems associated with infant care. None of the above practices, however, are *invariably* superior to their predecessors, and some of them (e.g., breast-feeding, late weaning) have not been shown to be superior at all to other alternatives. In either case it is clear that when used inflexibly or carried to extremes they create serious new

Caldwell (1964) has the most thorough and complete review of infant care practices to date.

problems of their own. In general it has not been demonstrated that any specific practice significantly improves health, nutrition, and general developments or experts lasting differential effects on personality or adjustment.

More important than the surface value of using a specific practice, consideration of the parental attitudes for use of a particular practice is exigent. It may turn out that:

> Underlying attitudes may influence not only the choice of a specific parent practice (such as decision to breastfeed) but also support the decision when personal needs (comfort, convenience) challenge the wisdom of the choice (Caldwell, 1964; p. 81).

For example, infant females with mothers characterized as "warm" did much better with breast feeding than with formula feeding, whereas the infant females of "cold" mothers showed less disturbance with formula feeding than with breast feeding. This finding did not appear in the case of infant males (Heinstein, 1963).

The fact that sex differences occur above hints at the possibility that interaction effects may be more important than either attitudes or practices considered separately (Caldwell, 1964). Interest in reciprocal interaction between mother and child however is just beginning to be taken seriously. The previous research has been "one tailed" in that the child's characteristics have been attributed to parental treatment and handling, and no consideration has been given to the possible effects that infant activities and characteristics have on the particular practices that the parent utilizes (Bell, 1964).

The demonstration that infants are *individually* different even from birth (e.g., activity level, irritability, etc., see p. 107) has encouraged recent studies on infant care practices to consider the effects of the individual infants on the mode and patterning of caretaking (Caldwell & Hersher, 1964; Yarrow, 1963; 1964). These studies rest on the assumption that the infant is an active organism influencing his immediate environment, rather than a passive-receptive creature receiving and reacting to the effects of caretaking (Blauvelt & McKenna, 1963). Thus, considering the infant as the initial stimulus to the social reaction helps to explain the differences in the caretaking behavior of the same foster mother toward two infants of the same sex and age (assigned almost simultaneously to her) (Yarrow, 1965). The infant who showed the higher levels of waking motoric activity and response to social stimuli produced more immediate gratification of his needs and more physical contact with the caretaker than did the other infant (Yarrow, 1965). The importance of this simple finding is that it illustrates the need for consideration both of the characteristics of the infant and of the characteristics and responses of the caretaker (Yarrow, 1965). (The results of the above study could be quite different if the parent or caretaker had a very low tolerance for high activity children.).

Research strategies in recent studies of mother-infant interaction appear to be following Caldwell's (1964) prescription which suggests that:

> Closer attention . . . be given to important subject variables which may mediate the effect of specific practices. Examining for effects of specific practices on boys and girls seems obligatory in future research, as does concern with individual differences in attributes other than those serving as dependent variables in a given study (p. 81).

INFANT TRAINING AND ADULT PERSONALITY

The influence of the psychoanalytic model has forced many theorists to make the unwarranted conclusion that infant care practices have a rather direct influence on later personality development. The evidence, in general, has not supported the widely-held belief that *specific practices in and of themselves* contribute significantly to enduring psychosocial and idosyncratic differences in personality development. Our purpose in the present section is to propose possible reasons for this absence or relationship and to suggest how and under what conditions infant and early childhood experience might conceivably influence the development of intracultural (idiosyncratic) differences in personality structure as well as the distinctive (psychosocial) patterning of personality traits in different cultures.

Psychosocial Traits

Since cultures obviously tend to perpetuate themselves, i.e., to produce adult individuals who develop ways of behavior that are consonant with prevailing norms, it is self-evident that cultural values must somehow be woven into the developing fabric of personality structure. In the course of growing up, for example, certain influences must be brought to bear on the Hopi child that reliably produce a Hopi adult who more nearly approximates the Hopi than the American or Japanese idea of adult personality. The issue under discussion here is whether the psychosocial aspects of personality are primarily transmitted (a) via *specific* infant care practices *as such* or as representative of broader cultural values, of (b) via more direct and recurrent exposure to implicit and explicit expressions of pervasive cultural norms during the *entire* period of development prior to adult life but subsequent to infancy.

Assuming for the moment that particular infant care practices do not exert any specific invariant influence on personality development simply because they impinge on given erogenous zones, is it possible nevertheless that such practices consistently reflect basic cultural values and hence give rise to predictable personality outcomes on this basis? On a priori grounds alone this does not appear very likely. Since the realization of the same cultural goals and the expression of the same cultural attitudes can be achieved through different and even antithetical methods, the presence or absence of a particular practice cannot possibly have uniform attitudinal significance from one culture to another (Fromm, 1949). In addition, child rearing practices are influenced by such non-attitudinal and non-value factors as customs of marriage and family organization, economic conditions, and historical accident (Clausen, 1966; 1968). Thus, in their cross cultural survey of child training practices, Whiting and Child (1953) found that societal practices for one system of behavior are rather independent from its practices with respect to another. This study suggests that aspects of child training do not grow out of cultural attitudes which "might produce a dimension of general laxness or general strictness, but rather out of antecedents specific to each system of behavior."

This leaves us with the remaining possibility that cultural attitudes toward children, as well as other pervasive values, might be reflected in the *manner of administering* different practices if not in the mere fact of their presence of absence. Although careful observation would probably confirm this hypothesis, at least in part, it is still unlikely that cultural attitudes expressed in this way play an important role in structuring personality. First, during infancy the individual's contact with the culture is largely indirect and buffered by his family group. In a general way, of course, the family serves as the representative of the culture in dealing with the child. But parents differ considerably in how they interpret cultural norms relative to child rearing and in their need for conforming to such norms; and in any event, they are probably less disposed to follow the cultural prescription slavishly when the child is young and his lapses are excusable than when he is older. Furthermore, the actual flavor of the cultural attitude that is conveyed to the infant is undoubtedly influenced by affective and temperamental dimensions of the parent-child relationship that are *inter*-cultural in distribution (e.g., acceptance-rejection, under- or overdomination). Second, even if the cultural attitudes reflected in the manner of administering infant care practices were expressed more proximately and less variably, they could still not be perceived and understood very effectively by the perceptually and cognitively immature infant. Hence, if this mechanism of transmission does function at all it probably first becomes a significant factor in the post-infantile period. Environmental stimulation is not irrelevant during the first year of life but it only plays a supportive role; within a wide range of cultural diversity in child rearing attitudes, developmental outcomes remain essentially constant.

Therefore, in seeking to identify the mechanisms whereby cultures transmit the psychosocial attributes of personality it would seem more fruitful to look beyond the limited field of infant care practices. We would expect that the transmission of values, goals, interpersonal roles, and ways of perceiving and thinking would take place directly, as appropriate occasions for indoctrination arise, rather than obliquely and symbolically in the way parents administer the routines of child care. * In addition, we could expect that the culture would not limit its major indoctrinating efforts to cognitively immature infants but would exert socializing pressures continuously, recurrently, and in mutually reinforcing situations. Lastly we would expect that psychosocial traits would reflect certain *institutionalized* aspects of handling and timing shifts in children's biosocial status, i.e., the amount and explicitness of recognition accorded different stages of development, the choice of socializing methods and agents, the degree of role and status discontinuity existing between children and adults, the extent to which new demands and expectations are geared to maturational readiness and to individual differences, and the abruptness, duration and anxiety level associated with transitional stages of development.

Idiosyncratic Traits

Similar kinds of questions may be raised about the impact of infantile experience on the development of idiosyncratic traits as were asked in considering the impact of such experience on psychosocial traits. Do idiosyncratic traits develop (a) as consequences of *specific* infant care practices per se, (b) as consequences of *general parent attitudes* expressed in the presence or absence of practices or in the manner in which they are administered, or (c) as consequences of recurrent interpersonal experiences in later childhood and adolescence?

Practices versus Attitudinal Substrate. Two basic assumptions underlie the psychoanalytic doctrine that particular infant care practices in and of themselves exert specific, invarient, point-to-point effects on adult personality structure. First, it is assumed that the excess, sufficiency, or deficiency of "erotic" satisfaction experienced with a given practice impinges on a particular stage of psychosexual development (and its associated libidinal drive and erogenous zone) and plays a crucial organizing and directional role in subsequent personality development. Second it is assumed that the type of neuromuscular activity associated with erogenous experience (contraction or relaxation, sucking or biting) influences in a predetermined way the kind of personality trait that emerges.

---

* This does not mean that all indoctrination is accomplished by means of explicit training procedures. As a matter of fact, the influence of culture is so pervasive that perhaps most indoctrination occurs incidentally and on an implicit basis. Nevertheless incidental learning occurs most effectively in children when it is not indirect (inferential from or tangential to immediate experience). As Ralph Piddington observes in his Introduction to Social Anthropology, Vol. 2, 1957, *much indoctrinaction occurs on an impersonal level and its effects depend as much on its content as on the way in which it is carried out. The actual psychological mechanisms whereby individuals acquire the psychosocial traits that the* **culture** *transmits will be discussed in Chapter 17.*

It is not at all clear, however, why the satisfactions and frustrations resulting from such experience should have more than *immediate* effects on behavior. No self-evident reasons are apparent why these effects should be lasting, generalized, or involve core aspects of personality. It is true, of course, that since such parent-child interaction occurs in relation to erogenous zones and to the satisfactions, demands, and expectations connected therewith this experience acquires wider significance for the child's biosocial status, his sense of security, and his feelings of volitional and executive dependence and independence. But if this is the case the impact of infant care practices on personality development must be attributed to the child's reactions to the variable attitudinal, role, and status implications of these practices and not to the experience of particular erogenous satisfactions and gratifications *per se* or to any inherent relationships between sucking and passivity, biting and hostility, or and retention and stinginess.

Acceptance of the orthodox psychoanalytic thesis required that one arbitrarily exclude many important sources of variability associated with the meaning of a particular child rearing practice. One has to assume that the feeling tones and attitudes connected with the administration of a practice and the general psychological context of role and status relationships in which it occurs make no difference; that the child's past experience and present expectations and the attitudinal tenor of other parent practices are irrelevant. Hence, the more credible hypothesis at this point would be that it is the attitudinal substrate of a practice and its implications for biosocial status rather than its immediate hedonistic consequences which influence later personality development.

Underlying parent attitudes, however, cannot be inferred directly from the presence or absence of a practice. In the first place it is quite conceivable that the choice of a particular practice in preference to another may have no attitudinal significance whatsoever. At any rate it rarely has any *exclusive* attitudinal significance that is patently self-evident, varying rather in meaning from one parent to another in accordance with individual differences in personality and experience. Second, it also depends upon many factors completely unrelated to parents' attitudes of personality trends, such as social class membership, family tradition, and child rearing ideology. Thus in a given parent the choice of a particular practice may not have much attitudinal significance or be reflective of characteristic and pervasive general attitudes; and except in extremely homogeneous populations it is unlikely that its attitudinal significance will be similar for different individuals. It is hardly surprising, therefore, that children's personality traits in general are not significantly related to the presence or absence of particular infant care practices in their early upbringing and that "favorable" techniques in different areas of child rearing are not highly associated with

each other (Sewell, Mussen & Harris, 1955). Low and generally nonsignificant intercorrelations are found among child rearing practices, even in a
quite homogeneous population indicating that parents may follow what
appears to be permissive treatment with respect to one practice or during one
period of the child's development but employ restrictive techniques in other
aspects of training (Sewell, *et al.*, 1955)*.

Evidence such as this, however, does not prove that parents do not manifest characteristic, generalized, and pervasive attitudes in their child rearing
practices. It merely indicates, for the reasons pointed out above, that lack
of generality and individual self-consistency is found with respect to such
formal aspects of these practices as presence or absence, duration, and age
of initiation and termination. If we were to observe carefully the *manner in
which different practices were administered* it is much more likely, that persistent
and pervasive attitudinal constellations characteristic of individual parents'
approaches to child rearing could be identified. Such generalized *individual*
attitudes reflected in child rearing practices are probably more effective
in influencing the development of idiosyncratic traits than *cultural* attitudes
are in influencing the development of psychosocial traits. A single parent
can be more consistent and less variable in expressing his own personality
trends than many different parents can be in interpreting and expressing
cultural values. Also, unstandardized temperamental and attitudinal aspects
of parent personality are communicable to children more readily and directly,
less inferentially, and at an earlier age in the daily routines of child care
than the stylized aspects of cultural values which ordinarily require more
appropriately structured occasions for effective indoctrination.

Regardless of whether child rearing practices per se or the parent attitudes
they reflect are considered as significant in influencing subsequent personality
development, it is important to avoid the frequently committed error of
confusing antecedence with causality. This is the error of assuming that a
particular practice (or the attitudes underlying it) *causes* a later personality
trait simply because it precedes the latter chronologically. In the first place,
it stands to reason that any generalized parent attitude will be expressed
in *many* rather than in only one child rearing practice. Hence, no single
practice can ever be crucially determinative by itself. If consistent with a
general attitudinal trend, it would merely constitute one of many supportive
practices serving the same end; if inconsistent, its influence would be nullified
by the cumulative weight of other practices. Second, at the same time that
the child is exposed to reflections of parent attitudes and values in child
rearing practices he is also exposed to these same attitudes and values in other

---

*To some extent these findings are substantiated in the study of Sears, Maccoby and Levin (1957).
For example, there is almost no relation between dependency and other infant rearing practices.*

contexts both within and outside the family circle. Thus it is clear that manner of administering child rearing practices represents only one facet through which parent attitudes may be expressed, and that these attitudes impinge on the child's personality development through other channels (e.g., formal and informal instruction, interpersonal climate within family, observation of parents interacting with other persons) not only simultaneously but also continuously and recurrently throughout the entire period of child-hood. Many anthropological generalizations regarding alleged causal rela-tionships between specific infant care practices and various features of adult personality are suspect both for these reasons and because either (a) they are frequently derived from a sample of only one culture, and hence it is not even possible to ascertain whether the observed concomitance between infant training and adult personality is statistically significant on a cross-cultural basis; or (b) in most cross-cultural comparisons, the cultures are not suffi-ciently well matched on all other variables (apart from the specific practices under investigation) to warrant the drawing of definitive causal inferences.

Limiting Factors. Even if we grant that the child's personality development may be influenced by bread, pervasive parent attitudes reflected in infant care practices, this statement of relationship must be qualified by three important limiting conditions: parent attitudes cannot be communicated until infants are sufficiently mature to perceive and react to them, the reac-tions they make are in part a function of constitutional factors, and the effects of early infantile experience on personality may be modified (rein-forced, altered, reversed) by subsequent experience in later childhood, adolescence and adult life.

We have good reason to believe that the young infant's perceptual and cognitive immaturity tends to insulate him from the influence of subtle parent attitudes. His relatively slow rate of perceptual-social development, in comparison to that of the young of infrahuman mammals, limits his ability to perceive attitudinal cues and to comprehend their significance, to make subtle discriminations among feeling tones, to generalize and concep-tualize his interpersonal experience, or even to remember it for any length of time. It is true that infants tend to be quiescent when handled by calm, relaxed and confident mothers and to cry and fuss when handled by tense and flustered mothers who have ambivalent feelings about motherhood (Stewart, *et al.*, 1954). But it is much more parsimonious to suppose that maternal attitudes affect the smoothness and pleasantness of handling procedures and that the infant reacts to the immediate hedonistic and frustrating properties of the handling practices as such than that he perceives and responds to the attitudes underlying them. Hence we would conclude that until he actually perceives the parent attitudes that are reflected in the daily routines of child care they influence his immediate behavior rather than his personality development.

It would be a serious mistake, however, to assume that even *perceived* parent attitudes in late infancy and early childhood exert an irreversible effect on adult personality or that early favorable or unfavorable experience predetermines the outcome of later crucial stages of personality development. Thus, although favorable infantile and early childhood experience undoubtedly does much to insure the development of a well-adjusted adult personality, the damaging impact of serious trauma in late childhood, adolescence, and adult life cannot be discounted. Later rejection by parents, exposure to overprotective and under- or over dominating attitudes, crippling disease, extreme somatic deviations in adolescence, problems of acculturation and culture conflict*, severe economic hardships, etc., all leave their mark in undoing part of the desirable foundation established in childhood.

An additional source of trauma affecting later personality development lies in the tremendous contrast that prevails in certain cultures between the permissiveness of early upbringing and the severity of the demands and expectations imposed upon the adult (Goldfrank, 1945). This consideration is vital in evaluating the suggestion advanced by many that we import into our own culture some of the maximally permissive practices employed by some primitive peoples. Thus, prolonged and extreme mothering might be quite appropriate in Okinawa where the culture as a whole is relatively simply organized, undemanding, and noncompetitive and might indeed constitute *one* of the reasons for the relatively low incidence of psychosis among the Okinawans. But when the same practices are employed by immigrant Okinawan parents in the highly stratified and competitive Hawaiian culture, the incidence of psychosis is significantly greater than among other ethnic immigrant groups of comparable socioeconomic status (Wedge, 1952).

Evidence regarding the apparently irreversible effects of certain infantile experiences on the later behavior of infrahuman mammals cannot be applied indiscriminately to human infants. In the first place young infrahuman infants are relatively more mature, perceptually and socially, and hence can be influenced more crucially by early infantile experience. Second, personality development is more complex in human beings: a larger number of component developmental processes is involved; and as the critical phases of the different processes succeed each other, the relative importance of different interpersonal variables keeps shifting. Lastly, the possibilities of reversing the direction of personality development are much enhanced in

---

Discussions of the variables affecting the impact of acculturation on personality are available in Clausen (1968) and Goslin (1969).

human beings because of their greater ability to verbalize and generalize their experience, and because of the more important role of the environment in patterning major aspects of their development.

A final consideration affecting the impact of infantile experience is the matter of constitutional differences. The active, self-assertive child, for example, neither perceives nor reacts in the same way to parental rejection or overdomination as does the phlegmatic, submissive child; and this reactive difference in turn differentially affects the perpetuation or modification of the parent attitude in question. Thus, constitutional factors not only provide for interindividual variability in response to similar infantile experience, but also account for much intraindividual continuity in personality structure. If a given personality trait remains stable over the years, its persistence need not necessarily be attributed to the indelible influence of infantile experience, but may be explained both by the stability of certain temperamental predispositions and by the recurrence of the same environmental factors.

PART III

Personality Development

CHAPTER 8

Ego Development*

THE INVESTIGATION of the self-concept in early infancy is obviously fraught with serious scientific hazards. In the absence of verbal reports from the child regarding his perceptions of self and universe, we must have recourse to speculation and inference from the way he is treated, from the demands made upon him, from his reactive capacities, and from a subjective estimate of the degree of cognitive sophistication that determines his perception of these things. In making such inferences, the greatest single source of error is an "adultomorphic" approach which can never be completely avoided (see p. 12). But despite this limitation and the improbability of ever obtaining objectively verifiable data, it is desirable to deal, even by means of speculation, with this period, in order to prevent gaps in our theory of personality. Later stages of ego development are naturally dependent in part upon beginning phases in the evolution of a notion of self—even if the infant cannot tell us what they are. Speculative formulations, provided that they possess some plausibility, and obey the law of parsimony, are logically reconcilable with related empirical data at a later stage of development. Uttered with the humility and tentativeness befitting their status as hypotheses rather than as definitively established facts, they are as permissable here as in other theoretical areas. However, in this particular instance there is the additional requirement that they be consistent with the presumed cognitive maturity of infants.

DEFINITION OF CONCEPTS

To avoid confusion later it is necessary to distinguish at the outset between the terms *self*, *self-concept*, *ego*, and *personality*. These constitute, in the order given, an ascending hierarchy of complexity and inclusiveness. The *self* is a constellation of individual perceptions and memories consisting of the visual image of the appearance of one's body, the auditory image of the sound of one's name, images of kinaesthetic sensations and visceral tension, memories of personal events, etc. The *self-concept*, on the other hand, is an abstraction of the essential and distinguishing characteristics of the self that differentiate an individual's "selfhood" from the environment and from other selves. In the

---

*The material in this chapter is largely a revised and highly abridged version of material presented in earlier publications of the first author (Ausubel, 1952, 1954, 1968).

course of development, various evaluative attitudes, values, aspirations, motives and obligations become associated with the self-concept. The organized system of interrelated self-attitudes, self-motives and self-values that results may be called the *ego*. This constellation of ego referents, in turn, undergoes conceptualization: a least common denominator is abstracted and, at any given stage of development, it constitutes the conceptual essence of the person's notion of himself as a functioning individual endowed with certain attributes related to role and status. Insofar as this abstraction is a discriminable content of awareness characterized by personal identifiability and some continuity over time, it enjoys a measure of psychological substantiveness. Hence, as long as one does not reify it (i.e., attribute corporeality, activity or motivation to it) it is justifiable to refer to the ego as an entity.

Personality is a still more inclusive term than ego. It includes *all* of the behavioral predispositions characteristic of the individual at a given point in his life history. Thus it embraces the peripheral, transitory, and trivial as well as the central aspects of his behavioral repertoire. This distinction between ego and personality highlights the crucial role of the ego in the individual's personality organization. His psychological world can be ordered in terms of degree of ego-involvement, with concentric zones of objects, persons, values and activities varying in distance of affective proximity to self. The more central zones are areas of concern and importance to him. He has a vital stake in them. What happens in these areas is a source of pride or shame, of feelings of success or failure. It is these central ego-implicated constituents of personality which give it continuity, consistency, and generality.

In the present chapter we propose to present a normative overview of ego development, to delineate the changes in ego structure that accompany shifts in the biosocial status of the developing individual. The remaining chapters will consider in greater detail various component aspects (emotions, values, and interests) and determinants (relationships with parents, peers, teachers, and the wider culture) of ego development. Other determinants of ego development (physical and motor capacity, language, and cognition), which also constitute important areas of child development in their own right, will be considered in the next part.

PREDETERMINISTIC APPROACHES TO EGO DEVELOPMENT

According to psychoanalytic doctrine, the ego is formed as a characterological precipitate of the id as the latter comes into contact with reality (Freud, 1952, 1935; Hartmann, 1952). It supposedly serves both as a subjugator of socially unacceptable id impulses and as an ally of the id in satisfying its libidinal drives through acceptable means (Freud, 1952, 1935). Thus psychoanalytic theory does not regard the ego as completely preformed but as an experiential derivative of innate drives (Loevinger, 1967). Nevertheless it is clear that this theory follows basically predeterministic lines: variability in ego development can only occur within the framework of an innately patterned sequence of prestructured libidinal drives; ego drives do not arise autonomously in the course of changing interpersonal experience but can only be derived (sublimated) from the original source of libidinal energy. Since individual and cultural variability in the unfolding of psycho-sexual drives is made coextensive with ego development the *only* kind of ex-perience that is considered relevant to this development is that which involves frustration and gratification of erogenous drives. *

The psychoanalytic view of ego development also contains elements of preformationism as well as of predeterminism. All properties of the ego are not considered to evolve from experiential modification of the id; the existence of a rudimentary ego and of some specific ego attributes is assumed at birth (i.e., before there is any opportunity for interpersonal experience) (Freud, 1952; Hartmann, 1935). Thus the neonate is said to react with anxiety to the "trauma" of placental separation from the mother (Freud, 1936), to be capable of volition, and to experience feelings of omnipotence (Ferenczi, 1916); and the male child is presumed to have innate attitudes of both hatred toward and identification with his father (Freud, 1935). In addition, even though psychoanalysis attributes the genesis of patterned psycho-sexual drives exclusively to a phylogenetic id, too many core aspects of personality related to the self-concept are implicated in the origins of sexual behavior to exclude such behavior arbitrarily from ego structure. Hence, psychoanalytic concepts of psychosexual drives actually constitute a preformationistic ap-proach to an integral component of ego development. †

AN INTERACTIONAL APPROACH TO EGO DEVELOPMENT

Ego development may be viewed as the resultant of a process of con-tinuous interaction between current social experience and existing person-ality structure that is mediated by perceptual responses. According to this

---

*Gesell's approach to ego development, as already pointed out (see p. 25), is also predeterministic. It presumes that (just as in the case of early motor development) the basic order and the general modality if not the specific outline of differentiations are determined by intrinsic factors (ancestral genes). Environ-mental factors allegedly account for only minor variations in ego development, whereas all basic uni-formities are attributed to internal "morphogenic" factors.

†Contemporary psychoanalytic ego psychology deviates from orthodox psychoanalytic psychology in its emphasis on autonomous ego functions. The major change in emphasis is the belief that the moving force of ego development resides in the ego itself. Ego functioning is independent of sexual and aggressive drives. For a general discussion of this change in viewpoint see Loevinger, 1967; White, 1959, 1960, 1963. To a greater or lesser extent these neoanalytic viewpoints concur with the interactionist approach propounded in this chapter.

interactional view, neither the direction nor the patterning of ego development is predetermined by endogenous genic factors or by the sequential unfolding of psychosexual drives. It is felt instead that a wide range of interpersonal experience (both current and internalized within personality) constitutes the major determinant of inter- and intracultural uniformities in ego development. * Such experience is prerequisite to the genesis of the ego and of ego attributes, including psychosexual drives, and its salient components are not infant care practices that impinge on erogenous zones but significant dimensions of parent attitudes, shifts in role and status, and changes in cultural demands and expectations. From exposure to influences such as these, ego drives are generated autonomously rather than being sublimated from prestructured libidinal drives.

Major Variables Affecting Ego Development

The more important variables that participate in ego development may be classified as social (external), endogenous (internal), and perceptual (mediating). *Social* variables include all aspects of institutional, inter-group, intra-group, and interpersonal relationships and organization that affect the course of ego development. They not only comprise the current stimulating conditions that help to determine the direction of behavior and development at any particular moment, but also, through a process of internalization, contribute significantly to the growing structure of personality. *Endogenous* (or internal) variables constitute the growth matrix (see p. 51) of ego development. They are a product of all previous relevant interactions between heredity and environment, and selectively predispose or limit the direction of change in response to current experience. Internal variables include personality and temperamental traits, level of motor and cognitive capacity, physiological factors, and, most important, the prevailing state of ego organization itself. Thus, it is clear that most significant personality development is not a simple and immediate function of social experience. Complicating the relationship are both the ego structure that the individual brings into the social situation and perceptual factors (Cronbach, 1957).

Perceptual variables play a mediating role in the interactional process underlying ego development. Before social experience (e.g., parent attitudes, cultural norms), various competencies related to self, and different ego needs, motives and attributes can be brought together in the same interactional field, they must first be reacted to perceptually (i.e., give rise to a clear content of awareness). The stimulus world, therefore, whether of internal or external

---

Various patterning predispositions and potentialities of genic origin (see table 1, p. 66) also give rise to intercultural uniformities in ego development. These genic factors, however, influence primarily those general features of human behavior that set limits to variability in ego development rather than determine the direction of such development in their own right.

origin, is not the proximate antecedent of behavior or development; the perceptual world is. * Thus although a child's role and status in the home and his parents' behavior toward him are objective social events in the real world, they affect his ego development only to the extent and in the form in which they are perceived. The importance of this proposition rests on the fact that children's person perceptions are realities which are quite different from the assessments based on observations of researchers (Dubin and Dubin, 1965). This does not imply that the perceived world *is* the real world but that perceptual reality is both psychological reality and the actual (mediating) variable that influences behavior and development.

Insofar as perception itself undergoes systematic developmental changes during the life cycle, level of perceptual maturity must be considered a determining as well as a mediating variable in ego development. We have already seen the extent to which perceptual immaturity insulates the young infant from awareness of environmental threat and from the attitudinal effects of parent practices. This same perceptual immaturity, for example, does not enable the child to appreciate fully his executive dependence and incompetence or the meaning of parental deference to his needs during infancy; it obscures awareness of subtle interpersonal attitudes and of the functional and reciprocal nature of social rules and obligations within the childhood peer group. On the other hand, increasing perceptual maturity makes it possible for the self-concept and the ego to become abstract conceptual entities. Also, many of the more complex constituents of the ego, such as self-esteem, self-critical ability, and the ability to set consistent levels of aspiration could only exist in very rudimentary fashion in the absence of verbal symbols.

How can we explain these evidences of growth in perceptual maturity? One obvious possibility is that perceptual maturity is a function of cognitive capacity and sophistication which, in turn, tend to increase with age and experience. Here we must consider the impact on perception of increased ability to verbalize, to manipulate symbols and abstractions, and to form categorical judgments; to make more subtle differentiations within the stimulus field, to avoid animistic thinking, and to disregard irrelevant instances of concomitance in reaching judgments of causality (see Chapter 16). Some aspects of perceptual maturation, however, are probably attributable to normative modifications of ego structure itself, e.g., changed perceptions of parents and peers following ego devaluation (see pp. 260-330).

The Nature and Acquisition of Biosocial Status

The term "biosocial status" is a convenient abstraction which makes it possible to refer to the generalized aspects of both role and status pertaining

---

*Perceptual reality considered as a dependent variable is itself an interactional product of stimulus content, cognitive maturity, and ego structure.

to an individual of given sex and functional age level in a relatively homogeneous cultural setting. Its *culturally standardized* attributes are anchored in the organizational procedures, requirements, values and traditions of social groupings and institutions. Thus infants, as a group in American middle-class culture, have a stereotyped biosocial status recognizably distinct from that of male and female children, adolescents and adults. The role aspects of biosocial status consist of significant interpersonal behavior functionally differentiated in part by adjustment to the demands and expectations of others; the status aspects delineate hierarchical position, defined by relative dominance, control, prerogatives, independence, prestige, etc., vis-à-vis others. However, the actual biosocial status that any *individual* enjoys is a *particular* interactional product that is a variant of the cultural stereotype. The latter serves as an external determinant entering into the formation of personal biosocial status by generating (through appropriate representatives) specific demands and expectations to which the individual carriers of the culture react (as they do to any social stimulus) in terms of existing ego structure, idiosyncratic personality traits, and perceptual maturity.

But it is not enough to say that individuals, in accordance with idiosyncratic personality dispositions and social situations, enact and enjoy variants of a perceived cultural stereotype of biosocial status. Because of an all-too-easy tendency to conceive of age level roles in a reified sense, as an ordered sequence of socially stylized masks and robes racked up in a cultural prop room all ready to don as the player moves across the stage of life, it is necessary to insist explicitly on the fact that biosocial status is for the most part an *individual achievement* in an interpersonal setting. Except for hereditary princes, few persons inherit a ready-made status; and except in the relatively rare instances of highly structured social situations, roles require considerable improvisation. Each of us must achieve our own biosocial status within the framework of the culturally standardized stereotype (Blumer, 1953).

This becomes more clear when one inquires as to how roles are learned. The formal concept of role implies that an individual acquires a role by learning from a model the actions, words, grimaces, and gestures appropriate for him in a given situation. But when one actually looks for this model in childhood it turns out to be little more than a reified abstraction. Does a child learn the child's role by attending the children's theatre, by reading books about children, or even by observing friends and siblings? No! In early childhood the cultural model becomes psychologically real mainly through the influence it exerts on the *parents'* child-rearing practices. In much the same manner as do the young of other mammalian species (Scott, 1967), the human infant, after highly variable initial contacts with parents, siblings, and others enters into increasingly standardized and stable relationships with them. The upshot of these repeated interactions are roles that he himself and his opposite numbers have *created*. It is only as the child grows older and is exposed more directly to the symbolic values of the culture that preconceived notions and models become important in the initial structuring of interpersonal "transactions" between human beings.

Primary and Derived Status. Whenever social life is characterized by differences in roles and status and by dependence of one person on another or on the group as a whole, one of the more basic kinds of human interaction that arises under such conditions is the reciprocal relationship of identification-acceptance. This type of relationship includes, in varying proportions, the elements of "dominance-subordination," "leadership-followership," and "care-dependency" (Bandura, 1962; Hartup, 1963; Mussen, 1967). Much confusion results, however, from the failure to distinguish between two essentially different kinds of identification-acceptance, each of which involves a reciprocal relationship between a relatively independent and dominant individual (or group) and a relatively dependent and subordinate individual (Ausubel, 1952).

One type of identification which is very common in the canine and simian worlds and very uncommon in the feline world may be called satellization (Ausubel, 1952). In a satellizing relationship the subordinate party acknowledges and accepts a subservient and deferential role, and the superordinate party in turn accepts him as an intrinsically valuable entity in his personal orbit. As the child acquires a stable sense of the superiority of the superordinate party, "look at me" develops into requests for approval, and for confirmation (Kohlberg, 1963); the child seeks approval of his performance primarily as confirmation that he is intrinsically valued rather than as evidence that he is intrinsically competent. The satellizer thereby acquires a vicarious or *derived* biosocial status (a) which is wholly a function of the dependent relationship and independent of his own competence or performance ability, and (b) which is bestowed upon him by the fiat of simple intrinsic valuation by a superordinate individual or group whose authority and power to do so are regarded as unchallengeable.

On the other hand, the two parties to the same "transaction" could relate to each other in quite a different way. The subordinate party could acknowledge his dependency as a temporary, regrettable, and much-to-be remedied fact of life requiring, as a matter of expediency, various *acts* of conformity and deference; but at the same time he does not have to accept a dependent and subservient status as a *person*. In turn, he could either be rejected outright or accorded qualified acceptance, i.e., not for intrinsic reasons (as a person for his own sake), but in terms of his current or potential competence of his usefulness to the superordinate party. The act of identification, if it occurs at all, consists solely in using the latter (superordinate) individual as an emulatory model so that he can learn his skills and methods of operation and thus eventually succeed to his enviable status; and accordingly, the only type of biosocial status that can be engendered in this situation is the *primary* status that reflects his actual functional competence, power, or control. This non-satellizing type of identification occurs for one of two reasons: either the superordinate party will not extend unqualified intrinsic acceptance (e.g., as in the case of the rejecting parent or the parent who values his child for ulterior self-enhancing purposes), or the subordinate party is unwilling to or incapable of satellizing.

The wider significance of primary and derived status for personality structure, as we shall hypothesize in detail later, is that each is associated with distinctive patterns of security (freedom from anticipated threat to physical integrity), adequacy (feelings of self-esteem, worth, importance), and other ego attributes (level of ego aspirations, dependence and independence, etc.). Corresponding to derived status in ego structure are both feelings of *intrinsic* security that inhere in the affectional aspects of a satellizing relationship, and feelings of *intrinsic* adequacy that are relatively immune to the vicissitudes of achievement and position. Corresponding in turn to primary status are (a) feelings of *extrinsic* security that depend upon biosocial competence or the possession of a competent executive arm in the person of an available super-ordinate figure, and (b) feelings of *extrinsic* adequacy that fluctuate with both absolute level of ego aspirations and the discrepancy between the latter and perceived accomplishment or hierarchical position (see p. 260).

Experienced versus "Objective" Dependency. It is important to realize that feelings of dependence and independence in ego structure do not correspond in point to point fashion to the theoretically expected "realities" of the environmental dependency situation. This is so because more proximate than these latter "realities" in determining dependency feelings are the actual attitudes and behaviors of parents and the child's perceptions of them. During early infancy, for example, when the child is most helpless and dependent "in fact," he is treated with most deference by his parents. Thus, despite his actual helplessness to gratify his needs or compel conformity to his wishes, considerable environmental support is given to his perception of self as volitionally independent. Perceptual immaturity adds further to the discrepancy between the child's actual biosocial incompetence and the minimal feelings of dependency he probably does experience (Sullivan, Grant, and Grant, 1957; see also p. 257).

Executive and Volitional Dependence. At this point it might be helpful to make more explicit the distinction between executive and volitional dependence. Both consist of affectively colored self-perceptions of limited self-sufficiency and freedom of action, but *executive* refers to the manipulative activity involved in completing a need-satisfaction sequence, whereas *volitional* refers solely to the act of willing the satisfaction of a given need apart from any consideration as to how this is to be consummated. As perceptions also they correspond only *more or less* to their relevant stimulus content. And although these two ego attributes tend to be positively related to each other, marked discrepancies may exist between them at any point in the life cycle, especially during infancy when it is reasonable to suppose that the child conceives of himself as both volitionally independent and executively dependent. *

In addition to constituting perceived ego attributes, volitional and executive dependence (or independence) also constitute ego *needs*. Their strength varies in relation to other ego attributes (such as notions of omnipotence), to needs for primary and derived status, and to parental and cultural demands, reinforcement and punishment. The need for executive dependence is compatible with and reinforced by the exalted (regal) self-concept of infants and with the benevolent, undemanding environment in which they live (see p. 257). The young child is coerced, by environmental pressures and by the need for derived status, both to surrender much volitional independence and to acquire more executive independence. During adolescence the attainment of executive independence is essential for achieving the volitional independence and primary status necessary for adult personality maturation.

Sources of Psychosocial and Idiosyncratic Differences

Psychosocial differences in ego development reflect both differences in the ways various cultures institutionalize interpersonal relationships on the basis of age, sex, and kinship, and differences in basic values and ideals of personality structure. These factors in turn influence such crucial aspects of ego development as the handling and timing of shifts in biosocial status (e.g., explicitness, abruptness, choice of socializing agents), the amounts and kinds of status that individuals are expected to seek, and the degree of personality maturity considered appropriate for different age levels. In our culture, for example, girls are expected to satellize more than boys, and women are expected to obtain a larger proportion of their current biosocial status than are men from derived rather than from primary sources. Thus, girls more than boys tend to perceive themselves as accepted and intrinsically valued by parents (Ausubel et al, 1954) and are more apt to be relatively docile, to conform to adult expectations, and to be good (Parsons, 1942). Boys' wishes and emotional responsiveness exceed girls' in the areas of self-aggrandizement, personal achievement, and possessions, and are surpassed by girls' in the direction of social and family relationships, physical appearance, and personal characteristics (Cobb, 1954; Crandall, 1967; Havighurst et al, 1954; Zeligs, 1942).

---

*Failure to make this distinction between volitional and executive dependence is responsible for the unexplained contradictory allegations in psychoanalytic literature that the infant both regards himself as omnipotent and feels overwhelmed by his dependence on parents.

Within the normative schema of ego development to be presented below, numerous opportunities also exist for the elaboration of idiosyncratic differences. First, it might be expected that children who are *temperamentally* more assertive, "thick-skinned," self-sufficient, energetic, or resistive to stress, would be less dependent on others' approval, more capable of maintaining self-esteem in the face of less primary or derived status, and in general less disposed to satellize than children with the opposite set of temperamental traits. It might also be expected that individuals genically predisposed to develop strong hedonistic needs would tend to be more resistive to pressures directed toward attenuation of these needs during the course of ego maturation; and that children who are accelerated in motor or cognitive development would be subjected to greater parental demands for mature behavior. Second, as will be seen shortly, differences in such basic dimensions of parent attitudes as acceptance-rejection, intrinsic-extrinsic valuation, and over- or under-domination, have important implications for variability in satellization, desatellization, needs for achievement, and mode of assimilating values. A third source of idiosyncratic differences in development lies in variability in perceptual sensitivity. It seems reasonable to suppose, for example, that the perceptually more sensitive child is more vulnerable to the detrimental effects of unfavorable parental attitudes and is more apt to be aware of his own limitations and the realities of the dependency situation. Finally, once differences in such ego attributes as relative propensity to satellize are established they themselves serve as important sources of variability in ego development. Thus we might predict that, everything else being equal, the more intrinsic self-esteem a child enjoys the less need he has to strive for ego aggrandizement and the more realistically he is able to adjust his current aspirational level to prior experience of failure (Ausubel *et al*, 1954).

NORMATIVE SEQUENCES IN EGO DEVELOPMENT*

In this section we propose to outline normative uniformities in the sequential course of ego development during childhood. Most of the evidence for this analysis comes from materials drawn from our own culture. Nevertheless, it is believed that sufficient intercultural commonality prevails in genic patterning predispositions, behavioral potentialities, and in intrafamilial and social needs, problems, and conditions of adaptation to make many of the hypothesized general features of ego development applicable to all cultural environments. This assumption, however, can only be verified by extensive cross-cultural investigation.

We wish to emphasize again that the theoretical propositions contained herein are frankly speculative and are offered as hypotheses only.

Differentiation of the Self-Concept

Preverbal Stage. As a unified abstraction of its essential properties, the self-concept is a complex ideational entity that is slow in developing and usually requires the facilitating influence of language. Nevertheless the child possesses a functional *perception of self*, i.e., of the distinction between that which is within and that which is beyond the borders of his own body, long before he acquires any language. As in the evolution of any new percept, the basic problem is that of defining boundaries between figure and ground. In the case of the self-percept, the boundaries of self must be delimited from the wider environment of objects and persons with which it is initially fused (Harvey *et al*, 1961; Murphy, 1947; Sherif, 1965).

This latter process occurs along multisensory lines as the infant comes into contact with his physical environment. The sense of touch acquaints him with the presence of objects outside himself; kinaesthetic sensations make him aware of his own movements in space; and the sense of pain vividly informs him that transgressions of the self-not-self boundary are unpleasant. The visual *body image* as manifested by self-recognition of a portrait or mirror reflection (Garai, 1966) and by correct identification of own age, size, sex, and skin color in a series of pictures first becomes a stable self-percept during the preschool period (Clark and Clark, 1947; Horowitz, 1943). Apparently, therefore, in the early years of childhood it serves more as an abstract symbol of self-identity than as a concrete functional datum helping the child to differentiate between himself and the environment.

Self-perception is facilitated further by the infant's reaction to the mother as a person. As early as six weeks he smiles differentially to the sound of the human voice even though it is not associated habitually with care and attention (Bühler, 1933; Dennis, 1941); and in the third month of life he smiles and vocalizes spontaneously in response to the human face (Dennis, 1941; Spitz, 1962). Thus mother's outline serves as an anchorage point for the slowly accumulating self-pattern (Murphy, 1947). It provides a scaffolding for the elaboration of his own self-portrait as a person, and as we shall see shortly, makes possible a perception of mother as a manipulator of his reality and as a causal agent in the satisfaction of his needs.

Perhaps the most poignant experience leading to the consciousness of self develops as an outgrowth of inevitable delays in the gratification of the infant's organic needs. Here the contrast between inner experience and the outside world is highlighted by the juxtaposition of awareness (a) of painful discomfort and pleasant satisfaction referable to the *body* and (b) of objects and persons in the *environment* that lead to dramatic change in the affective quality of consciousness. Later, when a sense of volition develops, the act of willing (as a directed expression of the self as an entity) and the assistance it invokes from other persons sharpens even more the distinction between self and environment. Further accentuation of the self-environment dichotomy accompanies the appreciation of cause-effect sequences and emerging perceptions of own helplessness, executive dependence, and volitional omnipotence to be described below.

Verbal Stage. The abstraction of a unified concept of self from its component percepts (cutaneous, visceral, visual, volitional, etc.) requires the intervention of language (Garai, 1966). Two preliminary steps precede the final emergence of the self-concept in its most highly developed verbal expression, the first-person singular: (a) the concept of possession, and (b) third-person reference to self. By the eighth month, "possessive emotions toward toys are manifested. . . . Between the tenth and twelfth months . . . a positive sense of property becomes observable" (Spitz, 1949). By 21 months* this is conceptualized as "mine," a generalized term that not only includes *all personal* possessions but also excludes the possessions of others. This concept of possession presupposes a sharpening of the distinction between self and others to the point where objects come to "belong" to the person habitually using them.

A slightly more advanced stage in the acquisition of a verbal concept of self is completed at 24 months. At this time, the child becomes aware of himself as an entity in the same sense that he perceives other persons as entities (Gesell *et al*, 1943). Before he referred to another child as "baby," now he uses this same term or his own given name in making third-person reference to himself, his possessions and his activities. The highest degree of nominative abstraction in relation to the self appears at 27 months when the child uses the personal pronoun "I" (Gesell *et al*, 1943). This "I" constitutes an abstraction of all the separate perceptions of self. It implies a genuine conceptual self-consciousness. In contrast to third-person usage which merely indicates cognizance of himself as a *person like other persons*, the use of the first-person singular means that he designates himself as a special and unique kind of personal entity, *distinct from all other persons* (Sherif, 1965). After this point is reached, self-reactions, at a new abstract level, become possible; these include identification with persons, goals and values, incorporation of standards, competitive behavior, and, finally, self-judgments, guilt feelings, and conscience.

The Yale norms reported here were obtained from a very specialized and unrepresentative group of children. As used in this chapter they are only intended to convey a rough notion of mean age and sequential order of development in an unrepresentative but relatively homogeneous sample of children in our culture. It is not implied that the same designated mean ages or sequences necessarily apply to all children everywhere.

The Omnipotent Phase

The stage of ego development that follows the emergence of a functional self-concept may be designated as the omnipotent phase (roughly, the period from six months to two and one-half years). It seems paradoxical and contradictory that feelings of omnipotence should coexist with the period of the child's greatest helplessness and dependence on adults. Yet, as we shall see shortly, the paradox is easily resolved if the nonunitary concept of dependence is first broken down into its easily discriminable executive and volitional components. When this is done self-perceptions of volitional independence and executive dependence are seen as quite compatible with each other under the biosocial conditions of infancy. Unlike the psycho-analytic doctrine of infantile omnipotence which assumes the existence both of a preformed ego and of volition at and even prior to birth (Ferenczi, 1916), the present theory conceives of omnipotent feelings in infants as a naturalistic product of actual interpersonal experience (parental deference) and cognitive immaturity. It is self-evident that the child's perception of his relative omnipotence cannot be demonstrated empirically prior to the advent of language; and even then it can only be inferred from the rampant expressions of imperiousness and possessiveness that are so prevalent during the latter portion of this age interval (Ames, 1952; Gesell *et al*, 1943).

Development of Executive Dependence. Although completely helpless and dependent *in fact*, it is highly improbable that the newborn infant appreciates his helplessness and executive dependence. Before he could conceivably recognize his helplessness, he would first have to be capable of deliberately willing the satisfaction of his needs and perceiving in a causal sense his own inability to do so. Similarly, to appreciate that he is dependent on *another* for the execution of his wishes requires that he perceive the latter as a person and the succorant acts of this person as causally related to his need-satisfaction sequences. In the first few months of life, however, crying is not volitional, mother is not perceived as a person, and the child probably has no conception of causality (Piaget, 1952; 1954). It is true, of course, that the mother is always present before and during the act of need reduction, and that after the first month of life merely holding the infant without offering him nourishment is sufficient to still his hunger cry. But at this early stage of development it is more credible (for the reasons given above) to suppose that the mother (by virtue of habitual association with need reduction) serves as a signal of imminent need satisfaction and perhaps as a substitutive satisfying object in her own right, than that the infant perceives his helplessness and the *causal* connection between mother's presence and the reduction of his hunger.

From the foregoing analysis it would seem that the development of a sense of volition is a prerequisite first step before a feeling of executive dependence can arise. How this development is brought about, however, must remain forever in the realm of speculation. The most credible hypothesis we can suggest here is that volition is a learned outgrowth of the innately determined pattern of general excitement in response to any intense internal or external stimulus (e.g., hunger). This reactive pattern, particularly crying, has adaptive value in that it frequently evokes maternal succorant activity which reduces the need responsible for the excitement. Eventually, after repeated observation of the efficacy of crying in relieving the tensions of need, it may be supposed that a causal connection is perceived between antecedent and consequent. At this point crying becomes a conscious, deliberately employed (volitional) device rather than an almost reflex response for relieving unpleasant sensations referable to self.

Once volition is acquired, it reciprocally facilitates the perception of causality, since the act of willing constitutes a vivid antecedent in many causal sequences. The child is now in a position to perceive that his expression of will does not lead to need satisfaction through his own manipulative activity (perception of own helplessness) but only through the intervention of an external agency (perception of executive dependence). In this instance ability to perceive the mother as a person facilitates the perception of causality inasmuch as it is undoubtedly less difficult to conceive of a person than of an object as a causal agent and manipulator or reality.

Environmental and Perceptual Supports of Omnipotence. But all the while that a conception of executive independence is being developed, a notion of *volitional* independence and omnipotence is concomitantly engendered. It is precisely when the child is most helpless that almost invariably in all cultures he is accorded more indulgence and deference by parents than at any other period of childhood (Whiting and Child, 1953). At this time parents tend to be most solicitous and eager to gratify his expressed needs. In general they make few demands upon him and usually accede to his legitimate requests. If training is instituted, it tends to be delayed, gradual and gentle (Leighton and Kluckhohn, 1947; Whiting and Child, 1953). In this benevolent environment, therefore, much support is provided, in external stimulus conditions, for a perception of parental subservience to his will. Furthermore, it is unlikely that he is sufficiently mature, cognitively speaking, to appreciate the relatively subtle motivations (i.e., love, duty, altruism) underlying their deference (Schaffer, 1963). The immaturity does not appear as a lack of ability to perceive the overt attitudes and behaviors of individuals in his interpersonal world; he does not expect to receive the same degree of deference from older siblings as he does from parents. It is manifested, rather, at the level of perceiving the more subtle, covert, or motivational aspects of attitudes. Thus the child has, quite understandably, the autistic misperception that because of his volitional power, the parent is *obliged* to serve him rather than the correct interpretation that the subservience is altruistic and performed in deference to his extreme helplessness (Sullivan *et al*, 1957).

The infant's appreciation of his *executive* dependence does not detract essentially from his self-concept of relative *volitional* omnipotence and independence. He perceives his helplessness and dependence on others, but nevertheless, when he wills the satisfaction of his needs, they seem to be satisfied. Hence his perception of dependency is limited to the executive sphere. A volitionally powerful individual has no need for executive competence as long as other competent persons are at his beck and call. In fact it may even enhance the child's notion of his own power that success in need gratification takes place *despite* the manifest handicap of executive incompetence. He might, therefore, legitimately think, "My will must be powerful indeed if a tiny, helpless creature like myself can compel omniscient adults to gratify my desires." At the very most, perceived executive dependence qualifies the regal scope of his will by making it subject to the availability of a compliant executive arm. Feelings of executive dependence thus become satisfactorily integrated as a subsidiary aspect of the more inclusive self-image of volitional omnipotence. And despite objective biosocial incompetency the infant's sense of adequacy (self-esteem) at this point—his feeling of personal worth, importance, and ability to control and manipulate the environment to his own ends—is predominantly of the *primary* type; that is, it depends upon a misinterpretation of early parental subservience to his needs and desires as a result of which he vastly exaggerates his volitional power and independence.

The self-perception of helplessness, however, constitutes a potential threat to the infant's physical safety and integrity. Hence it gives rise to an undercurrent of insecurity which can only be allayed by the continued availability of the executive arm upon which he is dependent (mother). Thus at this stage of development his sense of security—his level of confidence regarding the future benevolence of his interpersonal environment in providing for his basic needs—is closely allied with feelings of executive dependence; and inasmuch as a need for security exists it generates a parallel need for perpetuating executively dependent relationships. These dependency needs are reinforced both by (a) the perceived efficacy of such relationships in providing security, and in relieving hunger, discomfort, and insecurity (reward), and (b) by the undesirable consequences associated with unavailability of mother, i.e., insecurity, hunger, discomfort (frustration), the alleviation of which can only be accomplished through the highly canalized device of the dependency situation. Thus when the dependency needs of infancy are not satisfied because of abrupt separation from the mother, sudden change or ambiguity in the conditions of succorance, or premature demands for executive independence, there is some evidence of residual overdependence in young children (Hartup, 1963), and of overanxiety about dependence in adults.

The Ego Devaluation Crisis

As long as the infant is helpless in fact, parents are content to be indulgent and deferential in treating him, expecting only that he grow and realize the phylogenetic promise of infancy. In part this attitude is indicative of solicitousness and altruism; but it is also the only realistic expectation they could have in the light of his actual incapacity for responding to their direction. They are naturally desirous of being liberated from this subservience as soon as possible and of assuming the volitionally ascendent role that is warranted in the relationship. In addition they begin to feel the social pressure and the responsibility of training the child in the ways of his culture. But typically in all cultures they wait until he attains sufficient motor, cognitive, and social maturity to enable him to conform to their wishes.

The age deemed appropriate for ending the stage of volitional independence and executive dependence varies between two and four in different cultures. In our own middle-class society it is closer to two than four (Whiting, 1953). At this time parents become less deferential and attentive. They comfort the child less and demand more conformity to their own desires and to cultural norms. During this period the child is frequently weaned, is expected to acquire sphincter control, approved habits of eating and cleanliness, and to do more things for himself. Parents are less disposed to gratify his demands for immediate gratification, expect more frustration tolerance and responsible behavior, and may even require performance of some household chores. They also become less tolerant toward displays of childish aggression. In short, all of these radical changes in parent behavior tend to undermine environmental supports for infantile self-perceptions of volitional independence and omnipotence.

Increased cognitive sophistication also contributes to ego devaluation by enabling the child to perceive more accurately his relative insignificance and impotence in the household power structure. He begins to appreciate that his parents are free agents who are not obliged to defer to him, and only satisfy his needs out of altruism and good will, and that he is dependent upon them volitionally as well as executively. Now volitional independence is no longer perceived as compatible with executive dependence. As a consequence of ego devaluation, the situation is precisely reversed: increased *executive* independence is required along with greater *volitional* dependence. From this point on, perceived lack of executive independence is no longer regarded as a regal badge of omnipotence but as a condition necessitating dependence on the will of others.

The Satellizing Solution to Ego Devaluation

The devaluing pressures described above precipitate a crisis in ego-development that is conducive to rapid discontinuous change. They tend to render the infantile ego structure no longer tenable and to favor reorganization on a satellizing basis, since in no culture can the child compete with adults on better than marginal terms. The only stable, nonmarginal status to which he can aspire and still retain a reasonably high level of self-esteem requires the adoption of a volitionally dependent and subordinate role in relation to his parents. Since he cannot be omnipotent himself, the next best thing is to be a satellite of persons who *are*. By so doing he not only acquires a derived status which he enjoys by the fiat of being accepted and valued as important for himself (i.e., irrespective of his competence and performance ability), but also, by perceiving himself as allied with them, shares vicariously in their omnipotence. His sense of security now becomes less a function of having competent persons available to satisfy his physical needs than of maintaining an emotionally and volitionally dependent relationship with stronger, protective, and altruistic persons; such a relationship implies among other things, the provision of whatever succorance is necessary. He is also relieved of the burden of justifying his adequacy on the basis of hierarchical position or actual performance ability; these, at the very best, are marginal and, in any event, are subject to unpredictable fluctuations.

The satellizing solution to the ego devaluation crisis is more stable and realistic and less traumatic than any alternative solution open to the child at this time. Since feelings of adequacy (self-esteem) are largely a function of achieving status commensurate with level of ego aspiration, the retention of grandiose aspirations of volitional independence and omnipotence in the face of a reality which constantly belied these pretensions would obviously make him chronically vulnerable to serious deflation of self-esteem. On the other hand, there are limits to the degree of ego devaluation that is consonant with the maintenance of feelings of adequacy. If the child's ego aspirations had to be lowered to the point necessary to bring them into line with his *actual* ability to manipulate the environment, the resulting abrupt and precipitous trauma to self-esteem would probably be even greater than if the untenable pretensions to omnipotence were retained. Thus, by satellizing he avoids both unfavorable alternatives and maintains the maximal degree of self-esteem realistically compatible with the cultural status of children.

Prerequisites for Satellization. From the foregoing it is apparent that satellization cannot occur in just *any* kind of home environment. Before the child can accept volitional dependency and seek a derived status he must first perceive himself as genuinely accepted and valued for himself; for in the absence of these two parent attitudes, the potential advantages of satellization (i.e., the acquisition of a guaranteed and stable derived status and the assurance of intrinsic security and adequacy) are vitiated, and the child has little incentive for relinquishing the aspirations of volitional independence and becoming subservient to the will of another. Acceptance of volitional dependence on powerful figures is a hazardous venture indeed unless one feels assured in advance of their benevolent intentions. The rejected child also cannot acquire any derived status when his parents, instead of extending emotional support and protection, regard him as an unwanted burden. Rejection is the most extreme method of indicating to the child that the omnipotent and omniscient parents consider him unworthy.

Similarly, the advantages of a derived status cannot accrue if the parent only values the child in terms of his potential eminence.* Sooner or later the child realizes that he is not valued for himself but in terms of his potential capacity for gratifying frustrated parental ambitions. In this case, however, the infantile ego structure is more tenable and less subject to the usual pressures forcing devaluation. The over-valuing parent has no interest in deflating infantile notions of omnipotence and grandiosity. He interprets these characteristics as protentous of future greatness, and continues through indulgence and adulation to provide an environment which helps to maintain for some time the fiction of infantile omnipotence.

Several other variables related to the personality characteristics of parent and child tend to make the process of satellization more or less difficult or prolonged but do not affect ultimate outcome crucially. An unduly submissive or permissive parent who fails to impress the child with the distinction between their respective roles and prerogatives tends to prolong the phase of omnipotence. The child is spared the pressure of parental demands for conformity to their will and standards, and hence exhibits less need for ego devaluation. But if he is truly accepted and valued for his own sake he will eventually perceive his actual biosocial status and choose satellization as the most feasible solution to the problem of maintaining childhood self-esteem in an adult dominated society. Reference has already been made to the effect of temperamental variables in the child on tendency to satellize.

Consequences of Satellization. Satellization has profound consequences for all aspects of ego structure and for the future course of personality development. Part of the satellizing shift in source of biosocial status involves abandonment of notions both of volitional omnipotence and independence and of the centrality of self in the household social economy. But to compensate for this the child acquires a guaranteed source of derived status from which he obtains

---

Evidence from the study of children's perceptions of parent attitudes indicates that it is possible for extrinsically valuing parents to be perceived as accepting. The same evidence, however, supports the logical supposition that the rejecting parent cannot possibly extend intrinsic valuation to his child. In general, acceptance and intrinsic valuation are highly correlated. And since extrinsically valued children are almost invariably overvalued, the latter term alone will be used henceforth in referring to children who are overvalued for ulterior purposes. It is not rare, however, for accepted, intrinsically valued children to be overvalued. (Ausubel et al., 1954).

intrinsic feelings of security and adequacy. Thus children who perceive themselves as more intrinsically valued tend to undergo more ego devaluation:
they conceive of their capacities in less omnipotent terms and are less tenacious about maintaining unrealistically high levels of aspiration in a laboratory
task after cumulative experience of failure. (Ausubel *et al*, 1954). School
children ranked high on acceptance tend to be characterized by "willing
obedience" and relative lack of self-sufficiency and ego defensiveness (Sanford, 1943).

Another product of satellization that is related to but distinguishable from
its devaluing features (i.e., changes in status, aspiration level, volitional
independence) has to do with the *object* or *content* of the child's conformity to
parental volitional direction. It encompasses the training goals underlying
the new parental demands and expectations to which the child is conforming. These goals may be designated as *ego maturity* goals since (irrespective of
later changes in source of status, independence and volitional control) they
remain as constant objectives of personality maturation throughout the
desatellizing and adult as well as the satellizing period of ego development.
Although there is much intercultural variability in the ideals of personality
maturity, the needs of individual and cultural survival require that infantile
hedonism, executive dependency, and moral irresponsibility be attenuated
in all cultures. With respect to all of these components the infant is characteristically at one pole and the mature adult at the other.

Hence, as children increase in age beyond the period of infancy, they are
expected to grow in ability to develop nonhedonistic motivations, to plan in
terms of larger and more distant goals, and to forego immediate satisfactions
in order to gratify more important, long-term aspirations. Second, they are
expected to develop more executive independence. Growth in motor capacity for self-help is not always matched by equal *willingness* to carry out the
often tedious and time-consuming manipulations necessary in gratifying
needs. Parents, however, are unwilling to serve indefinitely as the executive
arm of their offspring's will, and demand that children acquire a certain
measure of self-sufficiency in the ordinary routines of living. In contrast to
younger children, for example, older children are less apt to request a helping
hand in walking a plank blindfolded (Heathers, 1953). Lastly, it is expected
that children will internalize parental standards, accept the moral obligation
to abide by them, and regard themselves as accountable to parents for lapses
therefrom.

During the satellizing period the child is motivated to undergo change in
these of personality development in order to obtain and retain parental
approval, since only in this way can he feel sure that the derived status he
enjoys will continue. His sense of security and adequacy becomes increasingly

dependent upon conformity to parental expectations of more mature behavior. Highly accepted children are judged as willing to exert much "conscientious effort" to hold the approval of "admired authorities" (Sanford, 1943); and children who perceive themselves as intrinsically valued at home are rated by teachers as more executively independent and more able to postpone the need for immediate hedonistic gratification (Ausubel *et al*, 1954). It has also been shown that task-oriented children (who presumably satellize more and have less need for ego aggrandizement) exhibit more emotional control and make fewer demands on adults (Gruber, 1954).

Finally, satellization has important implications for the mechanisms by which norms and values are assimilated from elders and from membership and reference groups. The essential motivation directing the satellizer's organization of his value system is the need to retain the acceptance and approval of the persons or groups that provide his derived status. Hence he develops a generalized set to perceive the world in the light of the values and expectations he attributes to the latter individuals. Children who perceive themselves as most intrinsically valued by parents are least apt to make value judgments deviating from perceived parent opinions (Ausubel *et al*, 1954). Later this orientation is reinforced by the desire to avoid the guilt feelings that are associated with repudiation of parental values. Value assimilation is thus an unconditional act of personal loyalty in which both considerations of expediency and the objective content of what is internalized are largely irrelevant from a motivational standpoint. The satellizing child identifies uncritically with the moral values and membership groups of his parents even when these are only meaningless symbols. Thus, irrespective of his actual experience with Negro children, the white child of five and six tends to assume his parents' attitudes (favorable or unfavorable) toward Negroes (Radke-Yarrow *et al*, 1952).

Negativistic Reactions to Devaluation. Ego devaluation is not usually brought about smoothly and painlessly. Typically (although not invariably) the child first resists the threatened loss of his infantile ego status by more vigorous and aggressive assertion of its grandiose-imperious features before acknowledging that the advantages of a derived status offer him a more tenable biosocial position (Ausubel, 1950). This leads to resistive or negativistic behavior which tends to reach a peak between two and three years of age (Harvey *et al*, 1961; Levy, 1955; White, 1960). The sources of resistance to ego devaluation are many: the inertia of existing personality organization; the insecurity and loss of immediate status involved in any rapid transition; the loss of advantages associated with present status and the disadvantages perceived in the new status; aggression and counteraggression.

The two- or three-year-old has been accustomed for some time to living with the prerogatives and immunities of his omnipotent ego structure. Hence, he is understandably reluctant to part with an orientation that places him at the center of his universe and to accept instead the role of dependent satellite. To retain parental approval he must inhibit hedonistic impulses, surrender volitional independence, and conform to parental standards; and until the prospects for satellization are entirely certain he must contend with the marginality and anxiety of transitional status. Rage, however, is more conspicuous than anxiety as a component of the child's response to ego devaluation, provided that the latter takes place in a generally benevolent and accepting atmosphere. Such an atmosphere alleviates anxiety by providing a pervasive sense of security and opportunity to satellize. Finally, negativism during this period constitutes a form of counteraggression against the often aggressive and interfering behaviors which parents use in pressing their training demands. Thus it tends to be less intense when either parent or child happens to be temperamentally unassertive or submissive.

Issues regarding self-help are frequent excitants of negativism. The child vigorously resists attempts to abolish the executive dependence and "baby ways" which are part of his omnipotent self-concept. On the other hand, denying him the opportunity for self-help is also a common precipitant of resistiveness. We may hypothesize here, however, that the child's ire is aroused not so much because desire for executive independence per se is frustrated but because of interference with his notion of volitional independence, i.e., with his perceived prerogative to do a particular task by himself *if he* so chooses (Ausubel, 1950). The birth of a sibling is often such a traumatic event because the dethroning and transfer of indulgent attention to a new child comes at a time when the ego is already bearing the brunt of a violent devaluing process. Thus sibling rivalry tends to be less severe if the younger child is born either before or after (i.e., less than 18 or more than 42 months) the crucial stage of devaluation in the older sibling (Sewall, 1930). Girls apparently manifest less negativism at this age than do boys* for two reasons: First, because they perceive themselves as more accepted and intrinsically valued by parents and have a more available like-sexed person with whom to identify, they can acquire more derived status (Ausubel *et al*, 1954). Second, they are able to obtain more subsidiary primary status than boys can by participating in female household tasks (Parsons, 1942).

In any particular instance of this kind of negativism, specific normative, temperamental, or situational factors are undoubtedly important. Because of volitional immaturity, compliance may be difficult without prior or simultaneous execution of the opposite alternative of refusal (Gesell *et al*, 1943). Misunderstanding of requests, disinterest in particular tasks, or requiring the child to exercise control and discrimination beyond his developmental

---

*See F. L. Goodenough, *Anger in young children*, Inst. Child Welf. Monogr. *No. 9, 1931.*

capacity also instigate negativistic behavior (Harvey *et al*, 1961). At any rate, children's negativism, when compared with that of adults, seems blatant since they lack a language repertoire of polite evasions and circumlocutions when aroused (Reynolds, 1928).

The Non-Satellizing Solution to Ego Devaluation

The satellizing solution, for the reasons given above, is hypothesized as the most acceptable and satisfactory, and hence as the most frequently chosen way in which children resolve the crisis of ego devaluation. It presupposes that they can acquire a derived status through the medium of a dependent parent-child relationship. In all cultures, however, a variable number of parents are psychologically incapable of or unwilling to extend acceptance and intrinsic valuation to their offspring. Thus, deprived of the self-esteem provided by the fiat of unconditional parental acceptance, such children must continue to seek primary status and feelings of adequacy on the basis of their *own* power to influence and control their environment. There is this important difference, however: whereas, before, a grandiose primary status could easily be assumed on the basis of a misinterpretation of parental subservience to their desires, increased cognitive maturity no longer makes this possible. Although the environment may continue to provide some support for the notions of volitional independence and omnipotence, these notions must be increasingly related to *actual* performance ability (executive competence) and hierarchical position.

If satellization is impossible, two alternatives now remain for resolving the crisis of ego devaluation: ego aspirations can still be maintained at the omnipotent level, or they can be drastically reduced so as to correspond to actual biosocial competence unenhanced by the derived status afforded by parental acceptance and prestige. In the first instance no devaluation of ego aspirations takes place; in the second, devaluation is complete. Although the latter alternative (complete devaluation) is conceivable under certain circumstances, it is not very probable. In the first place, it involves an overly drastic, abrupt, and traumatic depreciation of self-esteem. To aim high is in itself an enhancement of self-esteem, whereas immediate capitulation to the most unpalatable ego status available implies defeat and degradation. Second, various factors in the parent-child relationship operate against complete devaluation. An individual who fancies himself omnipotent does not react passively but with counter-aggression, bitterness, and vengeful fantasies to the hostility, aggression, and humiliating depreciation of his self-esteem implied by rejection by parents. By setting his sights on power and prestige, he hopes someday to obtain revenge and negate parental judgments regarding his worthlessness. In the case of the extrinsically valued (over-valued) child, complete devaluation is also an unlikely outcome. The parent who intends to aggrandize his own ego through the child's future eminence does all in his power to perpetuate the fiction of the latter's infantile omnipotence by maintaining a worshipful and deferential attitude. Thus, only where rejection takes the more passive form of prolonged emotional neglect and deprivation (as in foundling homes) is the child apt to undergo complete devaluation instead of attempting the preservation of omnipotent aspirations. If the neglect is sufficiently thoroughgoing, no real need for devaluation exists, since omnipotent fancies do not develop in the first place; and in the absence of overt parental aggression the maintenance of grandiose aspirations as a mechanism of counteraggression and revenge is unnecessary.

Consequences of Failure in Ego Devaluation. The child who fails to satellize generally fails also to undergo ego devaluation. The infantile personality structure that is not presented with the prerequisite conditions for reorganization tends to persist despite various shifts in biosocial status. Unable to achieve feelings of security and adequacy on a derived basis, he continues to seek their extrinsic counterparts. Feelings of adequacy continue to reflect primary status, whereas feelings of security remain a function of the parents' availability in providing for his basic needs until he possesses sufficient power, position, and prestige to feel unthreatened in facing the future.

Under these conditions the child is not obliged to relinquish aspirations for volitional independence, renunciation of which is implicit in the self-subordination of anyone who satellizes (i.e., who derives his status by the mere fact of dependent relationship to or acceptance by another). It is true that increased capacity to perceive the social environment more realistically compels him to revise somewhat both these aspirations and his self-estimate in a downward direction. But even though a discrepancy between aspirational level and current status is inevitable for some time, his high ego aspirations still tend to persist. In the absence of satellization which guarantees a derived intrinsic status, the acquisition of extrinsic (primary) status becomes a more compelling necessity. Hence, because of this compensatory need for high primary status, exaggeratedly high levels of ego aspiration remain tenaciously resistant to lowering despite their relative untenability in the present. The child hopes to close the gap in the future; and even in the meantime the maintenance of a high aspirational level in and of itself elevates self-esteem. Lending some empirical support to these speculations are the findings (a) that children who perceive themselves as extrinsically valued by parents tend to have more omnipotent conceptions of their capacities and to maintain a tenaciously high level of aspiration on a stylus maze task despite persistent failure (Ausubel *et al*, 1954); and (b) that low acceptance by parents tends to be associated with high scores on self-sufficiency and ego defensiveness and low scores on "willing obedience" in school children and with high need for achievement in college students (McClelland *et al*, 1953; Sanford, 1943; Schaefer and Bayley, 1963).

Although both rejected and overvalued children can enjoy no derived status and fail to undergo substantial devaluation in terms of aspirations for volitional independence and omnipotence, important differences between them are observable during the childhood years. In an austere and hostile home environment the rejected child cannot possibly acquire any primary status or entertain any immediate aspirations for same. Hence, not only is it impossible for him to enjoy any current self-esteem, but also all of his aspirations for power and prestige must either be projected outside the home (e.g., school, peer group) or into the more distant future. The need for survival also compels a humiliating outward acceptance of an authority and control he resents. In such generally insecure surroundings the catastrophic impairment of self-esteem to which he is subjected tends to make him over-react with fear to any new adjustive situation posing a threat to his sense of adequacy.* Nevertheless, hypertrophied ego aspirations are carefully nurtured within and there is no inner yielding of independence and no true subordination of self to others. The environment of the overvalued child, on the other hand, provides abundant satisfaction of both current needs for primary status and immediate aspirations for volitional independence and omnipotence. The child is installed in the home as an absolute monarch and is surrounded by adulation and obeisance. Hence he suffers no impairment of current self-esteem and has no current cause for neurotic anxiety. These eventualities first threaten when the protection offered by his unreal home environment is removed and his hypertrophied ego aspirations are confronted by peers and adults unbiased in his favor.

Satellizers and non-satellizers also differ markedly with respect to motivation for achieving ego maturity goals (i.e., executive independence, attenuation of hedonistic needs, development of moral responsibility). In contrast to the satellizing child who merely assimilates these goals and standards of parental training through a process of value assimilation (see p. 264), the non-satellizer is primarily motivated in his orientation to values by considerations of expediency and attainment of primary status. He responds to the prestige suggestion of authority figures not because of any need to agree unconditionally with them but because he acknowledges their suitability as emulatory models and stepping stones to power and prestige. Children who perceive themselves as extrinsically valued tend to disagree more with perceived parent opinions, and children who fail to identify emotionally with their parents only assimilate the latter's values superficially (Ausubel et al, 1954; Finney, 1961; Zuker, 1943).

The non-satellizer, therefore, does not accept the unconditional obligation to abide by *all* internalized values but tends to be selective in this regard.

This condition corresponds to neurotic auxiety *discussed in Chapter 12.*

The basis of this selectivity is the expediential criterion of potential usefulness for ego enhancement. Thus, the curbing of hedonistic impulses and the acquisition of executive independence are regarded as essential for ego enhancement and, therefore, become invested with moral obligation. Hence, with respect to these attributes of ego maturity, rejected school children tend to be rated just as favorably as their accepted contemporaries; whereas in the light of these same criteria extrinsically valued children (who are under little external pressure from parents to conform to standards of mature behavior) are temporarily retarded, probably until their status depends more on persons outside the home (Ausubel *et al*, 1954). On the other hand, values such as truthfulness and honesty do not always serve and sometimes oppose the interests of self-aggrandizement. In such instances, as suggested by the higher incidence of delinquency in children who are made to feel rejected, unloved and unwanted, the sense of obligation may selectively fail to operate unless buttressed by either strong convictions of equity or by coercive external sanctions.

The Satellizing Stage

After the negativistic reaction to ego devaluation subsides, the child who finds it possible to satellize is less self-assertive and more anxious to please and conform. He is more responsive to direction and can be bargained with or put off until "later" (Gesell *et al*, 1943). His appraisal of his own power and position is much depreciated and he feels quite dependent upon parental approval. In their eyes he is a "good boy," that is relatively docile, obedient, and manageable (Gesell *et al*, 1943; Harvey *et al*, 1961). But progress toward satellization does not proceed in a straight line. Changing capacities engender new self-perceptions with resulting fluctuations in disposition to remain content with a satellizing status.

Early Fluctuations. The four-year-old is more conscious of his own power and capacity. Marked strides have taken place in intellectual, motor, and social growth and he is much less dependent on his parents. He learns new ways of manipulating persons and social situations and establishes a modicum of independent status for himself outside the home in the world of his peers. With increased self-consciousness of capacity comes a resurgence of infantile ego characteristics; and possessing still a merely rudimentary self-critical faculty, he tends to exaggerate his newly acquired abilities. This tendency toward self-overestimation is facilitated by the intoxication accompanying initial success, by exposure to competitive cultural pressures, and by a past history, only recently abandoned, of grandiose thinking. Apparently there are times when he even believes he is capable enough to regain volitional independence and cast aside satellization in favor of seeking an extrinsic status on the basis of his own competence. Deference to parental authority can become burdensome, especially when it is so obvious to him that he "knows better." Parents are also always interfering with his desires for immediate pleasure.

Thus at four the child becomes expansive, boisterous, obstreperous and less anxious to please, obey, and conform, (Gesell *et al*, 1943). His behavior shows resistiveness to direction and is typically "out-of-bounds." He is "bigger" than everyone and can do everything (Gesell *et al*, 1943). Now for the first time he becomes intensely competitive in his play and desires to excel others (Mussen *et al*, 1963). Everything that he has or can do is compared with the possessions and abilities of others, and the decision regarding relative superiority is invariably made in his favor. He is acutely resentful of the privileges accorded older siblings. His concern with power and prestige is also manifested by his preoccupation with possession, by interference with and teasing of other children and household pets, and by snatching of toys (Mussen *et al*, 1963). With the growth of language his resistance assumes more verbal, subtle, and symbolic forms. Threats, boasts, contentiousness, deceit, and delaying and stalling tactics replace temper tantrums and open aggression.

It is important to distinguish between the negativism current at four and the variety prevailing at two and one-half. The goal of the latter is to perpetuate a highly autistic brand of omnipotence reflecting a very immature grasp of the social reality in which the child lives. The basis of parental subservience is completely misinterpreted and no incompatibility is perceived between executive dependence and volitional omnipotence. At four, however, omnipotent pretensions are given a more legitimate and realistic basis. Executive competence is accepted as prerequisite for volitional independence, but because of an inadequate self-critical faculty a very minimal degree of executive ability is inflated to the point of omniscience. Resistance is provoked when the exuberantly self-confident child tries to capture volitional control from the parent but meets with rebuff. At this age also self-assertion is no longer an end in itself; stimulated by competitive pressures, the child seeks to demonstrate his own superiority and reveal the weaknesses of others. But despite his bold front, the expression of negativism begins to acquire moral implications which were previously absent. This is revealed by a growing tendency to disclaim responsibility for resistive behavior; to ascribe it to accidental causes, to coercive agents operating on him, or to other persons; and to rationalize it as desirable or as a form of self-defense.

At other times, however, the four-year-old becomes painfully aware that he is only a child. When his bluff is called, his inescapably dependent biosocial position brings him back to reality with a thud. Thus he is torn between two opposing forces—a longing for volitional independence based on an exaggerated self-estimate of his executive competence, and a frightened desire to return to the protection of his dependent status as he stretches his wings too far and falls. This conflict is generally resolved in favor of the need to retain parental approval and derived status (that is, in the case of emotionally accepted, intrinsically valued children). The eventual triumph of satellization not only is aided by the development of a more realistic self-critical faculty but also is an almost inevitable product of the child's dependent biosocial status in all cultures. The acceptance of parental control is also facilitated by the growing prestige authority of the parent, by the child's unstructured attitudinal field, by the operation of guilt feelings in the child, by the child's rationalization of compulsory parental demands as elective desires of his own, and by the liberal application of rewards, threats, and punishment.

Later Aspects. Five, like three, is also a relatively quiet, well-conforming age that succeeds a period of negativism. As the child's self-critical faculty improves, his self-exuberance diminishes with a resulting loss of confidence in and enthusiasm for his own powers (Gesell *et al*, 1946). He is more dependent on adult emotional support, tends to be sympathetic, affectionate, and helpful, and is likely to invite supervision (Gesell *et al*, 1946). The parents are idealized and appear more omnipotent than ever. The extent to which the child accepts parental value judgments is indicated by his almost tearful sensitivity to approval. A minor threat or mild show of disapproval is remarkably successful in effecting compliance. But until identification with the parent reaches a maximum at about the age of eight, one more major fluctuation in level of satellization still has to occurr. It is precipitated by changes in biosocial status occasioned by the child's entrance into school.

The six-year-old tends to be aggressive, expansive, boastful, and resistive to direction (Gesell *et al*, 1946). His negativism follows the same pattern met with at age four: there is much of the same cockiness and blustering self-assurance based on an exaggerated notion of a recent gain in competence. But this time there is more real cause for crowing and ego inflation. For the first time now he is conceded an official status in the culture which is independent of the home: several hours every day he enjoys—at least in part—an extrinsic status which reflects his relative competence in mastering the curriculum. In addition, the authority of his parents is undermined by the termination of their reign as sole dispensers of truth and moral values. At the same time school exerts a sobering influence on the child since it also makes greater demands for mature behavior. Hence there is an improvement in such attributes of ego maturity as independence and reliability (Stendler and Young, 1950).

School does not have the same impact on all children. The satellizer tends to react to the teacher as a parent substitute, but the approval he receives from her is less unconditional and more related to performance ability than that which he receives from parents. In the total economy of his personality, also, the primary status he earns at school still plays a relatively peripheral role in comparison to the derived status provided by his home. The rejected child finds in school his first major opportunity to obtain any status whatsoever, whereas the overvalued child almost inevitably suffers a loss in appreciation at the hands of his classmates.

Satellizing and non-satellizing tendencies are not mutually exclusive or all-or-none characteristics. Superimposed on the satellizing child's quest for intrinsic status is a greater or lesser striving for a subsidiary extrinsic status. Similarly, non-satellizers are more or less able to form satellizing-like attachments to non-parent individuals who better qualify for this relationship. In addition to these individual differences, typical normative changes also take place in the balance between satellizing and non-satellizing tendencies. Despite periodic fluctuations, the general trend between three and eight years of age is toward greater satellization. Thereafter, rapid strides in social maturity, the new source of status available in the peer group, resentment over exclusion from the adult world, the impetus of sexual maturation, and changing expectations from adults all play a role in undermining the satellizing attitude. But even in adult life, as already pointed out, satellizing attitudes continue both to provide a subsidiary source of current status and to influence in substrate fashion level of ego aspirations, susceptibility to neurotic anxiety and mode of assimilating new values.

The Ego Maturation Crisis: Desatellization

Before ego development can be complete, one more important maturational step is necessary: emancipation from the home and preparation to assume the role of a volitionally independent adult in society. But before adult personality status can be attained, ego maturation must achieve a new balance between the dichotomous needs for independence and dependence— a balance which is closer to the volitional independence and self-assertiveness of infancy than to the docility and submissiveness of childhood. This involves largely a process of desatellization: the path away from volitional independence trod during early childhood must be largely retraced. Although the consummatory aspects of desatellization must be postponed until late adolescence, important preparatory aspects are accomplished during middle and late childhood.

In terms of the needs arising out of the child's dependent biosocial status, satellization is the most felicitous of all possible solutions to the crisis of ego devaluation. However, beginning in late childhood and extending throughout adolescence, a second major shift in biosocial status precipitates a new crisis in ego development, the maturation crisis, which demands a reorganization of comparable scope and significance. Confronted by changing bio-

social conditions and under pressure to become more volitionally independent and acquire more primary status, the satellizing organization of
personality becomes just as untenable and unadaptive as the omnipotent
organization was at an earlier date. But since the home and parents still
continue to function as the major status-giving influences in the child's life
until adolescence, the actual crisis phase (transitional disequilibrium, disorientation, marginality, and anxiety) is postponed until that time.

Despite much intercultural diversity in the specific content and method
of ego maturation, the *general* goals of personality maturation tend to be
similar in most cultures (see table 1, p. 66). Ego maturation encompasses
two essentially different kinds of personality changes—changes in (a) ego
maturity goals, and in (b) ego status goals. *Ego maturity* goals include the
attenuation of hedonistic motivation; the acquisition of increased executive
independence and frustration tolerance; the development of greater moral
responsibility, more realistic levels of aspiration, and more self-critical
ability; and the abandonment of special claims on others' indulgence. Beyond
infancy there is continuity of cultural expectation regarding these goals for
individuals of all ages, the only differences being in the purposes they serve
and in the *degree* of development expected. Thus, progress toward ego
maturity goals is made during the satellizing as well as the desatellizing
period. During the latter period the motivation underlying the attainment
of these goals tends to shift from the retention of derived status and parental
approval to the fact that such attainment is perceived as prerequisite to the
achievement of higher standards of volitional independence and primary
status. In deciding whether to assimilate new values, the desatellizing child is
more prone than the satellizing child to use criteria such as expediency and
capacity for enhancing ego aspirations rather than using the criterion of
blind personal allegiance (satellizing orientation). This new approach to
value assimilation (which also characterizes the non-satellizer at *all* ages) will
henceforth be referred to as the *incorporative* orientation.

The *status goals* of ego maturation, on the other hand, are discontinuous
from early childhood to late childhood, adolescence, and adult life. They
include the acquisition of greater volitional independence and primary
status; heightened levels of ego aspirations; the placement of moral responsibility on a societal basis; and the assimilation of new values on the basis
of their perceived intrinsic validity or their relation to the major goals of the
individual. With respect to these goals the child is not expected to be a
miniature adult. Volitional independence, for example, is high during
infancy, drops to a lower point during middle childhood and starts rising
again during late childhood. The child obtains the major portion of his
status from derived sources and the adult obtains his from primary sources;
and although this reversal is not completed until adolescence, the balance

begins to shift during middle and late childhood. Hence, insofar as the realization of ego status goals is concerned, the stage of satellization represents a period of retrogression rather than of progress. But even though desatellization restores many of the ego inflationary features of the infantile period, this does not mean that the adolescent is back in the same place which he left at the close of infancy; supporting this gain in ego enhancement are considerable growth in cognitive sophistication and executive competence, much real accomplishment in the goals of ego maturity, and fundamental changes in social pressures and expectations.

Pressures toward Desatellization. No sooner is the dependency of satellization achieved than new conditions are created which undermine it and alter the shifting balance of dependence-independence. First among the factors impelling change toward personality maturation is the cumulative impact of progress in cognitive and social capacities, which in turn induces modification of parental and societal expectations. During the period of middle childhood there is an unspectacular but steady gain in the child's ability to comprehend abstract relationships, to reason, and to generalize (Chapter 15). His level of sophistication in perceiving the attitudes, needs and feelings of others, the relative status positions of various persons (including himself) in the group, and the distinguishing criteria of social class status (see Chapter 11) is gradually pushed forward. Thus, understanding more thoroughly the nature of the environment in which he lives, he feels less awed by its complexity and more confident to navigate alone and unguided. He feels that he now possesses a sufficient fund of social and intellectual competence to qualify for a more mature and responsible role in the affairs of his culture and to engage in the status-giving activities that he formerly regarded as the exclusive prerogative of adults. Hence he tends to wish more than younger children do, for such status-conferring attributes as good looks, stature, mental ability and popularity, to prefer difficult tasks which he cannot complete to easier ones which he can, and to be less hedonistic and authority conscious in his emotional responsiveness to different situations (Mussen *et al*, 1963). But this time, unlike the situation at four, he really possesses sufficient executive competence to warrant a serious and legitimate quest for more primary status and greater volitional independence.

Neither the parent nor the culture is unaware of the growth in cognitive and social competence that takes place during the preadolescent years. In accordance with practical economic needs and the overall cultural training program, therefore, the child is expected to acquire a source of extrinsic status to supplement his role as dependent satellite in the family configuration.* Depending on the degree of cultural discontinuity prevailing between

---

Achievement motivation tends to be relatively high in children whose mothers make early demands for and reward independent accomplishment highly. There are also marked intercultural and social class differences in achievement motivation (see pp. 281 and 285).

children's and adult's roles, he either acquires a sub-adult, fringe status in adult society or primary status in peripheral activities (e.g., school, peer group) far removed from the main stream of status-giving operations in the adult world. In most primitive cultures the home serves as both the source of subsidiary extrinsic status and the training institution for developing more mature and responsible behavior. The child is assigned responsible tasks of considerable social and economic importance in agriculture, handicrafts, household arts, and looking after younger siblings; "the tasks that are expected of it are adapted to its capacity" (Benedict, 1938).

In complex modern cultures children have little opportunity for exercising independence, responsibility and identification with the world of adult concerns; this necessitates a complete separation of the activity and interest systems of child and adult. Such children are given no responsibilities in the workaday world of adult concerns, and evolve a complete set of prestige-giving values of their own. They are obliged to find sources of primary status in peripheral activities and to supplement this with the vicarious status that can be obtained through identification with the glamorous exploits of prominent figures in public life, and with whatever satisfaction can be gained by carrying on covert guerrilla warfare with adults and adult standards.

One undesirable consequence of excluding children from *genuine* responsibility in the adult world is that, deprived of this necessary role-playing experience, related aspects of ego maturation tend to lag behind. Study of children in grades four through twelve reveals little evidence of marked developmental progress in the child's amount of responsibility (Harris *et al*, 1954a), or of any relationship between his sense of responsibility and the number of home duties he assumes (Harris *et al*, 1954b). The fact that these relationships hold true for rural as well as urban children suggests that the child in our culture has no *real* opportunity for socially responsible participation. The routine assignments he carries out are so subordinate and expendable that they have little bearing on his primary status or volitional independence.

A second consequence of the displacement of the home as a training center for ego maturation is that the child becomes increasingly dependent on non-parental sources of primary and derived status. In his peer group he is given a chance to obtain the mature role-playing experience from which society excludes him and which his parents are unable to furnish. Identification with this group also provides a substitute source of derived status providing him with ego supports that reduce his dependence upon parental approval. By attributing the prerogatives of volitional independence and moral decision to a group fashioned in his own image he effectively demolishes his exclusive association of these powers with parental figures and thus paves the way for eventually assuming them himself. School serves a very similar function. It provides both a new subsidiary source of primary status based upon academic ability and a fresh source of derived status which challenges the parent's monopoly of this commodity and of omniscience as well.

All of these factors—the availability of other sources of derived status, the possession of subsidiary primary status, the need for going beyond the home for sources of extrinsic status, the child's own greater competence, exposure to a diversity of family and social climates with resulting awareness of alternative standards and ways of doing things, and the emergence of new authorities to challenge his parents' omniscience—tend to break down the child's deified picture of his parents. Thus, beginning with late childhood, glamorous figures such as movie stars and sports heroes, attractive visible adults, and composite portraits of admired adults start to displace parents as emulatory models (Havighurst *et al*, 1946). As the ties of dependency weaken and the perceived omnipotence of the parent diminishes, the latter's power to confer by fiat an absolute intrinsic value on the child begins to ebb; and as the parents' glory fades, less vicarious status can be reflected to the satellite.

Systematic observation of the eight-year-old indicates that he is already more outgoing and in greater contact with his environment. He resents being treated as a child and can't wait to grow up. The nine-year-old is more independent, responsible, cooperative, and dependable. After making a futile attempt to draw the adult into his world, he seems to accept the fact that fusion is impossible. He becomes very busy with his own concerns and doesn't have time for routines or parents' demands. There is much planning in great and practical detail. He may prefer work to play. But these concerns are now oriented more toward his contemporaries than toward his parents and he verbally expresses indifference to adult commands or adult standards (Gesell *et al*, 1946). Thus begins a long period of estrangement between children and adults which persists until the former attain adulthood themselves. Insurmountable barriers to commonality of feeling, to mutual understanding, and to ease of communication are often built up. This alienation is not unaccompanied by resentment and bitterness. Although outright resistance to adult authority is usually withheld until adolescence, there is reason to believe that the preadolescent's apparent conformity is only a veneer which hides the smoldering rebellion from view. This is suggested by the often contemptuous and sneering remarks he makes about adults in his own company; and perhaps were it not for compensatory outlets in movies, comics, and opportunities for fighting with peers and bullying younger children, it would come more into the open (Murphy, 1947). Because girls are able and expected to satellize more and longer than boys (see p. 253) and can also achieve more primary status at home and in school they tend to be more conforming to and less at war with adult standards and values.

Mechanisms of Desatellization. From the foregoing description of the nature and determinants of the desatellizing process it is apparent that three different kinds of mechanisms are involved. The first mechanism may be called *resatellization.* It involves gradual replacement of parents by agemates and others as the essential socializing agents of children and as the individuals in relation to whom the satellizing orientation is maintained. Resatellization follows the same pattern of dependent emotional identification with stronger, prestigeful individuals or groups as did satellization. The identifications are merely transferred in part from parents to teachers, parent surrogates, agemates, and others on whom the child is dependent for derived status. Values, goals and attitudes are now acquired from *these* individuals as by-products of personal loyalty. But although resatellization is a prominent feature of desatellization in our culture, it tends not to occur in most primitive cultures (Frank, 1944; Mead, 1940). Here the parents remain the chief socializing agents and the source of standards and derived status; the older child and adolescent merely acquires greater volitional independence and primary status within the family circle without revolting against the authority of the head of the household.

Thus, more important in bringing about desatellization than the issue of who (parents or peer group) becomes the object of residual satellizing trends are the child's increased needs for obtaining primary status and the sources from which it is available. The satellizing orientation is abrogated more effectively by the displacement of derived by primary status as the basis of self-esteem than by replacement of parents by peers, teachers and adult leaders as the source of derived status. Hence, the more crucial contribution of these latter individuals to the desatellizing process is the primary status they are able to furnish the preadolescent and adolescent child. At first, the opportunity of gaining parental approbation constitutes the child's chief motivation to acquire the primary status resulting from independent accomplishment; thus in the beginning the acquisition of extrinsic status is largely a modified form of satellization. Later, primary status becomes an end in itself; and accordingly there is a parallel shift in the child's orientation toward value assimilation and in his motivation for achieving the attributes of ego maturity (see p. 273).

A third but relatively minor mechanism through which desatellization is effected depends upon the operation of the *exploratory* orientation to value assimilation. This is a task-oriented approach to the problem of values that stresses such criteria as objective validity, logic, and equity, and de-emphasizes the status considerations, both derived and primary, that underlie the satellizing and incorporative orientations respectively. The utilization of the exploratory orientation is obviously limited during childhood since it conflicts with basic loyalties to parents and hence precipitates strong guilt feelings. But as subservience to parental values wanes it can be used more freely; and continued use in turn promotes desatellization. Extensive use, however, tends to be precluded by the fact that it also threatens the new sources of primary and derived status that becomes available at this time.

Facilitating and Retarding Factors. Desatellization is a difficult and conflictful phase of ego development. The child is expected to become more independent and self-assertive; and in achieving this goal he has to combat ambivalent tendencies in both himself and his parents. If he is too submissive and dependent he loses face in his own eyes and in the eyes of his peers; if he is too independent and aggressive, he feels guilty for excessive repudiation of his parents. Whether or not, and the extent to which, ego maturation actually occurs depends on the ways in which various factors of parent behavior, child temperament, and cultural expectations facilitate or retard the mechanisms whereby desatellization is effected. Desatellization, for example, is facilitated if the child (in contradistinction to his behavior) is accepted unconditionally, that is, if obedience and conformity are not made the price of acceptance. Similarly, the more impersonal the basis on which obedience and conformity are required the less likely is the desire for independence to be inhibited by feelings of personal loyalty and guilt. The dangers of excessive satellization may also be avoided if the child can find derived status in multiple sources rather than in the parents alone (Bronfenbrenner, 1962a; Campbell, 1964). Under such circumstances the one source is no longer so precious. Fortified by the ego support he receives from friends, grandparents, siblings, teachers, etc., he can afford more easily to assert his volitional and ideational independence.

For children to develop the skill and confidence necessary for competent exercise of volitional independence, they require opportunity for practicing self-direction, making plans and decisions, actually participating in mature role-playing experience, and learning from their own mistakes. Overdominated children, although mature in such respects as "conscientious effort" and "orderly production," tend to be shy, submissive, lacking in self-confidence, and deficient in the volitional aspects of independence (Becker, 1964). The latter outcome also holds true for overprotected children whose parents withhold the opportunity for independent decision-making lest it lead to injury or frustration (Becker, 1964).

It also seems reasonable to suppose that if children are to develop executive independence and frustration tolerance, learn how to set realistic goals for themselves and make reasonable demands on others, and acquire self-critical ability and capacity for restricting hedonistic urges, they must have first-hand experience in coping with frustration and must be confronted unambiguously with the expectations and limitations defining their biosocial position.

Overly permissive parents fail to develop frustration tolerance,* executive independence, and non-hedonistic motivation in the child, both because they fail to demand independent accomplishment and because they yield excessively to the child's demands for hedonistic gratification and help whenever he encounters difficulty (Levy, 1943; Symonds, 1949). They fail also to structure realistically the limiting and restrictive aspects of the child's world, thereby making difficult the setting of realistic goals and the accurate perception of self-role and the boundaries of acceptable behavior. The extremely underdominated child, therefore, tends to be aggressive, rebellious, and disobedient; he may develop the notion that he is a very precious and privileged person and that his parents and others *have* to do things for him because he has a special claim on their indulgence (Levy, 1943; Symonds, 1949). And insofar as the desire to protect the child from all frustration leads to similar kinds of parental behavior, comparable developmental outcomes may be expected in the overprotected child (Levy, 1943; Stendler, 1954; Symonds, 1949).

Ego maturation in response to parental expectations of more mature behavior may ordinarily be expected to lag initially because of the phenomenon of perceptual constancy in the child. The prepotency of habitual expectations may temporarily force *altered* parent behavior into *familiar* perceptual molds despite manifest changes in stimulus content. The rate of ego maturation is also held back by ambivalent feelings in the child, who is naturally reluctant to part with the protection and security of dependency. This ambivalence is probably greater in children with strong needs for hedonistic gratification (who find long-range striving difficult) and in sedentary, shy, "thin-skinned," and introverted children to whom self-assertion comes painfully.

Lastly, ego maturation is a function of cultural expectations and of the availability of mature role-playing experience. These latter factors reciprocally influence each other as well as generating pressure and opportunity for personality reorganization on a more mature basis. Largely for these reasons, when ego maturation in our culture is appraised in a cross-cultural context, the acquisition of ego status goals (e.g., volitional independence, primary status) is seen to lag markedly behind the acquisition of ego maturity goals (e.g., executive independence). Parents in our culture expect much executive independence and conformity to adult standards but allow children relatively little opportunity to fend for themselves (Winterbottom, 1953).

Preparatory and Consummatory Stages. The preparatory changes in ego maturation catalogued above as well as the factors bringing them about are

---

*For a study of frustration tolerance in "under-controlling" children, see J. Block and B. Martin, J. Abnorm. Soc. Psychol. 51: 281-285, 1955.

certainly important in the total scheme of personality maturation. Yet the transition to adult personality status cannot be consummated merely by the cumulative impact of these factors. The extrinsic status of childhood—even if achieved in economically significant activities—can constitute only a subsidiary source of status. The sexually immature (prepubescent) individual can nowhere acquire adult personality status; the primary status he enjoys must inevitably play a subordinate role in the larger Gestalt of volitional dependency and derived status which characterize the biosocial position of children the world over. Until adolescence, parents and home continue to function as the major status-giving influences in the child's life. The ego maturity of childhood remains qualitatively different from that of adolescence and adult life until derived and primary sources of status exchange positions as central and peripheral respectively in the total economy of ego organization.

Pubescence, therefore, plays the role of crucial catalytic agent in inaugurating the consummatory aspects of ego maturation. It constitutes a prerequisite condition for reversing social expectations and individual aspirations about the major type of status that the child may appropriately seek. For the pubescent individual the social value of derived status depreciates while the corresponding value of extrinsic status increases; and simultaneously social pressure is put on the parents to withdraw a large portion of the derived status which they had hitherto been extending to him.

Ego Maturation in Non-Satellizers. As already indicated, the non-satellizer never really surrenders his aspirations for volitional independence and exalted primary status. Hence in a sense the ego-status goals of maturation are already accomplished in advance; and since the main function of most ego-maturity goals is the enhancement of primary status, these tend to be acquired with little difficulty. The chief exception here relates to realistic goal development, which is largely precluded by the non-satellizer's insistent need to maintain high ego aspirations irrespective of the situation or his level of ability. It would also seem reasonable to question under certain conditions the stability of values that were never implicitly internalized on the basis of personal loyalty but solely for purposes of ego enhancement. The obligation to abide by all internalized moral values, for example, is threatened by the fact that many such values are often in conflict with the ends of ego enhancement.

SOME ASPECTS OF EGO FUNCTIONING

Once a verbal concept of self emerges, the stage is set for the development of ego goals, motives, and attitudes, and of subjective ego responses (e.g., self-esteem) to such changes in status as success or failure in goal achievement.

Ego-Involvement and Achievement Motivation

Ego-involvement is not synonymous with ego enhancement. It merely refers to the degree of self-implication in a given task or performance (i.e., whether or not the outcome is a matter of concern or importance to the individual) and does not make explicit the motives for his concern. Thus, non-ego-involved areas in the environment are relatively peripheral and undifferentiated; failure in such areas is easily sloughed off, and success does not inspire elation. As already pointed out, since the magnitude and tenacity of aspirations vary with degree of ego-involvement in a task (see pp. 114 and 166), the generality of aspirational (as well as of other) "trait" behavior depends upon holding ego-involvement constant. Even more than success or failure in performance, degree of ego-involvement also determines the extent to which children find tasks attractive (Nunally *et al*, 1965; Schpoont, 1955). Failure lowers the attractiveness of a task much less when children perceive themselves as "trying hard" to do well than when they are indifferent about performance (Schpoont, 1955).

The *motivation* underlying ego-involvement, however, is quite another matter. In many ego-involved tasks the chief object of the activity is ego enhancement, in which case we speak of *ego orientation*. Here the task is pursued as a source of either derived or primary status. On the other hand, the motivation for some ego-involved activities may be entirely unrelated to ego enhancement, being energized solely by a need to acquire mastery or to discover a valid solution to a problem. Thus human beings may become intensely ego-involved in tasks in which the outcome per se rather than its relation to self-enhancement is the major focus of concern (White, 1963). In such instances the person is *task-oriented*. He experiences feelings of success and failure, but not loss or gain in ego status or self-esteem.

It follows that before ego-involvement can arise developmentally, the child must first possess a functional concept of self in relation to which various objects and activities in his environment are ordered in a hierarchical arrangement. When this occurs he is able to experience success and failure whenever ego-involved goals are either gratified or frustrated. The capacity for ego enhancing motivation, on the other hand, requires in addition that the child be able to set ego aspirations and respond with fluctuations in self-esteem to success and failure affecting these aspirations. In our culture, this is illustrated by the competitive behavior which first appears in three-year-old children and becomes increasingly prominent thereafter (Ames, 1952; Gesell, 1954; Gesell *et al*, 1943; Greenberg, 1932; Leuba, 1933); such behavior presupposes comparison of own and others' performance, appreciation of the concept of surpassing others, and desire to excel. It is also illustrated in the practical setting of aspirational levels for self-help in informal situations;

in two- to three-year-olds these aspirations adhere quite closely to level of ability (Anderson, 1940). However, consistent levels of aspiration in more formal laboratory situations are not apparent until about the age of five (Gesell *et al*, 1943). For this kind of behavior the child requires a clear notion of the immediate future, some self-critical ability (Crandall, 1967; Greenberg, 1932), and acceptance of the cultural value of aspiring to goals that are less accessible (Wright, 1937), or somewhat beyond prior level of performance (Crandall, 1967; Rosenzweig, 1933).

Ego-enhancement motivation in our culture is clearly identified in the achievement motive (McClelland *et al*, 1953).* The *achievement motive* in children is characterized by their perception of performance in terms of standards of excellence (McClelland *et al*, 1953). Furthermore, the perception of standards of excellence is accompanied by the experience of pleasant or unpleasant feelings about meeting or failing to meet these standards (Crandall, 1967).

Achievement motivation is by no means the reflection of a unitary or homogeneous drive. It has at least three components. One of these is a cognitive drive, i.e., the need for acquiring knowledge and solving problems as ends in themselves. This drive certainly underlies the need for academic achievement to the extent that such achievement represents to the learner the attainment of the knowledge he seeks to acquire. It is completely *task-oriented* in the sense that the motive for becoming involved in the task in question (acquiring a particular segment of knowledge) is *intrinsic* to the task itself, i.e., is simply the need to know; and hence the reward (the actual attainment of this knowledge) also inheres completely in the task itself since it is capable of wholly satisfying the underlying motive.

A second component of achievement motivation, on the other hand, is not task-oriented at all. It may be termed *ego enhancing* because it is concerned with achievement as a source of primary or earned status, namely, the kind of status that an individual earns in proportion to this achievement or competence level. It is ego enhancing inasmuch as the degree of achievement determines how much primary status he enjoys, and, simultaneously, how *adequate* he feels (his level of self-esteem); feelings of adequacy in this case are always a direct reflection of relative primary status. The ego-enhancement component of achievement motivation is therefore directed both toward the attainment of current achievement, or prestige, and toward future goals (later sources of primary status) that depend on the latter.

The final or *affiliative* component of achievement motivation is neither task-oriented nor primarily ego enhancing. It is not oriented toward academic achievement as a source of primary status, but rather toward such

---

The most recent review of the literature on achievement motivation in children may be found in V. Crandall (1967).

achievement insofar as it assures the individual of the approval of a super-ordinate person or group with whom he identifies in a dependent sense, and from whose acceptance he acquires vicarious or *derived* status. The latter kind of status is not determined by the individual's own achievement level, but by the continuing intrinsic acceptance of him by the person(s) with whom he identifies. And the individual who enjoys derived status is motivated to obtain and retain the approval of the superordinate person—by meeting the latter's standards and expectations.

Some aspects of each of the cognitive, ego-enhancement, and affiliative components are normally represented in achievement motivation; however, their proportions vary, depending on such factors as age, sex, culture, social-class membership, ethnic origin, and personality structure. Affiliative drive is most prominent during early childhood when children largely seek and enjoy a derived status based on dependent identification with, and intrinsic acceptance by, their parents. During this period, their striving for achieve-ment is one way of meeting their parents' expectations and, hence, of retain-ing the approval they desire. Actual or threatened withdrawal of approval for poor performance therefore motivates them to work harder to retain or regain this approval. Since teachers are largely regarded as parent surrogates, they are related to in similar fashion.

Affiliative drive is thus an important source of motivation for achievement during childhood. However, children who are not accepted and intrinsically valued by their parents, and who therefore cannot enjoy any derived status, are compensatorily motivated to seek an inordinate amount of earned status through high achievement. Thus high levels of achievement motivation typically represent low affiliative drive that is more than compensated for by high-ego-enhancement drive.

During late childhood and adolescence, affiliative drive both diminishes in intensity and is redirected from parents toward age-mates. Desire for peer approval, however, may also depress academic achievement when such achievement is negatively valued by the peer group. This is a more common occurrence among lower-class and certain culturally deprived minority groups (Ausubel, 1965). Middle-class peer groups, as is pointed out later, place a high value on academic achievement and expect it from their members.

The significance of satellization versus nonsatellization in early personality development is associated with a distinctive pattern of achievement motiva-tion. Generally speaking, the nonsatellizer exhibits a much higher level of achievement motivation in which the ego-enhancement component is pre-dominant, whereas the satellizer exhibits both a lower level of achievement motivation and one in which the affiliative component tends to predominate prior to adolescence.

The satellizer identifies with his parents in a dependent sense and is accepted by them for himself. He enjoys, by virtue of this acceptance, both an assured derived status and the accompanying feelings of intrinsic adequacy or self-esteem that are relatively immune to the vicissitudes of achievement and competitive position. Thus he has relatively little need to seek the kind of status that he would have to earn through his own competence—the kind of status that would generate feelings of extrinsic adequacy commensurate with his degree of achievement. He does not, in other words, view achievement as the basis of his status or as the measure of his worth as a person; it is merely a means of meeting the expectations of his parents and of retaining thereby the approval that confirms for him his good standing in their eyes.

The non-satellizer, on the other hand, is either accepted on an extrinsic basis or rejected by his parents. Enjoying no derived status or intrinsic self-esteem, he has no choice but to aspire to a status that he earns through his own accomplishments. Since his feelings of adequacy are almost entirely a reflection of the degree of achievement he can attain, he necessarily exhibits a high level of aspiration for achievement and prestige—a level that is much higher, and more stable in the face of failure experience, than that of satellizers. This is obviously a compensatory reaction that reflects his lack of derived status and intrinsic self-esteem. Consistent with his higher aspirations for achievement, he manifests more volitional and executive independence than the satellizer, and is better able to defer the immediate gratification of hedonistic needs in order to strive for more long-term goals (Mischel, 1961). Similar personality differences between individuals manifesting ego-enhancement and affiliative drive orientations to learning, respectively, were reported by Atkinson and Litwin (1960) and by McClelland et al (1953). Consistent with the sex differences previously mentioned concerning satellization and intrinsic evaluation (see p. 253), female achievement performance is motivated more by affiliative needs, whereas male achievement motivation is primarily ego-enhancing (Crandall et al, 1964; Sears, 1962; Tyler, Rafferty and Tyler, 1962).

Other aspects of the parent-child relationship are also implicated in the development of achievement motivation. Achievement motivation tends to be higher in those children whose parents have high intellectual achievement aspirations both for themselves (Katkovsky et al, 1964a, 1964b) and for their offspring (Rosen and D'Andrade, 1959); whose parents stress independence training and high standards of excellence (McClelland et al, 1953; Winterbottom, 1958); and whose parents, when present in problem solving situations with their offspring, exhibit greater participation, instigation, encouragement, and disapproval (Katkovsky et al, 1964b; Rosen and D'Andrade, 1959). It is also apparently stronger in instances where an achievement-oriented mother is dominant in the home; a dominant, demanding, and successful father, on the other hand, is perceived by his sons as providing a competitive standard that is too overwhelmingly superlative to be challenged successfully (Strodtbeck, 1958). In summary, review of the literature on achievement motivation and parental determinants bears out the prediction that non-satellizing (i.e., extrinsically valued children) seek primary status through ego-enhancing motivation. The studies suggest:

> . . . that high levels of active parental involvement, particularly along cross-sex, parent-child lines provide the basis for achievement motivation performance on intelligence tests, and intellectual achievement behaviors in free play. . . . In each case, part of that involvement was reflected in negatively-valued parental behaviors or attitudes such as rejection, criticality, hostility, or "pushing" the child beyond his ability, and this was particularly true of mothers of achieving children of either sex (Crandall, 1967, pp. 179–180).

Significant normative fluctuations (as well as individual differences) in the balance between primary and derived status occur throughout the course of ego development. But, as already indicated, initial ways of relating to others tend to persist, especially if they occur at critical periods of socialization. Thus, although it is true that as the satellizing child grows older he increasingly strives for primary status, he will, even as an adult, continue to enjoy the residual sense of intrinsic worth which his parents earlier conferred on him, and will continue to satellize in some aspects of his current interpersonal relationships.

Level of Aspiration

Much insight into ego organization and functioning can be gained by observing the extent to which individuals take past performance into account in setting their level of aspiration for future performance. Children with adequate amounts of self-esteem (well-adjusted, academically successful children) respond to cultural pressure for achievement by aspiring to levels somewhat above the level of prior performance (Crandall, 1967; Ringness, 1961; Sears, 1940,). However, since they do not have compensatorily high ego aspirations, they neither respond beyond the range of present capacity, nor cling rigidly to high aspirations after failure experience. In this way, they minimize feelings of failure associated with a marked discrepancy between aspiration and performance levels.

Individuals with relatively little self-esteem (e.g., especially unsuccessful non-satellizers), on the other hand, are coerced by their high ego aspirations into maintaining tenaciously high levels of aspiration despite realistic considerations to the contrary. They find surrender of their high aspirations more traumatic than the immediate feelings of failure accompanying performance that is below aspirational level; also, merely in the maintenance of their high levels of aspirations, they find a source of ego enhancement. If they can manage to disinvolve their egos from the task, however, they tend to aspire to unrealistically low performance levels which they can always surpass, and thus at least spare themselves immediate failure experience (Sears, 1940).

In support of the above interpretation of level of aspiration behavior are the following findings: (a) since boys possess less derived status than do girls, they generally tend to set higher levels of aspiration and are more willing to take risks (Crandall and Rabson, 1960; Slovic, 1966; Walter and Marzolf, 1951); (b) handicapped or socially stigmatized children who presumably have a compensatory need for high extrinsic status, e.g., mentally retarded, physically handicapped and asthmatic children (Little and Cohen, 1951; Ringness, 1961; Wenar, 1953), Negro children (Boyd, 1952), individuals of low social and economic status (Gould, 1941), and children who fail chronically in school (Sears, 1940) tend more than control groups to aspire unrealistically beyond present level of performance; (c) children or adolescents who perceive themselves as extrinsically valued (Ausubel *et al*, 1954), who have high prestige needs (Ausubel, Schiff and Goldman, 1953; Ausubel, Schiff and Zeleny, 1953) and unrealistic ambitions (Hausmann, 1933, Sears, 1941) all tend to adhere to high levels of aspiration in the face of persistent failure experience.

Egocentricity, Egoism and Subjectivity

By egocentricity is meant the extent to which the individual's self (in contradistinction to *other* persons, things, and events) is central as an object of attention in his psychological field. At the superficial level of saliency of awareness it merely connotes preoccupation with self and relative indifference to external events. * At a deeper level of value, concern and importance, i.e., as indicative of high degree of ego-involvement in self and of relative inability to relate emotionally to others, it is more appropriate to speak of *egoism*. Although egocentricity and egoism are probably related positively to each other, they are determined by different kinds of factors. Egocentricity-sociocentricity depends upon social maturity, social poise and skill, sociability, introversion-extraversion, etc.; egoism is more a function of magnitude of ego aspirations. Thus, it is conceivable that an outgoing person may be sociocentric but egoistic (superficially interested in others and their affairs, yet not *really* concerned with their welfare), and that a shy, introverted person may be egocentric but capable of genuine concern for and warm attachments to others. In the course of intellectual, social, and personality maturation, both egocentrism and egoism tend to diminish with increasing

---

When the self and its attributes are the focus of psychological self-analysis the term introspection is applicable.

age. In communicating with others, children gradually increase in ability to perceive, pay sustained attention to, and take into account the feelings and viewpoints of others, and in ability to interchange ideas as well as talking to each other (see Chapter 14). In their play they tend, as they grow older, to become more aware of the presence and needs of others, more cooperative, considerate and altruistic (see p. 330).

Closely related to but distinguishable from egocentricity is the young child's overly *subjective* approach to the analysis of experience, his perceptual autism, and his lack of reality testing (Sullivan *et al.* 1967; Piaget, 1929, 1932). He is as yet relatively unable to dissociate what belongs to objective laws from what is bound up with the sum of subjective conditions (Piaget, 1932). As he advances in age he becomes increasingly able to approach questions of equity from a less personal and more detached point of view, and to argue from the standpoint of a hypothetical proposition (Inhelder and Piaget, 1958; Piaget, 1929). His pictorial representations of reality come to resemble more and more the model rather than the artist (Ausubel *et al*, 1954)

Self-Critical Capacity

A prerequisite condition for the growth of a mature self-critical capacity is the ability to appraise self on the same basis that is used in evaluating others. Of all the subjectivistic proclivities characterizing early childhood, the child finds it most difficult to liberate himself from the tendency to apply selectively preferential standards to his own capacities, productions, and behavior. This development depends on more than possession of sufficient intellectual capacity to make critical judgments, since children are able to perceive deviations from acceptable standards in *others* at a much earlier age than they can in themselves (Piaget, 1932; Gesell *et al*, 1943); in fact, prior to five years of age the latter ability is infrequently observed (Gesell *et al*, 1943).

Self-critical ability, therefore, is obviously important for the implementation of moral obligations. This presupposes that an individual does not selectively exempt himself from the standards he expects in others, and that he can become sufficiently aware of his own wrongdoing to experience feelings of guilt. We have also seen how immaturity of the self-critical capacity contributes to exaggerated notions of volitional power and executive independence, and how development of this capacity helps to promote ego devaluation and satellization. Further growth in self-critical ability is essential for acquiring primary status and for realistic exercise of volitional independence. At the operational level of ego functioning, a harsh self-critical faculty reduces the amount of self-esteem available to the individual, whereas an overly gentle self-critical faculty unwarrantedly enhances feelings of adequacy.

It also seems reasonable to suppose that the prevailing level of self-esteem influences self-critical ability. Although an individual with relatively little self-esteem may tend generally to take a harsh view of his accomplishments, he may at times be extremely reluctant to acknowledge shortcomings and culpability that would further depress his already damaged self-esteem. A person who enjoys adequate self-esteem, on the other hand, is less threatened by confrontation with unflattering aspects of his behavior. Thus, in line with findings for adult subjects, better adjusted children are able to accept significantly more disparaging statements about themselves than less well-adjusted children (Taylor and Combs, 1952). Moreover, children who are high in their accuracy of self-appraisal tend to be less defensive (Weiner, 1964). On logical grounds one could also expect a more severe self-critical faculty to develop when children are overdominated, overcriticized and underappreciated than when the opposite conditions prevail (Ausubel, 1952).

CHAPTER 9

Parent-Child Relationships

PARENTAL INFLUENCES are so crucial and pervasive in child developmen-
that it is almost impossible to discuss any aspect of this field without considering its relationship to parent attitudes and behavior. We have, for
example, already considered the origin of maternal *behavior* during the neonatal period (Chapter 7), the relationship between child rearing *practices* and
the development of psychosocial and idiosyncratic personality traits (Chapter 7), and the impact of specific parent *attitudes* on major phases of ego
development (Chapter 8). In the present chapter we propose to consider
some of the following more *general* aspects of parent-child relationships: the
individual and social sources of parent attitudes, and their continuity,
consistency and characteristics in relation to sex of the parent and ordinal
position of the child; the various dimensions of parent-child interaction; the
mechanisms through which parent attitudes shape the personality development of the child and the factors that limit their influence; the impact of
socialization in the home on later phases of socialization; and the characteristics of parental discipline and their effects on personality development.

Parent-child relationships deserve such extensive treatment because they
constitute perhaps the most important single category of variables impinging
on the personality development and socialization of the child. In their
capacity as socializing agents and representatives of the culture, parents
determine many intercultural uniformities (psychobiological traits) and
differences (psychosocial traits) in development; and in their capacity as
individuals with unique personalities of their own, parents determine a
large part of the personality variance in children within a given culture
(idiosyncratic traits). The family exhibits a variety of structural forms ranging from extended family, nuclear, polygamous, or communal (Whiting &
Whiting, 1960). In industrialized urban western culture the nuclear family
of father, mother and children has evolved as a universal cultural solution to
a common core of interpersonal problems, needs and conditions of adaptation to the physical and social environments (Clausen, 1966). In all societies,
the nuclear family is the initial social matrix within which personality is
rooted and cultivated (Clausen, 1966). Despite the myriad forms it adopts, it
performs everywhere the same basic functions of extending physical and
emotional succorance to children, taking responsibility for their socialization

and enculturation, and providing for mutual sharing of commodities and services in a continuing group structure marked by division of labor and differentiation of roles.

Although commonplace today, conceptions of personality development that emphasize the crucial role of the parent-child relationship in its broader aspects have appeared only relatively recently in the history of personality theory. The belated recognition accorded this factor can be attributed largely to the influence of Freud. He and his followers were among the first to stress the importance of early childhood experience and parental treatment for later personality formation. However, the earlier studies selected out of this experience only those specific child-rearing *practices* that impinge on the individual's alleged psychosexual development such as weaning, feeding, etc. (Medinnus, 1967), and more or less ignored the impact of broader emotional *attitudes* (e.g., rejection, overprotection) on the salient features of ego development traced in Chapter 8. They also exaggerated the communicability of parent attitudes to young infants and the importance of child rearing *practices* in determining psychosocial traits (see Chapter 7).

Parenthood involves both satisfactions and burdens for most persons, some of which are anticipated and some of which are not. It is self-evident, however, that the demands of parental role are more compatible with the needs and personality traits of some individuals than they are with those of others; but since the functions of the parent vary in content and emphasis with the age of the child, the congeniality of parental role is subject to change. Many parents enjoy only the early period of cuteness and dependence, and lose interest or feel at a loss when their children become more competent and independent individuals with concerns outside the home.

GENERAL DETERMINANTS OF PARENT ATTITUDES*

How do parents come to acquire the attitudes they hold in relation to their children? In general, four categories of determinants may be delineated: the wider culture, the parent's own family and childhood experience, his personality structure, and various situational variables. The first factor accounts for intercultural or subcultural (psychosocial) variability in parent attitudes, the latter three factors for idiosyncratic variability.

Determinants of Psychosocial Variability in Parent Attitudes

The extent to which parents are disposed to be accepting, protective, dominative, etc., in dealing with their children is obviously determined in part by the prevailing cultural ideology defining appropriate norms of parent-child interaction:

*For several discussions of this general topic see Glidewell (1961).

Society intrudes itself into the process in numerous ways. Indirectly its effect is felt by its shaping of the environment of the organism—influencing diet, physical comfort, the density of the population, the regularity of care, the presence or absence of the father. More directly, society shapes the socialization process by establishing the standard which the socialized individual is expected to achieve in physical development, in skills and capacities, in emotional expression, in intellective and cognitive activity, and in the patterning of his relation with significant others. In their efforts to socialize the child, parents are guided, however, fallibly, by their awareness of such social expectation and their image of what the child must become if he is to live successfully in the world as the parent's environment will be at the time the child becomes an adult (Inkeles, 1968, p. 75).*

The norms and values relating to parent-child interaction are therefore products of custom, tradition, ideological evolution, and historical accident; of economic, social, political, and religious beliefs and institutions; of institutionalized modes of timing and handling shifts in the biosocial status of the child; and the different ways of ordering marital relationships, family structure and intrafamilial roles (Clausen, 1966; Murdock & Whiting, 1951). In our own culture approved standards of parent behavior tend to correspond to shifts in attitudes and practices advocated in successive editions of such widely read manuals as the Children's Bureau Bulletin on *Infant Care* and Spock's *Baby and Child Care* (Bronfenbrenner, 1961). Conformity to these currently approved child-rearing fashions is more characteristic of middle-class parents (Bronfenbrenner, 1961; Caldwell, 1964; Hoffman & Lippitt, 1960; Kohn, 1963; Yarrow, 1963).

The cultural ideology influences parents' child-rearing attitudes because it serves as a major, prestigeful frame of reference in their evolution. It has been shown, for example, that parents' expectations of children's level of play are easily manipulated by "expert" opinion (Merrill, 1946). Parents also feel a sense of obligation to rear their children in conformity to prevailing social values, and fear both social censure and feelings of guilt if they deviate too much from what is expected of them. If alternative philosophies of child rearing are available, the parent is naturally more apt to choose one that is consonant with his temperamental preferences. His choice is also characterized respectively by varying degrees of intellectual objectivity or subjective rationalization, of independent thinking or uncritical acceptance of the current vogue, and of emotional or merely verbal identification. Irrespective of the basis on which they are chosen, as long as emotional involvement is present, such beliefs have the same impact on parent behavior as do

---

*The cultural ideology, as already suggested, helps to perpetuate the distinctive characterology of a given culture by contributing to the determination of psychosocial traits. It does this not so much by the selection of particular infant care practices nor by the manner in which such practices are administered, but by pervasively influencing parent attitudes. These attitudes in turn, reinforced by the child's direct contact with the culture, affect his personality formation recurrently throughout the entire period of development (see pp. 234-241).

attitudes derived from idiosyncratic personality factors. Purely verbal acceptance of child rearing beliefs is not entirely without effect on parent behavior but obviously leads to less spontaneous impulses as well as to impulses that are often negated by underlying attitudes.

The aforementioned factors relating to "cultural ideology" probably account for the cross-cultural differences observed in certain dimensions of child rearing. Cross-cultural differences are complexly organized into clusters of child rearing attitudes and practices. Thus, the general observation that German mothers are more *controlling* than American mothers (Rapp, 1961) must be qualified by the fact that German mothers control more than American mothers in behaviors such as table manners and toilet training, whereas the opposite obtains in sexual behavior (Karr & Wesley, 1966). In addition, German parents rely more on love-oriented discipline (e.g., withdrawal of affection) as compared to English and American parents (Bronfenbrenner, 1969). Cultural ideology probably also accounts for such differences in parental attitudes and practices as are observed in Japanese (Matsumoto and Smith, 1961), Israeli (Rabin, 1959; Rapaport, 1958), and Russian culture (Bronfenbrenner, 1968, 1969).*

Social Class Factors. Present-day investigations of social class differences in parent attitudes suggest that more middle-class than lower-class parents have assimilated the permissive approach in interacting with children and managing child care routines. They have especially moved away from the more strict styles of care and discipline advocated in the early twenties and thirties (Bronfenbrenner, 1961):

> Generally, the research has shown that middle-class parents provide more warmth and are more likely to use reasoning, isolation, show of disappointment, or guilt-arousing appeals in disciplining the child. They are also likely to be more permissive about demands for attention from the child, sex behavior, aggression to parent, table manners, neatness and orderliness, noise, bedtimes rules, and general disobedience. Working-class parents are more likely to use ridicule, shouting, or physical punishment in disciplining the child, and to be generally more restrictive (Becker, 1964, p. 171).

Social class differences in child rearing practices and attitudes have generally diminished in the past twenty years (Bronfenbrenner, 1958, 1961). In spite of these diminished differences, however, social class differences are still apparent between the middle- and lower-class stratas with regard to parent-child relationships. Middle-class mothers typically exercise much greater supervisory control and direction over their children's activities (Walters, Connor & Zunich, 1964). They extend this supervisory role outside the home by placing restrictions on the child's freedom to come and go as he pleases, to attend movies alone, to keep late hours, to choose his own asso-

---

Cross-national and cross-cultural differences are discussed in more detail in Clausen (1968), Elder (1965), Whiting & Whiting (1960).

ciates, and to explore the life of the streets (Davis & Havighurst, 1946; Havighurst & Taba, 1949; Maas, 1951; Short, 1966). Nevertheless, within the home middle-class parents value curiosity, happiness, consideration, and self-control more highly than do lower-class parents (Kohn, 1963). Lower-class parental values tend to center on conformity to external prescriptions, whereas middle-class parents place greater emphasis on self-direction (Kohn, 1963).

Where social class differences are present, it is very difficult to determine the mechanisms which mediate these differences. Social class studies that directly link social class status to behavioral consequences in the child are open to the criticism that the conceptual jump between class membership and behavioral differences leaves open many possible alternative explanations for any empirical relationship obtained (Hoffmann & Lippitt, 1960). Although social class differences are negligible at the present time, the same practices probably have a different basis in each class. In the lower-class they are more a matter of custom, tradition, and folklore acquired from parents, relatives, and friends. In the middle-class they are more an expression of belief in the formal ideology of child rearing currently approved of by the "experts" (Bronfenbrenner, 1958, 1961). Kohn (1963) takes a different slant on the differences observed, arguing they are a reflection of differences in values held by parents of different classes. The values held by parents of different classes reflect in turn the different life situations which are experienced by the members of these classes. For example, middle-class occupations deal more with interpersonal relations, ideas, and symbols, whereas working-class occupations deal more with the manipulation of things (Kohn, 1963). These types of differences create different value orientations which are reflected in the kinds of family interactions that develop (Kohn, 1963). Situational factors may also operate to account for the fact that there are no differences between social classes in frequency of physical punishment when size of family is controlled (Clausen, 1966).

Determinants of Idiosyncratic Variability in Parent Attitudes

Since all aspects of goal and method in child rearing are not culturally standardized, much room remains for the operation of situational factors and of genically and experientially determined differences in temperament, values, and resourcefulness. But even in those areas in which cultural prescriptions do exist, idiosyncratic variability in parent attitude may still occur. First, even in a relatively homogeneous subculture, parents perceive much heterogeneity in child-rearing practices and interpret them selectively in accordance with their own preferences. Whatever the degree of objective homogeneity that does exist (Brodbeck, Nogee, De Mascio, 1956; Kohn, 1963), the more heterogeneous the cultural norm is perceived to be, the less coercive is its influence on individual attitudes. Hence, in the absence of any clear-cut normative standard of discipline, mothers tend to rely more on their own experience and predilections than to conform to the perceived view (Brodbeck *et al*, 1956). Second, all cultures tolerate a certain degree of deliberate non-conformity from its members which is quite variable from one culture to another. In our own culture, the norms and ideal conceptions of what a good family should be are relatively diffuse, admitting of many alternatives and variations within different segments of the population; thus even marked deviations may draw only mild disapproval (Clausen, 1966). Generally speaking, greater individual latitude is permitted in matters of method than in matters of goal since it is often appreciated that different techniques may yield the same end result. Thus the culture makes fewer demands on parents for conformity during early childhood when the achievement of goals is still distant and when children are largely restricted to their own homes. On the other hand, parents may be more inclined to follow their own preferences when their children are older and they (the parents) have acquired a greater backlog of child-rearing experience. In any case the extent to which the individual parent is disposed to ignore social guideposts and expert opinion and follow his own notions is extremely variable (Merrill, 1946), and depends on such traits as self-sufficiency, self-confidence, independence of thought, suggestibility, critical sense, and need for public approval.

Idiosyncratic variability in parent attitudes is partly a function of family tradition and in some ways the family as a whole tends to evolve its own unique culture, norms, values, and role definitions (Handel, 1965). Idiosyncratic variability is also a function of parents' memories of their own childhood, and of their affective reactions to the practices of their own parents (see p. 202). The structure of the family may mediate unique interactions relating to size of the family and ordinal position (Clausen, 1966; Rosenberg & Sutton-Smith, 1966). For example, mothers of single-child families exhibit higher overall rates of talking to their infants than mothers in families of several children (Gewirtz & Gewirtz, 1968). The influence of situational factors such as current economic stresses and marital discord, must also be considered (Clausen, 1966). As discussed previously, the personality characteristics of the child may make it difficult to predict the outcome of certain forms of parent-child interaction (see pp. 189 and 196). The child's unique personality characteristics may contribute to the production of unique interaction patterns with his parents (Bell, 1964, 1968).

Also important, in relation to intracultural variation in child rearing, is the fact that parent attitudes are largely a characteristic manifestation of an individual's ego structure (e.g., feelings of adequacy and security, ego aspirations, level of anxiety, volitional and executive independence, moral obligation, self-preoccupation, ability to postpone hedonistic gratification, emotional relatedness to others) and of other personality traits such as ascendence, introversion-extroversion, motherliness, hostility, and acceptance of the female role. Observed parent behavior and measured parent personality characteristics are substantially related. "In the mother's social interaction with the child as she takes on the maternal role she . . . expresses . . . emotional needs" that are salient in the current economy of her personality organization (Behrens, 1954). The attitudes that are evoked by these needs are sometimes directly adjustive in the sense that they satisfy needs for ego enhancement (as in overvaluation) or reduce anxiety (as in over-protection). On the other hand, they may chiefly give vent to deep-seated feelings (e.g., hostility) or insulate the individual from parental obligations that interfere with the satisfaction of more pressing needs (as in rejection attributable to anxiety or narcissism).

CHARACTERISTICS OF PARENT ATTITUDES*

Attitudes and Practices

We have already taken the position that child-rearing practices in and of themselves can only affect the immediate behavior of the child unless they are reflective of broad, pervasive, and reasonably self-consistent parent attitudes. Although personality factors are undoubtedly prepotent in fashioning the major content of the more significant parent attitudes, cultural, familial, and situational determinants cannot be ignored. Regardless of their source, all parent attitudes affect child-rearing practices. Purely verbal and ego-peripheral beliefs, however, are associated with practices that tend to have a transitory effect on the behavior of the child rather than a more lasting influence on his personality devleopment. Thus the child's adjustment, as illustrated by his responses to parental socialization techniques, is a reflection of a cluster of maternal personality characteristics rather than of specific child-rearing practices (Bayley & Schaefer, 1960; Behrens, 1954) (see child care practices on pp. 237-241).

Because of other nonattitudinal determinants of child-rearing practices, and because of individual differences in the meaning which identical practices have for different parents, it is not possible to infer from the mere presence *of a practice in a given parent what* its attitudinal significance is. We have to look for the latter in the parent's manner of administering a large number of specific practices in recurrent situations. This very pervasiveness of parent attitudes renders any single practice relatively insignificant as a determining factor in personality development. It is also important to

*A current compendium of articles on the topic of parent-child relations is available (see Medinnus, 1967).

realize that parent attitudes can be communicated to children in other ways than through rearing practices, and that such attitudes are both reinforced and counteracted by other socializing agents.

Consistency and Continuity

Consistency is an important aspect of parent behavior because of its undoubted effect on the behavior and personality development of the child. Inconsistency generates confusion regarding what is expected, contributes to the production of antisocial behavior, and maladjustment (Becker, 1964), increases susceptibility to fear and anger (Chapter 12), and probably retards ego maturation and socialization. Although parents naturally vary greatly in the consistency of their child-rearing attitudes (Becker, 1964; Clausen, 1966), such attitudes (like any other meaningful expression of personality) must necessarily be characterized by considerable intersituational generality. Apart from reasons inherent in the very organization of personality, (see p. 111) a conscious need for self-consistency apparently operates in many persons. This, of course, does not preclude inconsistency stemming from situational factors, ambivalent feelings, or particular idiosyncrasies; inconsistency which the parent is unable to recognize; or genuinely high tolerance for self-perceived inconsistency.

Some direct evidence of intersituational consistency in parent attitudes has been found in studies of parent-child interaction (Lafore, 1945; Medinnus, 1967; Shirley, 1941). Such consistency can also be inferred from the fact that logically related parent behaviors intercorrelate meaningfully to form more inclusive attitudinal clusters (Baldwin, Kalhorn & Breese, 1945, 1949; Bayley & Schaefer, 1960; Becker, 1964; Cline, Richards & Needham, 1963; Nichols, 1962; Sears, Maccoby & Levin, 1957). Apparent evidence of inconsistency, on the other hand, i.e., non-significant intercorrelations among permissiveness scores on different child-rearing practices (Sewall, Mussen & Harris, 1955; Schaefer, 1965) is mostly phenotypic; it reflects the operation of non-attitudinal meanings associated with a given practice (see p. 237). Although mothers may employ seemingly contradictory practices, the attitudinal content permeating the *manner in which they are administered* may be highly uniform for both mother and child. This supposition is consistent with the finding that high positive correlations may exist between the child's adjustment and the mother's character structure and maternal role even though no significant relationships prevail between adjustment and specific child-rearing practices (Behrens, 1954).

Continuity. Despite the abundance of clinical impressions (Levy, 1943; Shirley, 1941; Symonds, 1949), systematic empirical evidence of longitudinal continuity in parent attitudes is extremely sparse. Nevertheless, since a parent's child-rearing attitudes might be expected to remain about as stable as his personality, it is plausible to suppose that within certain limits of variation a given parent tends to manifest the same general kinds of child-rearing attitudes throughout his parental tenure. The determinants of longitudinal continuity in personality structure have been discussed in detail elsewhere (see pp. 106-110). In addition to those factors that operate to keep personality functioning relatively stable, numerous cultural expectancies regarding parental role tend to constrict intra- as well as interindividual variability in the expression of parent attitudes.

However, considerable basis also exists for discontinuity in parent attitudes—both in the culture and in the personality functioning of the parent. Apart from the influence of changing fads and fashions, many culturally standardized modifications and reversals in parent attitudes are expected with shifts in the biosocial status of the child (Chapter 12); and even if no basic changes occur in the parent's personality structure, the manifest behavioral correlates of feelings of security and adequacy, of level of anxiety and ego aspiration, and of self-preoccupation all tend to vary with vicissitudes in life history. Because of the inescapable ambivalence in his feelings, the parent is also apt to be more impressed at certain times than at others with either the satisfactions or the burdens of child rearing. As more children are added to the family he may find one sex or temperament more or less congenial; he may also either adapt better to the responsibilities of parenthood or find them increasingly intolerable. For example, sex of the child interacts with dimensions of child-rearing; mothers of boys show more stability and continuity in the factor "loving versus hostile" and less stability in autonomy-control when compared with mothers of girls (Bayley, 1964; Shaefer & Bayley, 1960). In addition to the above, parents are more or less inclined to think of children as advantages during different segments of the life cycle (Pohlman, 1967). As already suggested (p. 290), because of marked preference or distaste for different age period aspects of parental role the parents' overall attitudinal orientation toward the child may undergo marked change. Finally, the child precipitates discontinuity by sometimes forcing parents to change their attitudes and values (Brim, 1967).

Difficulties in Measuring Parent Attitudes*

Inasmuch as parents are highly ego-involved in their role, it is extremely difficult to obtain valid measures of their child-rearing attitudes. Observational and self-report techniques are partly contaminated by the parent's natural hesitancy in revealing information or behavior that would give an unfavorable impression of his adequacy or intentions as a parent (Hoffman &

---

*No extensive discussion will be made here on the topic of methodology. The following sources should be consulted for a more thorough handling of the topic: Hoffman & Lippitt (1960), Whiting & Whiting (1960), Yarrow (1963).

Lippitt, 1960; Yarrow, 1963). It is especially difficult to overcome this methodological problem in the case of middle-class parents, since they are particularly well-informed about the kinds of attitudes and practices approved by the "experts" (Hoffman & Lippitt, 1960; Kohn, 1963; Yarrow, 1963). This may be one of the reasons why "approved" items on parent attitude scales tend to have little discriminating power (Schaefer & Bell, 1958). Distortions occurring in an interview with the mother can be partially counterbalanced by also interviewing the father and child (Yarrow, 1963). Retrospective reports are highly suspect (Yarrow, 1963) although there are individual differences in the accuracy of retrospective data (Wenar & Coulter, 1962). Retrospective reports of mothers also vary in accuracy across different content areas (Mednick & Schaffer, 1963). The problems with retrospective data make *observation* of parent-child interaction more attractive as a viable method of measuring parent attitudes (Yarrow, 1963).

Parent attitude research instruments have been devised (e.g., Schaefer & Bell, 1958), but they have not as yet been very successful in predicting parent or child behaviors in observed settings (Becker & Krug, 1965; Brody, 1965). In general most studies carried out on parent attitudes have considered the adult as the active agent of the interaction with the child serving as the passive recipient of these attitudes (Bell, 1968; Clausen, 1966; Medinnus, 1967). More sophisticated studies of parent-child interaction will have to develop designs which will assess interactions in a reciprocal manner (Bell, 1968). Evidence for reciprocal interactions between parent and child is indicated by the finding that scores on parent attitude are consistently higher in mothers with children who have congenital defects as compared with mothers of normal children (Bell, 1964). Finally, because self-report techniques with parents are contaminated and also because the personality development of children is influenced more proximately by the attitudes *they* perceive than by the objective properties of the latter (as reported by parents or observers), we have advocated that parent attitudes be measured by ascertaining how they are perceived by children (see p. 169). This can be done either through direct subjective inquiry or by using projective techniques. Although the former method is more transparent it enjoys the advantages of greater denotative specificity and intersituational generality.

Maternal and Paternal Roles

The bulk of the early literature on parent-child relationships has analyzed the roles of parents without any further specification of sex (Brim, 1957). The father, especially, has been ignored by psychologists when studying the relationships between parents and children (Nash, 1965).* Although ma-

---

*Recent reviews of literature have focused on the role of the father. See Clausen (1966), Nash (1965), Rogier (1967).

ternal and paternal roles overlap to a great extent, they are clearly differentiated in all cultural settings. The differentiation is naturally related to the
social sex roles, to the concepts of masculinity and femininity, and to the
division of labor prevailing in a given culture. The traditional family in
Western society during earlier centuries tended to be patriarchal with the
father having maximum power over both wife and children (Clausen, 1966).
Although this condition still prevails in Oriental, Moslem, and Latin
Catholic societies, the trends in contemporary American society are moving
in the direction where both law and public opinion put definite limits on the
husband relative to the wife (Clausen, 1966). Although marriage relationships in contemporary American society are characterized by joint family
decisions, there is nevertheless ample evidence to indicate that the father
still maintains priority and the stronger final voice (Clausen, 1966).

Although our culture is patriarchal in law, it is matricentric rather than
patricentric as regards child rearing (Ostrovnsky, 1959). It is interesting to
note here that as the allocation of authority is moving away from the father
and is being shared reciprocally by both husband and wife, there has been a
corresponding increase in the father's participation in child-rearing and
household tasks (Bronfenbrenner, 1961; Rogier, 1967). In general, the
mother's role remains more highly structured and culturally standardized
than the father's; for one thing fathers, unlike mothers, seldom compare
notes about their offspring. The father's role is also derived more completely
from learned concepts and interpersonal experience; it is reinforced at no
time by hormonal factors or by childbearing and lactation.

As mentioned previously, American culture is somewhat diffuse in terms of
its role allocation when compared with other societies. The relative power of
the spouses depends on the husband's occupational status, the couple's
comparative educational status, the wife's work participation, the involvement of the wife with small children, and the personalities of husband and
wife (Clausen, 1966). In general, there appears to be a division of parental
role functions in the family, the father exhibiting primarily instrumental
functions (e.g., economic support) and the mother expressive (nurturant and
affectional) functions (Clausen, 1966; Miller & Swanson, 1958; Nash, 1965;
Parsons & Bales, 1955).* The mother is perceived as providing most of the
routine nurturant care, emotional succorance, and discipline (Droppleman
& Schaefer, 1963; Emmerich, 1962; Ghosh & Sinha, 1966; Radke, 1946),
and is viewed as a more friendly and less threatening (Kagan, 1956a); for
these reasons she is more frequently the preferred parent, especially in times
of stress, and also occupies the central position in the child's image of the

---

*Parsons & Bales (1955) contend that this type of role differentiation is necessary for adequate
sexual identification of children. This position is disputed by Slater (1961).

family (Clausen, 1966; Matt, 1954). This position may be somewhat challenged if the mother is employed and the father takes a greater share in the
household tasks (Clausen, 1966). She is also perceived by girls as a model to
be emulated in growing up (Gardner, 1947).

In the early years of the child's life the father's role is more passive, but as
children grow older they discriminate male roles on the basis of power
(Emmerich, 1961). If the father has any special role in the family (apart from
economic provider), it is that of chief authority figure, moral arbiter, and
disciplinarian. Traditionally his discipline is more arbitrary and severe
(Kagan, 1956a; Radke, 1946) than the mother's; when mutiny is brewing it
is he who "lays down the law." * The father is conceptualized on the semantic differential as stronger, longer, and darker (Kagan, Hosken &
Watson, 1961). Studies on boys' moral development indicate that the father's
role in discipline take on greater significance with increasing age (Hoffman,
1963). If their reactions to thematic materials are truly reflective of real-life
behavior, children adopt more submissive attitudes toward the father than
toward the mother (Kates, 1951). This situation probably still prevails
despite the trend toward a more equalitarian type of father-child relationship
(Radke, 1946; Tasch, 1952). In addition, as far as their limited time permits,
fathers consciously play the roles of guide, teacher, companion, and affectionate rearer, influence the mother's practices, and help establish the value
structure of the home (Clausen, 1966; Hoffman, 1963; Tasch, 1952).
Extremely important in structuring the father-child relationship is the
mother's attitude toward her husband and his parental role. As the major
socializing influence in his life, the child takes his cue from her in responding
to his father, especially when the latter is separated from the home (Nash,
1965). The perception of the father is also related to social class, children
from middle-class families seeing their fathers as more powerful in the family
than lower-class fathers (Hess & Torney, 1967). This situation is partially a
reflection of the father's occupation; because as the male becomes more
dependent, passive, and conforming in the occupational world, the wife's
relative authority increases in the home (Clausen, 1966).

The father's role is also somewhat differentiated for the two sexes. He
helps the girl define her biological and social sex role by treating her en-
dearingly as a little woman (Colley, 1959). She, in turn, tends to find his
personality more congenial than the mother's (Gardner, 1947). In relation
to the boy, although not consciously recognizing it, the father serves as a
model of masculinity and of the male sex role, including acceptable forms of

---

*Mothers actually give more coercive responses than fathers to hypothetical problem stituations
because they bear the greater share of the responsibility in managing children's misbehavior. However,
to act consistently with cultural expectations of femininity they tend more to sugar-coat their aggressiveness (Jackson, 1956).

exhibiting male aggression (Gardner, 1947; Mischel, 1966; Sears, Pintler & Sears, 1946). Preschool boys, characterized as generous, perceive their fathers as warm and nurturant (Rutherford & Mussen, 1968). Nevertheless, the father ordinarily subjects his son to more rigorous disciplinary control than his daughter and is much less affectionate toward him; boys accordingly tend to regard their mother's disposition as more congenial (Gardner, 1947). Middle-class fathers tend to play a more active and supervisory role but at the same time are more supportive of their sons as compared to lower-class fathers (Clausen, 1966). Finally, several studies indicate, especially in the case of boys, that when the father rather than the mother is the disciplinarian, the child is more likely to be angry, assertive, and directly aggressive, whereas maternal discipline is more related to inhibition of anger and hostility and to psychosomatic ailments (Clausen, 1966).

Ordinal Position in the Family *

Parent attitudes toward and treatment of the child vary to some extent with the latter's ordinal position in the family constellation:

. . . Birth order, i.e., the position of an individual among his siblings, is obviously linked with family size. It is also linked with age of the parents since first-born children will tend to have younger and last-born children older parents. Moreover, the sex of siblings and their spacing may contribute substantially to the meaning of a given position. Being first, middle, or last may tend to have certain meanings and consequences, but so may being the only boy or girl in a family with several children of the opposite sex (Clausen, 1966, p. 15).

It is obvious that the above conditions make it difficult to draw clear con- clusions about birth order effects, but there are some tentative findings which are worthy of note. The positions of the oldest, youngest, and only child are most highly differentiated. The first child is more likely to be planned and wanted and to be the recipient of his mother's succorance for a longer period of time (Sears, Maccoby & Levin, 1957). Nevertheless, because of the parents' inexperience, they are more likely to be more anxious with the first child (Clausen, 1966; Warren, 1966). Although first-borns receive slightly greater warmth and affection than the second-born (Clausen, 1966), parents at the same time tend to be less relaxed and more interfering with first-born children (Hilton, 1967). Parents are less permissive with first-borns with respect to feeding and weaning, more worrisome about sickness and danger, and more nurturant at bedtime (Sears, 1950). The oldest child is often given responsibility for other siblings and is expected to "set a good example" (Bossard & Boll, 1955; Mauco & Rambaud, 1951); his early self-concept is based more on parents' appraisal, whereas later-borns' self-conceptions have a large component of peer reflection (Clausen, 1966).

*For more extensive reviews, see Bradley (1968), Clausen (1966), Sampson (1965), Warren (1966).

Because of his initial privileged status, he is more likely than later-born children to feel that a sibling is favored by one of his parents (Clausen, 1966). The youngest child receives a considerable amount of attention since he interacts with parents and older brothers and sisters. He is most likely to be called by affectionate names (Clausen, 1966), is most frequently the "spoiled one" in the family (Bossard & Boll, 1955), is most likely to display infantile home relationships (Wile & Davis, 1941), is most given to peculation (Wile & Davis, 1941), and exhibits more attention-seeking behavior (Mauco & Rambaud, 1951), school difficulty, and intersibling conflict (Wile & Davis, 1941). In larger families, the mother tends to be more closely involved in both affection and authority with the youngest child, whereas the father tends to play a relatively greater authority role with the oldest child (Clausen, 1966). In keeping with his greater possibility of being "spoiled," the youngest son or daughter at any age level is less likely to be spanked than is a first born son or daughter of the same age (Clausen, 1966). This difference between youngest and oldest children in amount of punishment increases as the size of the family increases (Clausen, 1966).

Although there are many inconclusive results in studies of birth order effects, it is safe to indicate some general, though tentative, conclusions. Measured intelligence (I.Q.) is not appreciably related to sibling order, although there is a tendency for first-borns to score slightly higher on verbal intelligence consistent with the finding that they speak earlier and receive more verbal stimulation (Clausen, 1966). First-borns score slightly lower on tests of perceptual discrimination when compared with later-borns (Clausen, 1966). Oldest male children have higher achievement needs than their siblings (Altus, 1965; Bartlett & Smith, 1966; Chittenden, Foan, Zweil & Smith, 1968; Clausen, 1966; Warren, 1966). There is also some evidence that oldest children are more susceptible to normative influence while later-born children are more susceptible to informational influence (Becker, Lerner & Carroll, 1966; Clausen, 1966; Warren, 1966). These findings, however, are not unequivocal (Clausen, 1966; Warren, 1966). For example, first-born males are more readily influenced by group pressures (Clausen, 1966), yet the findings for females are inconsistent with regard to this type of influence (Carrigan & Julian, 1966; Clausen, 1966). The positive findings on oldest children concerning susceptibility to influence may be partly attributed to their initial greater internalization of parental values (Altus, 1965; Palmer, 1966). Apart from intense anxiety situations there appears to be no clear-cut consistency relating affiliation needs or affiliative behavior to birth order (Clausen, 1966; Warren, 1966). In anxiety-provoking situations first-borns appear to be more affiliative and conforming (Carrigan & Julian, 1966; Clausen, 1966; Schachter, 1959, 1963). In the judgment of parents and teachers, later-born siblings are more comfortable and relaxed with peers than are first-borns (Clausen, 1966). Oldest children are also less likely to involve themselves in high-risk sports (Nisbett, 1968) and are more cautious in other aspects of play (Collard, 1968). Consistent with the greater pressures placed on oldest children, they exhibit more anxiety than later-born siblings (Clausen, 1966; Zucker, Manosevitz & Lanyon, 1968). This finding is clearer in younger children and is confounded with sex differences at older ages (Sutton-Smith & Rosenberg, 1965). Finally, although oldest children have demonstrated higher adjustment scores on personality tests (Lessing & Oberlander, 1967) there are several studies which report less behavior pathology for later-born children (Clausen, 1966). Part of the apparent inconsistencies in these findings is probably due to the lack of differentiation between younger and middle siblings in these studies (Warren, 1966).

There have been many studies in the past few years showing that first-borns demonstrate greater scholastic and vocational achievement (e.g., Bracileg, 1968).

IMPACT OF PARENT ATTITUDES ON PERSONALITY DEVELOPMENT

Basis of Impact

On what grounds is it postulated that during early childhood parent attitudes exert extremely important determining effects on later personality development? First, the parent is associated from the very beginning in a benevolent and altruistic light with the satisfaction of the child's visceral needs, biological survival, and emotional security; and throughout the entire period of childhood he continues to wield tremendous power in regulating the child's motivations, satisfactions, and standards, and in influencing the course and outcome of various stages of ego development (Clausen, 1968a, and Chapter 8). Since perception of persons and emotional response to their presence and absence antedate similar awareness of and reaction to inanimate objects (Tagiuri, 1969) the sense of self emerges and grows in an interpersonal context (Adams, 1967; Clausen, 1968a).

Second, early experience has a disproportionate effect on development because it enjoys the benefits of *primacy*. In the unstructured attitudinal field of children, from which most competing influences are excluded, the specific behavioral differentiations and value systems of parents soon become relatively pre-emptive in their patterning effects. These effects tend to perpetuate themselves by making the individual selectively reaction-sensitive to the conditions that bring them about; and once consolidation occurs, reorganization is resisted because of "perceptual constancy," the tendency to utilize existing orientations and habits before acquiring new ones, and the stability of ego-involved components of personality (see pp. 106-110). Further enhancing the effects of primacy is the fact that childhood embraces many critical periods of development in which maximum susceptibility to environmental influences prevails. During these periods when development is still not committed in a particular direction, the individual is extremely flexible; afterwards, the very fact that commitment has already occurred makes for rigidity.

Although less crucial in their contribution, Child (1954) has delineated several additional factors explaining the importance of parent attitudes for personality development: (a) increased susceptibility to trauma because of immature interpretive and adjustive capacities; (b) the insusceptibility of preverbal learning to counteractive verbal influences, (c) the resistance of inconsistently reinforced learning to extinction, and (d) the transferability of attitudes and habits acquired in early family life to later behavior as spouse and parent.

Factors Limiting the Impact of Parent Attitudes

The above statement regarding the impact of parent attitudes on personality development requires many serious qualifications. The effects of parent attitudes are dependent on their communicability to children; vary with normative and individual differences in cognitive capacity and perceptual acuity, with the particular developmental needs that are dominant at a given stage of personality growth, and with the temperamental characteristics of the child; and are modifiable for better or worse by concurrent or subsequent experience outside the home. Thus, since parent attitudes are not the sole determinants of personality development and are frequently not even communicable to children, the widespread tendency to blame parents for *all* behavior problems is not only unwarranted, but leads to unwholesome self-recriminatory and apologetic attitudes toward children.

There is some evidence of very early ability in children to distinguish certain emotions (e.g., the fact that babies cry when they are shown contorted faces) but their discriminative capacities do not go beyond this primitive level (Tagiuri, 1969). As we have already emphasized repeatedly, the infant's cognitive immaturity insulates him from all but the most overt and obvious manifestations of interpersonal attitudes. This insulation is seen in the striking lack of specificity in the stimuli capable of evoking a smile, since even scolding can elicit such a response (Tagiuri, 1969). Hence, the impact of the parent's attitudinal substrate first begins to overshadow the influence of his grosser feelings and actions when the child enters the post-infantile stage (Kagan, 1967). But even later it is highly questionable whether many covert and adequately screened attitudes that are only uncovered in the course of psychotherapy (e.g., hostility and underlying apparent over-solicitude) are ever perceived (even "unconsciously") by many children;

much depends here on individual differences in perceptual sensitivity or empathic ability:

> . . . Determination of whether a parent is rejecting or not cannot be answered by focusing primarily on the behaviors of the parents. Rejection is not a fixed invariant quality of behavior qua behavior. Like pleasure, pain, or beauty, rejection is in the mind of the rejectee. It is a belief held by the child; not an action by the parent (Kagan, 1967, p. 132).

Cognitive and verbal immaturity set limits on the child's ability to make fine distinctions among feeling tones, to conceptualize and generalize his impressions, and to retain his experiences over long periods of time. Furthermore, when he is mature enough to form categorical judgments, he often tends to dismiss the manifest content of immediately perceived experience (unless it is too obtrusive to be ignored), and to infer from a culturally standardized proposition (e.g., all parents are *supposed* to love and protect their children) that his parents must obviously love him.

Constitutional factors also limit and modify the influence of parent attitudes (Becker, 1964; Bell, 1968). Because of variable, genically determined temperamental predispositions in children, the *same* parent attitude may have different effects. Apathetic and submissive children tend to become passively dependent in response to overprotection, whereas self-assertive and ascendent children are more apt to react aggressively (Meyers, 1944). Depending on their strength such predispositions may prove very tenacious—even in the face of opposing environmental pressures (Bell, 1968). They not only *evoke* different kinds of behaviors in the parent, but may also modify the latter's child-rearing attitudes (Bell, 1968; Medinnus, 1967). For example, children who are characteristically "person oriented" reinforce social responses in parents, whereas children of "low person orientation" tend to induce less nurturant responses in their parents (Bell, 1968).

Apart from changes in the parent's needs, personality traits, insights and current level of adjustment, other influences both within and outside the home modify and counteract the impact of early parent attitudes on the child's personality development. Balancing forces are usually at hand to soften extreme attitudes and practices. The deviant parent must first contend with the objections of his spouse, and later with the opposition of relatives, neighbors, and friends. As the child grows older he is increasingly exposed to the direct influence of persons other than parents—to siblings, age mates, relatives, teachers, and other adults. Some children, who never manage to identify with their parents, find an almost satisfactory substitute in a relative, teacher, or parent of a playmate. By the same token, the beneficial influence of favorable intrafamilial experience in early childhood may be partly undone by detrimental parent attitudes in later childhood, or by crippling disease, delayed pubescence, economic hardship, racial discrimination, etc.

Unfavorable parent attitudes are also limited in their effects when they are not operative during the particular critical periods of developmental need or maximal growth for which they are especially relevant. In the pre-satellizing period all that is required for adequate personality development is a certain amount of succorance, personal attention, and overt affection. The other major dimensions of the parent-child relationship that are so crucial for later stages of ego development seem relatively unimportant for the essential developmental tasks of infancy. Overdominating and overprotecting parents, parents who value their children for ulterior motives, and parents who are basically rejecting despite a veneer of affection, all seem to provide an adequate enough environment for the development of the omnipotent ego structure. During the second and third years of life, however, genuine emotional acceptance and intrinsic valuation of the child are essential for satellization; and the child accordingly becomes selectively sensitized in perceiving these aspects of parent attitude. Hence it no longer suffices for a parent to exhibit the outward manifestations of affection; evidence of an intrinsically accepting attitude in the smaller and more subtle aspects of feeling and action is required. It is at this time therefore that rejection has the most damaging effects on personality development. At a later age the child's more versatile and mature ego structure and his well-established set of defenses protect him somewhat from the trauma of rejection; at this time also there is more opportunity of forming satellizing and satellizing-like relationships to other adults and to the peer group. Finally, the dominative, protective, motivating, and critical aspects of parent attitude are most crucial during the period of desatellization; and children are accordingly most susceptible to such influences during the middle years of childhood (McGuire, 1969). Unless the parent sets appropriate expectations, standards, and limits, applies necessary coercive pressures, allows sufficient freedom for exploration, goal setting and decision making, and shows appreciation of the child's progress in these directions, the ego status and ego maturity aspects of desatellization may be retarded.

A final limiting factor that should be considered is the *wide margin of safety* that applies to parent attitudes as to most regulatory conditions affecting human development. If the attitudes of parents are generally wholesome in relation to their children, considerable deviancy from the theoretical opti-mum and occasional "mistakes" are still compatible with normal personality development. In view of this fact and the probable noncommunicability of many attitudes, merciless self-recrimination about the underlying motivations and the possible irrevocable consequences of minor deviations from "ac-cepted" practices is not only unnecessary but also robs parenthood of much joy and spontaneity.

DIMENSIONS OF PARENT ATTITUDES*

The preceding discussion of the impact of parent attitudes on personality development points up the importance for theoretical and research purposes of identifying and defining clearly as many significant variables as possible that are encompassed by the parent-child relationship. In no other way will it be possible to determine unambiguously the antecedents and consequences of various parent attitudes. Much of the difficulty in the past can be ascribed to confusion between popular and scientific usage, overlapping of terms, and lack of clarity in defining the precise aspects of the parent-child relationship to which these terms refer. In the popular literature about child care, for example, "spoiled," "indulged," "overprotected," "underdominated" and "overvalued" are used almost interchangeably.

Early attempts at a more precise categorization of parent attitudes tended to oversimplify matters by using unidimensional (acceptance) or bi-dimensional (acceptance-domination) scales. With the growth of computers in the 1950's, larger samples and more complex statistical procedures have been increasingly utilized in attempting to distinguish between the multiple influences that parent attitudes have on the child's development (Becker, 1964). More explicit multiple scale approaches have emerged which initially were too unwieldly and atomistic in orientation to be useful in elucidating developmental sequences (e.g., Fels Parent Behavior Rating Scales; Champney, 1941). These multiple scales have been reduced in size by factor analysis or by interrelating variables meaningfully into naturally occurring syndromes (Baldwin, Kalhorn & Breese, 1949; Becker, 1964; Roff, 1949; Schaefer, 1961). Factorial structure of scales is dependent on the type of parent involved, experienced mothers revealing simpler patterns (Schaefer, 1961). The number of factors which emerge also depends on the types of scales utilized (Schaefer, 1961). Even when statistical techniques are utilized to reduce the number of dimensions, these scales still leave much to be desired from the standpoint of making significant predictions from parent-child relationships to child behavior or adult personality. Without differential weighting in terms of relationship to and significance for successive developmental tasks, they do not help us to understand how children in general progress from one sequential stage of personality to another or why a particular child acquires or fails to acquire the major attributes of ego structure characteristic of his age level. Thus it is not surprising that certain dimensions of parent attitudes are less stable over time than developmentally more sensitive dimensions. For example, the dimension of autonomy versus control

*Our discussion of dimensions of parent attitudes will be restricted to an interpretation which is consistent with our chapter on ego development. Recent discussion of this topic may be found in Becker (1964), Schaefer (1961), and Zigler & Child (1969).

is much more variable developmentally than the dimension of love-hostility (Schaefer, 1961):

> . . . Differential consistency appears reasonable since the child's need for love is constant through time but the child's need for autonomy changes greatly from infancy to adolescence (Schaefer, 1961).

Similar parent attitudes may have quite different outcomes depending on whether the individual is or is not a satellizer. Overprotection, overdomination, and rejection have very different effects in infancy, early childhood, and preadolescence. Hence, phenotypically different attitudes such as rejection and extrinsic valuation are both associated with the same outcome of nonsatellization. Without some conceptual scheme for systematizing the data one ends up with a bewildering maze of discrete and uninterpretable correlations.

Another source of confusion has arisen from the widespread tendency to subsume the dominative aspects of parent behavior under overprotection, i.e., to consider over- and underdomination as subtypes of overprotection (Levy, 1943). Although such combinations of attitudes are frequently encountered, they are by no means inevitable. Many overprotective parents are able to maintain a proper balance of domination; contrariwise, over- or underdominated children are not necessarily overprotected. The dimension of protectiveness refers to extent of parental care and solicitude. The overprotecting parent unduly prolongs infantile care, provides excessive personal contact and supervision, and seeks to furnish an environment for his child which is free of hurt, disappointment, failure, frustration, and exposure to the harsher realities of life. Its source inheres in projected anxiety: the parent mitigates his own unidentifiable anxiety by projecting threat onto the child and giving it more concrete reference. The dimension of dominance, on the other hand, refers to the relative balance of volitional self-assertiveness and deference between parent and child and is not related in origin to parent anxiety. Thus the confounding of the protective and the dominative aspects of parental attitudes is extremely unfortunate since each refers to clearly different roles and functions of parenthood. Only conceptual confusion can result when two discriminably different variables are treated as if they were coextensive. The confusion is even more regrettable when the entirely different origins and consequences of the two kinds of attitudes are considered.

It is true that overprotection and underdomination have an important point in common, namely, great reluctance in frustrating the child. In the overprotecting parent, however, it is part of the larger anxiety reducing goal of sparing the child psychological and physical trauma rather than a manifestation of unassertiveness; if deferring to the child's will exposes the latter to physical or social danger, the overprotective parent would sooner frustrate the child's volitional independence. Thus, although the underdominating parent tends to be consistently deferential, the overprotecting parent can be yielding only in situations which either increase the child's infantile dependency or which do not contain threats of illness, injury, or failure.

It would seem more fruitful and economical of effort, therefore, to start with a theoretical structure hypothesizing various stages of personality development with their component attributes and developmental tasks. By defining and categorizing parent-child relationships in terms of dimensions compatible with this structure, one could then test various hypotheses regarding the intrafamilial antecedents of various developmental outcomes by relating measurements of these dimensions to personality outcomes in children and adults. The dimensions of the parent-child relationship designated in Table 2 were formulated with this end in view. They are not the only dimensions that could possibly be identified, but they encompass the major aspects of this relationship that have relevance for the developmental tasks and processes described in Chapter 8.

Although the above dimensions are separate variables, permitting in theory an almost infinite number of combinations and permutations, the actual number of important combinations occurring in practice is sharply limited by hierarchical factors and psychological compatibility. Most important is the patterning influence of the key attitudes leading to satellization

TABLE 2.—*Dimensions of the Parent-Child Relationship* *

Dimension (Parent Attitude or Behavior)	Child's Position on Scale	
	Upper Extreme	Lower Extreme
1. Emotional acceptance	Accepted	Rejected
2. Valuation of child for self or in terms of parent's ego needs	Intrinsically valued	Extrinsically valued
3. Magnitude of valuation of child's importance	Overvalued	Undervalued
4. Protectiveness (care, solicitude)	Overprotected	Underprotected
5. Dominance (self-assertiveness or deference to child's will)	Overdominated	Underdominated
6. Level of aspiration for child	Overmotivated	Undermotivated
7. Criticism of child (overt or implied)	Overcriticized	Undercriticized
8. Appreciation (recognition of child's competence)	Overappreciated	Underappreciated

*Adapted from D. P. Ausubel, Ego Development and the Personality Disorders.

and non-satellization respectively. Satellizers are all both emotionally accepted and intrinsically valued, whereas non-satellizers are either rejected and extrinsically valued or accepted and extrinsically valued. The rejected group of non-satellizers is usually underprotected, overdominated, underappreciated, over-criticized and undervalued. The extrinsically valued group of non-satellizers is almost invariably overvalued, underdominated, overmotivated, under-criticized and overappreciated. For all practical purposes it is most convenient to refer to these two groups of non-satellizers as "rejected" and "overvalued" respectively. Greater variability in patterning prevails among parents of satellizing children. Except for the uniformity provided by the two prerequisite conditions, almost any combination of the remaining parent attitudes is possible.

ORIGIN OF SPECIFIC PARENT ATTITUDES

The attitudes which an adult displays as a parent go back in large part to his own childhood and the kind of relationship he enjoyed with his own parents. They reflect both the impact of the parent-child relationship on personality development and the influence which parents exert as models of parental role and function.

Rejection and Overvaluation

Both clinical experience and developmental logic suggest that non-satellizing children tend to have parents who themselves were non-satellizers. It is by no means true, however, that all non-satellizers have non-satellizing children. A history of rejection or extrinsic valuation in the parent's childhood predisposes him toward high ego aspirations and neurotic anxiety; and in such an individual, immersed in his own ambitions and harassed by constant threat to self-esteem, self-preoccupation is easily understandable. In the case of women it leads to reluctance to accept the feminine role in life and the compromises in prosecuting a career that motherhood necessarily entails. Under these circumstances, responsibility for the protective care and emotional succorance of a child may seem like such a formidable and burdensome duty that rejection becomes a very likely alternative. Other equally possible alternatives are attempts to achieve vicarious ego enhancement through projection of omnipotent ego aspirations onto the child (overvaluation) and efforts directed toward anxiety reduction through the mechanism of displacement, i.e., perceiving the child as the object of threat (overprotection). The tendency toward self-preoccupation is also enhanced by narcissism and the inability to relate emotionally to others that so frequently characterize non-satellizers. These traits are more pronounced in overvalued than in rejected persons, since they proceed more from habituation to a one-way flow of affection and interest than from dread of emotional involvement for fear of repeating an experience of rejection. In some instances the hostile attitudes of a rejecting parent seem to stem at least in part from an unresolved residue of hostility toward his own parents or siblings which in turn resulted from a situation of rejection or favoritism. By identifying with the role of his own rejecting parent he vicariously gives vent to these feelings.

Given all of these personality predispositions toward becoming an over-valuing or rejecting parent, however, it does not necessarily follow that the non-satellizing individual will actually become one. Much depends on other personality traits as well as on various situational factors. His level of anxiety, for example, can be kept under better control if he is an able, enterprising, organized, and socially perceptive person. The more self-indulgent and visceratonic he is, the more resentful he is of any responsibilities toward others which interfere with the gratification of his own hedonistic needs. If he has a strong sense of moral obligation he may endeavor to inhibit much of his hostility or even become oversolicitous in order to avoid guilt feelings. The unhampered expression of rejecting tendencies is also limited by the individual's sensitivity to prevailing cultural norms and to social censure. If he is concerned with appearances he can usually find "reputable excuses for hating a child" (Symonds, 1949); and only too frequently, the same narcissistic preoccupation with himself that causes him to neglect his child provides him with a thick skin in the face of public or private criticism.

The prevailing level of anxiety or hostility that becomes manifest from underlying personality trends is also affected by numerous situational factors. Latent residual hostility toward a parent is often reactivated by an unhappy marital relationship and then displaced onto the child. This is more likely to occur if the parent feels that he is being rejected by his spouse in favor of the child. Thus, a moderately positive correlation prevails between marital adjustment and the acceptance of children (Clausen, 1966; Porter, 1955). The entrance of an infant into the household, especially if he is ill or if his parents are confronted by vocational or financial difficulties, frequently exacerbates chronic anxiety. In any event the child's chances of being rejected are obviously increased if his sex, physique, or temperament are at variance with the parent's preferences. A docile child's reaction to rejection usually encourages a hostile or narcissistic parent to continue this treatment since the parent is not even required to placate his nuisance value. An irritable, self-assertive, and rebellious child, on the other hand, may destroy the equilibrium of an anxiety-torn parent who then utilizes the child's behavior as justification for the original rejection and the subsequent counter-aggression.

The probability of developing *consistently* rejecting parent attitudes is determined in part by the individual's capacity for relating himself emotionally to others. In rejected persons this capacity, which is ever latent but inhibited by fear of rejection, has an excellent opportunity for overt expression in the form of warm, accepting parent attitudes since little threat of rejection can be anticipated from a child. Self-preoccupation here is largely a function of anxiety and can be mitigated if other personality traits and situational factors are favorable for keeping the level of anxiety under control. In over-valued individuals, on the other hand, self-preoccupation seems to be more a reflection of narcissism and incapacity for relating emotionally to others, and hence is less apt to be favorably influenced by benign environmental conditions. For similar reasons, the overvalued parent is also more disposed than the rejected parent to extend a more *passive* kind of rejection to his children. Lack of concern for the needs of others stemming from narcissism leads to neglect and indifference which arouse little guilt feelings since they reflect an habitual orientation in interpersonal relations. If current exacerbations of anxiety were to induce self-preoccupation in rejected parents, passive neglect and avoidance of parental responsibility would more likely engender guilt feelings. Thus the rejected parent tends more to continue to care for and interact with the child—but resentfully and with evident hostility which he tries to rationalize as a form of counter-aggression made necessary by the latter's perverseness.

A final problem has to do with the basis of choice between rejecting and overvaluing attitudes. What differences might we anticipate between two parents, both non-satellizers with grandiose ego aspirations, one of whom finds the child a cumbersome and unwanted burden, while the other is able to utilize him as a principal vehicle for ego aggrandizement? Much seems to depend on the parent's capacity to perceive the dependent child as an extension of himself rather than as entity in his own right, and to react to his triumphs as if they were his own achievements. This capacity probably reflects in part some degree of pessimism in the parent's appraisal of his chances for ego aggrandizement through his own efforts. Also, everything else being equal, the parent faced with the choice of either rejecting or overvaluing his child is more likely to choose the latter alternative as he is less hostile, embittered, and withdrawn, and is more extroverted, socio-centric and better able to relate to others.

Overprotection

We have already suggested that the principal basis of overprotecting attitudes is a form of parental anxiety in which the object of threat is displaced from parent to child. The parent is anxious, insecure, fearful of impending disaster, and feels inadequate to cope with the ordinary adjustive problems of life. By projecting the object of threat onto the child he is able to mitigate his own anxiety in two ways: (a) some of the perceived threat to himself is deflected, thereby making the environment look less foreboding, and (b) he is better able to cope with the threats confronting the child than those besetting himself. He can isolate the child from painful experiences by using himself as a shield, since the frustrations facing a child are relatively concrete and avoidable; whereas he cannot insulate himself from the world and still maintain his own intense strivings. But the success he enjoys in protecting his child from danger and frustration is transferable to his own situation. Since the anxiety-ridden personality is also predisposed toward rejecting and overvaluing attitudes, overprotection may be regarded as an alternative to the latter orientations. Sometimes it occurs as a reaction-formation for covert rejecting tendencies or as a form of expiation for overt rejecting behavior. In some instances the predisposing anxiety is reinforced by such contributory factors as marital unhappiness, a long history of sterility or miscarriages, severe illness or injury in the child, and death of a previous child or close relative (Clausen, 1966; Levy, 1943; Staver, 1953).

Under-and Overdomination

The simplest explanation of the origin of under- and overdominating attitudes is that they reflect a temperamental disparity in self-assertiveness between parent and child. A combination of mild, self-effacing parent and aggressive, ascendent child (or vice versa) is not a statistical rarity. Frequently, however, the explanation is not as simple. A truly ascendent and self-reliant parent may have little need to assert himself with his children, whereas (as some evidence suggests) the submissive, ineffective parent who lacks self-assurance may use his relationship with the child as a means of compensating for lack of status, prestige, or authority vocationally or in the eyes of his spouse (Block, 1955). The overdominating or underdominating parent may sometimes pattern his behavior after his recollections of his own parents' way of dealing with him. On the other hand, if he believes that his parents' practices were undesirable, he may make a deliberate effort to veer to the opposite extreme. In some cases underdomination is a manifestation of passive rejection; the parent is only too happy to leave the child to his own devices as long as he himself is not bothered. Actively rejected children, however, are usually overdominated. In overvaluing parents underdomination is generally a projection of exaggerated ego aspirations. Since the parent hopes for vicarious ego enhancement through the accomplishments of a volitionally omnipotent child, he can hardly afford to frustrate the latter's will. Either orientation (but especially underdomination) may also represent adherence to a current philosophy of child rearing.

In terms of both source and expression, parental overdomination is largely the antithesis of underdomination. But although the general consequences of both attitudes are quite similar in their impact on ego maturation, much greater possibility for heterogeneity in the child's response exists in the case of the former. This heterogeneity results from variations (a) in the brusqueness or kindliness with which the overdomination is administered, and (b) in the self-assertiveness of the child. The first variable governs the acceptability of the overdomination to the child. The second variable determines the type of resistance that will be offered if overdomination is unacceptable, i.e., active (rebellion) or passive (sabotage).

EARLY SOCIAL DEVELOPMENT IN THE FAMILY*

Parents as Cultural Representatives

Especially during the early years, the child is not exposed directly to a representative sample of the culture at large but to a restricted, family-biased version of it. The parent is under obligation both to interpret the culture to the child and to serve as its official representative in dealing with him. He is under pressure to produce and deliver an individual who is a reasonable facsimile of the prevailing cultural pattern. If he himself—within acceptable limits of deviancy—has assimilated the values and expectations of his culture with respect to the goals of child rearing, relatively little difficulty ensues in playing the role of cultural representative. If, however, his personal values and attitudes are at variance with cultural norms he is often resentful and ambivalent about this role, sometimes showing open defiance, but more often conforming verbally while covertly following his own inclinations.

In what ways does the child's indirect exposure to the culture through his parents differ from the more direct kind of exposure that he later receives at the hands of other socializing agents? First, the family presents a highly idiosyncratic picture of the culture to the child. Parents are always selective in the cultural alternatives they choose to transmit and in their perceptions of cultural norms. Furthermore, they not only deviate deliberately in varying degrees from cultural prescriptions, but also improvise their own prescriptions in the more unstandardized aspects of parent-child relationships. In any event, salient features of their own idiosyncratic personality traits are always expressed in their dealings with the child. Second, the *specific* models of behavior presented by the parents differ qualitatively from *other* specific models the child perceives in the wider community. The idiosyncratic features of the latter tend to lose their individual identity in the composite role portraits that eventually emerge; but because of their *primacy*, the models provided by mother and father retain their idiosyncratic properties. Their particular specificity constitutes in itself and becomes equivalent to other

*Discussion of findings on parent-child relations relies heavily on reviews of the literature because of the enormous amount of literature on the topic. See Aronfreed (1968), Becker (1946), Baumrind (1966), Hoffman (1963), Zigler & Child (1969).

general categories or abstractions in which only commonalities are retained while nondistinguishing specificities are discarded. Finally, the home environment is not only a social one but is also intensely personal and intimate. Rewards and punishments come with simple directness from persons, never from abstract symbols (Cameron, 1947). Home, therefore, can never be more than a rough preview of what the child can anticipate from the wider culture. He can only predict that it (the culture) will treat him more objectively, casually, and impersonally; he can expect no special privileges, no special concern with his welfare, and no favored treatment. But apart from these negative forecasts, he is much more at a loss regarding the kinds of behavior he may anticipate from others, since he is confronted on the outside by a much larger array of persons about whose attitudes he knows substantially less.

Initial Social Behavior in the Home

The child's first social behavior occurs within the family circle in relation to adults rather than to other children. Considering his immaturity in other spheres—perceptual, cognitive, language, and motor—it is unusually well developed. This precocity reflects the operation of potent, genically determined capacities for social responsiveness, including specific predispositions for such stereotyped expressive characteristics as smiling, cooing, and gurgling in response to the human voice and face. Sensitization to the social environment is shown by earlier recognition and differentiation of and emotional responsiveness to persons than to inanimate objects (Tagiuri, 1969).

The child's social responsiveness is also facilitated by his dependency, which requires that his needs be satisfied from the very beginning in an interpersonal context. He becomes accustomed and responsive to the behavior and communicative acts of others in the course of having his needs satisfied by them. Initially, however, until the child becomes *psychologically* dependent, the objective dependency situation primarily influences the *parent's* social behavior. It is conceivable, nevertheless, that even before he appreciates the mother's causal relationship to the satisfaction of his needs, her status as substitutive reward and signal of imminent gratification facilitates his social responsiveness to and recognition of her. Once he perceives his helplessness and dependence on her availability for his continued physical survival his very sense of security acquires social reference. He now initiates social interaction with adults, responds affectively to their presence and absence, discriminates between friendly and angry expressions, and shows fear when a stranger approaches. During this time he also acquires needs for the affection and stimulation that parents provide; and during the satellizing period he becomes dependent on their acceptance and approval for security and adequacy feelings. It is little wonder then that social relationships with persons—through which all other needs are satisfied—should become important needs in their own right.

Impact of Intrafamilial Experience on Later Social Development

One of the most important consequences of early parent-child relationships is the pronounced tendency for the child's later interpersonal relations with peers and other adults to reflect the influence of social attitudes, expectancies, and adjustive techniques experienced in dealings with his first socializers, his parents. To the child the world of interpersonal relations is completely unstructured at first; and for the first few years of life most of the differentiation of this unstructured field occurs in the home. Hence, in the absence of any other frame of reference for basing his expectations of what people in the outside world are like and for reacting to them, it is most natural for him to use the model provided by his parents and to employ adaptive techniques previously utilized in the home situation. Moreover, habituation to *particular* satisfying features of the parent-child relationship creates needs for them in the child, needs which can only be satisfied by conditions analagous to those which produced them in the first place.

The child's capacity for forming wholesome interpersonal relationships outside the home, therefore, is influenced by the following aspects of the intrafamilial situations: (a) whether on the basis of friendly relations with parents he is led in advance to expect the best from people unless given cause to feel otherwise; (b) the extent to which his parents do not create unique or unrealistic needs and expectations in him which only they are willing and able to satisfy, or encourage the development of special adjustive techniques to the exclusion of the more usual and adaptive abilities necessary for most social situations; (c) the availability (neither insufficient nor excessive) of family support, assurance, and guidance should he encounter difficulties with others; (d) the absence of home attachments that are so strong as to be pre-emptive; (e) not acquiring personality traits or adjustive habits from the parent-child relationship that other children find offensive; and (f) not being predisposed by home training to withdraw from extrafamilial social experience to the point where the learning of realistic social roles becomes impossible.

The child's social behavior is also profoundly affected by whether or not he has undergone satellization, which in turn is an outcome of the parent-child relationship. To the satellizing child, group membership provides derived status and constitutes an intrinsic ego support. He experiences a certain spontaneous joy and enthusiasm in group activity which follows from the "we-feeling" associated with group relatedness. To the nonsatellizer, on the other hand, the field of interpersonal relations is just another arena in which he contends for extrinsic status and ego aggrandizement. There is no identification with or self-subordination to group interests, and no possibility of deriving spontaneous satisfaction out of gregarious activity. A similar type of dichotomy prevails in the relationships satellizers and non-satellizers respectively establish with teachers and other adults.

The rejected individual has strong needs for volitional autonomy but finds it difficult to assert himself effectively in interpersonal relationships. Not only has he failed to master customary roles and techniques necessary for adult self-assertion but he also *feels* incapable of playing these roles convincingly. This is partly a result of the low degree of empathy that rejecting parents manifest in relation to their children (Guerney, Stover & De Meritt, 1968) and a direct carry-over of the child's feeling of helplessness in coping with the ruthless domination of parents; but in part it also reflects feelings of unworthiness attributable to his parents' negative valuation of him, lack of intrinsic self-esteem, and chronic anxiety. Rejection and derogation by parents adversely affects cognitive and linguistic abilities in rejected children (Brodie & Winterbottom, 1967; Hurley, 1965; Kinstler, 1961). Because he does not appear adequate to protect his own interests and avoid being taken advantage of he invites aggression from others; but in view of his genuine needs for volitional independence he resents any subservience to which he is subjected and may eventually react explosively. More typically he withdraws from conflictful social situations and intellectualizes his aggression; and if he can overcome his haunting fear of further rejection he may even try to establish satellizing-like relationships with non-threatening persons.

During childhood, rejected individuals are alternatively described as shy and submissive on the one hand, and as aggressive, quarrelsome, noncompliant and resistive to adult guidance on the other hand (Baldwin *et al*, 1945; Baumrind, 1966; Becker, 1964; Hatfield, Ferguson & Alpert, 1967). Without a secure home base to which they can return they tend to adjust less successfully than accepted children to novel and stressful social situations (Becker, 1964; Heathers, 1954; Shirley, 1942). Juvenile delinquency is significantly more frequent in homes characterized by lack of parent warmth and rejection (Becker, 1964; Medinnus, 1965). Children's control over aggression and their reactions to their own transgressions are all characterized by a low degree of internalization when they have been exposed to extreme parental rejection or punitiveness (Bandura & Walters, 1963; Sears *et al*, 1957). Where rejection is prolonged but passive (e.g., as in foundling homes), children tend to establish emotionally shallow interpersonal relationships and to display social immaturity.

The underdominated child is encouraged to assert himself, but at the same time no demands are made on him to develop the mature personality traits necessary for realistic implementation of volitional independence. Because he has little direct experience with the restrictive features of reality and is not required to learn the limits of acceptable conduct, he cannot easily choose realistic roles and goals. As a result of being conditioned to a relationship in which all of the yielding is done by the other party, he comes to think of himself as a unique person to whom others just naturally defer. In his relations with other children and adults, he tends to be domineering, aggressive, disobedient, petulant, and capricious (Becker, 1964; Levy, 1943). He is unwilling to defer to the judgment and interests of others, always demanding his own way upon threat of unleashing unrestrained fits of temper (Levy, 1943). But despite his conspicuous lack of social success outside the home, he still tends to persist in this type of domineering behavior, partly because he is so thoroughly overtrained in it and partly because of the imperious need to dominate which he has acquired from the parent-child relationship (Cameron, 1947; Levy, 1943). The overvalued child for very similar reasons develops the same type of social behavior, but has stronger needs for volitional independence and ego aggrandizement. Hence, although he never basically abandons his grandiose aspirations and desire for deference, he is more highly motivated to modify the strategy of his interpersonal behavior in order to establish the overtly satisfactory social relationships he recognizes as important in the quest for status and power. The extrinsically valuing parent who over-values his (her) child's achievements is frequently characterized as rejecting, critical, hostile, and pushing his child beyond intrinsic ability levels (Crandall, 1967). Part of parents' overvalued striving for their children appears to be related to lack of self-acceptance in themselves (Medinnus & Curtis, 1963).

Because of constrictive and dominative home environments respectively, both overprotected and overdominated children fail to learn the social skills necessary for adequate self-assertion and self-defense. Unable to defend their rights successfully, they are continually fearful of being duped and exploited by others. Since the peer group is unwilling to satisfy their special needs for protection and direction, they tend to withdraw from peer relationships and to seek the company of parents and adults who can play the roles their needs demand. Overprotected children are generally submissive, dependent, compliant, shy, anxious (Becker, 1964; Levy, 1943; Radke, 1946), and inadequate in meeting stressful situations (Shirley, 1942). They are extremely dependent on their mothers and experience great difficulty in making friends (Levy, 1943). Overdominated children exhibit the same traits and in addition tend to be well-controlled, dependable, polite, self-conscious and introverted (Baldwin, 1948; Becker, 1964; Radke, 1946; Siegelman, 1966; Walsh, 1968). Autocratic, harsh, and capricious overdomination, however, may not be accepted by the child, and hence may lead to active rebellion in ascendent, extroverted children and to passive sabotage in docile, introverted children. These latter two groups probably account for the reported frequency of quarrelsome, uncooperative, uninhibited, and inconsiderate behavior in children from autocratic homes (Becker, 1964; Symonds, 1949). Children from "democratic homes" tend to be active, competitive, and socially outgoing, both in friendly and in aggressive and domineering ways, and to enjoy high acceptance from their age mates. In contrast to over-dominated children, they show originality, intellectual curiosity, and con-structiveness in school activities (Baldwin, 1948; Becker, 1964).

DISCIPLINE*

The Need for Discipline

Although much cultural diversity prevails in the severity and techniques of discipline, the phenomenon itself is encountered in all cultural settings. In the child's development, there are several authority holders who make differential demands on his behavior (Dubin & Dubin, 1963) but the earliest authority agents in our culture are clearly parents. The need for discipline occurs in those situations where the child is concerned with routines of daily living, in establishing sibling and adult relationships, and in displaying behavior that adults deem appropriate (Clifford, 1959). We have already elaborated on the reasons for believing that every noteworthy advance in personality maturation is accompanied by some change in the expectations of significant persons in the child's environment which is enforced in part by some coercive form of pressure. On both counts parents occupy a strategic position. Not only do their own expectations change as a result of altered needs and new perceptions of the child's behavioral capacity, but also chan-neled through them are changing cultural expectations of appropriately mature behavior at different age levels. In either case the parent is one of the most appropriate agents for applying whatever coercive measures are necessary for effecting conformity of the child's behavior to changed patterns of expectations. Direct experience with limiting and restrictive factors in the environment is necessary for learning a reasonable degree of conformity to social norms of acceptable behavior, for the learning of realistic roles and goals, for learning to make reasonable demands on others, and for the acquisition of responsibility, self-control, and the capacity for deferring need satisfaction. Since these aspects of socialization are not written into the genes, they would not be acquired spontaneously. To be sure, the removal of all pressures for conformity would undoubtedly eliminate most interpersonal conflict and negativism, but it still has to be demonstrated that normal per-

---

*As used in this section, discipline refers to the imposition of standards and controls by others on the child's behavior. The relative absence of discipline is equivalent to maximal permissiveness (under-domination) in the handling of children.

sonality maturation would also occur under these conditions. It is also profitable to distinguish between the effects on the child of restrictive, subjective authority and of an authority orientation which is warm and issue-oriented (Baumrind, 1966). The former is more likely to be associated in the child with negative affect, disaffilitiveness, and rebelliousness (Baumrind, 1966).

Discipline is also necessary from the standpoint of the child's emotional security. Without unambiguous standards of social reality in relation to which he can orient his behavior and control his impulses, he feels confused and insecure. The absence of external standards places too great a burden on his limited degree of self-control and attitudinal sophistication. In a completely permissive environment, he is afraid of the consequences of his own uninhibited behavior—of both the retribution and the guilt; and in the absence of punishment there is also very little opportunity for reducing guilt feelings.

Ambiguous control also cannot be avoided unless discipline consists of punishment as well as reward. It is unrealistic to expect that in the early and middle years of childhood approval for acceptable behavior automatically endows its logical opposite with negative valence. The child does not make inferences so easily and does not typically operate at the level of logical consistency that this approach assumes. Especially during the early years the positive valence of an attractive but forbidden activity is not effectively reduced until such time as explicit evidences of reproof are administered. Reproof can have a variety of consequences depending on the way it is administered (Aronfreed, 1968; Baumrind, 1966; Hoffman, 1963). The use of disciplinary techniques which attempt to change the child's behavior by appealing to his need for affection and self-esteem appear to foster a more internalized moral orientation, whereas physical coercion and shame lead to externally controlled and authority-regulated conduct in children (Aronfreed, 1968; Bronfenbrenner, 1961; Hoffman, 1963). More important than love withdrawal is the use of induction techniques where parents focus on the consequences of the child's actions for others (Aronfreed, 1968; Hoffman & Saltzstein, 1967).

Democratic Discipline

Proponents of extreme permissiveness frequently equate their philosophy with democratic discipline and assert that other forms of discipline are synonymous with authoritarianism. The arguments and evidence used in this latter connection (see Chapter 11) only discredit autocratic types of control (over-domination)—*not* all types of non-permissive discipline. This evidence merely supports the need for democratic methods of control rather than for maximally persmissive (laissez-faire) methods (underdomination), the effects of which are no more desirable than those of overdomination (see Chapter 11). There is also no rational basis for believing that the parent's authority role is necessarily incompatible with a relaxed and cordial parent-child relationship. Most children recognize their parents' right to impose controls and do not question the legitimacy of disciplinary measures. A democratic approach to discipline does not require the parent to renounce his prerogative of making final decisions or to refrain from imposing "external" standards and restraints on the child:

> Authoritarian control and permissive non-control may both shield the child from the opportunity to engage in vigorous interaction with people. Demands which cannot be met or no demands, suppression of conflict or sidestepping of conflict, refusal of help or too much help, unrealistically high or low standards all may curb or understimulate the child so that he fails to achieve the knowledge and experience which could realistically reduce his dependence upon the outside world. The authoritarian and permissive parent may both create, in different ways, a climate in which the child is not desensitized to the anxiety associated with nonconformity. Both models minimize dissent, the former by suppression and the latter by diversion or indulgence. To learn how to dissent, the child may need a strongly held position from which to diverge and then be allowed under some circumstances to pay the price for nonconformity by being punished. Spirited give and take within the home, if accompanied by respect and warmth, may teach the child how to express aggression in self-serving and prosocial causes and to accept the partially unpleasant consequences of such actions (Baumrind, 1966, p. 904).

Characteristics

In contrast to authoritarian discipline which is harsh, tyrannical, vengeful and power-oriented in terms of control measures (Becker, 1964; Brody, 1965; Hart, 1957; Hoffman, 1960), democratic discipline avoids any attempt to intimidate the child, and repudiates the use of punishment as an outlet for parental aggression. It does not propose to eradicate the distinction between parental and filial roles. The parent is recognized as the more mature and dominant party in the relationship; his judgments are given more weight and his demands more authority. Nevertheless, no exaggerated emphasis is placed on status differences, and all artificial barriers preventing free communication are removed. Respect is always a two-way proposition: the child's rights, opinions, and especially his dignity as a human being are never disregarded. The child is encouraged to participate in the determination of goals and standards whenever he is qualified to do so, and maximal reliance is placed on inner controls. Verbal exhortations are reinforced by personal example.

Democratic discipline is also as rational and as unarbitrary as possible. The parent provides explanations for decisions and permits the child to present his point of view; and even when the latter is too young to understand reasons, he (the parent) tries to use a reasonable tone of voice. For many reasons, however, a wholly rational approach is unfeasible since

(a) cognitive limitations make it impossible to render many explanations intelligible to the child; (b) many parental requests cannot be justified on the basis of reason but must nevertheless be heeded on the grounds of either necessary conformity to cultural tradition or of superior experience and judgment; and (c) many emergency situations in childhood require complete, immediate, and unquestioning obedience.

Other Aspects of Parental Discipline

Methods of parental control must obviously be adapted to meet changing conditions of personality organization and maturity. In the presatellizing period parents are largely dependent on physical restraint, reward, and punishment. During the satellizing stage they can rely more upon approval and disapproval, prestige suggestion, personal loyalty, and moral restraints of conscience and guilt feelings. Later, in the desatellizing period, the child is less disposed to conform on the basis of personal allegiance and desire for approval; considerations of expediency and ego enhancement become more salient at this time. With increasing age, therefore, effective discipline becomes more rational and less authoritarian. It is more acceptable to the older child if the parent acts as an impersonal agent of the culture in interpreting and enforcing social norms than if he continues to serve as a personal source of authority and to demand obedience as an axiomatic right. Parents also instigate less resistance if wherever possible they bring children into line by letting age mates apply "lateral sanctions" than by applying hierarchial sanctions themselves.

Although the effects of inconsistent discipline are difficult to assess because "inconsistency" refers to a multitude of different combinations and orderings of parental responses to children's behavior (Becker, 1964; Walters & Parke, 1966), it is nevertheless safe to suggest that effective discipline is unambiguous consistent, and relevant to the misbehavior to which it is applied. Arbitrary and inconsistent rules can exist within and between parents (Becker, 1964) and tend to be cognitively unclear (Baldwin, 1955); hence they are learned with great difficulty. Rules are also inevitably ambiguous if the parent fails to define the limits of acceptable behavior, does not differentiate clearly between filial and parental prerogatives, and handles every situation as a special case according to the demands of expediency. The ambiguity surrounding the limits of unacceptable behavior is further enhanced by an habitual tendency to avoid issues by distracting the child. Two other favorite techniques of the ineffectual parent are self-insulation (pretending unawareness) and empty verbalism when an occasion for discipline arises. Halfhearted verbal reproof that is not accompanied by effective disciplinary action actually reinforces misbehavior by guaranteeing to the child that he can expect no *real* interference from his parents. The behavioral outcome of inconsistent discipline is the high frequency of antisocial behavior, conflict, and aggression in the child (Becker, 1964; Walters & Parke, 1966). By contrast, consistent paternal discipline is associated with independence and assertiveness in boys and with affiliativeness in girls (Baumrind & Black, 1967).

CHAPTER 10

Relationships with Peers

ORIGINS OF PEER GROUPS*

IN MANY CULTURES, both primitive and complex, "wherever children and youth are together for any length of time and free to pursue their own purposes," a subculture of peers is operative (Tryon, 1944). Apart from cultural tradition and parental expectations that they join such groups, many other factors facilitate the formation of peer groupings. As a social being man cannot fully experience, develop, or express his own individuality or enjoy a biosocial status except through a system of relationships to constituted groups. A *group* is defined as a social unit of a number of individuals who stand in status and role relationships to one another and who possess a set of values or norms regulating the behavior of individual members (Sherif, 1964). The family, it is true, provides such a social identity for the child; and if it includes several siblings it even affords the opportunity for companionship with children approximately his own age. The same applies to the school. Nevertheless, neither one of these institutions can ever satisfy his need for an identity with persons of equal status (Parsons, 1959; Piaget, 1932b; Piaget, 1951). In the shadow of superordinate adults he cannot gain recognition, play differentiated roles, practice social skills, or interact with others, except as a dependent and subordinate figure. The peer group, of course, could also provide neither primary nor derived status unless it were a superordinate body, but in contrast to parents, teachers, and the adult community, its authority reflects a superordination by equals rather than by superiors.

At the very best, children can enjoy no more than a marginal, subadult status even in primitive and rural cultures. In complex, urban cultures, extreme discontinuity between child and adult roles does not permit them even this degree of fringe participation. Cultures with rapid social and technological change, therefore, tend to develop more discontinuity between generations (Keniston, 1962). Prolonged discontinuity and exclusion from the wider community, and the accompanying resentment and estrangement help to solidify the peer group (Eisenstadt, 1962). As children become more

*For general reviews on peer group relations see Campbell (1964), Swift (1964). Discussion of research designs and measures for studying peer groups may be found in Thompson (1960) and Wright (1960).

324

firmly anchored in the distinctive goals, values, and loyalties of their own subculture, its very separateness as a world apart serves to perpetuate its existence.

Individual Differences in Orientation to Group Experience

We have been saying that children in their peer group behavior seek to establish a social identity in relation to equals. But the acquisition of biosocial status, differentiated on the basis of age level and sex, does not exhaust the child's needs in this matter. He is also concerned with achieving self-actualization, self-expression, and competence in as benevolent an environment as possible (Brewster-Smith, 1968). Hence he also seeks a highly *personal identity* in the group, an identity that is most congruent with his fundamental personality trends and temperamental predispositions, that is particularized with respect to breadth of social responsiveness, motivational orientation to group participation, level of activity, introversion-extroversion, leadership-followership, etc. This is suggested by the marked variability in children's degree and quality of social responsiveness and by the stability of their choice behavior and sociometric status (Campbell, 1964; Glidewell *et al*, 1966; Swift, 1964).

Much interindividual variability in approach to peer group experience reflects the impact of early socializing experience within the family circle. Partly as a result of this experience the child is predisposed to welcome or avoid contact with his peers, to expect the best or worst from them, and to make realistic or unrealistic demands on them. His reaction to his peers is influenced by early upbringing in a foundling home, by ordinal position and sex of siblings, and by such parental attitudes as overprotection, rejection, overvaluation, and over- and underdomination. Even the extent to which he is traumatized by racial or ethnic discrimination is influenced in part by the amount of self-acceptance he can acquire from interaction with his parents.

We have also hypothesized that the pervasive difference between satellizers and non-satellizers in over-all orientation to interpersonal relations generalizes from home to peer group. The satellizing child expects to be accepted for himself by his peers. The group is more than a source of primary status to him. It also provides derived status in much the same way as the parent except that the status-giving authority resides in a corporate body of equals of which he himself is part. By relating to it he obtains the same spontaneous "we-feeling" that he experiences in the family group. The non-satellizer, on the other hand, is not accustomed to assuming an internalized attitude of self-subserviency in relation to the group. To compensate for his lack of intrinsic self-esteem, he has greater need for recognition and applause from his peers. The field of intra-group relations, like the home, is no place for spontaneous "we-feeling"; it is just another arena in which he contends for prestige, power, and self-aggrandizement. If he is a rejected child, his chances of acquiring primary status in the group are much better than at home; if he is overvalued by his parents, the reverse is true. The non-satellizer is quite capable, of course, of obtaining vicarious status from identification with prestigeful membership or reference groups; but since no subservience of self is involved, it bears little resemblance to the derived status of satellizers.

DEVELOPMENTAL FUNCTIONS OF THE PEER GROUP

An overview of the impact of the peer group on children's personality development can be accomplished most simply by listing briefly the various normative functions it performs:

1. Depending on the prevailing degree of cultural discontinuity between child and adult roles, the peer group furnishes a little to a goodly portion of the child's primary status. In any case it is the only cultural institution in which his position is not marginal, in which he is offered primary status and a social identity among a group of equals, and in which his own activities and concerns reign supreme. As a result his self-concept undergoes expansion and differentiation in terms other than as a child of his parents.

2. The peer group is also a subsidiary source of derived status for the satellizer during childhood. By achieving acceptance in the group, by subordinating himself to group interests, and by making himself dependent on group approval, the child gains a measure of intrinsic self-esteem that is independent of his achievement or relative status in the group. This "we-feeling" furnishes security and belongingness and is a powerful ego support and basis of loyalty to group norms.

3. By providing primary and derived status, a new source of values and standards, and experience in behaving as a sovereign person, the peer group devalues parents, transfers part of the child's loyalties from them to itself (resatellization), and hence promotes desatellization. As a result of the support the child receives from his peer group, he gains the courage to weaken the bonds of emotional anchorage to parents. By vesting in his peers the authority to set standards, he affirms his *own* right to self-determination since he is patently no different from them. No longer need he implicitly subscribe to the belief that only parents and adults can determine what is right. The peer group also serves as a field of exercise in independence from adult controls (Parsons, 1959). By creating precedents and then appealing to the prevailing group standards, the peer culture operates as a pressure group, obtains important concessions for individual members with restrictive parents, and emancipates itself from adult and institutional controls.

4. Like home and school, the peer group is an important socializing, enculturative and training institution. It is here that children learn much of their poise in dealing with persons outside the intimate family circle, acquire approved techniques of sociability, self-assertion, competition and cooperation, and develop sensitivity to cues indicative of group expectations, censure, and approval. By interacting with their peers they learn the functional and reciprocal basis of rules and obligations, how to play differentiated roles, and how to subordinate their own interests to group goals. As will be pointed out, however, the peer group influences moral development more by enforcing or discouraging conformity to values, norms, and goals originating in the particular adult community from which it stems than by generating moral values of its own. Only the peer group can furnish suitable models and occasions for children to observe and practice the social skills and behaviors they must know in order to enact their appropriate age and sex roles both in their own subculture and in the wider community. It constitutes a proving-ground where they can test the workability of techniques they observe elsewhere. Hence, such experience serves as a form of apprenticeship for adult social life. Through the peer group children also pick up much knowledge, misinformation and folklore regarding science, sex, sports, religion, etc.

5. Finally, the peer group provides a *particularized* social identity for the child insofar as it permits him to play roles that are most compatible with his personality orientation toward group experience. For many children it also serves as a corrective influence counteracting the undesirable social effects of such extreme parental attitudes as under- or overdomination and providing a substitutive source of derived and primary status for rejected children.

Differential Impact of Peer Relationships on Later Personality Development

Just as particular kinds of socializing experience in the home determine individual differences in children's initial orientation to the peer group, the type of interpersonal relationships they characteristically establish in their early experiences with peers differentially conditions their later personality development. The child's early pattern of peer relationships—breadth of social responsiveness, sociometric status, leadership-followership—tends to be remarkably stable from middle childhood through adolescence (see pp. 333 and 352). Similarly, on the basis of early acceptance or rejection by peers, he either acquires enhanced feelings of self-esteem and confidence about being intrinsically accepted by others, or suffers ego deflation and regards social acceptance as something to be won by impressing associates or buying their favor. If peer group experience tends to be habitually unsatisfying or downright threatening, it encourages introversion, retreat into the home, and withdrawal from participation in group life; and if the opportunity for social experience is sufficiently curtailed, it interferes with the acquisition of necessary skills of communication, self-assertion, and self-defense and with the enactment of realistic and effective interpersonal roles during adolescence and adulthood.

Longitudinal consistency in the child's peer group status may be attributed to several factors. First, we may assume some degree of continuity in the personality traits that make him attractive or unattractive to others and more or less capable of satisfying their interpersonal needs. Second, there is presumably some continuity in the relative degree of social skill he possesses and in his individual orientation to group experience. Third, even though he may shift his membership from one peer group to another, not only does the child tend to carry his reputation with him, but much generality over groups also prevails in the criteria determining social acceptability. The group's total impression of him is acquired in the early grades and is extremely difficult to change (Glidewell *et al*, 1966). In reacting to his rejection by others, he either withdraws further from group activities or develops obnoxiously aggressive traits, thereby increasing his unlikableness and social ineffectiveness. Such alterations in sociometric status as do occur reflect changes in the membership and purposes of the peer group, ego-inflating or deflating experiences outside the peer group, early or late pubescence, increasing sensitivity to social class membership, age level changes in the bases of peer status, and increased ability or incentive to conceal objectionable traits or curry favor with others.

Relationship of Peer Group to Home and Wider Community

In a very real sense the peer group may be considered a buffering medium between home and the wider community. As the child emerges from the sheltered confines of the home, he enjoys relatively little direct contact with the culture at large. He is inducted instead into two special training institutions—school and peer group. In the latter he becomes immersed in a peripheral subculture of his own making which pursues activities and establishes criteria for prestige that bear little resemblance to their counterparts in the adult community. Nevertheless such peer groups still reflect in a larger sense the major values, aspirations, developmental goals, and ethical norms of the social milieu in which they are formed (Campbell, 1964). In addition, many forms of peer group activity in our society (e.g., school clubs, scouts) do not arise spontaneously but are conceived and directed by adults.

In assessing the relative importance of the peer group for personality development in our culture, it would be fair to say that it generally plays only a subsidiary role to the family as a socializing and enculturative agency and as a source of values and derived status, but that it shares with the school the major responsibility of providing the child's primary status. As already pointed out this situation varies interculturally and with social class and urban-rural status within our culture. Also, in a rapidly changing and unstable culture the peer group becomes a more important source of values since family and school are preoccupied with transmitting the established cultural heritage and are less strategically placed for transmitting what is changing. Under any circumstances, the peer group is a less important source of values and derived status during childhood than during adolescence. And since primary status (unlike the situation at adolescence) constitutes only a relatively minor factor in the total economy of the child's ego organization, the derived status he obtains within the family circle must still be accounted the principal interpersonal influence impinging on his personality development.

DEVELOPMENTAL TRENDS IN PEER RELATIONSHIPS

As previously indicated, the dependency of the human infant facilitates the relatively precocious emergence of social behavior and explains why in the first two years of life it is largely restricted to adults. With increasing age, however, a shift occurs in nursery school children from *passive dependence* on adults to attention- and approval- seeking dependence on peers (Swift, 1964). In the strictest sense of the term, peer group behavior begins when the child, unmonitored by adults, is permitted to interact freely with his fellows. Initially, a substantial proportion of his contacts with peers are rather closely supervised; and even later when he is largely left on his own, much peer activity still occurs under the over-all supervision of adults.

Trends in Early Childhood

Limiting Factors in Early Peer Relationships. Apart from the pre-emptive influence of initial socialization in relation to adults, many other factors tend to retard the early development of peer relationships. First, motor incompetence restricts the child's ability to participate manually in many joint play activities. Second, because of cognitive immaturity he lacks adequate awareness of others' needs and feelings and experiences difficulty in perceiving group goals and expectations, in sharing common perspectives, and in assuming differentiated roles. Third, difficulties in communication hamper effective group interaction. Even after he acquires sufficient language skills to express his ideas, the young child fails to communicate clearly because he is preoccupied with his own point of view and because he tends to assume that his listeners have access to his thoughts and hence do not require explanatory information (Flavell, Botkin, Fry, Wright & Jarvis, 1968). Fourth, a low span of attention limits his ability to engage in group enterprises requiring continuity and sustained concentration. Fifth, ignorance of techniques of sharing, of property rights, and of the "rules of the game" precipitates much unnecessary conflict and prematurely terminates many interpersonal transactions.

Just as important perhaps as the foregoing limiting factors is an attitude of egocentricity that is not reflective of cognitive immaturity but of the prevailing state of ego organization.* During the omnipotent and negativistic phases of ego development the child is preoccupied with his own needs and activities. "He wants everything to come in to him. His chief interpersonal relation with other children is the acquisition of objects and the protection of any object which he is using, has used, or might use" (Ames, 1952). With satellization, the child's impulses are directed more "outward toward others," and he is "able to demand less for [himself] and to adapt to the needs of others. . . . He no longer seems to need to embellish self with many possessions. There is less domineering, less violence, and fewer threats of violence in his relations with other children. He can share, take turns, and make polite requests of others. He begins to say 'We' . . . and 'Me, too' " (Ames, 1952). The out-of-bounds, expansive four-year-old, on the other hand, is a quarrelsome, boastful, and self-assertive playmate (Ames, 1952; Gesell & Ilg, 1943). At five, more realistic self-appraisal makes him more cooperative, considerate and sympathetic, and less prone to interfere with the liberties of others (Bühler, 1933; Gesell & Ilg, 1943). Much of children's early egocentricity in peer relationships reflects their early socialization with parents. Accustomed to being on the receiving end of a nurturant relationship, to being favored and given special consideration, they are naturally reluctant to surrender their privileged positions or consider the needs of others. Under atypical conditions, however, where children become emotionally dependent on each other instead of on adults, egocentricity is less marked. Thus, studies of children who are reared together as orphans and kibbutz children indicate less sibling rivalry and stronger identification with one another (Swift, 1964).

Initial Responses to other Children. The infant's early responses to other children are primarily egocentric. During the first two years of life the majority of the child's reactions are to himself and his own activities (Ames, 1952; Swift, 1964). The child initially interacts sporadically and inconsistently with other children, frequently treating them impersonally as objects or play materials (Ames, 1952; Bühler, 1933; Maudry & Nekula, 1939). Many of his initial responses are negative and involve conflicts over possessions; but the aggression engendered in such situations also tends to be impersonal. He appears to react to the interfering child as though the latter were a frustrating agent rather than a hostile individual (Ames, 1952; Maudry & Nekula,

---

The decline in egocentricity with advancing age is also attributable to various aspects of perceptual, cognitive, moral, and social development.

1939). Toward the close of this period, however, positive social responses toward children increase and become both more personal and more integrated with play materials (Ames, 1952; Maudry & Nekula, 1939; Swift, 1964).

Social Participation in the Preschool Period. Both the quantity and the quality of social participation continue to improve during the preschool years as the inhibitory influence of the aforementioned limiting factors gradually declines. Although sharply demarcated stages cannot be drawn, certain types of social participation are clearly more characteristic of younger preschool children, whereas other types are found more frequently among older children of this age group. Observational studies of nursery school children support the generalization that peer group behavior proceeds from a "solitary" or "onlooker" stage to a stage of "associative" and "cooperative" play, with "parallel" play constituting an intermediate step. Quality of social participation is highly correlated with chronological age (Ames, 1952; Goodenough, 1930; Hattwick & Sanders, 1938; Raph, Thomas, Chess & Korn, 1968; Parten & Newall, 1943; Swift, 1964), but is unrelated to the extent of nursery school experience (Raph *et al*, 1968; Parten & Newhall, 1943). The young nursery school child is still preoccupied with his own activities. Self-initiated approaches to other children are less frequent than responses to the teacher but this diminishes with advancing age (Ames, 1952; Raph *et al*, 1968). Consistent with his hoarding proclivities and inability to share is the predominance either of solitary play (that goes on adjacent to but completely without reference to the activities of others) or of a passive type of onlooking (Ames, 1952; Dennis, 1940; Parten & Newhall, 1943; Swift, 1964). As peer relations increase in frequency and sharing and taking turns become more common, "parallel" play predominates. Here the child pursues the same activities or uses similar toys as his playmates, but plays "beside" rather than with them (Parten & Newhall, 1943). Finally, he participates more in a collaborative type of play which, at first, is mostly associative and later involves "division of labor, group censorship, centralization of control, and the subordination of individual desires" to some group purpose and to a sense of belongingness in the group (Parten & Newhall, 1943). With increasing age, he tends to play with a larger group of children and to become less emotionally upset upon exposure to a novel social situation (Swift, 1964).

Although "self-initiated reactions predominate" in the preschool period, the child gradually becomes more responsive to the approaches of other children (Ames, 1952; Swift, 1964). Children of this age "are more interested in themselves and their own relationships with other children but have a growing awareness of the playmate choices, likes, and dislikes of their fellows" (Harris, 1946). They are particularly aware of attention-getting and non-conforming behavior and of the activities of friends and popular children

(Harris, 1946). During the nursery school period, the degree of social awareness is related neither to chronological age nor to extent of group experience (Harris, 1946).

As relationships with contemporaries become less impersonal, the preschool child begins to react to "other children as individual persons with special individual characteristics. One child is no longer equally good as another as a playmate" (Ames, 1952). Thus mutually congenial children begin to pair off and the group tends to exclude children with overly aggressive, passive, or otherwise objectionable traits (Ames, 1952; Sorokin & Gove, 1950; Swift, 1964).

Leadership behavior also increases during the preschool years. The independent pursuit of activities is first replaced by following behavior, then by shared leadership, and finally by directing behavior (Parten & Newhall, 1942). Degree of leadership is highly correlated with chronological age but not with amount of nursery school experience; it is practically coextensive with degree of social participation (Parten & Newhall, 1943). The desire for social attention and applause and for bossing other children evidently becomes greater with increasing age (Hattwick & Sanders, 1938). Parten distinguishes between "artful" and "brute force" leaders in the nursery school and notes that "the technique of leadership is sometimes learned, perhaps, through following a forceful leader" (Parten & Newhall, 1943). It has also been suggested that the fabrication of imaginary playmates reflects a need to control playmates more completely than is possible in real life (Ames, 1952). Although the presence of rival leaders often has a disruptive influence on intra-group relationships, quarrels at this age tend to be self-terminating (Sorokin & Gove, 1950). Situational factors also have an important bearing on leadership. A child may be a leader in one group or type of activity and a follower in another. In breaking into new groups he also tends to revert to more primitive types of leadership and social participation (Sorokin & Gove, 1950).

Marked variability prevails in degree, quality, and breadth of social participation, social responsiveness, and leadership "among children of approximately the same social and educational status" (Harris, 1946; Sorokin & Gove, 1950). Children even show consistent individual differences from day to day in amount of upset to a novel social situation, the less socially adequate children reacting more violently (Heathers, 1954). Intelligence is correlated only slightly with leadership and degree of social participation (Parten & Newhall, 1943) and not at all with social responsiveness (Harris, 1946).

Some individual differences in social behavior remain quite stable from early to late childhood. Such characteristics as degree of social participation, leadership, cooperativeness, sensitivity to the feelings of others, respect for property rights, negativism, and flexibility show considerable consistency from nursery to elementary school (Stott, 1958; Van Alstyne & Hattwick, 1939). Interpersonal and impersonal orientations remain stable during the nursery school period and are correlated with positive and negative personality characteristics (Emmerich, 1964).

Effects of Nursery School Experience. * Attendance in nursery school obviously facilitates the development of peer relations by providing unusually good opportunities for child interaction, social participation, and the learning of the necessary techniques of self-assertion, cooperation, and adjustment. In the absence of such or equivalent experience, it could be reasonably anticipated that developmental changes in peer group behavior would be somewhat retarded. But although relevant experience is a necessary growth factor in this instance and influences the *rate* of development, it does not seem to account for either the particular direction (sequence of changes) that development takes or for enduring individual differences in peer relations. Thus, as already pointed out, after all children in the group have had a certain minimal amount of social experience, duration of nursery school attendance is *not* related to degree or quality of social participation, leadership, or social responsiveness (Harris, 1946; Parten & Newhall, 1943; Swift, 1964). The general findings on the effects of nursery school experience so far have been inconclusive and conflicting with respect to intellectual, social, and physical development of young children (Swift, 1964). At the same time, there is no evidence that children receiving nonresidential group care have been negatively affected in their development or adjustment as a result of the experience.

In comparing groups of children who do and do not attend nursery school, there appear to be divergent findings (Swift, 1964). Several studies indicate that nursery school attenders are more spontaneous and highly socialized (Walsh, 1931), show more initiative, self-reliance, and independence from adults (Hattwick & Sanders, 1938; Jersild & Fite, 1939; Kawin & Hoefer, 1931; Walsh, 1931), and are more self-assertive and aggressive (Caille, 1933; Ezekiel, 1931; Walsh, 1931). They are less shy and withdrawn in the presence of strangers and show more mature and persistent reactions when faced with frustrating tasks (Hattwick, 1936; Van Alstyne & Hattwick, 1939). In contrast, Brown & Hunt (1961) report that nursery school children are less comfortably adjusted in kindergarten when compared with non-attenders. Elementary-school children who had no preschool experience were rated equally well with preschool attenders by teachers and by sociometric techniques (Bonney & Nicholson, 1958). Also, no differences have been found

---

*A review of research on the effects of nursery school experience may be found in Swift (1964). The recent research on the effects of different types of preschools on the child's intellectual development is not directly relevant to a chapter on peer relationships. See the volume on early education edited by Hess and Bear (1968), the chapters by J. McV. Hunt, Bereiter, and Stendler-Lavatelli in the volume edited by Deutsch, Katz, and Jensen (1968), and the discussion by Hodges and Spicker (1967).

between the two groups in such traits and behaviors as social adaptability (Greene, 1930-31), over-sensitivity to criticism (Andrus & Horowitz, 1938), fears (Hattwick, 1936), temper tantrums (Andrus & Horowitz, 1938; Hattwick, 1936), crying and thumb-sucking (Hattwick, 1936). The equivocal results may be due to a variety of conditions both historical and contemporaneous. For example, there may be selective factors which determine which children do or do not attend preschool. Some preschool children will probably be enrolled because of their parents' active interest in their wider social development, whereas other children will be sent because they are burdens on the parents. Contemporaneous factors such as the ecological setting in which preschool assessment takes place may also contribute to equivocal findings. For example, constructive use of material occurs most frequently in art and book areas, whereas complex social interaction occurs most frequently in the doll corner (Shure, 1963). More careful assessment of the school's ecological settings may possibly resolve some of the discrepant findings. Finally, beneficial effects of nursery school attendance are also dependent in part upon the quality of the adult supervision, i.e., the warmth, friendliness and personal involvement of the teachers (Swift, 1964; Thompson, 1944). There is a need for more extensive studies defining the relationship between teacher behavior, classroom atmosphere, and the child's behavior and adjustment (Swift, 1964).

Trends in Later Childhood. The previously indicated trends in peer relations, begun during the preschool years, tend to undergo completion during middle childhood and adolescence. The child of "school age" continues to be highly dependent, emotionally as well as instrumentally, on his parents (Parsons, 1959). During this period, however, the peer group provides the setting for further desatellization from parents and resatellization on the peer group proper:

> . . . the peer group may be regarded as a field of exercise of independence from adult control; hence it is not surprising that it is often the focus of behavior which goes beyond independence from adults to the range of adult-disapproved behavior . . . But another very important function is to provide the child a source of non-adult approval and acceptance (Parsons, 1959, p. 305).

During the elementary school years, as children become increasingly involved in activities with peers, their orientation moves increasingly toward the peer group and away from parents, particularly with respect to association, and to a lesser extent, with respect to the acceptance of norms and values (Bowerman & Kinch, 1959). This shift in orientation is much more gradual and less discontinuous for girls than for boys (Bowerman & Kinch, 1959). Peer groups continue to grow in size, complexity of organization, and freedom from adult supervision (Campbell, 1964). Children become capable of sustained, spontaneously organized, and highly structured enterprises of their own (Bühler, 1933; Campbell, 1964; Furfey, 1930). Their play interests also reflect the trend toward greater social sensitivity and responsiveness (Lehman & Witty, 1927). Play activities involve increasingly greater division of labor, differentiation of roles and status, teamwork, loyalty to a larger group, and breadth of leadership. Highly characteristic is the emergence of strict and formal sets of rules in connection with competitive games. At first these "rules of the game" tend to be conceived as arbitrarily valid, "sacred," and immutable; later they are regarded more as functional contrivances, reached through mutual agreement, that facilitate the orderly and equitable regulation of play (see Chapter 13). Only when willingness to abide by the rules develops are children first able to think of "winning" and "losing" competitive activities in accordance with duly constituted law. They insist on strict compliance with and equalitarian application of the rules and are extremely punitive in dealing with infractions thereof (Mowrer, 1939). Only later, when their equalitarianism is tempered by considerations of equity (see Chapter 13), are they willing to be more flexible.

Underlying these changes in the child's peer relations are gradual gains in span of attention and ability to communicate, improved social techniques, a decline in egocentricity, and the experience of satisfactions associated with conformity to the demands of peer group membership. Even more important, perhaps, is unspectacular but steady improvement in cognitive sophistication enabling him to understand complex rules, appreciate subtle group expectations, and perceive the relative hierarchical status, including his own, of the various group members. Complex group structure first becomes possible when individuals are able to perceive the attitudes of others toward themselves and feel confident enough of their perceptions to hazard both predictions regarding their implications for future dealings and adaptive responses based on such predictions (de Jung & Meyer, 1963). The individual's adjustment to his peer group, therefore, is partly a function of how well he is able to perceive his own and others' hierarchical positions. Insofar as these perceptions are accurate, a more realistic basis for interpersonal relations is provided; more specifically, the child's aspirations with respect to assuming various roles in group activities, his expectations of the roles others might be induced to play, the demands he might legitimately make on others, and the attitudes he might adopt in dealing with them are more or less appropriate in accordance with the validity of his estimates of own and others' sociometric status. During the elementary school years the child not only shows more accurate estimation of his own and others' status (de Jung & Meyer, 1963) but also is more accurate in inferences regarding the feelings and thought of others (Flapan, 1965). When role behavior becomes more formalized, it is true that accurate perception of others' intentions becomes a less relevant determinant of the individual's social behavior (Steiner, 1955).

But highly stylized role behavior is hardly characteristic of children's groups; and in any case the perception of hierarchical status is still important, even in a relatively impersonal group setting.

During the preadolescent period children are more interested in joining formal and highly structured groups, both adult-sponsored organizations such as scouts (Jersild & Tasch, 1949), and spontaneously organized gangs. Gang activities at this age (unlike adolescence) are not necessarily indicative of a lower-class environment, social maladjustment or pre-delinquency. They reflect the older child's alienation from the wider community, an anti-adult orientation, and an aggressive bid for primary status through defiance of adult authority. By establishing their own distinctive norms, gang members increase group cohesiveness, test adult limits, and enhance the identity of the in-group. Except in urban-slum areas, gangs tend to be replaced in adolescence by more intimate and less predatory bisexual crowds and cliques. Decreasing identification with the gang is associated with increased identification with the adult male pattern (Crane, 1955).*

The preadolescent gang is a closely-knit, unisexual action group with a high degree of role and status differentiation and much intra-group solidarity. It maintains a hostile, rebellious and conspiratorial attitude toward adult society and frequently participates in socially disapproved activity. Great emphasis is placed on excitement and adventure, and on such formal trappings of organizational secrecy as special names, cryptic codes and signals, special meeting places, and unique initiation ceremonies. More so than in other preadolescent groups, leadership in gangs tends to be despotically wielded and based on toughness, daring, and fighting ability.

PERCEPTION OF PEER ATTITUDES AND RELATIONSHIPS

We have already suggested that growing sensitivity to interpersonal attitudes and relationships underlies much developmental progress in the differentiation of peer interactions. Although empirical evidence bearing on the development of interpersonal perception is sparse, it does seem clear that with increasing age children improve in the ability to interpret expressions of emotions (Flapan, 1965, see Chapter 11), to discriminate and verbalize traits they like or dislike in others (see Chapter 11), and to perceive the extent to which fellow group members accept them and other children (Ausubel, Schiff & Gasser, 1952; Dymond & Hughes & Raabe, 1952; Estvan, 1966). Even though this growth in social perceptual capacity presumably cuts across many different areas of interpersonal relations, there is no reason to believe that social sensitivity itself is a unitary personality

*There is some evidence of the importance of preadolescent identification for later adult adjustment. For example, adult males who are characterized as distant have been found to have no close friendships in preadolescence (Maas, 1968).

trait. The child's accuracy in perceiving how others react to him, for example, is not related to his accuracy in perceiving their attitudes toward or relationships with persons other than himself (e.g., their sociometric status or feelings about associates) (Ausubel & Schiff, 1955; Dymond & Hughes, Raabe, 1952). During late childhood children also become much more discriminating both in their own interpersonal preferences and in their perception of others' interpersonal attitudes. They tend to make less disproportionate use of the upper (favorable) portion of the rating and prediction scales in expressing and predicting sociometric choices (Ausubel *et al*, 1952).

Children's interpersonal perceptions are influenced by their feelings and attitudinal biases, especially when the objects of perception are relatively ambiguous. On unstructured tasks, and particularly in highly stable and cohesive groups, they tend to overestimate the performance of associates enjoying high status in the group and to underestimate the performance of age mates with low status (Redl, 1949). The need to have something in common with individuals they like also makes children perceive group members they prefer most both as more similar to themselves than they actually are and as more similar than group members they prefer least (Glidewell *et al*, 1966; Davitz, 1955). Reflecting their bias in favor of their own sex group, children perceive this group as possessing more favorable personality traits and as playing more positive social roles than do members of the opposite sex (Amatora, 1954; Bjerstedt, 1954).*

AGGRESSION AND CONFLICT

Conflicts and quarrels occur frequently among preschool children. In one observational study, the average rate of conflict reported was one per child every five minutes (Jersild & Markey, 1935). Characteristically quarrels are brief (about thirty seconds duration) (Dawe, 1934; Jersild & Markey, 1935), self-terminating (Sorokin & Gove, 1950), and resolved without lingering resentment or vindictiveness (Dawe, 1934; Jersild & Markey, 1935). Moreover, despite their apparent frequency, they are greatly exceeded in number by friendly, cooperative contacts (Anderson, 1937a, 1937b, 1939; Jersild & Markey, 1935; Mengert, 1939; Walters, Pearce & Dahms, 1957). For reasons given elsewhere (see Chapter 11 and Chapter 12), lower-class children tend to be physically more aggressive than middle-class children and to be involved more frequently in conflict with their peers both during the preschool period and during later childhood. We have also discussed elsewhere sex differences in the frequency and techniques of aggression and possible explanations for these differences (see Chapter 11 and Chapter 12).

---

*In spite of these findings boys are perceived by both sexes as being better at role-playing (Sutton-Smith & Rosenberg, 1967).

Age Trends

There is equivocal evidence concerning the incidence of conflicts and aggression in preschool children. Several studies indicate that, with increasing age, the incidence of conflict tends to decrease in frequency but last longer (Dawe, 1934; Jersild & Markey, 1935) and have prolonged after-effects (Appel, 1942). Walters, Pearce and Dahms (1957), however, report an increase in aggression during the preschool period. It is difficult to account for this discrepancy but there is further evidence that supports the notion that as social participation increases in preschool children, the frequency of conflict also increases (Dawe, 1934; Green, 1933a and b; Jersild & Markey, 1935). Although substitution of teasing and bullying and more covert and verbal aggression are increasingly utilized with age (see Chapter 12), there is little difference between physical and verbal aggression during the pre-school period (Walters *et al*, 1957).

The reduction in physical aggression which slowly leads to more verbal and symbolic forms is attributable both to cultural pressures against the direct expression of hostility and gains in cognitive, personality, and social maturity. The cognitively more mature child is more able to cope with difficulties, to appreciate that many hurts are inflicted unintentionally, to disguise his hostility, to avoid misunderstandings, and to use language as both an outlet for aggression and as a means of circumventing conflict. Such concurrent manifestations of personality growth as decreased egocentricity, increased frustration tolerance, and greater ability to accept inevitable delays and restrictions in the gratification of his needs also serve to reduce tensions leading to conflict. Finally the older child is more reconciled to the fact that he cannot take his privileged position in the home with him to the peer group. He has learned to share, to take turns, and to accept group norms. He has a better understanding of property rights, of the needs of others, of what is expected of him, of his relative status in the group, of what he can legitimately demand from others and of what they will tolerate from him, and of the retaliatory consequences of aggression. There is less need for grabbing, pushing, and outshouting others when he can appeal to a set of mutually accepted rules. It may be partly the result of the lack of appreciation of other children's rights which accounts for the finding that aggressive children seem to need and demand more space (Lebo, 1962). The relationship between aggression and popularity amongst peers is complex and difficult to assess (Moore, 1967). Research evidence tentatively indicates that popular children who are aggressive are more likely to be low to moderate in degree of aggression, with correspondingly more positive interactions with their peers; whereas unpopular children appear to be high on aggression and low on other positive interactions (Moore, 1967).

Increased exposure to and awareness of the wider community also creates new instigations for frustration and aggression. As the child enters the school and participates in competitive activities, new incitements to and outlets for aggressive behavior are provided. Fighting ability also becomes an important determinant of the "pecking order" in boys' groups. Boys also rate themselves as more aggressive than girls (Walker, 1967). The pecking order is ordinarily established in boys by common agreement after a few actual battles. Thereafter it remains relatively stable without recourse to violence unless marked changes occur in the relative status or physical prowess of the group members. Unstable children who are characterized as hyperaggressive, show a much more intense interaction with peers which is more hostile dominant than friendly dominant when compared with normal children (Dittman & Goodrich, 1961).

Determinants of Aggression

The occurrence of conflict in the peer group is influenced by a large variety of precipitating, situational, and intra-group factors. In addition, as is apparent from the wide range of individual differences in frequency of involvement in conflict (Jack, 1939; Jersild & Markey, 1935), such variables as temperament, personality, and family environment are important determinants of aggression in the peer group. The significance of the latter factors is highlighted by the fact that individual differences in aggressiveness are extremely stable over a 12-month period (Jersild & Markey, 1935).

The major precipitating causes of aggression during the preschool years are disputes over material possessions and interference by one child with another child's freedom of movement (Appel, 1942; Dawe, 1934; Green, 1933a; Jersild & Markey, 1935). Many quarrels are also precipitated by children working at cross-purposes or misunderstanding each other's motives and intentions, and by the discord engendered when a child tries to force his way into a group or activity where he is unwanted (Appel, 1942). Sometimes a child seems to provoke aggression for no other reason than to test the limits of a situation.

Conflict is more apt to occur between children of the same sex but different ages (Dawe, 1934) and in crowded play areas (Jersild & Markey, 1935). It is aggravated by ambiguity in the social situation and by hunger, fatigue and physical indispositions (see Chapter 12). The presence of permissive adults may increase the incidence of aggression since under these circumstances children rely more on the adults and less on their own internalized controls for keeping the peace (Siegel, 1956). Prior experience in solving their own conflicts without adult interference decreases the frequency of quarrels in the long run, even though such interference may prevent the outbreak of conflict at the moment (Jersild & Markey, 1935).

Since the opportunities for conflict are obviously enhanced by the frequency of peer interactions, children who are energetic, socially active, and friendly tend to be involved in more disputes than phlegmatic and socially unresponsive children (Appel, 1942; Jersild & Markey, 1935). It is not surprising, therefore, that close friends quarrel more with each other than with other children (Green, 1933a). Degree of temperamental self-assertiveness is also an important predisposing factor. Anderson (1937a, 1939) distinguishes between two varieties of ascendant tendencies in children—a tendency to be rigid and inflexible, to work against others and satisfy needs at their expense (dominative behavior), and a tendency to be flexible and receptive to change, to work with others toward improved understanding, mutually satisfying goals, and resolution of conflict (integrative behavior). The effect of each type of behavior, according to Anderson, is to evoke like behavior in others.

Acquired personality trends also influence frequency of involvement in conflict. Aggression in children is a manifestation of insecurity, poor ego control (Livson & Mussen, 1957), impaired self-esteem, or jealousy. Sometimes, especially in a previously insecure child, it is indicative of increased self-confidence. The effects of different parental attitudes such as permissiveness toward aggression and the use of physical punishment (Bandura & Walters, 1959; Lefkowitz, Walder & Eron, 1963; Lynn, 1961; McCord & Howard, 1961; Patterson, Littman & Bricker, 1967; (see Chapter 12) are apparently closely related to aggression and conflict in children. Rejected boys and girls are more aggressive than are their accepted peers (Gold, 1958; Glidewell et al, 1966; Moore, 1967). As expected, boys tend to depict themselves as, and are, generally more aggressive than girls (Hartup & Himeno, 1959; Walker, 1967; Walters et al, 1957). Relatively nonascendant children can be made more ascendant through training appropriate for increasing their self-confidence (Jack, 1939; Mummery, 1947; Page, 1936), whereas training in social perception and in techniques of cooperation can decrease the incidence of objectionable ascendance in overly dominative children (Chittenden, 1942).

COMPETITION AND COOPERATION

Competition is an ego-oriented, self-aggrandizing activity in which the individual vies with others for hierarchical pre-eminence. Cooperation is a group-oriented activity in which the individual collaborates with others to attain some common goal. Nevertheless, neither developmentally nor in terms of psychological content are these two activities wholly antithetical to each other: both imply a considerable degree of interaction within the group as opposed to individual behavior that is carried on with little reference to the activities of others. The child pursues a solitary course with his peers before he is either cooperative or competitive (see p. 330); both types of behavior increase as individualism subsides. Which becomes more prominent (as well as the extent to which individualism is superseded) varies greatly with cultural environment (Bronfenbrenner, 1969). Our own culture values both kinds of behavior, often inconsistently, and hence fosters much moral confusion. In general, in our culture, ego-oriented motivation has a self-aggrandizing (competitive) flavor (see p. 282), which varies from one social class to another. Although in play situations lower-class preschool children tend to be more competitive than middle-class children (Bonney, 1942a), the latter eventually internalize higher aspirations for academic and vocational prestige (see Chapter 11). According to L. B. Murphy (1937), lower-class preschool children also express more affection, are more helpful and assume more responsibility culturally. Russian children appear to assume more responsibility for other peers when compared with American children (Bronfenbrenner, 1969). Boys are consistently more competitive than girls in our culture during both early and late childhood (McKee & Leader, 1955; Vinacke & Gullickson, 1964; see Chapter 11). Surprisingly, boys also tend to be more cooperative than girls which is probably a result of greater task-orientation (Perrodin, 1960).*

Many activities in the peer group evoke cooperative and competitive behavior either simultaneously or alternately. Different activity settings affect the quality and quantity of cooperative or competitive activities (Gump, Schoggen & Redl, 1957; Raush, Farbman & Llewellyn, 1960). For example, food settings are associated with more cooperative and friendly activities (Raush et al, 1960). Team games are competitive contests between two cooperatively organized groups. However, members of the same team may compete against each other while striving jointly for a distinctive team goal, or several teams may compete against each other in furthering a cause common to all. Some children are competitive under cooperative conditions, others are cooperative under competitive conditions (Stendler, Damrin, and Haines, 1951), and still others are task-oriented under any conditions (Ausubel, 1951). Thus, despite the purportedly cooperative or competitive conditions characterizing a particular enterprise, the extent to which a given child is ego-oriented, task-oriented, or group-oriented can only be ascertained by individual motivational analysis.

Although aggressiveness may be expressed in many ways other than competitiveness, one would ordinarily anticipate a high relationship between the two traits since competition is the most acceptable outlet for aggression

---

There is conflicting evidence on this topic when social class is considered. For example, lower-class Negro boys appear to be less cooperative in their play than girls, but no differences in cooperativeness are evident between white middle-class boys and girls (Hartford & Cutter, 1966).

in our culture and almost inevitably involves some frustration, hostility, or jealousy. In preschool children the relationship is negligible (McKee & Leader, 1955). Evidently, then, it takes some time for young children first responding to the cultural pressures of competition to learn "to be angry when they are unsuccessful" (McKee & Leader, 1955).

Age Trends

Although younger children exhibit impersonal rivalry over possessions and personal rivalry over the affection and attention of adults (Adams, 1967), true competition in the sense of a performance contest first appears between the ages of three and four (Greenberg, 1932; Hirota, 1951; Leuba, 1933). Thereafter, as children gradually internalize, from the competitive norms of our culture, a desire to excel, competitiveness becomes an increasingly characteristic feature of their response to peer activities (Gesell & Ilg, 1943; Greenberg, 1932; Leuba, 1933; McKee & Leader, 1955). Such behavior presupposes the ability to become ego-involved in performance, to set levels of aspiration, and to experience fluctuations in self-esteem upon encountering success and failure. Preschool and kindergarten children display competitiveness by grabbing materials from others, cornering a supply, making favorable comments about their own work, withholding assistance, increasing their work output, and showing greater perseverance (Greenberg, 1932; Leuba, 1933; Wolf, 1938). As they acquire increasing appreciation of the concept of excelling others according to the rules of the game, and gain in ability realistically to compare their own performance with that of others, competition takes place on a more sophisticated plane. Children of elementary school age work harder both under competitive conditions than under anonymous conditions (Ausubel, 1951), and for individual rewards than for group prizes. Even so they are highly responsive to such natural group competitive situations as contests between boys and girls, teams, and classrooms (Maller, 1929).

Cooperation requires greater cognitive and personality maturity than competition. Rudimentary forms of cooperative play and of mutual aid in the solution of problems requiring collaborative efforts appear in older preschool children (Gottschaldt & Frühauf-Ziegler, 1958; Wolfe & Wolfe, 1939). There is also an increasing tendency with age for preschool children to seek out cooperative efforts with other children rather than adults (Stith & Connor, 1962). In one study, spontaneous understanding (on a conceptual level) of the nature of cooperative group work was not found prior to the age of six (Hirota, 1951). Cooperation presupposes considerable social responsiveness and capacity for self-subordinating and differentiated role behavior. The child must be able to perceive the possibilities for and advantages of cooperative action in enterprises where individual efforts are inadequate and must be capable of communicating effectively with his fellows (Wolfle & Wolfle, 1940). Cooperative communication and coordination increase with age during the elementary school years (Alvy, 1968; Fry, 1967). The development of cooperative behavior, therefore, is related to the growth of sympathy, affection, social sensitivity, language, and altruism. In human beings it is greatly facilitated by the interdependency of social living and by genic capacities for emotional identification with persons and groups.

Determinants

Tendencies toward competitive and cooperative-sympathetic behavior are influenced by numerous situational and personality variables and also show a wide range of individual differences (Ausubel, 1951; Glidewell et al, 1966; Greenberg, 1932; Maller, 1929; Moore, 1967; Murphy, 1937). Relatively low intersituational generality has been reported by Hartshorne and May for such traits as helpfulness (see p. 166). As previously indicated, however, much of this apparent lack of generality is a function of the child's varying degree of ego-involvement in different activities. The extent to which he is competitive in an arithmetic contest, for example, varies directly with his liking for and desire to do well in that subject (Ausubel, 1951). Moreover, despite the operation of such situational factors as the child's relationship to the person in distress and to the cause of his suffering (see Chapter 12), L. B. Murphy found considerable individual consistency in the expression of sympathetic behavior (Murphy, 1937). It is evident, nevertheless, that children's disposition to be cooperative or sympathetic (rather than competitive) in a given situation is greater (a) if their companions are considerably younger than themselves (Murphy, 1937), (b) if such companions are strangers instead of established friends,* and (c) if the general social atmosphere is cordial (Horrocks & Buker, 1951).

Temperamental and personality variables are presumably important determinants of cooperativeness and competitiveness but have received little systematic attention in developmental studies. Because socially active and responsive children have a relatively large amount of interaction with peers, they tend to be both more aggressive and more sympathetic than less active children (Murphy, 1937). Children from democratic homes tend to be more outgoing and competitive than children from authoritarian homes (see p. 319); I.Q., however, is only slightly related to sympathy and cooperativeness (Maller, 1929; Murphy, 1937). Turning to more central personality traits, one might hypothesize that since non-satellizers enjoy little intrinsic self-esteem and have high, tenacious ego aspirations (see p. 285), they would ordinarily be extremely competitive; whatever initial

---

*This was only true of eight year olds. The opposite tendency was found in a group of five year olds (Wright, 1942).

sympathetic and cooperative behavior they might manifest would reflect feelings of insecurity and inadequacy or an expedient bid for favor (rather than genuine "we feeling"), and would be superseded by competitiveness as their status in the group improved. Satellizers, on the other hand, feeling intrinsically more adequate, might be expected to be more group-minded, especially once their own positions in the group were secure. Consistent with this interpretation is the tendency for rejected peers to be low on cooperative activity (Moore, 1967).

Effects of Competition on Personality Development

Competition has both desirable and undesirable effects on personality development. On the credit side, it stimulates individual efforts and productivity, promotes higher standards and aspirations, and narrows the gap between capacity and performance. By enabling the individual to obtain a more realistic estimate of his own capacities in relation to those of others, it exerts a salutary effect on the self-critical faculty. Under the stimulus of competition the child is better able to discover both his own limitations and hitherto unrealized capacities and is motivated to overcome objectionable personality traits. Competition makes group games more interesting and everyday tasks less monotonous.

On the debit side, when carried to unwholesome extremes, competition fosters feelings of inadequacy in less able children and unduly depresses their status in the group. It may lead to a tense, hostile, vindictive, and negative group climate (Stendler et al, 1951) in which ruthlessness, unfairness, and dishonesty are condoned in the interests of emerging victorious. In such an atmosphere the demonstration of superiority per se becomes the primary goal, whereas the intrinsic value of the activity and the enjoyment of participation are deemphasized. When excessive value is placed on superior achievement, children become obsessed with the notion of self-aggrandizement and lose sight of human values. Prestigeful attainment becomes the sole criterion of human worth and source of self-esteem; and the perceived accomplishments of others constitute a threat and a competitive challenge, which must be bested or denied, to the individual's sense of adequacy.

ACCEPTANCE AND REJECTION *

Sociometric techniques provide the most objective and conveniently determined indices of the individual's status in or acceptance by the group. In addition, they provide data that have been shown to be related to several other important group dimensions of group processes, such as morale, group

*See Campbell (1964), Glidewell et al,, (1966), Moore (1967), and Swift (1964) for reviews.

effectiveness, and patterns of communication (Thompson, 1960). Although fairly good correspondence exists between such different methods of determining sociometric status as the paired-comparison and the rank-order method (Bjerstedt, 1956), a somewhat different picture emerges when social acceptability is measured by averaging the ratings of acceptance-rejection given an individual by *all* of the group members; when the latter scores are correlated with the more traditional measures of sociometric status, the resulting correlations are relatively lower (Ausubel, Schiff & Gasser, 1952; Bjerstedt, 1956). Hence it means one thing to achieve high popularity on the basis of being chosen frequently as a *preferred* associate for various activities and quite a different thing to achieve a high level of acceptance based on ratings from *all* members of a group. The latter method takes *negative* as well as positive feelings into account, discriminates between attitudes of rejection and indifference, is more representative of *total* group acceptance of the individual, and reflects more deep-seated emotional currents in interpersonal relations. The traditional method is more reflective of group structure and of actual functional relationships.

Sociometric status scores show some generality over different choice situations (e.g., work, play, seating arrangements) (Bjerstedt, 1956; Gronlund, 1955, Jennings, 1943) but this is partially a result of the type of sociometric measure utilized (Thompson, 1960). When situations are structured and their contents specified, as in the Syracuse Scale of Social Relations (see Thompson, 1960), the degree of correlation between different situations can diminish considerably; children differentially rank their classmates according to specific need situations under consideration (Meyer & De Jung, 1963). Stability (test-retest reliability) is also high over a period of several weeks to a year (Glidewell *et al*, 1966; Jennings, 1943; Lippitt & Gold, 1959; Toshimi, 1964); it is highest for the paired-comparison method, next highest for the rating scale method, and lowest for the partial rank-order (choice) method (Thompson & Powell, 1951; Witryol & Thompson, 1953). For reasons already mentioned (see p. 328), social acceptability scores tend to remain quite stable over months and years (Campbell, 1964; Glidewell *et al*, 1966). As might be expected, stability of relationships is positively related to age (Campbell, 1964). Between the ages of seven and ten they are almost as stable as intelligence and achievement scores (Bonney, 1943b). Cross-sex choices, however, are very unstable (Gronlund, 1955). Further evidence for stability is provided by the fact that attempts at manipulating change in classroom status are seldom self-substaining (Glidewell *et al*, 1966). The validity of sociometric status scores is demonstrated by their high degree of correspondence with actual behavior choices, even among preschool children (Biehler, 1954; Moore, 1967).

Correlates of High Peer Group Status

The following traits are for self-evident reasons positively related to high sociometric status in the peer group: (a) *personality traits:* alert, outgoing personality (Bonney, 1944a; Marshall & McCandless, 1957b; Moore, 1967; Northway, 1944; Tuddenham, 1951); cheerfulness (Bonney, 1944a, 1944b, Laughlin, 1954; Moore, 1967); emotional stability and dependability (Bonney, 1947a) and honesty (Bjerstedt, 1956); (b) *physical traits:* athletic ability (Bjerstedt, 1956; McCraw & Tolbert, 1953; Tuddenham, 1951); good looks and tidiness (Bonney, 1944a, 1944b; Laughlin, 1954; Tuddenham, 1951); (c) *social traits:* friendliness (Bonney, 1942, 1943b, 1944b; Laughlin, 1954; Marshall & McCandless, 1957b; Moore, 1967; Tuddenham, 1951); cooperativeness and helpfulness (Bonney, 1947; Bonney & Powell, 1953; Moore, 1967); social conformity (Bonney, 1947; Bonney & Powell, 1953; Koch, 1933); social adaptability (Bonney, 1947; Lippitt, 1941; Moore, 1967); positive social aggressiveness (Moore, 1967); good sportsmanship (Tuddenham, 1952) and respect for others' property (Koch, 1933). The weight of the evidence points to a low to moderate relationship between I.Q. and sociometric status (Barbe, 1954; Bjerstedt, 1956; Bonney, 1942, 1943b; Campbell, 1964; Glidewell *et al*, 1966; Taylor, 1952). The probable mediating factor here is the greater frequency of scholastic failure, non-promotion, truancy, and inarticulateness among intellectually dull children. All of these conditions also tend to increase emotional instability which, in turn, has detrimental effects on both learning capacity and interpersonal relationships (Schmuck & Van Egmond, 1965). Children who are above average scholastically and either regularly promoted or under-age for their grade level tend to enjoy a higher sociometric status than low achievers and over-age (non-promoted) pupils (Bjerstedt, 1956; Buswell, 1953; Glidewell *et al*, 1966; Goodlad, 1954; Taylor, 1952). In general, there is a consistently high relationship between sociometric status and social class status (Bonney, 1942a, 1942b, 1943b, 1944b; Glidewell *et al*, 1966). Lower-class membership apparently affects social acceptability adversely insofar as it is associated with untidiness, poor clothing, negative social aggressiveness and low school achievement.

Characteristics of Socially Rejected Children

Several clusters of socially unacceptable personality traits have been found in children who are rejected by their peer group (Campbell, 1964; Swift, 1964; Moore, 1967). First are traits associated with the overbearing, aggressive, and egocentric child who frequently gives a history of being underdominated or overvalued by his parents. Such children are described by their associates or by teachers as noisy, attention-seeking, demanding, rebellious, querulous, arrogant, and boastful (Dunnington, 1957; Hartup,

Glazer & Charlesworth, 1967; Jenkins, 1931; Koch, 1933; Moore, 1967; Northway, 1944; Sorokin & Gove, 1950). Aggressive behaviors, however, are not always perceived negatively (Marshall & McCandless, 1957a) so it is necessary to look at hostile behaviors within the context of other positive or negative personality traits (Moore, 1967). A second cluster of socially unacceptable traits is typified by apathetic children with few expressive interests. They are listless, lacking in physical vigor, slow-moving, and generally disinterested in their surroundings (Kerstetter, 1946; Northway, 1944). A third cluster of seriously unacceptable personality traits reflects a degree of introversion sufficiently disabling to interfere with spontaneous and uninhibited participation in group activities. Included in this group are such characteristics as shyness, overdependence on adults, timidity, and withdrawing behavior (Dunnington, 1957; Koch, 1933; McCandless, Bilous & Bennett, 1961; Moore, 1967; Northway, 1944). These children frequently play alone, and refuse or ignore the advances of other children (Moore, 1967). Many rejected children fail to learn the give-and-take techniques of peer group play and to develop social poise, skills, and effective methods of self-assertion and self-defense (see p. 317). Others regard them as excessively overdependent, fearful of being misunderstood, abused, or taken advantage of, and given to whining, nagging and complaining (Jennings, 1943; Moore, 1967).

Finally, there are children who by virtue of inappropriate group personality traits, or motor, intellectual and social incompetence (Campbell, 1964; Chennault, 1967), are rejected by the group. In addition to this last category, we must also consider two other subsidiary categories of children who enjoy little peer group status: (a) children who reject group experience because they find it traumatic or unrewarding as a result of their personality make-up or social incompetence; and (b) children who neither reject nor are rejected by the group but who are willing to accept ostracism, if need be, to satisfy other needs or pursue other interests. Included in the latter category are opportunists who flaunt group standards to gain adult approval, children who are too individualistic to conform to group expectations, and children with all-consuming interests in esoteric activities. In practice all three categories of low peer status are often found in the same person. For example, the overprotected child who tends to withdraw from group experience because he finds it traumatic may be rejected by his peers for reasons of excessive timidity and overdependence, and may develop strong non-social interests as a compensation for his social isolation.

Interpretation of Peer Acceptance and Rejection

Acceptance and high status in a group may be a source of positive self-conception and lack of status and security may be a source of dissatisfaction with oneself (Campbell, 1964). It is difficult, however, to determine the relation between status and self-conception and the direction of this relationship (Campbell, 1964). Nevertheless, children who are accepted by others appear to have a more realistic perception of themselves when compared to rejected children (Goslin, 1962). The psychological significance of sociometric status scores are, however, subject to several important qualifications. First, acceptance or rejection is seldom completely unanimous in any sizeable group, or even as unequivocal as it appears at first glance (Cunningham, 1951; Thompson, 1960). Because of the operation of halo effects, the status of "stars" is perceived as higher than it actually is, whereas the status of "isolates" tends to be under-estimated (Ausubel, 1955b). Second, popularity is not coextensive with adequate social adjustment. An ostensibly popular child may be little more than a "stranger in his group" in terms of the depth of his attachments (Wittenberg & Berg, 1952), or may be popular because he is docile, conforming, and willing to be directed and "used" by others (Alexander & Alexander, 1952). Moreover, popularity may also be associated with manipulative behavior which takes advantage of other members of the group (Moore, 1967). Contrariwise, the child who is unpopular because of temperamental shyness or strong personal interests is not necessarily socially maladjusted or inevitably fated to become so (Morris, Soroker, and Burruss, 1955). Overinfluenced by the modern cult of the outgoing personality, many mental hygienists presently fail to appreciate the wide range of variability in introversion-extroversion compatible with normal personality development.

The effects of rejection also depend on many factors that do not inhere in a child's objectively low sociometric status. Such status leads to feelings of inadequacy only to the extent that he is ego-involved in the group and aspires to greater acceptance than he enjoys. Since his acceptance of the group and the group's acceptance of him tend to be unrelated (Cunningham, 1951), the mere fact of rejection tells us nothing about his desire to be accepted. Many children rejected by their peers concomitantly reject the latter or *pretend* that their isolation is voluntary or admirable. Thus, in evaluating the significance of rejection, it is important to know the extent to which the individual desires to be accepted by the group and, if he does not, whether his expressed disdain for acceptance is genuine or rationalized. It should be appreciated, however, that even though unconcern with status in the group may (in rejection) be associated with relatively little deflation of self-esteem, it may be symptomatic of much graver defects in personality structure than is the rejection of a socially ineffective child who craves acceptance by his age mates.

Further appraisal of the seriousness of an individual case of rejection requires knowledge of (a) how widely shared the attitude of rejection is in the group, (b) whether it reflects active dislike of or passive indifference toward the person involved, (c) the modifiability of the factors on which the rejection is based, and (d) the availability of other compensatory attachments or interests. Finally much depends on whether the child perceives that he is being rejected. Rejection is not as self-evidently obvious as it may seem. Although many overrejected children perceive their low status in the group (Bjerstedt, 1956), others who are just as seriously rejected seem to be unaware of the fact.

FRIENDSHIP

Peer friendships involve very close, affective relations of equality in which children are enabled and encouraged to learn more about themselves (Schmuck, 1969). As such, friendships represent the ultimate step in the selective differentiation of interpersonal relations along a social distance scale. They satisfy the need for *particularized* social relationships most compatible with a given child's dominant personality traits. Under the best of circumstances where choice can be exercised, children select friends whose qualities furnish a basis for mutual satisfaction of interpersonal needs. Ordinarily this means that the friends they choose either resemble or complement them in ways most conducive to congeniality. Often however they are obliged to settle for whoever is available. The expression of preference in the choice of playmates is already evident by the preschool period (Abel & Sahinkaya, 1962; Challman, 1932; Green, 1933b; Moore, 1967; Parten, 1933; Swift, 1964). Indices of friendship increase during these years, first in the number of individuals the child plays with, and later (as he gradually learns that certain relationships are more satisfying than others) in the selective strengthening of particular attachments (Green, 1933b).

Selective factors in the determination of children's friendships can be inferred from two related lines of evidence: (a) from the extent to which pairs of friends are similar, and (b) from the statements of children about the qualities they seek in freinds. Unfortunately, the measuring devices currently available for ascertaining resemblances between friends are too gross to give adequate insight into the subtle factors that generate mutual attraction between individuals. At any rate the evidence we have indicates that friends are more similar than dissimilar to each other (Bogardus & Otto, 1936; Bonney, 1943b; Newstetter, Feldstein & Newcomb, 1938; Swift, 1964).

First, friends are similar in those characteristics necessary for adequate and equitable interaction between persons: in chronological age (Challman, 1932; Furfey, 1927; Jenkins, 1931; Wellman, 1926), I.Q. (Bonney, 1942b, 1946; Furfey, 1927; Wellman, 1926), socioeconomic status (Bonney, 1942b, 1946; Glidewell et al, 1966; Jenkins, 1931; Neugarten, 1946), school grade

(Jenkins, 1931; Yohsida, 1963), and height (Furfey, 1927). Preference for children of the same sex appears during the preschool years and becomes more pronounced with increasing age (Abel & Sahinkaya, 1962; Challman, 1932; Kanous, Daugherty & Cohn, 1962; Parten, 1933; Tuddenham, 1952). Most friends live in the same neighborhood or are in the same class in school* (Austin & Thompson, 1948; Furfey, 1927; Yohsida, 1963). Similarities in interests and tastes are frequent (Austin & Thompson, 1948; Bonney, 1946) but are not absolutely essential, since considerable dissimilarity in these areas is compatible with strong mutual friendship (Bogardus & Otto, 1936; Bonney, 1946). More important, perhaps, for children's friendships is similarity in orientation toward and competence in social relationships as judged by measures of social participation (Challman, 1932), social adjustment (Bonney, 9146), social maturity (Furfey, 1927), sociality (Bonney, 1946; Furfey, 1927), and leadership (Bonney, 1946). Verbal statements by elementary and junior high school children of the qualities desired in friends stress similarity of interests and taste (Austin & Thompson, 1948; Hicks & Hayes, 1938; Jenkins, 1931), friendliness and cheerfulness (Austin; & Thompson, 1948; Dymond, Hughes & Raabe, 1952), tidiness (Dymond et al, 1952), good manners and generosity (Austin & Thompson, 1948; Dymond et al, 1952). With increasing age, as children become more physically mobile and aware of the wider community, propinquity becomes less of a limiting condition in the choice of friends (Furfey, 1927; Jones, 1943). Other outstanding age level changes in children's friendships include increasing stability (Horrocks & Buker, 1951; Thompson & Horrocks, 1947) and increasing importance of socioeconomic status (especially for girls) and degree of physical maturity (Jones, 1943).

Consistent with their greater social orientation and interest in persons, girls are more socially active than boys during the preschool years, play with a large number of children, make higher friendship scores, and show greater mutuality of friendship (Challman, 1932; Green, 1933b; Parten, 1933). Their sociometric choices are also more stable at this time (Speroff, 1955). Girls continue to be more sociable than boys during the elementary-school period (Bonney, 1942b) and to establish more intimate and confidential relationships with each other. These differences can also be inferred from the greater frequency of clique formation among girls (Campbell, 1939), the greater mutuality of friendships (Bonney, 1942b), and the greater amount of time they spend with their friends. In choosing friends, girls pay more attention than boys to social class standing (Brown & Bond, 1955).

---

*Intra-neighborhood homogeneity in social class membership and social class uniformities in values and social behavior probably account for the obtained similarities in socioeconomic status and I.Q. between friends.

Children's friendships are relatively unstable even over such short periods of time as two weeks. Sixty per cent of sixth-grade pupils change at least one of their three "best friends" during this interval (Austin & Thompson, 1948). This suggests that the chief purpose of childhood friendships is to satisfy the need for a congenial companion in the prosecution of mutual interests rather than to obtain intimate interpersonal experience and mutual understanding. Principal reasons given by children for terminating friendships include quarrels, changes in interests, lack of recent contact, incompatibility, and charges of conceit, bossiness, disloyalty, and quarrelsomeness (Austin & Thompson, 1948). As previously indicated, the stability of friendships increases with age in both sexes and begins earlier in girls (Horrocks & Buker, 1951; Thompson & Horrocks, 1947).

LEADERSHIP

In contrast to friendship and popularity, which represent the outcome of the *feelings* (like-dislike, acceptance-rejection) that group members develop toward each other, leadership is more closely related to the *functional* properties of groups. This does not mean that the leader's personality and the group members' feelings toward him are irrelevant to the achievement and maintenance of leadership. It means rather that those aspects of the leader's personality that affect the functional effectiveness of the group and those particular feelings of group members toward the leader that are related to his functional efficacy are most relevant to these problems (Kobayashi & Saito, 1958). As groups become more highly structured in terms of role differentiation, leadership refers more to an effect on activities and working relationships than to an influence on persons. Thus in "sociogroups," where the emphasis is on the functional roles of persons in groups, popularity (high sociometric status) is tantamount to leadership; whereas in informal "psychogroups" popularity is more akin to friendship (Jennings, 1943).

The leader may be best described as the person who "moves the group to action" (Cunningham, 1951). Leadership, therefore, is bestowed by the group on that individual who in its judgment has the personality attributes, experience, and skills to organize, mobilize, and represent the group best in achieving its paramount needs and goals. In "sociogroups" the correlates of high sociometric status have great prestige value and hence are closely related to leadership. In "psychogroups" affectional attitudes toward others are important in their own right. Thus, an easygoing, ineffectual person may be popular by virtue of these very qualities, without necessarily possessing any of the prestige-giving characteristics associated with high sociometric status. And by the same token, although sustained unpopularity is seldom compatible with successful leadership, leaders are not obliged to be the most popular persons in the group or to have many close friends.

How Leadership is Achieved and Maintained

In accordance with its functional nature, "leadership is conferred by the group" (Cunningham, 1951). The popularly held belief that gangs are creatures of dynamic leaders is seldom true. Quite the contrary, "the gang forms and the leader emerges as a result of interaction" (Sherif *et al*, 1961; Thrasher, 1927). The "group-given nature of leadership is evident from the fact that the leader cannot successfully disregard the established traditions of the group or the common purposes that he is chosen to advance. He cannot wield his power capriciously or abusively (Thrasher, 1927). Nor can adult authorities impose a leader on the group by choosing a promising candidate and "training" him for leadership. If this is done, actual leadership power is withdrawn by the group and the adult-imposed individual retains at best a nominal status out of deference to his sponsors (Cunningham, 1951). The partly situational nature of leadership also points to its group-given origins. To a certain extent the prestige of leadership ability in one area carries over without any objective justification to an entirely unrelated area ("halo effect"). But the more sophisticated children become in group activities, the more they choose leaders on the basis of situational requirements, and the less they confuse the criteria for leadership with popularity or personal loyalty (Cunningham, 1951).

Leadership is acquired in many different ways. Among young children, one can observe both the aggressive, dominative and coercive "bully" and the more integrative and task-oriented "diplomat," who through perceptiveness, social skill, and a gift for compromise welds the group into a congenial, smoothly functioning unit (Anderson, 1937a, 1937b, 1939; Parten, 1933). Usually, however, the young leader is a mixture of both stereotypes. But even at the kindergarten age, children express preference for the latter kind of leader (Hanfmann, 1935), and from related evidence regarding (a) the effects of authoritarian and democratic social climates (see Chapter 11), (b) the correlates of sociometric status (see p. 346), and (c) the trend with increasing age toward more reciprocal and equalitarian notions of obligation (see Chapter 13), one can infer that older children increasingly favor the more integrative type of leadership.

In children's "sociogroups," most of the correlates of popularity are also qualities that are highly valued by the group, and hence are determinants of both prestige and leadership (Campbell, 1964; Schmuck, 1969). These prestige factors generally include among boys, superior height (Greenberg, 1932), strength (Polansky, Lippitt & Redl, 1950; Thrasher, 1927), and athletic prowess (Greenberg, 1932; Lippitt, Polansky & Rosen, 1952; Thrasher, 1927), intelligence (Campbell, 1964; Greenberg, 1932; Zwier, 1966), and such group-relevant aspects of personality as independence of adults and social pressure, sex sophistication, and "having ideas for fun"

(Campbell, 1964; Cunningham, 1951). Children with high attributed prestige in the group are more likely than low prestige children to attempt the more direct influencing of others and to be more successful in the attempt (Harvey & Rutherford, 1960; Patel & Gordon, 1960). Their approval is solicited by average group members (Lippitt *et al*, 1952); and since they are also more resistive to direct influence, others tend to approach them indirectly (Polansky *et al*, 1950). Children on their way to leadership can usually be identified by their tendency to seek out persons who are already leaders (Jennings, 1943).

Once attained, leadership is maintained in various ways. Control through fear of physical prowess is a significant factor in some groups, especially in lower-class groups (Short, 1966; Thrasher, 1927; Whyte, 1943).

Self-oriented leaders compared to group-oriented leaders tend to give fewer suggestions to their followers (Hare, 1957). More important, however, is the leader's ability to give or withdraw belongingness, to help the group achieve its aims by his special skills or general cleverness, and to influence the group to place high value on the activities in which he excels (Cunningham, 1951). Thus, children with power are perceived as possessing those characteristics that are highly valued by their peers (Gold, 1958; Schmuck, 1969). Leadership fluctuates with changes in the needs of groups as determined both by social maturation and by situational factors. It appears, however, that there is an increase in leadership and followership behavior with age (Kobayashi & Saito, 1958). Nevertheless, because of considerable constancy in the personality traits associated with leadership and in factors making for prestige, a good deal of stability prevails, particularly if leadership is acquired gradually rather than suddenly (Jennings, 1943; Stott & Ball, 1957). The leader's awareness of his high prestige position enables him to use it deliberately in influencing others; and success in this endeavor reinforces the very qualities responsible for his prestige as well as consolidating his position in the group (Polansky *et al*, 1950). Leadership in nursery school is fairly stable (Gellert, 1961) and somewhat prognostic of later leadership in elementary school (Van Alstyne & Hattwick, 1939). Between elementary school and junior high school, however, because of behavioral changes associated with the onset of pubescence, much of this continuity is lost and not regained until adolescence (Levi, 1930).

Behavioral Contagion

"Behavioral contagion" may be defined as "an event in which a person's behavior is changed to resemble that of another person" without any overt intention on the latter's part (Lippit *et al*, 1952; Polansky *et al*, 1951). It involves an act of social imitation or responsiveness to prestige suggestion in which the initiator's behavior serves as a stimulus triggering off comparable behavior in the imitator. Unlike leadership, no direct or deliberate attempt is made to influence another's decisions. As customarily used, the term does not imply an act of identification motivated by either satellizing or incorporative (non-satellizing) considerations (see Chapter 13). Presumably the initiator's actions structure the field differently for the imitator and provide direction and sanction for his behavior.

The capacity for initiating behavioral contagion is primarily a function of possessing a very high prestige position in the group and of accurately perceiving that position (Lippitt et al, 1952; Polansky et al, 1951). Apparently, awareness of his high status in the group provides the child with sufficient sense of security to act in the spontaneous manner that is necessary for generating contagion. The same freedom to act spontaneously also makes him more susceptible to contagion initiated by others (Lippitt et al, 1952). In situations of common frustration, however, the child's impulsiveness rather than his prestige position is a more important determinant of his ability to initiate contagion (Polansky et al, 1951). Contagion is facilitated if the suggested act is visualized as a satisfying means of escaping from a frustrating, conflictful, or ambiguous situation; if the restraining influence exercised by anticipation of disapproval or fear of reprisal is reduced(Grosser, Polansky & Lippitt, 1951); and if the behavior of the initiator is congruent with the goals, value system, and characteristic expressive techniques of the group (Polansky et al, 1951; Redl, 1949).

AGE AND SEX CLEAVAGE

The grouping of children in terms of age and sex limits the nature of peer relations (Campbell, 1964).

Membership in a given age-sex category appears to be a prerequisite for the occupation of almost any status in a society . . . Although such typings are universal throughout different societies, there is no universal agreement on the number and definition of such groupings. For example not all societies have a separate term for or give recognition to the period of adolescence nor do all give equal emphasis to the transition from one age grouping to another (Campbell, 1964, pp. 298-299).

In American society segregation is not only along lines of race and class, but also by age (Bronfenbrenner, 1969). The schools' use of homogeneous grouping by age and ability has set a pattern from preschool onward in which a child's contacts with other children are increasingly limited to youngsters of his own age (Bronfenbrenner, 1969). This trend is more typical of middle-class children than of lower-class children (Schmuck, 1969). With increasing age children's social attachments become more pronounced; social activities become increasingly differentiated and organized, and the effectiveness of the group in motivating behavior increases (Campbell,

1964). The organization of the school throughout the elementary-school years encourages interaction amongst peers to take place within restricted age levels (Schmuck, 1969).

Restricted peer interaction within rather confined age levels in American culture mitigates against youngsters of different age levels relating in a productive fashion (Elder, 1967; Lippitt & Lohman, 1965; Schmuck, 1969; Sullivan, 1968). Age differentiation frequently leads to distrust and animosity between older and younger children since many older youngsters perceive their younger peers as incompetent and unskillful (Lippitt & Lohman, 1965; Schmuck, 1969). Encouragement of older peers in tutorial work with younger children can lead to more positive interactions between children of different age levels (Lippitt & Lohman, 1965). When cross-age relationships are established on a more positive footing, younger children can learn expectations about different degrees of adulthood and what being older or younger means in terms of privilege, responsibility, and behavioral skills (Schmuck, 1969).

Cross-cultural evidence supports the view that, from the early years of childhood, cultural pressures also train the child in sex-differentiated behavior (Campbell, 1964). Our own culture clearly shows a progressive trend toward segregation of the sexes during the course of childhood. Although preschool boys and girls show some preference for their own sex in choosing favorite playmates (Challman, 1932; Koch, 1944; Lippitt et al, 1952; Parten, 1933; Walters et al, 1957), considerable cross-sex friendship and overlapping of activities still prevail. Even in the primary grades, a single boy will play unembarassedly with a group of girls (or vice versa) (Campbell, 1939). Preference for like sex companions increases markedly during the middle years of childhood and preadolescence. This is shown by the rarity of cross-sex sociometric choices (Koch, 1944; Lippitt et al, 1952; Reese, 1966), more favorable attitudes towards members of one's own sex (Harris & Tseng, 1957; Meyer, 1959), self-consciousness about and avoidance of physical contact with members of the opposite sex (Campbell, 1939), sex-typing of games and activities, and sex-biased perceptions of the personality traits and social roles of the sexes (Amatora, 1954; Bjerstedt, 1955). Sex appropriate game preferences are much more apparent in boys than in girls (Sutton-Smith, Rosenberg & Morgan, 1963; Walker, 1964), in keeping with the more intense sex-typing of boys in our culture. Girls are more influenced by boys in heterosexual choices, since they favor those boys that are accepted by other boys whereas the opposite does not hold true (Reese, 1962). Sociometric preference for individuals of the same sex is present even in high school, but declines rapidly; this trend occurs earlier and more prominently in girls (Campbell, 1939; Koch, 1944). After the kindergarten period and until adolescence, girls tend to show more preference for their own sex than boys do

(Amatora, 1954; Koch, 1944; Moreno, 1934). Nevertheless, during the same period as boys' opinions of their own sex gradually improve, their opinions of the opposite sex correspondingly worsen, with the reverse trends holding true for girls (Smith, 1939). Lower-class children are less markedly sex-cleaved when compared with middle-class children during this time (Kanous, Daugherty & Cohn, 1962).

As previously indicated, this segregation of the sexes during childhood is neither a manifestation of genic tendencies nor of a pre-determined stage of psychosexual development such as the so-called "latency period" (see Chapter 11). It is encouraged by such conditions as the sex-typing of peer interests and activities, the preferential status of girls in the school, and the school's emphasis on separation of and competition between the sexes. Hence, much variability is found in degree of segregation between different cultures (Mead, 1949) and social classes (Bonney, 1954; Kanous *et al*, 1962) and also when these conditions differ from one community to another (Bonney, 1954). Sex cleavage probably makes the transition to adolescent heterosexual behavior more difficult, especially where years of social antagonism precede adolescence. Contemporary American society is showing a trend away from the severe sex-cleavage which was heretofore characteristic of our culture (Kuhlen & Houlihan, 1965). There is an increase in cross-sex friendships in preadolescence (Broderick & Fowler, 1961) which may make the transition to young adolescence less discontinuous and less threatening in the domain of heterosexuality.

CONFORMITY BEHAVIOR

For two important reasons the peer group demands a certain degree of minimal conformity from its members. First, no institution, especially if it has status-giving functions, can exist for any length of time without due regard by its members for uniform, regular, and predictable adherence to a set of avowed rules and traditions. Hence, in its efforts to establish a new and distinctive subculture and to evolve a unique set of criteria for the determination of status and prestige, the peer society must do everything in its power to set itself off as recognizably distinct and separate from the adult society which refuses it membership. If this distinctiveness is to be actually attained, widespread nonconformity obviously cannot be tolerated. Second, conformity is also required to maintain the group solidarity that is necessary to offer effective and organized resistance to the encroachments of adult authority (Campbell, 1964).

The peer group is in an excellent position to demand conformity from the child as the price of its acceptance. No other institution can offer him a satisfactory social identity in relation to his equals; and to the extent that he enjoys a marginal position in the culture and is alienated form adult society, he is also beholden to the group for much of his primary and derived status. Thus, from middle childhood through adolescence, as the child's dependence on and stake in the effectiveness of the peer group increases, the latter's power to exact conformity is concomitantly enhanced (Campbell, 1964; Schmuck, 1969). Conforming tendencies are also reinforced by the fact that group approval brings a welcome reprieve from anxiety and that obligations to abide by group standards are internalized out of feelings of loyalty, belongingness, and gratitude. If these implicit group pressures and internalized restraints of the individual are insufficient to keep him in line, explicit sanctions are imposed. Depending on the seriousness of the offense and the nature and functions of the group, the punishment may vary from ridicule, censure, and rebuff to physical chastisement and complete ostracism. Sex differences in conformity behavior indicate that females conform more than males during the middle years of childhood (Iscoe, Williams & Harvey, 1963). Susceptibility to influence is greater when the influence agent is a peer with high-status in the group (Harvey & Rutherford, 1960).

In general, because of the present-day intolerance for deviancy in the wider culture and because of an exaggerated perception of the degree of conformity required for peer group acceptance, children tend to be over-impressed with the need for conforming to group standards. Some evidence (Newstetter *et al*, 1938) also points to the conclusion that apparent disregard for the group's approval tends to enhance the individual's sociometric status by making him appear above the need for currying favor with others. Hence many perfectly "safe" opportunities are lost for expressing individuality compatible with over-all group standards. In any case marked individual differences are evident in the need to conform. The highly self-assertive child, for example, can only restrain his individuality to a point, and the extreme introvert draws a line beyond which he refuses to participate in boisterous activities. The child who has a highly developed set of moral or religious activities may refuse to condone the practices of his group. Other individuals may have overwhelming interests that are regarded with scorn by their age mates. Finally, the non-satellizer's need for ego aggrandizement and his lack of loyalty and "we-feeling" may cause him to betray group interests for personal advantage.

IMPACT OF SOCIAL STRATIFICATION

In various other contexts we have pointed out that as children grow older social stratification in the wider culture has progressively greater influence on peer relationships. Children become increasingly aware of the symbols of social class status (see Chapter 11) and pay more attention to racial, social class, and ethnic requirements for membership in particular cliques. The parental and cultural pressures that draw caste and social class lines more sharply with increasing age and make children's racial and class attitudes gradually approximate those of their elders will be described in detail later (see Chapter 11). We will consider various reasons why girls are more status-conscious than boys (see Chapter 11).

INTER-GROUP BEHAVIOR

As members of particular *in*-groups, children also interact both individually and collectively with members of other groups (*out*-groups). In these instances they react less as individuals in their own right than in terms of their in-group identifications, the prevailing degree of social distance between their respective groups, and various situational factors affecting inter-group relations (Proshansky, 1966; Sherif & Sherif, 1954). In other words, they manifest *inter-group* behavior. Such behavior naturally presupposes a high degree of intra-group solidarity and of role and status differentiation, and hence cannot be expected much before middle childhood or preadolescence. Once such cohesive in-groups are formed, it is possible under experimentally controlled conditions of competition and reciprocal frustration to produce negative group attitudes, unfavorable stereotype perceptions, and hostile actions in relation to the out-group (Proshansky, 1966; Sherif & Sherif, 1953; Sherif, Harvey & White, 1954). These manifestations of hostility toward the out-group are accompanied (after some initial in-group bickering, scapegoating and changes in leadership) by an enhancement of in-group solidarity and friendships, and of favorable perceptions of in-group behavior (Proshansky, 1966; Sherif & Sherif, 1953; Sherif *et al*, 1954). However, when groups in this induced state of tension are brought together in a situation where the attainment of commonly desired, "superordinate" goals exceeds the energies and resources of a single group, inter-group cooperation results, with a concomitant reduction of hostility and negative stereotypes (Sherif *et al*, 1954).

CHAPTER 11

Psychosocial Aspects of Personality Development

WE HAVE USED the term "psychosocial" to refer to certain relatively plastic, socially determined aspects of development that are *approximately* uniform for all individuals sharing a common cultural tradition and are different for individuals coming from diverse cultural environments. Acceptance of such intracultural uniformities (or intercultural differences), however, does not imply endorsement of the extreme relativistic view that personality development is *completely* unique in every culture (that no intercultural uniformities exist), or that it is *completely* uniform for all individuals within a given culture. Inkeles (1968) remarks that . . .

. . . in contrasting socialization practices in societies with broadly different systems of economy or polity, we lose sight of the important fact of sub-system differentiation. In particular, large-scale and complex nation states often include subgroups whose life experience is sharply differentiated from others in a variety of ways. Sex and age may, of course, be the basis for discrimination. Generally, however, the most important differentiation is expressed in the systems of stratification, usually economic and sometimes based on status and power, and is manifest in concrete form in the differential allocation of resources to families and individuals. Such differential allocation may have profound effects on the individual's self-conception, effects which are evident very early and may be reinforced and emphasized throughout the life cycle (pp. 111-112).

Insistence on the only *approximately* uniform nature of psychosocial traits rests on more than the fact that each individual experiences a somewhat idiosyncratic version of cultural reality (see pp. 73-79). Few customs or institutions apply without exception to all members of a culture; and in complex cultures such as our own, the social environment is differentiated into a number of partially self-contained subcultures on the basis of caste, social class, and ethnic origin, each defining in distinctive and semi-restrictive ways both value alternatives and the determining conditions of personality development. Thus, for example, the concept of "national character's is valid only as long as (a) one appreciates that in addition to uniformities referable to a common heritage of customs, traditions, and social institutions, there is also much intranational subcultural variability, and (b) one does not assume in the absence of adequate control data that a specific item or constellation of childhood experiences is *causally* related to distinctive features of adult personality.

Our task in this chapter will be to consider: (1) certain general problems of psychosocial personality development (i.e., mediation of cultural influences; determinants and mechanisms of transmitting psychosocial traits); (2) the impact of specific socializing agencies and conditions other than family (Chapter 9) and peer group (Chapter 10) on the personality development of children, i.e., caste, social class, school; and (3) psychosocial aspects of biological and social sex role. Much of this material, of course, has already been discussed in detail in other contexts, and need only be referred to or summarized here in relation to these three issues. Generally speaking, we shall use our own American culture to illustrate development of psychosocial traits, since this culture is most familiar to the majority of readers. * Wherever necessary, for purposes of contrast, brief reference will be made to other cultures.

INDIRECT MEDIATION OF CULTURAL INFLUENCES

The relationship between social experience and personality development is seldom immediate or direct. Social variables exert their influence indirectly by implicating ego values and aspirations and by modifying ego structure. It is true, of course, that either social or physiological stimuli can instigate behavior directly without involving ego structure; but these effects merely constitute peripheral, transitory and situational fluctuations in the diurnal stream of behavior. Long-lasting normative change in personality development can result only when ego structure undergoes substantial modification or reorganization; and typically such reorganization becomes necessary following significant shifts in biosocial status.†

Perception (see p. 248) also acts as a mediating mechanism interposed between social stimulus content and the ultimate content of awareness that actually influences behavior and development. Cognitive maturity is one of the most crucial components of this perceptual process since it determines the child's capacity to respond to social stimuli of varying degrees of sophistication (Kohlberg, 1968). Cognitive immaturity either insulates him from a large portion of the social world that has relatively uniform perceptual significance for older individuals in his culture, or makes him misperceive it in ways that are congruent with his ego structure and existing level of

---

The same procedure has been and will continue to be followed in considering psychobiological problems. Universally distributed aspects of emotional, ego, moral, cognitive, and motor development can be rendered most comprehensible to the typical reader of this book by considering their manifestations in the contemporary American child.

†*A very similar position to ours is argued by Kohlberg (1968) in the area of imitation and identification and by Harvey, Hunt, & Schroder (1961) in personality development.*

sophistication (see p. 249). With advancing age and perceptual maturity, however, he is brought into more direct and realistic contact with the social environment (Kohlberg, 1968). His role-taking and empathic ability in interpreting interpersonal feelings (Dymond & Hughes, 1952) and expressions of emotion (Bowers & London, 1965; Gates, 1923; Harvey, Hunt, & Schroder, 1961; Walton, 1936) improves, as well as his ability to verbalize and discriminate traits he likes and dislikes in others (Amatora, 1952; Jersild, Markey & Jersild, 1933), to forecast his own and others' sociometric status (see p. 337), and to recognize the relevant symbols of social class status (Brown, 1965; Glidewell, Kantor, Smith & Stringer, 1966; Whiting & Child, 1953).

The influence of cultural variables on personality development may also be considered indirect in the sense that especially in his early formative years, when much socialization takes place, the child's exposure to his culture is largely buffered by the nuclear family group. Partly for this reason, but mostly because of perceptual immaturity and the centrality of psychobiological aspects of development, few differential effects of cultural influence are observable during the first year of life. Especially in contemporary urban society, the child moves outside of the family and is gradually introduced to play groups, school, and mass media (Clausen & Williams, 1963), and this tends to lessen the confining influence of the family circle and its biased interpretation of the culture. Through increased, broadened, and more direct contact with the wider community, he acquires more first-hand and sophisticated knowledge of social institutions and of caste and class differences in our mosaic-like culture. Acclimatization to the wider community takes place earlier and with greater ease and continuity in cultures where the child visits frequently and is warmly received in other households (e.g., Arapesh, Samoan), and in cultures characterized by an extended family group (e.g., Navaho).

SOURCES OF PSYCHOSOCIAL TRAITS

Two basic problems pervade the study of personality-in-culture. First, how is variability in cultural values, customs, and institutions related to significant intercultural variability in personality structure? What aspects of cultural diversity are related in what ways to characteristic intercultural differences in behavioral orientation? Second, what developmental mechanisms account for the *transmission* of such differences? Through what media do distinctive cultural factors operate to influence personality development differentially so that the child eventually becomes a reasonable facsimile of the modal adult in his culture? We are, in other words, inquiring into (a) the sources or determinants of psychosocial traits, and (b) the vehicles

through which such traits are transmitted in the process of enculturation.*
In a very real sense these two problems are interrelated. Differential child
rearing practices, for example, may simultaneously serve as a source and as
a means of transmitting intercultural variability in personality structure.
For purposes of analysis, however, it is helpful to consider each problem
separately. Since the limiting determinants of psychosocial variability are
rather self evident (see p. 73), the present discussion of the first problem
will be restricted to patterning sources.

The differential value system of a culture is a basic source of psychosocial
traits and of modal personality structure. It determines in part such culturally
conditioned aspects of motivation as level and object of striving; relative
need for primary as against derived status; desire for ego aggrandizement,
hierarchical status, and volitional independence; goal frustration tolerance;
and level of anxiety referable to ego enhancement. Cultures vary greatly with
respect to the kinds of personality traits that are idealized and encouraged
and the severity of expectations regarding criteria of adult maturity, i.e.,
expected degree of executive independence, responsibility, self-critical ability,
and ability to postpone hedonistic gratification. They also define the characteristic role attributes of age, sex, kinship, status, and occupation, and such
generalized dimensions of interpersonal relationships as cooperativeness-
competitiveness, egocentricity-sociocentricity, egoism-altruism, individualism-
group mindedness, introversion-extroversion, directness-indirectness, and
straightforwardness-duplicity. Such culturally distinctive role stereotypes
constitute the available models that children and adolescents use in fashioning their individual role behavior and thus participate in the transmission
of psychosocial traits. Lastly, stemming directly or indirectly from the
cultural value system is a general *Weltanschauung* or orientation to life. This
includes such items as primary life goals or interests (mercantile, spiritual,
aesthetic, military, etc.), criteria for evaluating the worth of a person,
general attitudes toward children, moral values and sanctions, responsiveness to time and conformity pressures, degree of reality testing, optimistic
or pessimistic and casual or somber views of life.

In addition to the pervasive modeling influence of its distinctive value
system, each culture exerts a characteristic *experiential* impact on the socialization of its members by virtue of the unique ways in which it institutionalizes
basic interpersonal relationships. Since children actually acquire primary
and derived status and feelings of security and adequacy as products of such

---

*Enculturation *refers to the processes whereby a child acquires the distinctive (psychosocial) behavior
patterns of his culture.* Socialization *is a more inclusive term encompassing the effects of* all *social
variables on personality development. Hence it includes the acquisition of culturally conditioned traits
that are distributed universally (psychobiological) as well as of psychosocial traits. Herskovits
(1951) uses the two terms to distinguish between adaptation to culture and society respectively.*

relationships, the "transactions" associated with the individual acquisition of biosocial status are probably a more important source and vehicle of transmitting psychosocial than is the observation of cultural role models (see p. 250). Both factors, however — satisfying role experience and the interiorization of cultural goals and values—account for the learning of new, socially appropriate behaviors. The majority of early identification theories assumed a strong deficit-state motivation for imitation and identification (Kohlberg, 1968). More recent formulations of imitative modeling postulate cognitive components which are not directly related to any deficits in the organism (Aronfreed, 1968; Bandura, 1968; Kohlberg, 1968).* Differential institutionalization of interpersonal experience leads to characteristic inter-cultural and subcultural differences in ego development. Caste and class membership and reference groups furnish an important basis for inflation or deflation of feelings of adequacy. It also makes much difference whether the young child acquires his derived status primarily from the parents as in our culture or from satellizing relationships to siblings and agemates as among the Kibbutzim children (Clausen & Williams, 1963); whether sources of primary status are available to the child at home or only in school and peer group (see p. 275); whether parents or agemates are the chief socializing agents in late childhood and adolescence (see p. 276); whether resatellization and devaluation are important aspects of desatellization and value assimilation during the latter periods (see p. 277); whether sanctions are applied laterally or by parents. Depending on various institutionalized aspects of handling and timing shifts in children's biosocial status, much or little discontinuity in role and status may prevail between age and sex groups, and transitional periods of development may either be abrupt, prolonged, and anxiety-ridden or gradual, brief, and relatively untraumatic. Cultures also presumably differ in the characteristic degree of parental acceptance-rejection extended to children; because of much intracultural personality variability among parents the mode of expression rather than content of this parent attitude is more likely to be successfully institutionalized.

At any particular stage in the historical development of a given culture, current political, economic and social vicissitudes exert considerable qualifying influence on the traditional pattern of psychosocial traits transmitted to

---

*There is still a considerable amount of controversy concerning the motives and mechanisms involved in imitation and identification learning. Although Aronfreed (1968), Bandura (1968), and Kohlberg (1968) emphasize "congnitive constructs", there is nevertheless a different developmental emphasis in Kohlberg (1968) which makes his "cognitive" emphasis clearly age related. In contrast to the above theorists, Gewirtz (1968) and Gewirtz & Stingle (1968) provide an instrumental learning analysis of generalized imitation which omits any use of "cognitive constructs". Because of our stage developmental emphasis in ego development, our position is most closely approximated in Kohlberg's (1968) interpretation without his emphasis on "competance motivation."

the growing generation (Clausen & Williams, 1963). War, depression, famine, social disorganization, acculturation pressures, technological advances, and rapid social change are only some of the more striking current factors that account for historical variation in culture patterns, in the prevailing level of frustration and anxiety, and in the quality of interpersonal relations.

We have already taken pains to indicate that the influence of culturally distinctive child rearing practices as a source and a vehicle of transmitting psychosocial traits has been greatly overrated. Child-rearing practices have received most attention because the family was given most attention in the formulation of the earlier socialization theories (Kohlberg, 1968). It seems plausible that child-rearing practices, to begin with, could only have lasting and generalized effects on core aspects of personality if they were reflective of pervasive cultural values—not because they happened to impinge on the gratification of alleged libidinal drives (see p. 273). It is very unlikely, however, that the selection of specific child rearing techniques would consistently have the same psychological significance or reflect the same social values from one culture to another. Many overtly dissimilar practices are compatible with the realization of the same aims of upbringing, and many specific aspects of child rearing are arbitrary products of custom or historical accident and hence have little or no attitudinal significance. It is entirely possible, of course, that the general manner of administering child care (if not the presence of absence of specific practices) in a particular culture is indicative of pervasive cultural attitudes towards children; but the interpretation of such attitudes underlying the cultural prescription undoubtedly varies greatly from parent to parent and in any case is considerably modified in practice by the personality trends of individual parents. Hence, since it is extremely difficult to institutionalize cultural values through the medium of subtle culture-wide common denominators of child handling, and since it is improbable that infants and young children would be sufficiently mature cognitively to perceive their significance even if they were uniformly expressed, general features of child rearing probably constitute a more important source of idiosyncratic than of psychosocial variability.

Parent attitudes, insofar as they are reflective of cultural values, do play an important role in transmitting psychosocial traits, especially during the early years when the child's direct contact with the wider culture is minimal. But it is more credible to suppose that they do so directly through recurrent explicit and implicit indoctrination (training, precept, example, incidental exposure), reinforced by appropriate external and internal sanctions and by later experience with other socializing agents, during the entire period of childhood and adolescence, than indirectly and inferentially through the tenor of child rearing practices during infancy and early childhood.*

TRANSMISSION OF PSYCHOSOCIAL TRAITS

We shall consider in another context the intracultural transmission of values in terms of external patterning factors, interiorization, and external and internal sanctions (see Chapter 13). In general the same explanatory principles apply to the transmission of psychosocial traits since the latter are inclusive of values. The present section is intended as an addendum to the previous discussion. In a broad sense, of course, the acquisition of particular cultural patterns (socially acquired needs) constitutes a relatively permanent incremental modification of behavior and hence can be considered a form of learning. Broadly conceived it involves cues, incentive, drives, responses, rewards and punishments. But since this kind of social learning is more complex and implicates more core aspects of personality than the learning of mazes, motor skills, or school information it would greatly oversimplify matters to abandon the specialized frame of reference previously adopted for this type of learning and revert to a more primitive type of analysis.

The first step in the transmission of psychosocial traits involves differential exposure to a restricted learning environment.† Children in diverse cultures develop into different kinds of adults because of the cumulative effects of (a) recurrent exposure to different value systems and role models and (b) participation in different kinds of role and status experience (Kohlberg, 1968). Interiorization and reinforcement by internal and external sanctions, as later described, (see Chapter 13), and the action of various self-perpetuating mechanisms complete the process of transmission. In the absence of appropriate role experience, however, a child cannot possibly acquire the distinguishing personality attributes of a given cultural or sub-cultural group. On an intercultural level, restriction of experience is usually a function of simple unawareness of the existence of alternatives available in other cultures; where such awareness is not lacking, the selective interiorization of our cultural values is favored by greater primacy, frequency, reward, and

---

*The vast majority of studies on imitation modeling have focused on simply dyadic relationships (Flanders, 1968). Flanders (1968) points out that it is essential to clarify and explore the research designs in dyadic relationships because they are the most fundamental and provide an empirical and theoretical base from which it will be possible to extrapolate more complex situations. Our position is that this phenomenon is not additive and that quadratic situations (e.g., two children families) as presented by Parsons & Bales (1955) are governed by qualitatively different interactions than a dyadic structure.

†See Goslin's (1968) "Handbook of Socialization" for the most recent and extensive coverage of this topic. Also Zigler and Child's chapter in Volume III of Lindsey and Aronson's "Handbook of Social Psychology", 1969 (2nd edition).

saliency, and by the prestige suggestion exercised by personally significant representatives of the individual's particular reference and membership groups. Intraculturally, where the availability of role experience is restricted to particular classes of persons on an institutionalized basis, not only is the necessary experience unavailable to other persons, but the latter also do not perceive it as within their grasp and fail to develop the motivation to obtain it:

> Such status differentiations as these have the effect of defining and limiting the developmental environment of the child. Within each of these participation levels with their cultural environments, a child learns characteristic behavior and values concerning family members, sexual and aggressive acts, work, education and a career . . . These restricted learning environments are maintained by powerful and firmly established taboos upon participation outside of one's status level, . . . (by pressures) exerted not only by those above . . . but also by persons below . . . and by those in one's particular class (Davis, 1944, pp. 200-203).

Appropriate age, sex, status and kinship role are learned both experientially and by observation of culturally stereotyped role models. The influence of the latter, however, first becomes important after a minimal level of cognitive maturity is achieved. It also tends to be vitiated whenever considerable heterogeneity in perceived social norms is present (see p. 291). With increasing age, despite growing ability to generalize from one situation to another, roles tend to become more specific and more rigidly defined. This trend reflects progressively greater differentiation of role behavior as well as the cultural tendency to compartmentalize roles and ignore contradictions between them. Hence the child is conditioned not to perceive role inconsistencies emanating from contradictory values of the different reference groups from which they are derived. Each role merely reigns supreme in its separate domain. If attempts at reconciliation are made, one role may be selected and the others repressed or rejected, or several conflicting roles may be subsumed under a more inclusive loyalty (Hartley, 1951).

> The transmission of differential class levels of aspiration * is achieved by the maintenance [in] the individual of a certain level of anxiety with regard to the attainment of the required behavior for *his status*. This socialized anxiety plays a major role in propelling him along that culture rout prescribed by his family, school, and later by adult society at his cultural level . . . Anxiety leads to striving because only thus can anxiety be reduced to a tolerable level . . . The anxiety which middle-status (children) learn is effective, first, because it involves the threat of loss of present status (and the severe social penalties associated therewith), and, second, because it leads as the individual may plainly see in 'successful persons' to the rewards of power (and) . . . social prestige (Davis, 1944, pp. 213-214) . . . The class goals in education, occupation, and status are made to appear real, valuable, and certain to him because he actually begins to experience in his school, clique,

---

Interiorization and other internal and external sanctions also operate similarly here as in the transmission of values (see Chapter 13).

and family life some of the prestige responses. The lower-class child, however, learns by *not* being rewarded in these prestige relationships that the middle-class goals and gains are neither likely nor desirable for one in his position (Davis, 1941, p. 353).

Finally, once established, psychosocial traits tend to be perpetuated by the same mechanisms that account for the long-range stability of idiosyncratic traits, i.e., continued exposure to the same environment, inertia, perceptual sensitization, "perceptual constancy," "categorical perception," symbolization, and the organizing effects of central dimensions of personality (see Chapter 14). Individuals in a particular culture become selectively sensitized to perceive only a restricted sphere of their physical and social environments, and because of a common set of values, beliefs and attitudes toward life tend to develop a characteristic way of perceiving reality and to structure the world along perceptually uniform lines (Brown, 1965). Part of this perceptual standardization is a function of common symbolical and conceptual categories into which raw sensory experience is fitted by cultural convention. These self-perpetuating mechanisms do more than just endow psychosocial traits with longitudinal consistency within individual members of the culture. Since the latter are carriers and transmitters of the cultural pattern as well, they also help in the perpetuation of the culture from one generation to the next.

IMPACT OF SOCIAL STRATIFICATION AND SOCIALIZING AGENCIES

In our heterogeneous society there is no such thing as a uniform social environment determining in the same way the developmental careers of all children. It seems rather that . . .

. . . participation of any given individual in the culture of his society is not a matter of chance. It is determined primarily and almost completely as far as the overt culture is concerned, by his place in the society and by the training he has received in his occupying this place . . . For the complex industrial society of the United States, social class—the way people are ranked in the hierarchy of prestige and power—is but one way of defining the individual's place (Clausen & Williams, 1963, pp. 67-68).

Listed in order of increasing degrees of in-marriage, prestige and status ranking can be on the basis of (1) social classes, (2) minority ethnic groups, and (3) castes (Davis, 1941). These status categories, of course, are not mutually exclusive. Negro children, for example, grow up under predominantly lower-class conditions. Class and caste are distinguished from one another, in that in the latter, membership is fixed at birth for life, whereas in the former membership can be changed in a man's life time (Brown, 1965). Because of social mobility in American society, there is an absence of caste except the apparent caste system imposed by American whites on American blacks (Brown, 1965).

Racial, Religious and Ethnic Attitudes*

Developmental Trends. Awareness of racial differences occurs relatively early. By the age of three, Hawaiian children clearly perceive the difference between orientals and non-orientals (Springer, 1950) and divide along racial lines in play in nursery schools (McCandless & Hoyt, 1961). American children by age three are aware of and correctly identify racial differences between white and Negroes (Clark & Clark, 1947; Goodman, 1952; Landreth & Johnson, 1953; Morland, 1958, 1966; Stevenson & Stevenson, 1960; Stevenson & Stewart, 1958; Vaughn, 1964). Awareness of ethnic and religious differences develops at a later age because the differences in question are more difficult to perceive in terms of both stimulus content and degree of social emphasis placed upon them. Ethnic self-recognition precedes ethnic recognition of others (Hartley, Rosenbaum & Schwartz, 1948a, 1948b); and, as might be reasonably anticipated, membership in an ethnic minority increases the saliency of this social datum and facilitates early development of ethnic awareness (Hartley, Rosenbaum & Schwartz, 1948a, 1948b). Regional differences in "racial awareness" of children appear; Northern Negro children show earlier racial awareness (Goodman, 1952; Porter, 1963), while Southern white children apparently show earlier racial awareness than their Negro counterparts (Morland, 1958; Stevenson & Stewart, 1958). Jewish children in the early elementary school grades are more highly aware of and strongly identified with their own membership group than are Catholic and Protestant children (Radke, Trager & Davis, 1949), and throughout the elementary school years they tend to be more extrapunitive and less impunitive when compared to Catholic and Protestant children on a picture frustration test (Kirchner, McGary & Moore, 1962).

Despite the evidence of awareness of racial and ethnic differences during the preschool period, children's concepts of racial and religious membership are understandably vague and confused at this time (Hartley, Rosenbaum & Schwartz, 1948a, 1948b; Landreth & Johnson, 1953; Proshansky, 1966). With increasing age not only does the extent of awareness increase, but also the relevance, abstractness, and subtlety of the differentiating criteria (Proshansky, 1966). Children first distinguish between different religious groups in terms of conspicuous concrete symbols and only later identify with evaluative statements made about *people* of different religions (Radke, Trager *et al*, 1949). The use of racial and ethnic designations (e.g., Negro, Jew) gradually replaces reference to specific persons (Proshansky, 1966) and to such gross characteristics as skin color (Clark & Clark, 1947).

Racial *self-identification* is a somewhat different matter than awareness of racial differences since it also involves knowledge of the favorable and unfavorable implications of racial membership. Thus, between the ages of

---

Recent reviews on these topics may be found in Proshansky (1966) and Stevenson (1967).

three and seven, 66 per cent of Negro children in one experimental sample identified themselves with a white rather than with a brown doll (Clark & Clark, 1947)*. This choice was not completely autistic or a function of ex-pediential considerations; reality pressures also enter the picture.† Signific-antly more Southern and dark-skinned Negro children identified with the colored doll than did Northern and light-skinned Negro children. Also, with increasing age (except between four and five), the percentage of identifica-tion with the colored doll increased (Clark & Clark, 1947).

Except for Negro children, who in general tend to show preference for white skin color (Proshansky, 1966), racial *self-preference* is well-established in white and Oriental preschool children (Goodman, 1952; Johnson, 1950; Landreth & Johnson, 1953; Springer, 1950). The majority of children in this age range, both Negro and white, are aware of the social significance of racial membership and value people differentially in terms of their color (Goodman, 1952). Even at the age of three, Negro children have learned that skin color is important and that white is to be desired, dark to be regretted (Landreth & Johnson, 1953). In nursery school, Negro children prefer white, while their white counterparts distinctly make preferences favoring their own color (Morland, 1962, 1966; Stevenson & Stewart, 1958). During the ego-expansive period of three to five (see Chapter 8), identification with the prestige of the culturally dominant class seems to be especially important, and the preference of Negro children for white skin color accordingly in-creases. During the next two years, as identification with parents and age-mates increases, expressed preference for white dolls, playmates and white skin color decreases (Clark & Clark, 1947; Morland, 1962; Stevenson & Stewart, 1958). Between six and seven years Southern Negro children prefer their own race in doll preference; but whereas the majority of white children said that the Negro doll was bad, none of the Negro children said the "white doll" was bad (Gregor & McPherson, 1966). Penniger & Williams (1966) also indicate that white preschoolers make similar negative evaluations of blackness. In contrast to lower-class white and Negro children, white upper-class children react more cognitively and less affectively to skin color. They are more accurate in matching skin colors and show no preference for one color over another (Landreth & Johnson, 1953).

---

*Greenwald (1968) questions these self-identification studies and by the inclusion of an intermediate (mullato) alternative reduced Negro misidentifications significantly. The finding may indicate the compromise that the black child must make in contemporary American society.

†These trends may be changing in the Negro community as a result of the emphasis on "black nationalism." As Essien-Udom (1964) points out: "the Negroes' consciousness, though slow, is awakening to their heritage of abuse and degradation, and, especially, to their possible destiny as human beings. It may well signal the beginning of the end of the Negroes' aimless and vain desire to hide their dark skins behind a white mask (p. 353)."

Behavioral or sociometric cleavage between the races occurs later than attitudinal cleavage (Proshansky, 1966) although there is indication that, even as early as the preschool, white children express a steady increase in preference for white playmates (Stevenson & Stewart, 1958). Despite marked verbally expressed preferences, there is little actual hostility; and cross-racial sociometric and behavior interactions occur relatively frequently during the preschool and early elementary school years (Crisswell, 1939; Goodman, 1952; Koch, 1946; Stevenson & Stevenson, 1960). From kindergarten to the twelfth grade, however, racial self-preference, as indicated by sociometric measures, continues to increase (Crisswell, 1939; Koch, 1946) and crossing of color lines practically ceases after the tenth grade (Koch, 1946). At all grade levels until the tenth, white children show more racial self-preference than Negroes (Crisswell, 1939; Koch, 1946). Until the sixth grade, as a matter of fact, the latter choose white children as often as children of their own race (Koch, 1946). This racial difference is consistent with the preschool trend. It indicates that Negro children are much more desirous of being assimilated by the culturally more prestigeful group than white children are willing to let them. On the other hand, a sociometric study of school children in Hawaii, where Caucasians constitute a minority group, indicates that racial self-preference is greater in Oriental than in white children and diminishes for cross-sex choices and as the size of the minority nationality in the classroom decreases (Springer, 1953). During the early elementary school years, children also exhibit preferential attitudes toward members of their own religious group (Radke, Trager, et al, 1949).

In accordance with general trends in value assimilation (see p. 464), the racial and ethnic attitudes of children become increasingly more homogeneous and gradually approach the prevailing adult norms in their community (Blake & Dennis, 1943; Zeligs, 1938, 1948). Their stereotypes become more sophisticated and discriminating as shown by the more highly rationalized arguments given for intolerant attitudes and by the attribution of some favorable traits to unfavored minorities (Blake & Dennis, 1943; Horowitz, 1936). Intraindividually also, prejudice gradually becomes a more highly generalized and self-consistent trait (Horowitz, 1936). Consistent with existing cultural contradictions between verbal ideals of democratic tolerance and actual standards of discriminatory behavior, the affective intensity of children's prejudicial *attitudes* toward minority groups tends to remain relatively constant (Blake & Dennis, 1943; Horowitz, 1936; Minard, 1931), whereas desire to exclude them from social participation increases sharply (Crisswell, 1939; Horowitz, 1936; Koch, 1946; Minard, 1931). The recent impetus of the civil rights movement may precipitate a change in the older finding since . . .

. . . this last decade was not merely the sharpened awareness of the dilemma but, more importantly, the unique and direct response to it. A grass roots civil rights movement was and continues to be sustained on the domestic scene by increasing urbanization and industrialization and by the growing emphasis in the international arena on the concept of self-determination for all peoples. A sustained challenge to the status quo invariably is met with greater resistance to the attempts to such change. . . . Out of the resulting intensification of conflict in local and broader community settings, there have emerged fundamental changes in national policy and in public attitudes (Proshansky, 1966, p. 312).

The specific effects of these changes on children's intergroup attitudes is, as yet, an unknown quantity.

Determinants. At least three broad assumptions about intergroup attitudes about which there is agreement are that: (a) intergroup attitudes are learned, (b) they are multicausally determined, and (c) they are functional or need satisfying in character for the individual (Proshansky, 1966). Parents are the primary agents of socialization and they are the most important agents for the transmission of cultural norms for intergroup attitudes (Proshansky, 1966). Thus, the first step in the acquisition of racial and ethnic attitudes begins in the home. Through explicit or implicit indoctrination by parents, or merely through recurrent exposure to and identification with parental attitudes, children acquire strong feelings about minority groups before they have any first-hand experience with them (Horowitz, 1936; Radke & Sutherland, 1949; Radke, Sutherland & Rosenberg, 1950; Radke, Trager & Paris, 1949). Thus Horowitz found that anti-Negro attitudes in white children were independent of degree of contact with negro children and were about as marked in New York City as in the South; but in particular instances were parents were favorably disposed toward Negroes on doctrinal grounds, their children were substantially free of anti-Negro bias (Horowitz, 1936).

As children approach pubescence and the game of life is conceived as being played more "for keeps," adult indulgence toward spontaneous manifestation of "childish" tolerance decreases. Parental admonitions about associating with the "wrong type" of children become more pointed, and (especially in girls) are reflected in increased attitudinal intolerance toward Negroes (Bird, Monachesi & Burdick, 1952). In the meantime, the attitudes learned at home are reinforced by exposure to the prevailing climate of opinion in the wider community (Horowitz, 1936; Radke & Sutherland, 1949; Radke, Trager & Davis, 1949; Trager & Yarrow, 1952; Zeligs, 1938, 1948), and to such officially sanctioned and institutionalized symbols of discrimination as segregated neighborhoods, schools, and churches. Current racial stereotypes, as reflected in folklore, jokes, mass-media, and everyday gossip, are easily assimilated when attitudinal conformity is habitually rewarded with social approval and nonconformity is punished with scorn and ridicule (Berelson

& Salter, 1946; Proshansky, 1966). Conformity to these cultural norms legitimizing prejudice is a factor in the formulation of intergroup attitudes (Pettigrew, 1958). Even if no explicit social approval is forthcoming, the belittlement of other persons is rewarding because it leads to ego enhancement.

In the light of these highly ingrained attitudes, actual contact with members of minority groups, even if favorable, probably does more to bolster than to counteract existing prejudices. The prejudiced child tends to force every aspect of minority group behavior into preconceived judgmental molds; hence, the resulting perceptual products all fit the same stereotype, irrespective of actual stimulus content (Radke, Sutherland & Rosenberg, 1950). He is sensitized to notice the bad, to ignore the good, and to misinterpret the innocuous as maliciously intended. Undesirable behavior or traits of particular out-group members, which would be overlooked or regarded as idiosyncratic in members of the in-group, are generalized as indigenous to the basic personality structure of the former group. The small "kernel of truth" in every stereotype is inevitably encountered and provides dramatic and irrefutable confirmation of the validity of his views. Pleasant social contacts, on the other hand, are regarded as exceptions to the general rule and seldom alter the prevailing stereotype (Radke, Trager & Davis, 1949). Furthermore, legalized or de facto segregation tends to bolster these emergent attitudes. Thus, if the child . . .

> . . . needs reasons for the observed segregation of these groups, then the perceived effects of both segregation and discrimination create a social reality for the child which indeed lends support to the view that "they are not like us and therefore must be kept separate." Certain objective qualities of some minority groups are, in fact, consistent with this kind of interpretation. In the case of Negroes, for example, the child in many instances can observe that they are less educated, work in menial occupations, live in substandard housing, dress poorly and so on (Proshansky, 1966, p. 333).

It is small wonder, therefore, that racial and ethnic attitudes constitute logic-tight compartments that are practically unassailable by ordinary experience and by commonly accepted rules of evidence.

All of these mechanisms are naturally intensified under conditions of chronic inter-group tension or competition for status (Bettleheim & Janowitz, 1964). The prejudiced child does not preceive his out-group competitior as just another individual with conflicting prestige needs but as a scheming and unscrupulous representative of his malevolent race. He justifies his aggressive impulses toward the latter by projecting his hostility. His aggressive actions provoke counter-aggression and provide in turn further justification for the original prejudice. Frequently the biased attitudes of in-group members are reinforced by the competitive advantage that accrues when discriminatory practices are applied to their out-group rivals. Direct competition, however, is not necessary to evoke hostile feelings toward members of minority groups. The latter represent convenient and constantly available scapegoats on whom aggression may be displaced and to whom misfortunes may be attributed when frustration from *any* source arises, especially if there is a prior history of inter-group tension. Miller and Bugelski (1948) demonstrated this mechanism experimentally in a *Northeastern* summer camp for boys by showing that the prejudice of the campers toward Mexicans and Japanese increased markedly following the imposition of frustrating conditions by the camp management. Similar findings against Negroes are also found under conditions of mild frustration (Cowan, Landes & Schaet, 1964).

Although the foregoing considerations apply generally to the development of biased attitudes toward minority group members, all children are not equally prone to acquire such attitudes under comparable circumstances. Consistently high intercorrelations among different forms of ethnic and racial prejudice in older children suggest that prejudice is in part an expression of personality structure (Frenkel-Brunswik & Havel, 1953; Gough, Harris, Martin & Edwards, 1950; Horowitz, 1936; Proshansky, 1966). Since expressions of prejudice provide an ample source of ego enhancement and a relatively safe outlet for aggressive impulses, it is hardly surprising that they are more intense among children who are psychologically insecure, hostile, suspicious, punitive, and distrustful of others (Ammons, 1950; Frenkel-Brunswik, 1951; Gough *et al*, 1950; Lyle & Levitt, 1955; Mussen, 1950; Radke, Truger *et al*, 1949; Tabachnick, 1962). Related ways of perceiving, thinking, and ordering knowledge in these children also predispose them toward racial bias. They are relatively incapable of tolerating ambiguity and suspending judgment (Frenkel-Brunswik, 1948; Levitt, 1953), tend to perceive social roles in excessively discontinuous, authoritarian, and hierarchical terms (Frenkel-Brunswik, 1948; 1951; Lyle & Levitt, 1955; Proshansky, 1966), and conform rigidly to conventional values (Frenkel-Brunswik, 1951). In addition, children who are more prejudiced appear to demonstrate lower-level abstract reasoning ability (Kutner, 1958; Kutner & Gordon, 1964).

Direct interracial contact increases racial prejudice in such individuals, whereas it reduces bias in children who are unaggressive and who hold favorable attitudes toward parents and agemates (Mussen, 1950). Under some inter-group conditions intense conflict can be reduced if the children are confronted with a common and compelling problem which demands cooperative versus competitive action (Sherif, 1958). It is important for the development of positive ethnic attitudes, however, that the members of the different ethnic groups are cooperatively engaged in the pursuit of common objectives under *equal-status* conditions or as functional equals (Proshansky,

1966). Strong racial and ethnic prejudice is also characteristic of "authoritarian personalities," i.e., adults who typically were rigidly disciplined as children by highly status-conscious parents, repressed their resentments, and later expressed them in the form of extreme ethnocentrism (Adorno, Frenkel-Brunswik, Levinson & Sanford, 1950). Consistent with these findings is the fact that mothers of highly prejudiced children lean toward authoritarian, punitive methods of control and lack tolerance for annoying aspects of children's behavior (Harris, Gough & Martin, 1950; Lyle & Levitt, 1955). Thus, parents not only transmit racial and ethnic biases directly, but also predispose children toward acquiring such biases by the kind of interpersonal relationships they maintain with them.

Effects on Personality Development. * The problem of investigating the effects of ethnic attitudes on the personality development of minority group children is frequently confounded with the socioeconomic status of that minority group (Pettigrew, 1964b; Proshansky & Newton, 1968). For example, the vast majority of self-identity studies on Negro children have been centered on lower-class populations with comparison groups drawn from the white middle-class (Proshansky & Newton, 1968). When class is held constant, it is clear that Negro lower-class homes have their own unique patterns and problems which are somewhat distinct from their white lower-class counterparts. Broken homes are more common in lower-class Negro families and despite continuing economic growth and declining national unemployment, Negro unemployment rates are more than double that of whites (National Commission on Civil Disorders, 1968). These peculiar findings and others concerning black lower-class populations have led this Commission to conclude that . . .

> . . . What white Americans have never fully understood—but what the Negro can never forget—is that the white society is deeply implicated in the ghetto. White institutions created it, white institutions maintain it, and white society condones it (National Commission on Civil Disorders, 1968, p. 2).

Racial and ethnic bias affects the personality development of both the prejudiced child and the victim of the prejudice. Indirectly, the latter is influenced by the impact of discriminatory practices on his parents' child-rearing attitudes and goals. It is not unreasonable to suppose that racially victimized parents in our culture are more highly prone than non-victimized parents either to (a) perpetuate through overvaluation the omnipotent phase of ego development and place undue stress on ego aggrandizement, or (b) so preoccupy themselves with their own frustrations as to reject their children. Other parents who are discriminated against may encourage attitudes of

---

*Extended treatments of this topic may be found in Deutsch, Katz & Jensen (1968) and Parsons & Clark 1967).

violent counter-aggression, passive sabotage, obsequious submission, or strident counter-chauvinism. As mentioned previously, lower-class Negro families are much more unstable than comparable lower-class white families and most authorities agree that well over 50 per cent of Negro families live at the very lowest level of the lower-class standard (Hill, 1957). In addition, Negro families have a disproportionate number of loosely connected unions (Hill, 1957; Proshansky & Newton, 1968). Illegitimacy is a very common phenomenon and is associated with relatively little social stigma in the Negro community (Cavan, 1959). Homes are more likely to be broken, fathers are more frequently absent, and a matriarchal and negative family atmosphere more commonly prevails (Dai, 1949; Deutsch et al, 1956; Gordon & Shea, 1967; Hill, 1957; Moynihan, 1965; Rainwater, 1966). Thus, the lower-class child is frequently denied the benefits of biparental affection and upbringing; he is often raised by his grandmother or older sister while his mother works to support the family deserted by the father (Deutsch et al, 1956; Moynihan, 1965). When compared with Negro children with intact families, father-absent Negro children feel more victimized and feel they have less control of their environment (Pettigrew, 1964). One consequence of the matriarchical family is an open preference for girls (Proshansky & Newton, 1968). Boys frequently attempt to adjust to this situation by adopting feminine traits and mannerisms (Dai, 1949; Pettigrew, 1964). Also, when the father is present, male identification suffers when the boy is faced with a strong role model while also confronted with an image of his future self (i.e., his father) as an economically inadequate male (Gordon & Shea, 1967; Rainwater, 1966). The Negro female child is in many instances more assertive (Proshansky & Newton, 1968) and, when compared with white children of the same age, is less conforming to pressures (Iscoe, Williams & Harvey, 1964).

Negro family life is even more authoritarian in nature than is that of the lower-class generally. "Children are expected to be obedient and submissive" (M. C. Hill, 1957), and insubordination is suppressed by harsh and often brutal physical punishment (Dai, 1949; Hill, 1957). "Southern Negro culture teaches obedience and respect for authority as a mainspring for survival" (Greenberg & Fane, 1959).

More directly, children who are victims of prejudice soon perceive that they are objects of disparagement and ridicule, and correspondingly experience deflation of self-esteem, shame, humiliation, and embarrassment. * The Negro child inherits an inferior caste status and almost inevitably acquires negative self-esteem that is a realistic reflection of his ego status. Through personal slights, blocked opportunities, and unpleasant contacts

---

* These reactions are more acute in Negro girls than boys (Goff, 1949; Trent, 1953), perhaps because this treatment contrasts more sharply with their more favored and sheltered position in the home. In completely segregated neighborhoods, however, the reverse appears to be true (Deutsch, 1956).

with white persons and with institutionalized symbols of race inferiority (segregated schools, neighborhoods, amusement areas) and more indirectly through the mass media and the reactions of his own family—as mentioned previously—he gradually becomes aware of the social significance of racial membership (Goff, 1949). The Negro child perceives himself as an object of derision and disparagement, as socially rejected by the prestigeful elements of society and as unworthy of succorance and affection (Coles, 1967; Deutsch *et al*, 1956); and having no compelling reasons for not accepting this officially sanctioned negative evaluation of himself, he develops a deeply ingrained negative self-image (Coles, 1967; Bernard, 1958; Proshansky, 1966; Proshansky & Newton, 1968).

In addition to suffering ego-deflation through awareness of his inferior status in society, the Negro child finds it more difficult to satellize and is denied much of the self-esteem advantages of satellization. The derived status that is the principal source of children's self-esteem is all cultures is largely discounted in his case since he can satellize only in relation to superordinate individuals or groups who themselves possess an inferior and degraded status. The middle-class Negro child does not escape this problem since even he does not participate in the cultural mainstream when compared to his white middle-class counterpart (Deutsch & Brown, 1964). Satellization under such conditions not only confers a very limited amount of derived status, but also has deflationary implications for self-esteem. We can understand, therefore, why young Negro children resist identifying with their own racial group, why they seek to shed their identities (Parsons & Clark, 1967), why they more frequently choose white rather than Negro playmates (Stevenson & Stewart, 1958), why they prefer the skin color of the culturally dominant caste (Clark & Clark, 1947; Goodman, 1952), and why they tend to assign negative roles to children of their own race (Coles, 1967; Stevenson & Stewart, 1958). Behaviorally, minority group children react to perceived prejudice with hyperactivity (Goodman, 1952), aggressiveness (Goodman, 1952; Hanmer, 1953), compensatory striving for symbols of prestige, unrealistic self-estimates (Gibby, 1967), lethargy, submission (Pettigrew, 1964), and passive sabotage (National Committee on Civil Disorders, 1968).* Not infrequently racial or ethnic prejudice is employed as an all-inclusive rationalization for personal shortcomings or incompetence. Negro children especially tend to perceive themselves as hopelessly stigmatized for what they are and not for what they do (Wertham, 1952), and since the stigma bears the ethical stamp of the state, it leads to doubts about the legitimacy of the moral authority of society. Sooner or later all minority group children are

---

Some of these reactions are fictionally depicted for Northern urban ghetto in Claude Brown's Manchild in the Promised Land.

confronted in varying degrees with the proposition that they must go through life with the primary status available to them subject to systematic discount on the basis of their racial or ethnic membership.

Only extreme cultural determinists would argue that all children in the incapsulated Negro community necessarily respond in substantially identical ways to the impact of their social environment. Although common factors in cultural conditioning obviously make for many uniformities in personality development, genically determined differences in temperamental and cognitive traits, as well as differential experience in the home and wider culture, account for much idiosyncratic variation. As previously noted, a considerable amount of interindividual variability prevails in the reactions of children to minority group status. Fortunately, sufficient time is available for establishing stable feelings of intrinsic adequacy within the home before the impact of caste, class, and ethnic stratification exerts a catastrophically destructive effect on ego development. Proshansky and Newton (1968) suggest that the Negro needs to view the social system and the white man, not himself, as the source of difficulties. Some of these attitudes are being expressed in contemporary Negro American fiction and autobiography (e.g., Cleaver, 1968; Malcolm X, 1966) and they may be filtering down into the Negro community. Martin Luther King (1968) speaks of a new and emerging self-conception in the Negro American in which he has . . .

> . . . acquired a new self-respect and a new sense of dignity. He lacks the fear which once characterized his behavior. He once used duplicity—a survival technique—but now he has developed an honesty (p. 91).

Depending on whether this foundation of intrinsic self-esteem is built in childhood the psychological consequences of identification with a stigmatized reference group can assume either central or relatively peripheral significance in ego structure. Thus it was found that Negro children who are most self-accepting also tend to exhibit more positive attitudes toward other Negro and white children (Trent, 1953). Presumably, then, the more intrinsic self-esteem a child enjoys the less traumatized he is by prejudice and the less need he has for counter-aggression.

Prejudice against Negroes is deeply rooted in the American culture (Cleaver, 1968; National Commission on Civil Disorders, 1968; Pettigrew, 1964b) and is reinforced by the socioeconomic gain and ego-enhancement it brings to those who manifest it (Bernard, 1958; Hen, 1959; National Committee on Civil Disorders, 1968; Rosen, 1959). The prejudiced child's personality development is also influenced directly by his own attitudes, feelings, and behavior, and indirectly by the interpretation of the social climate of his home and school which may foster prejudice. He exhibits snobbishness, denies human values, ignores the feelings of other human beings,* behaves cruelly and unfairly and is consumed by hostility, suspicion and jealousy. The opportunity for aggression and ego enhancement that prejudice provides diverts him from constructive solutions to his life problems. In yielding abjectly to social pressures and considerations of expediency he has little opportunity to develop moral courage and is deprived of many potentially worthwhile relationships. Finally, he is burdened with a heavy load of irrationality and inconsistency between his actual behavior and professed ideals of democratic tolerance. To preserve the latter as well as his prejudices, he is driven to tortuous rationalization, self-deception, and the erection of logic-tight ideational compartments.

Social Class Environment†

Social classes may be tentatively described as psychosocial groupings of the population of persons whose socioeconomic positions are objectively similar in the main and whose politico-economic interests tend to coincide (Centers, 1947).

Each class, to a greater or lesser extent, has its own ideology, characteristic patterns of overt behavior, and typical ways of rearing children. Thus, within a given social class environment, not only are there distinctive educational and vocational aspirations (Ausubel, 1968; Barow, 1966) and accepted forms of social participation for children (Clausen, 1968) but also characteristic moral values relating to sex, aggression, honesty, responsibility, etc. (Clausen, 1968). In addition, social class membership affects such practical matters as amount of play space and materials available to children and the degree of attention and supervision parents can afford to devote to them. It is important to realize, however, that although home, neighborhood, and peer group environments are reasonably well differentiated on the basis of social class, the official socializing institutions of our society—school, church, courts and social agencies—are middle-class in outlook. Their influence impinges on children of all social strata, reinforcing the teachings of middle-class parents and conflicting in part with the standards that lower-class children learn from parents and neighborhood associates.

American society is, in general, reluctant to recognize social class status differentiations and its presence within our social framework is denied by many (Brown, 1965). The notion of a stratified social system is alien to American democratic traditions and, if accepted at all, is regarded as peculiar to city life or to the remnants of plantation society in the south. Class membership is not a salient feature of the American's way of describing himself, although many occupational references are indirectly related to social class

---

*For an excellent fictional treatment of this as perceived by the black man see: Ralph Ellison's The Invisible Man.

†Reviews on this topic are available. See Bronfenbrenner, 1958; Clausen & Williams, 1961; Sewell, 1961.

definitions (Brown, 1965). When pressed to indicate their class membership, most persons prefer to be identified with the middle-class (Harris, Gough & Martin, 1950). Upper-class individuals, who benefit most from the class system, naturally try to persuade others that no class differences prevail in the United States; and regardless of their actual feelings in the matter, they carefully instruct their children to avoid any open show of superiority or snobbishness that would offend the sensibilities of their social "inferiors."

The fact that social-class status is not manifested by discontinuities between the classes in terms of class consciousness, interaction, and style of life has led some to question its relevance as a scientific concept (Brown, 1965). The utility of the concept of "social class" lies in the fact that it refers to more than simply educational level, or occupation, or any large number of correlated variables (Kohn, 1963):

> It is so useful because it captures the reality that the intricate interplay of all these variables creates in different basic conditions of life at different levels of the social order. Members of different social classes, by virtue of enjoying (or suffering) different conditions of life, come to see the world differently—to develop different conceptions of social reality, different aspirations and hopes and fears, different conceptions of the desirable (Kohn, 1963, p. 471).

Sociologists generally agree that there are three major social classes in our society with two subclasses in each. Social class differences cut across color, ethnic, and religious lines and although less rigid than the latter demarcations are probably more crucial in determining major values and behavior patterns (Davis & Havighurst, 1946). Considerable variability also prevails within each class with respect to income, occupation, educational status, social participation, political beliefs, and aspirations for social mobility. Social stratification is greater in certain regions of the country than in others, in older and urban communities, and in areas characterized by marked racial or ethnic heterogeneity.

Since the criteria of social class membership are necessarily multiple, perfect agreement among the various criteria does not always occur. Hence, considerable difficulty may be encountered in placing particular individuals. In practice, however, this situation arises relatively rarely. Because of the obliteration and even reversal in recent years of the wage differential between manual and white collar labor, family income is often a misleading criterion; greater stress must be placed on such factors as occupation, neighborhood, education, participation in community affairs, social aspirations, and value structure. Perception of social structure also varies with class membership, being more highly differentiated at the upper end of the continuum (Davis, 1944; Kohlberg, 1969). Members of a given class tend to think of themselves as a discriminable group, to maximize differences from and oppose the mobility of groups beneath them, and to minimize distinctions and resent exclusion from groups immediately above them. The latter tendency is presumably reflective of aspirations for higher social status (Davis, 1944).

Interaction between Social Classes. Social classes are not closed systems. The differentiation of values and behavior on the basis of social class membership does not imply complete homogeneity within a given class. Personal interaction between members of different classes, intercommunication of norms, the development of cross-class loyalties, and upward and downward mobility are commonplace phenomena. The American emphasis on "ascribed status" based on performance criteria insures a certain downward and upward mobility between classes (Brown, 1965). At the same time these evidences of overlapping and diffusion do not negate the existence of marked *mean* differences in ideology between classes.

Promoting the downward diffusion of middle-class ideology is the prolonged exposure of all children to school, church, mass media, and youth organizations. Lower-class parents also officially profess middle-class values even though they do not enforce them consistently (Havighurst & Taba, 1949). Social mobility is enhanced by the continuing trend toward higher working-class incomes and a wider dispersion of secondary school and college education. The preservation of class identities, on the other hand, is maintained through the medium of "restricted learning environments" (Ausubel, 1968). Purely on a physical basis, social distance between upper and lower classes is enforced by neighborhood segregation, large estates, nurses, governesses, private boarding schools, and chauffeured automobiles. Interaction is also discouraged by parental pressures and admonitions and by the gradual acquisition of class loyalties. "Taboos upon participation outside of one's status level" undoubtedly originate from above downwards but soon become retaliatory and reciprocal. They are reinforced by snobbishness and condescension from above and by resentment from persons at or below one's class level.

As segregation of children by social class is prolonged, its effects become increasingly irreversible. The longer a lower-class child is deprived of *intimate* contact with middle-class children the less opportunity he has of acquiring their values and sanctioned patterns of behavior. To rise above his class he must associate consistently with his "betters" and endure their patronizing ways as well as the outspoken resentment of his social peers.

Younger children from lower-class homes who have pleasing personalities and are willing to conform to middle-class standards may often find a measure of peripheral acceptance in middle-class groups. With the approach of adolescence, as class lines are accentuated under the impact of increasing parental and peer group pressures, this type of idiosyncratic social mobility becomes increasingly more difficult.

Perception of Social Class Differences. Development of the ability to perceive social class differences illustrates the general process of perceptual learning or cognitive maturation (see pp. 554-555) as applied to interpersonal and social phenomena. It involves growth in the capacity for abstraction and generalization, increased familiarity and differentiation of the perceptual field, and greater objectivity and less autism in the operation of judgment. Children gradually learn the more relevant symbols of social status and become more precise and discriminating in their awareness of their own and others' class membership (Jahoda, 1959). Perception of occupational differences tends to develop first in all children; later these are linked with differences in wealth, income and, in the case of middle-class children, style of life (Jahoda, 1959). First-graders tend both to perceive themselves as rich and to overestimate the opulence of their classmates. Fourth-graders are somewhat less euphoric in this regard, and sixth- and eighth-graders are still more conservative (Stendler, 1949). Paralleling the trend among adults, both poor and wealthy children tend to identify with the middle-class; the poor overrate their parents' financial status and the rich underrate it (Stendler, 1949). Although awareness of poverty is generally greater among lower- than among middle-class children, what is physically proximal to the child (e.g., squalor, overcrowding) has not always been found to be psychologically salient. With increasing age, as pressures from adults mount to maintain greater social class distance, awareness of class distinctions concomitantly increases (Meek, 1940).

Class Differences in Training, Personality and Behavior. A review of child-training techniques during the past twenty-five years indicates that differences in these practices between middle and lower-class families are steadily diminishing (Bronfenbrenner, 1958). The results of specific practices by one or both of the parents often reveals contradictory results. Davis & Havighurst (1946) indicate that middle-class mothers supervise and restrict more stringently the child's activities outside the home. At the same time, several studies indicate less restrictiveness in middle-class mothers (Bayley & Schaefer, 1960; Sears, Maccoby & Levin, 1957; White, 1957) or no difference generally between social classes in their socialization practices (Littman, Moore & Pierce-Jones, 1957). The fact that the data for these studies were gathered at different periods of time in various parts of the country may provide a few of the reasons for the discrepancies (Waters & Crandall, 1964). Lower-class parents, in controlling their children, resort to more authoritarian methods, applying more forceful and punitive methods (Bayley & Schaefer, 1960; Bronfenbrenner, 1958; Sears, Maccoby & Lenin, 1957; Waters & Crandall, 1964; White, 1957), whereas middle-class parents more often resort to love-oriented techniques such as reasoning, isolation and elicitation of guilt (Hoffman, 1963; Sears, Maccoby & Lenin, 1957).

Authoritarian control, as used by lower-class parents, tends to be relatively ineffective because of inconsistency, the long time lag between its administration and the occurrence of misbehavior, and the frequently poor example set by parents in matters of responsibility and control of aggressive and sexual impulses (Bandura & Walters, 1963; Davis, 1943). As working-class children grow older their parents grant greater freedom from control and supervision (Clausen & Williams, 1963). Division of child-rearing responsibilities appears to differ along social class lines. The working-class mother expects her husband to take a more salient role in the imposition of constraints, whereas middle-class mothers expect husbands to be less controlling and more supportive (Kohn & Carroll, 1960).

According to some researchers (Maas, 1951; Walters, Connor & Zunich, 1964) the greater pressures and restrictions on social exploration imposed upon middle-class children are compensated for in part by the opportunity for more open, spontaneous, and flexible psychological communication with peers and adults. In contrast, the interpersonal relationships of lower-class children are characterized as hierarchical, absolutistic, rigidly structured, and by dependent attitudes toward contemporaries and psychological distance from adults. Thus, the middle-class father is more available as an instrumental companion and authority (especially for the son) when compared with working-class fathers (Bronfenbrenner, 1958). Moreover, there is a greater emphasis in middle-class families on the instrumental companion aspects of the father while playing down his authority role (Clausen & Williams, 1963). At the same time, middle-class mothers are taking over some of the authoritarian functions (Clausen & Williams, 1963).

Middle-class parents place greater stress than lower-class parents on the maintenance of high aspirations for primary status and the achievement of high levels of academic and vocational success, financial independence and social recognition (Ausubel, 1968; Borow, 1966). To ensure the attainment of these ego enhancement goals, they encourage the development of supportive personality traits. These include (a) habits of initiative and responsibility (Aberle & Naegele, 1952); (b) the "deferred gratification pattern" of hard work, self-denial, long-range planning, high frustration tolerance, relentless self-criticism, thrift, prolonged education, vocational training, and economic dependence on parents (Davis, 1943; Havighurst & Taba, 1949; Kohn, 1959a, Kohn, 1959b; Renners, Horton & Lysgaard, 1952; Schneider & Lysgaard, 1953); (c) emphasis on punctuality, orderliness, honesty, respect for property, good manners, religious observance, and participation in civic affairs, curiosity for boys, consideration for girls (Davis, 1941, 1943; Davis & Havighurst, 1946; Havighurst, 1949; Hess, 1969; Kohn, 1959a). (d) respect (rather than fear) of adult authority and conformity to conventional standards of behavior (Griffiths, 1962; Kluckhohn & Kluckhohn,

1947; Pope, 1953; Schneider & Lysgaard, 1953). Since the majority of these traits are coextensive with the attributes of ego maturity in our culture, it seems plausible to hypothesize that maturational failure would be less common in middle- than in lower-class individuals. The latter should achieve earlier desatellization and volitional independence, should obtain a larger portion of their derived status from age mates, and should bear a lighter burden of impulse frustration and anxiety.

Middle-class children are willing to internalize these ego status goals and to acquire the necessary supportive traits because they perceive the eventual rewards of striving and self-denial as real and attainable for persons of their status. They can both observe the achievement of these rewards by their own parents and experience an early taste of them in their own family, neighborhood, and school life. Their efforts are encouraged by parental example, reinforced by the standards of school, church, and peer group, and sustained by the anxiety of forfeiting the advantages of present and future status should they fail in completing these tasks. In the case of lower-class children all of these considerations operate in the opposite direction.

Urban-Rural Differences

Rural life differs from urban life in many ways that affect the personality development of the child. It should not be imagined, however, that modern rural society is in any way comparable to preliterature cultures. In fact, many of the differences that have existed until relatively recently are being quickly eroded under the impact of mass media, levels of living, educational opportunities, and the fact that size of families continues to become equalized for rural and urban families (Burchinal, Hawkes & Gardner, 1957).

The rural mother tends to be more casual and permissive than the urban mother in her infant care routines and to place less emphasis on orderliness and cleanliness (Leninger & Murphy, 1946; Lewis, 1947). The pressure of farm work does not enable her to devote herself as single-mindedly to the care of her children. On the other hand, older farm children share more in the care of babies, and the father is a more constant and integral member of the household. Because of fewer environmental hazards, parents need not issue as many or as arbitrary prohibitory commands (Leninger & Murphy, 1946). The wider spaces and the lesser density of population affects the play patterns of the rural child in various self-evident ways and fosters greater communion with nature. Exposed less to mass media and other children his imaginative productions are necessarily structured more from within.

The rural home plays a more prominent and exclusive role than the urban home in socializing children, in interpreting the culture to them, and in enforcing the moral code. Rural parents are displaced more gradually as the principal source of their children's values and are devalued less rapidly than urban parents. Their children presumably desatellize more slowly and less prominently through the mechanism of resatellization to peers and parent surrogates. In general rural children live in a world of less rapid social change and are able to relate to a more stable and orthodox set of moral and religious values (Leninger & Murphy, 1946). Restrictions upon social experience of rural youth have an adverse impact on the range and ambitiousness of their occupational goals (Borow, 1966). Urban middle-class children are also much more competitive than their rural counterparts (Madsen, 1967).

The opportunity for rural children to participate in adult tasks and to make a more responsible contribution to the economy creates somewhat less discontinuity between their interest and activity concerns and those of adults than is typical of urban communities. Thus, the rural child is less dependent on school and peer group for his primary status than is the urban child. At the fifth grade level, rural children are more self-reliant than urban children (Werner, 1957). The significance of this difference, however, should not be overestimated. Many of the tasks he performs are highly routine and subordinate chores that contribute little to any real sense of responsibility or volitional independence. Furthermore, for both rural and urban children, derived status constitutes a much more central component of self-esteem than does primary status, and in both instances is chiefly available from parents.

IMPACT OF THE SCHOOL ON PERSONALITY DEVELOPMENT

Although the family constitutes an ideal unit for guiding and nurturing the child toward participation in the larger social life, it cannot impart the technical knowledge required by our own complex institutions (Clausen, 1968). In addition to its special functions of imparting knowledge and intellectual skills, the school in our society shares in many of the socializing and enculturative responsibilities exclusively exercised by the family in other cultures. It not only participates in the transmission of our particular cultural ideology and psychosocial traits, but also plays an important role in the development of ego status and ego maturity goals and in the acquisition of acceptable standards of social behavior. For all of these functions it is admirably suited by virtue of the prolonged and intensive contact it maintains with children during the formative years of their development.

School constitutes the first major source of primary status available to the majority of children in our culture. As a result of initial school attendance they acquire heretofore unrealized feelings of bigness and importance (Stendler & Young, 1950). Academic success not only reinforces objective learnings but also leads to ego enhancement and increased self-confidence. Chronic school failure, with its associated emotional trauma and social rejection, induces profound ego deflation (Pettigrew, 1967a; Sandin, 1944). The opportunity for acquiring primary status in school is somewhat greater for girls than for boys because of their superior verbal ability and greater conformity to adult authority, and because school success is less ambivalently prized by their peer group.

In the school environment the child is inescapably thrust into competition for the solitary kind of primary status (academic proficiency) available in the classroom. He is coerced by prevailing social pressures for high achievement to aspire to at least the class mean of academic performance. Middle-class children are prepared by their parents for this new experience; mothers of lower-class children, however, present the school as a much more threatening and unrewarding place (Hess & Shipman, 1967). In many instances the aims and demands of the teacher are strange and beyond the initial capabilities of some children and the teacher is seen as hostile and humiliating (Clausen, 1968). The objective failure of the low achiever is intensified subjectively by the forced maintenance of unrealistically high levels of aspiration and is only mitigated by the compensatory value of aiming high and conforming to the motivational norm. The only other alternative is ego disinvolvement from the competitive school situation and the setting of aspirational levels that are sufficiently low to guarantee empty feelings of success (see pp. 285 and 386). Hence, early in his school career anxiety becomes an important motivational spur to learning; and both goal tenacity and the affective properties of subject matter become less dependent on objective performance than on degree of ego-involvement and semester grades (Ausubel, 1968).

Although the socialization aims and activities of the teacher tend to overlap with those of the parents in the early elementary grades (Clausen, 1968), nevertheless, school attendance facilitates desatellization by providing both a major source of primary status and suitable adults (teachers) in relation to whom resatellization can occur (see p. 272). Under these circumstances the home source of derived status becomes less precious. Furthermore, parents become devalued and lose part of their halo of omniscience in the eyes of many children as teachers take over a substantial portion of the parental role of propounding truth and moral values (Stendler & Young, 1950). Counteracting the current fetish of permissiveness in middle-class homes, the school's greater demands for conformity to adult authority and for more mature behavior has two kinds of effects. It de-emphasizes volitional independence, initiative, and spontaneity in children (Stendler & Young, 1950) but brings about improvement in such aspects of ego maturity as executive independence and responsibility (Anderson & Brewer, 1946).

School does not affect the personality development of all children in the same way. Although the new emphasis on primary status and the devaluation of parents induce greater change in the satellizer's than in the non-satellizer's ego structure, two factors tend to limit the significance of this change. First, the primary status available in school plays only a relatively subsidiary role in relation to the derived status he obtains at home. Second, even though the teacher's valuation of the child is more contingent than the parent's upon satisfactory performance, the satellizer still attempts in part to establish an emotionally dependent, satellizing relationship to her. Her approval confers derived as well as primary status. The non-satellizer merely transfers his quest for primary status from home to school, and reacts to the teacher as an emulatory model and as the person to be propitiated if such status is to be won. Hence subservience to her is regarded more as expedientially necessary than as desirable, and her approval becomes important mostly as a symbol of academic success. Because his self-esteem is more completely dependent than the satellizer's on acquiring primary status, he is more anxious about his school progress and is less free to lower his level of aspiration in the face of failure. For reasons designated elsewhere (see p. 272), entrance into school significantly increases the self-esteem of many rejected children but almost invariably has an ego deflationary effect on overvalued children.

Social Class. Since the school reinforces middle-class values and often comes into opposition with lower-class values, it is commonly a source of ego enhancement for middle-class children and of failure, conflict, and ego deflation for lower-class children (Clausen, 1968; McCandless, 1967; Proshansky & Newton, 1968). Most teachers in American schools have middle-class backgrounds (Clausen, 1968; Glidewell and associates, 1966); McCandless, 1968). But even if they do originate from other social class environments, they still tend to identify with the school's implicit mission of encouraging the development of middle-class values (Clausen, 1968). Thus, quite apart from the issue of whether this mission is appropriate and desirable for our culture, teachers find it difficult to understand the goals, values, and behavior of pupils from other social class backgrounds. Normal ethnocentric bias predisposes them to believe that their own class values are self-evidently true and proper, and that deviations therefrom necessarily reflect wayward-ness. On the other hand, since middle-class boys and girls behave in accord-ance with their expectations and accept the standards of the school, teachers are usually as prejudiced in their favor as they are prejudiced against children from other social strata.

Understanding the background and values of lower-class children does not, of course, imply acceptance of their attitudes and behavior when these are in conflict with the objectives and standards of the school. It merely implies sufficient awareness of relevant background factors to make possible intelli-gent interpretation of the behavior of lower-class pupils and the avoidance of discriminatory attitudes and practices towards them.

In addition to their natural inclinations to reward conformity to middle-class ideology, teachers are influenced by other pressures, both explicit and implicit, in giving preferential treatment to pupils whose families enjoy high social status. Middle- and upper-class parents are active in civic and school affairs, members of school boards, and leaders in parent-teacher associations. Even if no explicit pressures are exerted, teachers and school administrators, knowing on what side their bread is buttered, are disposed to see things their way. Teachers are also intimidated somewhat from taking action against refractory but popular members of leading student cliques who, when supported by their clique-mates, may be surprisingly rebellious (Hollingshead, 1949). Under such circumstances, many teachers are reluctant to force a showdown that would provoke the enmity of pupils who are influential in their own right as well as through the position of their parents.

Teacher-Pupil Interaction. The school as a socializing agency receives far too little collaboration and feedback from other segments of the community and more than its fair share of criticism for failing to achieve its idealized standards (Lippitt, 1968). At the same time, the school has failed to utilize the resources of social research and theory to improve its functioning as a sub-system of the community (Lippitt, 1968). The school provides a large percentage of the occasions in which children interact with each other and with adults and, thus, plays an important role in the socialization of interpersonal behavior. It constitutes the major locus of operation for peer group activities under adult supervision. Under its auspices children learn much of their social skills, age, sex, class, and status roles, and adult sanctioned norms of aggression, competition, cooperation and fair play. The teacher also serves as a role model for the learning of interpersonal attitudes (Proshansky, 1966; Proshansky & Newton, 1968). Children, for example, quickly assimilate her attitudes toward particular children and racial and ethnic groups. Children praised randomly by the teacher are perceived as more competent by their peers (Flanders & Havumaki, 1960). In one experiment they even mimicked her prejudicial behavior toward an artificially created underprivileged sub-group (Thompson, 1940). There is also some evidence that the teacher exerts a more profound influence than the parent in the socializing of moral and academic values (Glidewell *et al*, 1966). Caution must be observed in interpreting these findings, however, since the studies were conducted in the classroom and the teacher's behavior may be more salient there than it would have been in the home (Glidewell *et al*, 1966).

An equally significant outcome of school experience is the learning of a typical pattern of volitional dependence on extrafamilial adults and of conformity to their authority. For purposes of optimal ego maturation in our culture, it is important to achieve a proper balance between realistic acknowledgement of children's biosocial dependence and need for external direction, on the one hand, and their actual capacity for exercising initiative, responsibility, and self-discipline, on the other. Although the school has been subject to changes in structure due to ideological and technical change, the prevailing educational milieu still leans too far toward the traditional "adult rule-child obedience" pattern (Anderson & Brewer, 1946; Cunningham *et al*, 1951; Glidewell *et al*, 1966) in which obedience and conformity are perceived by both teachers and pupils as ends in themselves (Biber & Lewis, 1949; Goodman, 1964). This type of atmosphere stifles initiative, spontaneity, and freedom of reality testing sufficiently to impair the development of volitional independence and of critical, independent thinking (Hunt, 1964; Minushin, 1964). The early experimental studies of authoritarian social climates in children's recreational groups by Lewin, Lippitt and White (1939) point to many socially undesirable effects on group morale and solidarity. These include generalized apathy; aggressive and dominative behavior toward peers; displaced aggression in the form of scapegoating; submissive, placatory, and attention-demanding behavior toward the adult leader; less "we-feeling," frustration tolerance, and task-oriented behavior; and the break-down of discipline when adult supervision is removed. The observation that students give the teacher what she wants (Henry, 1957) and that students perceive her as a "checker-upper" rather than a person to learn from (Ojemann & Snider, 1959) is indicative of an authoritarian school climate.

Studies such as these only suggest that excessively autocratic methods of handling children's groups in our culture have less beneficial effects on group morale than do more democratic procedures. They give no support to maximally permissive (laissez-faire) approaches that advocate freedom from discipline as an end in itself and removal of all externally imposed direction and restraints. Democracy is no more coextensive with laissez-faire methods than the realistic employment of necessary teacher controls is synonymous with autocracy. The need for discipline is no less urgent in the school than in the home (see p. 319). As a matter of fact, observation of laissez-faire school climates shows that they lead to "confusion, insecurity and keen competition for power among group members"; aggressive pupils become ruthless and retiring pupils become even more withdrawn (Cunningham, 1951). Children fail to learn the normative demands of society and how to operate within the limits these set, do not succeed in learning how to deal effectively with adults, and develop unrealistic perceptions of adult social structure. Other unfavorable effects of excessive permissiveness (under-domination) have been discussed elsewhere (see pp. 279 and 318).

The characteristics of democratic discipline that are appropriate in the home (see pp. 320-321) are also applicable to the school situation. A democratic climate of teacher-pupil interaction has been achieved in the classroom by emphasizing respect for the dignity and feelings of pupils as persons, by avoiding techniques of ridicule and intimidation, and by employing various devices that enable children to share in the planning and management of the curriculum and in the regulation of pupil activities and discipline. Although the distribution of the teacher's power and acceptance induces more social independence and flexibility of thought (Minuchin, 1964) this should not be construed as a laissez-faire group structure. A summary of the most recent research attests to the desirable outcomes of "democratically" generated group atmospheres (Glidewell et al, 1966). Glidewell's et al, (1966) review indicates that an atmosphere* where the teacher delegates part of her power to her pupils and generates a wide dispersion of emotional acceptance is found to . . .

. . . (a) stimulate more pupil-to-pupil interaction; (b) reduce interpersonal conflicts and anxieties; (c) increase mutual esteem, rapport, self-esteem; (d) induce a wider dispersion and flexibility of peer social power as manifested by a greater tolerance for divergent opinions in the initial phases of decision-making and a greater convergence of opinion in the late phases of decision making; (e) increase moral responsibility, self-initiated work, independence of opinion, and responsibility in implementing accepted assignments (p. 232).

Although these procedures are not directly related to academic achievement (Clausen, 1968), they do not necessarily ignore the impact of prior conditioning to anxiety reduction and other extrinsic motivations in the learning situation, and do not seek unrealistically to predicate all learning activity upon inherent desire for knowledge. When properly paced and geared to actual capacities for self-determination such procedures have been successful in improving group morale and in facilitating the development of mature, responsible, and realistically grounded volitional independence (Davis, 1949; Lewin, Lippitt & White, 1939). They can encourage greater personal responsibility in and group support for the teacher and, in some instances, tested achievement has also been enhanced (Clausen, 1968). By contrast, authoritarian teachers and those who wield their power to enhance popularity are unlikely to achieve solid group support for their educational objectives (Clausen, 1968).

Teachers' perceptions of and reactions to pupils depend both on their own personality traits and on the characteristics of the particular children (Hunt & Joyce, 1967). The extent to which they are generally tolerant of the annoying qualities of pupils' behavior varies inversely with their tendency to be authoritarian (McCandless, 1967). Low concrete teachers with more abstract belief systems, tend to be less dictatorial, less punitive, and more

---

*A more extensive discussion on research methods in children's groups may be found in Thompson (1966).

resourceful in developing different teaching environments for individual differences in their pupils (Harvey *et al*, 1966, 1968; Hunt & Joyce, 1967). The highly inequitable but consistent manner in which teachers distribute approval indicates that they react differentially to various aspects of children's personality and behavior (de Groat & Thompson, 1949). The classroom atmosphere in elementary school tends to be clearly oriented to the interests and dispositions of middle-class children and especially middle-class girls (Clausen, 1968). The social structure of the class is perceived by children as early as the second grade (Glidewell *et al*, 1966) and is partially contingent on the teacher's approval or disapproval (Flanders & Havumaki, 1960). For the most part, pupils who receive much teacher approval tend to rank highly on intelligence, academic achievement, and personality adjustment (de Groat & Thompson, 1949; Glidewell *et al*, 1966). Positive perceptions of teachers' feelings by the pupil are significantly related to academic achievement and more desirable classroom behavior (Proshansky & Newton, 1968). The marginal status of teachers, which is generally "upwardly mobile," makes it difficult for them to sympathize with lower-status children (Clausen, 1966; Proshansky & Newton, 1968). Even Negro teachers may express marked hostility toward Negro children because they are a reminder of their past and a threat to their newly won security (Proshansky & Newton, 1968). Teachers vary considerably in their ability to perceive the sociometric status of their pupils (Gage, Leavitt & Stone, 1955; Gronlund, 1960). In general, however, their perceptions, which are reasonably accurate in the middle grades (Ausubel, Schiff & Gasser, 1952; Bonney, 1947; Gage *et al*, 1955; Gronlund, 1950) become increasingly less accurate as the latter progress through the grades (Ausubel *et al*, 1952; Moreno, 1934); as might be expected they tend to overrate the popularity of children they prefer and vice-versa (Glidewell *et al*, 1966).

How pupils perceive and react to teachers also depends on the respective personality traits of the interacting parties. These perceptions define and limit the kinds of interpersonal relationships that can be established in the school. In general teachers are seen as playing three major kinds of roles—friends, opponents, and manipulators of status in learning situations (Cunningham, 1951). As friends they are "older and wiser" persons, helpful counselors, heroes, givers of security, and occasionally "pals." As opponents they are cast as "kill-joys" who arbitrarily interfere with legitimate pleasures, as "enemies" to be "fought" and "outwitted," and as demons of power to be feared, respected and placated. In the learning aspects of the school situation they are perceived as "necessary evils" in the acquisition of knowledge, efficient organizers in the direction of work projects, "stepping stones" to future status rewards, dispensers of approval and disapproval, and as moral arbiters who can absolve from guilt as well as point the accusing finger (Cunningham, 1951).

The affective reactions of pupils to teachers are as much a function of personality characteristics of the latter as of their teaching skills. Teachers who are warm and understanding tend to gratify the affiliative drive of pupils. This is particularly important for the many elementary-school pupils who seek in teachers a parent surrogate and a source of acceptance and approval indicative of derived status. It becomes less important in secondary school and university when affiliative drive constitutes a less salient motivation for learning than the growing need for ego enhancement and earned status. The warm teacher can be identified with easily by pupils. He provides emotional support, is sympathetically disposed toward pupils, and accepts them as persons. Characteristically he distributes much praise and encouragement and tends to interpret pupil behavior as charitably as possible. He is relatively unauthoritarian and is sensitive to pupils' feelings and affective responses. For all of these reasons he tends to score high on the Minnesota Teacher Attitude Inventory, which is keyed in this direction, and to promote more wholesome self-concepts in elementary-school pupils (Spaulding, 1963). Warm teachers tend to be rated more favorably by principals, supervisors, pupils and other observers (Cook et al, 1951; McGee, 1955; Ryans, 1960; Solomon et al, 1964).

At all grade levels teacher warmth is less important for pupils whose motivational orientation to learning is largely cognitive or ego enhancing rather than affiliative. For such pupils, liking of a teacher is not related to the latter's degree of warmth or to his score on the Minnesota Teacher Attitude Inventory (Della-Piana & Gage, 1955). In sharp contrast, pupils who are highly concerned with their interpersonal relationship to and feelings for a teacher tend to like teachers who are characterized by warmth (i.e., who make high scores on the Minnesota Teacher Attitude Inventory), and to dislike teachers who are not.

As a result of identifying with a warm teacher, a pupil is obviously more disposed to assimilate his values. Theoretically, also, he should be more highly motivated to learn and thus to attain a higher level of academic achievement. But the evidence tends to be equivocal on this point (Flanders, 1960; Medley & Mitzel, 1959).

Classroom Interaction and Racial Desegregation in the Schools. * All of the problems of teacher-pupil and pupil-pupil interactions associated with lower-class membership are further complicated when compounded with America's racial problem. Although "Black Americans" are represented in all social class strata, they are particularly concentrated at the lowest social class rung (Proshansky & Newton, 1968). Their relatively immobile position in

Recent normative findings, interpretive articles, and theorizing may be found in the following sources: The Coleman Report (Coleman and associates, 1966); the United States Commission on Civil Rights (1967); an edited volume by Deutsch, Katz & Jensen, 1968; and the Nebraska Symposium on Motivation (Levine, 1967), especially articles by Katz and Pettigrew.

America's class stratification has been comparable to an almost caste-like status (Brown, 1965). We have already reviewed some of the debilitating effects of chronic low-status group membership on the personality development of the Negro child. The social structure whose stratification habitually restricts a subgroup from power, respect, and opportunity within it leads not only to personality devaluation but also to deficits in executive independence and academic achievement (Brewster-Smith, 1968).

> Restriction of opportunity not only blights hope; it excludes the person from the chance to acquire the knowledge and skill that would in turn enable him to surmount barriers to effectiveness. Contempt and withheld respect may lead to "self-hatred' . . . and may necessitate debilitating postures of self-defense. Absence of power entails general vulnerability and creates dependence. When opportunities are offered without a sharing of power, we have paternalism, which undercuts respect, accentuates dependence, and breeds a lurking resentment that the powerful are likely to condemn in righteousness as ingratitude (Brewster-Smith, 1968, p. 313).

It is within the confines of these very complex problems that the recent emphasis on desegregation in the schools has evolved as one avenue of solution. *Educational desegregation* is a politico-legal concept referring to the elimination of racial separation within the school system (Katz, 1968). Its enactment rests partly on the assumption that good education is a partial solution to the elimination of the caste status of the Negro in the American society. It is clear that segregated schooling along racial lines has led to lower academic achievement among Negro children (Coleman *et al*, 1966; United States Commission on Civil Rights, 1967). A survey of American public school systems indicates that Negroes' achievement test scores are one standard deviation below white averages (Coleman *et al*, 1966). Moreover, the social-class climate of the school is markedly correlated with achievement test scores; children of all backgrounds do better when they are in a predominantly middle-class milieu (Coleman *et al*, 1966). The bulk of the research findings argues for desegregated education, yet despite the publicity there is relatively little research on the effects of school desegregation on black and white children (Proshansky, 1966; Proshansky & Newton, 1968; Katz, 1968).

Before Negroes can assume their rightful place in a desegregated American culture, important changes in the ego structure of Negro children must first take place. They must shed feelings of inferiority and self-derogation, acquire feelings of self-confidence and racial pride, develop realistic aspirations for occupations requiring greater education and training, and develop the personality traits necessary for implementing these aspirations. Such changes in ego structure can be accomplished in two different but complementary ways. First, all manifestations of the Negro's inferior and segregated caste status must be swept away—in education, housing, employment, religion, travel, and exercise of civil rights. This in itself will enhance the Negro's self-esteem and open new opportunities for self-fulfillment. Second, through various measures instituted in the family, school, and community, character structure, levels of aspiration, and actual standards of achievement can be altered in ways that will further enhance his self-esteem and make it possible for him to take advantage of new opportunities.

Desegregation in the schools, of course, is no panacea for the Negro child's personality difficulties. It is a necessary but not a sufficient condition for integration—integration involving in addition to a racial mix, a climate of interracial acceptance (Pettigrew, 1967b). In many instances, it tends to create new problems of adjustment, particularly when it follows in the wake of serious community conflict. In addition, it cannot quickly overcome various long-standing handicaps which Negro children bring with them to school "such as their cultural impoverishment, their helplessness or apathy toward learning, and their distrust of the majority group and their middle-class teachers;" nor can it compensate for "oversized classes, inappropriate curricula, inadequate counseling services, or poorly trained or demoralized teachers" (Bernard, 1958, p. 158). Even where teachers are not deeply prejudiced, their unidimensional view of the "culturally deprived" child* coupled with low expectations for academic performance may lead to a self-fulfilling prophesy due to their low expectations (Rosenthal, 1968; Rosenthal & Jacobson, 1968). Experimental studies on teachers' expectations of pupil performance indicate that when teachers expect that certain children will show greater intellectual development, those children do show greater intellectual development, especially in the lower grades (Rosenthal, 1968; Rosenthal & Jacobson, 1968). Clark (1965) believes that expectation is a key component of the deprivation that affects ghetto children in their school learning experience. Further complications may confront the bright Negro child because of the teacher's low expectations. For example, Rosenthal & Jacobson (1968) found that children who were not expected to show any growth in intellectual development were less favorably regarded the more they gained intellectually. Jonathan Kozol's *Death at an Early Age* gives several personal accounts of this type of teacher response made to ghetto children in the Boston public school system.

In spite of these hazards, desegregation remains an important and indispensable first step in the reconstitution of Negro personality, since the school is the most strategically placed social institution for effecting rapid change both in ego structure and in social status. A desegregated school offers the Negro child his first taste of social equality and his first experience

*Hunt & Dopyera (1966) argue that the description of the "culturally deprived" has emphasized his fairly uniform cognitive style in a rather oversimplified and global fashion. Their own assessment of "conceptual level" indicates a considerable amount of variability within lower-class populations.

of first-class citizenship. He can enjoy the stimulating effect of competition with white children and can use them as realistic yardsticks in measuring his own worth and chances for academic and vocational success. The inter-racial classroom also provides both Negro and white children with the possi-bilities of cross-racial evaluation, and a middle-class milieu furnishes higher comparison levels for achievement and aspirations. Higher levels of achieve-ment are especially influential for disadvantaged Negro children whose working referents would otherwise be much lower levels (Pettigrew, 1967b). The Coleman Report (1966) indicates that Negro children in more than half-white classrooms score higher on achievement tests than other Negro children, this result occurring most strongly in those situations where inter-racial schooling occurs in the early grades. In conditions where desegregation is graduated, it seems desirable to begin the process at the lowest grades where Negro children have smaller handicaps and where unfavorable racial attitudes are least strongly learned (Katz, 1968).

It is also reasonable to anticipate that white children will be prejudiced and continue to discriminate against their Negro classmates long after desegregation accords them equal legal status in the educational system. Attitudes toward Negroes in the South, for example, are remarkably stable, even in periods of rapid social change involving desegregation (Young *et al*, 1960), and are not highly correlated with anti-Semitic or other ethnocentric trends (Greenberg *et al*, 1957; Kelly, Ferson & Holtzman, 1958; Prothro, 1952). Prejudice against Negroes is deeply rooted in the American culture and is continually reinforced both by the socio-economic gain and by the vicarious ego enhancement it brings to those who manifest it (Bernard, 1958; Herr, 1959; Rosen, 1959). It is hardly surprising, therefore, that racial prejudice is most pronounced in lower social class groups (Westle, 1952), and that these groups constitute the hard core or resistance to desegregation (Killian & Haer, 1958; Tumin, 1958). Increased physical contact *per se* between white and Negro children does little to reduce prejudice (Neprash, 1958; Webster, 1961), but more intimate personal interaction under favor-able circumstances significantly reduces social distance between the two groups (Kelly *et al*, 1958; Mann, 1959; Yarrow *et al*, 1958).

Political Socialization and the School. * A topic that was virtually ignored in child psychology literature until recently, is the development of citizenship and political behavior in children (Hess & Torney, 1967). The American society has not, in the past, been characterized by any notable degree of political involvement and participation by most of its citizens (Brim, 1967). The whole process of political socialization involves the learning of political norms and behaviors acceptable to an ongoing political system in order to

---

*See the Harvard Educational Review, *Vol. 38, 1968 for an extended discussion.*

guarantee intergenerational stability in that system (Sigel, 1965). Rapid social and political changes in the contemporary world and their corresponding precipitation of instability in ongoing political structures have made this topic an important area in child development research (Sigel, 1965). The child's comprehension of political institutions is limited by many factors, one of which is his initial lack of cognitive sophistication. His limited social experience at six makes it difficult for him to clearly differentiate such concepts as "town" and "country" (Jahoda, 1963a). Conceptions of "nationality" are slowly differentiated during the elementary school years (Jahoda, 1963b), although ideological conflicts between certain nations are associated with earlier ideological differentiation (e.g., American and Russian flags) (Lawson, 1963). Political figures enjoy a choice status with children, American children viewing their nation, government and its representatives as wise, powerful, and benevolent (Greenstein, 1965; Hess, 1968, Hess & Easton, 1960; Hess & Torney, 1967). Uncritical, favorable attitudes toward representatives, however, decrease with age (Hess, 1969; Hess & Torney, 1967). Sex and I.Q. differences are apparent, boys acquiring attitudes more rapidly than girls and having more interest in political matters (Hess & Torney, 1967). More intelligent children regard the political system in less absolutistic terms and have more reservations about the competence and intentions of governmental figures and institutions (Hess & Torney, 1967). As the child grows older, his confidence in his ability to affect the Government increases but this increase is much more marked in middle-class children (Hess, 1968; Hess & Torney, 1967).*

These rather idealistic and fantasied ideas about government are encouraged by the socialization procedures of both home and school (Hess, 1968; Hess & Torney, 1967; Sigel, 1965). With the complex problems facing the American political system (e.g., racial, poverty, etc.), it is exigent that the school take a more active and realistic role in the child's development of more sophisticated political attitudes and behaviors:

Political socialization in the school is a form of political indoctrination, designed to perpetuate the dominant values of the present system. In the past, the schools have served an acculturating, melting-pot function, providing common allegiance and values to bring together in a single country immigrant groups from different ethnic and national backgrounds. It now seems, however, that the ethnic and cultural differences within the nation cannot be easily blended into unity. Divergences and inequities which have been ignored, particularly with respect to Negroes in the society, are dramatically apparent. It is evident to many citizens that the picture of unity, equality, and freedom that is so often presented is distorted, over-simplified, and, to a degree, false. Indeed, political

---

*Jennings & Niemi (1968) note the urban and white bias of the samples gathered. From our previous discussion of Negro identity, we would expect even more depressed confidence in these children about influencing political institutions.

socialization in the schools may have created an attitude of complacency, a willingness to accept the image of unity and freedom—as well as the actions of the government—and, in so doing, it may have contributed to feeling of disillusionment and the consequent climate of protest (Hess, 1968, p. 529).

THE SIGNIFICANCE OF SEX IN CHILD DEVELOPMENT*

Although this century has seen a broadening in the "range of prevailing attitudes toward social sex roles for men and women and sex-appropriate behavior for boys and girls" (Minuchin, 1965), it is nevertheless true that, in spite of these changing cultural standards concerning male and femaleness, children still demonstrate many of the traditional values (Kagan, 1964). Changing cultural standards do not alter the fact that sex differentiation constitutes almost a bifurcation in status and roles in almost all cultures from the very beginning of the socialization process.

> Aside from the facts that it is living, human, and helpless, the next most important observation that parents can make about an infant that will give them a basis for meaningful response to it, is that it is either male or female. Maleness-femaleness is the nearest thing to a dichotomy that man can discern in animate nature—and dichotomies are so satisfying (Colley, 1959, p. 169).

All known human populations appear to honor this dichotomy and all cultures distinguish males and females on the basis of primary and secondary sex characteristics (D'Andrade, 1966). Anatomically, males on the average, tend to have greater height, more massive skeletons, a higher ratio of muscle to fat, and more body hair (D'Andrade, 1966). In terms of psychological behavioral traits, males tend to be more sexually active, dominant, aggressive and less responsible, nurturant and emotional then females (D'Andrade, 1966).

Although sex membership is ultimately predicated upon anatomic sex criteria, the datum of organic sex differences is not of *intrinsic* psychological importance to the child. This does not mean that he would ordinarily ignore such differences or fail to be curious about them. However, were it not for the fact that they receive special social emphasis from the moment of birth as a principal basis for the differential structuring of role and status behavior in all cultures, he would be relatively indifferent to them. Anatomic sex differences, in other words, are chiefly important to the child because they are significant determinants of the erotic and social behavior of adults, and hence affect both his emulatory behavior and the expectations and socializing procedures of the latter in their dealings with him. For analogous reasons he pays

---

Reviews and theoretical discussions on the biological, psychological sociological and anthropological aspects of this topic are available. See Bakan (1966), Colley (1959), Garai & Scheinfeld, (1968), Kagan (1964), Maccoby (1966). The summary of the research literature here relies heavily on the reviews.

particular attention to skin color differences when these receive comparable emphasis as determinants of role and status in a given culture; and if his culture correspondingly used eye color as a basis for special stratification, the difference between brown and blue eyes would similarly acquire special saliency in his psychological field. That anatomic sex differences are primarily important to children for purposes of social categorization is further suggested by the fact that even preschool children who are well aware of them tend to place greater stress on hair-do and dress as the essential distinguishing criteria of sex membership (Kohlberg, 1966).

Sex organs, in addition to furnishing a more functional and universal basis for the patterning of social behavior than skin or eye color are also objects of somewhat greater interest in their own right (see p. 398). Nevertheless, they still lack critical importance to children because the prerequisite conditions for enacting a genuine biological (erotic) sex role are absent in their case. Under these circumstances their "sex behavior" only has peripheral significance in the total economy of personality organization, and concern with the ultimate objects of adult sex striving is correspondingly not very insistent.* But although the child's identification with his own sex group carries none of the implications of membership in a biological sex clan, there is no gainsaying the intensity of his sex loyalties and their significance for his social groupings, play interests, values, and aspirations. With some exceptions the social sex roles of boys and girls are miniature editions and precursors of the respective sex roles of men and women.

Infantile "Sexuality"

Genital Play. In the course of body exploration the infant inevitably discovers and manipulates his genitals. Upon experiencing the pleasurable effects of this activity, he may repeat it in order to reexperience the pleasant sensations involved, or (as in the case of thumb-sucking) to obtain a non-specific type of tension relief following frustration or anxiety of any origin. In some cultures, as a matter of fact, it is common for mothers to stroke the naked genitals of crying, fretful infants as a means of soothing them (Leighton & Kluckhohn, 1947; Whiting & Child, 1953). The incidence of self-stimulation (at one time or another) in children under three years is exceedingly high (Levy, 1928). Girls reportedly indulge much less frequently than do boys (Koch, 1935; Levy, 1928) but this difference may be misleading since the habit is appreciably more difficult to detect in girls. Toward the close of the preschool period, as more and more children become introduced to its pleasurable properties and become aware of its availability as a tension

---

* *These considerations, of course, would be so self-evident as hardly to require mentioning were it not for widespread acceptance (despite the absence of any convincing empirical evidence) of the psychoanalytic doctrine that the sexual behavior of children is qualitatively equivalent to that of adults.*

reducing device, the practice tends to become more widespread and persistent, especially in emotionally tense children; and in accordance with the imposition of parental and cultural taboos, indulgence tends to become more furtive (Dillon, 1934). Beginning at this age also, curiosity about sexual anatomy and differences may stimulate some children to "peek" and play genitally exhibitionistic and manipulative games with youngsters of the same or opposite sex. Although varying tremendously in extent from one culture or subculture to another, these interests and activities are still relatively sporadic and uninsistent in comparison with those of post-pubertal individuals (Kinsey *et al*, 1948; Malinowski, 1927).

The "Oedipus Situation." Subsumed under this designation is the Freudian doctrine that during the "genital phase" of psychosexual development the parent of opposite sex is the child's principal love object. Supposedly inherent in the "phylogenetic unconscious" of the male child is a potent libidinal drive for incestuous sexual union with the mother accompanied by hatred for the father as a sexual rival and desire for his death.* Giving this theory a certain measure of superficial plausibility is the fact (impressionistic to be sure) that among many (but not all) families in our culture the father-son relationship in early childhood appears to be marked by more hostility and less intense emotional attachment than either the mother-son or father-daughter relationships. Other explanations for these phenomena, however, are available that seem far more parsimonious and self-evidently valid.

Erotic Significance. What is the erotic significance of the several phenomena that psychoanalytic theory groups under the heading of "infantile sexuality"? To what extent is the meaning of the oral, anal and genital activities we have reviewed above qualitatively equivalent to that of adult sexuality? Our position here is that *adult sexuality (true eroticism) can only be conceived of as a form of self-expression in which the individual enacts and experiences himself in a biological sex role.* Prerequisite to such experience, we believe, is (a) either current hormonal facilitation or exposure to such facilitation in the past, and (b) social and self-recognition as a sexually mature person capable of desiring a sexual object as such, and of serving in this capacity himself. Since these conditions cannot possibly be fulfilled prior to puberty, the "erotic" behavior of children cannot be regarded as qualitatively comparable to adult sexuality. It lacks the social significance of adult eroticism, its significance in the total economy of personality organization, its rich feeling tones, its urgency and regularity, and its status as an absorbing interest in its own right separate from other play.

The oedipus situation in the female child corresponds to that described for the male except that the respective objects of love and hatred are reversed.

"Infantile sexuality," therefore, consists chiefly of erogenous *sensuality* that is both indulged in for its own sake and to relieve the tensions of frustration and anxiety. It also includes the elements of exploratory and manipulative activity, of curiosity about the anatomy and physiology of sex and reproduction, and of desire for affectional closeness with the parent, accompanied perhaps by feelings of rivalry for perceived competitors. As we shall see later, however, because the child lacks a true biological (erotic) sex role, sex differences are not intrinsically important to him. Their true significance for personality development in childhood inheres in the fact that they constitute one of the principal bases for the differential structuring of social roles and behavior.

The origin of the psychoanalytic confusion between infantile sensuality and adult sexuality is not difficult to locate. First, it is easy to be overimpressed with the obvious fact that the same bodily parts are involved in both phenomena. This superficial resemblance, however, is both irrelevant and misleading: masturbation, for example, does not have the same psychological significance for child and adult simply because both individuals stroke the same organs. Furthermore, the Freudian hypothesis that all children believe that both males and females have a "penis-organ" is not substantiated by cross-cultural study (Kreitter & Kreitter, 1966). The "castration complex" is therefore questioned and must rely on evidence other than "pan-penism" (Kreitter & Kreitter, 1966). Second, in adult life sensuous and sexual pleasure are interwoven in erotic experience (Ausubel, 1952). Hence, since adults find it extremely difficult to exclude their cumulative experiential perspective in interpreting the behavior of children (adultomorphism), they may confidently attribute erotic significance to the oral and genital play of the latter or "remember" that these same activities had sexual meaning in their own childhood. Even the sensual pleasure connected with anal and bladder evacuation, which ordinarily is not incorporated into adult sexual expression, may be "remembered" as having had erotic significance in early childhood years. This can be explained by the close association between eliminative and genital functions as a result of anatomical proximity, the shame and pleasure that is common to both, and their linkage in folklore and folk language. Thus, by virtue of this prior association, when genital activities are eroticized in adult life retrospective distortion may operate to superimpose some sexual significance on childhood memories of anal-urethral sensuality.

Some neo-Freudians recognize that "infantile" and adult sexuality are not phenomenologically comparable but argue nevertheless that *eroticism* or *sexuality* should be defined broadly enough to encompass both sensuality and expressions of affection as well as sexual behavior in the more literal sense. In our opinion this only results in unnecessary semantic confusion and in a lamentable loss of scientific precision. If three distinguishably different phenomena can be discriminated conceptually, what possible advantage could accrue from subsuming all of them under the same single term that is commonly understood as referring to only one of the three?

"Sex Behavior" in Childhood

Our discussion of "infantile sexuality" indicates that there are reasons for believing that the prerequisite conditions for enacting a true biological sex role are absent in childhood, and hence that adult and childhood sexuality are qualitatively discontinuous from each other. Generally speaking, "sex behavior" in middle childhood and preadolescence is similar to and has much the same significance as in infancy and early childhood. Abundant evidence from our own and other cultures (Broderick & Rowe, 1968; Ford & Bench, 1951; Whiting & Child, 1953) indicates that children continue to manifest the following kinds of "sexuality" during the elementary school years: (a) hedonistic sensuality (masturbation) as an end in itself or as a nonspecific form of tension reducing behavior; (b) curiosity about sexual anatomy and the physiology of reproduction (peeking, "creepitis," "show games," mutual genital manipulation, questions about procreation, interest in pornographic art and literature); and (c) desire for non-erotic bodily contacts as expressions of affectional closeness to parents. Particularly characteristic of "sex behavior" during this period is experimentation with the biological sex roles of adults, varying from attempted intercourse to crude imitations of romanticism. It includes flirtation with parents and age mates of the opposite sex, boy-girl "crushes," chasing and kissing, and the furtive passing of "I love you" notes in the classroom. Although the extent of such activity varies greatly both between and within cultures, the near universality of its occurrence provides little support for the psychoanalytic doctrine of a "latency" period in psychosexual development (Broderick & Rowe, 1968). Nevertheless, it is an assumption of quite another order to equate such behavior with adult sexuality when it lacks all of the distinguishing properties of the latter phenomenon.

Cross-cultural comparisons indicate that the participation of children in overt sex play is largely a function of cultural tolerance for such experimentation, but that surreptitious expression often occurs even when strong cultural taboos are operative (Ford & Beach, 1951; Whiting & Child, 1953). This suggests some degree of genic determination. The *differential* patterning of male and female biological sex roles by genic factors, on the other hand, does not occur prior to pubescence, and in any case is considerably modified by cultural norms of masculinity and femininity. In sexually mature individuals, genic factors either differentially influence perceptual and behavioral thresholds of sexual reactivity through some presently unknown mediating mechanisms or through the differential effects of androgens and estrogens on the nervous system.

In addition to regulating the child's overt sex activity, the culture also influences his general attitudes about sex and his degree of sophistication about sexual matters. The child assimilates much of the cultural folklore (four-letter words, "dirty" stories, etc.) and moral values about sex: that sex is ugly or beautiful, that it is a necessary evil or a saving grace, that it is equally desirable for both sexes or intended primarily for men. He elaborates in fantasy many unshared misperceptions and half-truths which frequently are not subject to social validation for many years. Finally, in our culture, he derives from sex a source of shame, guilt, conflict and anxiety, and a weapon with which to shock adult sensibilities and express defiance of adult authority.

Development of Sex Identity and Awareness

During the preschool and elementary school period sex role differentiation is an important aspect of ego development. Relatively early in their social careers, children learn to think of themselves as male or female. This awareness is absent in most two-year-olds but is present in many three-year-olds (Kagan, 1964; Kohlberg, 1966; Spencer, 1967). However, even when children are familiar with anatomic sex differences they frequently regard the latter as less basic differentiating criteria than hair style or clothing (Kohlberg, 1966). Until approximately the age of five, the child is not even certain of the constancy of gender (Kohlberg, 1966). The concept of male-female is not stably acquired until school age (Kagan, 1964; Kohlberg, 1966), boys acquiring the concept earlier than girls (Kagan, 1964). Because sexual identify is vastly more complex in humans as compared to subhuman species, it does not emerge exclusively from biological origins, and thus it cannot be discriminated on the basis of biological information alone (Colley, 1959). Human sexual identity involves not only biological components, since biology will interact with psychological and sociological factors (Colley, 1959). For purposes of clarity, we will treat total sexual identity under the three separate modes: biological, psychological, and sociological (see Colley, 1959). *Biological sexual identity* involves the characteristics of heredity and organic structure and function which distinguish the biologically male from the biologically female (e.g., primary and secondary sex characteristics and endocrine functions). *Psychological sexual identity* includes the characteristic ways of perceiving one's sexual interactions with others who are identified as being of the same or of opposite sexual identity. *Sociological sexual identity* relates to such things as dress, interests, attitudes, social standards of beauty and strength which, taken together, constitute what a particular society contributes to the concepts of maleness and femaleness (Colley, 1959). The separation of sexual identity into various components for discussion purposes in no way is indicative of a separation in nature.

Biological Sexual Identity

The biological differences between the sexes is indicated almost from birth. Hormones appear to play a significant role even during pre-natal development; for example, the secretion of androgens is necessary during the final embryonic stage of differentiation since failure of secretion results in a femininization of the external genitalia (Hamburg & Lunde, 1966). More dramatic, however, are the initial post-natal differences in behaviors of males and females (Garai & Scheinfeld, 1968; Hamburg & Lunde, 1966).

> From conception on, the female follows a different developmental path from that of the male organism as distinguished by (a) her earlier maturation; (b) much greater production of the estrogens with less production of the androgens [following pubescence], whereas males produce significantly more androgens than estrogens; (c) an anatomical structure characterized by a trend toward smaller bones, slighter muscles, and . . . [more] . . . fatty tissue as compared with the males more rugged bone and muscle structure; (d) much less genetic defectiveness in all "sex-linked" conditions and stronger overall resistance to most major diseases; and (e) with the advent of puberty, her exposure to the specific female processes of menstruation, ovulation, pregnancy, and menopause (Garai & Scheinfeld, 1968, p. 248).

It is obvious that these sex differences are going to have a profound effect on the biological and psychological behavior of the two sexes (Gerai & Scheinfeld, 1968). The fact that biology interacts with psychology in this differentiation is indicated by the fact that the onset of puberty is apparently triggered by the brain rather than simply the endocrine system (Hamburg & Lunde, 1966). Moreover, sociological aspects of the culture appear to promote or delay the "growth spurt" and is evident in the fact that the age of puberty in our culture has been occurring at increasingly earlier ages* (Hamburg & Lunde, 1966).

Psychological Sexual Identity

The development of psychological sexual identity is an intricate part of ego development in the child. The psychological component refers to the individual's concept of himself as male or female with a specific emphasis on the individual's perception of sexual interactions which are identified as being of the same or of opposite sexual identity. It is assumed that, like other types of concept formation, the development of a sexual self-conception is related to the child's expanding cognitive experience and buffered by sociological and biological conditions.

This trend may, of course, also be influenced by such biological factors as improved nutrition and general health. (Hamburg & Lunde, 1966).

Developmental Trends. A clear conception of sexual differences does not occur until the end of the preschool period. As noted previously, the child's conception of sexual identity "is rather vague at three years of age and children tend to label gender by general physical criteria" (Kohlberg, 1966). A stabilized conceptual identification of sex differences is not apparent until five years of age (Kohlberg, 1966). Thus, children under five, when asked whether a pictured girl could be a boy if she wanted to (by changing her hair and clothes, etc.), said it was possible to change gender (Kohlberg, 1966). Preschoolers have difficulty in learning that there are generalized differences between the sexes and their confusion about genital differences at five years suggests that psychoanalytic concepts of genital role are rather questionable in explaining the direct basis for sex role stereotypes (Kohlberg, 1966).

The acquisition of sex awareness and appropriate sex behavior is facilitated by the pervasive and recurrent exposure of boys and girls to differential experience, treatment, expectations, and norms of conduct. Some of these differences in handling are obvious: distinctive clothing and hair style; separate toilets, games, toys, books, and interests. Other differences—in valuation by parents, in discipline, and in expectations regarding achievement, conformity, deportment, and emotional expression—are more subtle but no less real. Pressures for learning an appropriate sex role originate in the home and are reinforced by identification with the like-sex parent and older siblings. Later, school, peer group, and mass media contribute greatly to the learning process by encouraging segregation of and rivalry between the sexes and by providing appropriate emulatory models. Boys and girls in our culture have many reasons for estrangement and mutual antagonism. First, gross differences in play interests necessitate the formation of unisexual play groups (Kagan, 1964). Second, because girls are more docile, obedient, and conforming to adult direction at home and in school (Garai *et al*, 1968; Vraegh, 1968), they tend to receive preferential treatment. This provides an endless source of rivalry, discord, resentment, aggression, and counter-aggression. Third, boys become indoctrinated with prevailing notions of male chauvinism and incite girls to retaliate in kind. Surprisingly, elementary school boys seem more favorable (sociometrically) toward girls than girls toward boys (Reese, 1966). Fourth, group competitions in school are frequently staged as contests between the sexes (Garai *et al*, 1968). All of these factors promote strong feelings of intra-sex solidarity and the utilization of the opposite sex as a convenient object for the displacement of hostile feelings of any origin.

Lower-class children become more clearly aware of sex differences and of appropriate sex role behavior at an earlier age than do middle-class children (Bronfenbrenner, 1961; Minuchin, 1965; Rabban, 1950; Spencer, 1967;

Weider & Waller, 1950). Middle-class parents, in general, have less dichotomous sex-typed expectations (Minuchin, 1965), while the lower-class child is exposed to more sharply and narrowly defined standards of masculinity and femininity and their conformity to such standards is more rigorously enforced. Middle-class fathers, in contrast, are not only home less but the nature of their work is also less concrete; hence their sons find it more difficult to identify with them, especially since they are surrounded by female models at home and in school. Furthermore, middle-class parents define and enforce sex appropriate behavior less rigidly (Minuchin, 1965; Rabban, 1950). Middle-class families can be further differentiated with respect to sex role attitudes and sex typed reactions of children when "traditional" and "modern" middle-class socialization standards are assessed (Minuchin, 1965). "Traditional" middle-class families (stressing socialization toward general standards) and "modern" middle-class families (stressing individualized development) have differential sexually expressive consequences in their children, the children of traditional families expressing relatively greater unequivocal commitment to their own sex role and sex typed play (Minuchin, 1966).

Boys become aware of their social sex roles earlier than do girls (Kagan, 1964; Kohlberg, 1966; Spencer, 1967), girls tending to reach a peak in awareness at five years and either maintain or decrease in feminine awareness during the elementary school years (Spencer, 1967). Despite the fact that girls have greater opportunities for identification with sex appropriate models and activities at home or in school (Parsons, 1942), boys seem to be more clearly aware of their social sex role than girls (Kagan, 1964; Rabban, 1950). This apparent paradox is largely a function of the fact that although the sex role of girls is more available and visible than that of boys it is less clearly defined. Boys are taught to view feminine pursuits with disdain and are severely ridiculed if they step out of line. The female sex role tends to be more ambiguous both in childhood and in adult life. It is more inclusive of masculine interests than the male role is inclusive of feminine interests. Thus, the participation of girls in cross-sex activities is regarded more tolerantly and is less subject to prohibition and reproof (Kagan, 1964). Finally, the child's conception of sex is, as might be expected, dependent on his advancing cognitive skills. In general, sex role attitudes tend to be developed earlier in brighter children; trends between the ages of four and eight show brighter children developing sex role attitudes chronologically earlier than average children (Kohlberg & Zigler, 1967).

Theories of Psychological Sexual Identity. In keeping with a rather consistent "male" bias in Western culture, psychological explanations of sexual identification have emphasized male sexual identity. To be sure, the female was accounted for in the Freudian "Electra complex" but the "Oedipus complex" has by far received more careful attention in psychoanalytic theorizing on sexual identification.

To his credit, Freud opened up and fostered investigation of sexual identity in children because, in psychoanalytic theory, the problems of later psychological pathology are sexually based in early childhood. His major theoretical statement on "sexual identification" of male and female were centered around the "instinctually" based conflicts (i.e., Oedipus or Electra), that were, if successfully resolved, the foundation for later adequate sexual identification. The timing of the conflicts in Western culture was between the ages of four and six years. Thus, in the case of the male child, identification and love in the early childhood years are centered around the mother and reaches "incestual proportions" at approximately five years of age. The "incest" conflict is counteracted by the child's fear of the father who is perceived as stronger and punitive. Partly as a result of infantile masturbation and partly because of the father's perception of his son's incest wishes, the paternal instinct is to threaten "castration." The young male's perception of this leads to "castration anxiety" and, because of fear of genital loss, he represses his incest wishes and identifies with the stronger and more aggressive male parent. This initial conflict and its successful resolution forms the basis of subsequent like-sexed male identification. In spite of the rather bizarre theorizing that has centered around Freudian theory concerning sexual identification, it has nevertheless formed the basis of later theory construction about sexual identification in social-learning theory, sociological-power explanations, and cognitive developmental models.

Social-learning explanations of sexual identification have summarily rejected the "instinctual" explanations that were advanced by psychoanalytic theorists (Bandura & Walters, 1963; Kagan, 1964; Mischel, 1966). The development of masculine and feminine identification like all other behaviors, is not a function of "instincts" but of reward and punishment contingencies. The fact that individuals whose original sex assignment was incorrect or ambiguous, due to initial confusion of their external genitalia, develop the roles and expectations of their culturally ascribed sexual status is an indication of the importance of cultural expectations in sex-role development (Mischel, 1966). The development of a specific sexual identity does not depend on the repression of incestual wishes but on the rewards and punishments of the culture. In normal family relationships, the child is increasingly rewarded for modeling his behavior on the father, and this type of imitation procedure is given wider reward significance in the culture at large. Both male and female sexual identification are, therefore, contingent on the differential reward systems given to boys and girls within the family and supported by the culture at large.

A "power" theory of sexual identification constitutes an amalgam of the Freudian theory of "punishment" with the social-learning stress on "reward" and "nurturance" (Parsons, 1955). * The "power" theory of identification sees male identification as a consequence of the child's perception of the father as not only a "punishing" agent but also as an effective rewarder. The male child does not simply identify with the father out of "fear" but also because he perceives the privileged status that the father has in the family. Kohlberg (1966) has criticized social-learning and power theories of sexual identification because they cannot explain the fact that adult forms of sexual pathology persist in spite of the fact that they are severely punished in cultural expectations and are rarely rewarded by the culture at large. Moreover, cross-cultural studies indicate that child training practices may not be an adequate explanation of sexual identification because the largest sex differences occur in the younger age levels (three to six years) rather than in the older (seven to ten years) giving less weight to the training hypothesis which would predict the opposite result (D'Andrade, 1966).

Most recently Kohlberg's (1966) "cognitive-developmental" theory clearly separates the biological, pyschological, and sociological aspects of sexual identification. Rejecting the previous explanations of sexual identity, he places the major burden of psychological sexual identity on the child's advancing cognitive development. Most crucial for sexual identity is the development of a clear concept of maleness or femaleness. As indicated previously, the child at approximately five years of age develops a concept of gender identity or self categorization as boy or girl which forms the basis of his subsequent sex-role attitudes. The development of this gender conception emerges slowly during the years from two to five when gender identity takes on more permanent characteristics. The child's self-conception of himself (or herself) as male or female becomes the basis of his subsequent sex role evaluations. In contrast to social learning theorists, Kohlberg's (1966) cognitive developmental viewpoint stresses the importance of a gender conception in determining what is to be a reward within the culture:

> The social-learning syllogism is: 'I want rewards, I am rewarded for doing boys' things, therefore I want to be a boy.' In contrast, a cognitive theory assumes this sequence: 'I am a boy, therefore, I want to do boys' things, therefore the opportunity to do boys' things (and to gain approval for doing them) is rewarding' (Kohlberg, 1966, p. 89).

The basic sex-role stereotypes develop early in children and are a consequence of the child's conception of body differences which are supported by visible differences in the sex assignment of social roles. After masculine and feminine conceptions of gender have developed, they become stabilized and form the irreversible basis of identification with like-sex figures, in particular

---

See Bronfenbrenner (1960) for a more thorough discussion of these theories.

the like-sex parent. The desire to be masculine leads to the desire to imitate a masculine model because of a need to value things that are consistent with or like the self (Kohlberg, 1966).

In general, theories of psychological sexual identity have not been generated from a more general theory of ego development and have thus stressed one or another particular aspect of general sexual identity. Freudian theory has emphasized the biological instinctual components while ignoring the more pervasive cultural determinants of sex role conception. Social-learning theorists in stressing the importance of cultural expectations and rewards have, in general, sidestepped the biological basis of sexual differentiation. All theories have been partial to explaining male identification and, by attempting to explain male and female identification separately, have fallen short in their explanatory power. We shall discuss this matter in greater detail shortly (see pp. 410 and 413) but it is first necessary to discuss the sociological basis of sexual identity.

Sociological Sexual Identity

In relative contrast to biological and psychological sex role, the sociological aspects of sexual identity refer to those differential functions, status and personality traits that are expected of the two sexes in a particular cultural setting. Cultural expectations may be biologically based and these differential expectations combine with biological determinants in the formation of the individual's psychological conception of himself (herself) as male or female. Since all cultures provide differential training for boys and girls that will enable them to assume their roles as men and women (D'Andrade, 1966), childhood social sex roles tend to mirror and foreshadow their adult counterparts. Because of varying degrees of cultural discontinuity, however, a point to point correlation never exists. Athletic prowess, for example, which is an important determinant of boys' prestige status in their peer group, is a negligible factor in determining the social standing of the adult male. Three component and interrelated aspects of social sex role may be considered here: (a) the hierarchical ordering of relations between the sexes in terms of the relative values placed by the culture on maleness and femaleness respectively and the degree of access each sex has to positions of social power and privilege; (b) social and vocational differences reflective of the division of labor along sex lines; and (c) norms of masculinity and femininity.

The hierarchical ordering of relations between the sexes is in some ways difficult to ascertain. First of all, girls initially perceive themselves as more highly accepted and intrinsically valued than boys and have a more available emulatory model in the mother. Their orientation to affiliation over achievement and mastery (Bakan, 1966; Garai *et al*, 1968) is seen in their tendency to satellize more and longer. The cultural emphasis on achievement and

mastery, however, creates certain discrepancies in the female's ego orientation. For example, boys tend to be ahead of girls in the development of sex
roles and preferences (Kagan, 1964; Kohlberg, 1966; Spencer, 1967). Young
boys more frequently and consistently choose masculine items on preference
tests than girls of the same age choose feminine items (Brown, 1957; Hartup &
Zook, 1960).* Girls are much more ambivalent, reaching a peak in femininity
preference at five years, and proceeding to maintain or decrease this level
during the elementary school years (Spencer, 1967). Boys, on the other hand,
continue to increase in male preference throughout the elementary school
years (Spencer, 1967). The ambivalence of the female occurs because the
culture awards superior prestige and competence values to the male role
(Kohlberg, 1966). However, the culture also awards a number of superior
attributes to the female role which, in comparison to male status, are not as
salient. Thus:

> As awareness of these prestige values and stereotypes develops in the years of four to
> eight, there is a tendency for both sexes to attribute greater power and prestige to the
> male role. However, the greater relative prestige of the adult male role does not imply
> the absence or decline of absolute prestige, or positive value, of the female role, a prestige
> that is sufficient to channel girls' competence strivings into feminine role values (Kohlberg,
> 1966, p. 165).

At all socioeconomic levels in our society girls are subjected to less pressure
to achieve primary status through achievement behaviors.† Whereas the
middle-class boy fully anticipates that he will be expected to create, through
his own vocational efforts and achievements, the social status of his future
family, few girls in the same social class expect as married women to compete
with men in their own fields or at occupational levels of equivalent social
prestige (Parsons, 1942). Girls are not *really* driven by the culture as are boys
to prove their adequacy and maintain their self-esteem by their accomplishments. Their fathers are satisfied if they are pretty, sweet, affectionate, and
well-liked (Aberle & Naegele, 1952). They expect to fall heir to a derived
status dependent upon their husbands' station in life, and to acquire primary
status in the roles of mother, housewife and supplementary wage earner,
augmented perhaps by participation in cultural and community welfare
activities (Bakan, 1966; Garai *et al*, 1968; Parsons, 1942). Largely for this
reason perhaps—because their status is more attributed than earned—girls
and women tend to be more conscious and jealous of status distinctions than
boys and men (Garai *et al*, 1968).

---

*Kohlberg (1966) questions the validity of Brown's (1957) stick figure preference, since it looks
much more like a boy in physical characteristics.

†There may be some exception to this in lower-class Negro families where the female is sometimes
expected to achieve in place of the male.

The superordinate position of men in our society (and the accompanying male chauvinism) is also reflected in childhood social sex roles. From an early age boys learn to be contemptuous of girls and their activities; and although girls retaliate in kind by finding reasons for deprecating the male sex, they tend to accept in part the prevailing view of their inferiority (Kitay, 1940). Whereas boys express scorn for girls' tasks, games, and future role in life (Kagan, 1964) and seldom, if ever, desire to change sex, girls not infrequently wish they were boys (Kagan, 1964; Spencer, 1967). Girls apparently express their hostility for superior male prestige by being less sociometrically acceptant of males than males are for females (Reese, 1966). The cultural importance of male characteristics is seen in the less frequent crossing of sex lines in male as opposed to female children. The male equivalent of "tomboy" who reads girls' books or plays with girls' toys is rare indeed in our culture (Kagan, 1964).

In some ways the acquisition of social sex role is more difficult for boys, but in other ways it is more difficult for girls. Sex-appropriate emulatory models and activities are less available to boys, and fewer of the sex-typed activities they learn in childhood can be carried over into adult life (e.g., athletic skills versus housekeeping skills). To acquire the male social sex role boys are also required to undergo greater personality change during late childhood and adolescence than girls undergo in acquiring their social sex role. The implications of desatellization—volitional independence, self-reliance, striving for primary status—are applied more thoroughly in their case; whereas to a very large degree, women (as wives) can retain many of the dependent and passive attributes of derived status. The female sex role is more ambiguous and inclusive, more productive of conflicting choices, and is changing more rapidly. Girls are understandably more confused than boys about the extent to which they can remain content with a derived status or must struggle for achievement in their own right (Bakan, 1966).

Sex differences in play and mass media interests affect both prevailing norms of masculinity and femininity as well as anticipated cleavage along vocational lines. The sex typing of games is well established during the pre-school period (Kagan, 1964). Boys choose objects related to sports, machines, aggression, whereas girls select games and objects associated with kitchen and home, baby, etc. (Kagan, 1964). In infancy, males exhibit a greater interest in objects and their manipulation, whereas females show a greater interest in the interpersonal domain (Garai et al, 1968). During the elementary school years boys excel in mechanical and athletic skills, verbal comprehension, verbal reasoning, arithmetic and mathematical reasoning, spatial perception and orientation and problem-solving ability; girls excel in verbal fluency, correct language usage, spelling, articulation, manual dexterity, perceptual speed, clerical skills and rote learning (Bakan, 1966; Garai et al, 1968; Olson,

1970; Maccoby, 1966). Boys are more oriented to "achievement" and task accomplishment, whereas girls are more oriented to affiliation tasks (Bakan, 1966; Garai et al, 1968). When "achievement" is being stressed, boys tend to be more "intrinsically" involved in the tasks, females' "achievement" motivation being more "extrinsic" and less task-oriented (Garai et al, 1968). Sex differences in vocational choice are evident by the fifth grade, girls being more realistic and less fantasy-oriented in their future goals (Borow, 1966). During the elementary years there is a gradual acquisition of dislike for occupations incongruous with sex role (Tyler, 1955).

In addition to sex differences in status and interest-ability patterns listed above, boys and girls in our culture typically differ in certain temperamental traits, emotional expression, and conformity to social controls. Boys tend to be more active, energetic, and versatile in their play activities (Bakan, 1966; Garai et al, 1966), more fearless, (Sheehy, 1948) and more overt in the expression of aggression, rebellion, and friendliness (Bakan, 1966; Garai et al, 1968; Kagan, 1964; Maccoby, 1966; Vroegh, 1968). Girls are more affectionate, interpersonal, passive, suspicious, affiliative, nurturant, and introverted (Bakan, 1966; Garai et al, 1968; Kagan, 1964; Maccoby, 1966; Vroegh, 1968). The greatest contrast between boys and girls lies in the area of aggressiveness-compliance. Boys are more aggressive, expressive of anger, rebellious and negativistic (Garai et al, 1968; Koch, 1955a, 1955b). Boys are also more dominant, boastful, exhibitionistic, and insistent on their rights (Koch, 1955a; Sheehy, 1938; Vroegh, 1968), more revengeful, extrapunitive and alibi building (Koch, 1955a), more quarrelsome, given to teasing, and uncooperative with peers and teachers (Glidewell et al, 1966; Koch, 1955a). Girls are more obedient and amenable to social controls (Bakan, 1966), more responsible (Koch, 1955a), friendlier to teachers, and more responsive to their approval (Bakan, 1966; Garai et al, 1968; Koch, 1955a, 1955b). They are more responsive to prestige suggestion, more sensitive to social expectations, more cooperative, and more discriminative of socially approved behavior (Bakan, 1966).

GENIC AND ENVIRONMENTAL DETERMINANTS:
A CONCLUDING PERSPECTIVE

Our general discussion of sexual identity involved separate discussion of the biological, psychological and sociological aspects of this phenomenon. The separation of "sexual identity" into three components was made in order to clarify some of the relative determinants of sex role identification in the developing child. A summary of animal studies indicates that there is biochemical, neurophysiological, and behavioral evidence suggesting that hormones influence the brain and thereby affect behavioral functioning, e.g., progesterone in females (Hamburg & Lunde, 1966). Moreover, in humans there are very early behavioral indications of initial sex differences which may be genically regulated (Garai et al, 1968). For example, the male organism is initially more susceptible to genetic defects and diseases, maturationally slowed in physical developments, etc. (Garai et al, 1960). Cross-cultural evidence indicates that males are more sexually active, more dominant, more deferred to, less nurturant, etc. (D'Andrade, 1966; Garai et al, 1968). To some extent it may therefore be said that sex differences are psychobiologically regulated.

The explanation of "psychobiological" regulation of sex differences, however, must be made with a considerable amount of reserve and qualification. It is difficult to determine the extent to which the child's learning of his sex role may be influenced by underlying biological disposition (Hamburg & Lunde, 1966). First of all, the tremendous variability in social sex role from one culture to another (D'Andrade, 1966) despite the operation of nearly identical genic variables in all cultures, strongly suggests that modal differences in behavior between the sexes is predominantly determined by environmental (cultural) factors, e.g., social, political and economic organization, value system, religion, custom complexes, historical accident. Secondly, the fact that individuals conform to the sex-role initially assigned by the culture in spite of the fact that the initial sex assignment was biologically incorrect, seems indicative of the fact that environmental determinants play an important role in sexual identity (Hampson & Hampson, 1961; Money, 1965). However, since certain behavioral and trait differences between the sexes seem to be differentially influenced by hormones[*] or sex-linked on a genic basis (and at least partially independent of differential experience) we cannot rule out the possibility of partial panhuman genic determination:

The evidence and arguments presented show that, primarily owing to prenatal, genic, and hormonal influences, human beings are definitely predisposed at birth to a male or female gender orientation. Sexual behavior of an individual, and thus gender role, are not neutral and without initial direction at birth. Nevertheless, sexual predisposition in only a potentiality setting limits to a pattern that is greatly modifiable by ontogenetic experiences. Life experiences most likely act to differentiate and direct a flexible sexual disposition and to mold the prenatal organization until an environmentally (socially and culturally) acceptable gender is formulated and established (Diamond, 1965, p. 167).

The component aspects of psychological and sociological sexual identity are probably transmitted experientially in much the same manner as any psychosocial trait. It is difficult to indicate at this time the inter relationship between the various components of sexual identity. For example, a person's

---

[*]See p. 77 for reference to the effects of androgens, estrogens, and prolactin on behavior.

"psychological" sexual identity is mediated through his experiences with cultural expectations of male-femaleness (i.e., sociological aspects). If Kohlberg (1966) is correct, however, once a stable psychological gender identity is formed, it feeds back and gives value to cultural prescriptions of maleness and femaleness. Thus a clear cognitive conception of maleness enables one to value and identify with male cultural norms. At present, this interpretation is more of a hypothesis than an established scientific fact and is questioned by some social learning theorists (Mischel, 1966). It cannot be denied, however, that a person's "psychological" sexual identity (i.e., that part of self-concept relating to male-female differentiation) is in some way developmentally related to the social expectations of his culture, since the culture (i.e., family, peers, school) is never neutral toward the person in regards to sex. Boys and girls are no doubt recipients of a double-edged feedback from parents and peers (Colley, 1959). The character of these early interactions may be differentiated into two general classes: (1) prosexual perceptual responses are perceptions that certain interpersonal situations are appropriate for sexual approach response patterns; (2) antisexual perceptual responses are perceptions that certain interpersonal situations are appropriate for sexual avoidance behavior (Colley, 1959). The mother and father enter into many types of interactions with their children, but differential feedback will be given due to the sexual nature of the interaction. In normal family arrangements it is expected that the "mother" will encourage prosexual responses from the male and antisexual responses from the female child. At the same time, the father will encourage prosexual responses from the female and antisexual responses from the male (Colley, 1959). An illustration of this situation in the case of the male in which this interaction is given wider cultural significance is as follows:

> As a male child matures, he is responded to by others, some of whom are similar to mother and some of whom are different and respond to him differently. From the ones similar to mother, he gets recurring patterns of response that are in many important ways like that of the mother. From a different sort of figure . . . he begins to get response patterns which are very unlike those of the mother. From these, the males, he gets responses which tell him that he is one who will be in competition with them—that they view him as inappropriate for the kind of emotional treatment that the mother provides. Thus it is that the male child learns the expectations which the two major classes of adult figures have for him (Colley, 1959, p. 172).

The female child's relationships are formed in an inverse manner with the father and other males encouraging prosexual responses from their female children and the mother and other females discouraging them.

A biosocial interpretation allows the development of "psychological" sexual identity to be based on more differential reciprocal role-taking skills demanding more mature cognitive differentiation. It may be contrasted with psychoanalytic theory where social sex differences in children are viewed as reflecting the possession of different sex organs (or reactions to same) or innate differences in libidinal drives. It differs from most social learning theories of identification because of its more complex interpretation of sexual identification. Identification theories place the major role of sex identification on some sex modeling (Colley, 1959) and do not differentiate the psychological, sociological and biological components of sexual identity.

It is understood that sexual identification involves more than just pro-sexual and antisexual responses. The culture also emphasizes vastly different patterns of behavior in areas of achievement, emotional expression, conformity, interests, etc. (Bakan, 1966; Kagan, 1964; Maccoby, 1966; Garai *et al*, 1968). Girls are more accepted and intrinsically valued by parents and are protected more from contact with other social classes. Boys are more severely disciplined by their fathers (see p. 301), are allowed more freedom in physical activity, rough play, hitting, getting dirty, swearing, roaming the neighborhood, sex experimentation, and bodily exposure, and less freedom in expressing sentiment, tenderness, fear, weakness, and hurt feelings. It is small wonder, therefore, that boys and girls have different conceptions of maternal and paternal roles.

The interaction of these various determinants of sexual identity are, at present, poorly defined. It is important to keep in mind that the conceptual distinctions between biological, psychological and sociological sexual identity were made in order to clarify the relative weight exerted by such determinants as heredity, environment, and the growth matrix. These distinctions may also help clarify certain conceptual difficulties encountered in discussing the general topic of sexual identity. Thus, a person may be correctly identified as a male in terms of his *biology* and social skills who is nevertheless afraid of females. Here, his biological and sociological components are correctly typed but through possible confused antisexual reactions from females he is psychologically unable to make prosexual responses toward the opposite sex. It is impossible to discuss the various ramifications of these distinctions, since it is outside the scope of this book. Suffice it to say, sex differences constitute a most important area of self-conception in general ego development, but at present there is no general theory which adequately links the various components and determinants together into an adequate theory of sex role identity.

CHAPTER 12

Emotional Development*

THE NATURE OF EMOTION

THE CONCEPT OF "emotions" appears to be universally held by laymen, yet the systematic study of this concept has lagged behind other apparently less appealing topics (Mandler, 1962). Emotion as such may be defined as a heightened state of subjective experience accompanied by skeletal-motor and autonomic-humoral responses and by a selectively generalized stage of lowered response thresholds. In this chapter we shall consider both the pleasant emotions that the child tries to prolong and the unpleasant emotions that he attempts to avoid or terminate, by respectively approaching and withdrawing from relevant stimulating conditions.

The following sequential steps are involved in the instigation of an emotional response: (a) *interpretive* phase—perception or anticipation of an event that is interpreted as threatening or enhancing an ego-involved need, goal, value, or attribute of self; (b) *preparatory reactive* phase consisting of a selectively generalized lowering of the particular response thresholds implicated in a given emotion; (c) *consummatory reactive* phase with subjective, autonomic-humoral, and skeletal-motor components; and (d) a *reflective reactive* phase involving subjective awareness of the drive state and of visceral and skeletal responses.

Genic and Environmental Determinants

A potentiality for developing patterned emotions is genically inherent in all human beings, although affective reactivity at birth is limited to undifferentiated excitement in response to any intense or prolonged stimulus. In addition, genically determined *patterning* predispositions exist, both with respect to the general categories of stimulation that evoke a particular emotion and with respect to the general ways in which such affect is expressed. Thus, frustration (at least in the early stages of emotional differentiation)primarily inspires rage and less frequently fear, whereas a perceived threat to personal safety more often evokes fear than anger. Smiling appears in the three-month-old infant as an unlearned response to

Current references covering a variety of dimensions of emotional development are available. See Candland, 1962; Cofer & Appley, 1964; Gellhorn, 1968; Mandler (1962); Plutchik, 1962; Freedman, Loring & Martin, 1967; Pribram, 1967; Riccuiti, 1968; Tomkins & Izard, 1965.

414

the human face and laughter typically accompanies tickling in the six-month-old (Leuba, 1941).

The hierarchy of responses that may be released in connection with a particular emotional state (i.e., the relative probability of their occurrence in accordance with the selective lowering of response thresholds) is also genically determined in part. Flight and avoidance tend to be associated with fear, and aggression with anger. The appearance in only ten-month-old infants of facial expressions that can be correctly identified (by adult judges) with specific emotional experiences suggests that the language of (emotional) expressions is built upon a core of native reaction patterns that can hardly be ascribed to training (Goodenough, 1931). Similar conclusions are indicated by findings that the facial expressions exhibited by normal and blind-deaf children in experiencing various emotions are highly comparable (Freedman, 1964; Goodenough, 1931; 1932), and by findings that indicate greater similarity in patterns of smiling and fear of strangers between identical twins than between fraternal twins (Freedman, 1965; Freedman & Keller, 1963).

Environmental factors help to determine both intercultural uniformities and differences in emotional patterning. Along with genic factors, universal kinds of interpersonal relationsips and conditions of adaptation to the personal and social environments (see Table 1, p. 66) account for *psychobiological* aspects of emotional behavior. Specific cultural variations in the conditions evoking particular emotions, institutionalized modes of elaborating affective expression, and culturally stylized preferences in the type of emotional response deemed appropriate for a given situation are responsible for *psychosocial* differences in emotional patterning. *Idiosyncratic* differences in emotional expression are determined both by variability in experience and by inter-individual differences in temperamental traits. Children not only differ in the patterning of autonomic responses to emotional stimuli, but also exhibit self-consistency in such patterning over different situations. Consistent individual differences also exist in the extent to which autonomic and visceral components are represented in the total emotional response. Some children respond most vigorously in the motor sphere, others most vigorously in the autonomic sphere, and still others with equal vigor in both spheres (Jones, 1950).

Because emotions are *multiply determined*, it is impossible, even in a designated cultural context, to predict from the eliciting stimulus alone what the emotional reaction will be. The individual's interpretation of the stimulus is always influenced by his idiosyncratic experience and temperamental make-up, and by such situational factors as current goal, the familiarity of the behavioral setting, and the relationship between instigating agent and reacting person. Lastly, as we shall show in a later section, emotional response is also determined in part by developmental (age level) differences in cognitive and social maturity and in ego structure.

Accessibility and Identifiability

Emotions vary both in the extent to which they are accessible to consciousness and in the degree of precision with which they can be identified. This variability applies to all phases of the emotional sequence. Sometimes it is the excitant (e.g., nature of the threat, cause of anger) that is relatively inaccessible or unidentifiable; at other times the child may be unaware of or unable to identify the area of personality concern to which the excitant refers (e.g., what is threatened). Still another possibility is that he might not be aware of his subjective feelings or of the relationship between these feelings, the excitant and the referent. This would tend to be especially true in the case of emotional situations and responses that are difficult to verbalize.

Because of cultural pressures to suppress certain kinds of emotional responses, the child is most apt to inhibit those aspects of emotional expression that have most social visibility, namely motor and vocal reactions. Subjective components of emotion are more difficult to inhibit; and since they can be hidden from public view, they are only coercible by such internal pressures as shame and guilt. Physiological aspects of emotional response are least inhibitable and under no pressure whatsoever to be inhibited; for these reasons, and when other outlets are blocked, they may constitute the chief channel for affective reactivity. Thus, visceral responsiveness to emotional stimuli (as measured by the galvanic skin reflex) is much greater in older than in younger children; and among adolescents an inverse relationship tends to prevail between autonomic reactivity, on the one hand, and motor activity, talkativeness, animation, and assertiveness, on the other (Jones, 1950, 1960). Also, high GSR reactions are correlated with low motor activity and less appropriate affect in emotionally disturbed children while the inverse is true of low reactors (Helper, Garfield & Wilcott, 1963). In the recollection of past emotional experience, inaccessibility may occur at any of these points in the emotional sequence, and inhibition of response may occur for any of the same reasons as occurred in the original arousal.

The notion of "free-floating" emotions, i.e., emotional states that are phenomenologically unrelated to particular excitants and selective patterns of response, is psychologically untenable. The illusion of "free-floatingness" is created by lack of accessibility and identifiability, and by delayed occurrence of the consummatory stage of response; this leaves the individual in a prolonged state of readiness or vigilance without tangible awareness of a relevant consummatory excitant.

Autonomic Patterning

One of the major questions in the study of emotions is the extent to which physiological patterns are correlated with different emotional responses. The autonomic patterning of the different emotional states is much more complex than the vastly oversimplified differentiation made between "vegetative" (parasympathetic) and "emergency" (sympathetic) reactions. The present state of knowledge suggests that the apparent control of emotional reactions by visceral events is rather diffuse and global in character. Several studies have demonstrated differential patterning between fear and hostility (Wolf & Wolf, 1947) and between fear and anger (Ax, 1953), but the differences are not such that one could predict a particular emotional behavior on the basis of these alone. Mandler (1962) demonstrated that subjects who are disturbed by sexual stimuli show a greater increase in body temperature than the less disturbed individuals. The available evidence, however, indicated that visceral changes do not produce emotions but are necessary concomitants of emotions (Mandler, 1962). Although emotional states may be generally characterized by a high level of sympathetic activity, there are few, if any, physiologically distinguishable aspects of the many emotional states (Izard, Nehmer, Livsey & Jennings, 1965). An adequate explanation of the phenomenon of differentiation of emotions requires inclusion of cognitive factors and central nervous processes (Arnold, 1960; Gellhorn, 1968; Mandler, 1962; Schachter & Singer, 1962).

Drive, Activation and Emotion

Drive is an inferred neurobehavioral state that accounts for transitory fluctuations in the organism's propensity for responding to stimulation with its available repertoire of reaction tendencies. This momentary difference in reactivity may be attributed to the existence of a state of drive (e.g., hunger or thirst) consisting of a partly generalized but nonetheless selective lowering of response and perceptual thresholds in accordance with their capacity for terminating the drive state that is operative. Although by no means synonymous, emotions and drives are closely related. *In the first place, many of the determinants of drive also (but not necessarily) tend to generate emotion;* but even if drives and emotions are not simultaneously determined by the same factors, subjective repercussions of drive states and of their associated responses and outcomes (need satisfaction or denial) are often productive of emotion. In any case the subjective and visceral components of emotion, and frequently the need or desire to prolong or terminate its affective qualities, constitute additional drive determinants influencing the continuation or cessation of drive states. In the second place, even when emotions are aroused independently of any connection with drives, one of their main consequences is to lower response thresholds in selectively generalized fashion. Thus, although the determinants of drives and emotions do not overlap completely, if emotion is aroused, whether in association with drive determinants or effects or entirely apart from drives, the emotion itself invariably serves as a drive determinant.

Similarly, the concept of *activation* also bears a close, yet distinct, relationship to emotion. Activation is defined as a continuum involving activity of the cerebral cortex, and, at the behavioral level as a state stretching from sleep to violent emotion (Mandler, 1962). The level of activation is usually neurologically related to the activity of the ascending reticular activating system (Mandler, 1962). It is clear that the expression of emotions is often accompanied by high levels of activation which is probably due to the recruitment of the sympathetic nervous system. The concept of activation is not an adequate explanation for emotional behavior since it does not exhaustively explain the events that control emotional behavior. As Mandler (1962) points out:

> We may say that one of the necessary conditions is an activated organism, and we may even go one step further and assume some correspondence (though not identity) between the activation concept and the drive concept in modern learning theory . . . But the statement that emotion usually involves activation does not, of course, imply that activation usually involves emotion. Thus, a man trying to lift a two-hundred pound weight is quite activated . . . but is he necessarily in an emotional state? (p. 322).

With the activation concept, as with autonomic patterning, other factors are required for an adequate explanation of emotional responsiveness.

Emotional and Cognitive Interaction

Emotional and cognitive development are interrelated in many intricate ways. In terms of priority of development, it is difficult to dispute the fact that young children exhibit intense and well-differentiated feelings long before a capacity for logical thought is prominent. Emotions similarly precede reasoning in the phyletic scale. Nevertheless, even in the earliest stages of emotional expressiveness, the cerebral hemispheres add two important features, differentiation and sensitization, to emotional responsiveness (Gellhorn, 1968). As noted previously, visceral changes and activation are conditions which accompany, but do not explain, emotional responses (Schachter & Singer, 1962). Cognitive expectancy appears to be a major determinant of emotional states, since a single state of epinephrine-induced sympathetic activation can produce euphoria or anger depending on the person's cognitive expectations. Cognitions arising from the immediate situation as interpreted by past experience provide the framework in which an individual comes to understand and label his feelings (Schachter & Singer, 1962).

The extent of the developmental gap between the emergence of differentiated emotions and that of logical thought has probably been exaggerated. Also, although thought undoubtedly tends to be liberated somewhat from autistic and subjectivistic influences with increasing age (see p. 563), abundant evidence indicates that attitudes and wishes continue to distort logical thinking in persons of all ages. Not only do feelings influence thought, but also level of cognitive sophistication, as we shall see shortly, has a profound influence on emotional reactivity. It is the cognitive interpretation of the perceived excitant, after all, rather than the latter per se which determines the nature of the emotional response.

GENERAL TRENDS IN EMOTIONAL DEVELOPMENT

Differentiation of Specific Emotions

One of the earliest features of affective development is the differentiation of specific emotions out of the state of general excitement that limits emotional reactivity at birth.* This development occurs, roughly speaking, between the second half of the first year and the third year; in subsequent sections it will be traced separately for each emotion. By way of general introduction, it will suffice to point out here that the process of differentiation affects excitants, feeling tones, and modes of expression, and depends for the most part on (a) the development of a self-concept and other ego attributes that provide sufficiently salient personality referents to warrant the instigation of emotional states, and (b) the growth of sufficient cognitive sophistication to make possible the differential interpretation of perceived and anticipated events that enhance or threaten the self. To some extent also, the emergence of new reactive capacities (e.g., volitional aggression and avoidance) and of differential autonomic responses contributes to the distinctive properties of differentiated emotions; but these contributions are only reflective and secondary, since the skeletal and visceral reactions accompanying emotional states are themselves determined by interpretive (cognitive) differences in response to excitants with self-reference. According to this view, the hypothalamus is not a primary determinant of emotional quality in its own right, but a coordinating center for the *expression* of emotional reactions already determined at a sophisticated cortical level.

Changes in Excitants

With increasing age, systematic changes occur in the properties of stimuli evoking emotional reactions or in the responsiveness of children to different categories of emotional stimulation. Some of these changes undoubtedly

---

*See pages 225 and 226 for a discussion of emotional experience in the neonate, the evidence against specific emotions, and the probable reasons for lack of differentiation.

reflect *specific* family and cultural training concerning the conditions under which the expression of particular emotions is considered appropriate. Many of these changes, however, are attributable to cumulative increments in cognitive and personality maturity resulting from neural maturation and incidental experience and training in these *other* (i.e., cognitive and personality) areas of development. As notions of omnipotence decline and as frustration tolerance increases, children react less vigorously to volitional constraint. As self-esteem and self-criticism become more prominent in the economy of personality organization, children become more susceptible to feelings of anxiety. And with increasing cognitive sophistication, we can expect that the scope of emotional reactivity will be extended to new situations and that some excitants of affective response at earlier stages of development will no longer be effective.

The range of stimuli instigating emotional reactions inevitably broadens in subtlety and complexity as children become more able to perceive, anticipate and imagine potential implications for self in more intricate life situations. Infants' susceptibility to fear increases as they become sufficiently mature to grasp the threatening implications of strangeness and other previously unrecognized hazards (Freedman, Loring & Martin, 1967). Thus, brighter preschool children become afraid of certain situations at an earlier age than their duller contemporaries (Holmes, 1935). Older children are more responsive than younger children to less tangible and more symbolic excitants of emotion (Jersild & Holmes, 1935); they react not only to the immediate perceptual properties of an emotional stimulus but also to its long range and deducible implications (Jersild & Meigs, 1943).

While the scope of emotional responsiveness is being extended to more subtle, abstract and complex excitants, the child is simultaneously desensitized to other kinds of emotional stimuli. By virtue of the same gain in cognitive maturity he is able to discount formerly adequate excitants based on misconceptions, misinformation, inexperience and lack of skill in coping with problems. As he becomes more critical and less suggestible (Anderson, 1950), and as he accumulates successful experience in handling various situations (Lacey & Vanlehn, 1952), he becomes less aroused emotionally by many previously provocative stimuli. With shifts in ego goals, ego-involvements, and internal endocrine states, as for example during adolescence, he becomes less responsive to some stimuli (e.g., thrills, adventure) and more responsive to others (e.g., heterosexual concerns) (Anderson, 1950).

Changes in Expression

Paralleling the age level changes in responsiveness to different kinds of excitants are developmental changes in mode of expression. In general, emotional responses become less diffuse and more specific, directed, and adaptive with increasing age (Freedman *et al*, 1967). Instead of reacting indiscriminately and with exaggerated and uniform intensity to all excitants, the older child tends to utilize a selective gradation of response intensity appropriate to the situation at hand. At the same time the response becomes more highly differentiated or distinctive in relation to the feeling tones involved. Newly acquired reactive capacities (avoidance, aggression) are superimposed upon a genically determined core pattern of expression. The young infant can only cry and thrash about; the young child can hide, run away, strike out, shout defiance, or argue contentiously. Later, culturally directed training further restricts the range of acceptable alternatives and specifies the appropriate type of response and the time, place, and conditions under which it may be legitimately made. In our culture lower-class children learn to express their emotions in motor activity; middle-class children, on the other hand, are taught to express their feelings in more abstract and ideational form (Davis & Havighurst, 1947; McNeil, 1956). In all children a tendency toward more subtle, symbolic, and devious affective expression is a regular accompaniment of emotional development. But despite selectively greater utilization of covert expressive components, the correspondence between the two kinds of reactions tends to improve with increasing age indicating a more integrated type of total organismic response.

Invariably, as children grow older, the culture demands greater suppression of overt emotionality, and accordingly, they gradually learn increased emotional control (Paulson, 1953). An inevitable concomitant of this trend is an increase in the strength of the autonomic component and a corresponding decrease in the strength of the skeletal-motor component of affective behavior—a state of affairs which tends to make emotional response less superficial and more long lasting in its effects. It is illustrated by the gradual decline of crying as a form of emotional expression. For a given age group, however, the incidence of crying varies considerably in accordance with situational factors; it is less at school than at home, when sympathetic observers are absent, and when hurts are accidental rather than deliberately inflicted. The pressure for control also varies from one culture, subculture, and family to another in the type of emotional expression that has to be suppressed and in the degree of suppression required. Middle-class children, for example, are under greater pressure than lower-class children to repress the physical components of aggression (Davis *et al*, 1947; McKee & Leader, 1955; McNeil, 1956). Boys are expected more than girls to repress fear and crying, but are permitted greater expression of physical aggression.

FEAR

Fear is in a generic sense a differentiated emotional experience that betokens cognitive awareness of threat to some highly ego-involved aspect of the individual's self-concept such as his physical well-being or his self-esteem. Regardless of how else they may be classified, all excitants of fear embody some such threat to self. Although fear stages usually include autonomic-humoral reactions, selective lowering of relevant perceptual and response thresholds, a somewhat variable pattern of motor responses, and the conscious repercussions of these different reactions, the only *essential* component of fear experience is subjective awareness of threat following cognitive interpretation of an adequate excitant. The autonomic-skeletal concomitants of fear, whether induced by direct hypothalamic stimulation, by injection of adrenalin, or by abrupt loss of physical support in older children, cannot by themselves (in the absence of perceived threat) generate genuine states of fear. Furthermore, because of cultural pressures, the somatic aspects of fear are either frequently repressed or else constitute highly modified and variable derivatives of original, genically patterned neuro-muscular and avoidance responses.

Although the maladaptive effects of intense fear on problem solving and delicate skills are not to be underestimated, we should not for this reason discount the important role of fear as a protective, motivating and socializing agent. Fear promotes the prudent avoidance of danger and the exercise of reasonable caution. It alerts the individual to potential threat and mobilizes his reactive capacities. And most important of all, fear of punishment, social censure, failure, guilt, and loss of status are ubiquitous and indispensable factors in the acquisition of socialized and moral behavior and the realization of ego status and ego maturity goals.

Classification of Fear States

By specifying whether the excitant evoking fear is a current or anticipated threat and whether the individual's physical well-being or self-esteem is being threatened, it is possible to classify generic fear experience into four subcategories (see table 3). *Fear* (in the specific sense) and *anxiety-fear* refer to fear states elicited in response to current threats, whereas *insecurity* and *anxiety* are referable to anticipated threats. Both *fear* and *insecurity* involve affective reactions to threats directed at the individual's physical safety or continuance as a biological and psychological entity, whereas in the case of *anxiety-fear* and *anxiety*, his self-esteem is perceived as under attack. The stimuli initiating anxiety are ordinarily more difficult to identify than the stimuli for fear reactions (Freedman *et al*, 1967).

Threats vary in their accessibility to consciousness and in their identifi-ability—both with respect to their source (the origin or nature of the threat) and their object (the aspect of self that is threatened). Repression of aware-ness (inaccessibility) temporarily reduces fear but is maladaptive in the long run since it does not permit the individual to cope constructively with the

TABLE 3.—*Classification of Fear States**

Temporal Position of Perceived Threat	What is Threatened	
	Physical Well-Being	Self-Esteem
Current	Fear	Anxiety-Fear
Anticipated	Insecurity	Anxiety

Adapted from D. P. Ausubel, Ego Development and the Personality Disorders.

threat confronting him. Unidentifiable threats tend to generate more fear than identifiable threats since the threatened individual cannot prepare his defenses adequately when he can specify neither the source nor the target of danger. Thus arises the common mechanism of displacement—giving a vague or unpalatable intrapersonal source of threat concrete external reference and shifting the object of threat from an unspecifiable aspect of self-esteem to a more tangible (and manageable)aspect of physical safety. *Phobias* are just such displaced fears.

The persistence of "irrational fears" in children, that is, fears of situations that are out of all proportion to the actual probability of their occurrence (fear of wild animals and ghosts and of failing in school) probably represent a form of phobia or displaced fear. Also frequently involved in such fears are intrapersonal sources of threat (e.h., feelings of inadequacy, guilt feelings, aggressive impulses) over and above the objective hazards confronting the individual. In certain instances the seemingly exaggerated fear response to an improbable catastrophe (e.g., failure in school) may not even be irrational if the child is reacting to the imagined calamitous consequences that would ensue if the improbable event actually *did* occur rather than to the statistical probabilities involved.

Development of Fear in Infants

In the first half year of life potentially harmful stimuli are not perceived as threats and hence elicit diffuse excitement or distress rather than fear. Before threat can be perceived as such, the infant must first be able to perceive and discriminate between persons and objects, and between the familiar and unfamiliar in his environment; he must also possess sufficient cognitive maturity to appreciate that certain persons and situations can threaten his continued existence as an individual. And it is obvious that threats can have no self-reference (and hence insufficient salience to instigate fear) until a functional notion of identity exists.

Once the prerequisites for experiencing fear are fulfilled, the adequate stimuli initially eliciting this emotion are practically coextensive with the factors instigating general excitement (i.e., any intense stimulation), provided that the elements of suddenness, unexpectedness, or unfamiliarity are also present. During early infancy fear is most commonly elicited by unexpected loud noises, rapid or abrupt displacement in space, pain, strange events, and sudden movements (Freedman *et al*, 1967).

However, such stimuli should not be conceived of as "original" in a reflex-like sense; it appears, rather, that at this primitive level of cognitive maturity *only* such gross, concrete, and immediate stimuli as these have threatening implications. A component of the fear response may be a result of maturation, and in its earliest stages a fear of strangers corresponds to flight reactions seen in lower mammals (Freedman, 1961). Genic factors may be operative in fear of strangers since identical twins show higher resemblance than do fraternal twins in the pattern and timing of fear (Freedman, 1966). Fear, however, emerges with increasing cognitive maturity. For example, fear of strangers demands habitual interaction with the environment, and its onset is between the sixth and ninth months (Bronson, 1968; Freedman, 1961; Morgan & Riccuiti, 1968; Polak, Emde & Spitz, 1964; Schaffer, 1966; Schaffer & Emerson, 1964); and fear of strangers also appears to be correlated with discrimination of familiar and unfamiliar individuals (Schaffer, 1966). The presence of the mother substantially decreases or inhibits the infant's fear response to strangers (Arsenian, 1943; Bronson, 1968). The ability to differentiate familiar and distorted faces may mark the beginning of this early discrimination process (Kagan *et al*, 1966).

Developmental Changes

Altered Responsiveness. Developmental shifts in responsiveness to fear are mirrored in the changing range and properties of fear excitants as children advance in age. Many stimuli that effectively instigate fear during earlier years become less adequate as children gain in experience, understanding, and the ability to cope with trying situations. Many other factors, on the other hand, simultaneously enhance susceptibility to fear. The broadening of the older child's physical and psychological experience with excitants with which he has relatively little direct experience (darkness, solitude, abandonment, wild animals, storms, criminal characters, supernatural figures, death, occult phenomena) increases his fear of these situations; in addition he learns to fear such new threats as school failure, social ridicule, and personal inadequacy. This trend continues into and becomes even more pronounced during the elementary school years (Alexander & Alderstern, 1958; Angelino, Dollins & Mech, 1956; Hagman, 1932; Jersild & Holmes, 1935; Jersild, Markey & Jersild, 1933; Maurer, 1965). The elementary school years are also characterized by an increase in the use of terms which indicate fears and in the mentioning of bodily states (Plutchik, 1962).

Expressive Characteristics. In accordance with general developmental trends in emotional expression, the expression of fear becomes more subtle, abstract and devious, and less transparent and overt with increasing age. Not only the gross motor components of fear (crying, trembling, shrinking, clinging, cringing, flight), but also its subjective content, are repressed. If subjective repression is impossible, the child may fail either to recognize his feelings as fear or to acknowledge any relationship between them and relevant excitants. In either case the autonomic-humoral component of the fear response is enhanced.

The reasons for these trends are rather self-evident. First, since the excitants of fear tend to become more imaginary, symbolic, unidentifiable, and intrapersonal in origin, overt response becomes less possible. Second, since in many cultures the expression of fear is regarded as opprobrious and as a confession of weakness or cowardice, it is treated with contempt and ridicule; as the child learns to fear ridicule he also learns to fear the expression of his own fears. Internalization of this cultural standard also makes self-acknowledgement of fear sufficient cause for self-contempt, thereby favoring suppression of subjective awareness.

Other Factors Affecting Responsiveness to Fear

Children's responsiveness to fear is affected by cultural influences, by individual differences in personality structure, and by situational factors. The form that fears take is largely molded by cultural stereotypes, that is, by social expectations, by traditional views of what constitutes an adequate stimulus, and by the particular uses adults make of fears in the socializing process. In our culture, in accordance with differential social expectations, girls exceed boys in almost all categories of fear expression (Hagman, 1932; Varma, 1957). Our culture, too, makes only oblique but highly suggestive references to bogeymen, witches, and goblins as instruments of retribution, whereas some North American Indian cultures rely upon actual enactment of these roles by masked and robed relatives as a principal means of disciplining children and exacting conformity to social norms (Wallis, 1954).

Interindividual differences in responsiveness to fear are related to such temperamental traits as timorousness and "toughness of skin," to actual incompetence or feelings of inadequacy, and to the extent that fear is utilized by children (or parents) as a means of obtaining attention and affection or of perpetuating executive dependence. Children are more responsive to fear in an atmosphere of fearfulness, insecurity, and hostility, when they are burdened prematurely with adult worries and problems, and when they are chronically subjected to threat, intimidation, harsh punishment, and demands beyond their capacity. They are also more fearful when parents are overprotective or set an example of fear, since not only is fear contagious but also in this instance it deprives them of their main source of support and reassurance. Thus, a high positive correlation prevails between the number of fears possessed by children and the number possessed by their mothers (Hagman, 1932). Firstborns, widely spaced children, and institutionalized orphans show more fear of strangers and objects (Collard, 1968; Dambiorska & Stepanova, 1962). Social class differences in both quality and quantity of fears have also been reported (Angelino *et al*, 1956; Sidana, 1967). In addition, children are more prone to be aroused by fear in unfamiliar physical settings and in unstructured social situations in which standards of acceptable behavior are ambiguous.

ANXIETY*

Anxiety is a special variety of fear experienced in response to an *anticipated* threat to self-esteem. It always includes the interpretive and preparatory reactive phases of an emotional experience. The consummatory phase, however, with its subjective, autonomic-humoral, and motor components (and their reflective repercussions) may either be experienced as an advance reaction to the anticipated threat, or may be delayed until the threat is current or self-esteem itself actually undergoes impairment. In the latter instances, the response is identical in content with that of *anxiety-fear* except that it is initiated by an anticipatory stimulus and involves a prolonged preparatory phase. Anxiety and insecurity thus include both a currently experienced emotion and a "set" to respond affectively to an anticipated threat; and since these reactions implicate such stable and salient features of ego structure as adequacy and security feelings, they too become conceptualized as ego attributes in relation to the self-concept. Hence, quite apart from the existence of *particular* anticipated threats, an individual tends to conceive of himself as *typically* manifesting a given affective level of anxiety and insecurity.

Except for these designated differences, anxiety and insecurity share all of the properties of fear states described above. They vary in degree of accessibility, identifiability and displacement, with respect to both source and object of threat; and the component aspects of the affective response may also undergo varying degrees of repression. In our opinion, therefore, the many attempts that have been made to differentiate between fear and anxiety on such grounds as the facts that in anxiety states the source of threat is allegedly less accessible, identifiable and exogenous, the object of threat is more central, and the response is more apt to be both disproportionately great and subjectively inaccessible are warranted neither by logic nor by

A review of the literature on anxiety discussing normative data theory and methodological problems is available. See Ruebush, 1963.

empirical data. The current threat to physical safety in fear states is always psychologically salient, is frequently unidentifiable, and may also inhere largely in feelings of inadaquacy, guilt and hostility, whereas, in many instances of anxiety, the threat is external and specifiable, the individual is completely aware of the feelings it evokes, and the response (except in neurotic anxiety) is wholly commensurate with the objective magnitude of the danger involved.

Varieties of Anxiety

The basic problem in classifying anxiety states is to distinguish between anxiety as a pathological entity (neurotic anxiety) and as a normal situational or developmental type of behavior that is warranted under certain conditions. Since every affect, neurotic or otherwise, must be instigated by a *subjectively* adequate stimulus, it is only possible to designate as *"neurotic"* that anxiety in which the exogenous or endogenous threat to self-esteem is not *objectively* adequate to instigate fear but appears *subjectively* adequate to the individual because of existing impairment of self-esteem (the very target of threat) itself. He overreacts with fear not because his self-esteem is threatened by objectively adequate hazards, failings, or feelings of guilt and hostility, but because *any* trivial threat to an ego-involved area of self-esteem is *actually* calamitous to an individual whose self-esteem is already impaired and lacks a reasonable margin of safety. Hence, in neurotic anxiety, the fear response is disproportionate to the objective degree of threat emanating from sources distinct from the object of threat itself (self-esteem).

It is reasonable to suppose that the degree of impairment of self-esteem predisposing toward neurotic anxiety is characteristically found only in children who have not undergone satellization in the course of development. First, they lack the background of derived status that provides a current or residual core of intrinsic self-esteem irrespective of environmental vicissitudes in the quest for primary status. Second, their extrinsic feelings of adequacy are extremely vulnerable to catastrophic impairment by virtue of chronic rejection, precipitous devaluation outside the home (in the case of overvalued children), and unrealistically high ego aspirations.

Normal *transitional* anxiety arises during periods of crisis in ego development. Its source lies in pressures that are inherent in the very nature of developmental transition (see p. 116). Hence it occurs more or less universally in all individuals and at every age when rapid personality change is required. The relevant factors entering into the threat are: new social expectations regarding the abandonment of an established, and the gaining of a new, biosocial status; the need to accomplish new developmental tasks; an intermediate period of attitudinal disorientation and marginal status; and uncertainty whether the new status will ever be attained—a state of affairs deliberately fostered by the culture to encourage a high and sustained level of motivation regarding the acquisition of new ego maturity and ego status goals.

Because of exposure to certain undesirable parent attitudes it is understandable that transitional anxiety may be more severe in some children than in others. Overprotected and overdominated children are especially threatened by the need to relinquish derived status and to strive for primary status and volitional independence (see p. 279). During the course of socialization the underdominated child must cope with the anxiety arising from the absence of effective internal and external control of his aggressive impulses. The children of underappreciating and hypercritical parents may experience serious doubts about their ability to meet the new requirements and standards of more mature personality status. In the case of rejected and overvalued children, the excitants of transitional anxiety may furnish the occasion for either the initial generation of or the release of existing neurotic anxiety.

Situational anxiety is the normal type of anxiety that arises in relation to exogenous threats to self-esteem. It is a self-protective reaction which is limited to the duration of the situation that elicits it and is proportionate to the objective magnitude of the threat involved. Situational anxiety is inherent in almost any new ego-involved task or problem that exposes the individual to the possibility of frustration, failure, or loss of self-esteem. Susceptibility to situational anxiety is increased by several factors; by any of the situational, personal, and interpersonal factors enhancing responsiveness to fear (see p. 425); by past experience with such traumatic events as accidents, operations, separations, vivid frights, and sudden privations; and by predispositions to neurotic anxiety. Also influencing general responsiveness to situational anxiety are such cultural factors as the extent to which society intrinsically values the individual as opposed to coercing him into competing for hierarchical status, the availability of the extrinsic status for which the culture motivates its members to strive, and the incidence of cultural crises and social disorganization.

Endogenous anxiety is similar to situational anxiety except for the fact that the threat arises from within the individual rather than from the environment. Unlike neurotic anxiety the threat is objectively adequate in relation to the response it evokes, and the source of the threat does not inhere in impaired self-esteem. A common type of endogenous anxiety is derived from objective physical, motor, intellectual and social disabilities which constitute a threat to self-esteem insofar as they expose the individual to ridicule and ostracism, loss of status, and failure in various adjustive situations. Hostility and other socially unacceptable impulses and attitudes generate anxiety by threatening the individual (if they are expressed) with loss of acceptance from the persons on whom he is dependent for derived status and with reprisals from authority figures who control his primary status. * Indirectly, by giving rise to guilt feelings (awareness of moral culpability, self-reproach), these impulses endanger self-esteem and induce anxiety.

Assessment of Anxiety. The assessment of anxiety in children is contingent on the age of the child and on the particular interest of the researcher. Anxiety in infancy demands observation of the behavior of the infant and clinical interview techniques with the parent or caretakers. Older children can respond to paper-and pencil tests designed to assess anxiety, so that these can be used in addition to direct observation techniques. The particular methods of assessment used depend on whether the anxiety being studied is general or specific, and neurotic or normal. Clinical techniques such as observation of classroom behavior, ratings by teachers, ratings by parents, interviews with parents and observation and interviews with children are available for use (Ruebush, 1963). Several objective measures of anxiety have also been devised for a variety of purposes. The Children's Manifest Anxiety Scale (CMAS) is administered by teachers to assess general or chronic states of anxiety rather than specific situational complaints (Castaneda, McCandless & Palermo, 1956). Sarason (1960) has devised a general anxiety scale for children which can also be used to measure the relationship between anxiety in specific situations and more general forms of anxiety. Test Anxiety Scales for Children (TASC) have been developed to measure anxiety in test-like situations (Sarason, 1960).†

Development of Anxiety

Precursors of anxiety responses are seen in neonates in the cycles of distress which occur in the absence of specific trauma (Kessen & Mandler, 1961). Insecurity is differentiated out of general excitement several months later than is fear since it requires the ability to anticipate danger or perceive future threat to safety in current cues. It is first manifested at approximately the eighth month in response to abrupt separation from the customary mother figure (Riccuiti, 1968). The infant is aware of his executive dependency and hence perceives the deprivation of his executive arm as a threat to his physical well-being. Concurrent increase in attachment behavior and stranger anxiety supports this interpretation (Ainsworth, 1963, 1964; Schaffer & Emerson, 1964), although there is some evidence that stranger anxiety occurs before separation anxiety (Tennes & Lampl, 1964). After satellization takes place and the child identifies his security with parental acceptance,

---

Fear of physical retaliation and loss of succorance engendered by aggressive impulses is really a form of insecurity.

†*Discussion of reliability and validity of these various techniques is beyond the scope of this book. See Ruebush, 1963.*

disapproval becomes a more salient precipitant of insecurity feelings. Thus, anxiety appears relatively late on the emotional horizon. It presupposes the child's ability to conceptualize his own biosocial status, to react to depreciation of such status with lowered feelings of adequacy, and to anticipate future threats to self-esteem. Anxiety, therefore, can make its first appearance only after the emergence of a primitive sense of adequacy which initially reflects the infant's tendency to perceive himself as volitionally omnipotent and independent. Serious challenges to this status, such as occur during the period of ego devaluation, threaten self-esteem sufficiently to instigate transitional anxiety; but since the devaluation is generally carried out in a setting of benevolence and affection, this anxiety tends to be overshadowed by negativism.

During the preschool and early elementary school years anxiety is instigated in relation to parent-child and peer-child conflicts (Dorkey & Amen, 1947; Temple & Amen, 1944). In preschoolers, the presence of high anxiety fosters dependency behavior in girls (Rosenthal, 1967). The anxiety and dependency are probably a result of the threatened loss of derived status. As cognitive sophistication increases with advancing age and ego functioning becomes more complex, the child becomes responsive to a wider, more subtle, abstract, remote, and unidentifiable array of situations threatening his self-esteem.* Threats to primary status (school failure, personal inadequacy) become more prominent excitants of anxiety (Ruebush, 1963) which, as in the case of fear, are increasingly subjected to repression. Children with low anxiety probably repress anxiety less and this is seen in their quicker reaction to emotionally charged words (Ruebush, 1963). Thus, anxiety may be linked with age-changing shifts in psychosocial pressures which may differ from one culture to another (Gotts, 1968).

Personality and Psychosocial Dimensions of Anxiety

The explanation for the development of different types of anxiety in children is as yet unknown. Neurotic anxiety in children is characterized by impairment of self-esteem and the consequent overreaction with fear to perceived threats to self-esteem. For example, high-anxiety children are much more sensitive to failure experiences than are low-anxiety children (Smock, 1963). Consideration of normal personality development, as well as clinical study, suggest that an individual can never develop neurotic anxiety as long as he enjoys intrinsic feelings of self-esteem, by which is meant a deep inner conviction that he is important and worthwhile for himself—apart from what he can do or accomplish, and apart from the

---

*The empirical measures of anxiety (e.g., CMAS) have not demonstrated any clear age differences in anxiety. See Ruebush (1963) for a thorough review of the normative data. The test anxiety scores (TASC) have been found to increase linearly with age (Ruebush, 1963).

position he holds in life (Ausubel, 1956). As long as he possesses this intrinsic self-esteem, failure in achieving superior competence or status is intense, deeply felt, discouraging—but always peripheral to basic self-esteem, and, hence, never catastrophic. If the child is extrinsically valued, he relies on his executive competence. When the child's self-esteem is impaired following some very traumatic failure experience he becomes increasingly sensitive to future possible experiences. If such failure occurs, it is not peripheral but central—since there is now no basis whatsoever (intrinsic or extrinsic) for a feeling of worth as a human being. Since the individual's sense of adequacy is purely a function of his competence or reputation, little self-regard can remain if these are seriously undermined.

Feelings of intrinsic self-esteem, as we have already seen, can develop only in one way—from a child identifying in a dependent sense with his parents. He can do this if he perceives that he is accepted and valued for himself. His all-powerful, omniscient parents can endow all objects, including him, with intrinsic value if they so desire. If they respond to him as a person who is worthwhile and important in his own right—just because they accept him as such—he tends to react to himself in the same way, since he has no other standards of value but theirs. He thus acquires an intrinsic sense of adequacy, a vicarious status which is derived from his dependent relationship to his parents, and which is independent of his actual competencies. As he becomes older, he will increasingly strive for a more primary status based upon his own accomplishments, and will develop feelings of self-esteem related to them. But there will always remain a residual sense of worth which his parents conferred on him by fiat, when, as a child, he perceived this to lie within their power.

As pointed out above, however, not all children are fortunate enough to be accepted and intrinsically valued by their parents. Some are rejected outright, and others are accepted but extrinsically valued, that is, accepted only in terms of their potential capacity for enhancing their parents' egos by becoming important and successful individuals (Crandall, 1967). Such children do not undergo dependent identification with their parents, since they cannot acquire any vicarious status or intrinsic feelings of self-esteem from such a relationship. From the very beginning, their self-esteem becomes a function of what they are able to do and accomplish, and their anxiety is compounded with both active and passive forms of dependency (Ruebush, 1963); this contradicts their attempts at independence. Of course, vulnerability to impairment of self-esteem does not, in itself, guarantee that such impairment must inevitably occur. In most instances, however, the anxiety aroused appears to correlate with negative self-concept, self-disparagement, clinical maladjustment, insecurity and negative peer status* (Cowen, Zax

---

*The generality of these findings is questioned by a study which indicates a negative relationship between anxiety and sociometric status when across-sex comparisons are made (Hill, 1963).

et al, 1965; Feldhusen & Thurston, 1964; Ruebush, 1963). The negative status probably occurs when self-enhancement is attempted by derogation of others (Phillips, 1968). Further evidence for the effects of extrinsic evaluation on children's anxiety is seen in the more prevalent occurrence of such states in Negro children. In our culture, in keeping with the more prominent satellization in females, threats to their self-esteem elicts less anxiety in a variety of situations than is the case for males (Crandall, 1967; Maccoby, 1966; Ruebush, 1963).

Behavioral Correlates of Anxiety

Intelligence. Research evidence indicates almost uniformly that there is a low but significant negative correlation between anxiety and intelligence (Cowen *et al*, 1965; Feldhusen, Denny & Condon, 1965; Penney, 1965; Ruebush, 1963; Sarason *et al*, 1964). Although stability of anxiety scores decreases as intervals between testings increase, marked changes in anxiety are inversely related to changes in I.Q. during the early elementary school years (Hill & Sarason, 1966). These findings are consistent with the inverse relationship between anxiety and novel problem solving; they suggest that, in a threatening test situation, the negative effects of anxiety on complex learning tasks overshadow its positive motivational effects on test performance. Another plausible interpretation is that the low-IQ individual may feel generally anxious as a result of his inferior school achievement. A less likely interpretation is that anxiety may actually depress the development of intelligence rather than merely depressing performance on an intelligence test.

*Effects of Anxiety on Learning.** We have postulated that neurotic anxiety is the overreaction of an individual with impaired self-esteem to the threat anticipated in adjustive situations. The threatening implications of the latter are derived from their capacity to further impair self-esteem in the face of an inner feeling of inadequacy to cope with them. Normal anxiety, on the other hand, is the fear evoked by anticipation of objectively hazardous threats to self-esteem. Normal subjects do not display anxiety when confronted with ordinarily adjustive situations, because they do not lack confidence in their ultimate capacity to acquire the necessary adaptive responses.

The relationship between anxiety and learning is complicated by the fact that although high-anxiety individuals exhibit more than average *motivation* (i.e., although they tend originally to manifest an excess of ego-enhancement drive and are further driven to achieve as the only practicable means of reducing anxiety), their high level of anxiety also tends to have a disruptive effect on *novel* problem solving (Ruebush, 1963). Thus, it has been generally

---

A more comprehensive review of the literature is available. See Ruebush, 1963.

found that anxiety facilitates rote and less difficult kinds of meaningful reception learning, but has an inhibitory effect on more complex types of learning tasks that are either highly unfamiliar or are more dependent on improvising skill than on persistence (Ausubel, Schiff & Goldman, 1953; Caron, 1963; Castenada et al, 1956; Lantz, 1945; McGuigan, Calvin & Richardson, 1959; Marks & Vestre, 1961; Palermo et al, 1956; Pickrel, 1958; Russel & Sarason, 1965; Sarason et al, 1960; Stevenson & Odom, 1965; Tomkins, 1943; Zander, 1944). These complex types of learning situations are obviously highly threatening to anxious individuals and tend to induce a disabling level of anxiety. It does appear, however, that anxiety may *enhance* the learning of complex tasks when they do not seriously threaten self-esteem, i.e., when they are not inordinately novel or significant (Van Buskirk, 1961; Wittrock & Husek, 1962), when the anxiety is only moderate in degree, or when the learner possesses effective anxiety-coping mechanisms (Cox, 1968; Horowitz & Armentraut, 1965; Suirn, 1965). The learning of complex verbal materials in a typical school setting, for example, seems to be a relatively familiar and nonthreatening task when compared to novel problem-solving situations. Consistent with these findings are the observations that highly anxious subjects, as compared to less anxious subjects, have poorer visual discrimination of pictures of social scenes (Knights, 1965), show less curiosity (Penney, 1965), exhibit more rigidity and earlier perceptual closure (Cohen, 1961; Smock, 1958), and evince less preference for novel toys (Mendel, 1965).*

Effects of Anxiety on School Achievement. As could be reasonably anticipated, the effect of anxiety on school achievement is comparable to its effect on learning, except that on a long-term basis its disruptive influence is much less intense. School achievement tasks, after all, tend to lose their threatening implications as students gain experience in coping with them. Nevertheless, highly anxious children are more negative in their attitudes to school-related concepts (Barnard, 1966). At the elementary-school level, anxiety generally depresses scholastic achievement (Cowen et al, 1965; Feldhusen & Klausmeier 1962; Hill & Sarason, 1966; Lunneborg, 1964; Reese, 1961; Sarason, et al, 1964). In high school, as the motivational effects of anxiety become stronger relative to its disruptive effects, the negative correlation between anxiety and academic achievement decreases, particularly in boys; it is either weaker or entirely absent when grades are used as an index of achievement (Sarason, 1961, 1963; Walter, Denzler & Sarason, 1964). In highly structured learning tasks such as programmed instruction, a positive relationship has been reported between anxiety and achievement (Kight & Sassenrath, 1966;

Mendel's (1965) interpretation as "generalized novelty preference" in low anxious children can be questioned since novelty does not always interact with a child's anxiety state to produce changes in toy preferences (e.g., see Gilmore, 1966).

Traweek, 1964). This finding is consistent with the fact that anxious pupils, particularly when compulsive, do much better in highly structured learning situations where novelty and the need for improvisation are minimal.

ANGER AND AGGRESSION*

Anger is a differentiated emotional experience instigated by threat to an ego-involved aspect of self in which awareness of threat (and its preparatory, autonomic-humoral and motor consequences) is partly or completely replaced by aggressive subjective content and corresponding activity in the autonomic-humoral and motor spheres. Anger is frequently aroused by threats to physical well-being and self-esteem, by attacks on property or on reputation, by frustration of volitional desires, or by interference with goal-directed physical activities. In the past frustration was considered to be the primary antecedent of anger and aggression, but contemporary research does not support this contention (Bandura & Walters, 1963a, Buss, 1961). Frustration can certainly increase anger and aggression (Bandura & Walters, 1963; Mallick & McCandless, 1966) but these states are not exclusively caused by frustration (Bandura & Walters, 1963a; Kuhn, Madsen and Becker, 1967). Whether a child responds to frustration with aggression apparently depends on his seeing both the nature of the response to frustration made by significant adults (Bandura & Huston, 1961; Bandura, Ross & Ross, 1961) and the behavioral outcome of this response. For example, children respond with more imitative aggression and anger if they have seen an adult model rewarded for aggression (Bandura & Walters, 1963a; Rosenkrans & Hartup, 1967). Peers can also serve as models for anger and aggression when a child is frustrated and victimized (Patterson, Littman & Bricker, 1967). But just as anger may be instigated by excitants other than frustration, frustration may also lead to outcomes other than rage and aggression. In the course of learning, frustration may become associated with fear, insecurity, and anxiety, with submission avoidance and dependency (Bandura & Walters, 1963a; Whiting, 1944), and with nonspecific compensatory satisfactions and regression (Bandura & Walters, 1963a; Barker, Dembo & Lewin, 1941).

Anger and fear are closely related. Similar factors are involved in instigating and increasing responsiveness to each, and either emotion may accompany or give rise to the other. An individual's awareness of his own hostility often precipitates fear and, contrariwise, many acts of aggression are prompted by fear. Anger, however, is encountered more frequently in

---

*Reviews on the topics of anger and aggression are available. See Bandura & Walters (1963a); Berkowitz (1964); Buss (1961).

children than is fear because it is aroused more easily, is less avoidable, and is more apt to be effective in gaining goal satisfaction (Felder, 1932).

Because parental and cultural tolerance for children's aggression almost invariably diminishes as they leave infancy, the expression of anger is subjected to varying degrees of inhibition (Whiting & Child, 1953). More commonly only the motor-verbal components of rage are inhibited; sometimes, however, the subjective component is also repressed. Frequently when the overt motor-verbal expression of aggression is inhibited because of fear of punishment or retaliation, indirect, disguised and covert outlets, such as passive sabotage, exaggerated friendliness, and imagining or wishing injury to others, are utilized. The amount of overt aggression a child displays is a poor indication of the amount he feels. Korner (1949) obtained only low positive correlations between real-life and different kinds of fantasy aggression, and Sears (1951) found that preschool children highly punished by their mothers for aggression tended to rank low on frequency of aggressive acts in school but high on doll play aggression. Results of other studies support the view that the amount of overt and fantasy aggression are positively related in children provided that they do not fear punishment excessively for their aggressive impulses (Mussen & Naylor, 1954).* Without additional interview data it is impossible to ascertain the extent to which such fantasy aggression is accessible to consciousness and is recognized as such. Subjective repression of the excitant and the referent, as well as of the feeling tones themselves, is especially apt to occur when hostility is accompanied by either guilt feelings or intense anxiety. Children may further protect themselves from the consequences of their own hostility by failing to perceive hostile acts directed against themselves.

All of the factors promoting the inhibition of aggression also favor the displacement of the object or person against whom anger is directed. The anger children feel toward parents and other persons in authority is frequently displaced to animals, siblings and classmates, or is expressed in the form of truancy, delinquency, antisocial attitudes, and racial prejudice (Bandura & Walters, 1963a; Buss, 1961; Lewin, Lippitt & White, 1939). Sometimes children turn their anger against themselves and court injury in order to provoke guilt feelings in parents or to involve them in personal and financial difficulties. Krall (1953) found that a group of accident-prone children exhibited significantly more aggression in doll play than did a matched group of accident-free children. Children also frequently project their aggressive feelings onto others as a means of both disowning and justifying them.

---

*Extent of overt and fantasy aggression are highly correlated when both have the same goal object and mode of expression. (J. Kagan, Journal of Abnormal and Social Psychology, 1956, 52, 390-393.

Differentiation from Excitement

As in the case of fear, the differentiation of rage from excitement presupposes the development of a functional concept of self and sufficient cognitive maturity to appreciate the significance of threat. In addition, before rage can be evoked in response to volitional frustration, a sense of volition must first exist. Thus restraint as such—even initial strapping to the cradle board—evokes no response whatsoever from neonates (Dennis, 1940a, 1940b) and rough restraint, like any intense stimulus, merely elicits undifferentiated excitement (see p. 226). Later, as the infant becomes more responsive to interference per se as a form of frustration, persistent restraint of motion evokes excitement (Dennis, 1940a; 1940b; Levy, 1944). If he is accustomed to the cradle board, he does not experience restraint as frustration; in fact he cries and is unable to sleep if he is kept off it (Dennis, 1940a).

True rage is not observed until about the tenth month of life, when needs are expressed in volitional form (Spitz, 1949). It is instigated most commonly at first by bodily restraint and delay in the gratification of visceral needs, but the adequate stimulus soon becomes generalized to include any interference with goal-directed activity (Goodenough, 1931). The violence of the affective response to volitional frustration is attributable in part to the anticipatory set of compliance associated with the omnipotent self-concept. * Because of its intensity, refractoriness to control, longevity, and self-perpetuating properties, anger easily gets out of hand and continues long after the aroused child has ceased being aware of the exciting cause. Rage also constitutes the core of negativistic reaction to ego devaluation since the pressures responsible for this shift in ego structure challenge the child's notion of volitional independence and the goal-directed activity predicated upon it.

Developmental Changes

Altered Responsiveness. Many factors operate both to increase and decrease responsiveness to excitants of rage as children advance in age. Thus the relative frequency of anger outbursts at a particular age is a result of these opposing influences. Partly for this reason and partly because the expression of overt anger tends to undergo increasingly greater inhibition with age, evidence regarding age trends is highly equivocal. Goodenough (1931a) found that outbursts of anger reach maximum frequency at 18 months and then decline regularly in frequency throughout the preschool period; after the age of four, however, the after-effects of anger were found to be more frequent and prolonged than in younger children (Appel, 1942). These findings are supported by Jersild and Markey's (1935) study of social con-

Chronically neglected children reared in foundling homes do not develop notions of omnipotence and hence exhibit shallow and superficial emotionality.

flicts in preschool children, but other investigators either fail to obtain a consistent trend with age or report a trend in the opposite direction (McKee & Leader, 1955; Muste & Sharpe, 1947; Roff & Roff, 1940). Doll play aggression tends to increase somewhat in frequency between three and four years of age but remains relatively constant between four and five years of age (Sears, 1951).

Cognitive maturation generally broadens the child's range of responsiveness to rage-producing stimuli. The widening of his intellectual and social horizons and the emergence of goal strivings in a social context provide many new occasions for the occurrence of frustration and anger. Bodily restraint and training routines thus become less important excitants of rage (Goodenough, 1931a), whereas conflict with peers and adult authority, opposition to ongoing activity, and perceptions of unfairness and inequity correspondingly gain in importance (Fawl, 1962; Goodenough, 1931a; Hicks, 1938). Increasing cognitive sophistication and motor competence, on the other hand, enable the child to cope more adequately with difficulties and hence decrease the likelihood of frustration (Douglas, 1965). With increased understanding of his environment and with greater self-critical ability he also becomes less easily inflamed by unintentional injury and better able to set realistic goals.

Normative changes in ego development also affect responsiveness to anger. As pretensions of omnipotence decline and as acceptance of parental authority increases children become less insistent on doing the impossible and more willing to tolerate delay in need-satisfaction, to accept realistic restrictions on their volitional desires, and to bow to the inevitable. Frustration tolerance also increases as the child gradually learns that, in a generally benevolent environment, denial of his legitimate needs is usually only temporary, and that initial frustration in problem solving situations can be endured until a successful solution is forthcoming. The older child learns to ignore many frustrating situations or to interpret them in ways less threatening to his volitional goals (Douglas, 1965).

Expressive Characteristics. The earliest expression of rage is typified by the diffuse, explosive, and uninhibited temper tantrum. With increasing age the rage becomes better controlled and tends to be more adaptively directed against the perceived excitant or obstacle. During the preschool period, crying, screaming and physical forms of attack (striking, pushing, kicking) decline in frequency and tend to be replaced by such verbal techniques as threatening, name-calling, scolding, fussing, belittling and teasing (Goodenough, 1931a; Jersild & Markey, 1935; Ricketts, 1934). To the extent that cultural tolerance and indulgence for aggression diminish as children grow older, direct and overt forms of aggression also give way to more devious manifestations (Inselberg, 1958).

Factors Affecting Responsiveness to Anger

Sex and Social Class Differences. Sex is an important determinant of the frequency and form of aggression in children. Practically all studies of overt (Bandura, 1965; Bandura & Walters, 1963a; Dawe, 1934; Goodenough, 1931a; Jersild & Markey, 1935; Maccoby, 1966; McCandless, Bilous & Bennett, 1961; Muste & Sharpe, 1947) and doll play (Bach, 1945; Bandura & Walters, 1963; Maccoby, 1966; Moore & Ucko, 1961; Sears, 1951; Sears, Rau & Alpert, 1965) aggression in preschool children indicate that boys are significantly more aggressive than girls. Similar findings are also obtained in ratings by parents, peers, and teachers and by experimental studies (Maccoby, 1966). The fact that these differences are not obtained prior to the age of two suggests that they originate in differential parental expectations (Radke, 1946), in differential modeling on the like-sexed parent (Bandura & Walters, 1963a, 1963b), and in differential availability of derived and extrinsic status and of the mother as an emulatory model (see p. 265). These factors account for the sex differences in the form of expression, as well as in the frequency of aggression after the age of two—the greater decline of physical aggression in girls (Bandura & Walters, 1963a) and of screaming and crying in boys (Dawe, 1934; Jersild & Markey, 1935), and the greater utilization of verbal forms of aggression by girls (Dawe, 1934; Hattwick, 1937; Sears, 1961). Sex differences in aggression increase during the preschool years but slowly decrease thereafter (Bandura & Walters, 1963a). That cultural expectations play an important part in the expression of aggression is shown by the finding that girls can be just as aggressive as boys if they are assured that no one will have knowledge of it (Mallick & McCandless, 1966). Probably because of greater parental tolerance of aggression, less parental supervision, and greater maternal deprivation, lower-class children tend to be physically more aggressive than middle-class children in play situations (Appel, 1942; Bandura & Walters, 1963a; Davis & Dollard, 1940; Jersild & Markey, 1935; McKee & Leader, 1955).

Parental Influences. The incidence of anger and aggression in children depends heavily on parental determinants (Berkowitz, 1964). Parents are the first agents to transmit cultural values and it is clear from cross-cultural studies that interpersonal aggression occurs in cultures where it is rewarded and is absent in cultures where it goes unrewarded (Bandura & Walters, 1963a). Habitual and excessive thwarting increases susceptibility to anger whereas training in frustration tolerance through gradual dosing has the opposite effect (Keister, 1937). Whether anger occurs, however, depends on how children have seen adults and peers cope with frustration (Bandura & Walters, 1963a). The occurrence of anger is dependent on the child's models for socialization, on rewards and punishments for, and on permissive attitudes toward aggression (Bandura & Walters, 1963a; Berkowitz, 1964). Anger occurs more frequently in children of parents who threaten, cajole or nag (Goodenough, 1931a), who encourage actively and condone aggression (Bandura & Walters, 1963), or who are permissive of aggression especially of the sort that occurs outside the home (Bandura & Walters, 1963a; Sears, Maccoby & Levin, 1957). Anger outbursts also occur more frequently in children with anxious, over-critical, absolutistic, inconsistent, or recriminating parents (Bandura & Walters, 1963a; Goodenough, 1931a; Hoffman, 1960) and in underdominated children where extreme permissiveness prevails and self-control is not required (Bandura & Walters, 1963a; Levy, 1937; Symonds, 1949).

Punishment is an important and complex antecedent of aggression in children. Its effects are difficult to interpret because (depending in part on the nature of the punishment) it both increases and decreases the strength of aggressive tendencies and, too, it inhibits their overt expression (Bandura & Walters, 1963a). Even under the best of circumstances children find the authority role of parents restrictive and frustrating. Hence they tend to react with some degree of aggression providing that it actually serves the retaliatory function of paining and annoying parents (as indicated by the latter's angry or punitive responses) (Sears, Whiting, Nowlis & Sears, 1953). Those children who are most severely punished at home exhibit the highest level of latent hostility in doll play aggression (Hollenberg & Sperry, 1951; Sears, 1951), whereas those children who are subjected to least maternal punishment exhibit the least amount of doll play aggression (Sears, 1951). Severe punitiveness toward aggression in the home is frequently associated with high incidence of aggression outside the home (Bandura & Walters, 1963a). The punishing adult here appears to serve as an imitative model for aggression in situations where punishment is not immediately forthcoming. Children who are very severely punished for aggression at home (Sears, 1951) or who show considerable fear of punishment for aggression (Mussen & Naylor, 1954) exhibit much fantasy aggression but relatively little overt aggression. Under such circumstances aggressive feelings against parents tend to be displaced to age mates (Sears et al, 1953; Wittenborn, 1956), especially if such behavior is approved of and rewarded by parents (Bandura & Walters, 1963a). Thus, in cultures where parents administer much punishment for aggression during early socialization, adults tend to be relatively aggressive and hence to manifest a great deal of anxiety about aggression (Whiting & Child, 1953). If, in particular cases, punishment is also unreasonably harsh, capricious, discriminatory or indicative of rejection, children develop a deep sense of resentment which may find indirect expression in bullying, cruelty to animals, and delinquency (Redl & Wineman, 1951). By the same token, insofar as punishment is administered benovolently and is accepted by children as rightful, it tends to stimulate remorse rather than aggression. In such instances the tendency to *acquire* aggressive impulses in response to parental punishment is weakened by fear of further punishment and by the need to avoid the guilt feelings that accompany aggression. Thus, Hopi children resent the formal authority role of the maternal uncle much more than they do that of their parents which is part of a larger affectional relationship (Dennis, 1940b).

Peer Influences. The effects of peer influences assume greater importance with age since the child is increasingly making social contacts outside of the family. Peers, in addition to parents, can act as modeling agents for aggressive behavior and can be effective as socializing agents of aggression (Bandura & Walters, 1963a). Male peer models appear to elicit greater imitative aggression in both boys and girls (Hicks, 1965). Peer imitation constitutes only one factor in aggressive behavior in children; interpersonal relations also are important determinants. Children who are considered less popular by their peers appear to demonstrate more anger, aggression and other types of anti-social behavior (Lesser, 1959; Schmidt, 1958). Lippitt & Gold (1959) found that rejected children in the fourth and sixth grades expressed less positive affect in their sociometric ratings of others and more often engaged in unfriendly behavior. Children who have high aggressive peer ratings are also found to be more punitive with other children when they are engaged in common tasks (Williams, Meyerson, Eran & Seinber, 1967). Both boys and girls agree that aggressive behavior is more objectionable than nonconformity; this increases the negative ratings, by peers, of children in whom aggressive outbursts frequently occur (Goerdzen, 1959). Aggressive behavior, however, is tolerated more in boys than it is in girls (Marshall, 1961). Finally, anger and aggression are more likely to occur in ambiguous social situations (Goodenough, 1931a), in physically crowded play areas (Jersild & Markey, 1935), and when many siblings and adults are present in the home (Goodenough, 1931a).

Other Aspects. Conditions such as fatigue, hunger, and transitory disturbances in health (Goodenough, 1931a) as well as such temperamental factors as ascendance and high energy output (Fries, 1946; Levy, 1944) increase susceptibility to frustration and rage. Catharsis, a mechanism for reducing aggression by acting out and draining off, has no basis in psychological research (Berkowitz, 1968; Bandura & Walters, 1963). Studies in which children have been exposed to film-mediated aggressive models have indicated that participation in aggressive activities increases, rather than decreases, the frequency and intensity of aggression (Bandura & Walters, 1963a; 1963b). As children grow older they are able to perceive more violence (Moore, 1966). Finally, adopted children are more likely than non-adopted children to be aggressive (Menlove, 1965).

JEALOUSY AND ENVY

Jealousy is a composite affective state, combining the elements of generic fear and anger, in which an individual feels threatened when he perceives his *exclusive* possession of a source of security, status, or affection challenged by the needs, aspirations, and activities of others. Envy is a related but more complex and later-developing emotion in which the threat to self-esteem emanates from a perception that other persons are superior in status, attainments, or possessions. As already pointed out, the mere quest for primary or derived status does not necessarily presuppose competition, jealousy, or envy (see p. 281). For jealousy to arise a special kind of competitive situation is required—one in which some restriction prevails in the availability of a desired object or relationship and in which possession tends to exist on a preclusive basis. Once this situation exists, jealousy develops if the individual desires or claims exclusive entitlement, perceives a challenge to his claim, and feels threatened by this perception. Later, even if he possesses ample exclusive sources of status and security and does not perceive anyone trying directly to share in or deprive him of these, he may still feel threatened by the perceived superior status of others (envy); it is as if his own worth and self-esteem were automatically depreciated by the very existence of competence in other persons and by the recognition accorded them. Thus, envy is predicated on the proposition that "the more and better selfhood a person has, the less is available for others—that no one can enhance or defend himself without encroaching upon the self-enhancement and self-defence of others." (Murphy, 1947).

The interpersonal and social conditions necessary for the generation of jealousy and envy exist almost universally, but obviously vary greatly, both inter- and intraculturally, in degree of extensiveness. Envy flourishes especially in a cultural milieu in which "the individual can . . . [not] rejoice naively in elementary physical or social selfhood . . . [but] must compare the self continually with a standard set up within or with an objective standard defined by the self-gratification available to others" (Murphy, 1947). But even in this type of highly competitive social climate, susceptibility to envy varies in accordance with many temperamental, personality, and interpersonal factors.

Sibling Jealousy

Sibling jealousy is the most common and important type of jealousy encountered during childhood. It emanates from the desire for exclusive possession of the parents' nurturant affection and of the source of derived status in the home. Inescapable conditions of family organization render this aspiration universally untenable whenever and wherever it exists—except, of course, in single-child families. Newborn infants require much protective care; and because of their greater helplessness and lesser frustration tolerance, their needs are given priority, and fewer demands are made on them than on their older siblings.* The latter, therefore, must not only share nurturance and affection with the newcomer but must also surrender the lion's share to him. It is no wonder then that sibling jealousy has been observed in a wide variety of cultures (Dennis, 1940b; Leighton & Kluckhohn, 1947; Mead, 1947). The intensity of the jealousy, however, varies greatly with cultural and familial practices and with the personality make-up of parent and child. Much depends on the abruptness and completeness with which the older child is "dethroned" and on whether other relatives are available (as in the extended family group) to provide care and solicitude. The Balinese lap baby, for example, is deliberately taunted and teased at the time of weaning with the fact that his former pre-eminent position is being usurped by a new sibling; and if an actual sibling is not available an infant is borrowed for this purpose (Mead, 1947).

It should be realized, though, that not all conflict and discord among siblings is indicative of rivalry over parental affection. Children in the same household invariably get in each other's way and compete for material things, for dominance, and for other forms of primary status. Teasing, tormenting, and bullying are also manifestations of exuberance, pecking order behavior, and of the mischievous fun and play found in the young of other primate species (Yerkes, 1943); they constitute, as well, part of an institutionalized pattern of jockeying for position in peer relationships. In any event, it is self-evident that the presence of rivalry and jealousy does not preclude the possibility of much genuine friendliness, affection, and loyalty in the relationship between siblings.

Expressive Outlets. Sibling jealousy is expressed directly (especially by younger children) in bodily assault (Sewall, 1930), or verbally in the form of belittling, teasing and tattling. Sometimes the parent as well as the rival sibling becomes the object of the jealous child's ire. With advancing age, as such behavior is subjected to increasingly greater punishment and disapproval, it tends to be replaced by more devious kinds of aggression. Latent hostility toward a baby sibling may be displaced to older siblings and age mates (Leighton *et al*, 1947; Sewall, 1930), or give rise to vengeful fantasies that are enacted in doll play settings (Levy, 1937; Sears, 1951). In older children, sibling jealousy often takes the form of extreme competitiveness over prestige and accomplishment; ostensibly no hostile feelings are intended, but secretly each rival may strive more for the other's humiliation than for his own success. Various withdrawal techniques are also frequently utilized—

This situation obviously facilitates the process of ego devaluation.

studied indifference, blustering nonchalance, and persistent obliviousness to and even outright denial of the younger sibling's existence (Neisser, 1951; Sewall, 1930). The older child may bid for the parents' attention by regressing to infantile habits of eating, dressing, sleeping and sphincter control (Sewall, 1930), by feigning fear, by resorting to silliness and naughtiness, and by strutting about and showing off (Neisser, 1951). He may try to win his parents' favor by being excessively submissive, obedient, and helpful, and even by showing extreme solicitude for his rival's well-being.

As children develop new interests, affiliations, and sources of status outside the home, sibling rivalry over parental affection tends to diminish in intensity; and as they compete more for status and prestige in school and peer group, siblings are replaced by age mates as objects of jealousy, and jealousy in turn is superseded by envy.

Factors Affecting Susceptibility to Jealousy. It seems reasonable to suppose that children who are genically and experientially predisposed toward dominance, self-sufficiency, and independence (and who therefore are less dependent on derived or primary status for feelings of adequacy) would be less threatened by others' status and by the need to share parental affection than would "thin-skinned," submissive, dependent and timorous children.* Children who are brought up in a Kibbutz show less sibling rivalry since they are more accustomed to diffuse social arrangements (Rabin, 1958). Less susceptibility to sibling jealousy might also be anticipated in girls who are predisposed temperamentally or by familial and cultural pressures to adopt maternal attitudes toward infants. On the other hand, children who are insecure or who lack intrinsic feelings of adequacy might be expected to feel especially threatened by loss of exclusive possession of parental nurturance and by the accomplishments of their siblings. Thus, excessive jealousy or envy is frequently only one of many indications of maladjustment in children (Foster, 1927). The stage of personality development through which the child is passing must also be considered. During the period of ego devaluation, dethronement merely adds insult to injury; whereas during the period of desatellization, when the child is less dependent himself on parental care and affection, he may actually vie with the parent in extending protection to the infant.

Intrafamilial variables are perhaps the most significant factors affecting responsiveness to sibling jealousy. Marital discord, favoritism, discrimination, and inequitable distribution of affection obviously tend to enhance the development of jealous feelings. A rejected child frequently displaces the resentment he feels toward parents onto a sibling, especially if the latter is perceived as favored. Jealousy is less apt to arise when the age difference

---

*Iatmul children, who are trained to be volitionally and executively independent from a very early age, show conspicuous lack of jealousy toward their infant siblings. (Mead, 1947).

between siblings is greater than 42 months (Sewall, 1930). By this age ego devaluation is more or less completed and the child begins to find interests outside the home. Furthermore, the new sibling is so much less competent as to lie outside his competitive range—at least during the phase of early infancy. Less jealousy develops when the age difference is small (less than 18 months), since the older child still requires and receives much protective care. Like twins, such siblings also make more compatible playmates. In large families where children are more accustomed to sharing parental affection and looking after each other, jealous behavior is less pronounced (Sewall, 1930). Under such circumstances, since dethronement is a fate that systematically befalls each new child in turn, his predecessors are less likely to interpret their own experiences in this regard as uniquely personal affronts.

AFFECTION

More systematic attention has been given to the impact of parental affection (or lack of affection) on children's development than to the development of affection in children themselves. In discussing ego development during early childhood, we have considered the importance of parental affection as part of a larger pattern of acceptance and intrinsic valuation necessary for satellization and for development of intrinsic feelings of security and adequacy. In the following section we would like to consider affection and attachment in a more specific developmental context.

Early Attachment

Although a potentiality for developing feelings of affection is undoubtedly inherent in all human beings, it is self-evident that the infant is first on the receiving rather than on the giving end. The infant is not passive, however, and it has been argued that the child possesses inborn behavior patterns such as following, clinging, sucking, smiling, etc., which enhance the possibilities for affective interchange (Ainsworth, 1964; Bowlby, 1958, 1960). The physically helpless child bridges the distance between himself and his caretakers by the use of vision and hearing and by such responses as looking, smiling and vocalizing (Ainsworth, 1963, 1964; Rheingold, 1966; Walters & Parke, 1965). The forming of attachments is not dependent upon the fact that the child is being fed by the mother since in many instances the child forms attachments to people who were never involved in caretaking and feeding (Ainsworth, 1963; Schaffer & Emerson, 1964). Animal studies also indicate that the feeding situation is not essential to the formation of attachments (Harlow, 1958, 1961, 1963; Harlow & Zimmermann, 1958; Scott, 1963).

The beginnings of a clear indication of affection and attachment occur at about the third quarter of the first year (Schaffer, 1958; Schaffer & Callender, 1959; Schaffer & Emerson, 1964; Wahler, 1967). Schaffer (1963) postulates a three-stage process in the formation of early attachment behavior. During the earliest stage, the infant is aroused by all parts of the environment. The second stage is characterized by a preference for human beings over inanimate objects. Finally, the last stage is marked by the infant's preference for specific persons in his environment. Thus, attachment behavior is first indiscriminate, and during the second and third months the infant protests the withdrawal of anyone's attention, familiar or strange (Schaffer & Emerson, 1964). At about seven months, the infant begins to fear strangers and cries in their presence (Morgan & Ricciuti, 1968; Schaffer & Emerson, 1964).

Another indication of the formation of bonds of affection and attachment is smiling in infants (Wahler, 1967).* Before six months of age, indiscriminate smiling can be elicited by anything resembling a human face (Ainsworth, 1963; Schaffer & Emerson, 1964; Spitz & Wolf, 1946). Smiling becomes much more discriminating during the latter part of the first year (Ainsworth, 1963; Schaffer & Emerson, 1964; Spitz & Wolf, 1946), and is usually made to only significant caretaking persons. Concomitant with discriminate smiling and stranger anxiety is the beginning of what Piaget calls object constancy (see p. 558). Schaffer & Emerson (1964) hypothesize that the infant must perceive entities as apart from himself and independent in time and space if attachments are to be formed. Up to the third quarter of the first year Piaget indicates that the child makes no distinction between self and environment and that objects do not exist in their own right. After a functional self-concept emerges and the child appreciates his executive incompetence, the causal role of his parents in gratifying his needs, and his dependence upon them for continued survival, then his sense of security becomes contingent upon their availability. Prior to this time, adults nevertheless can influence attachment behavior in infants through effective reinforcement (Gewirtz, 1965, 1968). When attachments have been clearly formed, the child's feelings toward attached adults are positively valenced since he perceives them as providing security and relief from insecurity. These events probably constitute the earliest manifestations of affection. But although he will eventually exhibit spontaneous affection toward those who care for him (Dennis, 1941), at this stage he is more apt to return affection than to assume the initiative in offering it. Feelings of affection become more spontaneous and prominent when the child derives his major source of security and adequacy from an affectionate, satellizing relationship

---

*A more extensive review of the literature on smiling in infants may be found in Freedman et al., 1967; Walters & Parke, 1965.

(see p. 260). One would hardly anticipate, therefore, that a rejected child would display much affection for his parents. And although overvalued children do receive considerable affection from their parents, the ulterior motives from which it stems neither allow satellization to occur nor inspire affectionate impulses in the child.

Later Manifestations of Affection

Beyond this point, everyday observation and logical inference (in the absence of empirical data) suggest certain developmental changes in affection. First, the conditions evoking affectionate responses broaden from simple receipt of succorance and derived status to include moral obligation, gratitude, loyalty, and helplessness in others (Hartup, 1963). Second, other emotional components are added to the expression of affection. With increasing age, the latter becomes coupled with altruistic, compassionate, and protective attitudes, with imitative displays of adult romanticism, and finally (after pubescence) with the enactment of a biological sex role. Third, the objects of affection are gradually expanded in scope. In addition to parents, affection is extended to siblings, other persons, pets and inanimate objects in the household, and later to adults and age mates outside the home. However, the development of such relationships beyond the family circle tends to be restricted if affectionate ties to parents are either lacking or excessively strong. The overprotected child is isolated emotionally from other persons by physical barriers, by induced fears, and by an overwhelming dose of parental love. The rejected child is desirous of entering into affectionate relationships with others but tends to regard himself as unworthy of love; hence he withdraws from emotional involvements in order to avoid further traumatic rebuff. The overvalued child, on the other hand, is so habituated to *receiving* affection and has such a grandiose self-concept that he develops little capacity for loving others.

DEPRIVATION OF AFFECTION*

The literature on the development of affection in children is eclipsed by the vast number of studies reporting the adverse effects of emotionally-depriving parents on the development of their children. Many of these studies were summarized by Bowlby (1951) and, although they were lacking in sophisticated design and extremely impressionistic and subjective in nature, they

---

*There are numerous excellent theoretical and methodological critiques and reviews of the literature on this topic over the past eighteen years. See Ainsworth (1966); Andry (1966); Bowlby (1951); Caldwell (1964); Clausen & Williams (1963); Freedman et al., (1967); Gewirtz (1961, 1968a); Gewirtz & Gewirtz (1968); Mead (1966); Pinneau (1955); Prugh & Harlow 1966); Schaffer & Emerson (1964); Scott (1963); Stone (1954); Walters & Parke (1965); Wooton (1966); Yarrow (1961, 1964b).

nevertheless ingeniously took advantage of uncontrived deprivation occurring in foundling homes or resulting from wartime dislocation.

Maternal Deprivation

The early studies on maternal deprivation report findings which indicate that after six to nine months of age, prolonged or severe deprivation of maternal care or abrupt separation from the accustomed mother figure during the first three years of life often (but not necessarily) leads to extremely serious developmental consequences. In the preschool period the immediate effects may be described as follows: (a) retardation in motor, language and intellectual development (Freud & Burlingham, 1944; Hasselmann Kahlert, 1953; Haggerty, 1959; Provence & Lipton, 1962; Spitz, 1945, 1949, 1951a, 1951b); (b) malnutrition and an unusually high infant mortality rate despite excellent medical care (Spitz, 1945, 1951b); and (c) a behavioral syndrome of agitation and weepiness followed by apathy, passivity, disinterest in the environment, stereotyped rocking movements, hostility and increased susceptibility to infection (Fischer, 1952; Roudinesco, 1952). The latter syndrome, designated as "anaclitic depression" (Spitz & Wolf, 1946) appears typically after abrupt separation from the mother and generally disappears shortly after her return (Fischer, 1952; Spitz & Wolf, 1946).

Before considering the long-term effects of deprivation or separation, several comments should be made concerning the conceptualization of the effects of deprivation. First of all, the earlier studies, because of their design problems, can be only considered suggestive in nature (Yarrow, 1964b). Secondly, the research literature has treated maternal deprivation and maternal separation as synonymous topics with the result that the effects attributed to maternal separation are often due to other deviating conditions of maternal care (Yarrow, 1961). Finally, the meaning of the deprivation or separation experience and subsequent experiences after separation will vary with individuals and with experiential factors (Yarrow, 1964b) such as the developmental stage of the child at the time of separation (Casler, 1961; Prugh & Harlow, 1966; Yarrow, 1964b), the character of the relationship with the mother prior to separation (Yarrow, 1964b), the nature of the institution and the possibilities for adequate caretaking (Ainsworth, 1966; Casler, 1961; Yarrow, 1964b), the reason for the separation (Ainsworth, 1966; Casler, 1961), and individual differences in vulnerability to separation (Yarrow, 1964b).

The early research literature on "maternal deprivation" has been applied to a variety of different conditions, which, singly or in combination, produce the general consequences already reported. At least three major conditions of deprivation have already been explored, but, in many instances, not distinguished from one another. First of all, deprivation can occur when an infant or young child lives in an institution where he receives no maternal care, and consequently has insufficient opportunity for interaction with a mother-figure (Ainsworth, 1966). Secondly, deprivation can also occur when an infant or a young child lives with a mother or caretaker, but does not have sufficient interaction with her (Ainsworth, 1966). This type of deprivation, where mother or caretaker is present but not interacting, has been labelled "masked deprivation" (Prugh & Harlow, 1966). Finally, deprivation may occur because of the child's inability to interact with a mother-figure—presumably the result of repeated breaches of ties with mother figures or previous deprivation experiences (Ainsworth, 1966).

The concept of "maternal deprivation" can now be distinguished from "maternal separation" if we consider the latter as covering those situations where there are discontinuities in a relationship already formed (Ainsworth, 1966). The distress due to discontinuities in attachments may, in many instances, be different from the effects of deprivation, unless the separation leads to a deprivation experience (Ainsworth, 1966).

Long-Term Effects of Separation and Institutionalization. When relationships are found between early separation experiences and later personality characteristics, a cautious attitude concerning statements about causality is required (Yarrow, 1964b). Most of the evidence on the long-term effects of deprivation is derived from studies which are retrospective in nature (Ainsworth, 1966). The retrospective study identifies a cluster of symptoms or personality characteristics and explores the history of the individual(s) displaying this syndrome to discover the likely antecedents or conditions that possibly led to these symptoms or personality characteristics (Ainsworth, 1966; Yarrow, 1964b). Bowlby (1944), with a sample of forty-four juvenile thieves, did the classic study relating delinquency to early deprivation experiences. Fourteen of these forty-four youths were characterized as "affectionless characters" and a retrospective historical analysis revealed that twelve of these fourteen children were separated from their mothers during infancy or early childhood. Several other studies have supported this finding, revealing a higher incidence of maternal deprivation in children characterized as psychopathic or sociopathic personalities (Bender, 1947; Earle & Earle, 1961). Summaries of the research literature which uses the retrospective design reveal a significantly higher incidence of separation in the diagnostic categories of schizophrenia, neurosis, depression, and psychoneurotic and psychosomatic disturbances (Ainsworth, 1966; Yarrow, 1964). At the same time, discrepant evidence mitigates against any general conclusion concerning deprivation and separation; several studies report no significant differences in the incidence of early separation experiences between disturbed patients and normal controls (Howells & Layng, 1955; Schofield & Ballan, 1959). The time of the separation may be an important consideration since the loss of the mother is only a factor in psychotic disturbances if it occurs before ten years (Gregory, 1958); and severely disturbed children usually have entered the institution before the end of the first year whereas more stable institutional children had the separation occurring after two years of age (Pringle & Bosio, 1958; Pringle, Kellmer & Bosio, 1960).

The follow-up study provides firmer evidence than the retrospective study because the separation experience can be carefully documented and a follow-up history charted (Yarrow, 1964b). However, follow-up studies reveal similar results and discrepancies as do the retrospective studies. Children hospitalized in foundling homes from the earliest months to three years of age and then placed with foster parents were followed through adolescence and compared with matched controls who had not been subjected to the institutional experience (Goldfarb, 1945). The former had several distinctive characteristics: they tended to have a persistently depressed IQ (median 75); they exhibited special retardation in language skills and conceptualization; they were severely distractable, unable to concentrate, hyperactive, and uncontrollable; they showed little ability to anticipate the consequences of their behavior or to acquire normal inhibitory control; and they displayed temper tantrums and aggressive, impulsive, antisocial behavior without appropriate anxiety. Their emotionality and interpersonal relationships were shallow, they demanded attention and affection indiscriminately, they adjusted poorly with their peers, and they showed conspicuous lack of executive and volitional independence (Goldfarb, 1945). Similarly, Provence and Lipton (1962) reported that children from adopted homes had difficulty in forming close affectional relationships and had problems with impulse control and conceptual thinking. However, as with the retrospective studies, the follow-up studies do not always reveal such severe outcomes. Several studies indicate that severe personality disturbance is not an inevitable outcome of maternal deprivation and is highly dependent on other factors in combination with the separation event (Beres & Obers, 1950; Bowlby, Ainsworth, Boston & Rosenblith, 1956; Freud & Burlingham, 1944; Hellman, 1962; Maas, 1963).

The present findings permit no general conclusions concerning the long-term effects of maternal separation on later personality characteristics. The varied and discrepant results that are obtained may be due to the fact that such studies involve many variables beside the simple event of maternal separation. The earlier conclusion that the young infant is sensitive to the most subtle nuances of parent attitudes, that permanent psychological damage results unless extremely high levels of mothering are maintained, must certainly be qualified in light of the ongoing research. The separation experience cannot be considered the sole etiological factor (Yarrow, 1964b) and several qualifications should be kept in mind. First, the effects of separation have not been established prior to six months of age, and most observers agree that the period from nine months to three years is the most crucial in this regard (Bender, 1950; Bowlby, 1946; Bowlby, 1951; Schaffer & Emerson, 1964; Spitz, 1945, Spitz; 1949; Spitz, 1951b; Yarrow, 1964b). Prior to this time insufficient perceptual and conceptual maturity exists for the infant to enter significant interpersonal relationships or to appreciate the meaning and consequences of loss of attachment (Schaffer & Emerson, 1964).

Second, the degree of trauma concurrent with separation appears as an important factor in the ultimate outcome (Yarrow, 1964b). The subsequent experiences may be crucial because separation can have mild consequences if the child is provided with a mother-figure rather than the insufficient interaction experiences characterized by institutional care (Trassler, 1960).

Finally, aside from the fact that the effects of deprivation and separation can be reversed (see p. 453), it is important to distinguish between rejection and outright neglect. The former attitude does not necessarily imply lack of personal attention or inadequate stimulation; and it can only be perceived by older, more perceptually mature infants.

The Critical-Periods Hypothesis and the Issue of Irreversibility of Deprivation and Separation Effects

The "critical periods hypothesis" has been advanced to explain the thesis that certain forms of deprivation and separation occurring at certain times in the child's development cause irreversible damage to this ongoing process. This hypothesis maintains that irreversibility of behavioral development is due to the extreme susceptibility to particular types of stimulation during those brief periods in individual development when certain types of behavior are shaped or molded for life. By the same token, if the individual is deprived of the necessary stimulation during the critical period, when he is maximally susceptible to it in terms of actualizing particular potential capacities or developing in new directions, some degree of permanent retardation is thought to be inevitable. Numerous examples of the existence of critical periods can be found in perceptual, motor, and social development of infrahuman mammals. Infant chimpanzees isolated from normal tactual stimulation exhibit defective kinesthetic learning and cautaneous localization (Nissen, Chow & Semmes, 1951); and if reared in darkness, they fail to fixate or recognize familiar objects or to blink in response to a threatening object (Riesen, 1947). Newborn domestic lambs, reared on a bottle and isolated from sheep for ten days, experience difficulty later in adjusting to the flock and tend to graze by themselves (Scott, Fredricson & Fuller, 1951). Puppies isolated for nine weeks or more are unable to adapt socially to other dogs, and if they are not removed from the litter by three months of age, they are extremely difficult to tame at a later date (Scott, 1963; Scott & Marston, 1950). Similarly, female chimpanzees who are maternally deprived later show bizarre sexual patterns and have extreme difficulty in copulating and caring for their young (Harlow, 1963). "Imprinting" in animals is also a manifestation of the "critical periods" phenomenon. An isolated newborn duck, for example, will slavishly follow the first object or creature that moves (Hess, 1959a, 1959b). High susceptibility to stimulation during this period accounts both for the nonspecific nature of the imprinted response and for its "canalization" (its preemption of the response category in question); the latter feature, of course, also reflects the animals isolation from competing stimuli.

The issue of "critical periods" in human infant development becomes important when one considers the reversibility or irreversibility of some of the symptoms produced by early deprivation and separation experiences. Psychoanalytic interpretations imply that these early adverse experiences set up certain dynamic processes that become entrenched or ingrained, and are therefore irreversible despite subsequent alteration of the reality situation (Ainsworth, 1966). More recently, ethological theories of "imprinting" have stimulated psychologists to consider the "critical periods" hypothesis in the areas of attachment and deprivation effects. The "imprinting" phenomenon in animals is considered analogous to the attachment behavior, of human infants (Ambrose, 1963; Bowlby, 1958; Caldwell, 1962; Gray 1958; Scott, 1963). For example, the visual following response in humans may be considered the equivalent of the following response in birds (Caldwell, 1962). The "critical periods" hypothesis appears to be utilized in two distinct ways: (1) there is a critical period *beyond* which a given phenomenon will not appear, and; (2) there is a critical period *during* which an organism is especially sensitive to various developmental modifiers, which, if introduced at a different time in the life cycle, would have little or no effect (i.e., a period of maximum susceptibility) (Caldwell, 1962). The "imprinting" studies on subhuman species have stressed the "beyond" aspect of a critical period and the extrapolation of this theoretical stance into the study of human deprivation and separation hints at the possibility of *irreversible* changes which may take place if these conditions prevail at certain stages of the child's development. Undoubtedly the age of the infant at the time of separation and the duration period are highly significant variables in relation to both the immediate effects of the disruption of the relationship and the long-term effects on the child's social-emotional development; but time must be considered with other factors which operate during the deprivation or separation periods (Ainsworth, 1966; Bowlby, 1951; Walters & Parke, 1965; Yarrow, 1964b). It appears unwarranted and confusing, therefore, to consider deprivation and separation effects as analogous to the "critical periods" hypothesis in "imprinting" because they are not similar phenomena.

The "imprinting" phenomenon assumes that learning is irreversible, that it takes place in a limited sensitive period, that it is supra-individual learning, and that it influences patterns of behavior which have not yet developed in the organism's repertoire (Hinde, 1963).

The studies on maternal deprivation which consider the *age* of the child as an important variable have been interpreted within the critical periods hypothesis (Yarrow, 1964b). For example, the normative data on attachment behavior and separation anxiety are somewhat age dependent, in that reactions to either temporary or permanent separations are apparently less severe in early infancy, before the establishment of a stable attachment relationship with a mother-figure, than after six months, when attachments have developed (Schaffer & Emerson, 1964; Yarrow, 1964b). The analogy has also been made with the imprinting concept, the hypothesis being that if the separation occurs before relationships are established and if the child has never had the opportunity to experience a warm personal relationship during this "critical period," he is permanently impaired in the capacity to establish relationships (Yarrow, 1964b).

However, the analogies drawn between *imprinting* and *critical periods* in lower mammals and deprivation and separation phenomena in humans appear to confuse rather than clarify the issues underlying the latter phenomena. First of all, the deprivation literature, even where parallels can be made with *imprinting*, in no way comes close to meeting the criteria for "imprinting" phenomena because the evidence for timing and *irreversibility* is tenuous and limited, and the supra-individuality of the phenomenon has not been demonstrated.* Secondly, preoccupation with *age* tends to make one ignore the interpersonal events which are occurring within these so-called critical time periods.

No one will deny that age and timing relationships exist as statistical phenomena in the deprivation literature. Rather, it is the irreversibility of the changes which supposedly occur during these "critical" time periods" which is being questioned. For example, Goldfarb (1943; 1945a; 1945b) provides the most evidence that damage incurred during severe early deprivation is resistent to reversal by subsequent relief from deprivation. He reports that children who were separated from parents starting in early infancy for three years were impaired in intellectual functions; this deficit was not overcome (reversed) after deprivation was relieved. Before interpreting *irreversible* changes as a consequence of *critical periods* however, it would be wise to consider a wider range of circumstances such as the type of stimulation offered in the institution, the conditions of life that have preceded or

---

*For example, Schaffer & Emerson (1964) indicate a considerable amount of variation in the timing and intensity of attachment behavior.

followed the separation experience, and specific individual differences related to vulnerability to separation experiences.

At present, it is safer to say that at least specific aspects of psychological functioning can be reversed or altered by changing certain morbid environmental effects. Rheingold (1956), working with six-month old institutional babies, was able, by, means of eight weeks of individual caretaking (as opposed to the normal multiple caretaking in institutions), to increase the responsiveness of these children to other people. Control group subjects of the same age did not vary in their social responsiveness over the same time period. However, there was no appreciable difference between experimental and control groups on postural control and intelligence assessments. The effect of more *individualized* interaction within the institution appears to be an important consideration, but the particular characteristics of the interaction must be carefully evaluated. It appears that it is not the number of caretakers per child but rather a consistent interaction with one or two caretaking adults that is important (David & Appell, 1961). It is reported that babies reared at home receive four and one-half times as much attention as do institutional babies (Rheingold, 1956). These findings support the recommendation that foster-home care is preferable to institutional care for very young infants (Ainsworth, 1966). However, it may be that institutional care can be made more individualized, and there do exist institutions where severe deprivation effects have not been reported (Dennis & Najarian, 1957; Rheingold & Bayley, 1959).

In conclusion, it should be realized that, like biological heredity, infant experiences, while placing certain constraints upon personality, give mainly potentialities. Whether or not these potentialities become actualized, and the extent to which they do so, will depend on later social and other conditions which structure the individual's experiences (Mowrer & Kluckhohn, 1944). External conditions of adult life actualize the behavior the predispositions for which have been learned in the experiences of infancy and early childhood (Mowrer & Kluckhohn, 1944).

Other Aspects

Multiple Mothering. The fact that separation from parents frequently leads to a new type of environment (i.e., institutional) in which there are several caretakers taking on the mother's role has led to a considerable amount of speculation concerning the diffusion of the mother's role (Yarrow, 1964b). The often deleterious effects of the institutional environment has fostered interest in the study of cultures where multiple-mothering is the rule rather than the exception, and in caretaking arrangements which exist outside institutional settings.

The Israeli kibbutzim offer a culturally acceptable way of raising children which involves a type of multiple-mothering arrangement. The kibbutz practice frequently involves the separation of the mother from child in early infancy where a substitute-mother (metapelet) takes over many of the mother's child-rearing duties. In contrast to the institutional living previously discussed, the mother maintains contact with her child (often breast-feeding him for several months) and the parents visit the infants regularly (Yarrow, 1964b). Kibbutz children do show early developmental retardation; but this may be the result of less stimulation in this setting as compared with the home (Rabin, 1958). However, from the late pre-school years onward, such children manifest no intellectual retardation and no apparent personality problems. Rabin (1958) also reports one study in which the children were considered more mature in their emotional control and had greater overall ego strength. It is likely that kibbutz children have as much contact and interaction with their parents after infancy as do children living at home (Spiro, 1955). It may be that this early communal living with sufficient parental interaction provides an adequate means of both satellization on parents and re-satellization on peers at much earlier ages than normally thought possible.

Another type of non-institutional setting where multiple-mothering is employed is the home management training house for students of home economics. Children are frequently taken out of institutions and put in these houses where they are cared for by several young women in training (Gardner, Hawkes, & Burchinal, 1961). The house mother (for the trainees) provides a sense of continuity as she shares some of the infant care responsibilities. The children are the objects of considerable attention by the trainees and eventually move to foster or adoptive homes. Follow-up study of these children during the preschool years reveals no evidence of intellectual retardation or gross personality disorder (Gardner *et al*, 1961). These apparently successful multiple-mothering arrangements have led some to question the view that single mother-child institutions are the only way to counteract or relieve deprivation and separation effects (Mead, 1962; 1966). Mead (1962) even suggests that multiple-mothering, when it is adequate, may help the child trust more people and therefore engender toleration for separation experiences. Ainsworth (1966) counterargues that even where multiple-mothering exists as a successful societal institution, it is likely that the infant himself is monatrophic (i.e., he tends to attach himself primarily to one specific figure even though he extends his attachments to other supplementary figures). More careful observational studies of specific family and multiple-mothering structures may help in resolving some of the present theoretical controversy (e.g., Gewirtz & Gewirtz, 1968).

Paternal Deprivation and Separation*

The vast majority of the research studies dealing with separation and deprivation have dealt primarily with the mother. Interest in the father's role in the socialization process has originated in the theoretical writing stressing sex role identification in pre-schoolers and in the middle years of childhood (Yarrow, 1964b). The influence of psychoanalytic theory on parental separation problems was first advanced when it was noticed that there was a strong attachment to father fantasy figures among pre-schoolers who had had meager contact with their fathers (Freud & Burlingham, 1944). Subsequent cross-cultural studies indicate that the boys raised in societies where the father is absent during infancy have sex-role identity conflicts and display strong overcompensatory masculine behaviors to threatened feminization (Burton & Whiting, 1961). Father absence appears to affect the sexes differentially (Lynn & Sawrey, 1959). In studying the eight- and nine-year old children of families of Norwegian sailors and in comparing them to intact families, it was found that the boys from the father-absent group showed immature and insecure satellization with the father and poor peer adjustment and that the girls from these families were highly dependent (Lynn & Sawrey, 1959). Father absence probably induces certain types of maternal behaviors since the mothers in the sailor families were more overprotective and authoritarian (Tiller, 1957).

Father absence has also been studied in situations where the father has been called for military duty. Stolz et al, (1954) studied families where the father was absent for the Second World War and found that boys in such families display more feminine fantasy and overt feminine behavior and poorer relations with their peers than do boys in intact families. The return of the father also caused friction, for the male child now had to compete for maternal affection and the father was frequently upset by the boy's feminine mannerisms. Aggressive fantasy in doll play has also been reported for boys in the father-absent families of World War Two (Bach, 1946; Sears, Pintler & Sears, 1946). Carlsmith (1964) found more feminine intellectual patterns (i.e., more stress on verbal, as opposed to mathematical items) for males coming from father-absent families, and the earlier the separation of father and son, the more feminine the patterns that were displayed.

An interesting problem is posed by the observation that there is a high incidence of delinquent behavior in children from father-absent homes (McCord, McCord & Thurber, 1962). Children in lower-class families where the father is absent by virture of death, desertion, divorce, or imprisonment show a much higher incidence of adult criminality (McCord

*See Nash (1965) for a review of studies on paternal deprivation.

et al, 1962) than do children from intact families. Even medical students report a much more antisocial history when the father has been absent during early childhood (Siegman, 1966). It is clear that other factors operate, along with father-absence per se, to produce antisocial behaviors, and that the presence of the father must be related to certain types of parent-child interaction for favorable outcomes (Andry, 1960). Andry (1960, 1966), in fact, indicates that delinquents tend to stay away from both parents and do not seek their advice when in trouble. A type of "masked paternal deprivation" may occur in father-present delinquent families since children in such families often prefer to deal with their mothers when they encounter trouble (Andry, 1966). Again, deprivation and separation appear to be necessary research distinctions.

The recent investigations into the families of lower-class Negroes reveals a family structure, essentially matriarchical in nature, where the father is absent or demoralized through habitual unemployment (Bronfenbrenner, 1967; Moynihan, 1965; White House Commission on Civil Disorders, 1968). Negro families are much more unstable than comparable white families (Hunt, 1966) and the child is frequently denied the benefits of bi-parental affection and upbringing; he is often raised by his grandmother or older sister while his mother works to support the family which has been deserted by the father (Deutsch *et al*, 1956). One consequence of this matriarchical family climate is an open preference for girls. Boys frequently attempt to adjust to this situation by adopting feminine traits and mannerisms (Dai, 1949). Even when the father is present in the Negro family, sexual identification may be difficult for the boy faced with a strong feminine figure while also confronted, for satellization, with a male who is economically inadequate (Gordon & Shea, 1967).

These studies point to the fact that the father should not be ignored in the discussion of deprivation and separation effects. The treatment of specific effects in a univariate manner (i.e., just paternal deprivation or maternal deprivation), however, leads to superficial relationships which appear and disappear from one study to another. As with maternal deprivation and separation, the effects of paternal deprivation and separation exist within a complex social matrix which can also change maternal behaviors toward the child. Future studies in this area increasingly will have to treat family interaction, or lack of it, as a multivariate process instead of treating mother and father as separate and independent variables. Moreover, sibling composition of the family also interacts in different ways with the father's absence (Sutton-Smith, Rosenberg, and Landy, 1968).

Short-Term Hospitalization. The experience of hospitalization may represent a type of separation phenomenon but the effects of separation may be compounded by many other concomitant factors. Frequently accompanying short-term separation from parents due to hospitalization is the threat of surgery, acute illness, and other fear-provoking phenomena (Yarrow, 1964b). Children under seven months of age are apparently less traumatized by hospitalization, and more responsive to strange adults, than are infants over seven months of age (Schaffer & Callender, 1959). Also, infants over seven months show desperate clinging to their mother and considerable departure crying (Schaffer & Callender, 1959). Early childhood is marked by developmental changes in hospital reactions; these are probably due to changes in ego-development, with the satellizing two- to three-year-old children showing the most severe reaction to hospitalization, and with this reaction decreasing with age as desatellization and resatellization take place (Prugh, Staub et al, 1953). School-age children (6 to 10 years) showed less anxiety about separation and their fears were focused on painful or potentially painful hospital experiences (Prugh, Staub et al, 1953). Return from hospital was accompanied by age differential reactions; the children under seven months stared with blank expressions and scanned the surroundings without interpersonal interests, and the older infants, who were more satellized, showed excessive anxiety about anticipated mother separation and a marked fear of strangers (Schaffer & Callender, 1959). The traumatic experiences of hospitalization can be alleviated if the hospital designs procedures to minimize separation anxiety and fear of bodily injury (Faust, Jackson et al, 1952). Robertson (1958) has suggested that the mother be given permission to "room-in" at the hospital before and following surgery. Obviously, the short-term effects of deprivation due to hospitalization are rarely similar to the effects of extended institutionalization.

In summary, at least three major conditions of deprivation have already been explored but, in many instances, not distinguished from one another. First of all, deprivation can occur when an infant or young child lives in an institution, where he receives no maternal care, and consequently has insufficient opportunity for interaction with a mother-figure (Ainsworth, 1966). Secondly, deprivation can also occur when an infant or a young child lives with a mother or caretaker but does not have sufficient interaction (Ainsworth, 1966; Prugh & Harlow, 1966). Finally, deprivation may occur because of the child's inability to interact with a mother-figure; this is presumably the result of repeated breaches of ties with mother figures or previous deprivation.

JOY AND BOREDOM

Between the second and third months of life, physiological satiety and relief of physical discomfort are accompanied by signs of emotion that are more positive than mere quiescence or absence of excitement. The smiling, laughter, cooing and gurgling that occur at this age and under these circumstances are the earliest manifestations of pleasure or delight (Bridges, 1932; Buhler, 1935; Goldstein, 1957). They constitute primitive hedonic responses to visceral satisfaction and require neither cortical involvement* nor the presence of a self-concept. When conditioned to the presence of other persons they are frequently mistaken for affection.

Following the emergence of the self-concept, pleasure-giving stimuli become more salient and instigate more intense and active signs of elation such as crowing and clapping of hands (Buhler, 1935). The eliciting stimuli are also extended to include exteroceptive and erogenous stimulation and uninhibited motor activity. During early childhood, joy and happiness are largely associated with such hedonic satisfactions and activities as accompany holidays and birthdays (Jersild & Tasch, 1949). But as children grow older, factors that enhance self-esteem through the acquisition of new capacities and primary status become increasingly important determinants of elation (Jersild & Tasch, 1949). More frequently encountered also is an ephemeral type of elation in which self-esteem is enhanced by grandiose daydreaming or by temporary depression of the self-critical faculty.

Boredom is a characteristic affective state induced by absence of challenging stimulation and activity or by oversatiation of a need (Lewin, 1954). As objects and activities satisfy the needs that instigate them, their current attractiveness diminishes, and unless they are temporarily discontinued, oversatiation or boredom results (Lewin, 1954). Repetition or monotony leads to boredom more rapidly in children than in older individuals because of their lesser attention span and frustration tolerance, because of the greater wholeheartedness with which they enter activities (Lewin, 1954), and because they are less capable of rigidly insulating one experience from another (Kounin, 1943). Thus, Kounin (1943) demonstrated that with mental age held constant, the satiation of both the same and related activities occurs more rapidly in younger than in older persons. Children, though, are less likely than adults to encounter monotony since the vast majority of life's experiences still lies before them.

SYMPATHY

Sympathy refers to sorrow induced by perceived distress in others. Because of the relatively mature capacities it presupposes, it does not appear much before the age of two (Murphy, 1937). Before sympathy can be felt a child must possess sufficient cognitive maturity to appreciate situational cues of distress when he himself is not threatened. If he had never experienced similar difficulties himself, he must be able to extrapolate from related

---

Expressions of pleasure can be elicited in decorticate but not in decerebrate animals.

experience and knowledge. Naturalistic and experimental assessments of sympathy in children indicate that both behavioral and verbal expressions of sympathy are directly related to the amount of actual or role-playing experience that the children have had as recipients of sympathetic behavior under conditions of stress (Aronfreed, 1968; Lenrow, 1965). Thus, a three year old is not moved to sympathy by black and blue marks, crutches, or funerals, but does respond sympathetically to such evidence of calamity as bandages, falls, confinement, and deprivation of toys, food, and mother (Murphy, 1937). Over and above this cognitive appreciation, susceptibility to sympathy is also a function of sensitivity to the feelings of others (empathy). Although wide interindividual differences undoubtedly prevail at all age levels, empathic ability partly depends on degree of social maturity and experience. Sex differences appear to be relevant in children, since boys are more empathetic to boys and girls to girls (Feshbach & Roe, 1968). Finally, the child must have the capacity for being affected by the perceived predicaments of others. In other words he must be capable of affection or emotional relatedness to others.

With increasing age the child reacts sympathetically to a wider and more subtle range of distress symbols (Murphy, 1937). As he grows in motor competence, verbal facility, and social experience, he is also able to respond more actively and helpfully—by comforting, soliciting aid, and removing the cause of distress—rather than just staring and whimpering (Murphy, 1937). The greater his interest in and responsiveness to others, the more sympathy he is apt to display; hence, because socially active children are more intensely involved in interpersonal concerns, they tend to be both more sympathetic and more aggressive than socially phlegmatic children (Murphy, 1937). Disposition toward sympathetic behavior is also affected by whether the child is merely a witness or the effective cause of another's distress. In the latter instance, the need to disclaim responsibility is obviously incompatible with the expression of sympathy. (McFarland, 1938). Some children tend to be less responsive to others' distress once their own position in the group is consolidated (Murphy, 1937). In their case, sympathy is largely a projection of anxiety or a bid for favor. Other children who are intrinsically more secure and capable of generosity tend to become more sympathetic as their own status improves. It is to be expected that a non-satellizing ego orientation leads to fewer displays of sympathy and altruism than does a satellizing orientation. Parents of non-satellizers are critical of their children's short-comings and frequently express contempt when the child is in distress, whereas satellizing parents express support and concern in distress situations (Tomkins, 1963). Moreover, parents who discipline children by emphasizing the needs of others have more considerate offspring than control- and power-oriented parents (Hoffman, 1963).

HUMOR*

Humor is a complex state of joy or elation instigated by cognitive appreciation of surprise or incongruity. It neither consists of a single emotional content that is invariable in all instances nor is its adequate stimulus reducible to any single psychological element. Subjectively there may only be elevation of mood in response to a cognitively amusing situation. Frequently, as when a prestigeful or authority figure is exposed to ridicule, humor enhances self-esteem or constitutes an expressive outlet for hostile feelings (Berlyne, 1969b; Justin, 1932; Wolfenstein, 1954). At other times it serves the adjustive purposes of minimizing failure and frustration, of providing release from strain and anxiety, and of expressing socially unacceptable interests (Justin, 1932; Wolfenstein, 1954).

Laughter has been reported, from the fourth month onward, in response to surprise stimuli (chirruping sounds, sudden movements, peek-a-boo games) and tickling (Bridges, 1932; Buhler, 1935; Leuba, 1941; Washburn, 1927). It is apparently an unlearned and stereotyped expressive manifestation of humor that is highly contagious at all age levels. During the preschool years, laughter occurs mostly in social situations (Ding & Jersild, 1932; Kenderdine, 1931) and frequently in the course of motor activities, particularly when the child is a participant (Ding & Jersild, 1932; Justin, 1932; Kenderdine, 1931). Also, during this period, socially unacceptable situations and appreciation of incongruity and of relative superiority over others become increasingly important excitants of laughter (Berlyne, 1966; Justin, 1932; Kenderdine, 1931). The crucial role of cognition in humor is born out by the fact that brighter children laugh more frequently, especially to absurd and incongruous situations than do children of average intelligence (Brumbough, 1939; Kenderdine, 1931). Also, humor and mirth are best elicited by cartoons which make moderate demands on the child's expanding cognitive abilities (Zigler, Levine & Gould, 1966, 1967). During middle and late childhood, adequate stimuli for humor are still predominantly visual and auditory and of the "slapstick" variety (Brumbough, 1939; Kappas, 1967). During the elementary school years the child's humor becomes increasingly individual. First graders show a much greater homogeneity in their perception of humor than do older children (Graham, 1958; Kappas, 1967). Incongruity, violations of rules, and tabooed topics are common instigants of a type of group merriment that is frequently disapproved of by adults (Brumbough, 1939). Appreciation of verbal humor, such as puns, requires considerable intellectual sophistication and occurs relatively late in development (Brumbough, 1939; Graham, 1958; Kappas, 1967; Wolfenstein, 1954). When such humor does become more prominent at the beginning of the adolescent period, favorite jokes become more subtle and pithy and employ more elaborate disguises for the expression of tabooed ideas (Wolfenstein, 1954).

*A general review of theories and research on humor is available. See Berlyne (1968b).

CHAPTER 13

Moral Development

VALUES REFER to ways of striving, believing, and doing whenever purpose and direction are involved or choice and judgment are exercised. Values are implied in the relative importance an individual attaches to different objectives and activities, in his moral, social and religious beliefs, and in his aesthetic preferences. They underlie sanctioned ways of behaving and interacting with people in a given culture and the kinds of personality traits that are idealized. Values therefore are important factors in determining goals and goal-seeking behavior, standards of conduct, and feelings of obligation to conform to such standards and to inhibit behavior at variance with them. They help to order the world of the child differentially in terms of degree of ego-involvement (i.e., to determine his interests), orient him to his cultural milieu, influence the content of his perceptions, and selectively sensitize him to perceive certain classes of objects and relationships.

THE TRANSMISSION OF VALUES*

Three component problems are involved in the intracultural transmission of values. First we must consider the external patterning factors to which the child is exposed and which influence him selectively to interiorize certain values in preference to others. Second, we must identify the mechanisms through which the external standards are interiorized. Third, we must reckon with the sanctions (both internal and external) that maintain values in relatively stable form once they are internalized.

External Patterning Factors

The young child's world of value judgments is largely unstructured for lack of relevant experiential frames of reference and, hence, is very susceptible to the influence of prestige suggestion from significant figures in his environment (see p. 303). First through his parents and later through other socializing agents, he is exposed to both explicit and implicit indoctrination. The latter occurs insidiously through recurrent and unobtrusive exposure to the underlying value assumptions of family and culture. Thus, young children

---

*This chapter makes no attempt to evaluate the methods used in assessing the development of moral and other value orientations. Methodological discussions may be found in the following sources: Pittel and Mendelsohn (1966); M. Yarrow (1960).

tend to identify with the value symbols of their parents' membership and reference groups long before they are sufficiently mature to comprehend the meaning of these symbols. Preschool and early school age children, for example, assimilate the racial and religious prejudices of their parents quite independently of any actual contact with the groups concerned (see p. 371), and identify with parental religious and political attitudes without any rational understanding of the issues involved (Hirschberg and Gilliland, 1942; Proshansky, 1966).

Several studies have provided experimental evidence of children's susceptibility to prestige suggestion. Direct person-to-person influence in the form of modeling has been shown to modify children's moral judgments (Bandura and McDonald, 1963) and self-imposed delay of gratification (Bandura and Mischel, 1965). Prestige suggestion is more effective (a) when the authority's opinion is rationalized rather than arbitrary, and (b) in ambiguous judgmental situations where the child has little past experience, an indefinite and unformed evaluative frame of reference, and no incontrovertible sensory evidence before him (Ausubel et al, 1956). Children naturally vary greatly in their susceptibility to prestige suggestion, but the question of whether suggestibility can be considered a general personality trait is still unsettled. Evidence from studies with adults indicated that degree of susceptibility is inversely related to self-sufficiency, self-assertiveness, and relative indifference to others' approval. In accordance with a social sex role which includes being more docile, conforming, and submissive to adult authority, girls tend to be more responsive than boys to prestige suggestion (Ausubel et al, 1956; Duncker, 1938; Messerschmidt, 1933; Patel and Gordon, 1960).

Mechanism of Interiorization

We may distinguish, on the basis of the degree of motivation involved, between two essentially different ways of interiorizing the values of other persons or of groups. As an individual simply habituates to a given set of norms, values underlying these norms may acquire an aura of axiomatic rightness and may be accepted as self-evidently valid. Here no particular needs of the individual are satisfied. A simple mechanical type of imitation belongs in the same category: the expressed values of one person serve as a stimulus instigating acceptance of comparable values by another. This process is facilitated in group situations and is very similar to behavioral "contagion". However, whenever such imitation involves a more active need to be like other persons or to conform to their expectations (apart from fear of punishment), it is more proper to speak of motivated interiorization or identification. Identification, therefore, is a motivated form of imitation in which both the *interpersonal relationship* (direct or fantasied) between imitator and imitatee and the imitated act itself are highly significant for the learning that ensues.*

Although identification implies an underlying motive in one person's acceptance of another's values the term itself without further qualification does not specify the type of motivation that is operative. In order to designate more precisely the individual's motivational orientation to value assimilation, the terms *satellizing* and *incorporative* (non-satellizing) will be used. In each case the child responds to prestige suggestion† but does so for different reasons (see p. 273). The non-satéllizer (in contrast to the satellizer) does not accept prestige authority blindly and uncritically from a person or group out of personal loyalty or desire for derived status, but because the authority of the suggester is respected as relevantly influencing the outcome of his quest for primary status. The purpose of his hero worship is not to be a loyal and devoted camp follower but to emulate and displace the hero, and to use him as a guide and stepping-stone to ego enhancement. Conformity to group norms in his case is more a matter of expediency, and of obtaining the status advantages of group reference or membership than a reflection of a need for self-subservient belongingness or "we-feeling" (Ausubel 1952; Kagan, 1958; Whiting, 1960). *The exploratory* orientation to value assimilation, on the other hand, is a more task-oriented, objective, problem-solving approach that ignores considerations of primary and derived status and places major emphasis on objective evidence, logical validity, and equity in determining the acceptability of different value positions.

External and Internal Sanctions

After the child is exposed to and assimilates values from significant persons in his environment, both external and internal sanctions operate to keep them relatively stable and to insure (in the case of moral values) that behavior is kept compatible with them. At the disposal of parents, teachers, and peer groups are such forms of control as reward and punishment, approval and disapproval, ridicule, withdrawal of love and respect, depreciation of status in the group, and ostracism. From within, a parallel set of controls is operative. The child feels apprehensive about the consequences (e.g., possible loss of present status and the threat of not attaining future status goals) of deviation from his internalized values. He learns gradually

---

*The mechanisms and motives which underlie imitative behavior have been discussed from a variety of theoretical viewpoints. The theoretical perspective proposed in this chapter is derived from the chapter on ego development. Psychoanalytic and social learning theories of identification may be found in the following sources; Bandura and Walters, 1963b; Bronfenbrenner, 1960, Kagan, 1958; Mussen, 1967; Sears, Rau, and Alpert, 1965; Whiting, 1960.

†No difference in responsiveness to prestige suggestion was obtained between children displaying satellizing and non-satellizing orientations (Ausubel et al., 1956).

to respond with feelings of shame to the negative evaluation of himself by others, acquires a feeling of *obligation* about inhibiting behavior that is at variance with his value structure, and feels guilty when he fails to do so. The need to avoid these highly unpleasant guilt feelings and to retain feelings of belongingness in and acceptance by the group eventually becomes one of the most effective of all behavioral sanctions. In the case of satellizing children, personal loyalty is also an important factor in preventing deviancy from internalized standards.

DEVELOPMENTAL TRENDS IN VALUE ASSIMILATION

Since socialization is a gradual and cumulative process, it is hardly surprising that with increasing age children show progressively closer approximation to adult moral, social (Cruse, 1963; Eberhart, 1942; Lockhard, 1930; Pressey & Robinson, 1944), and aesthetic norms (Thompson, 1962), and correspondingly greater agreement among themselves (Watson, 1965). Paralleling this trend is a gradual increase in the conformity aspects of personality as measured by Rorschach responses (Thetford, Molish, and Beck, 1951). This greater conformity to adult standards naturally depends in part upon increased ability to perceive what is expected and to discriminate between finer shadings of behavioral standards. There is progressive improvement in the ability to perceive another's sociometric status (Ausubel *et al*, 1952; Horowitz, 1962) and to discriminate between the behaviors that teachers approve and disapprove of (Witryol, 1950) and between different degrees of seriousness of offense against property (Eberhart, 1942). Children also become progressively more aware that they are expected to conform to adult roles, and to inhibit aggressive, socially deviant behavior (Griffiths, 1952). Further consequences of the growth in cognitive capacity are the increasing tendency for values to be organized on an abstract basis, thereby permitting greater generality and consistency from situation to situation (Hartshorne and May; Hoffman, 1963; Kohlberg, 1964; 1968), and the improving ability to differentiate value judgments from factual judgments (Weir, 1960).

Although much interindividual variability prevails at any given age level, the growing importance of attaining primary status during the desatellizing period increasingly tends to favor a shift from the satellizing to the incorporative and exploratory motivational orientations in value assimilation. In interiorizing new values and goals, therefore, such considerations as ego enhancement, expediency, social recognition, and status in the group become more relevant than adult approval or personal loyalty; and satisfaction of these considerations demands much more critical examination of values prior to internalization. Accordingly, the evidence indicates that suggestibility in children decreases as a function of age (Campbell, 1964;

Messerschmidt, 1933; Reymer and Kohn, 1940). The adoption of the exploratory orientation is also greatly facilitated during the desatellizing stage by the opportunity of following objective evidence and principles of equity to their logical conclusions without incurring such heavy burdens of guilt and disloyalty and without being so concerned about the possible loss of derived status.

Reflective of this shift in value assimilation is the increasing sensitivity of children to the disapproval of such authority figures outside the home as the school superintendent (Bavelas, 1942), the decreasing importance of the parents as emulatory models (Bray, 1962; Ugurel-Semin, 1952), and the increasing replacement, as models, of the parents by glamorous, historical and public figures (Engelmann, 1962; Havighurst and others, 1946). As shown by the steadily diminishing correlations from the age of 10 to 16 between children's reputations for various traits and the closeness of affectional ties with families (Brown and others, 1947), parents become increasingly less influential than other socializing agents in determining children's values (Campbell, 1964). Values acquire a wider social base as increased exposure to new social environments, coupled with less subservience to parental views, enables the older child to perceive the standards of his home as merely special variants of subcultural norms. Hence, with increasing age, his values tend to become more typical of the culture at large and less typical of his own family.

With increasing age children also tend to adopt a less subjectivistic approach to values. They consider them from a less personal and more detached point of view, show greater ability to argue from the standpoint of a hypothetical premise, and think more in terms that transcend their own immediate experience. There is a decline in egoism and an increase in altruism (Handlon and Gross, 1959; Ugurel-Semin, 1952; Wright, 1942); children become more aware of the needs, feelings, and interests of others and more able to consider a situation from another's point of view. For example, the reason offered for the unacceptability of stealing tends to shift from fear of apprehension and punishment to the perceived injury it causes others (Eberhart, 1942; Kohlberg, 1964).

MORAL DEVELOPMENT*

Morals constitute that part of our cultural and personal value systems concerned with the proper ends of man's activities and strivings, with questions of good and evil, and with responsibility or accountability for behavior.

---

*Our treatment of moral development will be couched in the framework of ego development. Reviews of the literature on moral development are available in the following sources; Aronfreed, (1968); Berkowitz, (1964); Bronfenbrenner, (1962); Edwards, (1965); Jones, (1954); Kohlberg, (1963a, 1964, 1968b).

Thus, the learning of moral values is only a component aspect of ego development and obeys all of the principles regulating the assimilation of any ego-related value (Kohlberg, 1964; Loevinger, 1966; Lorimer, 1968; McCullough, 1969; Wilson, Williams and Sugarman, 1967). From a developmental standpoint, we can see no theoretical advantage in divorcing moral development from ego development or in postulating the existence of a separate layer of personality such as the Freudian superego. Hence, in our analysis of the development of conscience, we shall be concerned with the same type of variables as those that determine the outcome of other aspects of ego development.

Importance for Child Development

During the past three decades or more, psychology—the science of behavior—has attempted to evade coming to terms with ethics, the science of ends, norms, good, right, and choice. The focus of psychological concern has been on adjustment as an end in itself, the contention being that moral values are subjective and unverifiable. According to this view moral judgments are matters of arbitrary preference and opinion beyond the pale of science; no objective psychological criterion is possible. Behavior may be appraised as constructive or antisocial, but never as good or evil. The purpose of psychology is to explain conduct, not to judge it; questions of accountability are held to be irrelevant in the light of psychological determinism, and hence the proper concern of only jurists and philosophers.

In reply to this line of argument, we would say first that to ignore ethical considerations is to overlook one of the most significant components of human conduct. Whether the psychologist chooses to recognize it or not, most purposeful behavior in human beings has a moral aspect, the psychological reality of which cannot be ignored. The goals of human development, insofar as they are determined by man and culture, are always predicated upon certain moral assumptions. Thus, the development of the individual is invariably influenced by coercive exposure to the particular set of assumptions which his culture espouses and which he himself eventually assimilates. Second, empirically validatable ethical propositions *can* be discovered once we accept certain basic philosophical value judgments regarding the proper ends of development which themselves are phenomenologically unverifiable. If, for example, we were to grant that self-realization were the highest goal toward with man could strive, it would be possible to establish which behavioral alternatives are most compatible with this goal and hence most ethical. But even if the primary value judgments are not empirically verifiable, they must still be predicated upon empirically determined human capacities for the kind of norms that are advocated. It is futile to speak of life goals that are motivationally unsupportable or of standards of maturity that only angels could reach. The same criterion obviously applies also to principles of accountability which must be grounded on attainable norms of moral development. Finally, moral behavior is of interest to the child development specialist because it has a developmental history. It undergoes orderly and systematic age level changes and manifests psychobiological uniformities and psychosocial as well as idiosyncratic variability. In terms of the underlying psychological processes involved in conscience development, we deal with genically determined potentialities. However, the actual acquisition of moral behavior, the normative sequences, and variability in development are largely determined by experiential and sociocultural factors.

By means of a developmental and cross-cultural approach, it becomes possible (a) to determine the limits that define man's capacity for acquiring moral behavior and the sequential steps involved in moral growth; (b) to predict the various types of delinquent behavior that may arise as a consequence of aberrant moral development; and (c) to determine under what conditions individuals may be held morally accountable for their misdeeds.

Importance for Socializing Process

Moral obligation is one of the most important psychological mechanisms through which an individual becomes socialized in the ways of his culture. It is also an important instrument for cultural survival since it constitutes a most efficient watchdog within each individual serving to keep his behavior compatible with his own moral values and the values of the society in which he lives. Without the aid it renders, child rearing would be a difficult matter indeed. If children felt no sense of accountability to curb their hedonistic and irresponsible impulses, to conform to accepted social norms, or to acquire self-control, the socializing process would be slow, arduous and incomplete. The methods of sheer physical force, threat of pain, deprivation and punishment, and withholding of love and approval, all used in combination with constant surveillance, would be the only available means for exacting conformity to cultural standards of acceptable behavior. And since it is plainly evident that the interests of personal expediency are not always in agreement with prescribed ethical norms, that the maintenance of perpetual vigilance is impractical, and that fear alone is never an effective deterrent against antisocial behavior, a social order unbuttressed by a sense of moral obligation in its members would enjoy precious little stability.

The need to conform to established cultural norms, however, is only one component of the more general problem of moral obligation. As it stands, this type of obligation refers only to those contemporaneous aspects of moral behavior which are subject to change as society itself changes. The process of simple cultural transmission of values is today complicated by the comparatively frequent influx of new values which challenge moral preconceptions (Hemming, 1957). Although many aspects of personal morality remain stable and *conformity* to established norms is maintained, it is nevertheless important to consider that:

> ... in a changing society, in fact, the habit of conformity is not enough. Once culturally standardized answers to any major ethical questions cease to exist, an element of selection becomes a feature of moral maturity. When existing values are likely to be tested again and again by the extension of knowledge, the capacity to *re-assess* values in the light of fresh evidence also becomes a necessary attribute of the morally mature persons. Indeed, perhaps the most pertinent question a psychologist can ask himself in the field under discussion is what the conditions are which permit a schema of values to be laid down in the growing mind while preserving flexibility of outlook (Hemming, 1957).

In more mature forms of morality, then, obligation stems more from a reasoned judgment based on some personal principles than from simple conformity to prevailing cultural norms. The cultural basis of conscience development in the individual may be found in the potent need of both parents and society to incultate a sense of responsibility in the child. Not only the physical survival of its members, but also the perpetuation of its selective way of life is contingent upon the culture's degree of success in this undertaking. Thus, the attenuation of infantile irresponsibility might be considered part of the necessary process of ego devaluation and maturation that presumably characterizes personality development in all cultures. Socialization demands the learning of self-control and self-discipline, the subordination of personal desires to the needs and wishes of others, the acquisition of skills and self-sufficiency, the curbing of hedonistic and aggressive impulses, and the assimilation of culturally sanctioned patterns of behavior. Moreover, in its most mature aspects, socialization demands that the individual govern his behavior by *rules* which he arrives at rationally before conforming to them. It seems highly unlikely that any of these propensities could become thoroughly stable before conscience is firmly established. Indeed, the very notion of *character* formation assumes adherence to the directive role of conscience in moral behavior.

Conscience and Character

The term *conscience* is an abstraction referring to the cognitive-emotional organization of an individual's moral values, to the feelings of obligation to abide by these values, and to other psychological processes involved in keeping conduct compatible with internalized moral standards. As such, it is a compound of two logically distinct elements: (1) what one might describe as a *feeling* of guilt, fear, taboo, etc.; and (2) some kind of propositional *belief* or judgment about what is right (Wilson, Williams and Sugarman, 1967). Psychologists, especially learning theorists and psychoanalysts, have placed greater emphasis on the emotional component of conscience (e.g., Bandura and Walters, 1963b; Eysenck, 1959-60; Freud, 1935), whereas philosophers have stressed the rational or cognitive component (Edel, 1955).* Although both components are operative at most stages of conscience development, the relative importance of the rational component tends to increase with increasing age. The younger child interiorizes norms of adult authority and adheres to them by force of habit, which is buttressed by guilt feelings and fear of adult authority (Peters, 1963). Older school age children demand reasons for adult norms and sanctions and are less bound by adult constraints because of their own emerging cognitive capacities (Peters, 1963; Piaget, 1932b).

The specific cognitive aspect of conscience development is the ability to generate *prescriptive* judgments (propositions) in making moral decisions. A brief discussion of the characteristics of *moral judgments* will be given here since it is pertinent to the discussion on normative changes in conscience development (see p. 474). Moral judgments share the following characteristics: (1) they are judgments which *prescribe* causes of actions that an individual must take or avoid and are accompanied by such statements, as ought, right, wrong, good, or bad; (2) they are judgments that are universalizable; that is, the judgment follows the Kantian Categorical Imperative "act only on that maxim whereby thou canst at the same time will that it should become a universal law." The conditions of universalizability are met if the consequences would be undesirable if everyone did it, and if all are equally entitled to engage in it (Baier, 1966); (3) finally, they are judgments that involve a *reversible* component, that is, the behavior in question must be acceptable to a person whether he is at the "giving" or "receiving" end of it (Baier, 1966).

It is obvious from this discussion that children do not inherently possess the required capabilities for making mature moral judgments. Moreover, these cognitive abilities are dependent on the child's advancing emotional, social and personality development. Thus, to meet the criteria of *universalizibility* and *reversibility*, it is necessary to possess advanced role-taking capabilities as well as the ability sympathetically to represent in imagination the interests of others and the effects of our actions on their lives (Frankena, 1958).

This picture of conscience development still remains incomplete, however, without the discussion of the concept of *character*. It is not enough merely to

---

It is apparent, in reading the work of psychologists interested in conscience development, that their treatment sidesteps the issues raised by moral philosophers on the rational decision-making component of conscience development. The notable exceptions among psychologists are Ausubel (1952) Kohlberg (1964) and Piaget (1932b). Rational philosophers, however, simply treat the cognitive aspects of the development of conscience, while ignoring many valuable findings of the psychologists on the emotional aspects (e.g., Baier, 1966; 1963, Nowell-Smith, 1954). The notable exceptions amongst philosophers are Edel (1955), Peters (1959-60, 1963), and Wilson et al., (1967).

generate moral judgments; it is also necessary to act in accordance with these prescriptions. In a sense, this consistency between judgment and action is part of the definition of *moral character*. Character, as discussed here, is the moral component of the person's developing ego. As such, character refers to the totality of enduring and relatively stable behavioral predispositions in an individual that are influenced by feelings of moral obligation. Mature character development involves several integrated developmental skills: (1) a legislative capacity to generate norms and rules for actions; (2) a judicial capacity to determine that the rules apply in a given situation; and (3) an executive capacity which enables the individual to consistently operate on these rules when he sees that they apply to the situation in question (Peters, 1962).

The development and use of these skills are integrally related to the expanding capacities of the ego. As the person's ego matures, there is an increasing integration of cognition, perception, and the mechanisms of behavior control. Parenthetically it should be noted that there is no inherent necessity for this integration to take place simply because the individual grows older. In a sense, the control mechanism of *guilt* is a goad to live consistently with one's rational (cognitive) judgments, but, nevertheless, errors in the socialization process lead people to feel guilty about actions that they believe to be good and appropriate. Here the control mechanism of *guilt* distorts legitimate moral actions and results in faulty character development. Obviously, many other distortions can result during the socialization process, which makes philosophical discussion of moral development incomplete, though necessary.

> It is just because things so often go wrong in this way that philosophical description is not enough: we need not only to describe rationality, but to find out and produce the psychological and social factors that make rationality tolerable and if possible enjoyable (Wilson *et al*, 1967, p. 116).

Because of the important psychological influences on character formation, it is necessary to consider in more detail the psychological components of conscience.

Psychological Components of Conscience Development*

Psychological treatments of conscience development have stressed three different aspects of internalization: the behavioral, emotional, and judgmental aspects of moral action (Kohlberg, 1964).

It would be virtually impossible, short of writing a book, to consider all of the psychological studies and theories which address themselves to the question of conscience. Exhaustive reviews are available however, and they provide excellent sources of a more detailed study of this phenomenon. See Berkowitz (1964), Bandura and Walters (1963b), Aronfreed (1968), Kohlberg (1963, 1964), Walters and Parke (1966), Turiel (1967). Social learning and experimentally oriented theory and research are emphasized in Aronfreed, Bandura and Walters, and Walters and Parke, cognitive developmental concepts in Kohlberg, and psychoanalytic concepts in Turiel.

The behavioral criterion of internalization is seen in intrinsically motivated conformity or resistance to temptation (Kohlberg, 1964). The famous Hartshorne and May (1930) character study, in which such traits as honesty and service were assessed, is an illustration of the type of research conducted in this tradition. Honesty was measured by observing the child's ability to resist temptation to break a rule (e.g., cheating) when there was little chance of being detected. Conformity studies assessing the effects of positive control of conduct through the imitation of adults who delay gratification (Bandura and Mischel, 1965; Stein, 1967), or contrived experimental inducements of sympathetic and altruistic responses (Aronfreed, 1968), and studies involving negative controls which induce conformity through the timing of different conditions of punishment (Parke and Walters, 1967; Walters and Parke, 1966) further illustrate this tradition.

The second criterion of internalized standards is the emotion of guilt, that is, the self-punitive, self-critical reactions of remorse and anxiety after transgression of cultural standards (Kohlberg, 1964). The types of research illustrating this specific kind of reaction to transgression are exemplified by studies on reparation, confession, self-criticism, and, reactions oriented toward external punishment (Aronfreed, 1968).

Finally, the judgmental aspects of moral development discussed previously (see p. 469) stress the cognitive component in this internalizing process. The theoretical impetus for studying these aspects stems mainly from philosophical traditions, but the recent work of Kohlberg (1964) and Piaget (1932), to be discussed later, has provided some measure of empirical psychological support for pertinent philosophical propositions.

For an adequate understanding of all of the factors involved in the development of conscience, it is clearly evident that all the above aspects must be taken into account. At present, however, the precise relationships between these several aspects are not clearly delineated. As Kohlberg (1964) points out:

> A common interest in the basic psychological processes of moral internalization has given direction to studies of moral conduct, moral judgment, and moral emotion. In addition, a certain degree of empirical consistency is to be found between the various aspects of children's moral character. Nevertheless, the findings and theories based on these various aspects of morality tend to lead in quite different directions (p. 384).

Accordingly, for purposes of clarity and consistency, we will discuss these various aspects within our own theoretical framework as set forth in the chapter on ego development. Obviously, the same tentativeness of interpretation is encouraged in our discussion on moral development.

Consistent with our previous definition of conscience (see p. 468), the relevant psychological research confirms the applicability of both cognitive and emotional variables to problems of moral development. To reiterate, *conscience* refers to the cognitive-emotional organization of an individual's moral values, feelings of to obligation abide by these values, and to other psychological processes involved in keeping conduct compatible with internalized moral standards. It presupposes, first, that he is able to assimilate certain external standards of right and wrong or good and evil and accept them as his *own* (see p. 462). However, the mere assimilation of moral values does not necessarily mean that these values will influence conduct in any stable and systematic fashion until a sense of *obligation* evolves to conform to them in his own *personal* behavior and to feel accountable for lapses therefrom. The sense of obligation is itself a moral value and must undergo internalization; developmentally, however, this step occurs *after* the interiorization of other ethical values. That is, the child believes that certain actions are good or bad and applies these designations to *other* persons' conduct before he feels that he ought or ought not do them himself. But unlike other values, moral obligation has the regulatory function of compelling adherence to internalized norms of behavior. Hence it is the core value of his moral system which not only makes possible the implementation of other values in actual conduct, but also welds them together into an organized system of behavior. It gives generality and genotypic consistency to moral conduct by entering into every moral decision he makes. For example, the disposition to refrain from commiting an act of dishonesty depends on more than the strength of honesty in a given context. The *total* inhibitory control that can be exercised in this situation is, rather, the strength of the particular moral value (honesty) weighted by a general factor represented by the strength of the moral obligation to abide by *all* internalized values.

The operation of conscience also presupposes the capacity to *anticipate* the consequences of actions in advance of their execution, and to exercise volitional and inhibitory control in order to bring these anticipated consequences into line with perceived obligation. The acquisition of such inhibitory self-control is naturally a very gradual process that parallels the growth of ability to endure postponement of immediate hedonistic gratification.

A final psychological component involved in the operation of conscience is *self-critical* capacity. Without this capacity for objectively appraising one's own intentions and behavior in the light of internalized moral principles, it is neither possible to inhibit immoral actions nor to experience guilt after they are committed. In the child, the development of this capacity is fostered by various parental determinants. One factor in the acquisition of self-critical ability is the administration of punishment which terminates in the utterance of self-critical responses by the child (Aronfreed, 1968). Thus, when parents give reasons for administering punishment, it is believed that the child adopts these reasons himself and, when the adult is no longer present, uses them in regulating his own conduct. For punishment to operate in this fashion, however, a warm parental relationship is essential, since children reject and withdraw from criticisms made by rejecting adults (Walters and Parke, 1966). The importance, then, of the self-critical faculty in the development of conscience can be seen in the fact that the latter remains in a rudimentary state until the former is reasonably well advanced. When self-criticism can be employed, guilt feelings become possible since these feelings are a reaction to the perception of a discrepancy between one's own behavior and the moral standards in relation to which a sense of obligation exists.

Guilt is a special kind of negative *self-evaluation* that occurs when an individual acknowledges that his behavior is at variance with a given moral value to which he feels obligated to conform. It always includes feelings of shame in perceiving or imagining the negative evaluation of himself *by others* for violating a moral obligation. It also involves other *self-reactions* that are at least partially independent of the actual or presumed censure of others, namely, self-reproach, self-disgust, self-contempt, remorse, lowered self-esteem, and various characteristic and subjectively identifiable visceral and vasomotor responses. Through the processes of retrospective association and anticipation, guilt tends to be incorporated into the behavioral system of conscience; and since it is an extremely uncomfortable, self-punishing and anxiety-producing phenomenon, the need to avoid it becomes a strong motivating force to keep behavior consistent with moral obligation. Behavior leading to guilt evokes the anticipation that retribution will be inevitable either through the suffering inherent in guilt feelings, the seeking out of social punishment as a means of guilt reduction, or through the medium of a supernatural agency. The perceived inevitability of punishment, therefore, is one of the characteristic properties of conscience reactions.

It is evident from the foregoing that conscience embodies several component psychological processes and is in no sense a single reified entity. It does, however, enjoy an apparent measure of psychological substantiveness reflective of: (a) generalized inhibitory potential (based on the strength of particular moral values and general feelings of obligation) which lowers the probability of occurrence of acts perceived as incompatible with internalized standards; and (b) anticipation of highly identifiable guilt reactions if such behavior should nevertheless occur. It only confuses the issue to postulate that a separate layer of personality (i.e., the superego) embodies in reified fashion the properties associated with conscience reactions and arises in an inevitably predetermined manner (apart from actual interpersonal experience) in relation to a single aspect of psychosexual development. The Freudian superego is not coextensive at all with the developmental concept of conscience described above. It restricts the genesis of conscience *solely* to the child's supposed identification with the moral values of the like-sexed parent as a means of repressing both sexual rivalry toward the latter and libidinal

(Oedipal) desires for the parent of opposite sex,* and assumes that this identification is facilitated by its postulated occurrence in the "prehistory (phylogenetic unconscious) of every person." Furthermore, it asserts that the moral values assimilated in this context are qualitatively different from other interiorized social norms, and makes no provision for the fact that the underlying bases of value assimilation and moral obligation undergo marked developmental changes.

Normative Changes in Conscience Development

Although none of the conditions necessary for the emergence of conscience can ever be satisfied at birth, all human beings are potentially capable of acquiring conscience behavior under minimally favorable circumstances. Culture may make a difference in the form which this behavior takes and in the specific kinds of stimuli which instigate it, but the capacity itself is so basically human and so fundamental to the sanctions by which social norms are maintained and transmitted to the young in *any* culture that differences among individuals within a culture would probably be as great as or greater than differences among cultures. Thus, despite the probable existence of many important culturally conditioned differences in children's acquisition of guilt behavior, there are presumptive grounds for believing that considerable communality prevails in the general patterning of sequential development. Such communality would be a product of various uniformities regarding (a) basic conditions of the parent-child relationship, (b) minimal cultural needs for socialization of the child, and (c) certain grows trends in cognitive and personality growth from one culture to the next (Ausubel, 1955).

Normative shifts in conscience development reflect both gains in cognitive maturity and age level changes in personality organization. Significant personality factors include alterations in dependency relationships, ego status needs, and mode of assimilating values. Significant cognitive factors include increased capacity for perceiving social expectations and the attributes of social roles, and increased ability to discriminate, generalize, formulate abstractions, and take multiple perspectives. Growth in self-critical ability and in capacity for a less egocentric and more objective approach to values involves both cognitive and personality variables. Interaction between these two sorts of variables is responsible for most developmental changes in the basis of moral obligation and in notions of moral law, justice, and culpa-

---

*The Freudian theory of conscience naturally assumes the reality of the so-called Oedipus complex. See the critique on pp. 398. It is evident that Freud's conception of morality changed frequently and he left many knots untied (Turiel 1967). The more recent neo-analytic discussions of moral development have de-emphasized the rule of the superego while placing greater stress on ego controls (Hartmann, 1960).

bility; because of the many psychological components of conscience, how-ever, it is entirely conceivable that some aspects of moral development are influenced more by one type of factor than by another. MacRae (1954), for example, found that children's disapproval of moral transgressions was positively related to measures of parental authority, whereas conceptions of equity and culpability were not. In general, cognitive capacities seem more important as prerequisites for reaching certain normative levels of moral functioning than as determinants of interindividual differences.

Cognitive Changes. The importance of cognitive factors in conscience de-velopment is seen in the capacity for making *moral judgments.* Consideration of the moral judgments (i.e., knowledge of the difference between right and wrong) of children stresses the fact that we are dealing with a conscious cognitive or intellectual process quite different from the Freudian uncon-scious superego (Wilson *et al*, 1967).

The pioneer work on normative changes in children's *moral judgments* was carried out by Piaget (1932). Piaget presented children with a series of paired short stories, centering on a moral issue, and asked the children to make judgments as to the naughtier action and the extent of culpability or guilt. The following is an example of one of the paired stories:

    a. There was once a little girl who was called Marie. She wanted to give her mother
        a nice surprise, and cut out a piece of sewing for her. But she didn't know how to use
        the scissors properly and cut a big hole in her dress.
    b. A little girl called Margaret went and took her mother's scissors one day when her
        mother was out. She played with them for a bit, and then, as she didn't know how to
        use them properly, cut a little hole in her dress.

Younger children judged Marie the naughtier child because she had done the most damage, whereas older children judged Margaret naughtier because of her intentions. On the basis of these age differences in response to these and other stories, Piaget formulated a two-stage theory of moral development.

A *heteronomous stage* (approximately four to about eight years) is based on an ethic of authority. The child views moral rules and restraints as laid down from above. The rules have a literal interpretation, are sacred, and cannot be changed. An act is morally wrong because it is defined in terms of adult sanctions (i.e., an act is wrong if it is punished by an adult). The child be-lieves in *"imminent justice"* in which the punishment follows invariably upon a violation; its severity varies directly with the magnitude of the consequences of the action, and ignores the motive which inspired it. Because of the child's intellectual limitations, moral rules are considered external (transcendental); this lack of an internalized rule system encourages adherence solely on the basis of external punishment by superordinate adults. Thus, moral duty is simply seen as obedience to adult authority.

Piaget calls his second stage of morality the *autonomous stage* (approximately eight years and above). This type of morality is egalitarian and democratic; the child operates on his "own moral rules" inspired by mutual respect and cooperation with others. Piaget (1932, 1951) maintains that this type of morality arises because of the child's interaction with his peers. The movement away from *unilateral respect* for adults (i.e., desatellization) and the increasing development of *mutual respect* and solidarity with peers helps the child realize that rules are compacts, arrived at and maintained by equals, in the common interest. Rules are no longer sacred and can be changed by mutual consent and in extenuating circumstances. Punishment is no longer an absolute necessity and, in place of being expiatory, it is now specific to the infraction. Moreover, when punishment is deemed necessary, it is aimed at reciprocity in kind or restitution; it is guided by a *principle of equity* which takes into consideration the motive underlying the act and the circumstances in which the transgression was committed.

Since the inception of Piaget's (1932) work on children's moral judgments, numerous replication studies have been carried out which confirm certain aspects of his findings, while disagreeing with others. * Several cross-cultural studies (Caruso, 1943; Lerner, 1937; MacRae, 1954; establish the fact that some of Piaget's dimensions are genuinely developmental and are present in several cultures (e.g., United States, Belgium, Italy). These dimensions are cognitive in import and include a shift from subjectivity to objectivity and from absolutism to relativism. Nevertheless,

. . . given that some such transition sometimes occurs, much more needs to be established about the conditions which favor or retard it. These would include a variety of social factors, but of particular importance would be the techniques for passing on the rules of a society (Peters, 1959-60, p. 252).

It appears that Piaget's proposed relationship between heteronomous morality and unilateral respect for authority and that between autonomous morality and mutual respect between peers has not been clearly validated by later research (Boehm, 1966; Kohlberg, 1963a).

One disturbing aspect of Piaget's two-stage theory of morality is the presence of *heteronomous* morality in adults (Peters, 1959-60; Wilson *et al*, 1967) Specifically in relation to moral judgment, it may be that Piaget's stages have been to gross to encompass all of the nuances of children's judgments after eight years of age. This possibility is supported by Kohlbert's (1957, 1963b, 1968) study of moral judgments in childhood and adolescence. Taking a broadly-based sample of 72 boys, aged 10, 13, and 16, with equal proportions of popular and socially isolated children, he presented 10 moral dilemma

---

A summary and discussion of these replication studies up to 1963 may be found in Kohlberg (1963a). Most recent Piagetian studies: Boehm (1966); Cudrin (1966); Whitman and Kosier (1964).

situations. These situations involved conflicts between particular kinds of values (e.g., a conflict between "legal-social rules" or the "commands of authority" and the needs or welfare of other individuals). Kohlberg, following the Piagetian tradition, asked children to judge the morality of conduct described in the stories. The following example is an illustration of the conflict stories presented for evaluation:

"In Europe, a woman was near death from a special kind of cancer. There was one drug that the doctors thought might save her. It was a form of radium that a druggist in the same town had recently discovered. The drug was expensive to make, but the druggist was charging ten times what the drug cost him to make. He paid $200 for the radium and charged $2000 for a small dose of the drug. The sick woman's husband, Heinz, went to everyone he knew to borrow the money but he could only get together about $1000 which is half of what it cost. He told the druggist that his wife was dying, and asked him to sell it cheaper or let him pay later. But the druggist said 'no. I discovered the drug and I'm going to make money from it.' So Heinz got desperate and broke into the man's store to steal the drug for his wife. Should the husband have done that? Why?" (Kohlberg, 1963b, p. 18-19).

On the basis of responses to these dilemma situations, Kohlberg (1958, 1969) suggested that the child's development of moral judgment falls into six stages, which can be grouped in three levels. The lowest level is characterized as *pre-moral* because of the rather primitive use of moral statements and the lack of sophistication of the judgments. Stage 1 is characterized by judgments which attempt to resolve the dilemma by recourse to a punishment and obedience orientation. An act is considered wrong because it results in punishment and not because of its own intrinsic merits. The second stage is more differentiated than the first and the child indicates that his conformity to rules is motivated by a desire to obtain rewards and so on. The judgments made of the dilemma situations reveal a main instrumental hedonism and an egoistic orientation which is indicative of the increasing self-other differentiation which is taking place at this time. The second level is characterized by a morality of conventional rule conformity. The third stage is labelled good boy-good girl morality because the child's response to the dilemma is an attempt at maintaining good relations with others and conformity to avoid disapproval. The rule orientation of the child at this time is constantly couched in a familial context which eventually gives way to the wide social frame of reference that characterizes stage 4. The morality which invests the conventional authority structures in the society with censure-giving powers constitutes the fourth stage. Legitimate authorities such as police, government, etc. are invested with censuring powers designed to elicit guilt and retaliation when transgressions are made against their societal prescriptions. Finally, level 5 marks the more autonomous stage where morality is based on self-accepted moral principles. Stage five is a morality of social contract and general avoidance of violations of the rights of others. The last stage (6) is exemplified by a morality of individual principles in which the child conforms not to carry out a contract, but to avoid his own self-condemnation when he perceives himself as violating his self-imposed principles.

Kohlberg's Stage 1 is similar in several respects to Piaget's heteronomous morality. It implies a concern for consequences rather than intentions, lack of awareness of relativity of value, and definition of right in terms of obedience to authority and in terms of punishment. However, Kohlberg (1963b) does not view this stage as indicative of heteronomous respect for rules but, rather, of an externalistic undifferentiated orientation. Stage II is equivalent to Piaget's autonomous morality; we see here the emergence of individualistic hedonism growing out of an increased differentiation in cognitive abilities. It is obvious from Kohlberg's data that the achievement of autonomous morality is not completed by age eight as Piaget would have it. Later childhood sees the development of a more abstract good-boy and authority-maintaining orientation; it is exemplified also by the moral judgments of many adults who are overimpressed by the importance of implicitly conforming to the rules promulgated by authority figures.

It is not ordinarily until adolescence is reached that the last developmental stage emerges (Stage VI). In this stage children begin to make judgments on the basis of moral principles which are *universilizable* and *reversible* (see p. 469). Conscience here is similar to the philosophical definition of a self-judging function rather than a feeling of guilt or dread. The child at this stage makes moral judgments of his own internal standards, and is increasingly less influenced by his immediate social environment.

It is clear from Kohlberg's data that the rational component of conscience development (i.e., cognitive moral judgments of right and wrong) reaches its peak after a long developmental process. This is contrary to the assertions of Piaget, who sets it at about eight years, and to those of Freud, who sees its completion by the age of five. Moreover, his data provide statistical evidence (something which is not found in Piaget's work) for the hypothesis that there exists a genuine developmental hierarchy in moral growth (Wilson *et al*, 1967). The sequence of these stages has been replicated in different cultures cross-sectionally (e.g., Kohlberg, 1969; Sullivan, 1969), and also longitudinally (Kohlberg, 1969). Finally, this developmental hierarchy assumes that a more advanced stage represents a reorganization of preceding stages (Rest, Turiel and Kohlberg, 1967; Turiel, 1966).

In both Piaget's and Kohlberg's stage formulations, the age-level changes in the development of the cognitive aspects of conscience are primarily reflective of qualitative shifts in the basis of moral obligation and in conceptions of moral law, rather than of quantitative improvement in moral conduct. Their findings illustrate developmental trends in the judicial and legislative components of conscience, but the executive or behavioral component rests on a variety of specific cultural factors. After conscience is stabilized by the development of an adequate self-critical faculty, total character (e.g., helpfulness, truthfulness) scores do not improve consistently; in fact, during this age period of 10 to 13, older children are significantly more deceitful than younger children (Hartshorne and May, 1930). Improvement is shown only in those aspects of conduct that depend on knowledge of societal moral standards and in motivational traits that are necessary for the acquisition of greater primary status (Hartshorne and May, 1930; Terman, 1925). This situation is probably reflective in part of the characteristic moral confusion and expediency of our culture. Children gradually learn that the triumph of honesty is not inevitable. Thus it does not follow that good deeds necessarily result from good words. To complete the picture of conscience development, therefore, we must view the impact of cognitive factors within the general framework of the child's socio-affectional relations. Our general discussion will follow along the lines previously developed in the chapter on ego development.

Related Changes in Ego Development. Our discussion of ego development in a moral context rests on the assumption that moral development is a subset of general ego development which can be independently conceptualized (Loevinger, 1966). The essential similarities between moral and ego development theorists are seen in the three-stage developmental process which all embrace (Kohlberg, 1969). This three-level process in moral and ego development implies: (1) a first level at which rules and the expectations of others are external to the self; (2) a second level at which the self is identified with or equated with the rules, stereotypes, and expectations of others, especially authorities; and (3) a third level at which the self is differentiated from conventional rules (Kohlberg, 1969).* In our ego development framework, level one is the pre-satellizing ego, level two involves early and late ego satellization, and level three is the desatellizing stage. The reason for discussing ego development here is that the *cognitive-judgmental* component of conscience development is incomplete without considering the *executive aspects* that are closely related to ego development considerations. The following discussion will therefore consider "conscience" development under our *general ego development* theory as advanced in Chapter 8.

In the *"Presatellizing Stage"*, *conscience* for the most part involves little more than the development of inhibitory control on the basis of learning to anticipate and avoid punishment. Previous experience with a given type of unacceptable behavior leads the child to expect pain, deprivation, isolation or disapproval if such behavior is repeated, and leads to feelings of insecurity in

---

This three-level developmental process is seen in several personality theorists (Ausubel, 1959; Harvey, Hunt and Schroder, 1961; Loevinger, 1966; Peck and Havighurst, 1960) and moral theorists (Baldwin, 1906; Kohlberg, 1969).

contemplating it. Inhibition of such behavior, therefore, is rewarding since it reduces insecurity. During this stage, children obey prohibitory commands but do not consistently honor unenforced positive requests. Such conduct is devoid of any moral implications since it only indicates submission to authority rather than genuine acceptance of it. Cognitively, the presatellizing period roughly corresponds to Piaget's egocentric stage and Kohlberg's premoral level. Thus consciousness of rules in terms of obligation has yet to be developed, and the primary motivating force is fear of punishment. Contrary to Piaget's interpretation, our own position agrees with Kohlberg's (1964) view that it is fear of punishment rather than respect for the rules of adults which is the primary motivating force at this stage. The premoral level of "punishment and obedience orientation" and early precursors of "naive instrumental hedonism," leads to a somewhat autistic definition of values in terms of private needs (Kohlberg, 1969).

During the "*Early Satellizing Stage*" the child acknowledges his dependence upon parents for volitional direction and decides to accept a satellizing role in relation to them, thereby gradually acquiring a need to assimilate their values. Acceptance of parental standards of rightness and wrongness depends upon this satellizing relationship to parents (Lerner, 1937; Piaget, 1932), and is facilitated by prestige suggestion and by the parent's altruistic role. But acceptance of these values does not obligate him—in the absence of a still undeveloped sense of moral responsibility—to regulate his own behavior accordingly (Ausubel, 1955). Hitting, for example, is perceived as "bad" when *other* persons do it but not when gratification of his *own* aggressive impulses are involved (Fite, 1940).

Behavior can first be regarded as manifesting moral properties when a sense of obligation is acquired. The child's need to retain his derived status makes him acquiesce to the proposition that disobedience is wrong, disloyal, and hurtful to his parents. At this point, guilt reactions become possible, and the child becomes motivated to conform to parental standards in order to avoid the negative self-evaluation, anxiety, and remorse associated with guilt. This development takes place in children who are accepted and intrinsically valued. Parents of delinquents are typically less accepting, affectionate, and solicitous than parents of nondelinquents (Kohlberg, 1964). Moral identification is facilitated in a democratic home atmosphere by firm, consistent, and love-oriented discipline (Hoffman, 1963). In general, strength of guilt feelings in adults tends to be correlated with love-oriented techniques of punishment (Hoffman, 1963; Kohlberg, 1964).

Early satellization corresponds to the latter phases of Piagetian "egocentrism" or to the beginning of the autonomous stage. Correspondingly, the "naive hedonistic orientation" (Kohlberg, 1969) involves sufficient reciprocity in interpersonal relations to foster the early development of guilt reactions. With this development there is a greater, but by no means over-whelming, probability that there will be greater consistency between moral judgments (i.e., legislation) and moral action, (i.e., execution). Thus the development of feelings of moral obligation is a gradual process. It is not only hampered by negativistic trends (see p. 264), but also by the slow growth of self-critical abilities and of the ability to generalize principles of right and wrong beyond specific situations. It does not arise spontaneously but, rather, under the pressure of the parent's new authority role and training demands. Furthermore, it is reinforced by the parents' physical presence and prestige suggestion, by the continued application of external sanction (reward, and punishment, threat, and ridicule), by the withdrawal of love and approval, and by the child's continued dependence on the parent for physical survival. The early stages of satellizing conscience represent a compromise between aggressive negativism and an unstable sense of moral responsibility. The preschool child strenuously attempts to rationalize his misdeeds by attribut-ing them to accident, forgetting, real or imaginary playmates, sensory deficiency, involuntary movements, and misunderstanding.

The "*Late-Satellizing Stage*" is marked by the completion of the internaliza-tion and assimilation of parental values. Stabilization of the sense of moral obligation occurs primarily as a result of gains in self-critical ability. Once the child is able to appraise himself and his situation realistically enough to accept the dependent biosocial status that is inevitably his in any culture, he can finally acknowledge parental authority as unquestionably and uncon-ditionally valid. Improved self-critical ability also enables him to perceive his own wrongdoing in the absence of external coercive agents. The child appears concerned with the spirit as well as the letter of moral duty, and threats of reprisal for punishment are less frequently uttered (Piaget, 1932). He is attuned to conventional moral roles, and the anticipation of praise or blame related to these roles begins to operate as a controlling force on con-duct. At first this role-taking ability is mainly based on natural and familial types of affection and sympathy, but then, it yields to a wider social radius where *justice* is based on regard for the rights and expectations of both rule-enforcers and rule-obeyers (Kohlberg, 1963a). Regard for rules is based on some form of organized social order (Kohlberg, 1968).

Because of the child's social inexperience, his satellizing orientation to value assimilation, and his cognitive inability to appreciate the functional basis of moral principles, the organization of conscience during the middle years of childhood remains somewhat absolutistic and depends heavily on the conventional wisdom of older family members and authorities in the com-munity (Kohlberg, 1964).

The "*Desatellizing-Stage*" is marked by significant changes focused on the basis of moral obligation and conceptions of moral law. During this phase, feelings of moral accountability are placed on a societal basis (Kohlberg's stage 4) instead of remaining a function of the parent-child relationship (Kohlberg's stage 3) and are referred to more abstract principles of justice and responsibility based on relationships outside the immediate family. The beginning of the desatellizing period remains conventional and "authority maintaining" in focus, but the notion of unilateral obligation and respect for adults (Piaget, 1932) gives way to reciprocal obligations which are stressed in conventional societal institutions (Kohlberg, 1964). Changes in the heterogeneity and differentiation of peer group organization and its status functions make possible a reformulation of the concept of moral law on a more reciprocal, functional, and exploratory basis.

The above changes are instigated by modification in the parent-child relationship, shifts in the child's needs for a more primary source of status, alteration in his group experience, and maturation of his perceptual and cognitive capacities. As he begins to lose his volitional dependence upon parents and to become more concerned with acquiring primary status, his satellizing orientation to value assimilation becomes increasingly less serviceable for the satisfaction of his ego needs (see p. 464). Since the inherent sacredness of moral standards also depends in part upon a perception of parents as infallible and omniscient beings, it begins to break down as he enters the school and community and discovers that there are other authorities, various moral alternatives, and different versions of the truth. The more he comes into contact with the variable moral beliefs of the culture at large, the more his parents' early monopoly on moral authority is challenged and the less axiomatic their values become.

The changing nature and organization of peer group experience also promotes developmental changes in moral behavior. A primary function of the early peer group is to provide a supplementary source of derived status; and the child accepts its authority on the same unilateral and absolutistic basis as he does the parents'. Prior to the age of eight he also operates in small, isolated, and informally organized groups in which roles are poorly differentiated and a lack of functional devision of labor exists. Later, groups become larger, less isolated, and more stable. Children experience membership in several different groups exhibiting a variety of rules, practices, and values, and begin to improvise their own rules to meet new situations. As individual roles are differentiated the need for cooperation and mutual obligations increases. The older the child becomes the more he looks to the group as a source of primary status and the more the group tends to supplant parents as the source of moral authority.

However, it is mostly in heterogeneous *urban* cultures that values (during preadolescence and especially adolescence) tend to acquire a wider social base and peers tend to replace parents as interpreters and enforcers of the moral code. But neither phenomenon is indispensable for the maturational changes in moral organization that occur at this time. Repudiation of parental authority and of filial ties is *not* necessary for the acquisition of mature conceptions of moral responsibility and culpability based on intention, interpersonal needs, and reciprocal obligations. All that is required from a personality standpoint is a change in status and dependency needs and sufficient social experience to appreciate the functional basis of existing authority relationships. The later phase of desatellization, therefore, differs from its predecessor only in intensity and completeness of desatellization. The transition into adolescent society makes it possible for the child to incorporate and explore more fully the gamut of moral values leading to greater tolerance and flexibility (McCullough, 1969). In some cases, the ego has achieved sufficient maturity to allow the self to become differentiated from conventional rules (Kohlberg, 1968). This increasing differentiation is marked by moral obligations and principles which are based on contract and democratically accepted laws (Kohlberg, 1969). Hence this development brings with it the ability to entertain and resolve conflicting norms, where previously conflicting norms are ignored or misunderstood (Kohlberg, 1969).

Acting conjunctively with personality factors in bringing about desatellizing changes in moral values are the various aforementioned facets of cognitive maturation. Increased ability to generalize and think in more logical and abstract terms makes possible a more objective and integrated approach to moral issues (Ausubel, 1952; Kohlberg, 1969). Much normative change in moral conduct can similarly be attributed to the fact that with increasing age, as he becomes more able to take multiple perspectives extensively, flexibly, and abstractly (Feffer and Gourevitch, 1960; Feffer and Suchotliff, 1966; Flavell, 1967; Strauss, 1954), the child's perception of social roles become more accurate (Flavell, 1967; Lerner, 1937b; Strauss, 1954), and built-in role conceptions become justifications of motivations for behavior appropriate or inappropriate to enactment of roles (Lerner, 1937b). With increasing age, children also tend to adopt a less subjectivistic approach to values. They consider them from a less personal and more detached point of view, show greater ability to argue from the standpoint of a hypothetical premise, and think more in terms that transcend their immediate experience (Ausubel, 1968). A corresponding trend in value assimilation is a decline in egoism and an increase in altruism (Van den Daele, 1967; Ugurel-Semin, 1952; Wright, 1942). Children become more aware of the needs, feelings, and interests of others and are more able to consider a situation from another's point of view (Kohlberg, 1963a). There is also an increasing facility in appreciating intentions over consequences in judgment (Breznitz & Kugelmass, 1967; Kohlberg, 1963a). Finally, intellectual development, in conjuncition with the decline in egocentricity and subjectivism, enhances self-critical ability, making possible both the perception of finer discrepancies between precept and conduct and the judgment of one's own moral behavior on the same basis as that of others (Ausubel, 1952; Kohlberg, 1969).

INDIVIDUAL DIFFERENCES IN MORAL DEVELOPMENT

In the foregoing sketch of age level changes in moral development we attempted to trace sequential stages that can presumably be found in all cultural settings. Still to be considered are the psychosocial aspects of moral development and personality and cognitive factors that account for inter-individual (idiosyncratic) differences within a culture.

Parental Variables and Personality Considerations

Our discussion thus far has not treated the effects of parental antecedents independently from ego development theory. Before considering idiosyncratic personality differences, it would be desirable briefly to summarize the relationships between moral development and parental training conditions in order to clarify the subsequent discussion.

Parental Antecedents. At present, summaries of studies exploring the relationship between moral development and parental antecedents allow few definitive conclusions (Aronfreed, 1968; Becker, 1964; Hoffman, 1963; Kohlberg, 1963a, 1968). Tentative generalizations, recognizing exceptions, indicate that frequent expression of warmth and affection toward the child promotes identification with parental values (Hoffman, 1963; Lidson, 1966; Mussen and Parker, 1965). Although threatening and punitive parents elicit identification in their children (Hoffman, 1963), it is found that this general approach to child rearing leads to external orientations in childrens' verbal expression and application of evaluative standards (Aronfreed, 1968). There is also evidence to indicate that physical punishment and direct power assertion of parents are conducive to a moral orientation based on fear of external detection and punishment (Hoffman, 1963). In contrast, an "internal orientation" toward compliance (e.g., appeals to the child's needs for affection and self-esteem) is seen in parents who have affectionate relationships with their children (Hoffman, 1963). Affectionate parental relationships, also, seem to be related to sympathetic behavior in children (Lenrow, 1965).

Although "love withdrawal" has been frequently cited as an important mechanism in the development of "internalized controls" (Hoffman, 1963), it now appears that the "induction" of certain cognitive constraints (e.g., explaining to the child the consequences of his actions before "love withdrawal") is also an important antecedent in developing internalized guilt and internalized moral judgment (Hoffman and Salzstein, 1967; Aronfreed, 1968; Kohlberg, 1968). At present, then, these tentative generalizations are subject to many reservations—a probable reflection of the fact that different theoretical accounts of moral development are at variance with one another. For example, social learning theory stresses the role of "imitation" in fostering mature moral judgments (Bandura and McDonald, 1963) whereas developmental theorists confine the phenomenon of "imitation" to very short-term, situational changes in moral orientation (Cowan, Langer and others, 1968; Crowley, 1968; Lorimer & Sullivan, 1968; Turiel, 1968). The tentative conclusions concerning parental warmth and acceptance, however, are not at variance with our ego development orientation. The evidence regarding the effects of warm-accepting parental attitudes is consistent with our previous interpretation of the relationship between these attitudes and the satellizing stage of conscience development. The absence of parental acceptance and its effect on moral development will now be discussed.

Personality Considerations. The non-satellizer obviously fails to undergo the various changes in conscience development associated with satellization, and similarly, the changes resulting from desatellization. His moral development is less discontinuous than that of the satellizer. During early and middle childhood the non-satellizer continues to conform to parental standards for the same expediential reasons as during infancy; he fails to develop a sense of moral obligation in relation to a general attitude of subservience, loyalty, and need for approval and retention of derived status. Fear of deprivation and loss of succorance rather than guilt avoidance keep him in line and check the overt expression of his hostility. Moral obligations are assimilated on a selective basis only, that is, if they are perceived as leading to ego enhancement. In moral judgment the saliency of this ego enhancement criterion is seen in the adoption of a naive-egoistic orientation (Kohlberg, 1964). The non-satellizer's conformity to moral rules is, therefore, based on the principle of expediency; those moral obligations which lead to the acquisition of primary status are selectively assimilated (McCullough, 1969). The non-satellizer's moral value system is thus functional and based on mutual obligations leading to ego enhancement (McCullough, 1969).

During late childhood the non-satellizer becomes capable of internalizing moral values and obligations on the basis of an exploratory orientation. Unhampered by satellizing loyalties he finds it easier to grasp functional concepts of moral law based on equity and reciprocal obligations. In this way he too acquires the prerequisites for a guilt-governed conscience. But the stability of moral obligations that circumvent a preliminary history of satellization is highly precarious because: (a) infantile irresponsibility has never been attenuated by strong, emotionally charged feelings of obligation toward significant figures in his interpersonal world, and (b) powerful needs for ego enhancement are often in conflict with the content and goals of ethical norms. Under these conditions, nevertheless, moral obligations are

seldom repudiated outright since this would require direct and inexpedient
conflict with cultural sanctions (Ausubel, 1952; Kohlberg, 1964). However,
two less drastic alternatives are available: (1) indirect evasion of the demands
of conscience and the punishment of guilt when the needs of ego aggrandizement are too strong to be denied; and (2) buttressing conscience by the
mechanism of reaction formation when moral obligations are too solidly
entrenched to be circumvented.

Moral obligation may be evaded either (a) by selectively inhibiting the
self-critical faculty so that, when expedient, even glaring discrepancies
between precept and practice cannot be perceived, of (b) by claiming
superior status so that one is *above* the law for *ordinary* people. Reaction
formation rigidly suppresses motives that are at variance with internalized
moral obligations and substitutes more acceptable motives in their place.
Nevertheless, many loopholes for surreptitious circumvention are still
present. Antisocial trends can often be expressed under the guise of lofty
ideals. At the very best, the moral behavior of the non-satellizer becomes
unspontaneous, stereotyped, and unduly circumscribed. Awareness of the
underlying strength of unacceptable motives encourages the erection of
exaggerated defenses.

The overvalued child who has never felt much pressure to conform to
parental standards frequently regards himself as exempt from ordinary moral
obligations. The rejected child, on the other hand, is not likely to claim such
unique exemptions since he has been subjected to rigorous discipline. In most
instances he will acquire a strong rational conscience buttressed by reaction
formation and permitting occasional moral lapses through impairment of the
self-critical faculty. However, the concomitance of harsh rejection by parents,
perhaps the doubling of the Y chromosome, and extreme self-assertiveness in
the child may result in the latter repudiating the entire fabric of parental
moral values; the resulting personality structure and correlated type of
delinquency is known as aggressive, antisocial psychopathy. When rejection
is expressed in parental neglect and self-love, the child displaces the hostility
he feels for his parents onto others. Such behavior is reinforced by the
parents' tendency to condone it as long as they themselves are not disturbed
(Bandura & Walters, 1963a). On the positive side, the rejected child possesses
a latent capacity for forming satellizing-like relationships which enable him
to experience the type of guilt feelings that occur in satellizing children.

Among *satellizers*, aberrations in conscience development are generally less
severe. The more serious problem is presented by the underdominated child
who has great difficulty acquiring a sense of moral obligation. To begin with,
he is not required to inhibit hedonistic motivations or to curb aggressive
impulses. The limits of unacceptable behavior are poorly defined and inadequately or inconsistently enforced (Hunt & Hardt, 1965). Second, like

the overvalued child, he is sometimes treated as a specially privileged person exempt from usual responsibilities toward others, and is not encouraged to develop a realistic self-critical faculty. Capricious and inconsistent parental discipline is associated with lack of self-discipline in children (Hunt & Hardt, 1965; Sanford et al, 1943) and is more characteristic of delinquents than of non-delinquents, (Glueck & Glueck, 1950; Hunt & Hardt, 1965; Kohlberg, 1964). Fortunately the motivation for immoral behavior is more likely to lie in hedonistic self-indulgence than in unprincipled ego-aggrandizement at the expense of others. The chief difficulty in moral development for overprotected and overdominated children, on the other hand, lies in transfering feelings of moral obligation from parents to society and in arriving at independent value judgments. Even when delinquent behavior is present, self-critical capacity and guilt are substantially correlated with more mature moral judgment levels (Kohlberg, 1968; Ruma & Mosher, 1967). This situation has less serious consequences if the parents are alive and do not subscribe to antisocial attitudes. However, if the parents are moral deviants, uncritical loyalty on the part of the child can lead to delinquent behavior; whereas the death or removal of the parents can create a vacuum in moral responsibility.

Ascendence and viscerotonia are probably important temperamental variables influencing the course of conscience development. The more self-assertive a child is the more likely he will be to resist the imposition of parental standards upon his behavior. Similarly, the greater his need for hedonistic satisfactions, the more reluctant he will be to accept the obligation of conforming to rules aimed at minimizing these satisfactions. Dishonest children tend to be impulsive, emotionally unstable, and suggestible (Hartshorne & May, 1930; Slaght, 1928). Delinquents may also be more prone, for temperamental reasons, to utilize aggression as a defense or status-gaining mechanism (Healey and Bronner, 1936). In contrast to nondelinquents they have been described as more restless, active, impulsive, and danger-loving (Glueck & Glueck, 1950; Healey & Bronner, 1936; Hunt & Hardt, 1965; Kohlberg, 1968).

Cognitive Factors

Since values and moral behavior obviously have a cognitive aspect, we could reasonably anticipate that they would be influenced by both intelligence and moral knowledge. A minimal degree of intelligence is required for acquiring abstract principles of moral value, for perceiving the moral expectations of the culture, for anticipating the consequences of behavior, and for appreciating the advantages of conforming to social norms. Moral conduct also presupposes moral knowledge. However, it seems that intelligence and moral knowledge are only significantly related to moral behavior when they fall below a certain critical level. Beyond this point, personality and motivational variables are probably crucial determining factors.

Intelligence correlates with those moral maturity scores obtained from Kohlberg- and Piaget-type tests (Boehm, 1962a, b: Kohlberg, 1963a, 1964, 1968; Whiteman & Kosier, 1964). As Kohlberg (1964) points out, however:

> moral judgment is [only] moderately correlated with IQ but quite highly related to age, with intelligence controlled . . . Intellectual development, then, is an important condition for the development of moral thought, but level of moral thought can be clearly distinguished from general intellectual level (pp. 404-405).

Substantial correlations between moral *conduct* and intelligence have also been obtained (Kohlberg, 1963a). Intellectually "superior" children surpass their "average" contemporaries in such traits as conscientiousness, perseverence, prudence, and truthfulness(Kohlberg, 1968; Terman *et al*, 1925). Their superiority, however, prevails mostly in regard to moral traits that either depend on moral knowledge or are important for achieving individual success rather than in regard to traits reflecting moral attitudes (Hartshorne and May, 1930; Jones, 1954; The following factors, therefore, probably contribute to the positive relationship found between intelligence and certain kinds of moral traits: (1) Brighter children are better able to perceive the expectations of their culture and to learn appropriate forms of conduct. They can also perceive more accurately which character traits are required for success. (2) The personality traits that correlate most highly with intelligence are also most highly prized by middleclass homes; and as already pointed out (Chapter 9), intelligence tests scores are positively related to social status. (3) Highly motivated children tend to be persistent, stable, and responsible, and to make the most of their intellectual endowment by continually exercising their cognitive capacities and by performing maximally on intelligence tests.

The moderately positive relationship between intelligence and honesty (Hartshorne and May *et al*, 1930; Jones, 1936), can be largely attributed to such extrinsic considerations as having less reason to cheat in order to do well in school work and being shrewd in avoiding detection or inadvisable opportunities for cheating. This interpretation is supported by the fact that intelligence correlates more highly with moral conduct than does moral knowledge (Hartshorne and May, 1930). Evidently then, intelligence affects such conduct less by influencing moral knowledge than in some extraneous fashion. Mental deficiency occurs more frequently among delinquents than nondelinquents, and the mean I.Q. of the former is also somewhat lower (Healey & Bronner, 1948; Owen, 1937; however, I.Q.'s are *generally* lower in the urban slum areas in which juvenile delinquency breeds, as shown by the negligible difference in mental test performance between delinquents and non-delinquent siblings (Healey & Browner, 1948). Scores on moral knowledge are not highly correlated with moral conduct (Hartshorne & May et al, 1930), and fail to differentiate between delinquents and nondelinquents. Thus, low I.Q. per se cannot be an important etiological factor in delinquency, but may constitute one of the larger constellation of variables associated with depressed socioeconomic conditions that contributes to the development of delinquent behavior. Intellectual deficit, for example, increases suggestability, the tendency to take unwise chances, and the probability of apprehension.

To summarize, it appears that the same gross variables which favor superiority in moral judgment also favor resistance to temptation and moral autonomy. These include intelligence and social class, where the findings on moral conduct, as well as on moral judgment, suggest a considerable convergence of influence of various social participation groups on development, though not on immediate reactions to moral situations (Kohlberg, 1964).

Sex Differences*

The significance of sex differences in several aspects of the child's moral development is presently unclear (Maccoby, 1966). Summaries of studies on Piagetian aspects of moral maturity reveal few differences between boys and girls (Maccoby, 1966). The one study that reports significant sex differences in this area favors girls—showing them to be less inclined toward immanent justice and moral realism, and less accepting of the efficacy of severe punishment (Porteus and Johnson, 1965). Studies indicating resistance to cheating are somewhat equivocal with regard to sex differences (Maccoby, 1966). Girls tend to resist breaking a prohibition longer (Walters & Demkow, 1963). Cheating on tests when surveillance is assumed absent has been found to be more prevalent in boys (Burton, Allinsmith and Maccoby, 1966; Rebelsky, Alinsmith & Grinder, 9163), with only one exception favoring boys (Hartshorne and May et al, 1930). The tendency to confess or become upset after deviating from some norm is greater in girls than in boys (Luria, Goldwasser and Goldwasser, 1963; Porteus and Johnson, 1965; Rebelsky et al, 1963; Sears, Rau and Alpert, 1965).

The possibility that girls are more intrinsically valued by their parents, and hence greater satellizers, may account for the rather consistent findings indicating their greater adherence to societal moral codes. Girls more than boys consider stealing categorically wrong in both public and private situations (McDonald, 1963), and mothers report girls as less deviant from moral norms (Sears, Maccoby and Levin, 1957; Sears, Rau and Alpert, 1965).

---

*Reviews on sex differences pertaining to moral development may be found in several sources (Bronfenbrenner, 1962a; Maccoby, 1966).

However, boys, in the self-reports, present themselves as less deviant (Lansky, Crandall and others, 1962); but this may be a reflection of their tendency not to confess wrongdoings as readily as girls. Finally, boys are slower in learning to share under incentive conditions when compared with girls (Doland & Adelberg, 1967).

CULTURAL FACTORS INFLUENCING MORAL DEVELOPMENT

Cultural and social class variables affect the development of conscience and account for intercultural differences (or intracultural uniformities) by influencing: (a) the particular moral values that are assimilated and their mode of transmission; (b) the kinds of internal and external sanctions that are imposed; and (c) the ways in which guilt feelings are instigated and expressed. The effects of both types of variables are exceedingly pervasive but differ in that individuals are typically influenced by the norms of other social classes but only rarely by the standards of other cultures.

A general problem arises in the impact of culture on conscience development when serious discrepancies or inconsistencies prevail between the professed (official) moral ideology and the ideology that is really believed and actually practiced. This situation is illustrated in our culture by the formal endorsement of humility, kindliness, helpfulness, and fair play, and the simultaneous overvaluation of aggressiveness, prestige, and success at any price. It is symptomatic of both a rate of social and economic change that has by far outstripped its ideological substrate and of widespread moral disintegration and confusion. In the struggle for material success, concern for moral values and traditional moral restraints are being swept aside. The form rather than the content and intention of behavior is becoming the chief criterion of moral judgment in our society. What it means for a child to grow up in such a moral climate is something that still requires considerable investigation. We can only predict on logical and historical grounds that it will encourage expediential lack of principle and cynical acceptance of moral depravity. We can expect children to grow up hypocritical, deceitful, unconcerned with human values and the welfare of others, indifferent to injustice, and sold on the principle of getting the most out of people and valuing them solely on the basis of their market price.

At the very best this situation leads to ethical confusion and inconsistency and a potentially heavy burden of guilt. However, because of the prestige suggestion inherent in the operation of social norms, and because of extremely high tolerance for moral ambiguity, inconsistent values may be assimilated in such a way that their incompatibility is never perceived. It is presumed by the perceiver that inconsistency in cultural values is inconceivable; hence, an advance "set" exists to perceive such values as consistent regardless of manifest content, and consequently, logic-tight compartments must be constructed. Even if perceived, awareness of moral inconsistency and culpability may be subsequently repressed or disowned. More direct forms of guilt reduction include confession, expiation, and reaction-formation. Various culturally stereotyped types of guilt reduction, such as verbal magic, pseudo-remorse, and hypocritical religious observance, are also available. It is not necessary to believe, however, that all guilt feelings are intolerable and must somehow be repressed, disowned, rationalized, expiated for, etc. Man's portrait of himself need not be free of all moral blemishes. Hence, a good deal of guilt can be tolerated on a conscious level without any efforts being made toward guilt reduction. In other instances, true guilt feelings may fail to develop because no *real* internalization of moral obligation has taken place, or because self-criticism is inhibited to the point where no discrepancy can be perceived between hehavior and obligation.

Thus, many children may fail to perceive that any problem of moral inconsistency exists, others may be acutely disillusioned, and still others may perceive the problem but fail to be disturbed by it. This type of moral climate is, in a sense, made to order for the ego needs of the non-satellizer, except when he happens to have a strong rational conscience. On the other hand, the satellizer who perceives what is going on is often unable to make the required adaptations without experiencing feelings of conflict, guilt, and resentment toward a culture that requires such moral compromises for the sake of survival and legitimate ego enhancement. Before considering intracultural social class differences in moral development, a brief discussion of intercultural differences is presented to dramatize the effects of varied social experiences on the child's moral development.

Cross-Cultural Differences

The findings of cross-cultural research in moral development are fraught with many of the methodological and conceptual difficulties characteristic of this type of research (see p. 158). Different kinship patterns, moral beliefs, moral attitudes, etc. make it exceedingly difficult to apply a common research instrument when making cross-cultural comparisons. The few studies that have been attempted, however, give us some indication of the differential impact of different socialization practices and expectancies on moral development. Although there is some evidence that the cognitive-evaluative stages of moral orientation are universal developmental processes common to all cultures (Kohlberg, 1968), (e.g., stage sequences appear to be the same in the cultures of Taiwan, Mexico, Turkey, and the United States), both cognitive and social factors may inhibit the achievement of the highest stages in certain cultures. However, the fact that some cultures do not reach these stages does not discredit the hypothesis of a universal developmental process.

The finding that more abstract levels of moral judgment appear earlier in some cultures than in others is indicative of the effects of their different socialization and educational practices (Aronfreed, 1968). For example, Swiss children are slower in moving from "moral realism" to "moral subjectivism" than are British children (Harrower, 1935). Similar trends are found when Swiss children are compared with American children (Boehm, 1966). American children emphasize intention over consequences earlier than do Swiss children (Boehm, 1957), and also take advice from peers in preference to parents at significantly earlier age than do their Swiss counterparts (Boehm, 1963). On the other hand Lebanese children demonstrate moral realism much later than do Swiss children (Najarian-Svjian, 1966). These differences appear to be a result of differential timing of "desatellization" within these cultures. The fact that American children accept peer advice earlier (Boehm, 1963) is indicative of the possibility that American children are encouraged to desatellize sooner than are European children. This is clearly seen when the socialization practices of Russian and American families are compared (Bronfenbrenner, 1968). Whereas American children are subjected to socialization procedures which encourage independence (i.e., desatellization) from parents, Russian children show greater conformity and obedience to adults, and parents discourage independence (i.e., desatellization). At present, these findings are only grossly indicative of the effects of differential socialization on the child's moral development. Concomitantly one can also note socialization differences in moral development within a particular culture when "*social class*" differences are considered.

Social Class Differences

General studies and reviews have reported positive relationships between lower social class status in children and both more absolutistic, rigid, and authoritarian conceptions of moral law (Boehm, 1962a, 1966, Bronfenbrenner, 1962; Dolger and Ginandes, 1946; Durkin, 1959; Harrower, 1934; Lerner, 1937b; Kohlberg, 1963a, 1968; MacRae, 1954) and more primitive and retaliatory notions of discipline. Middle-class children react to their own transgressions with more self-criticism than do their lower-class counterparts (Aronfreed, 1968). This situation is undoubtedly reflective, in part, of the authoritarian lower-class parent-child relationship and of inconsistent training in the "official" moral idealogy*; since the latter is accepted only halfheartedly and is inconsistently enforced, it must be adhered to rigidly if it is to be maintained at all. The effects of inconsistency are less compelling in middle-class families where there appears to be greater homogeneity of values than in lower-class families (Rosen, 1964). Middle-class parents behave in

---

Both honesty (Hartshorne and May, 1930) and truthfulness (Slaght; 1928) are positively correlated with socioeconomic status.

ways which would tend to produce an internal governor in their children and also use a verbal medium of discipline and explicit withdrawal of affection (Aronfreed, 1968). Moreover, lower-class parents exercise less immediate control over their childrens' activities, and seem to give their attention primarily to overt manifestations of transgression (Aronfreed, 1968). The more direct kind of punishment utilized in lower-class families seems to sensitize children to the external consequences of transgression (Aronfreed, 1968).

Middle-class children anticipate assuming responsibilities earlier than do lower-class children (Zunich, 1963), but this may be more reflective of social stratification than of parental upbringing. The fact is that the lower-class child does not and cannot feel as much of a sense of power in, and responsibility for, the institutions of government and economy as does the middle-class child (Kohlberg, 1968). This lack of participation generates a lesser disposition to view these institutions from a generalized, flexible, and organized perspective based on various roles as vantage points, i.e., law and government are perceived quite differently by the child if he feels a sense of potential participation in the social order than if he does not (Kohlberg, 1968).

Social class differences with respect to certain aspects of moral development appear to have been diminishing over the past 20 years (Bronfenbrenner, 1962a). In some cognitive aspects of conscience development, as a matter of fact, recently obtained differences are negligible (Boehm and Nass, 1962). This phenomenon may reflect the diminution of class differences, over this period of time, in child-rearing practices.

Religious Differences

Because religion is inextricably bound up with other environmental factors, it is difficult to isolate its impact on the moral development of children. Church membership and religious observance are intimately related to social class status and affect the social standing and character reputation of the child and his family (Havighurst and Taba, 1949). It is also virtually impossible to separate religious from moral values in most cultures. Even if a child receives no *formal* religious instruction, he is still influenced indirectly by religious precepts in his home training, secular schooling, peer group experience and exposure to mass media. Partly for this reason and partly because of problems of measurement it is extremely difficult to assess the effect of religion on childrens' moral conduct and development. If we attempt to use extent of religious instruction or observance as our measure of the independent variable in studying this relationship, this difficulty becomes immediately apparent. For some children religious observance is perfunctory, and religious doctrine is almost completely divorced from every-day life; for other children religion is an important consideration in determining moral choice and regulating interpersonal relationships. However, in American society, as compared to Turkish society, there appears to be remarkably little use of religious precepts in children's moral judgments (Kohlberg, 1967). At the same time, the development of moral reasoning appears to be much the same in many different religious communities (e.g., Protestants, Catholics, Moslems and Buddhists), (Kohlberg, 1967).

Religious orientation may affect the level of moral judgment through certain beliefs or practices. Thus, Catholic and Jewish parochial school children respond more to *intentions* (that is to distinguish between motivation of and results of actions), earlier than do public school children (Boehm, 1926, 1966). In certain judgmental situations, moreover, Jewish and Catholic children can be distinguished from one another (Boehm, 1966). For example, Catholic preschool children respond at a lower level of moral judgment in the situation where a child has hurt a peer accidentally (i.e., Jewish children are more concerned with the victim's feelings whereas Catholic children are more concerned with the guilt of the accidental offender (Boehm, 1966). These differences probably reflect different religious emphases regarding moral responsibility, since specific attendance at Sunday school appears to have a negligible effect on the child's moral reasoning (Whiteman and Kosier, 1964).

The behavioral correlates of religious observance present an equally complex picture. Hartshorne and May's (1930) finding that the child who attends Sunday school is only very slightly more honest and helpful than children who do not attend has yet to be challenged (Kohlberg, 1964). Cross-national comparisons suggest conclusions similar to the above (Kohlberg, 1967). As Kohlberg (1967) points out:

> Theft, deceit, and juvenile delinquency are low in some atheistic societies (Soviet Russia, Israeli atheistic kibbutzim) as well as in some Buddhist and Christian societies, while some strongly religious nations have high rates of dishonesty (Islamic Middle Eastern nations, Italy, Mexico, etc.). Although we should not conclude from these and other findings that there is no relation between religious experience and moral character, we can conclude that religion is not a necessary or highly important condition for the development of moral judgment, and conduct (p. 181).

This conclusion should be tempered by the fact that in general, the present accumulation of evidence only tells us that religious *observance* is not highly correlated with moral conduct—not that religious belief and moral behavior are intrinsically unrelated. In fact, just the opposite is indicated by the finding that Mennonite children ascribe more religious values to life situations and more moral authority to the church than do non-Mennonite children (Kalhorn, 1944), and by the finding that Lutheran adolescents in a particular closely-knit community have reputations for honesty and reliability despite relatively low social status (Havighurst & Taba, 1949).

Evidence is just beginning to accumulate regarding developmental changes in children's religious beliefs per se. As such, the trends indicated are congruent with the changes occurring in the child's intellectual and moral development. Children at age six can comprehend, to some extent, many religious concepts (Josephina, 1961), and the growth in many of these concepts appears to follow a developmental pattern. Thus, the meanings children attach to their religious denominations change systematically with increasing age (Elkind, 1966). Summaries of denominational studies of Jewish, Catholic, and Protestant children reveal three stages:

At the first stage (usually ages 5 to 7) the child had only a global, undifferentiated conception of denomination, as a kind of proper name . . . Children at the second stage (usually ages 7 to 9) had a concretely differentiated conception of their denomination . . . Third stage children (usually 10 to 12) demonstrated an abstract differentiated concept of their denomination. It was an abstract in the sense that these children no longer defined their denomination by mentioning names or observable activities, but rather by mentioning nonobservable mental attributes such as belief and understanding (Elkind, 1966; pp. 213-214).

The transistion into adolescence, characterized by increasing ability to reason critically, marks the onset of questioning or abandoning ideas about God (e.g., God's rewarding the good or punishing the bad (Hilliard, 1959-60). Thus, it would seem reasonable to suppose that with increasing age such beliefs become less concrete, literal, dogmatic, and ritualistic, and more abstract, tolerant, and concerned with intentions as opposed to consequences.

Peer Group

The child's peer group, apart from the wider adult culture, exerts a significant influence on his moral development. In some ways, it is the child's first introduction to the wider social groupings that exit outside of the family (Crane, 1958). It is to be expected that peer influences will have a differential impact within the context of different cultures. Thus in Russia the *peer group* functions as an agency of control that reinforces parental values, whereas in the United States it tends, somewhat, to undermine parental control (Bronfenbrenner, 1962b; 1968). According to Piaget's theory, the peer group provides a context in which the child can learn the rules of the game, principles of equity, and self-subordination to group goals based on mutual respect and reciprocity (Piaget, 1932; 1951). Evidence indicates that children with higher sociometric status are more autonomous in moral maturity scores (Kohlberg, 1964; 1970). The type of participation in the peer group may also be an important factor since children who are given an opportunity to be rule carriers in a game appear to have more positive attitudes toward the rules of conduct involved in the game (Borishevsky, 1965). This supports the thesis that greater social participation in and control over institutions leads to greater moral maturity (Kohlberg, 1964).

Specific types of peer participation appear to have different effects. Children who are members of character-building clubs (e.g., boy scouts) surpass non-club members in such traits as cooperativeness; however, in regard to general traits, such as honesty and judgmental maturity, which are less dependent on structured group experience, no significant difference prevails (Hartshorne & May *et al*, 1930; Whiteman & Kosier, 1964). This evidence supports the logical inference that the peer group does not constitute in itself an important source of moral values during childhood. Its values tend to mirror those held by significant adults (parents, teachers, clergy, etc.) in the subculture in which it is embedded. The influence of the peer group is more important in providing a *situational climate* that affects the child's in-hibitory control in *particular* instances in which relevant moral obligations are not thoroughly interiorized. Social stratification within some cultures affords the peer group in childhood varying degrees of influence. Thus, moral values are more peer-oriented for kibbutz children than for parent-raised children (Kohlberg, 1964;) behaviorly this appears to lead to more confession for transgressions in kibbutz children (Luria *et al*, 1963). In our own culture, the correlation of .23 between "best friends" on deception scores increases to .66 when they are members of the same classroom and can influence each other's behavior more directly (Hartshorne and May *et al*, 1930). Significant dif-ferences between different classes in the same school and between "progres-sive" and traditional schools also point to the influence of group morale (Ausubel, 1951; Hartshorne and May *et al*, 1930). Lower-class children become more independent of adults and more dependent on peers at earlier ages than do middle-class children (Ausubel and Ausubel, 1962; Boehm, 1962, 1966). This situational influence may be especially important in the instigation of delinquent activity. Bolstered by group suggestion and moral sanction the individual child will sometimes participate in aggressive anti-social behavior that he would never think of doing on his own. In such par-ticipation he also responds to implied threats of ostracism and to genuine feelings of loyalty to either intimate associates or to the groups as a whole. Hence, most juvenile delinquency is usually committed by groups of children rather than by individuals (Short, 1966).

MASS MEDIA*

Despite their unofficial status in our culture, the various mass media* probably exert more influence on moral development than do some of the

---

*A review of the literature on the effects of the mass media on children's attitudes and values may be found in Maccoby (1964).

socializing agencies, which have been more traditionally charged with this responsibility. The efficacy of these media in this regard can be attributed to the fact that, in addition to presenting a more dramatic version of life to children, they are also not bound by reality restraints. Because they provide unmatched opportunities for vicarious ego enhancement and satellizing hero worship, they may both influence the kinds of values that children interiorize, and affect the inhibitory potential of moral obligation and the development of guilt feelings.

The first type of effect is illustrated by the manipulation of children's ethical standards through the showing of selected motion pictures (Jones, 1936; Maccoby, 1964; Thurstone, 1931). For example, studies of the induction of changes in both favorable and unfavorable attitudes toward certain groups have been summarized in a recent review (Maccoby, 1964). In addition it was found that children who spend more time with the mass media are more stereotyped in their thinking (Maccoby, 1964). The second type of effect is illustrated by scattered findings that movies and cartoons (Bandura, Ross and Ross, 1961; Blumer and Hauser, 1934; Lovaas, 1961; Mussen and Rutherford, 1961), crime magazines (Healey and Bronner, 1936; Maccoby, 1964), and comic books (Hoult, 1949; Maccoby, 1964) may be contributory factors in causing aggression and juvenile delinquency. By suggesting that cleverly executed wrongdoing may go unpunished, stories of successful aggression may release the inhibitory restraints of conscience without necessarily affecting moral values or associated guilt feelings (Brodbeck, 1955; Maccoby, 1964). Other relevant factors in the influence of mass media on delinquency are (a) identification with glamorous or prestigeful figures who portray violence and ruthlessness in a laudable light (Maccoby, 1964), and (b) the suggestive presentation of detailed information necessary for the execution of criminal acts (Maccoby, 1964). In opposition to this line of reasoning, it has been argued that mass media do not create but only release delinquent and aggressive trends, and also provide a harmless outlet in fantasy for aggressive tendencies that might otherwise be expressed in real life (Maccoby, 1964). In most instances, furthermore, right is pictured as triumphant in the end, even though it is frequently associated with violence in the hero (Maccoby, 1964). Nevertheless, it is conceivable that, depending on the way themes of violence are handled and on the particular circumstances and individuals involved, mass media may have either an inhibitory or facilitating effect on delinquent behavior (Maccoby, 1964). The present contribution of the mass media, however, seems slanted toward the darker aspects of human nature with little exploration into its creative potentialities (Brodbeck, 1962).

OTHER ASPECTS OF MORAL DEVELOPMENT

Intersituational Consistency and Generality of Moral Conduct. *

This controversial issue has already been considered at great length in a more general theoretical context. The specific issue related to moral development centers around the question of whether there is sufficient consistency and generality of moral conduct in a variety of behavioral situations to justify a construct of moral character. Psychological studies have in general interpreted the notion of moral character to mean the sum total of a set of virtues (Kohlberg, 1964; 1968). Character traits or virtues are those personality traits which are subject to the moral sanctions of society (Kohlberg, 1964). The early studies of character development identified such traits as honesty, service, and self-control as the prominent virtues (Hartshorne & May *et al*, 1930). The focus on "actions" over "words" (e.g., judgments) has been the general approach that psychologists have employed when assessing the presence of "moral character" (Kohlberg, 1964). Thus the measurement of the character trait of "honesty" was accomplished by cumulating occurrences of obedience to rules in situation where cheating or stealing could be accomplished without apparent detection (Hartshorne & May *et al*, 1930). The presence of the character trait *honesty* would be indicated if there was high intersituational consistency and generality across temptation situations.

The earlier findings of Hartshorne and May *et al* (1930), however, revealed little intersituational consistency and generality across situations for any of the character traits assessed (e.g., honesty, service, etc.). These initial findings led to the pessimistic conclusions that there are no such things as stable character traits and that consistency of behavior from one situation to another is due to similarities in the situations and not to consistent personality traits in people (Hartshorne & May *et al*, 1930).† At present the evidence warrants the tentative conclusion that although many factors indigeneous to personality organization make moral conduct unusually susceptible to the influence of situational variables, much of the apparent lack of generality is a function of such measurement difficulties as variability in ego-involvement, different phenotypic expressions of the same genotypic tendency, and the masking effect of normative uniformities on individual differences. In support of this view is (a) evidence showing the close relationship between measurement of ego-involvement and scores on objective measures of character and personality (see Kohlberg, 1964, 1968); (b) the tendency for the generality coefficients of moral traits to be higher in older children and adolescents than in young children (Burton, 1963; Hartshorne & May *et al*, 1930; Havighurst &

A more comprehensive discussion of this topic may be found in the following sources. (Aronfreed, 1968; Berkowitz, 1964; Burton, 1963; Kohlberg, 1964; 1968).

†*More recent studies on "honesty" yield results similar to the above: (Sears, Rau and Alpert, 1965).*

Taba, 1949); and (c) evidence from several studies of moral conduct in children that show greater generality of function than was reported by Hartshorne & May (see p. 113) and especially the review and analysis by Burton, 1963, and the study by Nelsen, Grinder & Mutterer, 1965).

"These findings suggest a core of truth to common-sense notions of general good character, and provide some justification for adding up measures of various aspects of moral conduct into a total assessment of moral character. Common sense seems to exaggerate this consistency, however." (Kohlberg, 1964; p. 387).

The Relationship Between Moral Evaluative Judgments and Moral Conduct

Character has also been defined as the demonstration of congruence between a person's evaluative judgments and his conduct (Peters, 1959-60). Thus a person is said to "have character" if his actions are in keeping with what he judges to be morally good or bad. Consistency between judgment and conduct suffers from the same discrepancies in the data that are present in the studies on intersituational consistency and generality of moral conduct. Summaries of available data have reported variable findings (Aronfreed, 1968; Kohlberg, 1969). The earlier studies (e.g., Hartshorne & May *et al*, 1930) on honesty indicated that childrens' verbalized knowledge of social standards often seem discrepant with their behavior when they think they are not being observed (Aronfreed, 1968). Nevertheless a low correlation between knowledge of standards and internalized conduct was reported (Hartshorne & May *et al*, 1930). More recent studies correlating Piagetian judgment situations with conduct reveal negative results: increasing (with age) internalized orientation of conscience is not apparently accompanied by corresponding changes in conduct (Aronfreed, 1968), However, more detailed studies of childrens' moral judgment suggest that conscience and conduct are not as clearly divorced from one another as the previous findings would indicate (Aronfreed, 1968). Kohlberg (1964), and Hoffman (1963) report an inverse relationship between cheating, reaction to transgressions, and an internalized conscience orientation. The discrepancies in the data may be due to several factors. First, the inconsistencies may reflect the fact that the linkages between conduct and conscience are complex and variable in their operation (Aronfreed, 1968), or the fact that the relationship between the hypothetical judgment situation and the actual behavior situation may sometimes be quite tenuous and unrelated. Second, "expressed" beliefs and "true" beliefs may be at odds with one another.

Thus, there is good reason to suppose that the *true* moral beliefs of an individual are an excellent reflection of his character and are more significantly related to it than is his overt behavior (Ausubel, 1952). The contention that belief and character are unrelated springs from (a) confusion between moral *belief* and *moral knowledge*, (b) confusion between expressed and true belief;

and (c) confusion between deliberate insincerity and unavoidable lack of discriminative ability as determinants of the discrepancy between belief and conduct. As already indicated, moral knowledge involves only one cognitive aspect of moral belief and is a relatively minor factor in the total configuration of variables determining its development.

For various reasons either expressed belief or overt behavior may be at variance with true moral belief. For example, a child who wishes to make a good impression may state insincere beliefs which naturally are inconsistent with his actual behavior; but here, although expressed belief is inconsistent with both conduct and true belief, it is quite probable that behavior is consonant with *true* belief. In other instances, for reasons of legitimate expediency or conformity to social norms, both expressed belief and behavior may be incongruent with true belief. Under these conditions the discrepancy between true belief and conduct is not a reflection of inconsistency or weakness of character but of coercive factors preventing the translation of true belief into congruent behavior. In still other instances, where the disparity between true belief and conduct cannot be attributed to legitimate expediency, the true belief actually exists but is negated by competing behavioral tendencies which at a particular moment happen to undergo disinhibition or are actually more potent. This type of situation occurs when the judicial and legislative components of conscience are at odds with the *executive* component (Peters, 1959-60).

Lastly, conduct may be inconsistent with true belief not because of any insincerity or deliberate attempt at dissimulation but (a) because of cognitive limitations in logic, insufficient generalization of moral values, or inability to apply general principles to real-life situations (Ausubel, 1952, Peters, 1959-60); and (b) because of institutionalized inconsistencies in cultural values that the individual is either unable to perceive or obliged to accept (Kohlberg 1964; Ausubel, 1952).

Shame and Guilt

Several cultural anthropologists have advanced the paradoxally ethnocentric view that guilt is not universally present or prominent as a sanction in mediating and sustaining the culture (Benedict, 1946; Leighton and Kluckhohn, 1947; Mead, 1950). They contend that in some cultures sensitivity to shame largely takes the place that remorse and self-punishment have in preventing anti-social conduct in Western civilization (Leighton and Kluckhohn, 1947). Instead of acknowledging that guilt behavior can occur whenever and wherever an individual internalizes moral obligations and can exercise sufficient self-critical ability to perceive his own wrongdoing, they lay down three indispensable criteria for the development of guilt behavior. First, the child must accept the parent as omniscient and as the source of all moral authority. Second, genuine guilt feelings can only exist when shame and other external sanctions are not operative. Third, guilt must be characterized by conviction of sin and need for atonement. Behavior that does not conform to these requirements is categorized as shame.

If we accepted the first criterion, there could be no guilt behavior in the numerous cultures in which children do not regard parents as omniscient and in which the authority for moral sanctions is derived laterally or from the group as a whole (De Vos, 1960). However, actual examination of the moral behavior of children and adults in such cultures (e.g., Navaho) does not confirm this proposition (Ausubel, 1955; Aronfreed, 1968). The same criterion would also deny the observed occurrence of guilt among adolescents and adults in our own culture who accept the peer group and society (rather than parents) as the source of moral authority, and among non-satellizers who never accept the moral authority of parents, but who nevertheless interiorize moral obligations on the basis of abstract principles of equity (Ausubel, 1955). The second criterion ignores the fact (a) that guilt (a negative self-judgment for violating moral obligations) is invariably accompanied by shame (a self-deprecatory reaction to the actual or presumed judgments of others), and (b) that at all stages of development, internal sanctions are reinforced by external sanctions. Hence, although shame and guilt are distinguishable from each other, they are neither dichotomous nor mutually exclusive (Aronfreed, 1968; Ausubel, 1955). The third criterion is peculiarly specific to certain religious doctrines and beliefs about the original nature of man that prevail in cultures adhering to the Judeo-Christian tradition, and hardly applies to peoples like the Japanese who nevertheless show striking evidences of both guilt and shame in their moral behavior (Ausubel, 1955).

Moral Accountability

Although a philosophical discussion of moral accountability and "free will" versus determinism is obviously out of place in this volume* it should be noted that acceptance of the psychological schema of conscience organization and development presented above implies a belief in moral accountability. If we accept the fact that an individual has the power to inhibit immoral impulses and prevent the occurrence of wrongdoing, we can accept the notion of accountability for failure to do so without necessarily denying psychological determinism or asserting the existence of "free will." The *explanation* of his moral lapses on the basis of antecendent genic and environmental factors in his developmental history is a matter of psychological determinism; since he has no control over many of these factors no one can claim that he is a free agent in regulating his development. But the issue of

---

See Ausubel (1952) for a more complete discussion of this issue.

whether or not he is morally accountable is an entirely different matter: it refers to something which *is* under his control, namely, the power to regulate present behavior in accordance with perceived moral obligations. Thus, regardless of events beyond his control that once transpired, if he is *presently* capable of complying with moral obligations but fails to do so, he is accountable for his misdeeds. The vast majority of immoral and delinquent acts are committed under conditions where there is clear awareness of a moral issue and reasonable opportunity for exercising adequate inhibitory control.

This issue would hardly concern us except for the fact that liability to punishment for morally culpable behavior is an integral rather than an arbitrary component of the notion of moral obligation which children interiorize in the course of moral development. Hence, if we followed the prevailing opinion of social scientists and only instituted therapy for immorality, immoral behavior would be indistinguishable from other behavior disorders and the very basis of conscience would be jeopardized.

PART IV

Linguistic and Cognitive Aspects of Development

CHAPTER 14

The Development of Language*

DISTINCTIVE ROLE OF LANGUAGE IN HUMAN DEVELOPMENT

THE CAPACITY FOR INVENTING and acquiring language is one of the most distinctive features of human development. It is undoubtedly both a prerequisite for the original development of culture and a necessary condition for the subsequent acquisition by the individual of the complex cognitive, social and moral products of the culture in which he lives. Without language, the development and transmission of shared meanings, values, and traditions would be impossible. People would be unable to communicate with each other except in face-to-face situations, individual relatedness and interaction between groups could not take place in the absence of physical proximity, and all of the countless intellectual, interpersonal and institutional manifestations of cultural existence that depend on verbal conceptualization would be inconceivable.

Language may also be thought of as both a product or reflection of culture and as a patterning or limiting factor in the cognitive development of the individual carriers of the culture. It reflects the particular kinds of psychosocial standardization of word-object and word-idea relationships as well as the characteristic attitudes, values, and ways of thinking that prevail in a given culture. Once constituted, the structure of the language and the conceptual categories it contains definitely influence the perceptual and cognitive processes of the developing individual. He learns to perceive selectively in terms of the classificatory schemes available to him in his mother tongue; if the latter fails to recognize certain conceptual distinctions, he is greatly handicapped in making them himself. Thus, characteristic patterns of thought in a particular culture affect the nature of the language that evolves,

---

The tremendous growth of theory and research in language development makes it virtually impossible to give a complete summary of it in this chapter. General surveys of language development research are available (Carroll, 1964; Ervin-Tripp, 1966; Ervin & Miller, 1963: Ervin-Tripp & Slobin, 1966c; Jenkins, 1969, McCarthy, 1954, 1966; McNeill, 1966, 1968; Olson, 1968; Slobin, 1966). For the specific topic of research methodology in children's language development, the following references are appropriate: (Brown, 1958, 1965; Berko & Brown, 1960; McNeill, 1968; Irvin, 1960; Slobin, 1967). Edited books of readings which provide a general overview of some of the central issues in language development are also available (Hildum, 1967; Jakobovits & Miron, 1967; Lenneberg, 1964; Saporta, 1961).

and the language in turn patterns and limits the type of thinking in which individual members of the culture engage.

Human versus Infrahuman Speech*

In many respects the speech behavior of infrahuman organisms resembles that of children in the early stages of language development. Thus untutored animals vocalize spontaneously, mimic sounds in their environment, and communicate effectively with each other. Many animals can also be trained to react differently to different verbal cues, to mimic human words, and to make the latter responses to appropriate situations. Representational symbolism is only rudimentary in animals, however, and is restricted to relatively concrete and immediate situations. Verbal conceptualization and the use of symbols to represent ideas that transcend concrete experience are undoubtedly nonexistent at the infrahuman level. Furthermore, only humans can be said to possess a true language, the import of which is socially rather than genically determined, which possesses an organized structure, and which can communicate meaning without face-to-face contact.

Why only human beings have developed a true language is attributable to several factors. First, they possess an elaborate vocalizing mechanism capable of great versatility in sound production, tend to babble spontaneously as infants, and are relatively proficient at mimicry. Much more important is their immeasurably greater capacity for representational symbolism, for verbal conceptualization, and for handling abstract ideas. Lastly, because they live in *cultural* aggregations, they are able to standardize and perpetuate shared meanings for the verbal symbols they invent.

NATURE OF LANGUAGE

In order to further pursue the topic of language development in children, it is necessary to clarify the nature of language so that it is distinguished conceptually from other aspects of development. *Language* may be defined by certain design features which taken together make it possible for a creature with limited powers of discrimination learning and a limited memory to transmit and understand an infinite variety of messages, and do this in spite of noise or distraction (Brown, 1965). The language system involves three major components, phonology, syntax, and semantics. *Phonology* is the study of the most basic sounds which constitute spoken language. The particular

---

Discussions of infrahuman speech behavior are available in the following sources: DeVore, 1965; Frings & Frings, 1964; Hockett, 1959; Kalmus, 1966; Lanyon & Tanolga, 1960; Marler, 1961; Premack & Schwartz, 1966; Sebeok, 1965.

unit of analysis is the *phone* which designates any particular occurrence of a vowel or consonant. *Phonemes* are a category of phones that are distinctive for native speakers of a language. As Brown (1965) points out:

> Phonemes are for the most part vowels and consonants, and they correspond roughly to the letters of an alphabet writing system. Phonemes are not themselves meaningful; they are semantically empty. No language uses very many. The range in the languages of the world is from about fifteen to about eighty-five, with English using forty-five. Probably the number is small because it is advantageous to use only sounds that can be easily produced or identified (p. 247).

Phonemes can be combined in various ways and a more complex unit, called the *morpheme*, emerges. A morpheme is the smallest meaningful unit in a language represented by a sequence of one or more phonemes, as in "Chatauqua," "take," "ing," "-er" (Ervin-Tripp, 1966). *Syntax* is the study of a set of rules for combining morphemes into words and sentences. *Semantics* is the study of the meaning of words and sentences. To summarize the basic design features of the linguistic communication system, it may be said that all of these systems are inter-related and, thus, discussion of one feature may involve consideration of the other features. For example, the semantic meaning of a word is partially contingent on its place in a sentence (i.e., syntax). Before elaborating on these three systems in the language development of children, a brief discussion of the distinction between *competence* and *performance* and *comprehension* and *production* is necessary in order to adequately conclude the treatment of basic linguistic terminology.

Competence versus Performance

The difference between linguistic *competence* and *performance* is an important distinction made in current linguistic theorizing (Chomsky, 1965) especially where this current theorizing distinguishes itself from the older formulations stemming from S-R behaviorism (e.g., Skinner, 1957). *Competence* refers to the speaker-hearer's knowledge of his language, and *performance* is the actual use of language in concrete situations (Chomsky, 1965). *Competence* describes the knowledge that the speaker-hearer must have in order to understand or generate any of one of the infinitely large number of sentences permitted in the language. *Performance* is the actual use of part of this competence in talking and listening to speech. Performance may be hindered by such things as an excessive memory load, or fatigue, etc., whereas competence would not.* The importance of this distinction will become apparent in the discussion of the child's acquisition of syntax.

---

*A provocative extension of this competence-performance distinction to the area of subcultural language differences may be found in Cazden (1967).

Comprehension versus Production

The difference between *comprehension* and *production* centers around the distinction between active and passive linguistic skills (McNeill, 1966). *Comprehension* is the "passive skill" of the listener in decoding the language in the surrounding language community. *Production* is the "active skill" of the speaker in encoding messages to the surrounding language community. As a developmental phenomenon in language acquisition, comprehension often precedes production of speech (McNeill, 1966). Comprehension and production on the one hand, and competence and performance on the other, are different though related distinctions, and it is important to see the differences and the relations that obtain (McNeill, 1966). Noting the previous distinction between competence and performance above, it may be said that:

> Production and comprehension of speech are both categories of linguistic performance; both involve the expression of competence, the one in producing and encoding speech, the other in receiving and decoding speech. The claim that passive control precedes active control in development, therefore, can be rendered to mean that comprehending speech somehow involves fewer distorting and obstructing factors in the passage from competence to performance than producing speech does (McNeill, 1966, p. 77).

Thus, the only data available comes from performance, either comprehension or production. Yet the task of the linguist and the psychologist is to infer the speaker's competence and to show how these regularities in his actual speech result from regularities in his grammatical knowledge or competence (McNeill, 1966). The utility of these distinctions will become more apparent in the discussion of the child's acquisition of syntax.

PHONOLOGY

Pre-linguistic Utterances

The study of language development nautrally brings us back to the period before the first words are uttered by the child. Study of prelinguistic utterances during the first year of life is necessary because the child does not utter his first meaningful word (i.e., linguistic utterance) until he is about one year old (Darley & Winitz, 1961). An adequate understanding of language, then, demands that we study the relationship between prelinguistic speech and later stages of language development.

The prelinguistic speech of the first year of life includes (a) crying and other affective utterances and (b) phonemic utterances that are either spontaneous or responsive, and which may or may not have expressive significance. For the most part, except for volitional crying, gestures, and "private" words, prelinguistic speech is prerepresentational. Prelinguistic speech may be divided into three stages: first, the earliest period of organically based sounds; second, a period of extensive vocal play and babbling; and finally, a period of imitative behavior and speech which seems intentional because of its situational distribution (Ervin-Tripp, 1966).

Earliest Sounds

From a developmental standpoint it is important to remember that the organs used in speech are also implicated in the biologically more urgent functions of eating and breathing. Hence, practically no non-crying utterances are heard until breathing and feeding are well established (Irwin, 1946; McCarthy, 1960). During the first weeks respiration and feeding are mixed with other vocalizations (Ervin-Tripp, 1966). Studies by Lenneberg, Rebelsky, Nichols (1965) and Tischler (1965) indicate that during the first thirteen weeks vocalization categories, from most to least frequent, are fussing, crying, and cooing. Crying gradually decreases in frequency and cooing increases, even during hunger (Lenneberg, 1966).

Babbling. As the frequency of cooing increases, it begins to sound to adults more like human speech (Ervin-Tripp, 1966). The changes in speech toward more adult patterns of vocalization is labelled *babbling*. Babbling patterns change systematically with age, but this early development is largely organically based, since it occurs in both deaf and hearing children who cannot be distinguished by vocal output in the first six months (Lenneberg, 1964a, b, 1966).

Previous to the onset of babbling, vocalizations are mainly vowels, with infrequent consonants. The earliest appearing consonants are formed in the throat and back of the mouth and gradually decrease. Thus, contrary to popular belief, labials (e.g., m, b, p) are not the first consonants to appear. The early-appearing consonants are velars, glottals, and aspirates (associated with feeding and breathing), while the later-appearing consonants are labials, dentals, and postdentals (Irwin, 1947a; Irwin and Chen, 1947; Jersild and Ritzman, 1938). Plosives and fricatives are prominent during early infancy; afterwards the latter are largely displaced by nasal glides and semivowels (Irwin, 1947b). Reduplication is frequent in babbling; this is illustrated by the repetition of CVCV sequences (e.g., "dada," "bebe") (Ervin-Tripp, 1966).

Imitative Speech. The consistent and exclusive use of a particular combination of sounds ("private" words) to convey a particular meaning is a frequent precursor of linguistic speech that ordinarily persists long after the appearance of the conventional "first word." A parallel kind of nonvocal communication that also meets all of the criteria of representational symbolism is the use of expressive gestures. Children generally understand and employ such gestures before they understand and use conventional language. This does not mean however, that they respond to gestures before they comprehend the affective and intonational content of adult speech (Buhler and Hetzer, 1935; Leopold, 1939-49; Lewis, 1951). Gestures are most adequate for concrete and pictorial representation of signified objects, actions, and intentions, e.g., pointing, accepting, rejecting, questioning, commanding. They are frequently combined with intonations and introjections.

Evidently intonation is imitated very early (Pike, 1949). Intonational patterns change towards adult models in such a way that babbled sequences are uttered with assertive, interrogative, or exclamatory inflections (Shirley, 1933; Leopold, 1939-49). These inflections are expressive and they occur in correct context, even if they are non-referential. They are therefore, prelinguistic in form but mimic faithfully the expressive content of adult speech.

Distinctive Features Hypothesis of Phoneme Differentiation. The characterization of the phonological system in its developmental context has been attempted by Jakobson and Halle (1956) in their theory of differentiation of distinctive features. This theory attempts to analyze a given language into its ultimate constituents by seeking the smallest set of distinctive oppositions which allow the identification of each phoneme in the message framed in the language. They describe the distinctive features of a phoneme in terms of binary contrasts of a set of values such as vocalic-non-vocalic, compact-diffuse, nasal-oral, grave-acute. Thus, the first distinctive feature is between a vowel and a consonant, since vowels and consonants are more different than any other part of the system. Later, the child might learn to contrast a stop with a nonstop, e.g., /p/ and/m/ or /p/ and /f/ (Ervin and Miller, 1963). Theoretically, the child could double his set of consonants with each pair of contrasting features (Ervin and Miller, 1963). An example of contrasting features is given by Velten (1943) in analyzing the language features of his 2-year-old daughter Joan. He reports she had only nine phonemes, 7 consonants and 2 vowels, which she formed into monosyllabic words by linking either two or three phonemes together in the form CV or CVC, thus, a system limited to three phonemes could result in the words "black," "pat," "bark," "bite" being represented by the word "*pat*."

To summarize, at present there are few empirical studies exploring this hypothesis (McNeill, 1968), but the ones reported support the notion of the acquisition of features (Ervin and Miller, 1963). The theory posits an economical process of learning since the number of contrasting features is much smaller than the number of phonemes. Radical changes in the system therefore develop relatively abruptly rather than through the gradual approximation of the adult phonemes one by one (Ervin and Miller, 1963). Thus:

. . . it must be clear that phonemes are not discrete discriminated stimuli. Their detection and production is dependent on contrasted pairs of distinguishing features: the phonemes are therefore not simply and discretely acquired, rather the acquisition of one contrast may run through and divide into two the entire set or at least a subset of the phonemes (Olson, 1968, p. 39).

Factors Influencing Prelinguistic Vocalizations. Vocalizations during the prelinguistic period are partially organically based (Lenneberg, 1964a, b). The fact that prelinguistic utterances, during the first six months, undergo parallel developments for deaf and hearing children indicates the importance of biological factors.* At the same time, the importance of the general linguistic environment in language development is seen in findings which show that deaf children, if exposed for even short time intervals to adult speech before deafness ensues, develop a more normal phonological system (Fry, 1966).

The effect of social reinforcement on prelinguistic utterances appears to operate after the first three months (Rheingold, Gewirtz and Ross, 1959). Previous to the third month, there appears to be no appreciable differences in cooing between infants of hearing parents and infants of deaf parents (Lenneberg, 1966). The fact that deaf parents provide less vocal stimulation indicates that the overall impact of stimulation and reward on infant vocalization is not apparent during this period (Ervin-Tripp, 1966).† However, at the third month, vocalizations can be increased by smiling at babies, by touching their abdomens, and by providing a vocal click when the infant is making sounds that are neither fussing nor crying (Rheingold *et al*, 1959).

Imitation, through secondary reinforcement, has been suggested as the mechanism by which the child's speech becomes increasingly similar to adult speech (Mowrer, 1958). Sounds which the adult makes during caretaking and feeding have secondary reinforcement value and are repeated by the child because of their reinforcement value. This theory predicts that maternal warmth and vocalization frequency should be correlated with infant vocalization. Moreover, it should predict that the babbling sequences will begin to approximate the phonemic forms of the mother tongue (Olson, 1968). Present evidence, however, does not bear out this prediction, since there are no differences in such sequences between Japanese and American children until the ninth month, when speech is beginning (Nakazima, 1962). Thus although the volume of vocalizations can be increased by reinforcement

---

*It is interesting to note a parallel theory in prelinguistic speech which is quite similar to McGraw's theory of the maturation of motor behavior (see p. 86). Bever (1961) maintains that the earliest speech is a manifestation of a primary level of neurological organization of vocal behavior (reflex), which gives way to a second stage involving cortical inhibition of the reflex; and finally, the cortex gradually reorganizes the activity it had inhibited.

†This conclusion is questioned somewhat in light of the findings of Lewis (1959). He reports that a ten-week-old boy made a total of only 4 sounds in 3 minutes of observation when the father was silent and 18 sounds in 3 minutes when the father said "hello" every ten seconds. Thus further study on the effects of adult vocal reinforcement seems warranted.

(Lewis, 1959; Rheingold *et al*, 1959) during the prelinguistic stage, specific imitation of adult patterns is not apparent.

Imitation of various intonational patterns, however, indicates a change toward adult models such that babbled sequences are uttered with assertive, interrogative and exclamatory inflections (Olson, 1968). Thus, the effect of imitation, in less specific ways, is still an interesting topic in phonological development. A less stringent criterion of imitation may further reveal its importance in phonological development, expecially in the development of sound articulation:

> . . . When it comes to the articulation and the development of the phonological system, however, it seems that imitation does play a very important role. Imitation is here taken to mean simply that the child tries to produce a sound that strikes him as similar to the sound he hears coming in from outside. Doubts about the part played by imitation must, I believe, be dispelled by the fact that similarities in pronunciation do exist and are very strong. . . . Toward the end of the babbling stage, then, the child begins to copy specifically the sounds made by adults and especially, of course, by his mother. Since the control of motor speech activity through auditory feedback is already an established principle, he has at his disposal the means of making his own utterance match more nearly the pattern that is given to him (Fry, 1966, pp. 190-191).

Phonological development will continue until mastery at school age (Carroll, 1960; Olson, 1968), but for purposes of exposition and economy we will not consider it in any further detail. The utterance of the *first word* at about the tenth month leads the discussion to the development of the semantic system in children.

SEMANTICS

Early Linguistic Speech

There is no sharp developmental boundary between prelinguistic and linguistic speech.* Long after the child begins using conventional language, he continues to babble and employ incomprehensible and private words. The transition from prerepresentational to representational linguistic speech is also difficult to locate. Most observers agree that children comprehend conventional language in a representational sense before they produce language themselves (Ervin-Tripp, 1966; McCarthy, 1954; McNeill, 1966, 1968). The use of *representational symbols* depends on the development of perceptual and conceptual organization and thus obviously precedes the

---

*The evidence that the child's vocal output during the prelinguistic period has no formal relation to his later phonological and grammatical patterns has led some linguists to postulate a discontinuity between prelinguistic and linguistic speech (see McNeill, 1968). Ervin-Tripp (1966) acknowledges this discontinuity but maintains that there is no discontinuity in the functions of language, or in the social factors influencing fluency which continue without break from the prelinguistic into the linguistic period.

development of linguistic speech. At the same time, language gives the society a chance to bring the individual's conceptual system into conformity with the culture's (Ervin-Tripp, 1966).

> Deviance in connotations is more permissible than in denotations; a child who thought his mother "bad" would be tactless but one who called dogs "mother" after a certain point in time would be thought abnormal. Part of the socializing of word meanings occurs well before the child's first meaningful utterances but, because it is more obvious, the "first word" is commonly regarded as a significant milestone (p. 60).

First Words. Because of methodological ambiguities, most of the normative data on the appearance of the "first word" are almost impossible to interpret. Much depends, naturally, on the stringency of the criteria laid down for this phenomenon: whether the word is used meaningfully and consistently; whether its use is appropriately restricted; whether it is conventional or private, intelligible or unintelligible; whether the judge is a fond mother. Varying reports of first-word utterances also depend on who does the observations. Thus, the earliest reports range from 36 weeks (Cohen, in Ervin-Tripp, 1966; Darley and Winitz, 1961) to sixty weeks (Shirley, 1933). The commonest of such words are duplicated monosyllables (McCarthy, 1954; Shirley, 1933). Their meanings, however, are neither simple nor invariable. Depending on the situation and accompanying gestures and intonation, a single word may convey the import of an entire sentence as well as a large variety of meanings (Brown, 1965; Ervin-Tripp, 1966; McCarthy, 1954; McNeill, 1968; Olson, 1968; Shirley, 1933). Thus, the child's primitive phonology and his global meanings may lead to adult oversight of genuine first words; on the other hand, lenience in the criterion of consistency leads to underestimation of the age of first words by optimistic parents (Ervin-Tripp, 1966).

The meanings of early utterances are probably quite global, and because of their fluidity, bear little correspondence to adult categories (Ervin-Tripp, 1966; Werner and Kaplan, 1963). Early one-word utterances are called "holophrases" and precede the development of either words or sentences (Brown, 1965; McNeill, 1968; Werner and Kaplan, 1963). Holophrastic utterances fuse both noun and verb functions and refer to total happenings not precisely defined as things or actions (Olson, 1968). These utterances are not only expressive of reference to external events; they are also a reflection of the child's attitude states and reactions (Werner and Kaplan, 1963). Early one-word utterances may express at the same time a declarative or a command (Leopold, 1939-49); they may be highly specific (Liublinskaya, in Olson, 1968) or highly generalized (Guillaume, 1927; Pavolitch, 1920, in Ervin-Tripp, 1966; Velten, 1943; Werner and Kaplan, 1963).

Conventional Symbols. After the "first word" is uttered, vocabulary grows slowly for the next six months as the child seems preoccupied with the mastery of locomotion skills (Shirley, 1933). Between the ages of eighteen months and six years, however, growth is extremely rapid. The new oral vocabulary is built on an existing foundation of concrete concepts and pre-linguistic symbols. The problem is one of fitting conventional symbols with standardized meanings to individual conceptual experience until symbol-concept relationships for the individual come to approximate corresponding relationships holding for the culture at large. Initially when a new word is learned, it is applied both too inclusively and not inclusively enough (Brown, 1958). Generalization or extension of use occurs on the basis of the objective, affective, or functional similarity of a new object or situation to the object or situation originally designated by the word in question (Lewis, 1951). After the distinguishing properties of a class of concepts are properly abstracted, overinclusive applications are appropriately restricted and underinclusive applications are appropriately extended.

Methodological ambiguities also becloud interpretation of the normative findings regarding vocabulary growth. Different investigators have employed different methods of counting separate words and different criteria for crediting a child with knowledge of a given word. Some investigators have sampled spoken vocabulary, others have tested ability to define words verbally, and still others have required children to point to one of a group of pictures designated by the stimulus word or to say correctly the word repre-sented by a given picture (Ervin-Tripp, 1966; McNeill, 1968). In one study, in which a combination of picture and question techniques was used, the following estimates of total vocabulary were obtained: at 12 months—3 words; at 15 months—19 words; at 18 months—22 words; at 2 years—272 words; at 3 years—896 words; at 4 years—1540 words; at 5 years—2072 words; and at 6 years 2562 words (Smith, 1926). These estimates may differ according to the methods employed, and consideration of the semantic content or lack of it will vary according to the method utilized. For example, children use number-words without knowing their meaning (Miller and Ervin, 1964). Nevertheless, in spite of the methods employed, it appears that nouns occur first, followed by action verbs, adjectives, adverbs, and finally pronouns (Konishi, 1960; McCarthy, 1954; Shirley, 1933). Connectives or functors (prepositions, conjunctions) are the last parts of speech to appear and are rarely heard before the age of two since they presuppose some apprecia-tion of relationship between ideas (Brown, 1965; McCarthy, 1930).

Distinctive Dimensions of Preschool Speech. Two distinguishing aspects of pre-school speech are its concreteness and its focus on sounds (Ervin-Tripp, 1966). When compared to adults, children's nouns more often refer to items with characteristic sizes and visual contours, and verbs refer to animal and human movements (Brown, 1958b). Moreover, adults use more super-ordinates which appear more abstract (e.g., vertebrate, energy) (Brown,

1958a; Ervin-Tripp, 1966; Olver and Hornsby, 1966). The use of super-ordinate responses to word association tests increases until the sixth grade and declines thereafter (Palermo and Jenkins, 1963). The range of the child's early references may be quite wide. Preschool children may use the word "mama" for adult females before they reduce its range to their own particular mother. Later, the word "adult" will have a similar referential range to the primitive "mama" (Ervin-Tripp, 1966; Werner and Kaplan, 1963). Because of this finding, Brown (1958a) argues that the difference between the child and the adult is one of discriminative generalization.Thus, children exhibit more simple stimulus generalization than do adults (i.e., generalization not requiring prior discriminative analysis). Some authors have claimed that adults do not really use a wider range of abstract concepts in their thinking but merely employ a more highly differentiated repertoire of subcategories within existing categories (Brown, 1958a; Ervin-Tripp, 1966). Simple stimulus generalization, however, can hardly be considered a form of abstract thinking that reflects the use of abstract concepts. Thus, it seems more plausible to believe that older children and adults also char-acteristically use a greater number of *generic categories* than do children, as well as more differentiated sub-categories (Ausubel, 1968).

Another distinguishing aspect of preschool speech is its focus on sounds (Chukovsky, 1966; Ervin-Tripp, 1966). The salience of the sound of words over their meaning has been discussed in several studies (Chukovsky, 1966; Razran, 1961; Rice and Di Vesta, 1965). Rice *et al* (1965), for example, found generalization shifts in a paired-associate learning task from sound similarity at younger age levels to semantic (meaning) similarity at older age levels. Direct observation studies indicate that little children engage in nonsense word play, making up words and rhymes and associating by sound relations (Chukovsky, 1966).*

Comprehensibility. Much of the child's early linguistic speech, of course, is incomprehensible except perhaps to his parents and intimate associates. Not only does he have difficulty in articulating some individual sounds such as *s, t,* and *th,* but he also tends to contract polysyllabic words by dropping initial or final syllables and to make many mistakes in pronunciation, grammar, syntax, and diction. Although deliberate training measures have little effect at this stage, spontaneous correction occurs gradually in most instances if he is exposed to a reasonably good model of speech and is not encouraged in emotional infantilism. The correction of some mistakes in pronunciation must, of course, await the emergence and mastery of new sounds. Other errors in diction and syntax (e.g., "baby talk") are persistent

*A most interesting book written by the Russian child poet Kornei Chukovsky called "From Two to Five" gives numerous examples of this sound play with children. More systematic studies with English-speaking children are found in Weir (1962, 1966).

simply because the form in which they are used is perfectly adequate for purposes of communication even if grammatically and conventionally incorrect. Largely through habituation also, many words continue to be used inappropriately although the original conceptual confusion underlying the error no longer exists. On the other hand, numerous factors make for effective revision of infantile language habits. The child hears the correct pronunciation of words in the environment more frequently than he does his own mistakes. He also finds that more intelligible speech elicits more approval and is more efficacious in communicating his needs. Clarity of speech, however, is not highly correlated with understanding of language or extent of vocabulary.

Normative studies show a steady improvement with increasing age both in correctness of articulation (Templin, 1953, 1966; Wellman, 1931) and in overall comprehensibility of children's utterances (McCarthy, 1930; Templin 1966). By the time they enter school, children are able to articulate most sounds correctly and only rarely experience difficulty in making themselves understood. However, misarticulators in kindergarten appear to have articulation problems in the second grade (Templin, 1966). Differences in favor of children from upper socioeconomic levels are apparent in the preschool period, but sex differences before the age of seven are not significant (Sampson, 1959; Templin, 1953).

Later Linguistic Development

Throughout the elementary school years the vocabulary of children, particularly reading recognition vocabulary, continues to grow at a rapid rate (Russell, 1954; Smith, 1941). Older children have larger passive as well as active vocabularies than younger children (Riegel, 1966). In defining words, older children tend to employ explanations and synonyms whereas younger children typically offer descriptions, illustrations and uses (Feifel and Lorge, 1950). Older children respond more to abstract and categorical as opposed to concrete properties of words (Davis, 1937; Feifel et al, 1950). There are many indications that in the primary grades children do not really understand many of the abstractions they read and use in their school subjects unless they have a rich background of relatively concrete information in those particular areas (Serra, 1953). Older children, when presented with different phrases, tend more to utilize context in determining the meaning of individual words in the phrase (Braun et al, 1962). Between the ages of six and eight years, children come to distinguish between anomalous and fully grammatical sentences (McNeill, 1968). Individual differences in the comprehension of verbal abstractions are, of course, highly related to intelligence level (Serra, 1953).

Werner and Kaplan (1950, 1963) have reported an important developmental study of the ability to derive word meanings from their contextual reference. They not only found both gradual and saltatory improvement in this ability with advancing age, but also obtained interesting, qualitative differences between older and younger children (age range 8.5 to 13.5). The attribution of meaning to words involves a process of "signification in which the interdependence of word and sentence meaning" must be perceived.

> In order for the child to signify adequately he has to comprehend that a word has a relatively stable and self-contained meaning and that it is placed in a sentence which itself has a stable structure. He must further understand that the word and sentence, by being specifically related, form a meaningful whole (Werner and Kaplan, 1950, p. 77).

The younger child, more often than his older contemporary, fails to appreciate that a word possesses a circumscribed and differentiated meaning "relatively independent of the sentence context in which it appears." He is also more rigid in postulating contextual meaning, is less aware of his semantic inadequacies, and, rather than apprehending the sound pattern as an artificial or conventional symbol for an object, identifies sound and meaning (Werner and Kaplan, 1963).

In addition to learning many new words, the elementary school child learns new meanings and more subtle connotations for old words. The meanings he attributes to words increasingly approximate the meanings they evoke in the culture at large. The progressive trend toward the conventionalization of language is reflected in the decreasing variability of meanings ascribed to words that occurs as a function of increasing age (Werner and Kaplan, 1963). Meanings also tend to become more precise and less ambiguous. Misconceptions based on similarities between the sound and appearance of semantically unrelated words and on lack of background experience necessary for the comprehension of particular abstractions are gradually cleared up.

During this period the child is also expected to master many new linguistic skills in school such as reading, writing, spelling, punctuation, grammar and composition. Readiness for the acquisition of these skills is not simply a matter of "internal ripening" or genic determination, but depends to a large extent on intelligence level and on the background of language experience and motivation of a given child in a particular family, social class, and cultural environment. Readiness is also relative to the method of instruction employed, the level of abstraction involved and the specific skill the child is required to learn (see p. 90). Many of the language skills, such as articulation of speech sounds, word usage, length of sentence, and grammatical completeness and complexity of sentence structure are highly

intercorrelated (McCarthy, 1954). Vocabulary, however, is not substantially related to these latter criteria of language proficiency (McCarthy,
1954). Situational context is also important since such characteristic features
of individual language functioning as loquacity, egocentricity and emotional
tone are not very consistent from one situation to another (McCarthy, 1954).
In general, the mean number of words per sentence in written compositions
increases (Stormzand and O'Shea, 1924), and the mean number of inflectional errors decreases (Davis, 1939) during the elementary school years.

The Acquisition of Meaning *

The domain represented by semantics concerns the meaning of words or
sentences. At present, the state of theory construction in semantic development is rather meager (Katz, 1966; McNeill, 1968). The contribution of
linguistic theory has thus far focused on the domain of syntax (Chomsky,
1957, 1965, 1968), but the relationship between syntax and semantics is of
paramount importance in a linguistic account of language (Chomsky, 1968).
Present theoretical accounts of semantic development by linguists (Katz,
1966; Katz and Fodor, 1963; Weinreich, 1967) have emphasized the importance of defining meaning not so much in terms of reference as in terms of
wider linguistic relationships; the linguistic meaning of a word is described
by using other words (i.e., words have meaning by virtue of their place in the
linguistic system). This de-emphasis on the role of reference is justified on
the grounds that:

> In isolation most words can have many different meanings; which meaning they take
> in a particular sentence will depend on the context in which they occur. That is to say,
> their meaning will depend both on the other words and on their grammatical role in the
> sentence (Miller, 1964, p. 6).

The relation between syntax and semantics as emphasized by Chomsky
(1957) is apparent when the two systems must interact for an adequate
linguistic description of language (Katz and Fodor, 1963). However, the fact
that linguistic semantics de-emphasizes the study of denotation or reference
(Weinreich, 1967) leaves the whole area of *representational reference* open to
psychological theorizing. The present focus of our theorizing still rests on
representation until adequate linguistic theorizing deems otherwise. We
concur in our present discussion with the viewpoint that:

> . . . linguistic symbols whether "natural" or conventional are basically representational,
> that is, depictive — in a wider sense — of a referent (Werner and Kaplan, 1963, p. 106).

---

*Relevant discussions of contemporary semantic problems and theories may be found in the following
references: Olson, 1969; Hildum, 1967; Jakobovits and Miron, 1967; Saporta, 1961. These references contain selected readings from several authors on this topic.

Before presenting our particular viewpoint on semantic (meaning) development, a brief exposition of the most widely accepted representational theory will be given and criticized.

Present Controversy in Representational Theories of Meaning. The nature or meaning of meaning has long been a fruitful source of speculation and controversy among philosophers and psychologists. Before neobehaviorism achieved its current dominant position in American psychology, meaning was generally identified with the ideas or differentiated cognitive content elicited by symbols. Present-day cognitive theorists still espouse, more or less, the same point of view. This view of meaning, however, is commonly regarded by neobehaviorists as "mentalistic" in nature; and simply by applying this somewhat opprobrious label, members of the neobehavioristic camp tend to feel that they have adequately disposed of the competing theoretical conception of meaning. But the term "mentalistic," although used opprobiously, does not detract in any way from the theoretical cogency of the cognitive view—unless one assumes in advance the axiomatic validity of the behavioristic position. A psychological theory has no need to be apologetic about hypothesizing the existence of differentiated states of consciousness.

Mediational Theory of Meaning. The leading (mediational) neobehavioristic theory does not identify meaning with the differentiated cognitive experience elicited by symbols or with the cognitive operations that give rise to such experience. Meaning, rather, is conceived of as the implicit *behavior*, affective and motor, evoked by signs. According to Osgood's "mediational hypothesis," the acquisition of meanings involves a conditioning process in which signs, as a result of multiple contiguous presentations with their significates, eventually come to elicit an implicit fractional portion of the total *response* evoked by the significates (Osgood, Suci, and Tannenbaum, 1957). Signs, in other words, are said to represent significates because they elicit an implicit part of the total response made to significates, and the meaning of a sign is therefore held to be coextensive with this implicit fractional response which Osgood calls a "representational mediation process."

The principal difficulty with the mediational theory is its inability to account for the denotative aspects of meaning.* The word "dog," for example, elicits a sharply defined and precisely differentiated cognitive experience (meaning) embodying the distinctive or criterial attributes of dogs as distinguished from cats, wolves, human beings, and other creatures. At the very most, a representational mediation process reflective of the most conditionable aspects of the total behavior instigated by dogs, can identify the attitudinal and affective connotations of the word "dog." It cannot possibly define its denotative meaning. Despite the elicitation of markedly

---

Several other criticisms of Osgood's mediational hypothesis have been made by Brown (1958a), Chomsky (1959), and Fodor (1965).

different implicit responses or dispositions in persons who respectively fear, cherish, and despise dogs, the word "dog" has the same denotative meaning for all three individuals, that is, it instigates substantially the same differentiated cognitive content. These same implicit responses can also be instigated by many other signs (e.g., "hyena," "wolf") which have different denotative meanings. Thus, the same sign can instigate quite different implicit responses (motor, affective) consistent with the same denotative meaning, and the same implicit responses can be elicited by signs with quite different denotative meanings. It is clear therefore that an adequate theory of meaning must define the meaning of a sign in terms of differentiated cognitive content and the psychological operations that determine such content, even if this approach is opprobiously characterized as "mentalistic" by other theorists.

Although mediational processes are patently too indefinite, incomplete, and nondistinctive to identify meaning as a differentiated cognitive experience, they constitute for Osgood (1961) the *sole* basis of "psychological" meaning. Denotative meaning is dismissed as simply "a conventional, habitual correlation between a nonlinguistic perceptual pattern . . . and some particular linguistic response" (p. 102). Thus, two persons are said to be in denotative agreement when they use the same formal linguistic responses to refer to the same object or situation, even though the responses in question, in their capacity as signs, instigate quite different organismic processes in the two individuals. In other words, the distinctive features of cognitive experience that are coextensive with denotative meaning are arbitrarily excluded from the domain of psychological meaning, and denotative meaning itself is alleged to be concerned with nothing more than "the arbitrary 'rules of usage' which govern the vocabulary and grammar of a language" (p. 529).

Cognitive theorists concede, of course, that the connotative aspects of meaning can be plausibly conceptualized as a fractional implicit response, largely affective in nature. In fact, Staats and Staats (1957) were able, through simple conditioning procedures, to invest nonsense syllables with the connotative meanings of already meaningful words. However, by any standard, the more crucial and distinctive aspect of the acquisition of meaning is denotative in nature; and this aspect of the meaning phenomenon can hardly be explained by invoking the same mechanism that accounts for the connotative attributes of words.

Osgood's mediational theory of meaning has been broadened by both Mowrer (1960) and Staats (1961) to include "conditioned sensory responses." The word "apple," according to Mowrer, . . . "not only carries the implication of something liked or disliked but also of an object with certain purely sensory qualities." On the positive side, this modified mediational view approaches the cognitive position inasmuch as it maintains that words (conditioned stimuli) represent objects by virtue of eliciting part of the same cognitive content (images or conditioned sensory responses) evoked by the objects. Once the carrier of meaning is thus identified with substantive conscious content (images) rather than with implicit behavior, an adequate basis is established for the differentiated aspects of denotative meaning. Nevertheless, significant theoretical difficulties still remain. In the first place, it strains credulity to conceive of the cognitive content evoked by a sign or significate as a sensory *response*. If conscious experience must be equated phenomenologically with motor and glandular responses to fit cognitive events into the stimulus-response paradigm, only pseudo-rapprochement is achieved between the neobehavioristic and cognitive positions. Second, as will be seen shortly, the mechanism whereby meanings are acquired is not really very analogous to conditioning.

A second related difficulty on which mediational theories of meaning tend to founder concerns the very nature of symbolic representation. The very essence of a representational symbol is that, although it does not resemble its referent in any way, it signifies the same thing that the latter does after representational learning occurs. According to the mediational view, however, ". . . words represent things because they produce in human beings some replica of the actual *behavior* toward these things as a mediation process" (Osgood, Suci, and Tannenbaum, 1957, p. 7). But the fact that a given symbol evokes an implicit affective or motor response, that is, a fractional part of the total response that its referent elicits, does not imply in any way that the symbol actually signifies to the reacting individual what the referent does. In the first place, what anything, significate or symbol, primarily signifies to a person who knows it is the objective, explicit, sharply defined, and distinctive content of awareness it induces in him—in short, the kind of awareness that enables him to distinguish it (referent or symbol) from other things. There is no signification without this special kind of awareness.

Implicit affective or motor behavior, however, is either not accompanied by any awareness whatsoever or is accompanied by awareness that is typically vague, subjective, poorly defined, and nondistinctive. Further, what something signifies to a person, and what he does or feels about the thing signified, are related but by no means identical phenomena. He may not respond to it at all, either affectively or skeletally, and, if he does respond, the response can hardly be considered distinctive of what the particular significate or symbol signifies to him. All of this, of course, is just another and more explicit way both of saying that what representational symbols signify is essentially denotative in nature, and of explaining why this is the case.

Second, implicit in the very concept of a representational symbol is the notion that the person, who knows what it means, appreciates its representational character and function, i.e., appreciates that it *signifies* the same thing that the referent does but actually *is* not the same thing. However, if a symbol merely serves as a conditioned stimulus, that is, if through conditioning it acquires the power to elicit part of the same response that the unconditioned or originally adequate stimulus (the significate) does, thereby developing a capability it did not originally possess, it does not, as a result of this process, *represent* the significate but simply becomes an *adequate stimulus for it in its own right;* the conditioned individual, in other words, responds to the symbol as if it *were* the significate and has no appreciation whatsoever of its representational character. Indispensable, therefore, to the concept of symbolic representation is some degree of appreciation, on the part of the individual who knows what a particular symbol means, that the pattern of stimulation constituting the symbol is not the same pattern of stimulation constituting its significate.

Finally, it is evident that the use of the conditioning paradigm to explain the process whereby representational meaning is acquired, constitutes an unwarranted extension of principles that are valid for certain simple kinds of learning to a more complex and qualitatively different kind of learning. This is particularly unfortunate when a more parsimonious and satisfactory explanation with greater face validity is available.

There are at least three good empirically-grounded reasons for believing that the description of representational learning as an active *cognitive* process, exemplifying the basic features of meaningful learning (see below), is more tenable than the conditioning explanation favored by mediational theorists. (a) Human beings generally, apparently even in early childhood and unquestionably afterwards, understand that everything has a name and that any given name signifies the same things that its referent does. It would certainly be remarkable if this general insight were not put to good use in learning the meanings of particular symbols—if the learning of all particular word meanings did not involve some non-arbitrary reference to, and facilitation by, the presence of this stable generalization in cognitive structure. (b) In acquiring word meanings, learners give every indication of consciously and actively equating word and referent in meaning. They are also well aware of the fact that although symbol and significate signify the same things, each consists of an entirely different pattern of stimulation. (c) Even very young children can learn word meanings, and retain them for days and often weeks at a time, after only a single pairing of word and significate. These facts are wholly incompatible with either a conditioning or rote learning explanation of acquiring word meanings, but are entirely consistent with the available evidence regarding meaningful learning outcomes.

The cognitive interpretation of the acquisition of meanings conflicts in no way with the empirical fact that signs, like any conditioned stimuli, may *automatically* elicit conditioned *responses*. This latter phenomenon, as we have seen previously, probably accounts, in part, for the connotative meaning of words. Hence, in the acquisition of meanings, the *same* sign can become *both* a conditioned stimulus for the implicit affective responses associated with connotative meaning and a representational equivalent of concrete images or of more abstract cognitive content (denotative meaning). Contiguity in time between symbol and significate is an essential condition for learning each type of meaning, but plays a different role in the acquisition of representational equivalence or denotative meaning (meaningful learning) than in the acquisition of connotative meaning (conditioning).

A Mentalistic Theory of Meaningful Verbal Learning*

The essence of the meaningful verbal learning process is that symbolically expressed ideas are related in a nonarbitrary and substantive (nonverbatim) fashion to what the learner already knows, namely, to some existing relevant aspect of his structure of knowledge (i.e., an image, an already meaningful symbol, a concept, or a proposition). Meaningful learning presupposes *both* that the learner manifest a meaningful learning set (that is, a disposition to relate the new material nonarbitrarily and substantively to his cognitive structure), and that the material he learns be potentially meaningful to him, namely, relatable to his structure of knowledge on a nonarbitrary and non-verbatim basis (Ausubel, 1963). There are three distinct types of meaningful learning which are relevant to the discussion of semantic development. The most basic type of meaningful learning is *representational* learning, that is, learning the meanings of single symbols (typically words) or learning what they represent. Single words in any language, after all, are conventional or socially shared symbols, each of which represents a unitary object, event, situation, concept, or other symbol in the physical, social, and ideational worlds. To any *uninitiated* individual, however, what a given symbol means, or represents, is at first something completely unknown to him; it is something that he has to learn. The process whereby he learns this is called representational learning, and is coextensive with the process whereby new words come to represent for him the corresponding objects or ideas to which the words refer (their referents); that is, the new words come to signify to him the same things that the referents do or to elicit the same differentiated cognitive content that they do.

How representational learning actually occurs, and how children develop a capacity for such learning, will be discussed later in some detail under the

---

Most of the materials on this position have been thoroughly discussed in Ausubel, 1963, 1968.

heading of "vocabulary learning." At this point we wish only to distinguish between two basic kinds of meaningful learning, that is, between learning the meanings of unitary symbols or words (representational learning), on the one hand, and learning the meanings of ideas expressed by groups of word combined into *propositions* or sentences, on the other. In the first instance (as in naming, labelling, and defining activities), learning the meanings of single words involves learning what they represent, or in effect, learning specific propositions of representational equivalence, i.e., learning that particular symbols represent, or are equivalent in meaning to, particular referents. In the second instance or in *true propositional learning*, the meaningful learning task is not to learn what words singly, or in combination, *represent* but rather to learn *the meaning of new ideas expressed in propositional form.* In true propositional learning, in other words, the object of the learning is not to learn propositions of representational equivalence, but to learn the meaning of verbal propositions that express ideas other than those of representational equivalence.

In true verbal propositional learning, one is, of course, learning the meaning of a new *composite* idea in the sense (a) that the proposition itself is generated by combining or relating to each other multiple individual words, each representing a unitary referent, and (b) that the individual words are combined in such a way (i.e., in sentence form) that the resulting new idea is more than just the sum of the meanings of the component individual words. Obviously, before one can learn the meanings of verbal propositions one must first know the meanings of their component terms, i.e., know what the terms represent. Thus representational learning is basic to, or a prerequisite for, true propositional learning when propositions are expressed in verbal form.

A third type of meaningful learning consists of *concept* learning or of learning the meaning of concepts (unitary generic or categorical ideas), which, as stated above, are also represented by single symbols just as other unitary referents are. Except in very young learners, as a matter of fact, the individual words that are commonly combined in sentence form to constitute propositions actually represent concepts rather than objects or events; and hence propositional learning largely involves learning the meaning of a composite idea generated by combining into a sentence single words each of which represents a concept or a unitary generic idea.

At this point, it is obviously necessary to indicate how concept learning, or learning the meaning of concepts, is related to representational learning. Since concepts, as well as objects and events, are represented by words or names, learning what *concept words* mean (i.e., learning which concept is represented by a given new concept word, or learning that the new concept word is equivalent in meaning to whatever the concept itself means) is self-evidently a major type of *representational* learning. It typically follows concept learning itself, inasmuch as it is very convenient to be able to represent a newly-learned concept by a single word that is equivalent to it in meaning. But learning what the concept *itself* means, which, in effect, consists of learning what its criterial (distinguishing or identifying) attributes are, involves a very different type of meaningful learning that, like propositional learning, is substantive in nature and intent rather than nominalistic or representational. These two types of meaningful learning (conceptual and propositional) differ in that in the former instance the *criterial attributes* of a new concept are related to cognitive structure to yield a new generic but *unitary* meaning, whereas in the latter instance a new *proposition* (or composite idea) is related to cognitive structure to yield a new *composite* meaning. They are *both* very different from representational learning even though concept learning is typically followed by a form of representational learning in which the newly-learned concept is equated in meaning with the concept word that represents it.

Vocabulary or Representational Learning. We have already indicated that learning the meanings of single words, or learning what single words represent, involves the meaningful learning of particular propositions of representational equivalence, i.e., learning that particular words represent and thereby signify psychologically the same things that their referents do. It was also pointed out that, as a result of such learning, words come to elicit approximately the same differentiated cognitive content that their referents do. Our task at this point is to relate more explicitly this particular type of meaningful learning, namely, representational learning, to the previously presented paradigm of the meaningful learning process and to the previous discussion of the nature of meaning itself. In other words, how do human beings acquire vocabulary? How do they actually learn what single words mean, and how does such learning exemplify meaningful learning in general?

To begin with, there is the matter of genic endowment without which no amount of appropriate experience would suffice. Unlike subhuman species, human beings have a genically determined potentiality for representational learning, that is, for learning that a given pattern of stimulation (such as the distinctive pattern of sounds in the symbol "dog") represents and thereby signifies approximately the same thing (i.e., a dog-image) that an entirely unrelated pattern of stimulation (such as the referent dog-object) signifies. The principal step in actualizing this potentiality for representational learning is typically taken near the end of the first year of life, when the child acquires the *general insight* that it is possible to use a symbol to represent any referent that signifies something (i.e., any significate), and thus to signify the same thing that the significate does. He acquires this insight by generalizing, subverbally and intuitively, from multiple exposures to the two complementary forms of the proposition of representational equivalence that more proficient users of his native language arrange for him, i.e., that different referents have different names and that different exemplars of the same referent have the same name (Ausubel, 1968).

Once this insight is firmly established in cognitive structure, it lays the necessary foundation for all subsequent representational learning or for the meaningful learning of what single words represent. Thereafter, when a particular new proposition of representational equivalence is presented to him (e.g., that "dog" is representationally equivalent to different dog-objects and, hence, to their corresponding dog-images), he is able nonarbitrarily and substantively to relate such a proposition as an exemplar to the already established and more generalized version of the same proposition in his cognitive structure.* The resulting product of the interaction between the two propositions is the differentiated cognitive content that "dog" signifies, or is representationally equivalent to, a composite dog-image; and presentation of the word "dog" will subsequently elicit this image. At this stage of the game, a particular proposition of representational equivalence may often be learned, and retained, for a surprisingly long time, even though it is put to the child only once and in connection with only a single exemplar of the significate in question, provided of course, that the latter is familiar to him.†

Development of Vocabulary Learning. In the early stages of vocabulary learning, words tend to represent actual and noncategorical objects and events, and hence to be equated in meaning with the relatively concrete and specific images such referents signify. Thus "naming," the earliest form of vocabulary learning in children, involves the establishment of representational equivalence between first-order symbols and concrete images. Later on, as words begin to represent concepts or generic ideas, they become concept names and are equated in meaning with more abstract, generalized, and

---

*It is understood here, that propositions of representational equivalence are not always presented explicitly by the adult language community. While many adults name objects for children, it is probable that much semantic learning results from overheard adult speech (Ervin-Tripp, 1966). Adult speech samples indicate that objects which are directly at hand usually are referred to by pronouns, not nouns (Bresson, 1963). Thus, verbal context rather than association with visible referents must be a significant source of learning about the meaning of model words.

†It would seem that the naming process illustrated in our example could also explain how the child acquires the meaning of non-noun prepositions like "in" or "on" or of verbs like "run" or "eat". For example, the word "on" would be used by a parent when the child is perceiving the relationship between objects; for example, he might be observing the "on" relationship between dog and floor (i.e., the dog is on the floor). As in the earlier case, the verbal symbol (i.e., the spoken word "on") can, with repeated pairing, come to elicit an image of the relationship pertaining between these objects; this image, the differentiated cognitive content elicited by the word "on," would constitute the meaning of that symbol.

categorical cognitive content. The word "dog" to a toddler may just signify a composite image of his own pet and of the particular dogs in his neighborhood; to the older preschool child, however, it signifies the *criterial attributes* of a composite dog-image which he himself has discovered inductively from his own concrete-empirical experience with dogs. Correlated with the *denotative* meaning of "dog" that emerges when the criterial attributes of this concept are meaningfully learned are various idiosyncratic affective and attitudinal reactions that the term elicits in each child depending on his particular experience with the species. These reactions constitute the *connotative* meaning of "dog." It should be noted, however, that in older children the connotations of most words (e.g., divorce, alcohol, communism) are not acquired through first-hand experience, but are assimilated from prevailing evaluative attitudes in their immediate cultural environment.

After the preschool years, the meanings of most new words are learned by definition or by being encountered in appropriate and relatively explicit contexts. In this case, representational equivalence is established in cognitive structure between synonyms and already meaningful words or between new concept words and the meanings conveyed by their respective definitions or contexts. An adequate definition or context furnishes, in turn, the criterial attributes of the new concept expressed in already meaningful words or combinations of such words. For example, in learning the meaning of the new concept word "president" (a form of representational learning typically *following* concept learning itself) a pupil equates the word in meaning to whatever "chief of state or chief executive in a republic" means to him, that is, he does so *after* he learns what these attributes themselves, presented in the definition, mean (concept learning *per se*). However, only the representational learning that *follows* concept learning, namely, the process of equating the concept word in meaning with what the concept itself means, can be legitimately considered part of vocabulary learning since, by any reasonable standard, vocabulary learning is synonymous with representational learning. According to the generally accepted meaning of the expression, acquiring a vocabulary consists of learning a body of word meanings which, by definition, refers to learning what the words in question mean and not to learning what their referents (generic ideas) mean. Thus, using the term "vocabulary learning" to encompass concept learning *per se* as well as learning what concept words mean, although very commonly done, only generates conceptual confusion.

Learning what concept words mean obviously demands more sophisticated *prior* knowledge about their corresponding referents than do other forms of representational learning, since learning the meaning of concept words differs in one important respect from learning the meaning of words that do not represent concepts. Where the referent of a given word is an *actual* object or event, learning that the word signifies the same thing as the referent, does not really involve a prior *substantive* task of *learning* what the referent itself signifies. This is so because getting to know what an object or event signifies is a simple matter of perception; an object, for example, simply signifies the corresponding perceptual image it evokes when present, or the corresponding memory image that remains, and can be otherwise evoked, when the object is no longer present. However, when the referent of a word is a concept (i.e., an abstraction or a generic idea that does not actually exist as such) learning that the concept word signifies the same thing as the referent *does* involve a prior substantive task of learning what the referent itself (namely, the concept or generic idea) signifies; this is the case because one can get to know what the concept itself signifies only by *learning* what its criterial attributes are and what they mean, and this, by definition, is a substantive form of meaningful learning. Thus learning the meaning of a concept word always presupposes that the learner first meaningfully learns what its referent (the concept) signifies, even though the actual representational learning involved is essentially no different in process than that involved in learning the meaning of words that do not represent concepts.

Propositional Learning. The meaningful learning of verbal propositions, although somewhat more complex than learning the meaning of words, is similar to representational learning in that new meanings emerge after a potentially meaningful learning task is related to, and interacts with, relevant ideas in cognitive structure on a nonarbitrary and substantive basis. In this case, however, the learning task, or potentially meaningful proposition, consists of a composite idea and is expressed verbally in a sentence containing both denotative and connotative word meanings and the syntactic functions* of, and relations between, words; and the differentiated cognitive content resulting from the meaningful learning process, and constituting its meaning, is an interactional product of the particular way in which the content of the new proposition is related to the content of relevant established ideas in cognitive structure. The relationship in question may be either subordinate, superordinate, or combinatorial relative to these latter ideas.

It is in trying to explain how we acquire the meanings engendered by relating ideas to each other that neobehaviorists encounter their greatest difficulty. The only explanation they can offer to account for the acquisition of propositional meaning is that the meaning responses of subject and predicate are reciprocally conditioned to each other (Mowrer, 1954, 1960). One obvious difficulty with this view is that the conditioning paradigm cannot possibly explain the semantic information conveyed by the syntactic functions of words in a sentence. Most propositions are both logically and

---

The learning of syntax itself and the apprehension of syntactic relationships will be discussed in later sections of this chapter.

syntactically much more complicated with respect to the subject-predicate relationship than Mowrer's paradigm example of "Tom is a thief" would have us believe. For example, on the basis of simple contiguity and conditioning principles alone, "John hits Mary" and "Mary hits John" should elicit identical meanings.

Even more important is the fact that in understanding the meaning of "Tom is a thief," one is doing much more in a cogitive sense than merely "conditioning" the meaning response of "thief" to the subject. "Tom." We have already considered the shortcomings of the conditioning mechanism in explaining the acquisition of word meanings. In addition, it seems much more plausible to suppose that a specific proposition of this nature derives its meaning from the fact that it can be subsumed as an exemplar, under the more general existing proposition in cognitive structure, that *any* particular individual may be a thief. Further, as already pointed out, most propositions bear a much more complex relationship to established ideas in cognitive structure, and also involve the perception of much more complex syntactic relationships between the component words of a sentence than does Mowrer's illustration. For example, in judging the truth value of propositions, (1) it is more difficult to judge negative propositions than affirmative ones; (2) and judgments of 'false' are more difficult than judgments of 'true' when sentences are affirmative, but easier than judgments of true when sentences are negative (Slobin, 1966; Wason, 1965).

SYNTAX*

The distinction between competence and performance made previously although appropriate for consideration in phonology and semantics, becomes extremely important here because of its salience in directing present research in the area of syntax development. As Ervin-Tripp (1966) points out:

> Child development literature includes both studies of grammatical structure or knowledge and studies of behavior. When a child listens, imitates, or speaks, his behavior reflects his fundamental grammatical knowledge and also many other factors such as memory, personality, the person with whom he is speaking, and the setting and topic. Research which is concerned with inferring the sets of rules used by the child employs behavioral evidence, but merely for testing inference. . . . On the other hand, much research on children's language has been concerned instead with frequency counts of typical behavior (p. 73).

The normative research quoted previously under semantic development (i.e., vocabulary, length of utterance, etc.) can be considered frequency-oriented. The focus of syntax research is on underlying syntactic competence rather than on performance. Grammatical competence is an attempt to

---

*A most detailed discussion of syntactic development in children may be found in McNeill (1966, 1968).

assess from the child's linguistic performance (i.e., production and comprehension), the underlying rules which enable children to produce and understand novel sentences (Chomsky, 1965). Linguistically speaking, grammar
consists, in large part, of the particular set of syntactic rules that are generally
accepted by the users of a language for inflecting words and combining them
into sentences. It is in effect, a syntactic code consisting, among other things,
of (a) connecting words (prepositions, conjunctions); (b) designative words
(articles, demonstrative adjectives); (c) inflections indicating number,
gender, person, case, tense, mode and mood; and (d) word order rules adding
relational meaning to connected discourse.

The syntactic rule system, as illustrated in children's and adults' speech,
is ordinarily implicit and it is the rare adult who can explicitly formulate
these rules (Ervin-Tripp, 1966). Moreover, rules are not absolute laws, and
are therefore violated in everyday linguistic performance. These lapses in
performance can be attributed to such factors as memory or fatigue, etc., but
they do not negate the presence of underlying rule structures (McNeill,
1966). In fact, as we shall see, certain performance errors with irregular
constructions serve to dramatize the notion of underlying generative rules
(Berko, 1958; Ervin, 1964).

First Grammars—Sentence Generating Rules

The early one-word utterances seen in children's speech (i.e., holophrastic
speech) have been interpreted as equivalent to the full sentences of adult
grammar (Leopold, 1939-1949; McCarthy, 1954). The possibility that
predication may be implicit (McNeill, 1966, 1968) in holophrastic utterances
does not, however, allow one to infer syntactic rules from these utterances.
It is not until utterances can be broken down into syntactic classes, with
shared *"privileges of occurrence"* that we have the necessary condition for the
discussion of the child's first grammar (Olson, 1968).

Pivot-Open Class Distinction. The occurrence of two-word utterances at about
the eighteen months marks the beginning of a primitive grammar (McNeill,
1966, 1968). The inference from two-word utterances to some primitive
linguistic competence (i.e., underlying grammar) honors the important
distinction between competence and performance. The first grammars have
been described in several different independent research studies (Braine,
1963a; Brown and Bellugi, 1964; Brown and Fraser, 1963; Ervin, 1964; Miller
and Ervin, 1964) and show amazing similarities in their structure. These
studies have found that when the earliest multiword utterances appear, they
may be divided, because of privileges of occurrence, into two major classes;
"pivot" and *"open"* (Braine, 1963a). Words that are members of the pivot
class (P) are few in number but occur frequently, whereas words in the open
class (O) are greater in number but occur infrequently. Such utterances as

"this pretty," "this doll," "allgone boy," "allgone shoe," etc., are illustrations of this early primitive grammar. The position of (P) words in two-word
sentences is fixed, first for some children, and second for others, but never
both (McNeill, 1968). Analysis of the words which form both classes in the
several studies cited reveals that the members of these classes vary from child
to child and that they correspond to no single adult grammatical class.
Basically, a sentence is formed by taking one word from the pivot class and
combining it with one word from the open class (e.g., "allgone bye bye,"
"allgone sock" or "allgone boat"), the postulated primitive underlying
competence for these generations being P + O. These utterances are not
mere imitations of adult language (i.e., performance) because they do not
honor adult grammatical distinctions and are novel in relation to adult
speech. As McNeill (1966) concludes:

> It is more parsimonious to assume that children generate all these sentences according to
> rules and that the rules and word categories we infer from their speech reflect some kind of
> primitive competence (p. 24).*

Early Grammatical Differentiation. The pivot-open class distinction becomes
apparent as early as eighteen months and syntactic development proceeds by
the differentiation of these first classes (Brown and Bellugi, 1964; McNeill,
1966, 1968; Olson, 1968).† The description and analysis of the differentiated
pivot class (P) in a two-year-old at three points over a five-month interval,
indicates the emergence of five grammatical classes from the initial primitive
pivot class: articles, adjectives, demonstrative pronouns, possessive pronouns,
and a pivot that contains "other," "mother," "one," "all," and "more"
(McNeill, 1966). For example, at the outset, *my, that, two, a, big,* had identical
privilege of occurrence (e.g., *a* will now occur only before the pivot *my,* such
that "that a my car" occurred but not "that my a car").

With the appearance of three or more word utterances, two phenomena
appear. One is the nested construction, showing the beginnings of phrase
structure (Ervin-Tripp, 1966). Thus, *"a blue flower," "that flower"* have the
same privilege of occurrence as *"flower"* (Brown and Bellugi, 1964). The
second phenomenon is the appearance of "slot" grammars, in which no
higher-order structures are obligatory, but a series of optional positions is
present (Ervin-Tripp, 1966). Thus, a child might say "see truck," "see a
truck" or "truck" with no distinction in meaning, yet the relative position of

---

*Slobin (1966d) cites evidence for the pivot-open class distinction in the early speech of Russian,
Croation, French and German children. Weir (1962, 1966) also gives examples of this early P—O
distinction in her own two children's speech play.

†The following discussion of differentiation of early syntax is based on the linguistic development
of two boys and a girl beginning at approximately two years of age and continuing for one child until
the age of five (see Bellugi and Brown, 1964; Brown, Cazden and Bellugi, 1967; Brown and Fraser,
1963; McNeill, 1966, 1968).

the words remains consistent (Brown and Bellugi, 1964; Ervin, 1964). McNeill (1966, 1968) has postulated eight rules to account for virtually all of children's early sentences, and this is the first attempt at a competence model which involves developmental components. The systems described at this stage involve very few grammatical classes and constructions and no transformation rules are present (McNeill, 1966). Although attempts at assessing these early grammars, by finding what proportion of the utterances in a second sample could be accounted for by the rules from a first sample, have proved to be partially adequate (Fraser, Bellugi and Brown, 1963), it may nevertheless be concluded at present that the number of classes and their patterning into syntactical rules seems to be idiosyncratic, the determinants still being unknown (Ervin-Tripp, 1966).

Word-Generating Rules—Morphology

Grammatical competence is not only illustrated in rules for generating sentences. In addition, there is also a rule system which governs the construction of individual words. Morphemes are the smallest elements in speech to which meaning can be assigned, and morphology is the study of the rules which govern the construction of morphemes. More specifically, the rules involve the use of *markers* or *inflections* that are added to classes of words such as those involved in plural inflections ("s") and past tense inflections ("-ed") (Olson, 1968).

Early Inflection Rules. The clearest evidence for the presence of rules for the construction of words can be seen in the consistent errors children make in forming plurals and past tense for irregular parts of speech (e.g., goed, digged, brang, and oxes, sheeps, etc.). The first major attempt to explore inflection rules systematically is seen in a technique which involved asking children to make new formations using nonsense words (Berko, 1958). Children between the ages of four and seven were presented with a drawing in conjunction with a nonsense word such as "wug" and the following dialogue ensued: "This is a wug. Now there are two of them. There are two ———." If the child responded with "wugs" he was credited with the rule covering plural inflections. Past tense inflections of verbs involved such questions as the following: "This is a man who knows how to gling. Today he glings. Yesterday he ———." The results indicate that children between the ages of four and seven have mastered inflectional rules for plurals and past tense, the older children better than the younger children.* A similar study, with younger children, indicates the presence of rules for the plural before three years of age, but with large individual differences (Miller and Ervin,

*The discussion of inflectional rules for past tense and plurals is for purposes of illustration. The study also indicated the presence of rules for forming the plural and possessive for nouns and the past tense and third person singular for verb.

1964). The persistence of these rules is seen when children resist imitating the correct adult usage of an irregular plural in preference to their own incorrect inflection rule (Berko, 1958).

Brown and Berko (1963) studied the syntactic rules of children between grades one and three by combining certain nonsense syllables when these were presented in various contexts. For example, "wug" was presented as a transitive verb (i.e., "The little girl wants to wug something"), as a mass noun (i.e., "The little girl is thinking about a wug"), etc. The children, in constructing sentences, improved with age and performed better at all ages with the count nouns, adjectives, and transitive and intransitive verbs than with the mass nouns and adverbs. Thus, children show an ability, which increases with age, to construct grammatically correct sentences using new words (Berko and Brown, 1960).

Competence in sentence generation and word construction rules develops early; this partially accounts for the fact that there are few structural analyses of language in older children (Ervin and Miller, 1963). In summarizing the present studies available on early syntactic competence, Miller and Ervin (1963) suggest that:

> By the age of four most children have learned the fundamental structural features of their language and many of the details. There is then a long period of consolidation, a period of overlearning so that grammatical habits become automatic. Some irregular patterns are learned. Other irregular patterns already learned, still must become firmly established. A six-year-old often uses forms such as *buyed* and *bought*, or *brang* and *brought* interchangeably. When he corrects himself, changes *buyed* to *bought*, he indicates that he knows the adult norm but has not yet developed a firmly established habit. . . . The child must still acquire certain grammatical patterns that are associated with difficult semantic patterns, such as passive transformations and causal patterns with *why* and *because* (p. 125).

The Development of Transformations

Transformations involve the reordering and combining of phrase structure sequences by inversions, additions, deletions, or substitutions (Ervin-Tripp, 1966). Transformational operations produce such semantically related sentences as declaratives, passives, negatives and interrogatives. One of the most salient differences between pre-schoolers and school children is the increasing use of transformations (Menyuk, 1963a, 1963b, 1964a, 1964b). Specifically, significant decreases between nursery school children and first-grade children were found in the idiosyncratic rules which had produced omissions of articles and prepositions, and corresponding increases were found in the regularity of question inversions and verb inflections. Moreover first-grade children still exhibited unmastered patterns (i.e., "if" and "so" clauses, nominalizations, etc.).

Transformational studies have barely begun and have so far been confined to the acquisition of two transformational systems—negation and interrogation (Bellugi, 1965; Brown, Cazden and Bellugi, 1967; Klima and Bellugi, 1966; McNeill, 1968). The development of the negative transformation starts at the same time as the P + O construction and is first characterized by the use of a negative operator before or after the sentence (Klima and Bellugi, 1966). Similar constructions are found in Russian (Slobin, 1966), French (Gregoire, 1937) and Japanese (McNeill, 1968). An intermediate stage marks the beginning of negative forms and then proceeds to the use of the auxiliary verbs (Klima and Bellugi, 1966). Interrogative transformations emerge early, coinciding with P + O construction, and are characterized by the use of *wh* words and intonation. The *wh* questions are at first formed simply by using the *wh* word at the beginning of an undisturbed declarative sentence (Klima and Bellugi, 1966). *Why* and *why not* questions are more restricted and are usually made in response to a declarative statement made by the parent (Brown *et al*, 1967). Finally, an auxilliary system different from adults appears. The previously mentioned studies stop at the age of four, so further clarification at older ages is needed.

To summarize, the development of syntax starts with the appearance of two-word utterances occurring at about eighteen months, and, within two years from this starting point, the major syntactic forms are represented in the child's speech. During this period, the child develops a set of rules for combining classes of words into the two major sentence constituents, the noun phrase and the verb phrase, as well as rules for their combination. Three-word utterances mark the appearance of hierarchical structures that integrate phrases within phrases. Markers for plurals and verb tense are developed, over-generalized at first and then gradually differentiated. At four years of age, the only major syntactic forms that are not completed are the transformations for negatives, questions, and passives. The completion of these rules will occur during the elementary-school years. Because of the rapidity of the syntactic events which take place during this short period of time (preschool), it is difficult to assess the factors which operate in producing syntactic competence. Several factors deserve consideration, and it is to these factors that we will now turn.

Factors Affecting Syntactic Acquisition

Two questions must be asked concerning the factors which affect syntactic development: (1) what determines the difference between comprehension and production of syntactic forms, and (2) how does a child extract from the finite sample of speech to which he is exposed the rule structure that will generate an infinite set of sentences?

Comprehension versus Production. The distinction between active and passive linguistic skills is common in discussions of child language development (McNeill, 1966). The distinction is made because it is frequently stated that comprehension of language features (passive control) occurs earlier in development than does production (active control) (McNeill, 1966). An example of this difference is seen in the comparison between children's production and comprehension of grammatical contrasts (Fraser, Bellugi and Brown, 1963). Children were given pairs of sentences that differed on single grammatical features. For example, one pair of sentences contrasted *the sheep is jumping* with *the sheep are jumping.* The sentences were associated with two pictures; one sheep jumping while one looked on, and a second showing two sheep jumping. The two sentences differed only in whether the auxilliary verb *be* was singular or plural. Singular-plural inflections (e.g., the boy draws versus the boys draw), tense inflections, and active-passive transformations were also measured. Three different methods of assessment were utilized: (1) *comprehension* involved the selection of the picture that corresponded to the sentence, (2) *production* involved the generation of a sentence to describe contrasting pictures and (3) *imitation* which did not involve the child in seeing the pictures but only in hearing the sentences. The results indicated that all three functions improve with age and that children's *imitation* exceeds *comprehension* which in turn exceeds *production.* It should be remembered that both production and comprehension of speech are indicators of linguistic competence, the one producing or encoding speech, the other receiving and decoding speech (McNeill, 1966). Several theorists have concluded that the difference between passive and active controls which favors comprehension of speech probably occurs because of the larger load placed on memory in production (Fraser *et al*, 1963; McNeill, 1966).* As McNeill (1966) points out:

> In this framework, a distinction between active and passive *grammars*, which some have wanted to draw, is not necessary; a grammar is a statement of competence, whereas comprehension and production are parts of a theory of performance, and it can be assumed the grammar feeds into both kinds of performance (p. 77).

The fact that *imitation* exceeded comprehension on every contrast except one (Fraser *et al*, 1963), leads us to the consideration of the second question, i.e., the source of generative grammar. Because grammatical rules change upon exposure to the adult language, imitation is a common explanation given for this change (Ervin, 1964; Slobin, 1967).

The difference between comprehension and production in some cases may also be an experimental artifact. Anisfield and Tucker (1967) in studying pluralization rules hint at the possibility of the two procedures tapping different aspects of the child's linguistic knowledge. Their hypothesis is that in production tasks children depend mainly on the information contained in the rules governing English plurals, whereas in comprehension (recognition) they can draw on the generalization that in English, plurals are longer than singulars.

Imitation, Expansions, Approval-Disapproval. The role of imitation has been suggested by several theorists as a factor in language acquisition (Bandura and Harris, 1966; Mowrer, 1954). Imitation of adult speech is not sufficient to account for language development however, since children say more than they hear in adult speech (i.e., novel utterances) and also articulate non-adult forms. The fact that *imitations* emerge before comprehension and production in the Fraser *et al*, (1963) study may be due to the fact that these imitations were elicited (Ervin, 1964). An analysis of *spontaneous* imitations in one study indicated, for example, that they were not "grammatically progressive" (Ervin, 1964). Thus, the child who does not produce the progressive inflection will not imitate it (e.g., "Adam is running fast" might be imitated as "Adam run"). In these cases . . .

    . . . children assimilated the adult models to their current grammars; when there was no place for -ing in the grammar, -ing did not appear in imitation. But, of course, assimilating imitations to the current grammar means that imitation cannot change the grammar (McNeill, 1966, p. 69).

A noticeable phenomenon in parent-child linguistic interaction is the expanded imitations adults make of their children's utterances (Brown and Bellugi, 1964). Approximately 30 percent of the time, adults repeat the speech of children and *expand* their utterances into the nearest adult equivalent (Brown and Bellugi, 1964). Analysis of Brown and Bellugi's (1964) transcripts indicated that over half of the children's imitations of adult expansion were grammatically progressive, that is, the child in his speech added some feature of the adult expansion (Slobin, 1968). A systematic attempt at expansion of the speech of lower-class children, however, has yielded negligible findings (Cazden, 1966). Further studies on *expansions* seem warranted because of their salient presence in adult-child linguistic interaction. There may be a sort of critical age for expansions in which the child is most helped by an expanded model of his own utterance to imitate and is most prone to imitate it (Slobin, 1966, 1968).

    Approval and disapproval of children's grammatical statements have also been considered as factors in the development of grammatical competence (Brown *et al*, 1967). Analysis of their sample of three children seems to indicate that adults typically approve or disapprove of semantic quality rather than of syntactic quality in their children's speech. Beautifully stated:

    It seems, then, to be truth value rather than syntactic well-formedness that chiefly governs explicit verbal reinforcement by parents. Which renders mildly paradoxical the fact that the usual product of such a training schedule is an adult whose speech is highly grammatical but not notably truthful (Brown *et al.*, 1967, p. 58).

    Consideration of the above factors, although important, should not lead us away from the fact that the child's grammar is generative (i.e., rule-governed). Children produce many coherent sentences that they have never heard before, which precludes copying from an adult model. Before closing the discussion on syntactic development, it seems appropriate to briefly discuss present theoretical accounts of the mechanism(s) for the presence and acquisition of generative rules.

Mechanism(s) Underlying Syntactic Acquisition. Several learning theorists have advanced arguments that rely upon the ordinal sequences of words in adult language to account for the order of elements in children's sentences and for the formation of word classes (Braine, 1963a, 1963b, 1965; Jenkins and Palermo, 1964). Braine (1963b) explicates a "place contingency theory" which suggests that the child learns associations between morpheme pairs and locations of units (i.e., words and phrases) within higher-order units. For example, the pivot-open class distinction is illustration of the learning of positional rules. The term "pivot" is so named because it refers to only those words for which a child knows the proper temporal position in the sentence (i.e., pivot words occur first or last). Open class words occur and are positioned wherever pivot words are not, which means that in two-word sentences the positions of both pivot and open words are locked in place in the sentence frame (Braine, 1963a).

Theories which rely heavily on ordinal sequences of words in adult language to account for the order of elements in children's sentences and for the formation of word classes are open to several criticisms. First of all, word order in adult English is much more variable and idiosyncratic than "position" theorists realize (Bever, Fodor, Weksel, 1965). Second, even in a foreign language such as Russian, word order is more variable than English (Slobin, 1966a). In spite of this variability in adult Russian, however, the early stages of the acquisition of Russian (e.g., P + O class) as a native language bear a striking similarity to the acquisition of English (Slobin, 1966a).

A radically different alternative account of linguistic competence has been offered by transformational linguists (Chomsky, 1965; Katz, 1966; McNeill, 1966, 1968). They postulate an innate language acquisition device (L.A.D.) that governs the development of the major syntactic structures (e.g., grammatical relations between noun phrase and verb phrase and hierarchic integration). This theory stems from the observation that children acquire grammar in the remarkably short time period between the second and fourth years of life. McNeill (1966, 1968) postulates therefore that the child is preprogrammed with the L.A.D., which gives him much of the knowledge of a generative grammar. Thus, knowledge of the sentence relations called "subject," "predicate," and "object," and other possible linguistic universals may rely on innate factors since many syntactic structures are not particularly salient in adult speech.

The hypotheses of an innate component in language acquisition is reasonable if it can specify the interaction between the innate component and the environmental factors which obviously play an important role in language acquisition (i.e., children learn the language of their local community). As Brown (1968) points out:

> The child is always assumed to learn on the basis of principles not themselves learned. So long as psychology did not fully apprehend the complexity of adult linguistic knowledge it was possible to believe that theory might succeed with such simple "givens" as association by contiguity, response selection through reinforcement, and stimulus generalization. Now that the complexity of the terminal state is more fully appreciated it appears that we cannot get there by these means. We need a more powerful . . . innate component (p. 49).

The postulation of an innate component in language acquisition, however, poses a serious and difficult question as to just when to appeal to such a device as explanatory (Slobin, 1966b). A more tenable interactionist explanation is that the child is not pre-programmed with specific structural information but with an inferential capacity that enables him to discover in the speech sample of his community just the kinds of relationships that figure in linguistic descriptions (Brown and Fraser, 1964; Fodor, 1966; Jenkins, 1966; Slobin, 1966a). Thus, from the finite sample of adult speech to which he is exposed, he is able to infer the basic syntactical rules and forms found in his native language. And given both this acquired knowledge of the syntactic code and the presence of appropriate relevant propositions in his cognitive structure, he can easily decode or encode an infinite number of sentences whose propositional message is expressable in the code and relatable to his cognitive structure. What is probably innate therefore in the child is not an L.A.D. or core grammatical structure underlying syntactical universals, but rather an inferential capacity for abstracting the basic syntactical structure of his native language from prolonged exposure to multiple but finite exemplars of such structure.

The Relationship Between Semantics and Syntax

Thus far, we have considered syntactic development from a linguistic viewpoint. From a psychological standpoint, however, syntactical rules primarily serve the *transactional* function of bringing verbally expressed ideas (images and concepts) into relationship with each other, in a reliable fashion, for the purpose of generating and understanding new ideas. Hence, when a group of words are appropriately inflected and combined according to the designated rules, the resulting sequence is not only grammatically correct, but also communicates the idea that the speaker or writer intends to convey. Typically, therefore, a given word in a sentence both conveys a distinctive denotative meaning and, by virtue of its particular syntactical function in the sentence (e.g., subject, object, verb), furnishes additional *semantic* information that contributes to the understanding of propositional meaning. As a matter of fact, one often needs to know the syntactical function of a word before its denotative meaning can be apprehended, as in the case of words of different meaning that sound alike, or of certain words that can serve as both nouns and verbs.

GENERAL FACTORS INFLUENCING LANGUAGE DEVELOPMENT

The development of language exemplifies the operation of both maturation and learning. Genically determined capacities, neurophysiological growth, incidental experience, environmental stimulation, motivational factors, and deliberate training measures interact in complex ways in accounting for both normative changes and individual differences among children. Readiness for different phases of language is a function not only of genic determinants and neurophysiological growth but also of all the environmental variables indicated above.

Initial Acquisition of Language

What does it mean when a child begins to talk unusually early or unusually late? It is clear from the previous discussion on phonology, syntax, and semantics, that the factors influencing the speed of language acquisition are multidetermined and represent a complex interaction of genic sources and environmental support.

Intelligence is perhaps the most important determinant of precocity in speech since it affects both the ability to mimic and the ability to understand the meaning of verbal symbols. Earliness of onset of speech is positively correlated with I.Q. (Abt, Adler, and Bartelme, 1929) and is one of the most striking developmental characteristics of intellectually gifted children (McCarthy, 1960; Terman, 1925). Even in the first two years of life a small but reliably positive relationship prevails between attained level of infant speech and both current and later measures of intelligence (Catalona and McCarthy, 1954; Spiker and Irwin, 1949; Smith, 1957; Winitz, 1964). This is hardly surprising since the comprehension, use and manipulation of verbal symbols are conspicuous components of the capacities measured by intelligence tests.

The ability to mimic words is partly dependent on intellectual level (Sheridan, 1948), but other factors such as auditory discrimination (Kronvall and Diehl, 1954) and kinaesthetic imagery are also important. In any case, mimicry of speech is a less valid indicator of intelligence than is comprehension of language. Many precocious talkers are merely successful mimics who are able to parrot speech accurately without necessarily understanding it. Precocity in talking is a highly over-rated criterion of superior intelligence.

In some instances, "only" and overvalued children talk at an early age because of the surfeit of adult attention, affection, and stimulation they receive and because of the increased availability of adult speech models (Carroll, 1960; Davis, 1937). Early acquisition of speech in children is also stimulated sometimes by the competitive example and urging of older siblings. The earlier they learn to communicate verbally, the more opportunities they gain for participation in inter-sibling play.

Variability in the same factors, but at the opposite end of the distribution, accounts for initial retardation in language development. Mimicry may be impaired by such gross defects in the vocalizing apparatus as dysarthria and cleft palate (Morley, Court and Miller, 1950), by hearing disability (Doehring et al, 1960; Fry, 1966; Goldenberg, 1950; Hirsh, 1966; Kronvall et al, 1954; Morley et al, 1950; Sheridan, 1948), and by either the endogenous familial variety of intellectual deficit (Goldenberg, 1950; Loomis, 1960; Morley et al, 1950; Noel, 1953; Templin, 1957; Wood, 1946) or the organic type associated with such conditions as aphasia (Eisenson, 1960; Mercer, 1960; and Wood, 1960), paranatal asphyxia and birth trauma (Beckey, 1942; Sheridan, 1948), cerebral palsy (Lefevre, 1960), and premature birth (DeHirsch et al, 1964). Low intelligence is also a major handicap in acquiring the meaningful and conceptual aspects of language. But whereas precocity in talking is always indicative of at least average intelligence, delayed speech is not necessarily a sign of below average intelligence (McCarthy, 1960). It is true that feebleminded children are invariably retarded in language development; on the other hand, many normally intelligent and even intellectually gifted children are late talkers for reasons unconnected with either hearing disability or speech organ pathology (McCarthy, 1960; Terman, 1939).

Some bright children simply have poor auditory discrimination or kinaesthetic imagery. Others either rebel at parroting words until their meanings are clear or prefer to defer speech until their verbal ability catches up with their relatively advanced ideational processes. Environmental impoverishment, inadequate motivation, and personality disorder must also be considered. Delayed speech is more common among institutionalized and isolated children (see p. 542), among children from lower socioeconomic levels, and among twins (see p. 543). It is a result of over-protective parental attitudes and of child-rearing practices that anticipate the child's needs (see p. 312). Mutism is frequently a negativistic response to parental rejection and coerciveness (McCarthy, 1952, 1954). It is also characteristic of seclusive children who prefer to play alone (Beckey, 1942) and of schizoid and autistic personality trends (Despert, 1938; Loomis, 1960). In all these instances of delayed speech, less unwarranted concern would be manifested about the possibility of feeblemindedness if more attention were paid to the evidence of language comprehension and development than to indications of verbal facility (Newland, 1960). Moreover, research on early infantile speech would be benefited if it could be carried into the framework of theory. Menyuk's (1964a) finding which indicates that infantile speech is related to retarded sentence generating rules is a step in this direction.

Determinants of Individual Differences

Intelligence. The high positive correlations generally reported between measured intelligence and language proficiency throughout the entire period of childhood are somewhat difficult to interpret (McCarthy, 1954). To some extent, highly verbal children have a marked advantage and verbally retarded children a serious disadvantage in taking the typical verbal test of intelligence. Bilingual children make a relatively much better showing on nonverbal than on verbal intelligence tests (Darcy, 1946; Johnson, 1953; Jones, 1953). Part of the obtained correlation also reflects overlapping of content between tests of language and intelligence (e.g., vocabulary, opposites, dissected sentences). On both theoretical and empirical grounds it seems highly improbable that these artifacts can account for *all* of the relationships between language and intelligence. First, factorial analyses of intelligence indicate both that non-language abilities are represented and that the latter are positively correlated with various language components. Second, correlations between tests of vocabulary and intelligence are much too high to be explained simply on the basis of overlapping and test advantage (Dunsdon, and Roberts, 1953). It seems likely that the ability to acquire and utilize language is both a highly representative manifestation of general aspects of intelligence and is directly implicated in many of the operations of problem solving.

Sex. In the vast majority of earlier studies reviewed by McCarthy (1954), where boys and girls were reasonably well matched with respect to socioeconomic status and I.Q., girls proved superior on a majority of performance measures of language proficiency. In more recent studies, where sampling and design features have been improved, these sex differences are very slight (Templin, 1957). The earlier studies ordinarily proceeded to collect *performance* measures with no apparent attempts to assess underlying language *competence* (see p. 507). Thus, when grammatical competence is measured there are no salient differences between males and females (Menyuk, 1963, 1964a).

In those studies where performance differences do favor females, an adequate explanation for these differences may be the operation of consistent differential cultural expectations (i.e., sex-typing games, prevailing conceptions of masculinity and femininity, etc.). The fact that sex differences follow an erratic pattern in lower-class families points to the importance of socio-environmental factors, such as home stimulation and types of play (Ervin-Tripp, 1966). For example, a language study on Puerto Ricans in New York City indicates no sex differences in language (Anastasi & de Jesus, 1953), whereas studies of New York City Negroes favor boys (Anastasi & D'Angelo, 1952) and of Detroit Negroes favor girls (Thomas, 1962). In conclusion, it appears that complex environmental factors, which are at present difficult to delineate, play an important role when sex differences in language are found.

Environmental Stimulation. The degree of contact that children have with adults is a crucial determinant of their language development (Cazden, 1966). Cazden (1966) provides an excellent interpretive review of subcultural differences in children's language. A review specifically related to the socially disadvantaged child may be found in Ralph (1965). Numerous studies of "only" children indicate their language superiority; this is attributed to the opportunities these children have for conversation with parents. Several studies reveal the importance of peers in linguistic development (i.e., especially the detrimental effects of lower-class peer contacts); the relative influence of parents and peers may revolve around the importance of parental conversation in determining the complexity of the child's linguistic program for constructing and understanding sentences, and the importance of peer conversations in having more of an effect on specific details of those programs such as features of phonology and morphology (Cazden, 1966). In addition to the purely intellectual stimulation and reinforcement of children's speech, adult affection is correlated with higher language scores in children (Anastasi & de Jesus, 1953; Milner, 1951). Anastasi & de Jesus (1953) attribute the relative language superiority of Puerto Rican nursery school children over comparable white and Negro children in New York City slum areas—in the face of more severe socioeconomic handicaps—to the fact that they enjoy more contact with adults in the home. A high positive correlation also prevails between the scores of children and parents on language usage tests (Noel, 1953). Even on a purely situational basis, children tend to use more mature patterns of speech when conversing with adults than when communicating among themselves (Cazden, 1966).

At the opposite pole of the continuum is the retarded language development of institutionalized children; this becomes apparent as early as the second month of life in the variety and frequency of phonemes emitted (Brodbeck and Irwin, 1946). Comparisons of caretaking activities of parents in homes and adults in institutions reveal notably more talking to infants at home (Provence & Lipton, 1962; Rheingold, 1960). Differences between institutionalized and noninstitutionalized children in these respects are greater by far than corresponding differences between social class groups, and hence cannot be explained simply on the basis of socioeconomic selectivity in the institutional population (Brodbeck & Irwin, 1946). Goldfarb's (1945) longitudinal study of children who were and were not institutionalized during the first three years of life points to the continued language retardation of the institutionalized group throughout childhood and even through adolescence. The language development of institutionalized children *also lags* behind other aspects of their intellectual development. Their scores on vocabulary tests, for example, are consistently inferior to those of non-institutionalized children matched on either mental age or I.Q. (Little & Williams, 1937; Williams & McFarland, 1937). Some of this retardation can be offset by providing a special program of enriched language experience (Bereiter & Engelmann, 1967; Dawe, 1942).

The development of twins and "only" children furnish neat illustrations of the influence of adult contact on the acquisition of language. Between the ages of two and five, twins become increasingly retarded in all phases of language proficiency (Davis, 1937; Day, 1932). This not only is a reflection of relatively less attention from parents and of being less exposed to adult speech, but also attests to the adequacy of gestures and "private" language for purposes of communication between two children who are almost constantly in contact with each other. Kindergarten attendance leads to a marked spurt in social speech, but twins do not overcome their language handicap until they are almost 10 years of age, and then only if they come from middle- and upper-class homes (Davis, 1937). Quite the opposite conditions encourage precocious language development in "only" children, more so in the case of girls than of boys (Davis, 1937a; 1937b).

Language development shows the same positive correlation with social class status that is customarily found with I.Q. Studies indicate that social class differences in language proficiency are evident in the preschool period, tend to increase with age, and are quite marked by the elementary school years (Cazden, 1966; Ervin-Tripp, 1966). These differences reflect the influence of an enriched verbal environment, of greater parent-child contact, of superior language models in the home, and of higher parental expectations regarding verbal accomplishment in the middle-class family.* Correspondingly, lower-class children demonstrate language deprivation, particularly with respect to the abstract dimension of verbal functioning. Many factors contribute to this unfortunate outcome. The lower-class home, to begin with, lacks the large variety of objects, utensils, toys, pictures, etc., that require labeling and serve as referents for language acquisition in the middle-class home. The child is also not spoken to or read to very much by adults. Both for this reason and because of the high noise level of his home, his auditory discrimination tends to be poor. Unlike the middle-class child, he receives little

---

It is interesting to note the consistent finding in the literature of the verbal superiority of children coming from Jewish families (Lesser, Fifer & Clark, 1965).

corrective feed-back regarding his enunciation, pronunciation, and grammar (Deutsch, 1963; John and Goldstein, 1964), and the vocabulary and syntactical model provided him by his parents are typically impoverished and faulty.

Various interpersonal aspects of adult-child communication and social control in the lower-class home also contribute to language retardation (Hess and Shipman, 1965). The lower-class mother's verbal behavior style in communicating with her offspring is typically "restricted"; that is, her speech tends to be abbreviated, lacking in precision and explicitness, and undifferentiated with respect to person, topic, and circumstances. This tendency toward constriction is further compounded by a style of social control in which parental decisions are arbitrary and are justified by an appeal to authority and status differences, rather than explained and justified by an appeal to reason or equity. In a social environment that offers a very narrow range of alternatives of thought and action, there is little opportunity for learning precise and differentiated linguistic expression. But although the social use of language is constricted in lower-class families, it is at least more adequate than the virtually nonexistent cognitive use of language. Lower-class parents, unlike their middle-class counterparts, use language primarily as a means of expressing their feelings and controlling the behavior of their children, and not as a means of communicating ideas (e.g., naming, identifying, comparing, explaining, clarifying, differentiating) (Bereiter and Engelmann, 1966).

Later on, when new concepts and different transactional terms are largely acquired verbally, i.e., by definition and context from speech and reading, rather than by abstraction from direct concrete experience, the lower-class child suffers from the paucity of abstractions in the everyday vocabulary of his elders; from the rarity of stimulating conversation in the home; from the relative absence of books, magazines, and newspapers in his surroundings; and from the lack of example of a reading adult in the family setting.

It is small wonder, therefore, that the abstract vocabulary of the lower-class child is deficient in range and precision (Deutsch, 1963; McCarthy, 1930; Schulman and Havighurst, 1947; M. E. Smith, 1933), that his representational functioning is deficient (Sigel and McBane, 1966), that his grammar and language usage represent a non-standard form of English (Cazden, 1966), that his attentivity and memory are poorly developed, and that he is impoverished in such language-related knowledge as the number concepts, self-identity information, and understanding of the physical, geometric, and geographical environments (Deutsch, 1963; Sigel and McBane, 1966). Social-class differences in language and conceptual measures also tend to increase with increasing age (Deutsch, 1963), thus demonstrating the cumulative effects of both continued environmental deprivation and of early deficit in language development.

The lower-class child's entire orientation to language is also different from that of the middle-class child. He responds more to the concrete, tangible, immediate, and particularized properties of objects and situations rather than to their abstract, categorical and relational properties (Bernstein, 1958; 1960; Siller, 1957). His speech is instigated more by the objects and actions he sees than by abstract ideas emanating from within, and he makes more ancillary use of such nonverbal forms of communication as gestures and facial expressions (Bernstein, 1958; Riessman, 1962). In short, the language of the lower-class child is more concrete, expressive, and informal than that of the middle-class child, showing signs of impoverishment mainly in its formal, abstract, and syntactical aspects (Bernstein, 1960; Deutsch, 1963). His sentences are short, staccato-like, and heavily interlaced with slang and cliches; they are rarely compound or complex in structure (Bernstein, 1960; Deutsch, 1963; Loban, 1963). He uses few conjunctions, adjectives, adverbs, and qualifying phrases or clauses.

Merely stating that there are class differences in language development, however, does not tell us why they occur (Ervin-Tripp, 1966). Moreover, inferences about types of environmental stimulation associated with social class differences must be more stringently stated. At present, the effects of specific aspects of the linguistic environment can be assessed most unambiguously by intervention techniques (Olson, 1968). The importance of environmental stimulation in language deficit has also been questioned by reinforcement theorists (Rheingold et al, 1959; Weisberg, 1963). Infant vocalizations have been demonstrably influenced by reinforcing the child for his spontaneous vocal babbling, but Cazden (1966) questions whether these results should be generalized across the discontinuity which separates pre-linguistic babbling from true verbal behavior.

An interesting study with slightly older children hints at the importance of environmental stimulation (Irwin, 1960). Working-class mothers were provided with books for daily reading beginning at thirteen months. The results at thirty months indicated a significant increase in production of speech sounds compared to a working-class control group. These findings were attributed to a systematic increase in speech sound stimulation; yet it is possible that in the course of reading the mothers also responded to the vocalizations of the child which the reading may have induced (Cazden, 1966). Although the verbal measure in this study was "phoneme frequency" it may bear a low relationship to the structural properties of language (Olson,1968) and although the effects of exposing a child to language and of responding to his language become confounded, it nevertheless provides evidence of the effectiveness of verbal stimulation.

At present, only one attempt has been made to alter the measured "grammatical competence" of lower-class children. Cazden (1966) compared two experimental groups and a control group composed of Negro children aged twenty-eight to thirty-eight months, given two and one-half hours of treatment per week for three months. A "modeled group" received full grammatical sentences in reply to the child's utterances. An "expanded group" had their utterances expanded by an adult to the nearest full grammatical sentences. Both groups improved over the control on measures of grammatical development but the "modeled group" showed the most improvement. Although the study does not support the contention that direct corrective feedback in the form of expansions substantially enhances grammatical competence (Cazden, 1966), it nevertheless suggests that linguistic richness—verbal stimulation per se—may be more important than the reinforcement value of the adult's response to the preceding utterance of the child (Ervin-Tripp, 1966).

In summary, the few intervention studies executed have focused on different linguistic periods (e.g., babbling, verbal behavior) and on different aspects of the child's linguistic system. There is no indication that operant reinforcement training is important in altering phonology or grammar; its effects are probably strongest on fluency, vocabulary selection, etc. (Ervin-Tripp, 1966). Stimulation appears to succeed in areas of grammatical competence. A tentative resolution of the differential effects of stimulation versus reinforcement is attempted by Cazden (1966) in which she suggests that:

> . . . reinforcement, in the classical sense, probably operates to increase vocalizations at the babbling stage of infancy, but once true language begins to develop, there is no clear evidence that any specific kind of adult response, verbal or non-verbal, aids the child's progress. Natural observations and the few existing manipulative studies are consistent with the hypothesis that it is the amount and richness of language stimulation available in the context of face-to-face interaction which is most important. Differential access to such stimulation by children from different subcultural groups can be explained by differences in conditions of their lives (p. 202).

Obviously, the exploration of these differential conditions is at present in the germinal stage.

Bilingualism. The weight of the earlier evidence on bilingualism indicates that it is a retarding factor in language development (Anastasi & de Jesus, 1953; Carrow, 1957; Johnson, 1953; Smith, 1935, 1957). A bilingual environment apparently has little effect on the initial acquisition of language, but does lead to later confusion in idea-word relationships and in language structure and to less mature use of language (Smith, 1935, 1939, 1957). Bilingual Hawaiian children are retarded about three years at the time of school entrance and speak a type of pidgin English (Smith, 1939). Much of this language retardation reflects a loss of vocabulary in the first language that is not fully compensated for by a corresponding gain in the second language (Carrow, 1957; Leopold, 1939; Smith, 1957). Thus, bilingual children possess below average vocabularies in both languages and even their combined vocabulary is generally inferior to the vocabulary of their monolingual counterparts (Smith, 1949, 1957).

Although bilingualism clearly does not inhibit the development of non-verbal intelligence (Darcy, 1946; Johnson, 1953; Jones, 1953), it does have an adverse effect on the growth of functional intelligence as measured by verbal tests (Carrow, 1957). Some of this influence can undoubtedly be attributed to language handicap and to socioeconomic factors described above.

The bulk of the results summarized, however, should be examined from the perspective that, in some cases, in many of these studies, we are actually measuring monolingual children who are thrust into a second language in an entirely different social context (Bossard, 1954; Soffietti, 1955). The effect of this factor may account for the fact that much of the superiority of mono-lingual children in verbal tests of intelligence is retained even when these children are matched with bilinguals on the basis of social class status (Darcy, 1946), non-verbal I.Q., and English reading ability (Jones, 1953). Where the child uses one language at home and another in school, there is likely to be a separate development of vocabulary and syntax (Ervin-Tripp, 1966). The bifurcation can be diminished if the home has *information-exchanging habits* and a scholastic bent or if the school teaches the child to read in his home language, using the standardized literacy form of the home language, and making him familiar with its written traditions (Ervin-Tripp, 1966). Ervin-Tripp (1966) quotes several studies which suggest that in such situations, the child may have intellectual advantages and greater conceptual flexibility in both languages. In view of major gaps in our knowledge, how-ever, any conclusions regarding the effects of bilingualism on the develop-ment of language and intellectual development can only be accepted on a highly tentative basis.

LANGUAGE AND OTHER ASPECTS OF DEVELOPMENT

It is evident that language enters into almost every aspect of development and it would be impossible in this chapter to consider all of these relationships in detail. The role of language in relation to cognition will be considered in the next chapter, and the present discussion will limit itself to the psycho-social and interpersonal aspects of language.

Language and Ego Development

The importance of the impact of language on ego development stems from a variety of reasons. Language is necessary for the abstraction, consolidation, and differentiation of the self-concept, and for such complex aspects of ego functioning as self-criticism, ego involvement, the setting of levels of aspiration, competition, assimilation of values, and identification with various reference groups. It provides a medium for the expression of self-assertion, defiance, and negativism that becomes progressively more subtle, indirect, and circumlocutious with increasing age.

The language of the child also furnishes a window for observing changes in his feelings, self-concepts, ways of thinking, and *Weltanschauung*. As his interpersonal relationships become more stabilized and the expression of his feelings more restrained, the emotional tone of his language becomes less intense (McCarthy, 1954; Shirley, 1938). As the sphere of his interests and activity widens, the proper nouns in his conversation make increasingly greater reference to persons and places remote from home and the immediate neighborhood (Davis, 1937). As he becomes progressively less cocksure of his opinions during the elementary school years, he uses more and more expressions that are indicative of uncertainty (L'Abate, 1956).

Egocentric versus Sociocentric Communication

A more controversial topic in language development centers aroung the extent to which the young child's language may be considered "egocentric" or "socialized." In terms of the sheer frequency of ego reference (Fisher, 1934) and use of "I" (Jersild *et al*, 1938; Smith, 1926), there seems to be little question that he has a subjectivistic approach to experience. It is hardly surprising that his own activities are central in his psychological field, that he makes little reference to the experience of others, and that he fails to distinguish adequately between his own impressions and the objective properties of the situation (Sullivan and Hunt, 1967). Furthermore, unlike adults and older children, he has not yet learned to suppress the more obnoxious features of self-preoccupation or to confine his subjectivism to unvocalized thought (Vygotsky, 1962). Much more debatable is Piaget's (1926) assertion that the child's speech prior to the age of seven or eight is egocentric in the sense of being a monologue that disregards the point of view of the hearer and is not directed toward a genuine interchange of ideas. Early studies repeating Piaget's work have obtained a much smaller percentage of egocentric speech (McCarthy, 1930, 1954); in addition they have indicated that adults are also guilty of egocentric speech (Henle and Hubbell, 1938), and that there is no definite age at which egocentric speech is replaced by socialized speech. Nevertheless, even if children's speech is not as egocentric and the transition to socialized speech is not as abrupt as Piaget claimed, it is difficult to dismiss other independently obtained evidence which indicates that with increasing age children become aware of the needs, feelings, and viewpoints of others and are more able to consider situations from the standpoint of another person (see Chapter 15). Moreover, a recent replication study comes much closer to Piaget's original findings (Neville, 1967b).* That overlapping occurs between age groups does not in any way vitiate the reality of mean differences between these groups or render impossible the designation of stages of development (see p. 101).

More recently, these earlier findings on Piagetian "egocentrism" have been recast to answer questions about children's communication efficiency. Specifically, the research centers around the developmental aspects of children's *encoding* and *decoding* ability. Decoding ability focuses on comprehension and is seen in the translation of communicated messages. Encoding ability focuses on production and is seen in the transmission of communicated messages. The importance of these encoding skills is stressed by Brown (1965) when he states:

> . . . it is necessary to control a lexicon and also the grammar of the language. But something else is needed. The encoder must realistically assess the informational requirements of his decoder. Children are not very good at this last aspect of the game. They have a tendency to project their own information into their auditors, a tendency that Piaget has called "egocentric" (p. 340).

Current studies assessing communication abilities usually pair two children off with one another as encoder and decoder or study a child encoding to an adult. The tasks involve the encoding and decoding of real stories, visual discriminations, or object placements. The subject populations vary from preschool children to adolescents. In general, success at encoding and decoding messages increases with age (Cowan, 1967; Flavell, 1966; Fry, 1967; Glucksberg and Krauss, 1967; Neville, 1967b). With increasing age, children encoders utilize corrective feedback from the listener (decoder) (Fry, 1967), and take into consideration the informational requirements of the listener (Cowan, 1967; Flavell, 1966; Fry, 1967; Glucksberg et al, 1967). More specifically, social class differences when demonstrated depended on the specific pairs of encoders and decoders. Middle-class children encoded and decoded better among themselves when compared to lower-class children, but both of the above pairings fared better than middle-lower class pairs (Cowan, 1967). Upon completion of the task however, middle-lower class pairs had improved more than lower-class pairs (Cowan, 1967). Children encode more to adults than to other children (i.e., talk more to adults and use more subordinate clauses) (Frail, Lunberg, and Levin, 1967) and appear to decode messages better from adults (Glucksberg, Krauss, and Weisberg, 1966). Sex differences on Piagetian stories consistently, though nonsignificantly, favored females between the ages of six and eight years (Neville,

---

*As with other earlier replications of Piaget's work, the replication procedure may have been somewhat different than Piaget's original method. Neville (1967a) obtained different sets of results by varying the experimental procedures.

1967b), and were significant on an instruction placement task for children between the ages of ten and eleven (Cowan, 1967).

In summary, general trends in communication efficiency indicate increasing encoding and decoding ability with age. The trends in decoding ability are consistent with findings which indicate greater listening acuity with age (Maccoby and Konrad, 1966, 1967). Social class differences in communication efficiency deserve closer scrutiny, especially where these differences hamper effective communication between teacher and child (Peisach, 1965).

CHAPTER 15

General Aspects of Perceptual and Cognitive Development

THE TREATMENT OF PERCEPTION and cognition under one chapter heading rests on the assumption that there is a very close relationship between the two. In the broadest interpretation, "cognitive processes" refer to those processes through which "knowledge" is acquired and maintained (Berlyne, 1966). The most important problem defining the area of cognitive development is the attempt to comprehend how an organism of a particular kind, in its encounters with phenomena, constructs the world (Kessen, 1966). It is obvious from this definition of the problem that cognition must be intrinsically related to perceptual processes. Such terms as sensation, perception, imagery, retention, recall, problem-solving, and thinking, etc., are all aspects of cognition (Neisser, 1967). Thus in discussing perception and cognition:

> It is more logical to define the simplest act of perception as a process incorporating rudiments of ideation. The abstracting of attributes is almost necessarily integral to perception, while higher intellectual activities evolve from a process of combining the simpler perceptual acts (Fowler, 1962a, p. 116).

This chapter will consider the gross developmental changes in perception and cognition and the factors which facilitate or impede this development at different phases of the life cycle. The subsequent chapter will consider more specific aspects of cognitive development such as developmental trends in memory, concept acquisition, problem solving, etc.

INTERPRETING THE INFANT'S COGNITIVE EXPERIENCE

Before the infant is capable of giving verbal introspective reports we can only speculate on the nature of his cognitive experience. Such speculations, which must rest on inferences from behavior, on logical plausibility, and on estimates of prevailing cognitive sophistication, are obviously subject to all of the serious errors of "adultomorphism". In the past decade, several investigators have devised ingenious techniques in order to make initial assessment of the infant's perceptual and conceptual experiences (e.g., Bower, 1966; Fantz & Nevis, 1967; Piaget, 1952; White, 1965; White, Castle & Held, 1964).

Although it appears that the objective world has no conceptual existence for the neonate (Piaget, 1952), it may nevertheless serve to evoke innately organized responses such as grasping and pursuit (White, 1965). In spite of the lack of "representational" processes in the newborn, he is not a "tabula rasa" and demonstrates this in his early perceptual preferences for certain patterns and forms (Fantz & Nevis, 1967). Experiments on eight-week old infants indicate that they are capable of depth discrimination, orientation discrimination, size constancy, etc.; these findings appear to be at odds with an "empiricist's" interpretation of perception and cognition (Bower, 1966). However it would be unwise to overinterpret such evidence as indicative of psychological processes qualitatively similar to perception and cognition in the older individual. The conceptual bridge between early cognitive experiences and later cognitive manifestations involves a long and arduous route, as is illustrated by the massive developmental findings of Piaget and his followers. The course of cognitive development in infancy is also coextensive with the early development of self-concept, the differentiation between self and environment, and the emergence of differentiated emotions and notions of executive dependence and volitional omnipotence (see p. 252). Following the acquisition of language, more complex features of cognitive development (see p. 256), concept formation, (see p. 611), problem solving (see p. 630), and reasoning (see p. 570) become evident. The study of conceptual and perceptual processes in the infant alerts one to the problem to be encountered in later cognitive development. It is sobering to consider that:

> The discovery of such complexities and unknowns in the perceptual, motivational, and learning processes of young infants should remind us of the humorous side of our presumptuous though necessary attempts as experimental psychologists to reduce to a few scientifically elegant statements the behavior of adults, who presumably have not become less complex with age and experience (Fantz & Nevis, 1967, pp. 88-89.)

PERCEPTUAL DEVELOPMENT*

We have already considered perception as a process mediating the interaction of social and endogeneous factors in ego development (see p. 248). Level of perceptual maturity has also been regarded throughout as a crucial determining factor in ego, emotional, moral and social development. In this section we propose to consider perceptual development itself, that is, the factors that bring about age level changes in maturity of perceptual func-

---

*Reviews of the literature are available. See Gibson, 1963, 1969; Kidd & Rivoire, 1966; Pick, 1963; Von Fieandt & Wertheimer, 1969; Wohlwill, 1960. Discussion of methodology may be found in Gibson, 1969; Gibson & Olum, 1960.

tioning. Before turning to this task, however, it may be worthwhile to indicate briefly the various factors that determine the nature of any given perception.

A particular perceptual experience always reflects interaction between internal and external determinants. *External* determinants include such structural characteristics of the physical stimulus situation as figure-ground relationships, proximity, similarity, contrast, continuity, etc., as well as various contextual factors. Thus, when talking about "sense perception," it is necessary to distinguish it from merely sensing as in "having sensation"; the former is sensitivity to information as determined by the structural characteristics, while the latter is simply sensitivity to energy, or to receptors excited by energy (J. J. Gibson, 1966). *Internal* determinants include: (a) "contemporaneous" variables, such as the nature of receptor and central processes involved in sensation, (b) transitory states of the organism that influence perceptual thresholds (e.g., needs, values, expectancies, and sets), and (c) developmental factors. The *developmental* category of internal determinants refers to variables whose effects vary with the maturity level and experience of the child. It includes: (1) structural and functional maturation of the cerebral cortex, during the first few months of life, which provides the neural substrate necessary for more advanced perceptual development (Scheibel & Scheibel, 1964); (2) progressive enculturation and language development, resulting in the child's gradual acquisition of the perceptual sensitivities and patterning proclivities typical of the adult members of his culture (Vygotsky, 1966); (3) changes in personality organization (e.g., ego devaluation, decreased hedonism) that are responsible in part for such perceptual trends as the decline in autism and egocentricity (see Chapter 8); and (4) progressive cognitive sophistication, both in general and in particular areas of experience.

We are concerned in this chapter with those determinants of perception that change as a function of increasing age. Of these, the only one requiring extensive discussion is cognitive sophistication. However, the problem that will first receive some brief attention is a "non-developmental" one, namely, the way in which transitory need states influence perception. This exception is made in order to alert the reader to some motivational aspects of perception. In any case, the problem does have developmental aspects, for there is an apparent decline with advancing age in the effects of needs and desires on perceptual outcomes.

Effects of Transitory Need States on Perception

Despite some methodological ambiguities in experimental design (Bruner & Goodman, 1947; Carter & Schooler, 1949; Dukes, 1955; Gibson, 1963; Postman, 1953) there seems to be little doubt that transitory motivational states effect perceptual responses. It is likely that needs, likes, and dislikes affect perception by directing attention toward relevant aspects of incoming stimulation. This can be seen in accentuation, sensitization, and the increased tendency to perceive desired objects in ambiguous stimulus configurations under conditions of extreme need. For example, perceptual awareness can be enhanced by food deprivation (Crumpton, Wine & Drenick, 1967; Gordon & Spence, 1966). In addition, poor children are more prone than rich children to overestimate the size of coins when making their judgments from memory (Carter & Schooler, 1949). This finding, however is somewhat limited by the fact that the perceptual overestimation made by poor children tends to decrease with age (Rosenthal, 1968), perhaps because of the increasing operation of "cognitive dissonance" factors. In any case, the influence of motivational determinants seems to be proportional to the ambiguity of the external (stimulus) determinants (Carter & Schooler, 1949; Crumpton, et al, 1967; Gordon & Spence, 1966).

At present, it is still difficult to say what types of mechanisms mediate the effects of motivational factors. Does motivation influence perception directly by its selective function of making effective some of the potential stimulation (Gibson, 1963), or does its effect reflect the operation of such principles of associative learning as frequency, recency, and reinforcement? Postman (1953, 1963) believes that the latter possibility can account for all of the empirical findings in this area if the methodological and analytical language of perception and learning converge. These two possibilities concerning the way motivation affects perception however, are not necessarily mutually exclusive. If perceptual responses are regarded as analogous to behavioral responses, it follows that drive determinants could induce *transitory* and selectively generalized lowering of perceptual response thresholds. This does not in any way exclude the possibility that the more *permanent strength* of a given perceptual response disposition is governed by general principles of learning.

Perceptual Learning

Implicit in the notion that perception is a multi-determined phenomenon is a rejection of the nativistic view that the nature of the percept is inherent in the coercive organizational properties of the stimulus field and in the *predeterminedly* parallel organization of the neural traces of that field (Allport, 1955; Pronko, Ebert & Greenberg, 1966). This is not to deny that structural and functional properties of receptors influence perception or that perceptual patterning predispositions exist (i.e., some responses are inherently more relevant or elicitable than others under specified conditions of need and stimulation). Nevertheless, if what is perceived represents the outcome of interaction between sensory input and an experientially acquired and constantly developing cognitive and personality structure, it is impossible to escape the conclusion that percepts are largely learned. Perception is a process by which one gets information about the world around him (Gibson, 1969). Perceptual learning is an increase in the ability of an organism to get information from its environment, as a result of practice or experience (Gibson, 1969). Since perception includes all of the senses it may be interpreted as covering the awareness of complex environmental situations as well as single objects (Allport, 1955). Perceptual learning occurs in the sense that older children perceive the stimulus world differently than do younger children because the former have, as the major internal variable in the interactional process determining perception, a more sophisticated cognitive structure. Learning in this sense does not imply that perceptual development proceeds from a stable *tabula rasa* basis, that inherent perceptual capacities are nonexistant, or that one type of percept is as likely to occur as another irrespective of stimulus content, receptor and neural organization, or genically determined patterning predispositions.

Normal growth in perceptual capacity depends on progressive cognitive sophistication derived from cumulative experience with a wide range of stimulation. If such experience is unduly restricted, cognitive sophistication and hence perceptual learning fail to take place. This is demonstrated in dramatic fashion by the perceptual immaturity and the extremely slow development of discriminative abilities in individuals who first acquire vision in adult life as a result of successful operations on congenital cataracts. A preliminary period of orientation is necessary before they can organize visual experience, make even simple discriminations between geometrical figures, or recognize the same objects in different contexts (Hebb, 1949). Similar evidence has been presented for chimpanzees reared in darkness. Furthermore, repeated exposure to particular kinds of perceptual discrimination problems greatly enhances educability. As a consequence of interproblem learning and the formation of learning sets, discriminations are made rapidly and proficiently (Harlow, 1949; Reese, 1963). In this context, "learning how to learn" means learning how to perceive. Children show much more rapid and proficient perceptual discrimination learning as indicated by "learning set" capabilities, than do animals (Reese, 1963).

It is clear that in order to delineate developmental trends in perception (or progressive stages in perceptual learning) one must indicate what kinds of changes occur during the course of becoming more cognitively sophisticated. This, naturally, will not explain *how* perceptual learning actually occurs. It will merely identify component determinants of perceptual development and correlative age level changes in the nature of perception. The precise mechanisms mediating the effects of these determinants can only be uncovered by focusing research efforts on this particular aspect of perceptual learning.

In considering the nature of cognitive sophistication it is also necessary to distinguish between (a) *general* attributes that reflect the cumulative impact of *all* kinds of experience as well as the more advanced levels of ideational organization and functioning, and (b) cognitive sophistication in *particular* areas of experience. Thus, with increasing age, the child's cognitive structure becomes generally more sophisticated irrespective of the specific nature of his experience, and this increased sophistication affects in a general way the maturity level of any percept. On the other hand, his actual perceptual dispositions with respect to particular kinds of properties of stimulation mirror most directly the specific types of sophistication acquired in corresponding areas of experience.

GENERAL TRENDS IN THE ATTAINMENT OF COGNITIVE SOPHISTICATION

In this section we propose to specify the characteristics of cognitive sophistication during infancy and childhood.* These characteristics not only have relevance for developmental trends in perception, but also have an important bearing on age level changes in such other aspects of cognitive functioning as memory, concept formation, and problem solving.

Widening and Increasing Complexity of Cognitive Field. Kindergarten and first-grade children tend to be relatively oblivious of events in the environment which have no personal or immediate significance for them (Russell, 1940). During the elementary school years, however, the world of time and space is gradually extended beyond the confines of home, neighborhood, personal concern, and the immediate present to include the wider community, the globe, the historical past, and the historical future. For example, as the child grows older he begins to realize that his own nationality is considered foreign by other peoples and that foreigners are not foreigners at home (Lambert & Klineberg, 1967). The child's conception of national groupings seems to widen so that increasingly with age there is equal attention given to homeland and foreign groups; both of these can be thought of with a similar degree of objectivity (Lambert & Klineberg, 1967). An entirely new perceptual vista involving complex and subtle shades of meaning and relationship is opened to view as children become responsive to written symbols and abstractions. Their heroes tend to be drawn less from their immediate surroundings and more from historical, fictional, and public characters (Hill, 1930); and in free discussion periods they make increasing reference to national and international news in contradistinction to events which they witness or are

---

In any given instance of cognitive sophistication influencing an ideational process, no explicit designation concerning which attributes of sophistication are general and which reflect particular experience will be made, for the appropriate designation will be evident from the context.

involved in personally (Baker, 1942). Finally, widening of the temporal field also makes possible more long-range planning and anticipation of future consequences.

Increasing Familiarity of the Psychological World. One of the most important consequences of repeated encounters with the same array of stimulation is an increase in the familiarity or recognizability of the stimuli in question (Draguns and Multari, 1961; Gollin, 1965). This seems to be a necessary preliminary step before differentiation of the stimulus field is possible (Gibson & Gibson, 1955). As perception develops, there is a detection of variables of stimulation, which, even though they may have been present, were not previously registered (Gibson, 1969). Thus, perception becomes more differentiated and more precise with growth and continued exposure to the world of stimuli (Gibson, 1969). Much of the facilitation of perceptual discrimination that occurs as a result of the formation of "learning sets" (Harlow 1949; Reese, 1963) can undoubtedly be attributed to the acquisition of a general background of familiarity. Although certain types of stimulus patterns appear to be discriminated in early infancy (e.g., Fantz & Nevis, 1967), much of the stimulus world is unfamiliar to the infant, and this leads to a slow development of perceptual discrimination in many areas of experience.

Decreasing Dependence of Perception on the Stimulus Field. As the child's cognitive structure becomes increasingly more elaborate and systematized, the stimulus field correspondingly tends to become a decreasingly important determinant of perception (Witkin *et al*, 1962). Percepts become less stimulus-bound and less dependent on sensory information. Another way of conceptualizing this development is to say that the laws of field organization are much less compelling to older than to younger children (Baldwin & Wellman, 1928; Sullivan & Hunt, 1967). More accurate perception is correlated with advancing age, since the child is increasingly able to "decenter" his perceptual judgments from the pull of the stimulus field (Pollock, 1969). Four kinds of consequences are evident from this shift in the relative significance of stimulus conditions and cognitive organization in the determination of perception.

First, there appears to be evidence of a developmental shift in judgmental activity, between the ages of five and seven years, from dependence upon sensory-perceptual properties to a reliance upon more inferential conceptual manipulations (S. H. White, 1963). This shift can be seen in social judgments (Gollin, 1965), development of conceptual styles (Kagen, Moss & Sigel, 1963), and in Piagetian conservation tasks (Bruner, 1966; Piaget, 1960). In general, the shift can be considered as a movement away from a "perception bound" thinking to a more "deductive" orientation (Elkind & Scott, 1962; Halpern, 1965; Piaget, 1960; Wohlwill, 1962).

Second, as children grow older they become more independent of the immediate perceptual field and develop greater flexibility in dealing with perceptual input (Crandall & Sinkeldam, 1964; Falk, 1968; Sullivan & Hunt, 1967). Thus, as elementary school children grow older, they develop more sophisticated abilities for dealing with figure-ground problems in embedded figure tasks (Crandall & Sinkeldam, 1964), and greater facility for coordinating their own and others' spatial perspectives (Sullivan & Hunt, 1967).

Third, older children are better able to form complete percepts from only partial and indirectly relevant sensory input. Ability to recognize only partially complete representations of objects increases with advancing age (Gollin, 1956, 1958, 1965). By utilizing information from contextual and auxiliary cues, older children are able to make perceptual inferences that go beyond the information given in the immediate stimulus situation (Bruner, 1957). This tendency accounts in part for age-related changes in certain types of illusions, e.g., the size-weight illusion which appears to increase with age (Pollock, 1969; Wohlwill, 1960).

Finally, new stimulus information tends, if at all possible, to be subsumed under appropriate existing categories of objects and phenomena in the individual's cognitive organization. The formation of "concepts" increasingly demands that pertinent first-hand information be subsumed and integrated into the individual's "cognitive structure." In order to subsume information meaningfully it is frequently necessary to distort or disregard some of the stimulus input. Thus, the learning of controversial materials that are congruous or incongruous with the child's attitude structure is, respectively, enhanced or inhibited (Ausubel, 1968). When attitudes toward controversial material are favorable, children find it very easy to assimilate and learn the material since the cognitive component of the attitude is well-established and the children have clear, stable and relevant anchoring ideas for incorporating the new material. When, however, their attitudes toward the controversial material are unfavorable, all of these factors operate in precisely the opposite direction (Ausubel, 1968). Expectancies established on the basis of past experience also tend to force stimulus properties into preconceived perceptual molds even if the actual stimuli are partly incongruous with the anticipated percepts.

Acquisition of Object Permanence and Constancy. One of the earliest and most persistent controversies in the study of perception has been the question of the perceived constancy of objects and its development in the child (Gibson, 1969). Certainly an important aspect of cognitive sophistication is learning that objects have permanent properties despite fluctuations in sensory data (Piaget, 1954, Werner & Kaplan, 1956; Wohlwill, 1963). To take the example of vision, constancy here refers to the tendency for perceived sizes, shapes, and colors of objects to remain relatively invariant regardless of changes in the sizes, shapes and colors of their retinal images (Wohlwill, 1963). In order to perceive accurately the permanent properties of objects, the child must learn to discount contextual sensory information that would otherwise modify the essential identifying characteristics of such objects. If he thus learns to perceive the permanent external world as it actually exists rather than as it appears from the images it projects on his receptors, he acquires a significant advantage in adapting to physical reality. Although some aspects of perceptual size and shape constancy appear in the early months of life (Bower, 1966; Cruikshank, 1941), it may be said with some qualification that, with advancing age, objects tend to be increasingly perceived as possessing a constant size, form, and color.* Under certain conditions, however, there is a contradiction to this developmental trend toward increased constancy. For example, there is a tendency toward overestimation of objective size that increases with age (Gibson, 1969). These errors of overestimation occur only with respect to sizes of objects located far from the observer (Gibson, 1969; Pollock, 1969; Wohlwill, 1963). This lack of constancy is not reflective of confusion due to differential retinal images, as it is in children; overconstancy (overestimation) here is, rather, due to more sophisticated differentiation of independent dimensions of judgment from earlier perceptions of an unanalyzed object (Gibson, 1969). Thus, errors in size estimation are thought to result from the operation of more sophisticated analytic attitudes (Gibson, 1969), and this interpretation is partly supported by the fact that more intelligent children are more prone to errors of overestimation (Gibson, 1969; Pollock, 1969). Thus, for size (and in addition for shape), it may be said that cognitive sophistication does not always manifest itself in the acquisition of constancy.

Another manifestation of the acquisition of object permanence is the emergence, at about the latter part of the first year, of behavior (e.g., persistant searching) that reveals a belief in the continuing existence of objects even when they are partially or wholly removed from view (Piaget, 1954; Charlesworth, 1966; De-carie, 1965; Escalona & Corman, 1967; Hunt, Uzgiris & Wachs, 1967). As the child comes to appreciate the presence of objects independent of his perception, he is also constructing primitive concepts of space, time, causality, etc. (Sullivan, 1967a). The construction and development of object permanence is a precursor and prerequisite to the various manifestations of the "conservation" (Langer, 1969b) which will increasingly demonstrate the child's advancing ability to bring order and coherence into his phenomenal world (see p. 576). The development of object permanence, therefore, leads the child to postulate a world of enduring objects that can be explored through different senses, and to

---

*Several reviews and interpretive commentaries on perceptual constancy are available (See Gibson, 1963, 1969; Pollock, 1969; Wohlwill, 1960, 1963).

substitute this for the apparent fleeting experiences with which he seemed to begin (Wallach, 1963).

Another type of perceptual constancy is reflective of anticipatory "sets" and established categorical propositions. This tendency enables a child to maintain a relatively constant view of significant persons or things in his psychological world in the face of transitory, non-representative fluctuations in their behavior. This phenomena is seen in the increasing tendency with age to maintain the generic category of identity after apparent transformation (DeVries, 1969). If carried too far however, it interferes with the perception of actual (more permanent) changes in the demands and expectations of his social environment. Baldwin (1955) also speaks of "value constancy" by which he means the child's growing capacity to perceive the intrinsic value of a goal or incentive irrespective of such essentially irrelevant considerations as remoteness. However, the ability to strive for long-range goals also depends upon widening of the temporal field, possession of a sufficient backlog of experience as a basis for anticipation, facility in verbal pre-testing of alternatives, and interiorization of parental and cultural standards of maturity (Mischel, 1961a, 1961b, 1961c; Terrell, 1965.

Increasing Differentiation and Specificity of Cognition. Werner (1967) has advanced an orthogenetic principle of development which states that development proceeds from a state of relative globality and lack of differentiation to a state of increasing differentiation, articulation and hierarchic integration. It is difficult to say how pervasive this process is in all aspects of development, but it can certainly be demonstrated in several specific aspects of development. In the area of perception, differentiation refers to the increasing tendency with repeated exposures to a given array of stimulation to perceive distinctions, separate regions, and detailed structure in what originally appeared to be a global and homogeneous field (J. J. Gibson, 1953; E. J. Gibson, 1963, 1969; Gochman, 1966). As a result, stimuli that at first seem to be functionally identical gradually begin to acquire distinctiveness (Gibson, 1969). We have already referred to the young child's difficulty in discriminating between a smiling and scowling face, between subject and object, reality and fantasy, the self- and the not-self. With increasing age he not only learns to make these distinctions, but also shows a gradual improvement in his ability to make finer discriminations in such areas as form and auditory perception (Baldwin & Wellman, 1928; Gibson, 1969). Rorschach records reveal progress over the preschool and elementary school years in elaboration and specification of detail (Ames, Learned, Metraux & Walker, 1953; McLeod, 1950; Werner, 1957). Intersensory integration of equivalence judgments (e.g., integration of haptic-visual systems) increases with age, thus allowing a more flexible and differentiated response to the stimulus world (Abravanel, 1968; Birch & Lefford, 1967). Thus, differentiation of the perceptual-cognitive field appears to be related to the organism's adjust-ment capacities (Gochman, 1966). Lastly, as children grow in cognitive sophistication they tend less to use only the extreme categories of a judg-mental scale.

Two other more indirect manifestations of increasing differentiation might be mentioned briefly. First, older children are better able to distinguish boundaries between figure and ground and are less distracted by obtrusive background factors from perceiving the essential features of a configuration (Witkin *et al*, 1962). Hence, ability to isolate geometric and meaningful figures embedded in a complex background tends to improve with advancing age (Werner & Kaplan, 1963; Witkin *et al*, 1962). Correspondingly, older children reveal a diminished set to respond to the whole figure and a greater facility in fragmenting the total figure, in identifying sub-wholes, and in combining and reorganizing for the purpose of reconstructing the whole figure (Birch & Lefford, 1967). Second, as Baldwin (1955) points out, some part of young children's proclivity for animistic thinking must be attributed to their difficulty in discriminating between what is truly alive and what only apparently possesses some of the attributes of living organisms.

An important by-product of cognitive differentiation is an increase in the precision and specificity and a decrease in the diffuseness of perception after successive exposures to a designated stimulus field (Ames *et al*, 1953; McLeod, 1950; Werner, 1948). A given pattern of stimulation tends to evoke just one instead of several percepts, and a given percept tends to be instigated by only a particular instead of by many patterns of stimulation (J. J. Gibson, 1953; E. Gibson, 1963; 1969).

Transition from Concrete to Abstract. The concrete-abstract dimension will only be briefly discussed here since a more detailed discussion follows under the discussion of general stages of cognitive functioning (see p. 565). As such, cognitive development during childhood is characterized by an in-creasing ability to comprehend and manipulate verbal symbols and to employ abstract, classificatory schemata. This trend has several major, self-evident implications for perceptual and cognitive functioning. First, as already indicated, the anticipation of consequences and pretesting of alternatives is facilitated. Second, the child becomes more responsive to abstract features of his environment and, in turn, apprehends the world more in abstract and categorical terms than in terms of tangible, time-bound, and particularized contexts. Third, perception, imagery and ideation all become less dependent on the physical presence of objects. Finally, the child is able with the aid of verbal symbols and abstractions to handle much more complex problems of logic and reasoning and to generalize much more efficiently.

Transition from Specific to General. With advancing age children tend to perceive, think, and organize their cognitive worlds in increasingly general terms (Ausubel, 1963, 1968; Biber, Murphy, Woodcock & Black, 1942). They show greater understanding of general propositions (Ausubel, 1968; Inhelder & Piaget, 1958) and are less situation-bound in formulating their wishes (Jersild, Markey & Jersild, 1933), rules, and moral judgments (Kohlberg, 1964). This is also expressed in the growing trend to attribute properties to objects and situations on the basis of inference (generalization) rather than on the basis of direct experience (Olver & Hornsby, 1966). At the more complex level of generalizing from categorical propositions to specific instances and vice versa (i.e., in deductive and inductive reasoning), similar developmental trends are apparent (Ausubel, 1968).

Largely accounting for this trend toward increased generalization of cognitive phenomena is the older child's greater ability to use verbal symbols and abstract forms of categorization (Ausubel, 1963, 1968; Flavell, 1969). The availability of verbal symbols facilitates generalization because such symbols are more manipulable and have less particularized connotations than objects or concrete images and because they simplify the process of labelling or identifying a given situation. Abstract categorization facilitates generalization by making it less dependent on *tangibly* perceived similarities and differences (Ausubel, 1968). Hence, more remote degrees of transposition can be effected by older and more intelligent children and in instances where the distinctive properties of a situation can be characterized by a categorical symbol (Brackbill & Koltsova, 1967; Reese, 1963; Spiker, 1956; S. H. White, 1963).

Increasing Detection of Distinctive Features. After repeated exposure to a given array of stimulation, perception tends to become increasingly differentiated and distinctive features of the stimulus field are detected. Learning to detect differences is the defining characteristic of a theory of "distinctive features" in perceptual learning (Gibson, 1963, 1969). In this formulation, the percept only includes those aspects of the stimulus field that are selectively relevant for the particular motivational context currently dominating the individual's attention (Gibson, 1963, 1969). This suggests that with advancing age children learn to structure their percepts along less literal lines. The omission of irrelevant detail in the detection of crucial differences results in a representation of the stimulus field that is synopsized and diagrammatic and that is functionally more manipulable for the purposes of the moment. In other words, it is not the features of the object per se that are important, but rather those features which distinguish it from other objects in relevant ways (Gibson, 1969; Olson, 1969).

Decline in Egocentricity and Subjectivity. * An integral aspect of cognitive sophistication is the decreasing prominence of egocentricity and subjectivity in the child's approach to experience. The importance of this dimension of cognitive sophistication can be partially seen in the number of developmental studies which have recently focused on this aspect of cognitive growth. Moreover, the theoretical significance of a decline in egocentricity is seen in its pervasive significance very early in the life cycle. As Langer (1969b) points out:

> The basic hypothesis about the evolution of the child's interaction with his milieu is that it is directed toward the progressive elaboration of perspectivism. His development is directed toward (a) integrating himself as participant in and member of his social world, that is, acquiring the same type of objective status as other social beings, yet at the same time (b) differentiating himself as a subjective entity that is distinct from other social objects so that he feels and acts as an individual of a particular nature (Langer, 1969b, p. 109).

The differentiation of self from others follows a long progressive development which increasingly results in greater role-taking and perspective-taking abilities in several domains of experience (Sullivan & Hunt, 1967). Not surprisingly, Piaget has been a pioneer in this area of research. The decline in egocentricity and increase of perspectivism with age can be seen in several cognitive domains (Piaget, 1926, 1928, 1929, 1932c). For example, the earliest research on this topic indicates that as the child grows older he is more aware of the thoughts and feelings of others (Piaget, 1926), is more capable of viewing situations from the standpoint of other persons (Piaget, 1928), and effects a more genuine interchange of ideas in discussions (Baker, 1942; Piaget, 1926, 1929). Unlike his younger contemporary he is quite aware of and better able to communicate the workings of his thought processes (Piaget, 1928) and can transcend in his thinking the limits of his own experience (Piaget, 1928, 1929, 1932b). Hence, he tends less to argue from the premise of particular isolated cases and is more able, for purposes of discussion, both to argue from the perspective of another person and to assume the validity of a hypothetical proposition (Piaget, 1928, 1929).

Recent studies related to Piaget's earlier works on decline in egocentrism have tended to corroborate his earlier findings (Flavell, 1969). Studies of ego trends indicate that the child shows increasing ability in representing the perceptual experience of another individual as different from his own (Cowan, 1967; Piaget & Inhelder, 1956; Sullivan & Hunt, 1967), shows greater attention to the informational requirements of the listener or speaker in communication tasks (Cohen & Klein, 1968; Flavell, 1966, 1967, 1969;

**A general review of the literature of all aspects of research related to this topic may be found in Flavell, 1969.*

Flavell & Botkin *et al*, 1968; see also p. 548), demonstrates increasing role-taking, role-playing and empathic ability (Bowers & London, 1965; Burns & Cavey, 1957; Flavell, 1966, 1967, 1969; Flavell *et al*, 1968; Gratch, 1964; Sullivan & Hunt, 1967; Wolfe, 1963), and shows a substantial increase across the middle years of childhood in his ability to explain surface behavior in terms of subsurface cognitions and motives (Feffer, 1959; Feffer & Gourevitch, 1960; Flavell, 1969; Gollin, 1958; Sullivan & Hunt, 1967).

Piaget relates this decline in subjectivity to corresponding decreases with advancing age in animistic and magical thinking, in "nominal realism" and in "moral absolutism." Involved in part in animistic and anthropomorphic thinking is a subjectivistic attribution of the child's own characteristics to inanimate objects and non-humans (Laurendeau & Pinard, 1962; Piaget, 1929). Subjectivity (ethnocentrism) similarly enters into "nominal realism" (Piaget, 1929) and "moral absolutism" (Brooks & Sullivan, 1968; Flavell, 1969; Piaget, 1932a; Stuart, 1967) insofar as the child assumes that the names of objects and the content of moral law in *his* particular culture are inherently and axiomatically given rather than arbitrarily designated or chosen by mutual agreement. Magical thinking, on the other hand, is based on the autistic supposition that, by means of occult verbal formulas, will and desire can be successfully interposed between naturalistically related antecedents and consequences.

Increasing Attentional Capacities. In the past, attentional factors have occupied a peripheral position in accounting for children's learning (S. H. White, 1963) but there is ample current evidence to indicate its importance as a salient dimension in cognitive sophistication (Flavell & Hill, 1969; Lee, La Crosse, Litman, Ogilvie, Stodolsky & White, 1969). The notion of attention is approached in a variety of ways and it is therefore difficult to define (Lee *et al*, 1969). The research on attention has focused on orienting responses, stimulus properties, physiological indices, base rates of responding, techniques of gaining and maintaining attention, distractibility etc., (Lee *et al*, 1969). With qualification, it may be said that the child's "interest span" and "orienting reactions" with certain tasks increase and become more complex with age (Gibson, 1963; Gutteridge, 1935; Van Alstyne, 1932; Zaporozhets & Zinchenko, 1966). Age trends are not always apparent however, since there is both considerable overlapping between age groups and intra-group variability reflecting the influence of factors such as stimulus novelty and complexity (Berlyne, 1969a; Cantor, 1963; Lee *et al*, 1969; Zaporozchets & Zinchenko, 1966), personality (Lee *et al*, 1969), and motivation (Cantor, 1963; Berlyne, 1969a). In spite of these qualifications, it is nevertheless apparent in a summary of the recent literature on attention that older children have distinct advantages over younger children on some attentional tasks (Flavell & Hill, 1969). Thus, older elementary school children are better able to give accurate reproduction of one of two simultaneously presented messages (Flavell & Hill, 1969; Maccoby & Konrad, 1967), have less difficulty in identifying stimuli through visual as well as auditory noise (Flavell & Hill, 1969), and are better able to focus on the relevant versus irrelevant features in a display when the task demands it (Hagen, 1967; Maccoby & Hagen, 1965). Finally, older children seem more able to avoid an attentional commitment to any particular, salient feature before identification of the relevant cues have been established (Flavell & Hill, 1969).

GENERAL STAGES OF INTELLECTUAL DEVELOPMENT

We have already considered the more general criteria for developmental stage and our purpose here will be to explicate this construct within the domain of cognitive development. General theories of intellectual development, such as those advanced by Piaget and his collaborators (Inhelder & Piaget, 1958; Piaget, 1954, 1960), include age-level changes in at least four major areas of cognitive functioning, namely, perception, objectivity-subjectivity, the structure of ideas of knowledge, and the nature of thinking or problem solving. As indicated briefly earlier (see p. 556) cognitive sophistication is partially characterized by an age-related movement along a concrete-abstract dimension. It has been demonstrated that with increasing age, children tend to perceive the stimulus world more in general, abstract, and categorical terms and less in tangible, time-bound and particularized contexts (Gollin, 1958; Piaget, 1960, 1954; Serra, 1953); they demonstrate increasing ability to comprehend and manipulate abstract verbal symbols and relationships and to employ abstract classificatory schemata (Inhelder & Piaget, 1958; 1964; Piaget, 1954, 1960; Wallon, 1952); they are better able to understand ideational relationships without the benefit of direct, tangible experience, of concrete imagery, or of empirical exposure to numerous particular instances of a given concept or proposition (Goldman & Levine, 1963; Inhelder & Piaget, 1958; Szuman, 1951; Werner, 1948); they tend more to infer the properties of objects from their class membership rather than from direct experience or proximate sensory data (Gollin, 1958, 1965; Reichard, Schneider & Rapaport, 1944; Sigel, 1953; Wallon, 1952; Wohlwill, 1960); they are more disposed to use remote and abstract rather than immediate and concrete criterial attributes in classifying phenomena, and to use abstract symbols rather than concrete imagery to represent emerging concepts (Bruner, 1964, 1966; Inhelder & Piaget, 1958; Werner, 1948); and they acquire an ever-increasing repertoire of more inclusive and higher order abstractions (Inhelder & Piaget, 1958; Serra, 1953; Welch, 1940a & b; Werner, 1948).

The Piagetian Stage Construct

Piaget's delineation of qualitatively distinct stages of intellectual development has been a powerful stimulus to research in the area of stage theory constructs, as well as a perennial source of theoretical controversy. Despite the general cogency and heuristic promise of his formulations, however, the issue of stages remains unresolved for a number of reasons.* Some of these reasons, unfortunately, inhere in Piaget's unsystematic methods of conducting his research and reporting his findings.† In the first place, he is almost totally indifferent to problems of sampling, reliability, and statistical significance. He fails to present adequate normative data on age level, sex, and I.Q. differences, to use uniform experimental procedures for all subjects, to designate unambiguous criteria for classifying the responses of his subjects, or to determine inter-rater reliability. In place of statistical analysis of data and customary tests of statistical significance, he offers confirmatory illustrations culled from his protocols. Second, he tends to ignore such obvious and crucial considerations as extent of intersituational generality and relative degree of intra- and inter-stage variability in delineating stages of development. For example, it is not clear whether the inter-situational variability at a given stage is the result of a developmental lag or of task variability and difficulty (Flavell & Wohlwill, 1969). A considerable amount of investigation is required before it can be ascertained precisely which behavioral and conceptual landmarks in psychological development come in an inevitably fixed order and which do not (Hunt, 1969). On this account it is wise to

---

*The reader is encouraged to pursue discussions of Piagetian stage criteria because of the importance of this construct in his theoretical formulation. General references for stage theory criteria have already been given in Chapter 4. Primary references discussing criteria for Piagetian stages of intellectual development may be found in Piaget (1956, 1960, 1967) and Inhelder (1962). See the recent edited volume of Sigel & Hooper (1968), especially the articles by Kohnstamm and by Uzgiris, and the volume of Elkind & Flavell (1969), with attention to the articles by Flavell & Wohlwill and by Pinard & Laurendeau. Discussions by Langer (1969b); Flavell (1963); Furth (1969); Laurendeau & Pinard (1962); Hunt (1961, 1969); Sullivan (1967a, 1968); and Turiel (1968) are also appropriate to this topic.

†In the past few years, the findings of other investigators (Almy, Chittenden & Miller, 1966; Braine, 1959; Bruner et al., 1966; Case & Collinson, 1962; Dodwell, 1960, 1961; Dubreuil & Boisclair, 1960; Elkind, 1961; Ervin, 1960; Feigenbaum, 1963; R. J. Goldman, 1965; Hood, 1962; S. Jackson, 1965; Koolistra, 1963; Laurendeau & Pinard, 1962; Lovell, 1959a,b, 1961a; Lovell & Ogilvie, 1960; Lunzer, 1960; Mannix, 1960; Peel, 1959; Smedslund, 1960, 1961; Wohlwill, 1960; Yudin & Kates, 1963) have, on the whole, been in general agreement with Piaget's more recent formulations regarding stages of intellectual development. They differ from Piaget's findings less in terms of the development sequences identified than in the specification of different age levels for particular stages, in exhibiting greater intra-stage variability, and in manifesting less inter-situational and inter-task generality. Nevertheless, rigorous developmental data, especially of a longitudinal nature (such as that of Almy et al., 1966) are required to substantiate Piaget's conclusions, and to date, such data have rarely been presented.

consider that the particular stage breakdown that Piaget has described may be the result of his emphasis of certain aspects of cognitive experience. As Flavell and Wohlwill (1969) tersely put it:

> We wonder how much the current picture of uneven development owes to our current knowledge or, if you prefer, our current ignorance. It is largely based on Piaget's theory and research which, properly and inevitably, have been highly selective with regard to methods used and phenomena studied. We should not be at all surprised to find some future theorist making an excellent case for the simply momentous cognitive changes that take place, say during the three- to five-year-old span. Since his discoveries would not likely gainsay the hard core of Piaget's accomplishments, the outcome would be that apparent uneveness across one segment of childhood is effectively reduced. Developmentalists would then say that some very important things happen between three and five and that some other things, quite different, but equally important, happen between five and seven (pp. 81-82).

Third, the cross-sectional observations Piaget uses to measure developmental change (observations on *different* age groups of children) are particularly ill-adapted for his purposes. The transitional stages and qualitative discontinuities he purports to find can be convincingly demonstrated only by longitudinally extended studies of the *same* children. Logical inference is not an adequate substitute for empirical data in naturalistic investigation. To date, the only longitudinal information concerning Piagetian phenomena comes from observations of Piaget's own three children (Piaget, 1952, 1953, 1954) and from investigations on older children (Almy *et al*, 1966; Inhelder, 1962). Finally, Piaget refines, elaborates, and rationalizes the subdivision of his stages to a degree that goes beyond the data. For example, there seems to be no evidence that children use all of the concrete operational groupings or that this is necessary for the requirements of the theory (Baldwin, 1967). Hence, the psychological plausibility and freshness of the general outline of his theory tend to become engulfed by a welter of logical gymnastics and abstruse disorganized speculation.

Criteria of Piaget's Developmental Stages. Piaget and others have frequently delineated the formal characteristics which are essential to a stage theoretical construct (Inhelder, 1962; Kohlberg, 1968, 1969; Piaget, 1956, 1960, 1967; Pinard & Laurendeau, 1969; Sullivan, 1969; Turiel, 1968). Briefly, to recapitulate, stage criteria for a structural conception of cognitive development involve four parameters (Inhelder, 1962). First, each stage involves a period of formation (genesis) and a period of attainment. Attainment is characterized by a progressive organization of a composite structure of mental operations. Second, each structure constitutes at the same time the attainment of one stage and the starting point of the next stage. Third, the order of succession of stages is constant. Age of attainment can vary within certain limits as a function of factors of motivation, exercise, cultural milieu, etc. Finally, the transition from an earlier to a later stage follows a law of implication analogous to the process of integration, with preceding structures becoming a part of later structures (Inhelder, 1962).

Although many legitimate criticisms and questions can be made of these criteria (see for example, Flavell & Wohlwill, 1969; Pinard & Laurendeau, 1969), it would seem that critics' unwarranted or gratuitous assumptions regarding such criteria have done more to prevent the resolution of disagreement concerning stages of intellectual development than have Piaget's methodological shortcomings. Many American psychologists and educators, for example, have been sharply critical of Piaget's designation of stages for the concrete-abstract dimension of cognitive development. They argue that the transition between these stages occurs gradually rather than abruptly; variability exists, both between different cultures and within a given culture, with respect to the age at which the transition takes place; fluctuations occur over time in the level of cognitive functioning manifested by a given child; the transition to the formal stage occurs at different ages both for different subject-matter fields and for component sub-areas within a particular field; and that environmental as well as endogenous factors have a demonstrable influence on the rate of cognitive development. For all of these reasons, therefore, they deny the validity of Piaget's designated stages.

We have already considered (see p. 102) some of the criticisms which appear to be relevant to Piaget's stage criteria. These include the facts that stages of development need not succeed each other abruptly even though they are *qualitatively* discontinuous in process from one to another; that a given stage need not always occur at the *same* age in every culture; that certain amounts of overlapping among age groups are apparent; and that *complete* consistency and generality of stage behavior are lacking. We concluded (see p. 109) that none of these phenomena fail to fit a stage theory formulation.

It is also erroneous to consider Piaget's theory of developmental stages to be completely invalidated by the fact that they are sensitive to environmental influence (see p. 104) since Piaget recognizes this factor to a limited extent. However, it appears that he and his followers have not taken sufficient account of environment. Piaget states that four major factors influence changes in intellectual development, namely, maturation, physical experience, social experience and equilibration (see pp. 27-28). His emphasis on "equilibration" as a major *delineation* and his virtual denigration of learning has, from our perspective, forced him into a predeterministic position somewhat like that of Gesell, although strictly speaking Piaget is not a maturationist. Nevertheless, many of his less astute followers have by . . .

. . . attributing such discontinuities in behavior too readily to maturation [led to] . . . our traditional blind alley because it has long served to stop investigation of the role of experience in their occurrence. Despite the enlargement in the domain of learning implied by Piaget's observations and interpretations in terms of disequilibrium, accommodation, and assimilation, he has been satisfied with his descriptions and interpretations. He has been singularly unconcerned with determining the conditions of a disequilibrium and of testing experimentally the implications of his interpretations . . . (Hunt, 1969, p. 49).

This much is clearly evident from data indicating that schooled African Bush children acquire conservation of volume earlier and give fewer perceptual (as opposed to conceptual) reasons for conservation or nonconservation than do their unschooled counterparts (Greenfield, 1966). Urban living seems to have some of the same effect as schooling in this regard inasmuch as unschooled Hong Kong children do as well as schooled Hong Kong children on conservation tasks, but not as well on a task of combinatorial reasoning (Goodnow & Bethon, 1966).

Quantitative and Qualitative Changes in Intellectual Development

Still another reason for confusion and conflict about the problem of stages in intellectual development inheres in the tendency to adopt an all-or-none position regarding the existence of such stages. Actually, the evidence suggests that some aspects or dimensions of intellectual development are characterized by quantitative or continuous change, whereas others are characterized by qualitative or discontinuous change. It is necessary at the outset to distinguish between problems of continuity and in continuity of stages of intellectual development (Flavell & Wohlwill, 1969; Pinard & Laurendeau, 1969). It is clear that Piaget recognized that some aspects of development cannot be considered discontinuous (e.g., somatic and perceptual development) and therefore in these areas the stage construct is inappropriate (Inhelder, 1962). But the issue of continuity-discontinuity in stages of cognitive development should not be confused with the interpretation that development is without levels or without discernible pauses, since the question here consists only of asking if the changes that intervene in the course of development are of a qualitative nature or only quantitative (Pinard & Laurendeau, 1969).

Some types of logical operations (e.g., equivalence) and some approaches to problem solving (trial-and-error versus insightful) appear to differ in degree rather than in kind from one age level to another.* The evidence

---

*It is important not to confuse quantitative changes in these simple logical operations, from one age level to another, with those changes in logical operations that are reflective of qualitatively different stages along the concrete-abstract dimension of cognitive development (see p. 561). Thus the more significant logical operations (e.g., "reversibility") imply a capability to understand and meaningfully manipulate relationships between secondary obstractions—a capability that is not present in the preoperational (logically "nonoperational") child. Similarly, whether or not a given individual is dependent on concrete-empirical props in performing logical operations determines whether he is in the concrete or abstract stage of logical operations. (See Flavell & Wohlwill (1969) for a more detailed discussion of this issue).

indicates that these kinds of logical operations and problem-solving approaches are employed at all age levels, and differ principally in degree or complexity at different ages (Burt, 1919; Long & Welch, 1941a; Welch & Long, 1943). As Munn (1954) points out, the age differences are partly attributable to disparity in previous experience, motivation, and neuromuscular coordination. Perhaps an even more important source of these age level differences, however, is the child's growing ability to generalize and use abstract symbols. Both trial-and-error and insightful problem solving, for example, are found in preschool children, elementary-school children, adolescents, and adults; the choice between these two approaches at all ages depends on the inherent difficulty of the problem, on the individual's prior background of experience, and on the problem's amenability to logical analysis. It is true that insightful approaches tend to increase with age, but only because increasing ability to generalize and use abstract symbols permits a more hypothesis-oriented approach.

Two dimensions of intellectual development characterized by gradually occurring *qualitative* change, on the other hand, are the transition from subjective to objective thought and the transition from concrete to abstract operations. Acquisition of the ability to separate objective reality from subjective needs and preferences results in the gradual disappearance of autistic, animistic, anthropomorphic, magical, absolutistic, and nominalistic thinking (Piaget, 1928, 1929, 1932a & b). Reference has already been made to studies supporting Piaget's findings (Inhelder & Piaget, 1958; Piaget, 1954b, 1957b, 1960) concerning the transition from concrete to abstract thought.

THE CONCRETE-ABSTRACT DIMENSION OF COGNITIVE DEVELOPMENT*

The concrete-abstract dimension of intellectual development may be divided into four qualitatively distinct developmental stages—the sensorimotor stage, the pre-operational stage, the stage of concrete logical operations, and the stage of abstract logical operations. Before describing specific phenomenal characteristics of these stages it would be helpful to delineate several basic Piagetian concepts in order to inform later discussions on developmental change. Piaget (1960, 1965, 1967) defines intelligence as a

---

*The following description of this aspect of cognitive development is a modified and idiosyncratic interpretation of the account given by Piaget and Inhelder (Inhelder & Piaget, 1958, 1964; Piaget, 1954, 1960). The term "abstract" is used synonymously with Piaget's term "formal". Other descriptions and interpretations of Piaget's concrete-abstract dimensions are available in the following secondary sources: Baldwin, 1967; Berlyne, 1969; Brown, 1965; Elkind, 1967; Flavell, 1963, 1969; Fourth, 1969; Ginsburg & Opper, 1969; Langer, 1969b; Hunt, 1961; Sigel, 1964; Sullivan, 1967a; Wallach, 1963.

process of adaptation and organization. Adaptation is seen as an equilibration (equilibrium) in the organism's interaction with its environment. Organization is the structural side of intelligence and it involves coordination and integration of what Piaget calls schemas. Schemas are defined as essentially repeatable psychological units of intelligent action (Piaget, 1960). The best interpretation of this definition is that schemas are types of "programs" or "strategies" that the individual has at his disposal when interacting with the environment (Sullivan, 1967).

Adaptation involves two invarient processes called assimilation and accommodation. Assimilation is the incorporation of environment into present patterns of behavior. Accommodation is the change in the intellectual structures (schemas) which is necessary in order for the person to adjust to the demands which the external environment makes on him. Equilibration involves a balance between the two invariant processes of assimilation and accommodation. When imbalance occurs, the organism is forced to change its schemas (i.e., strategies) in order to adjust to the demands of the external environment (adaptation). When the organism attempts to adapt to the environment with the already existing schemas, assimilation is said to be in operation. The postulation of *schemas* as mental processes by which past experiences are stored and made partial determinants of present behavior is significant, because it implies that the organism perceives the environment in terms of its existing organization. Disequilibration or imbalance exists when assimilation is unsuccessful. Accommodation occurs as a result of disequilibration and this alteration causes the emergence of new *schemas*. Cognitive development is marked by a series of equilibration-disequilibration states. Stages in Piaget's theory may be considered as particular sets of strategies (schemas) which are in a relative state of equilibration at some point in the child's development (Sullivan, 1967a). The development from one stage to the next in Piaget's framework involves a hierarchial organization of preceding and successive stages. Simply stated, the lower stage is coordinated and integrated into the next higher stage.

Sensori-Motor Stage (Birth to Approximately 2 Years)

The *schemas* present at birth for adaptation and mediation with the environment are few and the coordination and integration between schematic structures are not apparent in the child's actions. The sensori-motor stage involves simple structures (schemas), starting with the inborn reflex mechanisms which increasingly become altered and complicated by the child's interaction with his environment. Characteristically the sensori-motor period is exemplified in those behaviors which are pre-verbal and are not mediated by signs and symbols. At birth, the child mediates with the world with inborn reflex schemas and has no conception of a permanent world outside of his own immediate perceptual experience. One of Piaget's basic assumptions about early sensori-motor development is that there is an expansion from the reflex to more complex modes of behavior, He postulates a functional comparability and developmental continuity between reflex and non-reflex behavioral sequences. Thus, more advanced forms of cortically controlled prehension are said to be derived from the primitive, subcortically regulated reflex (Piaget, 1952). We have already criticized this position since most behavioral change subsumed under motor development occurs in the area of non-reflex activity; this is not necessarily continuous with phenotypically similar reflex activities (Ausubel, 1966). Most of the development and coordination of the schemas results from the child's prolonged every-day contact with the physical environment (Charlesworth, 1969). This continued contact will inevitably lead to structures (schemas) which reflect the invariances and lawfulness characterizing physical phenomena (Charlesworth, 1969).

The fact that the child lacks object permanence (see p. 558 and p. 560) is an initial indication that he, at birth, lacks *representational* symbolic activity. During this period, the child is concerned with objects as objects. Thus, when a toy is hidden from his view, he shows no searching movements, since he has no internal representation of the objective world (i.e., object schemas) outside of immediate perception. Gradually, by the latter part of the first year the child develops object permanence through repeated experience with the environment (Décarie, 1965; Escalona & Corman, 1967; Charlesworth, 1969; Golden & Birns, 1967; Hunt, 1969; Hunt, Wachs & Uzgiris, 1967). As the child constructs object permanence through experience, primitive concepts of space, time, causality, and intentionality, which were not present at birth, develop and are incorporated into present patterns of behavior. These concepts are only distinct on a theoretical level, since they are intricately dependent on one another. In order to have spatial displacements, there must be an orderly, coherent world, which is provided by object constancy. Without object constancy, there could be no further development of objective causality, or objective time, since the relationships of before and after, and cause and effect demand a permanent stabilization and differentiation of environment.

During the sensori-motor stage, schema systems become increasingly differentiated and intercoordinated with one another, as is seen in the development of prehension (Bruner, 1969; Piaget, 1954b; White, 1969). At the earliest phase of sensori-motor intelligence there is the absence of that coordination of sensory systems (i.e., hand, eye, grasp, etc.) which eventually will be apparent in prehensive activity at later phases of sensori-motor intelligence. And, by the end of the sensori-motor stage, the possibility for more elaborate symbolic activity, characterized by language and symbolism, is enhanced by the elaboration and coordination of structures which are necessary prerequisites for more advanced forms of cognition.

Pre-operational Stage (Approximately 2 to 7 Years)

For purposes of clarity we divide the Piagetian stage of preoperational thought into pre-conceptual and intuitive sub-stages. The preoperational stage, in contrast to sensori-motor intelligence, involves the mediation of structures (schemas) which indicate the presence of symbolic representational activity. This symbolic activity is seen in the child's *symbolic play* as well as in his use of language (Piaget, 1952). With the appearance of language, the objective world is now symbolized by a thought process which can be retained by the mind (i.e., primitive symbolic structures). Despite the fact that the child's world is mediated by signs and symbols, in the form of words and images, the child nevertheless operates in a world of pre-concepts. In contrast to adult thought, which is characterized by inductive and deductive reasoning, the child's reasoning is transductive (preconceptual) since he makes no distinction between the general and the particular, and such a distinction is an essential prerequisite for advanced logical reasoning. Transduction is a logic which moves from particular instances to other particular instances. The transductive child demonstrates his logic in his uncertainty as to whether the same object is reappearing or there are different objects in different times and places. For example, walking through the woods, the child does not know whether he sees a succession of different snails, or whether the same snail keeps reappearing. This is an example of what Piaget calls the preconcept (Inhelder & Piaget, 1964; Piaget, 1952, 1960).

Intuitive thought (4 to 7 years) appears to mark the half-way house between preconceptual thought and the more advanced stage of concrete operations. The thought structures (schemas) exemplified in this stage are illustrated in the following problem. The child is presented with two small glasses, A1 and A2, which are identical in height and width dimensions. The child continues to place one bead in each glass until both are filled. The A2 is emptied into a taller but thinner glass B. The child in the preconceptual phase thinks that the amount of beads has changed in the process, even though he says no beads were removed or added. When glasses B and A1 are compared, the child says there are more beads in B, since it is taller than A, or that there are more beads in A1, since it is wider than B. The child is centered on one aspect of the situation, "height" or "width," and since he cannot hold the centerings simultaneously, he is unable to solve the problem. This type of focused centerings can also be seen in the observation of the child's eye movements (O'Bryan & Boersma, 1969; Zaporozhets, 1965; Zaporozhets & Zinchenko, 1966). The child in the "intuitive stage" still

remains prelogical, but decenterings can occur, where in the previous sub-
stage centerings led to absurd conclusions. Thus, for example, a child may
initially estimate that there are more beads in the taller glass because the
level has been raised, thus centering his attention on height and ignoring
width. If, however, the experimenter continues to empty the beads into
increasingly thinner and taller glasses, there will be a time when the child in
this stage replies that there are fewer beads in the taller glass, since it is too
narrow. This is an example of a transition from a single centering (pre-
conceptual thought) to two successive centerings (intuitive thought). When
the child is able to reason with respect to both relations at the *same* time, he
will, in fact, deduce "conservation," (i.e., state that the beads remain the
same and only the glasses change). This simultaneous reasoning does not
occur during the intuitive stage, and the above example indicates that there
is neither deduction nor true logical operations; an error is simply corrected
but the two relations are seen alternatively instead of simultaneously. All that
occurs is an intuitive regulation and not a truly operational mechanism.

The difference between the "intuitive" stage and the next stage, operational thought, is also seen in answers to questions regarding the formation
of classes (Inhelder & Piaget, 1964; Piaget, 1952, 1960). These interrogations
involve the child's understanding of the cardinal $(3 = 1 + 1 + 1)$ and
ordinal $(3 = 2 + 1)$ properties of number. Cardinal properties of number
involve the ability to classify and combine classes. Piaget (1960) placed 20
beads in a box, and the child acknowledged that they were all made of wood
(this constituted a class B). A small number of beads (3) were white in color
(this constituted a subclass A') and a larger number were brown (this constituted a subclass A). In order to determine whether the child is capable of
understanding an operation such as $A + A' = B$, the following question is
asked: "In this box (all of the beads are visible), which are there more of,
wooden beads or brown beads?" (i.e., B or A). Piaget found that up to about
7 years, the child invariably replies that there are more brown beads, "since
there are only three white ones." Then the child is asked further" "Are all
the brown ones made of wood?" The child usually responds, "Yes." Piaget
questions further: "If one takes away all the wooden beads and puts them in a
second box, will there be any beads left in the first box?" Most children
replied, "No, because they are all made of wood." The child is now asked the
following question: "If the brown ones are taken away, will there be any
beads left?" The child responds that, "Yes, the white ones." After this
interrogation is finished, the original question is repeated. The child, during
the intuitive phase, continues to state there are more brown beads than
wooden ones, etc. The mechanism for this response is that the subject finds no
difficulty in centering his attention on the whole Class B, or on the subclass
A or A'; however, he is unable to grasp both simultaneously, and thus cannot

understand the logical and mathematical truth that the whole is equal to the sum of its parts. The child in the stage of concrete operations can do so.

The problem of ordination or seriation, must also wait to be solved until the child attains concrete operational thought. Although the child during the intuitive stage is beginning to arrange things in a series, his arranging ability is only "global." The child is able to compare two members of a set within a series when they follow one another in a consecutive order. For example, the child knows that Monday comes after Sunday, that Tuesday comes after Monday. When asked whether Tuesday comes after Sunday, the child, however, becomes confused. The operational thought, involving the seeing of logical relations between things and events that are arranged in a series, is not yet possible to the child in the intuitive stage.

The cognitive structures that are elaborated during the preoperational stage enable the child to acquire *primary* abstractions (concepts) and to understand, use, and meaningfully manipulate for problem-solving purposes both primary abstractions and the relations between them (Ausubel, 1963, 1968). Primary concepts are those concepts whose meanings are given originally in relation to genuine concrete-empirical experience, that is, they are those of his concepts whose criterial attributes, whether discovered or presented, yield generic meanings during learning when they (the attributes) are *first* explicitly related to the exemplars from which they are derived, *before* they are related alone to his cognitive structure. Once concept meanings are acquired, the preoperational child can understand and use them apart from their particular exemplars, and he can also understand and manipulate in problem-solving operations, relationships between these primary abstractions, namely propositions composed of such abstractions.

But the fact that he is limited to dealing with primary abstractions, i.e., the fact that he cannot similarly handle *secondary* abstractions and relationships between secondary abstractions, obviously imposes severe constraints on the level at which he operates. (Secondary concepts are those concepts whose meaning a given individual does *not* learn in relation to genuine concrete-empirical experience, i.e., those of his concepts whose criterial attributes yields generic meanings during learning when they (the attributes) are related to his cognitive structure *without* being first explicitly related to the particular exemplars from which they are derived.) The preoperational child's understanding and manipulation of abstract concepts and propositions take place at a level of abstraction that is only slightly removed from the intimate participation of concrete-empirical experience in the acquisition of his primary concepts themselves.

One important manifestation of this constraint is that the preoperational child is unable to perform many significant logical operations; these operations, such as "reversibility," all imply a capability to understand and manipulate relationships between secondary abstractions. Thus, for example, because he cannot perform the logical operation of "reversibility" * (as shown by many of the studies cited on p. 557), he cannot, as the concrete or abstract operational child can, grasp the ideas of "conservation." Another consequence of his inability to perform true logical operations, and of the related fact that the meanings of many of his primary concepts (particularly those of familiar perceptible objects and events) are little more than idealized images embodying appropriate criterial attributes, is that problem solving at this stage involves much overt manipulation of objects and internal manipulation of near-images (Ausubel, 1963, 1968).

Concrete Operational State (7 through 11 Years)

Piaget (1965b) maintains that the emergence of concrete operations marks the beginning of rational activity in the child. Up to this time, the child demonstrates a logic (transductive) which is quite different from that (inductive and deductive) of the adult members of his species. The ability to reason inductively and deductively is due to the presence of thought structures (schemas) which are labelled operations. Operations are defined as internalized actions which can return to their starting point, and which can be integrated with other actions also possessing this feature of reversibility (Piaget, 1960). Stated simply, operations are "mental acts," which were formerly actions which had reversible properties. According to Piaget (1960), the stage of concrete operations is so characterized because the starting point of the operation is always some real system of objects and relations that the child perceives; that is, the operations are carried out on concrete objects. The emergence of concrete operations is often a sudden phenomenon in development. Piaget attributes these operations to a sudden thawing out of intuitive structures which were, up to now, more rigid, despite their progressive articulation (Piaget, 1960). The operations cited by Piaget (1960) are reversibility, combinitivity, associativity, identity, and tautology. The concrete operational structures (schemas) are analogus to particular operations which have been identified in mathematical and logical disciplines. Thus, the Piagetian thought structures at this stage are modelled after logico-mathematical operations. Piaget (1960) has stipulated that the various concrete operations develop in unison. This stipulation places an extremely heavy burden on the stage construct, and has received little if any research support (Flavell & Wohlwill, 1969; Shantz, 1967).

---

*Piaget's explanation of conservation is not that logical operations, such as reversibility, imply a capability to understand or manipulate relationships between secondary abstractions (a capability whose existence he denies at the stage of concrete logical operations), but rather that logical operations (which he defines as "internalized actions") do not exist, by definition, at the preoperational stage.

In order to understand what internal process brings about this transition from intuitive thought, it is necessary to see how concrete operational structures are brought to bear on the problems previously described in the intuitive stage. First the conservation problem (i.e., the pouring of the beads from one glass to another) will be reconsidered. In the intuitive stage, one sees slow-moving centerings and decenterings, such that the problem is first seen from one point of view (height) and then from another point of view (width). During the concrete operational stage, the child holds both centerings simultaneously, and thus deduces conservation. He explains his conviction by verbally pointing out that the quantity of beads in both glasses is the same, because if they were poured back into the other glass they would be the same height again (reversibility) or that they are the same now because they were the same when you started out (identity). Conservation is not a unitary concept and manifests itself, in several ways, and at different times. Conservation of discrete quantities (number) that is, the situation where two equivalent groups of discrete objects in one-to-one correspondence are moved to a new arrangement wherein correspondence is not perceptually evident, occurs slightly before conservation of continuous quantity (substance). Conservation of *weight* (i.e., downward force of an object) follows conservation of *quantity* and is in turn followed by conservation of *volume* (i.e., the space occupied by an object). Evidence confirming this sequential order of conservation has varied somewhat from Piaget's original findings but in general has confirmed his age trends (Almy *et al*, 1966; Elkind, 1961; Feigenbaum, 1963; Goldschimid, 1967; Kooistra, 1963; Lovell and Ogilvie, 1960; Pratoomraj & Johnson, 1966). Thus, the principles of conservation do not hold in all systems or ideas, emerging later in some systems than in others. In addition there is a considerable amount of intra-task specificity depending on the materials used in the measurement of conservation (Baker & Sullivan, 1966; Uzgiris, 1964; Zimiles, 1966).

The type of reasoning involved in concrete operations is illustrated in the class inclusion problem (e.g., brown beads-wooden beads problem). By the age of eight, the child understands class inclusion (combinatory operation) in the wooden beads experiment, yet is unable to solve a verbal test involving an identical structure until he reaches the age of formal operations. Although replications of Inhelder & Piaget's (1964) findings on classification and seriation have tended to support their results (Lovell, Mitchell, and Everett, 1962; Kofsky, 1966), individuals nevertheless vary in the sequence of some of these cognitive tasks and also in the steps to mastery of the tasks (Kofsky, 1966).

With specific reference to the concrete-abstract dimension of cognitive development, it can be noted that while the child during the concrete operational stage is capable of acquiring secondary abstractions and of under-standing, using, and meaningfully manipulating both *secondary* abstractions and the relations between them, he differs from the abstract operational individual in that he uses *concrete-empirical props*. His cognitive level conforms to the definition of a secondary concept given earlier, that is, he does *not* learn the meaning of a concept by *first* relating its criterial attributes to the particular exemplars from which they are derived, *before* relating them to his cognitive structure; he learns its meaning, rather, by relating the criterial attributes *directly* to his cognitive structure. However, and this is where he differs from the child at the abstract operational level, he typically does so with the benefit of concrete-empirical props, namely, exemplars of the various *attributes*. The use of such props in concept acquisition implies a more abstract process of learning than the actual use of "genuine" concrete-empirical experience itself (a) because the exemplars of attributes are ex-amples of the *abstracted* properties of a concept—not particular instances of the concept; (b) because a *single* example of an attribute, as opposed to the multiple exemplars of the concept that is given in concrete-empirical ex-perience, suffices as a prop, and (c) because the prop serves mainly as a "crutch" in relating the criterial attribute to cognitive structure rather than as the concrete-empirical matrix from which either the criterial attribute itself is derived or in relation to which it derives its potential meaningfulness.

For example, while the concept of "work" is being learned as a primary concept, the preoperational child may eventually hypothesize such attributes as "activity," "necessary," and "useful" as criterial, by abstracting them from farming, fixing cars, keeping house, nursing, etc., or he may be given these attributes. In either case, however, he tests each of the attributes against each of the exemplars *before* relating them to his cognitive structure. If, in elementary school, he learns the concept of "work" as a secondary concept, he is given its attributes in definitional form and may use an exemplar for one or more of the attributes in relating them to his cognitive structure. Finally, as a high-school student, in the abstract operational stage, he relates the criterial attributes directly to his cognitive structure without props, and if he does not know the meaning of a given attribute, it too need only be defined.

Once secondary concepts are acquired, the concrete operational child is no longer dependent on props in understanding or using their meanings. Understanding *relationships between secondary abstractions* (or meaningfully manipulating these relationships for problem-solving purposes), however, is quite another matter. In this kind of learning task he is dependent upon recently prior or concurrent concrete-empirical props consisting of a par-ticular exemplar for each of the abstractions in the relationship: when such props are not available he finds abstract relational propositions unrelatable to cognitive structure and hence devoid of meaning. This dependence upon concrete-empirical props self-evidently limits the generality and abstractness of his attempts meaningfully to grasp and manipulate relationships between abstractions; he can acquire only those relational understandings and perform only those relational problem-solving operations that do not go beyond the somewhat particularized representation of reality implicit in his use of these props. Thus, where complex propositions are involved, he is largely restricted to an intuitive or semi-abstract level of cognitive functioning, a level that falls far short of the clarity, precision, explicitness, and generality associated with the more advanced abstract stage of intellectual development.

During the elementary-school years (which roughly correspond to the stage of concrete operations), therefore, abstract verbal propositions (propositions consisting of relationships between secondary abstractions) that are presented on a purely expository basis are too remotely removed from concrete-empirical experience to be relatable to cognitive structure. This does not mean, however, that autonomous discovery is required before such propositions can be meaningfully learned; as long as concrete-empirical props are made an integral part of the learning situation, they (the propositions) are eminently learnable. Concrete-empirical props also need not necessarily be nonverbal or tangible (e.g., objects, pictures). "Concrete" and "nonrepresentational" are not synonymous; words that represent particular exemplars or attributes of a concept are very adequate concrete-empirical props in learning abstract propositions and secondary concepts respectively.

Hence, because the child can as mentioned earlier, perform logical operations such as conservation, and because the meanings of his concepts are more abstract in nature, problem-solving involves less overt manipulation of objects and internal manipulation of images.

It is important to realize that just because the concrete-operational child uses concrete-empirical props in understanding and thinking about relationships between abstractions, this stage of intellectual development is not really concrete in the sense that objects or *concrete images* of objects are relationally manipulated in meaningful reception or discovery learning. Contrary to Piaget's contention that the child at this stage conducts logical operations on concrete objects, and that his thought processes are closely tied to his concrete experience, the evidence suggests that he essentially understands and manipulates relations between the verbal representations of secondary abstractions. The concreteness of this stage inheres, rather, in the fact that relationships between abstractions can be understood and meaningfully manipulated *only* with the aid of current or recently prior concrete-empirical props. Logical operations are therefore constrained in the generality and abstractness of their implication by the particularity of the props in question; unlike the situation in the later stage of abstract logical operations, they do not involve logical transformations of all possible and hypothetical relationships between general abstract variables.* Nevertheless, they are more closely related in level of abstraction to the following than to the preceeding stage of cognitive development, and represent a very significant advance over the latter. It also appears that Piaget overstates his case, and gives children too little credit, when he does not differentiate between primary and secondary abstractions in asserting that only in the final stage can children understand and manipulate relationships between abstractions; as far as relationships between primary abstractions are concerned, this capability is evident without props in the concrete operational and even in the preoperational stage.

Abstract Logical Stage (11 years and up)

Beginning in the junior-high school period, the pupil becomes decreasingly dependent upon the availability of concrete-empirical props in meaningfully relating abstract relationships to cognitive structure. Eventually he no longer needs them at all in understanding and meaningfully manipulating any relationships between abstractions. He then assimilates abstract propositions and solves abstract problems in terms of all-inclusive hypothetical possibilities rather than in terms of these possibilities as constrained by their reference to "the here and now," (Glick & Wapner, 1968). In other words, he attains full conceptual and propositional generality. "Instead of just coordinating facts about the actual world, hypothetico-deductive reasoning draws out the implications of possible statements and thus gives rise to a unique synthesis of the possible and the necessary" (Piaget, 1957a, p. 19).

Inhelder and Piaget (1958) present considerable evidence indicating that "formal" (abstract) operations appear slightly before the onset of adolescence. On the whole their findings are corroborated by other investigators (R. J. Goldman, 1965; S. Jackson, 1965; Lovell, 1961a; Wynns, 1967; Yudin, 1966; Yudin and Kates, 1963). Lovell's subjects attained this stage of development somewhat later than Inhelder and Piaget's, and Case and Collinson's (1962) somewhat earlier. Both Goldman and Jackson reported greater age variability, and Jackson less intertask generality, than did Inhelder and Piaget. None

---

*R. Brown (1958) argues that the cognitive processes of adults are more abstract than those of children only in the sense that they manifest more discriminative generalization—that children actually exhibit more simple stimulus generalization than do adults (i.e., generalization not requiring prior discriminative analysis). Hence he claims that adults do not really use a wider range of abstract concepts in their thinking, but merely employ a more highly differentiated repertoire of subcategories within existing categories. Simple stimulus generalization, however, can hardly be considered a form of abstract thinking that reflects the use of abstract concepts. Thus, it seems more plausible to believe that adults also characteristically use a greater number of generic categories than do children, as well as more differentiated subcategories. In fact, it has been argued that children organize information into narrow concepts and overdiscriminate (Sigel, Saltz & Roskind, 1967).

of these findings, however, detract from the essential validity of Piaget's conclusion that the child entering this stage of cognitive development thinks, for the first time, in terms of all-inclusive hypothetical possibilities (instead of merely in terms of the "here and now").

Thus, eventually, after sufficient gradual change in this direction, a qualitatively new capacity emerges: the intellectually mature individual becomes capable of understanding and manipulating relationships between abstractions without any reference whatsoever to concrete-empirical reality. Instead of reasoning directly from a particular set of data, he uses indirect, second-order logical operations for structuring the data; instead of merely grouping data into classes or arranging them serially in terms of a given variable, he formulates and tests hypotheses based on all *possible* combinations of variables (see also Grodskaya, 1962). Since his logical operations are performed without props on abstract verbal prepositions, he can go beyond the operations that follow immediately from concrete-empirical reality, and deal with all possible or hypothetical relations between ideas. He can now transcend the previously achieved level of intuitive thought and understanding, and formulate general laws relating to each other general variables that are divorced from the concrete-empirical data at hand. His concepts and generalizations, therefore, tend increasingly to be second-order constructs derived from relationships between previously established verbal abstractions that are already one step removed from the data itself. And, since he is freed from dependence on non-abstract contact with empirical data in independently *discovering* meaningful new concepts and generalizations, he is obviously also liberated from this same dependence in the much less rigorous task of merely *apprehending* these constructs meaningfully when they are verbally presented to him.

Careful analysis of the experiments performed by Inhelder and Piaget, and by the other investigators cited above, does not substantiate the Piagetian position, which is also held by Lunzer (1965), that the *distinctive* feature of formal or abstract (as opposed to concrete) operations is that the older child is able to deal internally with ideas about ideas or to perform "second-order operations." The younger ("concrete operational") child can *also* do these things, as shown by the studies of Case and Collinson (1962), S. A. Hill (1961), and O'Brien & Shapiro (1968). The latter demonstrated, for example, that most children aged six to eight can easily draw correct inferences from hypothetical premises involving abstract relationships. It is rather the preadolescent's and adolescent's ability verbally to manipulate relationships between ideas *in the absence of recently prior or concurrently available concrete-empirical props* that is the distinctive attribute of formal operations. (Hill's subjects, after all, were given logical problems that were invariably stated in terms of particular instances). This new capability emerging at age 11 and beyond invests propositional thought with a genuinely abstract and non-intuitive quality. Ideas about ideas now achieve a truly general status that is freed from any dependence whatsoever on particular instances and concrete experience. It is for this reason that thinking becomes hypothetico-deductive in nature, that is, refers to all possible relationships between variables rather than to relationships constrained by reference to particular instances.

Determinants of Change

From the foregoing account of stages along the concrete-abstract dimension of cognitive development, it is hypothesized that the combined influence of three concomitant and mutually supportive developmental trends accounts for the transition from concrete to abstract cognitive functioning. In the first place, the developing individual gradually acquires a working vocabulary of "transactional" or mediating terms (e.g., conditional conjunctions, qualifying adjectives). This makes possible the more efficient juxtaposition and combination of different relatable abstractions into potentially meaningful propositions and their subsequent relationship to established ideas in cognitive structure. Second, he can relate these latter propositions more readily to cognitive structure, and hence render them more meaningful, because of his growing fund of stable, higher-order concepts and principles encompassed by, and made available within, that structure. Russell and Saadeh (1962), for example, found that between the sixth and ninth grades children's use of concrete definitions decreases and their use of abstract and functional definitions correspondingly increases. A sufficient body of abstract concepts that are clear and stable is obviously necessary before one can hope efficiently to manipulate relationships between them so as to generate meaningful general propositions. The possession of a working body of inclusive concepts also makes possible the formulation of more general statements of relationships that are less tied to specific instances, greater integration of related ideas and different aspects of the same problem, the elaboration of more precise distinctions and finer differentiations, and less dependence on complete concrete-empirical data in reaching warranted inferences (Bruner et al, 1966; Greenfield & Bruner, 1966).

Finally, it seems reasonable to suppose that after many years of practice in understanding, and meaningfully manipulating relationships between abstractions *with* the aid of concrete-empirical props, the older child gradually develops greater facility in performing these operations, so that eventually (after acquiring the necessary transactional and higher-order concepts) he can perform the same operations just as effectively *without* relying on these props. The same sequence of events is seen in acquiring many other neuro-muscular and cognitive skills, e.g., walking without "holding on," bicycling "without hands," speaking a foreign language without internal translation from one's mother tongue, transmitting Morse code in sentences rather than in word or letter units.

Piaget and Inhelder (Inhelder and Piaget, 1958; Piaget, 1953, 1957b, 1960, 1964) largely embrace a maturational position in explaining how developmental transition is effected during the various stages of intellectual development. Their view of maturation, however, which they call "equilibration," is inclusive of both internal (genic) factors and some aspects of *incidental* learning. It is therefore closer to the empirical concept of maturation than it is to Gesell's notion of maturation as a process of internal ripening. * According to Smedslund (1961), "conservation of weight is acquired by a process of internal equilibration, independently of external reinforcement. By equilibration is meant a change in the direction of increasing stability, consistency, and completeness of behavioral structures. Conflicts are eliminated and gaps are closed . . . [Equilibration] is heavily dependent on activity and experience, [but such experience] is not assumed to act through external reinforcement, but by a process of mutual influence of the child's activities on each other." Piaget's theory of knowledge at all levels is linked to biological internal organization, and thus, knowledge does not merely derive from taking in of external data (Furth, 1968, 1969).

Thus, according to Piaget, maturation (genic factors and general aspects of incidental experience) accounts for the universality of the sequential stages and the order in which they occur, whereas variability in the kind of incidental learning experience accounts for interindividual, intraindividual, and intercultural differences in the age at which stages occur and in the content area in which they are manifested. Piaget and others (e.g., Langer, 1969b; Smedslund, 1961) deny that specific learning experince or training (practice), particularly of a verbal nature, or, for that matter, education generally, has any significant influence on the emergence of stages of intellectual development. His theoretical stance on "equilibration," however, does not provide an adequate explanation for the obvious effect that schooling or non-schooling has on Piagetian cognitive tasks (Bruner, *et al*, 1966; Goodnow, 1969; Greenfield & Bruner, 1966; Olson, 1970; Sigel & Mermelstein, 1965). We shall return to this problem later in another context, i.e., in considering whether training can accelerate stages in cognitive development.

Both general and specific motivational explanations (Inhelder and Piaget, 1958) have been advanced to account for the transition from the concrete operational to the abstract operational stage. Desire to obtain greater meaning out of experience is not a convincing explanation since this desire does not arise suddenly or uniquely at adolescence. Furthermore, although motivation may energize and facilitate cognitive change, it cannot convincingly explain

---

*See also the related discussion of predeterminism and Piagetian theory on (pp. 27-30).

either its occurrence or direction. Desire to identify with and participate in the adult world has more specific relevance for this age period; but, again, no amount of motivation would suffice to effect the change in question in the absence of the necessary genic potentialities and supportive experience.

General and Specific Aspects of Transition

We have already rejected complete generality over content areas and levels of difficulty as a legitimate criterion for a developmental stage. Even Piaget and his collaborators have indicated "that the increasing reversibility of development and the schemas of the higher levels do not function identically in all situations and that the same child may be found at different stages depending on the problem," (Szeminska, 1965; p. 52). There is certainly ample evidence for this conclusion (Kofsky, 1966; M. A. Stone, 1966; Uzgiris, 1964; Wohlwill, 1968) since too much unevenness exists in any individual's experiential background and pattern of abilities for the transition from concrete to abstract functioning to occur *simultaneously* in all areas. A stage of development, also, is always referable to a typical range of difficulty and familiarity of the problem at hand; beyond this range, regression to an earlier stage of development commonly occurs. It is apparent, therefore, that the transition from concrete to abstract cognitive functioning takes place *specifically* in each subject-matter area, and presupposes a certain necessary amount of sophistication in each of the areas involved. This specificity, however, does not invalidate the existence of qualitatively distinct stages of development. It is still possible to designate an individual's *over-all* developmental status as concrete or abstract on the basis of an estimate of his *characteristic or predominant* mode of cognitive functioning. M. A. Stone (1966) found that, beginning with junior-high school students, the generality of abstract cognitive functioning increases with age (i.e., gradually encompasses more subject-matter fields in older pupils). This trend was evidenced by successively higher intercorrelations, with increasing age, among learning scores on tests of ability to learn abstract verbal material in different disciplines.

This distinction between specific and general aspects of developmental status is important for two reasons: First, the individual necessarily continues to undergo the same transition from concrete to abstract cognitive functioning in each *new* subject-matter area he encounters—even *after* he reaches the abstract stage of development on an over-all basis. Second, once he attains this latter general stage, however, the transition to abstract cognitive functioning in unfamiliar new subject-matter fields takes place much more readily than is the case at earlier phases of the transition. For example, a cognitively mature adult who has never studied astronomy is not completely in the same developmental position as an eleven- or twelve-year-old with respect to the concrete-abstract dimension when both begin an introductory course in astronomy.

Thus, even though an adolescent or adult characteristically functions at the abstract level of cognitive development, he tends *initially* to function at a concrete, intuitive level when he is first introduced to a wholly unfamiliar subject-matter field. But since he is able to draw on various transferable elements of his more *general* ability to function abstractly, he passes through the concrete stage of functioning in this particular subject-matter area much more rapidly than would be the case were he first emerging from the stage of concrete logical operations. These facilitating transferable elements presumably include transactional terms, higher-order concepts, and ability *directly* to understand and manipulate relationships between abstractions (i.e., without the benefit of concrete-empirical props), which, although acquired in other specific subject-matter contexts, are generally applicable to new learning situations (see below).

In other words, growth in cognitive development always proceeds at two separate levels concomitantly—specific and general. Experience in learning *any* subject matter produces general as well as specific *developmental* changes in cognitive capacity, in addition to specific changes in subject-matter readiness. As a result of experience in studying a given discipline, pupils not only learn particular ideas that facilitate the later learning of other particular ideas, but also acquire greater capacity meaningfully to process more abstract material of any nature in that particular discipline and *other* disciplines as well. General cognitive development, in any given dimension, therefore, occurs with increasing age and education, and is independent of particular kinds of subject-matter experience. It is these general and transferable aspects of changed cognitive capacity occurring in the transition from concrete to abstract intellectual functioning in any particular discipline that facilitate the same transition in *any* new subject-matter area. Thus, the cognitively mature adolescent, confronted with a learning or problem-solving task in an unfamiliar discipline, does not have the benefit of *specific* cognitive changes along the concrete-abstract dimension resulting from past experience with the subject-matter area. In this sense he is no better off than the immature child who has not undergone the over-all transition from the concrete to the abstract stage; he has to make this transition anew in the unfamiliar area. But he makes the transition more easily because of the *general* cognitive changes that have occurred along this dimension and which are transferable to the particular new subject-matter field.

Hence, in contrast to the cognitively immature child who continues to use concrete-empirical props in relating abstractions to each other as long as he is in the concrete stage, the adolescent uses the props only initially—to develop the necessary higher-order abstractions in the new discipline—and then proceeds to dispense with props entirely in acquiring addition abstractions. His dependence on concrete-empirical props, in other words, is temporary and reflective of circumscribed cognitive immaturity in particular subject-matter fields, rather than reflective of an over-all concrete level of cognitive functioning.

Accelerating Stages of Intellectual Development

The issue of acceleration of stages of intellectual development is sufficiently entrenched in ideological commitments to make a coherent statement on this topic difficult without entering into rhetoric or polemics. The most well known statement in America on the topic of acceleration was made by Bruner (1960) when he conjectured:

> At each stage of development the child has a characteristic way of viewing the world and explaining it to himself. The task of teaching a subject to a child at any particular age is one of representing the structure of that subject in terms of the child's way of viewing things. The task can be thought of as one of translation (Bruner, 1960, p. 33) . . . If one respects the ways of thought of the growing child, if one is courteous enough to translate material into his logical forms, and challenging enough to tempt him to advance, then it is possible to introduce him at any early age to the ideas and styles that in later years make an educated man (p. 54) . . . Any idea can be represented honestly and usefully in the thought forms of children of school age and . . . these first representations can later be made more powerful and precise the more easily by virtue of this early learning (p. 33) . . . Actually any subject can be taught effectively in some intellectually honest form to any child at any stage of development (p. 33).

Without entering in to the controversy engendered by this thesis it still seems legitimate to ask if it is possible to accelerate children's progress through stages of intellectual development . . .

> . . . by taking account of their characteristic cognitive limitations, and by providing suitably contrived experience geared to their cognitive capacity and mode of functioning. Can we, for example, train them, as Inhelder (Bruner, 1960; pp. 43-45) suggests, to focus on more than one aspect of a problem at a time or to acquire genuine appreciation of the concept of conservation of mass? If stages of development have any true meaning, the answer to this question can only be that although some acceleration is certainly possible, it is necessarily limited in extent.
> Developmental considerations inevitably impose a limit on the extent of acceleration that is possible, inasmuch as transition to the next higher stage is invariably an organic outgrowth of, and hence presupposes, the attainment of a certain level of consolidation of proficiency at the proceeding stage (Ausubel, 1968, p. 214).

Such consolidation, in turn, implies gradual and cumulative change over an extended period of time. It can however, be assumed, even within Piaget's "equilibration" model of stage transition, that stages of intellectual development can be accelerated by appropriate experiences. Even as early as the stage of sensori-motor development, it appears that certain behavioral manifestations characteristic of this period can be accelerated by appropriate environmental influence. For example, visually-directed reaching for objects (prehension) is facilitated, in normal infants reared in institutions, by an enrichment program (White, 1969; White & Held, 1966). Extra handling by nurses of these infants had a significant positive effect upon the growth of visual attention (White & Held, 1966). Object permanence seems to be facilitated by experiences characteristic of middle-class environments when compared with lower class environments (Hunt, 1969). Certain types of means-end problem solving situations, characteristic of the later phases of Piaget's sensori-motor stage, can be enhanced by appropriately contrived learning experiences (Henninger, 1968). Moreover, a guided program of cognitive stimulation was conducive to accelerated learning of conceptions of physical causality in three-year-old children (Fowler, 1968).

In accounting for the transition from the preoperational stage to the stage of concrete logical operations, Piaget (1957b), for example, emphasized such mechanisms as successive and contrasting "decentration" (less exclusive preoccupation with a particular aspect of a phenomenon) and gradual appreciation of the theory of probability. In our opinion, however, Piaget and others have unwarrantly excluded the role of verbal instruction in bringing about transition from one stage of intellectual development to another (by Kohlberg, 1958; Piaget, 1964; Sinclair-De-Zwart, 1969; Szeminska, 1965). As Vygotsky (1962) points out, the relationship between intellectual development and education is invariably reciprocal. On theoretical grounds there is no reason why *only* incidental (spontaneous, undirected, unexplained) experience must effect the gradual, cumulative change in intellectual capacity that makes transition to a higher stage possible; and since guided practice is demonstrably more efficient than are more kinds of incidental learning, it should be quite possible for suitable training to accelerate the rate at which the various stages of intellectual development succeed each other. In fact, evidence was presented earlier which indicated that schooling and urban living *per se* accelerate the acquisition of conservation and combinatorial reasoning. But it was also pointed out above (see p. 97) that the mere facts that a given type of learning task *can* be mastered before the age of readiness, or that the age of readiness itself *can* be accelerated, do not necessarily mean that stages of development *should* be accelerated or that maximum acceleration is desirable.

Generally speaking, simple drill or training, in which the preoperational child is exposed to contrived conservation experience and given reinforcement for correct responses, does not suffice to bring about stable acquisition of conservation concepts. Such training merely leads to the acquisition of an "empirical rule", which, unlike the stable and organized concept in the "natural conserver," cannot withstand (i.e., is easily extinguished by) the influence of such spurious disconfirmation experiences as countersuggestion and perceptually deceptive appearances (Smedslund, 1961). Similarly, in another area of intellectual functioning, kindergarten children who receive laboratory training in learning the principle of a teeter-totter (i.e., that the longer side from the fulcrum falls when both sides are equally weighted) fail to exhibit resistance to the later learning of a spurious causal relationship about the operation of a teeter-totter (i.e., that the color of the blocks placed at either end of the teeter-totter is the determining factor) (Ausubel and Schiff, 1954). Beilin and Franklin (1962) also report that "no first-grader achieves operational area measurement even with training"; and Wohlwill and Lowe (1962) found improvement in conservation behavior on a nonverbal posttest after three kinds of training, but no transfer of this conservation learning to a verbal posttest.

It is important to realize that the acceleration of the conservations has become the focal point of the theoretical controversy concerning the role of transition variables which influence the course of intellectual development. *

Piaget (1964) and other proponents of his "equilibration" (e.g., Kohlberg, 1968; Smedslund, 1961) have been peculiarly reluctant to admit the possibility of learning in the acceleration of the conservations. The earlier literature on conservation acquisition tended to favor the interpretation that conservation could not be induced with any stability and generality through direct teaching (Flavell, 1963).

> Almost all of the training methods reported impress one as sound and reasonable and well suited to the educative job at hand. And yet, most of them have had remarkably little success in producing cognitive change (Flavell, 1963; p. 377). †

The above conclusion was recently reiterated by Kohlberg (1968) whose "equilibration" interpretation of conservation closely parallels Piaget's (Piaget, 1964). In light of more recent evidence of success or partial success with acquisition procecures (Beilin, 1969; Brison, 1966; Brison & Bereiter, 1967; Bruner et al, 1966; Engelmann, 1967a; Murray, 1967, 1968; Sigel, Roeper and Hooper, 1966; Sullivan, 1967b; 1969; Smith, 1968; Waghorn and Sullivan, 1968; Winer, 1968) it is interesting to see Flavell's most recent conclusion:

---

*Theoretical discussions and research summaries of conservation research may be found in the following sources (Brison and Sullivan, 1967; Bruner et al., 1966; Elkind, 1969; Flavell, 1963; Flavell and Hill, 1969; Flavell and Wohlwill, 1969; Oléron and Thong (1968); Sigel and Hooper, 1968; M. Wallach, 1963; L. Wallach, 1969). Methodological discussion of Piagetian assessment techniques are also of interest in the conservation controversy (Braine, 1959; 1962; Braine and Shanks, 1965a; 1965b; Charlesworth, 1969; Flavell and Wohlwill, 1969; Griffiths, Shantz and Sigel, 1967; Siegel & Goldstein, 1969; Zimiles, 1964).

†Several recent studies have also reported failure to induce conservation (see Gruen, 1965; Sinclair-De-Zwart, 1969; Wallace, 1966; Wallach, 1969).

"If our reading of recent trends is correct, few on either side of the Atlantic would now maintain that one cannot by any pedagogic means measurably spur, solidify, or otherwise further the child's concrete-operational progress (Flavell & Hill, 1969; p. 19)."

The most recent reports of moderate success with the conservation acquisitions does not mean that the question of transition rules (Kessen, 1962) between stages has been answered or that many important theoretical questions have been adequately resolved by the research (Flavell & Hill, 1969; Flavell & Wohlwill, 1969; Pinard & Laurendeau, 1969). Nevertheless, there is at least now some evidence that indicates that the use of various verbal *didactic* procedures (e.g., prior verbalization of principles, the use of verbal rules, filmed verbal explanations, confronting the child verbally with his own contradictions), in conjunction with concrete-empirical props, *can* accelerate the acquisition of conservation and probability theory (Frank, in Bruner, 1964; Kohnstamm, 1966; Ojemann and Pritchett, 1963; Ojemann, Maxey, & Snider, 1966; Sullivan, 1967b). Such didactic teaching, combined with the use of concrete-empirical props, also induces generalization of conservation responses to other materials (Kohnstamm, 1966; Sullivan, 1967b), promotes retention of these responses over periods as long as six months (Kohnstamm, 1966), and makes them resistant to extinction after an interval of seven days (Sullivan, 1967b). All of these findings strongly suggest that since even short-term verbal training can bring about a limited degree of stable, sustained, and generalized transitional change from the preoperational stage to the stage of concrete logical operations, long-term training along similar lines would be even more effective. Several studies seem to support this interpretation with concrete operational class-inclusion problems (Kohnstamm, 1966, 1967; Langer, 1969a; Templen'Kaya, 1966).

Thus it appears that after a certain degree of consolidation of the preoperational stage occurs, one can anticipate, and thereby accelerate, the attainment of the next higher (concrete operational) stage by training the child under the learning conditions that apply to the latter stage, i.e., by requiring him to relate secondary abstractions and abstract verbal propositions to cognitive structure with the aid of concrete-empirical props. In a similar way, the transition from concrete to abstract logical operations can be facilitated by gradually withdrawing concrete-empirical props as the prior stage becomes consolidated, that is, by withdrawing the props well in advance of the actual attainment of abstract cognitive functioning.* Thus in Vygotsky's (1962) terms, didactic instruction can, and *normally* does, play a role in facilitating (accelerating) transition from one stage of cognitive development to another—both by providing suitably contrived, directed,

---

*Galperin (1957) describes a method of teaching arithmetic to slow-learning pupils in which concrete-empirical props are eliminated very gradually and are replaced by abstract verbal representations. Szeminska (1965) observes that, as grade level increases, the methods used in schools rely increasingly on abstract reasoning.

and explained learning experience, and by making intellectual demands on pupils that go beyond their current capabilities, i.e., that anticipate or are pointed toward the conditions of cognitive functioning at the next higher stage. Although there have been failures in teaching attempts to induce formal abstract modes of functioning (Szeminska, 1965), there is, nevertheless, some evidence that some aspects of formal abstract reasoning can be induced through guided learning procedures. (Englemann, 1967b; Templen'Kaya, 1966).

THE EFFECTS OF ENVIRONMENTAL DEPRIVATION ON COGNITIVE DEVELOPMENT

We have already discussed some dimensions of the environment which can facilitate or impede cognitive development (e.g., schooling, social class, etc.). The recent interest in compensatory education has focused on certain aspects of the child's environment which are instrumental in advancing or retarding his cognitive functioning. The notion of "environmental deprivation" is a term frequently used in explaining why certain groups of children are retarded in some aspects of cognitive functioning. Since there is considerable ambiguity in the use of the term, it seems appropriate here to consider it in more detail and with a critical perspective.

What theoretical grounds and relevant evidence do we have for believing that prolonged environmental deprivation induces retardation in intellectual development? It is reasonable to assume, in the first place, that whatever the individual's genic potentialities are, cognitive development occurs largely in response to a variable range of stimulation requiring incorporation, accommodation, adjustment, and reconciliation. The more variable the environment to which individuals are exposed, the higher is the resulting level of effective stimulation. Hebb (1949) stresses the importance of early sensory and perceptual experience for later problem solving, and Piaget (1952) similarly emphasizes the importance of such experience for the early stages of intellectual development.

A certain amount of semantic ambiguity exists, however, when using the term "environmental deprivation" since it appears that it is not the mere absence of stimulation per se, but rather the absence of variety and possibly certain types of redundancy in stimulation (Uzgiris, 1968) that is important. Looking at stimulation from this perspective it could be argued that retardation in sensory-motor skills is a result of chaotic overstimulation rather than of deficiency in stimulation (Uzgiris, 1968). The culturally deprived home is characterized by a conflicting array of stimulation, with the result that the child is unable to attend to those stimuli most relevant in terms of increased intellectual development (Gray & Klaus, 1965).* Stimulation in the culturally deprived environment appears to occur within a restricted range, and there is less adequate and systematic ordering of stimulation sequences (Deutsch, 1963). The effects of this restricted environment include poor perceptual discrimination skills; inability to use adults as sources of information, correction, and reality-testing, and as instruments for satisfying curiosity; an impoverished language-symbolic system; and a paucity of information, concepts, and relational propositions (Deutsch, 1963). Thus, the parents in culturally deprived homes are less likely to play verbal games with their children (Stendler-Lavatelli, 1968) and are less likely to label objects and point out the distinctive properties of stimuli and subtle differentiations between stimuli (C. Deutsch, 1968).

Both the animal and human evidence indicates that early environmental deprivation stunts intellectual development. Cage-reared rats (Forgus, 1954; Gibson and Walk, 1956; Hebb, 1949) and dogs (Thompson and Heron, 1954) who are deprived of visual and exploratory experience are significantly inferior to pet-reared control animals in later problem-solving ability. When monkeys are deprived of stimulation during infancy, they tend to become inactive, to avoid exploration of the environment, and to "prefer visual and manipulatory stimuli of low complexity" (Sackett, 1965); and when kittens are placed in a complex-free (simplified) environment, they exhibit inferior maze learning ability and less activity (Wilson, Warren & Abbott, 1965). The longer children remain in substandard environmental conditions, i.e., in foundling homes (Freud and Burlingham, 1944; Spitz, 1945, 1949), in orphanages (Dennis and Najarian, 1957; Skeels, and Filmore, 1937; Skeels et al, 1938), or with mentally retarded mothers (Speer, 1940), the progressively lower their I.Q.'s become in comparison with the I.Q.'s of control children placed in more favorable environments.

These findings are consistent with the reports of progressive decline in the intelligence test scores of isolated mountain and canal-boat children who also grow up in unstimulating and nondemanding intellectual environments (Asher, 1935; H. Gordon, 1923; Sherman and Key, 1932; Wheeler, 1942); with the lower I.Q.'s of rural than of urban children (Asher, 1935; Ausubel, 1965; Chapanis and Williams, 1945; Wheeler, 1942); with the social-class differential in I.Q. (Bayley and Jones, 1937; Terman and Merrill, 1937); with the upgrading effect of urban residence on Negro children's I.Q.'s (Klineberg, 1935); and with the high correlation between the intra-pair

---

*Hunt (1968) argues that the whole issue of stimulation must be looked at from a developmental perspective. Thus, crowding in the home may not be a handicap for the human infant in the early months of life but this condition may have a retarding effect on later phases of development.

discrepancies in the I.Q.'s of separated monozygotic twins and the discrepancies in their educational advantages (Newman, *et al*, 1937). Evidence of depressed I.Q., of special retardation in language skills and conceptualization, and of inability to concentrate is found as late as adolescence among children who spend varying periods of their early years in foundling homes (Goldfarb, 1945; Provence and Lipton, 1962).

A striking contrast to the above findings can be seen when children are raised in environments where intellectual stimulation is explicitly programmed (Moore & Anderson, 1968; 1969). When the environment is carefully geared to the child's level and interests, he can learn to read and write with proficiency (Moore & Anderson, 1968, 1969). It is one thing, however, to appreciate that lack of adequate intellectual stimulation in the preschool years may stunt later intellectual ability, and quite another to make assertions such as those stating that "critical periods" exist for the learning of particular intellectual skills (see p. 593), that young children are invariably better able than adolescents or adults to learn *any* subject-matter material, or that the human being is *extraordinarily* open and receptive to learning between the ages of two and five (Pines, 1963).

Language Retardation

The issue of language retardation and certain types of subcultural differences in language development is beset with important conceptual questions at the outset. As Cazden (1966) notes:

"The argument over whether children from Harlem of Appalachia should be called "culturally deprived" is more than an empty terminological dispute. It reflects a basic and important question. Is the concept of cultural relativity valid in this subcultural context or not? More specifically, in what ways is the language used by children in various subcultural groups simply different and to what extent can the language of any group be considered deficient by some criteria?" (p. 186).

It is our contention that children living in substandard environments, as previously discussed (see p. 542), suffer from language deficits particularly with respect to the abstract dimension of verbal functioning, and it is here that the "culturally deprived" child manifests his greatest degree of intellectual retardation.*

The most important consequence of the culturally deprived child's language retardation, however, is his slower and less complete transition from concrete to abstract modes of thought and understanding. This takes place for two reasons. First, the culturally deprived child lacks the repertoire of

---

*It is easy to forget the individual variation of children classified as "culturally deprived" when they are being compared with other groups of children. There is evidence however, indicating a considerable amount of variability within groups labelled as "culturally deprived" on linguistic abilities (Sigel & Perry, 1968) and conceptual development (Hunt & Dopyera, 1966).

clear and stable abstractions and "transactional" terms (e.g., conditional conjunctives, qualifying adjectives) that is obviously prerequisite for the direct manipulation and understanding of *relationships* between abstractions. Second, for lack of adequate practice, he has not acquired sufficient facility in relating abstractions to each other *with* the benefit of concrete-empirical props, and hence is less likely to be able to dispense with their assistance at the same age as his environmentally more favored contemporaries. Because he uses concrete thought operations, which are necessarily more time-consuming than their abstract-verbal counterparts, and because of his distractibility, unfamiliarity with formal language, impaired self-confidence, and unresponsiveness to time pressure, the culturally deprived child typically works more slowly than the middle class child in an academic setting (Chapanis and Williams, 1945).

Schooling and Intellectual Development

We still lack firm evidence concerning the influence of an optimal learning environment on the intellectual development of culturally deprived children, especially those who have been subjected for many years to the frustration and demoralization of inappropriate school experience (see p. 384). This is an extremely urgent research problem that should engage our immediate attention. We need to investigate the effects of an optimal learning environment on both IQ scores and on the acquisition of school knowledge, making special efforts to eliminate errors of measurement associated with test-content bias, test-taking skills, test rapport, and test motivation. On *a priori* grounds one might anticipate that school knowledge would be more amenable than intelligence level to the influence of environmental stimulation.

Mechanisms Mediating Irreversibility

The Critical Periods Hypothesis. The "critical periods" hypothesis already discussed under parental deprivation and the effects of institutionalization (see pp. 450-453) was implicitly applied to intellectual development many years ago by Montessori and her followers to justify the particular graded

---

The gross findings of the positive effects of school attendance on certain cognitive skills (Goodnow, 1962; Goodnow and Bethon, 1966; Greenfield and Bruner, 1966; Olson, 1970; Mermelstein and Shulman, 1967) can only be specified within a restricted domain of cognitive tasks. Some tangential evidence concerning the ameliorative effect of school experience on intellectual development also comes from studies showing that the resumption of regular schooling in Holland after World War II raised the mean IQ of children (de Groot, 1948, 1951), and that long-term improvement in substandard school conditions raised the mean IQ among Hawaiian (S. Smith, 1942) and East Tennessee mountain children (Wheeler, 1942). Current remedial programs for culturally deprived children at this age level, undertaken as part of the anti-poverty movement, tend to be global action programs rather than controlled research studies that can yield valid evidence regarding the efficacy of any particular cognitive or motivational aspect of remediation.

series of learning tasks which children are set in Montessori schools (Rambusch, 1962). More recently it has been invoked by advocates of the proposition that young children can learn many intellectual skills and kinds of subject matter more efficiently than adults can. The argument in both instances is that since there are allegedly optimal periods of readiness for all kinds of cognitive acquisitions, children who fail to learn the age-appropriate skills at the appropriate time are forever handicapped in acquiring them later (Fowler, 1966b).

Serious difficulties, however, lie in the path of applying the "critical periods" hypothesis to human cognitive development (Ausubel, 1965b). In the first place, it has been validated only for infant individuals in infrahuman species, and in relation to those kinds of rapidly developing perceptual, motor, and social traits that are largely regulated by genic factors. In humans, especially beyond the prenatal period and the first year of life, environmental determinants of development are more important and the rate of maturation is significantly slower. Second, it has never been empirically demonstrated that *optimal* readiness exists at particular age periods for specified kinds of *intellectual* activities, and that if adequate conditions for growth are not present during those periods, no future time will ever be an advantageous, and thus irreparable developmental deficit will be caused.

Hence, if specific intellectual skills or subject-matter content are not acquired at the earliest appearance of readiness, this does *not* mean that they cannot be acquired later just as well or even better. The same degree of cognitive capacity that establishes readiness at an earlier age would *still* be present at least in *equal* degree at some future date; the problem, therefore, is not that this degree of maturity disappears or *declines* in some mysterious fashion, but rather that it fails to *grow* at a normal rate in the interim because it is not appropriately exercised. The disadvantage of unnecessarily postponing such learning tasks thus inheres in the irreparable loss of precious years of opportunity when reasonably economical learning (and the concomitant growth in cognitive capacity) fail to occur simply because these kinds of tasks are not attempted. When this happens, the individual, in comparison with equally endowed peers, incurs a deficit in cognitive capacity which limits his current and future rate of intellectual development.

The Cumulative Nature of Developmental Deficit. This brings us to a second, somewhat more credible, explanation of the possible irreversibility in cognitive development that results from prolonged cultural deprivation (Ausubel 1965b). We refer to the tendency for existing developmental deficits to become cumulative in nature, since current and future rates of intellectual growth are always conditioned or limited by the attained level of development. The child who has an existing deficit in growth incurred from past deprivation is less able to profit developmentally from new and more advanced levels of environmental stimulation. Thus, irrespective of the adequacy of all other factors—both internal and external—his deficit tends to increase cumulatively and to lead to permanent retardation.

New growth, in other words, always proceeds from the existing phenotype, that is, from already actualized capacity, rather than from potentialities inherent in the genotype (genic structure). It makes no difference in terms of this limiting influence whether the attained deficiency is attributable to inferior genic endowment or to inadequate environment. If, as a result of a consistently deprived environment during the early formative years, potential intellectual endowment is not actualized, the attained functional capacity significantly limits the extent to which later environmental stimulation, even if normal in quantity and quality, can increase the rate of cognitive growth. Hence, an individual's prior success or failure in developing his intellectual capacities tends to keep his future rate of growth relatively constant. Initial failure to acquire adequate language, information-processing, and problem-solving abilities, for example, limits the later growth of cognitive capacities and functioning.

MOTIVATIONAL FACTORS IN LEARNING

Few theoretical issues in psychology provoke more heated controversy than the role of motivation in learning. Positions vary all the way from the assertion that no learning whatsoever takes place without motivation to a complete denial that motivation is a significant variable in the learning process. Much of this controversy bears on the nature of learning as a "contemporaneous" phenomenon and hence cannot properly receive any systematic consideration in a book on developmental psychology. We can only be concerned here with the distinctive role of motivation in the learning of children and with age level changes in this relationship.

The weight of the evidence indicates that although motivation is a highly significant factor in and greatly facilitates learning is by no means an indispensible condition. On theoretical grounds it may be hypothesized that motivation becomes a progressively less important factor in learning as children advance in age. As learning becomes easier and less effortful due to the growth of cognitive capacity, attention span, and ability to concentrate, less energization of the learning process is necessary. In addition, cognitive structure variables become increasingly more important as determinants of learning. Lastly, since the child is motivated more by cognitive, affiliative, and ego-enhancement drives, material reward and punishment become less salient factors. Considerable research suggests that much learning is apparently neither energized by motivation nor reinforced by drive satisfaction (reduction). Classical or Pavlovian conditioning, for example, merely depends on temporal contiguity of the conditioned and unconditioned stimuli.

A good deal of learning, as pointed out above, occurs incidentally without any explicit intention to learn. Appreciation of a means-end relationship is frequently acquired and selectively retained, either through insight or trial-and-error variation of responses, even if unaccompanied by the original existence and later reduction of a drive state.

Even where motivation is clearly operative in human learning, it is misleading to extrapolate the familiar paradigm of homeostatic drive reduction that is characteristically used to explain animal learning (Harlow, 1953). Such drives are quickly satiated and, when accompanied by intense effect, disrupt learning (Harlow, 1953). Hence, hunger, thirst, pain, and the like, rarely motivate human learning; and although material rewards are often effective, intrinsic (task-oriented) and ego-enhancing motives increasingly tend to dominate the motivational picture with advancing age. Material rewards also tend to become less ends in themselves than symbols of earned or attributed status and sources of self-esteem.

The trend in recent research and thinking has been to place greater emphasis on the motivational power of such intrinsic and positive motives as curiosity (Berlyne, 1960, 1965, 1969; Day & Berlyne, 1969), surprise and moderate disequilibrium (Chadesworth, 1969; Hunt, 1965), exploration (Montgomery, 1954), activity (W. F. Hill, 1956), manipulation (Harlow, 1950; Terrell, 1959), mastery or competence (White, 1959), and the need for stimulation (Butler, 1954). In addition, these latter drives have been elevated to the status of primary drives in their own right. Unlike other drives, they are, furthermore, gratified (reduced) merely by the very fact of successful learning itself. It is hardly surprising, therefore, that in many human learning situations the provision of explicit rewards makes relatively little (Abel, 1936) or no (Auble and Mech, 1953) difference in speed of learning or in performance level. Because so much learning attributable to task-oriented or ego-enhancing motives has already occurred, the later introduction of homeostatic or material rewards into the learning situation does not dramatically accelerate the rate of learning as it does in comparable animal ("latent learning") experiments.

Cognitive Drive

At the human level, cognitive drive (the desire for knowledge as an end in itself) is probably an important motivational component for learning. As E. C. Tolman (1932) had pointed out, motivation may facilitate learning in ways other than by energizing behavior and by reinforcing the successful variant through drive reduction. It also exerts a purely cognitive effect by highlighting or emphasizing what is to be learned, and by providing confirmatory and corrective feedback. This is evident both in meaningful discovery learning and in meaningful reception learning where the choice of correct alternatives is rewarded and the choice of incorrect alternatives is not. Because meaningful learning provides its own reward, cognitive drive takes on greater significance as a motivational determinant. It is probably derived, in a very general way, from curiosity tendencies and from related predispositions to explore, manipulate, understand, and cope with the environment (R. W. White, 1959). These latter predispositions, however, originally manifest potential rather than actual motivational properties, and are obviously nonspecific in content and direction. Their potential motivating power is actualized in expression and particularized in direction by the developing individual, both as a result of successful exercise and the anticipation of future satisfying consequences from further exercise, and as a result of internalization of the values of those significant persons in the familial and cultural environments with whom he identifies. Far from being largely endogenous in origin, therefore, specific cognitive drives or interests are primarily acquired and dependent upon particular experience. Hence, we observe again that the relationship between cognitive drive and learning, like the relationship between motivation and learning generally, is reciprocal from a cause-effect standpoint.

Many properties of the learning situation that foster cognitive drive facilitate learning by attracting and sustaining attention. These include novelty, incongruity, surprise, change, and conceptual conflict (Berlyne, 1960, 1965, 1969; Day & Berlyne, 1969; Hunt, 1965). A moderate amount of discrepancy, incongruity, or gap between existing knowledge and a new learning task is most effective in mobilizing attention, particularly when the learner is dissatisfied with what he knows. In Piaget's terms, a child is most attentive to new learning tasks when they require some degree of accommodation on his part before they can be assimilated—when existing schemas are not wholly adequate for understanding or problem solving and require some but not too much modification.

In addition to its energizing effects on meaningful reception learning (by enhancing effort, attention, and persistence), motivation also mobilizes nonspecifically the individual's immediate readiness for such learning by lowering the thresholds of those general kinds of perceptions and responses that are customarily implicated in the learning process. Exemplifying this latter mechanism is the lowering of reaction times that occurs in response to instructions to "work faster" (Owens, 1959) (as opposed to task-oriented instructions or instructions to relax). It is important, however, not to confuse this non-specific motivational facilitation with the more direct and specific influence on dissociability strength that is exerted by such variables as meaningful learning set, integrative drive, and self-critical attitudes. As a result of the operation of these latter, more specific quasi-motivational mechanisms during learning, clearer and more stable meanings are acquired

and retained, which, in turn, facilitate the sequential type of learning involved in the mastery of subject matter. For example, both L. Festinger
(1958) and D. E. Berlyne (1960) speak of the need to reduce dissonance,
incongruity, or conflict between two cognitions. This may lead to change in
one of the beliefs, to integrative reconciliation, or, as pointed out above to
summary dismissal or compartmentalization of the contradictory cognition.

An optimal level of motivation or ego-involvement (neither too high nor
too low) apparently exists for complex kinds of learning (Iverson and
Reuter, 1956). According to Bruner (1957), impelling drive states may
conceivably disrupt meaningful generic learning both by overemphasizing
the particularity of newly-learned concepts, and by limiting the learner's
ability to apply previously-learned principles to newly-learned tasks, and
hence "to go appropriately beyond the information given." In support of this
proposition he cites an experiment conducted by Postman and himself, in
which subjects under stress made less improvement than a nonstress group in
lowering their perceptual thresholds while learning to recognize tachisto-
scopically-presented three-word sentences. Stated in terms of an hypothesized
physiological basis of motivation, a moderate amount of activation or arousal
seems to have an optimal effect on learning (Malmo, 1959).

Age Level Trends in Motivational Orientation to Learning

Since little or no systematic research has been conducted on age level
changes in children's motivational orientation to learning or on the relative
efficacy of different kinds of incentives among different age groups, we must
resort to logical inferences from general principles of personality development (Chapter 8). We have already suggested that with increasing age
material reward and punishment motivate learning less in their own right
than as symbols of approval and disapproval, of enhanced and depreciated
self-esteem, and of derived and primary status. Second, as part of the trend
toward desatellization, values tend to be assimilated more on an *incorporative*
and explanatory than on a satellizing basis (see pp. 272-280), and the need
to excel in school or other performance becomes motivated more by desire for
personal prestige than for parental approbation (Ausubel, 1968). During this
period, therefore children become more responsive to the stimulus of competition (Ausubel, 1968). Third, as a reflection of their quest for greater
volitional independence and primary status children become more critical
and resistive to prestige suggestion, particularly to the kind related to
personal loyalty. They are more resistive to training and less willing docilely
to learn rote skills and arbitrarily presented information merely because an
authority figure thinks them important. The mouthing of meaningless
phrases is also more of an affront to minds that have a greater capacity to
understand abstract ideas. Finally, the effectiveness of cognitive drive as an

intrinsic task-oriented type of motivation is impaired as a consequence of the increasing, almost exclusive, association of intellectual interests and activities with ego-enhancing and anxiety-reduction motives. If the desire to learn and understand is almost invariably exercised in the context of competing for grades, obtaining degrees, preparing for a vocation, striving for advancement, and reducing the fear of academic and occupational failure, there is little warrant for believing that much of it survives as a goal in its own right. This trend is reflected in the progressive decline in school interests and intellectual enthusiasm as children move up the academic ladder (Jersild and Tasch, 1949). Theoretically, of course, it is true that some cognitive drive may be developed as a functionally autonomous by-product of successful learning, even though the intellectual activity in question is originally motivated by extrinsic considerations.

Individual Differences in Motivational Orientation

Coexistent with and probably exceeding age level differences in motivational orientation to learning are individual differences in the extent to which satellizing, incorporative and explanatory orientations are employed. * Depending upon individual differences in personality development, different motivational orientations toward learning receive varying emphasis over and above the influence exerted by general developmental trends. They not only affect the mode of assimilating goals and values but also the acquisition of academic skills and knowledge.

Although the incorporative and exploratory orientations generally become more conspicuous with increasing age they are only dominant in non-satellizers. Satellizers chiefly manifest a satellizing motivational orientation, at least until adolescence. In varying degrees, however, all three orientations are usually present in most individuals. Not infrequently, as a result of continued successful experience, motivations that are originally absent in a given learning activity are developed retroactively. A socially rejected child, for example, may seek originally to achieve competence in some academic field solely for compensatory ego enhancement. Eventually, however, he may develop genuine task-oriented interests that are functionally autonomous of his original motivation.

When ideas are accepted on a satellizing basis, resistence to new learning proceeds largely from conflicting ideological trends in the new set of values, which can only be accepted at the cost of repudiating prior loyalties and assuming the associated burden of guilt. Nevertheless, this must take place for resatellization to occur. The satellizer feels secure in his derived status only as long as approval is forthcoming. He finds disapproval threatening and, when

---

* The principle features of these different orientations are described in detail in Chapter 8.

incurred through disloyalty, productive of guilt feelings. In the case of the non-satellizer, new ideas are resisted because they constitute a potential threat to self-esteem by challenging (a) the existing system of values organized on an ego prestige basis, and (b) various presumptions of independence, originality, infallibility and omniscience. Because he lacks "sufficient confidence in the ultimate outcome of the learning process he is naturally reluctant to undertake new learning which could end in failure, or at any rate constitute a threat to his security while still incomplete and tentative" (Ausubel, 1949). Resistance is usually overcome when "the possibility of future ego aggrandizement by incorporation of the new value" is perceived (Ausubel, 1949).

Since non-satellizers are more likely to suffer from impaired self-esteem and from anxiety, they are more likely to feel inadequate in new learning situations, to over-respond with fear, and to avoid improvisation. Disapproval does not threaten a relationship from which vicarious status is derived or provoke feelings of guilt; it serves rather as an objective index of failure with attendant consequences to self-esteem. The motivation for learning is generally higher than in satellizers because self-esteem is dependent solely upon extrinsic considerations and is largely a function of superior accomplishment.

CHAPTER 16

Specific Aspects of Cognitive Development

WE HAVE JUST CONSIDERED the general aspects of perceptual-cognitive development and the factors operant in the expansion of cognitive experience. In this chapter we will consider more specific aspects of cognitive development such as the development of memory, problem solving, motivation, and the relation between language and cognitive growth.

DEVELOPMENTAL TRENDS IN MEMORY*

In its simplest sense, memory is the retention of what has been learned or experienced (Elkind, 1967). In order to account for the continuing representation of prior conscious experience in present cognitive structure, it is necessary to assume the existence of some hypothetical construct such as memory trace—even if the neurophysiological basis of the trace is currently unidentifiable. Cognitive functioning and organization may then be conceptualized in terms of various interrelationships between existing trace systems and between the latter and ongoing perceptual processes. Memory is not a static process where stored information is suspended in a quiescent state (Neisser, 1967); rather the processes involved in memory are constantly constructing and transforming the information to be remembered (Mandler, 1967; Neisser, 1967; Inhelder, 1969; Piaget, 1968; Piaget, Inhelder and Sinclair, 1968). *Memory* does not refer to all possible dimensions and interactions of memory traces, but only to their relative availability as measured by recognition, recall, or the facilitation of relearning. It does *not* include behavioral evidence of the residual neural effects of noncognitive experience, such as most instances of conditioning.

Cognitive structure may be defined as a nonspecific but organized representation of prior experience (Neisser, 1967) and it seems reasonable to suppose that cognitive structure is hierarchically organized in terms of highly stable and inclusive conceptual clusters under which are subsumed less stable and less inclusive illustrative materials. As new perceptual and ideational data are experienced, they too are appropriately "catalogued" under

See Fowler, 1962; Olson, 1968 and Smirnov, 1961 for partial reviews of the literature.

relevant conceptual foci, since this is the most orderly and efficient way of organizing large quantities of information for ready availability. At first, for a variable period of time, the recently catalogued materials can be dissociated from their subsuming concepts and are reproducible as individually identifiable entities. Because it is most economical and least burdensome to subsume as much material under as inclusive categories as possible, the import of many specific illustrative items is assimilated by the generalized meaning of the more established and highly conceptualized subsuming foci. When this happens these items are no longer dissociable or identifiable as entities in their own right and are said to be "forgotten." Hence, barring repetition or some other special reason (e.g., primacy, uniqueness, affective content) for the perpetuation of dissociability strength, specific items of experience that are supportive of an existing conceptual entity tend to be irreversibly assimilated by the generality of the latter. This process is very similar to the abstraction of particular experiences by virtue of which the concept itself is originally formed.

Before turning to developmental norms in memory it appears useful, since the literature on memory honors this distinction, to distinguish long-term from short-term memory. Most people think of memory and forgetting as occurring over a period of months and years. Nevertheless, it is clear that memory may operate on a much less extended time interval which can be measured in seconds rather than days or months. Short-term memory refers to those traces which are available for very short durations of time (e.g., memory for telephone digits from looking to dialing). Short-term memory seems to be a purely perceptual trace which runs its course in seconds or less (Deese & Hulse, 1967). It is also evident that short-term memory can be preempted by succeeding perceptual events but not by stored information (Deese & Hulse, 1967). At present, it is conjectured that without specific control processes, encoded information in short-term memory is not transferred to long-term memory and cannot be retrieved at a later time (Mussen, Conger & Kagan, 1969). In spite of its fragility, short-term memory can be used in certain types of problem-solving tasks where the solution only demands that the memory trace be present for short periods of time. For example, short-term memory could be utilized in the conservation task where brief memory of the pretransformation experience allows the child to reverse his thought on the transformed sensory data and deduce conservation.

Early Signs and Development of Memory

Once the infant experiences genuine percepts, crude forms of memory undoubtedly exist but are difficult to demonstrate convincingly. Sensori-motor memory involves the retention of early sensori-motor coordinations learned in the course of adapting to the immediate environment (Elkind, 1967). For example, retention of a variety of motor coordinations such as those involved in swimming, may be learned in early childhood and retained in later phases of the life cycle (Elkind, 1967). Other early signs include unequivocal evidence that the infant recognizes his mother (see p. 445) and persistent searching activity for objects hidden or removed from current view. More objective evidence has been obtained through the use of the delayed reaction experiment. As early as twelve weeks of age, a child demonstrates awareness of the contingency between the onset of a stimulus (auditory sound) and the later occurrence of an interesting event; the delayed time in the contingency may be as much as 5 seconds (Watson, 1967). Another type of delayed reaction experiment involves teaching the child to respond in a particular manner to a particular situation (Munn, 1954). After being isolated from it for varying intervals of time, he is re-exposed and tested for retention of the appropriate response. With advancing age the delayed reaction occurs after increasingly greater intervals between original learning and subsequent re-exposure. The maximum period for the one-year-old varies between 30 and 60 seconds. Longer delays are probably mediated by language and can be seen in two-year-olds who are able to find a goal object after a day-long interval (Skalet, 1931). As the delay interval lengthens, it seems unlikely that memory is mediated by transitory-kinesthetic imagery and more likely that it is verbally mediated (Elkind, 1967). The end of the sensori-motor period is partly characterized by the appearance of language and is a significant transition point in the study of memory in children:

"The beginning of the ontogenetic development of verbal memory should be considered as the second year of life when reproducing verbal memory appears. This type (simple reproduction) achieves highest force at the beginning of puberty, but its fastest development occurs in preschool age. The reproducing memory of even the 7-8 year old does not so sharply differ from the maximum of this memory (Smirnov, 1961; p. 394)."

One of the characteristics of infancy is the involuntary character of memory (Smirnov, 1961). Gradually however, memory is characterized by the gradual subordination of the processes of retention and reproduction to the intention of retaining or reproducing what has been noted (i.e., voluntary memory) (Smirnov, 1961). Several situational conditions are relevant in memory studies with pre-school children (Smirnov, 1961). Pre-school children retain more efficiently under game conditions when compared to laboratory conditions. It is also reported that a higher type of behavior in *reproduction* begins to be found earlier than a similar type of behavior in retention (Smirnov, 1961). Preschoolers also strongly adhere to the basic plot of a story and they are less likely to elaborate on the basic plot (Smirnov, 1961).

Three principal factors account for the relative instability of memory in early childhood. First, in the absence of an organized and differentiated cognitive structure, percepts tend to be vague and unclear and to have no stable, relevant conceptual foci under which they may be catalogued. Memory here is usually of the short-term variety. Second, memory also depends on the potential meaningfulness of the material that is to be related to the child's cognitive structure. There is ample evidence to indicate that retention of connected material intelligible to the child is much more likely to facilitate stable memory than is unconnected and unintelligible nonsense material (Ausubel, 1968; Fowler, 1962; Smirnov, 1961). Finally, in the absence of an adequate vocabulary much of the early experience remains unspecifiable and dependent on concrete imagery for its continuing cognitive representation. Verbal coding appears to facilitate recall by permitting the subject to produce some type of representation of the absent stimuli during the delay period between presentation of the stimuli and its subsequent recall (Mandler, 1967). Once a minimal cognitive structure is established, forgetting also reflects the operation of irreversible reduction. Because of their uniqueness and psychological salience, novel emotional experiences stand the best chance both of resisting this reduction and of being retained in a relatively impoverished, undifferentiated, and nonverbal cognitive field. However, disorganizing perception and being more susceptible to "repression," sometimes the more intense and disruptive of these experiences may later become less available to consciousness than more neutrally toned experiences.

Memory in early childhood, however, is not nearly as unstable as might be inferred from the paucity of adult recollections referable to the third and fourth years of life. A college student's inability to recall a particular striking event that occurred when he was two and one-half does not mean that he was similarly unable to do so when he was three years old. One might also question at this point how much he will remember of his college days after a comparable lapse of time. Furthermore, many early memories are not totally lost but are simply below the threshold of recall and could be demonstrated by using recognition and relearning methods or the techniques of hypnosis and free association. Burtt (1932) showed that an eight-year-old child required fewer repetitions to learn Greek passages that had been read repeatedly to him when he was only 15 months old than to learn comparable passages to which he had never been exposed. By the age of 18, no residual effects of childhood learning were apparent (Burtt, 1941).

With the growth of language and the establishment of more adequate cognitive structure during the elementary school years, memory gradually becomes more stable and increasingly enters into more advanced problem-solving abilities. It is difficult at this time to specify adequately the role that memory plays in cognitive sophistication (Olson, 1968), but it has been suggested, either implicitly or explicitly, that the development of *operational structures* is dependent on the child's immediate memory span (Flavell & Wohlwill, 1969; McLaughlin, 1963; Pasqual-Leone, 1967). At the same time, it is evident that improvement in memory is, in some way, dependent on the development of cognitive structure. Miller (1956) has suggested that memory is limited to 7 plus or minus 2 items or words, but he noted that a tremendous amplification of the ability to store and retrieve information could be accomplished by grouping words into sentences (i.e., chunking). The ability to organize large bodies of information for storage and retrieval has been suggested by many theorists when discussing memory (Ausubel, 1963, 1968; Bousfield, Esterson and Whitemarsh, 1958; Mandler, 1967; Miller, 1956). It is therefore expected that the development of more sophisticated cognitive structures that occurs with age will be instrumental in facilitating memory (Ausubel, 1968).

Piaget and his collaborators have recently advanced the thesis that memory cannot be dissociated as a separate ability from the functioning of intelligence as a whole (Inhelder, 1969; Piaget, 1968; Piaget, Inhelder and Sinclair, 1968). In several interesting experiments on visual recognition, recall, and reproduction of visual memory items, there appears to be an improvement instead of deterioration of memory which the Piagetians attribute to the development of more advanced operational structures. Thus memory of visual seriation items and problems of causality appear to improve as the child moves from the concrete to the formal operational stage (Inhelder 1969). It also appears that children moving into the stage of formal operations increasingly tend to use paradigmatic catagorization of verbal materials for recall (Mandler and Stephens, 1967). Correspondingly, in problems of short-term visual memory there appear to be certain qualitative differences between concrete and formal operational thinkers (Mishima and Inoue, 1966). Finally, Piagetian concrete operational schemas have been hypothesized to be structures which aid in the improvement of short-term memory in the early elementary-school years when compared to the preschool years (Crosbie, 1969). For example, superordinate categorization facilitates recall of verbal items; superordination ability here is considered as a typical concrete operational structure (Crosbie, 1969; Smirnov, 1961). More efficient recall of items can be produced not only by their superordinate classification, but also by their proximity in conceptual organization (Willner, 1967).

Flavell (1969a) has recently advanced the hypothesis that a memory task can profitably be regarded as a type of problem-solving situation in which effort at mnemonic mediation constitutes the means of problem-solving strategy and recall the goal or problem solution. It appears that with increasing age the child utilizes more effective mediators, but it is not always the case that ineffective mediators disappear with increasing age (Flavell,

1969). Of more particular interest here is the developmental conception that Flavell (1969) and co-workers (Corsini, Pick and Flavell, 1968; Flavell, Beach & Chinsky, 1966; Keeney, Cannizzo and Flavell, 1967) have advanced concerning younger and older children. They question the hypothesis that preschool children are mediationally deficient in memory tasks, but they find in comparison with school age children that they are less likely to produce spontaneous mediators in memory problems. Flavell (1969a) summarizes research evidence which indicates that there are developmental transitions from nonproduction to production of mediational activities between the ages of five and seven; such transitions are reversed in the developmental increase in detectable verbal rehearsal. Spontaneous use of rehearsal strategies follows a developmental course, with children under six years hardly ever employing spontaneous strategies (Flavell, 1969a; Hagen & Kingsley, 1968). Finally, there is some evidence that genuine verbal rehearsal is a later developing mediational tactic and that spontaneous and deliberate efforts at finding conceptual and associative linkages among items is a process which increases with age (Crosbie, 1969; Flavell, 1969).

Adult Recall of Childhood Events

The memory of events in the past is a rather elaborate *reconstruction* process in humans (Neisser, 1967). The long-term memory involved in adult recollections of childhood events throws some light on the reconstructions involved in early memory but these recollections must nevertheless be interpreted cautiously because they are subject to all of the errors of retrospective distortion. It should also be borne in mind that even if specific events cannot be recalled, a developmental precipitate of all past experience is represented in current cognitive and personality structure and in the prevailing level of cognitive sophistication. The "earliest memory" of both college and high school students dates back to the third or fourth year of life (Cameron, 1966; Dudycha and Dudycha, 1933, 1941). The contents of the early memories are normally visual, and pleasant (joy) or unpleasant (fear) rather than neutral (Cameron, 1966; Dudycha and Dudycha, 1933, 1941; Smith, 1952). In addition, they more often involve a pleasant than an unpleasant and a novel than a repetitive experience (Dudycha & Dudycha, 1933, 1941; M. E. Smith, 1952a). The earliness and number of childhood memories vary positively with success in formal education and with precocity in talking (M. E. Smith, 1925a). For the latter reason, perhaps, women tend to have more and earlier childhood memories than men (Dudycha & Dudycha, 1933, 1941; Smith, 1952). The actual nature of childhood and current experience is also a determining factor. Older children (age 10 to 14) who are better adjusted and who have been reared in favorable surroundings report more pleasant memories than do poorly adjusted children and children reared in unfavorable surroundings (Pattie and Cornett, 1952). The particular earliest event that happens to be remembered by a given adult depends on its importance for his life history, the kind of personality structure he had when it first occurred, and its relevance to current personality trends (Neisser, 1967).

Factors Influencing the Rate of Forgetting

In the absence of overlearning, children and adults forget memorized material very rapidly at first and then more slowly (Munn, 1954). It has been found, however, that when children only partially learn highly conceptualized material such as poetry, more is recalled after an interval of several days than immediately afterwards (Ausubel, 1963; 1968). This phenomenon of reminiscence is probably reflective of spontaneous recovery from the threshold-elevating effects of initial "learning shock" (Ausubel, 1968). It is postulated, in other words, that a certain amount of resistance and generalized cognitive confusion occur when unfamiliar new ideas are first introduced into cognitive structure; that this confusion and resistance are gradually dissipated as the new ideas become more familiar and less threatening; and that the existence of the initial resistance and confusion and their gradual dissipation are paralleled, respectively, by a corresponding initial elevation and a subsequent lowering of the threshold of availability. This interpretation is strengthened by the fact that reminiscence occurs only when material is partially learned or not overlearned, and when practice trials are massed; that is, it occurs only when opportunity for immediate confusion and later clarification exists (Ausubel, 1968).

The facts that reminiscence has been convincingly demonstrated only in elementary-school children (Sharpe, 1952; Stevenson and Langford, 1957; O. Williams, 1926), and declines (Sharpe, 1952) or is not manifested at all (O. Williams, 1926) in older subjects, suggest that initial "learning shock" tends to decrease with increasing age as cognitive structure becomes more stable and better organized. Moreover, reminiscence cannot be demonstrated for verbatim (Edwards and English, 1939; English et al, 1934) and rotely-learned (L. B. Ward, 1937) materials unless measured within minutes after learning, inasmuch as the retention span for such materials is exceedingly brief. Later increments in retention (i.e., increments other than a gain between an *immediate* and a subsequent test of memory) are, by definition, not indicative of reminiscence; they probably reflect the later removal of competing memories (or of negative motivational factors) temporarily raising the threshold of availability during the preceding retention test, rather than the dissipation of initial learning shock.

Many factors influence the rate of forgetting in children.* The facilitating effect of stable and relevant foci on retention has already been mentioned. Meaningful and highly conceptualized materials ("substance" items, explanations, generalizations) are more resistent to irretrievable reduction (assimilation) and, hence, are retained longer than "verbatim" items and specific information (Ausubel, 1963, 1968). Repetition with intention to learn is the time-honored method of minimizing proactive inhibition and irreversible reduction. It is most efficacious when distributed rather than massed, when recitation and passive reading are judiciously combined, and when the choice of whole or part methods is adapted to the nature and difficulty of material. Most studies show a moderate to high relationship between memory and I.Q. (Munn, 1954; Thompson, 1962).

Longevity of retention is also affected by various subjective factors. There is little doubt that the child's prevailing attitude structure differentially enhances or inhibits his retention. Other things being equal, children tend to selectively recall value-laden items that are consistent with rather than in opposition to their own attitudinal biases (McKillop, 1952; Taft, 1954). The cognitive mechanism that purportedly mediates the effects of attitude on retention is the complex of ideas, that together with related affective components (attitudinal bias), characterizes the structure of all attitudes. Controversial materials that instigate positive affect or attitudinal bias are generally relatable to a set of subsuming ideas that are clearer, more stable, more relevant, and more discriminable from the learning task than are the general run of subsumers in the learner's cognitive structure; the reverse holds true for controversial materials instigating negative affect or attitudinal bias (Ausubel, 1968).

INTELLECTUAL CURIOSITY

Intellectual curiosity, especially during the preschool years, is reflected in the number and kinds of questions children ask, and a question addressed to someone likely to know the answer is an epistemic response that often forms an alternative to directed thinking (Berlyne, 1965).† The frequency of questions naturally increases concomitantly with the spurt in language between the second and third years of life; thereafter they constitute about 10 to 15 percent of all linguistic utterances (Fisher, 1934). Boys appear to ask questions at a faster rate than girls, and the rate of asking questions (both for boys and girls) increases up to 30 months of age; questions occur much more frequently when the child is talking to an adult than when he is talking to

---

*A more complete discussion of this topic, which can only receive brief mention here is available in Ausubel, 1963; 1968.

†The most recent review of the literature on children's questions may be found in Berlyne, 1969a.

another child (Berlyne, 1969a; Davis, 1932). Early questions reflect an interest in learning the names of objects and persons in the environment. *Why* and *how* inquiries are a somewhat later development. Why questions about "human life" increase with age, while why questions about "things" and about plants and animals become gradually less frequent (Aikawa and Horuchi, cited in Berlyne, 1969a). More questions are asked about novel, surprising and incongruous events than about familiar occurrences (Berlyne & Frommer, 1966; Charlesworth, 1969; Davis, 1932). Consistent with previously mentioned findings, girls ask more questions than boys about interpersonal relations, whereas boys make more inquiries about causal relationships (Davis, 1932). The positive correlation between socioeconomic status and number of questions asked (Berlyne, 1969a; McCarthy, 1930) probably reflects social class differences in language proficiency, the amount of time parents spend with children, the value placed on intellectual achievement, and the probability of parents providing satisfactory answers and encouragement of further questions (Hess & Shipman, 1965).

In general, the study of children's questions during the school years has been accomplished by procedures that induce or invite questions (Berlyne, 1969a). As children advance in age during the elementary school years their questions become less *global* (e.g., Why?) and more *specific* (asking questions such as what?, where?, who?, which?, and finally the *definitive* how?) (Yamamato, 1962 cited in Berlyne, 1969). When trying to solve problems by asking questions, there is an increase with age in constraint-seeking questions which narrow down the range of alternatives (Mosher & Hornsby, 1966). Also, the probability of asking questions about the outcome of a story with an uncertain ending increases with age (Berlyne & Frommer, 1966).

Children's questions are motivated by more than desire for information. Just as frequently they are utilized as a technique for establishing and maintaining social contact. The child can feel more confident that he is holding his parents' attention when they are preoccupied with answering questions. Sometimes, also, he is less interested in obtaining information than in confirming his preconceptions, in receiving sanctions for his views, and in being reassured that his apprehensions are groundless. Many why questions in children are expressions of astonishment, disappointment, or dismay (Berlyne, 1965). Under certain conditions persistent questioning may be used as an attention-getting device or as a delaying tactic.

THE ROLE OF PLAY IN COGNITIVE DEVELOPMENT*

Recognition of the role of play in the achievement of more advanced forms of cognitive functioning is a recent phenomenon (Berlyne, 1969b).

Discussions of theories of play and reviews of the recent literature may be found in Berlyne, 1969b; Sutton-Smith, 1967.

Although there is considerable literature centering around the topic of play, there is very little known about what play accomplishes for the human organism (Sutton-Smith, 1967).

Following our discussion of *intellectual* curiosity it is interesting to note that both exploratory and play behavior in children correlate highly with information seeking in general (Maw & Maw, 1965). Although most play is probably exploratory behavior, it cannot be said that all play is exploration since exploration is ordinarily defined in terms of intrinsically rewarding or biologically neutral sensory consequences (Berlyne, 1969b). The difference between play and exploration probably revolves around the fact that the intrinsic motivation for the latter places greater emphasis on novel variation of responses according to internal criteria, whereas play is accompanied by traditional affective accompaniments of "fun" and "playfulness" (Sutton-Smith, 1967).

Piaget (1952) has recognized three types of games which are specifically related to the development of intellectual capacities, and which appear in succession developmentally: (1) practice games, (2) symbolic games, and (3) games with rules. *Practice games* are characteristic of the period of sensori-motor development (see p. 571); here the infant appears to involve himself in repetitive activity purely for the pleasure in doing it. In theory, *play activity* during the sensori-motor period stresses assimilation over accommodation, since the repetitive interesting activity appears to serve no clear accommodative function. The transition from the sensori-motor stage to the early stages of conceptual thought marks the beginning of *symbolic games* where the child's use of the sign and symbol enables him to accomplish games of make-believe and pretence. The "symbolic function" during the early pre-conceptual stage is exemplified in the "use of objects for the purposes of imaginative play" (e.g., the child making believe that his spoon is an airplane). During the "intuitive stage" (age four through seven), imaginative play wanes, probably because of the variety of other opportunities to exercise the symbolic functions and also because the child is starting to adapt more and more to external physical and social reality (Piaget, 1952). In the course of this stage the child increasingly becomes interested in social games which involve reciprocity and the differential use of rule regulation. The use and understanding of *rule games* also follows a developmental pattern which leads to more advanced forms of cooperation and respect for rule systems involved in the games throughout the stage of concrete operations.

The conception of play in Piagetian theory has mainly a compensatory function, with play permitting the child to make an intellectual response in fantasy when he cannot make one in reality (Sutton-Smith, 1967). Play can also be considered as a form of cognitive variation seeking (Sutton-Smith, 1967), and it is in this context that the relationship between play and other types of cognitive functioning will now be discussed. First of all, there are several lines of evidence indicating the relationship between playfulness and creativity (Sutton-Smith, 1967). Second, sex differences are apparent in novel uses of boys' and girls' toys; boys are able to give more usages and more unique usages for trucks and blocks than for dolls and dishes, while the opposite held true for girls (Sutton-Smith, 1967). Thus, play apparently increases the repertoire of available responses to certain parts of the stimulus world. Third, games requiring the exercise of a variety of self-controls seem to indicate social improvements in the players (Sutton-Smith, 1967). Finally, there is some evidence that there are functional interrelations between the skills learned in games and other aspects of the player's personality and cognitive style (Sutton-Smith, 1967). For example, boys who are winners at games are perceived as strategists by peers and apparently are disposed to persevere at intellectual tasks and make rapid decisions whereas boys who are less successful are less independent and more conventional in their intellectual aspirations.

CONCEPT ACQUISITION*

Although it is conceivable that infrahuman primates can acquire rudimentary concepts, their conceptual learnings, even compared to those of two-year-old children, are faltering, limited to simple, concrete representations, and not very transferable to analogous situations (Gellerman, 1931). It is largely because of their superior ability to formulate abstract concepts (which both makes possible and is dependent on language symbols) that human beings are singularly capable of solving complex relational problems without coming into direct contact with the objects and phenomena involved.

Concept formation consists essentially of a process of abstracting the essential common features of a class of objects or events that vary contextually, in other noncriterial respects, or along dimensions other than the particular ones under scrutiny. Typically these "common features" are not discrete elements shared by a number of stimulus patterns, but are comparable configurations or sets of relationships. Component psychological processes involved in the most highly developed form of concept formation include the following, more or less in the sequence given: (a) discriminative analysis of different stimulus patterns; (b) the formulation of hypotheses regarding abstracted common elements; (c) subsequent testing of these hypotheses in specific situations; (d) selective designation from among them

---

*The topic of concept acquisition is so broad that it is necessary to limit our discussion to our own theoretical viewpoint and to be selective in our review of the literature. Alternative interpretations of concept formation and recent reviews of literature may be found in the following sources (Bruner, et al., 1966; Elkind, 1967; Flavell, 1969; E. Gibson, 1969; Hershenson, 1967; Kidd & Rivoire, 1966; Lovell, 1961b; Michotte, 1963; Sigel, 1964; Stevenson, 1966; Wallach, 1963).

of one general category or set of common attributes under which all of the variants can be successfully subsumed; (e) relation of this set of attributes to relevant anchoring ideas in cognitive structure; (f) differentiation of the new concept from related, previously learned concepts; (g) generalization of the criterial attributes of the new concept to all members of the class; and (h) representation of the new categorical content by a language symbol that is congruent with conventional usage.

In concept formation, the child generates hypotheses or problem-solving propositions which aim at defining the abstracted criterial attributes of the concept to be learned. To be potentially meaningful, a given hypothesis must embody a means-end relationship; that is, the hypothesized criterial attributes must be exemplifiable in the specific exemplars. The actual process of explicitly confirming or disconfirming that such is the case occurs during hypothesis-testing. Finally, the confirmed criterial attributes are related to relevant ideas in cognitive structure and thereby become meaningful, i.e., constitute the meaning of the concept after they have been assimilated.

The anchoring ideas in cognitive structure to which the criterial attributes of new concepts are related, naturally vary with the abstractness and complexity of the concept in question. When the referent of a concept is a perceptible object or event, its criterial attributes are related to a common perceptual core of the object or event. In the case of a relatively simple but superordinate concept, such as "vegetable," the anchoring ideas, at least initially, are probably mere exemplars of the class (e.g., carrots, peas, turnips) which are simple concepts in their own right. The criterial attributes of the same concept at a later stage of development, or of more abstract concepts with nonperceptible referents, on the other hand, are assimilated by those anchoring ideas to which the set of abstracted attributes (e.g., "something edible," "not tasty but good for you," in the case of vegetable) is relatable.

The actual process of concept formation is undoubtedly facilitated by the child's acquisition of the *general idea* of categorization. The development of this insight is similar in nature, and, in fact, is related, to the acquisition of the insight that everything has a name. The latter insight, it will be remembered (see p. 512), is an outgrowth of the realizations (a) that all significates with approximately the same perceptual core have the same name, and (b) that significates with basically different perceptual cores have different names. Simple "naming" itself therefore constitutes a primitive (perceptual) or precategorical type of concept formation. The more advanced idea of categorization conceivably arises from the gradually-developing insight that adults also use words in a categorical sense, that is, to include exemplars that do not share a common perceptual core. As the child comes into contact with such categorical words as "vegetable," "fruit," "play," "work," "toy," etc., he acquires the insight that a given word can be used to represent a class of significates with perceptually dissimilar cores. This general insight, in turn, motivates him, first, to identify some physically dissimilar exemplars of simple categorical concepts (e.g., to discover that carrots, peas, and turnips are vegetables) and later, to discover the abstracted criterial attributes both of such concepts and of even more abstract generic ideas that have no perceptible referents. Once several categorical ideas are actually acquired, they obviously serve as models or paradigms for later instances of concept formation.

Contemporaneously as a concept is acquired, certain characteristic changes gradually take place (Vygotsky, 1962). It becomes increasingly less global, less impressionistic, and less diffuse (S. C. Fisher, 1916); the learner focuses progressively on more salient criterial attributes. Generic mental content also tends to be emptied of particularistic attributes and to become more abstract and general in nature. The identification of relevant criterial attributes similarly becomes more precise and refined; noncriterial attributes are sloughed off and new criterial attributes are added. Distinctions from related concepts also tend to become sharper. Idiosyncratic and subjectivistic elements become less prominent as the learner's version of the concept comes increasingly to conform to a culturally standardized consensus. Lastly, new contextual variants of the concept are acquired with the acquisition of greater sophistication in the same and related disciplines (Rowe, 1966). Nevertheless, unique individual experience still tends to give an idiosyncratic denotative and connotative flavor to most concepts.

Classification of Concepts

Perhaps the most important distinction that can be drawn among concepts is that between the conjunctive and disjunctive varieties. In the case of *conjunctive* concepts, *all* of the essential criterial attributes must *always* prevail. All of the criterial attributes of *disjunctive* concepts, on the other hand, need not always be present or may be present in varying degrees; they are, in other words, either-or in nature (e.g., A real number is either a rational number or an irrational number). A third type of concept, *relational*, is sometimes recognized; it, however, is really only a subtype of the other two major categories since many conjunctive and disjunctive concepts are characterized by relational attributes. Disjunctive concepts are understandably much more difficult to acquire than are conjunctive concepts (Bruner *et al*, 1956; Wallace and Sechrest, 1961). Concepts also vary in complexity, in breadth or inclusiveness, and in degree of abstractness (the tangibility or perceptibility of their referents).

Developmental Aspects of Concept Acquisition

General developmental changes in concept acquisition have been largely covered already in considering the concrete-abstract dimension of cognitive development (see pp. 570-590). From the sensori-motor stage to the abstract operational stage, there are progressive gains in the level of abstraction at which the process of concept acquisition occurs, in the level of abstraction of the concept meanings that emerge from this process, and in the abstractness and complexity of the kinds of concepts that lie within the child's grasp. As indicated earlier, these changes may be grouped under the qualitatively distinct stages of cognitive development delineated previously (see pp. 570-590).

During the stage of sensori-motor intelligence concepts are limited to certain *schemas* of actions that the child makes in response to his environment. Bruner *et al* (1966) have labelled this period the *enactive* mode; the child represents the world by his actions upon it. In the preoperational stage the child is limited to the acquisition of *primary* concepts—those concepts whose meanings he learns by *first* explicitly relating their criterial attributes to the exemplars from which they are derived, before relating these same attributes to cognitive structure. Generally speaking the first of these two operations is performed during the hypothesis-testing aspect of concept formation. It is theoretically possible, however, and it does occasionally happen, that he is presented with the criterial attributes of a new concept; but under these circumstances, however, the latter attributes would not be relatable to his cognitive structure unless he were first able to test them explicitly against particular exemplars of the concept. In any case, since intimate contact with multiple particular exemplars of the concept is necessary for concept acquisition, both the conceptualization process itself and its products (the acquired new concept meanings) take place at a low level of abstraction.

The preoperational child's dependence on concrete-empirical experience also typically limits him to the acquisition of those primary concepts whose referents consist of perceptible and familiar objects and events (e.g., "dog," "house"). This is the case because only with respect to such concepts are there both sufficient available exemplars, and exemplars at a sufficiently low level of abstraction for him to handle at his level of cognitive maturity. When he is an adolescent or an adult, he may, of course, discover new primary concepts whose exemplars are themselves highly esoteric abstractions; but at the pre-operational stage the exemplars of such concepts are neither available nor usable for purposes of concept formation. This does not mean that the exemplars of concepts must necessarily be nonrepresentational in nature, i.e., consist of actual objects or events. Exemplars may also be verbal (consist of concept names), as in the previously cited examples of such low-order superordinate concepts as "vegetable" and "work," providing (a) that the concepts they represent are known and have perceptible referents themselves (e.g., "carrot," "bean," "housekeeping," "nursing"), and (b) that the criterial attributes of the superordinate concept, whether discovered or presented, are explicitly related to them (the exemplars).

The concrete-operational child's acquisition of concepts proceeds at a much higher level of abstraction and yields correspondingly more abstract concept meanings. He is able to cope with *secondary* concepts whose meanings he learns without actually coming into contact with the concrete-empirical experience from which they are derived. Since such concepts are acquired by assimilation (i.e., by reception learning), he is merely presented with their criterial attributes, either definitionally or by context. But he does *not* have to first relate these attributes to particular exemplars of the concept before they (the attributes) become relatable to his cognitive structure; he depends instead on the use of concrete-empirical props (i.e., exemplars of the *attributes*). The use of such props implies a much higher level of conceptualizing operation than the corresponding use of exemplars of the concept itself. Nevertheless the process of conceptualization is constrained by the particularity of the input data, and typically yields a semi-abstract and subverbal type of concept meaning. Only the less complex kinds of secondary concepts, not too remotely removed from the child's orbit of personal and vicarious experience, can be acquired at this time.

The highest level of abstraction in concept acquisition is reached during the stage of abstract logical operations. The criterial attributes of complex and higher-order secondary concepts can be related directly to cognitive structure without any concrete-empirical props whatsoever; and the emerging products of conceptualization are refined by verbalization to yield precise, explicit, and genuinely abstract generic ideas.

Concepts are generally attained more rapidly and efficiently with increasing age (Flavell, 1969; Rossi, 1964; Yudin and Kates, 1963). In addition several qualitative trends consistent with the stages delineated above have been adequately established.

Increased Abstractness and Precision. One of the most significant developmental trends in children's conceptual development is the ontogenetic shift from concepts formed on the basis of concrete and immediately given perceptual, situational and functional attributes of objects to concepts of a more abstract nature (Flavell, 1969b). Part of this developmental trend in concept acquisition consists of a gradual shift from a precategorical to a categorical basis of classifying experience, or from a relatively concrete to a truly abstract basis of categorizing and designating generic meanings. Even in the precategorical stage, classificatory behavior can be taken to include similar reactions to nonidentical objects (Flavell, 1969). Thus, even in the sensori-motor stage it may be said that the young infant exhibits the earliest signs of classificatory behavior (Inhelder & Piaget, 1964; Ricciuti, 1965). There is also evidence indicating that the very young child tends to group related or associated items in recalling them, associative clustering increasing with age (Flavell, 1969b). However, in the precategorical stage, conceptualization does not proceed beyond the step of discriminative analysis (Bruner and Olver, 1963; Goldman & Levine, 1963; Reichard, *et al*, 1944; Russell & Saadeh, 1962; Sigel, 1953; Vygotsky, 1962; Wallon, 1952; Werner, 1948). As indicated before, objects and events are grouped in terms of their immediately perceived properties rather than in terms of their class membership. Thus preschool children are likely to classify objects on the basis of nonessential, incidental features, spatial and temporal contiguity, or similarity of action and location. During the elementary school years, similarity of structure and function becomes a more important classificatory criterion. With advancing age, however, as the child approaches adolescence, and as he becomes verbal-directed and freed from dependence on concrete-empirical experience in his conceptualizing operations, *categorical* classification on the basis of abstract criterial attributes becomes the dominant mode of organizing experience.

At first, concrete images are employed to represent a general class of perceptible objects. But these are gradually replaced by more abstract representational symbols detached from the stimulus properties they signify (Malrieu, 1955; Piaget, 1954, 1960; Werner, 1948). Various dimensional properties (e.g., size, form, color) also tend at first to be restricted to the particular objects in relation to which they are originally experienced. With increasing age they become conceptualized and attain independent status in their own right. They can then be applied to any relevant object or situation. Concomitantly, new and more inclusive higher-order abstractions tend to be formed out of existing first-order concepts (Bruner and Olver, 1963; Piaget, 1950; Welch, 1940b).

It is clear therefore that concepts are cumulative precipitates of cognitive experience and that "later meanings are not only built but absorb earlier and simpler ones" (Strauss, 1952). Conceptual development involves a continuous series of reorganizations in which existing concepts are modified as they interact with new perceptions, ideational processes, affective states, and value systems. Increasing cognitive sophistication also leaves its mark on conceptualization. Concepts become more elaborate, systematic, and flexible (Schuessler and Strauss, 1950; Vinacke, 1951) and less diffuse, syncretistic and subjectivistic (Spiegel, 1950; Vinacke, 1951). Older children, for example, are less disposed to regard conceptual opposites (e.g., ugliness and beauty) as reified entities than as opposite ends of a conceptual continuum. They not only generate concepts of much greater scope and inclusiveness but also make finer distinctions between closely related concepts (e.g., "dog," and "wolf"). In the same way subconcepts develop within concepts (e.g., "terrier" and "beagle" within "dog").

It is important to appreciate that children's use of culturally standardized conceptual terms does not necessarily imply that these terms represent the same generic meanings that they do for adults in the culture. The difficulty arises from the fact that children have no other terms to represent their immature conceptualizations and hence are obliged (and are encouraged) to use prevailing linguistic terms. Thus "dog" to a toddler is typically a proper noun (rather than a concept) designating one particular dog; and "Daddy" does not refer to an adult male who is paternally related to him but, rather, to the most familiar adult male in his social environment. Later on, as the child attempts to generalize his existing "concepts" to new experience, "dog" represents *any* quadruped and "Daddy" *any* adult male. Generalization or extension of use occurs on the basis of the objective, affective, or functional similarity of a new object or situation to the object or situation originally designated by the word in question (Lewis, 1951). Typically this extension is over-inclusive and requires differentiation and restriction; to a much lesser extent is it also under-inclusive and requires widening. After the true criterial attributes of a class are properly abstracted, overinclusive applications are appropriately restricted and underinclusive applications are appropriately extended. Developmentally speaking, therefore, this problem is one of fitting conventional symbols, which have culturally standardized generic meanings, to individual cognitive experience until symbol-concept relationships for the individual come to approximate corresponding relationships holding for the culture at large.

Brown (1958a) points out that the development of concepts does not necessarily proceed from the concrete (subordinate) to the abstract (superordinate). To the extent that part of the process of conceptual development consists of differentiating subconcepts out of more inclusive categories (for instance, "carp" and "perch" out of "fish"), this contention is undoubtedly valid. Nevertheless it must be appreciated that "fish" to a toddler is not the same superordinate concept that it is to an adult. Actually, at first, it is not a concept at all, but, rather, a particularistic term referring to one or more exemplars of "fish"; and, later, before a categorical concept emerges, the basis of classification is a common perceptual core. Thus, before subconcepts can be truly differentiated from a more inclusive concept, the latter itself must first be acquired by a conceptualizing process in which concrete (precategorical) criterial attributes are progressively replaced by attributes that are more abstract or categorical in nature.

More Concept Assimilation and Less Concept Formation. Paralleling general trends in cognitive development, reception learning gradually becomes ascendent over discovery learning in the acquisition of concepts. Beginning with the child's entrance into school, an increasing proportion of his concepts are acquired by definition or use in context. But it is only as he approaches adolescence that such nonspontaneous concepts manifest true categorical and generalized meaning. Prior to this time (during the stage of concrete logical operations) they are still somewhat particularistic and intuitive in nature because of their dependence during acquisition on concrete-empirical props.

It is not difficult to understand why concept assimilation gradually becomes the predominant mode of concept acquisition once the child reaches school age, whereas concept formation, although possible at any age level, is, generally speaking, most characteristic of the pre-operational or preschool stage of cognitive development. Concept assimilation characterizes the acquisition of secondary concepts; it presupposes sufficient intellectual maturity to relate to cognitive structure the abstracted criterial attributes of a new generic idea even though they (the attributes) are *not* first in intimate association with the multiple particular exemplars of the concept from which they are derived. Since this degree of maturity does not exist before school age, and only does then when the child has the benefit of concrete empirical props, the principal alternative open to the preschooler is to discover the criterial attributes of concepts by himself, using the necessary conceptualizing operations of abstraction, differentiation, hypothesis-generation and testing, and generalization. In so doing, he is obviously limited to the more simple kinds of primary concepts whose referents are either perceptible and familiar objects or events, or known concept words that represent such referents. But the criterial attributes of a concept that are discovered through concept formation obviously meet the developmental conditions for relatability to cognitive structure, inasmuch as they have been abstracted from and tested against particular exemplars of the concept during the process of conceptualization. Hence there is no problem with respect to the potential meaningfulness of criterial attributes that he discovers by himself.

However, once the child can meaningfully relate to his cognitive structure the criterial attributes of a new concept without first relating them to multiple particular instances that exemplify it, he can acquire concepts much more efficiently. By the time he reaches this stage of development, he has also already acquired, for the most part, the available supply of primary concepts with familiar and perceptible referents. He would thus find it relatively difficult to discover by himself (to acquire by concept formation) the more abstract and complex concepts he attains relatively easily through concept assimilation. Hence after discovering the body of simple everyday concepts that are available to them when they enter school, most individuals discover very few concepts by themselves thereafter. Contributions to culture's store of more difficult concepts are made by its more gifted members over the course of generations, and become readily available to all other adequately mature members through concept assimilation.

During the elementary-school years, it thus appears that progressive development of the ability to *assimilate* concepts depends on the same three aspects of cognitive and language development that generally bring about the transition from concrete to abstract cognitive functioning: (a) gradual acquisition of an adequate working body of higher-order abstractions that provide the component properties and relational elements constituting the criterial attributes of more difficult concepts; (b) gradual acquisition of "transactional" terms, that is, of substantive words such as "state," "condition," "basis," "property," "quality," and "relationship," and of functional or syntactical terms, such as conditional conjunctives and qualifying expressions, that are necessary for bringing abstractions into relationship with each other in ways characteristic of the dictionary definition of new concepts; and (c) gradual acquisition of the cognitive capacity itself, that makes possible the relation of abstract ideas to cognitive structure without the benefit of concrete-empirical props.

It is important to recognize and take account of the highly significant interaction that takes place between many assimilated concepts and their subverbal or intuitive precursors. As Vygotsky (1962) notes, the elementary-school child, in acquiring assimilated concepts, is greatly assisted by the existence in his cognitive structure of analogous spontaneous concepts at the preoperational level which he uses nondeliberately and with relatively little cognitive awareness.* These provide a springboard for the acquisition of "scientific" concepts† and for their "downward" exemplification and everyday reference. But although these spontaneous concepts undoubtedly enhance the meaningfulness of their analogous assimilated counterparts, and probably discourage rote reception learning, they may also, because of their primacy and vividness, interfere with the learning of more precise and categorical criterial attributes. The same kind of relationships also undoubtedly prevail between the more precise and abstract concepts acquired at the secondary-school level and their more intuitive elementary-school precursors.

In teaching scientific concepts therefore, it is essential to take account of the nature of their spontaneous precursors, that is explicitly to contrast the two sets of criterial attributes and to indicate why the adoption of the more abstract and precise set is preferable. Within the limits imposed by developmental readiness, systematic verbal instruction in abstract concepts at the elementary-school level, combined with appropriate use of concrete-empirical props, is pedagogically feasible and can greatly accelerate the acquisition of higher-order concepts (Arnsdorf, 1961; O. L. Davis, 1958). It is unnecessary and educationally wasteful to wait for such concepts to evolve

---

*"Work", for example, is both a spontaneous concept acquired from direct experience and a more formal, abstract concept with precise criterial attributes.

†Vygotsky's term for assimilated concepts in contradistinction to concepts acquired by concept formation ("spontaneous concepts").

spontaneously from direct experience. Further, many abstract concepts (for instance, "photosynthesis," "ionization") can only be acquired verbally since they are not susceptible to direct experience. Other, more concrete concepts ("house," "dog," "red," "hot"), on the other hand, are practically meaningless in the absence of actual experience with the objects or phenomena in question.

Increased Awareness of Conceptualizing Operations. Both Piaget and Vygotsky agree that awareness of the cognitive operations involved in concept acquisition does not develop until the child approaches adolescence and has been exposed to considerable systematic instruction in scientific concepts.

As Vygotsky states:

> In operating with spontaneous concepts the child is not conscious of them because his attention is always centered on the object to which the concept refers, never on the act of thought itself . . .
> A concept can become subject to consciousness and deliberate control only when it is part of a system . . . In the scientific concepts that the child acquires in school, the relationship to an object is mediated from the start by some other concept . . . A superordinate concept implies the existence of a series of subordinate concepts, and it also presupposes a hierarchy of concepts at different levels of generality . . . Thus the very notion of a scientific concept implies a certain position in relation to other concepts . . . The rudiments of systematization first enter the child's mind by way of his contact with scientific concepts and are transferred to everyday concepts, changing their psychological structure from the top down. (Vygotsky, 1962, pp. 92,93).

Awareness of concept acquisition develops late, Vygotsky (1962) believes, because it requires awareness of similarity. This, in turn, presupposes "a more advanced structure of generalization and conceptualization than awareness of difference." Nevertheless, even though a child cannot use a word like "because" deliberately in a test situation, and does not really grasp causal relations except in a very primitive and intuitive sense, he is able to use "because" correctly in everyday conversation. The rules of syntax too can generally be employed correctly by young children despite complete lack of awareness of the nature of these rules. However, deliberate use of such words as "because" is possible in relation to scientific concepts because the "teacher, working with the pupil, has explained, supplied information, questioned, corrected, and made the pupil explain" (Vygotsky, 1962, p. 107). It is hardly surprising therefore that awareness of concept acquisition and deliberate use of concepts arise earlier in relation to scientific than to spontaneous concepts.

Experience, Intelligence, Sex

By virtue of the very way in which concepts are generally formed, it is inevitable that the acquisition of particular concepts is dependent on a rich background of relevant experience (Serra, 1953). Concepts in early and middle childhood, especially, reflect the cumulative impact of first-hand, concrete-empirical experience over extended periods of time. Hence, there tends to be a higher relationship between degree of experience (as indicated by school grade and chronological age) and scores on concept tests than between the latter scores and I.Q. (Deutsche, 1937; Vinacke, 1951). For this reason also, genuine understanding of such concepts, as is involved in the appreciation of temporal and sociological relationships, cannot be materially increased by exposing children to *brief* special periods of essentially second-hand, verbal practice in school (Eaton, 1944; Pistor, 1940); at the very least, systematic didactic instruction using concrete-empirical props is necessary. When abstractions are introduced prematurely, some children become quite adept at mouthing them, and at the same time, concealing their lack of true understanding. This obviously becomes a fertile source for misconceptions and uncritical acceptance of ideas.

Although superior mental age, in the absence of corresponding life experience (chronological age), provides little advantage in comprehending abstractions, such comprehension is definitely related to I.Q. *within* a given grade level (Braun, 1963; Elkind, 1961a; Osler and Shapiro, 1964; Osler and Weiss, 1962; Serra, 1953). In the face of irrelevant information or more complex concept formation tasks, children with higher intellectual abilities appear to have longer latencies in forming the concept (Katz, 1968; Osler and Trautman, 1961; Wolff, 1967). The correlation between concept scores and either vocabulary or verbal intelligence is higher than the correlation between these scores and nonverbal intelligence (Deutsche, 1937; H. N. Hoffman, 1955). Apart from conditions of actual cultural deprivation, cultural or social class environment does not have much effect on ability to conceptualize (Deutsche, 1937), but does sensitize the individual to particular areas of conceptual experience. Thus it is likely that conceptual learning ability is not a unitary trait; it varies with differential patterns of experience. Whatever sex differences appear in concept acquisition appear to conform to this explanation (Elkind, 1961; L. A. Olson, 1963; Tagatz, 1967).

Development of Some Specific Concepts

Color and Form. The vast majority of research on the development of color discrimination in infancy has been inconsistent with control of the dimension of brightness being the most serious stumbling block for unequivocal interpretation of results (Hershenson, 1967; Spears & Hohle, 1967). There is, however, evidence to support the assumption of similar scotopic and photopic luminosity curves for infant and adults (Hershenson, 1967; Spears & Hohle, 1967). As a result of the foregoing, it can be demonstrated that infants shortly after birth are sensitive to light changes under conditions of light adaptation and by one month of age under conditions of dark adaptation (Spears & Hohle, 1967). The child's ability to discriminate colors in early infancy is highly questionable. A summary of the earlier studies on color discrimination indicates that color preference may not even be consistent for one child, and that there is an apparent lack of consensual agreement among infants except for a preference for colors over non-colors (Spears, 1966; Spears & Hohle, 1966).

The perception of form requires that the infant discriminate a figure consistently through changes in orientation, dimension, and context of figure (Spears & Hohle, 1967). The ability to perceive form requires attention to details and cues that are apparently beyond the capacity and experience of the very young infant (Spears & Hohle, 1967). Nevertheless, there is sufficient evidence to indicate that the neonate is provided with at least some sensory capacities with which to synthesize a perceptual product (Hershenson, 1966). Data collected concerning early ability to discriminate patterns (e.g., Fantz & Nevis, 1967), the presence of the requisite muscular control and detector apparatus to bring the image of an object onto the fovea and to hold it reasonably well (Hershenson, 1967), and the functional integrity of the neural pathways necessary for mediation of sensory information (Hershenson, 1967) have made the question of form discrimination in the neonate amenable to research; however, as yet this question is unanswered. The present attack on the problem of the perceptual development of form indicates that the mediational or symbolic processes relevant to form perception probably involve language (Spears & Hohle, 1967). By the age of two, it is evident that the child can discriminate certain shapes and forms despite changes in orientation, size, and context (Spears & Hohle, 1967).

Color and form preference in matching appears to follow a developmental trend (Rivoire & Kidd, 1966). The relative potency of color and form perception at different ages can be demonstrated by showing two objects that differ from a third in either color or form and then asking the children to place the third object with one just like it (Rivoire & Kidd, 1966). The earlier studies on this problem indicate that children under three years of age predominantly use form in preference to color as a basis for classifying objects. Between the ages of three and six there is a gradual shift to color, but after the age of six form becomes dominant again (Brian & Goodenough, 1929; Welsh, 1940a). Recent studies support the more conservative conclusion that preschoolers tend to select color more frequently than older children (Corah, 1964; 1966a, b; Corah & Gaspodinoff, 1966; Suchman & Trabasso, 1966) although at least one investigation has failed to report this consistency (Kagan & Lemkin, 1961). The movement from color to form preference appears to occur at a median transition age of four years two months (Suchman and Trabasso, 1966). Several studies show individual differences in preference for either color or form, with inconsistencies in some of the results

(Corah, 1964; Kagan & Lemkin, 1961; Suchman, 1966). There are inconsistent sex differences in color-form preferences (Corah, 1964; Kagan & Lemkin, 1961); nevertheless females appear to have a preference for lighter colors (Child, Hansen & Hornbeck, 1968). Deaf children in elementary school tend to discriminate more on a color dimension than do children with normal hearing (Suchman, 1966).

The dominance of color over form in preschool children, when compared with their elementary-school counterparts, may be interpreted in several ways. Colby and Robertson (1942) advance an "attentional" explanation for the young child's greater use of color. Thus, when two distinct shapes of the same color are presented to the child, they will cohere against a differential background with low attention, while perception of contour demands more elaborate attentional capacities characteristic of older children. Corah (1964) maintains that attention of the younger child to a dominant characteristic such as color in a stimulus configuration is analogous to the Piagetian process of centration.

Space. * The child's conception of space provides one framework in which reality is considered (Cassirer, 1944). It seems impossible to consider the real world without considering a spatial dimension (Cassirer, 1944). Nevertheless, a vast part of the child's conception of space is not imminent and appears to develop over time. In infancy, there are no such things as dimensions in space (e.g., near-far, right-left, up-down) in the sense of scaled or metric coordinates (Gibson, 1969). As such, these coordinates are sophisticated, abstracted, and differentiated very late developmentally (Gibson, 1969). Space for the young child is not a concept, nor are its dimensions perceived as such (Gibson, 1969). As we shall see, the child's conceptualization of space is in a sense coextensive with his cognitive representation of the external world. Using the Piagetian scheme of analysis (Piaget, 1954a), Baldwin (1955) has identified the following acquisitions as necessary for minimally mature and objective cognition of the spatial environment: (a) appreciation of the permanence of objects; (b) distinction between permanent properties of objects and their transitory spatial relations; (c) realization that movements are reversible and that the location of an object is independent of the path taken to reach it; (d) distinction between own and external movements; (e) ability to locate self in the spatial field; (f) perception of the spatial field as consisting of more than the objects relevant to the satisfaction of own needs; (g) the unification of information from different sensory modalities; and (h) ideational representation of absent objects. All of these are characteristically completed during the first 18 months of life (Piaget, 1954).

* *The literature on spatial concepts will not be extensive but, rather, representative of certain developmental dimensions. For more extensive reviews see: Flavell, 1963, 1969; Gibson, 1963, 1969; Lovell, 1964; Rivoire & Kidd, 1966.*

The above acquisitions provide the initial framework for the further development of spatial concepts, the child's spatial concepts following a continual evolution from topological to projective and Euclidean conceptions (Piaget & Inhelder, 1956). The earliest concepts of space, occurring in the preoperational stage of thought (see p. 573), are topological in nature (Piaget & Inhelder, 1956). Topological concepts involve only relationships of proximity, separation, order, enclosure and continuity. During the concrete operational stage of development, topological conceptions of space give way to projective and Euclidean conceptions. In projective space, objects are located relative to one another although there is no measurement (Piaget & Inhelder, 1956). Although there is some indication that the pre-operational child has an unverbalized "imaged" conception of right and left (Olson & Baker, 1969), it is evident that the concrete operational child shows an increasing ability with age to coordinate such relations as left-right and before-behind, so that he is able to see objects from another point of view (Piaget & Inhelder, 1956; Sullivan & Hunt, 1967). Children also appear to have greater difficulty in discrimination of left-right than they have with the up-down dimension (Huttenlocher, 1967). Euclidean conceptions add the dimension of measurement (e.g., objects are located by means of axes of reference as in length, breadth and height) and become more elaborate and sophisticated as the child grows older (Piaget and Inhelder, 1956). In general, the replications and extensions of Piaget's findings tend to roughly indicate the same varieties of age-related results, with several investigations reporting differences in major or minor detail in the age of acquisition, ease of response classification, inter-task and intra-child inconsistencies, etc. (Flavell, 1969; Lovell, 1964a; Wallace, 1965).

It is clear that the Piagetian conceptualization of spatial development does not place great stress on innate determinants of the child's ability to cope with spatial relationships (Wallace, 1965). Both Russian and Genevan research are probably correct in stressing the point that "space" becomes better differentiated with practice and extension of a child's sphere of activities (Gibson, 1969). For Piaget, action in space is essential to the development of the perception of space (Gibson, 1969), and he probably stresses this because the temptation is especially great to conceive space as something given immediately in experience, and immediately given *perceptually*, rather than otherwise (Flavell, 1963). As Flavell (1963) points out, Piaget stresses (1) that this effortless seeing is really the end product of long and arduous developmental construction, and (2) that the construction itself is more dependent upon actions than upon perception per se (p. 328). Some of the recent findings on perception (e.g., visual cliff experiments, with infants and animals, on depth perception), however, indicate that Piaget may be underestimating some innate perceptual determinants (Gibson, 1963;

1969; Walk, 1966). In addition, the role of "imagery," which takes a second place to action in the Piagetian system, may have been seriously underestimated (Olson & Baker, 1969; Wallace, 1965).

*Time.** The development of time concepts illustrates many age level trends in conceptualization, i.e., concrete to abstract, specific to general, current to remote, precategorical to categorical, subjective to objective (Goldstone & Goldfarb, 1966; Wallace, 1965). Sleep and feeding schedules are the first temporal events with social significance, but it is only when the young child can conceptualize before, now, and after that he shows instrumental temporal behavior rather than passive temporal adaptation (Goldstone & Goldfarb, 1966). The most important aspects of time conception are the experiences of duration and order since time experiences never exist on a level where nothing beyond the present moment is perceived. (Wallace, 1965). As the child begins to be conscious of duration, he begins to feel the duration of time as an experience (Wallace, 1965). The child first acquires a practical (precategorical) appreciation of time relations in coordinating his own movements sequentially, but at the early sensori-motor period there appears to be no concept of duration per se (Piaget, 1954a). During the latter part of the sensori-motor period the child gradually conceptualizes in concrete terms a notion of before-and-after relationships and of durational intervals between a series of ongoing, external events (Piaget, 1964). Finally, he is able to deal with concrete images of future and past events and eventually to represent them symbolically (Piaget, 1954a).

The capacity to perceive time directly as a quality with measurable and communicable magnitude is unique to the human species (Goldstone & Goldfarb, 1966). The development of verbal time concepts suggests a slow, predictable acquiring of the use and comprehension of time language and relations, with development proceeding from personal to conventional references and from specific to general concepts (Goldstone & Goldfarb, 1966). The child responds to time words before he uses them himself (Ames, 1946). Temporal concepts at the pre-school level are primarily related to the personal aspects of before and after without the capability of employing calender and clock concepts (Ames, 1946; Goldstone & Goldfarb, 1966; Springer, 1952). The word "today" appears at 24 months, "tomorrow" at thirty months, and "yesterday" at 36 months. At four the child distinguishes between "morning" and "afternoon," and at five he knows the days of the week. The seven-year-old is cognizant of the time of day, the month, and the season; and the eight-year-old usually knows the day of the month and is able to name all the months of the year. However, vagueness in comprehending the conventional time system, especially in regard to historical time and

*Reviews and summaries of replications are available. See Flavell, 1963, 1969; Goldstone & Goldfarb, 1966; Lovell, 1964b, 1966; Wallace, 1965.

sequence, is very common until at least the sixth grade (Friedman, 1944; Goldstone & Goldfarb, 1966; Oakden & Sturt, 1922). For example, the child finds historical events which have taken place before his time but in his parents' life-time just as distant as events which occurred several centuries earlier (Wallace, 1965). Lacking events occurring through experience, distant centuries appear short in comparison to the recent past (Wallace, 1965). As already pointed out, the acquisition of time concepts is mostly a cumulative product of incidental experience (Springer, 1952) and is not materially benefited by special instruction (Goldstone & Goldfarb, 1966; Pistor, 1940).

Individual differences in time conceptualization are evident in subjects as well as tasks. The rate and level of temporal conceptualization is a reflection of general intellectual growth; mental retardation ordinarily is accompanied by a deficiency in time conceptualization (Goldstone & Goldfarb, 1966). For example, the retarded child has little conception of sequence, relativity, or historical time and cannot comprehend time beyond his own activities (Goldstone & Goldfarb, 1966). Social class differences in time concepts have been demonstrated; lower class children and delinquents have shorter time spans (Goldstone and Goldfarb, 1966). When simple tasks are interposed, time estimation is more frequently overestimated by younger children, and females tend to overestimate time more than males (Goldstone & Goldfarb, 1966). Inter-sensory dimensions appear to be an important consideration in time estimation. For example, sounds are judged longer in duration than are lights (Goldstone and Goldfarb, 1966).

The studies quoted thus far have in general dealt with knowledge of time words, clock time, and universal or historical time. With exceptions, the vast majority of this type of research is empirically based with a minimum amount of theorizing (Flavell, 1969). Piaget (1946) has investigated the concept of time within his theoretical framework, stressing what scientists or mathematicians would term the concept of time proper. A typical experiment involves the presentation of two dolls who race across the table in front of the child. Both dolls start the race, at the same time, with a distinctive sound; however, one moves faster than the other. Both dolls stop simultaneously, again with a distinctive sound. As a result of their different speeds, one of the dolls has proceeded a greater distance. Preoperational children up to about six years admit that the dolls started at the same time but deny that they stopped at the same time and that they were running for the same length of time. As a consequence, they contend that the faster-moving doll took longer and stopped later. During the transition between preoperational and concrete operational thought (about 6 and 7 years) children agree that the dolls started and stopped at the same time, but insist that the faster moving doll took longer. By 7 and 8 years, children accept that the period of movement for each doll was the same. Thus, children in the preoperational stage do not differentiate time from space and speed; they maintain that *faster* means *more time*. Replications of Piaget's studies on time conception have generally confirmed his general conclusion with some minor reservations (Flavell, 1969; Lovell, 1966; Wallace, 1965).

Causality. The development of the conception of causality in the child has not received extensive attention in contemporary child development research (Flavell, 1969). Historically, earlier philosophical interpretations of the notion of causality stressed two general themes: first, the Lockeian claim that causality is an empirical assertion that is a result of repeated observation; and second, the Kantian notion that it involves a synthetic *a priori* mental category of thought (De Charms, 1968). Contemporary treatment of the notion of the development of causality in the child is, not surprisingly, dominated by Piaget (Piaget, 1929, 1952, 1954a). Both Piaget (1930) and Michotte (1963) have advanced the interpretation that *animate movement* is of a different order of causality than that involved in the inanimate physical world. Both these theorists see the necessity of conceptually distinguishing notions of *physical causality* and *causality* of animate organisms. Developmentally, however, as we shall see, the child slowly arrives at these subtle types of differentiations.

During the earliest phases of sensori-motor intelligence, psychological efficacy and physical force are undifferentiated and, for all intents and purposes, no conception of causality seems indicated (Piaget, 1954). At about the third month the child demonstrates what Piaget has coined magico-phenomenalistic causality (Piaget, 1952, 1954a). Through a process very similar to Skinner's "superstitious behavior," the infant appears to consider certain events that are concomitant with his actions to be caused by them. By the seventh month and extending to the latter half of the second year, there is a gradual attainment of an objective sense of causality (Piaget, 1954a). This development involves the distinction between physical and psychological causes (e.g., the child recognizes causes that are entirely external to his actions and establishes among events perceived links of causality independent of the action itself, (Piaget, 1954a).

These earlier sensori-motor differentiations, however, are really the beginning of a long process of development towards scientific conceptions of causality. The Piagetian exploration of the development of causal concepts after the sensori-motor stage involves asking children their explanations of such phenomena as wind, air, movement of different sorts, and the mechanisms of simple engines (Piaget, 1929). Piaget identified three main developmental stages and seventeen distinct modes of explanation, the first two stages extending from 3 to 8 years approximately (precausal) and the third stage appearing about 7 or 8 years (causal stage). Precausal thinking is an important manifestation of the child's cognitive egocentrism, i.e., inability to differentiate self-world, subjective-objective, psychological-physical. Particularly in relation to causality, this egocentrism results in the child's inability to differentiate between psychological and physical aspects of reality. In other words, there is a confusion between *physical causality* and *psychological causality*. This confusion results in the precausal child's contaminating explanations of natural phenomena with psychological properties (e.g., explaining a physical event by humanizing the inorganic world). Precausal explanations involve physical explanations couched in animistic, dynamistic, finalistic, and artificialistic terms (Piaget, 1930). Animistic explanations, for example, involve explanations of things and events by endowing physical objects with human feelings. It is not until 7 or 8 years of age that the child begins to explain physical events in terms of scientific and physical causality.

Earlier replications of Piaget's work on physical causality have subjected this part of his theory and observations to severe criticisms (Flavell, 1969; Laurendeau & Pinard, 1962; Wallace, 1965). For example, some of the studies failed to find any substantial amount of animistic, artificialistic, or dynamistic reasoning in young children, while others reported its presence in children and adults alike (Flavell, 1969; Laurendeau & Pinard, 1962; Wallace, 1965). Laurendeau and Pinard (1962), paying careful attention to methodological problems that could cause discrepancies, have in general replicated and extended Piaget's (1929) earlier finding on the developmental of causal notions in children. The studies quoted thus far have paid relatively minor attention to *psychological causality* in the strictest sense, e.g., asking the child "What makes people angry?" instead of "What makes clouds move?" (Whiteman, 1967). Significant differences also appear between the preoperational and concrete operational stages in psychological aspects of a person's motivation such as projection (Whiteman, 1967).

The above studies have treated causality as a naturally developing phenomenon without specification of the conditions that facilitate its growth. Ausubel and Schiff (1954) have attempted to investigate some conditions facilitating the growth of causal concepts in children. Their study indicates that kindergarten children who receive laboratory training in learning the principle of a teeter-totter (that the longer side of the fulcrum falls when both sides are equally weighted) fail to exhibit resistence to the later learning of a spurious causal relationship about the operation of a teeter-totter (that the color of the blocks placed at either end of the teeter-totter is the determining factor). This study on causality antedates the later acceleration training studies on Piagetian conservation problems.

Death. Age level changes in children's theories of death illustrate the interaction that occurs among cognitive, emotional, and personality factors in the development of concepts that have more than the ordinary degree of ego reference. The young child's idea of death is often spontaneously associated with birth, with sorrowful ideas of separation from things or people loved, or with violence, aggressive desires, and destruction (S. Anthony, 1967). Prior to the age of five, it appears that the child categorically denies the reality and irreversibility of death (Nagy, 1948; Safier, 1964). Between the ages of 5 and 9 he is only willing to accept death in a figurative sense as a person or spirit. By the ninth year and beyond, on the other hand, children reluctantly acknowledge death as an inevitable process and as the cessation of corporeal existence (Nagy, 1948; Safier, 1964).

The child's cognitive conception of death is intricately related to his conceptions of life; both conceptions parallel one another and become more sophisticated with age (Safier, 1964). In discussing causality, we alluded to the precausal child's use of animism in explaining all sorts of events. Animistic conceptions of life and death appear to be logically linked (Safier, 1964). Ascription of life-like qualities to an "inanimate" object has been termed *positive animism;* whereas the ascription of death to an object is called *negative animism* (Safier, 1964). Both types of animism decrease with increase in age; correlations between these types are positive in the preschool and elementary school years. At about age 7, there appears to be a gap in the trend, possibly due to the onset of the more analytic period of concrete operations (Safier, 1964). Other indications of cognitive determinants on the child's conception of death can be seen in the fact that children with high intellectual ability have more sophisticated conceptions of death at all ages (Peck, 1966).

From a purely cognitive standpoint the idea of death is undoubtedly enigmatic and perplexing. Moreover, it is shunned, deemphasized, and rationalized by adults, and shrouded in mystery and superstition (S. Anthony 1967). Nevertheless, it is difficult to discount completely the suggestion that underlying the child's resistence to the notion of death is the objective complexity of the concept itself and the usual degree of animism and personification characterizing thought at this level of sophistication. On the other hand, the idea of death seems at least in part to be rejected so strenuously because it constitutes a grave and unpalatable threat to ego identity (E. J. Anthony, 1967). When the child can no longer deny the inevitability of death he manages to forestall the insecurity feelings it would otherwise engender by repressing thoughts of it below the threshold of consciousness, by giving it third-person reference, and by relegating its occurrence to the vague and unforeseeable future. This repression can be successfully maintained as long as he possesses a certain minimal level of self-esteem. Morbid preoccupation with and fear of death, therefore, probably reflect impaired self-esteem and acute deep-seated anxiety.

Misconceptions

The commonness of misconceptions during childhood may be attributed to several factors. First, children do not have the cognitive sophistication and the cumulative background of experience necessary for the complete development of many concepts. The pressure on children to mouth inadequately understood concepts and at the same time to conceal their lack of understanding further encourages the development and perpetuation of misconceptions. Some children, who have inordinate "intolerance for ambiguity," are predisposed toward acquiring misconceptions since they are prone to reduce the threat and discomfort of tentativeness by resorting to premature conceptual closure (Levitt, 1953). Second, many of children's misconceptions are derived from erroneous and incomplete information and from misinterpretations or uncritical acceptance of what they read or are told. This is especially true in a socially taboo area such as sex which has both a rich folklore and a special mythology for children. Such misconceptions are highly resistive to extinction since they tend to be insulated from the corrective influences of social verification. Still another group of childhood misconceptions can be traced to confusion between words with different meanings that either look or sound alike.

Since there is often a time lag between the correction of misconceptions and the revision of language usage it cannot be assumed that conceptual confusion necessarily exists in all instances where words are used inappropriately. On the other hand, some instances of incorrect diction that seem to be largely linguistic in origin may have a conceptual basis. The common tendency for children to use "tell" instead of "ask," for example, may indicate lack of cognitive appreciation of the distinction involved. It may also indicate that although some ego-expansive children appreciate the distinction they conceive of themselves as "telling" in situations where others would be "asking."

PROBLEM SOLVING

Problem solving refers to any activity in which both the cognitive representation of prior experience and the components of a current problem situation are reorganized in order to achieve a designated objective. Such activity may consist of more or less trial-and-error variation of available alternatives or of a deliberate attempt to formulate a principle or discover a system of relations underlying the solution of a problem (insight). When the activity is limited to the manipulation of images, symbols, and symbolically formulated propositions, and does not involve overt manipulation of objects, it is conventional to use the term *thinking*. It is clear, however, that depending on the approach taken, thinking may either employ the method of insight or may be merely an implicit variety of the trial-and-error procedure. Whether insight or trial-and-error learning is employed in the solution of a particular problem is a function of both the kind of problem involved and of the age, prior experience, and intelligence of the subject.

The Nature of Problem Solving

In terms of approach, two principal kinds of problem solving may be distinguished, both of which occur at all age levels. The trial-and-error approach consists of random or systematic variations, approximation, and correction of responses until a successful variant emerges. The insightful approach, on the other hand, implies a "set" that is oriented toward discovery of a meaningful means-end relationship underlying the solution of a problem. It may involve either simple transposition of a previously-learned principle to an analogous new situation, or more fundamental cognitive restructuring and integration of prior and current experience to fit the demands of a designated goal. Characteristically, insightful solutions *appear* to emerge suddenly or discontinuously . They are also invariably accompanied by at least some implicit appreciation of the principle underlying the solution of a problem—even if it cannot be successfully verbalized. This understanding is demonstrated functionally both in being immediately reproducible upon subsequent exposure to the same problem, and in being transferable to related problems. Hence, not only is insightful solution frequently a reflection of transfer or application of relevant established principles to new variants of the same problem, but transferability itself is perhaps the most important *criterion* of insight. Precisely verbalized understanding of a general principle greatly facilitates (through transfer) the solution of particular problems exemplifying it.

The utilization of hypotheses is a necessary but not a sufficient condition of insightful problem solving. However, it does not, in and of itself, provide assurance that an insightful approach is being taken toward solving a particular problem. Unless hypotheses incorporate means-ends relationships, they may merely represent systematic trial-and-error elimination of available alternatives. The absence of overt trial-and-error also does not necessarily imply insightful problem solving; trial-and-error manipulation in this instance may simply be covert or implicit in thought. On the other hand, insightful solutions are not always complete, perfect or immediate. They often appear after a protracted period of inauspicious search consumed in pursuing unpromising leads.

Developmental Changes in Problem Solving

Developmental changes in problem solving reflect all of the age trends described for cognitive functioning (see pp. 570-590) as a whole, and, more particularly, those occurring in concept acquisition (see pp. 611–630). Especially in the area of thinking and problem solving, it is important to distinguish between those developmental changes that are qualitative nature and those that are merely quantitative. Despite Piaget's (Inhelder and Piaget, 1958) assertions to the contrary, the weight of the evidence points to the conclusion that *some* kinds of thought processes, logical operations, and problem-solving strategies are employed at all age levels, and differ principally in degree or complexity (Burt, 1919; Long and Welch, 1941a, b; Welch and Long, 1943; Werner, 1948). For example, equivalence, discriminative, and eliminative logical operations seem to be qualitatively similar at all age levels once they emerge. The older child's greater competence in using these operations largely depends on his superior ability to think abstractly and to generalize. Similarly the use of trial-and-error and insightful approaches to problem solving does not undergo qualitative change from one age level to the next. Neither approach can be said to be characteristic of children at a designated stage of intellectual development; both are found at all age levels. The choice between the two approaches depends, mainly, on the intrinsic difficulty and complexity of the problem, on the individual's prior background of experience and general degree of sophistication in the problem area, and on the susceptibility of the problem to logical analysis and a hypothesis-oriented mode of attack. It is true that older children, on the whole, tend more to use an insightful approach, but this is so only because their greater capacity for abstract thinking makes such an approach more feasible.

On the other hand, certain qualitative changes in thinking do occur with increasing age. These are gradually occurring changes in *kind* that emerge after a certain threshold value of change in *degree* has been reached. One such change consists of a gradual transition from subjective to objective thought, i.e., of an emergent ability to separate objective reality from subjective needs, wishes, and preferences. This trend is responsible for the striking decline that occurs during the elementary-school years in autistic, animistic, ethnocentric, magical, anthropomorphic, absolutistic, and nominalistic thinking. *

A second qualitative change in thought is reflective of the transition from concrete to abstract cognitive functioning, and illustrates all of the characteristic features of this transition (see pp. 576-580). Because the preoperational child cannot meaningfully manipulate relationships between secondary abstractions, his thought processes are necessarily conducted at a low level of abstraction and also yield products at a correspondingly low level. Thus he

---

Evidence of such thinking can, of course, be found at older age levels also, but is much less flagrant and tends to occur under more atypical conditions, such as confrontation with unfamiliar phenomena or problem areas.

cannot perform many significant logical operations that presuppose a capability of meaningfully manipulating relationships between secondary concepts. As a result of this developmental constraint, his thought does not exhibit "conservation," and his problem-solving efforts are relatively dependent both on the overt manipulation of objects and on the internal manipulation of near-images.

The concrete operational child can meaningfully manipulate relationships between secondary abstractions, and can, therefore, perform those logical operations reflective of this capability. However, he is dependent in so doing on the availability of concrete-empirical props (exemplars of the abstractions). His thought processes are thus conducted at a qualitatively higher level than those of the preoperational child, but are still constrained in their level of abstraction by the particularity inherent in the props he uses. The products of his thought are therefore only intuitive and semi-abstract in nature.

Only in the stage of abstract logical operations, when relationships between secondary concepts can be meaningfully manipulated without any reference whatsoever to particular instances, does the process of thought become genuinely abstract in the fullest sense of the term. The products of such thought can therefore be refined through verbalization to yield ideas that are truly explicit, precise, abstract, and general. The individual at this stage of development is capable of solving problems by formulating general principles in terms of general relationships between all possible and hypothetical combinations of abstract variables. Problem solving performance may sometimes decline during the transition to the abstract logical stage, as children become capable of entertaining complicated and hypothetical hypotheses which may become overly complicated and obscure, thereby depressing performance temporarily (King, 1968).

Age Level Trends in Problem-Solving Ability

The increasing ability of children to solve more complex problems with advancing age has been demonstrated both for trial-and-error learning (Munn, 1954) and for such tests of insightful learning as the double alternation problem (Gellerman, 1931; Hodges, 1954), transposition (Alberts and Ehrenfreund, 1951) and other relational problems (Elkind, 1966b); Heidbreder, 1928; Levinson & Reese, 1967; Odom & Coon, 1966; Roberts, 1940; Wohlwill, 1960a; Yudin, 1966; Yudin and Kates, 1963), inductive and eliminative reasoning (Burt, 1919), and various tool-utilization problems (Matheson, 1931). Younger children profit less from hints, constraints, or perceptual enhancement (Gollin, Saravo & Salten, 1967; Olson, 1966; Welch and Long, 1943) and are less able to generalize or transpose solutions to more abstract and remote situations (Spiker, 1956; Stevenson and Bitterman, 1955; Welch and Long, 1943). They have more difficulty with problems at higher levels of abstraction (Burt, 1919; Welch and Long, 1943), with more complex kinds of reasoning operations (Long and Welch, 1941b, 1942; Odom, 1967) and with problems demanding the integration of two isolated experiences (Maier, 1936). Much of the superiority of older children in these latter instances inheres in the advantages that the ability to use verbal symbols provides for the process of generalization, for generating hypotheses, for processing information, and for employing efficient strategies (Marsh & Sherman, 1966; Weir, 1964).

Age Level Trends in Problem-Solving Approach

With advancing age, as might readily be anticipated, the frequency of overt trial-and-error approaches to problem solving declines (G. V. N. Hamilton, 1916; Munn, 1954; Nelson, 1936). Hypothesis-oriented approaches become more evident (G. V. N. Hamilton, 1916) and insightful solutions become more complete (Alpert, 1928). Older children also develop and use more logical strategies in solving problems (Neimark & Lewis, 1967, 1968). These trends obviously reflect, in part, increasing ability to generalize and to manipulate abstract symbols. As Lewin (1954) points out, they also reflect the widening and greater differentiation of the child's "life space." In the "detour" problem, for example, older children focus less exclusively on the obtrusively obvious barrier and are better able to appreciate that the most direct route to the goal is not necessarily the shortest.

Older children are more aware than younger children of the existence of a problem when exposed to one (Heidbreder, 1928). Their plan of attack is more systematic and their solutions tend to be more flexible and less stereotyped and perseverative (Elkind, 1966; G. V. N. Hamilton, 1916; Lindley, 1897; Maier, 1936; Raaheim, 1965; Weir, 1967). Since their knowledge tends to be organized in terms of more highly systematized, inclusive, and self-consistent categories, they adopt a less fragmented approach to problem solving; and because they are better able to bring prior experience to bear on a current problem (Maier, 1936), they profit more from past mistakes (Lindley, 1897). Younger children, on the other hand, are limited by their inability to focus on more than one aspect of a problem at a time (Piaget, 1952a), by the diffuseness of their thinking (Piaget, 1954b), by their low frustration tolerance, and by their reluctance to accept the immutable givens of a problem. They are more situation-bound and less able to generalize beyond a particular context (Piaget, 1950, 1954b). Their formulations are more dependent on concrete imagery and the physical presence of objects, and derive less benefit from the use of abstract symbols, higher-order concepts, and categorical propositions (Piaget, 1954b; Welch and Long, 1943). Finally, after solving a problem they are less capable of verbalizing (and hence transferring) the underlying principles (Berlyne, 1969a; Heidbreder, 1928; Piaget, 1954b; Reese, 1963; Roberts, 1940).

Age Level Trends in the Objectivity of Thought

The progressive developmental decline in the egocentricity and subjectivism of children's thought is one of the two principal aspects of cognitive sophistication accounting for age-level changes in the quality of problem solving (see p. 563). The growing child becomes more aware of his own thought processes and better able to distinguish between external reality and his own experience, between "the sign and the thing signified," and between thought and the object thought about (Piaget, 1928, 1929). Logical inference becomes less a matter of subjective preference and less tied to autistic premises (Heidbreder, 1927; Piaget, 1928). The more important of these trends can be illustrated by considering changes in subjectivism associated with the child's development of notions of causality.

Considered in this light, the evidence regarding "stages" becomes less contradictory. In support of Piaget's view, children do seem to pass through gross qualitative stages of causal thinking (Dennis, 1942, 1943; Grigsby, 1932; Mogar, 1960; R. W. Russell, 1940), and rarely appreciate antecedent-consequent relationships in the adult sense of the term prior to the age of eight to ten (Cohen and Hansel, 1955; Lacey and Dallenbach, 1940). Even Piaget's severest critics concede that there is gradual improvement with increasing age in the *quality* of children's causal explanations (Deutsche, 1937; M. E. Oakes, 1946). On the other hand, much overlapping prevails between age groups. All kinds of causal explanations are found at all age levels (Deutsche, 1937; Grigsby, 1932; M. E. Oakes, 1946; R. W. Russell, 1940); some adolescents and adults even give responses characteristic of young children (Dennis, 1943; Hazlitt, 1930; M. E. Oakes, 1946). Furthermore, changes tend to occur gradually and the quality of causal thinking shows much specificity and dependence on particular relevant experience (Dennis, 1942; Deutsche, 1937; M. E. Oakes, 1946). None of these facts, however, is incompatible with the existence of certain qualitative stages in children's thinking as defined earlier.

As mentioned earlier, externalization and objectification are relatively early steps in the development of ideas of causality. The infant must learn to distinguish between independent systems of cause-and-effect in the external world and effects attributable to his own volition and action. He begins to do this when he appreciates that mere volitional wishing does not satisfy his needs, that parents are mediators of need satisfaction, and that he is executively dependent on them; but although magical thinking tends to delcine with increasing age (Dennis, 1942, 1943; Piaget, 1932; R. W. Russell, 1940), it by no means disappears, even in adults (Dennis, 1943; Hazlitt, 1930; M. E. Oakes, 1946). It does, however, become less naive and more highly formalized; that is, magical properties and powers are attributed more to special words, objects, rituals, and beings, and less to wishing *per se*. Concomitantly, mechanical and naturalistic interpretations of causality increase and animistic and "artificialistic" interpretations decrease in frequency.

The concept of artificialism, related to animism previously discussed, refers to a type of personification in which creative activity in nature is attributed to some human agency rather than to naturalistic phenomena. At first, according to Piaget, the child regards everything that is active, whole, and useful as alive. Later, life is attributed only to moving objects. The still more sophisticated child applies the criterion of spontaneous movement. Finally, only plants and animals, or only animals, are considered to be alive. Other investigators (Huang and Lee, 1945; Klingensmith, 1953) have shown that when a child states that something is "alive," he mostly means that it is active, and does not necessarily attribute to it the anthropomorphic characteristics of feeling, seeing, knowing, thinking, wanting, breathing, etc.

Animistic tendencies are also not restricted to children, but are manifested even by educated adults in our culture when required to explain events completely beyond their sphere of experience and competence (Hazlitt, 1930; M. E. Oakes, 1946). This suggests that the crucial factor in causal thinking is making a judgment of relevance between antecedent and consequent. For the unsophisticated child (or adult) antecedence per se, as well as animistic, magical, and artificialistic connections between antecedent and consequent, seem to be sufficient criteria of relevance (Piaget, 1932). Given the benefit of increased incidental experience and instruction, however, he learns to avoid attributing causal significance to irrelevant and purely temporal antecedents of consequences, and to avoid generalizing the expectation of similar consequences in all situations superficially similar to a particular cause-effect sequence (Ausubel and Schiff, 1954).

Factors Influencing Problem Solving

As can easily be deduced from the previous discussion, problem solving development is a multidimensional process and cannot be more or less syncronous with I.Q. performance (Gallagher, 1964). Nevertheless, intelligence is one of the most important determinants of problem-solving ability. For one thing, reasoning power is a prominent component of all intelligence tests. For another, many other intellectual abilities measured by the intelligence test (e.g., comprehension, memory, information processing, ability to analyze) affect problem solving. I.Q. is positively related to both trial-and-error (Munn, 1954; Nelson, 1936) and insightful problem solving (Gellerman,

1931; Harootunian and Tate, 1960; Munn, 1954; Stevenson *et al*, 1968). However, for those kinds of problem solving that depend on cumulative incidental experience, e.g., causal thinking (Deutsche, 1937) and applications of the lever principle (G. M. Peterson, 1932), grade in school is a more significant correlate of success than either I.Q. or socioeconomic status. Brightness level also affects approach to problem solving. When mental age is held constant in a categorization problem, older (and duller) children adopt a more concrete and less self-consistent approach, use more categories, and are more "immediate-minded." They also find it more difficult to shift from one basis of categorization to another (Kounin, 1943). Retarded children are also more likely to rely on misleading cues significantly longer than normal children (Achenbach and Zigler, 1968).

Other cognitive traits such as open-mindedness, flexibility, capacity for generating multiple and novel hypotheses, attentiveness, incisiveness, problem sensitivity, intellectual curiosity, and ability to integrate ideas influences problem solving in rather self-evident ways. Cognitive style (see pp. 638-641) is obviously a relevant factor, particularly with respect to general strategies of problem solving. Although evidence is lacking, it seems reasonable to suppose that problem-solving ability is not a highly generalized trait within a given individual; rather it varies on the basis of interest, experience, and aptitude in different areas of human endeavor.

Sex differences in verbal problem solving (Munn, 1954) and causal thinking (R. W. Russell, 1940) are not significant, but boys tend to surpass girls in mechanical puzzle problems (Munn, 1954) and in arithmetical reasoning. Motivational traits such as drive, energy level, persistence, and frustration tolerance affect problem-solving outcomes in a positive way (Alpert, 1928; French and Thomas, 1958), but excessive drive or emotionality tends to constrict the cognitive field and to promote rigidity and perseveration (Bahrick *et al*, 1952; Easterbrook, 1950). Many temperamental and personality traits such as high kinetic level, decisiveness, venturesomeness, causal orientation, self-confidence, and self-critical ability (Alpert, 1928; Avital & Shettleworth, 1968; Kempler, 1962; Muuss, 1960) facilitate problem solving when present in a moderate to high degree. But when venturesomeness or decisiveness approaches impulsiveness (Kagan, *et al*, 1966), when self-confidence borders on dogmatism or complacency, and when self-criticism becomes self-derogation, the opposite effect may be anticipated. Anxiety level, as pointed out earlier (see pp. 426-434), has a negative effect on problem solving, particularly, in the case of novel and difficult tasks, because of its relationship to rigidity, constriction of the cognitive field, perseveration, disposition to improvise, premature closure, and intolerance for ambiguity. Intolerance for ambiguity is also associated with a "low causal" orientation (Muuss, 1960).

Personality variables undoubtedly interact with such situational factors as success and failure. Success experience enhances self-confidence, venturesomeness, and disposition to improvise, whereas failure experience has the opposite effects (Rhine, 1955). A mild degree of failure, however, may prove salutory by increasing drive, attentiveness, and willingness to consider other alternatives (George, 1964).

COGNITIVE STYLE

We have already briefly considered "cognitive style" as evidence of limited consistency in children's personality organization (see pp. 112–113). Cognitive style dimensions refer to self-consistent and enduring individual differences in cognitive organization and functioning. However, a serious methodological weakness common to many of the studies in this area is the fact that the intra- or intertask generality of function of the measures which they use for cognitive style, its determinants, and its functional consequences has not been adequately established. It is questionable, therefore, whether these measures are actually indicative of stable and generalized cognitive traits.

Many cognitive-style variables reflect self-consistent individual differences with respect to certain general properties or attributes of cognitive organization and functioning that characterize human beings as information-storing and processing mechanisms. These tendencies occur in the same direction and apply to all individuals and all age levels, but are consistently more or less accentuated in particular persons. The following aspects of cognitive style have been identified and studied: intolerance for ambiguity (tendency toward premature closure) (Rokeach, 1960); intolerance for unrealistic experience; leveling-sharpening (Holzman and Gardner; 1960; Santastefano, 1964); need for simplification (skeletonizing, rationalizing) (Holzman and Gardner, 1960); degree of cognitive differentiation (Uhlmann and Saltz, 1965), field-dependence—field-independence (Witkin, 1969; Witkin et al, 1962; Witkin et al, 1967); explication and importing of detail in memory (embroidery); vividness of memory; long-term versus short-term memory; memory for particular kinds and sense modalities of experience; construction or flexibility in problem solving; preference for cognitive complexity or simplicity, for widely known or little known information; and preference for broad or narrow categorization. Other possible and suggested aspects of cognitive style include strategy preferences in problem solving (focusing or scanning; the use of whole or part hypotheses); strategy preferences in processing, acquiring and organizing information; memory for details or concepts; integration versus compartmentalization in memory; degree of openness to new information after closure is achieved.

Preference for cognitive complexity and for little known as against widely-known information are related aspects of cognitive style. Although preference for cognitive complexity cannot be reduced to any simple dimension of cognitive functioning, it does exhibit considerable generality (Vannoy, 1965). As one might reasonably anticipate, it increases in direct proportion to an individual's ability to process or code variability (Munsinger and Kessen, 1964). Individuals preferring cognitive simplicity are differentially more sensitive to new information, and are thus more likely to change initial impressions (Leventhal and Singer, 1964). Elementary-school pupils who prefer little known to more widely-known information are more attracted to novelty and challenge, and are also more likely to choose intellectual vocations (Teeter et al, 1964).

According to Bruner and Tajfel (1961), and to Tajfel, Richardson and Everstein (1964), learners seem to manifest a consistent preference for broad or narrow categorization. Narrow categorizers show greater preference than broad categorizers for taking the risk of being wrong as stimulus situations change. Kagan et al. (1963) describe self-consistent "analytic-descriptive," "inferential descriptive" and "relational" tendencies among children in grouping pictures. These styles of categorization are evident as early as four years of age (Sigel, Jarman & Hanesian, 1967). The first-named tendency increases with age and is more characteristic of boys than of girls. Children with analytic tendencies tend to be more reflective with respect to alternative classification possibilities, and to analyze visually presented materials more into their component parts (Kagan, 1966; Kagan et al, 1964). They also tend to be less hyperactive and distractible. Children who are conceptually reflective tend to make fewer errors in reading and inductive reasoning than do children who are conceptually impulsive (Kagan, 1965; Kagan et al, 1966). Style of categorization is influenced by teachers; children taught by a "reflective" teacher increase in *reflection* themselves over the course of an academic year (Yando & Kagan, 1968).

Although it is probably true that human beings tend to "organize the world of ideas, people, and authority basically along the lines of belief congruence, [and that] what is not congruent is further organized in terms of similarity to what is congruent" (Rokeach, 1960, p. 395), interindividual differences obviously exist with respect to the need for internal consistency within belief systems. Some individuals are undoubtedly more content than others to internalize contradictory propositions in logic-tight compartments rather than to subject them to integrative reconciliation. However, direct research evidence regarding the stability and generality of such individual differences is presently unavailable.

Intolerance of ambiguity is a characteristic manifestation of the relatively "closed mind" and is symptomatic of high anxiety level (Ausubel, 1949;

Smock, 1957). The anxious individual, who requires immediate and clear-cut answers and is impatient with conflicting evidence and tentative conclusions, tends to exhibit either excessive impulsiveness or excessive cautiousness in decision making (Smock, 1957). Both early and late decision makers "manifested significantly more response perseveration and shorter latency of response" on an object recognition test than did a middle group (Smock, 1957, p. 35). "High causally oriented children are more tolerant of such perceptually ambiguous materials as are presented in the Decision Location Test and have less of a tendency to arrive at premature closure than low causally oriented subjects" (Muuss, 1960, p. 534). The latter tend to make more guesses, and their guesses are more likely to be rigid and judgmental in character.

Individuals also differ consistently with respect to their tendency to use "affect labels" in categorizing stimuli. In an investigation of intra-individual consistency in the use of affect labels in describing and categorizing social and ink blot stimuli, Kagan et al, (1960) were able to demonstrate significantly positive intercorrelations among their four measures.

Gardner et al, (1959) employing a factor-analytic approach, isolated a limited number of "control principles" reflective of individual consistencies in cognitive behavior. This study was later broadened to include tests of intellectual ability and personality variables (Gardner et al, 1960). On the basis of their findings, these investigators conclude that "intellectual abilities and cognitive controls are not isolated aspects of cognitive organization but are mutually interrelated. The arbitrary distinction that has sometimes been maintained between intelligence and the broad scale organization of cognition thus seems inappropriate" (Gardner et al, 1960, p. 123).

"Retention style" was studied by Paul (1959), who found general and consistent individual differences with respect to importation, amount of material retained, and the use and retention of imagery:

> "Importing sometimes was clearly explicatory in function (assimilating and connecting), at other times merely decorative and extraneous (sharpening). Interestingly enough, for the nonimporters it *rarely* seemed to be the latter; most of the decorative importations were contributed by the importers (p. 144).
>
> The reproductions of nonimporters and importers were stylistically different: the former were generally leaner in structure, more disconnected and more abbreviated than those of the importers; the latter seemed more continuous and coherent (p. 135)."

It is quite probable that consistent individual differences exist with regard to strategy of and general approach to problem solving. Although a particular strategy of concept acquisition (simultaneous scanning, successive scanning, conservative focusing, or focus gambling) is generally more likely to occur under some experimental conditions than under others (Bruner et al, 1956), it is also possible that self-consistent and generalized individual preferences are concomitantly operative.

The issue of flexibility-rigidity in problem-solving has also received considerable attention. Luchins and Luchins (1959), in reviewing the literature on rigidity of behavior and the effect of *Einstellung* (advance cognitive sets), assert that no conclusions are possible at this time as to whether a general and self-consistent factor of rigidity exists. The intratask generality of individual differences in the Water-Jar *Einstellung* Test has not yet been determined, and the validity of this measure, and its relationship both to other measures of rigidity and to other personality traits, are highly equivocal.

LOGIC AND THOUGHT

A commonly-held position in psychology today—particularly among psychologists who have had some philosophical training—is that logic and thought are more or less coextensive, and that thought consists of the cognitive exemplification of abstract logical processes in particular individuals. It is true that by virtue of his cognitive capacities, man has both discovered logic and learned how to use it in drawing valid inferences from premises and data. Nevertheless, the position that logic and thought are one and the same constitutes an unwarranted superimposition of an abstract and idealized state of affairs onto the reality of cognitive functioning, i.e., it equates thought itself with one of its specialized tools and products. Although Piaget and collaborators (Piaget, 1957a; Inhelder & Piaget, 1958) deny that logic and thought are one and the same, both his extreme emphasis upon the purely logical aspects of thought, and the fidelity and symmetry with which the logical operations he identifies in children's thought parallel the formal structure of rules found in logic and mathematics, imply greater perceived coextensiveness between logic and thought than he explicitly acknowledges. For example, the Piagetian interpretation of "formal operational" thinking relies heavily on logical notation from propositional calculus in interpreting responses. Piaget has been severely criticized for ambiguity and obscurity in his use of logical symbolism, and also for not convincingly showing the occurrence of the truth-functional forms of logical inference in his subjects' thinking (Parsons, 1960). Braine (1962) is also critical of Piaget's equating logical operations with reasoning processes. As Wallace (1965) points out:

"The logical complexity of conceptual structures does not operate directly on the process of acquisition which they exhibit. Complexity of logical structure demands a parallel complexity in the corresponding psychological processes, but the two structures are not necessarily identical, and it is the second which is fundamental to the cognitive development of children. To deduce from the logical interdependence of certain concepts to their psychological relationship is, also, a dangerous process. The psychological processes involved in the elaboration of concepts need to be examined separately (p. 202)."

Actually, much thought involves very little logic. It is not *il*logical but *a*logical. That is, most persons can be reasonably logical about affectively neutral issues when the occasion arises for the application of logic, but in many everyday aspects of thought, the need for and the opportunity of exercising logic simply do not arise. Many of the problems with which human beings are typically confronted either cannot be reduced to terms that are susceptible to logical proof or cannot be solved merely by invoking the application of rules of inference to data (Abelson & Rosenberg, 1958). In many situations where attitudes are involved, a psychologic may be operating: this involves different inferences than ones that are ordinarily arrived at by formal logic. For example,

1. Canada opposes U.S. military policy in Asia,
2. U.S. Asian policy is directed against curtailment of Red Chinese communism,
3. Therefore Canada is in favor of the spread of Chinese communism.

The logic is fallacious, but the inference is psychologically compelling for some people. This type of inference is quite common and it is not implausible to suppose, therefore, that we have somewhat unrealistically oversold the role of logic, and have correspondingly underestimated the role of other factors in typical instances of human problem solving (a) by using the mathematical or logical problem, or the scientific experiment, as the paradigm for all problem-solving tasks, and (b) by modelling the general operations of thought after the more formal and specialized operations that serve as rules of inference in mathematics, logic, and science. The kinds of insightful problem solving in which human beings engage are both more extensive than the paradigm allows, and less abstract, formal, and rigorous than the model suggests.

LANGUAGE AND COGNITIVE FUNCTIONING

Language and Concept Acquisition

The capacity for inventing and acquiring language is one of the most distinctive features of human development. It is undoubtedly both a prerequisite for the original development of culture and a necessary condition for the subsequent acquisition by the individual of the complex cognitive, social, and moral products of the culture in which he lives. Without language the development and transmission of shared meanings, values, and traditions would be impossible. People would be unable to communicate with each other except in face-to-face situations, individual relatedness to and interaction between groups could not take place in the absence of physical proximity, and all of the countless intellectual, interpersonal, and institutional manifestations of cultural existence that depend on verbal conceptualization would be inconceivable.

It seems probable that both human infants and infrahuman primates develop rudimentary precategorical concepts that subsume significates with a common perceptual core. Because of the absence of language, however, the processes of abstraction, differentiation, and generalization are exceedingly primitive. Generic meanings largely consist of modal or generalized images abstracted from objects and events that are physically similar. Symbols are not used representationally either in the process of conceptualization, in the attainment of generic cognitive content, or in the labelling of concepts. It is largely because of their unique ability to acquire abstract concepts (which itself is so largely dependent on language) that human beings are singularly capable both of meaningful reception learning and of meaningfully solving complex relational problems without coming into direct contact with the objects and phenomena involved. The actual roles of: (a) representational symbols, in facilitating the transformational operations involved in con-ceptualization and thought, and (b) verbalization, in refining the product of these transformational operations will now be discussed. Evidence indicative of the facilitating effect of language on concept acquisition will also be cited.

Language and Thought

The developmental relationship between language and thought is still a controversial and unresolved "chicken or egg" type of problem. It is clear at any rate that language and thought are not coextensive. Language can obviously be exhibited without thought and vice versa (Berlyne, 1969a; Church, 1961; Piaget, 1960; Vygotsky, 1962). Historically, two extreme views have prevailed concerning the relationship between language and thinking (Church, 1961). The first viewpoint contends that thinking consists of verbalization, and that the thought and the words in which it is expressed are one and the same thing. The second viewpoint posits thought taking place independent of language, with language being merely the vehicle or con-tainer of already accomplished thought (Church, 1961).

Contemporary theorizing on the relationship between language and thought is usually in the direction of one or the other of these historical posi-tions, although it is not normally as extreme and frequently involves an attempt to integrate the two extreme viewpoints.

Piaget and his collaborators consider thought to be internalized actions. The beginnings of thought anticipate language and exist in what Piaget refers to as the "symbolic function." The child's language reflects the maturing of his "thought" processes and it is the coordination of sensori-motor schemas (built up during the first 18 months) which is the necessary condition for language acquisition (Sinclair-de-Zwart, 1967, 1969). Lan-guage, as such, in Piaget's theory is a means of sharing and communicating

about thought but is neither a means of thought nor formative in its development (Piaget, 1951; Sinclair-de-Zwart, 1967, 1969). This position has
made Piaget and his collaborators highly resistant to language training experiments which assume that they are creating instances of "operational
thought". Although "concrete operational" children have more sophisticated linguistic responses (Inhelder, Bovet, Sinclair and Smock, 1966;
Sinclair-de-Zwart, 1967, 1969) than their pre-operational counterparts, the
Genevian position on the relationship between language and thought
operations distinguishes between information which can be conveyed
through language and processes which are not influenced by language. They
conclude:

"Our general systematic conclusions with respect to language training are straightforward. First, language training, among other types of training, operates to direct the
child's interaction with the environment and thus to 'focus' on relevant dimensions of
task situations. Second, the observed changes in the justification given for answers in
the conservation task suggest that language does aid in the storage and retrieval of relevant
information (p. 163)."

This position on language and thought is maintained because of the failure in
linguistic training to induce operational progress (Inhelder *et al*, 1966;
Sinclair-de-Zwart, 1967, 1969). Thus language is not a source of logic but is
structured by logic (Sinclair-de-Zwart, 1969). In this context, Sinclair-de-
Zwart (1969) has been sharply critical of linguistic theorists, maintaining that
linguistic structures are derived from logical structures. The question here is
whether "cognition" automatically leads to expression or requires the
impetus of a specific linguistic ability (McNeill, 1969). At present this complex question of whether the structure of thought influences the structure of
language or vice versa is unresolved (Furth, 1969; McNeill, 1969). At any
rate, the present Piagetian position is in the direction of the second historical
position previously discussed.

Several contemporary cognitive theorists have assigned to language a more
prominent role in cognitive development (Ausubel, 1968; Bruner, 1964,
1966; Greenfield & Bruner, 1966; Olson, 1970; Vygotsky, 1962). For example, Bruner (1964) contents that

. . . Translation of experience into symbolic form, with its attendant means of achieving
remote reference, transformation, and combination, opens up realms of intellectual possibility that are orders of magnitude beyond the most powerful image forming system . . .
Once the child succeeds in internalizing language as a cognitive instrument, it becomes
possible for him to represent and systematically transform the regularities of experience
with greater power and flexibility (pp. 13-14).

The prominent role of language in cognitive functioning receives support
from the frequently quoted studies showing the effects of schooling or instruction on intellectual skills (Greenfield & Bruner, 1966; Luria & Yudovich

1959; Olson, 1970), the studies showing the intellectual advantage of the hearing over the deaf (Furth, 1964; Oleron & Herron, 1961), and the specific studies showing the effect of language mediation in facilitating cognitive performance (see summaries: Berlyne, 1969a; Ervin-Tripp, 1966; Kohlberg, Yeager and Hjertholm, 1968; Miller and McNeill, 1969; Olson, 1966).

The role of speech in the direction and regulation of cognitive functioning must be considered within a developmental perspective. Vygotsky (1962) maintains that the young child vocalizes to guide his behavior because he is not able to linguistically direct his actions in a correct manner as do older children and adults. As children grow older there is a decline in "overt" egocentric speech and apparently speech is internalized as verbal thought. The verbal thought developing from overt speech becomes the mechanism for self-guidance of the child's cognitive functioning (Vygotsky, 1962). It seems at this point that *thought* and *language* become somewhat confused with one another. Brown (1965) also wonders why overt language becomes covert or internalized. In spite of some ambiguity, Vygotsky's (1962) position on language and its relation to cognitive functioning is an attempt at developing a theory which demonstrates the importance of language as a directive and regulative mechanism in cognitive functioning. An attempt will now be made to cite some experimental evidence in support of this thesis.

Directive Functions of Speech and the Development of Verbal Control. The Russian research on language bears out the developmental finding that there is a tendency for direct control of behavior by external stimuli to gradually give way to the mediating influence of verbal stimuli (Berlyne, 1969a). For younger children, especially at the pre-operational stages, behavior is governed more intensely by immediate sensory input and to a lesser extent by ideational processes such as sets, plans and rules (Anisfeld, 1965). Evidence from various sources indicates that somewhere between the fourth and fifth year of life, language assumes a dominant role in cognitive functioning. A. R. Luria (1959, 1961) has shown that "internalization" of speech (that is, the ability to manifest speech on a nonvocal and noncommunicative basis) at this age coincides with the emergence of language as the principal directive factor in instigating, controlling, and organizing behavior. In addition, as the task demands become more difficult, there is a corresponding increase in private speech (Kohlberg *et al*, 1968). The same shift from stimulus to verbal-cognitive control of behavior is exhibited in discrimination learning (T. S. Kendler, 1963) and in the ability to transpose a learned relationship to an analogous pair of stimuli (Kuenne, 1946; Alberts and Ehrenfreund, 1951). For example, after the "verbal" child learns to choose the larger member of a pair of two blocks, he can transfer this learned relationship to similar pairs of any absolute size. Experimental findings in discrimination learning (Kendler and Kendler, 1961; Spiker, 1963), transposition learning (Spiker and Terrell, 1955), and concept formation (Lacey, 1961; Weir and Stevenson, 1959) suggest that the superiority of verbal learning to preverbal cognitive functioning is attributable to the fact that symbolic learnings can be identified, transformed, and differentially responded to much more efficiently than can the stimuli or situations represented by the symbols. By this age, the child has also mastered the syntax of language sufficiently well to understand and generate fairly complex propositional statements. Finally, there is a spontaneous use of verbal mediation in memory tasks which increases in frequency as children grow older.

Parallel analysis of the development of language and thought (Inhelder and Piaget, 1958; Vygotsky, 1962) also suggests that growth in logical thinking is, in large measure, tied to growth in language capability. On purely theoretical grounds, it would be difficult indeed to deny some degree of causal relationship between such linguistic developments as symbolical representation, the mastery of syntax, the internalization of language, and the acquisition of more abstract and relational terms, on the one hand, and such developments in cognitive functioning as the internalization of logical operations, emergence of the ability to understand and manipulate relationships between abstractions without the benefit of current or recent concrete-empirical experience, and attainment of the capacity to think in terms of hypothetical relations between variables, on the other hand. Although simpler kinds of reasoning depend merely on relatively concrete, perceptual, and imaginal operations—and are evident in action prior to the emergence of verbal thought—the ability to think in abstract terms obviously requires the use of abstract concepts and symbols; only the most primitive kinds of problem solving are possible without language. The role of manipulable representational symbols in facilitating the transformational aspects of thought, and the role of verbalization in refining the products of thought, have been discussed in another context. It is also possible that *premature* verbalization of insight may impair its transferability because incomplete, unclear, and unconsolidated verbalized solutions are obviously less functional for purposes of transfer than subverbal solutions that are more adequate in these respects.

Thus the role of language in the facilitation of thought is very similar to its role in concept acquisition. It facilitates not only ideational problem solving (Gagné and Dick, 1962) but also the solution of motor and perceptual problems (Egstrom, 1964; Ray, 1957). Hypotheses can be formulated and tested much more precisely and expeditiously when they are expressed in verbal form. In conclusion, therefore, it can be stated that language contributes in two important ways to concept formation and problem solving. First, the representational properties of words facilitate the transformational processes involved in thought. Second, verbalization of the emerging subverbal products of these operations, prior to naming them, refines and enhances their meanings and thereby increases their transfer power. In a larger sense, however, acquisition of language also enables developing human beings to acquire through reception learning, and to use in discovery learning, a vast repertoire of concepts and principles they could never discover by themselves in their own lifetimes. This is the case because the human capacity for representational symbolism and verbalization make possible both: (a) the original generation (discovery) of ideas at a uniquely high level of abstraction, generality, and precision, and (b) the cumulation and transmission of these ideas during the course of cultural history. The scope and complexity of the ideas acquired through reception learning make possible and foster, in turn, a level of individual cognitive development that would be utterly inconceivable in the absence of language.

CHAPTER 17

The Growth of Intelligence

IN THIS CHAPTER WE PROPOSE to discuss the nature and growth of intelligence considered as a *measurement construct designating general level of cognitive functioning*. Developmental changes in the actual psychological capacities and processes involved in cognitive functioning, namely, symbolization, language use, concept formation, and problem solving are considered in Chapters 14 and 16. When level of ability in performing these functions is measured by a graded series of tasks and regarded as representative of a *general* capacity for processing information and for utilizing abstract symbols in the solution of abstract problems, the construct designating this measured capacity may be referred to as intelligence. An intellectual ability, in other words, is really nothing more or less than a *functional* manifestation of a distinct and identifiable cognitive process as expressed in a range of individual performance or capacity differences. Since the nature of cognitive processes varies in accordance with stage of development, tests of intellectual ability should take account of and try to reflect stage-related, qualitative changes in cognitive functioning (Décarie, 1965; Flavell, 1963; Laurendeau and Pinard, 1962; Smedslund, 1964; Stott & Ball, 1965).

THE NATURE OF INTELLIGENCE

In the sense that the construct of intelligence is derived from a particular set of measurement operations, it is obviously an abstraction that has no real existence apart from these constituent operations. It is also an abstraction in the sense that a *general* level of cognitive functioning has no actual reality apart from the particular kinds of cognitive functioning represented in an intelligence test. Nevertheless, insofar as the construct is logically tenable, related to naturalistic data, and derived from relevant and technically appropriate operations, it is by no means merely an arbitrary and fictitious invention of psychologists. It is definitely related to an existing state of affairs in the real world (i.e., cognitive capacity) and has much theoretical and practical value both in explaining cognitive and other aspects of behavioral development, and in predicting the cognitive level at which individuals function.

The concept of intelligence, by definition, clearly excludes level of functioning in all *noncognitive* areas of behavior. This definition renders largely

648

irrelevant the commonly voiced criticism that the I.Q. is misleading because it does not indicate an individual's capacity for coping with non-representational, nonverbal, concrete, mechanical, or interpersonal problems. The I.Q. is not intended to represent these latter capacities, and no claim is made that it does. In fact, if the intelligence test were modified so that it *could* perform these functions, it would automatically lose whatever effectiveness it possesses as a measure of cognitive ability. The argument here is not that indices of maturity level in other noncognitive areas are theoretically or practically unimportant, but rather that it is utterly naive to expect a single instrument adequately to measure several largely unrelated kinds of abilities.

Also irrelevant in much the same sense is the criticism that the I.Q. does not indicate *particular* cognitive strengths and failings or *typical* ways of attacking problems. No single *summary* score could possibly do so. If such information is desired it is available in the detailed test protocol from which the I.Q. is derived and in the qualitative observations of the examiner. Quite beside the point, also, is the frequently-voiced complaint that the intelligence test fails to identify *creativity*. As will be pointed out later, creativity refers to a unique degree of originality in some *substantive* area of human endeavor, and not to the possession of a high degree either of general intelligence or of one of its component abilities.

Much futile controversy rages over the issue of whether or not the intelligence test measures *native* (genically determined) *cognitive endowment*. Although an effort is made to maximize the influence of *genic* factors by using test items that presuppose only very *generally available* kinds of experience, it is obviously impossible to rule out the differential effects of exposure to different types of cognitive experience, to different levels of cognitive stimulation, and to different personality and motivational variables. Hence, intelligence can be regarded only as a *multiply-determined* functional *capacity*, the level of which in a given individual reflects the relative potency of these various factors as they exist and interact in his particular case. Most general intelligence tests, e.g., of the Binet types, explicitly attempt to avoid the impact of *particular* kinds of past experience by presenting the subject with relatively *novel* tasks. Even so, however, many of the component subtests, such as vocabulary, obviously reflect the influence of environmental factors, for example, of social-class membership and cultural deprivation (see pp. 590 and 592). Special aptitude tests, such as language usage, are even more dependent on the nature of prior experience and social-class background.

Another equally pointless controversy is the argument over whether the intelligence test score is a measure of performance or capacity. Obviously, capacity cannot be measured directly and must therefore be *inferred* from performance; but if the I.Q. were only an index of how adequately an individual utilizes his cognitive capacity (i.e., performs) rather than an index of existing capacity *per se*, its theoretical and practical usefulness would be seriously limited. Hence, the more meaningful and relevant question here is whether capacity can be validly *inferred* from performance or whether test performance provides a *fair* sample of capacity. An affirmative answer to this question is indicated if (a) the test includes a representative sample of cognitive functions, (b) the specific items on the test are related to equally available experience, and (c) the individual is motivated to perform as well as he can. If the latter two conditions are not met, performance is an underestimate of capacity; and subsequent improvement in score that is attributable to correction of test disadvantage or inadequate test motivation reflects a gain in performance rather than a gain in capacity. All increments in I.Q., however, do not necessarily fall in this category of more efficient utilization or fairer opportunity of displaying unchanged capacity. If the change is brought about through significant alterations in level of cognitive stimulation or in personality structure, it is reflective of a *genuine change* in capacity, since cognitive capacity (according to the definition of intelligence adopted above) refers to a multiply-determined phenotype (actualized genic endowment) rather than to genic potentiality.

If we are primarily interested in using I.Q. scores as predictors of an individual's actual academic achievement, we would, perhaps, be better advised to obtain them under *typical* motivational conditions. In this case, they would be more reflective of performance than of capacity.

In this chapter we shall be concerned with such *general* issues as the nature of intelligence, what I.Q. tests purport to measure, the organization of intelligence in terms of its component abilities, and the distribution of I.Q. scores. We shall also discuss various *developmental* issues bearing on intelligence when intelligence is considered either in absolute terms, i.e., mental age, or relative to group norms, i.e., as a developmental quotient (I.Q. or brightness level). These issues include (a) quantitative and qualitative changes in intelligence with increasing age; (b) the constancy of individual rates of growth; and (c) the nature-nurture problem—the relative contributions of heredity and environment to the development of intelligence, and the extent to which intelligence is modifiable.

Intelligence Tests and Culturally Deprived Children

"Liberal" educators often unwarrantedly castigate the intelligence test as being "unfair" to the culturally deprived child, both because it emphasizes verbal ability, rather than the mechanical and social kinds of abilities in which lower-class children excel, and because the middle-class environment is more propitious than the lower-class environment for the development of verbal intelligence. Reasoning such as this, for example, led to the recent (1964) decision to ban group intelligence tests from the New York City

Public Schools. Actually, however, the intelligence test is not *really* unfair to the culturally deprived child on either count. In the first place, it purports only to measure verbal ability and to predict school performance—not ability or performance in the mechanical and social areas. Second, any intelligence test can hope only to measure *functional* or operating capacity at a given point of development (i.e., degree of actualized genic potentiality) rather than innate potentiality *per se*. Adequacy of environmental stimulation is always a significant determinant of functional capacity and hence affects performance on an intelligence test. If the environment is inadequately stimulating, then functional capacity is naturally impaired. But this does not mean that our measuring instrument, the intelligence test, is unfair, since its function is merely to identify and measure impaired operating capacity *irrespective* of the *origin of the impairment*. The intelligence test, in other words, purports to *measure* functional capacity rather than to *account* for it. If the culturally deprived child scores low on an intelligence test because of the inadequacy of his environment, it is not the test which is unfair but the social order which permits him to develop under such conditions.

By the same token, we would not say that the tuberculin test is unfair or invalid (a) because the lower-class child really does not have any greater genic susceptibility to tuberculosis, but happens to live in an environment that predisposes him to this disease, or (b) because it measures exposure to a particular disease which happens to be related to lower social class status rather than to one which is not so related. In terms of operating functional capacity, an intelligence test is no less fair or valid because a low score is reflective of cultural deprivation than because it is reflective of low genic endowment. Furthermore, to argue that intelligence test scores are valid is not to claim that they are necessarily immutable irrespective of future environmental conditions, or to defend those aspects of the social system that give rise to the culturally deprived environment.

Traditional verbal intelligence tests *are* unfair to culturally deprived children in the sense that such children, in comparison with their middle-class agemates, have fewer test-taking skills, are less responsive to speed pressure, are less highly motivated in taking tests, have less rapport with the examiner, and are less familiar with the specific vocabulary and tasks that make up the content of the test (Haggard, 1954; Riessman, 1962). The tests are, therefore, unfair in that they do not give the lower-class child a fair opportunity to demonstrate his true attained level of cognitive capacity. When these errors of measurement are eliminated, however, substantial social-class differences in I.Q. still remain (Coleman and Ward, 1955; Haggard, 1954; S. Huey, 1966). These may reflect both hereditary and environmental influences. Cattell (1963) postulates that "culture-free"tests, emphasizing "crystallized" as opposed to "fluid" abilities, are fairer to culturally deprived children.

Even if "culture-free" tests are devised which minimize the effects of cultural deprivation and give a theoretically truer picture both of the culturally deprived child's genic endowment and of his attained level of cognitive capacity, it is likely that these tests, in comparison with tests reflecting experiences within the culture, will predict less well those behaviors dependent upon cultural differences. Furthermore, one can argue that since the growth of intelligence does not occur in a vacuum but is nourished by the cultural milieu, the impact of the culture on tests should not be ignored (Millman and Glock, 1965, p. 21).

The Organization of Intelligence

How are intellectual abilities and scholastic aptitudes organized? The answer to this question is both complex and technical, and goes far beyond the scope of a textbook in child development. Suffice it to say that the organization of intelligence depends in large measure on the age of the pupil in question.

The weight of the evidence indicates that intelligence consists both of a *general* or unitary ability as well as of a constellation of discrete and separately measurable abilities or aptitudes. The relative importance of these two characteristic tipically varies as a function of age. Typically, the various sub-abilities measured by an I.Q. test intercorrelate about .40, that is, show a moderate degree of generality. This reflects both the general and specialized nature of the intellectual abilities comprising intelligence or general scholastic aptitude. Thus the significance and predictive value of a composite score on a general intelligence test depend both on the age of the subject and on the purpose for which predictions are made. The tendency in recent years, at least for older students, has been to place greater reliance on the measurement of diverse and relatively separate abilities. This approach, however, has undoubtedly been carried to an extreme by factor analysts such as Guilford (1959, 1966). The latter suggests that there are 120 separately identifiable mental abilities comprising the structure of intellect and that these consist of the various combinations and permutations relating to five classes of operations, four kinds of content, and six types of product. * Actually, only about a

---

*Guilford's factors are derived from a purely hypothetical three-dimensional model comparable to the periodic table of chemical elements except for the fact that it is wholly speculative rather than based on a projection from known expirical data. Not only has the existence of many of these factors never been empirically demonstrated, but also, most of the demonstrated factors have not been shown to have any predictive significance for academic achievement, vocational accomplishment, or anything else. The low intercorrelations among Guilford's tests purporting to measure the same factorially-pure ability (Guilford, 1964) suggest, in addition, that scores on these tests are reflective of highly specific situation-bound abilities, rather than of true intellectual sub-abilities that manifest generality of function and hence psychological reality and significance.

It should also be pointed out that factor analysis is merely a statistical method of reducing the number of abilities measured by a given tests(s) to the smallest number of common denominators

half-dozen factors such as vocabulary, spatial relations, number ability, numerical reasoning, and language usage, have been well established and shown to have predictive value for related aspects of academic achievement.

The distribution of I.Q. scores typically shows a characteristically wide and continuous range of variability. This distribution is consistent with the interpretation that intelligence (like most human traits) is *polygenically* determined, that is, determined in large part (but not exclusively) by the cumulative and additive effects of a large number of genes, each of which exerts a small positive or negative effect on the development of the trait. Approximately 64 per cent of all I.Q. scores fall between the range of 85 and 114 (Terman & Merrill, 1937). A somewhat smaller range of variability prevails with respect to achievement test scores inasmuch as the uneducable mentally handicapped do not attend school.

DEVELOPMENTAL CHANGES IN INTELLIGENCE

The measurement of age level changes in intelligence is beset by many complicating factors. First, growth curves vary simply because of differences in the respective content, measurement units, discriminating power, and ceiling of different intelligence scales. This difficulty is compounded by the fact that separate scales are commonly employed to measure the intelligence of infants, preschool children, and children of school age. Thus, before a continuous curve can be legitimately plotted from such data it is necessary to transpose scores into comparable units (Bayley, 1955). Second, even when a single scale is employed throughout the entire age range different types and combinations of sub-tests must be used to test intelligence at the various age levels. This procedure is defensible only if the changing composition of the test is truly reflective of actual developmental changes in the organization of intelligence. Only if this condition is met can we assume that different batteries of sub-tests, although patently dissimilar, are equally representative of general intelligence at their respective age levels. A third difficulty is the problem of constructing units of measurement that are equivalent at all points on the scale. It cannot be assumed, for example, that a mental age increment of three months at three years is equivalent to the same increment at six years and at twelve years; for one thing, intra-age group variability tends to increase with increasing age. Thurstone *et al*, (1929), have attempted by various statistical procedures (e.g., comparison of overlapping frequency distributions at adjacent age levels) to devise approximately equal mental growth units at different levels of maturity.

---

capable of accounting for most of the variance in a particular population. The number of factors that emerge from a given analysis depends in large measure, therefore, on the particular tests used, at what point the investigator chooses to stop the reduction process, and how he chooses to conceptualize, interpret, and name the least common denominators that emerge.

Still other factors complicate the task of arriving at a valid growth curve of intelligence. Using the same raw data, two investigators may come up with strikingly different growth curves simply on the basis of differences in the statistical procedures used in treating the scores and plotting the curves. Sampling discrepancies, particularly in cross-sectional studies are also important causes both of differences in the appearance of different growth curves and of distortions within a single curve. Finally, it should be realized that any growth curve of intelligence is based on averaged composite scores. Not only does every individual exhibit his own unique pattern of intellectual growth (see p. 000), but each component cognitive function also grows at a different rate. Vocabulary, general information, and arithmetical ability reach their peak of development at a later age than does rote memory (Conrad et al, 1944; Garrett et al, 1935), and during preadolescence and adolescence vocabulary and ability to dissect sentences grow at a more rapid rate than reasoning ability (Conrad, 1944).

Growth Curve of Intelligence

Most investigators agree that the growth of intelligence is most rapid in infancy and early childhood and tends to increase thereafter at a progressively decreasing rate. This conclusion is in accord with everyday experience and with the fact that overlapping between score distributions of adjacent age groups increases with advancing age (Bayley, 1933b). A linear growth curve of intelligence is simply an artifactual outcome of plotting mental age in terms of units that are deliberately calibrated so that one year of intellectual growth is, on the average, achieved during the course of a calendar year. In general, the growth curve of general intelligence is negatively accelerated (shows a progressively decreasing rate of growth) when based either on raw scores (Terman and Merrill, 1937), on absolutely scaled* scores, or on scaled scores transformed into percentages of adult attainment. Some investigators report a slight reversal in the rate of negative acceleration during the preadolescent period (Freeman and Flory, 1937; Terman and Merrill, 1937; Wechsler, 1950). On the basis of scaled intelligence test scores, Thorndike, et al (1926) postulated a parabolic growth curve according to which about half of mature intellectual status is attained by the age of three. More recently, Bloom (1964a) reached a very similar conclusion, placing the midpoint of attainment of adult intelligence at age four. Growth begins to taper off in middle adolescence and continues very slowly thereafter until ultimate capacity is achieved (Bayley, 1949; Freeman and Flory, 1937; Garrett et al, 1935).

---

*The purpose of scaling is to make raw scores from different tests and from different age groups comparable by expressing them in such a way that at any point of the scale, the distances between units of measurement are equal in difficulty value.

Cattell (1963, 1967) has isolated "fluid" and "crystallized" components of intelligence. The "crystallized" factor consists largely of "process" functions, presumably not much influenced by learning or educational experience, and reaches maturity at a relatively early age. The "fluid" factor, in contrast, consists more of "product" functions which are appreciably affected by education and experience, and therefore reach maturity later in life. The so-called "culturally deprived" are naturally much more deficient in the fluid than in the crystallized component of intelligence (Cattell, 1963).

Growth Curves of Bright and Dull Children

Available evidence indicates that bright, dull, and average children grow intellectually at different rates and differ with respect to organization and qualitative pattern of cognitive abilities. Although the terminal age of intellectual growth is the same for all three groups, dull children attain a disproportionately large percentage of their *ultimate* intellectual status during the early years (Bayley, 1956) and tend to grow step-wise in spurts and pauses (Cornell and Armstrong, 1955). Normal children exhibit a more constant rate of growth (Freeman and Flory, 1937), whereas bright children "show an accelerated rate of growth in later childhood" that slows down somewhat in middle and late adolescence (Cornell and Armstrong, 1955; Freeman and Flory, 1937). The net effect of these differences is that the bright tend to "grow away" from the dull (Conrad, et al, 1944; Thurstone and Ackerson, 1929). Duller individuals (as might reasonably be anticipated from their greater chronological age) also show greater differentiation of intelligence than do brighter younger children of the same mental age (Thompson and Magaret, 1949). Greater differentiation concomitantly makes for decreased plasticity or increased rigidity. When chronological age is held constant, however, differentiation of cognitive traits (Segal, 1948; Lienert, 1961) is more marked among bright children (higher mental age *and* higher I.Q.).

There are also good reasons—from analysis of intelligence test scores alone—for believing that normal (average) cognitive functioning at a given maturity level is *qualitatively* different from the performance of accelerated younger or retarded older individuals of the same mental age. First, sub-scale analysis of the Stanford-Binet test shows significant differences between old-dull and young-bright individuals of comparable mental age in the types of items handled successfully (H. E. Jones, 1931; Laycock and Clark, 1942; M. A. Merrill, 1924). Second, bright and dull children tend to exhibit more "scatter" (i.e., spread of successes and failures on component sub-tests over a wider range of difficulty) on this test than do average children (M. A. Merrill, 1924). Third, bright and dull children of equivalent mental age excel in different kinds of cognitive abilities. The bright are generally superior in tests demanding comprehension, imagination, use of language, reasoning, abstraction, and generalization (Aldrich, 1931; K. S. Cunningham, 1927; Gallagher and Lucito, 1961; Ramaseshan, 1950; Purvis, 1938; Witkin, Paterson *et al*, 1966); the dull are superior in spatial ability (Ramaseshan, 1950), word fluency (Ramaseshan, 1950), manipulation of concrete materials (Aldrich, 1931), and an analytic factor (Witkin *et al*, 1966). Fourth, normal children do better than mentally retarded children of the same mental age in such school skills as arithmetic reasoning (Dunn, 1954), spelling (Dunn, 1954), reading comprehension (Bliesmer, 1954; Dunn, 1954; M. A. Merrill, 1924), ability to profit from contextual cues (Dunn, 1954), memory for factual details (Bliesmer, 1954), and understanding of ideational relationships (Bliesmer, 1954). No significant differences were found in the simpler and more mechanical reading skills (Bliesmer, 1954) and in arithmetic fundamentals (Dunn, 1954). Finally, bright and dull children of the same mental age show characteristic differences in approach to problem solving.

Developmental Changes in Organization in Infancy and Preschool

Since there is much disagreement regarding the way in which intelligence is organized, it is obviously impossible to make any definitive statement about developmental changes in its organization. The weight of the evidence, however, points to: (a) an initial stage (infancy and the early preschool period) in which the abilities measured by intelligence tests are predominantly perceptual and sensori-motor in nature, and are largely unrelated both to each other and to later manifestations of abstract intelligence*; (b) an intermediate state (from approximately the late preschool period to preadolescence) in which abstract intelligence is highly general in nature, i.e., cognitive abilities are highly intercorrelated; and (c) a later stage (preadolescence and beyond) marked by increasing differentiation of intellectual abilities. The tentative conclusions expressed above, are partially the result of the types of intelligence tests given at different phases of the life cycle. Therefore, a brief description and analysis of intelligence tests from infancy to adolescence may clarify the reasons for the above conclusions and also point out more promising approaches for the future.

The most widely used intelligence tests, or developmental schedules for infants are the Cattell Infant Scale, the Gesell, and the Northwestern adaptation of the Stanford-Binet† (McCandless, 1967).† The possibility of

---

*A most extensive review and evaluation of infant and preschool mental tests may be found in Stott and Ball (1965).

†The above conclusion is based on a systematic analysis of infants scales (Stott and Ball, 1965) with the awareness of exceptions in terms of interrelations between different infant scales (Caldwell and Drachman, 1964; Pease et al., 1961) and later predictability (Escalona and Moriarity, 1961; MacRae, 1955).

tapping problem solving ability in infants is a most difficult task because of the absence of language and, at the outset, of primitive symbol formation. Thus the items built into a test at this time are sensori-motor in nature. Examples of infant items are respectively, turning head in search of source of sounds, smiling to the verbalizations or smiles of an adult, grasping directly for objects. Because of the type of subject being tested during this time, it is most difficult to attain tester-observer and test-retest reliability (Werner and Bayley, 1966). Mental scale items with high tester-observer and test-retest reliabilities deal with object-oriented behavior, whereas low test-retest reliabilities deal with social-interaction items (Werner *et al*, 1966).

The predictive ability of infant intelligence scales for later intelligence test scores is generally low and seems to reflect the infant scale's emphasis on sensori-motor capacities in comparison to the more verbally oriented later scales. On the basis of factor analysis of intercorrelations of intelligence tests items between birth and maturity, Hofstatter (1954) tentatively concluded that the major element tapped by the items in infant intelligence scales is *sensori-motor alertness*. Thus early differences in intelligence during infancy may not appear in later intelligence scales since the latter tap other factors besides sensori-motor alertness; these include factors such as *persistence* in the pre-school scales and manipulation of symbols in school-age scales (Hofstaetter, 1954). Cronbach (1967) has recently criticized Hofstaetter's analysis of mental tests because the locations of the factors with regard to age give no fundamental information on stages of development, since arbitrary decisions regarding the beginning and ending of the series produce radical shifts in the ages where new factors become prominent.

It is difficult, then, to explain the lack of correlation between infant and preschool test scores, on the one hand, and scores obtained during later childhood, on the other, in terms of the concept of *quantitative* change. Theoretical conceptions which assume that intellectual development involves a *qualitative* change may, in the future, offer a more feasible explanation for low predictability because of the assumption that mentality at different levels of development is different in its constituent qualities as well as in amount (Stott and Ball, 1965). The latter authors see Piaget's stage theory of intellectual development as a future alternative to present infant and preschool scales. Because:

> . . . the present tests are designed on the theory of a constant general-intelligence rather than a developmental sequence of qualitatively different levels of functioning, they fail to register adequately the developmental change taking place. It would seem, as a result, that a promising approach to the construction of metal tests for early childhood might be along the lines established by the work of Piaget (Stott and Ball, 1954, pp. 44-45).

Several other writers have argued for the possibility of using Piaget's observations as an assessment of intellectual capacities (Ausubel, 1968;

Décarie, 1965; Escalona & Corman, 1967; Flavell, 1963; Golden & Birns, 1967; Hunt, 1961; Hunt et al, 1967; Laurendeau & Pinard, 1962; Pinard, 1958; Sullivan, 1967) and simply for a structural conception of intelligence (Bayley, 1955). In order to explore the above possibility for infant scales it is necessary to briefly outline Piaget's notion of sensori-motor intelligence (Piaget, 1952, 1954).

Sensorimotor thought* (birth to about 2 years) refers to those behaviors which are preverbal and are not mediated by signs or symbols. At birth the child mediates with the world with inborn reflex schemas and has no conception of object permanence. During this period the child is concerned with objects as objects. Thus, when a toy is hidden from his view, he shows no searching movements, since he has no internal representation of the objective world (i.e., object schemas) when not perceiving it. Gradually object permanence develops through repeated experiences with the world. As the child constructs object permanence through experience, primitive concepts of space, time, causality, and intentionality, which were not present at birth, develop and are incorporated into present patterns of behavior.

Piaget (1960) has described sensorimotor intelligence as (1) a coordination of successive overt movements; these coordinations can themselves be only successive in nature, linked by brief anticipations and reconstructions, but never arriving at simultaneous representation. (2) Sensorimotor intelligence acts like a slow-motion film, in which all pictures are seen in succession, but without fusion, and so without continuous vision necessary for understanding the whole. (3) Sensorimotor intelligence deals only with real entities, and each of its actions thus involves only short distances between subjects and objects.

In the discussion of sensorimotor intelligence, the concepts of object permanence, time, space, intentionality, and causality were considered as if they were distinct. This is only a conceptual distinction, since they are intricately dependent on one another. In order to have spatial displacements, there must be an orderly, coherent world, which is provided by object constancy. Without object constancy there would be no objective causality, or objective time, since the relationship of before and after, and cause and effect, demand a certain permanent stabilization and differentiation of the environment.

The possible practical utility of a Piagetian-type test can be seen when it is contrasted with many of the presently standardized tests of infant intelligence. First of all, a Piagetian-type test would be more than an empirical sampling at different age levels because the item placement receives its rationale from Piaget's theory of intellectual development. Thus the place-

---

*Most of the material on sensorimotor intelligence comes from the following references: The construction of reality in the child (1954); Play, dreams and imitations in childhood (1951); and The origins of intelligence in children (1952).

ment of *object permanence tasks* at the sensori-motor levels is not done because children have empirically demonstrated by average performance norms that it is important to place them there, but rather because in Piaget's theoretical formulation they best illustrate cognitive functioning at that age level. Secondly, Piaget's test is not an *omnibus test* and the differentiation of item content is apparent, since each item is intended to show the presence or absence of certain stages of cognitive functioning. Thirdly, in contrast to standardized intelligence tests, a wrong answer on a Piagetian item provides as much information about the child's intellectual capacity as a correct answer. The child who does not have object permanence has not as yet internally represented the environment and this should also affect his conceptions of time, causality and intentionality. Finally, because of Piaget's theoretical conceptualizations of stage transition, interpretation of Piagetian items as illustrations of 'fixed intelligence' and 'predetermined development' is not valid. Although, the stages of development follow an invariant sequence, movement through these stages can be accelerated or retarded by the child's environmental experiences (Hunt, 1961).

Several studies have been attempted with the purpose of standardizing Piaget's early observations on sensori-motor intelligence. The intent is to set up an intelligence test which is couched in the Piagetian framework. Since Piaget's observations during the sensori-motor period are made on his own three children, the demonstration of his stages in a larger population constitutes an important contribution to the research literature. The construction of an *object scale* based on Piaget (1954), on a sample of 90 children, substantiates the observations made by Piaget on his own three children (Décarie 1965). The stage sequence of the construction of the object concept proved to be the same as that predicted by Piaget. It was further noted that none of the ninety subjects passed a stage which was considered to follow one on which he had failed. These findings are a partial substantiation of Piaget's notion of the hierarchical basis of intelligence in which each preceding stage is reorganized into the next higher stage. The correlation between Piagetian items and global mental age on the Griffith's Intelligence Scale was .916. The results contradict certain assertions made by psychologists that Piaget's theories are vague philosophical speculations divorced from reality (Décarie, 1965).

A similar and more inclusive attempt at standardization of Piaget's sensori-motor intelligence is being carried out by Uzgiris and Hunt (1966) who are using not only object permanence items but also other facets of sensori-motor development (causality, intentionality, etc.). The focus of their work is the assessment of the effects of cultural deprivation on sensori-motor intelligence. It is rather interesting in this connection to note the consistent finding that intellectual performance is highly correlated with social class after the second year of life (Bayley, 1965; Hindley, 1960). The fact that such a relationship has not heretofore been found during the preverbal period may be accounted for by the fact that previous studies of the relationship between social class and intellectual development during the preverbal period have relied on infant tests, which are probably not direct measures of problem-solving ability (Golden and Birns, 1967). Bayley (1958), in fact, has pointed out that the validity of current infant intelligence tests as predictors of later cognitive development is questionable because of the generally low correlations with later measures of intelligence. Thus, validation of scales of cognitive development based on Piaget's observations during the sensori-motor period may be most helpful because the behaviors measured by the Piaget scales seem more related to problem-solving ability, and hence may be more sensitive to social class differences (Golden and Birns, 1967).

In relation to this problem, Hunt, Uzgiris, and Wachs (1967) postulated that the effects of early stimulation promote or retard the development of certain processes or functions that are crucial for all later development. In Piagetian terminology these processes or functions may be the assimilation-accommodation equilibrium. The authors postulate that inadequate environmental stimulation (i.e., physical experience) will retard the development of these processes which are the foundation for later development. Their study was designed to answer the following questions.

(1) Will children reared in environments associated with later deficits in psychometric intelligence show any deficits during infancy?

(2) If early deficits are found, when during infancy will these deficits appear and what abilities will be most affected?

(3) What environmental factors are associated with the early development of intelligence?

Their study indicated that infants raised in slum environments show significantly slower development at a much earlier age than previously suspected and that later deficits may be based on earlier differences in intellectual development, differences that appear on Piagetian scales as early as 11 months, and which increase from 18 months on. This widening difference after 18 months is clearly consistent with the research showing measured differences in intellectual performance at three years of age between deprived and non-deprived children. It appears that Piagetian scales are more sensitive to these differences than are other infant scales. *

---

*Golden and Birns (1967), using an object permanence scale designed by Escalona, arrived at a conclusion which appears to contradict the previous conclusion of Hunt et al, (1967). The results of their study confirm the older findings that social class differences in intellectual development to not appear during the first two years of life. The implication of this study is that the home environment of slum children does not seem to interfere with the development of sensori-motor intelligence. The discrepancy between these two studies was the inclusion of an "object permanence scale" in both studies. It should be noted that the Hunt et al, (1967) results on the "object permanence items" are the least compelling in showing differences between the "culturally deprived" and normal children.

Although the results thus far are not clearcut it seems that further use of Piagetian items for infant assessment is warranted because they appear more sensitive than previous assessment scales at this age level. The particular implications of the previously quoted research for infant intellectual assessment are summarized by Décarie (1965):

> We are convinced that by adding to the first series of the construction of the object concept tests concerning space, time, causality, one would obtain an excellent working tool for testing the intellectual performance of infants. Yet we do not think of this testing in terms of intelligence quotients (as in most tests of this kind) but rather in terms of a constellation of stages. This seems to me much more in the spirit of a structural theory of intelligence (p. 192).

The more general implications of tests based on Piaget's observations are summarized by Stott and Ball (1965), when they maintain that

> . . . a true developmental sequence of levels of mental functioning, based upon these unique and characteristic features, is needed as a basis for the construction of better infant and pre-school-age mental-test scales. The final summation of the mental test would, from this point of view, express the levels of mental functioning for a broad band of abilities, each of which is possibly developing at a different rate depending upon its *genetic potentiality* and environmental stimulation. Thus, as a diagnostic tool it would be available for a differential analysis of the various aspects of the child's mental life (p. 45).

One note of caution should be sounded when treating Piaget's observations as a structural theory of intelligence. Piaget's theoretical model of intellectual development is a rather elaborate superstructure which is superimposed on his observations. More research is needed to clarify how these 'structures' account for the observations that Piaget has catalogued. His stages seem to be stable phenomena, as seen by the replication studies, but his ideas about the presence of 'cognitive structures' at particular stages are *post hoc* interpretations of empirical observation (Sullivan, 1967).

During the preschool years (i.e., between 2 and 5 years), intelligence tests are given individually and may be both verbal and performance tests. That is, some items require purely verbal responses; others, such as buttoning, cutting with scissors, manipulating cubes, do not require the child to use words. Different tests apparently emphasize one or the other of these dimensions. Thus, the Stanford-Binet is presumably oriented more toward verbal-intellectual tasks, whereas the Merrill-Palmer Scale has less language and more object-oriented tasks (Stott and Ball, 1965). Abilities are not organized around this dichotomy, and there is serious doubt that nonverbal tests are successful in identifying a unique dimension of intellectual functioning (Curtin, 1951). On the other hand, nonverbal items may be just as effective an indication of cognition as are tests using words (Stott and Ball, 1965). Thus differentiation of various sets of abilities await further development during the school years.

Developmental Changes in Organization During the Elementary School Years

During the elementary school years, intelligence assessment moves from "individual" to more "group" type tests. Similar to preschool tests, they fall into the same general categories—verbal or nonverbal or verbal and quantitative. Because of the characteristics of the tests, they yield a predominant factor of manipulation of symbols or symbolic reasoning (Hofstaetter, 1954; Smart, 1965) when compared with infant and preschool tests of intellectual assessment.

At the age of five, abstract abilities are much in evidence and are so highly intercorrelated that it is relatively difficult to isolate independent factors. In contrast to the eight "primary abilities" that he was able to identify in a population of adolescents and young adults, Thurstone was able to isolate only five comparable abilities among five- and six-year-olds (Thurstone, 1938; Thurstone and Thurstone, 1946). Greater divergence in abilities is seen in normal children (i.e., five factors) than in retarded children (i.e., four factors) (Meyers, Orpet, Attwell and Dingman, 1962; Meyers, Dingman, Orpet, Sitker and Watts, 1964) at the mental age of six. As children grow older, particularly during the preadolescent period and beyond, there is evidence from factor analysis* of increasing differentiation of intellectual ability (Garrett, 1946; Garrett *et al*, 1935; Green and Berkowitz, 1964; Guilford, 1966; Heinonen, 1963; Ljung, 1965; W. J. Meyer, 1960; Werdelin, 1966). Increased integration also occurs *within* the various component subabilities (Ljung, 1965).

By the time an individual reaches adolescence, differential factors of interest, relative ability, specialization of training, motivation, success and failure experience, and cultural expectation operate selectively to develop certain original abilities and to leave others relatively undeveloped. Children with highly "differentiated" mothers (Bing, 1963; Dyk and Witkin, 1965) tend to undergo most differentiation. Children from Jewish families show increasing facility on verbal factors (Levinson, 1958, 1961). Original aptitude and experience seem to reinforce each other in circular fashion since children who are gifted in a particular area benefit differentially from instruction in that area (Lesser, 1962). However, inasmuch as considerable interrelatedness among different cognitive functions still remains (Schulman and Havighurst, 1947), evidence of increasing differentiation at the older age levels does *not* render the concept of general intelligence completely untenable Furthermore, relatively high correlations between intelligence test scores obtained in the primary grades and retest scores obtained during adolescence indicate that there is much overlapping between the factors determining

---

Using other kinds of tests, Vernon (1950), J. Cohen (1959), and Hagen (1952) failed to obtain consistent evidence of increasing differentiation.

early level of general cognitive ability and later level of differentiated cognitive ability.

For practical purposes an intelligence test score has less utility during and after preadolescence than during the early elementary-school years. The older child's relative standing in one ability has relatively little predictive value for his relative standing in another ability; and *composite* scores on intelligence tests are not very useful for predicting performance in a *particular* school subject. Much more meaningful than a total score is a profile showing the relative standing of an individual on a wide variety of basis intellectual abilities (e.g., Jensen, 1968b, 1969; Lesser, Fifer and Clark, 1965; Stodolsky and Lesser, 1967). Thurstone's test of "primary mental abilities" is also an example which provides such a profile. By expressing intelligence in terms of the smallest number of relatively "pure" and independent factors, it gives a much more definitive, convenient, and quantifiable qualitative analysis of cognitive ability than could be obtained from examination of the protocol of the more traditional Binet-type scale composed of batteries of heterogeneous sub-tests.

In conclusion, therefore, it can be stated that when differential aptitude batteries, purporting to measure only the relatively few and well-established "primary mental abilities" are used, they probably have more predictive value for the *particular* kinds of subject-matter achievement for which they are relevant than do composite scores on tests of general intelligence or of general scholastic aptitude. However, the latter tests, as Q. McNemar (1964) points out, are not completely without psychological significance or predictive value. In fact, they are more useful for predicting complex criteria of academic achievement, involving the interaction among several abilities, than are even the well-established differential aptitude batteries, and are incomparably more useful than are differential batteries consisting of unvalidated factors or of factors manifesting little generality of function.

In contrast to standardized tests of intellectual assessment during the elementary school years, more recent attempts are being designed around Piaget's developmental stages of intellectual development. Laurendeau and Pinard (1962) have attempted to cast Piaget's concepts of development into a standardized test for the elementary-school years. They have devised scales based on Piaget's earlier findings on realism, animism, artificialism, finalism, and dynamism (Piaget, 1929). Specifically, the questionnaires were on the concept of the dream, life, night, movement of clouds, and floating and sinking of objects. They standardized their assessment device on groups of children between the ages of 4 and 11 years. Precausal explanations were all forms of responses which preceded those depending on physical and objective connections. Examples of precausal explanations are "objects have life because they move," "objects have names as part of them," "night comes because we go to sleep." The results of this systematic replication confirm the existence of primitive beliefs of the precausal type in younger children, yielding to more adult explanations in the older children.

The distinctive difference therefore between tests based on stages of intellectual development and presently standardized measures of intellectual growth is that the latter measure intellectual growth by comparing an individual to age norms, whereas the former attempt to assess where an individual stands on a scale of intellectual development (Hunt, 1961). The utility of a stage concept of intellectual development is discussed in more detail in Chapter 15 (pp. 565-570) and in this chapter under tests in infancy (p. 656). At present, the relationship of precausal thinking to other criteria of intelligence have not as yet been explored, and the usefulness of the test in clinical examination has not as yet been assessed (Levine, 1966).

CONSTANCY OF INDIVIDUAL RATES OF GROWTH

Quite apart from normative fluctuations in the rate of intellectual development (see p. 654), it is important to ascertain whether children tend to retain the same *relative* status in their age group as they grow older. To the extent that this type of constancy prevails the child's developmental quotient (I.Q.) will fluctuate little from one age level to another; and his score at an earlier stage of development will not only be indicative of his relative status at that age level, but will also have predictive value for his relative status at later stages of development. The constancy of the I.Q. may be expressed either in terms of its probable error, or in terms of the coefficient of correlation between the intelligence-test scores of a group of children that are determined on two separate occasions (the coefficient of stability).

Generally speaking, once the I.Q. approaches stability it tends to remain relatively constant, and existing degrees of inconstancy tend to be normally distributed. At the age of nine, for example, the probable error of an I.Q. (Terman and Merrill, 1937) is about five points* (varying with brightness level), and the coefficient of stability (with an interval of three years between tests) is approximately .85 (Honzik *et al*, 1948). The predictive value of the I.Q. is greatly influenced both by the age of the child at the time of initial testing and by the length of the interval between test and retest. The older the child when first tested, and the shorter the interval between tests, the greater will be the predictive accuracy of the initial test (J. E. Anderson, 1939; L. D. Anderson, 1939; Bayley, 1940; Bradway and Thompson, 1962; Honzik *et al*, 1948; W. J. Meyer, 1960). Intelligence test scores gradually

---

This means that one-half of the I.Q.-tested persons do not deviate more than five points on immediate retesting. Over an interval of six to eight years, approximately ten per cent of all I.Q. scores change at least one standard deviation (16 points).

become more stable with advancing age, and first acquire sufficient stability to be practically useful for predictive purposes when the child reaches school age (Bayley, 1949). Stability in *component* mental abilities, however, is not impressive until the fourth grade, and first becomes high enough to forecast adult aptitudes during the eighth grade for boys (Bennett and Doppelt, 1951; W. J. Meyer, 1960); among girls, the findings are more equivocal (Meyer and Bendig, 1961). In this section we shall consider age-level changes in the stability of the I.Q., as well as various measurement, genic, and environmental factors that account for both consistency and fluctuations in individual rates of growth. Consistency and fluctuations in intelligence assessment should be tempered by the perspective that

> . . . changes occurring over such periods are likely to be cumulative and progressive for each individual, rather than random. Moreover, they usually characterize a relatively broad area of behavior rather than being restricted to test items. Nor can such retest correlations be properly considered as validity coefficients. Whether the same or a different test is used as the "criterion", it is likely that somewhat different functions are sampled when testing is repeated at widely separated age levels (Anastasi, 1960, p. 475).

Age Level Changes in the Stability of the I.Q.

The scores children make on infant intelligence scales have very little predictive value for their later intellectual status. Prior to the age of six months these scores tend to be negatively correlated with intelligence test scores determined at the age of four; and between seven and nine months the correlation with six-year-old scores is generally about zero (Bayley, 1940, 1955).

Stability increases gradually. At 12 months the correlations with test scores subsequently determined at age five is .085, and the corresponding correlations at 18 and 24 months are .23 and .52 respectively (L. D. Anderson, 1939a). Scores at 21 months, however, have little or no predictive implications for terminal intellectual status; the correlation between these scores and I.Q. at 19 years (Honzik & Macfarlane, 1948) is only .08. The items on infant scales that have most predictive value also show no particular overlap with those items that are most satisfactory for measuring current intellectual status (Maurer, 1946).

Reasons for the instability of infant intelligence scores as well as for the increasing stability of test scores with advancing age are not difficult to find. First, because of the very rapid rate of growth and the exceedingly narrow range of individual differences during infancy, temporary acceleration or retardation in rate of growth results in much larger fluctuations in test scores than when the rate of growth is slower and greater interindividual variability prevails. Second, relatively much less overlap in test content exists between successive age levels during infancy than during later childhood. "Infant tests, as presently constituted, measure very little if at all the function which is called intelligence at later ages" (J. E. Anderson, 1939b). Third, errors of measurement are maximal during infancy because of difficulties in communication and rapport, misinterpretation of responses, fluctuations in attention and motivation, and often negativistic reactions, etc. Fourth, subabilities measured by infant scales are very specific (not highly intercorrelated). Hence they have very little predictive significance for any general ability that transcends the particular functions they measure. Finally, infant scales have not been validated as have the later tests against ratings of brightness, academic achievement, or criteria of internal consistency. The only criterion generally employed has been increase in score with advancing age (J. E. Anderson, 1939b). This is a necessary but not a sufficient criterion, especially since items that satisfy it are not necessarily the same items that have the most predictive value.

Although most of the shortcomings of infant scales are inherent in the task of measuring, under extremely difficult conditions, an ability that for the most part has yet to emerge, some steps can be taken to increase their predictive accuracy. MacRae (1955) has shown that infant tests have more predictive value if ratings on a five point scale (mentally defective, below average, average, above average, and superior) rather than specific scores are correlated with intellectual status at age nine. This is especially true if such ratings are based on more than one test and are supplemented by independent clinical observations and by a judgment as to whether "optimal functioning is elicited from the child" (Anderson, 1939b; Escalona, 1950; Gesell & Amatruda, 1941; Illingworth, 1961; Pinneau, 1960). Another approach has been to employ the criterion of correlation with intellectual status in selecting items (Blank, 1964). This method however, has thus far enjoyed only very limited success.

Preschool intelligence tests measure a larger portion of abstract intellectual ability than do infant scales and hence have greater predictive value. After the age of two, scores on preschool tests show a moderate (.46 to .66) and progressively increasing correlation with scores determined at the age of seven (J. E. Anderson, 1939; Honzik, et al, 1948); but it is not until the age of school entrance that scores on intelligence tests are reasonably well correlated with terminal intellectual status (Bayley, 1949; Honzik et al, 1948). If preschool tests are administered accurately and on more than one occasion, school-age status can be predicted with a degree of error that rarely exceeds one category on a five point scale. During the later elementary-school years, I.Q. remains relatively stable, both on a year-to-year basis and over a period of three or more years (Bayley, 1949; Gehman & Matyas, 1956; Honzik et al, 1948). Although some fluctuations in test scores do occur, most children tend to retain the same *relative* position in their age group.

Causes of Constancy and Fluctuation. Much of the constancy of the I.Q. can undoubtedly be attributed to genic factors. To the extent that the development of intelligence is determined by polygenic influences (see p. 671), some degree of constancy is inherent in the fact that the genotype of an individual remains invariable throughout his lifetime. The environment also accounts for some constancy, since for any particular individual it tends, within limits, to remain relatively stable. The relative contributions of heredity and environment to the constancy of the I.Q. are, of course, proportionate to their relative weights in determining cognitive development. A third factor making for constancy is the phenomenon of *developmental irreversibility* or the limiting influence of current developmental status on potentialities for future growth. New growth always proceeds from the existing phenotype rather than from potentialities inherent in the genotype. If, as a result of a consistently poor environment during the early formative years, existing genic endowment is not actualized, the *attained* level of functional capacity (although incommensurate with genic potentiality) significantly limits the extent to which *later* environmental improvement can increase the rate of cognitive growth. An individual's prior success in developing his intellectual potentialities, in other words, tends to keep his future rate of growth relatively constant despite fluctuation in relevant environmental variables. Finally, constancy is, in part, a reflection of the overlap that prevails in the intellectual abilities measure by intelligence tests at different age levels (J. E. Anderson, 1939).

Fluctuations in I.Q. are caused by measurement, genic, and environmental factors. Included under the first heading are: (a) errors of measurement inherent in the selection and placement of test items and in the use of items that are not equally representative of generally available experience— thereby leading to variable amounts of test disadvantage at different points in the life cycle and for different groups of children; (b) errors of test administration and scoring, especially during infancy and early childhood when difficulties of communication are maximal; (c) situational variability in such factors affecting test performance as personality of the test administrator, rapport (Pasamanick and Knobloch, 1955), fatigue, physical well-being, general attitude, motivation (Haggard, 1954; Zigler & Butterfield, 1968), attention span, frustration tolerance, self-confidence, level of aspiration, emotional stability, level of anxiety, reaction to failure, venturesomeness, and negativism (Hill & Sarason, 1966; Rust, 1931); (d) variation in the standardization sample over the age range; (e) variation among age groups in test ceiling and in degree of variability of test scores; and (f) variable exposure to practice and coaching on intelligence tests (Wiseman, 1954) and to test experience generally.

The most important measurement factor making for instability of the I.Q. are age-level changes in the composition of intelligence tests and in the degree of overlap of test content between adjacent age groups (J. E. Anderson, 1939; Bayley, 1955). Because infant intelligence scales measure a largely unrelated type of sensorimotor ability, instead of the cognitive ability tested at later age levels, a child with high genic endowment for abstract intelligence tends to score much closer to the mean on earlier than on later tests. Hence, he makes a spuriously low score on the initial test and registers a spurious gain on the second test; the reverse holds true for the child deficient in abstract intelligence (J. E. Anderson, 1939). Dissimilarity in test content, on the other hand, is necessary and desirable in instances where genuine developmental change occurs in the organization of children's intelligence. For example, intelligence tests should be more highly differentiated at age fifteen than at age five.

Just because the genotype remains constant, we cannot assume on *a priori* grounds that its effects on development necessarily lead to individual constancy in relative rate of growth. Since genic factors also determine *normative* fluctuations in rate of cognitive development over the life span (see p. 671), they may also conceivably give rise to *intraindividual variability* in rate of growth. Longitudinal analyses of individual growth curves of intelligence by Bayley (1940) and Cornell and Armstrong (1955) are consistent with this interpretation. The latter investigators were able to classify most growth curves under three main patterns—a continuous growth curve from age five to eighteen, a step-like curve consisting of alternate spurts and pauses, and a discontinuous curve breaking at puberty and showing either a steeper or more gradual slope thereafter.

Environmental factors contribute in two ways to fluctuations in the I.Q. First, physical and emotional vicissitudes of a transitory nature (e.g., illness, emotional trauma, separation from parents, rejection by peers) may impair a child's intelligence test *performance* without basically affecting his cognitive *capacity*. Second, radical and sustained changes in cognitive stimulation or motivation may modify actual capacity for intellectual functioning. However, as will be pointed out below, significant alterations in I.Q. of such origin can be anticipated only in young children who are removed from a markedly impoverished to a normally adequate or enriched environment.

Personality traits associated with parent attitudes influence the constancy of the I.Q. "Democratic" homes, encouraging the development of children's independence, tend to be associated with a rising I.Q. (Baldwin *et al*, 1945; E. I. Grant, 1939). Gains in I.Q. are correlated with independence (Sontag, *et al*, 1955) and high achievement motivation (Kagan *et al*, 1958; Sontag, 1958); whereas losses in I.Q., especially for girls, are correlated with dependence (Sontag *et al*, 1955). The greatest changes in I.Q. tend to occur in intellectually gifted children (Lindholm, 1964).

Developmental Differences in I.Q. Between the Sexes

Sex differences in general intelligence tend to be negligible in magnitude and inconsistent in direction (Terman and Tyler, 1954). The most widely-used individual tests of general intelligence—the Revised Stanford-Binet Scale and the Wechsler Intelligence Scale for Children—have, after all, been constructed so as to eliminate sex differences. Most of the obtained differences can be attributed to the fact that the particular tests used are differentially weighted with respect to the various component aspects of intelligence in which boys and girls differ in opposite directions, i.e., vocabulary, verbal fluency, rote memory, spatial and numerical abilities (Terman and Tyler, 1954).

Evidence regarding sex differences in variability also tends to be inconsistent and equivocal. These differences, when found, are most marked at the extremes of the distribution; but the operation of variables other than genic factors makes interpretation difficult. Although the incidence of intellectual eminence is indisputably higher among males than among females, differential conditions of cultural expectation, motivation, and opportunity cannot be ignored. Lending support to this interpretation are Terman's findings that, in a population of intellectually-gifted children, boys more frequently than girls retain their high status as they advance in age (Terman and Oden, 1949). Males also exhibit I.Q. gains more frequently from adolescence to adulthood than do females (Brodway and Thompson, 1962).

Other complicating factors raise similar questions of interpretation regarding the preponderance of boys in classes for mentally-retarded children and in institutions for the feebleminded. Not only does prenatal brain injury occur more frequently among male infants (Lillienfeld and Pasamanick, 1956; Pasamanick and Knobloch, 1967), but mental deficiency is also a socially more conspicuous and disabling handicap in the case of boys. Furthermore, parents are less reluctant to commit sons than daughters to institutions. We must conclude, therefore, that, until more definitive evidence is available, it is impossible to decide to what extent obtained sex differences in variability are attributable to such *genuine* determinants as genic and relevant enivronmental factors, on the one hand, and to purely extraneous considerations, on the other.

Differences between the sexes in *particular* cognitive abilities tend to be larger and more significant than in tests of general intelligence, and to increase with increasing age (Terman and Tyler, 1954). When boys and girls are compared on "primary mental abilities," clear differences in favor of girls are found in word fluency, rote memory, and reasoning (Carlsmith, 1964; Havighurst and Breese, 1947; Hobson, 1947). In other areas, findings are more equivocal. Most investigators (Carlsmith, 1964; Havighurst and Breese, 1947; Hobson, 1947; Lord, 1941) agree that boys are superior in spatial and quantitative ability, but Koch (1954) failed to find a significant sex difference at the ages of five and six. The situation with respect to vocabulary is even more confusing. Some investigators (Freeman and Flory, 1937; Hobson, 1947; Koch, 1954) report a difference in favor of boys, some (Conrad *et al*, 1944; Garrett *et al*, 1935) report a difference in favor of girls, and still others (Havighurst and Breese, 1947) find no difference.

In view of the fact that, with the exception of verbal fluency, most sex differences in cognitive abilities are not evident at the preschool level (Terman and Tyler, 1954), it seems reasonable to suppose that such differences are, for the most part, culturally determined (Kagan, 1964). Girls are superior to boys in categorizing ability in the first grade, but by the sixth grade this difference is no longer evident (Bruner and Olver, 1963). Although girls generally receive higher grades than boys do in school, achievement test differences tend to disappear beginning in junior high school.

Sex Differences and Parental Interaction. The consistent findings of male-female difference in performance on intellectual assessments, points toward the notion that there are different rates of development for the sexes (Honzik, 1963). Although the source of these different rates of development could well be genetic, there are nevertheless several pieces of research which point in the direction of parental-child interactions to account for the different rates and patterns of growth between the sexes. Growth rate, exclusive of sex differences, is affected by the type of interaction the mother has with her child. High verbal I.Q. children have mothers who form a closer relationship with their children and are more demanding and intrusive than mothers of children with low verbal intelligence (Bing, 1963). Nonverbal abilities in children are enhanced by allowing the child a considerable degree of freedom to experiment on his own (Bing, 1963). Sex differences in I.Q. indicate that girls' I.Q. tends to be related to parental ability (i.e., parents' education and mothers' I.Q.), whereas boys' I.Q. tends more to be related to how loving early maternal behavior is along a love-hostility dimension (Bayley and Schaefer, 1964; Bayley, 1965). Honzik (1967) found the increasing correlation between child and parental I.Q. related to parental ability, maternal concern, and the concern of both parents with achievement. The relationship between sexes is dependent on affectional milieu (Honzik, 1967). Her findings indicate that son's I.Q. was higher with a close mother-son relation and with the father's occupational success and satisfaction. The daughter's test performance was positively related to father's friendliness to his daughter and to parental compatibility. All of these studies point to the possible importance of the influence of the opposite-sex parent on the child's cognitive development. Further studies in this area may cast some light on the consistent finding of female superiority on cognitive tasks during the elementary-school years (Ames, 1964).

NATURE AND NURTURE

Various methods have been used in attempting to arrive at a *quantitative* estimate of the relative influence of heredity and of environment on the development of a given trait. Applying these methods to the study of twins (Newman *et al*, 1937), foster children (Burks, 1928; Leahy, 1935), and relationships between intelligence, schooling, and reasoning ability (Burt, 1955, 1966), different investigators have reached quite different conclusions regarding the proportionate contributions of nature and nurture to measured differences in expressed intelligence. However, both because of the many uncontrollable sources of error involved in making precise quantitative estimates, and because of the questionable validity of the assumptions underlying the statistical procedures employed (Loevinger, 1943), it seems preferable in the present stage of our knowledge merely to examine the various kinds of evidence bearing on the heredity-environment issue and to assay only roughly their relative effects on inter- and intra-group variability in intelligence test scores. In any case, any estimate of the relative influence of heredity and environment in determining the development of intelligence necessarily varies both from one culture to another and within a given culture. An equally important issue is how the respective effects of heredity and environment are mediated.

Heredity imposes *absolute* limits on level of cognitive attainment in the individual, influences the rate and patterning of his intellectual growth, and affects the differentiation of his intellectual abilities. Except for such relatively rare conditions as phenyl-pyruvic amentia, cerebral agenesis, and cretinism, the mechanisms mediating genic influences on intellectual development are not presently understood. As in the determination of any trait that varies among individuals, *environment* also plays a limiting and patterning role in the development of intelligence. Even if it could be held *constant* over individuals, it would still play this *active* regulatory role, rather than merely constituting a passive field for the unfolding of a trait completely determined by genic factors; its effects under such conditions would simply operate in a uniform way for all individuals. However, since it varies in important ways that affect the development of intelligence, it also contributes to inter- and intra-cultural variability, both in the patterning of intelligence and in the realization of genic potentialities for developing intelligence. It determines the extent to which existing genic endowment can be converted into overt functional capacity, and helps determine which *particular* components will be selectively emphasized as the latter capacity undergoes differentiation with advancing age.

Culture, social class, and family have many ways of influencing attained level of cognitive development. By providing more or less opportunity for training and experience, by offering more or less encouragement and stimulation, and by selectively valuing and rewarding intellectual attainment, the operation of these factors leads to substantial differences in ultimate outcome among individuals with comparable genic potentiality. Personality variables of temperamental and environmental origin play a similar role. Especially important in this connection are (a) such determinants of *task-oriented* motivation as intellectual curiosity, activity level, and venturesomeness; (b) intensity and area of ego-involvement; (c) such correlates of ego-enhancement motivation as need for achievement, competitiveness, responsiveness to prestige incentives, level of ego aspiration, goal tenacity, frustration tolerance, and anxiety level; and (d) need for volitional and executive independence.* Intellectually-gifted children tend to excel in most of these traits (Lightfoot, 1951; Terman and Oden, 1949). Although some of the positive relationship between motivational and intellectual superiority can be attributed to their common association with high socio-economic status, or to the better ability of more intelligent children to perceive the characteriological ingredients of success, it is entirely conceivable that level of motivation *directly* influences extent of actualization of genic potentialities for developing intelligence (Zigler & Butterfield, 1968). Independent and competitive children, for example, tend to show large increases in I.Q. in the period from six to ten years of age (Sontag and Kagan, 1963).

The Problem of Modifiability

Once we grant that the I.Q. represents a *multiply-determined functional capacity* in the development of which experiential and motivational factors play an important regulatory role, it is superfluous to inquire whether it can be modified by significant changes in such factors. The more relevant questions at this point are the extent of modification that is possible and the conditions under which it occurs. The most important limiting factors are: (a) irreversible loss in attainable capacity following prolonged failure to actualize genic potentiality (see p. 667); (b) diminished plasticity in older children; and (c) the crucial role of genic influences in setting absolute as well as relative restrictions on the amount of change that can occur. From these considerations it is apparent that significant environmental modification can be anticipated only in early childhood and after correction of serious deprivation. It is hardly likely that discriminable changes in I.Q. will be found following improvement in an environment that is already reasonably adequate from the standpoint of intellectual stimulation and motivation.

**When overprotecting parents try to keep their children emotionally dependent or when the latter attempt to retain an infantile, dependent status, failure to develop intellectual competence admirably serves both purposes (Stover, 1953). See also L. W. Sontag, et al., (1955). Children from homes characterized by warmth, freedom of exploration, and "acceleratory pressure" make the largest gains in IQ (Baldwin, et al., 1945).*

Before changes in I.Q. can be validly interpreted as evidence of environmental modification of cognitive capacity, it should be obvious that such changes must be reliably greater than fluctuations attributable to *measurement* factors alone. Failure to take this consideration into account has led to many unwarranted and exaggerated claims regarding the modifiability of the I.Q. Hence, before we review studies of the effects of such factors as foster-home placement, continued institutionalization, or nursery-school attendance on level of intellectual functioning, we would do well to consider various nonenvironmental sources of change.

First, because of very large errors of measurement in infancy and early childhood, infant and preschool scales are not even very reliable measures of current "intellectual" status. Many of these errors of measurement lead to underestimation of a given child's actual intelligence; in other instances intelligence is overestimated. In either case, there is a tendency toward regression to the mean upon subsequent testing (statistical regression). Relatively large changes in measured I.Q., reflective of test unreliability, therefore, occur irrespective of any concomitant alteration in environment. Instability of such origin should certainly not be confused with evidence of genuine plasticity (J. E. Anderson, 1939).

Second, because of their emphasis on neuromuscular and sensori-motor functions, infant scales do not really measure abstract verbal ability, and thus have very little predictive value for children's later intellectual status. Scores on infant scales, therefore, constitute neither an adequate baseline from which to measure subsequent gains or losses in relative intellectual standing, nor an adequate criterion in terms of which infant or preschool subjects may be matched for relative intellectual ability (J. E. Anderson, 1939). Simply on the basis of actual genotypic capacity for abstract cognitive functioning that is *not* measured by the initial test, large *spurious* increments and decrements in intelligence are registered in later years. For example, quite apart from any environmental influence, progressive decline in I.Q. may be anticipated from poorly-endowed orphanage children simply because of their spuriously high scores on infant scales; and contrariwise, progressive increases in I.Q. may be anticipated from well-endowed orphanage children simply because their genic potentialities for developing abstract intelligence are underestimated by the infant scales. Selective factors that operate in the adoption of orphanage children (e.g., greater likelihood of placing brighter, better-endowed children) may thus account, in part, for the retention or even improvement of the initial I.Q. status of adopted children. In evaluating the gains associated with a "good" foster-home or nursery-school environment, it is also important to realize that test disadvantage (relative unfamiliarity with specific test material or indifferent test motivation) is more likely to occur in an impoverished than in a reasonably adequate environment.

In appraising studies of attempted modification of the I.Q., attention should also be paid to the principle of filial regression * and to the possibility of genically-determined *intraindividual variation* in rate of growth. Thus, quite independently of any errors of measurement or of any change in the environment, the children of intellectually dull individuals tend to score higher than their parents on intelligence tests, and many children also show considerable spontaneous fluctuation in relative status during their growth careers.

Deprivation and Enrichment

Because of the great practical importance of the possibility of modifying intellectual capacity, a voluminous and highly controversial literature dealing with the effects of environmental deprivation and enrichment has arisen during the past three decades. Interpretation of this literature is extremely difficult since very few studies have been sufficiently well controlled to exclude many nonenvironmental sources of measured change in I.Q. In general, the weight of the evidence suggests two tentative conclusions: First, serious and prolonged deprivation, especially during late infancy and the preschool years, seems capable of inflicting *permanent* damage on intellectual growth. Second, enrichment of the existing environment can effect substantial improvement of intellectual status only in young children with a prior history of serious deprivation.

Effects of Deprivation. We have already considered evidence of the immediate and long-term detrimental effects of early cognitive deprivation on sensori-motor, language, and intellectual development. Such studies are obviously vulnerable to criticism on the grounds of the unreliability of the infant scales employed and on the basis of inadequate matching of control and experimental groups (Pinneau, 1955). Unqualified dismissal of these findings, on the other hand, is unwarranted when they are considered in the larger context of related evidence. In the first place, the very grossness of the findings, and their consistent replication by many independent investigators in different parts of the world, compensate, in part, for their methodological weaknesses. Second, they are consistent with observational and clinical data on the children concerned, with studies of animal deprivation, and with studies of older children growing up in orphanages and in depressed rural areas.

It seems highly probable, as stated previously that the longer children remain in substandard environmental conditions, e.g., orphanages (Skeels and Fillmore, 1937; Skeels *et al*, 1938) or with mentally retarded mothers (Speer, 1940), the progressively lower their I.Q.'s become in comparison with the I.Q.'s of comparable children reared in more favorable environ-

---

The tendency for children of parents manifesting deviant traits to score closer to the mean than their parents with respect to these traits.

ments. Providing greater credibility for these findings are reports of progressive decline in the intelligence test scores of isolated mountain and canalboat children who also grow up in intellectually nonstimulating and unchallenging environments (Asher, 1935; H. Gordon, 1923; Sherman and Key, 1932; Wheeler, 1942). The facilitating effect of migration to and prolonged residence in the North on the I.Q.'s of Southern Negro children has already been considered. In general, prolonged exposure to extremely deprived environments depresses the I.Q. about 20 points—more during the preschool years than in older children (Bloom, 1964a). However, some of the loss registered by children who remain in the less favorable environments, is attributable (a) to relatively poor genic endowment (as a result of *selective* adoption or migration) which, for psychometric reasons, is not manifested until *later* tests of intelligence are given, and (b) to progressively greater test disadvantage as intelligence tests place increasing emphasis on verbal abilities. Further, despite the so-called "leveling effect" of the institutional environment, variability in intelligence test scores does *not* decline with advancing age (J. E. Anderson, 1939), thereby demonstrating the prepotent influence of original differences in genic endowment.

When orphanage children from relatively poor hereditary and social backgrounds are placed at an early age in superior foster homes, there is evidence of either improvement in I.Q. (Freeman, *et al*, 1928) or of maintenance of an above-average rate of intellectual growth that is sustained over many years (Skodak, 1939; Skeels and Harms, 1948; Skodak and Skeels, 1949; Skeels, 1966). Although *part* of these changes may reflect the influence of an improved environment, any complete explanation must also take into account the effects of filial regression and selective adoption, as well as the greater probability of test disdavantage and unfavorable test conditions at the time of initial testing. Kirk (1958) and Sayegh and Dennis (1965) have demonstrated the value of systematic intellectual stimulation in raising the I.Q.'s of mentally retarded preschool children. Preschool and later training also increase the I.Q.'s of culturally deprived urban children (Deutsch & Brown, 1964; Zigler *et al*, 1968); this effect is cumulative, being greater at grade five than at grade one (Deutsch and Brown, 1964).

The provision of an enriched (experimental) nursery-school environment to orphanage children has much the same effect as placement in a good foster home: it raises intelligence level only in the very young among those who have been seriously deprived (Reymert and Hinton, 1940). In comparison with corresponding groups of control children, experimental children who initially test relatively high do not lose ground after a period of one-half to two and one-half years and experimental children who initially test relatively low make larger gains (Skeels, *et al*, 1938). In general, these findings are supported by the gain in mean I.Q. shown by Hawaiian (S. Smith, 1942) and

East Tennessee mountain (Wheeler, 1942) children which is coincident with long-term improvement in substandard school conditions.

Effects of Enrichment. Quite unlike its effects on children reared under substandard home or school conditions, a program of school enrichment cannot be expected to increase intelligence test scores when provided to children who *already* enjoy reasonably adequate educational opportunities. Although children attending preschool tend to have a slightly higher mean I.Q. than non-preschool children (Wellman, 1945), the difference is small enough to be accounted for on the basis of dissimilarity in parental I.Q., errors of measurement, and the advantage of superior test rapport.* In support of this interpretation are the facts that children who initially test higher tend to make lower scores on retesting, despite the intervening nursery-school experience (Goodenough, 1940), and that no significant differences are found when experimental and control groups are carefully matched with respect to home background (Goodenough, 1940; Olson & Hughes, 1940). Kindergarten children who receive an intensive program of training in activities related to the Primary Mental Abilities Tests make larger gains than control children on these latter tests but not on a different and more general test of intelligence (Holloway, 1954). This suggests that the improvement in mental test scores following such training is largely a specific practice effect rather than a genuine gain in intellectual status.

Parent-Child Resemblance

Correlations between parent and child I.Q. are initially about zero (H. E. Jones, 1954; Skodak, 1939) but increase gradually with advancing age as amount of overlap between the abilities measured by intelligence tests at successive age levels increases. By school age, parent-child correlations are in the neighborhood of .50 (Burks, 1928; Conrad and Jones, 1940; Leahy, 1935). However, since the existing degree of relationship could reflect the influence of either heredity or environment, these data shed little light on the nature-nurture problem. Nevertheless, two clues point to the greater weight of heredity. If environment were a highly significant factor, we would expect (a) that since mothers bear the major burden of child rearing in our society, the I.Q. would be more highly correlated with mothers' than with fathers' I.Q.; and (b) that since siblings share a more uniform developmental environment with each other than with their parents, inter-sibling resemblance would be greater than parent-child resemblance. Since available data (Conrad and Jones, 1940) confirm neither hypothesis, the environmentalist position is accordingly weakened.

The same general conclusion applies to studies of curriculum enrichment at the elementary school level (Goodenough, 1940).

More crucial evidence on the nature-nurture problem is provided by comparison of foster parent-foster child and true parent-true child resemblances in I.Q. Foster children share only their foster parents' environment, whereas true children share both heredity and environment with their parents. In the foster-home situation, where the genic basis of resemblance is removed, parent-child correlations (Burks, 1928; Leahy, 1935) are considerably lower* (approximately .20) than in the natural home situation (approximately .50). Similarly, intra-pair differences between children whose *own* fathers are at opposite extremes of the occupational hierarchy are markedly higher than intra-pair differences between children whose *foster* fathers are in comparable positions (Burks, 1938). It seems, therefore, that the greater part of the variance in children's I.Q.'s is attributable to genic rather than to environmental factors (Honzik, 1957). This conclusion is consistent with findings (Skodak, 1939; Skodak and Skeels, 1949) that, whereas the I.Q. of foster children is only negligibly related to their foster parents' educational status, it is moderately correlated at school age with true mothers' educational status (.35) and I.Q. (.40). The latter correlation is almost as high as that between children and true parents who are domiciled together.

Sibling and Twin Resemblance

We have already noted that the absence of significant differences between the parent-child and inter-sibling correlations in I.Q. lends support to the hereditarian position. Other related findings point in the same direction: (a) The resemblance between true siblings reared in the same home is substantially greater than the resemblance between foster siblings (Freeman *et al*, 1928); (b) Similarity with respect to age and sex does not increase inter-sibling resemblance in I.Q. as one might expect if environmental factors exercised considerable weight (H. E. Jones, 1954); (c) Resemblances between foster siblings are no greater than foster parent-foster child resemblances despite greater similiarity in environment (Burks, 1928; Freeman *et al*, 1928; Leahy, 1935); (d) Separation of siblings does not appreciably lower inter-sibling correlations (Burt, 1966; H. E. Jones, 1954); and (e) When interfamilial environmental variability is eliminated, as in the orphanage situation, neither the resemblance between sibling pairs nor the degree of variability in I.Q. scores is correspondingly reduced (H. E. Jones, 1954).

Comparative studies of identical and fraternal twins shed more light on the nature-nurture problem inasmuch as identical twins have approximately identical genotypes, whereas fraternal twins are genically no more similar

---

*Some of the resemblance between children and foster parents may also reflect the influence of selective adoption, i.e., the tendency to match foster and true parents in terms of IQ and occupational background (Conrad and Jones, 1940; Leahy, 1935).

than ordinary siblings. Here, too, the findings give little comfort to environmentalists. Identical twins are markedly more similar in I.Q. than fraternal twins (correlations of .80 to .90 as against .50 to .60); and even when identical twins are separated, differences in I.Q. are generally smaller than among fraternal twins reared together (Burt, 1958, 1966; Newman *et al*, 1937; Woodworth, 1941). Sizeable differences in the I.Q.'s of separated identical twins are only found when their educational backgrounds are highly dissimilar. On the basis of these small differences in I.Q. when heredity is held constant, while the usual degree of environmental variability prevails, Woodworth (1941) concludes that "the differences found among the children of an ordinary community are not accounted for, except in small measure, by differences in home and schooling."

Social-Class Differences

Prior to 18 months of age, zero or low negative correlations are found between scores on infant intelligence scales and various socioeconomic factors (Bayley and Jones, 1937). Thereafter the magnitude of correlational indices increases rapidly, and at school age varies between .3 and .5 for different educational, occupational and economic criteria of social-class status (Bayley and Jones, 1937). The early absence of relationship simply indicates that intelligence tests cannot possibly measure the same cognitive abilities during infancy as in later years. The increasing correspondence between I.Q. and socioeconomic variables, as degree of test overlap increases, may reflect either the cumulative impact of environmental influences or "an increasing manifestation of hereditary potentialities" (Bayley and Jones, 1937; Jensen, 1968).

Beginning with the preschool period, a range of about 20 points separates children of the highest and lowest socioeconomic groups (Deutsch and Brown, 1964; Kennedy *et al*, 1963; Schmuck and Schmuck, 1961; Terman and Merrill, 1937). The relationship between children's relative intellectual status and father's position in the occupational hierarchy is practically linear (Deutsch and Brown, 1964; Terman and Merrill, 1937), and in correlational terms, varies between .20 and .43 for different tests of intelligence (Eells and Davis, 1951). Upper socioeconomic groups also contribute a disproportionately large number of intellectually gifted and disproportionately small number of mentally retarded children to the total population (McGehee and Lewis, 1942). These relationships refer, of course, to group averages since differences within an occupational group are actually much larger than differences between the means of various groups. Although social-class differences are greatest in the area of verbal abilities (Eells and Davis, 1951), significant differences have also been found for all of Thurstone's primary mental abilities (Havighurst and Breese, 1947) as well as for other nonverbal tests.

The interpretation of these social-class differences in intelligence has led to much heated controversy between hereditarians and environmentalists. Actually, three different kinds of explanations based respectively on measurement, environmental, and genic factors seem equally plausible, but the evidence currently available is not sufficiently definitive to establish their relative weight. The measurement argument stems from a certain amount of middle-class bias in the construction of most intelligence tests. This creates test disadvantage for the lower-class child and results in an underestimate of his true level of cognitive functioning. In order to derive a valid and fair estimate of intellectual capacity from test performance, it is necessary (a) that specific test items be based on experiences and symbols that are equally available and familiar to individuals from all social-class strata; and (b) that test materials arouse comparable degrees of interest and motivation in persons of different social-class origin (A. Davis, 1948; Eells and Davis, 1951).

Most present-day tests are heavily weighted with specific items that are more familiar and appealing to middle-than lower-class children, and with the kinds of *cognitive functions* (e.g., vocabulary, linguistic skills) that are particularly emphasized in middle-class environments.* The tests are thus "unfair" in the sense that their specific item content does not give the lower-class child a fair opportunity to demonstrate his *attained* level of cognitive capacity. But since intelligence tests do not purport to measure either genic potentialities per se or noncognitive abilities, they are unfair neither because they fail to measure level of functioning in those noncognitive abilities in which lower-class children excel, nor because the middle-class environment is experientially or motivationally more propitious for the development of native cognitive endowment. The very fact that these tests favor middle-class children demonstrates that the environment *can* operate selectively to develop certain aspects of intellectual endowment. This conclusion is compatible with the findings that intelligence becomes more and more differentiated with increasing age (Garrett *et al*, 1935; Segel, 1948), and that sex differences in many specific intellectual functions increase or reverse themselves as children grow older (Kuhlen, 1952).

Acceptance of the test-bias explanation of social-class differences by no means rules out the genic or environmental interpretations.† Insofar as environmental factors contribute to some of the variance in intelligence test scores, it would not be unreasonable to expect that differential social-class levels of stimulation and motivation affect extent of *actualization* of genic

---

*As noted above, however, large socioeconomic differences also prevail for other nonverbal tests.

† The findings that approximately the same social-class differentials appear on the Davis-Eells "Culture fair" test as on the Kulhmann-Finch test (Coleman and Ward, 1955) casts doubt on the claim that the Davis-Eells test is culturally more fair, but does not necessarily invalidate the test-bias hypothesis of social-class differences.

endowment. Evidence for this type of mediation of environmental influence comes from the finding that children's I.Q.'s are more highly correlated with parents' education than with the economic status of their homes (Loevinger, 1940). Social-class environment also *selectively* influences the *differentiation* of intellectual and other abilities as shown by the fact that middle-class children are superior to their lower-class contemporaries in both verbal *and* mechanical abilities at age 10, but are only superior in the former ability at the age of 16. More specifically, children of Jewish parentage show increasing facility on items which emphasize verbal ability and this is attributed to the cultural influence of traditional Jewish values (Levinson, 1958, 1961). The environmentalist position is weakened, however, by the existence of large social-class differences in the *preschool* period (Terman and Merrill, 1937), by the failure of social-class differentials to increase with advancing age (Shuttleworth, 1940), and by the significantly greater correlation of foster children's I.Q.'s with *true* mothers' than with *foster* parents' educational status (Skodak, 1939; Skodak and Skeels, 1949).

The hereditarian position rests on the assumption that (a) since there is indisputable evidence of substantial genic contribution to individual differences in I.Q., and (b) since more intelligent persons, on the average, choose and are selectively successful in the intellectually more demanding occupations, it is reasonable to ascribe at least part of the consistently obtained social-class differences in I.Q. to genic variability in cognitive potential. The tendency for more highly endowed individuals to reach the higher rungs of the occupational ladder is especially evident in a society characterized by a fair degree of social mobility; and since such persons also tend to marry at their own intellectual level (H. E. Jones, 1954), their offspring acquire a genic advantage from both parents. Although logically tenable, it is understandably difficult to put this hypothesis to empirical test. It is supported, in part, by the applicability of the principle of filial regression to social class differences, i.e., children of professional parents tend to have a lower I.Q. than their parents, whereas the reverse holds true for children of unskilled laborers (Outhit, 1933).

Urban-Rural Differences

The mean I.Q. of rural children is consistently lower than that of urban children and also tends to diminish with increasing age (Asher, 1935; Chapanis and Williams, 1945; Wheeler, 1942). As in the case of lower-class children, this inferiority is most marked on verbal and speed items and is undoubtedly attributable, in part, to test bias (H. E. Jones, 1954). Intelligence scales are typically devised by urban-reared psychologists and are validated on urban school children. However, since rural children also do more poorly on items presenting no special experiential or motivational handicap, it is unwarranted to ascribe *all* urban-rural differences to test dis-advantage. Equally plausible are explanations based either on the cumulative impact of a low level of intellectual stimulation or on the selective migration of more highly-endowed individuals to urban areas. *

Intelligence and Family Size

In most investigations of the relationship between I.Q. and number of siblings in the family, a negative correlation is reported (Anastasi, 1956; Clausen, 1966; Nisbet and Entwistle, 1967). Since there is no evidence what-soever of any intrinsic relationship between I.Q. and procreative ability, only two other explanations seem plausible. First, the presence of a large number of children in the family may reduce the amount of cognitive stimulation available for each child (Clausen, 1966). The per capita expenditure on education, recreation, housing, medical care, etc., is ordinarily lower when there are many siblings in the family; and even more important, in terms of children's language development, the extent of parent-child contact is restricted (Nisbet, 1953). Second, I.Q. and size of family are indirectly re-lated by virtue of a common relationship to social-class status, i.e., persons in the upper economic strata tend to have both a higher I.Q. and to raise relatively small families.

To the extent that the intellectual superiority of their children is a function of either measurement or environmental factors, the inverse relationship between parents' fertility and social-class status obviously has no implications for eugenics. However, insofar as persons in the upper occupational strata may be presumed to possess a superior genic endowment with respect to cognitive capacity, their relatively low fertility rate may be expected, over the course of many generations (in the absence of compensatory genic factors), to contribute to a national decline in the genotypic basis of intelligence.

In spite of the ominous prediction based on this line of reasoning, there is some evidence of a slight but significant gain in the mean I.Q. of Scottish children from 1932 to 1947 (Scottish Council for Research in Education, 1953). Furthermore, despite the tremendous increase in high school enroll-ment from 1916 to 1940, with a corresponding elimination of the intellectual selectivity that formerly operated, there has been no drop in the mean I.Q. of the American high school population (Finch, 1946). The maintenance of phenotypic levels of intelligence under these circumstances can be explained perhaps by (a) compensatory changes in such environmental determinants of intelligence as the general standard of public education, (b) greater test

---

Kennedy et al., (1963) found no difference between urban and rural Negro children. This is not too surprising in view of the fact that Negro children's performance is depressed even in urban areas.

sophistication on the part of children, and (c) a trend in recent years toward a higher birth rate among upper socioeconomic groups (Anastasi, 1956; Hoffman and Wyatt, 1960).

CREATIVITY

Creativity is one of the vaguest, most ambiguous, and most confused terms in psychology and education today. Much of the semantic confusion regarding the term "creativity" stems from failure to distinguish between "creativity" as a trait inclusive of a wide and continuous range of indivdual differences, and the "creative person" as a unique individual possessing a rare and singular degree of this trait, i.e., a degree sufficient to set him off *qualitatively* from most other individuals in this regard. This same difficulty also exists with respect to "intelligence," but gives rise to less confusion because the term is more familiar. Everyone agrees that all degrees of intelligence exist, that even an imbecile exhibits some manifestations of intelligent behavior. But when we refer to an "intelligent person," we mean only someone who is at the upper end of the distribution of I.Q. scores, someone who exceeds a hypothetical cut-off point separating intelligent individuals from the general run of mankind. Thus, although creativity undoubtedly varies along a continuum, only the rare individual who makes a singularly original and significant contribution to art, science, literature, philosophy, government, etc., can be called a creative person. The creative person is, by definition, a much rarer individual than the intelligent person. Thousands of intelligent individuals exist for everyone who is truly creative.

It is important, therefore, to preserve the criterion of unique and singular originality in designating a person as creative. All discovery activity is not qualitatively of one piece. In the course of growing older, for example, every infant inevitably discovers that objects continue to exist even when they are out of sight; this discovery, however, hardly manifests the same *quality* of creativity as Einstein's formulation of the theory of relativity. Similarly, a sixth-grade pupil may exhibit some degree of creativity in composing a song or writing a poem, but this does not mean that his accomplishments differ from Bach's and Shakespeare's merely in degree rather than in kind. The fact that it is often difficult to measure originality, and that great discoveries may frequently go unrecognized for decades or centuries, does not detract in the least from the existence of qualitative differences in creative achievement. A creative person must do more than simply produce something that is novel or original in terms of his *own* life history.

A truly creative individual, therefore, is rare not primarily because he lacks appropriate experience to develop his creative potentialities, but because he is, by definition, at such an extreme point in the distribution of creative potentialities that he is qualitatively discontinuous from persons exhibiting lesser degrees of creativity. This is not to deny the important role of the environment in the development of creativity; many potential Mozarts, for example, have spent their lives as peasants and cobblers. But even assuming an optimal environment, creative individuals would still be extremely rare. The principle determinant of creative persons, in other words, is genic within a specified range of environmental influences. These latter influences function more as limiting than as directive factors. A good environment is less of a formative influence in the actualization of creative potentialities than a guarantee that the necessary opportunities for their development are present.

A second source of semantic confusion regarding the concept of creativity reflects the failure to distinguish between creativity as a highly *particularized* and *substantive* capacity (i.e., a rare and unique manifestation of a talent in a *particular* field of endeavor), and as a *general constellation of supportive intellectual abilities, personality variables, and problem-solving traits*. Typical of the latter conception of creativity is Torrance's definition of creative thinking as the "process of sensing gaps or disturbing, missing elements; forming ideas or hypotheses concerning them; testing these hypotheses, and communicating the results, possibly modifying and retesting the hypotheses" (Torrance *et al*, 1960). These latter aspects of intellectual functioning presumably include such component traits or abilities as originality, redefinition, adaptive flexibility, spontaneous flexibility, word fluency, expressional fluency, associational fluency, and problem sensitivity (Guilford and Merrifield, 1960; Guilford *et al*, 1951; Kettner *et al*, 1959). Much stress, also, is currently laid on divergent thinking as the distinctive attribute of creative thinking; and such Guilford-type tests as unusual uses, consequences, impossibilities, problem situations, and improvements (Guilford *et al*, 1951) have been employed to measure this ability.

However, without denying in any way the existence of general supportive abilities, it must be insisted that such abilities do not constitute the essence of creativity. It is true that they are probably more intrinsically related to creative achievement than is I.Q. Genuinely creative talent, nevertheless, is a particularized intellectual-personality capacity related to the *substantive* content of a given field of human endeavor, rather than a set of general, content-free intellectual and personality traits, and with increasing age it probably becomes increasingly particularized in its expression. Creative achievement, in other words, reflects a rare capacity for developing insights, sensitivities, and appreciations in a circumscribed content area of intellectual or artistic activity.*

It may sometimes happen, of course, that a single individual possesses more than one creative talent.

This capacity is obviously not coextensive with any one general ability such as divergent thinking, although the possession of this latter ability, and of other supportive abilities as well, undoubtedly facilitates the actualization of particularized and substantive creativity. It should also be recognized that high scores on tests that purportedly measure divergent thinking also reflect the influence of such contaminating factors as verbal fluency and glibness, uninhibited self-expression, and deficient self-critical ability.

To summarize, *creativity per se* is a particularized, substantive capacity, whereas the commonly measured *creative abilities* are supportive intellectual-personality functions which, like general intelligence and capacity for disciplined concentration, help implement the expression of creativity, i.e., convert creative potentialities into creative achievement. These supportive abilities are normally distributed in the population; differences among individuals, like differences in I.Q., are differences in degree rather than in kind. Varying degrees of creativity also exist, but the creative person differs *qualitatively* from individuals manifesting lesser degrees of creativity. Hence, although some supportive abilities manifest a modicum of intersituational generality (Getzels and Jackson, 1962; Kettner *et al*, 1959; Wallach and Kogan, 1965; Wilson *et al*, 1953), there is no reason to believe that creativity *per se* exhibits any generality of function (Eisner, 1965). Because of their implementing or enabling function, high scores on tests both of general intelligence and of general supportive traits are more generously distributed among creative than noncreative individuals (Drevdahl, 1956; Roe, 1960). Neither type of test, however, measures creativity itself. As a matter of fact, by definition, no general test of creativity is possible. Assessments of creative potentiality can only be based on expert judgments of actual work products, suitably tempered by considerations of age and experience (Eisner, 1965).

Creativity and Intelligence

The relationship between creativity and intelligence is exceedingly complex and is further complicated by difficult problems of measurement. Creativity measures emphasizing divergent thinking tend to correlate only moderately ($r = .25 - .30$) with measures of intelligence (Cline *et al*, 1962; Cline *et al*, 1963a; Drevdahl, 1956; Getzels and Jackson, 1962; Guilford, 1950; J. L. Holland, 1961; Klausmeier and Wiersma, 1965; McGuire *et al*, 1961; Torrance, 1960a; Torrance *et al*, 1960; Yamamoto, 1964a,b,c). At first blush this suggests that these supportive cognitive traits associated with creativity tap a somewhat different spectrum of intellectual abilities than do traditional tests of intelligence. However, the evidence that these supportive traits correlate just as highly with intelligence as they do among each other (Cline *et al*, 1962; Getzels and Jackson, 1962; Ohnmacht, 1966; Piers *et al*, 1960; R. L. Thorndike, 1963) clearly indicates that they cannot be considered representative of a common attribute of creativity that is independent of intelligence. For all practical purposes, therefore, most commonly used batteries of creativity tests measure cognitive abilities that are not reliably distinguishable from intelligence; this fact undoubtedly accounts, in part, for their positive correlation with academic achievement.

In contrast to these findings, two investigators (Flescher, 1963; Wallach and Kogan, 1965) have reported negligible correlations between intelligence and creativity. But although Flesher's battery of tests are presumably measuring some cognitive abilities that are independent of intelligence, the negligible intercorrelations among them indicate that they can hardly be considered representative of a unitary trait of creativity. Additive treatment of scores on this battery and the derivation of a composite score are therefore unwarranted. Wallach and Kogan's (1965) more homogeneous measures of creative aptitude, on the other hand, exhibit satisfactory generality over component elements, and can, therefore, be considered reflective of a stable cognitive trait that is independent of intelligence. Even here, however, their measures of creativity may have limited psychological significance because there is little evidence that high creative children produce responses of superior quality in any situation (with the exception that the measures of creativity are correlated with other measures of social responsiveness) (Cronbach, 1968).

Much more important than the relationship between intelligence and supportive measures of creativity is the relationship between intelligence and true substantive creativity. The evidence invariably shows that creative individuals in art, literature, and science are more intelligent than non-creative individuals (Drevdahl and Cattell, 1958; Hitt and Stock, 1965), and that high-I.Q. persons contribute much more than their share of notable and original discoveries in the various disciplines (Terman and Oden, 1959). This suggests, of course, that intelligence, like other supportive cognitive traits, makes possible and implements the expression of substantive creativity (Price and Bell, 1965). In other words, a certain minimal degree of intelligence above the average is necessary for the actualization of creative potentialities. But above this critical level the relationship between intelligence and true creativity is approximately zero (Drevdahl, 1956; MacKinnon, 1962; Terman and Oden, 1959). The noncreative high I.Q. individual who does very well on academic tasks and is vocationally successful, but who never generates an original idea, is a very familiar figure in our culture. Contrariwise, many highly creative individuals do not sport spectacularly high I.Q.'s.

Personality Correlates of Creativity

Considerable research has been conducted on the personality characteristics of persons who have been rated by competent judges as creative in such areas as art, architecture, literature, and science. In general, these traits are consistent with what one would expect of original and talented individuals who have achieved success and recognition in their chosen fields. On the cognitive side, creative individuals tend to be original, perceptive, insightful, independent in judgment, open to new experience (especially from within), skeptical, and verbally facile. They are flexible, open-minded, and tolerant of ambiguity; they have wide-ranging interests; they prefer complexity; and they are less interested in small details and in the practical and concrete than in theoretical ideas and symbolic transformations (Barron, 1963; Drevdahl, 1956; Drevdahl and Cattell, 1958; MacKinnon, 1960, 1961, 1962). In general they delight in paradoxes and in reconciling opposites. From a motivational standpoint they are ambitious, achievement-oriented, dominant, and have a sense of destiny about themselves. They tend to be emotionally mature, venturesome, self-sufficient, and emotionally and aesthetically sensitive. Their self-image abounds in such traits as inventiveness, determination, industry, independence, individualism, and enthusiasm. On the whole, they exhibit higher ego strength and self-acceptance, more introspectiveness, and greater femininity than noncreative individuals. In their relations with others they are unconventional, rebellious, disorderly, self-centered, exhibitionistic, and prone to retreat to the role of observer. They tend to make deviant scores on the Minnesota Multiphasic Personality Inventory, but this is undoubtedly more reflective of complexity of personality, candor, lack of defensiveness, and openness to experience than of genuine personality distortion (Barron, 1963; Drevdahl, 1956; Drevdahl and Cattell, 1958; Hammer, 1961; MacKinnon, 1960, 1961, 1962).

Of somewhat less psychological significance are the personality characteristics associated with the supportive cognitive criteria of creativity. Wallach and Kogan (1965) found that their high creatives tended to be broad rather than narrow categorizers, to be tolerant of an unconventional type of hypothesizing about the world, and to be responsive to affective aspects of the environment. Their high-creative-high-intelligence group were high in self-confidence and self-esteem and low in defensiveness enjoyed a high sociometric status, actively sought the companionship of others, and exhibited a high attention span and ability to concentrate; however at the same time, they tended to display more than their fair share of attention-seeking and disruptive behavior. On the other hand, high-creatives who were low in intelligence exhibited the opposite set of characteristics except for the considerable attention-seeking, disruptive behavior in the classroom. Anxiety level was middling for the high creative groups; when it was either very high or very low, it appeared to depress creativity. This suggests either that a moderate degree of anxiety is necessary to generate creative behavior or that the expression of creativity is productive of moderate anxiety.

PART V

Physical and Motor Aspects of Development

CHAPTER 18

Physical Growth and Motor Development

PHYSICAL GROWTH IN CHILDREN

SINCE THIS BOOK IS PRIMARILY concerned with problems of psychological development we cannot undertake a definitive discussion of physical growth. *

Yet for several reasons it is important that we at least consider some major theoretical issues and developmental trends. First, physical growth is one of the more overt and impressive indications of children's development. Thus, a well-rounded view of the child and how he develops requires some discussion of normative growth changes and of the interpretation of individual physical status. Second, physical growth clearly illustrates many of the general principles of development discussed in Chapters 3 and 4. Finally, physical growth has an important impact on motor and other aspects of development.

Normative treatment of physical growth data reveals many age level uniformities as well as the orderliness of growth in the form of predictable age level changes in various quantitative, qualitative, and sequential aspects of development. Such data are also extremely useful as a standard for evaluating the current status of a given child and for ascertaining whether he maintains his relative position in his age group from one year to the next. When used for this purpose it is obviously necessary to consider the range of variability around the mean. Furthermore, since longitudinal studies show many individual patterns of growth (Bayley, 1956), it is also useful to have an *individual* standard for evaluating the child's current progress and for prognosticating physical development. Generally speaking, for reasons indicated elsewhere (see p. 695), the child's rate of growth in relation to that of his fellows tends to remain relatively constant until adolescence (Bayley & Pinneau, 1952; Stuart & Meredith, 1946; Wetzel, 1941). Although deviations from a predictable growth pattern are hardly rare in physical development (Garn, 1952), they tend to be normally distributed in magnitude.

A more complete treatment of the topics related to physical growth may be found in the following sources. (Bayer & Bayley, 1959; Garn, 1966; Garn and Shamir, 1958; Meredeth, 1960; Tanner, 1961; Ten-Bosch, Van der Werff, & Haak, 1966). Problems of childrens' health, nutrition and diseases are also beyond the scope of this book.

In appraising the physical growth status of a particular child, therefore, two mutually complementary methods are available. We can either compare him to the mean child of his own age and sex or we can use him as his own unique yardstick by relating his currently attained status to his own terminal (adult) status. Obviously, employment of the latter method must await the determination of adult status; thus, while useful for longitudinal analysis of *completed* growth cycles, it cannot be used for current evaluation of a growing child. On the other hand, it is often quite misleading to use simple age-sex norms in judging a child's growth status. For example, a tall, stocky, rapidly maturing, or pubescent child should presumably weigh more than a short, slender, slowly maturing, or prepubescent child. Hence, we would also want to consider such factors as height, skeletal maturity, pubescent status, and such indices of physique as could be calculated by relating height to various transverse dimensions of the body (chest circumference, shoulder width, hip width, calf girth) (Garn, 1966; Meredith, 1960; McCloy, 1938; Massler and Suher, 1951; Wetzel, 1941). If we wanted to be even more precise we could ascertain the respective contributions of fat, water, muscle, bone, and subcutaneous tissues to a given child's weight (McCloy, 1938).

Since it would be extremely cumbersome to consider all of the above factors in appraising individual growth progress, such modern techniques as the Wetzel Grid and the Massler Nomograms (see p. 695) identify the most significant variables affecting status in a particular function, divide children into various subgroups on the basis of their standing relative to these latter variables, and appraise a particular child's growth sequentially in terms of the subgroup to which he belongs. This approach represents a compromise between the gross normative and the multiple differential methods of individual appraisal. It also effects a compromise between the normative and individual yardsticks since it makes possible a comparison between the child's current status and the adult level achieved by his subgroup.

Dimensions of Growth

In addition to considering quantitative increments in height and weight, an overview of physical development must also include changes in such other dimensions of bodily growth as separate organ systems, qualitative aspects of the skeletal system, body proportions, and physiological maturity. Since rates of growth of different body parts are not highly intercorrelated, it is unlikely that any theoretical growth curve will be generally applicable over long periods of time (Thompson, 1954).

Separate Organ Systems. The body does not grow as a whole and in all directions at once (Thompson, 1954). In comparing the relative growth of the various organ systems, Scammon's grouping of their growth trends in four main categories (neural, lymphoid, general [skeletal and visceral], and genital) is useful (Harris, Jackson, Paterson and Scammon, 1930). After following parallel paths in the prenatal period, these four kinds of growth diverge markedly after birth. Neural growth is most rapid; 80 per cent complete by the age of four, it tapers off greatly thereafter. Growth of lymphoid tissues (e.g., thymus, lymph nodes) reaches the adult level at age six, more than doubles the adult level by age 12, and then declines until maturity. Genital growth is negligible between birth and pubescence because of the absence of functional levels of sex hormone stimulation. Growth of the skeletal system is marked by two spurts, one during infancy and the other beginning before pubescence; each spurt is followed by a period of decelerating growth. Growth of the respiratory and vascular organs tends to keep pace with growth in bone and muscle tissue (Maresh, 1948), thereby obviating the possibility of physiological imbalance in meeting the enhanced nutritive needs of an expanding body frame. Throughout childhood, and especially during adolescence, the heart grows more rapidly than the arterial system; as a result, relative cardiac competency increases, heart rate decreases and blood pressure increases.

Qualitative Changes in the Skeletal System. Important qualitative changes take place in the bones during the course of skeletal development. First, with increasing age, osseous tissue gradually replaces both connective tissue in the bones of the face and cranium and cartilageneous tissue in the other bones of the skeleton. The process of ossification is then completed by the deposition of calcium salts. Vitamin C is necessary for the first step and vitamin D is required for the latter step. As the percentage of calcium increases and of water and soft tissues decreases, the bones become harder, less pliable, and more brittle. Many new centers of ossification also appear in an orderly, predictable fashion.* By the end of childhood the diaphyses (shafts) and epiphyses (expanded terminal portions) of the long bones are completely ossified except for a strip of cartilage at their junction. Thereafter, all longitudinal growth takes place in these epiphysial cartilages until complete ossification at the end of adolescence results in fusion and forever terminates the possibility of increase in stature.

Since ossification of the hand and wrist parallels general skeletal growth, it furnishes a convenient index of a child's skeletal maturity. Also, the degree of calcification of the mandibular third molar is highly related to skeletal age (Demesch and Wartmann, 1956). A number of age level standards have been prepared by various investigators for determining skeletal age (Flory, 1936; Greulich, and Pyle, 1959; Todd, 1937). Degree of skeletal maturity is

---

Ossification also follows a cephalo-caudal trend. Since the bones undergoing ossification most rapidly are most affected by nutritional deficiencies, the principal site of rickets during the first year of life is in the cranium. During the second year the site shifts to the thorax, and during the third year to the extremities.

affected by hereditary factors (Flory, 1936; Garn, 1966) and is positively related to social class status (Low, Chan, Chan, and Lee, 1964; Todd, 1937). Girls are consistently more mature in their skeletal development, the sex difference tending to increase with age (Flory, 1936; Greulich & Pyle, 1950; Johnston, 1964; Terman & Tyler, 1954). Despite uniformly earlier ages of appearance for the ossification centers in girls, intercorrelations between ossification centers in the hand and wrist were greater for girls than for boys (Garn & Rohmann, 1959). Muscular growth parallels general body and skeletal growth throughout childhood and also shows a marked spurt at pubescence. The fat-bone ratio decreases with age for boys and increases with age in girls (Reynolds, 1949). Between the ages of 1.5 and 12.5 years, children who are one standard deviation above the average in fat are approximately one-half a year advanced in growth (Garn and Haskell, 1960).

The fact that skeletal maturation is sensitive to social class, cultural, and regional factors (Johnston, 1964; Low et al, 1964) warrants the possible compilation of separate growth curves for distinct groups (Johnston, 1964). Although skeletal age measures are subject to the above shortcomings, they are nevertheless more accurate predictors of adult status than chronological age (Garn, 1966).

Body Proportions. Because of the cephalo-caudal and proximo-distal trends in physical growth during the *fetal period*, the head and trunk are disproportionately large and the extremities are disproportionately short at birth. The rate of increase in head circumference is greater in males from birth through 15 months, and in females from the second through the twelfth year (Eichorn & Bayley, 1962). After the first year, the head grows most slowly, the proportion of its length to total body length progressively diminishes. The legs grow more rapidly than the trunk through childhood and especially during preadolescence. Beginning with adolescence, however, the reverse trend sets in (Bayley, 1935). During childhood the face also grows much more rapidly than the rest of the cranium.

The neonate is slender except for his head. He broadens out during the first year of life and then becomes progressively more slender until the age of seven or eight (Bayley, 1935). A broadening trend begins as the child approaches pubescence, being concentrated in the shoulder girdle among boys and in the hip region among girls. The pubertal growth spurt is also marked by a significant increase in head circumference (Eichorn & Bayley, 1962).

The foregoing changes in children's body proportions reflect age level shifts in the relative dominance of the different factors regulating their skeletal growth (Bayley, 1935). Ordinarily broad-built children tend to be physically accelerated and slender-built children physically retarded. The former also tend to progress through these sequential changes in body proportions more rapidly (Bayley, 1935).

Anatomical and Physiological Maturity. In general, the degree of anatomical and physiological maturity is represented by the extent to which attained status in a given structure or function approaches the adult level. Although not perfectly intercorrelated, different measures of physical maturity tend to be substantially related to each other (Nicholson & Hanley, 1953). Hence, degree of physical maturity may be expressed in terms of pubescent status (Greulich, 1950), skeletal maturity (Greulich, 1950), percentage of adult height (Nicholson & Handley, 1953), or developmental growth level achieved at a given age (Wetzel, 1941). Other functions that advance or decline regularly from birth to adulthood, such as increments in blood pressure, vital capacity, and dental age, or decrements in body temperature, pulse, respiratory and basal metabolic rates, are less useful indices of maturity because they are more variable and less highly intercorrelated (Iliff and Lee, 1952; Thompson, 1954).

The most commonly used measure of developmental age is skeletal age or bone age as measured by the postero-anterior hand radiograph (Garn, 1966; Greulich & Pyle, 1959). Skeletal age is an extremely useful general index of physical maturity since it is highly correlated with all measures of pubescent status (Garn, 1966; Greulich, 1950; Nicholson & Hanley, 1953). It indicates with certain qualifications, whether the child's skeletal development is proceeding at an average, accelerated, or retarded rate (Garn, 1966). Although reasonably independent of sheer bodily size (Greulich, 1950), in the sense that acceleration or retardation of pubescence (unless very extreme) does not materially affect terminal stature, it does indicate how close the child has progressed toward adult status (Bayley, 1956; Garn, 1966). Hence, from measures of present height and skeletal age it is possible to make predictions of adult stature with a reasonable degree of accuracy (Bayley & Pinneau, 1952), providing that pubescence does not occur abnormally early or late. Greater precision can be achieved for individual predictions by the knowledge that the child comes from either tall or short parents (Garn, 1966).

Growth in Height*

Growth in height is not evenly distributed over the approximately twenty year period in which it occurs. After an interval of rapid growth during the first two years, yearly increments in stature are small and relatively constant until the second growth spurt in pre- and early adolescence (Krogman, 1943; Watson and Lowrey, 1951). Boys are slightly taller than girls until the age of 11 when the earlier occurrence of the preadolescent growth spurt in the latter puts them ahead temporarily (Krogman, 1943; Watson & Lowrey, 1951). However, since this second spurt is more intense and longer lasting in boys, they regain their superiority at about the age of 15.

*See Garn, 1966 for a recent review of this topic.

Height is a typical example of a normally distributed, polygenically determined ontogenetic trait (see p. 57) in which genic influences account for the greater portion of phenotypic variability (Garn, 1966).* Where genotypes are identical, as among monozygotic twins, environmental differences give rise to relatively small differences in their ultimate height. The degree of resemblance between siblings and between parents and children, although substantial, is appreciably less because of greater genotypic diversity, (Harris et al, 1930). The influence of genic factors is undoubtedly mediated through the secretion of differential amounts of growth hormone (anterior pituitary), thyroxin, and sex hormones, and through the differential responsiveness of skeletal tissues to their stimulation (Garn, 1966). Growth hormone and thyroxin stimulate skeletal growth from the prenatal period to maturity. The adolescent growth spurt is largely attributable to the early proliferative effect of sex hormones on the epiphysial cartilages. Final ossification of the epiphyses (and the termination of growth) is caused by the later ossifying action of high concentrations of these hormones (Ausubel, 1954).

Since height is a polygenically determined trait it is somewhat susceptible to the influence of environmental factors. The adequacy of nutrition—especially the intake of protein, calcium, and vitamin D—plays an important role in determining whether the individual attains the maximum height that is possible within his genic limitations (Dreizen et al, 1953). It is not clear in some cases, however, whether the fact that a child is taller causes him to eat more (Garn, 1966). Taller children have larger bones and in consequence their needs for calcium and phosphorous during growth are proportionately larger (Garn, 1966). It is also plausible to attribute greater growth to nutritional factors by noting that from the last quarter of the 19th century change in stature has been upward in direction in infancy, early and middle years of childhood (Garn, 1966; Hale, 1958; Meredeth, 1963), and that substantial increases in height have occurred among children of American immigrants (Garn, 1966). Nutritional factors may also account for the positive relationship between height and social status (Garn, 1966) and for decrements and increments in the height of children coincident with periods of war and prosperity (Howe & Schiller, 1952).

Recent studies on protein-calorie malnutrition have suggested that inadequate size attainment results from this deficit (Garn, 1966). Geographic region (Johnston, 1964; Whitacre and Grimes, 1959) and exposure to atomic radiation also appears to affect height and skeletal maturity (Greulich et al,

---

*It is true, of course, that the range in which human stature occurs is a species characteristic. Consistent differences are also found between the mean heights of children of different racial stocks growing up in the same environment, e.g. Chinese, Japanese, South European, and North European on the islands of Hawaii. However, much overlapping occurs between groups (Wissler, 1930).

1953). At present these factors are only correlates associated with stature; the causes of these changes are unknown and plausible conjecture is frequently mistaken for explanation (Meredith, 1963). For example, the fact that children achieve higher adult stature in cultures where infant innoculation is practiced (Whiting, Landauer and Jones, 1968) in no way explains this phenomena.

Because the influence of genic factors on skeletal growth operates with considerable uniformity throughout the growth span, a child who is tall or short at birth also tends to be similarly tall or short at ages six and nineteen. The prediction of adult stature is frequently attempted by assessment of present height and rate of growth (as indicated by skeletal maturity) (Bayley & Pinneau, 1952). Size at a given age however is only a partial indication of size at later age—especially in cases of extreme parent-child size discrepancies (Garn, 1966). Thus, in prediction of human stature, then, the following generalization should be born in mind:

"The later the projection is made, the more it makes use of skeletal rather than chronological age, and the more nearly the child conforms to the characteristics of the group, the better the prediction. Conversely, the earlier the size prediction is made, the more it depends on chronological age alone (or early skeletal age estimates), and the more the child deviates from the averages for the group, the poorer the size prediction will necessarily be. (Garn, 1966, p. 538)."

Finally, the interpretation of the positive relationship reported between height and intelligence (Ketcham, 1960) is an open question. The fact that taller children, in many instances, come from more prosperous families is a possible indication that both these variables are influenced by family socio-economic background (Laycock and Taylor, 1964). Thus holding family background constant negates the positive relationship between height and intelligence (Laycock & Taylor, 1964).

Body Weight and Nutritional Status

The child's body weight is the most frequently studied index of growth (Meredith, 1960). Along with being a correlate of growth, it is also an index of nutritional status. Optimal weight depends on age, sex, physical and pubescent status; it can be calculated most conveniently from the Massler Nomograms which utilize a prediction formula based on the relationship of weight to height and calf girth (Massler and Suher, 1951). The general shape of the growth curve for weight closely parallels that for height, but the rate of gain is more rapid (Baer, Torgoff & Harris, 1962). Predictability of weight across age is most difficult during infancy and adolescence because of rapid growth during these periods (Meredith, 1965). The child ordinarily doubles his birth weight in six months or less, but requires four years, to double his height. Boys weigh more than girls during infancy and childhood; a reversal occurs between the ages of ten and thirteen during the female growth spurt, and another reversal, again favoring boys, at about thirteen occurs during their growth spurt (Peckos, 1957; Rauh, Schumsky and Witt, 1967; Singer *et al*, 1968). The same trends are seen in non-whites except that the reversal favoring girls occurs at age ten and lasts until fourteen years (Rauh, Schumsky, and Witt, 1967). Like the corresponding spurt in height the adolescent spurt in weight occurs earlier in children who mature early, and tends to precede other signs of sexual maturation. The heavier child, like the taller child, also tends to become pubescent earlier. Characteristic sex differences in the distribution of fat do not appear prior to pubescence.

Weight is also a normally distributed polygenically determined trait, but genic factors are much less prepotent than in the case of height. Mediating mechanisms include a polyglandular system of control (thyroid, anterior pituitary, adrenal cortex and gonads) as well as differential tissue responsiveness to hormonal stimulation. Genic factors related to body build are also significant determinants of weight. Ectomorphic children, for example, tend to be skinny despite the fact that their daily caloric intake greatly exceeds that of endomorphs (Peckos, 1953). Weight, however, is much more influenced than height by such environmental variables as exercise, disease, socio-emotional adjustment, and nutrition. The latter factor accounts for weight lag in undernourished children (Dreizen *et al*, 1953), for the long-term increase in mean weight of children over the past seven decades (Clements, 1953; Meredith, 1963), for fluctuations in mean weight during war and prosperity, (Howe & Schiller, 1952), and for the positive relationship between weight and socioeconomic status (Berry & Cowin, 1954). Weight lag has also been noted as a concomitant of disease, operations, and emotional stress (Binning, 1948; Fried & Mayer, 1948).

The Wetzel Grid is a useful technique for appraising the adequacy of a child's growth in weight relative to his height and physique (Wetzel, 1941). It indicates rate and consistency of growth, degree of maturity status currently attained, and deviations from the expected pattern. Ordinarily, a child's growth parallels, within rather narrowly defined limits of variation, the growth curve formed by plotting successive increments in weight and height of children in his own physique group. Nonpathological deviations from this "channelwise" progression, however, are less uncommon than Wetzel believed, especially among early and late maturing girls and children with unique body builds (Garn, 1952). Wetzel's (1941) grid progressions are more similar in pattern for weight variations than for variations in height, which in some instances may demand supplementary developmental age grid norms with separate assessments of height and weight (Baer, Torgoff and Harris, 1962). Furthermore, although the Wetzel Grid is an excellent clinical tool for revealing pathological aberrations in growth due to disease, malnutrition, or emotional stress, it neither indicates per se the cause of the disturbance nor the relative contributions of fat, bone, muscle, and subcutaneous tissue to an increment in weight. Hence, adequate interpretation of irregularity in a child's growth pattern also presupposes knowledge of his pubescent status, optimal weight, health, nutrition, and socioemotional history.

The Body Image

The body image is the mental picture that each individual has of his own appearance in space. It includes such factors as height, weight, body build, and facial appearance. Ordinarily, during most periods of life (e.g., from childhood to preadolescence), the body image changes imperceptibly because the body itself changes in this way. The small changes in appearance and quantitative increments in height and weight are easily absorbed in the prevailing image the child has of his own body; no radical revisions are necessary. During adolescence, however, conscious and wholesale restructuring of the body image is necessary to account for drastic changes in size, body proportions, primary and secondary sex characteristics, and facial appearance.

As a salient component of the ego, the body image usually has positive or negative rather than neutral affective valence. Whether it contributes positively or negatively to self-esteem depends on the social valuation of particular physical traits, deviations, and disabilities, i.e., whether the latter give rise to approval or disapproval, admiration, or ridicule. For example, teachers and parents rate endomorphic (plump) girls high in cooperativeness and ectomorphic (thin) boys and girls as uncooperative, emotionally restrained, aloof, etc. (Walker, 1962, 1963). The height of important figures tends to be overestimated and there is a positive correlation between peer status and body size for boys (Clarke & Clarke, 1961). Also, mesomorphic (athletic) boys are rated as more desirable from pictures in comparison with endomorphs (McCandless, 1967). Individuals are usually regarded as ugly or attractive insofar as they conform to or deviate from the idealized anatomic measurements of their own sex group. In our culture shortness and puniness in boys and obesity in either sex tend to detract from a child's status in his peer group. It should be noted, however, that somatic defects and deviations have a less disastrous effect on children's than on adolescents' self-concepts. Among the latter, physical attractiveness is a more crucial determinant of sociometric status and is also important for heterosexual effectiveness; furthermore, during childhood the individual is less dependent on the peer group for status and approval. He can still retain a flattering self-image if he is intrinsically valued by his parents.

Psychological Effects of Somatic Defects and Deviations

Physical defects and deviations constitute first of all an *objective* handicap in adapting to the social environment. Shortness, ectomorphy, obesity, and retarded pubescent development place a boy at a serious competitive disadvantage in athletic activity. Mesomorphic (muscular) boys enjoy the reputation among their fellows of being "real boys," daring, leaders, good at games, and grown-up, whereas ectomorphic boys have the reputation of being bashful, submissive and unhappy and aloof (Hanley, 1951; Walker, 1962). Boys also prefer the mesomorphic over the endomorphic physique (McCandless, 1967). Cardiac and orthopedic disabilities limit participation in physical and social activities, and visual and auditory defects restrict the range of sensitivity and responsiveness to important intellectual and social stimuli. When unsuspected and uncorrected they make school learning difficult and simulate mental deficiency; indirectly, they may lead to failure in school by placing too great a strain on the individual's capacity for attentiveness. Chronic strain, pain, fatigue, and hormonal imbalance associated with many physical and sensory defects may also give rise to behavioral disturbance by lowering the general threshold of reactivity. When this happens the affected child manifests undue irritability, restlessness, and distractibility, and responds to trifling stimuli with exaggerated, undirected, inappropriate, and frequently aggressive responses (McGraw, 1949).

More important than the objective handicap inherent in physical defects is the *social* disadvantage at which they place the deviant individual. Significant deviancy from group physical norms tends to elicit a negative response from his peers and almost guarantees that he will be treated differently from his fellows. The least common denominators of this differential treatment are devaluation, avoidance, rejection, and accordance of a lower status. Children prefer drawings of five different physical handicaps and the absence of handicap in the following order: no physical handicap, a child with crutches, a child in a wheelchair, a child with an amputation, a child with a slight facial disfigurement, and an obese child (Richardson, Goodman, Hastorf, and Dornbusch, 1961; Goodman, Richardson, Dormbusch & Hastoff, 1963). Boys preferences are based more on physical impairment whereas girls focus more on visual cues based on appearance (Richardson and Royce, 1968). Physical handicap is a more powerful cue in establishing preference than skin color (Richardson & Royce, 1968). Physically accelerated children, on the other hand are accepted and treated by adults and other children as more mature (Jones & Bayley, 1959). Although they may sometimes be the victims of excessive adult expectations, they appear to have relatively little need to strive for status. From their ranks come the outstanding student body leaders. In contrast, because others tend to treat them as the little boys they appear to be, physically retarded boys exhibit many forms of relatively immature behavior (Jones & Bayley, 1950).

The individual's ego response to his own physical disability is largely a reflection of the social reaction it elicits. If the latter is negative, therefore, he responds with feelings of self-depreciation, guilt, hypersensitivity, self-consciousness, and anxiety in facing new or competitive situations (Carter & Chess, 1951; Cruickshank, 1951; Mohr, 1948). Many children seek to compensate for their physical disadvantage with excessive activity and attention-getting behavior (Jones and Bayley, 1950); others become demanding and egocentric or exhibit regressive behavior. The most serious reaction to the ego-deflating implications of somatic defect is self-protective withdrawal from social situations. Persistent avoidance of interpersonal relations may lead to irreversible retardation in the socialization process.

It need not be imagined, however, that self-depreciation is an inevitable accompaniment of organic defect. Much depends on the seriousness of the disability or the extent of the deviation, both from the norm of the peer group and from the child's ideal; on its probable duration and its obviousness to others; on its relation to other physical defects and to problems of adjustment arising from nonsomatic sources; and on the availability of other compensatory and status-giving traits. Most important, perhaps, is the attitude of the child's parents toward the condition (MacFarlane, 1939). If they are rejecting, overprotective, embarrassed, or have unrealistic expectations, ego damage is unavoidable. If they handle the situation realistically, take it in stride, and extend unqualified acceptance, the worst features of impaired self-esteem may be largely circumvented (Carter & Chess, 1951).

Impact of Physical Growth on Motor Development

Skeletal and muscular development self-evidently provide the anatomic substrate for the development of strength and motor skill. Increment in muscle mass tends to precede growth in strength and skill since the latter not only presupposes the structural wherewithall but also the neurophysiological maturity and experience necessary for functional utilization and motor coordination. It is understandable, therefore, why gross physical development is accompanied by the ability to manipulate the parts of the body that have grown (Govatos, 1959), and why gross motor skills are positively related to such factors as mesomorphy (Sills, 1950), skeletal maturity (Sills, 1951), and development of the abdominal musculature (Vickers, Poyntz & Baum, 1942). Although motor learning of a more complex sort depends on sensori-motor intelligence (Blank, 1964) and is unrelated to gross motor skills and physical ability (McGraw, 1949), a correlation nevertheless exists between height, weight, and complex motor skills (Ghesquere, 1958).

Contrary to popular belief, individual differences in the emergence of locomotor abilities are not determined by weight or body build but by genic factors concerned with their development and by such temperamental characteristics as eagerness, venturesomeness, persistence and curiosity (Peatman & Higgins, 1942). Children who sit, stand, and walk late tend to be heavier and taller than individuals more advanced in these respects simply because they are older; they are not heavier or taller *for their age* than the latter (Peatman & Higgins, 1942). Also, under uniform conditions of pediatric and home care, the age at which these functions appear is not affected by general health status (Peatman and Higgins, 1940).

MOTOR DEVELOPMENT IN INFANCY AND EARLY CHILDHOOD

The motor ability of a child constitutes an important component of his feeling of competence in coping with the environment. It enables him to feel either executively independent and capable of looking after his own needs or relatively dependent on the physical assistance of others. It also constitutes an important source of primary status in the home, school and peer group as well as a basic prerequisite for ultimately attaining *volitional* independence. The precise effects on personality development of a gain in motor competence, however, depend on the prevailing state of ego organization. During the stage of omnipotence, the child feels volitionally independent *despite* and possibly even because of his executive dependence (see p. 259). Increased executive independence at this time may therefore result in further feelings of self-enhancement but is certainly not basic to current notions of volitional power; as a matter of fact since it leads to greater parental demands on the child, it tends to be associated with increased volitional dependence, ego devaluation, and satellization. This situation also prevails during most of the satellizing period since the attained level of motor competence is still insufficient to instigate demands for greater volitional independence.* Beginning with middle childhood enhanced motor competence becomes a major source of primary status and instrument of desatellization. The executively independent child is more free to explore the wider community with some feelings of assurance. Children with motor handicaps not only feel more timorous in this respect but also find it difficult to maintain a realistic level of aspiration when faced with motor tasks (Wenar, 1953).

Motor activity is an important outlet for emotional expression (fear, flight, rage, aggression) and source of basic satisfactions and self-expression. Increased motor competence helps reduce frustrations in childhood that are

---

Misperceptions of executive competence between the ages of four and five do *commonly instigate expansive, out-of-bounds behavior reflective of such demands (see p. 269).*

occasioned by inability to manipulate objects and play materials as desired. The way in which a child expresses himself in motor performance is also an excellent reflection of such temperamental and personality characteristics as venturesomeness, energy level, aggressiveness, sociality, and self-confidence.

Not the least important aspect of motor development is its implications for social participation and adjustment. We have already indicated how early participation in cooperative peer activities is limited by the infant's motor incompetence (see p. 330), the extent to which athletic prowess determines a boy's prestige and leadership status in his peer group (see p. 346), and how socially ascendant behavior may be increased by improving a child's motor skills (see p. 340). Strength and motor skill are integral components of the body image that impinge on self-esteem since they and their reciprocals are socially admired and disparaged in much the same way as tallness and shortness, mesomorphy and obesity. Retardation in motor competence forms the beginning of a vicious cycle in social maladjustment that is difficult to break. Boys with poor physical abilities tend to enjoy low social prestige in the group. Hence they have reason to shun both motor activities and group participation, because both are associated with failure. Their reluctance to participate, in turn, not only increases their poor reputation but also, through lack of practice, further depresses their relative standing in these very motor abilities that are so crucial for group status. The upshot may be a compensatory absorption in nonsocial activities that results in social isolation and failure to acquire the skills necessary for successful interpersonal relationships.

Organizational Trends

The principal organizational trends in the development of early motor behavior have already been discussed in Chapter 7 (see p. 205). Particularly striking as the child passes through the various, relatively uniform developmental sequences in the acquisition of postural, locomotor, and prehensile functions is the influence of the cephalo-caudal and proximo-distal trends. For example, the development of cortical control over eye-limb coordination proceeds in a cephalocaudal trend. Correlation of eye-arm coordination and eye-hand coordination reverses with development of the infant (Zagora, 1959). Proximo-distal development is also illustrated by the earlier development of eye-palm coordination as compared to eye-finger coordination (Zagora, 1959). Also, as might be reasonably anticipated, postural control of a given part always precedes controlled movements of the part (Shirley, 1931); and since the acquisition of upright posture requires dominance of muscles with an anti-gravity function, the balance between flexor and extensor tonus gradually shifts in favor of the later (Shirley, 1931). To some extent what has often been referred to as the "large to small muscle" and the "mass to specific" trends is in part a reflection of the proximo-distal trend since smaller muscles and the muscles involved in more specific functions tend to be distally located. The "mass to specific" trend also reflects a general tendency already evident in the neonatal period, toward the elimination of generalized, superfluous, and exaggerated movements irrelevant to the execution of a particular task.

Consistent with the trend toward minimal muscular involvement and economy of effort, bilateral performance of many motor activities is gradually superseded by consistent preference for a single hand (Gesell & Ames, 1947; Karr, 1934, Lederer, 1939). During infancy and childhood, however, unilateral preference tends to be relatively unstable and to alternate with bilateral proclivities (Cohen, 1966; Belmont & Birch, 1963; Flament, 1963; Gesell & Ames, 1947). One early manifestation of asymmetrical unilaterality is the tonic neck reflex (rotation of the head to one side when the infant lies in the supine position) which commonly persists for the first three months of life (Gesell, 1954). Various forms of "reciprocal interweaving" also characterized integration of the four extremities during the course of postural and locomotor development. These include ipsilateral and contralateral coordination of synergetic muscle groups, reciprocal opposition of antagonists, and diagonal alternation. Finally, motor development, like physical development, follows an asynchronous pattern. For example, two motor functions can develop at remarkably nonparallel rates, sucking varying much less with age than does manual strength (Bergman, Malasky, & Zohn, 1966).

Postural-Locomotor Development *

Postural-locomotor development is characterized by a sequence of stages which are relatively uniform for all children despite individual differences in age of occurrence. Occasionally some steps are omitted by individual children or even by most children in a particular culture. The following is a brief timetable of the more salient landmarks and their median age of emergence (Shirley, 1931a): lifting the chin from the prone position (three weeks); raising the head and chest from the prone position (nine weeks); sitting alone for one minute (31 weeks); crawling (37 weeks); standing, holding on (42 weeks); creeping (44 weeks); standing alone (62 weeks); walking alone (64 weeks).† These stages encompass non-reflex motor activities that are functionally discontinuous with subcortically regulated locomotor reflexes elicitable in the first few months of life.

Ames (1937) has identified fourteen successive stages of prone progression which coalesce and coexist before replacing each other in turn. The three most important precursors of walking are *crawling* (moving with the abdomen

---

More detailed accounts of postural-locomotor development are available. See Ames 1937; Bayley, 1935; Burnside, 1927; Crowell, 1967; Illingworth, 1962; Gesell & Amatruda, 1947.

†*Bayley (1935) reports the same sequence of steps with slightly different age norms.*

in contact with floor), *creeping* (moving on hands and knees with abdomen parallel to floor), and *hitching* (locomotion in a sitting position). Beginning walkers tend to flex their knees, take short, wide steps, and keep their arms elevated (Burnside, 1927). There appears to be a latent period between standing and independent walking (Shapiro, 1962) and the possibility that further cortical regulation is occurring is indicated by the disappearance of the plantar reflex about the time of standing (Dietrich, 1957).

As indicated previously, the age of occurrence varies from one study to another and some of the steps are omitted from the sequence. Thus children who spend their day on their backs in nursery (institutions) do not walk until four years and appear to skip the creeping stage entirely (Dennis & Najarian, 1957). Differences in mean age for walking in different European samples may be a result of genetic, nutritional, and parental factors (Hindley *et al*, 1966). Genetic differences, between different groups of children, in motor facility is more credible as a hypothesis in motor development than in other areas of development. For example, African infants are superior in motor development to European children in the control of their head movements and in exhibiting a lesser degree of flexion and the frequent absence of subcortically regulated reflex activities (Geber and Dean, 1957). The effects of environmental influences in African children is seen in the exceptionally early walking of Uganda infants (i.e., as early as seven months) whose parents encourage motor activity (Geber, 1958). Walking, however, appears to be less variable cross-culturally and intraculturally than other types of infant skills (i.e., language functions, body equilibrium, etc.) (Kohen-Raz, 1968).

Development of Prehension

The development of prehension involves the coordination of relatively distinct sensori-motor systems, namely visual-motor systems of eye, arm, and hand, and the tactual-motor system of the hands (White, Castle and Held, 1964). The development of these systems is asynchronous and occurs at different times before they are gradually coordinated into a complex super-ordinate system in prehension (White *et al*, 1964). At 2 months of age object-oriented movements are observed by babies in their cribs, illustrated by a swiping movement with no attempt at grasping (White *et al*, 1964). During this period hand movements occur basically to visual and visual-auditory stimuli (Kistyakovskaya, 1962). During the third and fourth months of age unilateral arm approaches decrease in favor of bilateral patterns, with the hands to the midline and clasped (White *et al*, 1964). At 16 weeks the child attempts to reach and grasp a cube placed before him on a table (Halverson, 1931). Unilateral responses reappear at about four months but the hand is no longer fisted; the open hand is raised to the vicinity of the object until the object is crudely grasped (White *et al*, 1964). At about 20 months, the infant begins to reach for and successfully grasp the test object in one quick, direct motion of the hand from out of his visual field (White *et al*, 1964). The 24-week-old infant uses a corralling and scooping approach with his palm and fingers. At 28 weeks he begins to oppose his thumb to his palm and other fingers. Finally, at 36 weeks coordinated grasping occurs between the tips of the thumb and forefinger (Halverson, 1931).

This developmental sequence, which is functionally discontinuous from the infant's grasp reflex is marked by the following noteworthy features: progressive improvement in aim, precision and smoothness of execution; decreasing bilateral involvement and use of shoulder and elbow movements; increasing rotation of the wrist and opposition of the thumb; and gradual replacement of the gross palmer-digital and palmar-thumb approaches by the more localized tip of thumb and forefinger technique.

Handedness *

We have already referred to the tendency for bilaterality in motor functioning to be gradually replaced by unilaterality during infancy and early childhood (see p. 702). Consistent preference for a *particular* hand however, develops slowly. It is not evident at all during the first six months of life, and is quite unstable at the end of the first year (Flament, 1963; Hildreth, 1949; Lederer, 1939). By the end of the second year about 85 per cent of all children are predominantly right handed (Hildreth, 1949) although ambilaterality is not uncommon (Belmont & Birch, 1963). Stability of preference, however, is not established until the age of six, at which time the percentage of left-handedness (7 per cent) roughly approximates that found in the adult population (Hildreth, 1949). Males show a slightly higher percentage of left-handedness than females (Flick, 1966).

Hand preference seems to be part of a general lateral dominance, but intraindividual discrepancies with respect to different body parts and even with respect to different activities performed by a single part (e.g.,writing, throwing, batting) are not uncommon (Eyre, 1933).

Left-handedness is somewhat of a motor handicap since most tools are designed for right-handed persons, and because the latter find it relatively difficult to demonstrate motor skills to left-handed individuals. More important perhaps is the fact that left-handed children are frequently made to feel self-conscious about their condition and are often subjected to strong pressures to shift hand preference. However, this is little evidence to indicate that changing handedness per se contributes to stuttering. Most stutterers give no history of changing handedness, and few children who do shift handedness subsequently develop this speech defect.

See Palmer (1964) for a review of the literature.

The determination of handedness is still a matter of conjecture. The bimodal distribution of unimanuality suggests that genic predispositions toward lateral dominance probably exist (Ojemann, 1930); and since there are few left-handed cultures, one might infer that the typical genic predispositions among human beings is toward right handedness. Genic predispositions, however, are seldom strong enough to be determinative or to offer effective resistance to potent cultural pressures. Right-handed predispositions are presumably reinforced by the culture, and left-handed predispositions are converted to right except in those rare instances when they are extremely tenacious. The most important determinants of handedness, therefore, are deliberate training measures* and the cumulative impact of innumerable environmental cues. Occasional cases of left-handedness are attributable to strong genic predispositions, absence of or resistance to training, unresponsiveness to environmental cues, and direct teaching by, or imitation of, left-handed parents or teachers.

Children with a suspected history of brain damage before or during birth show no clear preference for handedness when compared to normal children (Pasamanick & Knobloch, 1966). In contrast to brain-damaged children, early preference in infants is associated with advanced developmental status (Cohen, 1966).

There is little doubt that cerebral and lateral dominance are associated. Even the motor speech area is located in the same cerebral hemisphere that controls the preferred hand. It is more logical to suppose, however, that cerebral dominance is a consequence rather than a cause of handedness. Anatomically it is well established that each cerebral hemisphere controls the voluntary musculature on the opposite side of the body. If, because of genic predispositions and cultural pressures most motor skills are performed by the right hand, it stands to reason that the neuroanatomical and neurophysiological substrate (stimulus-response connections) of these skills will be located in the same hemisphere (left) that regulates voluntary motion in the right hand. On the other hand, if cerebral dominance were innately determined and caused handedness, it would be difficult to explain the not infrequent occurrence of differential, eye, hand, and foot preference. In fact, left hand-left eye dominance is associated with poor perceptual-motor performance (Flick, 1966).†

At present, the literature on handedness presents more questions than it answers. Hand lateralization is probably multiply and complexly determined, thus arguing against the notion of a unitary factor or dimension underlying

---

*Change in preference probably occur through direct influence rather than imitation, at least in infancy, since there is no relationship between hand preference of infants and their mothers (Cohen, 1966).

†Right-handed individuals seem to make better use of the left leg in static equilibrium tasks but use the right leg for initiating motor acts (Wallon, 1958).

all manifestations of lateralization (Palmer, 1964). Further study of these phenomena may reveal that:

> Measures of hand lateralization involving fairly gross arm-shoulder musculature and movement skills may have somewhat different dimensional properties and significance from measures based upon more discrete hand skills since, according to the proximo-distal principle of development, control of movements of large muscle groups proximal to the body axis tends to occur earlier in ontogenesis than independent movements of more distal parts (Palmer, 1964; p. 269).

Thus, lateralization of more proximal arm/shoulder movement patterns might possibly create stronger pressures for an accompanying coordination of subfunctions than would lateralization of peripheral skills (Palmer, 1964).

Preschool Motor Development

After rudimentary locomotion and prehension are established, the child acquires a repertoire of other motor skills. During late infancy and the preschool years he learns to walk backwards and upstairs, jump, hop, skip, operate a tricycle, and throw, catch and bounce a ball (Bayley, 1935; 1965; Gutteridge, 1939). He acquires such skills as drinking from a cup (18 months), pouring from a pitcher (36 months), and eating with a spoon (15-36 months) (Gesell, 1940). Two- and three-year olds button and unbutton and begin undressing themselves, and a year later they are capable of dressing themselves (Wagoner & Armstrong, 1928). A characteristic sequence is followed in the use of wheel toys. Between 21 and 24 months the child merely pushes and pulls them repeatedly. Shortly thereafter he concentrates on separate parts and acquires greater muscular control (Jones, 1939). Between 24 and 48 months more complex skills are practiced and integrated into larger wholes (Bayley, 1965). At 48 months the skills themselves are subordinated to various imaginative and social activities in which they are embedded. Writing skills are also developed during the preschool period, beginning with crude marks and scribbles at the age of two (Hildreth, 1936). During the third and fourth years the child adds some horizontal and systematic vertical lines to his repertoire and later some discrete symbols. At five and six he is able to form recognizable letters.

Motor skills involved in such artistic activities as drawing and block building also develop at this time. The youthful artist only makes random and exploratory strokes. After he acquires greater control he is able to manage simple designs, and finally, at about the age of four, crude figures and objects (Biber, 1934). A typical developmental sequence is seen in the use of blocks (Johnson, 1933). Before he is two, the child merely carries them about and arranges them in amorphous piles. The two- and three-year-old makes simple structures such as rows and towers, and the three- and four-year-old more complex structures (e.g., bridges, enclosures). Between four and five, blocks are used more in dramatic play to represent objects such as trains and ships, and the five- and six-year-old uses them to reproduce actual structures.

Maturation and Learning

The relative importance of maturation and learning in the acquisition of motor skills is largely a function of whether the latter are phylogenetic or ontogenetic in nature (see p. 213). Phylogenetic skills develop "autogeneously" in orderly, uniform sequence despite marked cultural differences in child-rearing practices. Environmental stimulation does not accelerate and deprivation of use (within limits) does not seem to retard their rate of development. The most important factor determining the emergence of a given phylogenetic skill is the adequacy of its neuroanatomical and neurophysiological substrate as determined by genic influences. Hence the overt appearance of earlier stages is a particular locomotor or prehensile sequence that is not prerequisite for the development of later stages and may be omitted if opportunities for expression are curtailed under conditions of cradling or cultural taboo. Individual differences in rate of development are largely determined by genic factors; intra-pair differences in the acquisition of phylogenetic skills, for example are much smaller among monozygotic than among dizygotic twins (Stern, 1949). As previously indicated, temperamental factors may affect age of emergence of some of these skills, but socioeconomic variables generally play no role. Only extreme emotional deprivation has been found to retard the rate of early (phylogentic) motor development.

In the case of ontogenetic motor skills, particularly those which are psychosocial or specialized in nature, rate and extent of development are largely dependent on opportunities for practice and on motive-incentive conditions. Advanced states in the development of ontogenetic skills presuppose the prior advancement of lower levels of performance (Fowler, 1966). Much of the deceleration in the rate of motor development that sets in about the age of three in our culture is attributed to the lack of challenging environmental stimulation and to steretyped playground equipment (Gutteridge, 1939; Jones, 1939). Manus children, in contrast, reach a much higher level of motor accomplishment in response to an environment which is much more demanding in terms of manual dexterity (Mead, 1939). Provision of environmental experiences which encourage accelerated motor behavior can also be successful at very early ages in our own culture. Visually-directed reaching has been accelerated in infants under six months through proper types of environmental experiences (White and Held, 1966). Climbing behavior in pre-school children can be increased when it is reinforced and encouraged with adult attention (Johnston, Kelley, Harris & Wolf, 1966).

The effects of practice are naturally more evident in relatively complex and specific activities such as maze learning, ball throwing, and roller skating than in skills that would ordinarily be learned in the course of incidental experience, e.g., jumping or climbing (Fowler, 1966). Guided practice or coaching also takes maximal advantage of whatever readiness is available (Dusenberry, 1952) and has facilitated retarded motor performance in institutional children (Dennis & Sayegh, 1965). In the case of certain skills (e.g., roller skating as against tricycling), however, the effects of practice are not carried over from one age period to another (in the absence of intervening practice), because original patterns of neuromuscular coordination are disrupted by marked changes in size, strength, and body proportions. When an older child is deprived of early experience in a particular skill commonly available to younger children, he generally begins at the same primitive level as the latter but progresses more rapidly through the intervening stages (Johnson, 1933).

Maturation also plays an important role in the learning of ontogenetic skills. The child cannot profit from practice in a given activity if his overall level of neuromuscular ability is not equal to the task. Hence, practice that is postponed until he is ready is much more efficacious than premature practice. The age of motor readiness, however, is quite specific and cannot be predicted on a priori grounds. At 18 months, for example, he is ready to learn roller skating but not tricycling. The above conclusion on maturation should be tempered with the knowledge that the early studies that have failed to demonstrate of effects of practice suffer from serious methodological difficulties (e.g., they fail to measure the effect of pre-experimental experience upon abilities) (Fowler, 1962).

Individual differences in the acquisition of ontogenetic motor skills are determined by genic factors, by motivational, emotional, and personality variables, and by opportunities for practice. For example, first-borns have higher motor performance scores compared to subsequent children, possibly because the mother spends more time with the first child (Solomons & Solomons, 1964). Although differences between identical twins tend to be less marked than corresponding differences between fraternal twins (Stern, 1949) environmental variability is associated with greater phenotypic variability than in the case of phylogenetic traits. Such motivational factors as material and psychological incentives (Chase, 1932, Johnston et al, 1966) and differential cultural expectations relating to the child's sex membership have an important effect on the acquisition of various motor skills. In general, little or no relationship exists between children's socioeconomic status and rate of development of gross or fine motor skills (Bayley & Jones, 1937); evidently the upper socioeconomic group does not have the same experiential advantage here that it has in the development of intellectual skills.

MOTOR DEVELOPMENT IN LATER CHILDHOOD

During the elementary school years the child learns many new motor skills and also improves on those previously acquired. Changes are generally in the direction of increased strength, speed, versatility, precision, and smoothness of execution. Progressive gains are registered in the speed of running, accuracy and distance of throwing, height and distance of jumping, balance, etc. (Cron & Pronko, 1957; Jenkins, 1930; Seils, 1951). A two-fold increase in strength occurs between the ages of six and eleven (Baldwin, 1921), as well as an impressive increase in speed of eye-hand coordination (Moore, 1937) and decrease in motor reaction time (Goodenough, 1935).

Fine motor skills and sensori-motor learning, as illustrated by maze and rotary pursuit performance, also improve during this period (Ammons, Alprin & Ammons, 1955; Davol, Hastings & Klein, 1965; Munn, 1954; Stachnik, 1964), but percentage of improvement resulting from given amounts of practice do not appear to change in any consistent way as a function of age (Munn, 1954). The ability to modulate motor performance through mediating cues increases with age (Luria, 1961). Continued improvement occurs in the writing of letters, numbers and words, and tends to follow an orderly developmental sequence (Ames & Ilg, 1951). In general, adult expectations regarding writing skills are out of line with prevailing developmental progress. Children cannot be expected to write with good slant, alignment and proportion before the age of nine. Current emphasis on manuscript writing in the primary grades is in accord with the finding that children are not ready for cursive writing until the age of eight or nine (Ames & Ilg, 1951).

Generality of Motor Skills

Low intercorrelations among different gross motor skills suggest that motor ability tends to be relatively specific in nature (Bayley, 1935; Gates & Scott, 1931; Hartman, 1943). Factor analysis also shows that speed and strength are relatively independent factors (Carpenter, 1941). There is, however, a correlation between strength of grip and weight which increases with age in boys and decreases in girls (Kawahara, 1963). Thus although various tests of strength (or speed) tend to be moderately intercorrelated, correlations between the two factors (or between abilities involving both factors) are relatively low. Furthermore, intercorrelations among various motor abilities tend to decrease with increasing age (Bayley, 1935). Hence, either little actual generality of motor ability exists or great variability prevails in opportunity for practicing different motor skills. Some of the existing generality of function must also be attributed to the self-confidence which success in one activity contributes to success in another activity.

Sex Differences

Boys are stronger than girls at all ages but the difference in strength first becomes significant for practical purposes during adolescence (Baldwin, 1921; Kawahara, 1963). At this time the growth curves which were hitherto parallel begin to diverge. Throughout childhood boys are superior to girls in most gross motor skills such as climbing, jumping, sliding, skipping, ball throwing, and ball kicking (Gutteridge, 1939; Jenkins, 1930).* However, preschool girls are superior to boys in tricycling, hopping, and bouncing and catching ball (Gutteridge, 1939; Jenkins, 1930). Females have better balance in early elementary school years, but this difference reverses itself in later childhood (Cron & Pronko, 1957). Boys' reaction time is shorter than girls' and they tend to be a year in advance. During adolescence the divergence in gross motor skills becomes even greater than that in strength. Under conditions of relatively equal opportunity for practice, sex differences in *fine* motor skills and sensori-motor learning tend to be small, statistically unreliable, and inconsistent in direction for most laboratory tasks (Goodenough, 1935; Munn, 1954). In everyday mechanical skills relative superiority is almost completely a function of differential opportunities for practice.

Sex differences in strength and gross motor skills during childhood reflect cultural expectations and the sex typing of games. Even the slight advantage that boys have in muscle mass and vital capacity is attributable to the influence of greater physical exertion. During adolescence a more substantial physical basis exists for these sex differences. Muscular hypertrophy caused by androgenic stimulation is much greater in boys, and their superior height, weight, limb length and shoulder breadth give them the advantage of greater leverage (Ausubel, 1954). In addition, differences in vital and cardiac capacity, although partly a reflection of differential participation in athletic activities, become sufficiently great to account for marked differences in tolerance for physical exertion (Ausubel, 1954). After pubescence, therefore, competitive athletic contests between the sexes are hardly feasible. During childhood, however, sex typing of games and segregation between the sexes in athletic activities cannot be defended on physical grounds.

Effects of Intellectual, Emotional and Personality Factors

The extent to which a child develops his genic potentialities for motor skills obviously depends somewhat on such temperamental and personality factors as energy level, venturesomeness, aggressiveness, and persistence. For example, motor characteristics in the young (e.g., activity, rapidity) are correlated with later measures of extroversion and aggressiveness (Schaefer & Bayley, 1963). Since motor skills are primarily developed in a peer-group

---

*Govatos (1959) reports that females excel males in standing broad jump at 6 years of age.

context, much also depends on his sociality and eagerness for group participation and competition. During the elementary school years the child increasingly manifests more active attitudes towards his human environment which can be observed in his increasingly rich emotional life (Missiuro, 1963). Home environment is also important. Children from over-protecting homes tend to be physically apprehensive and relatively retarded in gross motor development (Baldwin, 1949; Jones, 1939). Difficulties in perceptual-motor functioning are associated with low frustration tolerance and anxiety— a relationship which may be the result of particular parental attitudes (Williams, 1965). Williams and Scott (1953) attribute the acceleration of Negro children in motor abilities to the permissive child rearing practices which are partially evident in lower-class Negro homes. High levels of personality anxiety have been found to inhibit trial-and-error learning in children (Palermo, Castenada & McCandless; 1956). Finally, intelligence test scores are correlated with grip strength (Dawson & Edwards, 1965), and low positive, and in some cases, significant relationships are found between intellectual ability tests and perceptual-motor tests (Singer & Brunk, 1967).

References

Abel, H., and Sahinkaya, R.: Emergence of sex and race friendship preferences. *Child Develop. 33:* 939–943, 1962.

Abel, L. B.: The effects of shift in motivation upon the learning of a sensori-motor task. *Archives de Psychologie. 29:* No. 205, 1936.

Abelson, R. T., and Rosenberg, N. J.: Symbolic psycho-logic: A model of attitudinal cognition. *Behav. Sci.* 3: 1–13, 1958.

Aberle, D. F., and Naegele, K. D.: Middle-class fathers' occupational role and attitudes toward children. *Amer. J. Orthopsychiat. 22:* 366–378, 1952.

Abernathy, E. H.: Relationships between mental and physical growth. *Monogr. Soc. Res. Child Develop. 1(7):* 1936.

Abravanel, E.: The development of inter-sensory patterning with regard to selected spatial dimensions. *Monogr. Soc. Res. Child Develop. 23(2):* 1968.

Abt, I. A., Adler, H. M., and Bartelme, P.: The relationship between the onset of speech and intelligence. *JAMA. 93:* 1351–1355, 1929.

Achenbach, T., and Zigler, E.: Cue-learning and problem-learning strategies in normal and retarded children. *Child Develop.* 39: 827–848, 1968.

Adams, D. K.: The development of social behavior. *In* Y. Brackbill (Ed.), *Infancy and Early Childhood: A Handbook and Guide to Human Development.* Ch. 7., The Free Press, New York, 1967.

Adorno, T. W., Frenkel-Brunswik, E., Levinson, D. J., and Sanford, R. N.: *The Authoritarian Personality.* Harper, New York, 1950.

Ainsworth, M. D.: The development of infant-mother interaction among the Ganda. *In* B. M. Foss (Ed.), *Determinants of Infant Behavior.* Vol. II, pp. 67–112, Methuen Press, London, 1963.

Ainsworth, M. D.: Patterns of attachment behavior shown by the infant through action with his mother. *Merrill-Palmer Quarterly, 10:* 51–58, 1964.

Ainsworth, M. D.: The effects of maternal deprivation: A review of findings and controversy in the context of research strategy. *In* J. Bowlby (Ed.), *Deprivation and Maternal Care: A Reassessment of its Effects.* Pp. 289–357, Schocken Books, New York, 1966.

Alberts, C. A., and Ehrenfreund, D.: Transposition in children as a function of age. *J. Exptl. Psychol. 41:* 30–38, 1951.

Aldrich, C. A., Sung, C., and Knop, C.: The crying of newly born babies. I. The community phase. *J. Pediat. 26:* 313–326, 1945. (a).

———, ———, ———: The crying of newly born babies. II. The individual phase. *J. Pediat. 27:* 89–96, 1945 (b).

Aldrich, C. G., and Doll, E. A.: Comparative intelligence of idiots and of normal infants. *J. Genet. Psychol. 39:* 227–257, 1931.

Alexander, I. E., and Alderstein, A. M.: Affective responses to the concept of death in a population of children and early adolescents. *J. Genet. Psychol.: 93:* 167–177, 1958.

Alexander, T., and Alexander, M.: A study of personality and social status. *Child Develop.* 23: 207–213, 1952.

Allman, T. S., and White, W. F.: Birth-order categories as predictors of select personality characteristics. *Psychol. Rep. 22(3),* 857–860, 1968.

Allport, F.: Theories of Perception and the Concept of Structure. Wiley, New York, 1955.

Almy, M., Chittenden, E., and Miller, P.: Young Children's Thinking. Columbia University, Teachers College Press, New York, 1966.

Alpert, A.: The solving of problem situations by pre-school children. Teachers College, Columbia University, New York, 1928.

Altus, W. D.: Birth order and its sequelae. *Science. 151(3706):* 44–49, 1965.

Alvy, K. T.: Relation of age to children's egocentric and cooperative communication. *J. Genet. Psychol. 112(2):* 275–286, 1968.

Amatora, S. M.: Can elementary school children discriminate certain traits in their teacher? *Child Develop. 23:* 76–80, 1952.

Amatora, S. M.: Contrasts in boys' and girls' judgments in personality. *Child Develop. 25:* 51–62, 1954.

Ambrose, A.: The age of onset of ambivalence in early infancy: Indications from the study of laughing. *J. Child Psychol. and Psychiat. 4(3–4):* 167–181, 1963.

Ambrose, J. A.: The development of the smiling response in early infancy. *In* B. M. Foss (Ed.), *Determinants of Infant Behavior.* Pp. 179–196, Wiley, New York, 1961.

Ames, L. B.: The sequential patterning of prone progression in the human infant. *Genet. Psychol. Monogr. 19:* 409–460, 1937.

————: Motor correlates of infant crying. *J. Genet. Psychol. 59:* 239–247, 1941.

————: The development of the sense of time in young children. *J. Genet. Psychol. 68:* 97–125, 1946.

————: The sense of self of nursery school children as manifested by their verbal behavior. *J. Genet. Psychol. 81:* 193–232, 1952.

————: Constancy of content in Rorschach responses. *J. Genet. Psychol. 96:* 145–164, 1960.

————, and August, J.: Rorschach responses of Negro and white five- to ten-year-olds. *J. Genet. Psychol. 109:* 297–309, 1966.

Ames, L. B., and Ilg, F. L.: Developmental trends in writing behavior. *J. Genet. Psychol. 79:* 29–46, 1951.

————, and ————: *Mosaic Patterns of American Children.* Harper, New York, 1962.

————, and ————: Age changes in children's mosaic responses from five to ten years. *Genet. Psychol. Monog. 69:* 195–245, 1964, (a).

————, and ————: Sex differences in test performance of matched girl-boy pairs in the five-to-nine year old range. *J. Genet. Psychol. 104:* 25–34, 1964.

————, Learned, J., Metraux, R. W., and Walker, R. N.: *Child Rorschach Responses.* Hoeber, New York, 1952.

————, ————, ————, and ————: Development of perception in the young child as observed in responses to the Rorschach test blots. *J. Genet. Psychol. 82:* 183–204, 1953.

————, ————, ————, and ————: *Adolescent Rorschach Responses.* Hoeber-Harper, New York, 1959.

Ammons, R. B.: Reactions in a projective doll-play interview of white males two to six years of age to differences in skin color and facial features. *J. Genet. Psychol. 76:* 323–341, 1950.

————, Alprin, S. I., and Ammons, C. H.: Rotary pursuit performance as related to sex and age of pre-adult subjects. *J. Exptl. Psychol. 49:* 127–133, 1955.

Anastasi, A.: Intelligence and family size. *Psychol. Bull. 53:* 187–209, 1956.

————: *Differential Psychology.* (3rd ed.). Macmillan, New York, 1958, (a).

————: Heredity, environment and the question "How". *Psychol. Rev. 65:* 197–208, 1958, (b).

————: Standardized ability testing. *In* P. Mussen (Ed.), *Handbook of Research Methods in Child Development.* Pp. 456–486, Wiley, New York, 1960.

————: *Psychological Testing.* (2nd ed.). Macmillan, New York, 1961.

————: *Psychological Testing.* (3rd ed.). Macmillan, New York, 1968.

————, and Cordova, F. A.: Some effects of bilingualism upon the intelligence test performance of Puerto Rican children in New York City. *J. Educ. Psychol. 44:* 1–19, 1953.

————, and D'Angelo, R. Y.: A comparison of Negro and white preschool children in language development. *In* Goodenough Draw a Man I.Q. *J. Genet. Psychol. 81:* 147–165, 1952.

————, and de Jesus, C.: Language development and non-verbal I.Q. of Puerto Rican preschool children in New York City. *J. Abnor. Soc. Psychol. 48:* 357–366, 1953.

Anderson, C.: The development of a level of aspiration in young children. Unpublished doctoral dissertation, University of Iowa, 1940.

Anderson, H. H.: An experimental study of dominative and integrative behavior in children of preschool age. *J. Soc. Psychol. 8:* 335–345, 1937, (a).

————: Domination and integration in the social behavior of young children in an experimental play situation. *Genet. Psychol. Monogr. 19:* 343–408, 1937, (b).

————: Domination and social integration in the behavior of kindergarten children in an experimental play situation. *J. Exptl. Educ. 8:* 123–131, 1939.

————, and Brewer, J. E.: Effects of teachers' dominative and integrative contacts on children's classroom behavior. *App. Psychol. Monogr.* No. 8, 1946.

Anderson, J. E.: The limitations of infant and preschool tests in the measurement of intelligence. *J. Psychol. 8:* 351–379, 1939.

————: The prediction of terminal intelligence. *In* G. M. Whipple (Ed.), *Thirty-ninth Yearbook, National Society for Studies in Education.* Part 1. *Intelligence: Its Nature and Nurture.* Pp. 385–442, University of Chicago Press, Chicago, 1940.

————: Personality organization in children. *Amer. Psychol. 3:* 409–416, 1948.

————: Changes in emotional responses with age. *In* M. L. Reymert (Ed.), *Feelings and Emotions.* Pp. 418–428, McGraw-Hill, New York, 1950.

————: Methods of child psychology. *In* L. Carmichael (Ed.), *Manual of Child Psychology.* (2nd ed.). Pp. 1–59, Wiley, New York, 1954.

Anderson, L. D.: The predictive value of infancy tests in relation to intelligence at five years. *Child Develop. 10:* 203–212, 1939.

Andrus, R., and Horowitz, E. L.: The effect of nursery school training: Insecurity feeling. *Child Develop. 9:* 169–174, 1938.

Andry, R. G.: *Delinquency and Parental Pathology.* Methuen, London, 1960.

————: Paternal and maternal roles in delinquency. *In* J. Bowlby (Ed.), *Deprivation of Maternal Care: A Re-assessment of Its Effects.* Pp. 223–236, Shocken Books, New York, 1966.

Angelino, H., Dollins, J., and Mech, E. V.: Trends in the "fears and worries" of school children as related to socio-economic status and age. *J. Genet. Psychol. 89:* 263–276, 1956.

Anisfeld, M.: Language and cognition in the young child. Paper presented at the Symposium on the Psycho-Linguistic Nature of Reading Process. Wayne State University, May, 1965.

————, and Tucker, G. R.: English pluralizations of six-year-old children. *Child Develop. 38:* 1201–1217, 1967.

Anthony, E. J.: Psycho-neurotic disorders. *In* A. M. Fredman and H. I. Kaplan (Eds.), *Comprehensive Textbooks of Psychiatry.* Williams and Wilkins, Baltimore, 1967.

Anthony, S.: The child's idea of death. *In* T. Talbot (Ed.), *The World of the Child: Essays on Childhood.* Pp. 325–339, Doubleday and Company, New York, 1967.

Appel, M. H.: Aggressive behavior of nursery school children and adult procedures in dealing with such behavior. *J. Exptl. Educ. 11:* 185–199, 1942.

Archer, J.: Concept identification as a function of obviousness of relevant and irrelevant information. *J. Exptl. Psychol. 63:* 616–620, 1962.

Arey, J. B., and Dent, J.: Pathologic findings in premature infants. *Amer. J. Clin. Path. 20:* 1016–1025, 1950.

Arnold, Magda: *Emotion and Personality.* 2 volumes, Columbia University, New York, 1960.

Arnsdorf, V. E.: An investigation of the teaching of chronology in the sixth grade. *J. Exptl. Educ. 29:* 207–214, 1961.

Aronfreed, J.: The concept of internalization. *In* D. A. Goslin (Ed.), *Handbook of Socialization Theory and Research.* Ch. 4, Rand-McNally, Chicago, 1968, (a).

Aronfreed, J.: *Conduct and Conscience: Socialization of Internalized Control over Behavior.* Academic Press, New York, 1968, (b).

Arsenian, J. M.: Young children in an insecure situation. *J. Abnor. Soc. Psychol. 38:* 235–249, 1943.

Aserinsky, E., and Kleitman, N.: Regularly occurring periods of eye motility and concomitant phenomena during sleep. *Science 118:* 273–274, 1953.

————, and ————: Two types of ocular motility occurring in sleep. *J. App. Psychol. 8:* 1–10, 1955, (a).

————, and ————: The motility cycle in sleeping infants as manifested by occular and gross bodily activity. *J. App. Physiol. 8:* 11–18, 1955, (b).

Asher, E. J.: The inadequacy of current intelligence tests for testing Kentucky mountain children. *J. Genet. Psychol. 46:* 480–486, 1935.

Atkinson, J. W., and Litwin, G. H.: Achievement motive and test anxiety conceived as motive to approach success and motive to avoid failure. *J. Abnor. Soc. Psychol. 60:* 52–63, 1960.

Auble, D., and Mech, E. V.: Partial verbal reinforcement related to distributed practice in a classroom situation. *J. Psychol. 36:* 165–186, 1953.

Austin, M. C., and Thompson, G. G.: Children's friendships: A study of the bases on which children select and reject their best friends. *J. Educ.Psychol. 39:* 101–116, 1948.

Ausubel, D. P.: Ego development and the learning process. *Child Develop. 20:* 173–190, 1949.

————: Negativism as a phase of ego development. *Amer. J. Orthopsychiat. 20:* 796–805, 1950.

————: Prestige motivation of gifted children. *Genet. Psychol. Monogr. 43:* 53–117, 1951.

————: *Ego Development and the Personality Disorders.* Grune & Stratton, New York, 1952.

————: Reciprocity and assumed reciprocity of acceptance in an adolescent group: A sociometric study. *Sociometry, 16:* 339–348, 1953.

————: *Theory and Problems of Adolescent Development.* Grune & Stratton, New York, 1954.

————: Relationships between shame and guilt in the socializing process. *Psychol. Rev. 62:* 378–390, 1955, (a).

————: Socioempathy as a function of sociometric status in an adolescent group. *Human Relations 8:* 75–84, 1955, (b).

————: Some comments on the nature, diagnosis, and prognosis of neurotic anxiety. *Psychiat. Quart. 30:* 77–88, 1956.

————: The relationship between social variables and ego development and functioning. *In* M. Sherif and M. O. Wilson (Eds.), *Emerging Problems in Social Psychology.* Norman: University of Oklahoma Book Exchange, pp. 55–96, 1957.

————: *The Psychology of Meaningful Verbal Learning.* Grune & Stratton, New York, 1963.

————: *The Fern and the Tiki: An American View of New Zealand National Character, Social Attitudes and Race Relations.* Holt, Rinehart and Winston, New York, 1965(a).

————: The influence of experience in the development of intelligence. *In* M. J. Aschner and C. E. Bisch (Eds.), *Productive Thinking in Education.* Washington, D.C., National Education Association, pp. 45–62, 1965, (b).

————: *Maori Youth: A Psychoethnological Study of Cultural Deprivation.* Holt, Rinehart and Winston, New York, 1965, (c).

————: A critique of Piaget's theory of the ontogenesis of motor behavior. *J. Genet. Psychol. 109:* 119–122, 1966.

————: *Educational Psychology: A Cognitive View.* Holt, Rinehart and Winston, New York, 1968.

————, and Ausubel, P.: Research on ego development among segregated Negro children: Implications for education. Work Conference on Curriculum and Teaching in depressed urban areas. Teachers College, Columbia University, New York, July, 1962.

————, Balthazar, E. E., Rosenthal, I., Blackman, L., Schpoont, S. H., and Welkowitz, J.: Perceived parent attitudes as determinants of children's ego structure. *Child Develop. 25:* 173–183, 1954.

————, DeWit, F., Goldens, B., and Schpoont, S. H.: Prestige suggestion in children's art preference. *J. Genet. Psychol. 89:* 85–93, 1956.

————, and Schiff, H. M.: The effect of incidental and experimentally induced experience in the learning of relevant and irrelevant causal relationships by children. *J. Genet. Psychol. 84:* 109–123, 1954.

————, and ————: Some intrapersonal and interpersonal determinants of individual differences in socioempathic ability among adolescents. *J. Soc. Psychol. 41:* 39–56, 1955.

————, ————, and Gasser, E. B.: A preliminary study of developmental trends in socio-empathy: Accuracy of perception of own and others' sociometric status. *Child Develop. 23:* 111–128, 1952.

————, ————, and Goldman, M.: Qualitative characteristics in the learning process associated with anxiety. *J. Abnor. Soc. Psychol. 48:* 537–547, 1953.

——, ——, and Zeleny, M. P.: "Real-life" measures of level of academic and vocational aspiration in adolescents: Relation to laboratory measures and to adjustment. *Child Develop. 24:* 155–168, 1953.

——, ——, and ——: Prestige suggestions in children's art preferences. *J. Genet. Psychol.* 85–93, 1956.

Avital, S. M., and Shettleworth, S. J.: Objectives for mathematics learning: Some ideas for the teacher. *Bulletin No. 3.* The Ontario Institute for Studies in Education, 1968.

Ax, A. F.: The physiological differentiation between fear and anger in humans. *Psychoso. Med. 15:* 433–442, 1953.

Bach, G. R.: Young children's play fantasies. *Psychol. Monogr. 59(2):* 1945.

——: Father-fantasies and father-typing in father-separated children. *Child Develop. 17:* 63–80, 1946.

Baer, M. J., Torgoff, I. H., and Harris, D. J.: Differential impact of weight and height on Wetzel developmental age. *Child Develop. 33:* 737–750, 1962.

Bahrick, H. P., Fitts, P. M., and Rankin, R. E.: Effects of incentives upon reactions to peripheral stimuli. *J. Exptl. Psychol. 44:* 400–406, 1952.

Baier, K.: *The Moral Point of View: A Rational Basis of Ethics.* Random House, New York, 1966.

Bakan, D.: *The Duality of Human Existence: An Essay on Psychology and Religion.* Rand-McNally, Chicago, 1966.

Baker, H. V.: Children's contributions in elementary school general discussion. *Child Develop. Monogr.* No. 29, 1942.

Baker, N., and Sullivan, E. V.: The influence of some task variables and of socio-economic class on the manifestation of conservation of number. *J. Genet. Psychol.,* in press, 1969.

Baldwin, A. L.: Socialization and the parent-child relationship. *Child Develop. 19:* 127–136, 1948.

——: The effect of home environment on nursery school behavior. *Child Develop. 20:* 49–62, 1949.

——: *Behavior and Development in Childhood.* Dryden, New York, 1955.

——: The study of child behavior and development. *In* P. H. Mussen (Ed.), *Handbook of Research Methods in Child Development.* Pp. 3–35, Wiley, New York, 1960.

——: *Theories of Child Development.* Wiley, New York, 1967.

——, Kalhorn, J., and Breese, F. H.: Patterns of parent behavior. *Psychol. Monogr. 58(3,* Whole No. 268), 1945.

——, ——, and ——: The appraisal of parent behavior. *Psychol. Monogr. 63(299):* 1949.

Baldwin, B. T.: The physical growth of children from birth to maturity. *University of Iowa Studies in Child Welfare.* No. 1, 1921.

——, and Wellman, B. L.: The pegboard as a means of analyzing form perception and motor control in young children. *J. Genet. Psychol. 35:* 387–414, 1928.

Baldwin, J. M.: *Social and Ethical Interpretation in Mental Development.* Macmillan, New York, 1906.

Bandura, A.: Social learning through imitation. *In* M. R. Jones (Ed.), *Nebraska Symposium on Motivation.* University of Nebraska Press, Lincoln, pp. 211–269, 1962.

——: Influence of model's reinforcement contingencies on the acquisition of imitative responses. *J. Personal. Soc. Psychol. 1:* 589–595, 1965.

——: Social-learning theory of identificatory processes. *In* D. A. Goslin (Ed.), *Handbook of Socialization Theory and Research.* Ch. 3, Rand-McNally, Chicago, 1968.

——, and Harris, M. B.: Modification of syntactic style. *J. Exptl. Child Psychol. 4(4):* 341–352, 1966.

——, and Huston, A.: Identification as a process of incidental learning. *J. Abnor. Soc. Psychol. 18:* 311–318, 1961.

——, and McDonald, F. J.: The influence of social reinforcement in the behavior of models in shaping children's moral judgments. *J. Abnor. Soc. Psychol. 67:* 274–281, 1963.

——, and Mischel, W.: Modification of self-imposed delay of reward through exposure to live and symbolic models. *J. Personal. Soc. Psychol. 2:* 698–705, 1965.

————, Ross, D., and Ross, S. A.: Transmission of aggression through imitation of aggressive models. *J. Abnor. Soc. Psychol. 18:* 575–582, 1961.

————, and Walters, R.: *Adolescent Aggression: A Study of the Influence of Child-Training Practices and Family Inter-relationships.* Ronald Press, New York, 1959.

————, and ————: Aggression. *In* H. W. Stevenson (Ed.), *Sixty-Second Yearbook, National Society for the Study of Education.* Part 1. *Child psychology.* Chicago: University of Chicago Press, pp. 364–415, 1963, (a).

————, and ————: *Social Learning and Personality Development.* Holt, Rinehart and Winston, New York, 1963, (b).

Barbe, W. B.: Peer relationships of children of different intelligence levels. *School and Sociology. 80:* 60–62, 1954.

Barbu, Z.: Studies in children's honesty. *Quart. Bull. Brit. Psychol. Soc. 2:* 53–57, 1951.

Barker, R. G.: On the nature of the environment. *J. Soc. Issues. 19(4):* 17–38, 1963.

————: Observation of behavior: Ecological approaches. *Journal of the Mount Sinai Hospital. 31(4):* 268–284, 1964.

————: Explorations in ecological psychology. *Amer. Psychol. 20(1):* 1–14, 1965.

————, Dembo, T., and Lewin, K.: Frustration and regression: An experiment with young children. *University of Iowa Studies in Child Welfare. 18(1):* 1941.

————, and Wright, H. F.: Psychological ecology and the problem of psychosocial development. *Child Develop. 20:* 131–143, 1949.

Barnard, J. W.: The effects of anxiety on connotative meaning. *Child Develop. 37:* 461–472, 1966.

Barnet, A. B., Lodge, A., and Armington, J. C.: Electroretinogram in newborn human infants. *Science. 148:* 651–654, 1965.

Barns, H. H. F., and Morgans, M. E.: Prediabetic pregnancy. *Brit. J. Obs. Gyn. 55:* 449–454, 1948.

Barron, F.: *Creativity and Psychological Health.* Van Nostrand, Princeton, New Jersey, 1963.

Bartlett, E. W., and Smith, C. P.: Childrearing practices, birth order and the development of achievement-related motives. *Psychol. Rep. 19(3):* 1207–1216, 1966.

Bartoshuk, A. K.: Response decrement with repeated elicitation of human neonatal cardiac acceleration to sound. *J. Comp. Physiol. Psychol. 55:* 9–12, 1962, (a).

————: Human neonatal cardiac acceleration to sound: Habituation and dishabituation. *Percept. Motor Skills.* 15–27, 1962 ,(b).

————: Human neonatal cardiac responses to sound: A power function. *Psychonomic Science. 1:* 151–152, 1964.

Baumrind, D.: Effects of authoritative control on child behavior. *Child Development. 37(4):* 887–907, 1966.

————, and Black, A. E.: Socialization practices associated with dimensions of competence in preschool boys and girls. *Child Develop. 38:* 291–327, 1967.

Bavelas, A.: A method for investigating individual and group ideology. *Sociometry. 5:* 371–377, 1942.

Bayer, L. N., and Bayley, N.: Growth diagnosis. University of Chicago Press, Chicago, Illinois, 1959.

Bayer, M., and Reichard, S.: Androgyny, weight and personality. *Psychosom. Med. 13:* 358–374, 1951.

Bayley, N.: *The California First Year Mental Scale.* University of California Press, Berkeley, 1933, (a).

————: Mental growth during the first three years. A developmental study of 61 children by repeated tests. *Genet. Psychol. Monogr. 14:* 7–92, 1933, (b).

————: The development of motor abilities during the first three years. *Monogr. Soc. Res. Child Develop. (1):* 1935.

————: Factors influencing growth of intelligence in young children. *In* G. M. Whipple (Ed.), *Thirty-Ninth Yearbook, National Society for the Study of Education.* Part II. *Intelligence: Its Nature and Nurture: Original Studies and Experiments.* Pp. 49–79, University of Chicago Press, Chicago, 1940, (a).

————: Mental growth in young children. *In* G. M. Whipple (Ed.), *Thirty-ninth Yearbook, National Society for the Study of Education.* Part II. *Intelligence, Its Nature and Nurture: Original Studies and Experiments.* Pp. 11–47, University of Chicago Press, Chicago, 1940, (b).

————: Consistency and variability in the growth of intelligence from birth to eighteen years. *J. Genet. Psychol. 75:* 165–196, 1949.

————: On the growth of intelligence. *Amer. Psychol. 10:* 805–818, 1955.

————: Individual patterns of development. *Child Develop. 27:* 45–74, 1956.

————: Value and limitations of infant testing. *Children. 5:* 129, 1958.

————: Consistency of maternal and child behaviors in the Berkeley Growth Study. *Vita Humana. 7(2):* 73–95, 1964.

————: Comparisons of mental and motor test scores for ages 1–15 months by sex, birth order, race, geographical location, and education of parents. *Child Develop. 36(2):* 379–412, 1965, (a).

————: Research in child development: A longitudinal perspective. *Merrill-Palmer Quarterly. 11:* 183–208, 1965, (b).

————: Learning in adulthood: The role of intelligence. *In* H. J. Klausmeier and C. W. Harris (Eds.), *Analyses of Concept Learning.* Pp. 117–138, Academic Press, New York, 1966.

————, and Jones, H. E.: Environmental correlates of mental and motor development. *Child Develop. 8:* 329–341, 1937.

————, and Oden, M. H.: The maintenance of intellectual ability in gifted adults. *J. Geront. 10:* 91–107, 1955.

————, and Pinneau, S. R.: Tables for predicting adult height from skeletal age. Revised for use with the Grenlich-Pyle hand standards. *J. Ped. 40:* 423–444, 1952.

————, and Schaefer, E. S.: Maternal behavior and personality development: Data from the Berkeley Growth Study. *Psychiat. Res. Rep. 13:* 155–173, 1960, (a).

————, and Schaefer, E.: Relationships between socio-economic variables and the behavior of mothers towards young children. *J. Genet. Psychol. 96:* 61–77, 1960, (b).

————, and ————: Correlations of maternal and child behaviors with the development of mental abilities. *Monogr. Soc. Res. Child Develop. 29(6):* 1964.

Becker, S. W., Lerner, M. J., and Carroll, J.: Conformity as a function of birth order and type of group pressure. *J. Personal. Soc. Psychol. 3:* 242–244, 1966.

Becker, W. C.: Consequences of different kinds of parental discipline. *In* M. L. Hoffman and L. W. Hoffman (Eds.), *Review of Child Development Research.* Pp. 169–208, Russell Sage Foundation, New York, 1964.

————, and Krug, R. S.: The parent attitude research instrument: A research review. *Child Develop. 36:* 329–365, 1965.

Beckey, R. E.: A study of certain factors related to retardation of speech. *J. Speech Dis. 7:* 223–249, 1942.

Behrens, M. L.: Child rearing and the character structure of the mother. *Child Develop. 25:* 225–238, 1954.

Beilin, H.: Stimulus and cognitive transformation in conservation. *In* D. Elkind and J. H. Flavell (Eds.), *Studies in Cognitive Development: Essays in Honour of Jean Piaget.* Pp. 409–438, Oxford University Press, New York, 1969.

————, and Franklin, I. C.: Logical operations in area and length measurement: Age and training effects. *Child Develop. 33:* 607–618, 1962.

Bell, D. A., Taylor, W. C., and Dockrell, W. B.: A ten year follow-up of low birth weight infants: Intellectual functioning. *Alberta J. Educ. Res. 11(4):* 220–225, 1965.

Bell, R. Q.: Convergence: An accelerated longitudinal approach. *Child Develop. 24:* 145–152, 1953.

————: Retrospective and prospective views of early personality development. *Merrill-Palmer Quarterly. 6:* 131–144, 1960.

————: Structuring parent-child interaction situations for direct observation. *Child Develop. 35:* 1009–1020, 1964, (a).

————: The effect on the family of a limitation in coping ability in the child: A research approach and a finding. *Merrill Palmer Quarterly. 10:* 129–142, 1964, (b).

————: Level of arousal in breast-fed and bottle-fed human newborns. *Psychoso. Med. 28:* 177–180, 1966.

————: A reinterpretation of effects in studies of socialization. *Psychol. Rev. 75(2):* 81–95, 1968.

————, and Darling, J. F.: The prone head reaction in the human neonate: Relation with sex and tactile sensitivity. *Child Develop. 36:* 943–149, 1965.

Bellugi, U.: The development of interrogative structures in children's speech. *In* K. Rietal (Ed.), *The Development of Language Functions.* Report No. 8. University of Michigan Language Development Program, 1965.

Belmont, L., and Birch, H. G.: Lateral dominance and right-left awareness in normal children. *Child Develop. 34:* 257–270, 1963.

Benda, C. E.: Prenatal maternal factors in mongolism. *JAMA. 139:* 979–985, 1949.

Bender, L. Psychopathic behavior disorders in children. *In* R. M. Lindner (Ed.), *Handbook of Correctional Psychology.* Pp. 360–377, Philosophical Library, New York, 1947.

————: Anxiety in disturbed children. *In* P. H. Hoch and J. Zubin (Eds.), *Anxiety.* Pp. 119–139, Grune & Stratton, New York, 1950.

————, and Grudelt, A. E.: A study of certain epidemological factors in a group of children with childhood schizophrenia. *Amer. J. Orthopsychiat. 26:* 131–143, 1956.

Benedict, R.: Continuities and discontinuities in cultural conditioning. *Psychiatry. 1:* 161–167, 1938.

————: *The Chrysanthemum and the Sword.* Houghton Mifflin, Boston, 1946.

Bennett, G. K., and Doppelt, J. E. A longitudinal study of the Differential Aptitude Tests. *Educ. Psychol Meas. 11:* 228–237, 1951.

Bereiter, C.: A non-psychological approach to early education. *In* M. Deutsch, I. Katz, and A. R. Jensen (Eds.), *Social Class, Race and Psychological Development.* Ch. 9, Holt, Rinehart and Winston, New York, 1968.

————, and Engelmann, S. E.: *Teaching Disadvantaged Children.* Prentice-Hall, New York, 1966.

Berelson, B. R., and Salter, P. J.: Majority and minority Americans: An analysis of magazine fiction. *Public Opinion Quarterly. 10:* 168–190, 1946.

Beres, D., and Obers, S.: The effects of extreme deprivation in infancy on psychic structure in adolescence. *Psychoanal. Study Child. 5:* 121–140, 1950.

Bergman, P., Malasky, C., and Zahn, T. P.: Developmental changes in sucking strength and manual strength. *Percept. and Motor Skills. 23(2):* 595–606, 1966.

Berko, J.: The child's learning of English morphology. *Word. 14:* 150–177, 1958.

Berko, J., and Brown, R.: Psycholinguistic research methods. *In* P. H. Mussen (Ed.), *Handbook of Research Methods in Child Development.* Pp. 517–557, Wiley & Sons, New York, 1960.

Berkowitz, L.: *Development of Motives and Values in the Child.* Basic Books, New York, 1964.

————: Impulse, aggression and the gun. *Psychol. Today. 2(4):* 18–23, 1968.

Berlyne, D. E.: The influence of the albedo and complexity of stimuli on visual fixation in the infant. *Brit. J. Psychol. 49:* 315–318, 1958.

Berlyne, D. E.: *Conflict, Arousal and Curiosity.* McGraw-Hill, New York, 1960.

————: *Structure and Direction in Thinking.* John Wiley & Sons, New York, 1965.

————, and Frommer, F. D.: Some determinants of the incidence and content of children's questions. *Child Develop. 37(1):* 177–189, 1966.

————: The delimitation of cognitive development: Discussion. *In* H. W. Stevenson (Ed.), *The Concept of Development. Monogr. Soc. Res. Child Develop. 31(5):* 71–81, 1966.

————: Children's reasoning and thinking. *In* P. H. Mussen (Ed.), Revised edition of *Carmichael's Manual of Child Psychology.* In press, Wiley, New York, 1969, (a).

————: Laughter, humor and play. *In* G. Lindzey and E. Aronson (Eds.), *Handbook of Social Psychology,* 2nd ed. Addison-Wesley, Reading, Mass., 1969, (b).

Bernard, J.: Predictions from human fetal measures: *Child Develop. 35:* 1243–1248, 1964.

————, and Sontag, L. W.: Fetal reactivity to tonal stimulation: A preliminary report. *J. Genet. Psychol. 70:* 205–210, 1947.

Bernard, V. W.: School desegregation: Some psychiatric implications. *Psychiatry 21:* 149–158, 1958.

Bernstein, B.: Some sociological determinants of perception: An enquiry into subcultural differences. *Brit. J. Sociol. 9:* 159–174, 1958.

———: Language and social class. *Brit. J. Psychol. 11:* 271–276, 1960.

Berrien, F. K.: Methodological and related problems in cross-cultural research. *Internat. J. Psychol. 2(1):* 33–34, 1967.

Berry, W. T., and Cowin, P. J.: Conditions associated with the growth of boys, 1950–1951. *Brit. Med. J. 1:* 847–851, 1954.

Bettleheim, B., and Janowitz, M.: *Social Change and Prejudice:* (Including *"Dynamics of Prejudice."*) Free Press, New York, 1964.

Bever, T. G.: Pre-linguistic behavior. Unpublished honors thesis, Department of Linguistics, Harvard University, 1961.

———, Fodor, J. A., and Weksel, W.: On the acquisition of syntax: A critique of (contextual) generalization. *Psychological Rev. 72:* 467–482, 1965.

Bharucha-Reid, R. P.: Appearance and reality in culture. *J. Soc. Psychol. 57:* 169–193, 1962.

Biber, B.: *Children's Drawings: From Lines to Pictures.* Bureau of Educational Experiments, New York, 1934.

———, and Lewis, C.: An experimental study of what young children expect from their teachers. *Genet. Psychol. Monogr. 40:* 3–97, 1949.

———, Murphy, L. B., Woodcock, L. P., and Black, I. S.: *Child Life in School.* Dutton, New York, 1942.

Bibring, G. L., Dwyer, T. F., Huntington, D. S., and Valenstein, A. S.: A study of the psychological processes in pregnancy and of the earliest mother-child relationship. *Psychoanal. Study Child. 16:* 9–72, 1961.

Biehler, R. F.: Companion choice behavior in the kindergarten. *Child Develop. 25:* 45–51, 1954.

Bijou, S. W.: Ages, stages and the naturalization of human development. *Amer. Psychol. 23:* 419–427, 1968.

———, and Baer, D. M.: The laboratory-experimental study of child behavior. *In* P. H. Mussen (Ed.), *Handbook of Research Methods in Child Development.* Pp. 140–200, Wiley, New York, 1960.

———, and ———: *Child Development.* Vol. I, Appleton-Century-Crofts, New York, 1961.

Bing, E.: Effect of childrearing practices on development of differential cognitive abilities. *Child Develop. 34:* 631–648, 1963.

Binning, G.: Peace be on thy house. *Health.* P. 6, 1948.

Birch, H. G., and Lefford, A.: Visual differentiation, intersensory integration and voluntary motor control. *Monogr. Soc. Res. Child Develop. 32(2):* 1967.

Bird, C., Monachesi, E. D., and Burdick, H.: Studies of group tensions: III. The effect of parental discouragement of play attitudes upon the attitudes of white children toward Negroes. *Child Develop. 23:* 295–306, 1952.

Birney, R. C., and Teevan, R. C.: (Eds.), *Instinct.* Van Nostrand, New York, 1961.

Bjerstedt, A.: A double-directed analysis of preference motivations and other pal-description statements: Studies in socio-perceptual selectivity. *Acta Psychologica. 11:* 257–268, 1955.

———: The interpretation of socio-metric scores in the classroom. *Acta Psychologica. 12:* 1–14, 1956.

Blake, R., and Dennis, W.: The development of stereotypes concerning the Negro. *J. Abnor. Soc. Psychol. 38:* 525–531, 1943.

Blank, M.: Focal periods hypothesis in sensori motor development. *Child Develop. 35:* 817–859, 1964.

Blanton, M. G.: Behavior of the human infant during the first thirty days of life. *Psychol. Rev. 24:* 456–483, 1917.

Blauvelt, H., and McKenna, J.: Mother-neonate interaction: Capacity of the human newborn for orientation. *In* B. M. Foss (Ed.), *Determinants of Infant Behavior.* Pp. 2–29, Wiley, New York, 1963.

Blewett, D. B.: An experimental study of the inheritance of intelligence. *J. Men. Sci. 100:* 922–933, 1954.

Bliesmer, P.: Reading abilities of bright and dull children of comparable mental ages. *J. Educ. Psychol. 45:* 321–331, 1954.

Bloch, H., Lippsett, H., Redner, B., and Hirschl, D.: Reduction of mortality in the premature nursery. 2. Incidence and causes of prematurity: Ethnic, socioeconomic and obstetric factors. *J. Pediat. 41:* 300–304, 1952.

Block, J.: Personality characteristics associated with fathers' attitudes toward child-rearing. *Child Develop. 26:* 41–48, 1955.

Blommers, P., Knief, M., and Stroud, J. B.: The organismic age concept. *J. Educ. Psychol. 46:* 142–150, 1955.

Bloom, B. S.: *Stability and Change in Human Characteristics.* Wiley & Sons, New York, 1964.

Blumer, H.: Psychological import of the human group. *In* M. Sherif and M. O. Wilson (Eds.), *Group Relations at the Crossroads.* Pp. 182–202, Harper, New York, 1953.

Blumer, H., and Hauser, P. M.: *Movies, Delinquency and Crime.* Macmillan, New York, 1934.

Boas, F.: Changes in bodily form of descendants of immigrants. U.S. Government Printing Office, Washington, D.C., 1911.

Boehm, L.: The development of independence: A comparative study. *Child Develop. 28:* 85–92, 1957.

———: The development of conscience: A comparison of American children of different mental and socioeconomic levels. *Child Develop. 33:* 575–590, 1962, (a).

———: The development of conscience: A comparison of students in Catholic parochial schools and in public schools. *Child Develop. 33:* 591–602, 1962, (b).

———: The development of conscience of preschool children: A cultural and sub-cultural comparison. *J. Soc. Psychol. 59(2):* 355–360, 1963.

———: Moral judgment: A cultural and sub-cultural comparison with some of Piaget's research conclusions. *Internat. J. Psychol. 1(2):* 143–150, 1966.

———, and Nass, N. L.: Social class differences in conscience development. *Child Develop. 33:* 565–574, 1962.

Bogardus, R., and Otto, P.: Social psychology of chums. *Social. Soc. Res. 20:* 260–270, 1936.

Bonney, M. E.: A study of social status on the second grade level. *J. Genet. Psychol. 60:* 271–305, 1942, (a).

Bonney, M. E.: A study of the relation of intelligence, family size, and sex differences with mutual friendships in the primary grades. *Child Develop. 13:* 79–100, 1942, (b).

———: The constancy of sociometric scores and their relationship to teacher judgments of social success and to personality self-ratings. *Sociometry. 6:* 409–424, 1943, (a).

———: The relative stability of social, intellectual and academic status in grades II to IV, and the interrelationships between these various forms of growth. *J. Educ. Psychol. 34:* 88–102, 1943, (b).

———: Relationships between social success, family size, socioeconomic background, and intelligence among school children in grades III to V. *Sociometry. 7:* 26–39, 1944, (a).

———: Sex differences in social success and personality traits. *Child Develop. 15:* 63–79, 1944, (b).

———: A sociometric study of the relationship of some factors to mutual friendships in the elementary, secondary, and college levels. *Sociometry. 7:* 26–39, 1946.

———: Popular and unpopular children: A sociometric study. *Sociometric Monogr. (9):* 1947, (a).

———: Sociometric study of agreement between teacher judgments and student choices. *Sociometry. 10:* 133–146, 1947, (b).

———: Choosing between the sexes on a sociometric measurement. *J. Soc. Psychol. 39:* 99–114, 1954.

———, and Nicholson, E. L.: Comparative school adjustments of elementary school pupils with and without preschool training. *Child Develop. 29:* 125–133, 1958.

———, and Powell, J.: Differences in social behavior between sociometrically high and sociometrically low children. *J. Educ. Res. 46:* 481–495, 1953.

Borishevsky, M. I.: Characteristics of children's attitudes toward rules of conduct in game situations. *Voprosy Psikhologii. 4:* 44–54, 1965.

Borow, H.: Development of occupational motives and roles. *In* L. W. Hoffman and M. L. Hoffman (Eds.), *Review of Child Development Research*. Pp. 373–422, Russell Sage Foundation, New York, Vol. 2, 1966.

Bossard, J. H.: The bilingual as a person: Linguistic identification with status. *Amer. Sociol. Rev. 10:* 699–709, 1945.

———, and Boll, E. S.: Personality roles in the large family. *Child Develop. 26:* 71–78, 1955.

Bottschaldt, K., and Fruhauf-Ziegler, C.: On the development of cooperative behavior in children. *Zeitschrift fur Psychologie. 162:* 254–278, 1958.

Bourne, L. E., Goldstein, S., and Link, W. E.: Concept learning as a function of availability of previously presented information. *J. Exptl. Psychol. 67:* 439–448, 1964.

———, and Jennings, P.: The relationship between response contiguity and classification learning. *J. Genet. Psychol. 69:* 335–338, 1963.

———, and Parker, B. K.: Differences among modes for portraying stimulus information in concept identification. *Psychonomic Sci. 1:* 209–210, 1964.

Bousfield, W. H., Esterson, J., and Whitemarsh, G. A.: A study of developmental changes in conceptual and perceptual associate clustering. *J. Genet. Psychol. 92:* 95–102, 1958.

Bower, T. G.: The visual world of infants. *Scientific American, 215(6):* 80–92, 1966.

Bowerman, C. E., and Kinch, J. W.: Change in family and peer orientations of children between the fourth and tenth grades. *Soc. Forces. 37:* 206–211, 1959.

Bowers, P., and London, P.: Developmental correlates of role-playing ability. *Child Develop. 36:* 499–508, 1965.

Bowlby, J.: Forty-four juvenile thieves. *Internat. J. Psychoanal. 25:* 1–57, 1944.

———: *Forty-four Juvenile Thieves: Their Characters and Home Lives*. Balliere, Tindall and Cox, London, 1946.

———: Maternal care and mental health. *World Health Organization Monogr.* (2): 1952.

———: The nature of the child's tie to his mother. *Internat. J. Psychoanal. 39:* 350–373, 1958.

———: Ethology and the development of object relations. *Internat. J. Psychoanal. 41:* 313–317, 1960.

———, Ainsworth, M., Boston, M., and Rosenbluth, D.: The effects of mother-child separation: A follow-up study. *Brit. J. Med. Psychol. 29:* 211–247, 1956.

Boyd, G. F.: The levels of aspiration of white and Negro children in a non-segregated elementary school. *J. Soc. Psychol. 36:* 191–196, 1952.

Boyd, W. C.: *Genetics and the Races of Man*. Little Brown, Boston, 1953.

Brackbill, Y.: *Infancy and Early Childhood: A Handbook and Guide to Human Development*. The Free Press, New York, 1967.

———, Adams, G., Crowell, D. H., and Gray, N. L.: Arousal level in neonates and preschool children under continuous auditory stimulation. *J. Exptl. Child Psychol. 4:* 177–188, 1966.

———, and Koltsova, N. N.: Conditioning and learning. *In* Y. Brackbill (Ed.), *Infancy and Early Childhood: A Handbook and Guide to Human Development*. Pp. 205–286, The Free Press, New York, 1967.

———, and Thompson, G. (Eds.): *Behavior in Infancy and Early Childhood: A Book of Readings*. The Free Press, New York, 1967.

Bradley, R. W.: Birth order and school-related behavior: A heuristic review. *Psychol. Bull. 70(1):* 45–51, 1968.

Bradway, K. P., and Thompson, C. W.: Intelligence at adulthood: A twenty-five year follow-up. *J. Educ. Psychol. 5:* 1–14, 1962.

Braine, M. D.: The ontogeny of logical operations: Piaget's formulations examined by nonverbal methods. *Psychological Mongr. 73(4*, Whole No. 475), 1959.

———: Piaget on reasoning: A methodological critique and alternative proposal. *In* W. Kessen and C. Kuhlman (Eds.), Thought in the young child. *Monogr. Soc. Res. Child Develop. 27(2):* 1962.

———: The ontogeny of English phrase structure: The first phrase. *Language. 39:* 1–13, 1963, (a).

———: On learning the grammatical order of words. *Psychol. Rev. 70:* 323–348, 1963 (b).

————, Heimer, C. B., Wortis, H., and Freedman, A. M.: Factors associated with impairment of the early development of prematures. *Monogr. Soc. Res. Child Develop. 31(4,* Serial No. 106), 1966.

————, and Shanks, B. L.: The conservation of shape, property, and a proposal about the origin of conservation. *Canad. J. Psychol. 19:* 187–207, 1965, (a).

————, and ————: The development of conservation of size. *J. Verbal Learning and Verbal Behavior. 4:* 227–242, 1965, (b).

Braun, J. S.: Relation between concept formation ability and reading achievement at three developmental levels. *Child Develop. 34:* 675–682, 1963.

Braun-Lamesch, M.: Le rôle du contexte dans la compréhension du language chez l'enfant (The role of context in the child's comprehension of language). *Psychologie Francaise. 7:* 180–189, 1962.

Braley, L. S.: Strategy selection and negative instances in concept learning. *J. Educ. Psychol. 54:* 154–159, 1963.

Bray, D. H.: A study of children's writing on an admired person. *Educ. Rev. 15:* 44–53, 1962.

Brekstad, A.: Factors influencing the reliability of an amnestic recall. *Child Develop. 37:* 603–612, 1966.

Brennan, W., Ames, E. W., and Moore, R. W.: Age differences in infants' attention to patterns of different complexities. *Science. 151:* 354–356, 1966.

Bresson, F.: La signification. *In Problèmes de Psycho-Linquistique.* Pp. 9–45, Presses Universitaire de France, Paris, 1963.

Brewster-Smith, M.: Competence and socialization. *In* J. A. Clausen (Ed.), *Socialization and Society.* Pp. 270–320, Little Brown and Co., Boston, 1968.

Breznitz, S., and Kugelmass, S.: Intentionality in moral judgment: Development stages. *Child Develop. 38(2):* 469–479, 1967.

Brian, C. R., and Goodenough, F. L.: The relative potency of color and form perception at various ages. *J. Exptl. Psychol. 12:* 197–213, 1929.

Bridger, W. H.: Ethological concepts in human development. *In* J. Wortis (Ed.), *Recent Advances in Biological Psychiatry.* Vol. 4, pp. 95–107, Plenum Press, New York, 1962.

Bridges, K. M.: *The School and Emotional Development of the Preschool Child.* Kegan Paul, London, 1931.

————: Emotional development in early infancy. *Child Develop. 3:* 324–341, 1932.

Brim, O. G.: The parent-child relation as a social system: I. Parent and child roles. *Child Develop. 28(3):* 343–364, 1957.

————: Personality development as role learning. *In* I. I. Scol and H. W. Stevenson (Eds.), *Personality Development in Children.* University of Texas Press, Austin, 1960.

————: Adult socialization. *In* J. A. Clausen (Ed.), *Socialization and Society.* Ch. 5, Little, Brown and Co., Boston, 1967.

Brison, D. W.: Acceleration of conservation of substance. *J. Genet. Psychol. 109:* 311–322, 1966.

————, and Bereiter, C.: Acquisition of conservation of substance in normal, retarded, and gifted children. *In* D. W. Brison and E. V. Sullivan (Eds.), Recent research in the acquisition of conservation of substance. *Educ. Mongr.,* Ontario Institute for Studies in Education, 1967.

————, and Sullivan, E. V. (Eds.): Recent research on the acquisition of conservation of substance. *Educ. Mongr.* Ontario Institute for Studies in Education, 1967.

Brodbeck, A. J.: The mass media as a socializing agency. Paper read at American Psychology Association, San Francisco, September, 1955.

————: Eminent psychologist challenges TV writers and producers. *National Association for Better Radio and Television Quarterly. 2(3):* 1 and 4, 1962.

————, and Irwin, O. C.: The speech behavior of infants without families. *Child Develop. 17:* 145–156, 1946.

————, Nogee, P., and DeMascio, A.: Two kinds of conformity: A study of the Riesman typology applied to standards of parental discipline. *J. Psychol. 41:* 23–45, 1956.

Broderick, C., and Fowler, S. E.: New patterns of relationships between the sexes among preadolescents. *Marriage and Family Living. 23:* 27–30, 1961.

————, and Rowe, G. P.: A scale of preadolescent heterosexual development. *Journal of Marriage and the Family. 30:* 97–101, 1968.

Brodie, R. D., and Winterbottom, M. R.: Failure in elementary school boys as a function of traumata, secrecy and derogation. *Child Develop. 38(3):* 701–711, 1967.

Brody, G. F.: Relationship between maternal attitudes and behavior. *J. Personal. Soc. Psychol. 2(3):* 317–323, 1965.

Bronfenbrenner, U.: Socialization and social class through time and space. *In* E. Maccoby, T. Newcomb, and E. Hartley (Eds.), *Readings in Social Psychology.* Pp. 400–425, Henry Holt and Co., New York, 1958.

————: Freudian theories of identification and their derivatives. *Child Develop. 31:* 15–40, 1960.

————: The changing American child: A speculative analysis. *J. Soc. Issues. 17:* 6–17, 1961.

————: The role of age, sex, class, and culture in studies of moral development. *Religious Educ. 57(4):* 3–17, 1962, (a).

————: Soviet methods of character education: Some implications for research. *Amer. Psychol. 17:* 560–564, 1962, (b).

————: Developmental theory in transition. *In* H. W. Stevenson (Ed.), *Sixty-second Yearbook, National Society for the Study of Education.* Part I. *Child Psychology.* Pp. 517–542, University of Chicago Press, Chicago, 1963.

————: The psychological costs of quality and equality in education. *Child Develop. 38(4):* 909–925, 1967.

————: Soviet methods of upbringing and their effects. A social-psychological analysis. Paper read at a Conference on Studies of the Acquisition and Development of Values. National Institute of Child Health and Human Development, May, 1968.

————: On the making of new men: Some extrapolations from research. *Canad. J. Behav. Sci. 1(1):* 4–24, 1969.

————, and Ricciuti, H. N.: Appraisal of personality characteristics of children. *In* P. H. Mussen (Ed.), *Handbook of Research Methods in Child Development.* Pp. 770–820, Wiley, New York, 1960.

Bronshtein, A. I., and Petrova, E. P.: The auditory analyzer in young infants. *In* Y. Brackbill and G. G. Thompson (Eds.), *Behavior in Infancy and Early Childhood: A Book of Readings.* Pp. 163–172, Free Press, New York, 1967.

Bronson, G. W.: The development of fear in man and other animals. *Child Develop. 39:* 409–431, 1968.

————: Central orientations: A study of behavior organization from childhood to adolescence. *Child Develop. 37(1):* 125–155, 1966.

————: Adult derivatives of emotional expressiveness and reactivity control: Developmental continuities from childhood to adulthood. *Child Develop. 38(3):* 801–818, 1967.

Brooks, I. M., and Sullivan, E. V.: A comparison of relative structural levels on a variety of cognitive tasks. Unpublished research Paper. The Ontario Institute for Studies in Education, 1968.

Brown, A. W., and Hunt, R. G.: Relations between nursery school attendance and teachers' ratings of some aspects of children's adjustment in kindergarten. *Child Develop. 32:* 585–596, 1961.

————, Morrison, J., and Couch, G. B.: Influence of affectional family relationships on character development. *J. Abnor. Soc. Psychol. 42:* 422–428, 1947.

————, Stafford, R. E., and Vandenberg, S. G.: Twins: behavioral differences. *Child Develop. 38:* 1055–1064, 1967.

Brown, C.: *Manchild in the Promised Land.* Signet Books, New York, 1965.

Brown, D. G.: Masculinity-femininity development in children. *J. Consult. Psychol. 21:* 197–202, 1957.

Brown, J.: States in newborn infants. *Merrill-Palmer Quarterly. 10:* 313–327, 1964.

Brown, R. W.: *Words and Things.* Free Press, New York, 1958, (a).

————: How shall a thing be called? *Psychol. Rev. 65:* 14–21, 1958, (b).

————: *Social Psychology.* Free Press, New York, 1965.

————: In the beginning was the grammar. *In* a review of F. Smith, and G. A. Miller (Eds.), *The Genesis of Language: A Psycholinguistic Approach. Contemporary Psychology. 13(2):* 49–51, 1968.

————, and Bellugi, U.: Three processes in the child's acquisition of syntax. *Harvard Educ. Rev. 34:* 133–151, 1964.

————, Cazden, C., and Bellugi, U.: The child's grammar from one to three. *In* J. P. Hill (Ed.), *The 1967 Minnesota Symposium on Child Psychology.* University of Minnesota Press, Minneapolis, 1967.

————, and Fraser, C.: The acquisition of syntax. *In* C. N. Cofer and B. S. Musgrave (Eds.), *Verbal Behavior and Learning.* Pp. 158–209, McGraw-Hill, New York, 1963.

————, and ————: The acquisition of syntax. *In* U. Bellugi and R. Brown (Eds.), The acquisition of language. *Monogr. Soc. Res. Child Develop. 29(92):* 43–78, 1964.

Brown, S., Lieberman, J., Winston, J., and Pleshette, N.: Studies in choice of infant feeding by primiparas: I. Attitudinal factors and extraneous influences. *Psychoso. Med. 22:* 421–429, 1960.

Brown, W. H., and Bond, L. B.: Social stratification in a sixth-grade class. *J. Educ. Res. 48:* 539–543, 1955.

Brownell, W. A.: Observations of instruction in lower-grade arithmetic in English and Scottish schools. *Arithmetic Teacher. 7:* 165–177, 1960.

Brownfield, E. D.: An investigation of the activity and sensory responses of healthy newborn infants. *Visitation Abstracts. 16:* 1288–1289, 1956.

Brumbaugh, F. N.: Stimuli which cause laughter in children. Unpublished doctoral dissertation, New York University, 1939.

Bruner, J. S.: Going beyond the information given. A University of Colorado Symposium. Contemporary approaches to cognition. Pp. 41–69, Harvard University Press, Cambridge, Mass., 1957.

————: *The Process of Education.* Harvard University Press, Cambridge, Mass., 1960.

————: The course of cognitive growth. *Amer. Psychol. 19:* 1–15, 1964.

————: On cognitive growth. *In* J. S. Bruner, R. R. Olver et al., (Eds.), *Studies in Cognitive Growth.* Ch. 1, Wiley, New York, 1966.

————: Processes of cognitive growth in infancy. Heinz Werner Lectures, Clark University, Worcester, February, 1968.

————: Eye, hand, and mind. *In* D. Elkind and J. H. Flavell (Eds.), *Studies in Cognitive Development: Essays in Honor of Jean Piaget.* Pp. 223–235, Oxford University Press, Toronto, 1969.

————, and Goodman, C. C.: Value and need as organizing factors in perception. *J. Abnor. Soc. Psychol. 42:* 33–44, 1947.

————, Goodnow, J. J., and Austin, G. A.: A Study of Thinking. Wiley, New York, 1956.

————, and Olver, R. R.: Development of equivalence transformations in children. *Monogr. Soc. Res. Child Develop. 28:* (Whole No. 86), 125–141, 1963.

———— et al.: *Studies in Cognitive Growth.* Wiley, New York, 1966.

————, and Tajfel, H.: Cognitive risk and environmental change. *J. Abnor. Soc. Psychol. 62:* 231–241, 1961.

Buhler, C.: *The First Year of Life.* John Day, New York, 1930.

————: The social behavior of children. *In* C. Murchison (Ed.), *A Handbook of Child Psychology.* 2nd ed., pp. 374–416, Clark University Press, Worcester, Mass., 1933.

————: *From Birth to Maturity.* Routledge and Kegan Paul, Trench Trubner, London, 1935.

————, and Hertzer, H.: *Testing Children's Development from Birth to School Age.* Farrar and Rinehart, New York, 1935.

Bundesen, H. N.: Natal day deaths: The long neglected field of infant mortality. *JAMA. 153:* 446–473, 1953.

Burchinall, L. G., Hawkes, G. R., and Gardner, B.: Adjustment characteristics of rural and urban children. *Amer. Soc. Rev. 22:* 81–87, 1957.

Burke, B. S., Beal, V. A., Kirkwood, S. B., and Stuart, H. C.: Nutrition studies during pregnancy. *Amer. J. Obst. Gyn. 46:* 38–52, 1943.

Burks, B. S.: The relative influence of nature and nurture upon mental development: A comparative study of foster parent-foster child resemblance and true parent-true child resemblance. *In 27th Yearbook, National Society for Studies in Education.* Pp. 219–316, Part I, University of Chicago Press, Chicago, 1928.

Burley, L., Dobell, H. C., and Farrell, B. J.: Relations of power, speed, flexibility, and certain anthropometric measures of junior high school girls. *Res. Quart. Amer. Assoc. Health, Phys. Educ. Rec. 32:* 443–448, 1961.

Burns, N., and Cavey, L.: Age differences in empathic ability among children. *Canad. J. Psychol. 11:* 227–230, 1957.

Burnside, L. H.: Coordination in the locomotion of infants. *Genet. Psychol. Monogr. 2:* 281–372, 1927.

Burt, C.: The development of reasoning in children. *J. Exptl. Pedagogy. 5:* 68–77, 1919.

———: The evidence for the concept of intelligence. *Brit. J. Educ. Psychol. 25:* 158–177, 1955.

———: The inheritance of mental ability. *Amer. Psychol. 13:* 1–15, 1958.

———: The genetic determination of differences in intelligence: A study of monozygotic twins reared together and apart. *Brit. J. Psychol. 57:* 137–153, 1966.

Burton, R. V.: Generality of honesty reconsidered. *Psychol. Rev. 70(6):* 481–499, 1963.

———, Allinsmith, W., and Maccoby, E. E.: Resistance to temptation in relation to sex of child, sex of experimenter, and withdrawal of attention. *J. Personal Soc. Psychol. 3(3):* 253–258, 1966.

———, and Whiting, J. W.: The absent father and cross-sex identity. *Merrill-Palmer Quarterly. 7:* 85–95, 1961.

Burtt, H. E.: An experimental study of early childhood memory. *J. Genet. Psychol. 40:* 287–295, 1932.

———: An experimental study of early childhood memory: Final report. *J. Genet. Psychol. 58:* 435–439, 1941.

Buss, A. H.: *Psychology of Aggression.* Wiley, New York, 1961.

Buswell, M. M.: The relationship between the social structure of the classroom and the academic success of the pupils. *J. Exptl. Educ. 22:* 37–52, 1953.

Butler, R. A.: Incentive conditions which influence visual exploration. *J. Exptl. Psychol. 48:* 19–32, 1954.

Caille, R. K.: Resistant behavior of preschool children. *Child Develop. Monogr. (13):* 1933.

Caldwell, B. M.: The usefulness of the critical period hypothesis in the study of filiative behavior. *Merrill-Palmer Quarterly of Behavior and Development. 8(4):* 229–242, 1962.

———: The effects of infant care. *In* M. L. Hoffman and L. W. Hoffman (Eds.), *Review of Child Development Research.* Vol. I, pp. 9–87, Russell Sage Foundation, New York, 1964.

———, and Drachman, R. H.: Comparability of three methods of assessing the developmental level of young infants. *Pediat. 34:* 51–57, 1964.

———, and Hersher, L.: Mother-infant interaction during the first year of life. *Merrill-Palmer Quarterly. 10(2):* 119–128, 1964.

Callantine, M. F., and Warren, J. M.: Learning sets in human concept formation. *Psychol. Rep. 1:* 363–367, 1955.

Cameron, C. L.: Early memories as recorded by 7, 9 and 11 grade boys and girls. Teachers College, Columbia, Dr. of Education Project Report, New York, 1966.

Cameron, N.: *The Psychology of Behavior Disorders: A Biosocial Interpretation.* Houghton Mifflin, Boston, 1947.

Campbell, D., and Thompson, W. R.: Developmental psychology. *Annual Rev. Psychol. 19:* 251–292, 1968.

Campbell, E. H.: The social-sex development of children. *Genet. Psychol. Monogr. 21:* 461–552, 1939.

Campbell, H., and Kalafat, J.: The cardiac response as a correlate of attention in infants. *Child Develop. 37:* 63–71, 1966.

Campbell, J. D.: Peer relations in childhood. *In* M. L. Hoffman and L. W. Hoffman (Eds.), *Review of Child Development Research.* Pp. 289–322, Russell Sage Foundation, New York, 1964.

Candland, D. K.: *Emotion: Bodily Change.* Van Nostrand, New York, 1962.

Cantor, G. N.: Responses of infants and children to complex and novel stimulation. *In* L. P. Lipsitt and C. C. Spiker (Eds.), *Advances in Child Development and Behavior.* Vol. I, Pp. 1–29, Academic Press, New York, 1963.

Caplan, H., Bibace, R., and Rabinovitch, M. S.: Paranatal stress, cognitive organization and ego function: A controlled follow-up study of children born prematurely. *J. Child Psychiat. 2:* 434–450, 1963.

Cappon, D.: Some psychodynamic aspects of pregnancy. *Canad. Med. Assoc. J. 70:* 147–156, 1954.

Carismith, L.: Effect of early father absence upon scholastic aptitude. *Harvard Educ. Rev. 34:* 3–21, 1964.

Carmichael, L.: The onset and early development of behavior. *In* L. Carmichael (Ed.), *Manual of Child Psychol.* (2nd ed.). Pp. 60–185, Wiley, New York, 1954.

Caron, A. J.: Curiosity, achievement, and avoidant motivation as determinants of epistemic behavior. *J. Abnor. Soc. Psychol. 67:* 535–549, 1963.

Carpenter, A.: The differential measurement of speed in primary school children. *Child Develop. 12:* 1–7, 1941.

Carrigan, W. C., and Julian, J. W.: Sex and birth-order differences in conformity as a function of need affiliation arousal. *J. Personal. Soc. Psychol. 3:* 479–493, 1966.

Carroll, J. B.: Language development. *In* C. W. Harris (Ed.), *Encyclopaedia of Educational Research.* Pp. 744–757, Macmillan, New York, 1960.

———: Language acquisition, bilingualism and language change. *In* S. Saporta (Ed.), *Psycholinguistics: A Book of Readings.* Pp. 331–345, Holt, Rinehart and Winston, New York, 1961.

———: *Language and Thought.* Prentice Hall, New York, 1964.

Carrow, M. A.: Linguistic functioning of bilingual and monolingual children. *J. Speech Hearing Dis. 22:* 371, 1957.

Carter, V. E., and Chess, S.: Factors influencing the adaptations of organically handicapped children. *Amer. J. Orthopsychiat. 21:* 827–837, 1951.

Carter, L. F., and Schooler, K.: Value, need and other factors in perception. *Psychol. Rev. 56:* 200–208, 1949.

Caruso, I. H.: La notion de responsibilité et du justice immanent chez l'enfance. *Archives de Psychologie. 29:* Whole No. 114, 1943.

Case, D., and Collinson, J. M.: The development of formal thinking in verbal comprehension. *Brit. J. Educ. Psychol. 32:* 103–111, 1962.

Casler, L.: Maternal deprivation: A critical review of the literature. *Monogr. Soc. Res. Child Develop. 26(2):* 1961.

Cassirer, E.: *An Essay on Man: An Introduction to a Philosophy of Human Culture.* Yale University Press, New Haven, 1944.

Castenada, A., McCandless, B. R., and Palermo, D. S.: The children's form of the Manifest Anxiety Scale. *Child Develop. 17:* 317–326, 1956.

Catalona, F. L., and McCarthy, D.: Infant speech as a possible predictor of later intelligence. *J. Psychol. 38:* 203–209, 1954.

Cates, H. A., and Goodwin, J. C.: The twelve-day-old baby. *Human Biol. 8:* 433–450, 1936.

Cattell, R. B.: The interaction of hereditary and environmental influence. *Brit. J. Stat. Psychol. 16:* 191–221, 1963, (a).

———: Theory of fluid and crystallized intelligence. *J. Educ. Psychol. 54:* 1–22, 1963, (b).

———: Methodological and conceptual advances in evaluating hereditary and environmental influences and their interaction. *In* S. G. Vandenberg (Ed.), *Methods and Goals in Human Behavior Genetics.* Academic Press, New York, 1965.

———: The theory of fluid and crystallized general intelligence checked at the 5–6 year-old level. *Brit. J. Educ. Psychol. 37(2):* 209–224, 1967.

Cavan, R. S.: Negro family disorganization and juvenile delinquency. *J. Negro Educ. 28:* 230–239, 1959.

Cavanaugh, M. C., Cohen, I., Dunphy, D., Ringwall, E. A., and Goldberg, I. D.: Prediction from the Cattell Infant Intelligence Scale. *J. Consult. Psychol. 21:* 33–37, 1957.

Cazden, C. B.: Subcultural differences in child languages: An inter-disciplinary review. *Merrill-Palmer Quart. 12(3):* 185–219, 1966.

———: On individual differences in language competence and performance. *J. Spec. Educ. 1(2):* 135–150, 1967.

Centers, R.: The American class structure: A psychological analysis. *In* T. M. Newcomb and E. L. Hartley (Eds.), *Readings in Social Psychology.* Pp. 481–493, Holt, Rinehart and Winston, New York, 1947.

Cesa-Bianchi, M.: The development of social attitudes as studied in two cross-cultural research projects. *Internat. J. Psychol. 1(1,* No. 62), 1966.

Challman, R. C.: Factors influencing friendship among preschool children. *Child Develop. 3:* 146–158, 1932.

Champney, H.: The variables of parent behavior. *J. Abnor. Soc. Psychol. 36:* 525–542, 1941.

Chapanis, A., and Williams, W. C.: Results of a mental survey with the Kuhlmann-Anderson intelligence tests in Williamson County, Tennessee. *J. Genet. Psychol. 67:* 27–55 1945.

Charlesworth, W. R.: The development of the object concept: A methodological concept. Paper presented at the meeting of the American Psychological Association, New York, September, 1966.

———: Cognition in infancy: Where do we stand in the mid-sixties? *Merrill-Palmer Quart. 14:* 25–46, 1968.

———: The role of surprise in cognitive development. *In* D. Elkind, J. H. Flavell (Eds.), *Studies in Cognitive Development: Essays in Honour of Jean Piaget.* Pp. 257–314, Oxford University Press, New York, 1969.

Chase, L.: Motivation of young children: An experimental study of the influence of certain types of external incentives upon the performance of a task. *University of Iowa Studies in Child Welfare. 5(3):* 1932.

Chase, W. P.: Color vision in infants. *J. Exptl. Psychol. 20:* 203–222, 1937.

Chennault, N.: Improving the social acceptance of unpopular, educable mentally retarded pupils in special classes. *Amer. J. Men. Def. 72:* 455–458, 1967.

Chesley, L. C., and Annetto, J. E.: Pregnancy in the patient with hypertensive disease. *Amer. J. Obs. Gyn. 53:* 372–381, 1947.

Chess, S., Thomas, A., Birch, H. G., and Hertzig, M.: Implications of a longitudinal study of child development for child psychiatry. *Amer. J. Psychiat. 117:* 434–441, 1960.

Child, I. L.: Socialization. *In* G. Lindzey (Ed.), *Handbook of Social Psychology.* Vol. II. *Special Fields and Applications.* Pp. 655–692, Addison-Wesley, Cambridge, Mass., 1964.

———, Hansen, J. A., and Hornbeck, F. W.: Age and sex differences in children's color preferences. *Child Develop. 39:* 237–247, 1968.

Chittenden, E. A., Foan, M. W., Zweil, D. M., and Smith, J. R.: School achievement of first- and second-born siblings. *Child Develop. 39:* 1223–1228, 1968.

Chittenden, G. E.: An experimental study in measuring and modifying assertive behavior in young children. *Monogr. Soc. Res. Child Develop. 7(1):* 1942.

Chomsky, N. A.: Syntactic Structures. Mouton, The Hague, 1957.

———: A review of Skinner's verbal behavior. *Language. 35:* 20–58, 1959.

———: *Aspects of the Theory of Syntax.* M.I.T. Press, Cambridge, 1965.

———: Language and the mind. *Psychology Today.* 48–51, 1968.

Chukovsky, K.: *From Two to Five.* University of California Press, Berkeley, 1966.

Church, J.: *Language and the Discovery of Reality: A Developmental Psychology of Cognition.* Random House, New York, 1961.

Clark, K. B.: *Dark Ghetto: Dilemmas of Social Power.* Harper and Row, New York, 1965.

———: and Clark, M. P.: Racial identification and preference in Negro children. *In* T. M. Newcomb and E. L. Hartley (Eds.), *Readings in Social Psychology.* Pp. 169–178, Holt, Rinehart and Winston, New York, 1947.

Clarke, F. M.: A developmental study of the bodily reaction of infants to an auditory startle stimulus. *J. Genet. Psychol. 55:* 415–427, 1939.

Clarke, H. H., and Clarke, D. H.: Social status and mental health of boys as related to their maturity, structural, and strength characteristics. *Res. Quart. Amer. Assoc. Health and Phys. Educ. 32:* 326–334, 1961.

Clausen, J. A.: Family structure, socialization and personality. *In* L. W. Hoffman and M. L. Hoffman (Eds.), *Review of Child Development Research.* Vol. 2, pp. 1–54, Russell Sage Foundation, New York, 1966.

——: Perspectives on childhood socialization. *In* J. A. Clausen (Ed.), *Socialization and Society.* Ch. 4, Little, Brown Co., Boston, 1968, (a).

—— (Ed.): *Socialization and Society.* Little, Brown Co., Boston, 1968, (b).

——: and Williams, J. R.: Sociological correlates of child behavior. *In* H. W. Stevenson (Ed.), *Child Psychology. The Sixty-second Yearbook of the National Society for Studies in Education.* Ch. 2, University of Chicago Press, Chicago, 1963.

Cleaver, E.: *Soul on Ice.* McGraw-Hill, New York, 1968.

Clements, E. M.: Changes in the mean stature and weight of British children over the past seventy years. *Brit. Med. J. 2:* 897–902, 1953.

Clifford, E.: Discipline in the home: A controlled observational study of parental practices. *J. Genet. Psychol. 95:* 45–82, 1959.

——: Expressed attitudes in pregnancy of unwed women and married primagravida and multigravida. *Child Develop. 33:* 945–951, 1962.

Clifford, S. H.: Postmaturity with placental dysfunction. *J. Pediat. 44:* 1–13, 1954.

Cline, V. B., Richards, J. M., and Abe, C.: The validity of a battery of creativity tests in a high school sample. *Educ. Psychol. Meas. 22:* 781–784, 1962.

——, ——, and Needham, W. E.: Creativity tests and achievement in high school science. *J. App. Psychol. 47:* 184–189, 1963, (a).

——, ——, and ——: A factor analytic study of the father form of the parental attitude research instrument. *Psychol. Rec. 13:* 65–72, 1963, (b).

Cobb, H. V.: Role-wishes and general wishes of children and adolescents. *Child Develop. 25:* 161–171, 1954.

Cofer, C. N., and Appley, M. H.: *Motivation: Theory and Research.* Wiley, New York, 1964.

Coghill, G. E.: *Anatomy and the Problem of Behavior.* Macmillan, New York, 1929.

——: Integration and motivation of behavior as problems of growth. *J. Genet. Psychol. 48:* 3–19, 1936.

Cohen, A. I.: Hand preference and developmental status of infants. *J. Genet. Psychol. 108:* 337–345, 1966.

Cohen, B. D., and Klein, J. F.: Referent communication in school age children. *Child Develop. 39:* 597–609, 1968.

Cohen, I. S.: Rigidity and anxiety in a motor response. *Percept. and Motor Skills. 12:* 127–130, 1961.

Cohen, J.: The factorial structure of the WISC at age 7–6, 10–6, and 13–6. *J. Consult. Psychol. 23:* 285–289, 1959.

——, and Hansel, C. E.: The idea of independence. *Brit. J. Psychol. 46:* 178–190, 1955.

Colby, M. C., and Robertson, J. V.: Genetic studies in abstraction. *J. Comp. Psychol. 33:* 385–401, 1942.

Coleman, J. S., Campbell, E. Q., Hobson, C. J., McPartland, J., Mood, A. M., Weinfeld, F. D., and Tork, R. L.: *Equality of Educational Opportunity.* United States Government Printing Office, Washington (No. OE-38001), 1966.

Coleman, W., and Ward, A. H.: A comparison of Davis-Eells and Kuhlmann-Finch scores of children from high and low socioeconomic status. *J. Educ. Psychol. 46:* 465–469, 1955.

Coles, R.: It's the same, but it's different. *In* T. Parsons, and K. B. Clark (Eds.), *The Negro American.* Pp. 254–279, Beacon Press, Boston, 1967.

Collard, R. R.: Social and play responses of first-born and later-born infants in an unfamiliar situation. *Child Develop. 39(1):* 325–334, 1968.

Colley, T.: The nature and origins of psychological sexual identity. *Psychol. Rev. 66(3):* 165–177, 1959.

Conel, J. Le R.: *The Postnatal Development of the Human Cerebral Cortex. The Cortex of the Newborn.* Harvard University Press, Cambridge, Mass., 1939.

——: *The Postnatal Development of the Human Cerebral Cortex. The Cortex of the Three-Month Infant.* Harvard University Press, Cambridge, Mass., 1947.

————: *The Postnatal Development of the Human Cerebral Cortex. Cortex of the Six-Month Infant.* Harvard University Press, Cambridge, Mass., 1955, (b).

————: *The Postnatal Development of the Human Cerebral Cortex. Cortex of the Fifteen-Month Infant.* Harvard University Press, Cambridge, Mass., 1955, (b).

————: *The Postnatal Development of the Human Cerebral Cortex: Cortex of the Twenty-Four month Infant.* Harvard University Press, Cambridge, Mass., 1959.

Conrad, H. S., Freeman, F. N., and Jones, H. E.: Differential mental growth. *In* N. B. Henry (Ed.), *Adolescence, Forty-third Yearbook, National Society for the Study of Education.* Part I, pp. 164–184, University of Chicago Press, Chicago, 1944.

————, and Jones, H. E.: A second study of familial resemblance in intelligence: Environmental and genetic implications of parent-child and sibling correlations in the total sample. *In* G. M. Whipple (Ed.), *Thirty-ninth Yearbook, National Society for the Study of Education.* Part 2, pp. 97–141, University of Chicago Press, Chicago, 1940.

Cook, W. W., Leeds, C. H., and Callis, R.: *The Minnesota Teacher Attitude Inventory.* Psychological Corporation, New York, 1951.

Corah, N. L.: Color and form in children's perceptual behavior. *Perceptual and Motor Skills. 18(1):* 313–316, 1964.

————: The effect of instruction and performance set on color-form perception in young children. *J. Genet. Psychol. 108(2):* 351–356, 1966, (a).

————: The influence of some stimulus characteristics on color and form perception in nursery school children. *Child Develop. 37:* 205–211, 1966, (b).

————, Anthony, E. J., Painter, P., Stern, J. A., and Thurston, D.: Effect of perinatal anoxia after seven years. *Psychol Monogr. Gen. App. 79(3,* Whole No. 596), 1965.

————, and Gostodinoff, E. J.: Color-form and whole-part perception in children. *Child Develop. 37(4):* 837–842, 1966.

Cornell, E. L., and Armstrong, C. M.: Forms of mental growth patterns revealed by reanalysis of the Harvard growth data. *Child Develop. 26:* 169–204, 1955.

Corsini, D. A., Pick, A. D., and Flavell, J. H.: Production deficiency of nonverbal mediators in young children. *Child Develop. 39:* 53–58, 1968.

Cott, W. A.: Attitude measurement. *In* G. Lindzey and E. Aronson (Eds.), *Handbook of Social Psychology,* 2nd ed., Vol. 2, pp. 204–273, Addison-Wesley, Reading, Mass., 1968.

Cowan, E., Landes, S. J., and Schaet, D. E.: The effect of mild frustration on the expression of prejudiced attitudes. *J. Abnor. Soc. Psychol. 58:* 33–38, 1959.

Cowan, P. A.: The link between cognitive structure and social structure. Language development. Symposium presented at the Society for Research in Child Develop. March, 1967.

————, Langer, J., Hesvenrich, J., and Nathanson, M.: Has social learning theory refuted Piaget's theory of moral development? Unpublished draft, University of California, Berkeley, 1968.

Cowen, E. L., Zax, M., Klein, R., Izzo, L. D., and Trost, M. A.: The relation of anxiety in school children to school record, achievement and behavioral measures. *Child Develop. 36:* 685–695, 1965.

Cox, F. N.: Test anxiety and achievement behavior systems related to examination performance in children. *Child Develop. 35:* 909–915, 1964.

————: Some relationships between test anxiety, presence or absence of male persons, and boys' performance on a repetitive motor test. *J. Exptl. Child Psychol. 6(1):* 1–12, 1968.

Crandall, V.: Achievement behavior in young children. *In* W. W. Hartup and N. L. Smothergill (Eds.), *The Young Child: Review of Research.* Pp. 165–185, Publication Department, National Association for the Education of Young Children, Washington, D.C., 1967.

————: Achievement. *In* H. W. Stevenson (Ed.), *Sixty-second Yearbook, National Society for the Study of Education.* Part I. *Child Psychology.* Pp. 416–459, University of Chicago Press, Chicago, 1963.

————, Dewey, R., Katkovsky, W., and Preston, A.: Parents' attitudes and behaviors and grade school children's academic achievements. *J. Genet. Psychol. 104:* 53–66, 1964.

————, and Rabson, A.: Children's repetition choices in an intellectual achievement situation following success and failure. *J. Genet. Psychol. 97:* 161–168, 1960.

————, and Sinkeldam, C.: Children's dependent and achievement behaviors in social situations and their perceptual field dependence. *J. Personal. 32:* 1–22, 1964.

Crane, A.: Pre-adolescent gangs: A socio-psychological interpretation. *J. Genet. Psychol. 86:* 275–279, 1955.

————: Symposium. The development of moral values in children. IV: Pre-adolescent gangs and moral development of children. *Brit. J. Educ. Psychol. 28:* 201–208, 1958.

Crisswell, J. H.: Sociometric study of race cleavage in the classroom. *Arch. Psychol. 33:* No. 235, 1939.

Cron, G. W., and Pronko, N. H.: Development of the sense of balance in school children. *J. Educ. Res. 51:* 33–37, 1957.

Cronbach, L. J.: The two disciplines of scientific psychology. *Amer. Psychol. 12:* 671–684. 1957.

————: *Essentials of Psychological Testing*. Harper, New York, 1960.

————: Year-to-year correlations of mental tests: A review of the Hofstaetter analysis. *Child Develop. 38(2):* 283–289, 1967.

————: A parsimonious reinterpretation of the Wallach-Kogan data. *Amer. Educ. Res. J. 5(4):* 491–511, 1968.

————, Meehl, P. E.: Construct validity in psychological tests. *Psychol. Bull. 52:* 281–302, 1955.

Crosbie, D.: Defects of organization, both grouping and superordinate classification, on the development of memory in young children. Masters Thesis, University of Toronto, 1969.

Crosse, V. M.: *The Premature Baby*. (5th ed.), Little, Brown, New York, 1961.

Crowell, D. H.: Infant motor development. *In* Y. Brackbill (Ed.), *Infancy and Early Childhood: A Handbook and Guide to Human Development*. Pp. 123–203, Free Press, New York, 1967.

————, Yasaka, E., and Crowell, D. C.: Infants stabilimeter. *Child Develop. 35:* 525–532, 1964.

Crowley, T. M.: Effect of training upon objectivity of moral judgment of grade-school children. *J. Personal. Soc. Psychol. 8(3):* 228–232, 1968.

Cruikshank, R. M.: The development of visual size constancy in early infancy. *J. Genet. Psychol. 58:* 327–351, 1941.

Cruickshank, W. M.: The relation of physical disability to fear and guilt feelings. *Child Develop. 22:* 291–298, 1951.

Crump, E. P., Gore, P. M., and Horton, C. P.: The sucking behavior in premature infants. *Human Biol. 30:* 128–141, 1958.

Crumpton, E., Wine, D. B., and Drenick, E. J.: Effects of prolonged food deprivation on food responses to skeleton words. *J. Genet. Psychol. 76:* 179–182, 1967.

Cruse, D. P.: Socially desirable responses in relation to grade level. *Child Develop. 34:* 777–789, 1963.

Cudrin, J. M.: The relationship of chronological age, mental age, social behavior and number of siblings to the Piagetian concept of moral judgment development. *Dissertation Abstracts. 26(7):* 4072–4073, 1966.

Cunningham, K. S.: *The Measurement of Early Levels of Intelligence*. Teachers College, Columbia University, New York, 1927.

Cunningham, R.: *Understanding Group Behavior of Boys and Girls*. Teachers College, Columbia University, New York, 1951.

Curtin, J. T.: *A Factor Analysis of Verbal and Non-Verbal Tests of Intelligence*. Washington, D.C.: Catholic University of America, 1951.

Cutler, R., Heimer, C. B., Wortis, H., and Freedman, E. M.: The effects of prenatal and neonatal complications on the development of premature children at age 2½ years. *J. Genet. Psychol. 107(2):* 261–276, 1965.

Dai, B.: Some problems of personality development in Negro children. *In* C. Kluckhohn and H. A. Murray (Eds.), *Personality and Nature, Society and Culture*. Pp. 437–458, Knopf, New York, 1949.

Damborska, M., and Stepanova, P.: Problems of adaptability of institutionalized children. *Cesk. Pediat. 17:* 600–606, 1962.

D'Andrade, R. G.: Sex differences and cultural institutions. *In* E. E. Maccoby (Ed.), *The Development of Sex Differences.* Pp. 173–203, Stanford University Press, Stanford, Calif., 1966.

Darcy, N. T.: The effect of bilingualism upon the measurement of the intelligence of children of preschool age. *J. Educ. Psychol. 37:* 21–44, 1946.

Darley, F. L., and Winitz, H.: Age of first word: Review of research. *J. Speech Hearing Dis. 26:* 272–290, 1961.

David, M., and Appell, G.: A study of nursing care and nurse-infant interaction. *In* B. M. Foss (Ed.), *Determinants of Infant Behavior.* Pp. 121–135, Methuen, London, 1961.

David, P. R., and Snyder, L. H.: Genetic variability and human behavior. *In* J. H. Rohrer and M. Sherif (Eds.), *Social Psychology at the Crossroads.* Pp. 53–82, Harper, New York, 1951.

Davids, A., Holden, R. H., and Gray, G. B.: Maternal anxiety during pregnancy and adequacy of mother and child adjustment 8 months following childbirth. *Child Develop. 34:* 993–1002, 1963.

Davidson, A., and Fay, J.: Phantasy in childhood. Philosophical Library, New York, 1953.

Davis, A.: American status systems and the socialization of the child. *Amer. Sociol. Rev. 6:* 345–354, 1941, (a).

————: *Deep South: A Social Anthropological Study of Caste and Class.* University of Chicago Press, Chicago, 1941, (b).

————: Child training and social class. *In* R. G. Barker, J. S. Kounin, and H. F. Wright (Eds.), *Child Behavior and Development.* Pp. 607–620, McGraw-Hill, New York, 1943.

————: Socialization and adolescent personality. *In Adolescence. Forty-third Yearbook National Society for Studies in Education.* Part I, University of Chicago Press, Chicago, 1944.

————: *Social Class Influences Upon Learning.* Harvard University Press, Cambridge, 1948.

————, and Dollard, J.: *Children of Bondage.* American Council on Education, Washington, D.C., 1940.

————, and Havighurst, R. J.: Social class and color differences in child rearing. *Amer. Sociol. Rev. 11:* 698–710, 1946.

————, and Havighurst, R. J.: *Father of the Man.* Houghton Mifflin, Boston, 1947.

Davis, D. M.: Development in the use of proper names. *Child Develop. 8:* 270–272, 1937.

Davis, E. A.: The form and function of children's questions. *Child Develop. 3:* 57–74, 1932.

————: *The Development of Linguistic Skill in Twins, Singletons with Siblings, and Only Children from Age 5 to 10 Years.* University of Minnesota Press, Minneapolis, 1937, (a).

————: The mental and linguistic superiority of only girls. *Child Develop. 8:* 139–142, 1937, (b).

————: Accuracy versus error as a criterion in children's speech. *J. Educ. Psychol. 30:* 365–371, 1939.

Davis, O. L.: Learning about time zones: An experiment in the development of certain time and space concepts. Unpublished doctoral dissertation, Nashville, Tennessee, George Peabody College for Teachers, 1958.

Davitz, J. R.: Social perception and sociometric choice of children. *J. of Abnor. Soc. Psychol. 50:* 173–176, 1955.

Davol, S. H., Hastings, N. L., and Klein, D. A.: Effect of age, sex and speed of rotation on rotary pursuit performance by young children. *Percept. and Motor Skills. 21:* 351–357, 1965.

Dawe, H. C.: An analysis of two hundred quarrels of preschool children. *Child Develop. 5:* 139–156, 1934.

————: A study of the effect of an educational program upon language development and related mental functions in young children. *J. Exptl. Educ. 11:* 200–209, 1942.

Dawkins, N., and MacGregor, W. G.: *Gestational Age, Size and Maturity.* (Clinics in developmental medicine, No. 19). London: Spastics Society, 1965.

Dawson, W. W., and Edwards, R. W.: Motor development of retarded children. *Percept. and Motor Skills. 21:* 223–226, 1965.

Day, E. J.: The development of language in twins. *Child Develop. 3:* 179–199, 1932.

Day, H., and Berlyne, D. E.: Intrinsic motivation. *In* J. Lesser (Ed.), *Psychology and the Educational Process.* In press, Scott-Foresman Co., New York, 1969.

Dayton, G., and Jones, M.: Analysis of characteristics of fixation reflected in infants by use of direct current electro-oculography. *Neurology. 14(12):* 1152–1156, 1964.

Décarie, T. G.: *Intelligence and Affectivity in Early Childhood.* International Universities Press, New York, 1965.

De Chardin, P. T.: *The Phenomenon of Man.* Harper Torchbooks, New York, 1961.

De Charmes, R. *Personal Causation: The Affective Determinants of Behavior.* Academic Press, New York, 1968.

Deese, J., and Hulse, S. H.: *The Psychology of Learning.* (3rd ed.). McGraw-Hill, New York, 1967.

de Groat, A. F., and Thompson, G. G.: A study of the distribution of teacher approval and disapproval among sixth-grade children. *J. Exptl. Educ. 18:* 57–75, 1949.

de Groot, A. D.: The effects of war upon the intelligence of youth. *J. Abnor. Soc. Psychol. 43:* 311–317,1948.

————: War and the intelligence of youth. *J. Abnor. Soc. Psychol. 46:* 596–597, 1951.

De Guimps, R.: *Pestalozzi: His Life and Work.* Appleton, New York, 1906.

De Hirsch, K., Jansky, J., and Langford, W. S.: The oral language performance of premature children and controls. *J. Speech and Hearing Res. 29:* 60–69, 1964.

————, ————, and ————: Comparisons between prematurely and maturely born children at three age levels. *Amer. J. Orthopsychiat. 36(4):* 616–628, 1966.

Deitrich, H. F.: A longitudinal study of the Babinski and Plantar grasp reflexes. *Amer. J. Disturbed Children. 94:* 265–271, 1967.

De Jung, and Meyer, W. J.: Expected reciprocity: Grade trends in correlates. *Child Develop. 34:* 127–139, 1963.

Dell, R. Q.: Relations between behavior manifestations in the human neonate. *Child Develop. 31:* 463–477, 1960.

Della-Piana, G. M.: Searching orientation and concept learning. *J. Educ. Psychol. 48:* 245–253, 1957.

————, and Gage, N. L.: Pupils' values and the validity of the Minnesota Teacher Attitude Inventory. *J. Educ. Psychol. 46:* 167–178, 1955.

Delman, L.: The order of participation of limbs in responses to tactical stimulation of the newborn infant. *Child Develop. 6:* 98–109, 1935.

Delton, H. B.: The growth of phonemic and lexical patterns in infant language. *Language. 19:* 281–292, 1943.

Demesch, A., and Wartmann, P.: Calcification of the mandibular third molar and its relation to skeletal and chronological age in children. *Child Develop. 27:* 459–473, 1956.

Dennis, W.: A description and classification of the responses of newborn infant. *Psychol. Bull. 31:* 5–22, 1934.

————: Infant reaction to restraint: An evaluation of Watson's theory. *New York Acad. Sci. Trans. 2:* 202–217, 1940, (a).

————: *The Hopi Child.* Appleton-Century-Crofts, New York, 1940, (b).

————: The effect of cradling practices upon the onset of walking in Hopi children. *J. Genet. Psychol. 56:* 77–86, 1940, (c).

————: Infant development under conditions of restricted practice and minimum social stimulation. *Genet. Psychol. Monogr. 23:* 143–189, 1941.

————: Piaget's questions applied to a child of known environment. *J. Genet. Psychol. 60:* 307–320, 1942.

————: Animism and related tendencies in hopeless children. *J. Abnor. and Soc. Psychol. 38:* 21–36, 1943, (a).

————: Is the newborn infant's repertoire learned or instinctive? *Psychol. Rev. 50:* 203–218, 1943, (b).

————: Is the newborn infant's repertoire learned or unlearned? *In* W. Dennis (Ed.), *Readings in Child Psychology.* Pp. 46–53, Prentice-Hall, New York, 1951.

————: Cultural and developmental factors in perception. *In* R. R. Blake, and G. V. Ramsey (Eds.), *Perception: An Approach to Personality.* Pp. 148–169, Ronald Press, New York, 1952.

————, and Najarian, P.: Infant development under environmental handicap. *Psychol. Monogr. 71* (Whole No. 436), 1957.

————, and Dennis, M. G.: Does culture appreciably affect patterns of infant behavior? *J. Soc. Psychol. 12:* 305–317, 1940.

————, and Sayegh, Y.: The effect of supplementary experience on the behavioral development of infants in institutions. *Child Develop. 36:* 81–90, 1965.

Despert, J. L.: Schizophrenia in children. *Psychiat. Quart. 12:* 366–371, 1938.

————, and Pierce, H. O.: The relation of emotional adjustment to intellectual function. *Genet. Psychol. Monogr. 34:* 1–56, 1949.

Deutsch, C.: Environment and perception. *In* M. Deutsch, I. Katz, and A. R. Jensen (Eds.), *Social Class, Race, and Psychological Development.* Ch. 2, Holt, Rinehart and Winston, New York, 1968.

Deutsch, H.: *The Psychology of Women.* Grune & Stratton, New York, 1944.

————: An introduction to the discussion of the psychological problems of pregnancy. *In* M. J. Senn (Ed.), *Problems of Early Infancy.* Transactions of Second Conference, 1948. Pp. 11–17, Josiah Macy, Jr. Foundation, New York, 1949.

Deutsch, M.: Some social and personality factors in scholastic performance of minority group children. Paper read at American Psychological Association, Chicago, September, 1956.

————: The disadvantaged child and the learning process: Some social psychological and developmental considerations. *In* A. H. Passow (Ed.), *Education in Depressed Areas.* Pp. 163–179, Teachers College, Columbia University, New York, 1963.

————, and Brown, B.: Social influences in Negro-white intelligence differences. *J. Soc. Issues. 20:* 24–35, 1964.

————, Clark, K. B., Lee, R. S., and Pasamanick, B.: Some considerations as to the contributions of social, personality and racial factors to school retardation in minority group children. Paper read at the American Psychological Association Convention, Chicago, September, 1956.

————, Katz, I., and Jensen, A. R. (Eds.), *Social Class, Race, and Psychological Development.* Holt, Rinehart and Winston, New York, 1968.

Deutsche, J. M.: *The Development of Children's Concepts of Causal Relationships.* University of Minnesota Press, Minneapolis, 1937.

De Virs, R.: Constancy of generic identity in the years three to six. *Monogr. Soc. Res. Child Develop. 34(3):* 1969.

De Vore, I. (Ed.): *Primate Behavior: Field Studies on Monkeys and Apes.* Holt, Rinehart and Winston, New York, 1965.

De Vos, G.: The relation of guilt toward parents to achievement and arranged marriage among the Japanese. *Psychiat. 23:* 287–301, 1960.

Diamond, M.: A critical evaluation of the ontogeny of human sexual behavior. *Quart. Rev. Biol. 40:* 147–175, 1965.

Dienes, Z. P.: Insight into arithmetical processes. *School Rev. 72:* 183–200, 1964.

Dietrich, H. F.: A longitudinal study of the Babinsky and plantar graph reflexes in infancy. *Amer. J. Dis. Children. 94:* 265–271, 1957.

Dillon, M. S.: Attitudes of children toward their own bodies and those of other children. *Child Develop. 5:* 165–176, 1934.

Ding, G. F., and Jersild, A. T.: A study of laughing and smiling of preschool children. *J. Genet. Psychol. 40:* 452–472, 1932.

Dittman, A. T., and Goodrich, D. W.: A comparison of social behavior in normal and hyperaggressive preadolescent boys. *Child Develop. 32:* 315–327, 1961.

Dittrichova, J.: Nature of sleep in young infants. *J. App. Psychol. 17:* 543–546, 1962.

————, and Lapockava, Z.: Development of waking state in young infants. *Child Develop. 35:* 365–370, 1964.

Dobzhansky, T.: *Mankind Evolving.* Yale University Press, New Haven, 1962.

Dodwell, P. C.: Children's understanding of number and related concepts. *Canad. J. Psychol. 14:* 191–205, 1960.

Dodwell, P. C.: Children's understanding of number concepts: Characteristics of an individual and a group test. *Canad. J. Psychol. 15:* 29–36, 1961.

Doehring, D. G., and Rosenstein, J.: Visual word recognition by deaf and hearing children. *J. Speech Hearing Res. 3:* 320–326, 1960.

Doland, D. J., and Adelberg, K.: The learning of sharing behavior. *Child Develop. 38:* 695–700, 1967.

Dolger, L., and Ginandes, J.: Children's attitude toward discipline as related to socio-economic status. *J. Exptl. Educ. 15:* 161–165, 1946.

Doll, E. A.: The feeble-minded child. *In* L. Carmichael (Ed.), *Manual of Child Psychology.* Pp. 845–885, Wiley, New York, 1946.

Doris, J., and Cooper, L.: Brightness discrimination in infancy. *J. Exptl. Child Psychol. 3:* 331–339, 1966.

———, and Sarason, S. B., and Berkowitz, L.: Test anxiety and performance on projective tests. *Child Develop. 34:* 751–766, 1963.

Dorkey, M., and Amen, E. W.: A continuation study of anxiety reactions in young children by means of a projective technique. *Genet. Psychol. Monogr. 35:* 139–183, 1947.

Douglas, B. I.: Children's response to frustration: A developmental study. *Canad. J. Psychol. 19:* 161–171, 1965.

Douglas, J. W., Ross, J. M., and Simpson, H. R.: The relation between height and measured educational ability in school children of the same social class, family size and stage of physical development. *Human Biol. 37:* 178–186, 1965.

Draguns, J. G., and Multari, G.: Recognition of perceptually ambiguous stimuli in grade school children. *Child Develop. 32:* 521–550, 1961.

Dreizen, S. C., et al.: The effect of nutritive failure on the growth patterns of white children in Alabama. *Child Develop. 24:* 189–202, 1953.

Drevdahl, J. E.: Factors of importance for creativity. *J. Clin. Psychol. 12:* 21–26, 1956.

———, and Cattell, R. B.: Personality and creativity in artists and writers. *J. Clin. Psychol. 14:* 107–111, 1958.

Drillien, C. M.: Obstetric hazard, mental retardation and behavior disturbance in primary school. *Develop. Med. Child Neurology. 5:* 3–13, 1963.

———: *The Growth and Development of the Prematurely Born Infant.* Williams & Wilkins, Baltimore, 1964, (a).

———: The social and economic factors affecting the incidence of premature birth. I. Premature births without complications of pregnancy. *J. Obs. Gyn. Brit. Empire. 64:* 161–184, 1964, (b.)

———, and Ellis, R. W.: *The Growth and Development of the Prematurely Born Infant.* Williams & Wilkins, Baltimore, 1964.

Droppleman, L. F., and Schaefer, E. S.: Boys' and girls' reports of maternal and paternal behavior. *J. Abnor. Soc. Psychol. 67(6):* 648–654, 1963.

Dubin, E. R., and Dubin, R.: The authority inception period in socialization. *Child Develop. 34:* 885–898, 1963.

Dubin, R., and Dubin, E. R.: Children's social perceptions: A review of research. *Child Develop. 36(3):* 809–838, 1965.

Dubreuil, G., and Boisclair, C.: Le réalisme enfantin à la Martinique et au Canada francais: Etude génétique et expérimentale. *In Thought from the Learned Societies of Canada.* Pp. 83–95, Gage, Toronto, 1960.

Dudycha, G. J., and Dudycha, M. M.: Adolescents' memories of preschool experiences. *J. Genet. Psychol. 42:* 468–480, 1933.

——— and ———: Childhood memories: A review of the literature. *Psychol Bull. 38:* 669–681, 1941.

Dukes, W. F.: Psychological studies of values. *Psychol. Bull. 52:* 24–50, 1955.

Duncan, C. P.: Transfer after training with single versus multiple tasks. *J. Exptl. Psychol. 55:* 63–72, 1958.

Duncker, K.: Modification of children's food preferences through social suggestion. *J. Abnor. Soc. Psychol. 33:* 487–507, 1938.

Dunn, L. M.: A comparison of the reading processes of mentally retarded and normal boys of the same mental age. *Monogr. Soc. Res. Child Develop. 19:* 8–99, 1954.

Dunnington, M.: Behavior differences of sociometric status groups in a nursery school. *Child Develop. 28:* 103–111, 1957.

Dunsdon, M. I., and Roberts, J. A.: The relation of the Terman-Merrill vocabulary test to mental age in a sample of English children. *Brit. J. Stat. Psychol. 6:* 61–70, 1953.

Durkin, D.: Children's concepts of justice: A comparison with the Piaget data. *Child Develop. 30:* 59–67, 1959.

Dusenberry, L.: A study of the effects of training on ball throwing by children ages three to seven. *Res. Quart. Amer. Assoc. Health. 23:* 9–14, 1952.

Dustman, R. E., and Beck, E. C.: Visually evoked potentials: Aptitude changes with age. *Science. 151:* 1113–1115, 1966.

Dwornicka, B., Jasienska, A., Smolarz, W., and Wawryk, R.: Attempt of determining the fetal reaction to acoustic stimulation. *Acta Oto-Laryngologica. 57:* 571–574, 1964.

Dyk, R. B., and Witkin, H. B.: Family experience related to the development of differentiation in children. *Child Develop. 36:* 21–55, 1965.

Dymond, R. F., Hughes, A. S., and Raabe, V. L.: Measurable changes in empathy with age. *J. Consult. Psychol. 16:* 202–206, 1952.

Earle, A. M., and Earle, B. V.: Early maternal deprivation and later psychiatric illness. *Amer. J. Orthopsychiat. 31:* 181, 1961.

Easterbrook, J. A.: The effect of emotion on cue utilization of behavior. *Psychol. Rev. 56:* 183–201, 1950.

Eaton, M. T.: *A Survey of the Achievement in Social Studies of 10,220 Sixth Grade Pupils in 464 Schools in Indiana.* Bloomington, University of Indiana, 1944.

Eberhart, J. C.: Attitudes toward property: A genetic study by the paired-comparisons rating of offenses. *J. Genet. Psychol. 60:* 3–35, 1942.

Edel, A.: *Ethical Judgment: The Use of Science in Ethics.* The Free Press of Glencoe, Collier, Macmillan, London, 1955.

——: Scientific research and moral judgments: A philosophical perspective. Paper presented at the Conference on Studies of the Acquisition and Development of Values. National Institute of Child Health and Human Development. May, 1968.

Edwards, A. L., and English, H. B.: Reminiscence in relation to differential difficulty. *J. Exptl. Psychol. 25:* 100–108, 1939.

Edwards, J. B.: Some studies of moral development of children. *Educ. Res. 7(3):* 200–211, 1965.

Eell, K., Davis, A., Havighurst, R. J., Herrick, V. E., and Tyler, R. W.: *Intelligence and Cultural Differences: A Study of Cultural Learning and Problem-Solving.* University of Chicago Press, Chicago, 1951.

Egstrom, G. H.: Effects of an emphasis on conceptualizing techniques during early learning of a gross motor skill. *Res. Quart. 35:* 472–481, 1964.

Eichorn, D. H.: Biological correlates of behavior. *In* H. W. Stevenson (Ed.), *Sixty-second Yearbook, National Society for the Study of Education.* Part I. *Child Psychology.* Pp. 4–53, University of Chicago Press, Chicago, 1963.

——, and Bayley, N.: Growth in head circumference from birth through young adulthood. *Child Develop. 33:* 257–271, 1962.

Eisenberg, R. B., Coursin, D. B., and Rupp, N. R.: Habituation to an accoustic pattern and an index of differences among human neonates. *J. Auditory Res. 6(3):* 239–248, 1966.

——, Griffen, E. G., Coursin, D. B., and Hunter, N. A.: Auditory behavior in the human neonate: A preliminary report. *J. Speech Hearing Res. 7:* 245–269, 1964.

Eisenson, J.: When and what is aphasia? *Monogr. Soc. Res. Child Develop. 25*(3, Whole No. 77), 90–95, 1960.

Eisenstadt, S. N.: Archetypal patterns of youth. *Daedalus,* 28–46, 1962.

Eisner, E. W.: Children's creativity in art: A study of types. *Amer. Educ. Res. J. 2:* 125–136, 1965.

Elder, G. H.: Role relations, sociocultural environments and autocratic family ideology. *Sociometry. 28:* 173–196, 1965.

———: Age integration and socialization in an educational setting. *Harvard Educ. Rev. 37(4):* 594–619, 1967.

Elkind, D.: The development of quantitative thinking: A systematic replication of Piaget's studies. *J. Genet. Psychol. 98:* 37–48, 1961, (a).

———: Quantity conceptions in junior and senior high school students. *Child Develop. 32:* 551–560, 1961, (b).

———: The developmental psychology of religion. *In* A. H. Kidd, and J. L. Rivoire (Eds.), *Perceptual Development in Children.* Ch. 8, International Universities Press, New York, 1966, (a).

———: Conceptual orientation shifts in children and adolescents. *Child Develop. 37:* 493–498, 1966, (b).

———: Cognition in infancy and early childhood. *In* Y. Brackbill (Ed.), *Infancy and Early Childhood.* Pp. 361–396, The Free Press, New York, 1967.

———: Conservation in concept formation. *In* D. Elkind, and J. H. Flavell (Eds.), *Studies in Cognitive Development: Essays in Honour of Jean Piaget.* Pp. 171–190, Oxford University Press, New York, 1969.

———, and Flavell, J. H. (Eds.): *Studies in Cognitive Development: Essays in Honor of Jean Piaget.* Oxford University Press, New York, 1969.

———, and Scott, L.: Studies in perceptual development: I. The centering of perception. *Child Develop. 33:* 619–630, 1962.

Ellingson, R. J.: Response to physiological stress in normal and behavioral problem children. *J. Genet. Psychol. 83:* 19–29, 1953.

———: Electroencephalograms of normal, full-term new-borns immediately after birth with observation on arousal and visual evoked responses. *Electroencephalogram Clinic of Neurophysiology. 10:* 31–50, 1958.

———: Cortical electrical responses to visual stimulation in the human infant. *Electroencephalography and Clinical Neurophysiology*, 1960, *12:* 663–677. Reprinted *in* Y. Brackbill and G. G. Thompson (Eds.), *Behavior in Infancy and Early Childhood: A Book of Readings.* Free Press, New York, 1967.

Ellis, R. W.: Assessment of prematurity by birth weight, crown-rump length, and head circumference. *Arch. Dis. Childhood. 26:* 411–422, 1951.

Ellison, R.: *The Invisible Man.* Signet Books, New York, 1960.

Emmerich, W.: Family role concepts of children ages six to ten. *Child Develop. 32:* 609–624, 1961.

———: Variations in the parent role as a function of the parent's sex and the child's sex and age. *Merrill-Palmer Quart. 8:* 3–11, 1962.

———: Continuity and stability in early social development. *Child Develop. 35:* 311–332, 1964.

———: Continuity and stability in early social development. II. Teacher ratings. *Child Develop. 37:* 17–27, 1966.

———: Stability and change in early personality development. *In* W. W. Hartup and N. L. Smothergill (Eds.), *The Young Child: Reviews of Research.* Pp. 248–261, National Association for the Education of Young Children, Washington, 1967.

Engel, R., and Butler, B. V.: Appraisal of conceptual age in newborn infants by electro-encephalographic methods. *J. Pediat.* 386–393, 1963.

Englemann, S.: Cognitive structures related to the principle of conservation. *In* D. W. Brison, and E. V. Sullivan (Eds.), *Recent Research in the Acquisition of the Conservation of Substance.* Educational Monograph, Ontario Institute for Studies in Education, Toronto, 1967, (a).

———: Teaching formal operations to preschool advantaged and disadvantaged children. *Ontario J. Educ. Res. 9(3):* 193–207, 1967, (b).

Engen, T., and Lipsitt, L. P.: Decrement and recovery response to olfactory stimuli in the human neonate. *J. Comp. Physiol Psychol. 59:* 312–316, 1965.

————, ————, and Kaye, H.: Olfactory responses and adaptation in the human neonate. *J. Comp. Physiol. Psychol. 56(1):* 73–77, 1963.

English, H. B., Welborn, E. L., and Kilian, C. D.: Studies in substance memorization. *J. Genet. Psychol. 11:* 233–260, 1934.

Erikson, E. H.: Studies in the interpretation of play. *Genet. Psychol. Monogr. 22:* 557–671, 1940.

————: Sex differences in the play configurations of preadolescents. *Amer. J. Orthopsychiat. 21:* 667–692, 1951.

Ervin, S. M.: Training and logical operations by children. *Child Develop. 31:* 555–563, 1960.

————: Imitation and structural change in children's language. *In* E. Lenneberg (Ed.), *New Directions in the Study of Language.* Pp. 163–189, M.I.T. Press, Cambridge, Mass., 1964.

————, and Miller, W. R.: Language development. *In* H. W. Stevenson (Ed.), *Sixty-second Yearbook, National Society for the Study of Education.* Part I. *Child Psychology.* Pp. 108–143, University of Chicago Press, Chicago, 1963.

Ervin-Tripp, S.: Language development. *In* L. W. Hoffman, and M. L. Hoffman (Eds.), *Review of Child Development Research.* Vol. 2, pp. 55–106, Russell Sage Foundation, New York, 1966.

————, and Slobin, D. I.: Psycholinguistics. *Ann. Rev. Psychol. 17:* 435–474, 1966.

Escalona, S. K.: The psychological situation of mother and child upon return to the hospital. *In* M. J. Senn (Ed.), *Problems of Infancy and Early Childhood.* Transactions of the Third Conference, 1949. New York, Josiah Macy Jr. Foundation, pp. 30–51, 1950.

————: Patterns of infantile experience and the developmental process. *Psychoanalytic Study of the Child. 18:* 197–244, 1963.

————: Some determinants of individual differences. *Transactions of the New York Academy of Sciences. 27(7):* 802–816, 1965.

————, and Corman, H. M.: The validation of Piaget's hypotheses concerning the development of sensori-motor intelligence: Methodological issues. Paper presented at the Meeting of the Society for Research in Child Development. New York, 1967.

————, and Heider, G. M.: *Prediction and Outcome.* Basic Books, New York, 1959.

————, and Leitch, M.: Early phases of personality development: A non-normative study of infant behavior. *Monogr. Soc. Res. Child Develop. 17(1):* 1952.

————, and Moriarty, A.: Prediction of school-age intelligence from infant tests. *Child Develop. 32:* 597–605, 1961.

Essien-Udom, E. U.: *Black Nationalism: A Search for an Identity in America.* Laurel edition, Dell Books, New York, 1964.

Estvan, F. J.: Stability of nursery school children's social perception. *J. Exptl. Educ. 34(4):* 48–54, 1966.

Eyre, M. B., and Schmeckle, M. M.: A study of handedness, eyedness, and footedness. *Child Develop. 4:* 73–78, 1933.

Eysenck, H. J.: The contribution of learning theory. Symposium: Development of moral values in children. *Brit. J. Educ. Psychol. 29–30:* 11–21, 1959–60.

Ezekiel, L. F.: Changes in egocentricity of young children. *Child Develop. 2:* 74–75, 1931.

Falk, C. T.: Object and pattern discrimination learning by young children as a function of availability of cues. *Child Develop. 39:* 923–931, 1968.

Fantz, R. L.: Patterned vision in newborn infants. *Sci. 140:* 296–297, 1963.

————: Visual perception from birth as shown by pattern selectivity. *Ann. New York Acad. Sci. 118(21):* 793–814, 1965.

————, and Nevis, S.: Pattern preferences and perceptual-cognitive development in early infancy. *Merrill-Palmer Quart. 13(1):* 77–108, 1967.

————, Ordy, J. N., and Udelf, N. S.: Maturation of pattern vision in infants during the first six months. *J. Comp. Phsysiol. Psychol. 55:* 907–917, 1962.

Faust, O. A., Jackson, K., Cermak, E. G., Burtt, M. M., and Winkley, R.: Reducing emotional trauma in hospitalized children. Albany Research Project, Albany Medical College, Albany, N.Y., 1952.

Fawl, C.: A developmental analysis of the frequency in causal types of disturbance experienced by children. *Merrill-Palmer Quart. 8:* 13–18, 1962.

———: Disturbances experienced by children in their natural habitats. *In* R. G. Barker (Ed.), *The Stream of Behavior.* Pp. 99–126, Appleton-Century-Crofts, New York, 1963.

Feffer, N. H.: The cognitive implications of role-taking behavior. *J. Personal. 27:* 152–168, 1959.

———, and Gourevitch, V.: Cognitive aspects of role-taking in children. *J. Personal. 28:* 383–396, 1960.

———, and Suchotliff, L.: Decentering implications of social interaction. *J. Personal Soc. Psychol. 4:* 415–422, 1966.

Feifel, H., and Lorge, I.: Qualitative differences in the vocabulary responses of children. *J. Educ. Psychol. 41:* 1–18, 1950.

Felder, J. G.: Some factors determining the nature and frequency of anger and fear outbreaks in preschool children. *J. Juvenile Res. 16:* 278–290, 1932.

Feigenbaum, K. D.: Task complexity and I.Q. variables in Paiget's problem of conservation. *Child Develop. 34:* 423–432, 1963.

Feldhusen, J. F., Denny, T., and Condon, C. F.: Anxiety, divergent thinking and achievement. *J. Educ. Psychol. 56:* 40–45, 1965.

———, and Klausmeier, H. J.: Anxiety, intelligence and achievement in children of low, average, and high intelligence. *Child Develop. 33:* 403–409, 1962.

———, and Thurston, J. R.: Personality and adjustment of high and low-anxious children. *J. Educ. Res. 57:* 265–267, 1964.

Ferenczi, S.: Steps in the development of a sense of reality. *In Sex in Psychoanalysis.* Badger, Boston, 1916.

Ferguson, L. R., and Maccoby, E. E.: Interpersonal correlates of differential abilities. *Child Develop. 37(3):* 549–572, 1966.

Ferneira, A. J.: The pregnant woman's emotional attitude and its reflection on the newborn. *Amer. J. Orthopsychiat. 30:* 553–561, 1960.

Feshbach, N. D., and Roe, K.: Empathy in six- and seven-year-olds. *Child Develop. 39:* 133–145, 1968.

Festinger, L.: The motivating effect of cognitive dissonance. *In* G. Lindsley (Ed.), *Assessment of Human Motives.* Pp. 65–86, Grove, New York, 1958.

Finch, F. H.: Enrollment increases and changes in the mental level of the high school population. *App. Psychol. Monogr.* No. 10, 1946.

Finney, J. C.: Some maternal influences on children's personality and character. *Genet. Psychol. Monogr. 63:* 199–278, 1961.

Fischer, L. K.: Hospitalism in six-month-old infants. *Amer. J. Orthopsychiat. 22:* 522–533, 1952.

Fisher, M. S.: Language patterns of preschool children. *Child Develop. Monogr. 15:* 1934.

Fisher, S. C.: The process of generalizing abstraction and its product the general concept. *Psychol. Monogr. 21:* 1916.

Fisichelli, V. R., and Karelitz, S.: The cry latencies of normal infants and those with brain damage. *J. Pediat. 62:* 724–734, 1963.

———, and ———: Frequency spectra of the cries of normal infants and those with Down's Syndromes. *Psychonomic Sci. 6:* 195–196, 1966.

Fite, M. D.: Aggressive behavior in young children and children's attitudes toward aggression. *Genet. Psychol. Monogr. 22:* 151–319, 1940.

Flament, F.: Développement de la préférence manuelle de la naissance à six mois. *Enfance. 3:* 241–262, 1963.

Flanders, J. P.: A review of research on imitative behavior. *Psychol. Bull. 69(5):* 316–337, 1968.

Flanders, M. A.: *Teacher Influence, Pupil Attitudes and Achievement.* College of Education, University of Minnesota, Minneapolis, 1960.

———, and Havumaki, S.: The effect of teacher-pupil contacts involving praise on the sociometric choices of students. *J. Educ. Psychol. 51:* 65–68, 1960.

Flapan, D.: Children's understanding of social interaction. Unpublished doctoral dissertation, Columbia University, 1965.

Flavell, J. H.: Discussion of stage and structure. *In* W. Kessen and C. Kuhlman (Eds.), Thought in the young child. *Monogr. Soc. Res. Child Develop. 27:* 65–82, 1962.

————: *The Developmental Psychology of Jean Piaget.* Van Nostrand, Princeton, New Jersey, 1963.

————: The development of two related forms of social cognition: Role-taking and verbal communication. *In* A. Kidd and J. L. Rivoire (Eds.), *Perceptual Development in Children.* Pp. 246–272, International Universities Press, New York, 1966.

————: Role-taking and communication skills in children. *In* W. W. Hartup and N. L. Smothergill (Eds.), *The Young Child: Reviews of Research.* Pp. 59–76, National Association for the Education of Young Children, Washington, D.C., 1967.

————: Developmental studies of mediated memory. *In* L. P. Lipsitt and W. Reese (Eds.), *Advances in Child Development and Behavior.* Vol. 5, in press, Academic Press, New York, 1969, (a).

————: Concept development. *In* P. H. Mussen (Ed.), *Revised Edition of Carmichael's Manual of Child Psychology.* In press, Wiley, New York, 1969, (b).

————, Beach, D. R., and Chinsky, J. M.: Spontaneous verbal rehearsal in a memory test as a function of age. *Child Develop. 37(2):* 283–299, 1966.

————, Botkin, P. T., Fry, C. L., Wright, J. W., and Jarvis, P. E.: *The Development of Role-Taking and Communication Skills in Children.* Wiley, New York, 1968.

————, and Hill, J. P.: Developmental psychology. *Ann. Rev. Psychol. 20:* 1–56, 1969.

————, and Wohlwill, J. F.: Formal and functional aspects of cognitive development. *In* D. Elkind, and J. H. Flavell (Eds.), *Studies in Cognitive Development: Essays in Honor of Jean Piaget.* Pp. 67–120, Oxford University Press, Toronto, 1969.

Flescher, I.: Anxiety and achievement of intellectually gifted and creatively gifted children. *J. Psychol. 56:* 251–268, 1963.

Flick, G. L.: Sinistrality revisited: A perceptual-motor approach. *Child Develop. 37(3):* 613–622, 1966.

Flory, C. D.: Osseous development in the hand as an index of skeletal development. *Monogr. Soc. Res. Child Develop. 1(3):* 1936.

Fodor, J. A.: Could meaning be an Rm? *J. Verbal Learning Verbal Behavior. 4:* 73–81, 1965.

————: How to learn to talk: Some simple ways. *In* F. Smith and G. A. Miller (Eds.), *The Genesis of Language: A Psycholinguistic Approach.* Pp. 105–122, M.I.T. Press, Cambridge, 1966.

Fodor, N.: *In Search of the Beloved: A Clinical Study of the Trauma of Birth and Prenatal Conditioning.* Hermitage, New York, 1949.

Ford, C. S., and Beach, F. A.: *Patterns of Sexual Behavior.* Harper Hoeber, New York, 1951.

Forgus, R. H.: The effect of early perceptual learning on the behavioral organization of adult rats. *J. Comp. Physiol. Psychol. 47:* 331–336, 1954.

Forrest, T.: Paternal roots of male character development. *Psychoanalytic Rev. 54(1):* 51–68, 1967.

Foss, B. M. (Ed.): *Determinants of Infant Behavior.* Vol. I. John Wiley, New York, 1961.

———— (Ed.): *Determinants of Infant Behavior.* Vol. II, John Wiley, New York, 1963.

———— (Ed.): *Determinants of Infant Behavior.* Vol. III. John Wiley, New York, 1966.

Foster, S.: A study of personality make-up and social setting of fifty jealous children. *Men. Hygiene. 11:* 53–77, 1927.

Fowler, W.: Cognitive learning in infancy and early childhood. *Psychol. Bull. 59(2):* 116–152, 1962, (a).

Fowler, W.: Teaching a two-year-old to read: An experiment in early childhood learning. *Genet. Psychol. Monogr. 66:* 181–283, 1962, (b).

————: Concept learning in early childhood. *Young Children. 21(2):* 81–91, 1965.

————: Longitudinal study of early stimulation in the emergence of cognitive processes. Paper delivered at the Conference on Preschool Education, sponsored by the Social Science Research Council, University of Chicago, February, 1966, (a).

————: Dimensions and directions in the development of affecto-cognitive systems. *Human Develop. 9:* 18–29, 1966, (b).

————: Developmental cognitive stimulation of 3-year-old identical twins and triplets. Unpublished manuscript. The Ontario Institute for Studies in Education, Toronto, 1968.

Frail, C. M., Lundberg, S. V., and Levin, H. A.: Comparison of child-child and child-adult interaction. Paper delivered at the 1967 Annual Convention of the American Psychological Association,, September, 1967.

Frank, L. K.: The adolescent and the family. *In* N. B. Henry (Ed.), *Forty-third Yearbook, National Society for the Study of Education.* Part I. *Adolescence.* Pp. 1–7, University of Chicago Press, Chicago, 1944.

Frankena, W. K.: Toward a philosophy of moral education. *Harvard Educ. Rev. 28(4):* 300–313, 1958.

————: Toward a philosophy of moral education. *In* I. Scheffler (Ed.), *Philosophy and Education* (2nd ed.). Pp. 225–244, Allyn and Bacon, Boston, 1966.

Fraser, C., Bellugi, U., and Brown, R.: Control of grammar in imitation, comprehension and production. *J. Verbal Learning Verbal Behavior. 2:* 121–135, 1963.

Freedman, D. G.: The infant's fear of strangers and the flight response. *J. Child Psychol. Psychiat. 2:* 242–248, 1961.

————: Smiling in blind infants and the issue of innate versus acquired. *J. Child Psychol. Psychiat. 5:* 171–184, 1964.

————: An ethological approach to the genetical study of human behavior. *In* S. Vandenberg (Ed.), *Methods and Goals in Human Behavior Genetics.* Academic Press, New York, 1965.

————: Longitudinal studies in the social behavior of twins: Birth through five years. Paper presented at the American Psychological Association, 74th Annual Convention, New York, September, 1966.

————, and Keller, B.: Inheritance of behavior in infants. *Sci. 140:* 196–198, 1963.

————, Loring, C. B., and Martin, R. N.: Emotional behavior and personality development. *In* Y. Brackbill (Ed.), *Infancy and Early Childhood: A Handbook and Guide to Human Development.* Ch. 8, Free Press, New York, 1967.

Freeman, F. N., and Flory, C. D.: Growth in intellectual ability as measured by repeated tests. *Monogr. Soc. Res. Child Develop. 2(2):* 1937.

————, Holzinger, K. J., and Mitchell, C. B.: The influence of environment on the intelligence, school achievement, and conduct of foster children. *In* G. M. Whipple (Ed.), *Twenty-seventh Yearbook, National Society for the Study of Education.* Part I, pp. 103–217, University of Chicago Press, Chicago, 1928.

Freibergs, V., and Tulving, E.: The effect of practice on utilization of information from positive and negative instances in concept identification. *Canad. J. Psychol. 15:* 101–106, 1961.

French, E. G., and Thomas, F. H.: The relation of achievement motivation to problem solving. *J. Abnor Soc. Psychol. 56:* 45–48, 1958.

Frenkel-Brunswik, E.: A study of prejudice in children. *Human Relations. 1:* 295–306, 1948.

————: Pattern of social and cognitive outlooks in children and parents. *Amer. J. Orthopsychiat. 21:* 543–558, 1951.

————, and Havel, J.: Prejudice in the interviews of children. I. Attitudes toward minority groups. *J. Genet. Psychol. 82:* 91–136, 1953.

Freud, A.: *Introduction to the Technique of Child Analysis.* Nervous and Mental Disease Publishing Co., New York, 1928.

————: The mutual influences in the development of the ego and the id: Introduction to the discussion. *Psychoanalytic Study of the Child. 7:* 42–50, 1952.

————, and Burlingham, D.: *Infants Without Families.* International Universities Press, New York, 1944.

Freud, S.: *The Ego and the Id.* Hogarth, London, 1935.

————: *The Problem of Anxiety.* Norton, New York, 1936.

Fried, R. L., and Mayer, M. F.: Socio-emotional factors accounting for growth failure in children living in an institution. *J. Pediat. 33:* 444–456, 1948.

Friedlander, J. H.: Some comments on the relationship of the responsivity of the adrenal cortex in schizophrenia. *Psychiat. Quart. Suppl.*, Part I, *25:* 76–80, 1951.

Friedman, K. C.: Time concepts of elementary school children. *Elementary School Journal. 44:* 337–342, 1944.

Fries, M. E.: Play techniques in the analysis of young children. *Psychoanalytic Rev. 24:* 233–245, 1937.

————: The child's ego development and the training of adults in his environment. *Psychoanalytic Study of The Child. 2:* 85–112, 1946.

Frings, H., and Frings, M. *Animal Communication.* Blaisdell, New York, 1964.

Froebel, F.: *The Education of Man.* Appleton-Century-Crofts, New York, 1896.

Fromm, E.: Psychoanalytic characterology and its application to the understanding of culture. *In* S. S. Sargent, and M. W. Smith (Eds.), *Culture and Personality.* Pp. 1–10, Basic Books, New York, 1949.

Fry, C. L.: A developmental examination of performance in a tacit coordination game situation. *J. Personal Soc. Psychol. 5:* 277–281, 1967.

Fry, D. B.: Development of the phonological system. *In* F. Smith and G. A. Miller (Eds.), *The Genesis of Language.* Pp. 187–206, M.I.T. Press, Cambridge, 1966.

Fryatt, M. J., and Tulving, E.: Interproblem transfer in identification of concepts involving positive and negative instances. *Canad. J. Psychol. 17:* 106–117, 1963.

Fuller, J. L.: *Nature and Nurture.* Doubleday, New York, 1954.

————, and Thompson, W. R.: *Behavior Genetics.* John Wiley, New York, 1960.

Furfey, P. H.: Some factors influencing the selection of boys' chums. *J. App. Psychol. 11:* 47–51, 1927.

————: *The Growing Boy.* Macmillan, New York, 1930.

Furth, H.: Conservation of weight in deaf and hearing children. *Child Develop. 35:* 143–150, 1964.

————: Piaget's theory of knowledge: The nature of representation and interiorization. *Psychol. Rev. 75:* 143–154, 1968.

————: *Piaget and Knowledge: Theoretical Foundations.* Prentice Hall, Englewood Cliffs, New Jersey, 1969.

Gage, N. L., Leavitt, G. S., and Stone, G. C.: Teachers' understanding of their pupils and pupils' ratings of their teachers. *Psychol. Monogr. 69: (27):* 1955.

Gagné, R. M.: Instruction and the conditions of learning. *In* L. Siegel (Ed.), *Instruction: Some Contemporary Viewpoints.* Pp. 291–313, Chandler, San Francisco, 1967.

————, and Dick, W.: Learning measures in a self-instructional problem in solving equations. *Psychological Rep. 10:* 131–146, 1962.

Gairdner, D. (Ed.): *Recent Advances in Pediatrics.* 2nd ed. Little, Brown Co., Boston, 1958.

Gallagher, J. J.: Productive thinking. *In* M. L. Hoffman and L. W. Hoffman (Eds.), *Review of Child Development Research.* Vol. 1, pp. 349–381, Russell Sage Foundation, New York, 1964.

————, and Lucito, L. J.: Intellectual patterns of gifted compared with average and retarded children. *Exceptional Children. 27:* 479–482, 1961.

Galperin, P. Y.: An experimental study in the formation of mental actions. *In* B. Simon (Ed.), *Psychology in the Soviet Union.* Pp. 213–225, Stanford University Press, Stanford, California, 1957.

Garai, J. E.: Formation of the concept of self and development of sex identification. *In* A. H. Kidd and J. L. Rivoire (Eds.), *Perceptual Development in Children.* Ch. 13, International Universities Press, New York, 1966.

————, and Scheinfeld, A.: Sex differences in mental and behavioral traits. *Genet. Psychol. Monogr. 77(2):* 169–299, 1968.

Gardner, D. B., Hawkes, G. R., and Burchinal, L. G.: Noncontinuous mothering in infancy and development in later childhood. *Child Develop. 32:* 225–234, 1961.

Gardner, L. P.: An analysis of children's attitudes toward fathers. *J. Genet. Psychol. 70:* 3–28, 1947.

Gardner, R. W., Holzman, P. S., Klein, G. S., Linton, H. B., and Spence, D. P.: *A Study of Individual Consistencies in Cognitive Behavior: Psychological Issues. 1*, No. 4, International Universities Press, New York, 1959.

———, Jackson, D. N., and Messick, S. J.: Personality organization in cognitive controls and intellectual abilities. *Psychological Issues, 2*, No. 4, International Universities Press, New York, 1960.

Garn, S. M.: Individual and group deviations from 'channelwise' grid progression in girls. *Child Develop. 23:* 193–206, 1952.

———: Determinants of size and growth during the first three years. *In* S. Karger (Ed.), *Modern Problems in Pediatrics.* Pp. 50–54, Basel, New York, 1962.

———: Body size and its implications. *In* L. W. Hoffman and N. L. Hoffman (Eds.), *Review of Child Development Research.* Pp. 529–561, Russell Sage Foundation, NewYork, 1966.

———, Clark, A., Lankof, N., and Newell, L.: Parental body build and developmental progress in the offspring. *Science. 132:* 1555–1556, 1960.

———, Haskell, J. A.: Fat thickness and developmental status in childhood and adolescence. *Amer. Med. Assoc. J. Dis. Children. 99:* 746–751, 1960.

———, and Rohmann, C. G.: Communalities of the ossification centers of the hand and wrist. *The Amer. J. Phys. Anthrop. 17(4):* 319–323, 1959.

———, and Shamir, Z.: *Methods for Research in Human Growth.* Charles C Thomas Co., Springfield, Illinois, 1958.

Garrett, H. E., Bryan, A. I., and Perl, R. E.: The age factor in mental organization. *Arch. Psychol.* (Whole No. 175), 1935.

Gaspar, J. L.: Diabetes mellitus and pregnancy: Survey of 49 deliveries. *West. J. Surg., Obs. and Gyn. 53:* 21–27, 1945.

Gates, A. I.: The necessary mental age for beginning reading. *Elementary School Journal. 37:* 497–508, 1937.

———, and Scott, A. W.: Characteristics and relations of motor speed and dexterity among young children. *J. Genet. Psychol. 39:* 423–454, 1931.

———, and Taylor, G. A.: An experimental study of the nature of improvement resulting from practice on a mental function. *J. Educ. Psychol. 16:* 583–592, 1925.

Gates, G. S.: An experimental study of the growth of social perception. *J. Educ. Psychol. 14:* 449–462, 1923.

Geber, M.: The psychomotor development of African children in the first year, and the influence of maternal behavior. *J. Soc. Psychol. 47:* 185–195, 1958.

———, and Dean, R. F.: The state of development of newborn African children. *Lancet. 1:* 1216–1219, 1957.

Gehman, I. H., and Matyas, R. P.: Stability of the WISC and Binet Tests. *J. Consult. Psychol. 20:* 150–152, 1956.

Gellerman, L. W.: The double alternation problem: II. The behavior of children and human adults in a double alternation temporal maze. *J. Genet. Psychol. 39:* 197–226, 1931.

Gellert, E.: Stability and fluctuation in the power relationships of young children. *J. Abnor. and Soc. Psychol. 62:* 8–15, 1961.

Gellhorn, E.: *Biological Foundations of Emotion: Research and Commentary.* Scotts Foresman Co., Illinois, 1968.

———, and Loofbourrow, G. N.: *Emotions and Emotional Disorders.* Harper and Row, New York, 1963.

George, C.: L'anticipation dans la résolution d'une tâche complexe. *Année Psychologique. 64:* 83–100, 1964.

Gesell, A.: *Infancy and Human Growth.* Macmillan, New York, 1928.

———: Maturation and the patterning of behavior. *In* C. Murchinson (Ed.), *A Handbook of Child Psychology* (2nd ed.). Pp. 209–235, Clark University Press, Worcester, Mass., 1933.

———: *The First Five Years of Life.* Harper, New York, 1940.

———: *The Embryology of Behavior.* Harper, New York, 1945.

————: The ontogenesis of infant behavior. *In* L. Carmichael (Ed.), *Manual of Child Psychology* (2nd ed.). Pp. 335–373, Wiley, New York, 1954.

————, and Amatruda, C. S.: *Developmental Diagnosis: Normal and Abnormal Child Development.* Hoeber, New York, 1947.

————, and Ames, L. B.: Early evidences of individuality in the human infant. *J. Genet. Psychol. 47:* 339–361, 1937.

————, and ————: The development of handedness. *J. Genet. Psychol. 70:* 155–175, 1947.

————, and Halverson, H. M.: The daily maturation of infant behavior. *J. Genet. Psychol. 61:* 3–32, 1942.

————, and Ilg, F. L.: *Feeding Behavior of Infants: A Pediatric Approach to the Mental Hygiene of Early Life.* Lippincott, Philadelphia, 1937.

————, and ————: *Infant and Child in the Culture of Today.* Harper and Row, New York, 1943.

————, and ————: *The Child from Five to Ten.* Harper and Row, New York, 1946.

————, and Thompson, H.: Learning and growth in identical infant twins. *Genet. Psychol. Monogr. 6:* 1–24, 1929.

————, and ————: Twins T and C from infancy to adolescence: A biogenetic study of individual differences by the method of co-twin control. *Genet. Psychol Monogr. 24:* 3–121, 1941.

Getzels, J. W., and Jackson, P. W.: *Creativity and Intelligence: Explorations with Gifted Students.* Wiley, New York, 1962.

Gevlawiczowa, N. C.: Reaction time as a developmental trait connected with sex. *Psychologia Wychowawcza. 18:* 39–45, 1961.

Gewirtz, H. B., and Gewirtz, J. L.: Caretaking settings, background events, and behavior differences in four Israeli child-rearing environments: Some preliminary trends. *In* B. M. Foss (Ed.), *Determinants of Infant Behavior.* Methuen, London, 1968.

Gewirtz, J. L.: A learning analysis of the effects of normal stimulation, privation and deprivation on the acquisition of social motivation and attachment. *In* B. M. Foss (Ed.), *Determinants of Behavior.* Pp. 213–299, Methuen, London (Wiley, New York), 1961.

————: The cause of infant smiling in four child-rearing environments in Israel. *In* B. Foss (Ed.), *Determinants of Infant Behavior,* III. Pp. 205–260, Methuen, London (Wiley, New York), 1965.

————: Mechanisms of social learning: Some roles of stimulation in behavior in early human development. *In* D. A. Goslin (Ed.), *Handbook of Socialization Theory and Research.* Ch. 2, Rand-McNally, Chicago, 1968, (a).

————: The role of stimulation in models for child development. *In* L. L. Dittmann (Ed.), *Early Child Care: The New Perspectives.* Atherton Press, New York, 1968, (b).

————, and Stingle, K. G.: Learning of generalized imitation as the basis for identification. *Psychol. Rev. 75(5):* 374–397, 1968.

Ghesquiere, J. L.: Interdependence analysis of physical performance and growth in boys. *Annales Paediatriae Fenniae. 4:* Suppl. 11, 1958.

Ghosh, E. S., and Sinha, D.: A study of parental role-perception in siblings. *J. Psychol. Res. 10(1):* 8–18, 1966.

Gibby, R. G., and Gabler, R.: The self-concept of Negro and white children. *J. Clin. Psychol. 23(2):* 144–148, 1967.

Gibson, E. J.: Perceptual development. *In* H. W. Stevenson (Ed.), *Child Psychology. Sixty-second Yearbook, National Society for the Study of Education,* Part I. Ch. 4, University of Chicago Press, Chicago, Ill., 1963.

Gibson, E.: *Perceptual Learning.* In press, Prentice-Hall, Englewood-Cliffs, N.J., 1969.

Gibson, E. J., and Olum, V.: Experimental methods of studying perception in children. *In* P. Mussen (Ed.), *Handbook of Research Methods in Child Development.* Ch. 8, Wiley, New York, 1960.

————, and Walk, R. D.: The effect of prolonged exposure to visually presented patterns on learning to discriminate between them. *J. Comp. Physiol. and Psychol. 49:* 239–242, 1956.

Gibson, J. J.: Social psychology and the psychology of perceptual learning. *In* M. Sherif and M. O. Wilson (Eds.), *Group Relations at the Crossroads*. Pp. 120–138, Harper, New York, 1953.

————: *The Senses Considered as Perceptual Systems*. Houghton Mifflin Co., Boston, 1966.

————, and ————: Perceptual learning: Differentiation or enrichment? *Psychol. Rev. 62:* 32–41, 1955.

Gilinsky, A. S.: Relative self-estimate and the level of aspiration. *J. Exptl. Psychol. 39:* 256–259, 1949.

Gilliland, A. R.: Socio-economic status and race as factors in infant intelligence test scores. *Child Develop. 22:* 271–273, 1951.

Gilmore, J. B.: The role of anxiety and cognitive factors in children's play behavior. *Child Develop. 37:* 397–416, 1966.

Ginzburg, H., and Opper, S.: *Piaget's Theory of Intellectual Development: An Introduction*. Prentice Hall, Englewood Cliffs, N.J., 1969.

Glick, J., and Wapner, S.: Development of transitivity: Some findings and problems of analysis. *Child Develop. 39:* 621–638, 1968.

Glidewell, J. C. (Ed.): *Parental Attitudes and Child Behavior*. Charles C Thomas, Springfield, Ill., 1961.

————, Kantor, M. C., Smith, L. M., and Stringer, L. A.: Socialization and social structure in the classroom. *In* M. L. Hoffman and L. W. Hoffman (Eds.), *Review of Child Development Research*. Vol. 2, pp. 221–256, Russell Sage Foundation, New York, 1966.

Glucksberg, S., and Krauss, R. M.: Studies of the development of interpersonal communication. Paper read at Symposium on Language Development, Society for Research on Child Development, New York, March, 1967.

————, Krauss, R. M., and Weisberg, R.: Referential communication in nursery school children: Method and some preliminary findings. *J. Exptl. Child Psychol. 3:* 333–342, 1966.

Glueck, S., and Glueck, E.: *Unravelling Juvenile Delinquency*. Commonwealth Fund, New York, 1950.

Gobatos, L. A.: Relationships and age differences in growth measures and motor skills. *Child Develop. 30:* 333–340, 1959.

Gochman, D. S.: A systematic approach to adaptability. *Percept. and Motor Skills. 23:* 759–769, 1966.

Goddard, H. H.: *The Kallikak Family*. Macmillan, New York, 1912.

Goerdzen, S. N.: Factors relating to opinions of seventh grade children regarding the acceptability of certain behaviors in the peer group. *J. Genet. Psychol. 94:* 29–34, 1959.

Goff, R. M.: *Problems and Emotional Difficulties of Negro Children*. Teachers College, Columbia University, New York, 1949.

Gold, M.: Power in the classroom. *Sociometry. 21:* 50–60, 1958.

Golden, M., and Birns, B.: Social class and cognitive development in infancy. Paper presented at the Meeting of the Society for Research in Child development, New York, 1967.

Goldenberg, S.: An exploratory study of some aspects of idiopathic language retardation. *J. Speech Hearing Dis. 15:* 221–223, 1950.

Goldfarb, W.: Effects of early institutional care on adolescent personality. *J. Exptl. Educ. 12:* 106, 1943.

————: Effects of psychological deprivation in infancy and subsequent stimulation. *Amer. J. Psychiat. 102:* 18–33, 1945, (a).

————: Psychological privation in infancy and subsequent adjustment. *Amer. J. Orthopsychiat. 15:* 247–255, 1945, (b).

Goldfrank, E.: Socialization, personality, and the structure of Pueblo society. *Amer. Anthrop. 47:* 516–539, 1945.

Goldman, A. E., and Levine, M.: A developmental study of object sorting. *Child Develop. 34:* 649–666, 1963.

Goldman, R. J.: The application of Piaget's schema of operational thinking to religious story data by means of the Guttman scalogram. *Brit. J. Educ. Psychol. 35:* 158–170, 1965.

Goldschmid, M. L.: Different types of conservation and nonconservation and their relation to age, sex, I.Q., MA, and vocabulary. *Child Develop. 38:* 1229–1246, 1967.

Goldstein, K.: The smiling of the infant and the problem of understanding the 'other'.
Child Psychol. 44: 175–191, 1957.

Goldstone, S., and Goldfarb, J. L.: The perception of time by children. *In* A. H. Kidd and
J. L. Rivoire (Eds.), *Perceptual Development in Children.* Ch. 16, International Universities
Press, New York, 1966.

Gollin, E. S.: Some research problems for developmental psychology. *Child Develop. 27:*
223–235, 1956.

————: Organizational characteristics of social judgments: A developmental investigation.
J. Personal. 26: 139–154, 1958.

————: Organizational characteristics of social judgment: A developmental investigation.
J. Personal. 26: 139–154, 1958.

————: Developmental approach to learning and cognition. *In* L. P. Lipsitt and C. C.
Spiker (Eds.), *Advances in Child Development and Behavior.* Vol. 2, pp. 159–186, Academic
Press, New York, 1965.

————, Saravo, A., and Salten, C.: Perceptual distinctiveness and oddity-problem solving
in children. *J. Exptl. Child Psychol. 5:* 586–596, 1967.

Goodenough, F. L.: Inter-relationships in the behavior of young children. *Child Develop. 1:*
29–47, 1930.

————: Anger in young children. *Inst. Child Welfare Monogr.* (9): 1931, (a).

————: The expression of the emotions in infancy. *Child Develop. 2:* 96–101, 1931, (b).

————: Expression of the emotions in a blind-deaf child. *J. Abnor. and Soc. Psychol. 27:*
328–333, 1932.

————: The development of the reactive process from early childhood to maturity. *J.
Exptl. Psychol. 18:* 431–450, 1935.

————: New evidence on environmental influence on intelligence. *In* G. M. Whipple (Ed.),
Thirty-ninth Yearbook, National Society for the Study of Education. Part I, pp. 307–365,
University of Chicago Press, Chicago, 1940.

Goodlad, J. I.: Some effects of promotion and non-promotion upon the social and personal
adjustment of children. *J. Exptl. Educ. 22:* 301–328, 1954.

Goodman, M. E.: *Race Awareness in Young Children.* Addison-Wesley, Cambridge, Mass.,
1952.

Goodman, N., Richardson, S. A., Dornbusch, S. N., and Hastorf, A. H.: Variant reactions
to physical disabilities. *Amer. Soc. Rev. 28:* 429–435, 1963.

Goodman, P.: *Compulsory Mis-Education.* Horizon Press, New York, 1964.

Goodnow, J. J.: A test for milieu effects with some of Piaget's tasks. Paper read at the
Eastern Psychological Association, Atlantic City, April, 1962.

————: Problems in research on culture and source. *In* D. Elkind and J. H. Flavell (Eds.),
Studies in Cognitive Development: Essays in Honor of Jean Piaget. Pp. 429–462, Oxford
University Press, New York, 1969.

————, and Bethon, G.: Piaget's tasks: The effects of schooling and intelligence. *Child
Develop. 37:* 574–582, 1966.

Goodrich, F. W., Jr.: *Natural Childbirth.* Prentice-Hall, New York, 1950.

Gordon, C., and Shea, P. D.: Self-conceptions in family structures of disadvantaged
youths. An interim report for the Director of Upward Bound. Prepared for presentation
during Session 89 on Poverty at the Sixty-second Annual Meeting of the American
Sociological Association in San Francisco, California, August, 1967.

————, and Spence, D. P.: The facilitating effects of food set and food deprivation on
responses to a subliminal food stimulus. *J. Personal. 34:* 406–415, 1966.

Gordon, H.: Mental and scholastic tests among retarded children: An enquiry into the
effects of schooling on the various tests. *Educ. Pamphlets, Board of Educ.* London, No. 44,
1923.

Gordon, N. S., and Bell, R. Q.: Activity in the human newborn. *Psychol. Rep. 9:* 103–116,
1961.

Goslin, D. A.: Accuracy of self-perception and social acceptance. *Sociometry. 25(3):* 283–296, 1962.

—— (Ed.): *Handbook of Socialization Theory and Research.* Rand McNally, Chicago, 1968.

Gotts, E. E.: A note on cross-cultural by age-group comparisons of anxiety scores. *Child Develop. 39:* 945–947, 1968.

Gottschaldt, K., and Frühauf-Ziegler, C.: Über die Entwicklung der Zusammenarbeit im Kleinkinderalter. (On the development of cooperative behavior in young children.) *Zeitschrift für Psychologie. 162:* 254–278, 1958.

Gough, H. G., and Delcourt, N. J.: Developmental increments in perceptual activity among Swiss and American school children. *Develop. Psychol. 1(3):* 265–279, 1969.

——, Barris, D. B., Martin, W. E., and Edwards, M.: Children's ethnic attitudes: I. Relationship to certain personality factors. *Child Develop. 21:* 83–91, 1950.

Gould, R.: Some sociological determinants of goal strivings. *J. Soc. Psychol. 13:* 461–473, 1941.

Goussis, A.: Influence des accouchements rapides sans douleurs sur l'état cérébral de l'enfant (Influence of painless type labor on the mental state of infants). *Acta Neurologica Belgica. 58:* 512–520, 1958.

Govatos, A.: Relationships and age differences in growth measures and motor skills. *Child Develop. 30:* 333–340, 1959.

Graham, F. K., Caldwell, B. M., Ernhart, C. B., Pennoyer, M. M., and Hartmann, A. F.: Anoxia as a significant perinatal experience: A critique. *J. Pediat. 50:* 556–569, 1957.

——, Matarazzo, R. G., and Caldwell, D. M.: Behavioral differences between normals and traumatized newborns: II. Standardization, reliability and validity. *Psychol. Monogr. 70(21),* 1956.

Graham, L. R.: The maturational factor in humans. *J. Clin. Psychol. 14:* 326–328, 1958.

Graham, S. K., Pennoyer, N. M., Caldwell, B. M., Greenman, N., and Hartmann, A. F.: Relationship between clinical status and behavior test performance in the newborn group with histories suggesting anoxia. *J. Pediat. 50:* 177–189, 1957.

Grant, E. I.: The effect of certain factors in the home environment upon child behavior. *University of Iowa Studies in Child Welfare, 17:* 61–94, 1939.

Gratch, G.: Response alteration in children: A developmental study of orientations to uncertainty. *Vita Humana. 7:* 49–69, 1964.

Gray, P. H.: Theory and evidence of imprinting in human infants. *J. Psychol. 46:* 155–166, 1958.

Gray, S. W., and Klaus, R. A.: An experimental preschool program for culturally deprived children. *Child Develop. 36:* 887–898, 1965.

Green, E. H.: Friendships and quarrels among preschool children. *Child Develop. 4:* 237–252, 1933, (a).

——: Group play and quarreling among preschool children. *Child Develop. 4:* 302–307, 1933 (b).

Greenberg, H., Chase, A. L., and Cannon, T. M.: Attitudes of white and Negro high school students in a west Texas town toward school integration. *J. App. Psychol. 41:* 27–31, 1957.

——, and Fane, D.: An investigation of several variables as determinants of authoritarianism. *J. Soc. Psychol. 49:* 195–211, 1959.

Greenberg, P. J.: Competition in children: An experimental study. *Amer. J. Psychol. 44:* 221–248, 1932.

Greene, E. B.: *Measurements of Human Behavior.* Odyssey, New York, 1952.

Greene, K. B.: Relations between kindergarten and nursery school. *Childhood Educ. 7:* 352–355, 1930.

Greenfield, P. M.: On culture and conservation. *In* J. S. Bruner (Ed.), *Studies in Cognitive Growth.* Pp. 225–256, Wiley, New York, 1966.

——, and Bruner, J. S.: Culture and cognitive growth. *Internat. J. Psychol. 1(2):* 89–107, 1966.

Greenstein, F. E.: *Children and Politics.* Yale University Press, New Haven, 1965.

Greenwald, H. J.: Reported magnitude of self-misidentification among Negro children—artifact? *J. Personal. Soc. Psychol. 8:* 49–52, 1968.

Gregoire, A.: *L'apprentissage du langage. I: Les deux premières années.* Droz, Paris, 1937.

Gregor, H. J., and McPherson, B. A.: Racial attitudes among white and Negro children in a deep-south standard metropolitan area. *J. Soc. Psychol. 68:* 95–106, 1966.

Gregory, I.: Studies of parental deprivation in psychiatric patients. *Amer. J. Psychiat. 115:* 432–442, 1958.

Greulich, W. W.: The rationale of assessing the developmental status of children from roentgenograms of the hand and wrist. *Child Develop. 21:* 33–44, 1950.

———, Crimson, C. S., and Turner, M. L.: The physical growth and development of children who survived the atomic bombing of Hiroshima and Nagasaki. *J. Pediat. 43:* 121–145, 1953.

———, and Pyle, S. I.: *Radiograph Atlas of the Skeletal Development of the Hand and Wrist.* (2nd ed.) Stanford University Press, Stanford, California, 1959.

Griffiths, J. A., Shantz, T. A., and Sigel, I. E.: A methodological problem in conservation studies: The use of relational terms. *Child Develop. 38(3):* 841–848, 1967.

Griffiths, W.: *Behavior Difficulties of Children as Perceived and Judged by Parents, Teachers and Children Themselves.* University of Minnesota Press, Minneapolis, 1952.

Grigsby, O. J.: An experimental study of the development of concepts of relationship in preschool children as evidenced by their expressive ability. *J. Exptl. Educ. 1:* 144–162, 1932.

Grodskaya, N. V.: On the development of thinking of pupils in the process of mastery of homogeneous concepts. *Voprosy Psikhologii. 3:* 106–116, 1962.

Gronlund, N. E.: The accuracy of teachers' judgments concerning the sociometric status of sixth-grade pupils. *Sociometry. 13:* 197–225, 329–357, 1950.

———: Generality of sociometric status over criteria in measurement of social acceptability. *Elementary School J. 56:* 173–176, 1955, (a).

———: The relative stability of classroom social status with unweighted and weighted sociometric choices. *J. Educ. Psychol. 46:* 345–354, 1955, (b).

Grosser, D., Polansky, N., and Lippitt, R.: A laboratory study of behavioral contagion. *Human Relations. 4:* 115–142, 1951.

Gruber, S.: The concept of task orientation in the analysis of play behavior of children entering kindergarten. *Amer. J. Orthopsychiat. 24:* 326–335, 1954.

Gruen, G. E.: Experiences affecting the development of number conservation in children. *Child Develop. 36:* 964–979, 1965.

Guerney, B., Stover, L., and De Meritt, S.: A measurement of empathy in parent-child interaction. *J. Genet. Psychol. 112(1):* 49–55, 1968.

Guilford, J. P.: Creativity. *Amer. Psychol. 9:* 444–454, 1950.

———: Three faces of intellect. *Amer. Psychol. 14:* 469–479, 1959.

———: Zero correlations among tests of intellectual abilities. *Psychol. Bull. 61:* 401–404, 1964.

———: Intelligence: 1965 model. *Amer. Psychol. 21:* 20–26, 1966.

———, and Merrifield, P. R.: The structure of the intellect model: Its uses and implications. *Reps. Psychol. Lab.* University of Southern California, Los Angeles, *24:* 1960.

———, Wilson, R. C., Christensen, P. R., and Lewis, D. J.: A factor-analytic study of creative thinking. I: Hypotheses and description of tests. *Reps. Psychol. Lab.* University of Southern California, Los Angeles, *4:* 1951.

Guillaume, P.: Les débuts de la phrase dans le language de l'enfant. *Journal de Psychologie Normale et Pathologique. 24:* 1–26, 1927.

Gullickson, G. R., and Corwell, D. H.: Neonatal habituation to electro-tactual stimulation. *J. Exptl. Child Psychol. 1:* 388–396, 1964.

Gump, P., Schoggen, P., and Redl, F.: The camp milieu and its immediate effects. *J. Soc. Issues. 13(1):* 40–46, 1957.

Gutteridge, M. V.: *The Duration of Attention in Young Children.* University of Melbourne Press, Melbourne, Australia, 1935.

———: A study of motor achievements of young children. *Arch. Psychol. 244:* 1939.

Hagen, J. W.: The effect of distraction on selective attention. *Child Develop. 38:* 685–694, 1967.

———, and Kingsley, P. R.: Labelling effects in a short-term memory. *Child Develop. 39:* 113–121, 1968.

Hagen, P. E.: A factor analysis of the Weschler Intelligence Scale for Children. *Dissertation Abstracts. 12:* 722–723, 1952.

Hagerman, D. D., and Villier, C. A.: The transfer of fructose by human placenta. *J. Clin. Investigation. 31:* 911–913, 1952.

Haggard, E. A.: Social status and intelligence: An experimental study of certain cultural determinants of measured intelligence. *Genet. Psychol. Monogr. 49:* 141–186, 1954.

Haggerty, A. D.: The effects of long-term hospitalization or institutionalization upon language development of children. *J. Genet. Psychol. 94:* 205–209, 1959.

Hagman, R. R.: A study of fears of children of preschool age. *J. Exptl. Educ. 1:* 110–130, 1932.

Haith, M. M.: The response of the human newborn to visual movement. *J. Exptl. Child Psychol. 3(3):* 235–243, 1966.

Hale, C. J.: Changing growth patterns of the American child. *Educ. 78:* 467–470, 1953.

Hall, C., and Lindsey, G.: *Theories of Personality*. Wiley, New York, 1957.

Hall, G. S.: *Adolescence*. 2 vols. Appleton-Century-Crofts, New York, 1904.

Haller, N. W.: The reactions of infants to changes in the intensity and pitch of pure tone. *J. Genet. Psychol. 40:* 162–180. 1932.

Halliday, J. L.: *Psychosocial Medicine*. Norton, New York, 1948.

Hallowell, A. I.: Culture, personality, and society. *In* A. L. Kroeber (Ed.), *Anthropology Today*. Pp. 507–523, University of Chicago Press, Chicago, 1953.

Halpern, E.: The effects of incompatibility between perception and logic in Piaget's stage of concrete operations. *Child Develop. 36(2):* 491–497, 1965.

Halverson, H. M.: An experimental study of prehension in infants by means of systematic cinema records. *Genet. Psychol. Monogr. 10:* 110–286, 1931.

———: Studies of the grasping responses of early infancy. (I, II, III). *J. Genet. Psychol. 51:* 371–449, 1937.

———: Genital and sphincter behavior of the male infant. *J. Genet. Psychol. 56:* 95–136, 1940.

———: Variations in pulse and respiration during different phases of infant behavior. *J. Genet. Psychol. 59:* 259–330, 1941.

———: Mechanisms of early infant feeding. *J. Genet. Psychol. 64:* 185–223, 1944.

Hamburg, D. A., and Lunde, D. T.: Sex hormones in the development of sex differences in human behavior. *In* E. E. Maccoby (Ed.), *The Development of Sex Differences*. Pp. 1–24, Stanford University Press, Stanford, California, 1966.

Hamilton, G. V.: A study of perseverance reactions in primates and rodents. *Behavior Monogr. 3(2):* 1916.

Hammer, E. F.: Frustration-aggression hypothesis extended to socioracial areas: Comparison of Negro and white children's H-T-P's. *Psychiat. Quart. 27:* 596–607, 1953.

———: *Creativity: An Exploratory Investigation of the Personalities of Gifted Adolescent Artists*. Random House, New York, 1961.

Hampson, J. L., and Hampson, J. G.: The ontogenesis of sexual behavior in man. *In* W. C. Young (Ed.), *Sex and Internal Secretions*. Vol. II. Pp. 1401–1432, Williams & Wilkins, Baltimore, 1961.

Handel, G.: Psychological study of whole families. *Psychol. Bull. 63:* 19–41, 1965.

Handlon, B. J., and Gross, P.: The development of sharing behavior. *J. Abnor. Soc. Psychol. 59:* 425–428, 1959.

Hanfmann, E.: Social structure of a group of kindergarten children. *Amer. J. Orthopsychiat. 5:* 407–410, 1935.

Hanks, L.: The locus of individual differences in certain primitive cultures. *In* S. S. Sargent, and M. W. Smith (Eds.), *Culture and Personality*. Pp. 107–123, Basic Books, New York, 1949.

Hanley, C.: Physique and reputation of junior high school boys. *Child Develop. 22:* 247–260, 1951.

Hare, P. A.: Situational differences in leisure behavior. *J. Abnor. and Soc. Psychol. 55:* 132–135, 1957.

Hare, R. N.: *The Language of Morals.* Oxford University Press, New York, 1952.

————: *Freedom and Reason.* Oxford University Press, New York, 1963.

Harlow, H. F.: The formation of learning sets. *Psychol. Bull. 56:* 51–65, 1949.

————: Learning and satiation of response in intrinsically motivated complex puzzle performance by monkeys. *J. Comp. and Phsysiol. Psychol. 43:* 289–294, 1950.

————: Levels of integration along the phyletic scale: Learning aspect. *In* J. H. Rohrer and M. Sherif (Eds.), *Social Psychology at the Crossroads.* Pp. 121–141, Harper, New York, 1953.

————: The nature of love. *Amer. Psychol. 13:* 673–685, 1958.

————: The development of affectional patterns in infant monkeys. *In* B. Foss (Ed.), *Determinants of Infant Behavior.* Pp. 75–89, Methuen, London, 1961.

————: The maternal affectional system. *In* B. Foss (Ed.), *Determinants of Infant Behavior.* II. Pp. 3–33, Methuen, London, 1963.

————, and Zimmermann, R. R.: Affectional responses in the infant monkey. *Science. 130:* 421–432, 1959.

Harootunian, B., and Tate, M.: The relationship of certain selected variables to problem solving ability. *J. Educ. Psychol. 51:* 326–333, 1960.

Harris, D. B., Clark, K. E., Rose, A. M., and Valasek, F.: The measurement of responsibility in children. *Child Develop. 25:* 21–28, 1954, (a).

————, Clark, K. E., Rose, A. M., and Valasek, F.: The relationship of children's home duties to an attitude of responsibility. *Child Develop. 25:* 29–33, 1954, (b).

————, Gough, H. G., and Martin, W. E.: Children's ethnic attitudes: II. Relationship to parental beliefs concerning child training. *Child Develop. 21:* 169–181, 1950.

————, and Tseng, S. C.: Children's attitudes towards peers and parents as revealed by sentence completions. *Child Develop. 28:* 401–411, 1957.

Harris, E. K.: The responsiveness of kindergarten children to the behavior of their fellows. *Monogr. Soc. Res. Child Develop. 11(2):* 1946.

Harris, J. A., Jackson, C. M., Paterson, D. G., and Scammon, R. F.: *The Measurement of Man.* University of Minnesota Press, Minneapolis, 1930.

Harris, R. E., and Thompson, C. W.: The relation of emotional adjustment to intellectual function. *Psychol. Bull. 44:* 283–287, 1947.

Harrower, N. R.: Social status and moral development. *Brit. J. Educ. Psychol. 4:* 75–95, 1935.

Hart, I.: Maternal child-rearing practices and authoritarian ideology. *J. Abnor. and Soc. Psychol. 55:* 232–237, 1957.

Hartford, T., and Cutter, H. S.: Cooperation among Negro and white boys and girls. *Psychol. Rep. 18:* 818, 1966.

Hartley, E. L.: Psychological problems of multiple group membership. *In* J. H. Rohrer, and M. Sherif (Eds.), *Social Psychology at the Crossroads.* Pp. 381–387, Harper and Row, New York, 1951.

Hartley, E. L., Rosenbaum, M., and Schwartz, S.: Children's use of ethnic frames of reference: An exploratory study of children's conceptualization of multiple ethnic membership. *J. Psychol. 26:* 367–386, 1948, (a).

————, ————, and ————,: Schwartz, S.: Children's perception of ethnic group membership. *J. Psychol. 26:* 387–398, 1948, (b).

Hartman, D. M.: The hurdle jump as a measure of the motor proficiency of young children. *Child Develop. 14:* 201–211, 1943.

Hartmann, H.: The mutual influences in the development of the ego and the id. *Psychoan. Study Child. 7:* 9–30, 1952.

————: *Psychoanalysis in Moral Values.* International Universities Press, New York, 1960.

Hartshorne, H., and May, M. A.: *Studies in the Nature of Character*. Vol. I: *Studies in Deceit*. Vol. II: *Studies in Self-Control*. Vol. III: *Studies in the Organization of Character*. Macmillan, New York, 1928–1930.

Hartson, L.: Does college training influence test intelligence? *J. Educ. Psychol. 27:* 481–491, 1936.

Hartup, W. W.: Dependence and independence. *In* H. W. Stevenson (Ed.), *Sixty-second Yearbook, National Society for the Study of Education*. Part I. *Child Psychology*. Pp. 333–363, University of Chicago Press, Chicago, 1963.

———, Glazer, J. A., and Charlesworth, R.: Peer reinforcement and sociometric status. *Child Develop. 38:* 1917–1924, 1967.

———, and Himeno, Y.: Social isolation versus interaction with adults in relation to aggression in preschool children. *J. Abnor. and Soc. Psychol. 59:* 17–22, 1959.

———, and Zook, E. A.: Sex-role preference in three- and four-year-old children. *J. Consult. Psychol. 24:* 420–426, 1960.

Harvey, O. J., Hunt, D. E., and Schroder, H. M.: *Conceptual Systems and Personality Organization*. Wiley, New York, 1961.

———, Prather, M., White, B. J., and Hoffmeister, J. K.: Teachers' beliefs, classroom atmosphere and student behavior. *Amer. Educ. Res. J. 5:* 151–166, 1968.

———, and Rutherford, J.: Status in the informal group: Influence and influencibility at differing age levels. *Child Develop. 31:* 377–385, 1960.

———, and Sherif, M.: Level of aspiration as a case of judgmental activity in which ego-involvements operate as factors. *Sociometry. 14:* 121–147, 1951.

———, White. B. J., Prather, M., Alter, R. D., and Hoffmeister, J. K.: Teachers' belief systems and preschool atmosphere. *J. Educ. Psychol. 57:* 373–381, 1966.

Harvey, W. A., and Sherfey, M. J.: Vomiting in pregnancy, a psychiatric study. *Psychosom. Med. 16:* 1–9, 1954.

Hasselmann-Kahlert, M.: Einige Beobachtungen bei entwurzelten Kleinst-und Klein-kindern. *Praxis de Kinderpsychologie und Kinderpsychiatrie. 2:* 15–18, 1953.

Hatfield, J. S., Ferguson, L. R., and Alpert, R.: Mother-child interaction and the socialization process. *Child Develop. 38:* 365–414, 1967.

Hattwick, B. W.: The influence of nursery school attendance upon the behavior and personality of the preschool child. *J. Expt.. Educ. 5:* 180–190, 1936.

Hattwick, L.: Sex differences in behavior of nursery school children. *Child Develop. 8:* 343–350, 1937.

Hattwick, L. A., and Sanders, M. K.: Age differences in behavior at the nursery school level. *Child Develop. 9:* 27–47, 1938.

Hausmann, M. F.: A test to evaluate some personality traits. *J. Genet. Psychol. 9:* 179–189, 1933.

Havighurst, R. J., and Janke, L. I.: Relations between ability and social status in a mid-Western community. I. Ten-year-old children. *J. Educ. Psychol. 35:* 357–368, 1944.

———, and Breese, F. H.: Relation between ability and social status in a mid-Western community. III. Primary mental abilities. *J. Educ. Psychol. 38:* 241–247, 1947.

———, Robinson, M. Z., and Dorr, M.: The development of the ideal self in childhood and adolescence. *J, Educ. Res. 40:* 241–257, 1946.

———, and Taba, H.: *Adolescent Character and Personality*. Wiley, New York, 1949.

Hayes, C.: *The Ape in Our House*. Harper and Row, New York, 1951.

Haygood, R. C., and Bourne, L. E.: Forms of relevant stimulus redundancy in concept identification. *J. Exptl. Psychol. 67:* 392–397, 1964.

Haynes, H., White, B. L., and Held, R.: Visual accommodation in human infants. *Science. 148:* 528–530, 1965.

Hays, W. L.: *Statistics for Psychologists*. Holt, Rinehart and Winston, New York, 1963.

Haworth, M. R.: Repeat study with a projective film for children. *J. Consult. Psychol. 25:* 78–83, 1961.

———: Responses of children to a group projective film and to the Rorschach, CAT, Despert Fables and the D-A-P. *Journal of Projective Techniques. 26:* 47–60, 1962.

Hazlitt, V.: Children's thinking. *Brit. J. Psychol. 20:* 354–361, 1930.

Healey, W., and Bronner, A. F.: *New Light on Delinquency and Its Treatment*. Yale University Press, New Haven, 1936.

——, and Bronner, A. F.: What makes a child delinquent? *In* N. B. Henry (Ed.), *Juvenile Delinquency and the Schools. Forty-seventh Yearbook, National Society for the Study of Education*. Pp. 30–47, University of Chicago Press, Chicago, 1948.

Heathers, G.: Emotional dependence and independence in a physical threat situation. *Child Develop. 24:* 169–179, 1953.

——: The adjustment of two-year-olds in a novel social situation. *Child Develop. 25:* 147–148, 1954.

Hebb, D. O.: *The Organization of Behavior*. Wiley, New York, 1949.

Heidbreder, E. F.: Reasons used in solving problems. *J. Exptl. Psychol. 10:* 397–414, 1927.

——: Problem-solving in children and adults. *J. Genet. Psychol. 35:* 522–545, 1928.

Heilbrun, A. B., Orr, H. K., and Harrell, S. M.: Patterns of parental child-rearing and subsequent vulnerability to cognitive disturbance. *J. Consult. Psychol. 30(1):* 51–59, 1966.

Heinstein, M. I.: Behavioral correlates of breast-bottle regimes under varying parent-infant relationships. *Monogr. Soc. Res. Child Develop. 88(28, Whole No. 4), 1963.

Hellman, I.: Sudden separation and its effect followed over twenty years: Hampstead Nursery follow-up studies. *Psychoanal. Study Child. 17:* 159–174, 1962.

Helper, M. N., Garfield, S. L., and Wilcott, R. C.: Electrodermal reactivity and rated behavior in emotionally disturbed children. *J. Abnor. and Soc Psychol. 66:* 600–603, 1963.

Hemming, J.: Some aspects of moral development in a changing society. Symposium: The development of children's moral values. *Brit. J. Educ. Psychol. 27(2):* 77–88, 1957.

Hendry, L. S., and Kessen, W.: Oral behavior of newborn infants as a function of age and time since feeding. *Child Develop. 35:* 201–208, 1964.

Henle, M., and Hubbell, M. B.: "Egocentricity" in adult conversation. *J. Soc. Psychol. 9:* 227–234, 1938.

Henley, C.: Physique and reputation of junior high school boys. *Child Develop. 22:* 247–260, 1951.

Henninger, P.: Infant problem-solving. Master's thesis, University of Toronto, 1968.

Henry, J.: Attitude organization in elementary school classrooms. *Amer. J. Orthopsychiat. 27:* 117–133, 1957.

Henry, W. E.: Projective techniques. *In* P. H. Mussen (Ed.), *Handbook of Research Methods in Child Development*. Pp. 603–604, Wiley, New York, 1960.

——, and Farley, J.: The validity of Thematic Apperception Test in the study of adolescent personality. *Psychol. Monogr. 73(17):* 1959.

Herr, D. M.: The sentiment of white supremacy: An ecological study. *Amer. J. Soc. 64:* 592–598, 1959.

Herr, S. E.: The effect of pre-first grade training upon reading readiness and reading achievement among Spanish-American children. *J. Educ. Psychol. 37:* 87–102, 1945.

Hershenson, M.: Visual discrimination in the human newborn. *J. Comp. and Physiol. Psychol. 58:* 270–276, 1964.

——: Development of the perception of form. *Psychol. Bull. 67(5):* 326–336, 1967.

Herskovitz, M. J.: *Man and His Works*. Harper and Row, New York, 1948.

——: On cultural and psychological reality. *In* J. H. Rohrer and M. Sherif (Eds.), *Social Psychology at the Crossroads*. Pp. 145–163, Harper and Row, New York, 1951.

Hess, E. H.: Imprinting. *Science. 130:* 133–141, 1959, (a).

——: Two conditions limiting critical age for imprinting. *J. Comp. and Physiol. Psychol. 52:* 515–518, 1959, (b).

——: Ethology: An approach toward the complete analysis of behavior. *In* Mandler et al. (Eds.), *New Directions in Psychology*. Pp. 157–266, Holt, Rinehart and Winston, New York, 1962.

Hess, R. D., and Shipman, V. C.: Early experience and the socialization of cognitive modes in children. *Child Develop. 36:* 869–886, 1965.

——, and Shipman, D. T.: Maternal influences upon early learning: The primitive environments of urban preschool children. *In* R. D. Hess and R. M. Bear (Eds.), *Early Education: A Comprehensive Evaluation of Current Theory, Research, and Practice*. Ch. 8, Aldine, Chicago, 1968.

————: Political socialization in the schools. *Harvard Educ. Rev. 38(3):* 528–536, 1968.

————: Political attitudes and children: Do our school teachers subvert solid social growth? *Psychol. Today. 2:* 24–28, 1969.

————, and Bear, R. N. (Eds.): *Early Education: A Comprehensive Evaluation of Current Theory, Research, and Practice.* Aldine Publishing Co., Chicago, 1968.

————, and Easton, D.: The child's changing image of the President. *Public Opinion Quart. 24:* 632–644, 1960.

————, and Torney, J.: *The Development of Political Attitudes in Children.* Aldine Press, Chicago, 1967.

Hicks, D. J.: Imitation and retention of film-mediated aggressive peer and adult models. *J. Personal. and Soc. Psychol. 2:* 97–100, 1965.

Hicks, J. A.: The acquisition of motor skill in young children: A study of the effects of practice in throwing at a moving target. *Child Development. 1:* 90–105, 1930.

————, and Hayes, M.: Study of the characteristics of 250 junior high school children. *Child Develop. 9:* 219–242, 1938.

————, and Ralph, D. W.: The effects of practice in tracing the Porteus diamond maze. *Child Develop. 2:* 156–158, 1931.

Hildreth, G.: Development sequences in name writing. *Child Develop. 7:* 291–303, 1936.

————: The development and training of hand dominance: II. Developmental tendencies in handedness. *J. Genet. Psychol. 75:* 221–254, 1949.

Hildum, D. C. (Ed.): *Language and Thought.* Van Nostrand, New Jersey, 1967.

Hilgard, J. R.: Learning and maturation in preschool children. *J. Genet. Psychol. 41:* 36–56, 1932.

————: The effect of early and delayed practice on memory and motor performances studied by the method of co-twin control. *Genet. Psychol. Monogr. 14:* 493–567, 1933.

Hill, D. S.: Personification of ideals by urban children. *J. Soc. Psychol. 1:* 379–392, 1930.

Hill, K. T.: Relation of test anxiety, defensiveness and intelligence to sociometric status. *Child Develop. 34:* 767–776, 1963.

————, and Sarason, S. B.: The relation of test anxiety and defensiveness to test and school performance over the elementary school years: A further longitudinal study. *Monogr. Soc. Res. Child Develop. 31(2):* 1966.

Hill, M. C.: Research on the Negro family. *Marriage and Family Living. 19:* 25–31, 1957.

Hill, S. A.: A study of the logical abilities of children. Doctor's thesis. Stanford University, 1961.

Hill, W. F.: Activity as an autonomous drive. *J. Comp. Physiol. Psychol. 49:* 15–19, 1956.

Hilliard, M. H.: The influence of religious education on the development of children's moral ideas. *Brit. J. Educ. Psychol. 29–30:* 50–59, 1959–1960.

Hilton, I.: Differences in the behavior of mothers toward first- and later-born children. *J. Personal. Soc. Psychol. 7(3):* 282–290, 1967.

Hinde, R. A.: The nature of imprinting. *In* B. M. Foss (Ed.), *Determinants of Infant Behavior.* Pp. 227–230, Methuen, New York, 1963.

Hindley, C. B.: The Griffiths Scale of Infant Development scores and predictions from three to eighteen months. *J. Child Psychol. and Psychiat. 1:* 99–112, 1950.

————, Filliozat, A. M., Klackenberg, G. et al.: Differences in age of walking in five European longitudinal samples. *Human Biol. 38:* 364–379, 1966.

Hirota, K.: Experimental studies of competition. *Jap. J. Psychol. 21:* 70–81, 1951.

Hirsch, I. J.: Teaching the deaf child to speak. *In* F. Smith, and G. A. Miller (Eds.), *The Genesis of Language: A Psycholinguistic Approach.* Pp. 207–216, M.I.T. Press, Cambridge, Mass.

Hirsch, J.: Behavior genetics and individuality understood. *Sci. 142:* 1436–1442, 1963.

———— (Ed.): *Behavior-Genetic Analysis.* McGraw-Hill, New York, 1967.

Hirschberg, G., and Gilliland, A. J.: Parent-child relationships in attitude. *J. Abnor. and Soc. Psychol. 37:* 125–130, 1942.

Hirschl, D., Levy, H., and Litvak, A. M.: The physical and mental development of premature infants: A statistical survey with a five-year follow-up. *Arch. Pediat. 65:* 648–653, 1948.

Hitt, W. D., and Stock, J. R.: The relationship between psychological characteristics and creative behavior. *Psychol. Record. 15:* 133–140, 1965.

Hobson, J. R.: Sex differences in primary mental abilities. *J. Educ. Res. 41:* 126–132, 1947.

Hockett, C. F.: Animal "languages" as human languages. *In* J. N. Spuhler (Ed.), *The Evolution of Man's Capacity for Culture.* Pp. 32–39, Wayne State University Press, Detroit, 1959.

Hodges, A.: A developmental study of symbolic behavior. *Child Develop. 25:* 277–280, 1954.

Hodges, W. L., and Spicker, H. H.: The effects of preschool experiences on culturally deprived children. *In* W. W. Hartup and N. L. Smothergill (Eds.), *The Young Child: Reviews and Research.* National Association for the Education of Young Children, Washington, 1967.

Hoffman, H. N.: A study in an aspect of concept formation with subnormal, average, and superior adolescents. *Genet. Psychol. Monogr. 52:* 191–239, 1955.

Hoffman, L. W., and Lippitt, R.: The measurement of family life variables. *In* P. Mussen (Ed.), *Handbook of Research Methods in Child Development.* Ch. 22, Wiley, New York, 1960.

———, and Wyatt, F.: Social change and motivations for having larger families: Some theoretical considerations. *Merrill-Palmer Quart. 6:* 235–244, 1960.

Hoffman, M. L.: Power assertion by the parent and its impact on the child. *Child Develop. 31:* 129–143, 1960.

———: Child-rearing practices and moral development: Generalizations from empirical research. *Child Develop. 34:* 295–318, 1963.

———, and Saltzstein, H. D.: Parent practice and the child's moral orientation. Paper read at the American Psychological Association, Chicago, September, 1960.

———, and Saltzstein, H. D.: Parent discipline and the child's moral development. *J. Personal. and Soc. Psychol. 5(1):* 45–57, 1967.

Hofstaetter, P. R.: The rate of maturation and the cephalization coefficient: A hypothesis. *J. Psychol. 31:* 271–280, 1951.

———: The changing composition of "intelligence": A study in T-technique. *J. Genet. Psychol. 85:* 159–164, 1954.

Holland, J. L.: Creative and academic performance among talented adolescents. *J. Educ. Psychol. 52:* 136–147, 1961.

Hollenberg, E., and Sperry, M.: Some antecedents of aggression and effects of frustration in doll play. *Personal. 1:* 32–43, 1951.

Hollingshead, A. B.: *Elmtown's Youth.* Wiley, New York, 1949.

Holloway, H. D.: Effects of training on the SRA primary mental abilities and the WISC. *Child Develop. 25:* 253–263, 1954.

Holmes, F. B.: An experimental study of the fears of young children. *In* A. T. Jersild and F. B. Holmes (Eds.), Children's Fears. *Child Develop. Monogr. 20:* 167–296, 1935.

Holt, E. B.: *Animal Drive and the Learning Process.* Holt, Rinehart and Winston, New York, 1931.

Holzman, P. S., and Gardner, R. W.: Leveling-sharpening and memory reorganization. *J. Abnor. Soc. Psychol. 61:* 176–180, 1960.

Honzik, M. P.: Developmental studies of parent-child resemblance in intelligence. *Child Develop. 28:* 215–228, 1957.

———: A sex difference in the age of onset of the parent-child resemblance in intelligence. *J. Educ. Psychol. 54:* 231–237, 1963.

———: Personality consistency and change: Some comments on papers by Bayley, Macfarlane, Moss and Kagen and Murphy. *Vita Humana. 7(2):* 139–142, 1964.

———: Environmental correlates of mental growth: Prediction from the family setting at 21 months. *Child Develop. 38(2):* 337–364, 1967.

———, Hutchings, J. J., and Burnip, S. R.: Birth record assessments and test performance at eight months. *Amer. J. Dis. Children. 109:* 416–426, 1965.

———, Macfarlane, J. W., and Allen, L.: The stability of mental test performance between two and eighteen years. *J. Exptl. Educ. 17:* 309–324, 1948.

Hood, H. B.: An experimental study of Piaget's theory of the development of numbers in children. *Brit. J. Psychol. 53:* 273–286, 1962.

Hooker, D.: Reflex activities in the human fetus. *In* R. G. Barker, J. S. Kounin, and H. F. Wright (Eds.), *Child Behavior and Development*. Pp. 17–28, McGraw-Hill, New York, 1943.

————: The development of behavior in the human fetus. *In* W. Dennis (Ed.), *Readings in Child Psychology*. Pp. 1–14, Prentice-Hall, New York, 1951.

————: *The Prenatal Origin of Behavior*. University of Kansas Press, Lawrence, 1952.

————: *Evidence of Prenatal Function of the Central Nervous System in Man*. American Museum of Natural History, New York, 1958.

Horowitz, E. L.: The development of attitude toward the Negro. *Arch. Psychol. 28(194):* 1936.

Horowitz, F. D.: The relationship of anxiety, self-concept, and sociometric status among fourth, fifth, and sixth grade children. *J. Abnor. and Soc. Psychol. 65:* 212–214, 1962.

————: Infant learning and development: Retrospect and prospect. *Merrill-Palmer Quart. 14(1):* 101–120, 1968.

Horowitz, R. E.: A pictorial method for study of self-identification in preschool children. *J. Genet. Psychol. 62:* 135–148, 1943.

Horowitz, S. G., and Armantrout, J.: Discrimination-learning, manifest anxiety, and effects of reinforcement. *Child Develop. 36:* 731–748, 1965.

Horrocks, J. E., and Buker, M. E.: A study of the friendship fluctuations of preadolescents. *J. Genet. Psychol. 78:* 131–144, 1951.

Hottinger, A., and Berger, H.: (Eds.), *Modern Problems in Pediatrics*. Vol. VII. *The Growth of the Normal Child During the First Three Years of Life*. Karger, 1962.

Hoult, T. F.: Comic books and juvenile delinquency. *Sociology and Soc. Res. 33:* 279–384, 1949.

Hovland, C. I.: A communication analysis of concept formation. *Psychol. Rev. 59:* 461–472, 1952.

————, and Weiss, W.: Transmission of information concerning concepts through positive and negative instances. *J. Exptl. Psychol. 45:* 175–182, 1953.

Howe, P. E., and Schiller, M.: Growth responses of the school child to changes in diet and environmental factors. *J. App. Physiol. 5:* 51–61, 1952.

Howells, J. G., and Layng, J.: Separation experiences and mental health. *Lancet. 2:* 285–288, 1955.

Huang, I., and Lee, H. W.: Experimental analysis of child animism. *J. Genet. Psychol. 66:* 69–74, 1945.

Hull, C. L.: Quantitative aspects of the evolution of concepts. *Psychol. Monogr. 28* (Whole No. 123), 1920.

Hunt, D. E.: A conceptual systems change model and its application to education. Paper presented at ONR Symposium on "Developmental determinants of flexibility". Pp. 19–21, Boulder, Colorado, March, 1964.

————: Adolescence: Cultural deprivation, poverty and the drop-out. *Rev. Educ. Res. 36:* 463–473, 1966.

————, and Dopyera, J.: Personality variation in lower-class children. *J. Psychol. 62:* 47–54, 1966.

————, and Hardt, R. H.: Developmental stage, delinquency, and differential treatment. *J. Res. Crime and Delinquency. 2:* 20–31, 1965.

————, and Joyce, R.: Teacher-trainee personality and initial teaching style. *Amer. Educ. Res. J. 4(3):* 253–259, 1967.

Hunt, J. McV.: *Intelligence and Experience*. Ronald Press, New York, 1961.

————: Intrinsic motivation and its role in psychological development. *In* D. Levine (Ed.), *Nebraska Symposium on Motivation*. Pp. 189–282, University of Nebraska Press, Lincoln, 1965.

————: Environment, development and scholastic achievement. *In* M. Deutsch, I. Katz, and A. R. Jensen (Eds.), *Social Class, Race, and Psychological Development*. Ch. 8, Holt, Rinehart and Winston, New York, 1968.

————: The impact and limitations of the giant of developmental psychology. *In* D. Elkind, and J. H. Flavell (Eds.), *Studies in Cognitive Development: Essays in Honor of Jean Piaget*. Pp. 3–66, Oxford University Press, Toronto, 1969.

————, Uzgiris, I., and Wachs, T.: Cognitive development in infants of different age levels. Paper presented to the Society for Research in Child Development, New York, 1967.

Hurley, J. R.: Parental acceptance-rejection and childrdn's intelligence. *Merrill-Palmer Quart. 11:* 19–31, 1965.

Huttenlocher, J.: Some effects of negative instances on the formation of simple concepts. *Psychol. Rep. 11:* 35–42, 1962.

————: Discrimination of figure orientation: Effects of relative positions. *J. Comp. and Physiol. Psychol. 63(2):* 359–361, 1967.

Hyde, D. N.: An investigation of Piaget's theories of the development of the concept of number. Unpublished doctoral dissertation, University of London, 1959.

Iliff, A., and Lee, V. A.: Pulse rate, respiratory rate, and body temperature of children between two months and eighteen years of age. *Child Develop. 23:* 238–245, 1952.

Illingworth, R. S.: The predictive value of developmental tests in the first year, with special reference to the diagnosis of mental subnormality. *J. Child Psychol. and Psychiat. 2:* 210–215, 1961.

————: *An Introduction to Developmental Assessment in the First Year.* William Heinemann, London, 1962.

Ingalls, T. H., and Bibring, G. L.: Some considerations of the psychological processes in pregnancy. *Psychoanalytic Study of the Child. 14:* 113–121, 1959.

Inhelder, B.: Criteria of the stages of mental development. *In* J. M. Tanner and B. Inhelder (Eds.), *Discussions on Child Development: A Consideration of the Biological, Psychological and Cultural Approaches to the Understanding of Human Development and Behavior.* Vol. I. Proceedings of the First Meeting of the World Health Organization Study Group on the Psychological Development of the Child. Geneva, 1953. Pp. 75–96, International Universities Press, New York, 1953.

————: Some aspects of Piaget's genetic approach to cognition. *In* W. Kessen and C. Kuhlman (Eds.), *Thought in the Young Child. Monogr. Soc. Res. Child Develop. 27:* 19–40, 1962.

————: Memory and intelligence in the child. *In* D. Elkind, and J. H. Flavell (Eds.), *Studies in Cognitive Development: Essays in Honor of Jean Piaget.* Oxford University Press, New York, 1969.

————, Bovet, M., Sinclair, H., and Smock, C. D.: On cognitive development. *Amer. Psychol. 21:* 160–164, 1966.

————, and Piaget, J.: *The Growth of Logical Thinking from Childhood to Adolescence.* Basic Books, New York, 1958.

————, and Piaget, J.: *The Early Growth of Logic in the Child (Classification and Seriation).* Harper and Row, New York, 1964.

Inkeles, A.: Society, social structure, and child socialization. *In* J. A. Clausen (Ed.), *Socialization and Society.* Ch. 3, Little, Brown Co., Boston, 1968.

Inselberg, R. N.: The causation and manifestation of emotional behavior in Filipino children. *Child Develop. 29:* 249–254, 1958.

Irwin, O. C.: The amount and nature of activities of newborn infants under constant external stimulating conditions during the first ten days of life. *Genet. Psychol. Monogr. 8:* 1–92, 1930.

————: Infant responses to vertical movements. *Child Develop. 3:* 167–169, 1932, (a).

————: The distribution of the amount of motility in young infants between two nursing periods. *J. Comp. Psychol. 14:* 415–428, 1932, (b).

————: Infant speech: Consonantal sounds according to place of articulation. *J. Speech Dis. 12:* 397–401, 1947, (a).

————: Infant speech: Consonant sounds according to manner of articulation. *J. Speech Dis. 12:* 402–404, 1947, (b).

————: Language and communication. *In* P. H. Mussen (Ed.), *Review of Research Methods in Child Development.* Pp. 487–516, Wiley, New York, 1960.

————, and Chen, H. P.: Infant speech: Vowel and consonant frequency. *J. Speech Dis. 11:* 123–125, 1946.

————, and Curry, T.: Vowel elements in the crying vocalization of infants under ten days of age. *Child Develop.* *12:* 99–109, 1941.

————, and Weiss, L. A.: The effect of clothing on the general and vocal activity of newborn infants. *University of Iowa Studies in Child Welfare.* *9:* 149–162, 1934, (a).

————, and ————: The effect of darkness on the activity of newborn infants. *University of Iowa Studies in Child Welfare.* *9:* 163–175, 1934, (b).

Iscoe, I., Williams, M., and Harvey, J.: Modification of children's judgments by a simulated group technique: A normative developmental study. *Child Develop.* *34:*963–978, 1963.

————, ————, and ————: Age, intelligence and sex as variables in the conformity behavior of Negro and white children. *Child Develop.* *35:* 451–560, 1964.

Iverson, M. A., and Reuter, M. E.: Ego development as an experimental variable. *Psychol. Rep.* *2:* 147–181, 1956.

Izard, C. E., Wehmer, G. M., Livsey, W., and Jennings, J. R.: Affect, awareness, and performance. *In* S. Tomkins, and C. E. Izard (Eds.), *Affect, Cognition and Personality: Empirical Studies.* Pp. 2–41, Springer Co., New York, 1965.

Izmozi, H.: Studies of premature children. *Japanese J. Educ. Psychol.* *11:* 43–47, 1963.

Jack, L. M.: An experimental study of ascendent behavior in preschool children. *University of Iowa Studies in Child Welfare.* *9(3):* 7–65, 1939.

Jackson, P. W.: Verbal solutions to parent-child problems. *Child Develop.* 339–349, 1956.

Jackson, S.: The growth of logical thinking in normal and subnormal children. *Brit. J. Educ. Psychol.* *35:* 255–258, 1954.

Jahoda, G.: Development of the perception of social differences in children from six to ten. *Brit. J. Psychol.* *50:* 159–175, 1959.

————: The development of children's ideas about country and nationality. Part I: The conceptual framework. *Brit. J. Educ. Psychol.* *33:* 47–60, 1963, (a).

————: The development of children's ideas about country and nationality. Part II: National symbols and themes. *Brit. J. Educ. Psychol.* *33:* 143–153, 1963, (b).

Jaiswal, S.: Early childhood and adult personality. *Manasi,* *2:* 12–15, 1955.

Jakobovits, L. A., and Miron, M. S.: *Readings in the Psychology of Language.* Prentice-Hall, New York, 1967.

Jakobson, R., and Halle, M.: *Fundamentals of Language.* Mouton, The Hague, 1956.

Janke, L. L., and Havighurst, R. J.: Relations between ability and social status in a midWestern community. II. Sixteen-year-old boys and girls. *J. Educ. Psychol.* *36:* 499–509, 1945.

Jayaswal, S. R., and Stott, L. H.: Persistence and change in personality from childhood to adulthood. *Merrill-Palmer Quart.* *1:* 47–56, 1955.

Jenkins, G. G.: Factors involved in children's friendships. *J. Educ. Psychol.* *22:* 440–448, 1931.

Jenkins, J. J.: The acquisition of language. *In* D. A. Goslin (Ed.), *Handbook of Socialization Theory and Research.* Ch. 13, Rand McNally, Chicago, 1969.

————, and Palermo, D. S.: Mediation processes and the acquisition of linguistic structure. *In* U. Bellugi and R. Brown (Eds.), The Acquisition of Language. *Monogr. Soc. Res. Child Develop.* *29(1):* 141–149, 1964.

Jenkins, L. M.: *A Comparative Study of Motor Achievements of Children at Five, Six, and Seven Years of Age.* Teachers College, Columbia University, New York, 1930.

Jennings, H. H.: *Leadership and Isolation.* Longmans Green, New York, 1943.

Jennings, H. S.: Sociometric structure in personality and group formation. *In* M. Sherif and M. O. Wilson (Eds.), *Group Relations at the Crossroads.* Pp. 332–365, Harper, New York, 1953.

Jennings, M. K., and Niemi, R. G.: Patterns of political learning. *Harvard Educ. Rev.* *38(3):* 443–467, 1968.

Jensen, A. R.: Learning ability in retarded, average, and gifted children. *Merrill-Palmer Quart.* *9:* 123–140, 1963.

————: Social class in verbal learning. *In* M. Deutsch, I. Katz, and A. R. Jensen (Eds.), *Social Class, Race, and Psychological Development.* Ch. 4, Holt, Rinehart and Winston, New York, 1968, (a).

————: Social class, race, and genetics: Implications for education. *Amer. Educ. Res. J.* *5(1):* 1968, (b).

————: How much can we boost IQ and scholastic achievement? *Harvard Educ. Rev. 39:* No. 1, 1–123, 1969.

————, and Rohwer, W. D.: Syntactical mediation of serial and paired-associate learning as a function of age. *Child Develop. 36:* 601–608, 1965.

Jensen, K.: Differential reactions to taste and temperature stimuli in newborn infants. *Genet. Psychol. Monogr. 12:* 361–479, 1932.

Jersild, A. T.: *Child Psychology* (4th ed.). Prentice-Hall, New York, 1954.

————, and Fite, M. D.: The influence of nursery school experience on children's social adjustments. *Child Develop. Monogr.* No. 25, 1939.

————, and Holmes, F. B.: Children's fears. *Child Develop. Monogr. 20:* 1935.

————, Markey, F. V., and Jersild, C. L.: Children's fears, dreams, wishes, daydreams, likes, dislikes, pleasant and unpleasant memories. *Child Develop. Monogr. 12:* 1933.

————, and Markey, F. V.: Conflicts between preschool children. *Child Develop. Monogr. 21:* 1935.

————, and Meigs, M. L.: Children and war. *Psychol. Bull. 40:* 541–573, 1943.

————, and Ritzman, R.: Aspects of language development. I. The growth of loquacity and vocabulary. *Child Develop. 9:* 243–259, 1938.

————, and Tasch, R. J.: *Children's Interests and What They Suggest for Education.* Teachers College, Columbia University, 1949.

————, Chayer, M. E., Fehlman, C., Haldreth, G., and Young, M.: *Child Development and the Curriculum.* Teachers College, Columbia University, New York, 1946.

————, Woodyard, E. S., and del Solar, C.: *Joys and Problems of Child-Rearing.* Teachers College, Columbia University, New York, 1949.

Johansson, V. B., Wedenberg, E., and Westin, B.: Measurement of tone response by human fetus. *Acta Oto-Laryngologica. 57:* 188–192, 1964.

John, V. P., and Goldstein, L. S.: The social context of language acquisition. *Merrill-Palmer Quart. 10:* 265–276, 1964.

Johnson, G. B., Jr.: The origin and development of the Spanish attitude toward the Anglo and the Anglo attitude toward the Spanish. *J. Educ. Psychol. 41:* 428–439, 1950.

————: Bilingualism as measured by a reaction-time technique and the relationship between a language and a nonlanguage intelligence quotient. *J. Genet. Psychol. 82:* 3–9, 1953.

Johnson, H. M.: *The Art of Block Building.* John Day, New York, 1933.

Johnson, R. C., and Zara, R. C.: Relational learning in young children. *J. Comp. and Physiol. Psychol. 53:* 594–597, 1960.

Johnston, F. E.: Individual variation in the rate of skeletal maturation between five and eighteen years. *Child Develop. 35(1):* 775–780, 1964.

Johnston, M. K., Kelley, C. S., Harris, F. R., and Wolf, M. M.: An application of reinforcement principles to development of motor skills of a young child. *Child Develop. 37:* 379–387, 1966.

Jones, H. E.: The galvanic skin reflex. *Child Develop. 1:* 106–110, 1930.

————: The pattern of abilities in juvenile and adult defectives. *University of California Publications in Psychology. 5:* 47–61, 1931.

————: The galvanic skin reflex as related to overt emotional expression. *Amer. J. Psychol. 47:* 241–251, 1935.

————: The study of patterns of emotional expression. *In* M. L. Reymert (Ed.). *Feelings and Emotions.* Pp. 161–168, McGraw-Hill, New York, 1950.

————: The environment and mental development. *In* L. Carmichael (Ed.), *Manual of Child Psychology* (2nd ed.). Pp. 631–696, Wiley, New York, 1954.

————: Problems of method in longitudinal research. *Vita Humana. 1(2):* 93–99, 1958.

————: The longitudinal method in the study of personality. *In* I. Iscoe and H. W. Stevenson (Eds.), *Personality Development in Children.* Pp. 3–27, University of Texas Press, Austin, 1960.

————, and Conrad, H. S.: The growth and decline of intelligence: A study of a homogeneous group between the ages of ten and sixty. *Genet. Psychol. Monogr. 13(3):* 1933.

————, and ————: Mental development in adolescence. *In* N. B. Henry (Ed.), *Forty-third Yearbook, National Society for the Study of Education.* Part I, pp. 146–163, University of Chicago Press, Chicago, 1944.

Jones, M. C.: Adolescent friendships. *Amer. Psychol. 3:* 352, 1943.

————, and Bayley, N.: Physical maturity among boys as related to behavior. *J. Educ. Psychol. 41:* 129–148, 1950.

Jones, T. D.: The development of certain motor skills and play activities in young children. *Child Develop. Monogr. 6:* 1939.

Jones, V.: *Character and Citizenship Gaining in the Public School.* University of Chicago Press, Chicago, 1936.

————: Character development in children: An objective approach. *In* L. Carmichael (Ed.), *Manual of Child Psychology* (2nd ed.). Pp. 781–832, Wiley, New York, 1954.

Jones, W. R.: The influence of reading ability in English on the intelligence test scores of Welsh speaking children. *Brit. J. Educ. Psychol. 23:* 114–120, 1953.

Josephina, E.: A study of some religious terms for six-year-old children. *Religious Educ. 56:* 24–25, 1961.

Jost, H., and Sontag, L. W.: The genetic factor in autonomic nervous-system function. *Psychoso. Med. 6:* 308–310, 1944.

Jung, C. G.: *Contributions to Analytical Psychology.* Harcourt Brace, New York, 1928.

Justin, F.: A genetic study of laughter provoking stimuli. *Child Develop. 3:* 114–136, 1932.

Kagan, J.: The child's perception of the parent. *J. Abnor. and Soc. Psychol. 53:* 257–258, 1956, (a).

————: The measurement of aggression from fantasy. *J. Abnor. and Soc. Psychol. 52:* 390–393, 1956, (b).

————: The concept of identification. *Psychol. Rev. 65:* 296–305, 1958.

————: The stability of TAT fantasy and stimulus ambiguity. *J. Consult. Psychol. 23:* 266–271, 1959.

————: The long-term stability of selected Rorschach responses. *J. Consult. Psychol. 24:* 67–73, 1960.

————: American longitudinal research on psychological development. *Child Develop. 35:* 1–32, 1964, (a).

————: The acquisition and significance of sex-typing and sex-role identity. *In* M. Hoffman and L. Hoffman (Eds.), *Review of Child Development Research.* Vol. I. Pp. 137–167, Russell Sage Foundation, New York, 1964, (b).

————: Reflection-impulsivity and reading ability in primary grade children. *Child Develop. 36:* 609–628, 1965.

————: Developmental studies in reflection and analysis. *In* A. H. Kidd and J. L. Rivoire (Eds.), *Perceptual Development in Children.* Ch. 17, International Universities Press, New York, 1966.

————: On the need for relativism. *Amer. Psychol. 22(2):* 131–142, 1967.

————, and Henker, B. A.: Developmental psychology. *Ann. Rev. Psychol. 17:* 1–50, 1966.

————, Henker, B. A., Hen-Tov, A., Levine, J., and Lewis, N.: Infants' differential reactions to familiar and distorted faces. *Child Develop. 37:* 519–532, 1966.

————, Hosken, B., and Watson, S.: Child's symbolic conceptualization of parents. *Child Develop. 32:* 625–636, 1961.

————, and Lemkin, J.: Form, color and size in children's conceptual behavior. *Child Develop. 32:* 25–28, 1961.

————, and Lewis, M.: Studies of attention in the human infant. Unpublished manuscript, Fells Research Institute, Yellow Springs, Ohio, 1964.

————, and Moss, H. A.: Stability and validity of achievement fantasy. *J. Abnor. and Soc. Psychol. 58:* 357–364, 1959.

———, and ———: The stability of passive and dependent behavior from childhood through adulthood. *Child Develop. 31:* 577–591, 1960.

———, and ———: The availability of conflictful ideas: A neglected parameter in assessing projective test responses. *J. Personal. 29:* 217–234, 1961.

———, and ———: *Birth to Maturity: A Study in Psychological Development.* Wiley, New York, 1962.

———, ———, and Sigel, I. E.: Conceptual style and the use of affect labels. *Merrill-Palmer Quart. 6:* 261–278, 1960.

———, ———, and ———: Psychological significance of styles of conceptualization. *Monogr. Soc. Res. Child Develop. 28(2):* 73–112, 1963.

———, Pearson, L., and Welch, L.: Conceptual impulsivity and inductive reasoning. *Child Development. 37(3):* 583–594, 1966.

———, and Rosman, B. L.: Cardiac and respiratory correlates of attention and analytic attitude. *J. Exptl. Child Psychol. 1:* 50–63, 1964.

———, ———, Kay, D., Albert, J., and Phillips, W.: Information processing in the child: Significance of analytic and reflective attitudes. *Psychol. Monogr. 78* (Whole No. 578), 1964.

———, Sontag, L. W., Baker, C. T., and Nelson, V.: Personality and I.Q. change. *J. Abnor. and Soc. Psychol. 56:* 261–266, 1958.

Kalhorn, J.: Values and sources of authority among rural children. *University of Iowa Studies in Child Welfare. 20:* 99–151, 1944.

Kallman, F. J.: Modern concepts of genetics in relation to mental health and abnormal personality development. *Psychiatric Quart. 21:* 535, 553, 1947.

———: Comparative twin studies on the genetic aspects of male homosexuality. *J. Nerv. Men. Dis. 115:* 283–298, 1952.

———: *Heredity in Health and Mental Disorder.* Norton, New York, 1953.

———, and Roth, B.: Genetic aspects of preadolescent schizophrenia. *Amer. J. Psychiat. 112:* 599–606, 1956.

Kalmus, H.: Ontogenetic, genetical, and phylogenetic parallels between animal communication and pre-linguistic child behavior. *In* F. Smith and G. A. Miller (Eds.), *The Genesis of Language: A Psycholinguistic Approach.* Pp. 273–294, M.I.T. Press, Cambridge, 1966.

Kanous, L. E., Daughterty, R. A., and Cohn, T. S.: Relation between heterosexual friendship choices and socioeconomic level. *Child Develop. 33:* 251–255, 1962.

Kantrow, R. W.: An investigation of conditioned feeding responses and concomitant adaptive behavior in young infants. *University of Iowa Studies in Child Welfare. 13(3):* 1937.

Kappas, K. H.: A developmental analysis of children's responses to humor. *In* S. I. Fenwick (Ed.), *A Critical Approach to Children's Literature.* University of Chicago Press, Chicago, 1967.

Karelitz, S., and Fisichelli, V. R.: The cry thresholds of normal infants and those with brain damage. An aid in the early diagnosis of severe brain damage. *J. Pediat. 61:* 679–685, 1962.

———, Karelitz, R., and Rosenfeld, L. S.: Infant vocalizations and their significance. *In* P. W. Bowman and H. V. Mautner (Eds.), *Mental Retardation: First International Medical Conference.* Pp. 439–446, Grune & Stratton, New York, 1960.

Karr, C., Wesley, F.: Comparison of German and U.S. child-rearing practices. *Child Develop. 37:* 715–723, 1966.

Karr, M.: Development of motor control in young children: Coordinated movements of the fingers. *Child Develop. 5:* 381–387, 1934.

Kasatkin, N. I.: Early conditioned reflexes in the child. *J. Higher Nerv. Activity. 2:* 572–581, 1952.

Kates, S. L.: Suggestibility, submission to parents and peers, and extrapunitiveness, intropunitiveness, and impunitiveness in children. *J. Psychol. 31:* 233–241, 1951.

———, and Yudin, L.: Concept attainment and memory. *J. Educ. Psychol. 55:* 193–108, 1964.

Katkovsky, W., Preston, A., and Crandall, V. J.: Parents' attitudes toward their personal achievements and toward the achievement behaviors of their children. *J. Genet. Psychol. 104:* 67–82, 1964, (a).

———, Preston, A., and Crandall, V. J.: Parents' achievement attitudes and their behavior with their children in achievement situations. *J. Genet. Psychol. 104:* 105–121, 1964, (b).

Katz, I.: The socialization of academic motivation in minority group children. *In* D. Levine (Ed.), *Nebraska Symposium on Motivation.* Pp. 133–191, University of Nebraska Press, Lincoln, Nebraska, 1967.

———: Factors influencing Negro performance in the desegregated school. *In* M. Deutsch, I. Katz, and A. R. Jensen (Eds.), *Social Class, Race, and Psychological Development.* Ch. 7. Holt, Rinehart and Winston, New York, 1968.

Katz, J. J.: *The Philosophy of Language.* Harper and Row, New York, 1966.

———, and Fodor, J. A.: The structure of semantic theory. *Language. 39:* 170–210, 1963.

Katz, P.: Role of the relevant cues in the formation of concepts by lower-class children. *J. Educ. Psychol. 59(4):* 233–238, 1968.

Kawahara, A.: A study of the development of manual dexterity. III. Educational Studies, Faculty of Education, Hiroshima University. *11(1):* 241–247, 1963.

Kawin, E., and Hoefer, C.: *A Comparative Study of a Nursery School Versus a Non-Nursery School Group.* University of Chicago Press, Chicago, 1931.

Kaye, H.: The conditioned Babkin reflex in human newborns. *Psychonomic Sci. 2:* 287–288, 1965.

———, and Levin, G. R.: Two attempts to demonstrate tonal suppression of non-nutritive sucking in neonates. *Percept. Motor Skills. 17:* 521–522, 1963.

———, and Lipsitt, L. P.: Relation of electrotactual threshold to basal skin conductance. *Child Develop. 35:* 1307–1312, 1964.

Keeney, T. J., Cannizzo, S. R., and Flavell, J. H.: Spontaneous and induced verbal rehearsal in a recall task. *Child Develop. 38(4):* 953–966, 1967.

Keister, M. E.: The behavior of young children in failure: An experimental attempt to discover and to modify undesirable responses of preschool children to failure. *University of Iowa Studies of Child Welfare. 14:* 29–82, 1937.

Keitel, H. G., Cohen, R., and Hornish, D.: Diaper rash, self-inflicted excoriations, and crying in full-term newborn infants kept in the prone or supine position. *J. Pediat. 57:* 884–886, 1960.

Kellogg, W. N., and Kellogg, L. A.: *The Ape and the Child.* McGraw-Hill, New York, 1933.

Kelly, J. G., Ferson, J. E., and Holtzman, W. H.: The measurement of attitudes toward the Negro in the South. *J. Soc. Psychol. 48:* 305–317, 1958.

Kempler, H. L.: Self-confidence and problem solving rigidity. *J. Clin. Psychol. 18:* 51, 1962.

Kenderdine, M.: Laughter in the preschool child. *Child Develop. 2:* 228–230, 1931.

Kendler, H. H., and Kendler, T. S.: Effect of verbalization on reversal shifts in children. *Sci. 134:* 1619–1620, 1961.

Kendler, T. S.: Development of mediating responses in children. *Monogr. Soc. Res. Child Develop. 28(2):* 33–48, 1963.

Keniston, K.: Social change and youth in America. *Daedalus,* 145–171, 1962.

Kennedy, W. A., Van De Riet, V., and White, J. C., Jr.: A normative sample of intelligence and achievement of Negro elementary school children in the Southeastern United States. *Monogr. Soc. Res. Child Develop. 28(6):* 1963.

Kerstetter, L.: Exploring the environment in a classroom situation. *Sociometry. 9:* 149–150, 1946.

Kessen, W.: Research design in the study of developmental problems. *In* P. H. Mussen (Ed.), *Handbook of Research Methods in Child Development.* Pp. 36–70, Wiley, New York, 1960.

———: "Stage" and "structure" in the study of children. *In* W. Kessen and C. Kuhlman (Eds.), Thought in the Young Child. *Monogr. Soc. Res. Child Develop. 27:* 65–82, 1962.

———: Research in the psychological development of infants: An overview. *Merrill-Palmer Quart. 9:* 83–94, 1963.

————: Questions for a theory of cognitive development. *In* H. W. Stevenson (Ed.), Concept of development. *Monogr. Soc. Res. Child Develop. 31(5):* 1966.

————, Leutzendorff, A., and Stoutsenberger, U.: Age, food-deprivation, non-nutritive sucking and movement in the human newborn. *J. Comp. and Physiol. Pyschol. 63:* 82–86, 1967.

————, and Mandler, G.: Anxiety, pain, and the inhibition of distress. *Psychol. Rev. 68(6):* 396–404, 1961.

————, Williams, E. J., and Williams, J. P.: Selection and test of response measures in the study of the human newborn. *Child Develop. 32:* 7–24, 1961.

Ketcham, W. A.: Relationship of physical traits and mental traits in intellectually gifted and mentally retarded boys. *Merrill-Palmer Quart. 6:* 171–177, 1960.

Kettner, N. W., Guilford, J. P., and Christensen, P. R.: A factor-analytic study across the domains of reasoning, creativity, and evaluation. *Psychol. Monogr. 73:* No. 9 (Whole No. 479), 1959.

Kidd, A. H., and Rivoire, J. L.: (Eds.), *Perceptual Development in Children.* International Universities Press, New York, 1966.

Kight, H. R., and Sassenrath, J. M.: Relation of achievement motivation and test anxiety to performance in programmed instruction. *J. Educ. Psychol. 57:* 14–17, 1966.

Killian, L. M., and Haer, J. L.: Variables related to attitudes regarding school desegregation among white southerners. *Sociometry. 21:* 159–164, 1958.

King, M. L.: *I Have A Dream.* Grosset and Dunlap Co., New York, 1968.

King, W.: Rule learning and transfer as a function of age and stimulus structure. *Child Develop. 39:* 311–324, 1968.

Kingsley, R. G., and Hall, D. C.: Training conservation through the use of learning sets. *Child Develop. 38(4):* 1111–1126, 1967.

Kinsella, P. J.: A close look at preschool reading in instruction. *Illinois J. Educ. 58:* 7–10, 1965.

Kinsey, A. C., Momeroy, W. B., and Martin, C. E.: *Sexual Behavior in the Human Male.* Saunders, Philadelphia, 1948.

Kinstler, D. B.: Covert and overt maternal rejection in stuttering. *J. Speech and Hearing Dis. 26:* 145–155, 1961.

Kirk, S. A.: *Early Education of the Retarded Child: An experimental Study.* University of Illinois Press, Urbana, 1958.

Kirschner, R., McCary, J. L., and Moore, C. W.: A comparison of differences among several religious groups of children on various measures of the Rosenzweig picture-frustration study. *J. Clin. Psychol. 18:* 352–353, 1962.

Kistyakovskaya, M. I.: Development of hand and arm movements in children in the first six months of life. *Voprosky Psikhologii. 1:* 89–100, 1962.

Kistiakovskaia, M. I.: Stimuli evoking positive emotions in infants in the first months of life. *Soviet Psychol. and Psychiat. 3:* 39–48, 1965.

Kitay, P. M.: A comparison of the sexes in their attitudes and beliefs about women: A study of prestige groups. *Sociometry. 3:* 399–407, 1940.

Klatskin, E. H., McGarry, M. E., and Steward, M. S.: Variability in developmental test patterns as a sequel of neonatal stress. *Child Develop. 37:* 819–826, 1966.

Klausmeier, H. J., and Wiersma, W.: The effects of I.Q. level and sex on divergent thinking of 7th grade pupils of low, average, and high I.Q. *J. Educ. Res. 58:* 300–302, 1965.

Klein, G. S., and Schoenfeld, N.: The influence of ego-involvement on confidence. *J. Abnor. and Soc. Psychol. 36:* 249–258, 1941.

Klein, M.: *The Psychoanalysis of Children.* Norton, New York, 1932.

Klima, E. S., and Bellugi, U.: Syntactic regularities in the speech of children. *In* J. Lyons and R. Wales (Eds.), *Psycholinguistics Papers.* University of Edinburgh Press, Edinburgh, 1966.

Klineberg, O.: *Negro Intelligence and Selective Migration.* Columbia University Press, New York, 1935, (a).

————: *Race Differences.* Harper, New York, 1935, (b).

Klingensmith, S. W.: Child animism: What the child means by "alive". *Child Develop. 24:* 51–61, 1953.

Kluckhohn, C.: Universal categories of culture. *In* A. L. Kroeber (Ed.): *Anthropology Today.* Pp. 507–523, University of Chicago Press, Chicago, 1953.

———, and Kluckhohn, F. R.: American culture: Generalized orientations and class patterns. *In* L. Bryson, L. Finkelstein, and R. M. MacIver (Eds.), *Conflicts of Power in Modern Culture.* Harper, New York, 1947.

———, and Murray, H. A.: Personality formation: The determinants. *In* C. Kluckhohn and H. A. Murray (Eds.), *Personality in Nature, Society and Culture.* Pp. 35–48, Knopf, New York, 1949.

Knights, R. M.: Test anxiety and visual discrimination of social scenes. *Child Develop. 36(4):* 1083–1090, 1965.

Knobloch, H., and Pasamanick, B.: Prospective studies on the epidemiology of reproductive causality: Methods, findings, and some implications. *Merrill-Palmer Quart. 12(1):* 27–44, 1966.

Kobayashi, S., and Saito, M.: An experimental study of leadership function in young children's groups. *Jap. J. Educ. Psychol. 5:* 195–199, 1958.

Koch, H. L.: Popularity in school children: Some related factors and a technique for its measurement. *Child Develop. 5:* 164–175, 1933.

———: An analysis of certain forms of so-called "nervous habits" in young children. *J. Genet. Psychol. 46:* 139–170, 1935.

———: A study of some factors conditioning the social distance between the sexes. *J. Soc Psychol. 20:* 79–107, 1944.

———: The social distance between certain racial, nationality, and skin-pigmentation groups in selected populations of American school children. *J. Genet. Psychol. 68:* 63–95, 1946.

———: The relation of "primary mental abilities" in five- and six-year-olds to sex of child and characteristics of his sibling. *Child Develop. 25:* 209–223, 1954.

———: Some personality correlates of sex, sibling position and sex of sibling among five- and six-year-old children. *Genet. Psychol. Monogr. 52:* 3–51, 1955, (a).

———: The relation of certain family constellation characteristics and attitudes of children toward adults. *Child Develop. 26:* 13–40, 1955, (b).

———: A study of twins born at different levels of maturity. *Child Develop. 35:* 1265–1282, 1964.

Kodlin, D., and Thompson, D. J.: An appraisal of the longitudinal approach to studies of growth and development. *Monogr. Soc. Res. Child Develop. 23(1):* 1958.

Kofsky, E.: A scalogram study of classificatory development. *Child Develop. 37(1):* 181–204, 1966.

Kohen-Raz, R.: Mental and motor development of Kibbutz, institutionalized, and home-reared infants in Israel. *Child Develop. 39:* 489–504, 1968.

Kohlberg, L.: The development of modes of moral thinking and choice in the years ten to sixteen. Unpublished doctoral dissertation, University of Chicago, 1958.

———: The development of children's orientation to the moral order: I. Sequence in the development of moral thought. *Vita Humana. 6:* 11–33, 1963, (a).

———: Moral development and identification. *In* H. Stevenson (Ed.), *Sixty-second Yearbook, National Society for the Study of Education.* Part I. *Child Psychology.* Pp. 277–332, Chicago University Press, Chicago, 1963, (b).

———: Development of moral character and moral ideology. *In* M. L. Hoffman and L. W. Hoffman (Eds.), *Review of Child Development Research.* Pp. 383–431, Russell Sage Foundation, New York, 1964.

———: Relationships between the development of moral judgment and moral conduct. Paper presented at the Symposium on Behavioral and Cognitive Concepts in the Study of Internalization at the Society for Research in Child Development, Minneapolis, Minnesota, March, 1965.

———: A cognitive-developmental analysis of children's sex-role concepts and attitudes. *In* E. E. Maccoby (Ed.), *The Development of Sex Differences.* Pp. 82–173, Stanford University Press, Stanford, 1966.

———: Moral and religious education and the public schools: A developmental view. *In* T. R. Sizer (Ed.), *Religion and Public Education.* Houghton Mifflin, New York, 1967.

———: Early education: A cognitive developmental view. *Child Develop. 39:* 1013–1062, 1968.

———: Stage and sequence: The cognitive-developmental approach to socialization. *In* D. Goslin (Ed.), *Handbook of Socialization.* Rand-McNally, New York, 1968.

———: *Stages in the Development of Moral Thought and Action.* In preparation, Holt, Rinehart and Winston, New York. 1969.

———: The developmental approach to moral education. *In* C. Beck, B. Crittenden, and E. Sullivan (Eds.), *Moral Education: Interdisciplinary Approaches.* In press, University of Toronto, Press, Toronto, 1970.

———, Yaeger, J., and Hjertholm, E.: Private speech: Four studies and a review of theories. *Child Develop. 39(3):* 691–736, 1968.

———, and Zigler, E.: The impact of cognitive maturity on the development of sex-role attitudes in the years four to eight. *Genet. Psychol. Monogr. 75:* 89–165, 1967.

Kohn, M. L.: Social class and parental values. *Amer. J. Soc. 64:* 337–351, 1959, (a).

———: Social class and the exercise of parental authority. *Amer. Soc. Rev. 24:* 352–366, 1959, (b).

———: Social class and parent-child relationships: An interpretation. *Amer. J. Soc. 68:* 471–480, 1963.

———: The child as a determinant of his peers' approach to him. *J. Genet. Psychol. 109:* 91–100, 1966.

———, and Carroll, E.: Social class and allocation of parental responsibilities. *Sociometry. 23:* 372–392, 1960.

Kohnstamm, G. A.: Experiments on teaching Piagetian thought operations. Paper presented at the Conference on Guided Learning at the Educational Research Council of Greater Cleveland, 1966.

———: *Piaget's Analysis of Class-Inclusion: Right or Wrong?* Mouton, The Hague, 1967.

Konishi, T.: On the development of language in infants. *Jap. J. Child Psychiat. 1:* 62–74, 1960.

Kooistra, W.: Developmental trends in the attainment of conservation, transitivity and relativism in the thinking of children: A replication and extension of Piaget's ontogenetic formulations. Unpublished doctoral dissertation, Wayne State University, 1963.

Korner, A. F.: *Some Aspects of Hostility in Young Children.* Grune & Stratton, New York, 1949.

Kotaskova, J.: Methodological problems in longitudinal research of psychological development. *Psychologia a Patopsychologia Dietata,* No. 2, 15–35, 1966.

Kounin, J. S.: Intellectual development and rigidity. *In* R. G. Barker, J. S. Kounin, and W. F. Wright (Eds.), *Child Behavior and Development.* Pp. 179–188, McGraw-Hill, New York, 1943.

Kozol, J.: *Death at an Early Age: Destruction of the Hearts and Minds of Negro Children in the Boston Public Schools.* Houghton Mifflin Co., Boston, 1967.

Krall, V.: Personality characteristics of accident repeating children. *J. Abnor. Soc. Psychol. 48:* 99–107, 1953.

Kreitler, H., and Kreitler, S.: Children's concepts of sexuality and birth. *Child Develop. 37(2):* 363–378, 1966.

Kresch, D.: The chemistry of learning. *Saturday Rev.* 48–50, 1968.

Krogman, W. M.: A handbook of the measurement and interpretation of height and weight in the growing child. *Monogr. Soc. Res. Child Develop. 13(3)* (Whole No. 48), 1943.

Kronvall, E., and Diehl, C.: The relationship of auditory discrimination to articulatory defect of children with no known organic impairment. *J. Speech Hearing Dis. 19:* 335–338, 1954.

Kuder, K., and Johnson, D. G.: The elderly primipara. *Amer. J. Obs. Gyn. 47:* 794–807, 1944.

Kuenne, M. R.: Experimental investigation of the relation of language to transposition behavior in young children. *J. Exptl. Psychol. 36:* 471–490, 1946.

Kuhlen, R. G.: *The Psychology of Adolescent Development.* Harper, New York, 1952.

——: Age and intelligence: Significance of cultural change in longitudinal versus cross-sectional findings. *Vita Humana. 6(3):* 113–124, 1963.

——, and Houlihan, M. B.: Adolescent heterosexual interests in 1942 and 1963. *Child Develop. 36:* 1049–1052, 1965.

——, and Lee, B. J.: Personality characteristics and social acceptability in adolescence. *J. Educ. Psychol. 34:* 321–340, 1943.

Kuhn, D. Z., Madsen, C. H., and Becker, W. C.: Effects of exposure to an aggressive model and frustration on children's aggressive behavior. *Child Develop. 38(3):* 739–745, 1967.

Kutner, B.: Patterns of mental functioning associated with prejudice in children. *Psychol. Monogr. 72(7,* Whole No. 460), 1958.

——, and Gordon, N. V.: Cognitive functioning in prejudice: A nine-year follow-up study. *Sociometry. 27:* 66–74, 1964.

La Barre, W.: *The Human Animal.* University of Chicago Press, Chicago, 1954.

L'Abate, L.: Sanford's uncertainty hypothesis in children. Paper read at the meeting of the American Psychological Association, Chicago, September, 1956.

Labovici, S.: The concept of maternal deprivation: A review of research. *In* J. Bowlby (Ed.), *Deprivation and Maternal Care: A Re-Assessment of Its Effects.* Pp. 267–288, Schocken Books, New York, 1966.

Lacey, H. M.: Mediating verbal responses and stimulus similarity as factors in conceptual naming by school age children. *J. Exptl. Psychol. 62:* 113–121, 1961.

Lacey, J. I., Bateman, D. E., and Vanlehn, R.: Autonomic response specificity and Rorschach color responses. *Psychoso. Med. 14:* 256–260, 1952.

——, and Dallenbach, K. M.: Acquisition by children of the cause-effect relationship. *Amer. J. Psychol. 53:* 575–578, 1940.

——, and Vanlehn, R.: Differential emphasis in somatic response to stress. *Psychoso. Med. 14:* 71–81, 1952.

Lafkowitz, M. N., Walder, L., and Eron, L.: Punishment, identification and aggression. *Merrill-Palmer Quart. 9:* 159–173, 1963.

Lafore, G. G.: Practices of parents in dealing with preschool children. *Child Develop. Monogr. 31:* 1945.

Lambert, W. E., and Klineberg, O.: *Children's Views of Foreign Peoples: A Cross-National Study.* Appleton-Century-Crofts, New York, 1967.

Landis, C., and Hunt, W. A.: *The Startle Pattern.* Rinehart, New York, 1939.

Landreth, C.: *Early Childhood.* Alfred A. Knopf Co., New York, 1967.

——, and Johnson, B. C.: Young children's responses to a picture and inset test designed to reveal reactions to persons of different skin color. *Child Develop. 24:* 63–79, 1953.

Lang, A.: Perceptual behavior of 8- to 10-week-old infants. *Psychonomic Sci. 4:* 203–204, 1966.

Langer, J.: Disequilibrium as a source of development. *In* P. Mussen, J. Langer, and N. Covington (Eds.), *New Directions in Developmental Psychology.* Holt, Rinehart and Winston, New York, 1969, (a).

——: *Theories of Development.* Holt, Rinehart and Winston, New York, 1969, (b).

Lansky, L. M.: Crandall, V. J., Kagan, J., and Baker, C. T.: Sex differences in aggression and its correlates in middle-class adolescents. *Child Develop. 32:* 45–58, 1961.

Lantz, B.: Some dynamic aspects of success and failure. *Psychol. Monogr. 59(1):* (Whole No. 271), 1945.

Lanyon, W. E., and Tavolga, W. N.: (Eds.), *Animal Sound and Communication.* American Institute of Biological Sciences, Washington, 1960.

Lasswell, H. D.: The method of interlapping observation in the study of personality and culture. *J. Abnor. Soc. Psychol. 32:* 240–243, 1937.

Laughlin, F.: *The Peer Status of Sixth and Seventh Grade Children.* Teachers College, Columbia University, New York, 1954.

Laurendeau, M., and Pinard, A.: *Causal Thinking in the Child: A Genetic and Experimental Approach.* International Universities Press, New York, 1962.

Lawson, E. D.: Development of patriotism in children: A second look. *J. Psychol. 55(2):* 279–286, 1963.

Laycock, F., and Taylor, J. S.: Physiques of gifted children and their less gifted siblings. *Child Develop. 35:* 63–74, 1964.

Laycock, S. R., and Clark, S.: The comparative performance of a group of old-dull and young-bright children on some items of the Revised Stanford-Binet Scale of Intelligence, Form L. *J. Educ. Psychol. 33:* 1–12, 1942.

Leahy, A. M.: Nature-nurture and intelligence. *Genet. Psychol. Monogr. 17:* 235–308, 1935.

Lebo, D.: Aggressiveness and expansiveness in children. *J. Genet. Psychol. 100(2):* 227–240, 1962.

Lecine, I.: Le developement psychomoteur des jeunes prematures. *Etudes Neonatales. 7:* 1–50, 1958.

Lederer, R. K.: An exploratory investigation of handed status in the first two years of life. *University of Iowa Studies in Child Welfare. 15:* 5–103, 1939.

Ledwith, N. H.: *Rorschach Responses of Elementary School Children. A Normative Study.* University of Pittsburgh Press, Pittsburgh, 1959.

Lee, P.: The activation and generalization of conservation of substance. Unpublished doctoral dissertation, Syracuse University, 1966.

Lee, P. C., La Crosse, E. R., Litman, F., Ogilvie, D. M., Stodolsky, S. S., and White, B. L.: The first six years of life: A report on current research and educational practice. *Genet. Psychol. Monogr.* In press, 1969.

Lefevre, M. C.: Language problems of the child with cerebral palsy. *Monogr. Soc. Res. Child Develop. 25(3,* Whole No. 77), 59–69, 1960.

Lefkowitz, M. M., Walder, L., and Eron, L.: Punishment, identification, and aggression. *Merrill-Palmer Quart. 9:* 159–173, 1963.

Lehman, H. C., and Witty, P. A.: *The Psychology of Play Activities.* A. S. Barnes, New York, 1927.

Leighton, D., and Kluckhohn, C.: *Children of the People.* Harvard University Press, Cambridge, 1947.

Lenneberg, E. H.: Language disorders in childhood. *Harvard Educ. Rev. 34:* 152–177, 1964, (a).

————: *New Directions in the Study of Language.* M.I.T. Press, Cambridge, Mass., 1964, (b).

————: Speech as a motor skill with special reference to nonaphasic disorders. *In* U. Bellugi, and R. W. Brown (Eds.), The acquisition of language. *Monogr. Soc. Res. Child Develop. 1:* 115–127, 1964, (c).

————: The natural history of language. *In* F. Smith, and G. A. Miller (Eds.), *The Genesis of Language.* Pp. 219–252, M.I.T. Press, Cambridge, 1966.

————, Rebelsky, F., and Nichols, I.: The vocalization of infants born to deaf and hearing parents. *Human Develop. 8:* 23–37, 1965.

Lenrow, P. B.: Studies of sympathy. *In* S. S. Tomkins and C. E. Izard (Eds.), *Affect, Cognition, and Personality: Empirical Studies.* Pp. 264–294, Springer, New York, 1965.

Leopold, W. F.: *Speech Development of a Bilingual Child: A Linguist's Record.* Northwestern University Press, Evanston, 1939–1949.

Lerner, E.: *Constraint Areas and the Moral Judgment of Children.* Banta, Menasha, Wisconsin, 1937, (a).

————: The problem of perspective in moral reasoning. *Amer. J. Soc. 43:* 249–269, 1937,(b)

Lesser, G. S.: Relationship between various forms of aggression and popularity among lower-class children. *J. Educ. Psychol. 50:* 20–25, 1959.

————: Recent revisions and educational applications of the concepts of intelligence and giftedness. Address at Institute for School Psychologists, University of Wisconsin, 1962.

————, Fifer, G., and Clark, D. H.: Mental abilities of children in different social and cultural groups. *Monogr. Soc. Res. Child Develop. 30(4,* Serial No. 102), 1965.

Lessing, E. E., and Oberlander, M.: Developmental study of ordinal position and personality adjustment of the child as evaluated by the California Test of Personality. *J. Personal. 35(3):* 487–497, 1967.

Leuba, C.: An experimental study of rivalry in young children. *J. Comp. Psychol. 16:* 367–378, 1933.

———: Tickling and laughter: Two genetic studies. *J. Genet. Psychol. 58:* 201–209, 1941.

———: *The Natural Man.* Doubleday, New York, 1954.

Levenstein, T., and Sunley, R.: Stimulation of verbal interaction between disadvantaged mothers and children. *Amer. J. Orthopsychiat. 38(1):* 116–121, 1968.

Leventhal, A. S., and Lipsitt, L. W.: Adaptation, pitch discrimination and sound localization in the neonate. *Child Develop. 35:* 759–767, 1964.

Leventhal, H., and Singer, D. L.: Cognitive complexity, impression formation and impression change. *J. Personal. 32:* 210–226, 1964.

Levi, I. J.: Student leadership in elementary and junior high school and its transfer into senior high school. *J. Educ. Res. 22:* 135–139, 1930.

Levin, T. R., and Kaye, H.: Non-nutritive sucking by human neonates. *Child Develop. 35:* 749–758, 1964.

Levine, D.: (Ed.), *Nebraska Symposium on Motivation.* University of Nebraska Press, Lincoln, 1967.

Levine, M.: Psychological testing of children. *In* L. W. Hoffman and M. L. Hoffman (Eds.), *Review of Child Development Research.* Vol. 2, pp. 257–310, Russell Sage Foundation, New York, 1966.

Levinger, L., and Murphy, L. B.: Implications of the social scene for the education of young children. *Yearbook of the National Society for Studies in Education. 46:* 15–43, part 2, 1947.

Levinson, B. M.: Cultural pressure and WAIS scatter in a traditional Jewish setting. *J. Genet. Psychol. 93:* 277–286, 1958.

———: Subcultural values and IQ stability. *J. Genet. Psychol. 98:* 69–82, 1961.

Levinson, B., and Reese, H. W.: Patterns of discrimination learning set in preschool children, 5th graders, college freshmen and the aged. *Monogr. Soc. Res. Child Develop. 32* (Serial No. 115), 1967.

Levitt, E. E.: Studies in intolerance of ambiguity: I. The decision-location test with grade school children. *Child Develop. 24:* 263–268, 1935.

Levy, D. M.: Finger sucking and accessory movements in early infancy. *Amer. J. Psychiat. 7:* 881–918, 1928.

———: Studies in sibling rivalry. *Res. Monogr. Amer. Orthopsychiat. Assoc. 2:* 1937.

———: Psychosomatic studies of some aspects of maternal behavior. *Psychoso. Med. 4:* 223–227, 1942.

———: *Maternal Overprotection.* Columbia University Press, New York, 1943.

———: On the problem of movement restraint. *Amer. J. Orthopsychiat. 14:* 644–671, 1944.

———: Observations of attitudes and behavior in child health centers. *Amer. J. Public Health. 41:* 182–190, 1951.

———: Oppositional syndromes and oppositional behavior. *In* P. H. Hoch and J. Zubin (Eds.), *Psychopathology of Childhood.* Pp. 204–226, Grune & Stratton, New York, 1955.

Lewin, K.: Behavior and development as a function of the total situation. *In* L. Carmichael (Ed.), *Manual of Child Psychology.* (2nd ed.), pp. 918–970. Wiley, New York, 1954.

———: Lippitt, R., and White, R. K.: Patterns of aggressive behavior in experimentally created "social climates." *J. Soc. Psychol. 10:* 271–299, 1939.

Lewis, C.: *Children of the Cumberland.* Columbia University Press, New York, 1946.

Lewis, M. M.: *Infant Speech: A Study of Beginning of Language.* (2nd ed.). Routledge and Kegan Paul, London, 1951.

———: *How Children Learn to Speak.* Basic Books, New York, 1959.

———: The meaning of a response, or why researchers in infant behavior should be oriental metaphysicians. *Merrill-Palmer Quart.* Vol. 13, *1:* 7–18, 1967.

———, Bartels, B., Campbell, H., and Goldberg, S.: Individual differences in attention: The relation between infants' condition at birth and attention distribution within the first year. *Amer. J. Dis. Child. 113:* 461–465, 1967.

———, Kagan, J., and Kalafat, J.: Patterns of fixation in the young infant. *Child Develop. 37(2):* 331–341, 1966.

Lidson, N.: Parental behavior and children's involvement with their parents. *J. Genet. Psychol. 109:* 173–194, 1966.

Lienert, G. A.: Uberprufung und genetische Interpretation der Divergenz-hypotheses von Wewtzer (Verification and genetic interpretation of Wewtzer's divergence hypothesis). *Vita Humana, 4:* 112–124, 1961.

Lightfoot, G. F.: *Personality Characteristics of Bright and Dull Children.* Teachers College, Columbia University, New York, 1951.

Lillienfeld, A. M., and Pasamanick, B.: The association of maternal and fetal factors with the development of mental deficiency. II. Relationship to maternal age, birth order, previous reproductive loss and degree of mental deficiency. *Amer. J. Men. Def. 60:* 557–569, 1956.

Lindholm, B. W.: Changes in conventional and deviation IQ's. *J. Educ. Psychol. 55:* 110–113, 1964.

Lindley, E. H.: A study of puzzles with special reference to the psychology of mental adaptation. *Amer. J. Psychol. 8:* 431–493, 1897.

Lindzey, G.: *Projective Techniques and Their Application in Cross-Cultural Research.* Appleton-Century-Crofts, New York, 1960.

————: Some remarks concerning incest, the incest taboo, and psychoanalytic theory. *Amer. Psychol. 22:* 1051–1059, 1967.

Linton, R.: *The Study of Man.* Appleton-Century-Crofts, New York, 1936.

Lippitt, R.: An experimental study of the effect of democratic and authoritarian group atmospheres. *University of Iowa Studies in Child Welfare. 16:* 43–195, 1940.

————: Popularity among preschool children. *Child Develop. 12:* 305–322, 1941.

————: Improving the socialization process. *In* J. A. Clausen (Ed.), *Socialization and Society.* Ch. 8, Little Brown Co., Boston, 1968.

————, and Gold, N.: Classroom social structure as a mental health problem. *J. Soc. Issues. 15:* 40–58, 1959.

————, Polansky, N., and Rosen, S.: The dynamics of power: A field study of social influence in groups of children. *Human Relations. 5:* 37–64, 1952.

Lippitt, T., and Lohman, J. E.: Cross-age relationships—An educational resource. *Children. 12:* 113–117, 1965.

Lipsitt, L. P.: Learning in the first year of life. *In* L. P. Lipsitt and C. C. Spiker (Eds.), *Advances in Child Development and Behavior.* Pp. 147–195, Academic Press, New York, 1963.

————: Learning processes of newborns. *Merrill-Palmer Quart.* Vol. 1, *1:* 45–72, 1966.

————, Engen, T., and Kaye, H.: The developmental changes in the olfactory threshold of the neonate. *Child Develop. 34(2):* 371–376, 1963.

————, and Kaye, H.: Conditioned sucking in the human newborn. *Psychonomic Sci. 1:* 29–30, 1964.

————, ————, and Bosack, T. N.: Enhancement of neonatal sucking through reinforcement. *J. Exptl. Child Psychol. 4(2):* 163–168, 1966.

————, and Levy, N.: Electrotactual threshold in the neonate. *Child Develop. 30:* 547–554, 1959.

Lipton, E. L., and Steinschneider, A.: Studies on the psychophysiology of infancy. *Merrill-Palmer Quart. 10:* 102–117, 1964.

————, ————, and Richmond, J. B.: Autonomic functions in the neonate. II. Physiological effects of motor restraint. *Psychoso. Med. 22:* 57–65, 1960.

————, ————, and ————: Swaddling, a childcare practice: Historical, cultural and experimental observations. *Pediat.* (Suppl.), *35:* 521–567, 1965.

————, ————, and ————: Psychophysiologic disorders in children. *In* L. W. Hoffman and M. L. Hoffman (Eds.), *Review of Child Development Research.* Vol. II. pp. 169–220, Russell Sage Foundation, New York, 1966.

Little, M. F., and Williams, H. M.: An analytical scale of language achievement. *University of Iowa Studies in Child Welfare. 13(2):* 49–94, 1937.

Little, S. W., and Cohen, L. D.: Goal setting behavior of asthmatic children and of their mothers for them. *J. Personal. 19:* 376–389, 1951.

Livson, N., and Mussen, P. H.: The relation of ego control to overt aggression and dependency. *J. Abnor. and Soc. Psychol. 55(1):* 56–71, 1957.

Ljung, D.: The adolescent spurt in mental growth. *Studies in Educ. and Psychol.* Almquist and Wiksell, Upsala, 1965.

Lloyd, K. E.: Supplementary report: Retention and transfer of responses to stimulus classes. *J. Exptl. Psychol. 59:* 207–208, 1960.

Loban, W. D.: *The Language of Elementary School Children.* National Council of Teachers of English, Champaign, Ill., 1963.

Lockhard, E. G.: The attitude of children toward certain laws. *Religious Educ. 25:* 144–149, 1930.

Loevinger, J.: On the proportional contributions of differences in nature and nurture to differences in intelligence. *Psychol. Bull. 40:* 725–756, 1943.

————: The meaning and measurement of ego development. *Amer. Psychol. 21(3):* 195–206, 1966.

————: *Theories of Ego Development.* The Social Science Institute, Washington University, St. Louis, Missouri, 1967.

Lohman, E.: Mothers' perceptions of relative advantages and disadvantages of children at different ages and of various characteristics. *Percept. Motor Skills. 24:* 1311–1314, 1967.

Long, L., and Welch, L.: The development of the ability to discriminate and match numbers. *J. Genet. Psychol. 59:* 377–387, 1941, (a).

————, and ————: Reasoning ability in young children. *J. Psychol. 12:* 21–44, 1941, (b).

————, and ————: Influence of level of abstractness on reasoning ability. *J. Psychol. 13:* 41–59, 1942.

Loomis, E. A., Jr.: Autistic and symbiotic syndromes in children. *Monogr. Soc. Res. Child Develop. 25* (Whole No. 77), 39–48, 1960.

Lord, F. E.: A study of spatial orientation of children. *J. Educ. Res. 34:* 481–505, 1941.

Lorenz, K.: Der Kumpan in der Umwelt des Vogels. Der Artgenosse als ausiosendes moment sozialer Verhaltungsweisen. *J. Orn. Lpz., 83:* 137–213, 289–413, 1935.

Lorge, I.: Schooling makes a difference. *Teachers College Record, 46:* 483–492, 1945.

Lorimer, R. M.: Change in developmental level of moral judgment of adolescents: The influence of an exposition of basic ethical concepts versus social imitation. Unpublished doctoral dissertation, University of Toronto, 1968.

————, and Sullivan, E. V.: A psychological interpretation of the structure of moral judgment. Paper presented to Moral Development Conference, Ontario Institute for Studies in Education, June, 1968.

Lovaas, O. I.: Effect of exposure to symbolic aggression on aggressive behavior. *Child Develop. 32:* 37–44, 1961.

Lovell, K.: A follow-up study of some aspects of the work of Piaget and Inhelder on the child's conception of space. *Brit. J. Educ. Psychol. 29:* 104–117, 1959, (a).

————: Jean Piaget's views on conservation of quantity. *Indian Psychological Bull. 4:* 16–19, 1959, (b).

————: A follow-up study of Inhelder and Piaget's "The growth of logical thinking." *Brit. J. Psychol. 52:* 143–153, 1961, (a).

————: *The Growth of Basic Mathematical and Scientific Concepts in Children.* Philosophical Library, New York, 1961, (b).

————, Mitchell, B., and Everett, I. R.: An experimental study of the growth of some logical structures. *Brit. J. Psychol. 53:* 175–188, 1962.

————: The development of scientific concepts. *In* A. H. Kidd and J. L. Rivoire (Eds.), *Perceptual Development in Children.* Ch. 15, International Universities Press, New York, 1966.

————, and Ogilvie, E.: A study of the conservation of substance in the junior school child. *Brit. J. Educ. Psychol. 30:* 109–118, 1960.

Low, W. D., Chan, S. T., Chan, K. S., and Lee, M. M.: Skeletal maturation of Southern Chinese children. *Child Develop. 35:* 1313–1335, 1964.

Lubchenco, L. O., Horner, F. A., Reed, L. H., Hix, I. E., Metcalf, D., Cohig, R., Elliott, H. C., and Bourg, M.: Sequelae of premature birth. *Amer. J. Dis. Children. 106(1):* 101–115, 1963.

Luchins, A. S., and Luchins, E. H.: *Rigidity of Behavior: A Variational Approach to the Effect of Einstellung.* University of Oregon Books, Oregon, 1959.

Lunneborg, P. W.: Relations among social desirability, achievement, and anxiety measures in children. *Child Develop. 35:* 169–182, 1964.

Lunzer, E. A.: Some points of Piagetian theory in the light of experimental criticism. *Child Psychol. and Psychiat. 1:* 192–202, 1960.

——: Problems of formal reasoning in test situations. *Monogr. Soc. Res. Child Develop. 30:(2):* 19–46, 1965.

Luria, A. R.: The directive function of speech and development and disillusion. Part I. Development of the directive function of speech in early childhood. *Word. 15:* 341–352, 1959.

——: *The Role of Speech in the Regulation of Normal and Abnormal Behavior.* Liveright, New York, 1961.

——, and Yudovich, F.: *Speech and Development of Mental Processes in the Child.* Staples, London, 1959.

Luria, Z., Goldwasser, M., and Goldwasser, A.: Response to transgression in stories by Israeli children. *Child Develop. 34:* 271–280, 1963.

Lyle, W. H., Jr., and Levitt, E. E.: Punitiveness, authoritarianism, and parental discipline of grade school children. *J. Abnor. and Soc. Psychol. 51:* 42–46, 1955.

Lynd, R. S., and Lynd, H. M.: *Middletown in Transition.* Harcourt Brace, New York, 1937.

Lynn, D., and Sawrey, W. L.: The effects of father-absence on Norwegian boys and girls. *J. Abnor. Soc. Psychol. 59:* 258–262, 1959.

Lynn, R.: Personality characteristics of the mothers of aggressive and unaggressive children. *J. Genet. Psychol. 99:* 159–164, 1961.

Maas, H.: Some social class differences in the family systems and group relations of pre- and early adolescents. *Child Develop. 22:* 145–152, 1951.

——: Long-term effects of early childhood separation and group care. *Vita Humana. 6:* 34–56, 1963.

——: Preadolescent peer relations and adult intimacy. *Psychiat. 31(2):* 161–172, 1968.

Maccoby, E. E.: Effects of the mass media. *In* M. L. Hoffman and L. W. Hoffman (Eds.), *Review of Child Development Research.* Pp. 323–348, Russell Sage Foundation, New York, 1964.

——: Sex differences in intellectual functioning. *In* E. E. Maccoby (Ed.), *The Development of Sex Differences.* Pp. 25–55, Stanford University Press, Stanford, California, 1966, (a).

——: (Ed.), *The Development of Sex Differences.* Stanford University Press, Stanford, California, 1966, (b).

——, and Hagen, J. W.: Effects of distraction upon simple versus incidental recall: Developmental trends. *J. Exptl. Child Psychol. 2(3):* 280–289, 1965.

——, and Konrad, K. W.: Age trends and selective listening. *J. Exptl. Child Psychol. 3:* 113–122, 1966.

——, and ——: The effects of preparatory set on selective listening: Developmental trends. *Monogr. Soc. Res. Child Develop. 4(532):* 1967.

MacFarlane, J. W.: The guidance study. *Sociometry. 2:* 1–23, 1939.

——: Perspective on personality consistency and change from the guidance study. *Vita Humana. 7(2):* 115–126, 1964.

MacKinnon, D. W.: The highly effective individual. *Teachers College Record. 61:* 367–378, 1960.

——: The personality correlates of creativity. A study of American architects. *In* G. S. Nielson (Ed.), *Pro. XIV Internat. Congress Appl. Psychol.* Copenhagen, 1961.

——: The nature and nurture of creative talent. *Amer. Psychol. 17:* 484–495, 1962.

MacRae, D.: A test of Piaget's theories of moral development. *J. Abnor. and Soc. Psychol. 49:* 14–18, 1954.

MacRae, J. M.: Retests of children given mental tests as infants. *J. Genet. Psychol. 87:* 111–119, 1955.

Madsen, M.: Cooperative and competitive motivation of children in three Mexican subcultures. *Psychol. Rep. 20:* 1307–1320, 1967.

Magnussen, M. G., and Cole, J. K.: Further evidence of the Rorschach card stimulus values for children: A partial replication (and generalization). *J. Projective Techniques and Personal. Assessment. 30:* 44–47, 1967.

Maier, N. R.: Reasoning in children. *J. Comp. Psychol. 21:* 357–366, 1936.

Malinowski, B.: *Sex and Repression in Savage Society.* Harcourt Brace, New York, 1927.

Maller, J. B.: *Cooperation and Competition: An Experimental Study in Motivation.* Teachers College, Columbia University, New York, 1929.

Mallick, S. K., and McCandless, B. R.: A study of catharsis of aggression. *J. Personal. and Soc. Psychol. 4(6):* 591–596, 1966.

Malmo, R. B.: Activation: A neuropsychological dimension. *Psychol. Rev. 66:* 367–386, 1959.

Malrieu, P.: Some problems of color vision in children. *Journal de Psychologie Normale et Pathologique. 52:* 222–231, 1955.

Malzberg, B.: Some statistical aspects of Mongolism. *Amer. J. Men. Def. 54:* 266–281, 1950.

Mandler, G.: Emotion. *In* E. Galanter, G. Mandler, R. Brown, and E. H. Hess (Eds.), *New Directions in Psychology.* Pp. 265–343, Holt, Rinehart and Winston, New York, 1962.

————: Verbal learning. *In* E. Galanter, G. Mandler, R. Brown, and E. H. Hess (Eds.), *New Directions in Psychology.* III. Pp. 1–50, Holt, Rinehart and Winston, New York, 1967.

————, and Kessen, W.: *The Language of Psychology.* Wiley, New York, 1959.

————, and Stephens, D.: The development of free and constrained conceptualizaiton in subsequent verbal memory. *J. Exptl. Child Psychol. 5:* 86–93, 1967.

Mandy, A. J.: *An Introduction to Physical Anthropology.* (2nd ed.). C. C Thomas, Springfield, Ill., 1951.

————, Mandy, T. E., Farkas, R., and Scher, E.: Is natural childbirth natural? *Psychoso. Med. 14:* 431–438, 1952.

Manheimer, D. I., and Mellinger, G. D.: Personality characteristics of the child accident repeater. *Child Develop. 38:* 491–513, 1967.

Mann, J. H.: The effect of interracial contact on sociometric choices and perceptions. *J. Soc. Psychol. 50:* 143–152, 1959.

Mannix, J. B.: The number concepts of a group of E.S.N. children. *Brit. J. Educ. Psychol. 30:* 180–181, 1960.

Maresh, M. M.: Growth of the heart related to bodily growth during childhood and adolescence. *Pediat. 2:* 382–404, 1948.

Marks, P. A., and Vestre, N.: Relative effects of drive level and irrelevant responses on performance of a complex task. *Psychol. Rec. 11:* 177–180, 1961.

Marier, P.: A logical analysis of animal communication. *J. Theoretical Biol. 1:* 259–317, 1961.

Marquis, D. P.: Can conditioned responses be established in the newborn infant? *J. Genet. Psychol. 39:* 479–492, 1931.

————: Learning in the neonate: The modification of behavior under three feeding schedules. *J. Exptl. Psychol. 29:* 263–282, 1941.

————: A study of frustration in newborn infants. *J. Exptl. Psychol. 32:* 123–138, 1943.

Marsh, G., and Sherman, M.: Verbal mediation of transposition as a function of age level. *J. Exptl. Child Psychol. 4(1):* 90–98, 1966.

Marshall, H. R.: An evaluation of sociometric-social behavior research with preschool children. *Child Develop. 28:* 131–137, 1957.

————: Relations between home experiences and children's use of language and play interactions with peers. *Psychol. Monogr. 25(5):* 1961.

————, and McCandless, B. R.: A study of prediction of social behavior of preschool children. *Child Develop. 28:* 149–159, 1957, (a).

————, and ————: Relationship between dependence on adults and social acceptance by peers. *Child Develop. 28:* 413–419, 1957, (b).

Marx, M. N.: (Ed.), *Theories in Contemporary Psychology.* Macmillan, New York, 1963.

Massler, M., and Suher, T.: Calculation of "normal" weight in children. *Child Develop. 22:* 75–94, 1951.

Matheson, E.: A study of problem solving behavior in preschool children. *Child Develop.* 2: 242–262, 1931.

Matsumoto, M., and Smith, H. T.: Japanese and American children's perception of parents. *J. Genet. Psychol. 98:* 83–88, 1961.

Mauco, G., and Rambaud, P.: Le rang de l'enfant dans la famille. *Revue Francaise du Psychanalyse. 15:* 253–260, 1951.

Maudry, M., and Nekula, M.: Social relations between children of the same age during the first two years of life. *J. Genet. Psychol. 54:* 193–215, 1939.

Maurer, A.: What children fear. *J. Genet. Psychol. 106(2):* 265–277, 1965.

Maurer, K. M.: Intellectual status at maturity as a criterion of selecting items in preschool tests. *University of Minnesota Institute of Child Welfare Monographs. 21:* 1946.

Maw, W. H., and Maw, E. W.: Personal and social variables differentiating children with high and low curiosity. Cooperative research project No. 1511. Pp. 1–181, University of Delaware, Wilmington, 1965.

Mead, M.: *From the South Seas.* William Morrow, New York, 1939.

———: Social change and cultural surrogates. *J. Educ. Soc. 14:* 92–100, 1940.

———: Anthropological data on the problem of instinct. *Psychoso. Med. 4:* 396–397, 1942.

———: Age patterning in personality development. *Amer. J. Orthopsychiat. 17:* 231–240, 1947.

———: On the implications for anthropology of the Gesell-Ilg approach to maturation. *In* D. Haring (Ed.), *Personal Character and Cultural Milieu.* Pp. 508–517, Syracuse University Press, Syracuse, 1949, (a).

———: *Male and Female: A Study of the Sexes in a Changing World.* William Morrow, New York, 1949, (b).

———: Some anthropological considerations concerning guilt. *In* M. L. Reymert (Ed.), *Feelings and Emotions.* Pp. 362–373, McGraw-Hill, New York, 1950.

———: Research on primitive children. *In* L. Carmichael (Ed.), *Manual of Child Psychology* (2nd ed.). Pp. 735–780, Wiley, New York, 1954.

———: A cultural anthropologist's approach to maternal deprivation. *In Deprivation of Maternal Care.* Public Health Paper No. 14. Pp. 45–62, World Health Organization, Geneva, 1962.

———: A cultural anthropologist's approach to maternal deprivation. *In* J. Bowlby (Ed.), *Deprivation and Maternal Care: A Re-assessment of the Effects.* Pp. 237–254, Schocken Books, New York, 1966.

———, and Macgregor, F. C.: *Growth and Culture.* Putnam, New York, 1951.

Medinnus, G. R.: Q-sort descriptions of five-year-old children by their parents. *Child Develop. 32:* 473–489, 1961.

———: Delinquents' perceptions of their parents. *J. Consult. Psychol. 29:* 592–593, 1965.

———: *Readings in the Psychology of Parent-Child Relations.* Wiley, New York, 1967.

———, and Curtis, F. J.: The relation between maternal self-acceptance and child acceptance. *J. Consult. Psychol. 27:* 542–544, 1963.

Medley, D. M., and Mitzel, H. E.: Some behavioral correlates of teacher effectiveness. *J. Educ. Psychol. 50:* 239–246, 1959.

Mednick, S. A., and Schaffer, J. B.: Mothers' retrospective reports in child-rearing research. *Amer. J. Orthopsychiat. 33:* 457–461, 1963.

Meek, L. H.: *Personal-social Development of Boys and Girls with Implications for Secondary Education.* Progressive Education Association, New York, 1940.

Mendel, G.: Children's preferences for differing degrees of novelty. *Child Develop. 36:* 453–465, 1965.

Mengert, I. G.: A preliminary study of the reactions of two-year-old children to each other when paired in a semi-controlled situation. *J. Genet. Psychol. 39:* 393–398, 1939.

Menlove, F. L.: Aggressive symptoms in emotionally disturbed adopted children. *Child Develop. 36:* 519–532, 1965.

Menyuk, P.: Syntactic structures in the language of children. *Child Develop. 34:* 407–422, 1963, (a).

————: A preliminary evaluation of grammatical capacity in children. *J. Verb. Learning and Verb. Behav. 2:* 429–000, 1963, (b).

————: Comparison of grammar of children with functionally deviant and normal speech. *J. Speech and Hearing Res. 7:* 109–121, 1964, (a).

————: Syntactic rules used by children from preschool through first grade. *Child Develop. 18(2):* 533–546, 1964 (b).

Mercer, R. D.: Organic brain syndromes and speech disorders in children. *Monogr. Soc. Res. Child Develop. 25(3,* Whole No. 77), 25–34, 1960.

Meredith, H. V.: Birth order and body size. II. Neonatal and childhood materials. *Amer. J. Phys. Anthrop. 8:* 195–224, 1950.

————: Methods of studying physical growth. *In* P. Mussen (Ed.), *Handbook of Research Methods in Child Development.* Ch. 5, Wiley, New York, 1960.

————: Change in the stature and body weight of North American boys during the last eighty years. *In* L. P. Lipsitt and C. C. Spiker (Eds.), *Advances in Child Development and Behavior.* Vol. 1, pp. 69–114, Academic Press, New York, 1963.

————: Selected anotomic variables analyzed for interage relationships and the size-size, size-gain, and gain-gain varieties. *In* L. P. Lipsitt and C. C. Spiker (Eds.), *Advances in Child Development and Behavior.* Vol. II, pp. 221–257, Academic Press, New York, 1965.

Mermelstein, E., and Shulman, L. S.: Lack of formal schooling and the acquisition of conservation. *Child Develop. 38:* 39–52, 1967.

Merrill, B.: A measurement of mother-child interaction. *J. Abnor. and Soc. Psychol. 41:* 37–49, 1946.

Merrill, M. A.: On the relation of intelligence to achievement in the case of mentally retarded children. *Comp. Psychol. Monogr. 11:* 1924.

Messerschmidt, R.: The suggestibility of boys and girls between the ages of six and sixteen years. *J. Genet. Psychol. 43:* 422–437, 1933.

Mestyan, G., and Varga, F.: Chemical thermal regulation of full-term and premature newborn infants. *J. Pediat. 56:* 623–629, 1960.

Meyer, S. R.: A test of the principles of "activity", "immediate reinforcement", and "guidance" as instrumented by Skinner's teaching machines. *Dissertation Abstracts. 20:* 4729–4730, 1960, (a).

————: Report on the initial test of a junior high school program. *In* A. A. Lumsdaine and R. Glaser (Eds.), *Teaching Machines and Programmed Learning.* P. 229–246, National Educational Association, Washington, D.C., 1960, (b).

Meyer, W. J.: Relationship between social need strivings for the development of heterosexual affiliations. *J. Abnor. and Soc. Psychol. 59:* 51–57, 1959.

————: The stability of patterns of primary mental abilities among junior high and senior school students. *Educ. Psychol. Meas. 20:* 795–800, 1960.

————, and Bendig, A. W.: A longitudinal study of the Primary Mental Abilities Test. *J. Educ. Psychol. 52:* 50–60, 1961.

————, and De Jung, J. E.: Consistency of pupil rating behavior over two social-psychological need situations. *Child Develop. 34:* 791–798, 1963.

Meyers, C. E.: The effect of conflicting authority on the child. *University of Iowa Studies on Child Welfare. 20:* 31–98, 1944.

————, Dingman, H. S., Orpet, R. E., Sitkei, E. G., and Watts, C. A.: Four ability-factor hypotheses and three pre-literate levels in normal and retarded children. *Monogr. Soc. Res. Child Develop. 96:* Vol. 29, No. 5, 1964.

————, Orpet, R. E., Attwell, A. A., and Dingman, H. F.: Primary mental abilities at mental age six. *Monogr. Soc. Res. Child Develop. 27(1):* 1962.

Michotte, A.: *The Perception of Causality.* Basic Books, New York, 1963.

Midlirsky, E., and Bryan, J. H.: Training charity in children. *J. Personal. and Soc. Psychol. 5(4):* 408–415, 1967.

Millen, J. W.: Timing of human congenital malformations. *Develop. Med. Child Neurol. 5(4):* 343, 350, 1963.

Miller, D. R.: Motivation and affect. *In* P. H. Mussen (Ed.), *Handbook of Research Methods in Child Development.* Pp. 688–769, Wiley, New York, 1960.

————, and Swanson, G. E.: *The Changing American Parent.* Wiley, New York, 1958.

Miller, G. A.: Some preliminaries to psycholinguistics. Paper read at the meeting of the American Psychological Association, Los Angeles, California, September, 1964.
——: The magical number seven plus or minus two: Some limits in our ability for processing information. *Psychol. Rev. 63:* 81–97, 1956.
——, and McNeill, D.: Psycholinguistics. *In* G. Lindzey and E. Aronson (Eds.), *Handbook of Social Psychology* (2nd ed.), Vol. 3. Ch. 26, Addison-Wesley Co., Reading, Mass., 1969.
Miller, N. E., and Bugelski, R.: Minor studies in aggression: The influence of frustrations imposed by the in-group on attitudes expressed toward out-groups. *J. Psychol. 25:* 437–442, 1948.
Miller, W. R., and Ervin, S. M.: The development of grammar in child language. *In* U. Bellugi and R. W. Brown (Eds.), The acquisition of language. *Monogr. Soc. Res. Child Develop. 29(1):* 9–35, 1964.
Millman, J., and Glock, M. D.: Trends in the measurement of general mental ability. *Rev. Educ. Res. 35:* 17–24, 1965.
Milner, E.: A study of the relationships between reading readiness in grade one school children and patterns of parent-child interaction. *Child Develop. 22:* 95–112, 1951.
——: *Neural and Behavioral Development: A Relational Enquiry, with Implications for Personality.* Thomas Books, Springfield, Ill., 1967.
Minard, R. D.: Race attitudes of Iowa children. *University of Iowa Studies in Character. 4(2):* 1931.
Minuchin, P.: Children's sex role concepts as a function of school and home. Paper read at the American Orthopsychiatric Association, Chicago, March, 1964.
——: Sex-role concepts and sex-typing in childhood as a function of school and home environments. *Child Develop. 36(4):* 1033–1048, 1965.
Mischel, W.: Preference for delayed reinforcement and social responsibility. *J. Abnor. Psychol. 62:* 1–7, 1961, (a).
——: Delay of gratification, need for achievement, and acquiescence in another culture. *J. Abnor. Soc. Psychol. 62:* 543–552, 1961, (b).
——: Father absence and delay of gratification: Cross-cultural comparisons. *J. Abnor. Soc. Psychol. 63:* 116–124, 1961, (c).
——: Delay of gratification and deviant behavior. Paper read at meeting of the Society for Research in Child Development, Berkeley, California, April, 1963.
——: A social-learning review of sex differences and behavior. *In* E. E. Maccoby (Ed.), *The Development of Sex Differences.* Pp. 56–81, Stanford University Press, Stanford, California, 1966.
Mishima, J., and Inoe, K.: A study on development of visual memory. *Jap. Psychol. Res. 8(2):* 62–71, 1966.
Missiuro, W.: Studies on developmental stages of children's reflex reactivity. *Child Develop. 34:* 33–41, 1963.
Mogar, M.: Children's causal thinking about natural phenomena. *Child Develop. 31:* 59–65, 1960.
Mohr, G. J.: Psychosomatic problems in childhood. *Child Develop. 19:* 137–147, 1948.
Money, J.: Psychosexual differentiation. *In* J. Money (Ed.), *Sex Research: New Developments.* Holt, Rinehart and Winston, New York, 1965.
Montagu, A.: *An Introduction to Physical Anthropology* (2nd ed.). C. C. Thomas, Springfield, Ill., 1951.
Montagu, N. F.: *Prenatal Influences.* C. C Thomas, Springfield, Ill., 1962.
Montgomery, K. C.: The role of exploratory drive in learning. *J. Comp. and Physiol. Psychol. 47:* 60–64, 1954.
Moore, B. C.: Relationship getween prematurity and intelligence in mental retardates. *Amer. J. Men. Def. 70:* 448–453, 1965.
Moore, J. E.: A test of eye-hand coordination. *J. App. Psychol. 21:* 668–672, 1937.
Moore, M.: Aggression themes in a binocular rivalry situation. *J. Personal. and Soc. Psychol. 3:* 685–688, 1966.

Moore, O. K., and Anderson, A. R.: Some principles for the design of clarifying educational environments. *In* D. A. Goslin (Ed.), *Handbook of Socialization Theory and Research.* Ch. 10, Rand McNally, Chicago, 1969.

———, and ———: Responsive environments project. *In* R. D. Hess, and R. M. Baer (Eds.), *Early Education.* Aldine, Chicago, 1968.

Moore, S.: Correlates of peer acceptance in nursery school children. *In* W. W. Hartup and N. L. Smothergill (Eds.), *The Young Child: Reviews of Research.* Pp. 229–247, National Association for the Education of Young Children, Washington, 1967.

Moore, T., and Ucko, L. E.: Four to six: Constructiveness and conflict in meeting doll play problems. *J. Child Psychol and Psychiat. 2:* 21–47, 1961.

Moreno, J. L.: *Who Shall Survive?* Nervous and Mental Disorders Publishing Co., Washington, D.C., 1934.

Morgan, C. T., and Stellar, E.: *Physiological Psychology.* (2nd ed.). McGraw-Hill, New York, 1950.

Morgan, G., and Ricciuti, H. N.: Infants' responses to strangers during the first year. *In* B. M. Foss (Ed.), *Determinants of Infant Behavior.* Vol. IV. In press, Methuen, London (Wiley, New York), 1968.

Morgan, J. J., and Morgan, S. S.: Infant learning as a development index. *J. Genet. Psychol. 65:* 281–289, 1944.

Morland, J. K.: Racial recognition by nursery school children in Lynchburg, Virginia. *Soc. Forces. 37:* 132–137, 1958.

———: Racial acceptance and preference of nursery school children in the southern city. *Merrill-Palmer Quart. 8:* 271–280, 19621.

———: A comparison of race awareness in Northern and Southern children. *Amer. J. Orthopsychiat. 36:* 22–31, 1966.

Morlar, T.: A logical analysis of animal communication. *J. Theoret. Biol. 1:* 295–317, 1961.

Morley, M., Court, D., and Miller, H.: Childhood speech disorders and the family doctor. *Brit. Med. J. 4653:* 574–578, 1950.

Morphett, M. V., and Washburne, C.: When should chilren begin to read? *Elem. School J. 31:* 496–503, 1931.

Morris, D. P., Soroker, E., and Burruss, G.: Follow-up studies of shy, withdrawn children. I. Evaluation of later adjustment. *Amer. J. Orthopsychiat. 24:* 743–754, 1954.

Morrisett, L., and Hovland, C. I.: A comparison of three kinds of training in human problem solving. *J. Exptl. Psychol. 58:* 52–55, 1959.

Mosher, S. A., and Hornsby, K. R.: On asking questions. *In* J. Bruner et al. (Eds.), *Studies in Cognitive Growth.* Wiley, New York, 1966.

Moss, H. A., and Kagan, J.: Stability of achievement and recognition seeking behaviors from early childhood through adulthood. *J. Abnor. and Soc. Psychol. 62:* 504–513, 1961.

———, and ———: Report on personality consistency and change from the Fels Longitudinal Study. *Vita Humana. 7:* 127–139, 1964.

Mott, S. M.: Concept of a mother: A study of four- and five-year-old children. *Child Develop. 25:* 99–106, 1954.

Mowrer, O. H.: Authoritarianism versus "self-government" in the management of children's aggressive (anti-social) reactions as a preparation for citizenship in a democracy. *J. Soc. Psychol. 10:* 121–126, 1939.

———: "Maturation" versus "learning" in the development of vestibular and optokinetic nystagmus. *J. Genet. Psychol. 48:* 383–404, 1946.

———: The psychologist looks at language. *Amer. Psychologist. 9:* 660–692, 1954.

———: Hearing and speaking: An analysis of language learning. *J. Speech and Hearing Dis. 23:* 143–152, 1968.

———: *Learning Theory and the Symbolic Processes.* Wiley, New York, 1960.

———, and Kluckhohn, C.: Dynamic theory of personality. *In* J. McV. Hunt (Ed.), *Personality and the Behavior Disorders.* Vol. I, pp. 69–135, Ronald Press, New York, 1944.

Moynihan, D. D.: The Negro family: A case for national action. United States Department of Labor, Office of Policy Planning and Research, Washington, D.C., 1965.

Mummery, D. V.: An analytical study of ascendant behavior of preschool children. *Child Develop. 18:* 40–81, 1947.

Munn, N. L.: Learning in children. *In* L. Carmichael (Ed.), *Manual of Child Psychology* (2nd ed.). Pp. 374–458, Wiley, New York, 1954.

———: *The Evolution and Growth of Human Behavior.* (2nd ed.). Houghton Mifflin, Boston, 1965.

Munsinger, H., and Kessen, W.: Uncertainty, structure, and preference. *Pscyhol. Monogr. 78(9):* (Whole No. 586), 1964.

Murdock, G. P.: The common denominator of cultures. *In* R. Linton (Ed.), *The Science of Man in the World Crisis.* Pp. 123–142, Columbia University Press, New York, 1945.

———, and Whiting, J. W.: Cultural determination of parental attitudes: The relationship between the social structure, particularly family structure and parental behavior. *In* M. J. Senn (Ed.), *Problems of Infancy and Childhood.* Pp. 13–34, Josiah Macy, Jr. Foundation, New York, 1951.

Murphy, D. P.: The outcome of 625 pregnancies in women subjected to pelvic radium roentgen irradiation. *Amer. J. Obstet. and Gyn. 18:* 179–187, 1929.

———: *Congenital Malformation* (2nd ed.). University of Pennsylvania Press, Philadelphia, 1947.

Murphy, G.: *Personality: A Biosocial Approach to its Origins and Structure.* Harper, New York, 1947.

———: The psychology of 1975: An extrapolation. *Amer. Psychol. 18:* 689–695, 1963.

Murphy, L. B.: *Social Behavior and Child Personality: An Exploratory Study of Some Roots of Sympathy.* Columbia University Press, New York, 1937.

———: Social factors in child development. *In* T. Newcomb and E. L. Hartley (Eds.), *Readings in Social Psychology.* Pp. 129–138, Holt, New York, 1947.

———: Factors in continuity and change in the development of adaptational style in children. *Vita Humana. 7(2):* 96–114, 1964.

Murray, F.: Training in the acquisition of the conservation of length in children. *Proceedings of the 75th Annual Convention of the American Psychological Association. 2:* 297–298, 1967.

———: Cognitive conflict and reversibility training in the acquisition of length conservation. *J. Educ. Psychol. 59(2):* 82–87, 1968.

Murstein, B. I.: *Theory and Research in Projective Techniques.* Wiley, New York, 1963.

Mussen, P. H.: Some personality and social factors related to changes in children's attitudes toward Negroes. *J. Abnor. and Soc. Psychol. 45:* 423–441, 1950.

———: (Ed.), *Handbook of Research Methods in Child Development.* Wiley, New York, 1960.

———: Early socialization: Learning and identification. *In* G. Mandler, B. Mussen, N. Kogan, and M. A. Wallach, *New Directions in Psychology.* III. Pp. 51–110, Holt, Rinehart and Winston, New York, 1967.

———, Conger, J. J., and Kagan, J.: *Child Development and Personality.* (2nd ed.). Harper and Row, New York, 1963.

———, ———, and ———: *Child Development and Personality* (3rd ed.). Harper and Row, New York, 1969.

———, and Naylor, H. K.: The relationships between overt and fantasy aggression. *J. Abnor. and Soc. Psychol. 49:* 235–240, 1954.

———, and Rutherford, E.: Effects of aggressive cartoons on children's aggressive play. *J. Abnor. and Soc. Psychol. 62:* 461–464, 1961.

Muste, M. J., and Sharpe, D. F.: Some influential factors in the determination of aggressive behavior in preschool children. *Child Develop. 18:* 11–28, 1947.

Muus, R. E.: A comparison of "high causally" and "low causally" oriented sixth grade children in respect to a perceptual intolerance of ambiguity test. *Child Develop. 31:* 521–536, 1960.

McCall, R. W., and Kagan, J.: Attention in the infant: Effects of complexity contour, perimeter, and familiarity. *Child Develop. 38:* 939–952, 1967.

McCandless, B. R.: *Children: Behavior and Development* (2nd ed.). Holt, Rinehart and Winston, New York, 1967.

————, Bilous, C. B., and Bennett, H. L.: Peer popularity and dependence on adults in preschool socialization. *Child Develop. 32:* 511–518,1961.

————, and Hoyt, J. M.: Sex, ethnicity, and play preferences of preschool children. *J. Abnor. and Soc. Psychol. 62:* 683–685, 1961.

————, and Marshall, H. R.: A picture sociometric technique for preschool children and its relation to teacher judgment of friendship. *Child Develop. 28(2):* 139–147, 1957, (a).

————, and ————: Sex differences in social acceptance and participation in preschool children. *Child Develop. 28:* 421–425, 1957, (b).

————, and Spiker, C. C.: Experimental research in child psychology. *Child Develop. 27:* 75–80, 1956.

McCarthy, D.: *The Language Development of the Preschool Child.* University of Minnesota Press, Minneapolis, 1930.

————: Language and personality disorder. *Reading Teacher. 6:* 28–36, 1952.

————: Language development in children. In L. Carmichael (Ed.), *Manual of Child Psychology* (2nd ed.). Pp. 492–630, Wiley, New York, 1954.

————: Language development. *Monogr. Soc. Res. Child Develop. 25(3,* Whole No. 77), 5–14, 1960.

————: Affective aspects of language learning. In A. H. Kidd and J. L. Rivoire (Eds.), *Perceptual Development in Children.* Pp. 305–343, International Universities Press, New York, 1966.

McClearn, G. E.: The inheritance of behavior. In L. J. Postman (Ed.), *Psychology in the Making.* Pp. 144–252, Knopf, New York, 1962.

————: Genetics and behavior development. In M. L. Hoffman and L. W. Hoffman (Eds.), *Review of Child Development Research.* Vol. I, pp. 433–480, Russell Sage Foundation, New York, 1964.

McClelland, D. C., Atkinson, J. W., Clark, R. A., and Lowell, E. L.: *The Achievement Motive.* Appleton-Century-Crofts, New York, 1953.

McCloy, C. H.: Appraising physical status: Methods and norms. *University of Iowa Studies in Child Welfare. 15:* 1–260, 1938.

McConnell, O. H.: Perceptual versus verbal mediation in the concept learning of children. *Child Develop. 35:* 1373–1383, 1964.

McCord, J., and Howard, A.: Familial correlates of aggression in non-delinquent male children. *J. Abnor. and Soc. Psychol. 62:* 79–93, 1961.

————, McCord, W., and Thurber, E.: Some effects of paternal absence on male children. *J. Abnor. and Soc. Psychol.* 361–369, 1962.

McCraw, L. W., and Tolbert, J. W.: Sociometric status and athletic ability of junior high school boys. *Res. Quart. Amer. Assoc. Health, Phys. Educ. and Recreation, 24:* 72–80, 1953.

McCullough, G.: The role of developmental stages in reasoning in the counselling process. Unpublished doctoral dissertation, University of Toronto, 1969.

McDonald, F.: Children's judgment of stealing from individual and corporate owners. *Child Develop. 34(1):* 141–150, 1963.

McDonald, R. L.: Lunar and seasonal variations in obstetric factors. *J. Genet. Psychol. 108(1):* 81–87, 1966.

McDougall, W.: *An Introduction to Social Psychology.* Luce, Boston, 1914.

McFarland, M. B.: Relationships between young sisters as revealed in their overt responses. *Child Develop. Monogr. 39:* 1938.

McGee, H. M.: Measurement of authoritarianism and its relation to teachers' classroom behavior. *Genet. Psychol. Monogr. 52:* 89–146, 1955.

McGehee, W.: Judgment and the level of aspiration. *J. Genet. Psychol. 22:* 3–15, 1940.

————, and Lewis, W. D.: The socio-economic status of the homes of mentally superior and retarded children and the occupational rank of their parents. *J. Genet. Psychol. 60:* 375–380, 1942.

McGrade, B. J., Kessen, W., and Leutzendorff, A.: Activity in the human newborn as related to delivery difficulty. *Child Develop. 36(1):* 73–79, 1965.

McGraw, L. W.: A factor analysis of motor learning. *Res. Quart. Amer. Assoc. Health, Phys. Educ. Recreation. 20:* 316–335, 1949.

McGraw, M. B.: *Growth: A Study of Johnny and Jimmy.* Appleton-Century-Crofts, New York, 1935.

———: Development of the plantar response in healthy infants. *Amer. J. Disturbed Children. 54:* 240–251, 1937.

———: Neural maturation as exemplified in achievement of bladder control. *J. Pediat. 16:* 580–590, 1940.

———: *The Neuromuscular Maturation of the Human Infant.* Columbia University Press, New York, 1943.

———: Maturation of behavior. *In* L. Carmichael (Ed.), *Manual of Child Psychology.* Pp. 332–369, Wiley, New York, 1946.

McGuigan, F. J., Calvin, A. D., and Richardson, E. C.: Manifest anxiety, palmar perspiration-index, and stylus maze learning. *Amer. J. Psychol. 72:* 434–438, 1959.

McGuire, C. et al.: Dimensions of talented behavior. *Educ. Psychol. Meas. 21:* 3–38, 1961.

McGuire, W. J.: The nature of attitudes and attitude change. *In* G. Lindzey and E. Aronson (Eds.), *The Handbook of Social Psychology* (2nd ed.). Vol. III, ch. 21, Addison Wesley, Reading, Mass., 1969.

McKee, J. P., and Leader, F. B.: The relationships of socioeconomic status and aggression to the competitive behavior of preschool children. *Child Develop. 26:* 135–142, 1955.

McKhann, C. F., Belnap, W. D., and Beck, C. S.: Late effects of cerebral birth injury. *J. Michigan Med. Soc. 50:* 149–152, 1951.

McKillop, A. S.: *The Relationship Between the Reader's Attitude and Certain Types of Reading Response.* Teachers College, Columbia University, New York, 1952.

McKinnon, K. M.: Consistency and change in personality and behavior manifestations as observed in a group of 16 children during a five-year period. *Child Develop. Monogr.* Teachers College, Columbia University, New York, 1942.

McLaughlin, G. H.: Psychologic: A possible alternative to Piaget's formulation. *Brit. J. Educ. Psychol. 33(1):* 61–67, 1963.

McLeod, H.: A Rorschach study with preschool children. *J. Projec. Tech. 14:* 453–463, 1950.

McNeil, E. B.: Social class and the expression of emotion. *Michigan Acad. Sci., Arts and Letters. 41:* 341–348, 1956.

McNeill, D.: Developmental psycholinguistics. *In* F. Smith and G. A. Miller (Eds.), *The Genesis of Language.* Pp. 15–84, M.I.T. Press, Cambridge, Mass., 1966.

———: The development of language. *In* P. A. Mussen (Ed.), *Carmichael's Manual of Child Psychology.* In press, 1969.

———: Explaining linguistic universals. Paper presented to the 19th International Congress of Psychologists, as part of the Symposium on Biological, Social and Linguistic Factors in Psycholinguistics, April, 1969.

McNemar, Q.: Lost: Our intelligence? Why? *Amer. Psychol. 19:* 871–882, 1964.

Nagy, M.: The child's theories concerning death. *J. Genet. Psychol. 73:* 3–27, 1948.

Nakazima, S. A.: A comparative study of the speech development of Japanese and American English in childhood. I. A comparison of the development of voices at the prelinguistic period. *Studia Phonologica. 2:* 27–46, 1962.

Nash, J.: The father in contemporary culture and current psychological literature. *Child Develop. 36(1):* 261–297, 1965.

Neill, A. S.: *Summerhill: A Radical Approach to Child Rearing.* Hart Publishing Co., New York, 1960.

Neimark, E. D., and Lewis, N.: The development of logical problem-solving strategies. *Child Develop. 38:* 107–117, 1967.

———, and ———: Development of logical problem-solving: A one-year retest. *Child Develop. 39:* 527–536, 1968.

Neisser, E. G.: *Brothers and Sisters.* Harper, New York, 1951.

Neisser, U.: *Cognitive Psychology.* Appleton-Century-Crofts, New York, 1967.

Nelson, V. L.: An analytical study of child rearing. *Child Develop. 7:* 95–114, 1936.

Neprash, J. A.: Minority group contacts and social distance. *Phylon. 14:* 207–212, 1953.

Neugarten, B. L.: Social class and friendship among school children. *Amer. J. Soc. 51:* 305–313, 1946.

Neville, M. H.: Factors affecting the listening comprehension. *Alberta J. Educ. Res. 13(3):* 201–210, 1967, (a).

———: Understanding between children of the same age. *Alberta J. Educ. Res. 13(3):* 221–230, 1967, (b).

Newland, T. E.: Language development of the mentally retarded child. *Monogr. Soc. Res. Child Develop. 25(3,* Whole No. 77), 71–87, 1960.

Newman, H. H., Freeman, F. N., and Holzinger, K. J.: *Twins: A Study of Heredity and Environment.* University of Chicago Press, Chicago, 1937.

Newsletter, W. J., Feldstein, M. J., and Newcomb, T. M.: *Group Adjustment: A Study in Experimental Sociology.* Western Reserve University, Cleveland, 1938.

Newton, N.: Breastfeeding. *Psychology Today. 2(1):* 34, and 68–70, 1968.

———, and Newton, M.: Relationship of ability to breastfeed and maternal attitudes toward breastfeeding. *Pediat. 5:* 869–875, 1950.

Nichols, R. C.: A factor analysis of parental attitudes of fathers. *Child. Develop. 33:* 791–802, 1962.

Nicholson, A. N., and Hanley, C.: Indices of physiological maturity: Deviation and inter-relationships. *Child Develop. 24:* 3–38, 1953.

Nisbet, J.: Family environment and intelligence. *Eugen. Rev. 45:* 31–40, 1953.

Nisbet, J. D., and Entwistle, N. J.: Intelligence and family size, 1949–1965. *Brit. J. Educ. Psychol. 37(2):* 188–193, 1967.

Nisbett, R. E.: Birth order and participation in dangerous sports. *J. Personal. and Soc. Psychol. 8(4):* 351–353, 1968.

Nissen, H. W., Chow, K. L., and Semmes, J.: Effects of restricted opportunity for tactual, kinesthetic and manipulative experience on the behavior of a chimpanzee. *Amer. J. Psychol. 64:* 485–507, 1951.

Noel, D.: A comparative study of the relationship between the quality of the child's language usage and the quality and the type of language used in the home. *J. Educ. Res. 47:* 161–167, 1953.

Northway, M. L.: Outsiders: A study of the personality patterns of children least accept-able to their age mates. *Sociometry. 7:* 10–25, 1944.

Norval, N. A.: Relationship of weight and length of infants at birth to the age at which they begin to walk alone. *J. Pediat. 30:* 676–678, 1947.

Nowell-Smith, A. H.: *Ethics.* Penguin Books, London, 1954.

Nunally, J. C., Duchnowski, A. J., and Parker, R. K.: Association of neutral objects with reward: Effects on verbal evaluation, reward expectancy, and selective attention. *J. Personal. and Soc. Psychol. 1:* 270–274, 1965.

Nye, F. I., and Hoffman, L. W. (Eds.), *The Employed Mother in America.* Rand McNally, Chicago, 1963.

Najarian-Svajian, P. H.: The idea of immanent justice among Lebanese children and adults. *J. Genet. Psychol. 109:* 57–66, 1966.

Oakden, E. C., and Sturt, M.: Development of the knowledge of time in children. *Brit. J. Psychol. 12:* 309–336, 1922.

Oakes, M. E.: *Children's Explanations of Natural Phenomena.* Teachers College, Columbia University, New York, 1946.

O'Brien, T. C., and Shapiro, B. J.: The development of logical thinking in children. *Amer. Educ. Res. J. 5(4):* 531–542, 1968.

O'Bryan, K. G., and Boersma, F. J.: Eye movements: Their relationship to the develop-ment of conservation of length, area, and continuous quantity. Paper read to the Society for Research in Child Development, Santa Monica, March, 1969.

Odom, C. L.: A study of the mental growth curve with special reference to the results of group intelligence tests. *J. Educ. Psychol. 20:* 401–416, 1929.

Odom, R. D.: Problem-solving strategies as a function of age and socio-economic level. *Child Develop. 38:* 347–352, 1967.

———, and Coon, R. C.: The development of hypothesis testing. *J. Exptl. Child Psychol. 4:* 285–291, 1966.

Oetzel, R. M.: Annotated bibliography of sex difference literature. *In* E. E. Maccoby (Ed.), *The Development of Sex Differences*. Pp. 223–321, Stanford University Press, Stanford, California, 1966.

Ohnmacht, F. W.: Achievement, anxiety, and creative thinking. *Amer. Educ. Res. J. 3:* 131–138, 1966.

Ojemann, R. H.: Studies in handedness: I. A technique for testing unimanual handedness. *J. Educ. Psychol. 21:* 597–611, 1930.

———, Maxey, E. J., and Snider, B. C.: Further study of guided learning experience in developing probability concepts in grade 5. *Percept. and Motor Skills. 23:* 97–98, 1966.

———, and Pritchett, K.: Piaget and the role of guided experiences in human development. *Percept. and Motor Skills. 17:* 927–940, 1963.

———, and Snider, B.: An approach to the teaching of human relations. *J. Teacher Educ. 10:* 235–240, 1959.

Oleron, P., and Herren, H. L.: L'acquisition des conservations et la langage. *Enfance. 3:* 210–219, 1961.

———, and Thong, T.: L'Acquisition des conservations et l'apprentissage. *L'Annee Psychologique. 2:* 1968.

Olson, D. R.: The role of speech in the behavior of children: A theoretical overview. *Ontario J. Educ. Res. 8(3):* 249–259, 1966.

———: Language acquisition and cognitive development. Paper prepared for the International Conference on Social-Cultural Aspects of Mental Retardation, Nashville, June, 1968.

———: Language and thought: Aspects of a cognitive theory of semantics. Paper presented at the Conference on Human Learning, Prague, Czechoslovakia, July, 1969.

———: *The Development of Operational Thought: The Child's Acquisition of Diagonality.* In press, Academic Press, New York, 1970.

———, and Baker, N. E.: Children's recall of spatial orientation of objects. *J. Genet. Psychol.* In press, 1969.

Olson, L. A.: Concept attainment of high school sophomores. *J. Educ. Psychol. 54:* 213–216, 1963.

Olson, W. C., and Hughes, B. O.: Subsequent growth of children with and without nursery school experience. *In* G. M. Whipple (Ed.), *Thirty-ninth Yearbook, National Society for the Study of Education.* Part I. Pp. 237–244, University of Chicago Press, Chicago, 1940.

———, and ———: Growth of the child as a whole. *In* R. G. Barker, J. S. Kounin, and H. F. Wright (Eds.), *Child Behavior and Development.* Pp. 199–208, McGraw-Hill, New York, 1943.

Oltman, J., McGarry, J., and Friedman, S.: Parental deprivation and the "broken home" in dementia praecox and other mental disorders. *Amer. J. Psychiat. 108:* 685–694, 1952.

Olver, R. R., and Hornsby, J. R.: On equivalence. *In* J. S. Bruner (Ed.), *Studies in Cognitive Growth.* Pp. 68–86, Wiley, New York, 1966.

Oppe, T.: The emotional aspects of prematurity. *Cerebral Palsy Bull. 2:* 233–237, 1960.

Orlansky, H.: Infant care and personality. *Psychol. Bull. 46:* 1–48, 1949.

Ortar, G. R.: Transfer of psychological diagnostic measures. *Acta Psychologica. 21:* 218–230, 1963.

Osborne, R. H., and De George, F. V.: *Genetic Basis of Morphological Variation.* Harvard University Press, Cambridge, 1959.

Osgood, C. E.: A behavioristic analysis of perception and language as cognitive phenomena. *In Contemporary Approaches to Cognition.* Pp. 75–118, Harvard University Press, Cambridge, 1957.

———: Comment on Professor Bousfield's paper. *In* C. N. Cofer (Ed.), *Verbal Learning and Verbal Behavior.* Pp. 91–106, McGraw-Hill, New York, 1961.

———, Suci, G. J., and Tannenbaum, P. H.: *The Measurement of Meaning.* University of Illinois Press, Urbana, 1957.

Osler, S. F., and Shapiro, S. L.: Studies in concept attainment: IV. The role of partial reinforcement as a function of age and intelligence. *Child Develop. 35:* 623–633, 1964.

————, and Trautman, G. E.: Concept attainment: II. Effect of stimulus complexity upon concept attainment at two levels of intelligence. *J. Exptl. Psychol. 62:* 9–13, 1961.

————, and Weiss, S. A.: Studies in concept attainment: III. Effect of instruction at two levels of intelligence. *J. Exptl. Psychol. 63:* 528–533, 1962.

Osterkamp, A. M., and Sands, D. J.: Early feeding and birth difficulties in childhood schizophrenia: A brief study. *J. Genet. Psychol. 101:* 363–366, 1962.

Ostrovsky, E. S.: *Father to the Child: Case Studies of the Experiences of a Male Teacher.* Putnam, New York, 1959.

Ottinger, D. R., and Simmons, J. E.: Behavior of human neonates and prenatal maternal anxieties. *Psychol. Rep. 14:* 391–394, 1964.

Outhit, M. C.: A study of the resemblance of parents and children in general intelligence. *Arch. Psychol. 149:* 1933.

Owen, M. B.: The intelligence of the institutionalized juvenile delinquent. *J. Juv. Res. 21:* 199–206, 1937.

Owen, W. A.: Effects of motivating instructions on reaction time in grade school children. *Child Develop. 30:* 261–268, 1959.

Page, M. L.: The modification of ascendant behavior in preschool children. *University of Iowa Studies in Child Welfare. 11(3):* 1936.

Palermo, D. S., Castaneda, A., and McCandless, B. R.: The relationship of anxiety in children to performance in a complex learning task. *Child Develop. 27:* 333–337, 1956.

————, and Jenkins, J. J.: Frequency of superordinate responses to a word association test as a function of age. *J. Verbal Learning and Verbal Behavior. 1:* 378–383, 1963.

Palmer, R. D.: Development of a differentiated handedness. *Psychol. Bull. 62(4):* 257–272, 1964.

————: Birth order and identification. *J. Consult. Psychol. 30(2):* 129–135, 1966.

Parke, R. D., and Walters, R. H.: Some factors influencing the efficacy of punishment training for inducing response inhibition. *Monogr. Soc. Res. Child Develop. 32(1,* Whole No. 109), 1967.

Parks, J.: Emotional factors in early pregnancy. *In* J. E. Senn (Ed.), *Problems of Early Infancy. Transactions of Second Conference, 1948.* Pp. 22–27, Josiah Macy, Jr. Foundation, New York, 1949.

Parmelee, A. H.: The palmomental reflex in premature infants. *Develop. Med. and Child Neurol. 5:* 381–387, 1963.

————: A critical evaluation of the Moro reflex. *Pediat. 33:* 773–778, 1964.

————, Schulz, H. R., and Disbrow, N. A.: Sleep patterns in the newborn. *J. Pediat. 58:* 241–250, 1961.

————, Schultz, N. A., Akiyama, Y., Wenner, W. H., and Stern, D.: A fundamental periodacy in sleep in infants. Paper presented at the Association for Psychophysiological Study of Sleep, Annual Conference, 1967.

————, Wenner, W. H., and Schulz, H. R.: Infants' sleep patterns: From birth to 16 weeks of age. *J. Pediat. 65:* 576–582, 1964.

Parsons, C.: Inhelder and Piaget's "Growth of logical thinking." II. A logician's viewpoint. *Brit. J. Psychol. 51:* 75–84, 1960.

Parsons, T.: Age and sex in the culture of the United States. *Amer. Soc. Rev. 7:* 604–616, 1942.

————: Family structure and socialization of the child. *In* T. Parsons and R. F. Bales (Eds.), *Family, Socialization, and Interaction Process.* The Free Press, Glencoe, Illinois, 1955.

————: The school class as a social system: Some of its functions in American society. *Harvard Educ. Rev. 29(4):* 297–318, 1959.

Parsons, T., and Bales, R. F. Family, socialization and interaction process. Glencoe, Illinois: Free Press, 1955

————, and Clark, J. B.: *The Negro American.* Beacon Press, Boston, 1966.

Parten, M. B.: Leadership among preschool children. *J. Abnor. and Soc. Psychol. 28:* 430–440, 1933, (a).

——: Social play among preschool children. *J. Abnor. aud Soc. Psychol. 28:* 136–147, 1933, (b).

Parten, M., and Newhall, S.: Social behavior of preschool children. *In* R. G. Barker, J. S. Kounin, and H. F. Wright (Eds.), *Child Behavior and Development.* Pp. 509–525, McGraw-Hill, New York, 1943.

Pasamanick, B., and Knobloch, H.: Early language behavior in Negro children and the testing of intelligence. *J. Abnor. and Soc. Psychol. 50:* 410–420, 1955.

——, and ——: Retrospective studies on the epidemiology of reproductive causality: Old and new. *Merrill-Palmer Quart. 12(1):* 7–26, 1966.

Pasqual-Leone, J. A.: Mathematical model for the transition rule in Piaget's developmental stages. Unpublished manuscript. University of British Columbia, Vancouver, 1967.

Patel, A. S., and Gordon, J. E.: Some personal and situation determinants of yielding to influence. *J. Abnor. and Soc. Psychol. 61:* 411–418, 1960.

Patterson, G. R., Littman, R. A., and Bricker, W.: Assertive behavior in children: A step toward a theory of aggression. *Monogr. Soc. Res. Child Develop. 32(5):* 1967.

Pattie, F. A., and Cornett, S.: Unpleasantness of early memories and maladjustment of children. *J. Personal. 20:* 315–321, 1952.

Paul, I. H.: Studies in remembering: The reproduction of connected and extended verbal material. *Psychol. Issues. 1(2):* 1959.

Paulsen, A. A.: Personality development in the middle childhood years. A ten-year longitudinal study of 30 public school children by means of Rorschach tests and social history. *Microfilm Abstracts. 13:* 592–593, 1953.

Pavlovitch, M.: Le langage enfantin: Acquisition du serbe et du Francais par un enfant serbe. Champion, Paris, 1920.

Pease, D., Rosauer, J. K., and Wallins, L.: Reliability of three infant developmental scales administered during the first year of life. *J. Genet. Psychol. 98:* 295–598, 1961.

Peatman, J. G., and Higgins, R. A.: Development of sitting, standing and walking of children reared with optimum pediatric care. *Amer. J. Orthopsychiat. 10:* 88–110, 1940.

——, and ——: Relation of infants' weight and body build to locomotor development. *Amer. J. Orthopsychiat. 12:* 234–240, 1942.

Peck, R. S., and Havighurst, R. J.: *The Psychology of Character Development.* Wiley, New York, 1960.

Peck, R.: The development of the concept of death in selected male children: An experimental investigation of the development of the concept of death in selected children from the point of no concept to the point where a fully developed concept is attained with an investigation of some factors which may affect the course of concept development. *Dissertation Abstracts, 27:* 1294, 1966B.

Peckos, P. S.: Caloric intake in relation to physique in children. *Sci. 117:* 631–633, 1953.

——: Nutrition during growth and development. *Child Develop. 28(3):* 273–285, 1957.

Peel, E. A.: Experimental examination of some of Piaget's schemata concerning children's perception and thinking, and a discussion of their educational significance. *Brit. J. Educ. Psychol. 29:* 89–103, 1959.

Peiper, A.: Cerebral function in infancy and childhood. *The International Behavioral Sciences Series,* New York, 1963.

Peisach, E. C.: Children's comprehension of teacher and peer speech. *Child Develop. 36:* 467–480, 1965.

Penney, R. K.: Reactive curiosity and manifest anxiety in children. *Child Develop. 36:* 697–702, 1965.

Penrose, L. S.: (Ed.), *Recent Advances in Human Genetics.* Little, Brown, Boston, 1961.

Pepinsky, P. N.: The meaning of "validity" and "reliability" as applied to sociometric tests. *Educ. Psychol. Meas. 9:* 39–51, 1949.

Perrodin, A. F.: Factors affecting the development of cooperation in children. *J. Educ. Res. 53:* 283–288, 1960.

Pestalozzi, J. H.: *Leonard and Gertrude*. D. C. Heath, Boston, 1895.

Peters, R. S.: Freud's theory of moral development in relation to that of Piaget. Symposium: Development of moral values in children. *Brit. J. Educ. Psychol. 29–30:* 250–258, 1959–1960.

———: Moral education and the psychology of character. *In Philosophy: The Journal of the Royal Institute of Philosophy. 37(139):* 37–56, 1962.

———: Reason and habit: The paradox of moral education. *In* W. R. Niblett (Ed.), *Moral Education in a Changing Society.* Pp. 46–65, Faber and Faber, London, 1963.

Peterson, G. M.: An empirical study of the ability to generalize. *J. Genet. Psychol. 6:* 90–114, 1932.

Pettigrew, T.: Personality and sociocultural factors in inter-group attitudes: A cross-national comparison. *J. Conflict Resolution. 2:* 29–42, 1958

Pettigrew, T. F.: Negro American personality: Why isn't more known? *J. Soc. Issues. (2):* 4–23, 1964.

———: Race and equal educational opportunity. Paper presented at the Symposium on "Implications of Coleman Report on Equality of Educational Opportunity". American Psychological Association, Washington, D.C., 1967, (a).

———: Social evaluation theory: Convergences and applications. *In* D. Levine (Ed.), *Nebraska Symposium on Motivation.* Pp. 241–311, University of Nebraska Press, Lincoln, Nebraska, 1967, (b).

Phillips, B. N.: Problem behavior in the elementary school. *Child Develop. 39:* 895–903, 1968.

Piaget, J.: *The Language and Thought of the Child*. Harcourt, Brace, New York, 1926.

———: *Judgment and Reasoning in the Child*. Harcourt, Brace, New York, 1928.

———: *The Child's Conception of the World*. Harcourt, Brace, New York, 1929.

———: *The Language and Thought of the Child*. (2nd ed.). Harcourt, Brace, New York, 1932, (a).

———: *Moral Judgment of the Child*. Harcourt, Brace, New York, 1932, (b).

———: *The Child's Conception of Physical Causality*. Harcourt, Brace, New York, 1932, (c).

———: *Le Développement de la Notion de Temps chez L'Enfant*. Presses Universities de France, Paris, 1946.

———: *Play Dreams and Imitation in Childhood*. Norton, New York, 1951.

———: The right to education in the modern world. *In* UNESCO, *In Freedom and Culture.* Pp. 67–116, Columbia Unviersity Press, New York, 1951.

———: *The Origins of Intelligence in Children*. International Universities Press, New York, 1952, (a).

———: *The Child's Conception of Number*. Humanities Press, New York, 1952, (b).

———: How children form mathematical concepts. *Sci. Amer. 189(5):* 74–79, 1953.

———: *The Construction of Reality in the Child*. Basic Books, New York, 1954, (a).

———: Language and thought from the genetic point of view. *Acta Psychologica. 10:* 51–60, 1954, (b).

———: Les stades du développement intellectuel de l'enfant et de l'adolescent. *In* P. Osterrieth et al., *Le Problème des Stades en Psychologie de L'Enfant.* Pp. 33–41, Presses Universities de France, Paris, 1956.

———: *Logic and Psychology*. Basic Books, New York, 1957, (a).

———: Logique et équilibre dans les comportements du sujet. *Etudes d'Epistémologie génétique. 2:* 27–117, 1957, (b).

———: The general problems of the psychobiological development of the child. *In* J. M. Tanner and Barbel Inhelder (Eds.), *Discussion on Child Development.* Vol. IV. The fourth meeting of the World Health Organization Study Group on the psychobiological development of the child, Geneva, 1956. Pp. 3–27 and passim, Tavistock Publications, London, 1960, (a).

———: *The Psychology of Intelligence*. Littlefield, Adams, New Jersey, 1960, (b).

———: Development and learning. *In* R. E. Ripple and V. N. Rockcastle (Eds.), *Piaget Rediscovered.* A report of the Conference on Cognitive Studies and Curriculum Development. Pp. 7–20, Cornell, 1964.

————: Psychology and philosophy. *In* B. B. Wolman and E. Nagel (Eds.), *Scientific Psychology*. Pp. 28–43, Basic Books, New York, 1965.

————: *The Child's Conception of Number*. Norton, New York, 1965, (b).

————: Nécessité et signification des recherches comparatives en psychologie génétique. *Internat. J. Psychol. 1(1):* 3–13, 1966.

————: *Six Psychological Studies*. Random House, New York, 1967.

————: On the development of memory and identity. *Heinz Werner Lecture Series*. Vol. 2, 1967. Clark University Press, 1968.

————, and Inhelder, B. *The Child's Conception of Space*. Routledge and Kegan, Paul, London, 1956.

————, and ————: *La genese des structures elémentaires: Classifications et Seriations*. Editions Delachaux and Niestlé, Neuchâtel, 1939.

————, ————, and Sinclair, H.: *Memoire et Intelligence*. Presses Universites de France, Paris, 1968.

Pick, H.: Some Soviet research on learning and perception in children. *In* J. C. Wright and J. Kagan (Eds.), Basic Cognitive Processes in Children. *Monogr. Soc. Res. Child Develop. 28(2):* 185–196, 1963.

Pickrel, E. W.: The differential effect of manifest anxiety on test performance. *J. Educ. Psychol. 49:* 43–46, 1958.

Piers, Ellen V., Daniels, Jacqueline, M., and Quackenbush, J. F.: The identification of creativity in adolescents. *J. Educ. Psychol. 51:* 346–351,1960.

Pike, E. G.: Controlled infant intonation. *Language Learning. 2:* 21–24, 1949.

Pinard, A.: An experimental study based on Piaget's theory. Paper presented at a colloquium. New Haven, Connecticut, Yale University, December, 1958.

————, and Laurendeau, M.: "Stage" in Piaget's cognitive development theory: Exegesis of a concept. *In* D. Elkind and J. H. Flavell (Eds.), *Studies in Cognitive Development: Essays in Honor of Jean Piaget*. Pp. 121–170, Oxford University Press, Toronto, 1969.

Pines, M.: How three-year-olds teach themselves to read and love it. *Harpers. 226:* 58–64, May, 1963.

Pinneau, S.: The infantile disorders of hospitalism and anaclitic depression. *Psychol. Bull. 52:* 429–452, 1955.

Pinneau, S. R.: *Changes in Intelligence Quotient—Infancy to Maturity*. Houghton Mifflin, New York, 1960.

Pistor, F.: How time concepts are acquired by children. *Educ. Method. 20:* 107–112, 1940.

Pittel, S. N., and Mendelssohn, G. A.: Measurement of moral values. *Psychol. Bull. 66(1):* 22–35, 1966.

Plutchik, R.: *The Emotions: Fact, Theories, the New Model*. Random House, New York, 1962.

Pohlman, E.: Mothers' perceptions of relative advantages and disadvantages of children at different ages and of various characteristics. *Percept. Motor Skills. 24:* 1311–1314, 1967.

Polak, P. R., Emde, R. A., and Spitz, R. A.: The smiling response to the human face. I. Methodology, quantification and natural history. *J. Nerv. Men. Dis. 139:* 103–109, 1964, (a).

————, ————, and ————: The smiling response. II. Visual discrimination and the onset of depth perception. *J. Nerv. Men. Dis. 139:* 407–415, 1964, (b).

Polansky, N., Lippitt, R., and Redl, F.: An investigation of behavioral contagion in groups. *Human Relations. 3:* 319–348, 1950.

Polikanina, R. I.: The relation between autonomic and somatic components in the development of the conditioned reflex in premature infants. *Pavlov. J. Higher Nerv. Activ. 11:* 51–58, 1961.

Pollack, R. H.: Some implications of ontogenetic changes in perception. *In* D. Elkind and J. H. Flavell (Eds.), *Studies in Cognitive Development: Essays in Honor of Jean Piaget*. Pp. 365–407, Oxford University Press, Toronto, 1969.

Polyani, M.: Object and psychology. *Amer. Psychol. 23(1):* 27–43, 1968.

Pope, B.: Socio-economic contrasts in children's peer culture prestige values. *Genet. Psychol. Monogr. 48:* 157–220, 1953.

Popper, K. R.: Back to the pre-Socratics. Paper read at the meeting of the Aristotelian Society, London, October 13, 1958.

———: *The Open Society and Its Enemies*. Vol. 2. Harper Torchbooks, New York, 1963.

Porter, B. M.: The relationship between marital adjustment and parental acceptance of children. *J. Home Econ. 47:* 157–164, 1955.

Porteus, B. D., and Johnson, R. C.: Children's responses to two measures of conscience development and the relations of sociometric nomination. *Child Develop. 36:* 703–711, 1965.

Postman, L.: Experimental analysis of motivational factors in perception. *In Current Theory and Research in Motivation*. Pp. 59–108, University of Nebraska Press, Lincoln, 1953.

———: Perception and learning. *In* S. Koch (Ed.), *Psychology: A Study of a Science*. Vol. 5. Pp. 30–113, McGraw-Hill, New York, 1963.

Pratoomraj, S., and Johnston, R. C.: Kinds of questions and types of conservation tasks as related to children's conservation responses. *Child Develop. 37:* 343–353, 1966.

Pratt, K. C.: The neonate. *In* L. Carmichael (Ed.), *Manual of Child Psychology*. (2nd ed.). Pp. 215–291, Wiley, New York, 1954.

———, Nelson, A. K., and Sun, K. H.: The behavior of the newborn infant. *Contributions Psychol*. Ohio State University, No. 10, 1930.

Prechtl, H. F. R.: The directed head turning response and allied movements of the human baby. *Behavior. 13:* 212–241, 1958.

———: Neurological sequelae of prenatal and paranatal complications. *In* B. M. Foss (Ed.), *Determinants of Infant Behavior*. Pp. 45–46, Methuen and Co., London, 1961.

———: The mother-child interaction in babies with minimal brain damage. *In* B. M. Foss (Ed.), *Determinants of Infant Behavior*. II. Pp. 53–66, Wiley, New York, 1963.

———, and Beintema, D.: The neurological examination of the full-term newborn infant. The Spastic Society Medical Education and Information Unit, in association with Heinemann, London, 1964.

———, and Dijkstra, J.: Neurological diagnosis of cerebral injury in the new-born. *In* B. S. Berge (Ed.), *Prenatal Care*. Pp. 222–231, P. Noordhoff, Groningen, The Netherlands, 1960.

Prekstad, A.: Factors influencing the reliability of anamnestic recall. *Child Develop. 37:* 603–612, 1966.

Premack, D., and Schwartz, A.: Preparations for discussing behaviorism with chimpanzee. *In* F. Smith and G. A. Miller (Eds.), *The Genesis of Language: A Psycholinguistic Approach*. Pp. 295–335, M.I.T. Press, Cambridge, 1966.

Pressey, S. L., and Robinson, F. P.: *Psychology and the New Education*. Harper, New York, 1944.

Preston, M. G., and Bayton, J. A.: Correlations between levels of aspiration. *J. Psychol. 13:* 369–373, 1952.

Preyer, W.: *The Mind of the Child*. Appleton-Century, New York, 1888.

Pribram, K. H.: Emotion: Steps toward a neuropsychological theory. *In* D. C. Glass (Ed.), *Neurophysiology and Emotion*. Pp. 3–40, The Rockefeller University Press, New York, 1967.

Price, B. Marian, and Bell, B. G.: The relationship of chronological age, mental age, IQ, and sex to divergent thinking test. *J. Psychol. Res. 9:* 1–9, 1965.

Price-Williams, R. R. A.: A study concerning concepts of conservation of quantities amongst primitive children. *Acta Psychologica. 18:* 293–305, 1961.

Pringle, M. L., and Bossio, V. A.: A study of deprived children. I. Intellectual, emotional and social development. *Vita Humana. 1:* 65–92, 1958.

———, and ———: Early prolonged separation and emotional maladjustment. *J. Child Psychol. and Psychiat. 1:* 37–48, 1960.

Probst, C. A.: A general information test for kindergarten children. *Child Develop. 2:* 81–95, 1931.

Pronko, N. H., Ebert, R., and Greenberg, G.: A critical review of theories of perception. *In* A. H. Kidd and J. L. Rivoire (Eds.), *Perceptual Development in Children*. Pp. 57–78, International Universities Press, New York, 1966.

Proshansky, H. M.: The development of intergroup attitudes. *In* L. W. Hoffman and M. L. Hoffman (Eds.), *Review of Child Development Research.* Vol. 2, pp. 311–372, Russell Sage Foundation, New York, 1966.

———, and Newton, P.: The nature and meaning of Negro self-identity. *In* M. Deutsch, I. Katz, and A. Jensen (Eds.), *Social Class, Race, and Psychological Development.* Ch. 5, Holt, Rinehart and Winston, New York, 1968.

Prothro, E. T.: Ethnocentrism and anti-Negro attitudes in the deep south. *J. Abnor. and Soc. Psychol. 47:* 105–108, 1952.

Provence, S., and Lipton, R. C.: *Infants in Institutions.* International Universities Press, New York, 1962.

Prugh, D. G., and Harlow, R. G.: "Masked deprivation" in infants and young children. *In* J. Bowlby (Ed.), *Deprivation and Maternal Care: A Re-assessment of the Effects.* Pp.201–222, Schocken Books, New York, 1966.

———, Staub, E., Sands, H., Kirschbaum, R., and Lenihan, E.: A study of the emotional reactions of children and families to hospitalization and illness. *Amer. J. Orthopsychiat. 23:* 70–106, 1953.

Purvis, A. W.: An analysis of the abilities of different intelligence levels of secondary-school pupils. Unpublished Ed.D. Thesis, Harvard University, 1938.

Raaheim, K.: Problem solving and past experience. *Monogr. Soc. Res. Child Develop. 30:* 58–67 (Ser. No. 100), 1965.

Rabban, M.: Sex-role identification in young children in two diverse social groups. *Genet. Psychol. Monogr. 42:* 81–158, 1950.

Rabin, A. I.: Some psychosexual differences between kibbutz and non-kibbutz Israeli boys. *J. Project. Tech. 22:* 328–332, 1958.

———: Attitudes of kibbutz children to family and parents. *Amer. J. Orthopsychiat. 29:* 172–179, 1959.

———, and Hayworth, M. R.: (Eds.), *Projective Techniques with Children.* Grune & Stratton, New York, 1960.

Radke, M. J.: The relation of parental authority to children's behavior and attitudes. *University of Minnesota Institute of Child Welfare Monographs,* No. 22, 1946.

———, and Sutherland, J.: Children's concepts and attitudes about minority and majority American groups. *J. Educ. Psychol. 40:* 449–468, 1949.

———, Trager, H. G., and Davis, H.: Social perceptions and attitudes of children. *Genet. Psychol. Monogr. 40:* 327–447, 1949.

———, Sutherland, J., and Rosenberg, P.: Racial attitudes of children. *Sociometry. 13:* 154–171, 1950.

Radke-Yarrow, M., Trager, H. G., and Miller, J.: The role of parents in the development of children's ethnic attitudes. *Child Develop. 23:* 13–53, 1952.

Rainwater, L.: Crucible of identity: The Negro lower-class family. *In* T. Parsons and J. B. Clark (Eds.), *The Negro American.* Pp. 166–204, Beacon Press, Boston, 1966.

Ralph, J. B.: Language development in socially disadvantaged children. *Rev. Educ. Res. 35(5):* 389–400, 1965.

Ramaseshan, R. S.: A note on the validity of the mental age concept. *J. Educ. Psychol. 41:* 56–58, 1950.

Rambusch, N. M.: *Learning How to Learn: An American Approach to Montessori.* Helicon, Baltimore, 1962.

Rank, O.: The Trauma of Birth. Harcourt, Brace, New York, 1929.

Rapaport, D.: Behavior research in collective settlements in Israel: A study of kibbutz education and its bearing on the theory of development. *Amer. J. Orthopsychiat. 28:* 587–597, 1958.

Raph, J., Thomas, A., Chess, S., and Korn, S. J.: The influence of nursery school on social interactions. *Amer. J. Orthopsychiat. 38(1):* 144–152, 1968.

Rapp, D. W.: Child rearing attitudes of mothers in Germany and the United States. *Child Develop. 32:* 669–678, 1961.

Rasmussen, Elizabeth A., and Archer, E. J.: Concept identification as a function of language pretraining and task complexity. *J. Exptl. Psychol. 61:* 437–441, 1961.

Rauh, J. L., Schumsky, D. A., and Witt, M. T.: Heights, weights, and obesity in urban school children. *Child Develop. 38(2):* 515–530, 1967.

Raush, H. L., Farbman, I., and Llewellyn, L. G.: Person, setting, and change in social interaction: II. A normal control study. *Human Relations. 13:* 305–322, 1960.

Ray, W. S.: Verbal compared with manipulative solution of an apparatus problem. *Amer. J. Psychol. 70:* 289–290, 1957.

Raymert, M., and Hinton, R., Jr.: The effect of a change to a relatively superior environment upon the IQ's of one hundred children. *In* G. M. Whipple (Ed.), *Thirty-ninth Yearbook, National Society for the Study of Education.* Part I, pp. 255–268, University of Chicago Press, Chicago, 1940.

Razran, G.: The observable unconscious and the inferable conscious in current Soviet psychophysiology: Interoceptive conditioning, semantic conditioning, and the orienting reflex. *Psychol. Rev. 68:* 81–147, 1961.

Read, G. D.: *Childbirth Without Fear.* Rev. ed. Harper, New York, 1953.

Rebelsky, G., Allinsmith, W., and Grinder, R. E.: Resistance to temptation and sex differences in children's use of fantasy concession. *Child Develop. 34:* 955–962, 1963.

Rebelsky, F. G., Starr, R. H., and Luria, Z.: Language development: The first four years. *In* Y. Brackbill (Ed.), *Infancy and Early Childhood: A Handbook Guide to Human Development.* Pp. 287–357, Free Press, New York, 1967.

Redl, F.: The phenomenon of contagion and shock effect in group therapy. *In* K. R. Eissler (Ed.), *Searchlight on Delinquency.* International Universities Press, New York, 1949.

————, and Wineman, D.: *Children Who Hate.* The Free Press, Glencoe, Illinois, 1951.

Rees, L.: Body build, personality and neurosis in women. *J. Men. Sci. 96:* 426–434, 1950.

Reese, H. W.: Manifest anxiety and achievement test performance. *J. Educ. Psychol. 52:* 132–135, 1961.

————: Sociometric choices of the same and opposite sex in late childhood. *Merrill-Palmer Quart. 8(3):* 173–174, 1962.

————: Discrimination learning set in children. *In* L. P. Lipsitt, and C. C. Spiker (Eds.), *Advances in Child Development and Behavior.* Vol. I, pp. 115–145, Academic Press, New York, 1963.

————: Attitudes toward the opposite sex in late childhood. *Merrill-Palmer Quart. 12(2):* 157–163, 1966.

Reichard, S., Schneider, M., and Rapaport, D.: The development of concept formation in children. *Amer. J. Orthopsychiat. 14:* 156–162, 1944.

Remmers, H. H., Horton, R. E., and Lysgaard, S.: Teen-age personality in our culture. Report of Poll No. 32. *Purdue Opinion Panel,* 1952.

Rendle-Short, J.: The puff test. *Arch. Dis. Childhood. 36:* 50–57, 1961,

Renninger, Cheryl, and Williams, J. E.: Black-white color connotations and racial awareness in preschool children. *Percept. Motor Skills. 22:* 771–785, 1966.

Rest, J., Turiel, E., and Kohlberg, L.: Level of moral development as a determinant of preference and comprehension of moral judgments made by others. Unpublished research report, 1967.

Reymert, M. L., and Kohn, H. A.: An objective investigation of suggestibility. *Character and Personal. 9:* 44–48, 1940.

Reynolds, E. L.: The fat/bone index as a sex differentiating character in man. *Hum. Biol. 21:* 199–204, 1949.

Reynolds, M. M.: *Negativism of Preschool Children.* Teachers College, Columbia University, New York, 1928.

Rheingold, H. L.: The modification of social responsiveness in infant babies. *Monogr. Soc. Res. Child Develop. 21(2):* 1956.

————: The measurement of maternal care. *Child Develop. 31:* 565–575, 1960.

————: The development of social behavior in the human infant. *Monogr. Soc. Res. Child Develop.* No. 107, *31(5):* 1–17, 1966.

————, and Bayley, N.: The later effects of an experimental modification of mothering. *Child Develop. 30:* 363, 1959.

————, Gewirtz, J. L., and Ross, H. W.: Social conditioning of vocalization in the infant. *J. Comp. Physiol. Psychol. 52:* 68–73, 1959.

Rhine, R. J.: *The Effect on Problem Solving of Success or Failure as a Function of Cue Specificity.* Technical Report No. 8, NR 150-149. Department of Psychology, Stanford University, 1955.

Ricciuti, H. N.: Object grouping and selective ordering in infants 12 to 24 months old. *Merrill-Palmer Quart. 11:* 129–148, 1965.

———: Social and emotional behavior in infancy: Some developmental issues and problems. *Merrill-Palmer Quart. 14(1):* 82–100, 1968.

Rice, U. M., and Di Vesta, F. J.: A developmental study of semantic and phonetic generalization in paired-associate learning. *Child Develop. 36:* 721–730, 1965.

Richards, T. W.: The importance of hunger in the bodily activity of the neonate. *Psychol. Bull. 33:* 817–835, 1936.

———, and Irwin, O. C.: Plantar responses of infants and young children: An examination of the literature and reports of new experiments. *University of Iowa Studies in Child Welfare. 2(1):* 1934.

———, and Nelson, V. L.: Abilities of infants during the first eighteen months. *J. Genet. Psychol. 55:* 299–318, 1939.

———, and Newberry, H.: Studies in fetal behavior. III. Can performance on test items at six months postnatally be predicted on the basis of fetal activity? *Child Develop. 9:* 79–86, 1938.

Richardson, C. A., and Stokes, C. W.: Growth and variability of intelligence. *Brit. J. Psychol. 18:* 1935.

Richardson, S. A., Goodman, N., Hastorf, A. H., and Dornbusch, S. M.: Cultural uniformity in reaction to physical disabilities. *Amer. Sociol. Rev. 26:* 241–247, 1961.

———, and Royce, J.: Race and physical handicap in children's preference for other children. *Child Develop. 39:* 467–480, 1968.

Richmond, J. B.: Observations of infant development and psychological aspects. *Merrill-Palmer Quart. 10(2):* 59–101, 1964.

———, and Lipton, E. L.: Some aspects of the neurophysiology of the newborn and their implications for child development. *In* L. Jessner and E. Pavenstedt (Eds.), *Dynamic Psychopathology in Childhood.* Pp. 79–105, Grune & Stratton, New York, 1959.

Rickers-Ovsiankina, N. A.: (Ed.), *Rorschach Psychology.* Wiley, New York, 1960.

Ricketts, A. F.: A study of the behavior of young children in anger. *University of Iowa Studies in Child Welfare. 9(3):* 159–171, 1934.

Riegel, K. S.: Development of language: Suggestions for a verbal fallout model. *Human Develop. 9:* 97–120, 1966.

Riesen, A. H.: The development of visual perception in man and chimpanzee. *Sci. 106:* 107–108, 1947.

Riessman, F.: *The Culturally Derpived Child.* Harper, New York, 1962.

Riever, N.: Deviational aids and motor skill learning in children. *Child Develop. 39:* 559–567, 1968.

Ringness, T. A.: Self-concept of children of low, average, and high intelligence. *Amer. J. Men. Def. 65:* 453–461, 1961.

Rivoire, J. L., and Kidd, A. H.: The development of perception of colour, space, and movement in children. *In* A. H. Kidd and J. L. Rivoire (Eds.), *Perceptual Development in Children.* Ch. 4, International Universities Press, New York, 1966.

Roberts, K. E.: The ability of preschool children to solve problems in which a simple principle of relationship is kept constant. *J. Genet. Psychol. 56:* 353–366, 1940.

Robertson, J.: *Young Children in Hospitals.* Basic Books, New York, 1958.

Robinson, Nancy N., and Robinson, H. B.: A follow-up study of children of low birth weight and control children at school age. *Pediat. 35:* 425–433, 1965.

Roe, Anne.: Crucial life experiences in the development of scientists. *In* E. P. Torrance (Ed.), *Education and Talent.* University of Minnesota Press, Minneapolis, 1960.

Roff, M.: A factorial study of the Fels Parent Behavior Scales. *Child Develop. 20:* 29–45, 1949.

———, and Roff, L.: An analysis of the variance of conflict behavior in preschool children. *Child Develop. 11:* 43–60, 1940.

Roffwarg, H. P., Muzio, J. N., and Dement, W. C.: Ontogenetic development of the human sleep-dream cycle. *Sci. 152:* 604–618, 1966.

Rogers, A. L.: The growth of intelligence at the college level. *School and Society. 31:* 693–699, 1930.

Rogers, C. R.: *Client-Centered Therapy.* Houghton Mifflin, New York, 1951.

Rogier, A.: Psychologische gezichtpunten met betrekking tot de vader-zoon relatie. (Psychological viewpoints with reference to father-son relationship.) *Gawein. 15(3):* 137–148, 1967.

Rokeach, M.: *The Open and Closed Mind.* Basic Books, New York, 1960.

Rosen, B. C.: Race, ethnicity and the achievement syndrome. *Amer. Sociol. Rev. 24:* 47–60, 1959.

———, and D'Andrade, R.: The psychosocial origins of achievement motivation. *Sociometry. 22:* 185–218,1959.

Rosen, D. C.: Family structure and value transmission. *Merrill-Palmer Quart. 10:* 59–76, 1964.

Rosenberg, B. G., and Sutton-Smith, B.: Sibling association, family size and cognitive abilities. *J. Genet. Psychol. 109:* 271–279, 1966.

Rosenblith, J.: The modified Graham behavior test for neonates: Test-Retest reliability, normative data and hypotheses for future work. *Biologia Neonatorum. 3:* 174–192, 1961.

———: Prognostic value of neonatal assessment. *Child Develop. 37:* 623–631, 1966.

Rosenkrans, M. A., and Hartup, W. W.: Imitative influences of consistent and inconsistent response consequences to a model on aggressive behavior in children. *J. Personal. and Soc. Psychol. 7(4):* 429–434, 1967.

Rosenthal, B. G.: Attitude toward money, need, and methods of presentation as determinants of perception of coins from six to ten years of age. *J. Gen. Psychol. 78(1):* 85–103, 1968.

Rosenthal, M. K.: The generalization of dependency behavior from mother to stranger. *J. Child Psychol. and Psychiat. 8(2):* 117–133, 1967.

Rosenthal, R.: *Pygmalion in the Classroom: Teacher Expectation and Pupils' Intellectual Development.* Holt, Rinehart and Winston, New York, 1968.

———, and Jacobson, Lenore: Self-fulfilling prophesies in the classroom: Teachers' expectation as unintended determinants of pupils' intellectual competence. *In* M. Deutsch, I. Katz, and A. R. Jensen (Eds.), *Social Class, Race, and Psychological Development.* Ch. 6, Holt, Rinehart and Winston, New York, 1968.

Rosenzweig, S.: Preference in the repetition of successful and unsuccessful activities as a function of age and personality. *J. Genet. Psychol. 42:* 423–441, 1933.

———: Babies are taught to cry: A hypothesis. *Men. Hyg. 38:* 81–84, 1954.

Rossi, E.: Development of classificatory behavior. *Child Develop. 35:* 137–142, 1964.

Rossier, A.: The future of the premature infant. *Develop. Med. and Child Neurol. 4(5):* 483–487, 1962.

Rothschild, Barbara F.: Incubator isolation as a possible contributing factor to the high incidence of emotional disturbance among prematurely born persons. *J. Genet. Psychol. 110(2):* 287–304, 1967.

Roudinesco, J.: Severe maternal deprivation and personality development in early childhood. *Understanding the Child. 21:* 104–108, 1952.

Rousseau, J. J.: *Emile.* Appleton, New York, 1895.

Rowe, Mary B.: Some properties of content learning in elementary school science. Paper presented to the American Educational Research Association, Chicago, February 17, 1966.

Ruebush, B. K.: Anxiety. *In* H. W. Stevenson (Ed.), Child Psychology. Part I. *Sixty-second Yearbook of the National Society for the Study of Education.* Pp. 460–516, University of Chicago Press, Chicago, 1963.

Ruma, D. H., and Mosher, D. L.: General relationship between moral judgment and guilt in delinquent boys. *J. Abnor. Psychol. 72(2):* 122–127, 1967.

Russell, D. G., and Sarason, I. G.: Test anxiety, sex, and experimental conditions in relation to anagram solution. *J. Personal. and Soc. Psychol. 1:* 493–496, 1965.

Russell, D. H.: The dimensions of children's meaning vocabularies in grades four through twelve. *University of California Publications in Education, 11:* 315–414, 1954.

———, and Saadeh, I. Q.: Qualitative levels in children's vocabularies. *J. Educ. Psychol. 53:* 170–174, 1962.

Russell, R. W.: Studies in animism. II. The development of animism. *J. Genet. Psychol. 56:* 353–366, 1940.

Russell, W. A.: An experimental psychology of development: Pipe dream or possibility? *In* D. B. Barris (Ed.), *The Concept of Development: An Issue in the Study of Human Behavior.* Pp. 162–174, University of Minnesota Press, Minneapolis, 1957.

Rust, M. M.: The effect of resistance on intelligence test scores of young children. *Child Develop. Monogr. 6:* 1931.

Rutherford, E., and Mussen, P.: Generosity in nursery school boys. *Child Develop. 39:* 755–765, 1968.

Ryans, D. G.: *Characteristics of Teachers.* American Council on Education, Washington, D.C., 1960.

Ryans, D. G.: Some relationships between pupil behavior and certain teacher characteristics. *J. Educ. Psychol. 52:* 82–90, 1961.

Sackett, G. P.: Effects of rearing conditions upon the behavior of rhesus monkeys (macaca mulatta). *Child Develop. 36:* 855–868, 1965.

Safier, G.: A study in relationships between the life and death concepts in children. *J. Genet. Psychol. 105:* 283–294, 1964.

Saint-Anne Dargassies, S.: Neurologic development of the infant. The contributions of Andre Thomas. *World Neurology,* 1960, *1:* 71–77. Reprinted in Brackbill and Thompson (Eds.), *Behavior in Infancy and Early Childhood.* The Free Press, New York, 1967.

Salapatek, P., and Kessen, W.: Visual scanning of triangles of the human newborn. *J. Exptl. Child Psychol. 3(2):* 155–167, 1966.

Salk, L.: Mothers' heartbeat as an imprinting stimulus. *Transactions of the New York Academy of Sciences. 24:* 753–763, 1962.

Sameroff, A.: Can conditioned responses be established in the newborn infant? Paper presented at the Eastern Regional Meeting of the Society for Research in Child Development, Worcester, Mass., 1968.

Sampson, E. E.: A study of the ordinal position: Antecedents and outcomes. *In* B. Maher (Ed.), *Progress in Experimental Personality Research.* Vol. 2, pp. 175–228, Academic Press, New York, 1965.

Sampson, O. C.: Speech and language development of five-year-old children. *Brit. J. Educ. Psychol. 29:* 217–222, 1959.

Sandin, A. A.: Social and emotional adjustments of regularly promoted and nonpromoted pupils. *Child Develop. Monogr. 32:* 1944.

Sanford R. N.: Physical and physiological correlates of personality structure. *In* C. Kluckhohn and H. A. Murray (Eds.), *Personality in Nature, Society and Culture.* Knopf, New York, 1949.

Sanford, N.: Will psychologists study human problems? *Amer. Psychol. 20(3):* 192–202, 1965.

Sanford, R., Adkins, M. M., Miller, R. B., Cobb, E. A., Aub, J. C., Burke, B. S., Nathanson, I. T., Stuart, H. C., and Towne, L.: Physique, personality and scholarship. A cooperative study of school children. *Monogr. Soc. Res. Child Develop. 8(1):* 1943.

Santostefano, S. G.: A developmental study of the cognitive control "Levelling-sharpening". *Merrill-Palmer Quart. 10:* 343–360, 1964.

Saporta, S.: *Psycholinguistics: A Book of Readings.* Holt, Rinehart and Winston, New York, 1961.

Sarason, I. G.: Test anxiety and the intellectual performance of college students. *J. Educ. Psychol. 52:* 201–206, 1961.

———: *Contemporary Research in Personality.* Van Nostrand, New York, 1962.

———: Test anxiety and intellectual performance. *J. Abnor. and Soc. Psychol. 66:* 73–75, 1963.

Sarason, S. B., Davidson, K. S., Lighthall, F. F., Waite, R. R., and Ruebush, B. K.: *Anxiety in Elementary School Children.* Wiley, New York, 1960.

——, Hill, K. T., and Zimbardo, P. G.: A longitudinal study of the relation of test anxiety to performance on intelligence and achievement tests. *Monogr. Soc. Res. Child Develop. 29:* (Whole No. 98), 1964.

Sark, Lee.: Thoughts on the concept of imprinting and its place in early human development. *Canad. Psychiat. Assoc. J. 11* (Suppl.): 295–305, 1966.

Sassenrath, J. M.: Learning without awareness and transfer of learning sets. *J. Educ. Psychol. 50:* 205–211, 1959.

Sax, G., and Ottina, J. P.: The arithmetic reasoning of pupils differing in school experience. *California J. Educ. Res. 9:* 15–19, 1958.

Sayegh, Y., and Dennis, W.: The effect of supplementary experiences upon the behavioral development of infants in institutions. *Child Develop. 36:* 82–90, 1965.

Scarr, S.: Genetic factors in activity motivation. *Child Develop. 37:* 663–673, 1966.

Schachter, S.: *The Psychology of Affiliation.* Stanford University Press, Stanford, 1959.

——: Birth order, eminence and higher education. *Amer. Soc. Rev. 28:* 757–767, 1963.

——, and Singer, J. E.: Cognitive, social and physiological determinants of emotional state. *Psychol. Rev. 69:* 379–399, 1962.

Schaefer, E. S.: Converging conceptual models for maternal behavior and for child behavior. *In* J. C. Glidewell (Ed.), *Parental Attitudes and Child Behavior.* Pp. 124–146, Charles C Thomas, Springfield, Illinois, 1961.

——: A configurational analysis of children's reports of parent behavior. *J. Consult. Psychol. 29:* 552–557, 1965.

——, and Bayley, N.: Consistency of maternal behavior from infancy to preadolescence. *J. Abnor. and Soc. Psychol. 61:* 1–6, 1960.

——, and ——: Maternal behavior, child behavior, and their intercorrelations from infancy through adolescence. *Monogr. Soc. Res. Child Develop. 28(3):* (Whole No. 87), 1963.

——, and Bell, R. Q.: Development of a parental attitude research instrument. *Child Develop. 29(3):* 339–361, 1958.

Schaeffer, H. R.: Objective observations of personality development in early infancy. *Brit. J. Med. Psychol. 31:* 174–184, 1958.

——: Some issues for research in the study of attachment behavior. *In* B. Foss (Ed.), *Determinants of Infant Behavior.* II. Pp. 179–196, Methuen Press, London, 1963.

——: The onset of fear of strangers and the incongruity hypothesis. *J. Child Psychol. and Psychiat. 7(2):* 95–106, 1966.

——: Activity level as a constitutional determinant of infantile reaction to deprivation. *Child Develop. 37:* 595–602, 1966.

——, and Callender, W. N.: Psychologic effects of hospitalization in infancy. *Pediat. 24:* 528–539, 1959.

——, and Emerson, P. E.: The development of social attachments in infancy. *Monogr. Soc. Res. Child Develop. 29(3):* No. 94, 1964.

Schaie, K. W.: A general model for the study of development problems. *Psychol. Bull. 64(2):* 92–107, 1965.

Sharpe, J. F.: The retention of meaningful material. *Catholic University of Amer. Educ. Res. Monogr. 16:* No. 8, 1952.

Scheibel, M. E., and Scheibel, A. B.: Some neural substrates of postnatal development. *In* L. W. Hoffman and M. L. Hoffman (Eds.), *Review of Child Development Research.* Vol. I. Pp. 481–519, Russell Sage Foundation, New York, 1964.

Schiff, H. M.: Judgmental response sets in the perception of sociometric status. Unpublished doctoral dissertation, University of Illinois, 1953.

Schmidt, B. A.: Relationship between social status and classroom behavior. Unpublished study. Washington University, St. Louis, Missouri, 1958.

Schmuck, R. A.: Influence of the peer group. *In* G. S. Lesser (Ed.), *Psychology and the Educational Process.* In press, Scott, Foresman, Chicago, 1969.

——, and Schmuck, R. W.: Upward mobility and IQ performance. *J. Educ. Res. 55:* 123–127, 1961.

————, and Van Egmond, E.: Sex differences in the relationship of interpersonal perception to academic performance. *Psychology in the Schools. 2:* 32–40, 1965.

Schneider, L., and Lysgaard, S.: The deferred gratification pattern: A preliminary study. *Amer. Soc. Rev. 18:* 142–149, 1953.

Schneirla, T. C.: A consideration of some problems in the ontogeny of family life and social adjustments in various infra-human animals. *In* M. J. E. Senn (Ed.), *Problems of Infancy and Childhood.* Transactions of Fourth Conference, 1950. Pp. 81–124, Josiah Macy, Jr. Foundation, New York, 1951.

Schofield, W., and Ballan, L. A.: A comparative study of the personal histories of schizophrenic and non-psychiatric patients. *J. Abnor. Soc. Psychol. 59:* 216–225, 1959.

Schopbach, R. R., Fried, P. H., and Rackoff, A. E.: Pseudocyesis: A psychosomatic disorder. *Psychoso. Med. 14:* 129–134, 1952.

Schpoont, S. H.: Some relationships between task attractiveness, self-evaluated motivation, and success or failure. Unpublished doctoral dissertation, University of Illinois, 1955.

Schroeder, P. L.: Behavior difficulties in children associated with the results of birth trauma. *JAMA. 92:* 100–104, 1929.

Schuessler, K., and Strauss, A.: A study of concept learning by scale analysis. *Amer. Soc. Rev. 15:* 752–762, 1950.

Schulman, M. J., and Havighurst, R. J.: Relations between ability and social status in a mid-Western community. IV. Size of vocabulary. *J. Educ. Psychol. 38:* 437–442, 1947.

Scott, J. P.: Implications of infra-human social behavior for problems of human relations. *In* M. Sherif and M. O. Wilson (Eds.), *Group Relations at the Cross-Roads.* Pp. 33–73, Harper, New York, 1953.

————: The process of primary socialization in canine and human infants. *Monogr. Soc. Res. Child Develop. 28(1):* 1963.

————: The development of social motivation. *In* M. R. Jones (Ed.), *Nebraska Symposium on Motivation.* Pp. 111–132, University of Nebraska Press, Lincoln, 1967.

————, Fredericson, E., and Fuller, J. L.: Experimental exploration of the critical period hypothesis. *J. Personal. 1:* 162–183, 1951.

————, and Marston, M.: Critical periods affecting the development of normal and maladjustive social behavior of puppies. *J. Genet. Psychol. 77:* 25–60, 1950.

Scottish Council for Research in Education. *Social implications of the 1947 Scottish mental survey.* University of London Press, London, 1953.

Sears, P. S.: Levels of aspiration in academically successful and unsuccessful children. *J. Abnor. and Soc. Psychol. 35:* 498–536, 1940.

————: Level of aspiration in relation to some variables of personality: Clinical studies. *J. Soc. Psychol. 14:* 311–336, 1941.

————: Doll play aggression in normal young children: Influence of sex, age, sibling status, father's absence. *Psychol. Monogr. 65(223):* 1951.

————: Correlates of need achievement and need affiliation and classroom management, self-concept and creativity. Unpublished manuscript, Laboratory of Human Development, Stanford University, 1962.

Sears, R. R.: Influence of methodological factors on doll play performance. *Child Develop. 18:* 190–197, 1947.

————: Ordinal position in the family as a psychological variable. *Amer. Soc. Rev. 15:* 397–401, 1950, (a).

————: Relation of fantasy aggression to interpersonal aggression. *Child Develop. 21:* 5–6, 1950, (b).

————: A theoretical framework for personality and social behavior. *Amer. Psychol. 6:* 476–483, 1951.

————: The growth of conscience. *In* I. Iscoe and H. W. Stevenson (Eds.), *Personality Development in Children.* Pp. 92–111, University of Texas Press, Austin, 1960.

————: Relation of early socialization experiences to aggression in middle childhood. *J. Abnor. and Soc. Psychol. 63:* 466–492, 1961.

————, Maccoby, E., and Levin, H.: *Patterns of Child Rearing*. Row Peterson and Co., Evanston, Ill., 1957.

————, Pintler, M., and Sears, P. S.: Effect of father separation on preschool children's doll play aggression. *Child Develop. 17:* 219–243, 1946.

————, Rau, L., and Alpert, R.: *Identification and Child Rearing*. Stanford University Press, Stanford, California, 1965.

————, Whiting, J. W. M., Nowlis, V., and Sears, P. S.: Some child-rearing antecedents of aggression and dependency in young children. *Genet. Psychol. Monogr. 47:* 135–254, 1953.

Sebeok, T. A.: Animal communication. *Sci. 147:* 1006–1014, 1965.

Sechrest, L., and Kaas, Judith S.: Concept difficulty as a function of stimulus similarity. *J. Educ. Psychol. 56:* 327–333, 1965.

Segel, D.: *Intellectual Abilities in the Adolescence Period*. Federal Security Agency, Washington, D.C., 1948.

Seils, L. P.: The relationship between measures of physical growth and gross motor performance of primary-grade school children. *Res. Quart. Amer. Assoc Health, Phys. Educ. and Recreation. 22:* 244–260, 1951.

Sells, S. B.: An interactionist looks at the environment. *Amer. Psychol. 18:* 696–702, 1963.

Selye, H.: Stress and the general adaptation syndrome. *Brit. Med. J. 1:* 1383–1392, 1950.

Selzer, C. C.: The relationship between the masculine component and personality. *Amer. J. Phys. Anthropol. 3:* 33–47, 1945.

Serra, M. C.: A study of fourth grade children's comprehension of certain verbal abstractions. *J. Exptl. Educ. 22:* 103–118, 1953.

Sewall, M.: Two studies in sibling rivalry. I. Some causes of jealousy in young children. *Smith College of Studies in Social Work. 1:* 6–22, 1930.

Sewell, W. H.: Social class and childhood personality. *Sociometry. 24:* 340–356, 1961.

————, Mussen, P. H., and Harris, C. W.: Relationships among child training practices. *Amer. Soc. Rev. 20:* 137–148, 1955.

Shaffer, J. P.: Social and personality correlates of children's estimates of height. *Genetic Psychol. Monogr. 70:* 97–134, 1964.

Shaffer, L. H.: Concept formation in an ordering task. *Brit. J. Psychol. 42:* 361–369, 1961.

Shantz, C. U.: A developmental study of Piaget's theory of logical multiplication. *Merrill-Palmer Quart. 13:* 121–137, 1967.

Shapiro, H.: The development of walking in a child. *J. Genet. Psychol. 100(2):* 221–226, 1962.

Sheehy, L. M.: A study of preadolescents by means of a personality inventory. Catholic University Press, Washington, D.C., 1938.

Sheldon, W. H.: *The Varieties of Temperament*. Harper, New York, 1942.

Sheridan, M. D.: *The Child's Hearing for Speech*. Methuen, London, 1948.

Sherif, M.: Introduction. *In* J. H. Rohrer and M. Sherif (Eds.), *Social Psychology at the Crossroads*. Harper, New York, 1951.

————: The concept of reference groups in human relations. *In* M. Sherif and M. O. Wilson (Eds.), *Group Relations at the Crossroads*. Harper, New York, 1953.

————: Some superordinate goals in the reduction of inter-group conflicts. *Amer. J. Soc. 63:* 349–356, 1958.

————: Theoretical analysis of the individual-group relationship in a social situation. Paper for Symposium on Conceptual Definition in the Behavioral Sciences, Fairfield University, Fairfield, Connecticut, April 22, 1964.

————: Self concept. Paper prepared for the New International Encyclopedia of the Social Sciences, 1965.

————, Harvey, O. J., White, B. J., Hood, W. R., and Sherif, C. W.: *Experimental Study of Positive and Negative Intergroup Attitudes Between Experimentally Produced Groups: Robber's Cave Study*. University of Oklahoma Press, Norman, 1954.

————, ————, ————, ————, and ————: *Intergroup Conflict and Cooperation: The Robber's Cave Experiment*. University of Oklahoma Press, Norman, 1961.

————, and Sherif, C. W.: *Groups in Harmony and Tension*. Harper, New York, 1953.

Sherman, M.: The differentiation of emotional responses in infants. I. Judgments of emotional responses from motion picture views and from actual observations. *J. Comp. Psychol. 7:* 265–284, 1927, (a).

————: The differentiation of emotional responses in infants. II. The ability of observers to judge the emotional characteristics of the crying of infants and the voice of an adult. *J. Comp. Psychol. 7:* 335–351, 1927 (b).

————: The differentiation of emotional responses in infants. III. A proposed theory of the development of emotional responses in infants. *J. Comp. Psychol. 8:* 385–394, 1928.

————, and Key, C. B.: The intelligence of isolated mountain children. *Child Develop. 3:* 279–290, 1932.

————, and Sherman, I. C.: Sensori-motor responses in infants. *J. Comp. Psychol. 5:* 53–68, 1925.

————, Sherman, I. C., and Flory, C.: Infant behavior. *Comp. Psychol. Monogr. 12(4):* 1936.

Shinn, M. W.: *The Biography of a Baby.* Houghton Mifflin, Boston, 1900.

Shirley, M. M.: *The First Two Years: A Study of Twenty-Five Babies.* Vol. I. *Postural and Locomotor Development.* University of Minnesota Press, Minneapolis, 1931, (a).

————: The sequential method for the studying of maturing behavior patterns. *Psychol. Rev. 38:* 507–528, 1931, (b).

————: *The First Two Years: A Study of Twenty-Five Babies.* Vol. II. *Intellectual Development.* University of Minnesota Press, Minneapolis, 1933.

————: *The First Two Years: A Study of Twenty-Five Babies.* Vol. III. *Personality Manifestations.* University of Minnesota Press, Minneapolis, 1933.

————: Common content in the speech of preschool children. *Child Develop. 9:* 333–346, 1938, (a).

————: Development of immature babies during their first two years. *Child Develop. 9:* 347–360, 1938, (b).

————: A behavior syndrome characterizing prematurely-born children. *Child Devleop. 10:* 115–128, 1939.

————: Impact of mother's personality on the young child. *Smith College Studies in Social Work. 12:* 15–64, 1941.

————: Children's adjustments to a strange situation. *J. Abnor. and Soc. Psychol. 37:* 201–217, 1942.

Shore, E., and Sechrest, L.: Concept attainment as a function of number of positive instances presented. *J. Educ. Psychol. 52:* 303–307, 1961.

Short, J. F.: Juvenile delinquency: The socio-cultural context. *In* L. W. Hoffman and M. L. Hoffman (Eds.): *Review of Child Development Research. 2:* 423–468, Russell Sage Foundation, New York, 1966.

Shrader, W. K., and Leventhal, T.: Birth order of children and parental report of problems. *Child Develop. 39:* 1165–1175, 1968.

Shuey, A. M.: Improvement in scores on the American Council Psychological Examination from freshman to senior year. *J. Educ. Psychol. 39:* 417–426, 1948.

————: *The Testing of Negro Intelligence.* 2nd ed. Social Science Press, New York, 1966.

Shure, M. B.: Psychological ecology of a nursery school. *Child.Develop. 34:* 979–992, 1963.

Shuttleworth, F. K.: The cumulative influence on intelligence of socio-economic differentials operating on the same children over a period of ten years. *In* G. M. Whipple (Ed.), *Thirty-ninth Yearbook, National Society for the Study of Education.* Part 2, pp. 275–280, University of Chicago Press, Chicago, 1940.

Sidana, U. R.: A comparative study of fears in children. *J. Psychol. Res. 11(1):* 1–6, 1967.

Sielel, A. E.: Session differences in aggression in children's play in the absence of an adult. Paper read at American Psychological Association, Chicago, September, 1956.

Siegel, L. S., and Goldstein, A. G.: Conservation of number in young children: Recency versus relational response strategies. *Develop. Psychol.* Vol. I, No. 2, pp. 128–130, 1969.

Siegel, L., and Siegel, Lila C.: Educational set: A determinant of acquisition. *J. Educ. Psychol. 56:* 1–12, 1965.

Siegelman, M.: Loving and punishing parental behavior and introversion tendencies in sons. *Child Develop. 37:* 985–992, 1966.

Siegman, A. W.: Father absence during early childhood and antisocial behavior. *J. Abnor. Psychol. 71:* 71–74, 1966.

Sieve, B. F.: Vitamins and hormones in nutrition. V. Emotional upset and trauma. *Amer. J. Dig. Dis. 16:* 14–25, 1949.

Sigel, I. E.: Developmental trends in the abstraction ability of children. *Child Develop. 24:* 131–144, 1952.

———: The dominance of meaning. *J. Genet. Psychol. 85:* 201–207, 1954.

———: The attainment of concepts. *In* M. L. Hoffman and L. W. Hoffman (Eds.), *Review of Child Development Research.* Vol. I, pp. 209–248, Russell Sage Foundation, New York, 1964.

———, and Hooper, F. H.: *Logical Thinking in Children: Research Based on Piaget's Theory.* Holt, Rinehart and Winston, New York, 1968.

———, Jarman, P., and Hanesian, H.: Styles of categorization and intellectual and personality correlates in young children. *Hum. Develop. 10:* 1–17, 1967.

———, and McBane, B.: Cognitive competence and level of symbolization among five-year-old children. Paper presented at the American Psychological Association Convention, New York City, September, 1966.

———, and Mermelstein, E.: Effects of non-schooling on Paigetian tasks of conservation. Paper presented at APA meeting, September, 1965.

———, and Perry, C.: Psycholinguistic diversity among "culturally deprived" children. *Amer. J. Orthopsychiat. 38(1):* 122–126, 1968.

———, Roeper, A., and Hooper, S. H.: A training procedure for acquisition of Piaget's conservation of quantity: A pilot study and its replication. *Brit. J. Educ. Psychol. 36:* 301–311, 1966.

———, Saltz, E., and Rosking, W.: Variables determining concept conservation in children. *J. Exptl. Psychol. 74:* 471–475, 1967.

Sigel, R.: Assumptions about the learning of political values. *Annals Amer. Acad. Polit. and Soc. Sci. 361:* 1–9, 1965.

Siller, J.: Socio-economic status and conceptual thinking. *J. Abnor. Soc. Psychol. 55:* 365–371, 1957.

Sills, F. D.: A factor analysis of somatotypes and of their relationship to achievement in motor skills. *Res. Quart. Amer. Assoc. Health. 21:* 424–437, 1950.

Silver, A. A.: Behavioral syndrome associated with brain damage in children. *Pediat. Clin. N. Amer.* Pp. 687–698, 1958.

Silverman, W. A., Fertig, J. W., and Berger, A. P.: The influence of the thermal environment on the survival of the newly born premature infant. *Pediat. 22:* 876–886, 1958.

Simnel, M. L.: Developmental aspects of the body scheme. *Child Develop. 37:* 83–95, 1966.

Simsarian, F. P., and McLendon, P. A.: Feeding behavior of an infant during the first twelve weeks of life on a self-demand schedule. *J. Pediat. 20:* 93–103, 1942.

Simsarian, F. P., and McLendon, P. A.: Further records of the self-demand schedule in infant feeding. *J. Pediat. 27:* 109–114, 1945.

Sinclair-de-Zwart, H.: Acquisition du language et developpement de la pensee. Dunod, Paris, 1967.

———: Developmental cycle linguistics. *In* D. Elkind and J. H. Flavell (Eds.), *Studies in Cognitive Development: Essays in Honour of Jean Piaget.* Pp. 315–336, Oxford University Press, New York, 1969.

Singer, J. E., Westphal, M., and Niswander, K. R.: Sex differences in the incidence of neonatal abnormalities and abnormal performance in early childhood. *Child Develop. 39(1):* 103–112, 1968.

Singer, R. N., and Brunk, J. W.: Relation of perceptual-motor ability and intellectual ability in elementary school children. *Percept. Motor Skills. 24(3, Pt. 1),* 967–970, 1967.

Siqueland, Einar, and Lipsitt, L. P.: Conditioned head-turning in human newborns. *J. Exptl. Child Psychol. 3(4):* 356–376, 1966.

Sivan, C.: Rubella in pregnancy as aetiological factor in stillbirth. *Lancet 1.* Pp. 744–746, 1948.

Skalet, M.: The significance of delayed reactions in young children. *Comp. Psychol. Monogr.* *7(34):* 1931.

Skeels, H. M.: Adult status of children with contrasting life experiences. *Monogr. Soc. Res. Child Develop. 31(65):* 1966.

———, and Fillmore, E. A.: Mental development of children from underprivileged homes. *J. Genet. Psychol. 50:* 427–439, 1937.

———, et al.: A study of environmental stimulation. An orphanage preschool project. *University of Iowa Studies in Child Welfare. 4:* 1938.

———, and Harms, I. E.: Children with inferior social histories: Their mental development in adoptive homes. *J. Genet. Psychol. 72:* 283–294, 1948.

Skinner, B. F.: *Science and Human Behavior.* MacMillan, New York, 1953.

———: *Verbal Behavior.* Appleton-Century-Crofts, New York, 1957.

Skodak, M.: Children in foster homes: A study of mental development. *University of Iowa Studies in Child Welfare. 16(1):* 1939.

———, and Skeels, H. M.: A final follow-up of one hundred adopted children. *J. Genet. Psychol. 75:* 85–125, 1949.

Slaght, W. E.: Untruthfulness in children: Its conditioning factors and its setting in child nature. *University of Iowa Studies in Character. 1(4):* 1928.

Slater, E.: Genetic investigations in twins. *J. Men. Sci. 99:* 44–52, 1953.

Slater, P. E.: Parental role differentiation. *Amer. J. Soc. 67:* 296–308, 1961.

Slobin, D. I.: Comments on developmental psycholinguistics. *In* F. Smith and G. A. Miller (Eds.), *The Genesis of Language: A Psycholinguistic Approach.* Pp. 85–92, M.I.T. Press, Cambridge, 1966, (a).

———: Grammatical transformations and sense comprehension in childhood and adulthood. *J. Verb. Learning and Verb. Behav. 5:* 219–277, 1966, (b).

———: Soviet methods of investigating child language: A topical guide to "abstracts of Soviet studies of child language". *In* F. Smith and G. A. Miller (Eds.), *The Genesis of Language: A Psycholinguistic Approach.* Pp. 361–386, M.I.T. Press, Cambridge, 1966, (c).

———: The acquisition of Russian as a native language. *In* F. Smith and G. A. Miller (Eds.), *The Genesis of Language: A Psycholinguistic Approach.* Pp. 129–152, M.I.T. Press, Cambridge, 1966, (d).

———: (Ed.), *A Field Manual for Cross-Cultural Study of the Acquisition of Communicative Competence.* Berkeley: University of California, 1967.

———: Imitation and grammatical development in children. *In* N. S. Endler, L. R. Boulter, and H. Osser (Eds.), *Contemporary Issues in Developmental Psychology.* Pp. 437–443, Holt, Rinehart and Winston, New York, 1967.

Slovic, T.: Risk-taking in children: Age and sex differences. *Child Develop. 37:* 169–176, 1966.

Smart, R.: The changing composition of intelligence: A replication of a factor analysis. *J. Genet. Psychol. 107:* 111–116, 1965.

Smedslund, J.: Transitivity of preference patterns as seen by pre-school children. *Scand. J. Psychol. 1:* 49–54, 1960.

———: The acquisition of conservation of substance and weight in children. *Scand. J. Psychol. 2:* 11–20; 71–87; 153-16-; 2-3–210, 1961.

———: The acquisition of conservation of substance and weight in children: VII. Conservation of discontinuous quantity and the operations of adding and taking away. *Scand. J. Psychol. 3:* 69–77, 1962.

———: The effect of observation on children's representation of the spatial orientation of a water surface. *J. Genet. Psychol. 102:* 195–201, 1963.

———: Concrete reasoning: A study of intellectual development. *Monogr. Soc. Res. Child Develop. 29(93):* 1–39, 1964.

Smirnov, A. A.: The development of memory. *In Psychological Science of the USSR,* Vol. I. Pp. 346–420, United States joint publication research service, Washington, D.C., 1961.

Smith, I. D.: The effects of training procedures upon the acquisition of conservation of weight. *Child Develop. 39:* 515–526, 1968.

Smith, M.: Relation between word variety and mean letter length of words with chronological and mental ages. *J. Genet. Psychol. 56:* 27–43, 1957.

Smith, M. E.: An investigation of the development of the sentence and the extent of vocabulary in young children. *University of Iowa Studies in Child Welfare. 3(5):* 1926.

———: A study of some factors influencing the development of the sentence in preschool children. *J. Genet. Psychol. 46:* 182–212, 1933.

———: A study of the speech of eight bilingual children of the same family. *Child Develop. 6:* 19–25, 1935.

———: Some light on the problem of bilingualism as found from a study of the progress in mastery of English among preschool children of non-American ancestry in Hawaii. *Genet. Psychol. Monogr. 21:* 119–284, 1939.

———: Measurement of vocabularies of young bilingual children in both the languages used. *J. Genet. Psychol. 74:* 305–315, 1949.

———: Childhood memories compared with those of adult life. *J. Genet. Psychol. 80:* 151–182, 1952, (a).

———: A comparison of certain personality traits as rated in the same individuals in childhood and fifty years later. *Child Develop. 23:* 159–180, 1952, (b).

———: Word variety as a measure of bilingualism in preschool children. *J. Genet. Psychol. 90:* 143–150, 1957.

Smith, M. K.: Measurement of the size of general English vocabulary through the elementary grades and high school. *Genet. Psychol. Monogr. 24:* 311–345, 1941.

Smith, R. T.: Socio-environmental factors in twins. *In Methods and Goals in Human Behavior Genetics.* Pp. 45–61, Academic Press, New York, 1965.

Smith, S.: Age and sex differences in children's opinion concerning sex differences. *J. Genet. Psychol. 54:* 17–25, 1939.

———: Language and non-verbal test performance of racial groups in Honolulu before and after a fourteen-year interval. *J. Genet. Psychol. 26:* 51–93, 1942.

Smock, C. D.: The relationship between "intolerance of ambiguity", generalization and speed of perceptual closure. *Child Develop. 28:* 27–36, 1957.

———: Perceptual rigidity and closure phenomenon as a function of manifest anxiety in children. *Child Develop. 29:* 237–247, 1958.

———: Perceptual sensitization to threat objects as a function of manifest anxiety. *Child Develop. 34:* 161–167, 1963.

Snyder, L. H., and David, P. R.: *The Principles of Heredity.* (5th ed.). Heath, Boston, 1957.

Snyder, S.: Toward an evolutionary theory of dreaming. *Amer. J. Psychiat. 123:* 121–136, 1966.

Soffietti, J. P.: Bilingualism and biculturalism. *J. Educ. Psychol. 46:* 222–227, 1955.

Solley, C. M.: Affective processes in perceptual development. *In* A. H. Kidd and J. L. Rivoire (Eds.), *Perceptual Development in Children.* Ch. 11, International Universities Press, New York, 1966.

Solomon, D., Rosenberg, L., and Bezdek, W. E.: Teacher behavior and student leaning. *J. Educ. Psychol. 55:* 23–30, 1964.

Solomons, G., and Solomons, H. C.: Factors affecting motor performance in four-month-old infants. *Child Develop. 35:* 1283–1296, 1964.

Sontag, L. W.: The significance of fetal environmental differences. *Amer. J. Obst. and Gyn. 42:* 996–1003, 1941.

———: Differences in modifiability of fetal behavior and physiology. *Psychoso. Med. 6:* 151–154, 1964.

———: Some psychosomatic aspects of childhood. *Nervous Child. 5:* 296–304, 1946.

———: A critique of longitudinal methods of the study of personality. Proceedings of the 15th International Congress of Psychology, *Acta Psychologica.* P. 422, North Holland Publishing Co., Amsterdam, 1958.

———: The possible relationship of prenatal environment to schizophrenia. *The Etiology of Schizophrenia.* Basic Books, New York, 1960.

———: Somatophysics of personality and body function. *Vita Humana. 6:* 1–10, 1963.

————: Implications of fetal behavior and environment for adult personalities. *Ann. New York Acad. Sci. 134(2):* 782–786, 1966.

————, Baker, C. T., and Nelson, V.: Personality as a determinant of performance. *Amer. J. Orthopsychiat. 25:* 555–563, 1955.

————, Baker, C. T., and Nelson, V. L.: Mental growth and personality development: A longitudinal study. *Monogr. Soc. Res. Child Develop. 2(143):* 1958.

————, and Harris, L. M.: Evidence of disturbed prenatal and neonatal growth in bones of infants aged one month. *Amer. J. Dist. Children. 56:* 1248–1255, 1938.

————, and Kagan, J.: The emergence of intellectual achievement motives. *Amer. J. Orthopsychiat. 13:* 175–178, 1963.

————, and Richards, T. W.: Studies in fetal behavior: I. Fetal heart rate as a behavioral indicator. *Child Develop. Monogr. 3 (4):* 1938.

Sorokin, P. A., and Gove, D. S.: Notes on the friendly and antagonistic behavior of nursery school children. *In* P. A. Sorokin (Ed.), *Explorations in Altruistic Love and Behavior.* Beacon Press, Boston, 1950.

Spaulding, R.: Achievement, creativity and self-concept correlates of teacher-pupil transactions in elementary schools. University of Illinois, Urbana, 1963. (Mimeographed).

Spears, W. C.: Visual preference in the 4-month old infant. *Psychoso. Sci. 4(6):* 237–238, 1966.

————, and Hohle, R. H.: Sensory and perceptual processes in infants. *In* Y. Brackbill (Ed.), *Infancy and Early Childhood: A Handbook and Guide to Human Development.* Ch. 2, pp. 50–121, Free Press, New York, 1967.

Speer, G. S.: The mental development of children of feeble-minded and normal mothers. *In* G. M. Whipple (Ed.), *Thirty-ninth Yearbook, National Society for the Study of Education.* Part 2, pp. 309–314, Chicago University Press, Chicago, 1940.

Spelt, D. K.: The conditioning of the human fetus in utero. *J. Exptl. Psychol. 38:* 338–346, 1948.

Spencer, T. D.: Sex role learning in early childhood. *In* W. W. Hartup and N. L. Smothergill (Eds.), *The Young Child: Reviews of Research.* National Association for the Education of Young Children, Washington, D.C., 1967.

Speroff, B. J.: The stability of sociometric choice among kindergarten children. *Sociometry. 18:* 129–131, 1955.

Sperry, R. W.: Mechanisms of neural maturation. *In* S. S. Stevens (Ed.), *Handbook of Experimental Psychology.* Pp. 236–280, Wiley, New York, 1951.

Spiegel, L. H.: The child's concept of beauty: A study in concept formation. *J. Genet. Psychol. 77:* 11–23, 1950.

Spiker, C. C.: Experiments with children on the hypotheses of acquired distinctiveness of cues. *Child Develop. 27:* 253–263, 1956.

————: Verbal factors in the discrimination learning of children. *Monogr. Soc. Res. Child Development. 28:* (Whole No. 86), 53–69, 1953.

————: The concept of development: Relevant and irrelevant issues. *In* H. W. Stevenson (Ed.), Concept of Development. *Monogr. Soc. Res. Child Develop. 31(5):* 40–54, 1966.

————, and Irwin, O. C.: The relationship between I.Q. and indices of infant speech sound development. *J. Speech and Hearing Dis. 14:* 335–343, 1949.

————, and Terrell, G.: Factors associated with transposition behavior of preschool children. *J. Genet. Psychol. 86:* 143–158, 1955.

Spiro, M. E.: Culture and personality: The natural history of a false dichotomy. *Psychiat. 14:* 19–56, 1951.

————: Education in a communal village in Israel. *Amer. J. Orthopsychiat. 25:* 283, 1955.

Spitz, R. A.: Hospitalism: An inquiry into the genesis of psychiatric conditions in early childhood. *Psychoanal. Study Child. 1:* 53–74, 1945.

————: The role of ecological factors in emotional development in infancy. *Child Develop. 20:* 145–154, 1949.

————: Relevancy of direct infant observation. *Psychoanal. Study Child. 5:* 66–73, 1950.

————: Environment versus race: Environment as an etiological factor in psychiatric disturbances in infancy. *In* G. B. Wilbur and W. Muensterberger (Eds.), *Psychoanalysis and Culture.* Pp. 32–41, International Universities Press, New York, 1951.

————: The psychogenic diseases in infancy. *Psychoanal. Study Child. 6:* 255–275, 1951, (b).

————: The role of ecological factors in emotional development in infancy. *Child Develop. 25:* 125–146, 1954.

————: *A Genetic Field Theory of Ego Formation.* International Universities Press, New York, 1962.

————, and Wolf, K. M.: The smiling response: A contribution to the ontogenesis of social relations. *Genet. Psychol. Monogr. 34:* 57–125, 1946.

Spitz, Rene: *The First Year of Life: A Psychoanalytic Study of Normal and Deviant Development of Object Relations.* International Universities Press, New York, 1965.

Springer, D. V.: Awareness of racial differences by preschool children in Hawaii. *Genet. Psychol. Monogr. 41:* 215–270, 1950.

————: Development in young children of an understanding of time and the clock. *J. Genet. Psychol. 80:* 83–96, 1952.

————: National-racial preferences of fifth-grade children in Hawaii. *J. Genet. Psychol. 83:* 121–136, 1953.

Staats, A. W.: Verbal habit-families, concepts, and the operant conditioning of word classes. *Psychol. Rev. 68:* 190–204, 1961.

Staats, C. K., and Staats, A. W.: Meaning established by classical conditioning. *J. Exptl. Psychol. 54:* 74–80, 1957.

Stachnik, T. J.: Cross-validation of psychomotor tests for children. *Percept. Motor Skills. 18:* 913–916, 1964.

Standskov, H. H.: Some aspects of the genetics of human behavior. Paper read at a meeting of the American Psychological Association, New York, September, 1954.

Staver, N.: The child's learning difficulty as related to the emotional problem of the mother. *Amer. J. Orthopsychiat. 23:* 131–141, 1953.

Stechler, G.: A longitudinal follow-up of neonatal apnea. *Child Develop. 35:* 333–348, 1964.

————: New-born attention as affected by medication during labor. *Sci. 144:* Whole No. 3616, 315–317, 1964.

Stein, A. H.: Imitation of resistance to temptation. *Child Develop. 38:* 167–169, 1967.

Steiner, I. D.: Interpersonal behavior as influenced by accuracy of social perception. *Psychol. Rev. 62:* 268–274, 1955.

Steinschneider, A.: Developmental psychophysiology. *In* Y. Brackbill (Ed.), *Infancy and Early Childhood: A Handbook and Guide to Human Development.* Ch. 1, pp. 3–50, Free Press, New York, 1967.

————, Lipton, E. L., and Richmond, J. A.: Auditory sensitivity in the infant: Effect of intensity on cardiac and motor responsivity. *Child Develop. 37(2):* 233–252, 1966.

Stendler, C. B.: *Children of Brasstown.* University of Illinois Press, Urbana, 1949.

————: Possible causes of overdependency in young children. *Child Develop. 25:* 125–146, 1954.

————, Camrin, D., and Haines, A. C.: Studies in cooperation and competition: I. The effect of working for group and individual rewards on the social climate of children's groups. *J. Genet. Psychol. 79:* 173–197, 1951.

————, and Young, N.: The impact of beginning first grade upon socialization as reported by mothers. *Child Develop. 21:* 241–260, 1950.

Stendler-Lavatelli, C.: Environmental intervention in infancy and early childhood. *In* M. Deutsch, I. Katz, and A. R. Jensen (Eds.), *Social Class, Race and Psychological Development.* Ch. 10, Holt, Rinehart and Winston, New York, 1968.

Stern, C.: *Principles of Human Genetics.* Freeman, San Fransisco, 1949.

Stern, Carolyn: Labelling and variety in concept identification with young children. *J. Educ. Psychol. 56:* 235–240, 1965.

Stevenson, H. W.: (Ed.), Concept of development: A report of a conference commemorating the 40th anniversary of the Institute of Child Development, University of Minnesota. *Monogr. Soc. Res. Child Develop. 531(5):* 1966.

————: Studies of racial awareness in children. *In* W. W. Hartup and N. L. Smothergill (Eds.), *The Young Child: Reviews of Research.* Pp. 206–213, National Association for the Education of Young Children, Washington, D.C., 1967.

————, and Bitterman, M. E.: The distance-effect in the transposition of intermediate size of children. *Amer. J. Psychol. 68:* 274–279, 1955.

————, Hale, G. A., Klein, R. E., and Miller, L. K.: Interrelations and correlates in children's learning and problem solving. *Monogr. Soc. Res. Child Develop.* Serial No. 123, Vol. 33 (No. 7), 1968.

————, and Langford, T.: Time as a variable in transposition by children. *Child Develop. 28:* 365–370, 1957.

————, and Odom, R. D.: The relation of anxiety to children's performance on learning and problem-solving tasks. *Child Develop. 36:* 1003–1012, 1965.

————, and Stevenson, M. G.: Social interaction in an interracial nursery school. *Genet. Psychol. Monogr. 61:* 37–75, 1960.

————, and Stewart, E. C.: A developmental study of race awareness in young children. *Child Develop. 29:* 399–410, 1958.

Steward, J. H.: Evolution and process. *In* A. L. Kroeber (Ed.), *Anthropology Today.* Pp. 313–326, University of Chicago Press, Chicago, 1953.

Stewart, A. H., et al.: Excessive infant crying (colic) in relation to parent behavior. *Amer. J. Psychiat. 110:* 687–694, 1954.

Stith, M., and Connor, R.: Dependency and helpfulness in young children. *Child Develop. 33:* 15–20, 1962.

Stodosky, S. S., and Lesser, G. S.: Learning patterns in the disadvantaged. *Harvard Educ. Rev. 37(4):* 546–593, 1967.

Stolz, L. M., et al.: *Father Relations of War-Born Children.* Stanford University Press, Stanford, California, 1954.

Stone, A. A., and Onque, G.: *Longitudinal Studies of Child Personality.* Harvard University Press, Cambridge, 1959.

Stone, L. J.: A critique of studies of infant isolation. *Child Develop. 25:* 9–20, 1954.

Stone, Mary Ann: The development of the intersituational generality of formal thought. Unpublished Ph.D. Dissertation. University of Illinois, Urbana, 1966.

Stormzand, J. J., and O'Shea, M. V.: *How Much English Grammar?* Warwick and York, Baltimore, 1924.

Stott, D. H.: Evidence for prenatal impairment of temperament in mentally retarded children. *Vita Humana. 2:* 125–148, 1959.

Stott, L. H.: *A Longitudinal Study of Individual Development.* Merrill-Palmer School, Detroit, 1955.

————: The nature and development of social behavior. *Merrill-Palmer Quart. 4:* 62–78, 1958.

————, and Ball, R. S.: Consistency and change in ascendence-submission in the social interaction of children. *Child Develop. 28:* 259–272, 1957.

————, and ————: Infant and preschool mental tests: Review and evaluation. *Monogr. Soc. Res. Child Develop. 30(3):* 1965.

Strauss, A.: The development and transformation of monetary meaning in the child. *Amer. Soc. Rev. 17:* 275–286, 1952.

————: The development of conceptions of rules in children. *Child Develop. 25:* 193–204, 1954.

Strodtbeck, F. L.: Family interaction, values, and achievement. *In* D. C. McClelland (Ed.), *Talent and Society.* Pp. 135–194, Van Nostrand, Princeton, 1958.

————: Considerations of meta-method in cross-cultural studies. *In* H. K. Romney and R. G. D'Andrade (Eds.), Transcultural Studies in Cognition. *Amer. Anthropol.* Special publication. *66:* 223–229, 1964.

Stuart, H. C., and Meredith, H. V.: Use of body measurements in the school health program. *Amer. J. Pub. Health. 36:* 1365–1381, 1946.

Stuart, R. D.: Decentration in the development of children's concept of moral and casual judgments, *J. Genet. Psychol. 111(1):* 59–68, 1967.

Stubbs, E. M.: The effect of the factors of duration, intensity, and pitch of sound stimuli on the responses of newborn infants. *University of Iowa Studies on Child Welfare. 9(4):* 1934.

Suchman, Rosslyn G.: Colour-form preference, discriminative accuracy in learning of deaf and hearing children. *Child Develop. 37:* 439–451, 1956.

————, and Trabasso, T.: Colour and form preference in young children. *J. Exptl. Child Psychol. 3(2):* 177–187, 1966.

Sugawara, S.: Studies on correlation between mental development and birth injury. *Jap. J. Child Psychiat. 6(4):* 184–203, 1965.

Suinn, R. M.: A factor modifying the concept of anxiety as an interfering drive. *J. Gen. Psychol. 73:* 43–46, 1965.

Sullivan, C., Grant, M. Q., and Grant, J. A.: Development of interpersonal maturity; Applications to delinquency. *Psychiat. 20:* 373–385, 1957.

Sullivan, E. V.: Experiments in the acquisition of conservation of substance: An overview. *In* D. W. Brison and E. V. Sullivan (Eds.), *Recent Research on the Acquisition of Conservation of Substance.* Education Monograph, Ontario Institute for Studies in Education, 1967, (a).

————: The acquisition of conservation of substance through film-mediated models. *In* D. W. Brison and E. V. Sullivan (Eds.), *Recent Research on the Acquisition of Conservation of Substance.* Education Monograph, Ontario Institute for Studies in Education, 1967, (b).

————: Piaget and the school curriculum. A critical appraisal. *Ontario Institute for Studies in Education Bulletin. 2:* 1967.

————: The role of inter- and intra-age individual differences in planning teacher training programs. An invited chapter for Teachers College, Columbia University. Supported by the United States Office of Education. RFP No. 68-4, June, 1968.

————: Developmental change in moral judgments in adolescents. Unpublished paper, Ontario Institute for Studies in Education, 1969.

————: Transition problems in conservation research. *J. Genet. Psychol.* In press, 1969.

————, and Hunt, D. E.: Interpersonal and objective decentering as a function of age and social class. *J. Genet. Psychol. 110:* 199–210, 1967.

Sutton, H. E.: *Genes, Enzymes and Inherited Diseases.* Holt, Rinehart and Winston, New York, 1961.

————: Biochemical genetics and gene action. *In* S. Vandenberg (Ed.), *Methods and Goals in Human Behavior Genetics.* Pp. 1–15, Academic Press, New York, 1965.

Sutton-Smith, Brian. The role of play in cognitive development. *In* W. W. Hartup and N. L. Smothergill (Eds.), *The Young Child: Reviews of Research.* National Association for the Education of Young Children, Washington, D.C., 1967.

————, and Rosenberg, B. G.: Age changes in the effects of ordinal position on sex-role identification. *J. Genet. Psychol. 107(1):* 61–73, 1965.

————, and ————: The dramatic boy. *Percept. Motor Skills. 25(1):* 247–248, 1967.

————, ————, and Landy, F.: Father-absence effects in families of different sibling compositions. *Child Develop. 39(4):* 1213–1221, 1968.

————, ————, and Morgan, E. F.: Development of sex differences in play choices during pre-adolescence. *Child Develop. 34:* 119–126, 1963.

Swift, J. W.: Effects of early group experience: The nursery school and day nursery. *In* M. L. Hoffman and L. W. Hoffman (Eds.), *Review of Child Development Research.* Pp. 249–288, Russell Sage Foundation, New York, 1964.

Symonds, P. M.: *The Dynamics of Parent-Child Relationships.* Teachers College, Columbia University, New York, 1949.

Szeminska, A.: The evolution of thought: Some applications of research findings to educational practice. *In* P. H. Mussen (Ed.), European Research in Cognitive Development. *Monogr. Soc. Res. Child Develop.* Pp. 46–57, *30(2):* (No. 100), 1965.

Szuman, S.: Comparison, abstraction, and analytic thought in the child. *Enfance. 4:* 189–216, 1951.

Tabachnick, B.: Some correlates of prejudice towards Negroes in elementary age children. *J. Genet. Psychol. 100(2):* 193–203, 1962.

Taft, L., and Goldfard, W.: Prenatal and perinatal factors in childhood schizophrenia. *Develop. Med. Child Neurol. 6:* 32–43, 1964.

Taft, R.: Selective recall and memory distortion of favorable and unfavorable material. *J. Abnor. and Soc. Psychol. 49:* 23–28, 1954.

Tagatz, G. E.: Effects of strategy, sex, and age on conceptual behavior of elementary school children. *J. Educ. Psychol. 58(2):* 103–109, 1967.

Tagiuri, R.: Person perception. *In* G. Lindzey and E. Aronson (Eds.), *The Handbook of Social Psychology*, 2nd ed. Vol. 3, pp. 395–449, Addison Wesley, Reading, Mass., 1969.

Tajfel, H., Richardson, A., and Everstein, L.: Individual consistencies in categorizing: A study of judgment behavior. *J. Personal. 32:* 19–108, 1964.

Tanner, J. M.: (Ed.), *Human Growth.* Pergamon Press, Oxford, 1960.

——: *Education and Physical Growth.* University of London Press, London, 1961.

——: *Growth at Adolescence*, (2nd ed.). Blackwell Scientific Publications, Oxford, 1962.

Tasch, R. J.: The role of the father in the family. *J. Exptl. Educ. 20:* 319–361, 1952.

Tauber, E. S., and Koffler, S.: Optomotor response in human infants to apparent motion: Evidence of innateness. *Sci. 152:* 382–383, 1966.

Taylor, C., and Combs, A. W.: Self-acceptance and adjustment. *J. Consult. Psychol. 16:* 89–91, 1952.

Taylor, E. A.: Some factors relating to social acceptance in eighth grade classrooms. *J. Educ. Psychol. 43:* 257–272, 1952.

Taylor, J. H.: Innate emotional responses in infants. Ohio State University, *Stud. Con. Psychol. 12:* 69–81, 1934.

Taylor, R.: Hunger in the infant. *Amer. J. Dis. Children. 14:* 233–257, 1917.

Teeter, Barbara, Rouzer, D. L., and Rosen, E.: Development of cognitive motivation: Preference for widely known information. *Child Develop. 35:* 1105–1111, 1964.

Temple, R., and Amen, E. W.: A study of anxiety reactions in young children by means of a projective technique. *Genet. Psychol. Monogr. 30:* 59–113, 1944.

Templin, M. C.: Norms on a screening test of articulation for ages three through eight. *J. Speech and Hearing Dis. 18:* 323–330, 1953.

——: Certain language skills in children: The development and interrelationship. *University of Minnesota Institute of Child Welfare Monograph. 26:* 1957.

——: The study of articulation and language development during the early school years. *In* F. Smith and G. A. Miller (Eds.), *The Genesis of Language: A Psycholinguistic Approach.* Pp. 173–180, M.I.T. Press, Cambridge, 1966.

Ten-Bosch, J., Van Der Werff, J., and Haak, A.: (Ed.), *Somatic Growth of the Child.* Charles C Thomas, Springfield, Illinois, 1966.

Tennes, K. H., and Lampl, E. E.: Stranger and separation anxiety in infancy. *J. Nerv. and Men. Dis. 139(3):* 247–254, 1964.

Teplen'kaya, Kh.M.: Formirovanie ponyatii o prinadlezhnosti k klassu i sootnosheniyakh klassov i podklassov u detei 6–7 let. (The development of concepts of class membership and relationships between classes and subclasses in 6–7 year old children.) *Voprosy Psikhologii. 5:* 138–141, 1966.

Terman, L. M. et al.: Genetic studies of genius. Vol. 1. Mental and physical traits of a thousand gifted children. Stanford University Press, Stanford, 1925.

——, and Merrill, M. A.: *Measuring Intelligence.* Houghton Mifflin, Boston, 1937.

——, and Oden, M. H.: *The Gifted Child Grows Up: 25 Years Follow-up of a Superior Group.* Stanford University Press, Stanford, California, 1949.

——, and ——: *The Gifted Group at Mid-Life.* Stanford University Press, Stanford, 1959.

——, and Tyler, L. E.: Psychological sex differences. *In* L. Carmichael (Ed.), *Manual of Child Psychology*, (2nd ed.). Pp. 1004–1114, Wiley, New York, 1954.

Terrell, G.: Manipulatory motivation in children. *J. Comp. Psychol. 52:* 705–709, 1959.

——: Delayed reinforcement effects. *In* L. P. Lipsitt and C. C. Spiker (Eds.), *Advances in Child Development and Behavior.* Vol. 2, pp. 127–158, Academic Press, New York, 1965.

The hazardous first months of life. *Statistical Bulletin of the Metropolitan Life Insurance Company. 33:* 1–4, 1952.

Thetford, W. N., Molish, H. B., and Beck, S. J.: Developmental aspects of personality structure in normal children. *J. Project. Tech. 15:* 58–78, 1951.

Thiesen, J. W., and Meister, R. K.: A laboratory investigation of measures of frustration tolerance of pre-adolescent children. *J. Gent. Psychol. 75:* 277–291, 1949.

Thomas, A., Chess, S., Birch, H., and Hertzig, T. H.: A longitudinal study of primary action patterns in children. *Comp. Psychiat. 1:* 103–112, 1960.

———, ———, ———, ———, and Korn, S.: *Behavioral Individuality in Early Childhood.* New York University Press, New York, 1963.

Thomas, D. R.: Oral sentence structure and vocabulary of kindergarten children living in low socio-economic urban areas. Unpublished doctoral dissertation. Wayne State University, 1962.

Thomas, H.: *Training for Childbirth.* McGraw-Hill, New York, 1950.

———: Visual-fixation responses of infants to stimuli of varying complexity. *Child Develop. 36:* 629–638, 1965.

Thompson, C. W., and Margaret, A.: Differential test responses of normals and mental defectives. *J. Abnor. and Soc. Psychol. 42:* 285–293, 1949.

Thompson, G. G.: The social and emotional development of preschool children under two types of educational programs. *Psychol. Monogr. 56(5):* 1944.

———: Children's groups. *In* P. H. Mussen (Ed.), *Handbook of Research Methods in Child Development.* Pp. 821–853, Wiley, New York, 1960.

———: *Child Psychology* (2nd ed.). Houghton Mifflin Co., Boston, 1962.

———, and Horrocks, J. E.: A study of the friendship fluctuations of urban boys and girls. *J. Genet. Psychol. 70:* 53–63, 1947.

———, and Powell, M.: An investigation of the rating scale approach to the measurement of social status. *Educ. Psychol. Meas. 11:* 440–455, 1951.

Thompson, H.: Physical growth. *In* L. Carmichael (Ed.), *Manual of Child Psychology* (2nd ed.). Pp. 292–334, Wiley, New York, 1954.

Thompson, J.: Development of facial expression of emotion in blind and seeing children. *Arch. Pshych. 37 (264):* 1941.

Thompson, L. J.: Attitudes of primiparae as observed in a prenatal clinic. *Mental Hygiene. 26:* 243–256, 1942.

Thompson, M. M.: The effect of discriminatory leadership on the relations between the more and less privileged subgroups. Unpublished doctor's dissertation, University of Iowa, 1940.

Thompson, W. R., and Heron, W.: The effects of restricting early experience on the problem solving capacity of dogs. *Canad. J. Psychol. 8:* 17–31, 1954.

Thorndike, E. L.: *Educational Psychology.* Vol. I. *The Original Nature of Man.* Teachers College, Columbia University, New York, 1919.

———: On the improvement of intelligence scores from thirteen to nineteen. *J. Educ. Psychol. 17:* 73–76, 1926.

Thorndike, E. L. et al.: *The Measurement of Intelligence.* Teachers College, Columbia University, New York, 1926.

Thorndike, R. L.: Growth of intelligence during adolescence. *J. Genet. Psychol. 72:* 11–15, 1948.

———: *The Concepts of Over- and Under-Achievement.* Teachers College, Columbia University, New York, 1963.

Thrasher, F. M.: *The Gang.* University of Chicago Press, Chicago, 1927.

Thurstone, L. L.: Influence of motion pictures on children's attitudes. *J. Soc. Psychol. 2:* 291–305, 1931.

———, and Ackerson, L.: The mental growth curve for the Binet tests. *J. Educ. Psychol. 20:* 569–583, 1929.

Thysell, R. V., and Schulz, R. W.: Concept-utilization as a function of strength of relevant and irrelevant associations. *J. Verb. Behav. 3:* 203–258, 1964.

Tiedemann, D.: *Beobachtungen über die Entwicklung der Seelenfahrigkeiten bei Kindern.* Altenburg, Bonde, 1787.

Tiller, P. O.: Father absence and personality development of children in sailor families. A preliminary research report. *In* N. Anderson (Ed.), *Studies of the Family.* Pp. 115–137, Vanderhoeck and Ruprecht, Gottingen, Germany, 1957.

Tisdall, F. F.: The role of nutrition in preventive medicine. *Milbank Memorial Fund Quart.* 23: 1–15, 1945.

Todd, T. W.: *Atlas of Skeletal Maturation.* Mosby, St. Louis, 1937.

Tolman, E. C.: *Purposive Behavior in Animals and Men.* Century, New York, 1932.

Tomkins, S. S.: An experimental study of anxiety. *J. Psychol. 15:* 307–313, 1943.

———: *Affect, Imagery, Consciousness.* Vol. 2. *The Negative Affects.* Springer, New York, 1963.

———, Izard, C. D.: *Affect, Cognition and Personality: Empirical Studies.* Springer Co., New York, 1965.

Torrance, E. P.: Eight partial replications of the Getzels-Jackson study. *Research Memorandum,* BER-60-15. Bureau of Educational Research, University of Minnesota, Minneapolis, 1960, (a).

———, Yamamoto, K., Schenetski, D., Palamutlu, N., and Luther, B.: *Assessing the Creative Thinking Abilities of Children.* Bureau of Educational Research, University of Minnesota, Minneapolis, 1960.

Toshimi, U.: A study of the stability of children's sociometric status: An analysis of stability of choices given to others. *Jap. J. Educ. Psychol. 12:* 20–27, 1964.

Trager, H. G., and Yarrow, M. R.: *They Learn What They Live: Prejudice in Young Children.* Harper, New York, 1952.

Trasler, G.: *In Place of Parents.* Routledge and Kegan, Paul, London, 1960.

Traweek, M. W.: The relationship between certain personality variables and achievement through programmed instruction. *California J. Educ. Res. 15:* 215–220, 1964.

Trent, R.: An analysis of expressed self-acceptance among Negro children. Unpublished doctor's dissertation, Teachers College, Columbia University, 1953.

Tryon, C. M.: Evaluations of adolescent personality by adolescents. *Monogr. Soc. Res. Child Develop. 4(4):* 1939.

———: The adolescent peer culture. *In Adolescence, Forty-third Yearbook, National Society for the Study of Education.* Part I, University of Chicago Press, Chicago, 1944.

Tuddenham, R. D.: Studies in reputation. I. Sex and grade differences in school children's evaluation of their peers. *Psychol. Monogr. 66(1),* (Whole No. 333), 1951.

———: Studies in reputation. III. Correlates of popularity among elementary school children. *J. Educ. Pscyhol. 42:* 257–276, 1951.

———: The constancy of personality ratings over two decades. *Genet. Psychol. Monogr. 60:* 3–29, 1951.

Tumin, M. M.: Readiness and resistance to desegregation: A social portrait of the hard core. *Soc. Forces. 36:* 256–263, 1958.

Turiel, E.: An experimental test of the sequentiality of developmental stages in the child's moral judgments. *J. Personal. Soc. Psychol. 3:* 611–618, 1966.

———: An historical analysis of the Freudian conception of the superego. *Psychoanal. Rev. 54(1):* 118–140, 1967.

———: Developmental processes in the child's moral thinking. *In* P. Mussen, J. Langer, and N. Covington (Eds.), *New Directions in Developmental Psychology.* Holt, Rinehart and Winston, New York, 1968.

Turkewitz, G., Gordon, E. W., and Birch, H. G.: Head turning in the human neonate: Effect of pradial condition and lateral preference. *J. Comp. Physiol. Psychol. 59:* 189–192, 1965.

Tyler, F. T.: Issues related to readiness. *In* D. E. Griffiths (Ed.), *Sixty-third Yearbook, National Society for the Study of Education.* Part II, pp. 210–239, University of Chicago Press, Chicago, 1964.

———, Rafferty, J., and Tyler, B. B.: Relationships among motivations of parents and their children. *J. Genet. Psychol. 101:* 69–81, 1962.

Tyler, L. E.: The development of "vocational interests": I. The organization of likes and dislikes in ten-year-old children. *J. Genet. Psychol. 86:* 33–44, 1955.

Ucko, L. E.: A comparative study of asphyxiated and non-asphyxiated boys from birth to 5 years. *Develop. Med. and Child Neurol. 7(6):* 643–657, 1965.

Ugurel-Semin, R.: Moral behavior and moral judgment of children. *J. Abnor. and Soc. Psychol. 47:* 463–474, 1952.

Uhlmann, F. W., and Saltz, E.: Retention of anxiety material as a function of cognitive differentiation. *J. Personal. and Soc. Psychol. 1:* 55–62, 1965.

Underwood, B. J.: *Psychological Research.* Appleton-Century-Crofts, New York, 1957.

United States Commission on Civil Rights. *Racial Isolation in the Public Schools.* United States Government Printing Office, Washington, D.C., 1967.

Uzgiris, I. C.: Situational generality of conservation. *Child Develop. 35:* 831–841, 1964.

———: Socio-cultural factors in cognitive development. Paper presented at the Peabody NIMH Conference on Socio-cultural Aspects of Mental Retardation, Nashville, Tennessee, June 10–12, 1968.

———, and Hunt, J. McV.: An instrument for assessing infant psychological development. Paper presented at the International Congress of Psychology, 1966.

Vahlquist, B., Lagercrantz, R., and Nordbring, F.: Maternal and foetal titres of anti-strepolysin and antistaphylolysin at different stages of gestation. *Lancet, 259:* 851–853, 1950.

Vallbona, C., Desmond, M. M., Rudolph, A. J., Pap, L. F., Hill, R. M., Franklin, R. R., and Rush, J. B.: Cardiodynamic studies in the newborn. II. Regulation of the heart-rate. *Biol. Neonat. 5:* 159–199, 1963.

Van Alstyne, D.: *Play Behavior and Choice of Play Materials of Preschool Children.* University of Chicago Press, Chicago, 1932.

———, and Hattwick, L. A.: A follow-up study of the behavior of nursery school children. *Child Develop. 19:* 43–72, 1939.

Van Buskirk, C.: Performance on complex reasoning tasks as a function of anxiety. *J. Abnor. and Soc. Psychol. 62:* 200–209, 1962.

Vandenberg, S. G.: *Methods and Goals in Human Behavior Genetics.* Academic Press, New York, 1965.

Van den Daele, L.: A developmental study of the ego-ideal. Unpublished paper, Child Development Laboratory, University of Illinois, 1967.

———: Qualitative models in developmental analysis. *Develop. Psychol.* In press, 1969.

Vannoy, J. S.: Generality of cognitive complexity-simplicity as a personality construct. *J. Personal. and Soc. Psychol. 2:* 385–396, 1965.

Varma, R.: A study of children's fear. *J. Psychol Res. 1:* 46–48, 1957.

Vaughn, G. M.: Ethnic awareness in relation to minority group membership. *J. Genet. Psychol. 105:* 119–130, 1964.

Velten, H. B.: The growth of phonemic and lexical patterns in language. *Language. 19:* 281–292, 1943.

Vickers, V. S., Poyntz, L., and Baum, M. P.: The Brace Scale used with Young Children. *Res. Quart. Amer. Assoc. Health, Phys. Educ. and Recreation. 13:* 299–308, 1942.

Victoroff, V. M.: Dynamics and management of para-partum neuropathic reactions. *Dis. Nerv. Syst. 13:* 291–298, 1952.

Vinacke, W. E.: The investigation of concept formation. *Psychol. Bull. 48:* 1–32, 1951.

———, and Gullickson, G. R.: Age and sex differences in the formation of coalitions. *Child Develop. 35:* 1217–1231, 1964.

Vincent, C. E.: Trends in infant care ideas. *Child Develop. 22:* 199–209, 1951.

Volokhov, A. A.: Development of unconditioned and conditioned reflexes in ontogenesis. *21st International Congress of Physiological Science,* 248–254, 1959.

Von Fieandt, K., and Wertheimer, M.: Perception. *Ann. Rev. Psychol. 20:* 159–192, 1969.

Vroegh, Karen.: Masculinity and femininity in the preschool years. *Child Develop. 39(4):* 1253–1257, 1968.

Vygotsky, L. S.: *Thought and Language.* (Ed. and Trans., E. Hanfmann, and G. Vakar). M.I.T. Press, Cambridge, Mass, 1962.

———: Development of the higher mental functions. *In* A. Leontyev, A. Luria, and A. Smirnov (Eds.), *Psychological Research in the U.S.S.R.* Vol. 1, pp. 11–45, Progress Publishers, Moscow, 1966.

Waddington, C. H.: *The Strategy of the Genes*. Macmillan, New York, 1957.

Waghorn, L., and Sullivan, E. V.: The exploration of transition roles in conservation of quantity using film mediated modelling. Unpublished manuscript, Ontario Institute for Studies in Education, 1968.

Wagner, I. F.: The establishment of a criterion of depth of sleep in the newborn infant. *J. Genet. Psychol. 51:* 17–59, 1937.

Wagoner, L. C., and Armstrong, E. M.: The motor control of children as involved in the dressing process. *J. Genet. Psychol. 35:* 84–97, 1928.

Wahler, R. G.: Infant social attachments: A reinforcement theory interpretation and investigation. *Child Develop. 38:* 1079–1088, 1967.

Waldrop, N. S., and Bell, R. Q.: Effects of family size and density on newborn characteristics. *Amer. J. Orthopsychiat. 36:* 544–550, 1966.

Walk, R. D.: The development of depth perception in animals and human infants. *Monogr. Soc. Res. Child Develop. 31(5):* 82–106, 1966.

Walker, C. M., and Bourne, L. E.: The identification of concepts as a function of amount of relevant and irrelevant information. *Amer. J. Psychol. 74:* 410–417, 1961.

Walker, R. N.: Body build and behavior in young children: I. Body build and nursery school teachers' ratings. *Monogr. Soc. Res. Child Develop. 27(3):* 1962.

———: Body build and behavior in young children: II. Body build and parents' ratings. *Child Develop. 34:* 1–23, 1963.

———: Measuring masculinity and femininity by children's games choices. *Child Develop. 35:* 961–971, 1964.

———: Some temperament traits in children as viewed by their peers, their teachers and themselves. *Monogr. Soc. Res. Child Develop. 32(6):* 1967.

Wallace, J. G.: Concept growth and the education of the child. National Foundation for Educational Research in England and Wales: Occasional publication series No. 12, 1965.

———: Some issues raised by a non-verbal test of number concepts. *Educ. Rev. 18:* 122–135, 1966.

———, and Sechrest, L.: Relative difficulty of conjunctive and disjunctive concepts. *J. Psychol. Stud. 12:* 97–104, 1961.

Wallach, L.: On the bases of conservation. *In* D. Elkind and J. H. Flavell (Eds.), *Studies in Cognitive Development: Essays in Honour of Jean Piaget*. Pp. 191–219, Oxford University Press, New York, 1969.

Wallach, M. A.: Research on children's thinking. *In* H. W. Stevenson (Ed.), *Child Psychology. Sixty-second Yearbook of the National Society for the Study of Education*. Part I, Ch. 6, University of Chicago Press, Chicago, 1963.

———, and Kogan, N.: *Modes of Thinking in Young Children*. Holt, Rinehart and Winston, New York, 1965.

Wallis, R. S.: The overt fears of Dakota Indian children. *Child Develop. 25:* 185–192, 1954.

Wallon, H.: Pre-categorical thinking in the child. *Enfance. 5:* 97–101, 1952.

———, Ebart-Chemielinski, E., and Sauterey, R.: Static equilibrium, dynamic equilibrium: Double lateralization between five and fifteen years. *Enfance. 1:* 1–29, 1958.

Walsh, M. E.: The relation of nursery school training to the development of certain personality traits. *Child Develop. 2:* 72–73, 1931.

Walsh, R. P.: Parental rejecting attitudes and control in children. *J. Clin. Psychol. 24(2):* 185–186, 1968.

Walter, D., Denzler, L. S., and Sarason, I. G.: Anxiety and the intellectual performance of high school students. *Child Develop. 35:* 917–926, 1964.

Walter, L. M., and Marzolf, S. S.: The relation of sex, age and school achievement to levels of aspiration. *J. Educ. Psychol. 42:* 285–292, 1951.

Walters, C. E.: Reliability and comparison of four types of fetal activity and of total activity. *Child Develop. 35:* 1249–1256, 1964.

———: Prediction of postnatal development from fetal activity. *Child Develop. 36:* 801–808, 1965.

Walters, J., Conner, R., and Zunich, M.: Interaction of mothers and children from lower-class families. *Child Develop. 35:* 433–440, 1964.

———, Pearce, D., and Dahms, L.: Affectional and aggressive behavior of preschool children. *Child Develop. 28:* 15–26, 1957.

Walters, R. H., and Demkow, L.: Timing of punishment as a determinant of response inhibition. *Child Develop. 34:* 207–214, 1963.

———, and Parke, R. D.: The role of the distance receptors in the development of social responsiveness. *In* L. P. Lipsitt and C. C. Spiker (Eds.), *Advances in Child Development and Behavior.* II. Pp. 59–126, Academic Press, New York, 1965.

———, and Parke, R. D.: Progress in experimental personality research. *In* B. A. Maher (Ed.), *The Influence of Punishment and Related Disciplinary Techniques on the Social Behavior of Children: Theory and Empirical Findings.* Vol. 3, Academic Press, New York, 1966.

Walton, W. E.: Empathic responses in children. *Psychol. Monogr. 48:* 40–67, 1936.

Wann, K. D., Dorn, M. S., and Liddle, E. A.: *Fostering Intellectual Development in Young Children.* Bureau of Publications, Teachers College, Columbia University, New York, 1962.

Ward, L. B.: Reminiscence and rote learning. *Psychol. Monogr. 49(220),* 1937.

Warkany, J.: Etiology of congenital malformations. *In Advance in Pediatrics.* Interscience, New York, 1947.

Warner, W. L., and Lunt, P. S.: *The Social Life of a Modern Community.* Yale University Press, New Haven, 1941.

Warren, J. R.: Birth order and social behavior. *Psychol. Bull. 65(1):* 38–49, 1966.

Washburn, R. W.: A study of the smiling and laughing of infants in the first year of life. *Genet. Psychol. Monogr. 6:* 397–537, 1927.

Wason, P. C.: The contexts of plausible denial. *J. Verb. Learning and Verb. Behav. 4:* 7–11, 1965.

Waters, Eleanor, and Crandall, V. J.: Social class and observed maternal behavior from 1940–1960. *Child Develop. 35:* 1021–1032, 1964.

Watson, E. H., and Lowrey, G. H.: *Growth and Development of Children.* Year Book Publishers, Chicago, 1951.

Watson, G.: Some personality differences in children related to strict or permissive parental discipline. *J. Psychol. 44:* 227–249, 1957.

Watson, J. B.: *Psychology from the Standpoint of a Behaviorist.* Lippincott, Philadelphia, 1919.

———: *Psychological Care of Infant and Child.* Norton, New York, 1928.

Watson, J. S.: Memory and "contingency analysis" in infant learning. *Merrill-Palmer Quart. 13(1):* 55–76, 1967.

Watson, R.: *Psychology of the Child.* John Wiley and Sons, New York, 1958.

———: *Psychology of the Child* (2nd ed.). John Wiley and Sons, New York, 1965.

Webster, S. W.: The influence of interracial contact on social acceptance in a newly integrated school. *J. Educ. Psychol. 52:* 292–296, 1961.

Wechsler, D.: *The Measurement of Adult Intelligence.* (3rd ed.). Williams & Wilkins, Baltimore, 1944.

———: Intellectual development and psychological maturity. *Child Develop. 21:* 45–50, 1950.

Wedge, B. M.: Occurrence of psychosis among Okinawans in Hawaii. *J. Psychiat. 109:* 255–258, 1952.

Weider, A., and Noller, P. A.: Objective studies of children's drawings of human figures. I. Sex awareness and socioeconomic level. *J. Clin. Psychol. 6:* 319–325, 1950.

Weiner, G.: Psychologic correlates of premature birth: A review. *J. Nerv. and Men. Dis. 134:* 129–144, 1962.

Weiner, P. S.: Personality correlates of accuracy of self-appraisal in four-year-old children. *Genet. Psychol. Monogr. 70:* 329–365, 1964.

Weinreich, U.: Semantic structure of language. *In* D. C. Hildum (Ed.), *Language and Thought.* Pp. 152–167, 1967.

Weir, A. J.: A developmental measure of fact-value differentiation. *Vita Humana. 3:* 65–82, 1960.

Weir, M. W.: Developmental changes in problem-solving strategies. *Psychol. Rev. 71:* 473–490, 1964.

————: Children's behavior in probabilistic tasks. *In* W. W. Hartup and N. L. Smothergill (Eds.), *The Young Child: Reviews of Research.* Pp. 136–154, National Assoication for the Education of Young Children. Washington, D.C., 1967.

————, and Stevenson, H. W.: The effect of verbalization in children on learning as a function of chronological age. *Child Develop. 30:* 143–149, 1959.

Weir, R. H.: *Language in the Crib.* Mouton, The Hague, 1962.

————: Some questions on the child's learning of phonology. *In* F. Smith and G. A. Miller (Eds.), *The Genesis of Language: A Psycholinguistic Approach.* Pp. 153–172, M.I.T. Press, Cambridge, 1966.

Weisberg, P.: Social and non-social conditioning of infant vocalizations. *Child Develop. 34:* 377–388, 1963.

Weiss, L. A.: Differential variations in the amount of activity of newborn infants under continuous light and sound stimulation. *University of Iowa Studies in Child Welfare. 9:* 1–74, 1934.

Weitzman, E. D., Fishbein, W., and Graziani, L.: Auditory evoked responses obtained from the scalp electroencephalogram of the full-term human neonate during sleep. *Pediat. 35(3):* 458–468, 1965.

Welch, L.: The genetic development of the associational structures of abstract thinking. *J. Psychol. 10:* 211–220, 1940, (a).

————: A preliminary investigation of some aspects of the hierarchical development of concepts. *J. Gen. Psychol. 22:* 359–378, 1940, (b).

————, and Long, L.: Comparison of the reasoning ability of two age groups. *J. Genet. Psychol. 62:* 63–76, 1943.

Well, T.: The social development of some rhesus monkeys. *In* B. Foss (Ed.), *Determinants of Infant Behavior.* II. Pp. 35–49, Wiley, New York, 1963.

Wellman, B.: The school child's choice of companions. *J. Educ. Res. 14:* 126–132, 1926.

Wellman, B. L.: IQ changes of preschool and non-preschool groups during the preschool years: A summary of the literature. *J. Psychol. 20:* 347–368, 1945.

————, Case, I. M., Mengert, I. G., and Bradbury, D. E.: Speech sounds of young children. *University of Iowa Studies in Child Welfare. 5(2):* 1931.

Wenar, C., and Coulter, J. B.: A reliability study of developmental histories. *Child Develop. 33:* 453–462, 1962.

————: The effects of a motor handicap on personality: I. The effects on level of aspiration. *Child Develop. 24:* 123–130, 1953.

Wenger, M. A.: An investigation of conditioned responses in human infants. *University of Iowa Studies in Child Welfare. 12:* 9–90, 1936.

————: Preliminary study of the significance of measures of autonomic balance. *Psychoso. Med. 9:* 301–309, 1947.

Werdelin, I.: A study of age differences in factorial structure. *Didakometry.* (Malmo, Sweden, School of Education). No. 6, 1966.

Werner, E.: Milieu differences in social competence. *J. Genet. Psychol. 91:* 239–249, 1957.

Werner, E. E., and Bayley, N.: The reliability of Bayley's revised scale of mental and motor development during the first year of life. *Child Develop. 37(1):* 39–50, 1966.

Werner, H.: *Comparative Psychology of Mental Development.* Follet, Chicago, 1948.

————: The concept of development from a comparative and organismic point of view. *In* D. Harris (Ed.), *The Concept of Development: An Issue in the Study of Human Behavior.* Pp. 499–518, University of Minnesota Press, Minneapolis, 1957.

————, and Kaplan, B.: The developmental approach to cognition: Its relevance to the psychological interpretation of anthropological and ethnolinguistic data. *Amer. Anthropol. 58:* 866–880, 1956.

————, and ————: *Symbol Formation.* John Wiley and Sons, New York, 1963.

————, and Kaplan, E.: The acquisition of word meanings: A developmental study. *Monogr. Soc. Res. Child Develop. 15(1),* Whole No. 51, 1950.

Wertham, F.: Psychological effects of school segregation. *Amer. J. Psycho. 6:* 94–103, 1952.

809

Wertheimer, N.: Psychomotor coordination of auditory and visual space at birth. *Sci. 134:* 16–92, 1961.

Wesley, F., and Carr, C.: Problems in establishing norms for cross-cultural comparisons. *Int. J. Psychol. 1(3):* 257–262, 1966.

Wesselhoeft, C.: Rubella (German measles) and congenital deformities. *New Eng. J. Med. 240:* 258–261, 1949.

Westie, F. R.: Negro-white status differentials and social distance. *Amer. Soc. Rev. 17:* 550–558, 1952.

Wetzel, W. C.: Physical fitness in terms of physique, development and basal metabolism. *JAMA. 116:* 1187–1195, 1941.

Wheeler, L. R.: A comparative study of the intelligence of East Tennessee Mountain Children. *J. Educ. Psychol. 33:* 321–334, 1942.

Whitacre, J., and Grimes, E. T.: Some body measurements of native-born white children of seven to fourteen years in different climatic regions of Texas. *Child Develop. 30:* 177–209, 1959.

White, B. L.: Second-order problems in the studies of perceptual development. Paper presented at the Institute for Juvenile Research. Chicago, September 1, 1965.

———: The initial coordination of sensori-motor schemas in human infants—Piaget's ideas and the role of experience. *In* D. Elkind and J. H. Flavell (Eds.), *Studies in Cognitive Development: Essays in Honour of Jean Piaget.* Pp. 237–256, Oxford University Press, Toronto, 1969.

———, Castle, P., and Held, R.: Observations on the development of visually-directed reaching. *Child Develop. 35:* 349–364, 1964.

———, and Held, R.: Plasticity of sensori-motor development in the human infant. *In* Judy S. Rosenblith and W. Allinsmith (Eds.), *The Causes of Behavior: Readings in Child Development and Educational Psychology.* 2nd ed. Allyn and Bacon, Boston, 1966.

White, M.: Social class, child rearing practices and child behavior. *Amer. Soc. Rev. 22:* 704–712, 1957.

White, R. W.: *Lives in Progress: A Study of the Natural Growth of Personality.* Holt, Rinehart and Winston, New York, 1952.

———: Motivation reconsidered: The concept of competence. *Psychol. Rev. 66:* 297–233, 1959.

———: Competence in psychosexual stages of development. *In* M. R. Jones (Ed.), *Nebraska Symposium on Motivation.* Pp. 97–141, University of Nebraska Press, Lincoln, 1960.

———: Ego and reality in psychoanalytic theory. *Psychol. Issues. 3:* 182–196, 1963.

White, S. H.: Learning. *In* H. W. Stevenson (Ed.), *Child Psychology. Sixty-second Yearbook, National Society for the Study of Education.* Part I. University of Chicago Press, Chicago, 1963.

White House Commission Report: The report of the National Advisory Committee on Civil Disorders. Bantom Books, New York, March, 1968.

Whiteman, M.: Children's conception of psychological causality. *Child Develop. 38(1):* 143–156, 1967.

Whiteman, N., and Deutsch, M.: Social disadvantage as related to intellective and language development. *In* M. Deutsch, I. Katz, and A. R. Jensen (Eds.), *Social Class, Race, and Psychological Development.* Ch. 3, Holt, Rinehart and Winston, New York, 1968.

Whiteman, T. H., and Kosier, K. P.: Development of children's moralistic judgments: Age, sex, I.Q., and certain personal-experiential variables. *Child Develop. 35(8):* 843–850, 1964.

Whiting, J. W. M.: The frustration complex in Kwoma society. *Man 44:* 140–144, 1944.

———: Resource mediation in learning by identification. *In* I. Iscoe and H. W. Stevenson (Eds.), *Personality Development in Children.* Pp. 112–126, University of Texas Press, Boston, 1960.

———, and Child, I. L.: *Child-Training and Personality: A Cross-Cultural Study.* Yale University Press, New Haven, 1953.

———, Landauer, T. K., and Jones, T. M.: Infantile immunization and adult stature. *Child Develop. 39:* 59–67, 1968.

Whiting, J. W., and Whiting, B. B.: Contributions of anthropology to the methods of studying child rearing. *In* P. M. Mussen (Ed.), *Handbook of Research Methods in Child Development*. Ch. 21, Wiley, New York, 1960.

Whyte, W. F.: *Street Corner Society*. University of Chicago Press, Chicago, 1943.

Wickelgren, L.: Convergence in the human newborn. *J. Exptl. Child Psychol. 5(1):* 74–85, 1967.

Wiener, G. et al.: Correlates of low birth weight: Psychological status at 6–7 years of age. *Pediat.* 434–444, 1965.

Wile, I. S., and Davis, R.: The relation of birth to behavior. *Amer. J. Orthopsychiat. 11:* 320–334, 1941.

Williams, H. M., and McFarland, M. L.: A revision of the Smith vocabulary test for preschool children. Part III. Development of language and vocabulary in young children. *University of Iowa Studies in Child Welfare. 13(2):* 35–46, 1937.

Williams, J. F., Meyerson, L. J., Eron, L. D., and Sempler, I. J.: Peer-rated aggression and aggressive responses elicited in an experimental situation. *Child Develop. 38:* 181–190, 1967.

Williams, J. M.: Study of the effect of visuo-perceptual disorders on the emotional adjustment and early learning of young children. Unpublished report, 1965.

Williams, J. R., and Scott, R. B.: Growth and development of Negro infants: IV. Motor development and its relationship to child rearing practices in two groups of Negro infants. *Child Develop. 24:* 103–121, 1953.

Williams, O.: A study of the phenomenon of reminiscence. *J. Exptl. Psychol. 9:* 368–389, 1926.

Willner, Allan E.: Associate neighbourhoods and developmental changes in the conceptual organization of recall. *Child Develop. 38(4):* 1127–1138, 1967.

Wilson, J., Williams, N., and Sugarman, B.: *Introduction to Moral Education*. Penguin Books, Harmondsworth, Middlesex, 1967.

Wilson, Margaret, Warren, J. M., and Abbott, L.: Infantile stimulation, activity, and learning by cats. *Child Develop. 36:* 843–853, 1965.

Wilson, R. C., Guilford, J. P., and Christensen, P. R.: The measurement of individual differences in originality. *Psychol. Bull. 50:* 362–370, 1953.

Wilson, W.: The effect of competition on the speed and accuracy of syllogistic reasoning. *J. Soc. Psychol. 65:* 27–32, 1965.

Windle, W. F.: *Physiology of the Fetus: Origin and Extent of Function in Prenatal Life*. Saunders, Philadelphia, 1940.

Winer, B. J.: *Statistical Principles in Experimental Design*. McGraw-Hill, New York, 1962.

Winer, G. A.: Induced set and acquisition of number conservation. *Child Develop. 39:* 195–205, 1968.

Winitz, H.: Research in articulation and intelligence. *Child Develop. 35:* 287–297, 1964.

Winnicott, D. W.: *The Maturational Processes and the Facilitating Environment: Studies in the Theory of Emotional Development*. International Universities Press, New York, 1965.

————: *The Family and Individual Development*. Basic Books, New York, 1965.

Winstel, B.: The use of a controlled play situation in determining certain effects of maternal attitudes on children. *Child Develop. 22:* 299–311, 1951.

Winterbottom, M. R.: The relation of childhood training in independence to achievement motivation. Unpublished doctoral dissertation, University of Michigan, 1953.

Winterbottom, M. M.: The relation of need for achievement to learning experiences in independence and mastery. *In* J. W. Atkinson (Ed.), *Motives in Fantasy, Action and Society*. Pp. 453–478, Van Nostrand, Princeton, 1958.

Wiseman, S.: Symposium on the effects of coaching and practice in intelligence tests. IV. The Manchester experiment. *Brit. J. Educ. Psychol. 24:* 5–8, 1954.

Wissler, C.: Growth of children in Hawaii based on observations of Louis R. Sullivan. *Memoirs of the Bernice P. Bishop Museum. 11:* 109–257, 1930.

Witkin, H. A.: Social influences in the development of cognitive style. *In* D. E. Goslin (Ed.), *Handbook of Socialization Theory and Research*. Ch. 14, Rand-McNally, Chicago, 1969.

——, Dyk, R. V., Faterson, H. F., Goodenough, D. R., and Karp, S. A.: *Psychological Differentiation: Studies of Development*. Wiley, New York, 1962.

——, Goodenough, D. R., and Karp, S. A.: Stability of cognitive style from childhood to young adulthood. *J. Personal. and Soc. Psychol. 7:* 291–300, 1967.

——, Paterson, H. F., Goodenough, D. R., and Birnbaum, J.: Cognitive patterning in mildly retarded boys. *Child Develop. 37:* 301–316, 1966.

Witryol, S. L.: Age trends in children's evaluation of teacher-approved and teacher-disapproved behavior. *Genet. Psychol. Monogr. 41:* 271–326, 1950.

——, and Thompson, G. G.: A critical review of the stability of social acceptability scores obtained with the partial-rank-order and the paired-comparison scales. *Genet. Psychol. Monogr. 48:* 221–260, 1953.

Wittenberg, R. M., and Berg, J.: The stranger in the group. *Amer. J. Orthopsychiat. 22:* 89–97, 1952.

Wittenborn, J. R.: A study of adoptive children. *Psychol. Monogr. 70:* No. 1–3, 1956.

Wittrock, M. C., and Husek, T. R.: Effects of anxiety upon retention of verbal learning. *Psychol. Rep. 10:* 78, 1962.

——, and Twelker, P. A.: Verbal cues and variety of classes of problems in transfer of training. *Psychol. Rep. 14:* 827–830, 1964.

Wohlwill, J. F.: Absolute versus relational discrimination on the dimension of number. *J. Genet. Psychol. 96:* 353–363, 1960, (a).

——: A study of the development of the number concept by scalogram analysis. *J. Genet. Psychol. 97:* 345–377, 1960, (b).

——: Developmental studies of perception. *Psychol. Bull. 57:* 249–288, 1960.

——: From perception to inference: A dimension of cognitive development. *Monogr. Soc. Res Child Develop. 27(2):* 87–107, 1962.

——: The development of "over-constancy" in space perception. In L .P. Lipsitt and C. C. Spiker (Eds.), *Advances in Child Development and Behavior*. Vol. I, pp. 265–312, Academic Press, New York, 1963.

——: Responses to class-inclusion questions for verbally and pictorially presented items. *Child Develop. 30:* 449–465, 1968.

——, and Lowe, R. C.: An experimental analysis of the development of the conservation of number. *Child Develop. 33:* 153–167, 1962.

Wolf, T. H.: *The Effect of Praise and Competition on the Persisting Behavior of Kindergarten Children*. University of Minnesota Press, Minneapolis, 1938.

Wolfe, R.: The role of conceptual systems in cognitive functioning at varying levels of age and intelligence. *J. Personal. 31:* 108–123, 1963.

Wolfenstein, M.: Trends in infant care. *Amer. J. Orthopsychiat. 23:* 120–130, 1953.

——: *Children's Humor: A Psychological Analysis*. Free Press, Glencoe, Illinois, 1954.

Wolf, S., and Wolf, H. G.: *Human Gastric Function: An Experimental Study of a Man and His Stomach*. Oxford, New York, 1947.

Wolff, J. L.: Concept attainment, intelligence, and stimulus complexity: Attempts to replicate Osler and Trautman (1961). *J. Exptl. Psychol. 73(3):* 488–490, 1967.

Wolff, P. H.: Observations on newborn infants. *Psychoso. Med. 21:* 110–118, 1959.

——: Observations on the early development of smiling. In D. M. Foss (Ed.), *Determinants of Infant Behavior*. II. Pp. 113–133, Wiley, New York, 1963.

——: The development of attention in young infants. *Ann. New York Acad. Sci. 118(21):* 815–830, 1965.

——: The causes, controls, and organization of behavior in the neonate. *Psychol. Issues*. Vol. 5, No. 1, Monograph 17. International Universities Press, New York, 1966.

——, and Simmons, N. A.: Non-nutritive sucking and response thresholds in young infants. *Child Develop. 38:* 631–638, 1967.

Wolfle, D. L., and Wolfle, H. M.: The development of cooperative behavior in monkeys and young children. *J .Genet. Psychol. 55:* 137–175, 1939.

Wood, B. D., and Freeman, F. N.: *An Experimental Study of the Educational Influence of the Typewriter in the Elementary School Classroom*. Macmillan, New York, 1932.

Wood, K. S.: Parental maladjustment and functional articulatory defects in children. *J. Speech and Hearing Dis. 11:* 255–275, 1946.

Wood, N. E.: Language development and disorders: A compendium of lectures. *Monogr. Soc. Res Child Develop.* 1960.

Woodworth, R. S.: *Heredity and Environment: A Critical Survey of Recently Published Materials on Twins and Foster Children.* Social Science Research Council, New York, 1941.

Wooton, D.: A social scientists's approach to maternal deprivation. *In* J. Bowlby (Ed.), *Deprivation and Maternal Care: A Re-Assessment of Its Effects.* Pp. 255–266, Schocken Books, New York, 1966.

Wortis, H., and Freedman, A.: The contribution of social environment to the development of premature children. *Amer. J. Orthopsychiat. 35(1):* 1965.

———, Heimer, C. B., Braine, M., Redlo, M., and Rue, R.: Growing up in Brooklyn: The early history of the premature child. *Amer. J. Orthopsychiat. 33(3):* 535–539, 1963.

Wright, B. A.: Altruism in children and the perceived conduct of others. *J. Abnor. and Soc. Psychol. 37:* 218–233, 1942.

Wright, H. F.: The influence of barriers upon strength of motivation. *Duke University Series, Contributions to Psychological Theories. 1(3):* 1937.

———: Observational child study. *In* P. H. Mussen (Ed.), *Handbook of Research Methods in Child Development.* Pp. 71–139, Wiley, New York, 1960.

Wunderlin, R. J., and McPherson, M. H.: Sensitivity to imbalance in normal and anoxic damaged children. *J. Clin. Psychol. 18:* 410–413, 1962.

Wynns, F. C.: A developmental study of problem solving requiring use of a combinatorial system: A Piaget replication. Paper read at the Society for Research in Child Development, New York, March, 1967.

X, Malcolm: *The Autobiography of Malcolm X.* Grove Press, New York, 1966.

Yamamoto, K.: Role of creative thinking and intelligence in high school achievement. *Psychol. Rep. 14:* 783–789, 1964 (a).

———: Threshold of intelligence in academic achievement of highly creative students. *J. Exptl. Educ. 32:* 401–405, 1964, (b).

———: A further analysis of the role of creative thinking in high-school achievement. *J. Psychol. 58:* 277–283, 1964, (c).

Yando, R. M., and Kagan, J.: Defective teacher tempo on the child. *Child Develop. 39:* 27–34, 1968.

Yarrow, L.: Interviewing children. *In* P. H. Mussen (Ed.), *Handbook of Research Methods in Child Development.* Pp. 561–602, Wiley, New York, 1960.

———: Maternal deprivation: Toward an empirical and conceptual reevaluation. *Psychol. Bull. 58:* 459–490, 1961.

———: Research in dimensions of early maternal care. *Merrill-Palmer Quart. 9(2):* 101–114, 1963.

———: Personality consistency and change: An overview of some conceptual and methodological issues, *Vita Humana. 7(2):* 67–72, 1964, (a).

———: Separation from parents during early childhood. *In* L. Hoffman and M. Hoffman (Eds.), *Review of Child Development Research,* Vol. I. Pp. 89–136, Russell Sage Foundation, New York, 1964, (b).

———: An approach to the study of reciprocal interactions in infancy: Infant-caretaker pairs in foster care and adoption. Paper presented at the Biennial meeting of the Society for Research in Child Development, Minneapolis, Minnesota, March 25, 1965.

———, and Yarrow, M. R.: Personality continuity and change in family context. *In* P. Worchel and D. Byrne (Eds.), *Personality Change.* Pp. 489–523, Wiley, New York, 1964.

Yarrow, M. R.: The measurement of children's attitudes and values. *In* P. H. Mussen (Ed.), *Handbook of Research Methods in Child Development.* Pp. 645–687, Wiley, New York, 1960.

———: Problems of methods in parent-child research. *Child Develop. 34:* 215–226, 1963.

———, Campbell, J. O., and Yarrow, L. J.: Acquisition of new norms: A study of racial desegregation. *J. Soc. Issues. 14:* 8–28, 1958.

———, and Rauch, H. L.: (Eds.), *A Report of a Conference on Observational Methods in Research on Socialization Processes.* New York, 1962.

Yerkes, R. M.: *Chimpanzees.* Yale University Press, New Haven, 1943.

Yohsida, H.: Study on some determinants in the formation of friendship (II). Memoirs of the Faculty of Education, No. 11, 12–21, Toyama University, 1963.

Young, R. K., Benson, W. M., and Holtzman, W. H.: Change in attitudes toward the Negro in a southern university. *J. Abnor. Soc. Psychol. 60:* 131–133, 1960.

Yudin, L. W.: Formal thought in adolescence as a function of intelligence. *Child Develop. 37:* 697–708, 1966.

——, and Kates, S. L.: Concept attainment and adolescent development. *J. Educ. Psychol. 55:* 1–9, 1963.

Zagora, E.: Observations on the evolution and neurophysiology of eye-limb coordination. *Ophthalmologica. 138:* 241–254, 1959.

Zander, A.: A study of experimental frustration. *Psychol. Monogr. 56:* No. 3, (Whole No. 256), 1944.

Zapella, Michele.: The placing reaction in the newborn. *Develop. Med. and Child Neurol. 5(5):* 497–503, 1963.

Zaporozhets, A. D.: The development of perception in the pre-school child. *In* P. H. Mussen (Ed.), European Research in Cognitive Development. *Monogr. Soc. Res. Child Develop. 30(2):* 82–101, 1965.

——, and Zinchenko, V. P.: Development of perceptual activity and formation of a sensory image in the child. *In* A. Leontyev, A. Luria, and A. Smirnov (Eds.), *Psychological Research in the USSR.* Pp. 393–421, Progress Publishers, Moscow, 1966.

Zeligs, R.: Tracing racial attitudes through adolescence. *Sociology and Social Res. 23:* 45–54, 1938.

——: Children's wishes. *J. App. Psychol. 26:* 231–240, 1942.

——: Children's intergroup attitudes. *J. Genet. Psychol. 72:* 101–110, 1948.

Zemlick, M. J., and Watson, R. I.: Maternal attitudes of acceptance and rejection during and after pregnancy. *Amer. J. Orthopsychiat. 23:* 570–584, 1953.

Ziegelman, M.: Loving and punishing parental behavior and introversion tendencies in sons. *Child Develoop. 37:* 985–992, 1966.

Zigler, E.: Metatheoretical issues in developmental psychology. *In* M. H. Marx (Ed.), *Theories in Contemporary Psychology.* Pp. 341–369, Macmillan, New York, 1963.

——: Mental retardation: Current issues and approaches. *In* L. W. Hoffman and M. L. Hoffman (Eds.), *Child Development Research,* Vol. 2. Pp. 107–168, Russell Sage Foundation, New York, 1966.

——, and Butterfield, E. C.: Motivational aspects of changes in IQ test performance of culturally deprived nursery school children. *Child Develop. 29(1):* 1–14, 1968.

——, and Child, I. L.: Socialization. *In* G. Lindzey and E. Aronson (Eds.), *The Handbook of Social Psychology.* 2nd ed. Vol. 3, pp. 450–489, Addison-Wesley, Reading, Mass., 1969.

——, Levine, J., and Gould, L.: Cognitive processes in the development of children's appreciation of humor. *Child Develop. 37:* 507–518, 1966.

——, ——, and ——: Cognitive challenge as a factor in children's humor appreciation. *J. Personal and Soc. Psychol. 6(3):* 332–336, 1967.

Ziller, R., and Behringer, R.: A longitudinal study of assimilation of the new child in a group. *Human Relations. 14:* 121–133, 1961.

Zimiles, H.: A note on Piaget's concept of conservation. *Child Develop. 34:* 691–695, 1964.

——: The development of conservation and differentiation of number. *Monogr. Soc. Res. Child Develop. 31(6):* 1966.

Zucker, R. A., Manosevitz, M., and Lanyon, R. L.: Birth order, anxiety, and affiliation during a crisis. *J. Personal. and Soc. Psychol. 8(4):* 354–359, 1968.

Zuker, H. J.: Affectional identification and delinquency. *Arch. Psychol. 286:* 1943.

Zunich, M.: Development of responsibility perceptions of lower and middle class children. *J. Educ. Res. 56:* 497–499, 1963.

Zwerdling, M. A.: Factors pertaining to prolonged pregnancy and its outcome. *Pediat.* In press.

Zweir, M. D.: Interrelations among measured and perceived psychosocial variables. *Concept and Motor Skills. 22(3):* 910, 1966.

Index

820

Cognition
    differentiation increase, 560–561
    specificity increase, 560–561
Cognitive development, 90–93, 551–660
    abstract logical stage, 580–582
    accelerating stages, 586–590
    aspects of transition, 584–586
    concept acquisition, 611–630; causality,
        627–628; classification of, 613; color
        discrimination, 621–623; death, 628–
        629; developmental aspects, 614–620;
        experience, 620–621; intelligence, 620–
        621; language, 642–643; misconcep-
        tions, 630; sex, 620–621; space con-
        ception, 623–625; time conception,
        625–627
    concrete operational stage, 576–580
    determinants of change, 582–584
    intellectual curiosity, 608–609
    language, 642–647
    logic, 641–642
    perceptual development and attainment
        of cognitive sophistication, 556–565;
        concrete-abstract dimension, 570–590;
        egocentricity decline, 563–564; en-
        vironmental deprivation effects, 590–
        595; increasing attentional capacities,
        564–565; interpreting infant's ex-
        perience, 551–552; motivational fac-
        tors, 595–600; stages of intellectual
        development, 565–570; subjectivity
        decline, 563–564; transition from
        concrete to abstract, 561; transition
        from specific to general, 562
    pre-operational stage, 573–576
    problem solving, 630–638; age level
        trends, 633–636; changes in, 631–633;
        factors influencing, 636–638; nature
        of, 631
    role of play in, 609–611
    sensori-motor stage, 571–573
    style in, 638–641
    thought, 641–642
    trends in memory, 601–608; adult recall
        of childhood events, 606–607; de-
        velopment of memory, 602–606; early
        signs, 602–606; rate of forgetting,
        607–608
    See also Intellectual development
Cognitive drive, 596–598
Cognitive interaction, 418–419
Cognitive readiness, 90–93
Cognitive style, 112–113, 638–641
Cohen (1960), 214–215, 286, 433, 513, 563,
    635, 702, 705
Cohen, J. (1959), 662

Cohn, 350, 356
Cohorts, 147
Colby, M. C., 623
Cole, 167
Coleman, 391, 392, 651, 679
Coles, R., 376
Collard, R. R., 303, 426
Colley, T., 300, 396, 401, 412, 413
Collinson, 566, 580, 581
Combs, 288
Communication
    egocentric versus sociocentric, 548–550
    through the placenta, 178–180
    See also Language
Community, peer group relationship to,
    328–329
Competition, 340–344
    age trends, 342–343
    determinants, 343–344
    effects on personality development, 344
Concept acquisition, 611–630
    causality, 627–628
    classification of, 613
    color discrimination, 621–623
    death, 628–629
    developmental aspects, 614–620
    experience, 620–621
    intelligence, 620–621
    language, 642–643
    misconceptions, 630
    sex, 620–621
    space conception, 623–625
    time conception, 625–627
Concepts
    conjunctive, 613
    disjunctive, 613
    relational, 613
Conditioning
    appetitive, 228–229
    aversive, 227–228
    classical, 227–230
Conditioning stimulus (CS), 227, 229
Condon, 432
Conel, J. L., 84, 85
Conflicts, 337–340
    age trends, 338–339
Conformity behavior in peer relationships,
    356–357
Conger, 26, 602
Conjunctive concept, 613
Connor, 292, 342, 382
Conrad, H. S., 139, 654, 655, 670, 676, 677
Conscience, 468–470
    desatellizing-stage, 481–482
    early satellizing stage, 480–481
    late-satellizing stage, 481